Charles W. Eliot

THE HARVARD CLASSICS
EDITED BY CHARLES W ELIOT LL D

꙳

THE EDITOR'S INTRODUCTION

READER'S GUIDE

INDEX TO THE FIRST LINES OF POEMS SONGS & CHORUSES HYMNS & PSALMS

GENERAL INDEX

CHRONOLOGICAL INDEX

WITH A FRONTISPIECE

VOLUME 50

P F COLLIER & SON
NEW YORK

Designed, Printed, and Bound at
The Collier Press, New York

CONTENTS

PAGE

THE EDITOR'S INTRODUCTION TO THE HARVARD CLASSICS...   3

READER'S GUIDE TO THE HARVARD CLASSICS................   17

CLASS I A THE HISTORY OF CIVILIZATION..............   18

　　　　　B RELIGION AND PHILOSOPHY   31

　　　　　C EDUCATION   41

　　　　　D SCIENCE   44

　　　　　E POLITICS   48

　　　　　F VOYAGES AND TRAVELS   52

　　　　　G CRITICISM OF LITERATURE AND THE FINE ARTS   54

CLASS II A DRAMA   61

　　　　　B BIOGRAPHY AND LETTERS....................   64

　　　　　C ESSAYS   66

　　　　　D NARRATIVE POETRY AND PROSE FICTION......   70

AN INDEX TO THE FIRST LINES OF POEMS, SONGS AND
　　CHORUSES, HYMNS AND PSALMS......................   73

GENERAL INDEX   129

CHRONOLOGICAL INDEX   447

THE
EDITOR'S INTRODUCTION
TO THE
HARVARD CLASSICS

MY PURPOSE in selecting The Harvard Classics was to provide the literary materials from which a careful and persistent reader might gain a fair view of the progress of man observing, recording, inventing, and imagining from the earliest historical times to the close of the nineteenth century. Within the limits of fifty volumes, containing about 22,000 pages, I was to provide the means of obtaining such a knowledge of ancient and modern literature as seems essential to the twentieth century idea of a cultivated man. The best acquisition of a cultivated man is a liberal frame of mind or way of thinking; but there must be added to that possession acquaintance with the prodigious store of recorded discoveries, experiences, and reflections which humanity in its intermittent and irregular progress from barbarism to civilization has acquired and laid up. From that store I proposed to make such a selection as any intellectually ambitious American family might use to advantage, even if their early opportunities of education had been scanty. The purpose of The Harvard

Classics is, therefore, one very different from that of the many collections in which the editor's aim has been to select the hundred or the fifty best books in the world; it is nothing less than the purpose to present so ample and characteristic a record of the stream of the world's thought that the observant reader's mind shall be enriched, refined, and fertilized by it.

With such objects in view it was essential that the whole series should be in the English language; and this limitation to English necessitated the free use of translations, in spite of the fact that it is impossible to reproduce perfectly in a translation the style and flavor of the original. The reader of this collection must not imagine that he can find in an English translation of Homer, Dante, Cervantes, or Goethe, all the beauty and charm of the original. Nevertheless, translations can yield much genuine cultivation to the student who attends to the substance of the author's thought, although he knows all the time that he is missing some of the elegance and beauty of the original form. Since it is impossible to give in translation the rhythm and sweetness of poetry—and particularly of lyric poetry—far the larger part of the poetry in The Harvard Classics will be found to be poetry which was written in English.

While with very few exceptions every piece of writing included in the series is complete in itself—that is, is a whole book, narrative, document, essay, or poem—there are many volumes which are made up of numerous short, though complete, works. Thus, three volumes contain an anthology of English poetry comprising specimens of the work of over two hundred writers. There is also a volume of memorable prefaces, and an-

other of important American historical documents.
Five volumes are made up of essays, representing several centuries and several nationalities. The principal
subjects embraced in the series are history, biography, philosophy, religion, voyages and travels, natural
science, government and politics, education, criticism,
the drama, epic and lyric poetry, and prose fiction—in
short, all the main subdivisions of literature. The
principal literatures represented in the collection are
those of Greece, Rome, France, Italy, Spain, England,
Scotland, Germany, and the United States; but important contributions have been drawn also from Chinese, Hindu, Hebrew, Arabian, Scandinavian, and Irish
sources. Since the series is intended primarily for
American readers, it contains a somewhat disproportionate amount of English and American literature, and
of documents and discussions relating to American
history and to the development of American social
and political ideas.

Chronologically considered, the series begins with
portions of the sacred books of the oldest religions,
proceeds with specimens of the literature of Greece
and Rome, then makes selections from the literature of
the Middle Ages in the Orient, Italy, France, Scandinavia, Ireland, England, Germany, and the Latin
Church, includes a considerable representation of the
literature of the Renaissance in Italy, France, Germany, England, Scotland, and Spain, and, arriving at
modern times, comprehends selections derived from
Italy, three centuries of France, two centuries of Germany, three centuries of England, and something more
than a century of the United States.

Nothing has been included in the series which does

not possess good literary form; but the collection illustrates the variations of literary form and taste from century to century, the wide separation in time of the recurrent climaxes in the various forms of literary expression in both prose and verse, and the immense widening of the range and scope of both letters and science during the seventeenth, eighteenth, and nineteenth centuries.

At the very outset of the work unexpected difficulties arose, some of which, although almost mechanical, proved to be insurmountable. Many famous books were too long to be included in the set, that is, they would have taken a disproportionate number of the fifty volumes. Thus, the English Bible could not be included as a whole, because it was too long; and for the same reason only selections from Shakespeare, and the first part of "Don Quixote," could be included. Many famous and desirable books on history had to be excluded because of their length. The works of living authors were in general excluded, because the verdict of the educated world has not yet been pronounced upon them.

Finally, the whole of nineteenth century fiction, with two exceptions, was excluded; partly because of its great bulk, and partly because it is easily accessible. It proved to be possible, however, to represent by selections complete in themselves the English Bible, Shakespeare, and some other works of the highest order. Some authors whose greatest works were too long to be included in the series could be represented by one or more of their shorter works. It was hard to make up an adequate representation of the scientific thought of the nineteenth century, because much of the most

productive scientific thought has not yet been given a literary form. The discoverers' original papers on chemistry, physics, geology, and biology have usually been presented to some scientific society, and have naturally been expressed in technical language, or have been filled with details indispensable from the scientific point of view but not instructive for the public in general.

Although a good part of the reading provided in The Harvard Classics may fairly be called interesting, there are also volumes or portions of volumes which make hard reading, even for a practised student. In the literature of other days some of the topics treated are unfamiliar, and, moreover, the state of mind of the authors is apt to be strange to the present generation. The sentiments and opinions these authors express are frequently not acceptable to present-day readers, who have to be often saying to themselves: "This is not true, or not correct, or not in accordance with our beliefs." It is, however, precisely this encounter with the mental states of other generations which enlarges the outlook and sympathies of the cultivated man, and persuades him of the upward tendency of the human race. The Harvard Classics, as a whole, require close attention and a resolute spirit on the part of the reader. Nevertheless large parts of the collection were undoubtedly composed just to give delight, or to show people how to win rational pleasures. Thus, the real values of almost all the tales, dramas, fiction, and poetry in the series are esthetic, not didactic, values. The interested reader ought to gain from them enjoyment and new power to enjoy.

There is no mode of using The Harvard Classics

which can be recommended as the best for all readers. Every student who proposes to master the series must choose his own way through it. Some readers may be inclined to follow the chronological order; but shall they begin with the oldest book and read down through the centuries, or begin with the youngest and read backward? Another method would be to read by subjects, and under each subject chronologically. A good field for this method is the collection of voyages and travels. There is also merit in the chronological order in reading the documents taken from the sacred books of the world. Still another method is that of comparison or of contrast. The collection gives many opportunities of comparing the views of contemporaneous writers on the same subject, and also of contrasting the prevailing opinions in different nations or different social states at the same epoch. In government and politics, for example, the collection supplies much material for comparing the opinions of writers nearly contemporary but of different nationality, and for contrasting the different social states at the same epoch in nations not far apart geographically, but distinct as regards their history, traditions, and habits.

Another way of dealing with the collection would be to read first an essay or a group of essays on related subjects, and then to search through the collection to discover all the material it contains within the field of that essay or group of essays. The essays in the collection are numerous, and deal with a great variety of topics both old and new. Whoever should follow the various leadings of the essays in the collection would ultimately cover far the greater part of the fifty volumes.

The biographies, letters, and prefaces contained in the collection will also afford much good guidance to other material. The student who likes the comparative method will naturally read consecutively all the dramas the collection contains; and it will not make much difference at which chronological end he begins, for some persons find the climax of drama in Shakespeare, but others in the Greek tragedies.

The anthology of English poetry is one of the most important parts of the collection, in respect to its function of providing reading competent to impart liberal culture to a devoted reader; but those volumes should not be read in course, but rather by authors, and a little at a time. The poems of John Milton and Robert Burns are given in full; because the works of these two very unlike poets contain social, religious, and governmental teachings of vital concern for modern democracies. Milton was the great poet of civil and religious liberty, Puritanism, and the English Commonwealth, and Burns was the great poet of democracy. The two together cover the fundamental principles of free government, education, and democratic social structure, and will serve as guides to much good reading on those subjects provided in the collection. The poetry contained in The Harvard Classics from Homer to Tennyson will by itself give any appreciative reader a vivid conception of the permanent, elemental sentiments and passions of mankind, and of the gradually developed ethical means of purifying those sentiments and controlling those passions.

In order to make the best use of The Harvard Classics it will be desirable for the young reader to reread those volumes or passages which he finds most

interesting, and to commit to memory many of the pieces of poetry which stir or uplift him. It is a source of exquisite and enduring delight to have one's mind stored with many melodious expressions of high thoughts and beautiful imagery.

I hope that many readers who are obliged to give eight or ten hours a day to the labors through which they earn their livelihood will use The Harvard Classics, and particularly young men and women whose early education was cut short, and who must therefore reach the standing of a cultivated man or woman through the pleasurable devotion of a few minutes a day through many years to the reading of good literature.

The main function of the collection should be to develop and foster in many thousands of people a taste for serious reading of the highest quality, outside of The Harvard Classics as well as within them.

It remains to describe the manner in which The Harvard Classics have been made up. I had more than once stated in public that in my opinion a five-foot shelf would hold books enough to give in the course of years a good substitute for a liberal education in youth to any one who would read them with devotion, even if he could spare but fifteen minutes a day for reading. Rather more than a year ago the firm of P. F. Collier & Son proposed that I undertake to make a selection of fifty volumes, containing from four hundred to four hundred and fifty pages each, which would approximately fill my five-foot shelf, and be well adapted to accomplish the educational object I had in mind.

I was invited to take the entire responsibility of mak-

ing the selection, and was to be provided with a competent assistant of my own choice. In February, 1909, I accepted the proposal of the publishers, and secured the services of Dr. William A. Neilson, Professor of English in Harvard University, as my assistant. I decided what should be included, and what should be excluded. Professor Neilson wrote all the introductions and notes, made the choice among different editions of the same work, and offered many suggestions concerning available material. It also fell to him to make all the computations needed to decide the question whether a work desired was too long to be included. The most arduous part of his work was the final making up of the composite volumes from available material which had commended itself to us both.

It would have been impossible to perform the task satisfactorily if the treasures of the general library and of the department libraries of Harvard University had not been at our disposal. The range of the topics in the series was so wide, and the number of languages in which the desired books were originally written so great, that the advice of specialists, each in some portion of the field, had frequently to be sought. We obtained much valuable advice of this sort from scholarly friends and neighbors.

We are under obligations to the following Harvard professors and instructors, whose advice we obtained on questions connected with their several specialties:

Crawford Howell Toy, Hancock Professor of Hebrew; George Herbert Palmer, Alford Professor of Natural Religion; William James, Professor of Phi-

losophy; William Morris Davis, Sturgis-Hooper Professor of Geology; Ephraim Emerton, Winn Professor of Ecclesiastical History; Charles Rockwell Lanman, Wales Professor of Sanscrit; Edward Laurens Mark, Hersey Professor of Anatomy; George Foot Moore, Frothingham Professor of the History of Religion; Edward Stevens Sheldon, Professor of Romance Philology; Horatio Stevens White, Professor of German; Josiah Royce, Professor of the History of Philosophy; Harold Clarence Ernst, Professor of Bacteriology; Herbert Weir Smyth, Eliot Professor of Greek Literature; Frank William Taussig, Henry Lee Professor of Economics; Albert Bushnell Hart, Professor of History; Morris Hicky Morgan, Professor of Classical Philology; Theobald Smith, George Fabyan Professor of Comparative Pathology; Albert Andrew Howard, Pope Professor of Latin; George Lyman Kittredge, Professor of English; Samuel Williston, Weld Professor of Law; Charles Hall Grandgent, Professor of Romance Languages; Hugo Münsterberg, Professor of Psychology; Leo Wiener, Assistant Professor of Slavic Languages and Literatures; Heinrich Conrad Bierwirth, Assistant Professor of German; Theodore William Richards, Professor of Chemistry; George Pierce Baker, Professor of English; James Haughton Woods, Assistant Professor of Philosophy; Irving Babbitt, Assistant Professor of French; Charles Jesse Bullock, Professor of Economics; Edwin Francis Gay, Professor of Economics; Charles Burton Gulick, Professor of Greek; William Zebina Ripley, Professor of Political Economy; Thomas Nixon Carver, David A. Wells Professor of Political Economy; William Guild Howard,

Assistant Professor of German; Fred Norris Robinson, Professor of English; Charles H. C. Wright, Assistant Professor of French; William Rosenzweig Arnold, Andover Professor of the Hebrew Language and Literature; John Albrecht Walz, Professor of the German Language and Literature; Jeremiah D. M. Ford, Smith Professor of the French and Spanish Languages; Edward Kennard Rand, Professor of Latin; Oliver M. W. Sprague, Assistant Professor of Banking and Finance; Jay Backus Woodworth, Assistant Professor of Geology; George Henry Chase, Assistant Professor of Classical Archæology; William Scott Ferguson, Assistant Professor of History; Roger Bigelow Merriman, Assistant Professor of History; Ralph Barton Perry, Assistant Professor of Philosophy; Louis Allard, Instructor in French; Harold de Wolf Fuller, Instructor in Comparative Literature; Lawrence Joseph Henderson, Assistant Professor of Biological Chemistry; F. W. C. Hersey, Instructor in English; F. W. C. Lieder, Instructor in German; C. R. Post, Instructor in Romance Languages; R. W. Pettengill, Instructor in German; H. W. L. Dana, Assistant in English.

Many other scholars answered specific questions which we laid before them, among whom should be mentioned:

Jefferson Butler Fletcher, Professor of Comparative Literature, Columbia University; A. A. Young, Professor of Economics, Leland Stanford Jr. University; G. R. Noyes, Assistant Professor of Slavic, University of California; Lucien Foulet Professor of French, University of California; Francis B. Gummere, Professor of English, Haverford College;

Curtis Hidden Page, Professor of English Literature, Northwestern University; William Draper Lewis, Dean of the Law Department, University of Pennsylvania; James Ford Rhodes, LL.D. (Harvard), Historian; Henry Pickering Walcott, Chairman of the Massachusetts Board of Health; William Belmont Parker, New York; John A. Lester, Ph.D., the Hill School, Pennsylvania; Alfred Dwight Sheffield, Cambridge, Massachusetts.

The staff of the Harvard Library have also given valuable assistance.

In illustrating the volumes with portraits and facsimiles the publishers are under great obligations to the following owners of valuable prints, manuscripts, and autograph letters, who kindly permitted the publishers to use precious objects from their collections:

J. Pierpont Morgan, Esq.; R. H. Dana, Esq.; Wymberley Jones De Renne, Esq.; Harvard University Library; New York Public Library; Boston Public Library; Library of Congress; Library of the Metropolitan Museum of Art; Fogg Art Museum of Harvard University.

The elaborate alphabetical index is intended to give any person who knows the art of using indexes or concordances, or will acquire it in this instance, immediate access to any author or any subject mentioned in the entire collection, and indeed to any passage in the fifty volumes to which the inquirer has a good clue. This full index should make The Harvard Classics convenient books of reference.

March 10, 1910.   Charles W. Eliot

LIST OF VOLUME NUMBERS

AS DESIGNATED IN THE FOLLOWING INDEXES

Volume I	Benjamin Franklin, John Woolman, William Penn
Volume II	Plato, Epictetus, Marcus Aurelius
Volume III	Bacon, Milton's Prose, Thomas Browne
Volume IV	Complete Poems in English, Milton
Volume V	Essays and English Traits, Emerson
Volume VI	Poems and Songs, Burns
Volume VII	The Confessions of St. Augustine, The Imitation of Christ
Volume VIII	Nine Greek Dramas
Volume IX	Letters and Treatises of Cicero and Pliny
Volume X	Wealth of Nations, Adam Smith
Volume XI	Origin of Species, Darwin
Volume XII	Plutarch's Lives
Volume XIII	Æneid, Virgil
Volume XIV	Don Quixote, Part I, Cervantes
Volume XV	Pilgrim's Progress, Donne and Herbert, Walton
Volume XVI	The Thousand and One Nights
Volume XVII	Folk-Lore and Fable, Æsop, Grimm, Andersen
Volume XVIII	Modern English Drama
Volume XIX	Faust, Egmont, etc., Goethe, Doctor Faustus, Marlowe
Volume XX	The Divine Comedy, Dante
Volume XXI	I Promessi Sposi, Manzoni
Volume XXII	The Odyssey, Homer

15

Volume XXIII   Two Years Before the Mast, Dana

Volume XXIV   On the Sublime, French Revolution, etc., Burke

Volume XXV   J. S. Mill and Thomas Carlyle

Volume XXVI   Continental Drama

Volume XXVII   English Essays, Sidney to Macaulay

Volume XXVIII   Essays, English and American

Volume XXIX   Voyage of the Beagle, Darwin

Volume XXX   Faraday, Helmholtz, Kelvin, Newcomb, etc.

Volume XXXI   Autobiography, Cellini

Volume XXXII   Montaigne, Sainte-Beuve, Renan, etc.

Volume XXXIII   Voyages and Travels

Volume XXXIV   Descartes, Voltaire, Rousseau, Hobbes

Volume XXXV   Froissart, Malory, Holinshed

Volume XXXVI   Machiavelli, More, Luther

Volume XXXVII   Locke, Berkeley, Hume

Volume XXXVIII   Harvey, Jenner, Lister, Pasteur

Volume XXXIX   Famous Prefaces

Volume XL   English Poetry, 1

Volume XLI   English Poetry, 2

Volume XLII   English Poetry, 3

Volume XLIII   American Historical Documents

Volume XLIV   Sacred Writings, 1

Volume XLV   Sacred Writings, 2

Volume XLVI   Elizabethan Drama, 1

Volume XLVII   Elizabethan Drama, 2

Volume XLVIII   Thoughts and Minor Works, Pascal

Volume XLIX   Epic and Saga

Volume L   Introduction, Reader's Guide, Indexes

READER'S GUIDE TO THE
HARVARD CLASSICS

THE following lists have been prepared in order to enable the reader more easily to choose and arrange for himself such courses of study as have been suggested in the Introduction. They fall into two classes, the first being selected with respect to subject-matter, as History, Philosophy, or Science; the second with respect to literary form, as the Drama or Essay. Within each group the arrangement is in general chronological, but this has been occasionally departed from when it seemed wise to introduce national or geographical cross-divisions. While most of the volumes can be most profitably read in some chronological or other sequence, many others, such as the collections of English Poetry and of Essays, are equally suited for more desultory browsing.

These lists are not intended to relieve the reader from the use of the General Index, which has purposely been made so ample that it is possible by its intelligent use to track almost any line of interest through the entire set of volumes.

CLASS I

A

THE
HISTORY OF CIVILIZATION

THE following list is by no means confined to works regarded by their authors as history, but includes letters, dramas, novels, and the like, which, by virtue of their character, period, or scene, throw light upon social and intellectual conditions, enriching and making vivid the picture of human progress which is outlined in the more strictly historical narratives.

Professor Freeman's essay, which is suggested as a general introduction to this division, deals in a highly illuminating fashion with the much misunderstood term, "Race"; and by definition and illustration brings out the elements according to which the historian and the anthropologist determine the relationships among the families of mankind.

The oldest civilization with which the ordinary reader has any acquaintance is that of Egypt, and his knowledge of this is usually confined to the dealings of the Egyptians with the Israelites, as narrated in the first books of the Old Testament. The account of Egypt by Herodotus gives a picture of this people from the point of view of a Greek, and is made entertaining by the skill of one of the best story-tellers in the world. A glimpse of life in the days of the patriarchs, in the countries surrounding Palestine, is given in the nar-

rative portions of "The Book of Job," where Job himself is concerned as a powerful and wealthy sheik.

With Homer we come to the civilization which, more than any other, has affected the culture of modern Europe. The wanderings of Odysseus in the "Odyssey" and the account of the fall of Troy in the "Æneid" contain, of course, a large mythical element; but they leave, nevertheless, a vivid picture which must represent with much essential truth the way of life of the Greeks before the historic period. The two poems by Tennyson named here were suggested by the "Odyssey," and express with remarkable power and beauty the modern poet's conception of the Greek hero's character, and the mood of reaction from the life of effort and suffering. The pieces by Wordsworth and Landor are modern retellings of stories from the same treasure-house from which the Greek tragedians drew the plots of those great dramas which, with the dialogues of Plato, represent the height of intellectual achievement in the ancient world. The five Greek lives by Plutarch give portraits of a group of the most distinguished men of affairs in the same period.

Plutarch again, in his "Lives" of famous Romans, brings before us several of the greatest figures of Republican Rome. His main interest was in personality; but incidentally he gives much information as to the political history of this period. For the years immediately preceding the end of the Republic, the "Letters" of Cicero give a detailed picture of Roman politics from the inside. In spite of the frequent allusions to events and persons now known only to the scholar, the general reader may easily find interest in the similarities between the political methods of

antiquity and those of our own day. Dryden's "All for Love" is a thorough making-over of Shakespeare's "Antony and Cleopatra," which in turn is based on Plutarch's "Life of Antony." It is interesting, not only as an excellent example of Dryden's work as a dramatist, but as affording, along with Shakespeare's tragedy, a suggestive study of two of the most picturesque figures of ancient times. From the Alexandrian scenes one can gain an impression of the luxury that was beginning to sap the foundations of the old Roman virtue.

Pliny's "Letters" picture the life of a cultivated Roman under the Empire. Among them, special interest attaches to that giving a graphic account of the eruption of Vesuvius which destroyed Pompeii, and in which the elder Pliny perished, and to those in which Pliny as proconsul consults with the Emperor Trajan about the policy of persecuting the early Christians. The story of the "Æneid" does not deal with this period; but its patriotic purpose makes it important in judging the spirit of the times. Tennyson's tribute to Virgil is a superb appreciation of the literary quality of the Roman writer, with whom the Englishman had many points of kinship. In the writings of the Emperor Marcus Aurelius and the slave Epictetus, the moral philosophy of paganism reaches its highest level.

The condition of our Teutonic ancestors during the period of Roman supremacy is admirably described by the historian Tacitus in his account of Germany. The description is external, but well-informed, and is the work of an acute and highly trained observer of society and politics. More intimate are the poems that

have come down from the early period of Germanic culture, represented here by the Old English "Beowulf," and the Icelandic "Song of the Volsungs." These stories deal with incidents and personages whose historic bases belong to continental Europe, though the earliest extant literary poems of both happen to be insular. "Beowulf" is the more circumstantial as a picture of life and manners; the Volsung story in its various versions, through the "Nibelungenlied" down to Wagner's operas, has made a more profound appeal to the imagination. The splendid though grotesque specimen of Irish saga-writing given in "The Destruction of Dá Derga's Hostel" belongs to nearly the same period. In the case of all three, the material represents a stage of culture considerably earlier than the date of writing, and still essentially pagan.

The books from the New Testament are selected to give the story of the founding of Christianity; St. Augustine's "Confessions" exhibit the development, after a few centuries, of Christian doctrine, Christian standards of conduct, and Christian ways of thinking; while the Hymns of the Early Church, East and West, represent the lyrical expression of the devotional feeling of the young religion.

While Christianity was gradually overcoming the paganism of Europe, Mohammed appeared in Arabia; and from the chapters of the "Koran," which he claimed to have received by inspiration, we can form an idea of the teaching which, with the aid of the sword, so rapidly conquered the East. "The Arabian Nights" are Mohammedan in background, the multiplicity of angels and genii which the Prophet admitted into his system playing a large part in the mechanism

of the tales. The representation of the social life of the East is, however, more important than the religious element in these. Omar Khayyám is the free-thinking philosopher in a Mohammedan society, and his quatrains are given here in the free paraphrase of Fitzgerald, a work which ranks higher as an original poem than as an exact translation.

The Middle Ages denotes a period with somewhat vague boundaries; and some of the books already touched on might well be placed within it. Here it includes representative literary products of Western Europe from the time of Charlemagne to the middle of the fifteenth century. "The Song of Roland" begins, on a slight historical foundation, the great structure of French epic, and is itself a simple and vigorous celebration of heroic loyalty. In the passages from the Norse "Saga of Eric the Red" which describes the discovery of America by Icelanders about 1000 A. D., we get a glimpse of the hardy life of the Vikings. In "The Divine Comedy" Dante summed up the essential characteristics of the spiritual and intellectual life of the Middle Ages, and by his emotional intensity and the extraordinary distinctness of his imaginative vision gave his result an artistic preeminence that makes it the supreme creation of the epoch.

The pageantry and pomp of the military and court life of this age are seen at their best in the pages of Froissart; and in Marlowe's "Edward the Second" a dramatic genius of the next period interprets a typical tragedy of the medieval contest between king and nobles. Drayton, Marlowe's contemporary, celebrates, in one of our greatest war-songs, the victory of Agincourt. In contrast with these pictures of the

more exciting sides of medieval life is the exquisite
series of portraits of typical English men and women
which give Chaucer's "Prologue" its unique place
among the works, literary and historical, of the time.

Malory, Tennyson, and Morris deal with parts of
the great Arthurian legend, the most wide-spread and
characteristic of the themes which entranced the imagination of the Middle Ages, and one which con-
tinues to attract the modern writer.   Romantic in tone,
historical in incident, Rossetti's poem on the death of
James I. of Scots is one of the most successful modern
attempts to render a medieval theme in ballad form;
yet its essential literary quality will be apparent at once
when it is compared with the popular tone of the
genuine traditional ballads.

Our list of the productions of the Renaissance naturally begins with Italy, the country in which the great
revival of interest in pagan antiquity first showed itself, and from which came in large measure the im-
pulse to throw off the traditional bonds that had fet-
tered the human spirit in the Middle Ages, and to
seek a fuller scope for individual development.   Machiavelli and Cellini represent respectively the political
and the artistic sides of the Italy of this period; and
the impression to be derived from them may be made
more distinct by Browning's pictures of the scholar,
the painter, and the worldly ecclesiastic, and by Webster's and Shelley's dramas, with their lurid light on
the passion and crime which reigned in much of the
courtly life of the time.   A pleasing contrast is af-
forded by Roper's Life of the saintly Sir Thomas
More, and by More's own "Utopia," with its vision
of a perfect society.   Later in the sixteenth century

came the struggle of Spain to subjugate the Netherlands, an incident of which forms the plot of Goethe's "Egmont." Sir Walter Raleigh, compiling in his prison his vast "History of the World," prefixed to it a long preface which gives us a most interesting conception of the attitude of an Englishman who had lived and thought not only upon the history of past times, but upon the whole problem of man's relation to God and the universe. About the same time, in Spain, the great novelist, Cervantes, was showing in his masterpiece how quickly the world was passing from under the domination of the chivalrous ideals of the previous age.

So far we have been enumerating documents representative of the secular Renaissance. But a religious revolution had also taken place, and in the works of Luther, of Calvin, and of Knox, we have a statement in the words of the leaders themselves of the fundamental principles of the Protestant Reformation.

In Science also a new beginning had been made. In the "Journeys" of Ambroise Paré we have, incidentally, a picture of the armies of the sixteenth century in the field, and also, of more importance to posterity, the beginnings of a new and more humane surgery. Copernicus introduced his revolutionary theory by which the sun took the place of the earth as the center of our system, and Columbus, Vespucci, and the great English navigators opened up the Western world and circumnavigated the globe.

In England itself this exploration of the West brought on the conflict with Spain celebrated with fiery patriotism in the poems by Drayton, Macaulay, and Tennyson. How Englishmen lived at home is told

in intimate detail in Harrison's "Description," and
more dramatically represented by Dekker, Jonson, and
Beaumont; while in Keats's lines we have a later poet
harking back to those literary triumphs which are perhaps the most permanent of the achievements of the
"spacious times of great Elizabeth."

In the seventeenth century we find ourselves in
what may be regarded as modern times, though the
picture of the plague in Manzoni's great novel still
suggests a period far remote from modern science.
In the "Areopagitica," however, Milton is arguing
for that freedom of the press which is a very living
question in many modern states; and in the poems
of Marvell and Scott we have echoes of the struggle
for constitutional liberty through which modern
Britain came into existence. Voltaire's "Letters" re-
flect not only the impressions derived by an acute
Frenchman from a visit to England, but describe
many important phases of the life and thought of the
eighteenth century. Burke's "Reflections" recall the
excesses through which some of the things which Voltaire envied the English were achieved by France; and
Goethe in his exquisite idyl, "Hermann and Dorothea,"
lets us hear the echoes of the great Revolution in the
quiet life of a German village. In Byron's famous
lyric we have a lament over the spirit of liberty not
yet reawakened in Greece. Throughout all these later
pieces there appear, more or less distinctly, evidences
of the gradual spread over the world of the struggle
for freedom and equality.

Of this struggle in America the records collected in
the "American Historical Documents" and the other
works here enumerated need no interpretation.

Subject and Author	Vol.	Page
Race and Language:		
Edward Augustus Freeman	28	235
Ancient Egypt:		
Herodotus, Egypt	33	1
The East in Patriarchal Times:		
The Book of Job	44	73
Ancient Greece: *Legendary*		
Homer, the Odyssey	22	9
Dramas of Æschylus	8	5
Sophocles	8	197
Euripides	8	287
Fall of Troy, Virgil's Æneid, Book II . .	13	103
Tennyson, Ulysses	42	1007
The Lotus-Eaters	42	1026
Landor, Death of Artemidora	41	926
Iphigeneia	41	927
Wordsworth, Laodamia	41	678
Ancient Greece: *Historic*		
Plato, The Apology of Socrates	2	3
Plutarch, Life of Pericles	12	36
Life of Themistocles	12	5
Life of Aristides	12	80
Life of Alcibiades	12	110
Life of Demosthenes	12	197
Ancient Rome: *Republican*		
Plutarch, Life of Coriolanus	12	152
Life of Cicero	12	225
Cicero, Letters and Treatises	9	7
Plutarch, Life of Cæsar	12	274
Life of Antony	12	334
Dryden, All for Love	18	21

Subject and Author	Vol.	Page
Ancient Rome: *Imperial*		
Pliny the Younger, Letters	9	195
Virgil, Æneid	13	75
Tennyson, To Virgil	42	1051
Marcus Aurelius, Meditations	2	193
Epictetus, Golden Thoughts	2	117
Germanic Peoples in Primitive Times:		
Tacitus, Germany	33	95
Song of the Volsungs	49	265
Beowulf	49	5
Ireland in Primitive Times:		
Destruction of Dá Derga's Hostel	49	211
The Early Christian Church:		
The Gospel according to Luke	44	357
The Acts of the Apostles	44	429
The Epistles to the Corinthians	45	501
St. Augustine, Confessions	7	5
Hymns of the Greek Church	45	553
Hymns of the Latin Church	45	558
The Mohammedan East:		
Koran	45	885
The Arabian Nights	16	17
Rubaiyat of Omar Khayyám	41	970
The Middle Ages:		
The Song of Roland	49	97
Voyages to Vinland	43	5
Dante, The Divine Comedy	20	5
Marlowe, Edward the Second	46	5
Froissart, Chronicles	35	5
Chaucer, Prologue to Canterbury Tales	40	11
Drayton, Agincourt	40	226
Malory, The Holy Grail	35	107

SUBJECT AND AUTHOR	VOL.	PAGE
THE MIDDLE AGES:		
Tennyson, Morte d'Arthur	42	1019
Galahad	42	1036
William Morris, Defence of Guinevere	42	1230
Rossetti, The King's Tragedy	42	1200
A Gest of Robyn Hode	40	130
Traditional Ballads, especially	40	51
The Battle of Otterburn	40	89
Chevy Chase	40	94
Johnie Armstrong	40	102
Kinmont Willie	40	109
THE RENAISSANCE:		
Machiavelli, The Prince	36	7
Macaulay, Machiavelli	27	381
Benvenuto Cellini, Autobiography	31	5
Browning, A Grammarian's Funeral	42	1126
Andrea del Sarto	42	1130
The Bishop Orders his Tomb	42	1117
Webster, The Duchess of Malfi	47	721
Shelley, The Cenci	18	281
Sir Thomas More, Utopia	36	143
Roper, Life of Sir T. More	36	93
Goethe, Egmont	19	247
Raleigh, Preface to History of the World	39	69
Cervantes, Don Quixote	14	19
Luther, Ninety-five Theses	36	265
Address to the German Nobility	36	276
Concerning Christian Liberty	36	353
Calvin, Dedication of the Institutes	39	29
Knox, Preface to History of the Reformation in Scotland	39	61
Paré, Journeys in Diverse Places	38	9
Copernicus, Dedication of Revolutions of Heavenly Bodies	39	55
Columbus, Letter Announcing Discovery of America	43	22

Subject and Author	Vol.	Page
The Renaissance:		
Amerigo Vespucci, Account of his First Voyage	43	29
Cabot, Discovery of North America	43	47
Sir H. Gilbert's Voyage to Newfoundland	33	271
Sir Francis Drake Revived	33	133
Drake's Famous Voyage Round the World	33	207
Drake's Great Armada	33	237
Ralegh, Discovery of Guiana	33	321
Drayton, To the Virginian Voyage	40	230
Macaulay, The Armada	41	940
Tennyson, The Revenge	42	1041
Harrison, Elizabethan England	35	229
Dekker, The Shoemaker's Holiday	47	447
Jonson, The Alchemist	47	521
Beaumont, Letter to Ben Jonson	40	328
Keats, The Mermaid Tavern	41	898
Modern Europe:		
Manzoni, I Promessi Sposi	21	7
Milton, Areopagitica	3	193
Marvell, Horatian Ode upon Cromwell's Return	40	381
Scott, Here's a Health to King Charles	41	773
Bonnie Dundee	41	770
Voltaire, Letters on the English	34	65
Burke, Reflections on the French Revolution	24	151
Goethe, Hermann and Dorothea	19	335
Byron, The Isles of Greece	41	833

(For the history of recent European thought, see under headings, "Science," "Religion and Philosophy," "Politics," "Education," and the various literary types.)

Subject and Author	Vol.	Page
AMERICA:		
First Charter of Virginia	43	51
And the later items in volume of American		
Historical Documents	43	5
Franklin, Autobiography	1	5
John Woolman, Journal	1	177
Dana, Two Years before the Mast	23	7
Bryant, The Death of Lincoln	42	1272
Emerson, Concord Hymn	42	1296
Boston Hymn	42	1313
Longfellow, Evangeline	42	1353
Paul Revere's Ride	42	1348
Whittier, Randolph of Roanoke	42	1416
Massachusetts to Virginia . . .	42	1419
Barbara Frietchie	42	1439
Holmes, Old Ironsides	42	1443
Lowell, The Present Crisis	42	1447
Ode Recited at Harvard Commemora-		
tion	42	1458
Abraham Lincoln	28	441
Whitman, War Poems	42	1483
Pioneers	42	1486
Poems on Death of Lincoln . . .	42	1497

B

RELIGION AND PHILOSOPHY

IN THIS division are represented the sacred writings of the chief religions of the world, and characteristic works of the most important philosophers, so far as these can be expected to be intelligible to readers without technical training in philosophy. Here, as elsewhere in The Harvard Classics, the interest and profit of the reader have been preferred to formal completeness; yet it has been possible to bring together a selection of the attempts of thinkers to solve the problems of life for twenty-five centuries, with surprisingly few important omissions.

In I. Λ. we noted the historical interest of the narrative setting of "The Book of Job." The speeches themselves show the Hebrew mind wrestling with the problem of reconciling the justice of God with the misfortunes of the righteous. "Ecclesiastes" consists mainly of a collection of pungent and, for the most part, pessimistic comments on life, interspersed with passages of a more inspiring nature, which may be due to a different author. Both books are marvels of literary beauty. "The Psalms" gave utterance to the religious emotions of the people of Israel through many generations, and have appealed to the devout of races and periods far beyond the limits of their origin.

Plato is at once a philosopher and a great man of

letters; and the three dialogues given here not only present some of the main ideas about conduct and the future world which he received from Socrates or developed himself, but also draw a distinct and attractive portrait of his master during the closing scenes of his life. The plays of the Greek tragedians, though ostensibly dramatic entertainments, deal profoundly and impressively with some of the vital questions of religion, as these presented themselves to the Greek mind.

In Marcus Aurelius and Epictetus we have the loftiest expression of the Stoic doctrine in its application to the conduct of life; and in the treatises of Cicero the working philosophy of a great lawyer and politician.

The "Sayings" of Confucius, like these Roman writings, are ethical rather than religious; and while to the Western mind they appear curiously concerned with ceremonial, they still appeal to us through their note of aspiration toward a lofty and disinterested scheme of life. Equally remote in their religious and philosophical background are the examples of Hindu and Buddhist teaching, but here again there is much that is inspiring in the moral ideals.

In the previous section, "The Gospel of Luke," "The Acts of the Apostles," and "The Epistles to the Corinthians" were regarded as giving the history of the founding of the Christian Church. Here they should be read as giving a statement of its principles as laid down by its Founder and His immediate followers. Its development after four centuries is shown in the "Confessions" of one of the greatest of the Fathers; and the height of medieval devoutness is beautifully

exhibited in "The Imitation of Christ," ascribed to
Thomas à Kempis, one of the most widely circulated books in the history of literature. The Hymns
of the Early Churches bring out those features of
Christian belief which obtained prominence in public
worship.

Mohammedanism, with its curious borrowings from
Hebrew and Christian scripture and tradition, is more
interesting as the religion of many millions of people
than as a source of spiritual inspiration. An interesting
comparison may be made between Omar Khayyám in
his relation to Mohammedanism and the author of
"Ecclesiastes" in his relation to Judaism.

With the Reformation opens a new chapter in the
history of religion, and the figures of Luther, Calvin,
and Knox appropriately represent militant Protestantism in Germany, Switzerland, and Scotland. Raleigh
is a Protestant layman, a man of action rather than a
theologian or philosopher, yet his "Preface" is a remark-
ably enlightening presentation of the attitude of a de-
tached thinker at the beginning of the seventeenth century. His poems, with those of Southwell, Habington, Rowlands, Herbert, Donne, Quarles, Vaughan,
Crashaw, Drummond, Wotton, Watts, Addison, and
Christopher Smart, and the collection of modern
hymns, still further express, with varieties of em-
phasis and shade of opinion, the more popular aspects of modern Christianity. In Walton's "Lives"
of George Herbert and John Donne, Christian ideals
are exhibited in the history of two men of strongly
marked character and lofty spirituality. Sir Thomas
Browne was a member of the Church of England and
a physician, and the splendid prose of his "Religio

Medici" conveys a quaint mixture of orthodoxy and independent thought. "The Pilgrim's Progress" is the great popular presentation of Puritan theology in imaginative form; and this theology is again the background of the great religious lyrics and epics of John Milton.

Roman Catholic thought on religion and life is brilliantly represented in the writings of Pascal, one of the most acute minds and most intensely religious spirits of his age. The "Thoughts," collected and arranged after his death, suffer from lack of sequence; but their fragmentary nature cannot disguise from the careful reader the astounding keenness of the intellect behind them.

In the "Fruits of Solitude" of William Penn, and in John Woolman's "Journal," we have a representation of the views and ideals of the Quakers, who contributed so important a stream of spiritual influence to the Colonial life of America.

Modern philosophy is often said to begin with Bacon, and, though the fresh attack upon the problems of the universe made in the seventeenth century can not be credited to any one person, Bacon as much as any has a right to be regarded as the herald of the new era. The prefatory documents listed here indicate not only the nature and scope of his intellectual ambitions, but present in considerable detail his program for the conquest of nature and his "new instrument" for the advancement of science. The "Essays" deal with a thousand points of practical philosophy; and "The New Atlantis" outlines his view of a model state and foreshadows the modern research university.

For philosophy in its more technical sense Descartes is more important than Bacon, and his influence on succeeding thought is more clearly traceable. Hobbes, Locke, Berkeley, and Hume carried on the quest for philosophical truth in England, and were able to express their views in language that is still intelligible to the ordinary man. Pope, in his "Essay on Man," put into polished and elegant verse, the more obvious principles of a group of thinkers of his day; but the ideas are more memorable on account of their quotable form than their profundity or subtlety.

Voltaire, writing on many aspects of English life, includes in his "Letters" a condensed account of the philosophy of Locke and the investigations of Newton. Rousseau in his "Discourse," one of the earliest of his writings, expounds the fundamentals of that social philosophy which he expanded later in the "Social Contract" and elsewhere, and which had so important a place among the influences leading up to the French Revolution. Lessing, clinging much closer to essential Christianity than Voltaire or Rousseau, elaborates in his "Education of the Human Race" the views he upheld in opposition to the less liberal theologians of Protestant Germany.

With Kant and his successors philosophy becomes more a professional subject, and with an increase in depth and subtlety it loses in breadth of appeal to the world at large. Yet the treatises mentioned in this list will yield to the reader who cares to apply his mind an idea of a view of ethics of immense possibilities of influence over his thought and conduct.

A large part of the remaining titles are of poems whose philosophical bearing it is scarcely necessary to

point out. More and more during the last hundred years poetry has been made the medium of serious thought on the problems of life; and if one wishes to learn what earnest and cultivated people have thought on such matters in our day and that of our fathers, as much is to be gained from the poets as from the professional metaphysicians or moralists. In Carlyle and Emerson we have two writers who can not be regarded as systematic philosophers, and who yet have been among the most influential of modern thinkers. Mill has a more definite place in the history of philosophy; but in his fascinating account of his own development, and in his essay "On Liberty," we need have no fear of technical jargon, and may find a clear picture of a mind finely representative of English thought in the middle of the nineteenth century, and an abundance of ideas capable of application to the problems of our own day.

Subject and Author	Vol.	Page
HEBREW: The Book of Job	44	73
Ecclesiastes	44	339
The Psalms	44	147
GREEK: Plato, Apology of Socrates	2	3
Phædo	2	45
Crito	2	31
The Greek Drama: Æschylus, Sophocles, Euripides	8	5
ROMAN: Marcus Aurelius, Meditations	2	193
Epictetus, Golden Thoughts	2	117
Cicero, On Friendship	9	7
On Old Age	9	45

Subject and Author	Vol.	Page
CHINESE: Confucius, Analects or Sayings . . .	44	5
HINDU: Bhagavad-Gîtâ, or Song Celestial . . .	45	799
Buddhist Writings	45	587
CHRISTIAN: *Primitive and Medieval*		
The Gospel of Luke	44	357
The Acts of the Apostles	44	429
The Epistles to the Corinthians	45	501
St. Augustine, Confessions	7	5
The Imitation of Christ	7	213
Hymns of the Early Churches	45	545
MOHAMMEDAN: The Koran	45	885
Rubaiyat of Omar Khayyám	41	970
CHRISTIAN: *Modern*		
Luther, Ninety-five Theses	36	265
Address to the German Nobility . .	36	276
Concerning Christian Liberty . . .	36	353
Calvin, Dedication of the Institutes of the Christian Religion	39	29
Knox, Preface to History of the Reformation in Scotland	39	61
Raleigh, Preface to History of the World . .	39	69
Poems	40	206
Southwell, The Burning Babe	40	222
Habington, Nox Nocti	40	258
Rowlands, Our Blessed Lady's Lullaby . .	40	261
Walton, Life of George Herbert	15	377
Herbert, Poems	40	351
Walton, Life of John Donne	15	327
Donne, Hymn to God the Father	40	311
Quarles, Poems	40	350
Vaughan, Poems	40	356
Crashaw, Saint Theresa	40	372
Drummond, St. John Baptist	40	335

Subject and Author	Vol.	Page
CHRISTIAN: *Modern*		
Wotton, Character of a Happy Life	40	295
Sir Thomas Browne, Religio Medici . . .	3	261
Bunyan, The Pilgrim's Progress	15	13
Milton, Ode on the Nativity	4	7
Ode on the Passion	4	24
Paradise Lost	4	89
Paradise Regained	4	363
Pascal, Thoughts	48	7
Minor Works	48	369
Penn, Fruits of Solitude	1	329
Watts, True Greatness	40	408
Addison, Hymn	40	410
Smart, Song to David	41	496
Woolman, Journal	1	177
Hymns of the Modern Churches	45	570
MODERN PHILOSOPHERS:		
Bacon, Procemium, Epistle Dedicatory, Preface and Plan of the Instauratio Magna	39	122
Preface to the Novum Organum . .	39	150
Essays	3	7
The New Atlantis	3	151
Descartes, Discourse on Method	34	5
Hobbes, On Man (Bk. I of the Leviathan) .	34	323
Locke, Some Thoughts on Education . . .	37	9
Berkeley, Three Dialogues	37	201
Pope, Essay on Man	40	417
Voltaire, Letters on the English	34	65
Rousseau, Discourse on the Causes of Inequality	34	167
Lessing, Education of the Human Race . .	32	195
Hume, Enquiry concerning Human Understanding	37	305
Kant, Fundamental Principles of the Metaphysic of Morals	32	32?

Subject and Author	Vol.	Page
MODERN PHILOSOPHERS:		
Kant, Transition from Popular Moral Philosophy to the Metaphysic of Morals . .	32	337
Wordsworth, Ode on Intimations of Immortality	41	609
Ode to Duty	41	665
Lines Written above Tintern Abbey	41	650
Character of a Happy Warrior . .	41	672
Shelley, Adonais	41	879
Written among the Euganean Hills	41	858
Mill, Autobiography	25	7
On Liberty	25	203
Carlyle, Characteristics	25	333
Emerson, Essays	5	5
Poems	42	1292
Tennyson, The Higher Pantheism	42	1038
Flower in the Crannied Wall .	42	1039
Wages	42	1039
Maud	42	1052
Crossing the Bar	42	1098
Thackeray, The End of the Play	42	1099
Browning, Prospice	42	1106
Abt Vogler	42	1144
Rabbi Ben Ezra	42	1148
Epilogue	42	1155
Emily Brontë, Last Lines	42	1156
The Old Stoic	42	1157
Clough, Poems	42	1165
Arnold, Rugby Chapel	42	1176
Dover Beach	42	1183
The Better Part	42	1184
The Last Word	42	1185
Henley, To R. T. H. B.	42	1258
Stevenson, The Celestial Surgeon	42	1261
Bryant, Thanatopsis	42	1262
Whittier, The Eternal Goodness	42	1414

C
EDUCATION

THE earlier discussions on education differ from most modern writings on the subject in one important respect: the author had his eye on the single youth, the son of a family of birth and wealth, who was to be educated alone; while the educational theorist of to-day, even when he is not dealing with popular elementary education, is usually concerned with institutions for training pupils in large groups. This distinction has inevitably a profound effect upon the nature of the principles laid down.

Montaigne, Locke, and Milton are all examples of this earlier kind of discussion. It is assumed that all resources are at command, and the only questions to be settled are the comparative value of subjects and the best order and method of learning. On these points the opinions of these men are still valuable; and all three, but especially Locke, give incidentally much information on the manners and state of culture of their times.

The five "Essays" by Bacon named here do not form an attempt to construct a scheme of education, but deal suggestively with single points of importance in the training of children. "The New Atlantis" describes in "Solomon's House" an elaborate institution for advancing knowledge, which anticipates in many respects the departments for research in modern universities.

Swift's so-called "Treatise" deals lightly with social rather than intellectual culture; and the chapter on the "Education of Women" by his contemporary, Defoe, shows how long it is since some views which we are apt to regard as entirely modern have been put forward.

Lessing's treatise is more philosophical than educational in the ordinary sense, being rather an interpretation of history as the record of the development of the race than a plan for the future. The letters in which Schiller discussed the "Æsthetic Education of Man" contain the essence of his views on art.

It is characteristic of American democracy that the lectures by Channing should be on the elevation of the laboring classes, and should take up an educational problem at the end of the social scale most remote from that where Montaigne and Locke found their interest.

Mill's "Autobiography" is an account of great interest of the education of a remarkable son by a remarkable father; and though containing much that has no direct bearing upon the training of the average child, it is valuable as showing what extraordinary results can be achieved under exceptional conditions.

Newman's discussion of "The Idea of a University" deals with the ultimate aims of university education, and some of the more important considerations affecting the means of attaining them. Carlyle's address, delivered at Edinburgh while he was Lord Rector of his own University, is a sort of summary of an old man's wisdom on questions of a student's use of his time and the choice of his reading. Ruskin's well-known lectures, "Sesame and Lilies," deal in very dif-

ferent, but equally characteristic fashion with similar topics.

In "Science and Culture," Huxley presents from the point of view of the scientist his side of the standing question of modern education: the comparative value of science and the classics as a means of culture.

Subject and Author	Vol.	Page
Montaigne, On the Institution and Education of Children	32	29
Bacon, Of Travel	3	48
Of Nature in Men	3	101
Of Custom and Education	3	103
Of Studies	3	128
Of Parents and Children	3	20
The New Atlantis	3	151
Milton, Tractate on Education	3	245
Locke, Some Thoughts on Education	37	9
Swift, Treatise on Good Manners and Good Breeding	27	106
Defoe, Education of Women	27	158
Lessing, On the Education of the Human Race	32	195
Schiller, Letters upon the Æsthetic Education of Man	32	221
Channing, On the Elevation of the Laboring Classes	28	321
Mill, Autobiography	25	7
Newman, The Idea of a University	28	31
Carlyle, Inaugural Address at Edinburgh University	25	375
Ruskin, Sesame and Lilies	28	95
Huxley, Science and Culture	28	217

D

SCIENCE

THE writings of ancient times on physical science are now mainly of historical and curious interest; but from Greek times have come down these two interesting formulas to which the name of Hippocrates is attached, which show how loftly a conception the ancient physician held of his function, and which form the basis of the professional ethics of the modern doctor.

The army surgeon is a modern official. In the sixteenth century, even an officer who wished medical or surgical attendance had to take his personal doctor with him, or trust to the quacks who swindled the rank and file. Paré was such a personal surgeon to several distinguished generals through many campaigns; and the account of his improvements in the treatment of wounds vies in interest with his description of the battles themselves.

Few single scientific discoveries have influenced the world so profoundly as that which showed that the earth was not the center of the universe. The treatise in which Copernicus put forth the new theory is filled with arguments which are often preposterous, so that for the true explanation of the motions of the heavenly bodies the book is practically useless. But from his "Dedication" we gather something of the spirit of the man who led the way in this momentous reform. The

"Principia" of Newton has immeasurably greater scientific value, but the reasoning is highly technical, so that the ordinary reader is glad to get the great physicist's own statement of the purpose and method of the work which first expounded the law of gravitation.

The papers by Harvey and Jenner are landmarks in the history of physiology and medicine, the one explaining for the first time the true theory of the circulation of the blood; the other putting forward the method of vaccination which has relieved the world of the scourge of smallpox.

Faraday was not only a great investigator but also a great teacher, and these two books by him are classical expositions of fundamental laws in physics and chemistry.

Dr Holmes's paper is an interesting scientific argument, which proved of immense value in saving life; it is also an inspiring instance of the courage of a young scientist in risking professional disaster by attacking the practices and prejudices of his colleagues.

The theories which lie behind Lord Lister's application of the antiseptic principle in surgery are expounded in the fascinating papers in which Pasteur makes the original argument for the germ theory of disease, and founds the science of bacteriology.

In the chapters included in the following list from Sir Charles Lyell's "Principles of Geology," he combats the notion that to explain the present condition of the earth it is necessary to assume a series of great catastrophes. A more comprehensive view of a modern geologist's theory of how the physical world arrived

at its present form is given in Geikie's essay on "Geographical Evolution."

The great German physicist, von Helmholtz, is here represented by a lecture on the fundamental principle of the conservation of energy, and one on the theory of glaciers, while his colleague in Britain, Sir William Thomson, Lord Kelvin, expounds the wave theory of light and the movement of the tides.

It was on the voyage of the "Beagle" that Darwin collected the material which suggested to him the great generalization later set forth in "The Origin of Species," and gave currency to a theory of development that has proved to be the most pervasive and influential force in the intellectual progress of modern times.

How enormously modern astronomical investigation has increased our notion of the universe, of which we form so minute a part, is expounded by Newcomb in his essay on "The Extent of the Universe."

Thus in the scientific section of these volumes the reader may gain from the pens of the leaders and discoverers themselves an idea of many of the most important conceptions in the sciences of Medicine, Surgery, Physiology, Biology, Bacteriology, Physics, Chemistry, Geology, and Astronomy.

Subject and Author	Vol.	Page
The Oath of Hippocrates	38	3
The Law of Hippocrates	38	4
Paré, Journeys in Diverse Places	38	9
Copernicus, Dedication of Revolutions of the Heavenly Bodies	39	55
Harvey, On the Motion of the Heart and Blood of Animals	38	63

Subject and Author	Vol.	Page
Newton, Preface to the Principia	39	157
Jenner, The Three Original Publications on Vaccination against Smallpox	38	153
Faraday, The Forces of Matter	30	5
The Chemical History of a Candle	30	89
Holmes, The Contagiousness of Puerperal Fever	38	235
Lister, On the Antiseptic Principle in the Practice of Surgery	38	271
Pasteur, The Physiological Theory of Fermentation	38	289
The Germ Theory and its Applications to Medicine and Surgery	38	382
On the Extension of the Germ Theory to the Etiology of Certain Common Diseases	38	390
Lyell, Prejudices which have Retarded the Progress of Geology	38	405
Uniformity in the Series of Past Changes in the Animate and Inanimate Worlds	38	419
Von Helmholtz, On the Conservation of Force	30	181
Ice and Glaciers	30	221
Darwin, The Voyage of the "Beagle"	29	11
The Origin of Species	11	25
Kelvin, The Wave Theory of Light	30	263
The Tides	30	287
Newcomb, The Extent of the Universe	30	325
Geikie, Geographical Evolution	30	339

E
POLITICS

FROM the point of view that "history is past politics," it is evident that such historical documents as those in the "Lives" of Plutarch and the "Letters" of Cicero and Pliny are also of value from the political point of view. Many of the problems of politics change their form rather than their essence from age to age, and in these records of the political struggles and principles of antiquity there are many illuminating parallelisms to the conditions of our own day. Even the contrast to modern democratic ideas of government which the theories of Machiavelli afford is suggestive; and in the institutions of Elizabethan England as described by William Harrison we may often find the germ of practices which persist here to-day.

More's "Utopia" and Bacon's "New Atlantis" have the value belonging to any sketch of ideal conditions drawn up by men of capacity and experience; and, with much that is fantastic, both books still afford considerable practical suggestion for political progress. Those of Bacon's "Essays" which touch political topics contain abundance of acute observations on the conduct of public men, though the advice is sometimes, but not always, more suited to forming politicians than statesmen.

Though dealing with the special subject of un-

licensed printing, Milton, in his "Areopagitica," handles with a noble eloquence many of the fundamental questions affecting free government. Defoe's pamphlet treats in ironical strain the situation during a later period in the progress of England towards freedom and equality—in this case, religious equality; while Voltaire, coming from France a few years later, expresses his admiration for English tolerance. Of Rousseau's "Discourse" we have already spoken (I. A).

"The Wealth of Nations" may be regarded as founding the modern science of political economy; and it remains the greatest general treatise on the subject. The present edition has been relieved of those passages which are out of date and no longer of value.

In Burke's eloquent "Reflections" we get the view taken by an English constitutionalist of the principles of the French Revolution while it was still in progress; and in his "Letter to a Noble Lord" a vivid glimpse of the workings of politics in England at the same period.

Mill's treatise "On Liberty" is a classical argument on the relation of the individual to the state.

The poetry of the nineteenth century contains much political as well as philosophical thinking; and the pieces by Goldsmith, Wordsworth, and Tennyson are favorable examples of the impassioned treatment of these themes in verse.

The interest and importance of the American Documents here collected are obvious; and a careful study of these alone will go far to give a basis for an intelligent understanding of contemporary politics.

Subject and Author	Vol.	Page
Plutarch, Lives of Greeks and Romans	12	5
Cicero, Letters	9	83
Pliny the Younger, Letters to Trajan	9	195
Machiavelli, The Prince	36	7
Macaulay, Machiavelli	27	381
More, Utopia	36	143
Harrison, Elizabethan England	35	229
Bacon, The New Atlantis	3	151
Essays: Of Unity in Religion, Of Great Place, Of Nobility, Of Seditions and Troubles, Of Empire, Of Counsel, Of Delays, Of Cunning, Of Innovations, Of Despatch, Of the True Greatness of Kingdoms and Estates, Of Plantations, Of Ambition, Of Usury, Of Negotiating, Of Followers and Friends, Of Suitors, Of Faction, Of Judicature, Of Vicissitudes of Things	3	7
Milton, Areopagitica	3	193
Defoe, The Shortest Way with Dissenters . . .	27	143
Voltaire, Letters on the English	34	65
Rousseau, Discourse on the Causes of Inequality .	34	167
Smith, The Wealth of Nations	10	9
Burke, Reflections on the French Revolution . . .	24	151
Letter to a Noble Lord	24	401
Goldsmith, The Deserted Village	41	521
Wordsworth, Political Sonnets	41	690
Tennyson, Locksley Hall	42	1009
Maud	42	1052
Sydney Smith, Fallacies of Anti-Reformers . . .	27	237
Mill, On Liberty	25	203
Emerson, Politics	5	249
Lowell, Democracy	28	464
The Present Crisis	42	1447
American Historical Documents, especially . . .	43	5
The First Charter of Virginia	43	51

SUBJECT AND AUTHOR	VOL.	PAGE
American Historical Documents:		
The Mayflower Compact	43	62
The Fundamental Orders of Connecticut . .	43	63
The Massachusetts Body of Liberties . . .	43	70
Winthrop, Arbitrary Government Described .	43	90
The Instrument of Government	43	113
Sir Henry Vane, a Healing Question . . .	43	126
Declaration of Rights	43	157
Declaration of Independence	43	160
Constitution of the United States	43	192
The Federalist, I and II	43	212
Opinion of Chief Justice Marshall . . .	43	222
Washington, First Inaugural Address . . .	43	241
Washington, Farewell Address	43	250
The Monroe Doctrine	43	296
Lincoln, Gettysburg Address	43	441

F

VOYAGES AND TRAVELS

THE story of travel has always held a general fascination; and little is needed to introduce to the reader such a list as follows. Beginning with the account of ancient Egypt by Herodotus, the collection gives the narratives of the early voyages to America of Leif Ericsson, Columbus, Amerigo Vespucci, and Cabot; the campaigns followed by the French surgeon, Ambroise Paré, in the sixteenth century; the voyages, partly for exploration, largely for plunder, of the great seamen of Elizabeth's time, Drake, Gilbert, and Raleigh; and, in striking contrast, John Eliot's "Brief Narrative" of his travels in the attempt to propagate the Gospel among the American Indians. Goldsmith's "Traveller" describes many scenes in eighteenth century Europe; and in Dana's absorbing "Two Years Before the Mast" we have the double interest of a picture of life on a sailing vessel two generations ago, and an admirable account of California as it was under the Spaniards, and before '49.

Darwin's "Voyage of the Beagle," apart from its scientific importance, is a highly interesting and modestly told story of exploration in remote seas. Emerson's "English Traits" is a penetrating description and criticism of England, its people and its institutions, as the American philosopher saw it in the middle of the nineteenth century.

SUBJECT AND AUTHOR	VOL.	PAGE
Herodotus, Egypt	33	5
Voyages to Vinland from Saga of Eric the Red	43	5
Paré, Journeys in Diverse Places	38	9
Columbus, Letter Announcing Discovery of America	43	22
Amerigo Vespucci, Account of his First Voyage	43	29
Cabot, Discovery of North America	43	47
Sir Francis Drake Revived	33	133
Drake's Famous Voyage Round the World	33	207
Drake's Great Armada	33	237
Sir Humphrey Gilbert's Voyage to Newfoundland	33	271
Raleigh, Discovery of Guiana	33	321
Eliot, Brief Narrative	43	147
Goldsmith, The Traveller	41	532
Dana, Two Years Before the Mast	23	7
Darwin, The Voyage of the "Beagle"	29	11
Emerson, English Traits	5	327

G

CRITICISM OF LITERATURE AND THE FINE ARTS

WILLIAM CAXTON, the first printer in England, took a much more personal interest in the productions of his press than does the modern publisher. He himself made several of the translations which he printed; and to other books he attached Prologues and Epilogues, which, if not quite literary criticism after the modern manner, are yet interesting indications of the qualities which made the works which Caxton selected for publication the favorite reading of the end of the Middle Ages.

Of the three critical writings selected from the sixteenth century, Montaigne's is a delightful talk on his personal tastes (see essay by Sainte-Beuve below); Sidney defends imaginative literature against the assaults of an extreme Puritan; and Spenser explains to his friend Raleigh the plan and purpose of "The Faerie Queene."

Shakespeare, as is well known, paid no attention to the printing of his plays; and it was left for two of his fellow actors to make the first collected edition of them, seven years after his death. The unique importance of the volume makes the address of its editors to the readers a matter of curious interest. Of more real significance are the opinions, friendly yet candid,

which Ben Jonson has left of his great fellow dramatist, and of his patron, Bacon.

But it is with Dryden that we come to the first English critic on a large scale; and in his discussions on
Chaucer and on Heroic Poetry we have him, both for
style and matter, at his best. Swift's "Advice" is
slighter, and, like all his work, displays his ironic temper. Fielding, in a prefatory chapter, defines and expounds his idea of a novel. Dr. Johnson's famous
essay on Shakespeare originally formed the Preface to
his edition of the plays; and it remains one of the most
important estimates of the genius of our greatest
writer. In the "Life of Addison," Johnson was dealing with a subject where his eighteenth century limitations hampered him less, and the result is a delightful
piece of appreciative criticism.

So far the criticism in this list has been wholly
literary. The next four writers are concerned with
æsthetic principles in general, with, perhaps, a special
interest in painting and sculpture. Goethe, in this man-
festo of a new periodical to be devoted to the Fine
Arts, gives impressively his view of the fundamentals
of artistic training. Schiller, on a more extensive
scale, treats of the cultivation of taste and the nature
of the pleasure to be derived from art; while Hume
and Burke deal with similar problems from different
points of view.

The "Prefaces" of Wordsworth and Hugo express
in different but equally characteristic terms the revolt of
the romantic poets of England and France respectively
against the classical conventions that dominated poetry
and the drama. Coleridge discourses in his own profound and often illuminating fashion on the essentials

of poetry, as does Shelley in his eloquent and philosophical "Defense." Those who know Shelley only as the most exquisite of lyric poets will find that this essay will increase enormously their respect for his intellectual power. In the essay "On the Tragedies of Shakespeare" Lamb utters some of the most penetrating criticism ever passed upon the tragedy of "King Lear," and presses to an extreme his view of the inferiority of the stage to the study for the enjoyment of Shakespeare.

Thackeray's lecture on Swift is a fine example of the biographical essay, and may be compared with Carlyle's estimate of Scott with interesting results. Both men deal more with character than style, and both care passionately for moral quality.

Walt Whitman's "Preface," like his poems, stands by itself, the outspoken plea for an astounding extension of the limits of form and matter in poetry. His poems in the third volume of "English Poetry" in The Harvard Classics should be read in connection with this "Preface."

Sainte-Beuve is generally placed at the head of European criticism in the nineteenth century; and the two papers here given are good examples of his manner. Renan, one of the most eloquent of modern writers in any country, discourses on "The Poetry of the Celtic Races" to which he himself belonged. Mazzini, purest of patriots, is represented by a paper which shows his fine power of generalization and of taking large views. An Italian nationalist in feeling, Mazzini was continental in the range of his intellect. Taine's famous "Introduction" expounds his formula for explaining the characteristics of a literature. What-

ever objections may be raised to his theory, there is no question of the brilliance of the presentation.

Few critical writings of our own day have influenced the study of poetry so much as this of Matthew Arnold's. It is an excellent example of his style, and exhibits both the strength and the weakness of his critical thinking.

"Sesame and Lilies" consists of two lectures, largely hortatory, but incidentally containing some notable criticism. Bagehot, best known as a writer on finance, appears here as a specimen of a strong non-literary intellect applying itself to the discussion of a literary topic. At the opposite extreme is the paper in which Poe, a master of the technical side of his art, treats of what he regards as its essence. In three essays, Emerson discourses suggestively, if unsystematically, on "The Poet," on "Beauty," and on "Literature." Finally, in Stevenson's essay on "Samuel Pepys," one of the most expert of literary craftsmen of modern times sketches the personality of the writer who wrote the most remarkable "Diary" in English Literature.

SUBJECT AND AUTHOR	VOL.	PAGE
Caxton, Prologue and Epilogue to the Histories of Troy	39	5
Epilogue to Dictes and Sayings of the Philosophers	39	10
Prologue to the Golden Legend	39	14
Prologue to Caton	39	15
Epilogue to Æsop	39	18
Proem to Chaucer's Canterbury Tales	39	19
Prologue to Malory's King Arthur	39	21
Prologue to Virgil's Eneydos	39	25
Montaigne, Of Books	32	89

Subject and Author	Vol.	Page
Sidney, Defense of Poetry	27	7
Spenser, Prefatory Letter to Sir Walter Raleigh on the Faerie Queene	39	64
Heminge and Condell, Preface to the First Folio Edition of Shakespeare's Plays	39	155
Jonson, On Shakespeare	27	59
On Bacon	27	60
To the Memory of Mr. William Shakespeare	40	308
Dryden, Preface to Fables (On Chaucer)	39	160
Dedication of the Æneis (On Heroic Poetry)	13	5
Swift, Advice to a Young Poet	27	112
Fielding, Preface to Joseph Andrews (On the Comic Epic in Prose)	39	184
Johnson, Preface to Shakespeare	39	218
Life of Addison	27	165
Goethe, Introduction to the Propyläen (On Fine Art)	39	264
Schiller, Letters upon the Æsthetic Education of Man	32	221
Hume, On the Standard of Taste	27	215
Burke, On Taste	24	11
On the Sublime and Beautiful	24	29
Wordsworth, Prefaces to Various Volumes of Poems	39	281
Appendix to Lyrical Ballads	39	307
Essay Supplementary to Preface	39	327
Coleridge, On Poesy or Art	27	269
Lamb, On the Tragedies of Shakespeare	27	313
Shelley, A Defence of Poetry	27	345
Hugo, Preface to "Cromwell" (On Romanticism)	39	354
Thackeray, Jonathan Swift	28	5
Carlyle, Sir Walter Scott	25	409
Inaugural Address (On Books and Reading)	25	375
Whitman, Preface to Leaves of Grass	39	409
Sainte-Beuve, Montaigne	32	109
What is a Classic?	32	126
Renan, The Poetry of the Celtic Races	32	143

Subject and Author	Vol.	Page
Mazzini, Byron and Goethe	32	399
Taine, Introduction to History of English Literature	39	433
Arnold, The Study of Poetry	28	65
Ruskin, Sesame and Lilies	28	95
Bagehot, John Milton	28	171
Poe, The Poetic Principle	28	383
Emerson, The Poet	5	167
Beauty	5	307
Literature	5	449
Stevenson, Samuel Pepys	28	295

CLASS II

O F the large variety of literary types represented in The Harvard Classics, only a few of the more prominent have been selected for classification here. Others stand already grouped in the volumes: for, example, the three volumes of English Poetry, along with the works of Milton and Burns, contain most of the Lyric Poetry in the collection; and the Prefaces regarded as independent documents, are in one volume. Still others, such as Allegory, Oratory, the Dialogue, occur in the lists made up according to subject matter; and readers interested in these as forms can easily collect them from the Tables of Contents and the General Index.

A

DRAMA

In dramatic literature the palm of supremacy lies between Greece and England, and it is natural that these two countries should be most fully represented here. Both countries at a culminating point in their history expressed themselves in this form, and much of the intellectual and imaginative vitality of the Age of Pericles in Greece and the Age of Elizabeth in England can be apprehended from these dramas. Eight of the most distinguished masterpieces of the

other countries of Europe have been added; so that the present list represents not unworthily the best in this form that the world has produced.

These thirty-seven plays exhibit a great variety of dramatic form—classical and romantic tragedy, satirical and romantic comedy, chronicle history, masque, and cantata. No less varied are the themes; from gods to beggars all types of character appear, and every variety of human motive, human effort, and human suffering is shown. No other literary form could present in so few pages so just and so impressive a reflection of the pageant of human life.

SUBJECT AND AUTHOR	VOL.	PAGE
GREEK : Æschylus, Prometheus Bound	8	156
Agamemnon	8	5
The Libation-Bearers	8	71
The Furies	8	115
Sophocles, Œdipus the King	8	197
Antigone	8	243
Euripides, Hippolytus	8	287
The Bacchæ	8	349
Aristophanes, The Frogs	8	419
ENGLISH : Marlowe, Doctor Faustus	19	199
Edward the Second	46	5
Shakespeare, Hamlet	46	87
King Lear	46	203
Macbeth	46	305
The Tempest	46	379
Dekker, The Shoemaker's Holiday	47	447
Jonson, The Alchemist	47	521
Beaumont and Fletcher, Philaster	47	639
Webster, The Duchess of Malfi	47	721
Massinger, A New Way to Pay Old Debts .	47	819

Subject and Author	Vol.	Page
English: Milton, Comus	4	46
Samson Agonistes	4	418
Dryden, All for Love	18	21
Sheridan, The School for Scandal	18	105
Goldsmith, She Stoops to Conquer	18	203
Burns, The Jolly Beggars	6	129
Shelley, The Cenci	18	281
Byron, Manfred	18	403
Browning, A Blot in the 'Scutcheon	18	357
Spanish: Calderon, Life is a Dream	26	5
French: Corneille, Polyeucte	26	71
Racine, Phædra	26	125
Molière, Tartuffe	26	189
German: Lessing, Minna von Barnhelm	26	287
Goethe, Faust	19	21
Egmont	19	247
Schiller, Wilhelm Tell	26	369

B

BIOGRAPHY AND LETTERS

MOST of the titles in this list have already been the subject of comment; those that remain speak for themselves. Here are a number of records of actual human lives, all of them of notable people, chosen either for their representative or for their intrinsic value. Some of these records are by skilled biographers like Plutarch; in other cases, by letters, or confessions, or in set narratives, the story is told by the man himself; still others are summaries and estimates rather than detailed biographies. Perhaps the formal autobiographies are the most interesting and significant of all; and of these the personal revelations of St. Augustine, of Benvenuto Cellini, of Benjamin Franklin, and of John Stuart Mill stand in the first rank.

SUBJECT AND AUTHOR	VOL.	PAGE
Plutarch, Life of Themistocles	12	5
Pericles	12	36
Aristides	12	80
Alcibiades	12	110
Demosthenes	12	197
Coriolanus	12	152
Cicero	12	225
Cæsar	12	274
Antony	12	334

Subject and Author	Vol.	Page
Cicero, Letters	9	83
Pliny the Younger, Letters	9	195
St. Augustine, Confessions	7	5
Benvenuto Cellini, Autobiography	31	5
Roper, Life of Sir Thomas More	36	93
Walton, Life of Dr. Donne	15	327
Life of George Herbert	15	377
Johnson, Life of Addison	27	165
Burke, Letter to a Noble Lord	24	401
Franklin, Autobiography	1	5
Woolman, Journal	1	177
Macaulay, Machiavelli	27	381
Thackeray, Jonathan Swift	28	5
Carlyle, Sir Walter Scott	25	409
Mill, Autobiography	25	7
Lowell, Abraham Lincoln	28	441
Stevenson, Samuel Pepys	28	295

C

ESSAYS

THERE is almost no limit to the variety of theme which may be treated in the essay, and few rules can be laid down to regulate its form. Montaigne, who may be said to have originated this type of literature, remains one of the greatest masters of it; and in the specimens from his work in the present list one can find the ease and grace and the pleasant flavor of personal intimacy which constitute much of its charm.

A large proportion of these essays deal with books, and of these something has already been said in the section on Criticism. Some, like those of Milton, Swift, Defoe, Newman, and Huxley, fall also under the heading of Education. A few treat of political matters; such are those of Sydney Smith, Mill, and Lowell. Others, such as some of Montaigne's, Ruskin's, Carlyle's, Emerson's, and Stevenson's, deal with matters of conduct, though not in the formal manner of the ethical philosopher. Bacon's "Essays" are concerned with so great a variety of subjects that classification is difficult; but the largest group form a sort of handbook of the principles on which success in public life was achieved in his time. Yet these more severe themes are mingled with others of more charm, where he chats pleasantly on an ideal palace or garden, or on the contriving of courtly entertainments.

Of all prose forms, the essay is that which gives most scope for pure expression of personality. Those in the present list which rank highest as essays do so, not by virtue of the weight of their opinions, or arguments, or information, but by the spontaneity with which the author gives utterance to his mood or fancy. Thus the delightful essay of Cowley "Of Agriculture" is hardly to be recommended as a guide to farming; but as a quarter of an hour of graceful conversation it is charming. Hazlitt, Leigh Hunt, Lamb, De Quincey, Thoreau, and Stevenson (in "Truth of Intercourse") all exhibit this individual quality, and reveal personalities of different kinds and degrees of attractiveness, but none without a high degree of interest.

SUBJECT AND AUTHOR	VOL.	PAGE
Montaigne, That We Should not Judge of our Happiness until after our Death . . .	32	5
That to Philosophize is to Learn how to Die	32	9
Of the Institution and Education of Children	32	29
Of Friendship	32	74
Of Books	32	89
Sidney, Defense of Poetry	27	7
Bacon, Essays	3	7
Milton, Tractate on Education	3	245
Cowley, Of Agriculture	27	65
Dryden, Preface to Fables	39	160
Dedication of the Æneis	13	5
Addison, Westminster Abbey	27	82
Steele, The Spectator Club	27	89
Swift, Hints towards an Essay on Conversation . .	27	97
On Good Manners and Good Breeding . .	27	106
A Letter of Advice to a Young Poet . . .	27	112

Subject and Author	Vol.	Page
Swift, On the Death of Esther Johnson (Stella) .	27	131
Defoe, The Shortest Way with Dissenters . . .	27	143
The Education of Women	27	158
Fielding, Preface to Joseph Andrews	39	184
Johnson, Preface to Shakespeare	39	218
Preface to English Dictionary	39	191
Life of Addison	27	165
Hume, On the Standard of Taste	27	215
Burke, On Taste	24	11
Goethe, Introduction to the Propyläen	39	264
Sydney Smith, Fallacies of Anti-Reformers . . .	27	237
Wordsworth, Preface to Various Volumes of Poems	39	281
Appendix to Lyrical Ballads . . .	39	307
Essay Supplementary to Preface . .	39	327
Coleridge, On Poesy or Art	27	269
Hazlitt, On Persons One would Wish to have Seen .	27	281
Leigh Hunt, Deaths of Little Children	27	299
On the Realities of Imagination . .	27	304
Lamb, On the Tragedies of Shakespeare	27	313
De Quincey, Levana and Our Ladies of Sorrow . .	27	335
Shelley, A Defence of Poetry	27	345
Channing, On the Elevation of the Laboring Classes	28	321
Hugo, Preface to Cromwell	39	354
Macaulay, Machiavelli	27	381
Sainte-Beuve, Montaigne	32	109
What is a Classic?	32	126
Thackeray, Jonathan Swift	28	5
Renan, The Poetry of the Celtic Races	32	143
Mazzini, Byron and Goethe	32	399
Newman, The Idea of a University	28	31
Arnold, The Study of Poetry	28	65
Ruskin, Sesame and Lilies	28	95
Taine, Introduction to the History of English Literature	39	433
Bagehot, John Milton	28	171
Poe, The Poetic Principle	28	383

Subject and Author	Vol.	Page
Carlyle, Characteristics	25	333
Sir Walter Scott	25	409
Whitman, Preface to Leaves of Grass	39	409
Emerson, Essays	5	5
English Traits	5	327
Mill, On Liberty	25	203
Huxley, Science and Culture	28	217
Freeman, Race and Language	28	235
Thoreau, Walking	28	407
Lowell, Abraham Lincoln	28	441
Democracy	28	464
Stevenson, Truth of Intercourse	28	287
Samuel Pepys	28	295

D

NARRATIVE POETRY AND PROSE FICTION

IN this section we have the largest proportion of what frankly professes to be the literature of entertainment. All these titles belong to works which are in the first place good stories; and most of them have lived largely by virtue of this quality. They come from all centuries within the historic period, and from all the countries within our range. They deal with war and peace, love and hate, gods and men and animals, angels and demons, historic fact, modern observation, and pure fancy; some mean no more than they seem to—simple tales of the action and suffering of men; others carry mystical significations hidden under the surface.

But, though they may profess no more than a power to entertain, they, in fact, do far more for us. Each of these tales, in proportion to its truth to human nature and the effectiveness with which it is told, helps to make us more fully acquainted with our kind, broadens our sympathies, deepens our insight, serves us, in fact, as a kind of experience obtained at second hand. No less than the most weighty philosophy or the most informing history or science, then, do these stories in prose and poetry deserve their place among the essential instruments of mental and moral culture.

Subject and Author	Vol.	Page
Homer, The Odyssey	22	9
Virgil, The Æneid	13	75
Æsop's Fables	17	9
Beowulf	49	5
The Song of Roland	49	97
The Song of the Volsungs	49	265
The Destruction of Dá Derga's Hostel	49	211
The Arabian Nights	16	17
Dante, The Divine Comedy	20	5
Chaucer, Prologue to the Canterbury Tales	40	11
The Nun's Priest's Tale	40	35
The Gest of Robyn Hode	40	130
Traditional Ballads	40	51
Malory, The Holy Grail	35	107
Cervantes, Don Quixote	14	19
Drayton, Agincourt	40	226
To the Virginian Voyage	40	230
Milton, Paradise Lost	4	89
Paradise Regained	4	363
Bunyan, The Pilgrim's Progress	15	13
Addison, The Vision of Mirza	27	77
Steele, The Spectator Club	27	89
Goethe, Hermann and Dorothea	19	335
Cowper, The Diverting History of John Gilpin	41	559
Burns, Tam o' Shanter	6	411
Manzoni, I Promessi Sposi	21	7
Wordsworth, Michael	41	630
Ruth	41	622
Laodamia	41	678
Coleridge, The Ancient Mariner	41	698
Christabel	41	726
Love	41	721
Scott, Rosabelle	41	766
Lochinvar	41	769
Hogg, Kilmeny	41	774
Byron, The Prisoner of Chillon	41	821

Subject and Author	Vol.	Page
Byron, The Destruction of Sennacherib	41	804
Campbell, Lord Ullin's Daughter	41	792
Battle of the Baltic	41	798
Hohenlinden	41	800
Keats, The Eve of St. Agnes	41	907
Landor, The Death of Artemidora	41	926
Iphigeneia	41	927
Grimm, Household Tales	17	51
Andersen, Tales	17	237
Tennyson, Maud	42	1052
Morte d'Arthur	42	1019
The Lady of Shalott	42	997
The Revenge	42	1041
Rizpah	42	1046
Locksley Hall	42	1009
Browning, My Last Duchess	42	1115
How They Brought the Good News . .	42	1107
Macaulay, The Armada	41	940
D. G. Rossetti, The King's Tragedy	42	1200
C. Rossetti, In the Round Tower at Jhansi . . .	42	1229
W. Morris, The Defence of Guinevere	42	1230
Dobell, The Ballad of Keith of Ravelston . . .	42	1160
Poe, The Raven	42	1276
Longfellow, Evangeline	42	1353
The Wreck of the "Hesperus" . . .	42	1321
Paul Revere's Ride	42	1348
Whittier, Randolph of Roanoke	42	1416
Barclay of Ury	42	1424
Maud Muller	42	1427
Skipper Ireson's Ride	42	1434
The Pipes of Lucknow	42	1437
Barbara Frietchie	42	1439
Lowell, The Courtin'	42	1455
Lanier, The Revenge of Hamish	42	1474

AN INDEX TO THE FIRST LINES
OF POEMS, SONGS AND CHORUSES,
HYMNS AND PSALMS

INDEX TO THE FIRST LINES	VOL.	PAGE
A batter'd, wreck'd old man	42	1506
A book was writ of late called Tetrachordon . .	4	81
A chieftain to the Highlands bound	41	792
A feeling of sadness and longing	28	394
A fig for those by law protected	6	139
A flock of sheep that leisurely pass by	41	696
A garden is a lovesome thing, God wot	42	1195
A good sword and a trusty hand	42	1157
A grief without a pang, void, dark, and drear . .	25	89
A guid New-Year I wish thee, Maggie	6	155
A head, pure, sinless quite of brain and soul . . .	6	343
A heavy heart, Belovèd, have I borne	41	960
A high hall is there	49	318
A Highland lad my love was born	6	133
A hundred, a thousand to one; even so	42	1229
A hundred thousand cycles vast	45	591
A king there was once reigning	19	86
A lassie all alone, was making her moan . . .	6	512
A late lark twitters from the quiet skies	42	1257
A little onward lend thy guiding hand	4	418
A man in prosperity resembleth a tree	16	213
A may of all mays	49	422
A mighty fortress is our God	45	570
A million emeralds break from the ruby-budded lime	42	1057
A moody child and wildly wise	5	167
A pick-axe and a spade, a spade	46	182
A plenteous place is Ireland for hospitable cheer .	41	947

73

Index to the First Lines	Vol.	Page
A povre widwe somdel stope in age	40	35
A prince can mak' a belted knight	28	86
A robe of seeming truth and trust	6	101
A rose-bud by my early walk	6	302
A School for Scandal! tell me, I beseech you . .	18	109
A simple child	41	683
A slave to Love's unbounded sway	6	590
A slumber did my spirit seal	41	688
A sweet disorder in the dress	40	345
A voice by the cedar tree	42	1060
A weary lot is thine, fair maid	41	761
A wet sheet and a flowing sea	41	803
A widow bird sate mourning for her Love . . .	41	870
A wise priest knows he now must reap	45	687
Abide with me! fast falls the eventide	45	580
Abou Ben Adhem (may his tribe increase) . . .	41	893
Absence, hear thou my protestation	40	321
Abstain from censure; for it will strengthen the censured	16	11
Accuse me not, beseech thee, that I wear . . .	41	956
Adieu! a heart-warm fond adieu	6	225
Adieu, farewell earth's bliss	40	265
Admiring Nature in her wildest grace	6	291
Adopted in God's family, and so	15	359
Adown winding Nith I did wander	6	500
Ae day, as Death, that gruesome care	6	64
Ae fond kiss, and then we sever	6	455
Afar the illustrious Exile roams	6	306
Afflicted regents of my soul	31	246
Again rejoicing Nature sees	6	200
Again the silent wheels of time	6	267
Again yourselves compose	5	207
Ah, broken is the golden bowl! the spirit flown forever	42	1273
Ah, Chloris! could I now but sit	40	392
Ah, Chloris, since it may not be . . . . . ○ .	6	535
Ah! County Guy, the hour is nigh	41	760
Ah, did you once see Shelley plain	42	1124
Ah, rich in sorrow thou	19	151
Ah, sun-flower! weary of time	41	598
Ah, wasteful woman!—she who may	28	148

INDEX TO THE FIRST LINES	VOL.	PAGE
Ah, what avails the sceptred race	41	922
Ah, woe is me, my mother dear	6	25
Airly Beacon, Airly Beacon	42	1101
Alas, 'tis true I have gone here and there . . .	40	286
Alexis, here she stayed; among these pines . . .	40	338
All along the valley, stream that flashest white . .	42	1006
All hail, inexorable lord	6	203
All in the Downs the fleet was moor'd	40	412
All people that on earth do dwell	45	551
A' the lads o' Thorniebank	6	298
All they who thoughtless are, nor heed	45	705
All things are hush'd as Nature's self lay dead . .	39	340
All thoughts, all passions, all delights	41	721
All villain as I am, a damnèd wretch	6	23
A' ye wha live by sowps o' drink	6	226
All-conquering have I now become, all-knowing . .	45	740
All's over, then: does truth sound bitter	42	1111
Altho' he has left me for greed o' the siller . . .	6	440
Altho' my back be at the wa'	6	191
Altho' my bed were in yon muir	6	25
Altho' thou maun never be mine	6	590
Although the Cross could not here Christ detain .	15	360
Amang the trees where humming bees	6	511
Amidst the silence of the darkest night	14	348
Among the heathy hills and ragged woods . . .	6	296
An honest man here lies at rest	6	53
An somebody were come again	6	367
An old man bending I come among new faces . .	42	1491
An ye had been whare I hae been	6	381
Ance crowdie, twice crowdie	6	581
Ance mair I hail thee, thou gloomy December . .	6	456
An' Charlie, he's my darling	6	522
And I'll kiss thee yet, yet	6	31
And is this—Yarrow?—This the stream	41	644
And maun I still on Menie doat	6	200
An' O for ane an' twenty, Tam	6	441
An' O my Eppie, my jewel, my Eppie	6	369
And therefore if to love can be desert, I am not all unworthy	41	954
And thou art dead, as young and fair	41	805
And will he not come again	46	172

INDEX TO THE FIRST LINES	VOL.	PAGE
And wilt thou have me fashion into speech . . .	41	955
And wilt thou leave me thus	40	195
And ye shall walk in silk attire	41	593
And yet, because thou overcomest so	41	956
And yet I cannot reprehend the flight	40	224
Anna, thy charms my bosom fire	6	326
Answer me when I call, O God of my righteousness	44	149
Apples were they with which we were beguiled . .	15	270
Ariel to Miranda:—Take	41	870
Arms, and the man I sing, who, forc'd by fate . .	13	75
Art thou pale for weariness	41	870
Art thou poor, yet hast thou golden slumbers? . .	40	326
Art thou weary, art thou languid	45	556
Artemidora! Gods invisible	41	926
As a huge stone is sometimes seen to lie	39	319
As cauld a wind as ever blew	6	453
As down the burn they took their way	6	504
As father Adam first was fooled	6	62
As flowers in rich profusion piled	45	770
As Heaven and Earth are fairer far	5	222
As I cam by Crochallan	6	268
As I gaed down the water-side	6	377
As I gaed up by yon gate-end	6	534
As I in hoary winter's night	40	222
As I stood by yon roofless tower	6	512
As I stood by yon roofless tower	6	513
As I was a-wand'ring ae morning in spring . . .	6	26
As I was walking all alane	40	75
As I was walking up the street	6	581
As it fell upon a day	40	290
As Mailie, an' her lambs thegither	6	43
As oft as she names Phaedria, you retort . . .	9	132
As on the banks of winding Nith	6	435
As one that for a weary space has lain	22	7
As ships, becalmed at eve, that lay	42	1167
As slow our ship her foamy track	41	841
As sunbeams stream through liberal space . . .	42	1305
As Tam the chapman on a day	6	63
As the hart panteth after the water brooks . . .	44	198
As virtuous men pass mildly away	15	342
As virtuous men pass mildly away	40	312

Index to the First Lines	Vol.	Page
As well might corn, as verse, in cities grow . .	27	70
As when a wretch, who, conscious of his crime . .	24	32
As when it happeneth that some lovely town . .	40	338
As when the laboring Sun hath wrought his track .	3	297
As when 'tis said, 'The tree bears fruit'	45	699
As yielding wax the artist's skill commands . . .	9	317
Ascribe unto Jehovah, O ye sons of the mighty . .	44	178
Ask me no more where Jove bestows	40	361
Ask not the cause why sullen Spring	40	397
Ask why God made the gem so small	6	429
At Brownhill we always get dainty good cheer . .	6	437
At Flores in the Azores, Sir Richard Grenville lay .	42	1041
At the corner of Wood Street, when daylight appears	41	671
At the last day, men shall wear	5	301
At the last, tenderly	42	1508
At the mid hour of night, when stars are weeping, I fly	41	843
At the midnight in the silence of the sleep-time . .	42	1155
Attend, all ye who list to hear our noble England's praise	41	940
Auld chuckie Reekie's sair distrest	6	281
Auld comrade dear, and brither sinner	6	353
Avenge, O Lord, thy slaughtered Saints, whose bones	4	86
Awake, Aeolian lyre, awake	40	465
Awake, awake, my Lyre	40	374
Awake, my St. John! leave all meaner things . .	40	418
Away! the moor is dark beneath the moon . . .	41	877
Awa' Whigs, awa'	6	381
Awa' wi' your belles and your beauties	6	500
Awa' wi' your witchcraft o' Beauty's alarms . . .	6	586
Ay, flattering fortune, look you never so fair . .	36	130
Ay, tear her tattered ensign down	42	1443
Back and side go bare, go bare	40	192
Balow, my babe, lie still and sleep	40	189
Bannocks o' bear meal	6	523
Bards of Passion and of Mirth	41	896
Be merciful unto me, O God, be merciful unto me .	44	216
Be merciful unto me, O God; for man would swallow me up	44	215

INDEX TO THE FIRST LINES	VOL.	PAGE
Be not dismayed, thou little flock	45	572
Be your words made, good Sir, of Indian ware . .	40	216
Bear, lady nightingale above	19	81
Beat! beat! drums!—blow! bugles! blow	42	1484
Beauteous Rosebud, young and gay	6	350
Beautiful Evelyn Hope is dead	42	1120
Beauty like hers is genius. Not the call	42	1226
Beauty sat bathing by a spring	40	203
Beauty, sweet Love, is like the morning dew . .	40	225
Because I feel that, in the Heavens above . . .	42	1286
Because the few with signal virtue crowned . . .	42	1098
Because thou hast the power and own'st the grace .	41	966
Because you have thrown off your Prelate Lord .	4	82
Beer bring I to thee	49	321
Before the starry threshold of Jove's court . . .	4	46
Behind yon hills where Lugar flows	6	49
Behold, bless ye Jehovah, all ye servants of Jehovah	44	319
Behold her, single in the field	41	670
Behold, how fitly are the stages set	15	298
Behold, how good and how pleasant it is . . .	44	319
Behold, my love, how green the groves	6	538
Behold the hour, the boat, arrive	6	456
Behold the hour, the boat, arrive	6	503
Being your slave, what should I do but tend . . .	40	279
Belovèd, my Belovèd, when I think	41	958
Belovèd, thou hast brought me many flowers . .	41	968
Below thir stanes lie Jamie's banes	6	62
Beneath these fruit-tree boughs that shed . . .	41	657
Best and Brightest, come away	41	866
Between the dark and the daylight	42	1347
Beyond thee, dearie, beyond thee, dearie	6	427
Bid me to live, and I will live	40	346
Bird of the wilderness	41	785
Birds in the high Hall-garden	42	1068
Bless Jehovah, O my soul	44	276
Bless Jehovah, O my soul	44	277
Bless Jesus Christ, O Cardoness	6	533
Blessed are they that are perfect in the way . . .	44	299
Blessed be Jehovah, my rock	44	330
Blessed is every one that feareth Jehovah . . .	44	315
Blessed is he that considereth the poor	44	196

Index to the First Lines	Vol.	Page
Blessed is he whose transgression is forgiven . .	44	182
Blessed is the man that walketh not in the counsel of the wicked	44	147
Bless'd be the day that I began	15	198
Blessings on thee, little man	42	1431
Blest be M'Murdo to his latest day	6	496
Blest pair of Sirens, pledges of Heaven's joy . .	4	41
Blow, blow, thou winter wind	40	273
Blythe, blythe, and merry was she	6	301
Blythe hae I been on yon hill	6	493
Bonie lassie, will ye go	6	292
Bonie wee thing, cannie wee thing	6	428
Bonnie Kilmeny gaed up the glen	41	774
Borders of kohl enhance the witchery of her glance	16	381
Borgia, thou once wert almost too august . . .	41	929
Bow down thine ear, O Jehovah, and answer me .	44	256
Braw, braw lads on Yarrow-braes	6	481
Break, break, break	42	1006
Brief life is here our portion	45	560
Bright Star! would I were steadfast as thou art .	41	922
Brightest and best of the sons of the morning . .	45	578
Bring the bowl which you boast	41	773
Build me straight, O worthy Master	42	1332
Burly, dozing humble-bee	42	1297
Busk ye, busk ye, my bonnie, bonnie bride . . .	41	586
But do not let us quarrel any more	42	1130
But, knowing now that they would have her speak .	42	1230
But lately seen in gladsome green	6	538
But only three in all God's universe	41	950
But rarely seen since Nature's birth	6	589
But souls that of his own good life partake . .	5	137
But warily tent when ye come to court me . . .	6	499
But your allowance, and in that our all	47	899
Buy braw troggin frae the banks o' Dee	6	587
By all I lov'd, neglected and forgot	6	345
By Allah! good sir, I was not a robber	16	137
By Allan stream I chanc'd to rove	6	498
By cool Siloam's shady rill	45	577
By love, and by beauty, by law, and by duty . .	6	369
By Oughtertyre grows the aik	6	302
By our first strange and fatal interview	27	284

Index to the First Lines	Vol.	Page
By the cross, on which suspended	45	565
By the rivers of Babylon	44	323
By the rude bridge that arched the flood	42	1296
By what word's power, the key of paths untrod . .	42	1225
By yon Castle wa', at the close of the day . . .	6	421
Ca' the yowes to the knowes	6	376
Ca' the yowes to the knowes	6	530
Ca' the yowes to the knowes	41	569
Call for the robin-redbreast and the wren	40	331
Calm was the day, and through the trembling air .	40	233
Can I cease to care	6	569
Can it be right to give what I can give	41	953
Canst thou leave me thus, my Katie	6	544
Captain, or colonel, or knight in arms	4	80
Care-charmer Sleep, son of the sable Night . . .	40	226
Carle, an the King come	6	367
Cast the bantling on the rocks	5	63
Cauld blaws the wind frae east to west	6	316
Cauld is the e'enin blast	6	549
Cease, ye prudes, your envious railing	6	278
Cheer up, my mates, the wind does fairly blow . .	40	375
Cherry-ripe, ripe, ripe, I cry	40	343
Chiefest glory of deathless Gods, Almighty for ever	2	185
Child of Adam, let not hope make game of thee . .	16	335
Christ is arisen	19	33
Circulate it in the large cup	16	228
Clarinda, mistress of my soul	6	311
Cold and clear-cut face, why come you so cruelly meek	42	1057
Cold's the wind, and wet's the rain	40	326
Cold's the wind, and wet's the rain	47	507
Coldly, sadly descends	42	1176
Come all ye jolly shepherds	41	783
Come away, come away, Death	40	274
Come, bumpers high, express your joy	6	438
Come, dear children, let us away	42	1168
Come, gie's sang, Montgomerie cried	41	581
Come hither, lads, and harken, for a tale there is to tell	42	1242
Come hither, you that walk along the way . . .	15	139
Come into the garden, Maud	28	167

Index to the First Lines	Vol.	Page
Come into the garden, Maud	42	1082
Come, let me take thee to my breast	6	501
Come little babe, come silly soul	40	200
Come live with me and be my Love	40	259
Come my tan-faced children	42	1486
Come, rest in this bosom, my own stricken deer .	28	396
Come, Sleep; O sleep! the certain knot of peace .	40	217
Come to me, O ye children	42	1331
Come under my plaidie, the night's gaun to fa' . .	41	591
Come unto these yellow sands	46	393
Comrades, leave me here a little	42	1009
Condemn'd to Hope's delusive mine	41	515
Consider mine affliction, and deliver me	44	309
Consider what thou beholdest, O man	16	331
Contented wi' little, and cantie wi' mair	6	542
"Courage!" he said, and pointed toward the land .	42	1026
Courage, poor heart of stone	42	1089
Crabbed Age and Youth	40	273
Creator Spirit, by whose aid	45	559
Creep into thy narrow bed	42	1185
Criticks, I saw, that others' names efface	39	259
Cromwell, our chief of men, who through a cloud .	4	85
Cupid and Campaspe play'd	40	212
Curse on ungrateful man, that can be pleased . .	6	270
Curs'd be the man, the poorest wretch in life . .	6	343
Cyriack, this three years' day these eyes, though clear	4	88
Cyriack, whose grandsire on the royal bench . .	4	87
Daughter of Chaos' doting years	6	351
Daughter of Jove, relentless power	40	462
Daughter of that good Earl, once President . . .	4	81
Daughter of Time, the hypocritic Days	42	1294
Day of wrath, that day whose knelling	45	563
Dead, long dead	42	1092
Deal bountifully with thy servant, that I may live .	44	300
Dear ——, I'll gie ye some advice	6	276
Dear love, for nothing less than thee	40	313
Dear Myra, the captive ribband's mine	6	383
Dear Sir, at ony time or tide	6	348
Dear Smith, the slee'st pawkie thief	6	175
Death, be not proud, though some have callèd thee .	40	313

Index to the First Lines	Vol.	Page
Death stands above me, whispering low	41	930
Degenerate Douglas! oh, the unworthy lord . . .	41	695
Deliberate, and haste not	16	164
Deliver me from mine enemies, O my God . . .	44	218
Deliver me, O Jehovah, from the evil man . . .	44	326
Deluded swain, the pleasure	6	506
Depart from a place wherein is oppression . . .	16	300
Diaphenia like the daffadowndilly	40	233
Did I hear it half in a doze	42	1064
Dire was the hate at old Harlaw	6	584
Dizzied faith and guilt and woe	28	176
Do ye indeed in silence speak righteousness . . .	44	217
Do you remember me? or are you proud	41	929
Does haughty Gaul invasion threat	6	567
Does the road wind up-hill all the way	42	1229
Dost thou not rise, indignant shade	6	475
Doth then the world go thus, doth all thus move .	40	336
Doubt thou the stars are fire	46	120
Doubt you to whom my Muse these notes intendeth .	40	213
Down in yon garden sweet and gay	41	510
Drink to me only with thine eyes	40	298
Dulcinea here beneath	14	542
Duncan Gray cam' here to woo	6	476
Dweller in yon dungeon dark	6	344
Each altar had his fire	15	347
Earl March look'd on his dying child	41	796
Earth has not anything to show more fair . . .	41	689
Earth'd up, here lies an imp o' hell	6	533
Edina! Scotia's darling seat	6	264
E'en like two little bank-dividing brooks	40	350
England, my England	42	1259
Erewhile of music, and ethereal mirth	4	24
Eternal Spirit of the chainless Mind	41	832
Ethereal minstrel! pilgrim of the sky	41	659
Even as the dense and solid rock	45	718
Even as the word of chariot means	45	671
Even in a palace life may be led well	42	1185
Even such is time, that takes in trust	40	210
Ever let the Fancy roam	41	894
Except Jehovah build the house	44	315
Excuse me, sirs, I pray—I can't yet speak . . .	18	201

Index to the First Lines	Vol.	Page
Expect na, sir, in this narration	6	221
Faintly as tolls the evening chime	41	840
Fair and fair, and twice so fair	40	221
Fair Daffodils, we weep to see	40	347
Fair Empress of the poet's soul	6	321
Fair fa' your honest, sonsie face	6	266
Fair is my Love and cruel as she's fair . . .	40	223
Fair is my love, when her fair golden hairs . .	40	255
Fair maid, you need not take the hint . . .	6	280
Fair pledges of a fruitful tree	40	348
Fair stood the wind for France	40	226
Fair the face of orient day	6	360
Fairest maid on Devon banks	6	592
Fairfax, whose name in arms through Europe rings .	4	84
False friend, wilt thou smile or weep	18	348
False world, good night! since thou hast brought .	40	299
Fare thee well! and if for ever	41	819
Farewell to a' our Scottish fame	6	445
Farewell, dear friend, may guid luck hit you . .	6	232
Farewell, master; farewell, farewell	46	412
Farewell, old Scotia's bleak domains	6	235
Farewell, rewards and fairies	40	323
Farewell! thou art too dear for my possessing . .	40	282
Farewell, thou fair day, thou green earth and ye skies	6	452
Farewell, thou stream that winding flows . . .	6	543
Farewell to the Highlands, farewell to the north .	6	384
Farewell, ye dungeons dark and strong	6	313
Farewell, ye green meadows	26	370
Fate gave the word, the arrow sped	6	333
Father of light and life, thou Good Supreme . .	1	87
Fathers that wear rags	46	240
Fear death?—to feel the fog in my throat . . .	42	1106
Fear no more the heat o' the sun	40	275
Fill me with the rosy wine	6	588
Fintry, my stay in worldly strife	6	402
First time he kissed me, he but only kissed . . .	41	965
First when Maggie was my care	6	368
Five years have past; five summers, with the length	41	650
Flee with thy life if thou fearest oppression . . .	16	75
Flow gently, sweet Afton! among thy green braes .	6	443
Flower in the crannied wall	42	1039

INDEX TO THE FIRST LINES	VOL.	PAGE
Fly, envious Time, till thou run out thy race . .	4	40
Follow thy fair sun, unhappy shadow	40	292
Follow your saint, follow with accents sweet . .	40	291
For a' that, an' a' that	6	137
For a' that, an' a' that	6	138
For a' that, an' a' that	6	140
For auld lang syne, my dear	6	335
For ever, Fortune, wilt thou prove	40	454
For ever, O Jehovah	44	305
For he that can have good and evil doth choose .	14	310
For lack of gold she's left me, O	41	545
For lo! thy law is passed	28	145
For lords or kings I dinna mourn	6	341
For never yet hath any one attained	38	80
For oh, her lanely nights are lang	6	536
For sense, they little owe to frugal Heav'n . . .	6	171
For the tired slave, song lifts the languid oar . .	23	141
Fortress with turrets	19	39
Forlorn, my love, no comfort near	6	572
Forget not yet the tried intent	40	194
For us, down beaten by the storms of fate . . .	9	49
For thee is laughing Nature gay	6	310
Fortune, that favors fools, these two short hours .	47	520
Four and twenty bonny boys	40	83
Four seasons fill the measure of the year . . .	41	920
Frae the friends and land I love	6	445
Fresh from the dewy hill, the merry year . . .	41	606
Fret not thyself because of evil-doers	44	189
Friday first's the day appointed	6	224
Friend of the Poet, tried and leal	6	582
Friendship, mysterious cement of the soul . . .	6	175
From Harmony, from heavenly Harmony . . .	40	398
From midst the barren earth, here overthrown . .	14	410
From Sterling Castle we had seen	41	642
From the forests and highlands	41	845
From the white-blossom'd sloe my dear Chloris requested	6	532
From thee, Eliza, I must go	6	228
From those drear solitudes and frowsy cells . . .	6	517
From you have I been absent in the spring . . .	40	284
Full fathom five my father lies	40	275

Index to the First Lines	Vol.	Page
Full fathom five my father lies	46	394
Full many a glorious morning have I seen . . .	40	278
Full well thou know'st I love thee dear	6	592
Fy, let us a' to Kirkcudbright	6	558
Gane is the day, and mirk's the night	6	401
Gat ye me, O gat ye me	6	552
Gather ye rose-buds while ye may	40	345
Gazing from each low bulwark of this bridge . .	41	936
Gem of the crimson-colour'd Even	41	795
Get up, get up for shame! The blooming morn . .	40	348
Gie him strong drink until he wink	6	151
Gifts of one who loved me	5	229
Give a man a horse he can ride	42	1195
Give all to love	42	1295
Give ear, O my people, to my law	44	243
Give ear, O shepherd of Israel	44	249
Give ear to my prayer, O God	44	213
Give ear to my words, O Jehovah	44	150
Give me more love, or more disdain	40	362
Give me my scallop-shell of quiet	40	206
Give me patience, O Allah	16	55
Give me the splendid silent sun with all his beams	42	1295
full-dazzling	42	1494
Give the king thy judgments, O God	44	235
Gloom of the live-oaks, beautiful-braided and woven	42	1470
Gloomy winter's now awa'	41	608
Glory be to God on high	45	553
Glory of warrior, glory of orator, glory of song .	42	1039
Go and catch a falling star	40	314
Go, fetch to me a pint o' wine	6	336
Go from me. Yet I feel that I shall stand . . .	41	952
Go, lovely Rose	40	367
Go not, happy day	42	1074
Go now my little Book, to every place	15	171
Go, Soul, the body's guest	40	207
Go, wanton muse, but go with care	9	259
God be merciful unto us, and bless us	44	226
God is our refuge and strength	44	203
God makes sech nights, all white an' still . . .	42	1455
God moves in a mysterious way	45	575
God prosper long our noble king	40	94

INDEX TO THE FIRST LINES	VOL.	PAGE
God standeth in the Congregation of God . . .	44	252
Goethe in Weimar sleeps, and Greece	42	1181
Gold and iron are good	5	249
Good-bye, proud world! I'm going home . . .	42	1292
Good-morrow to the day so fair	40	344
Gracie, thou art a man of worth	6	549
Grant me, indulgent Heaven, that I may live . .	6	488
Great deeds of bale	49	450
Great is Jehovah, and greatly to be praised . . .	44	205
Great spirits now on earth are sojourning . . .	41	921
Green grow the rashes, O	6	50
Grow old along with me	42	1148
Gude pity me, because I'm little	6	127
Gudrun of old days	49	351
Guid mornin' to your Majesty	6	217
Guid speed and furder to you, Johnie	6	108
Ha! whaur ye gaun, ye crowlin ferlie	6	198
Had I a cave on some wild distant shore	6	498
Had I the wyte, had I the wyte	6	566
Had I wept before she did	16	351
Had we never loved sae kindly	28	88
Hail! beauteous Stranger of the wood	41	583
Hail, famous man, whom fortune hath so blist . .	14	17
Hail, Native Language that by sinews weak . . .	4	21
Hail, Poesie! thou Nymph reserv'd	6	434
Hail, thairm-inspirin, rattlin Willie	6	257
Hail to thee, blithe Spirit	41	851
Half a league, half a league	42	1039
Hallow the threshold, crown the posts anew . . .	40	368
Hame, hame, hame, O hame fain wad I be . . .	41	802
Happy the man whose wish and care	40	415
Happy those early days, when I	40	357
Happy those which, for more commodity	14	17
Happy were he could finish forth his fate . . .	40	294
Hard Texts are Nuts (I will not call them cheaters)	15	271
Hark, hark, my soul! angelic songs are swelling . .	45	584
Hark! hark! the lark at heaven's gate sings . . .	40	274
Hark! how all the welkin rings	45	574
Hark! I hear the tramp of thousands	42	1482
Hark the mavis' e'ening sang	6	530
Harp of the North, farewell! The hills grow dark .	41	773

INDEX TO THE FIRST LINES	VOL.	PAGE
Harry, whose tuneful and well-measured song . .	4	83
Has auld Kilmarnock seen the deil	6	254
Hast thou a charm to stay the morning-star . . .	41	724
Hasten, ye faithful, glad, joyful, and holy	45	567
Have mercy upon me, O God, according to thy loving-kindness	44	209
Have more than thou showest	46	221
Haymakers, rakers, reapers, and mowers	40	325
He clenched his pamphlet in his fist	6	269
He first by grace must conquer'd be	15	273
He is dead, the beautiful youth	42	1352
He is gone on the mountain	41	765
He that dwelleth in the secret place of the Most High	44	264
He that has and a little tiny wit	46	252
He that is down needs fear no fall	15	245
He that loves a rosy cheek	40	360
He used his lances as pens	16	203
He who of Rankine sang, lies stiff and dead . . .	6	64
He whom we mourned as dead	19	35
He's ower the hills that I lo'e weel	41	573
Health to the Maxwell's veteran Chief	6	448
Hear, land o' Cakes and brither Scots	6	369
Hear my cry, O God	44	220
Hear my prayer, O Jehovah	44	274
Hear my prayer, O Jehovah; give ear to my supplications	44	329
Hear my voice, O God, in my complaint	44	223
Hear the right, O Jehovah, attend unto my cry .	44	161
Hear the sledges with the bells	42	1283
Hear this, all ye peoples	44	206
Hear what God, the Lord, hath spoken	45	576
Hee balow, my sweet wee Donald	6	523
Helen, thy beauty is to me	42	1275
Help, Jehovah; for the godly man ceaseth . . .	44	158
Hence, all yon vain delights	40	330
Hence, loathèd Melancholy	4	31
Hence, overshadowing gloom	19	58
Hence, vain deluding joys	4	35
Hengist had verament	5	286
Her brother is coming back to-night	42	1077

Index to the First Lines	Vol.	Page
Her daddie forbad, her minnie forbad	6	318
Her flowing locks, the raven's wing	6	116
Her of your name whose fair inheritance . . .	15	382
Her skin is like silk and her speech is soft . . .	16	204
Here a little child I stand	40	343
Here, a sheer hulk, lies poor Tom Bowling . . .	41	514
Here am I laid, my life of misery done	12	391
Here awa, there awa, wandering Willie	6	482
Here Brewer Gabriel's fire's extinct	6	549
Here cursing, swearing Burton lies	6	534
Here, ever since you went abroad	41	923
Here Holy Willie's sair worn clay	6	78
Here is the glen and here the bower	6	515
Here lie Willie Michie's banes	6	278
Here lies a mock Marquis whose titles were shamm'd	6	534
Here lies Boghead amang the dead	6	53
Here lies John Busby, honest man	6	520
Here lies Johnie Pigeon	6	126
Here lies, now a prey to insulting neglect . . .	6	517
Here lies old Hobson. Death hath broke his girt .	4	26
Here lies our Sovereign Lord the King	40	392
Here lieth Bernardone, ass and pig	31	416
Here lieth one who did most truly prove . . .	4	27
Here, of a loving swain	14	117
Here Souter Hood in death doth sleep	6	53
Here Stuarts once in glory reigned	6	290
Here was a people whom after their works . . .	16	315
Here, where the Scottish Muse immortal lives . .	6	528
Here, where the world is quiet	42	1251
Here will I hold. If there's a power above us . .	1	86
Here's a bottle and an honest friend	6	277
Here's a health to ane I loe dear	6	590
Here's a health to them tha's awa	6	477
Here's to the maiden of bashful fifteen	18	149
Here's to the maiden of bashful fifteen	41	567
Here's to the year that's awa'	41	595
Here's to thy health, my bonie lass	6	28
Hey, ca' thro', ca' thro'	6	279
Hey, the dusty Miller	6	317
Hie upon Hielands	40	115

Index to the First Lines	Vol.	Page
High grace, the dower of queens; and therewithal .	42	1227
His face with smile eternal drest	6	343
His foundation is in the holy mountains . . .	44	257
Hnikar I hight	49	309
Hold, mighty man, I cry all this we know . . .	34	147
Hold not thy peace, O God of my praise . . .	44	289
Holy amity! which, with nimble wings . . .	14	251
Holy, holy, holy! Lord God Almighty . . .	45	577
Home they brought her warrior dead	42	1004
Homer, thy song men liken to the sea . . .	22	347
Honest Will to Heaven's away	6	303
Honor, riches, marriage-blessing	46	427
How amiable are thy tabernacles	44	254
How blest the happy solitude	45	642
How can my poor heart be glad	6	528
How cold is that bosom which folly once fired . .	6	516
How cruel are the parents	6	570
How daur ye ca' me "Howlet-face"	6	453
How delicious is the winning	41	801
How do I love thee? Let me count the ways . .	41	967
How fresh, O Lord, how sweet and clean . . .	40	354
How good is it to pardon one able to resist . . .	16	70
How happy is he born and taught	40	295
How haps it, Rozinante, thou art so lean	14	17
How hath time made me to tremble	16	205
How lang and dreary is the night	6	536
How, Liberty! girl, can it be by thee named . . .	6	532
How like a winter hath my absence been	40	284
How long and dreary is the night	6	316
How long, O Jehovah? wilt thou forget me for ever	44	158
How many companies have alighted	16	315
How many wretched persons are destitute of ease .	16	243
How near to good is what is fair	5	207
How often have I stood in fight	16	315
How pleasant the banks of the clear winding Devon	6	303
How should I your true love know	40	271
How should I your true love know	46	166
How sleep the Brave, who sink to rest . . .	41	488
How soon hath Time, the subtle thief of youth . .	4	30
How sweet the answer Echo makes	41	842
How vainly men themselves amaze	40	386

INDEX TO THE FIRST LINES	VOL.	PAGE
How Wisdom and Folly meet, mix and unite . .	6	357
Humid seal of soft affections	6	336
"Husband, husband, cease your strife"	6	507
I am a bard of no regard	6	137
I am a fiddler to my trade	6	135
I am a keeper of the law	6	56
I am a mariner to love	14	453
I am a son of Mars who have been in many wars .	6	129
I am enamoured of her	16	340
I am monarch of all I survey	41	548
I am my mammy's ae bairn	6	311
I am not of the noble Grecian race	12	5
I arise from dreams of Thee	41	850
I arise from dreams of Thee	28	385
I bought my wife a stane o' lint	6	458
I bring fresh showers for the thirsting flowers . .	41	875
I call no Goddess to inspire my strains . . .	6	375
I Catherine am a Douglas born	42	1200
I coft a stane o' haslock woo	6	563
I cry with my voice unto Jehovah	44	328
I did but prompt the age to quit their clogs . .	4	82
I die, and if I cannot be believed	14	348
I do confess thou art sae fair	6	457
I dream'd I lay where flowers were springing . .	6	21
I dream'd that as I wander'd by the way . . .	41	865
I du believe in Freedom's cause	42	1452
I fear thy kisses, gentle maiden	41	849
I fee'd a man at Michaelmas	6	466
I fill this cup to one made up	28	394
I gaed a waefu' gate yestreen	6	377
I gaed up to Dunse	6	342
I gat your letter, winsome Willie	6	92
I gazed upon the glorious sky	42	1268
I got me flowers to strew Thy way	40	355
I had a dream, which was not all a dream . . .	41	816
I had sax owsen in a pleugh	6	551
I hae a wife of my ain	6	324
I hae been at Crookieden	6	447
I hate the dreadful hollow behind the little wood .	42	1052
I hate them that are of a double mind	44	306
I have called with my whole heart	44	309

Index to the First Lines	Vol.	Page
I have done justice and righteousness	44	307
I have had playmates, I have had companions . .	41	752
I have heard tell	49	457
I have led her home, my love, my only friend . .	42	1074
I heard a thousand blended notes	41	659
I heard the trailing garments of the Night . . .	42	1318
I hold it, sir, my bounden duty	6	208
I know a little garden-close	42	1241
I know, Olalia, thou dost me adore	14	89
I know the thing that's most uncommon	40	416
I lang hae thought, my youthfu' friend	6	212
I lift my heavy heart up solemnly	41	951
I like a church; I like a cowl	42	1299
I lived with visions for my company	41	960
I lo'ed ne'er a laddie but ane	41	590
I long to talk with some old lover's ghost . . .	40	317
I love, and he loves me again	40	300
I love Jehovah, because he heareth	44	296
I love thee, O Jehovah, my strength	44	162
I loved a lass, a fair one	40	340
I met a traveller from an antique land . . .	41	873
I mind it weel in early date	6	270
I murder hate by flood or field	6	400
I must not grieve my Love, whose eyes would read .	40	225
I never gave a lock of hair away	41	957
I never saw a fairer	6	472
I once was a maid, tho' I cannot tell when . . .	6	130
I put my hat upon my head	39	303
I rede you, beware at the hunting, young men . .	6	274
I remember, I remember	41	935
I said, I will take heed to my ways	44	193
I said—Then, dearest, since 'tis so	42	1112
I saw him once before	42	1444
I saw where in the shroud did lurk	41	754
I see a form, I see a face	6	575
I see thine image through my tears to-night . . .	41	962
I sing of a Whistle, a Whistle of worth	6	384
I sprang to the stirrup, and Joris, and he	42	1107
I stood on the bridge at midnight	42	1328
I strove with none; for none was worth the strife .	41	929
I struck the board and cried, No more	40	353

Index to the First Lines	Vol.	Page
I thank all who have loved me in their hearts . .	41	966
I think of thee!—my thoughts do twine and bud . .	41	961
I thought of Thee, my partner and my guide . .	41	694
I thought once how Theocritus had sung . . .	41	950
I tore, I hackt, abolish'd, said and did	14	15
I travell'd among unknown men	41	686
I waited patiently for Jehovah	44	195
I wander'd lonely as a cloud	41	654
I was glad when they said unto me	44	312
I was thy neighbour once, thou rugged Pile . .	41	620
I was walking a mile	42	1065
I weep for Adonais—he is dead	41	879
I, who erewhile the happy Garden sung	4	363
I, who was late so volatile and gay	18	195
I will bless Jehovah at all times	44	184
I will cry unto God with my voice	44	242
I will extol thee, my God, O King	44	331
I will extol thee, O Jehovah; for thou hast raised me up	44	179
I will give thanks unto Jehovah with my whole heart	44	154
I will give thee thanks with my whole heart . .	44	323
I will lift up mine eyes unto the mountains . . .	44	311
I will sing of lovingkindness and justice . . .	44	273
I will sing of the lovingkindness of Jehovah for ever	44	259
I wish I were where Helen lies	40	333
I wonder, by my troth, what thou and I . . .	40	320
I'll aye ca' in by yon town	6	554
I'm now arrived—thanks to the gods	6	249
I'm o'er young, I'm o'er young	6	311
I'm sittin' on the stile, Mary	41	945
I'm three times doubly o'er your debtor	6	113
I'm wearing awa', Jean	41	573
I've heard them lilting at our ewe-milking . . .	41	495
I've seen the smiling	41	494
If age brought nothing worse than this . . .	9	54
If all the world and love were young	40	260
If aught of oaten stop or pastoral song	41	491
If doughty deeds my lady please	41	544
If from the public way you turn your steps . . .	41	630

Index to the First Lines	Vol.	Page
If I be possessed of wealth and be not liberal . .	16	211
If I fail any day to render thee due thanks . . .	16	40
If I freely can discover	40	307
If I have faltered more or less	42	1261
If I leave all for thee, wilt thou exchange . . .	41	964
If I, my lord, could show to you the truth . . .	31	255
If it had not been Jehovah who was on our side . .	44	313
If love were what the rose is	42	1254
If of love we complain, what shall we say . . .	16	68
If one says "No," I answer "No"	9	40
If the red slayer think he slays	42	1294
If thou chance for to find	15	402
If thou must love me, let it be for nought . . .	41	955
If thou should ask my love	6	363
If Thou survive my well-contented day . . .	40	277
If to be absent were to be	40	366
If women could be fair, and yet not fond . . .	40	296
If ye gae up to yon hill-top	6	24
If yet I have not all thy love	40	316
If you rattle along like your Mistress's tongue .	6	517
Ilk care and fear, when thou art near	6	31
Ill-fated genius! Heaven-taught Fergusson . . .	6	458
In a coign of the cliff between lowland and highland	42	1255
In a drear-nighted December	41	898
In close intrigue, their faculty's but weak . . .	5	393
In comin' by the brig o' Dye	6	298
In days long gone	49	433
In death for life I seek	14	341
In going to my naked bed as one that would have slept	40	204
In Jehovah do I take refuge	44	157
In Judah is God known	44	241
In London city was Bicham born	40	85
In Love, if Love be Love, if Love be ours . . .	42	1006
In Manchline there dwells six proper young belles .	6	62
In my distress I cried unto Jehovah	44	311
In Politics if thou would'st mix	6	480
In proportion to one's labor, eminences are gained .	16	246
In Scotland there was a babie born	40	59
In se'enteen hundred 'n forty-nine	6	534
In simmer, when the hay was mawn	6	467

Index to the First Lines	Vol.	Page
In Tarbolton, ye ken, there are proper young men .	6	26
In the downhill of life, when I find I'm declining .	41	607
In the greenest of our valleys	42	1274
In the highlands, in the country places	42	1260
In the merry month of May	40	199
In the midway of this our mortal life	20	5
In the sweet shire of Cardigan	41	662
In thee, O Jehovah, do I take refuge	44	180
In thee, O Jehovah, do I take refuge	44	233
In this strange land, this uncouth clime	6	322
In unploughed Maine he sought the lumberers' gang	42	1302
In vain to me the smiling mornings shine . . .	39	290
In wood and wild, ye warbling throng	6	496
In Xanadu did Kubla Khan	41	718
In youth, when I did love, did love	46	181
Indeed this very love which is my boast . . .	41	954
Inhuman man! curse on thy barb'rous art . . .	6	359
Instead of a song, boys, I'll give you a toast . .	6	489
Into the proud erected diamond stock	14	541
Inverey cam doun Deeside, whistlin and playin . .	40	120
Iphigeneia, when she heard her doom	41	927
Is it indeed so? If I lay here dead	41	959
Is it not better at an early hour	41	930
Is there a whim-inspirèd fool	6	228
Is there for honest Poverty . . ˙.	6	546
Is this thy plighted, fond regard	6	544
It befell at Martynmas	40	105
It fell about the Lammus time	40	89
It fell about the Martinmas time	40	88
It fell upon a holly eve	40	252
It is a beauteous evening, calm and free	41	688
It is a good thing to give thanks unto Jehovah . .	44	265
It is an ancient Mariner	41	698
It is na, Jean, thy bonie face	6	334
It is not beauty I demand	41	938
It is not growing like a tree	40	298
It is not to be thought of that the flood	41	690
It little profits that an idle king	42	1007
It was a dismal and a fearful night . . ˙. . .	40	376
It was a lover and his lass	40	269
It was a summer evening	41	749

Index to the First Lines	Vol.	Page
It was a' for our rightfu' King	6	525
It was fifty years ago	42	1346
It was in and about the Martinmas time	40	69
It was in sweet Senegal that my foes did me enthral	6	465
It was many and many a year ago	42	1290
It was not like your great and gracious ways . .	42	1158
It was roses, roses, all the way	42	1125
It was the charming month of May	6	539
It was the schooner Hesperus	42	1321
It was the winter wild	4	8
It was three slim does and a ten-tined buck in the bracken lay	42	1474
It was upon a Lammas night	6	47
Ithers seek they ken na what	6	469
Jamie, come try me	6	363
Jehovah answer thee in the day of trouble . . .	44	167
Jehovah, how are mine adversaries increased . .	44	148
Jehovah, I have called upon thee; make haste unto me	44	327
Jehovah is my light and my salvation	44	175
Jehovah is my portion	44	303
Jehovah is my shepherd	44	171
Jehovah, my heart is not haughty	44	317
Jehovah reigneth; he is clothed with majesty . .	44	266
Jehovah reigneth; let the earth rejoice	44	270
Jehovah reigneth; let the peoples tremble	44	271
Jehovah, remember for David	44	318
Jehovah saith unto my lord, Sit thou at my right hand	44	291
Jehovah, thou hast been favorable unto thy land .	44	255
Jehovah, who shall sojourn in thy tabernacle . .	44	160
Jenny kiss'd me when we met	41	893
Jerusalem the golden	45	561
Jesu, the very thought of thee	45	562
Jesus, lover of my soul	45	572
Jesus shall reign where'er the sun	45	549
Jesus, Thou Joy of loving hearts	45	563
Jockey's taen the parting kiss	6	582
John Anderson, my jo, John	6	365
John Gilpin was a citizen	41	559
Judge me, O God, and plead my cause against an ungodly nation	44	199

INDEX TO THE FIRST LINES	VOL.	PAGE
Judge me, O Jehovah, for I have walked in mine integrity	44	174
Just for a handful of silver he left us	42	1109
Kathrina say	19	155
Kemble, thou cur'st my unbelief	6	532
Ken ye ought o' Captain Grose?—Igo and ago	6	411
Kilmarnock wabsters, fidge an' claw	6	171
Kind gentlemen and ladies fair	19	38
Kind Sir, I've read your paper through	6	397
Know, Celia, since thou art so proud	40	361
Know thou, O stranger to the fame	6	229
Lady Onlie, honest lucky	6	298
Lady! that in the prime of earliest youth	4	80
Lament him, Mauchline husbands a'	6	127
Lament in rhyme, lament in prose	6	45
Lassie wi' the lint-white locks	6	540
Last May, a braw wooer cam doun the lang glen	6	574
Late at e'en, drinkin the wine	40	116
Late crippl'd of an arm, and now a leg	6	449
Late, late yestreen I saw the new Moon	41	745
Lawrence, of virtuous father virtuous son	4	87
Lay a garland on my hearse	40	330
Lead, kindly Light, amid the encircling gloom	45	581
Lead me, O God, and Thou, O Destiny	2	179
Leeze me on drink! it gies us mair	28	86
Let God arise, let his enemies be scattered	44	227
Let half-starv'd slaves in warmer skies	6	170
Let ignorance a little while now muse	15	129
Let India boast her palms, nor envy we	5	376
Let me not to the marriage of true minds	40	287
Let me ryke up to dight that tear	6	134
Let my cry come near before thee, O Jehovah	44	310
Let not ambition mock their useful toil	6	142
Let not Woman e'er complain	6	536
Let other heroes boast their scars	6	236
Let other poets raise a frácas	6	151
Let others sing of Knights and Paladines	40	225
Let schoolmasters puzzle their brain	18	209
Let the Most Blessed be my guide	15	192
Let the toast pass	18	149
Let the world's sharpness, like a clasping knife	41	959

Index to the First Lines	Vol.	Page
Let thy lovingkindnesses also come unto me, O Jehovah	44	302
Let us begin and carry up this corpse	42	1126
Let us drink and be merry, dance, joke, and rejoice	40	373
Let us with a gladsome mind	4	16
Life! I know not what thou art	41	568
Life ne'er exulted in so rich a prize	6	419
Life of Life! Thy lips enkindle	41	864
Light lay the earth on Billy's breast	6	520
Like as the Culver, on the barèd bough	40	257
Like as the waves make towards the pebbled shore	40	280
Like some brave steeds that oft before	9	50
Like to the clear in highest sphere	40	219
Listen, my children, and you shall hear	42	1348
Listen to me, as when ye heard our father	42	1105
Little I ask; my wants are few	42	1445
Little think'st thou, poor flower	40	319
Live in these conquering leaves	40	372
Lo, praise of the prowess of people-kings	49	5
Lo! 'tis a gala night	42	1291
Lo! where the four mimosas blend their shade	41	929
Lo! where the rosy-bosom'd Hours	40	463
Lock the door, Lariston, lion of Liddisdale	41	786
Lone on the bleaky hills the straying flocks	6	307
Long expected one-and-twenty	41	516
Long fed on boundless hopes, O race of man	42	1184
Long have I sighed for a calm	42	1056
Long have I slept	49	320
Long life, my lord, an' health be yours	6	215
Long, long the night	6	569
Look not thou on beauty's charming	41	765
Look, Nymphs and Shepherds, look	4	43
Lord of all being, throned afar	45	584
Lord Thomas and Fair Annet	40	61
Lord, thou hast been our dwelling-place	44	262
Lord, to account who dares thee call	6	488
Lord, we thank, and thee adore	6	490
Lords, knights, and squires, the numerous band	40	406
Loth am I, sister	49	385
Loud blaw the frosty breezes	6	305
Louis, what reck I by thee	6	334

Index to the First Lines	Vol.	Page
Love bade me welcome; yet my soul drew back . .	40	351
Love guards the roses of thy lips	40	220
Love in her eyes sits playing	40	412
Love in my bosom like a bee	40	218
Love not me for comely grace	40	334
Love thou thy land, with love far-brought . . .	42	1033
Love thy country, wish it well	40	475
Lovely was she by the dawn	6	539
Loving in truth, and fain in verse my love to show .	40	216
Lythe and listin, gentilmen	40	130
Maid of Athens, ere we part	41	815
Make a joyful noise unto God, all the earth . . .	44	225
Make a joyful noise unto Jehovah, all ye lands . .	44	272
Make haste, O God, to deliver me	44	232
Maker of all, the Lord	7	163
Mally's meek, Mally's sweet	6	581
Man is his own star; and the soul that can . . .	5	63
Many a green isle needs must be	41	858
Many a time have they afflicted me from my youth up	44	316
March, march, Ettrick and Teviotdale	41	764
Mark yonder pomp of costly fashion	6	570
Martial, the things that do attain	40	197
Mary! I want a lyre with other strings	41	549
Maud has a garden of roses	42	1071
Maud Muller on a summer's day	42	1427
Maugre the ravings that are set abroach	14	16
Maxwell, if here you merit crave	6	532
May I lose my heart if it cease to love you . . .	16	143
Meet me on the warlock knowe	6	502
Merrily swinging on brier and weed	42	1264
Methought I saw my late espousèd saint	4	88
Milton! Thou shouldst be living at this hour . .	41	692
Mine adventure to the Meek One	43	6
Mine be a cot beside the hill	41	596
Morning arises stormy and pale	42	1061
Mortality, behold and fear	40	327
Most glorious Lord of Lyfe! that, on this day . .	40	254
Most sweet it is with unuplifted eyes	41	688
Mother, I cannot mind my wheel	41	925
Much have I travell'd in the realms of gold . .	41	919

Index to the First Lines	Vol.	Page
Music, when soft voices die	41	878
Musing on the roaring ocean	6	319
My blessings on ye, honest wife	6	276
My blessins upon thy sweet wee lippie	6	268
My bonie lass, I work in brass	6	136
My curse upon your venom'd stang	6	251
My days among the Dead are past	41	751
My dear and only Love, I pray	40	368
My faith looks up to thee	45	583
My father was a farmer upon the Carrick border, O	6	39
My future will not copy fair my past	41	967
My girl she's airy, she's buxom and gay . . .	6	62
My God, I love thee; not because	45	568
My God, my God	15	421
My God, my God, why hast thou forsaken me . .	44	169
My God, where is that ancient heat toward thee . .	15	383
My godlike friend—nay, do not stare	6	326
My good blade carves the casques of men . . .	42	1036
My hair is gray, but not with years	41	821
My Harry was a gallant gay	6	378
My heart aches, and a drowsy numbness pains . .	41	899
My heart is a-breaking, dear tittie	6	366
My heart is fixed, O God	44	288
My heart is sair—I dare na tell	6	545
My heart is wae, and unco wae	6	299
My heart leaps up when I behold	41	615
My heart overfloweth with a goodly matter . . .	44	202
My heart was ance as blithe and free	6	312
My heart's in the Highlands, my heart is not here .	6	384
My honor'd Colonel, deep I feel	6	585
My lady's gown, there's gairs upon't	6	275
My letters! all dead paper, mute and white . . .	41	961
My life has crept so long on a broken wing . . .	42	1096
My lord a-hunting he is gane	6	275
My lord, I know, your noble ear	6	293
My Love in her attire doth shew her wit	40	334
My love, she's but a lassie yet	6	365
My lov'd, my honor'd, much respected friend . .	6	142
My lute, be as thou wert when thou didst grow . .	40	337
My mind to me a kingdom is	40	211
My minnie does constantly deave me	28	90

Index to the First Lines	Vol.	Page
My mother bids me bind my hair	41	594
My mother, the harlot	19	187
My own belovèd, who hast lifted me	41	961
My peace is gone	19	142
My Peggy is a young thing	40	411
My Peggy's face, my Peggy's form	6	304
My poet, thou canst touch on all the notes . . .	41	956
My Sandy gied to me a ring	6	363
My Sandy O, my Sandy O, ...	6	364
My sister! my sweet sister! if a name	41	812
My son, these maxims make a rule	6	192
My soul cleaveth unto the dust	44	301
My soul fainteth for thy salvation	44	304
My soul waiteth in silence for God only	44	221
My spotless love hovers with purest wings . . .	40	223
My sword could not at all compare with thine . .	14	16
My thoughts hold mortal strife	40	335
My true-love hath my heart, and I have his . .	40	215
Mysterious Night! when our first parent knew . .	41	938
Nae gentle dames, tho' ne'er sae fair	6	211
Nae heathen name shall I prefix	6	289
Nae shoon to hide her tiny taes	41	944
Nay, with my goodwill	49	413
Nearer, my God, to thee	45	582
Never the time and the place	42	1154
Never trust in women; nor rely upon their vows .	16	10
No churchman am I for to rail and to write . . .	6	38
No cold approach, no altered mien	6	471
No coward soul is mine	42	1156
No longer mourn for me when I am dead	40	281
No more of your guests, be they titled or not . .	6	549
No more, ye warblers of the wood! no more . .	6	521
No, my own love of other years	41	926
No, no! go not to Lethe, neither twist	41	906
No sculptured marble here, nor pompous lay . .	6	269
No song nor dance I bring from yon great city .	6	393
No Spartan tube, no Attic shell	6	526
No Stewart art thou, Galloway	6	496
Nobly, nobly Cape Saint Vincent to the North-west died away	42	1110
None keepeth a secret but a faithful person . . .	16	63

Index to the First Lines	Vol.	Page
Nor grain, nor wealth, nor store of gold and silver .	45	692
Not a drum was heard, not a funeral note . . .	41	843
Not, Celia, that I juster am	40	393
Not here and there, but everywhere	9	137
Not marble, nor the gilded monuments . . .	40	279
Not mine own fears, nor the prophetic soul . .	40	285
Not to know vice at all, and keep true state . .	40	301
Not unto us, O Jehovah, not unto us	44	295
Now daye was gone, and night was come . . .	39	343
Now haply down yon gay green shaw	6	555
Now in her green mantle blythe Nature arrays . .	6	544
Now, Kennedy, if foot or horse	6	196
Now Nature cleeds the flowery lea	6	540
Now Nature hangs her mantle green	6	420
Now, Reader, I have told my Dream to thee . . .	15	168
Now Robin lies in his last lair	6	99
Now rosy May comes in wi' flowers	6	502
Now Simmer blinks on flowery braes	6	292
Now sleeps the crimson petal, now the white . .	42	1004
Now spring has clad the grove in green	6	576
Now thank we all our God	45	571
Now the bright morning-star, Day's harbinger . .	4	40
Now the golden Morn aloft	40	472
Now the last day of many days	41	867
Now this is my first counsel	49	393
Now westlin winds and slaught'ring guns . . .	6	48
Nuns fret not at their convent's narrow room . .	41	696
O a' ye pious godly flocks	6	67
O angry fate, forbear	16	29
O aye my wife she dang me	6	551
O blithe new-comer! I have heard	41	656
O bonie was yon rosy brier	6	576
O Brignall banks are wild and fair	41	755
O brother, rest from miserable me	32	87
O cam ye here the fight to shun	6	379
O can ye labour lea, young man	6	465
O Captain! my Captain! our fearful trip is done .	42	1496
O could I give thee India's wealth	6	348
O Death, had'st thou but spar'd his life . . .	6	63
O Death! thou tyrant fell and bloody	6	406
O fairest flower, no sooner blown but blasted . .	4	18

Index to the First Lines	Vol.	Page
O for him back again	6	378
O, for my sake do you with Fortune chide . . .	40	287
O Friend! I know not which way I must look . .	41	692
O Friends! with whom my feet have trod . . .	42	1414
O give thanks unto Jehovah; for he is good . . .	44	285
O God, keep not thou silence	44	252
O God, the nations are come into thine inheritance .	44	248
O God, thou art my God; earnestly will I seek thee .	44	222
O God, thou hast cast us off, thou hast broken us down	44	219
O God, why hast thou cast us off for ever . . .	44	238
O goddess! hear these tuneless numbers, wrung .	41	904
O Gowdie, terror o' the whigs	6	100
O gude ale comes and gude ale goes	6	551
O had each Scot of ancient times	6	286
O had the malt thy strength of mind	6	548
O happy dames! that may embrace	40	196
O happy shades! to me unblest	41	555
O happy souls, which from this mortal vale . . .	14	410
O have ye na heard o' the fause Sakelde	40	109
O hearken, ye who speak the English Tongue . .	49	272
O how can I be blythe and glad	6	320
O how much more doth beauty beauteous seem . .	40	278
O how shall I, unskilfu,' try	6	429
O if thou knew'st how thou thyself dost harm . .	40	322
O Jehovah, my God, in thee do I take refuge . .	44	152
O Jehovah, our Lord	44	153
O Jehovah, rebuke me not in thine anger . . .	44	151
O Jehovah, rebuke me not in thy wrath	44	192
O Jehovah, the God of my salvation	44	258
O Jehovah, thou God to whom vengeance belongeth	44	266
O Jehovah, thou hast searched me, and known me .	44	324
O ken ye what Meg o' the Mill has gotten . . .	6	485
O Kenmure's on and awa, Willie	6	447
O Lady Mary Ann looks o'er the Castle wa' . . .	6	462
O lassie, are ye sleepin yet	6	553
O lay thy loof in mine, lass	6	589
O leave novels, ye Mauchline belles	6	61
O leeze me on my spinnin-wheel	6	468
O let me in this ae night	6	553
O let the solid ground	42	1068

INDEX TO THE FIRST LINES	VOL.	PAGE
O let us howl some heavy note	47	783
O listen, listen, ladies gay	41	766
O Logan, sweetly didst thou glide	6	492
O Logie o' Buchan, O Logie the laird	41	585
O Lord, since we have feasted thus	6	490
O Lord, when hunger pinches sore	6	490
O lovely Polly Stewart	6	438
O lovers' eyes are sharp to see	41	761
O luve will venture in where it daur na weel be seen	6	431
O lyric Love, half angel and half bird	42	1154
O Mary, at thy window be	6	32
O Mary, go and call the cattle home	42	1102
O May, thy morn was ne'er so sweet	6	454
O me! what eyes hath love put in my head . . .	40	289
O meikle thinks my luve o' my beauty	6	440
O merry hae I been teethin a heckle	6	141
O mirk, mirk is this midnight hour	6	483
O Mistress mine, where are you roaming	40	267
O Mother Earth! upon thy lap	42	1416
O mount and go, mount and make you ready . .	6	364
O my Luve's like a red, red rose	6	514
O never say that I was false of heart	40	286
O Nightingale that on yon blooming spray . . .	4	39
O once I lov'd a bonie lass	6	19
O Philly, happy be that day	6	541
O poortith cauld, and restless love	6	479
O praise Jehovah, all ye nations	44	297
O raging Fortune's withering blast	6	38
O rough, rude, ready-witted Rankine	6	57
O rowan tree, O rowan tree! thou'lt aye be dear to me	41	577
O sad and heavy, should I part	6	457
O saw ye bonie Lesley	6	470
O saw ye my Dear, my Philly	6	535
O saw ye my dearie, my Eppie Macnab	6	439
O saw ye not fair Ines	41	930
O saw ye not fair Ines	28	397
O say what is that thing call'd Light	40	452
O sing a new song to the Lord	6	356
O sing unto my roundelay	41	571

INDEX TO THE FIRST LINES	VOL.	PAGE
O snatch'd away in beauty's bloom	41	810
O soft embalmer of the still midnight	41	920
O stay, sweet warbling woodlark, stay	6	569
O steer her up, an' haud her gaun	6	552
O stream descending to the sea	42	1165
O swallow, swallow, flying, flying South	42	1005
O sweet and constant hope	14	454
O talk not to me of a name great in story	41	809
O that I had ne'er been married	6	581
O that 'twere possible	42	1089
O that's the lassie o' my heart	6	578
O the month of May, the merry month of May	47	480
O Thou dread Power, who reign'st above	6	249
O Thou Great Being! what Thou art	6	33
O Thou, in whom we live and move	6	454
O thou pale orb that silent shines	6	204
O thou, that sitt'st upon a throne	41	496
O Thou, the first, the greatest friend	6	35
O Thou unknown, Almighty Cause	6	36
O Thou! whatever title suit thee	6	147
O Thou, who in the heavens does dwell	6	75
O Thou who kindly dost provide	6	454
O thou whom Poesy abhors	6	277
O thou with dewy locks, who lookest down	41	598
O Tibbie, I hae seen the day	6	20
O, to be in England	42	1110
O waly waly up the bank	40	331
O wat ye wha that loes me	6	578
O wat ye wha's in yon town	6	555
"O well's me o' my gay goss-hawk"	40	70
O were I on Parnassus hill	6	332
O were my love yon Lilac fair	6	494
O wert thou in the cauld blast	6	591
O wert thou, Love, but near me	6	573
O wha my babie-clouts will buy?	6	191
O wha will shoe my fu fair foot	40	65
O wha will to Saint Stephen's House	6	327
O what a plague is love	40	389
O what can ail thee, knight-at-arms	41	917
O when shall I a mansion give	45	796
O when she cam' ben she bobbed fu' law	6	459

INDEX TO THE FIRST LINES	VOL.	PAGE
O whistle an' I'll come to ye, my lad	6	499
O why should Fate sic pleasure have	6	480
O why should the deuce should I repine	6	38
O wild West Wind, thou breath of Autumn's being .	41	856
O, Willie brew'd a peck o' maut	6	376
O wilt thou go wi' me, sweet Tibbie Dunbar . . .	6	364
O World! O Life! O Time	41	864
O world of wonders! (I can say no less) . . .	15	70
O worship the King all glorious above	45	552
O ye plants, ye herbs, and ye trees	14	239
O ye wha are sae guid yoursel'	6	192
O ye whose cheek the tear of pity stains	6	54
Obscurest night involved the sky	41	553
Of a' the airts the wind can blaw	6	323
Of all the girls that are so smart	40	414
Of all the numerous ills that hurt our peace . . .	6	52
Of all the rides since the birth of time	42	1434
Of all the thoughts of God that are	41	968
Of Heaven or Hell I have no power to sing . . .	42	1240
Of Lordly acquaintance you boast	6	453
Of man's first disobedience and the fruit	4	90
Of Nelson and the North	41	798
Of old, when Scarron his companions invited . .	41	517
Of this fair volume which we World do name . .	40	336
Oft in the stilly night	41	837
Often I think of the beautiful town	42	1343
Oh, a dainty plant is the Ivy green	42	1194
Oh clap your hands, all ye peoples	44	204
Oh come, let us sing unto Jehovah	44	268
Oh for my sake do you with Fortune chide . . .	27	322
Oh Galuppi, Baldassare, this is very sad to find .	42	1122
Oh give thanks unto Jehovah, call upon his name .	44	279
Oh give thanks unto Jehovah; for he is good . .	44	297
Oh give thanks unto Jehovah; for he is good . .	44	321
Oh how love I thy law	44	305
Oh I am come to the low Countrie	6	524
Oh, open the door, some pity to shew	6	484
Oh sing unto Jehovah a new song	44	269
Oh sing unto Jehovah a new song	44	271
Oh, slow to smite and swift to spare	42	1272
Oh that those lips had language!	41	556

INDEX TO THE FIRST LINES	VOL.	PAGE
Oh, the auld house, the auld house	41	574
Oh, yes! They love through all this world of ours .	41	966
Oh! young Lochinvar is come out of the West . .	41	769
Old Chronos once took queen Sedition to wife . .	12	39
Old Grahame he is to Carlisle gone	40	123
Old Winter, with his frosty beard	6	507
On a bank of flowers on a summer day	6	361
On a day, alack the day!	40	272
On a Poet's lips I slept	41	878
On Cessnock banks a lassie dwells	6	29
On either side the river lie	42	997
On his lips Persuasion hung	9	217
On Linden, when the sun was low	41	800
On parent knees, a naked new-born child	41	593
On peace an' rest my mind was bent	6	551
On the brink of the night and the morning . . .	28	90
On the heights peals the thunder, and trembles the bridge	26	370
On the Sabbath-day	42	1192
On the seas and far away	6	528
On these white cliffs, that calm above the flood . .	41	697
Once did She hold the gorgeous East in fee . . .	41	691
Once fondly lov'd, and still remembered dear . .	6	231
Once in a cellar lived a rat	19	82
Once upon a midnight dreary, while I pondered, weak and weary	42	1276
One day I wrote her name upon the strand . . .	40	256
One more Unfortunate	41	932
One more Unfortunate	28	398
One night as I did wander	6	97
One Queen Artemisia, as old stories tell	6	63
One word is too often profaned	41	873
One's-self I sing, a simple separate person . . .	42	1483
Oppress'd with grief, oppress'd with care	6	206
Or love of understanding quite is void	14	202
Orthodox! orthodox, who believe in John Knox . .	6	371
Others abide our question. Thou art free	42	1175
Our band is few but true and tried	42	1266
Our bugles sang truce, for the night-cloud had lower'd	41	789
Our God, our help in ages past	45	550

INDEX TO THE FIRST LINES	VOL.	PAGE
Our signal in love is the glance of our eyes . . .	16	83
Our thrissles flourish'd fresh and fair	6	381
Out of the depths have I cried unto thee, O Jehovah	44	317
Out of the night that covers me	42	1258
Out over the Forth, I look to the North	6	422
Out upon it, I have loved	40	363
Over the mountains	40	388
Pack, clouds, away, and welcome day	40	324
Pardon, oh, pardon, that my soul should make . .	41	965
Pausanias you may praise, and Xanthippus he be for	12	24
Peg Nicholson was a good bay mare	6	399
Phoebus, arise	40	339
Pibroch of Donuil Dhu	41	762
Pipes of the misty moorlands	42	1437
Piping down the valleys wild	41	599
Poets, like disputants, when reasons fail	18	101
Poor, little, pretty, fluttering thing	40	408
Poor Little-faith! Hast been among the Thieves .	15	137
Poor naked wretches, whereso'er you are	6	260
Poor Soul, the centre of my sinful earth	40	288
Poverty causeth the lustre of a man to grow dim .	16	136
Praise waiteth for thee, O God, in Zion	44	224
"Praise Woman still," his lordship roars	6	510
Praise ye Jehovah		
Blessed is the man that feareth Jehovah	44	293
Praise ye Jehovah		
For it is good to sing praises	44	333
Praise ye Jehovah		
I will give thanks unto Jehovah	44	292
Praise ye Jehovah		
Oh give thanks unto Jehovah	44	282
Praise ye Jehovah		
Praise God in his sanctuary	44	336
Praise ye Jehovah		
Praise Jehovah, O my soul	44	332
Praise ye Jehovah		
Praise, O ye servants of Jehovah	44	293
Praise ye Jehovah		
Praise ye Jehovah from the heavens	44	334
Praise ye Jehovah		
Praise ye the name of Jehovah	44	320

Index to the First Lines	Vol.	Page
Praise ye Jehovah		
Sing unto Jehovah a new song	44	335
Preserve me, O God; for in thee do I take refuge .	44	160
Princes have persecuted me without a cause . . .	44	310
Proud Maisie is in the wood	41	764
Proud word you never spoke, but you will speak .	41	923
Put forth thy leaf, thou lofty plane	42	1166
Queen and Huntress, chaste and fair	40	306
Ranged thus for battle on the sacred plain . . .	45	801
Rarely, rarely comest thou	41	847
Rash mortal, and slanderous poet, thy name . . .	6	291
Raving winds around her blowing	6	315
Reader, I am to let thee know	15	373
Rejoice in Jehovah, O ye righteous	44	183
Religion! what treasure untold	39	310
Remember me when I am gone away	42	1228
Remember the word unto thy servant	44	302
Remote, unfriended, melancholy, slow	41	532
Restore to my eyelids the sleep which hath been ravished	16	68
Revered defender of beauteous Stuart	6	279
Riches I hold in light esteem	42	1157
Right, sir! your text I'll prove it true	6	235
Righteous art thou, O Jehovah	44	308
Ring out, your bells, let mourning shews be spread .	40	214
"Rise up, rise up, now, Lord Douglas," she says . .	40	51
Rivulet crossing my ground	42	1082
Robin shure in hairst	6	342
Robin was a roving boy	6	98
Roman Virgil, thou that singest Ilion's lofty temples robed in fire	42	1051
Round the cape of a sudden came the sea . . .	42	1111
Rudely thou wrongest my dear heart's desire . .	40	256
Ruin seize thee, ruthless King	40	468
Rusticity's ungainly form	6	260
Sabrina fair	4	69
Sad thy tale, thou idle page	6	286
Sae flaxen were her ringlets	6	531
Sae rantingly, sae wantonly	6	313
Satyr-king, instead of swords	12	73
Save me, O God	44	230

INDEX TO THE FIRST LINES	VOL.	PAGE
Save me, O God, by thy name	44	212
Say not the struggle naught availeth	42	1165
Say over again, and yet once over again	41	958
Say, sages, what's the charm on earth	6	589
Scorn'd, to be scorn'd by one that I scorn	42	1070
Scots, wha hae wi' Wallace bled	6	502
Search while thou wilt, and let thy reason go . .	3	277
Searching auld wives' barrels	6	375
Season of mists and mellow fruitfulness	41	903
See how the flowers, as at parade	40	379
See the Chariot at hand here of Love	40	297
See the smoking bowl before us	6	139
See what a lovely shell	42	1086
See where she sits upon the grassie greene . . .	40	250
See with what simplicity	40	379
Sensibility, how charming	6	452
Shall I compare thee to a summer's day?	40	276
Shall I, wasting in despair	40	341
Shall they who wrong begin yet rightly end . . .	15	46
She came to the village church	42	1065
She dwelt among the untrodden ways	41	685
She is a winsome wee thing	6	472
She is not fair to outward view	41	937
She walks in beauty, like the night	41	809
She was a phantom of delight	41	667
She was so fair	5	287
She which you view, with triple face and sheen . .	14	540
She's fair and fause that causes my smart . . .	6	347
Shepherd of tender youth	45	553
Should auld acquaintance be forgot	6	335
Shouldst thou think upon me after the length of my age	16	318
Shrewd Willie Smellie to Crochallan came . . .	6	268
Sic a reptile was Wat, sic a miscreant slave . . .	6	517
Sick, am I sick of a jealous dread	42	1066
Sigurd of yore	49	396
Since all that I can ever do for thee	42	1165
Since brass, nor stone, nor earth, nor boundless sea .	40	280
Since cruel thou (I publish) dost desire	14	109
Since I am coming to that holy room	15	360
Since, then, such blessings manifold	45	755

Index to the First Lines	Vol.	Page
Since there's no help, come let us kiss and part . .	40	232
Sing aloud unto God our strength	44	251
Sing hey my braw John Highlandman	6	133
Sing lullaby, as women do	40	198
Sing on, sweet thrush, upon the leafless bough . .	6	481
Sir, as your mandate did request	6	194
Sir, o'er a gill I gat your card	6	197
Sir Wisdom's a fool when he's fou	6	132
Sir, yours this moment I unseal . . . . ,, . .	6	210
Sleep on, and dream of Heaven awhile . . .	41	596
Sleep'st thou, or wak'st thou, fairest creature . .	6	537
So all day long the noise of battle roll'd . . .	42	1019
So dark a mind within me dwells	42	1072
So every spirit, as it is most pure	5	173
So oft as I her beauty do behold	40	255
Soft on the fell	49	318
Some books are lies frae end to end	6	79
Some say the Pilgrim's Progress is not mine . .	15	323
Sometimes thou seem'st not as thyself alone . .	42	1227
Souls of Poets, dead and gone	41	898
Sound, sound the clarion, fill the fife	41	766
Spring, the sweet Spring, is the year's pleasant king	40	266
St. Agnes's Eve!—ah, bitter chill it was . . .	41	907
Stand close around, ye Stygian set	41	924
Star that bringest home the bee	41	790
Stars of the summer night	42	1325
Stay, my charmer, can you leave me	6	314
Stay, O sweet, and do not rise	40	318
Stern Daughter of the voice of God	41	665
Still anxious to secure your partial favour . . .	6	508
Still to be neat, still to be drest	40	297
"Stop thief!" dame Nature call'd to Death . . .	6	520
Strait is the spot and green the sod	6	283
Strange, that I felt so gay	42	1080
Streams that glide in orient plains	6	297
Strew on her roses, roses	42	1175
Strive thou, O Jehovah, with them that strive with me	44	186
Sun of my soul, Thou Saviour dear	45	579
Sunset and evening star	42	1098
Sunshine was he	5	60
Sure never were seen two such beautiful ponies .	18	128

INDEX TO THE FIRST LINES	VOL.	PAGE
Surely God is good to Israel	44	236
Surprised by joy—impatient as the wind	41	690
Swallow, my sister, O sister swallow	42	1249
Sweet and low, sweet and low	42	1002
Sweet are the banks—the banks o' Doon	6	422
Sweet are the thoughts that savour of content	40	289
Sweet Auburn! loveliest village of the plain	41	521
Sweet, be not proud of those two eyes	40	345
Sweet closes the ev'ning on Craigieburn Wood	6	427
Sweet day, so cool, so calm, so bright	40	351
Sweet dimness of her loosened hair's downfall	42	1227
Sweet Echo, sweetest Nymph, that liv'st unseen	4	52
Sweet fa's the eve on Craigieburn	6	547
Sweet flow'ret, pledge o' meikle love	6	418
Sweet Highland Girl, a very shower	41	668
Sweet naiveté of feature	6	475
Sweet stream, that winds through yonder glade	41	547
Sweetest love, I do not go	40	315
Swiftly walk over the western wave	41	854
Symmetrical, and square in shape	45	704
Take, O take those lips away	40	273
Talk not to me of savages	6	589
Tam Samson's weel-worn clay here lies	6	257
Tanagra, think not I forget	41	924
Tax not the royal Saint with vain expense	41	694
Teach me, my God and King	40	352
Teach me, O Jehovah, the way of thy statutes	44	301
Tears, idle tears, I know not what they mean	42	1002
Tears, idle tears, I know not what they mean	28	402
Tell me, Muse, of that man	22	9
Tell me not, in mournful numbers	42	1316
Tell me not of a face that's fair	40	378
Tell me not, Sweet, I am unkind	40	364
Tell me, thou Star, whose wings of light	41	879
Tell me where is Fancy bred	40	268
Tell me, ye prim adepts in Scandal's school	18	105
Thank Heaven! the crisis	42	1287
That sir which serves and seeks for gain	46	241
That there is a falsehood in his looks	6	533
That time of year thou may'st in me behold	40	282
That which her slender waist confined	40	366

Index to the First Lines	Vol.	Page
That's my last Duchess painted on the wall . . .	42	1115
The Assyrian came down like the wolf on the fold .	41	804
The bairns gat out wi' an unco shout	6	466
The battle on Thermodon that shall be	12	212
The blast from Freedom's Northern hills, upon its Southern way	42	1419
The blear-eyed escapeth a pit into which the clear-sighted falleth	1C	130
The blessèd Damozel lean'd out	42	1196
The blude-red rose at Yule may blaw	6	319
The bonie lass made the bed to me	6	565
The Brahman who his evil traits hath banished . .	45	641
The bride cam' out o' the byre	41	580
The cardin o't, the spinnin o't	6	563
The castled crag of Drachenfels	41	818
The Catrine woods were yellow seen	6	115
The clatt'ring thunderbolt that did adorn	14	540
The cock is crowing	41	619
The cod-piece that will house	46	251
The Cooper o' Cuddy came here awa	6	564
The crimson light of sunset falls	42	1247
The curfew tolls the knell of parting day . . .	40	455
The day is cold, and dark, and dreary	42	1326
The day is done, and the darkness	42	1326
The day is done, and the darkness	28	391
The day is past and over	45	554
The day returns, my bosom burns	6	331
The deil cam fiddlin thro' the town	6	467
The deil's awa, the deil's awa	6	467
The Devil got notice that Grose was a-dying . .	6	371
The dusky night rides down the sky	41	513
The earth is Jehovah's; and the fulness thereof . .	44	172
Th' expense of Spirit in a waste of shame . . .	40	288
The face of all the world is changed, I think . .	41	952
The fault was mine, the fault was mine . . .	42	1085
The first time that the sun rose on thine oath . .	41	963
The flame flared at its maddest	49	337
The flower it blaws, it fades, it fa's	6	438
The fool hath said in his heart, There is no God .	44	159
The fool hath said in his heart, There is no God .	44	211
The forward youth that would appear	40	381

Index to the First Lines	Vol.	Page
The fountains mingle with the river	41	854
The friend whom, wild from Wisdom's way . . .	6	510
The future hides in it	25	404
The gallant Youth, who may have gained . . .	41	647
The gloomy night is gath'ring fast	6	250
The glories of our blood and state	40	359
The Greeks, when by their courage and their might	12	101
The grief increaseth, and withal the shame . . .	14	331
The Groups break up, and only they, the wise say .	45	700
The harp that once through Tara's halls	41	840
The heather was blooming, the meadows were mawn	6	274
The heavens declare the glory of God	44	166
The Hill, tho' high, I covet to ascend	15	46
The isles of Greece! the isles of Greece	41	833
The King of love my shepherd is	45	548
The king our Emperor Carlemaine	49	97
The King shall joy in thy strength, O Jehovah . .	44	168
The king sits in Dumferling toune	40	75
The King's most humble servant I	6	490
The Laddies by the banks o' Nith	6	392
The Laird o' Cockpen, he's proud and he's great .	41	576
The lamp of day with ill-presaging glare	6	287
The lang lad they ca' Jumpin John	6	318
The lark now leaves his wat'ry nest	40	364
The last and greatest Herald of Heaven's King . .	40	335
The last time I came o'er the moor	6	491
The lazy mist hangs from the brow of the hill . .	6	333
The Lord is only my support	15	210
The lovely lass of Inverness	6	521
The Magadhaus hold hitherto a doctrine	45	738
The man, in life wherever plac'd	6	34
The man of life upright	40	293
The man whose mind, like to a rock	45	728
The master, the swabber, the boatswain and I . .	46	408
The merchant, to secure his treasure	40	407
The Mighty One, God, Jehovah, hath spoken . . .	44	207
The moon becometh perfect once each month . .	16	345
The more we live, more brief appear	41	794
The murmur of the mourning ghost	42	1160
The news frae Moidart cam' yestereen	41	578
The night is come, but not too soon	42	1317

Index to the First Lines	Vol.	Page
The night is come, like to the day	3	343
The night was still, and o'er the hill	6	249
The noble Maxwells and their powers	6	444
The play is done; the curtain drops	42	1099
The poetry of earth is never dead	41	919
The poor man weeps—here Gavin sleeps	6	230
The poplars are fell'd, farewell to the shade . . .	41	547
The red rose whispers of passion	42	1246
The Robin to the Wren's nest	6	580
The rounded world is fair to see	5	233
The sacred lowe o' weel-placed love	28	86
The sea is calm to-night	42	1183
The series which doth bear a fruit	45	699
The shadows lay along Broadway	28	386
The shepherd for the dance was dress'd	19	41
The simple bard, rough at the rustic plough . . .	6	242
The simple bard, unbroke by rules of art	6	232
The skies they were ashen and sober	42	1281
The small birds rejoice in the green leaves returning	6	322
The smile-dimpled lake woo'd to bathe in its deep .	26	370
The smiling Spring comes in rejoicing	6	442
The Solemn League and Covenant	6	548
The soul's Rialto hath its merchandise	41	957
The spacious firmament on high	40	410
The spacious firmament on high	45	547
The splendor falls on castle walls	42	1003
The sun descending in the west	41	599
The sun had clos'd the winter day	6	180
The sun has gane down o'er the lofty Benlomond .	41	608
The sun he is sunk in the west	6	22
The sun, in ancient guise, competing	19	16
The sun is warm, the sky is clear	41	848
The sun set; but set not his hope	5	191
The sun, the moon, the stars, the seas, the hills and the plains	42	1038
The sun upon the lake is low	41	772
The sun (which doth the greatest comfort bring,) .	40	328
The Sundays of man's life	15	421
The Thames flows proudly to the sea	6	362
The thirsty earth soaks up the rain	40	375

Index to the First Lines	Vol.	Page
The transgression of the wicked saith within my heart	44	188
The tree of deepest root is found	45	705
The tryals that those men do meet withal	15	78
The twentieth year is well-nigh past	41	550
The valiant, in himself, what can he suffer	6	234
The valiant warrior famoused for fight	5	114
The victory now hath this illustrious Buddha won	45	636
The wean wants a cradle	6	580
The weary pund, the weary pund	6	458
The whole world was not half so wide	25	455
The wind blew hollow frae the hills	6	424
The winter it is past, and the summer comes at last	6	320
The wintry west extends his blast	6	32
The word of the Lord by night	42	1313
The World is too much with us; late and soon	41	693
The world's a bubble and the life of Man	40	358
The world's great age begins anew	41	846
The worthy knight lies here	14	542
The year's at the spring	42	1115
The young May moon is beaming, love	41	842
Their groves o' sweet myrtle let Foreign Lands reckon	6	572
Then, gudewife, count the lawin	6	401
Then hate me when thou wilt; if ever, now	40	283
Then hey, for a lass wi' a tocher	6	586
Then mounte, then mounte, brave gallants all	28	404
Theniel Menzies' bonie Mary	6	299
There ance was a may, and she lo'ed na men	40	409
There be none of Beauty's daughters	41	808
There dwelt a man in faire Westmerland	40	102
There is a flower, the Lesser Celandine	41	629
There is a garden in her face	40	290
There is delight in singing, though none hear	41	926
There is no flock, however watched and tended	42	1329
There is no writer that shall not perish	16	88
There is not in the wide world a valley so sweet	41	838
There is sweet music here that softer falls	42	1028
There lived a carl in Kelly Burn Braes	6	463
There lived a wife at Usher's Well	40	81
There shall be seen upon a day	3	97

INDEX TO THE FIRST LINES	VOL.	PAGE
There they are, my fifty men and women	42	1137
There, through the long, long summer hours . .	28	393
There was a bonie lass, and a bonie, bonie lass . .	6	550
There was a boor from Gelderland	47	459
There was a king in Thule	19	113
There was a lad was born in Kyle	6	98
There was a lass, and she was fair	6	494
There was a lass, they ca'd her Meg	6	317
There was a roaring in the wind all night . . .	41	674
There was a time when meadow, grove, and stream	41	609
There was a wife wonn'd in Cockpen	6	460
There was five Carlins in the South	6	389
There was once a time, but old Time was then young	6	349
There was three kings into the east	6	41
There was twa sisters in a bow'r	40	54
There were three ladies lived in a bower	40	58
There were three rauens sat on a tree	40	74
There's a woman like a dew-drop, she's so purer than the purest	18	369
There's a youth in this city, it were a great pity . .	6	368
There's Auld Rob Morris that wons in yon glen .	6	473
There's Death in the cup, so beware	6	548
There's nane sall ken, there's nane can guess . . .	6	554
There's nane that's blest of human kind	6	277
There's news, lassies, news	6	580
There's not a joy the world can give like that it takes away	41	803
There's nought but care on ev'ry han'	6	51
These are the five donations great	45	635
These eyes, dear Lord, once brandous of desire . .	40	337
They all were looking for a king	42	1163
They are all gone into the world of light	40	356
They bore him barefac'd on the bier	46	171
They made use of their power	16	43
They shot him dead on the Nine-Stone rig . . .	41	788
They snool me sair, and haud me down	6	441
They that have power to hurt, and will do none . .	40	283
They that trust in Jehovah	44	314
They told me, Heraclitus, they told me you were dead	42	1159

Index to the First Lines	Vol.	Page
Thickest night, surround my dwelling	6	296
Thine am I, my faithful Fair	6	506
Thine be the volumes, Jessy fair	6	591
Think me not unkind and rude	42	1293
This day, Time winds th' exhausted chain . . .	6	394
This Doctrine out of toil begot	45	737
This is he, who felled by foes	5	283
This is no my ain lassie	6	575
This is the forest primeval	42	1353
This is the month, and this the happy morn . . .	4	7
This is the ship of pearl, which, poets feign . . .	42	1442
This is true Liberty when free born men	3	193
This Life, which seems so fair	40	335
This lump of earth has left his estate	42	1073
This morning timely wrapt with holy fire . . .	40	304
This rich marble doth inter	4	28
This Sancho Panza is of body little	14	541
This tale of my sore-troubled life I write . . .	31	3
This winter's weather it waxeth cold	40	190
This wot ye all whom it concerns	6	252
Thou comest! all is said without a word . . .	41	962
Thou flatt'ring mark of friendship kind	6	200
Thou greybeard, old Wisdom! may boast of thy treasures	6	489
Thou hast dealt well with thy servant	44	303
Thou hast left me ever, Jamie	6	504
Thou hast thy calling to some palace-floor . . .	41	951
Thou, Liberty, thou art my theme	6	432
Thou ling'ring star, with less'ning ray	6	386
Thou, Nature, partial Nature, I arraign	6	338
Thou of an independent mind	6	563
Thou Power Supreme, whose mighty scheme . .	28	88
Thou still unravish'd bride of quietness	41	901
Thou that my doleful life didst imitate	14	15
Thou thoughtest well of the days	16	211
Thou unrelenting past	42	1269
Thou, who thy honor as thy God rever'st . . .	6	427
Thou whom chance may hither lead	6	325
Thou whom chance may hither lead	6	337
Thou, Whose Almighty word	45	586
Thou youngest virgin-daughter of the skies . . .	40	394

INDEX TO THE FIRST LINES	VOL.	PAGE
Thou's welcome, wean; mishanter fa' me	6	59
Tho' cruel fate should bid us part	6	98
Though fickle Fortune has deceived me	6	37
Though the day of my destiny's over	41	810
Though the day of my destiny's over	28	401
Though thou art not a peer, thou hast no peer . .	14	16
Tho' women's minds, like winter winds	6	140
Thoughts, words, and deeds, the Statute blames with reason	6	217
Three poets, in three distant ages born	40	406
Three years she grew in sun and shower	41	686
Three years she grew in sun and shower	28	151
Through and through th' inspir'd leaves	6	277
Through birth and rebirth's endless round . . .	45	638
Through the black, rushing smokebursts	42	1172
Thy bosom is endearèd with all hearts	40	277
Thy braes were bonny, Yarrow stream	41	512
Thy hands have made me and fashioned me . . .	44	304
Thy hue, dear pledge, is pure and bright	41	757
Thy testimonies are wonderful	44	308
Thy tomb is fairly placed upon the strand . . .	12	35
Thy word is a lamp unto my feet	44	306
Tiger, tiger, burning bright	41	597
Time consists of two days; this bright and that gloomy	16	18
Timely blossom, Infant fair	40	451
Timon, the misanthrope, am I below	12	391
Tired with all these, for restful death I cry . . .	40	281
'Tis Friendship's pledge, my young fair Friend . .	6	579
'Tis that, that gives the poet rage	39	325
'Tis the day of resurrection	45	555
'Tis the last rose of summer	41	839
'Tis the middle of night by the castle clock . . .	41	726
'Tis time this heart should be unmoved	41	836
To be or not to be? That is the question	34	135
To draw no envy, Shakespeare, on thy name . . .	40	308
To fair Fidele's grassy tomb	41	487
To heal his heart of long-time pain	42	1479
To him who in the love of Nature holds	42	1262
To John I owed great obligation	40	408
To make a happy fireside clime	28	87

Index to the First Lines	Vol.	Page
To me, fair Friend, you never can be old	40	284
To Megara some of our madcaps ran	12	69
To Mercy, Pity, Peace, and Love	41	605
To my ninth decade I have totter'd on	41	929
To my true king I offered, free from stain	41	943
To paint fair Nature, by divine command	27	313
To Riddell, much lamented man	6	550
To see a world in a grain of sand	41	601
To the Lords of Convention 'twas Claver'se who spoke	41	770
To the weaver's gin ye go, fair maids	6	312
To you, sir, this summons I've sent	6	233
Toll for the Brave	41	546
To-morrow is Saint Valentine's day	46	167
Too many leaders are not well; the way	12	399
Toussaint, the most unhappy man of men	41	671
True hearted was he, the sad swain o' the Yarrow	6	484
True Thomas lay o'er yond grassy bank	40	77
Truly, I never have seen the market and street so deserted	19	335
Truly woman is of glass	14	333
Turn again, thou fair Eliza	6	441
Turn all thy thoughts to eyes	40	293
Turn, Fortune, turn thy wheel, and lower the proud	42	1007
Turn on the prudent Ant thy heedless eyes	39	309
'Twas at the royal feast for Persia won	40	400
'Twas even,—the dewy fields were green	6	230
'Twas in that place o' Scotland's isle	6	158
'Twas in the seventeen hunder year	6	561
'Twas na her bonie blue e'e was my ruin	6	571
'Twas on a Holy Thursday, their innocent faces clean	41	605
'Twas on a lofty vase's side	40	473
'Twas on a Monday morning	6	522
'Twas on a Monday morning	41	579
'Twas one of the charmèd days	42	1303
'Twas when the stacks get on their winter hap	6	242
Twenty years hence my eyes may grow	41	923
Two Voices are there, one is of the Sea	41	691
Umbriel, a dusky, melancholy sprite	34	153
Under a spreading chestnut-tree	42	1323

Index to the First Lines	Vol.	Page
Under the greenwood tree	40	268
Under the wide and starry sky	42	1261
Under yonder beech-tree single on the green-sward	42	1186
Underneath this sable hearse	40	343
Unhappy they, to whom God ha'n't reveal'd . . .	27	71
Unlike are we, unlike, O princely Heart	41	950
Unto thee do I lift up mine eyes	44	313
Unto thee, O Jehovah, do I lift up my soul . . .	44	173
Unto thee, O Jehovah, will I call	44	177
Up and waur them a', Jamie	6	393
Up from the meadows rich with corn	42	1439
Up in the morning's no for me	6	316
Up the airy mountain	42	1162
Up the streets of Aberdeen	42	1424
Up wi' the carls o' Dysart	6	278
Upon a simmer Sunday morn	6	102
Upon my lap, my Sovereign sits	40	261
Upon that night, when fairies light	6	117
Vane, young in years but in sage counsel old . .	4	85
Vanity, saith the preacher, vanity	42	1117
Verse, a breeze 'mid blossoms straying	41	719
Victorious men of earth, no more	40	360
Vigil strange I kept on the field one night . . .	42	1485
Virupakkhas, I love them all	45	724
Wae is my heart, and the tear's in my e'e . . .	6	545
Wae worth thy power, thou cursed leaf	6	232
Wailing, wailing, wailing, the wind over land and sea	42	1046
Wake! For the Sun behind yon Eastern bright . .	41	970
Waken, lords and ladies gay	41	768
Warriors and chiefs! should the shaft or the sword	41	832
We are na fou, we're nae that fou	6	376
We are the music-makers	42	1246
We cam na here to view your warks	6	289
We give thanks unto thee, O God	44	240
We grant they're thine, those beauties all	6	533
We have heard with our ears, O God	44	200
We must resign! heaven his great soul does claim .	34	149
We praise thee, O God, we acknowledge thee to be the Lord	45	558
We talk'd with open heart, and tongue	41	617

Index to the First Lines	Vol.	Page
We trod the steps appointed for us	16	74
We twa hae paidl't i' the burn	28	89
We walk'd along, while bright and red	41	615
We watched her breathing thro' the night	41	935
We'll hide the Cooper behint the door	6	564
We're all deluded, vainly searching ways	3	308
Weak-winged is song	42	1458
Wee, modest, crimson-tippèd flow'r	6	201
Wee, sleekit, cowrin, tim'rous beastie	6	125
Wee Willie Gray, and his leather wallet	6	550
Weep with me, all you that read	40	307
Welcome, wild North-easter	42	1103
Well I remember how you smiled	41	925
Well! If the Bard was weather-wise, who made	41	745
Were I as base as is the lowly plain	40	322
Were I so tall to reach the pole	40	408
Wha, in a brulyie, will	6	523
Wha is that at my bower-door?	6	51
Wha will buy my troggin, fine election ware	6	587
Whan bells war rung, an mass was sung	40	79
Whan that Aprille with his shoures soote	40	11
Whare are you gaun, my bonie lass	6	382
Whare live ye, my bonie lass	6	460
What ails ye now, ye lousie bitch	6	239
What bird so sings, yet so does wail?	40	213
What can a young lassie, what shall a young lassie	6	430
What can I give thee back, O liberal	41	953
What constitutes a state	41	592
What danger is the Pilgrim in	15	313
What dost thou in that mansion fair?	6	496
What flocks of critics hover here to-day	18	19
What guile is this, that those her golden tresses	40	254
What hath wrought Sigurd	49	417
What I have left, I left not from generosity	16	316
What is our life? The play of passion	40	210
What man his conduct guardeth, and hath wisdom	45	755
What needs my Shakespeare, for his honored bones	4	26
What needs this din about the town o' Lon'on	6	390
What one would think doth seek to slay outright	15	277
What time my age was twenty-nine, Subhadda	45	657
What was he doing, the great god Pan	41	948

Index to the First Lines	Vol.	Page
What will I do gin my Hoggie die	6	314
Whatever is, is right. Though purblind man . .	1	57
When a deed is done for Freedom, through the broad earth's aching breast	42	1447
When all the world is young, lad	42	1103
When at the first I took my pen in hand	15	5
When biting Boreas, fell and dour	6	260
When Britain first at Heaven's command	40	453
When, by a generous Public's kind acclaim . . .	6	273
When chapman billies leave the street	6	411
When chill November's surly blast	6	64
When Christians unto carnal men give ear . . .	15	24
When daisies pied and violets blue	40	270
When dear Clarinda, matchless fair	6	309
When Death's dark stream I ferry o'er	6	296
When do I see thee most, beloved one	42	1225
When Faith and Love, which parted from thee never	4	84
When first I came to Stewart Kyle	6	61
When first my brave Johnie lad came to the town .	6	439
When first the fiery-mantled Sun	41	790
When fortune is liberal to thee	16	212
When God at first made man	40	355
When God willeth an event	16	138
When Guilford good our pilot stood	6	54
When he came to grene wode	28	409
When he who adores thee has left but the name . .	41	838
When I am dead, my dearest	42	1228
When I consider how my light is spent	4	86
When I consider life, 'tis all a cheat	34	137
When I have borne in memory what has tamed . .	41	693
When I have fears that I may cease to be . . .	41	921
When I have seen by Time's fell hand defaced . .	40	280
When I survey the bright	40	258
When icicles hang by the wall	40	267
When in disgrace with fortune and men's eyes . .	40	276
When in the chronicle of wasted time	40	285
When Israel went forth out of Egypt	44	294
When Januar' wind was blawing cauld	6	564
When Jehovah brought back those that returned to Zion	44	314

INDEX TO THE FIRST LINES	VOL.	PAGE
When Lascelles thought fit from this world to depart	6	520
When Letty had scarce pass'd her third glad year	41	947
When lilacs last in the dooryard bloom'd	42	1497
When Love with unconfinèd wings	40	365
When lovely woman stoops to folly	41	517
When lyart leaves bestrow the yird	6	129
When maidens such as Hester die	41	753
When men shall find thy flow'r, thy glory, pass	40	224
When Morine, deceas'd, to the devil went down	6	497
When Music, heavenly maid, was young	41	488
When Nature her great master-piece design'd	6	329
When o'er the rill the e'ening star	6	471
When on my sickly couch I lay	28	24
When our two souls stand up erect and strong	41	958
When priests are more in word than matter	46	252
When Princes and Prelates	6	479
When rosy May comes in wi' flowers	6	360
When Ruth was left half desolate	41	622
When Saints do sleepy grow, let them come hither	15	141
When the blest seed of Terah's faithful Son	4	15
When the British warrior queen	41	551
When the drums do beat, and the cannons rattle	6	364
When the hounds of spring are on winter's traces	42	1247
When the hours of Day are numbered	42	1319
When the lamp is shatter'd	41	874
When the pine tosses its cones	42	1301
When the sheep are in the fauld, and the kye at hame	41	570
When the voices of children are heard on the green	41	604
When to her lute Corinna sings	40	291
When to the sessions of sweet silent thought	40	276
When to the strenuous, meditative Brahman	45	640
When we met first and loved, I did not build	41	964
When we two parted	41	807
When wild war's deadly blast was blawn	6	486
Whenas in silks my Julia goes	40	346
Where are the joys I have met in the morning	6	505
Where are the Kings and the peoples of the earth	16	327
Where art thou, my beloved Son	41	660
Where, braving angry winter's storms	6	304

Index to the First Lines	Vol.	Page
Where Cart rins rowin to the sea	6	437
Where did you come from, baby dear	42	1164
Where dost thou careless lie	40	305
Where hae ye been sae braw, lad	6	381
Where is the Home for me	8	364
Where lies the land to which the ship would go .	42	1168
Where shall the lover rest	41	759
Where the bee sucks, there suck I	46	435
Where the bee sucks, there suck I	40	272
Where the remote Bermudas ride	40	385
Where they once dug for money	28	414
Whereas my birth and spirit rather took	15	389
Whereas the wise who cultivate	45	753
Wherewith shall a young man cleanse his way . .	44	300
Whether is better, the gift or the donor	42	1305
Which that the sun with his beams hot	40	202
While at the stook the shearers cow'r	6	110
While briers an' woodbines budding green . . .	6	84
While eagerly man culls life's flowers	45	711
While Europe's eye is fixed on mighty things . .	6	474
While larks, with little wing	6	497
While new-ca'd kye rowt at the stake	6	88
While virgin Spring by Eden's flood	6	443
While winds frae aff Ben-Lomond blaw	6	70
While you here do snoring lie	46	406
Whiles in the early winter eve	42	1245
Whither, midst falling dew	42	1271
Who are you, dusky woman, so ancient hardly hu-		
man.	42	1490
Who doth my weal diminish thus and stain . . .	14	250
Who is it worships at my feet	45	722
Who is Silvia? What is she?	40	269
Who is the happy Warrior? Who is he	41	672
Who made the heart, 'tis He alone	28	87
Who shall, Mattio, yield our pain relief	31	175
Who would true valour see	15	305
Whoe'er he be that sojourns here	6	286
Whoe'er she be	40	369
Whoe'er thou art, O reader, know	6	230
Whoever comes to shroud me, do not harm . . .	40	310
Whom will you send to London town	6	556

Index to the First Lines	Vol.	Page
Whose is that noble, dauntless brow	6	272
Whoso would know the power of God's dominion .	31	263
Why am I loth to leave this earthly scene	6	36
Why art thou silent? Is thy love a plant . . .	41	689
Why boastest thou thyself in mischief, O mighty man	44	210
Why, Damon, with the forward day	41	493
Why do the nations rage	44	147
Why dois your brand sae drap wi' bluid . . .	40	56
Why, let the strucken deer go weep	46	146
Why look the distant mountains	41	943
Why so pale and wan, fond lover	40	363
Who standest thou afar off, O Jehovah	44	155
Why weep ye by the tide, ladie	41	758
Why, why tell the lover	6	573
Why, ye tenants of the lake	6	300
Will ye go to the Hielands, Leezie Lindsay . . .	6	580
Will ye go to the Indies, my Mary	6	210
Willie Wastle dwalt on Tweed	6	461
Wilt thou be my Dearie?	6	511
Wilt Thou forgive that sin where I begun . . .	40	311
Wilt Thou forgive that sin where I begun . . .	15	357
Winds blow and waters roll	5	102
Wishfully I look and languish	6	428
Wi' braw new branks in mickle pride	6	238
With Esop's lion, Burns says, sore I feel	6	290
With food and drinks and cunning magic arts . .	2	252
With his cross-bow, and his quiver	26	416
With how sad steps, O Moon, thou climb'st the skies	40	217
With little here to do or see	41	655
With numerous tribes from Asia's regions brought	12	12
With Pegasus upon a day	6	345
With sacrifice before the rising morn	41	678
With secret throes I marked that earth	6	188
With the same heart, I said, I'll answer thee . .	41	963
Within the glen sae bushy, O	6	211
Word's gane to the kitchen	40	118
Words of strife heard I	49	444
Work of his hand	5	191
Would that the structure brave, the manifold music I build	42	1144

INDEX TO THE FIRST LINES	VOL.	PAGE
Would'st thou hear what man can say	40	304
Wow, but your letter made me vauntie	6	387
Ye banks and braes and streams around	6	472
Ye banks and braes o' bonie Doon	6	424
Ye blushing virgins happy are	40	257
Ye distant spires, ye antique towers	40	459
Ye flaming Powers, and wingèd Warriors bright .	4	42
Ye flowery banks o' bonie Doon	6	423
Ye gallants bright, I rede you right	6	351
Ye Highlands, and ye Lawlands	40	109
Ye hypocrites! are these your pranks	6	489
Ye Irish lords, ye knights an' squires	6	165
Ye Jacobites by name, give an ear, give an ear . .	6	446
Ye learnèd sisters, which have oftentimes . . .	40	238
Ye maggots, feed on Nicol's brain	6	278
Ye Mariners of England	41	797
Ye men of wit and wealth, why all this sneering .	6	489
Ye sons of old Killie, assembled by Willie . . .	6	254
Ye true "Loyal Natives" attend my song	6	488
Ye twain, in trouble and distress	19	9
Ye wavering shapes, again ye do enfold me . . .	19	7
Yes, call me by my pet-name! Let me hear . . .	41	963
Yes; in the sea of life enisled	42	1174
Yes, let the rich deride, the proud disdain . . .	6	116
Yes, there is holy pleasure in thine eye	41	695
Yestreen I had a pint o' wine	6	399
Yestreen I met you on the moor	6	20
Yet if His Majesty, our sovereign lord	40	201
Yet, love, mere love, is beautiful indeed	41	953
Yet once more, O ye Laurels, and once more . .	4	74
Yet pleased with idle whimsies of his brain . . .	34	146
Yon wandering rill that marks the hill	6	439
Yon wild mossy mountains sae lofty and wide .	6	263
You ask me why, tho' ill at ease	42	1032
You brave heroic minds	40	230
You meaner beauties of the night	40	294
You promise heavens free from strife	42	1159
You render me lovelorn and remain at ease . . .	16	118
You spotted snakes with double tongue	40	270
You'll love me yet!—and I can tarry	42	1115
You're welcome to Despots, Dumourier	6	491

EXPLANATORY NOTE ON GENERAL INDEX

Titles of books, essays, dramas, poems, etc., are indexed under the significant subject word where there is one (as TRUTH, ESSAY ON, *Bacon's.* IMMORTALITY, ODE ON INTIMATIONS OF).

Where there is no principal subject word, the title is indexed in its proper order, omitting initial articles, prepositions, or interjections (HARP THAT ONCE THROUGH TARA'S HALLS, THE).

Titles of works included in The Harvard Classics are entered in small capitals (ÆNEID, THE). *Works discussed in the Classics, but not included therein, are entered in italics* (Percy's Reliques), *and will be found as a rule only as subtitles under the author's name. Where the author is unknown or uncertain, or where there is a multiple authorship, the work is entered under its own title.*

Titles of many poems are merely the first lines repeated. The exact titles of such poems will therefore be found in the INDEX TO THE FIRST LINES OF POEMS, SONGS, CHORUSES, HYMNS AND PSALMS. *Any other entry likely to be of use has been put into the* GENERAL INDEX.

GENERAL INDEX

Aaron, references to, in Psalms, xliv, 243 (20), 272 (6), 281 (26), 283 (16); beard of, 319 (2); and the golden calf, 444 (40-1); breastplate of, iv, 153, 388; Calvin on, xxxix, 45; Browning on, xlii, 1143; Mohammed on, xlv, 922

Abano, Pietro d', xix, 205, note 35

Abas, in the ÆNEID, xlii, 79, 332, 341

Abascantius, L. Satrius, ix, 379

Abbagliato, Dante on, xx, 124, and note 7

Abbati, Bocca degli, xx, 135, note 8

Abaddon, Hebrew for destruction, xliv, 116, note 13; Milton on, iv, 415

Abbondio, Don, in THE BETROTHED, meets the bravoes, xxi, 9-15; character and times of, 16-20; tells Perpetua his mishap, 21-4; plans to put Renzo off, 25-6; with Renzo, 27-30; owns truth to Renzo, 31-3, his fever, 34; on night of Renzo's intended marriage, 119-24, 132; ordered to go to Lucia, 385-9; with the Unnamed on the way, 390-5; returns with Lucia, 396-404; complained of, by Agnese, 415; with the Cardinal, 425-7; reprimanded by Cardinal, 433-44; during German invasion, 493-502, 508-13; at castle of Unnamed, 515-17; returns home, 517-20; with Renzo on latter's return, 569-71; anxieties about marrying Renzo, 645, 651-4; consents to perform ceremony, 655-8; advises Marquis how to aid lovers, 658-61

Abbott, T. K., translator of Kant, xxxii, 315

Abbott, Capt., at Gettysburg, xliii, 409, 411

Abdallah ibn Umm Maktûm, xlv, 895 note

Abd-el-Melik, xvi, 310, 339

Abd-es-Samad, the sheik, xvi, 313-37

Abdication, Rousseau on right of, xxxiv, 225

Abdiel, in PARADISE LOST, rebukes Satan, iv, 204; leaves the rebel

angels, 205-6; arrival among the faithful, 207-8; combat with Satan, 209-12; in the battle, 216; Bagehot on Milton's, xxviii, 204-5

A Becket (see Becket)

Abel and Cain, Milton on, iv, 333-4; Mohammed on, xlv, 1011; taken from Limbo by Christ, xx, 18; and the tree of Eve, xxxv, 196

Abelard, Carlyle on, xxv, 379

ABERFELDY, THE BIRKS OF, vi, 292-3

Aberrant species, xi, 468

Abiathar, Winthrop on, xliii, 100

ABIDE WITH ME, xlv, 580-1

Abihu, Browning on, xlii, 1143

Ability, Penn on, worldly, i, 392-5; with humility, i, 411, (247); M. Aurelius on low natural, ii, 225 (5), 246 (5), 252 (52), 255 (67), 258 (8); generally accompanied by frankness, iii, 18; certain to make itself felt, v, 297

Abime, the Saracen, xlix, 157, 158

Abimelech, and David, his, 184

Abindarracz, story of, xiv, 47

Abishag, reference to, xli, 499

Abolitionism, Lowell on, xxviii, 459

Abortion, Hippocrates on, xxxviii, 3

ABOU BEN ADHEM, xli, 893-4

Abra, Pompein's maid, xii, 282

Abradatas, xxvii, 23

Abraham, Milton on, iv, 348-9; and Ephron, x, 32; Bunyan on, xv, 107, 240-1; and Sarah, xxxvi, 285; Paul on, 370; the covenant with, xliv, 280 (9); Stephen on, 442 (2-8); Mohammed on, xlv, 915, 921-2, 967, 993; and Iblis, 965, note 5; Pascal on, xlviii, 167 (502), 202, 205, 207, 220 (644), 289 (822); 303; taken from Limbo, xx, 18

Abraxa, early name of Utopia, xxxvi, 182

Abridgments, Swift on, xxvii, 119

Abriorix, Gaulish chief, xii, 295

Abrotonon, mother of Themistocles, xii, 5

Absalom, and David, xx, 120; Psalm when David fled from, xliv, 148-9; Bunyan on, xv, 313; David's grief for, 423

Abscesses, antiseptic treatment of, xxxviii, 277-80

ABSENCE, by Landor, xli, 923

ABSENCE, PRESENT IN, xl, 321

Absence, Lovelace on, xl, 366; Confucius on, xliv, 30-1

Absentees, taxation of, x, 560

Absolutes, Plato on knowledge of, ii, 64-6; participation in, 94-6; further remarks on, 97-8; Schiller on search for, xxxii, 252; Mazzini on, xxxii, 401

Absolution, Luther on unjust, xxxvi, 289; Pascal on, xlviii, 309 (870), 316 (904-5), 322 (923)

Abstemiousness, Pliny on, ix, 312-13

Abstinence, Comus on folly of, iv, 65-6; Hindu doctrine of, xlv, 876-7

Abstract ideas, Plato on, ii, 64-6; Epictetus on, 157 (109); Schiller on, xxxii, 252; Rousseau on, xxxiv, 257; Berkeley on, xxxvii, 225-6; Hume on, 436, 438 note

Abstract names, Hobbes on, xxxiv, 341

Abstract philosophy, Hume on, xxxvii, 306-15, 370

Abstract reasoning, Hume on, xxxvii, 437-8, 443

Abstract sciences, Pascal on, xlviii, 58 (144)

Absurdities, Hobbes on, xxxiv, 346-7

ABT VOGLER, xlii, 1144-8

Abu Bekr, xlv, 977, note 24

Abu Ghal, xlv, 889, note 3

Abu-l-Abbas El-Khidr, xvi, 338

Abu Laheb, xlv, 1003, note 20

Abu Sufiân, xlv, 955, note 2

Abuses, Sidney on, xxvii, 38; Luther on, xxxvi, 324-5; Dryden on, xxxix, 183, note 36; Pascal on, xlviii, 318 (916)

Abyssinia, salt as money in, x, 30

Academic philosophy, Hume on, xxxvii, 337-8, 431-45

Academics, St. Augustine on the, vii, 77; on nature, xxxix, 114

Academy, Milton's design of an, iii, 251-9

Academy of Plato, ii, 1; first formed by Cimon, xxviii, 41; Milton on, iv, 405; Newman on, xxviii, 58-9

Acadie, A Tale of (see Evangeline)

Acamacari, town of, xxxiii, 373

Acception of persons, xxxiv, 426

Acciu works of, lost, xxvii, 361

Acclimatisation, Darwin on, xi, 152-5

Accolti, Benedetto, xxxi, 76, note 285, note 4

Accomplishments, Locke on, xxxvii, 182

Accorso, Francesco, xx, 66 and note 4

Accounting, as part of female education, i, 97-8; importance of punctual, 102-3; Locke on knowledge and practise of, xxxvii, 190-1

Accuracy, essential to beauty, v, 219; Hume on, xxxvii, 309-10; Goethe on, xxxix, 269

Accusations, kill innocent names, xviii, 333; Bentham on public, xxvii, 253-4; in law, Hobbes on, xxxiv, 415; of children, xxxvii, 96; Calvin on, xxxix, 30

Accusers, false, in ancient Rome, ix, 310, note 8

Acedophagi, xxxv, 367

Acelin, Count, xlix, 103, 191

Acestes, King of Sicily, xiii, 94; welcomes Æneas, 183; at games, 184; the arrow of, 199-200

Acetate of lead, under voltaic current, xxx, 134 note

Acetate of soda, xxx, 39 and note

Acevedo, Pietro de, on bravoes, xxi, 12

Achæmenides, xiii, 151-3

Achaia, Pliny on, ix, 349

Achaicus, xlv, 526 (17)

Achan, Dante on, xx, 230; Vane on, xliii, 137

Achates, faithful, xiii, 79; references to, 81, 86, 95, 98, 148, 212, 287

Achelons River, Herodotus on, xxxiii, 9

Acheron, Plato on the, ii, 109, 110; sooty flag of, iv, 62; Milton on the, 125; blood-bedabbled peak of, viii, 433; Virgil on, xiii, 215, 221; Dante on the, xx, 15, 62; Homer on the, xxii, 150; Burke on exhalation of, xxiv, 75 (see xiii, 219-20)

Acherusia Lake, ii, 109, 110

Achievement, Browning on, xlii, 1140

Achillas, and Cæsar, xii, 316

Achilles, Socrates on, ii, 15; and Patroclus, iii, 332; xxxii, 79; xlvi, 25; Milton on wrath of, iv, 264; heel of, v, 96; Dryden on, xiii, 9, 15, 28; xxxix, 166; father of Pyrrhus, and Priam, xiii, 121-2; imitated by Alexander, xxxvi, 52; brought up by Chiron, 60; flight from Chiron, xx, 182; in Dante's Hell, 23; javelin of, 129; his quarrel with Ulysses, xxii, 106; Homer on death and funeral of, xxii, 332-3; in Hades, 164-5, 331; Burke on, xxiv, 133; Tom Brown on, xxvii, 328; Shelley on Homer's, 352-3; and the twenty-five cities, xxxv, 246; and the captive, xxxix, 251

Achillini, and King Louis, xxi, 487

Achoriens, More on the, xxxvi, 168-9

Acilius, friend of Pliny, ix, 251; soldier of Cæsar, xii, 287
Acmon, in the ÆNEID, xiii, 331
Acoetes, servant of Pallas, xiii, 361, 363
Aconcagua, volcano of, xxix, 269, 309-10; height of, 261, note 11
Aconteus, in the ÆNEID, xiii, 383
Acoustics, in NEW ATLANTIS, iii, 187
Acquiescence, Burns on, vi, 73; Emerson's doctrine of, v, 64-5, 151-2; Epictetus on, ii, 126 (26, 29), 130 (37), 136 (58), 138 (61), 143 (71), 149 (84), 164 (131), 165 (133, 134), 167 (138, 139), 172 (152), 174 (159, 160), 179 (184, 186); Hume on doctrine of, xxxvii, 389-90; Jesus on, xli, 503; Job on, xliv, 75 (10); Kempis on, vii, 287-8, 289-90, 313-4, 316, 330-3; M. Aurelius on, ii, 205 (17), 212 (16), 217 (23), 220 (34), 226 (8), 228 (10), 231 (27), 242 (44), 251 (41), 252 (51, 54), 253 (58), 261 (32), 265 (50), 273 (28), 283 (14), 285 (28), 290 (6), 301 (14); Pascal's doctrine, xlviii, 345-6, 358, 377; Pascal on Epictetus's doctrine, 393-4; Pope on, xl, 422, 425; Raleigh on, xxxix, 102; Rousseau on, xxxiv, 288; Tennyson on, xlii, 1059; Thackeray on, xlii, 1100-1
Acrasia, the enchantress, xxxix, 68
Acron, death of, xiii, 351-2
Acropolis, propylæa of the, xii, 52
Acta Sanctorum, Carlyle on, v, 475
Actæon, son of Autonoë, viii, 406; and Artemis, 361-2; reference to, xlvii, 683 note
Actilius, Caxton on, 16
Actinic light, xxx, 272
Actinism, xxviii, 431
Action (see also Acts, Activity); Demosthenes on, iii, 33; the value of, to the scholar, v, 12-15; Kant on principles of, xxxii, 345-70; two ways of, xxxix, 123; Longfellow on, xlii, 1316, 1317; Hindu doctrine of, xlv, 809-10, 813-15, 819-20, 823-4, 826, 876-8; Webster on want of, xlvii, 723; Pascal on necessity of, xlviii, 51 (131); sources of, 117 (334); and love, 423, 425
Action and reaction (see Polarity)
Actium, battle of, xii, 385-9; Bacon on, iii, 83; Dryden on Antony at, xviii, 30; Virgil on, xiii, 294-5
Actius, razor of, iii, 329, note 9
Activity, Cicero on, ix, 52; Epictetus on, and meditation, ii, 125; M. Aurelius on, 271 (16); Hindu Krishna on, xlv, 813; man prone

to shirk, xix, 19; in perceptions, xxxvii, 228-9
Actor, the lance of, xiii, 398
Actors, attitude of, toward the drama, xix, 10, 12-13; as teachers, 27; high rewards of, reason for, x, 113; Lamb on, xxvii, 314-22; legal, xxxiv, 430-1; Montaigne on, xxxii, 72; Shakespeare on, xlvi, 130-1, 138-9; Voltaire on, xxxiv, 156
Acts, better than knowledge, xv, 87; xxxii, 60-1; xliv, 9 (24), 375 (47-9); better than words, ii, 177 (175), 283 (16), 292 (15); Browning on, and intentions, xlii, 1113; Confucius on, and words, xliv, 8 (13), 14 (24), 16 (9), 50 (29); consequences of, xlviii, 168 (505); effect of, on faculties and habits, ii, 144 (75); explain themselves, v, 71; carry own rewards, 94, 300; hidden, most noble, xlviii, 61 (159); Hindu doctrine of, xlv, 877-8; Hume on, and motives, xxxvii, 373-81, 383 note, 386-7; Kant on moral worth of, xxxii, 327-34, 370-1; Kempis on judgment of, vii, 308; kind of words, v, 170; not motives, to be judged, xxv, 37; our angels, v, 63; our epochs, xviii, 416; our only possessions, xlv, 692; religiousness of, 874; unsocial, ii, 272 (23)
Acts of the Apostles, authorship of, xliv, 356, 429-95; editorial remarks on, 428
Acts of settlement, succession, etc. (see Settlement, Succession)
Acuto, Giovanni, xxxvi, 44
Ad, xlv, 902, 916
Adam, awakening of, iv, 183-4; 253-7; Bacon on fall of, xxxix, 135; Bagehot on Milton's, xxviii, 210; Browne on, iii, 286-7; 304, 331; Burns on, vi, 150; Chaucer on, xl, 46; confesses his sin and is judged, iv, 297-9; creation explained to, 251; inquiries of, on creation, 231-3, 243; curse of, xxxvi, 349; Dante on, xx, 398-400; earth, kingdoms of, seen by, in vision, iv, 332-3; Eden, departure of, from, 360-2; Eden, Life in, described by, 253-7; Eden, loss of, dreaded by, 330-1; Eden, sentenced to leave, 325; Eve, accused by, 290-3; Eve, discourse with, on laboring apart, 268-73; Eve, love of, for, 259-62; Eve, meeting of, with, 258-9; Eve, supper of, with, 165-6; Eve, tree of, and, xxxv, 196; Eve, wrath of, at, iv, 316-18; fall of, through own fault, 294-5; future, vision of, by, 333-

59; HAMLET, mentions of, in, xlvi, 180; hides from God, iv, 297; Hobbes on language of, xxxiv, 335-6; labors of, iv, 189; Lamb on pictures of, xxvii, 327 note; lament of, iv, 312-16; Luther on, xxxvi, 380; Michael, meeting of, with, iv, 328-9; morning hymn, 187-9; Omens, evil, seen by, 327; PARADISE LOST, Description of, in, 164-5; supper with Eve, 165-6; Pascal on state of, xlviii, 187 (560); prayers relieve, iv, 326; Raphael discourses with, 195-7; Raphael parts with, 262-3; Raphael welcomed by, 191-3; rest suggested by, 173; retires to rest with Eve, 175-6; saved by Christ, xx, 18; his place in Paradise, 423; Savior promised to, xlviii, 219-220; stars, discourse of, on, 174; stars, inquiries of, on, iv, 247; submission advised by, 320-2; tree of knowledge, described to Eve by, 167-8; wisdom of, xx, 341, note 6; Eve tempts, iv, 285-90; waking, accuses Eve, 290-3

Adam and Eve, Woolman on, i, 223

Adam and Eve's Pools, iii, 179

Adam the First, and his daughters, xv, 74

Adamo of Brescia, xx, 126, note 2; Simon of Troy, and, 128

Adams, John, Americanism of, v, 71; American independence, and, xliii, 160 note, 164; treaty with England and, 185-6

Adams, John Quincy, treaty of 1814 and, xliii, 273; treaty with Spain and, xliii, 286

Adams, Matthew, i, 15

Adams, Samuel, signer of Declaration, xliii, 164; in Articles of Confederation, 177

Adams, Sarah Flower, hymn by, xlv, 582

Adams, William, xliii, 273

Adamus, in Utopia, xxxvi, 192

Adaptability, Marcus Aurelius on, ii, 241 (39); Montaigne on, xxxii, 59-60; to times, Machiavelli on, xxxvi, 84-6

Adaptation, in nature, xi, 90-1; examples of, 76-7, 98, 208, 235; xxix, 488; never perfect, 96; to atmospheric conditions, xxxviii, 355-6; to climate, xi, 152-3

Adder, Harrison on the, xxxv, 362-364

Addison, Joseph, birth and education, 165-7; Campaign, 169-70, 193-5; Cato of, 169, 176-9, 189-90; Cato, quotation from, i, 86; character and habits of, xxvii, 187-92; Commissioner of Appeals, 170; critical abilities of, 208-10;

death of, 186-7; defense of Christianity, 183-4; Dennis on Cato of, 197-208; descriptions of life, 210-11; the Drummer, 180; Dryden on translations of, xiii, 432; early writings of, xxvii, 167-8; Esther Johnson and, 132-3; Freeholder, 182; Hume on, xxxvii, 307; HYMN by, xl, 410; xlv, 547; Johnson on Cato of, xxvii, 196-7; xxxix, 238; Latin compositions of, early, 167; Letter to Halifax, 169, 193; Life and works of, 76; LIFE by Johnson, 165-211; marriage of, 182-183; Old Whig papers, 185, 186; on Chaucer, xxviii, 81; on criticism of art, xxiv, 28; on love of beauty in animals, 39; on the rotund in building, 65 note; papers for the Guardian, xxvii, 179-80; Peerage Bill Pamphlet, 184-5; plans a dictionary, 184; Poems, early, 167-8; poetry of, estimate on, 192-208; Political Papers, 180-1; Prose, 211; Regent, secretary to, 181-2; religion, 115; Rosamond, 170, 195-6; Sainte-Beuve on, xxxii, 137; Secretary of State, xxvii, 183; Shelley on Cato, 357-8; The Spectator, 88, 172, 174-5, 179, 181; Steele, relations with, 166, 170, 176, 177, 184-6; The Tatler, 171-2; Tender Husband, part in, 170; Thackeray on, xxviii, 7; Tragedy on Socrates, xxvii, 183; travels, 168-9; Under-Secretary, 170; VISION OF MIRZA, 77-81; Voltaire on Cato, xxxiv, 138; xxxix, 238; WESTMINSTER ABBEY, xxvii, 82-5; Wharton, Lord, secretary to, 170-1

Addison, Lancelot, father of Joseph, xxvii, 165

Adeimantus, son of Ariston, ii, 21

Adeimantus, son of Leucolophus, viii, 466

Adeodatus, son of St. Augustine, vii, 3, 100, 152; grief of, over Monica, 161

Ades, reference to, iv, 135

ADESTE FIDELES, xlv, 567-8

Adhibhuta, Adhidaiva, etc., xlv, 835

Adhyâtman, xlv, 835, 846

Adimantus, Athenian general, xii, 148

Admetus, king of Molossians, xii, 27

Administratio, defined, xxxvi, 298

Admirable Crichton, (see Crichton)

Admiral, origin of name, xxxv, 377

Admiralty Cases, (U. S.), xliii, 202 (Sec. 2)

Admiration, Byron on, xli, 813; caused by ignorance, xxiv, 55;

defined by Hobbes, xxxiv, 355; degrees of, ii, 236 (14); excited by the perilous, ix, 364; inferior degree of astonishment, xxiv, 51; Pascal on love of, xlviii, 60, (150-1); unknown to animals, xlviii, 132 (401)

Admlithe, the jester, xlix, 258

Admonition, Winthrop on use of, xliii, 99-100

Adœdatus (see Adeodatus)

Adolius, xxxviii, 412

ADONAIS, Shelley's, xli, 879-93

Adonijah, and Solomon, xliii, 99

Adonis, references to, iv, 73, 101, 274

Adoration, David on, xli, 504-8; "pure, which God likes best," iv, 176

Adoxa, Darwin on the, xi, 225

Adramelech, Milton on, iv, 216

Adrastos, viii, 188 note

Adrastus, king of Argos, xii, 248 note; in Hades, xiii, 227

Adrian, Roman Emperor (see Hadrian)

Adrian V, Pope, Dante on, xx, 225-6, note 8

Adrian VI, Pope, xxxvi, 106-7

Adrian, in THE TEMPEST xlvi, 398, 399, 423

ADRIAN, DYING TO HIS SOUL, xl, 408

Adulation, Burke on, xxiv, 157

Adultery in biblical times, xliii, 100; in Dante's Hell, xx, 22-5; in old England, xxxv, 384-5; in old Massachusetts, xliii, 85 (9); in Utopia, xxxvi, 223, 224, Jesus on, xliv, 404 (18); Job on, 191 (9-12); Mohammed on, xlv, 982; punishment of, in ancient Germany, xxxiii, 106

Advancement in Life, Channing on, xxviii, 324-31; Confucius on, xliv, 52 (5); Ruskin on, xxviii, 96-7, 131-2

Adversity, Christ's sake, for, vii, 249 (5), 263-7; Cicero, on, ix, 15, 16, 31; despair in, vii, 278, 306 (6), 343; Ecclesiastes on, xliv, 348 (14); Kempis on, vii, 224, 283 (2), 306 (4); love and, viii, 29; Pascal on, xlviii, 46 (107), 361; Penn on, i, 360 (239); prosperity of greatness, v, 301; Raleigh on, xxxix, 70, 100-3; religion and, iii, 46; strength proved by, vii, 229, (4); truth's sake, for, i, 200

ADVERSITY, ESSAY ON, Bacon's, iii, 16-17

ADVERSITY, HYMN TO, Gray's, xl, 462

Advice, Æsop on interested, xvii, 38; Bacon on, of friends, iii, 73-4, 126; Carlyle on, xxv, 377; Cicero

on, ix, 24, 39; in difficulties, xvii, 46; Kempis on giving and receiving, vii, 221 (3); Mill on liberty of, xxv, 307; of parents, xxxvii, 87; Pliny on seeking, ix, 356 (see also Counsel)

Advocates and judges, iii, 138-9

AE FOND KISS AND THEN WE SEVER, vi, 455

Æacus, judge in Hades, ii, 28

Æacus, porter in THE FROGS, viii, 432-3, 437-9, 441-3

Æantodorus, ii, 21

Æetes, brother of Circe, xxii, 140

Ægæon, and Jove, xiii, 346 (see also Briareus)

Ægina, in Persian war, xii, 21; Pericles on, 44-5

Ægisthus, in AGAMEMNON, viii, 65-70; Clytemnestra on, 60; Homer on, xxii, 10, 17, 39, 40-2, 62; in THE LIBATION-BEARERS, viii, 104-6; Orestes on, 84, 111

Ægospotami, battle of, xii, 148-9

Ægyptus, in the ODYSSEY, xxii, 22-3

Ælius, Sextus, Cicero on, ix, 55

Ælla, SONG FROM, xli, 571-2

Ælroth, xlix, 139

Æmilianus, Minutius, ix, 209-11

Æmilianus, Scipio (see Scipio)

Æmilius, Papus, ix, 22

Æmilius, Paulus, and the king of Macedon, xxxii, 16; Pascal on, xlviii, 134 (409, 410)

Æneas, adventures related by, xiii, 103-55; Africa, landing of, in, 81-2; Anchises's funeral games celebrated by, 184-202; Anchises rescued by, 125-8; arms of, brought by Venus, 292-6; arms of, made by Vulcan, 286-7; Cervantes on, xiv, 224; Carthage, entered by, xiii, 90-2; Carthage, prepares to sail from, 170-1; Carthage, second warning to fly from, 176-7; Carthage, warned to leave, 164-7; Chaonia, voyage of, to, 148; Circe, settles in, 134 0, Creusa, ghost of, and, 129-30; Dante places, in Limbo, xx, 20; Dido and, go hunting, xiii, 161-2; Dido, first meeting with, 93, 96-102; Dido, love of, for, 156-9; Dido reproaches, 167-70; Dryden on Virgil's, xiii, 9, 19, 20-39; xxxix, 165, 166; Evander's aid sought by, xiii, 274-84; 287-92; fire on ships of, 205; Hades visited by, 215-42; Helenus and Andromache receive, 141-7; hell, visit to, referred to, xx, 9-10, note 1; Italy, first landing in, xiii, 148-9; Italy, warned to seek, 136-7; Jove prophesies success of, 84; Juno persecutes, 75; Latium, arrival

in, 243-8; Mezentius and Lausus killed by, 353-9; Pallas, body of, sent back by, 361-4; parents of, Venus and Anchises, 97; prayer and agreement of, 400-1; ships of, turned to nymphs, 299-302; Sibyl visited by, 211-15; Sicily, driven to, by storm, 182-3; Sicily, first landing in, 150-5; Sicily, leaves settlement in (cf. Dante, p. 222), 206-7; Sidney on, xxvii, 13, 20, 26, 32; Spenser on, xxxix, 65; storm overtakes, xiii, 78-9; Strophades, landing of, in the, 138-40; Thrace in, 132-3; Trojan war, in, 371; trophy erected by, 360-1; Troy, in sack of, 112-24; Troy, sets sail from, 131; Troy, withdrawal from, xxxix, 235; Turnus challenged to single combat by, xiii, 364; Turnus, final combat with, 419-28; Turnus, prepares for combat with, 398; Turnus, war with, 263-4; Turnus, war with, renewed, 410-15; Venus heals, wounded, 406-9; Venus, meeting of, with, 86-9

Æneas, palsied man healed by apostles, xliv, 450 (33-5)

Æneid, The, Dryden's translation, xiii, 75-428; Arguments of, written by Addison, xxvii, 167; Burke on, xxiv, 20, 57, 63, 75, 143; Caxton's Prologue to, xxxix, 25-8; Dryden on machinery of, xiii, 48-52; Dryden on his translation of, 52-72; Dryden's defence of, 14-44; editorial remarks on, 4; Homer's influence on, xxxix, 165; Milton on, iv, 264; Montaigne on, xxxii, 92, 95; time of, 44-8; time of composition, 54; willed by Virgil to be burned, 19

Ænobarbus, Domitius, xii, 367

Æolus, called Hippotades, iv, 76; in the ÆNEID, xiii, 77-9; jailer of the winds, 80; Ulysses and, xxii, 136-8

Aeronautics, in NEW ATLANTIS, iii, 188

Æschere, xlix, 43, 45, 65

Æschines, the orator, xii, 209-10, 217-18; metaphors of, ix, 367; on Demosthenes, xii, 199, 207; ix, 224-5, 366

Æschines, son of Lysanias, ii, 21, 47

Æschylus, Aristophanes on, viii, 465-6; on Artemis, xxxiii, 81; Euripides's dispute with, in THE FROGS, viii, 441-65; on the hereafter, ii, 104; HOUSE OF ATREUS, viii, 5-155; Hugo on, xxxix, 365; life and works of, viii, 3-4; Milton on, iv, 417; Montaigne on death of, xxxii, 13-14; on Per-

sians, numbers of, xii, 18; PROMETHEUS BOUND, viii, 156-94; Shelley on choruses of, xxvii, 348; Sophocles beats, in contest, viii, 196; Sophocles and, compared, 196; Suppliants of, xxxix, 359; Taine on, and Euripides, 450; Voltaire on tragedies of, 382

Æsculapius, son of Apollo, xxxviii, 2; Æschylus on death of, viii, 41; Jonson on, xlvii, 589; Virgil on death of, xiii, 269

Æsion, on Demosthenes, xii, 206 and note

Æsir, northern gods, xlix, 315 note

Æson, son of Tyro, xxii, 158; Medea and, xli, 680

Æsop, author of Fables, xvii, 2; Bacon on, iii, 113; Herodotus on, xxxiii, 68

Æsop, the tragedian, xii, 229; Cicero on, ix, 112

ÆSOP'S FABLES, xvii, 9-46; CAXTON'S EPILOGUE TO, xxxix, 18-19; editorial remarks on, xvii, 2, 3; Emerson on, v, 183; Locke on, xxxvii, 141, 172; Montaigne on, xxxii, 92; Sidney on, xxvii, 21; versified by Socrates, ii, 48, 49

ÆSTHETIC EDUCATION, LETTERS ON, Schiller's, xxxii, 219-313

Æsthetics (see Art, Beauty, Taste)

Æstivation, of animals, xxix, 111

Æstyans, Tacitus on the, xxxiii, 121-2

Æthiops, river, viii, 184, note 56

Ætna, Æschylus on, viii, 168-9; Milton on, iv, 96; Virgil on, xiii, 150

Afer, Domitius, Pliny on, ix, 230-1; will of, 344

Affability, a source of power, xxxiv, 375

Affairs, great, by what performed, ix, 52

Affectation, Fielding on, xxxix, 188-9; Locke on, xxxvii, 48-50; of simplicity, ii, 293 (15)

Affectation, in speech, i, 401 (121); of wisdom, iii, 67-9

Affection, never wasted, xlii, 1385; "oft the spring of woe," vi, 204; praises of, xl, 308; (see also Love)

Affliction, Browne on, iii, 318; David's prayer in, xliv, 158-9; Elihu on, 131 (8-11, 15-16); Eliphaz on, 79 (6, 7), 80 (17-19); Emerson on compensation for, v, 107; Herbert on, xv, 393, 394-5; Kempis on patience under, vii, 226 (8), 291-2, 304-5, 312 (2); Longfellow on, xlii, 1330; Mohammedan proverb on, xvi, 82; Pascal on temporal, xlviii, 355; "sons of, brothers in distress," vi, 263; wisdom learned

by, viii, 11; Woolman on, i, 206-7, 246-7

AFFLICTION OF MARGARET, xli, 660-2

Affronts, Penn on bearing, i, 356 (182-5)

Afranius, Lucius, Cicero on, ix, 99, 165; in civil war, xii, 306, 310, 318-19

Africa, backward state of, cause of, x, 28; Herodotus on, xxxiii, 20; vegetation and animals of, xxix, 97-9

Africanus, Julius, ix, 315

Africanus, Scipio (see Scipio)

After-games, i, 365 (302)

AFTON, SWEET, vi, 443

Agabus, xliv, 455 (28), 478 (10-11)

Agace, Gobin, xxxv, 19-20, 21

Agag, Samuel on, xxxix, 82

Agamemnon, Achilles and, xiii, 15; burial of, viii, 88-9; Cassandra foresees death of, 44-54; Homer on return and death of, xxii, 38, 39, 40, 61-2, 162-3; in Hades, 162-4, 331-3; Iphigenia, sacrifice of, by, viii, 12-14; murder of, 55-65; Orestes on, 133; Sidney on, xxvii, 20; Spenser on, xxxix, 65; in Trojan war, viii, 7-11, 23-4; xxii, 106; Virgil on death of, xiii, 370

AGAMEMNON, TRAGEDY OF, Æschylus's, viii, 5-70; compared with LEAR, xxvii, 356

Agapetus, Bishop, xx, 308, note 6

Agariste, mother of Pericles, xii, 38

Agassiz, Alexander, on echinodermata, xi, 246, 247

Agassiz, Louis, on amblyopsis, xi, 152; on embryological characters, 456; on embryos, 388, 489; on his first lecture, xxviii, 465; on glacial period, xi, 412; on immutability of species, 363; on movement of glaciers, xxx, 235; on synthetic types, xi, 378; on tertiary species, 350

AGASSIZ [Louis], FIFTIETH BIRTHDAY OF, Longfellow's, xlii, 1346

Agatha, St., Kempis on, vii, 321, note 2

Agatharchus, Alcibiades and, xii, 124; Zeuxis and, 51

Agathocles, Machiavelli on, xxxvi, 30-1, 33

Agathon, Aristophanes on, viii, 421; in Dante's Limbo, xx, 238; quoted, ii, 216 (18)

Agathonius, age of, ix, 71

Agave, mother of King Pentheus in the BACCHÆ, viii, 349-415; doom of, 412-15; leader of Bacchanals, 379-81; slays Pentheus, 399-400

Age (see also Old Age); not to be regarded, viii, 265; legal, in Massachusetts, xliii, 78 (53)

Agelaus, in the ODYSSEY, xxii, 292-3, 310, 313, 314, 315

Agents, Bacon on choice of, iii, 124; Hobbes on, xxxiv, 430-1

Agesilaus, Bacon on, iii, 24, 113; Cicero on, ix, 107; on happiness, xxxii, 5

Aggravation, punishment of priests, xxxvi, 323 note

AGINCOURT, Drayton's, xl, 226-30

Agincourt, Macaulay on, xli, 940-1

Agio, defined, x, 376; of Amsterdam Bank, 267-8

Agis I of Sparta, and Alcibiades, xii, 132-3

Agis II of Sparta, xii, 217

Agis III, Emerson on, v, 191

Agis the Lycian, xiii, 352-3

Aglauros, in Dante's Purgatory, xx, 205

Agli, Lotto degli, xx, 59 note

Aglovale, Sir, xxxv, 134

Agnes, St., Luther on, xxxvi, 316, 342

AGNES, ST., EVE OF, Keats's, xli, 907

Agnese, in THE BETROTHED (see Mondella, Agnese)

Agnolo, Baccio d', xxxi, 430 note 3

Agnolo, Giuliano di Baccio d', xxxi, 409, 430

Agnolo, Michel, father of Bandinello, xxxi, 14-15

Agnolo, Michel, the Sienese, xxxi, 57 note 1, 62

Agnolo, Michel (Buonarroti) (see Michelangelo)

Agnosticism, Huxley on, xxviii, 316

Agostino, xx, 339 note 31

Agouti, Darwin on the, xxix, 81

Agrarian Laws, of Rome, xxxv, 319

Agravaine, reference to, xlii, 1235

Agreeableness, Pascal on, xlviii, 426

Agreement, always silent, xxv, 333; a way of honoring, xxxiv, 379

Agrican, and Angelica, iv, 396-7

Agricola, Julius, Milton on, iii, 234; Tacitus and, xxxiii, 94

Agricultural schools, Cowley on, xxvii, 69-70; Ticknor on, xxviii, 380

Agricultural systems, of political economy, x, 446-67

Agriculture, capital, best employment for, x, 305-6, 321

Agriculture, Cicero on pleasures of, ix, 64-8; combinations in, x, 134; effect of, on prices of bread and meat, 157-9; Emerson on, v, 52; European policy not favorable to, x, 6, 136; improvement in, 191-4; in Utopia, xxxvi, 183-4, 188-9; labor, division of, in, x, 11-12; Locke on, xxxvii, 186-7; Luther on, xxxvi, 349; manufactures compared with, x, 11-12; manufactures, relation to, 230-1, 319-22,

465-6; military spirit and, xxvii,
391; Milton on study of, iii, 252-3;
prices in general, x, 200; protective tariffs and, 355; Rousseau on,
xxxiv, 182-3, 211-12; skill re-
quired in, high, x, 134-6; taxes
on profits of, 526; wealth, best
source of, iii, 93; Woolman on,
i, 204 note

AGRICULTURE, ESSAY ON, Cowley's,
xxvii, 65-74

Agrippa, King, St. Paul and, xliv,
487 (13-27), 488 (1), 490 (27-32)

Agrippa, Cornelius, Emerson on, v,
183; in FAUSTUS, xix, 203-5; on
science, xxvii, 33

Agrippa, Marcus, Antony and, xviii,
23; at Actium, xii, 386-7; xiii,
295; Augustus and, iii, 71; marriages of, xii, 403; Octavia and,
361

Agrippa, Menenius, xii, 157; Sidney
on, xxvii, 27

Agrippina, daughter of Antony, xviii,
60-1; daughter of Germanicus, xii,
403

Agrippinus, Florus and, ii, 119

Aguarus, xxxv, 156

Aguecheek, Sir Andrew, Macaulay
on, xxvii, 404

Aguilar, Pedro de, xiv, 408-9; sonnets of, 410

Aguirre, Lope de, xxxiii, 333-4

Ahab, reference to, iv, 372

Ahala, C. Servilius, ix, 66

Ahasuerus, Dante on, xx, 215

Ahauton, the Indian, xliii, 152

Ahaz, Rimmon and, iv, 102

Ahenobarbus, Domitius, xii, 403

Ahitophel, Dante on, xx, 120

Ahriman (see Arimanes)

Ai, Duke, xliv, 8 (19), 11 (21), 18
(2), 40 (9), 49 (22)

Aias (see Ajax)

Aiguillon, siege of, xxxv, 5, 7

Aiguillon, Duke d', Burke on, xxiv,
262

Aiken, Robert, Burns's inscription
to, vi, 142; EPITAPH FOR, vi, 229;
references to, vi, 75, 77, 235, 372,
note 4

Aims, high, Browning on, xlii, 1133;
Johnson on, xxxix, 208

AINSLIE, MISS, EPIGRAM TO, Burns's,
vi, 280

Air, composition of, xxx, 150-1;
elasticity of, 155-6; life without
(see Anaërobian Life); needed
for combustion, 107-8; pressure
of, 152-5; resistance of, 18, 155;
temperature dependent on pressure, 222; weight of, 52, 151-2

Air-burner, the, xxx, 114 note

AIRLY BEACON, xlii, 1101-2

Ajax (Aias), son of Telamon, xxii,
164, 331; Hector and, v, 97; mad-

ness of, xxvii, 20; Socrates on, ii,
28; Ulysses and, xxii, 166; son
of Oileus, xxii, 61

Ajib, King, xvi, 99

Akber Khan, pigeons of, xi, 43

A Kempis (see Kempis, Thomas à)

Aladdin (see Ala-ed-Din)

Alæan Twins, xiii, 231 (see Ephialtes and Otus)

ALA-ED-DIN AND THE WONDERFUL
LAMP, xvi, 355-443; manuscripts
of, 3

Alagia, wife of Malaspina, xx, 226
note

Alamanni, Luigi, xxxi, 90 note 4;
Cellini and, 90, 95, 270, 271, 272,
288, 312, 333

Alam-ed-in Senjer, xvi, 218-19

Alaopolitanes, Nephelogetes and,
xxxvi, 229

Alāra Kālāma, xlv, 732-4, 739

Alaska Purchase, xliii, 459-63

Alaskie, Albert, v, 433

Alba Longa, Virgil on, xiii, 84

Albanians, Freeman on the, xxviii,
273-4, 275-6

ALBANY, THE BONIE LASS OF,
Burns', vi, 299

Albany, Duke of, in LEAR, xlvi, 203,
205, 207; before battle, 289; Cornwall, war with, 229, 249; Edgar
with, 297; Edmund with, 293-5;
France, war against, 275; Gloucester's wrongs, 271-2; Goneril's
death and, 299; Goneril denounced by, 296; Goneril's letter
to, 290; Goneril with, 226-8, 270-1;
Lear and Cordelia sent for, by,
299; Lear with, 225, 226; plot
against, 284; resigns power, 301

Albany Convention, Franklin on, i,
129-31

Albatross, Dana on the, xxiii, 37-8;
food of the, xxix, 176

Albemarle Island, Darwin on, xxix,
398

Alberigo, the friar, xx, 141 and
note 4

Alberigo of Como, xxxvi, 46

Albero of Sienna, xx, 124 note 5

Albert I, Emperor, Dante on, xx,
170, 369 notes 5 and 6; Switzerland, conduct of, toward, xxvi,
466; murder of, 463-4

Albert, Archbishop of Mayence,
xxxvi, 295 note; Luther's address
to, 261

Alberti, Alessandro and Napoleone,
xx, 134 and note 2

Alberto, Abbot, xx, 221, note 8

Albertus Magnus, xx, 329, note 15

Albin, in POLYEUCTE, xxvi, 78-9,
97-100, 111-12, 118

Albinus, Clodius, governor of Britain, xxvii, 11; rival of Severus,
xxxvi, 68

Albinus, Spurius, ix, 47
Albinus, D. Brutus surnamed, xii, 327
Albinus, correspondent of Pliny, ix, 296
Albizzi, Girolamo degli, xxxi, 425 and note
Al-Borák, reference to, xlii, 1434
Albracca, siege of, iv, 396; xiv, 82
Albret, Perducas d', xxxv, 72, 80
Albuquergues, killed by Don Pedro, xxxix, 88
ALCÆUS, ODE IN IMITATION OF, xli, 592-3
Alcandrê, her gifts to Helen, xxii, 51
Alcanor, xiii, 320, 338
Alcavala, of Spain, x, 565
Alcestis, Milton on, iv, 88; Ruskin on, xxviii, 146; Wordsworth on, xli, 680
ALCHEMIST, THE, xlvii, 519-635; remarks on, 518
Alchemy, Emerson on, v, 307-8; metal, the, xxxv, 341-2; punishment of, in Dante's Hell, xx, 124-5
Alcibiades, accused of impiety, xii, 127-9; Andros expedition and, 146; Aristophanes on, viii, 463; Athenian government, attempts to change, made by, xii, 134-6; Athens' power of, strengthened by, 123; Athens, return of, to, 143-5; at Potidæa, 115-16; Anytus and, 113-14; Bacon on, iii, 112; birth of, xii, 110; Bithynia and Phrygia, retires to, 149; childhood anecdotes of, 111; condemned, 131; Coriolanus and, compared, 192-6; death of, 150-1; Emerson on, v, 275; Eupolis and, ix, 154; excesses of, endured by Athenians, xii, 124; General, 136-7; Hipponicus and, 116; league broken by, 121; marriage of, 116-17; Montaigne on, xxxii, 59-60; naval victory of, xii, 137; Nicias's jealousy of, 120-1; Olympic games, success of, at, 118-19; Pericles and, 110, 112, 115; rivals of, in public life, 119-20; Socrates's relations with, 112-16 (see also xlvi, 25); Sparta, life of, at, 132-3; Syracuse, expedition of, to, 125, 130; Thrasybulus's accusation against, 147; Timon of Athens and, 124, 391; Tisaphernes with, 133, 138; treason of, 131; warns the generals, 148
ALCIBIADES, LIFE OF, Plutarch's, xii, 110-51
Alcidamas, Molière on, xxvi, 204-5
Alcides (see Hercules)
Alcinous, king of Phæacia, xxii, 85; Poseidon and, 185-6; descent and marriage of, 95; gardens of, iv,

274; Milton on feast of, 22; Ulysses received by, xxii, 98-119; Ulysses sent on way, 181-2
Alcis, German god, xxxiii, 120
Alcmæon, son of Amphiaraus, xxii, 214; Dante on, xx, 194, 302
Alcmena, Heracles's mother, xxii, 158; xl, 247; Homer on, xxii, 25; Herodotus on, xxxiii, 26
Alcohol, produced by fruits in carbonic acid gas, xxxviii, 318-25
Alcoholic fermentation, xxxviii, 290-317, 324-5 note, 327-32, 356, 362-79
Alcoholic liquors, Burke on taste for, xxiv, 16; Locke on, xxxvii, 20-1
Alda, Roland betrothed, xlix, 96, 162, 198-9
Aldobrandesco, Omberto, xx, 190-1 note 1
Aldobrandi, Bertino, xxxi, 103-4
Aldobrandi, Tegghiaio, xx, 68 and note 2
Aldobrandino, Clement VIII called, xviii, 283
Ale, Harrison on English, xxxv, 300
ALE, JOLLY GOOD, AND OLD, xl, 192-4
Alecto, in the ÆNEID, xiii, 254-63; Dante on, xx, 38
Alençon, Earl of, at Cressy, xxxv, 26, 28, 30
Aleotti, Giovanni, xxxi, 125 note 2
Alesia, siege of, xii, 297-8
Alessio, in Dante's Hell, xx, 78; in THE BETROTHED, xxi, 447, 449
Alethes, in the ÆNEID, xiii, 79, 305, 307
Alexander, Helen and, xxxiii, 55-7
Alexander, of Antioch, xii, 372, 373
Alexander, of Syria, xii, 387
Alexander, the grammarian, ii, 195 (10)
Alexander, the Jew, xliv, 474 (33-4)
Alexander, the Platonic, ii, 195 (12)
Alexander, the false prophet, xxxvii, 405-6
Alexander, king of Macedonia, at Platæa, xii, 95-6
Alexander the Great, Achilles and, xiii, 28; xv, 373; xxvii, 39; xxxvi, 52; age of, at conquest of Asia, iv, 389; Apelles and, ix, 107; Aristotle and, xxxii, 55; at Arbela, iii, 78; Athens, orators of, and, 216-7; attitude toward arts and sciences, xxxii, 55; M. Aurelius on, ii, 207 (3), 238 (24), 257 (3), 274 (29); Browne on, iii, 291; Cervantes on, xiv, 513; chastity and drunkenness of, xlviii, 45 (103); Curtius on, xxxvii, 375; Dante on, xx, 53; Darius's box and, xiv, 54; dogs of, xxxv, 375; Emerson on, v, 211, 275; Hephestion and, xlvi, 25; his wish for

more worlds to conquer, xxxix, 333; Pindar and, iv, 80; liberality of, xxxvi, 56; Marlowe on, xix, 230; melancholy of, iii, 51; Montaigne on, xxxii, 13; one of nine worthies, xxxix, 21; Pascal on, xlviii, 51 (132), 239 (701); the Platæans and, xii, 93; reproved for playing well, 37; reason of security of his conquests, xxxvi, 16-18; Sidney on, xxvii, 39; the shower of flame and, xx, 60; supposed prophecy of, xlviii, 252-3

Alexander III, Pope, exile of, xxvii, 386

Alexander VI, Pope, Cæsar Borgia, father of, xxxvi, 15; church, aggrandizement of the, 41; frauds of, 60; King Louis and, 14, 15, 25; son, efforts to aggrandize his, 24-5, 28

Alexander, James, i, 130
Alexander Pheræus, xxvii, 30
Alexander Severus, Machiavelli on, xxxvi, 66, 67, 71
Alexander, Wilhelmina, vi, 190, note 7
Alexander, William, To AURORA, xl, 322-3
ALEXANDER'S FEAST, xl, 400-6
Alexandridas, Montaigne on, xxxii, 46
Alexandrine philosophy, Taine on the, xxxix, 451, 455 note
Alexandrine verse, Dryden on, xiii, 56
Alexas of Laodicea, xii, 393; character in ALL FOR LOVE, xviii, 21-100; Antony told by, of Cleopatra's death, 90; Antony's messenger, 40; Cleopatra denounced, 84-5; on Ventidius, 51; Ventidius with, 26; with the priests, 22-4
ALEXIS, HERE SHE STAYED, xl, 338-9
Alf, son of Hjalprek, xlix, 300-1, 360-1; remarks on story of, 267
Alfonso X (The Wise), Bacon on, iii, 136
Alfred the Great, called the truth-speaker, v, 388; crowned and buried at Winchester, 480-1; Emerson on, 15; book, how he won the, 419
Algalif, the, xlix, 113, 114, 168, 169
Algarsife, reference to, iv, 38
Algebra, Descartes on, xxxiv, 17, 19
Ali, in Dante's Hell, xx, 117; quotation from, v, 87; and Mohammed, xlv, 1002 note 17
ALI-BABA AND THE FORTY THIEVES, xvi, 443-60
Alichino, the demon, xx, 90, 94
Alicorno, Traiano, xxxi, 96 note, 126, 151, 153
Alidosi, Lito, degli, xx, 352 note 12

Alienations, in Massachusetts, xliii, 72 (10, 11, 14, 15)
Alifamfaron, Pentapolin and, xiv, 146-7
Alighieri, grandfather of Dante, xx, 351 note 2
Alisto of Cos, alluded to, ix, 46
ALL FOR LOVE, Dryden's, xviii, 11-101; remarks on, 4; Byron's poem, xli, 809-10
A' THE AIRTS THE WIND CAN BLAW, vi, 323-4
All-Prayer, weapon of Christian, xv, 67
Allan, John, Poe and, xxviii, 382
Allan, Dr., on Diodon, xxix, 24; on Holuthuriæ, 490
ALLAN STREAM, BY, vi, 498-9
Allegories, barbarous nations among, xxiv, 18; Bunyan on, xv, 8; Spenser on, xxxix, 65
Allegretti, Antonio, xxxi, 101 note 5, 169, 173
Allemand, François l', xxxi, 293 note
Allen, John, translator of Calvin, xxxix, 1
Allen, Richard, xxxiii, 170
Allen, William, i, 111
ALLERLEIRAUH, story of, xvii, 172-7
Alliances, provision for, under Confederation, xliii, 172, 175; under constitution, 198 (10), 199 (3); Machiavelli on, xxxvi, 76-8; More on, 226; Washington on, xliii, 263-4
Alligators, fights of male, xi, 101
Allingham, William, THE FAIRIES, xlii, 1162-3
Allori, Angelo (Il Bronzino), xxxi, 418 note, 428
Allston, Washington, Coleridge on, v, 331, 333
Alluvium, land made of, xxxiii, 9-10; saliferous, in Peru, xxix, 385; stratified, in Andes valleys, 334-5
Allworth, Lady, in NEW WAY TO PAY OLD DEBTS, in mourning, xlvii, 823, 826; at home, 827-8; with Tom, 828-30; scene with Wellborn, 833-5; welcomes Wellborn and Marrall to dinner, 843-4; after dinner, 846; thought to be in love with Wellborn, 849-50; at Overreach's, 863-4, 866, 867; at home, with Lovell, 873-6; reconciliation with Lovell, 885-7; with Wellborn, 887-8; with Overreach, 889, 890, 891, 893, 895-6; in final scene, 896, 897
Allworth, Tom, in NEW WAY TO PAY OLD DEBTS, xlvii, with Wellborn at Tapwell's, 822-5; at home, with servants, 827; with Lady Allworth, 828-30; shuns Wellborn, 832; parting with servants, 840-1;

reconciled to Wellborn, 842; with Lovell on way to Overreach's, 851-4; at Overreach's, 859, 860, 862-3, 867; discharged from service, 869; as messenger to Margaret, 870; scene with Margaret, 881-5; Lovell on, 886; married to Margaret, 894; in final scene, 896, 898

Almagro, Diego, xxxiii, 327

Almaris, King, xlix, 125, 146

Almasour, in ROLAND, xlix, 129, 141

Almeni, Sforza, xxxi, 381 note

Almon, son of Tyrrheus, xiii, 261-2

Alms, Buddha on, xlv, 607; Krishna on, 876; Mohammed on, 893 note 1, 894, 970, 985; never impoverish, v, 27

Alnaschar, story of, xvi, 187-94

Alœus, and Iphimedeia, xxii, 160

Alonso, king of Naples, in THE TEMPEST, in shipwreck, xlvi, 380, 381; his previous conspiracy with Antonio, 385; in island after wreck, 397-403; plot against, 405-6; awakened by Ariel, 406-7; in search for Ferdinand, 419-20; at the banquet, 420-1; denounced by Ariel, 422-3; imprisoned by Ariel, 432; in final scene, 434-42

Alonso, Peter, and Don Quixote, xiv, 48

Alonzo III, of Arragon, Dante on, xx, 176 and note 12

Alpha Centauri, distance of, xxx, 330

Alphabet, methods of teaching, xxxvii, 138-9, 140

Alphebo, to Don Quixote, xiv, 16

Alphel, Sir Edmund, xxxv, 85

Alpheus and Arethusa, iv, 44; xiii, 154

Alphonsus of Castile, Bacon on, iii, 136

Alps, Byron on the, xli, 813; Goldsmith on states seen from, 533; Helmholtz on the, xxx, 221-4; glaciers of, 226-41

Alps, Witch of the, in MANFRED, xviii, 418-22

Alric, and Eric, v, 357

Alsus, and Podalirius, xiii, 405-6

Alswid, xlix, 327, 328, 329

Altabin, king of Atlantis, iii, 166-7

Alternate generation, Darwin on, xi, 478

Alternation, the law of nature, v, 112

Althea, Æschylus on, viii, 96

ALTHEA, TO, FROM PRISON, xl, 365-6

ALTHO' HE HAS LEFT ME, vi, 440

Altmayer, in FAUST, xix, 80-94

Altoviti, Bindo, xxxi, 399 note 1, 401

Altruism, Kant on duty of, xxxii, 354, 361, 372; Locke on, xxxvii,

126; Luther on, 384-6, 387, 391; Mill on, xxv, 5; More on, xxxvi, 210; St. Paul on, xlv, 515 (24)

Alum, crystallization of, xxx, 26-7, 36; fireproofing qualities of, xxxv, 336

Aluminium, weight of, xxx, 9 note 2

Alva, Duke of, at Metz, xxxviii, 29; EGMONT, character in Goethe's, xix, 247-331; Egmont's arrest planned by, 299-302; Egmont on, 323; Egmont with, 303-11; Gomez on, 297-8; in the Netherlands, 246; Netherlands, ruler of, 292-3; Netherlands, sent to, 281, 285-6; Orange, arrest of, planned by, 299-302; Orange thwarts, 302-3; Raleigh on, xxxix, 91

Alypius, student under St. Augustine, vii, 90-2; at the gladiatorial show, 92-3; apprehended as thief, 93-4; as assessor, 94-5; advises against marriage, 97-8; as lawyer, 131; his conversion, 120, 142, 148; baptized with Augustine, 152

Amadeus, Cardinal, xxxix, 45-6

Amadis of Gaul, Arcalaus and, xiv, 123; Cervantes on romance of, 52; Don Quixote on, 101, 224-5; Don Quixote, supposed sonnet of, to, 15; Montaigne on, xxxii, 91; Oriana and, xiv, 125, 224-5, 239; Sidney on romance of, xxvii, 26; squire of, xiv, 522; sword of, 145

Amadis of Greece, xiv, 52

Amalthea, and Jove, iv, 164; horn of, 385; vi, 339

Amana River, xxxiii, 353

AMANTIUM IRAE, xl, 204-6

Amantius, friend of Cæsar, xii, 317 note

Amapaia, xxxiii, 339-41, 373-4

Amara, Mount, iv, 164

Amara, town of, xlv, 591

Amarant, iv, 147

Amaryllis, reference to, iv, 76

Amasis, king of Egypt, xxxiii, 83-91; Ionian guard of, 79

Amastris, city of, ix, 428-9

Amata, in the ÆNEID, xiii; Æneas, rage against, 255-7; Dante on, xx, 215 note 2; death of, xiii, 416; Turnus tries to dissuade, 396

Amaurote, capital of Utopia, xxxvi, 182-3, 185-6

Amazon River, discovered by Orellana, xxxiii, 330; Thoreau on forests of the, xxviii, 418

Amazons, Æschylus on their war against Athens, viii, 142; home of the, 170 note 25, 181 note 45; Columbus on Indian, xliii, 27; Raleigh on, xxxiii, 337-8

Ambassadors (U. S.), appointed by President, xliii, 201 (2); foreign, received by President, 202; cases

affecting, 202 (2); under the Confederation, 172

Amber, Tacitus on, xxxiii, 122

Ambiorix, xii, 295 note

Ambition, Augustine, St., on, vii, 29, 199-200; Bacon on enviousness of, iii, 25; Burke on, xxiv, 45-6; Burns on, vi, 233, 262, 325, 337; Carlyle on, xxv, 401, 437, 465; Epictetus on, ii, 131 (43), 146 (79); Hobbes on, xxxiv, 354, 381, 387; Milton on, iv, 97, 268; Montaigne on, xxxii, 120; Pascal on, xlviii, 417-18, 421; Penn on, i, 399-400; Pope on, xl, 430-1; Rousseau on, xxxiv, 229; Ruskin on common, xxviii, 96-8; Shakespeare on, xlvi, 124, 332; Webster on, xlvii, 735

AMBITION, ESSAY ON, Bacon's, iii, 98-100

Amble, in NEW WAY TO PAY OLD DEBTS, xlvii, 825-7, 830, 832, 841, 842, 845-6, 874, 897

Amblyrhynchus, Darwin on the, xxix, 408-13, 418

Amboise, Cardinal d', xxxvi, 15, 29

Ambrogio, in THE BETROTHED, xxi, 124-5, 131

Ambrose, St., Augustine, St., on, vii, 80, 84-5; Donne, Dr., comparison of, with, xv, 346; Justina persecutes, vii, 153; Luther on, xxxvi, 280; Simplicianus, father of, vii, 125; verses by, 163

Ambrosio, the student, xiv, 92, 93, 106, 112, 117

Ameipsias, Aristophanes on, viii, 419-20

Amendment, Confucius on, xliv, 6 (8), 30 (23), 41 (21); Kempis on, vii, 244-7; Penn on, i, 362 (262)

Amendments, Constitutional, xliii, 204 (5); Lincoln on, 342

America, Bacon on ancient, iii, 143, 165-7; Browne on animals of, iii, 287-8; discovery of original documents concerning, xliii, 5-50; Emerson on, v, 473, 480; English colonies in, first, xxxiii, 234, 235 (see also Roanoke, St. John's); foreign powers in (see Monroe Doctrine); natives of, iii, 167-8; probable geological changes in, xxix, 144; glacial period in, xi, 418; Hayes on exploration and settlement of, xxxiii, 271-5; Hunt on, xxvii, 309; Irish monks in, xxxii, 183; Paré on Spaniards in, xxxviii, 34; Senecas's prophecy of, iii, 95, 97; Smith on discovery of, x, 343-4, 416-23; Thoreau on, xxviii, 418-20; zoology of North and South, xxix, 143-4; zoology of, changes in, 187-9 (see also

North America, South America, United States)

American art, Emerson on, v, 84

American Civil War, documents of, original, xliii, 334-458; Lowell on, xxviii, 441-5, 455-60; Mill on, xxv, 170-3

American colonies, agriculture and cattle in, x, 194-5; currencies in, 261, 262, 265-7; documents in history of, original, xliii, 51-112, 147-59; England's trade laws for, x, 444-5; xliii, 158; exportations of meat from, x, 201; Franklin's plan to unite, i, 129-31; Granville on royal government of, 166-7; interest, rates of, in, x, 97-8; Jefferson on wrongs of, xliii, 161-3; manufactures in, x, 322; newspapers in, i, 20; books in, i, 77-8; population in, increase of, x, 74-5; settlement of, motives of, 416-23; settlements in, situation of, 26; slavery in, i, 215-16; trade of, bounties on, x, 426-9; wages in, 73-4; wealth in, progress of, 308-9; Woolman on state of, i, 272

American flag, Haskell on the, xliii, 404; Longfellow on the, xlii, 1339

AMERICAN HISTORICAL DOCUMENTS, xliii

American Indians (see Indians)

American literature, Emerson on possibilities of, v, 5, 186; Whitman on, xxxix, 409-32

American mythology, possibilities of an, xxviii, 427

American Philosophical Society, founded by Franklin, i, 3, 109, 172

American poets, xlii, 1262-1508

American political institutions, Emerson on, v, 253-6

American Revolution, Burke and the, xxiv, 5-6; Burns on, vi, 54-6; documents of, original, xliii, 160-91; Franklin's part in, i, 4, 76, 173-4; Franklin's plan of union and, 131; French in the, 142; public libraries, influence of, on, 70; Sheridan on, xviii, 104

AMERICAN SCHOLAR, Emerson's, v, 5-24

AMERICAN WAR, BALLAD ON THE, Burns's, vi, 54-6

Americans, cant of, v, 448; Emerson on interest in, 52; in England, 472; faith and hope lacking in, 57; materialism of, 287-8; Mill on political abilities of, xxv, 322; morals and religion of, v, 290; Thoreau on, xxviii, 420; Whitman on, xxxix, 409-10

Amerigo, the enameler, xxxi, 50

Amerzene, Andrew, first mate on "Pilgrim," xxiii, 419

Ames, Fisher, on republics and monarchies, v, 256

Ames's *Mariner's Sketches,* xxiii, 5

Amici, Professor, v, 330

AMIENS'S SONG, xl, 273-4

Aminias, the Decelean, xii, 19

Amity, sonnet on, xiv, 251

Ammanato, Bartolommeo, xxxi, 432 note 2, 438, 439, 445, 446

Ammon, the Libyan Jove, iv, 164 (see also Amun); Alexander called son of, xx, 60; xl, 422; oracle of, founding of, xxxiii, 32

Ammonia, production of, by moulds, xxxviii, 313 note; test of organisms, 358

Ammonians, Herodotus on the, xxxiii, 26

AMNESTY PROCLAMATION, LINCOLN'S, xliii, 442-5

Amompharetus, xii, 97

Amoretta, and Busirane, xxxix, 68

Amos, prophecy of, xlviii, 259

Amphialus, in the ODYSSEY, xxii, 107

Amphiaraüs, Dante on, xx, 84 and note 1; Eriphyle and, 302 note 11; Homer on, xxii, 214; lines on, xii, 83

Amphilochus, son of Amphiaraüs, xxii, 214

Amphimedon, wooer of Penelope, xxii, 313, 314; death of, 315; in Hades, 334-6

Amphinomus, suitor of Penelope, xxii, 234; advises against killing Telemachus, 234-5, 290-1; death of, 309; with Odysseus, 258-9, 266; sees ship of conspirators, 233

Amphion, founder of Thebes, xxii, 158; Dante on, xx, 133; reference to, v, 249; Sidney on, xxvii, 8, 14

Amphithea, grandmother of Ulysses, xxii, 278

Amphitrite, references to, iv, 71; viii, 203; xxii, 82, 170

Amphitryon, husband of Alcmene, xxii, 158; Herodotus on, xxxiii, 26; name used to express a good host, v, 215

Amposte, chatelain of, xxxv, 42, 46, 60

Amputations, Paré on cauterizing after, xxxviii, 8, 20, 22

Amram, father of Mary, xlv, 964 note 4

Amsanctus, Lake, xiii, 262-3

Amsdorff, Nicolaus von, xxxvi, 274 note

Amun, Zeus called, xxxiii, 26 (see also Ammon)

Amusements, Pascal on, xlviii, 11 (11), 56

Amycla, nurse of Alcibiades, xii, 110

Amyclas, the fisherman, xx, 333 note 16

Amycus, in the ÆNEID, xiii, 83, 323, 412

Amyntas, king of Lycaonia, xii, 383, 384

Amythaon, Homer on, xxii, 158

Anabaptists, Bacon on, iii, 14; of Munster, xxiv, 301

Anachronisms, Dryden on, of Virgil, xiii, 35-7; in Shakespeare and Sidney, xxxix, 228

Anacreon, Byron on, xli, 834; in Dante's Limbo, xx, 238 note 7

Anaërobian life, xxxviii, 292 note, 333, 340, 349-52, 355-6, 361-2, 383-5

Analogical resemblances, xl, 462-7

Analogous variations, xi, 168-71

Analogy, Emerson on, v, 453; Hume on reasoning by, xxxvii, 392, 595 (7), 427-8

Analysis, Marcus Aurelius on, ii, 302 (18); Mill on habit of, xxv, 91; Pascal on, xlviii, 428

Ananda, servant of Buddha, xlv, 600, 647-60, 673-6, 716, 729-30, 791, 795

Ananias, husband of Sapphira, xliv, 438 (1-6); Bunyan on, xv, 127; "varlet that cozened apostles," the, xlvii, 563

Ananias, the disciple, and Paul, xliv, 449 (10-18), 481 (12-16); Dante on, xx, 396 note

Ananias, the high priest, xliv, 482 (2), 484 (1)

Ananias, prince of Babylon, xxxvi, 346

Ananias, in THE ALCHEMIST, xlvii, 560-3, 567-73, 611-13, 621, 630-1, 633

Anarchy, Sophocles on, viii, 264

Anastasius II, in Dante's Hell, xx, 46 note

Anastasius IV, and Bernard, xxxvi, 356

Anathemas, Burns on, vi, 234

Anatolius, St., hymn by, xlv, 554

Anatomy, Locke on study of, xxxvii, 147, 157; study of, necessary for artists, xxxvii, 309; xxxix, 269

Anaxagoras, a native of Ionia, xxviii, 60; Creator, his idea of the, xxxix, 106; Euripides and, viii, 286; in Dante's Limbo, xx, 20; Pericles and, v, 454; xii, 40-2, 44, 56-7, 71; Socrates on doctrines of, ii, 13, 92-3; Themistocles and, xii, 6; Voltaire on teachings of, xxxiv, 104

Anaxarete, Webster on, xlvii, 758

Anaxenor, harper of Antony, xii, 351

Anaxilaus, at Byzantium, xii, 142

Anaximander, on the world, xxxix, 109-10

Anaximenes, letter to Pythagoras, xxxii, 49; mention of his doctrines, vii, 171; xxxix, 106

Ancestors, Bentham on veneration of, xxvii, 238-41; Huxley on, xxviii, 232; Lowell on, xlii, 1451; More on, xxxvi, 150; Tennyson on, xlii, 1035; Tseng-tzu on, xliv, 6 (9)

Anchemolus, death of, xiii, 339-40

Anchises, father of Æneas, xiii, 97; Crete, advises settlement of, 134-5; death in Sicily, 154-5; Dante on, xx, 349; Evander and, xiii, 277-8; funeral games of, 184-202; ghost of, advises Æneas, 206; in Hades, 234-42; Priam, relationship to, 21; Sidney on, xxvii, 20; Troy, in sack of, xiii, 125-8

ANCIENT MARINER, RIME OF THE, xli, 698-718; Wordsworth on the, xxxix, 282

Ancus, Marcius, Virgil on, xiii, 239

Andersen, Hans Christian, life and works of, xvii, 234; remarks on stories of, 2; TALES OF, 237-383

Andes Mountains, appearance and scenery, xxix, 269-70, 274-5, 293, 337, 341-2, 353; Darwin on his passage of, 332-56; geology of, 338-40, 351-3; mines of, 336-7; rain, absence of, in, 343; shingle terraces of, 334-5; snow-line of, 261; stone, crumbling, of, 338; torrents of, 335-6; upheaval of, 335, 339-40; vegetation and zoology of, 337, 346-7; winds and storms of, 342-3, 381-2

Andocides, impiety, accused of, xii, 35; on Themistocles, 35

Andrea, in THE CENCI, xviii, 284, 285, 321

ANDREA DEL SARTO, xlii, 1130-7

Andrew, the apostle, xliv, 373 (14), 430 (13); in PARADISE REGAINED, iv, 376-7

Andrew, the boy, in DON QUIXOTE, xiv, 40-2, 312-15

Andrews, Dr., bishop of Winchester, xv, 344, 387-8

Andrews, Isaac, Woolman and, i, 189-91

Andrews, Jacob, i, 192

Andrews, Peter, i, 191-2, 192-4

Androcles, Alcibiades's accuser, xii, 127

ANDROCLES, FABLE OF, xvii, 19

Androgeos, death of, xiii, 116

Andromache, in Greece, xiii, 141-2, 147; dream of, xl, 43; Ruskin on, xxviii, 146

Andromachus, a Syrian, xxviii, 60

Andromeda, constellation, iv, 152

Andronicus, Livius, date of, ix, 64; Sidney on, xxvii, 9

Andros, Themistocles at, xii, 24

Andvari, the dwarf, xlix, 304-6

ANE AN' TWENTY, TAM, vi, 441

Anemolians, ambassadors of the, xxxvi, 203-5

Aneurin, Celtic bard, xxxii, 174

Aneurism, defined, xxxviii, 85

ANGEL, THE, a story, xvii, 362-4

Angelica, Agrican and, iv, 396-7; xiv, 82; Orlando Furioso and, xiv, 16, 225, 238; xxxii, 52 note

Angelo, Michael (see Michelangelo)

Angels, Bagehot on Milton's, xxviii, 207-8; bowers of the, iv, 324; Browne on creation of, iii, 298; chorus of, in FAUST, xix, 33-5; creation of, xx, 315 note 9, 408-9 notes; Dante on rank among, xx, 300 note 6; habitation of, iii, 300; in FAUSTUS, xix, 202, 212-3, 217-8, 219; in PARADISE LOST, iv, 198-200 (see also Michael, Raphael, etc.); rebellion of the, 200-29 (see also Fallen Angels); love among, 262; Milton on nature of, 215-16; number of, xx, 411-12; Smart on, xli, 499; Tutelary (see Tutelary Angels)

ANGELS, FOOTSTEPS OF, xlii, 1319

Anger, Augustine, St., on, vii, 30; Bacon on, iii, 141-2; Collins on, in music, xli, 489; in Dante's HELL, xx, 32, 48; Dante's examples of, 215; Ecclesiastes on, xliv, 347 (9); Epictetus on, ii, 144 (75); Hobbes's definition of, xxxiv, 353; Krishna on, xlv, 872; Manzoni on, xxi, 540; Marcus Aurelius on, ii, 202 (10), 205 (16), 231 (28), 239 (26), 284 (25), 295; Pascal on, xlviii, 167 (502); Penn on, i, 363 (270, 271); Plutarch on, xii, 172; Walton on, xv, 332; Webster on, xlvii, 753

Angle, Guichard d', xxxv, 47, 48, 52

Angles, Tacitus on the, xxxiii, 118

Angrivarians, Tacitus on the, xxxiii, 114

Anguillotto of Lucca, xxxi, 103-4

Angular figures, not beautiful, xxiv, 99; why unpleasant, 104, 127

Angus, in MACBETH, xlvi, 311, 365

Angustia, Donna, xxiii, 249-50, 404, 406

Aniause, King, xxxv, 173, 182

Anicius, Titus, ix, 122

Animal kingdom, how distinguished from vegetable, xxxviii, 358-9

Animalculæ, perfection of, v, 93; xlviii, 26

Animals, acclimatisation of, xi, 153-4; Bacon's experiments on, iii,

184; beauty in, proportion as cause of, xxiv, 81-2; beauty sense of, xxxvi, 215-16; Blake on cruelty to, xli, 601-2; Buddhist ideas of, xlv, 722-5; Burke on cries of, xxiv, 74; Burke on mating of, 38-9; care of, in Massachusetts, xliii, 84; Carlyle on, xxv, 453 note; death, no fear of, in, xxxiv, 181; Descartes on reason in, 47-8; domestic (see Domestic Animals); Emerson on, v, 240; extinction of large, cause of, xxix, 187-9; fertilisation of, xi, 113-14; habits, diversity of, 123-4; Hume on reason of, xxxvii, 392-5; Locke on cruelty to, 108-9; love of offspring among, xl, 436; Marcus Aurelius on kindness to, ii, 238 (23), 254 (65); Pascal on mind in, xlviii, 119 (340-3); admiration among, 132 (401); plants and, complex relations of, xi, 85-8; Rousseau on distinction between men and, xxxiv, 178-9; size of, disadvantages in, xi, 370; size of, in relation to vegetation, xxix, 97-101; social instincts of, ii, 270 (9); souls of, xxxvi, 241; truth, love of, among, v, 388; Voltaire on souls in, xxxiv, 108-9; Woolman on kindness to, i, 314 (see also Organic Beings, Species)

Animism, defined, xvii, 1

Animosities, teach value of friendship, ix, 16

Anius, king of Delos, xiii, 134

Anna, St., in Dante's PARADISE, xx, 423; Jesus found by, iv, 369

Anna, the prophetess, xliv, 364 (36-8)

Anna, sister of Dido, xiii, 156-8; Æneas sought for by, xiii, 171-2; at Dido's death, xiii, 180-1

ANNA, THY CHARMS, vi, 326

ANNABEL LEE, xlii, 1290-1

Annas, the high priest, xliv, 365 (2), 436 (6); Dante on, xx, 99 note 7

Annates, Luther on, xxxvi, 292-4, 302

Anne, St. (see Anna)

Annebault, Claude d', xxxi, 335 note 2, 342; Paré and, xxxviii, 13

Anneius, M., legate of Cicero, ix, 140, 143

Annibale, the surgeon, xxxi, 32

ANNIE, FOR, xlii, 1287-90

Annotations, Cervantes on, xiv, 8, 10-11; Hugo on, xxxix, 354; Johnson on, 259, 261

Ansârs, xlv, 961 note 14, 980 note

Anseïs, in SONG OF ROLAND, xlix, 100, 125, 142, 154

Anselm, Bacon on, iii, 53; Harrison on, xxxv, 265-6; in Dante's PARADISE, xx, 340; life of, 340 note 36

Anselmo, Lothario and, story of, xiv, 323-63, 368-73

Anselmo, in the goatherd's story, xiv, 526-30

Anson's Voyages, Mill on, xxv, 12

ANSWER, THE, Scott's, xli, 766

ANT AND GRASSHOPPER, fable of, xvii, 25

Antæus, Dante on, xx, 132-3 note 6; family of, xlix, 287 note; Hercules and, iv, 413; xiv, 21

Antæus, chief of Turnus, xiii, 345-6

Antagoras, of Chios, xii, 104

Antarctic islands, climate and productions of, xxix, 264-7

Anteia, wife of Helvidius, ix, 355

Antenor, founder of Padua, xiii, 83-4; xx, 165 note 7

Anteon (see Antæus)

Anterigoli, Piermaria d' (see Sbietta)

Anteros, and Eros, xii, 113 note 3; xviii, 420

ANTHEA, TO, xl, 346-7

Anthemocritus, xii, 69

Anthony, St. (see Antony, St.)

Anthony, the goatherd, xiv, 88-90

Anthores, death of, xiii, 354

Anthrax, Pasteur on, xxxviii, 383, 387-8

Anthylla, city of, xxxiii, 48

Antichrist, Browne on, iii, 311; legend of birth of, 295; Luther on, xxxvi, 310; Pascal on, xlviii, 290-1, 298, 300 (846); Paul, St., on, xxxvi, 288

Anticleia, mother of Odysseus, xxii, 154, 156-7; her death of grief, 217

Anticlus, in the Trojan horse, xxii, 55

Antigone, condemned to perish in cave, viii, 267; death of, 268-72, 281; fate bewailed by people, 264; in Dante's Limbo, xx, 239; Œdipus with, viii, 240-1; in The Phœnicians, xxxix, 358; Polynices's burial by, viii, 243-6; Ruskin on, xxviii, 146

ANTIGONE, TRAGEDY OF, Sophocles's, viii, 243-84

Antigonus, of Judæa, xii, 362; and the Parthians, iv, 397

Antilochus, son of Nestor, xxii, 37; Achilles and, 333; death of, 53; in Hades, 164, 331

Antinous, with the ODYSSEY, with Telemachus, xxii, 19

Antinous, complains of Penelope, xxii, 24-5; counsels suitors to heed Telemachus, 291; death of, 307; Irus, encouraged by, to fight with Ulysses, 256, 257; contest with the bow, 297, 299, 300, 302-3; Penelope, his gifts to, 262-3; Penelope rebukes, 235; Telemachus invited to feast by, 30;

Telemachus plotted against by, 64-5, 68, 233-4; Ulysses and, as beggars, 248-51

Antioch, Christian Church at, xliv, 455 (26-30), 457 (1)

Antiochus of Ascalon, xii, 227

Antiochus, Athenian admiral, xii, 147

Antiochus, king of Commagene, xii, 360-1

Antiochus Deus, xlviii, 253

Antiochus Epiphanes, and the Jews, iv, 392

Antiochus the Great, Ætolians and, iii, 134; anecdote of, v, 304; prophecy of, xlviii, 253-4; the Romans and, xxxvi, 12, 13, 77

Antiochus Hierax, xii, 86 note

Antiochus, the pilot, and Alcibiades, xii, 117

Antiope, Homer on, xxii, 158; mentioned, iv, 380

Antipater, the Edomite, iv, 386

Antipater, general of Alexander, xii, 220; and the Athenian orators, 221

Antipathies, national, Browne on, iii, 330; Pascal on, xlviii, 104; Washington on, xliii, 261-2

Antiphates, in the ÆNEID, xiii, 321

Antiphates, the Læstrygonian, xxii, 139

Antiphates, son of Melampus, xxii, 214

Antiphates, and Themistocles, xii, 21

Antiphon, Athenian orator, on Alcibiades, xii, 112; condemnation of, 209

Antiphon of Cephisus, ii, 21

Antiphus, son of Ægyptus, xxii, 22; friend of Ulysses, 240

Antipodes, Darwin on the, xxix, 440

Antiquity, Bentham on, xxvii, 238-41; Browne on, iii, 294; Harvey on, xxxviii, 66; Hobbes on, xxxiv, 385; Hugo on, xxxix, 380; Johnson on, 218-19; More on, xxxvi, 150; Pascal on, xlviii, 108 (301), 444-51; not the rule of belief, 95 (260)

Anti-Reformers, Fallacies of, Sydney Smith on, xxvii, 237-65

Antiseptic principle, Pasteur on the, xxxviii, 400-1

Antiseptic Principle, Lister's, xxxviii, 271-82

Antisthenes, on detraction, ii, 119 (7), 250 (36); on the piper, xii, 37; Pascal on, xlviii, 15 (27); with Socrates, ii, 47

Antonia, daughter of Antony, xii, 403; xviii, 60-1

Antoninus, Marcus Aurelius (see Aurelius, Marcus)

Antoninus, T. Aurelius (Pius), ii, 192; M. Aurelius on, 196 (16); 239 (30)

Antonio, in DUCHESS OF MALFI, xlvii; Ancona, banished from, 770-1; Bosola with, 722-3, 740, 746-7, 773, 810-11; Bosola on, 764-6; Cardinal, relations with, 728, 799-800, 806; Delio, scenes with, 721-2, 724, 726-7, 740, 742-3, 745, 754-5, 793-4, 795-6, 807-8; Duchess, scenes with, 733-7, 741, 742, 757-9, 761-2, 763-4, 772, 774-5; Duchess, steward of, 724; Ferdinand, relations with, 725, 770, 773; orders palace closed, 724; son of, born, 745

Antonio, in TEMPEST, xlvi; Ariel denounces, 421-3; banquet, at the, 420; Prospero and, 383-5, 434, 436; Sebastian, plot with, 403-7, 420

Antonius, Caius, Roman consul, xii, 234, 235; Catiline conspiracy, 238, 244; Mark Antony, relationship to, 340; Cicero mentions, ix, 83

Antonius, Lucius, Cicero on, ix, 179

Antonius, Marcus, the orator, grandfather of Mark Antony, xii, 334; Sidney on, xxvii, 51-2

Antonius, Marcus, the Triumvir (see Antony)

Antonius, Publius, and Cæsar, xii, 276

Antonius of Florence, xxxvi, 327

Antony, Caius, brother of Marcus, xii, 350

Antony, Mark, Actium, flight from, xii, 387-8; Antiochus, war with, 360-1; appearance and dress of, 336; Artavasdes seized by, 375; in Asia, 350-2; Bacon on, iii, 28; his relations with Octavius, 130; burial of, xii, 399; Cæsar and Pompey, contest of, 337-40, 301-2, 308, 312; Cæsar, favorite of, 342; after Cæsar's death, 262-3, 344, 345; character of, 352; children of, 403; Cicero, relations with, 261, 262-3, 264-5, 267-8, 334, 348; Cicero on his relations with, ix, 96, 185, 186, 188; Cleopatra and, Dryden on, xviii, 11; Cleopatra and sons honored by, xii, 378; Cleopatra, first meeting of, with, 352-7; Cleopatra prevents, from renewing war, 375-7; Cleopatra renews relations with, 362-3; Cleopatra, slave of, charged with being, 381-2; death of, 395-6; Dolabella and, 340, 342; East, campaigns in, early, 335-6; in Egypt after Actium, 390, 391-3; Fulvia, marriage to, 341-2; in Greece, 350, 359-60; Ides of March, at, 329, 330, 343-4; Italy, driven from, 264-5, 346; LIFE OF,

Plutarch's, 334-403; Lupercalia, at the, 325, 343; master of horse, 340; Octavia, marriage of, to, 357-8; Octavia neglected by, 376-7; Octavius and, meet at Tarentum, 361-2; Octavius, break of, with, 345-6; Octavius, charges against, made by, 378; Octavius, contest with, 383-7; Octavius's growing jealousy of, 359; parentage and youth, 334-5; Parthia invaded by, 363-75; Pompey's house bought by, 341; popularity and liberality of, 336-7; prodigies preceding the war, 382-3 (cf. xviii, 21); Sextus Pompey and, 358-9; statues and honors to, abolished, 268; triumvir, 348-9; Virgil on, at Actium, xiii, 295; war of, with republicans, xii, 349-50 (cf. xviii, 35); world divided by, to triumvirs, 357

Antony, in ALL FOR LOVE, xviii, 19; in Egypt after Actium, 23, 25, 26-7; his lamentation, 27-8; scene with Ventidius, 28, 35; remarks on scene with Ventidius, 18; his reply to Cleopatra's appeal, 37-8; on Octavius, prepares to march, 39-40; receives Cleopatra's gift, 41-2; meeting with Cleopatra, 43-9; with Cleopatra in the palace, 50-1; advised by Ventidius, 51-2; with Dolabella, 53-7; scene with Octavia, 57-61; sends farewell to Cleopatra by Dolabella, 65-6; hears Dolabella's falseness, 73-8; accuses Dolabella and Cleopatra, 79-83; betrayed by Egyptian fleet, 86-7; plans to fight it out, 88-9; hears Cleopatra dead, 90-1; death of, 92-6

Antony, surnamed Creticus, father of Marcus, xii, 334

Antony, the Younger, xii, 403

Antony, St., Augustine on, vii, 132; Burke on pictures of, xxiv, 56; conversion of, vii, 142; Newman on, xxviii, 38

Ant(s), aphides and, xi, 265; Brazilian, xxix, 45; Browne on, iii, 278 (15); Johnson on, xxxix, 309-10; Milton on, iv, 242; Pope on, xl, 438; slave-making instinct of, xi, 275-9; worker castes of, 61, 290-5

Antyllus, son of Antony, xii, 392, 398, 403

Anubis, called the dog, iv, 14; barking deity, vii, 125

Anuruddha, xlv, 660-1

Anuweekin, the Indian, xliii, 152

Anville, Marshal d', xxxviii, 26

Anxiety, Arabian verses on, xvi, 11; Hobbes on, xxxiv, 389, 391-2; mean and noble, xxviii, 117;

physical effects of, xxxviii, 131; Pliny on, ix, 342-3

Anxur, in the ÆNEID, xiii, 345

Anyder River, in UTOPIA, xxxvi, 185

Anysis, king of Egypt, xxxiii, 70, 71-2

Anything, Mr., in PILGRIM'S PROGRESS, xv, 104

Anytus, Alcibiades and, xii, 113-14; first briber in Athens, 165; Socrates's accuser, ii, 4, 10, 16, 17, 21, 134 (52)

Aorta, Harvey on the, xxxviii, 91, 94, 96, 108, 146

Apathy, in Dante's Hell, xx, 13-15; Pope on, xl, 428

Ape(s), intellectual powers of, xi, 234-5

Apelles, Alexander and, ix, 107; method of, iii, 112; the "Venus" of, ix, 130; xiii, 12

Apemantus, Timon and, xii, 391

Aphides, and ants, xi, 265; development of, 482

Aphrodite, Ares and, xxii, 111-13

Aphrodite, in HIPPOLYTUS, viii, 287-9; Cyrene's image of, xxxiii, 91; home of, viii, 364; queen of rapture, 123; "she whom none subdues," 268; (see also Venus)

Apires, Chilian miners, xxix, 361

Apis, court of, at Memphis, xxxiii, 79

Aplysia, Darwin on the, xxix, 16-17

Apocalyptics, Pascal on the, xlviii, 221 (650, 651)

Apodictic Principles, xxxii, 345

Apollinarian Heresy, vii, 120

Apollinarii, Milton on the, iii, 209

Apollinaris, Domitius, letter to, ix, 278

Apollo, Cassandra and, viii, 43-4, 49; Daphne and, xl, 386; Delphi, (Phœbus), fourth prophet of, viii, 115-16; Egypt, king of, xxxiii, 74; god of music, iv, 22, 59; viii, 426; Hyacinth and, iv, 19; in Egyptian mythology, xxxiii, 80-1; Latona's son, iv, 82; Loxias, called, viii, 94, 113, 116; Lyceian king, 203; Marsyas and, xx, 287; Phlegyas and, 33 note 1; Phœbus, called, viii, 115; Thymbræan god, xx, 193 note; Virgil on, xiii, 161; Zoilus and, xxviii, 395; (see also Delphian Oracle)

Apollo, in THE FURIES, viii, protector of Orestes, 117-18, 121-4; witness for Orestes, 136-7, 139-41; altercation with the Furies, 143-4

Apollo Belvedere, Cellini on the, xxxi, 332 note; not impossible in life, v, 202

Apollodorus, Socrates's friend, ii, 21, 25, 46-7, 114

Apollodorus, the orator, and Demosthenes, xii, 209

Apollodorus, Greek writer, on Chrysippus, xxxii, 31

Apollodorus, the Sicilian, with Cleopatra, xii, 315-16

Apollonius, Molon, and Cicero, xii, 228; Cæsar and, 275

Apollonius, the Stoic, M. Aurelius on, ii, 194 (8), 199; on self-discipline, 154 (100)

Apollonius, of Tyana, Bacon on, iii, 69

Apollos, the Alexandrian, xliv, 472 (24-8); St. Paul on, xlv, 504 (5-6), 505 (6), 526 (12)

Apollyon, and Christian, xv, 60-5

Apologies, Bacon on, iii, 67; Emerson on, v, 72; new actions the only, 198-9; Pascal on, xlviii, 21 (57)

APOLOGY OF SOCRATES, Plato's, ii, 3-29

APOLOGY, THE, Emerson's poem, xlii, 1293-4

Apostasy, Bunyan on, xv, 156-8

Apostles, Calvin on, xxxix, 47, 48; choosing of the, xliv, 373 (13-16); community of goods among, 438; council of, on circumcision, 463-4, xlviii, 227 (672); deacons appointed by the, xliv, 441 (1-6); Holy Spirit received, 431; imprisoned and miraculously freed, 439 (17-20), renew teachings, 439 (21-42); in Jerusalem, 446 (1, 14); with Paul, 450 (27); Jesus's appearances to, after death, 425 (36-53), 429 (3-11), xlv, 522 (5, 7); Jesus with, 379 (1, 9), 380 (22-5), 383 (10), 383 (18), 385 (43-6), 389 (1), 392 (1), 395 (41), 405 (5-10), 408 (31), 417 (14-40, 45-6); Judas's place supplied, 430-1; Kempis on the, vii, 297 (4), 306 (6); Lessing on the, xxxii, 209; Luther on the, xxxvi, 304, 361; Luther on council, 286; Milton on the, iv, 356-7, 358; miracles done by, xliv, 433 (43), 439 (12-16); Mohammed on the, xlv, 966, 980, 1020-1; Pascal on the, xlviii, 274 (770), 282-3, 294 (838); Paul, St., on the, xlv, 506 (9-13); power and authority given to, xliv, 382 (1); sent forth to preach, 382 (2-6)

APOSTLES, ACTS OF THE, xliv, 427-95

Apostles' Creed, xxxix, 51

Apothecaries, Chaucer on, doctors and, xl, 23; profits of, x, 118

Apparel, Penn on, i, 346; Woolman on, 262-4

Apparitions, Hobbes on, xxxiv, 328-9

Apparitor, Chaucer's, xl, 28-9 note 314

Appeal, right of, in Massachusetts, xliii, 76 (36)

Appearances, Emerson on regard for, v, 71; fable of deceptiveness of, xvii, 26; Goethe on, xix, 394; Machiavelli on care of, xxxvi, 61; Marcus Aurelius on, ii, 236 (13); Pascal on, xlviii, 112 (319); Paul, St., on, xxxvi, 289-90; Schiller on æsthetic, xxxii, 301-6

Appetite, Locke on tempting the, xxxvii, 32

Appius Claudius (see Claudius)

Appius, Marcus, Cæsar and, xii, 293; Cicero and, 248; ix, 124, 132, 147-8, 152; provincial governor, 136, 147-8; propylæum of, 157

Applauders, professional, in Rome, ix, 230

Applause (see Praise)

Apple-growing, in Chiloe, xxix, 316

Apples, Locke on eating of, xxxvii, 22

Appointments, Confucius on, xliv, 42-3; Koran on, xxv, 254; Presidential, xliii, 201 (2, 3)

Appomattox, terms of surrender at, xliii, 447-8

Apprehensions, Pliny on, ix, 343

Apprenticeships, limitation of, x, 127; long, 127-31; Smith on, 108; unknown to ancients, 130

Appropriations, in Massachusetts, xliii, 82 (78); (U. S.) under the Confederation, 175; under Constitution, 197 (12), 198 (7)

Apries, king of Egypt, xxxiii, 83-6

April, Chaucer on, xl, 11; Shakespeare on, 284

Apteryx, wings of the, xi, 186

Apuleius, Golden Ass of, xxxix, 368; xlii, 1434

Aquila of Pontus, xliv, 470 (2-4), 471 (18-19), 472 (26)

Aquila, P. Attius, ix, 431

Aquleia, Freeman on, xxviii, 265

Aquilius, Cicero on, ix, 83

Aquilo, charioteer of Winter, iv, 18

Aquinas, Thomas, St., angels, reference to, xx, 409 note; death of, 229 note 11; Hazlitt on, xxvii, 292; Dante places in Paradise, xx, 329; life of, sketch of, 329 note 16; pupil of Albertus Magnus, 329 note 15

Aquinius, Marcus, Cicero on, xii, 248

Arabella, Lady (see Stuart, Arabella)

Arabesques, Cellini on, xxxi, 62-3

Arabian heresy, iii, 270 (7)

ARABIAN NIGHTS' ENTERTAINMENTS, xvi

Arabs, adopted children among, xlv, 999 note 2, 1003 note; beaconfires of, 1015 note; chase, ideas

of, **v**, 363; divorce among, xlv, 999 note; Emerson on conquests of the, **v**, 58; hospitality among, xlv, 1004 note 28; religion of, 886; Schiller on civilization of, xxxii, 251; sheiks, habits of, **v**, 143-4; swords as mirrors among, xx, 344 note 22

Arachne, Dante on, xx, 194; reference to loom of, 72

Aratus, Pliny on, ix, 284

Araviscans, Tacitus on the, xxxiii, 111

Arbela, battle of, iii, 78

ARBITRARY GOVERNMENT, Winthrop on, xliii, 90-112

Arbitration, Hobbes on legal, xxxiv, 427; Pascal on international, xlviii, 106 (296); U. S. and Mexico, agreement between, for, xliii, 323-4

Arc, Joan of (see Joan of Arc)

ARCADES, MILTON'S, iv, 43-46

Arcadia, Johnson on first inhabitants of, xxxix, 209; Spartan invasion of, xii, 154 note; the "thesmophoria" in, xxxiii, 86-7

Arcalaus, the enchanter, xiv, 123

Arcas, Callisto's son, xx, 417 note 5

Arceisius, father of Laertes, xxii, 227

Arcens, son of, xiii, 317

Arcesilaus, method of teaching, xxxii, 36; Pascal on, xlviii, 126 (375)

Archander, Herodotus on, xxxiii, 48

Archangels, in FAUST, xix, 16-17

Archedemus, Aristophanes on, viii, 431, 436

Archelaus, Antony and, xii, 336; the tower of, xxxv, 336

Archenomus, Aristophanes on, viii, 465-6

Archeopteryx, xi, 356-7

Archiac, M. d', on changes in species, xi, 374-5

Archias, the exile-hunter, xii, 221-2

Archibius, Cleopatra's friend, xii, 402

Archidamus, king of Sparta, xii, 68, 71-2

Archidiche, Herodotus on, xxxiii, 69

Archilochus, banished from Sparta, iii, 204

Archimedes, Huxley on, xxviii, 227; Manzoni on, xxi, 119; Marcus Aurelius on, ii, 244 (47); Pascal on, xlviii, 280

Archipelagoes, Darwin on, xi, 362

Archippe, wife of Themistocles, xii, 34

Archippus, Flavius, ix, 408-11, 420-1

Architecture, Burke on colors in, xxiv, 72; Coleridge on, xxvii, 276; effects, its means of producing, **xxiv**, 136; figures in, various, xxiv,

66-7; Greenough's theory of, **v**, 329; Hobbes on, xxxiv, 377; Hugo on mediæval, xxxix, 368; human body as model in, xxiv, 85; light and shade in, 71; magnitude in, 67; Vitruvius on study of, **v**, 182; xxxi, 8

Architeles, Themistocles and, xii, 11-12

Archytas of Tarentum, on isolation, ix, 38; on sensual pleasure, 60

Arcite and Palamon, story of, xxxix, 167, 169, 180

Areius and Octavius, xii, 398, 399

AREOPAGITICA, MILTON'S, iii, 193-244

Areopagus, Council of, Æschylus on ordaining of, viii, 142; Burke on, xxiv, 355; its composition, xii, 46; its powers reduced, 43, 46

Ares, Æschylus on, viii, 20-1; Aphrodite and, xxii, 111-13; Phineus's sons and, viii, 273; worshipped in Egypt, xxxiii, 33, 34-5, 42; (see also Mars)

Arete, wife of Alcinous, xxii, 95-6; Ulysses with, 97-8, 115-16, 160; Ulysses's farewell to, 182

Aretheus, Eudamidas and, 83-4

Arethusa, Alpheus and, Milton on, iv, 44; Dante on story of, xx, 106; Jupiter and, xix, 239; Virgil on, xiii, 154

Arethusa, in PHILASTER, xlvii, Bellario sent to, 655-7, 661; Bellario scenes with, 662-3; 682-3, 691, 718; hunt, at, 683, 684; king, scenes with, 678-9, 704-5; lost in wood, 688-90; Megra denounces, 668-9, 713; Pharamond and, 639-40, 641-3, 653-5, 661-2, 663-4, 694-5; Philaster, letter to, 674; Philaster, scenes with, 649-53, 680-2, 691-3, 699, 700-2, 703

Arethusa on river, iii, 269

Aretino, Pietro, Milton on, iii, 214 note 43; pictures of, reference to, xlvii, 545; portrait by Titian, 286

Argand, Aimé, inventor of hollow wick, xxx, 108, 163

Argas, friend of Orgon, xxvi, 266

Argas, the poet, xii, 200

Argent, Dr., Harvey to, xxxviii, 65

Argenti, Filippo, in Dante's Hell, xx, 34

Argia, in Limbo, xx, 239

Arginusæ, battle of, ii, 19

Argo, Homer on ship, xxii, 171; Milton on ship, iv, 136; Stukeley on, v, 477

Argonauts, date of expedition of, xxxiv, 132-3

Argos, eyes of, references to, **iv**, 326; xlvii, 543

Argos, Hermes, slayer of, viii, **176** note 37; xxii, 10

Argos, Io and, viii, **176**, **179**

Argos, dog of Ulysses, xxii, 246
Argument, Franklin on habit of, i,
15-16, 132; Penn on, 352 (133-6);
Socrates on, ii, 83-4; varieties of,
xxxvii, 351 note
Argus, Evander and, xiii, 283; (see
also Argos)
Argustus, Eliazar and, xxxv, 162
Ariadne, sister of Minotaur, xx, 50
note 5; placed among stars, 341;
Homer on, xxii, 160; Theseus and,
xxvi, 128, 135
Ariamenes, Xerxes's admiral, xii,
19
Arians, Bacon on the, iii, 145;
Browne on the, 271 (8); Pascal
on the, xlviii, 299, 306; Voltaire
on, xxxiv, 84-5
Aricia, mother of Virbius, xiii, 269
Aricia, in PHÆDRA, Hippolytus and,
xxvi, 127-9, 139-47, 174, 175-6,
182-3; Theseus and, 177-8, 185
Ariel, in FAUST, xix, 177, 183
Ariel, in PARADISE LOST, iv, 216
Ariel, in THE TEMPEST, xlvi, at
banquet, 421-2; Caliban and, 416-
19; Ferdinand and, 393-4, 397;
Gonzalo and, 402, 406; Prospero
and, 387-91, 424-5, 429, 430, 431-
2, 432-3, 435, 439, 440, 442; Hugo
on, xxxix, 372; Hunt on Shakespeare's, xxvii, 309; Shelley on
Miranda and, xli, 871
Aries, Dante on sign of, xx, 181;
sun started in, 6 note 5
Arimanes, in MANFRED, xviii, 426
Arimaspians, Æschylus on the, viii,
184 and note 55; and gryfons, iv,
134
Arimnestus, at Platæa, xii, 92, 100
Ariobarzanes, Cicero and, ix, 141-2,
148-9; Plutarch on, xii, 256
Arioch, in PARADISE LOST, iv, 216
Ariosto, Lodovic, Cervantes on, xiv,
53; Dryden on, xiii, 5, 13, 27, 57;
Hugo on, xxxix, 369; Hume on,
xxvii, 219; Montaigne on, xxxii,
93; Renan on, 168; Sainte-Beuve
on, 137; Spenser on, xxxix, 65;
Titian's portrait of, xxvii, 286;
Wordsworth on, xxxix, 333
Ariovistus, xii, 290-1
Ariphron, guardian of Alcibiades,
xii, 110, 112
Aristarchus, friend of Paul, xliv,
474 (29), 475 (4), 490 (2)
Aristarchus of Samos, referred to,
xlvi, 75
Aristides, archon, xii, 85-6; assess-
ment made by, 105; Athenian democracy proposed by, 103; banishment of, 87-8; birth and condition of, 80-1, 106-7, 108; children of, 108-9; commissioner, as,
104; constancy and justice, 83-4,
86; death of, 107-8; Eleutheria

proposed by, 102; levy of Greeks
proposed by, 102; LIFE OF, Plutarch's, 80-109; Marathon, at, 84-
5; Persian wars, in, 17, 20, 88-
101; public conduct guided by
expediency, 106; resentment, freedom from, 195-6; Themistocles
and, 7, 15, 17, 20, 23, 81-3, 84,
87, 88-90, 103, 105-6, 107
Aristippus, Horace on, xxxii, 60;
not with Socrates in prison, ii,
47; on children, xxxii, 76; quotation from, 64
Aristo, Titus, letters to, ix, 274, 335;
Pliny on, 219-21
Aristobulus and Antony, xii, 335
Aristocracy, Channing on, xxviii,
357; Mill on government by, xxv,
112; natural and actual, 222; of
Europe, v, 223; origin of, xxxv,
226
Aristocrates, Antony and, xii, 390
Aristodicus, the Tanagræan, xii, 48
Aristogiton, grand-daughter of, xii,
109; Hermodius and, xxxii, 79
Ariston, Claudius, ix, 309
Ariston, of Ceos, xii, 82 note 1
Ariston, Greek tragedian, xxxii, 72
Aristonicus, death of, xii, 221
Aristophanes, Dryden on, xxxix,
182; Euripides and, viii, 286;
THE FROGS, 419-66; Hugo on,
xxxix, 365; life and works, viii,
418; Milton on, iii, 204, 216;
Samians on the, xii, 5; Socrates
on, ii, 5; Taine on comedies of,
xxxix, 460
Aristophanes, the grammarian, on
Epicurus, xxxii, 66
Aristophon, the painter, xii, 124
Aristotle, air and rain, on, xxxviii,
107; Alexander's tutor, iv, 405,
xxxii, 55; animals, motion of,
xxxviii, 142-3; Antipater on per-
suasiveness of, xii, 194; Art of
Poesy, xxvii, 42; Augustine on
Predicaments of, vii, 62; Bacon
on ostentation of, iii, 134; Browne
on, 275 (12), 278, 300, 320, 336-7;
Cicero on, xii, 245; comedy on,
xxvii, 49; comets on, xxxiv, 120;
Dante's Limbo in, xx, 20 note 8;
death, on, xxxviii, 89; democracy,
on, xxiv, 273 and note; Don Ferrante on, xxi, 465; drama, on
the, xiii, 6-7; xxxix, 231; Emerson on, v, 159; Euripus, flux of,
xxxviii, 79; friendship, on, xxxii.
75, 82, 83; heart and blood, on
the, xxxviii, 85, 88, 98, 130, 135,
138, 139, 141, 145; human understanding, on, xxxiv, 104; Hume
on, xxxvii, 307; imitation, on,
xxiv, 45; inequality, on, xxxiv,
425; Lowell on, xxviii, 465; Luther
on, xxxvi, 338-9; Mill on, xxv,

227; medicine, on study of, xix, 201 notes 12 and 13; Milton on Lyceum of, iii, 256; iv, 405; Montaigne on, xxxii, 29; natural selection, his idea of, xi, 9 note; Newman on Lyceum of, xxviii, 59; Pascal on, xlviii, 116; Plato's pupil, ii, 1; poetry, on, xiii, 36-7; xxvii, 54; xxviii, 80; xxxix, 294, 408; poetry and history, on, xxvii, 21-2; xxviii, 74; Raleigh on his doctrine of eternity, xxxix, 104, 105, 106, 109-10; *Rhetoric* of, xxv, 13; ridicule, on, xxxix, 188; soul, on the, 106; space, on, v, 182; state, on members of, xx, 320 note 14; summum bonum of, iii, 346 (15); Taine on, xxxix, 455 note; teacher, profits as, x, 142-3; taste, on, xxviii, 388; things to be avoided, on, xx, 48 note; tragedy, on, iv, 416; xiii, 8; viper, on the, xxxv, 363

Arithmetic, Descartes on, xxxiv, 19; Hobbes on, xxxiv, 377; Hume on, xxxvii, 324; Locke on study of, 164, 165

Arius, Dante on, xx, 344 note 21; Pascal on, xlviii, 293 (832)

Arjuna, Prince (see BHAGAVAD-GITA)

Ark, Browne on story of the, iii, 287; on pigeon sent from, 286; Milton on the, iv, 341

Arkansas River, sediment of, xxxviii, 424

Arkwright, the spinning-jenny and, v, 410, 411

ARMADA, THE, by Macaulay, xli, 940-3

Armadillo, Darwin on the, xxix, 108; Raleigh on the, xxxiii, 366

Armado, fish, xxix, 149

Armagnac, Earl of, xxxix, 100

Armenians, Freeman on the, xxviii, 281

Armgart, in WILHELM TELL, xxvi, 453, 454-9

Armies, Machiavelli on, xxxvi, 42-50; mediæval Italy, of, xxvii, 392-3; 16th century, xxxviii, 8; standing (see Standing Armies)

Arminians, Bacon on the, iii, 145

Arminius, Milton on, iii, 214

ARMOUR, ADAM, PRAYER OF, vi, 127-8

Armour, Jean, farewell to, vi, 235; lines on, 62, 73-4, 98, 323-4, 334-5; references to, 150 note, 182; Robert Burns and, 15, 16

Arms, Don Quixote on profession of, xiv, 393-4, 396-8; Machiavelli on practice and study of, xxxvi, 42, 50-2; Milton on lack of training in, iv, 351; More on practice of, xxxvi, 153-4; profession of, necessary to empire, iii, 81-2; right of, in U. S., xliii, 207 (2)

Armstead, Gen., at Gettysburg, xliii, 414

Armstrong, Dr., on puerperal fever, xxxviii, 240-1

ARMSTRONG, JOHNIE, xl, 102-4

Army, U. S., under the Confederation, xliii, 171, 174, 175-6; under Constitution, 197 (12, 14); President commander-in-chief of U. S., 201 (1)

Army of the Potomac, Haskell on, xliii, 348-9, 428

Arnaces, the eunuch, xii, 20, 90

Arnæus, the beggar, xxii, 255

Arnauld, M., references to, xlviii, 352 note 3, 392

Arnold, Sir Edwin, translator of BHAGAVAD-GITA, xlv, 799

Arnold, Matthew, on culture, xxviii, 222; life and writings, 64; POEMS by, xlii, 1168-86; STUDY OF POETRY, xxviii, 65-91

Arnold, Sir Nicholas, xxxv, 346

Arnold, Thomas, Matthew Arnold on, xlii, 1176-81

Arnold, Bishop of Liege, xxxv, 104-5

Arnold's Battery, at Gettysburg, xliii, 359, 373, 405

Aromaia, Raleigh on, xxxiii, 344-5, 365

Aroras, Raleigh on the, xxxiii, 364

Arouet, François-Marie (see Voltaire)

Arowacai, town of, xxxiii, 361

Arragon, Cardinal of, in DUCHESS OF MALFI, xlvii, 721-816; Antonio, relations with, 726, 728, 795; Bosola, scenes with, 722, 799-800, 805-6, 812-15; Duchess and, 730-2; Ferdinand and, 728, 751-4, 769-70, 797, 798-9; Julia and, 748-50, 802-5; keeps watch alone, 809-10; Loretto, at, 770; Malatesti and, 767-8

Arrangement, Pascal on, xlviii, 14 (22-3)

Arrests, in U. S., xliii, 207 (4)

Arria, wife of Pætus, ix, 253-5; Certus, in case of, 355, 358; exile of, 250; Pliny and, 355

Arrian, Epictetus and, ii, 116

Arrianus, Maturus, letters to, ix, 195, 263, 291, 347

Arrigo, Cardinal, xx, 338 note 20

Arrigo, Florentine nobleman, xx, 27 note 12

Arrius, Quintus, xii, 237; Cicero on, ix, 91, 96

Arrogance, Dante places, in Hell, xx, 34; Hobbes on, xxxiv, 378, 426; Marcus Aurelius on, ii, 28 (13, 19)

Arrows, Raleigh on poisoned, xxxiii, 364-5

Arruntius, at Actium, xii, 387 note

Arsaces, Parthian empire, founder, iv, 395

Arsago, Pagolo, xxxi, 28

Art, ancient and modern, contrasted, xxviii, 198; Aurelius on nature and, ii, 291 (10); Browne on, and nature, iii, 280; Browning on, xlii, 1114; Burke on, xxiv, 49, 67-9, 91-3; Coleridge on, xxvii, 269-77; Confucius on nature and, xliv, 20 (16), 39 (8); Emerson on, v, 186, 311; Goethe on, xxv, 399; xxxix, 264-80; Goldsmith on blessings of, xli, 534-5; Greenough's ideas of, v, 328; Hugo on, xxxix, 362-4, 366-7, 369-70, 373, 374, 383, 385-7; human and divine, ii, 138 (61); Hume on, xxvii, 220; xxxvii, 309; "is long" (original saying), xxxviii, 2; Morley on principles of, xxiv, 28; Pascal on, and nature, xlviii, 49 (120); Penn on, i, 360; public attitude toward, xxviii, 123; purism in, satirized, xix, 179; Ruskin on, xxviii, 157; Schiller on, xxxii, 221, 224, 244-52, 268-70, 282-4, 284-91; Sidney on nature and, xxvii, 12; Taine on, xxxix, 453-4, 455-6, 458-9; unity the vital requisite of, xxviii, 383; utility and, xxxii, 223; "weaker than necessity," viii, 174; Whitman on reality in, xxxix, 424 (see also Beauty, Taste)

ART THOU WEARY, xlv, 556-7

Artabanus, Themistocles and, xii, 29-30

Artavasdes, king of Armenia, xii, 363, 364, 375

ARTEMIDORA, THE DEATH OF, xli, 926-7

Artemidorus, Cæsar and, xii, 328; Pliny on, ix, 249-51

Artemis, Actæon and, viii, 361-2; Atridæ and, 10; Egyptian mythology, in, xxxiii, 81; Bubastis, festival of, 33-4; oracle of, 42; temple of, 70-1; Homer on, xxii, 88; reference to, viii, 203; Thebes, goddess of, 202, 203 (see also Diana)

Artemisia, Burns on, vi, 63

Artemisium, battle of, xii, 12-13

Artemon, the engineer, xii, 65-6

Arteries, Harvey on the, xxxviii, 68-73, 77, 84-6, 92, 94, 108, 116, 120, 122, 145, 147

Arthmius of Zelea, xii, 10

Arthur, King, Caxton on, xxxix, 21-5; Cervantes on, xiv, 100, 515; drinking-cup and arms of, xxxii, 152; Eliwlod and, 176-7; Guenevere and, xlii, 1233; Mordred and, xx, 135 note 3; Renan on, xxxii, 155-6, 162-4; Spenser on, xxxix,

65-6; university at Cærleon, xxxv, 391; Uther's son, iv, 105

Arthur, King, in HOLY GRAIL, xxxv, 109-10; his custom of adventure, 112; and the marvelous sword, 112-13; welcomes Galahad, 113-14, 115; and the Sangreal, 116; his tourney at Camelot, 116-17; at Holy Grail feast, 118; grief at departure of knights, 118-19, 120, 121; orders chronicles of the Grail, 226

ARTHUR, MORTE D', by Tennyson, xlii, 1019-26

Arthur, Prince, son of Henry VII, xxxix, 28

Arthur's hunting, xxxii, 160 note 9

Arthurian legends, Caxton on, xxxix, 22-5; Renan on, xxxii, 153, 155-73 (see also HOLY GRAIL)

Artichoke, compared with cardoon, xxix, 131 note 9; Jerusalem, xi, 154

Article, Dryden on the, xiii, 63

ARTICLES OF CONFEDERATION, xliii, 168-79; Lincoln on, 337

Articulate speech, man and nature, the distinction between, xxvii, 270

Artificers, in agricultural system, x, 450-6, 459-63; in policy of Europe, 107-8

Artificial, Carlyle on the, xxv, 344

Artisans, anciently inferior to warriors, xxxiii, 85; Socrates on, ii, 8-9

ARTIST, EPIGRAM TO AN, vi, 276-7

Artist, Northern, in FAUST, xix, 179

Artists, Browning on, xlii, 1139; Emerson on duty of, v, 53-4; Goethe on training and duty of, 265, 268-70; xxxix, 274-5, 277, 278-9; relations to public, 272-3

Arts, Burke on the, xxiv, 41, 45, 49; Dante on, xx, 49; Emerson on the, v, 84, 314; Raleigh on the, xl, 209; progress in, due to wants, xxxiv, 181; relations of various, xxxix, 274 (see also Architecture, Music, Painting, Poetry, Sculpture)

Arulenus, Rusticus (see Rusticus)

Arundel, Earl of, in Crecy campaign, xxxv, 8, 23, 26

Arundel, Thomas of, xxxv, 267

Arundel, in EDWARD II, xlvi, 40-2, 46, 55

Aruns, Camilla and, xiii, 388-90; doomed by Diana, 391; his death, 391; in Dante's HELL, xx, 84

Auspicy, defined, xxxiv, 397

Arwacas, Raleigh on the, xxxiii, 352, 388

Aryan Races, Freeman on the, xxviii, 249-51; Taine on the, xxxix, 444, 445, 446, 448

Aryans, Tacitus on the, xxxiii, 120

Arybas, the daughter of, xxii, 219-21

Asaf, son of Barkhiya, xvi, 29 note, 31, 322

Asaph, Psalms attributed to, xliv, 146, 207, 236-53

Ascanio, servant of Cellini, xxxi, 193-6, 197, 201, 206, 222-3, 269, 273, 276, 289, 290, 291, 317, 341, 350, 363, 366

Ascanius (Iulus), in sack of Troy, xiii, 126, 128; Dido's hunt at, 161, 162; Anchises's funeral games, 200-1; in fire of the ships, 204; kills stag of Silvia, 260; his fight with Tyrrheus, 261-2; Nisus and Euryalus, with, 305-6; in defence of the town, 317-19, 331; prophecy of his future reign, 84, 274

Ascension Island, Darwin on, xxix, 517-21; rock incrustations at, 19; species of, xi, 432

Ascension Day, Walton on, xv, 408

Ascetic goodness, Bagehot on, xxviii, 177-9; disagreeable to women, 189

Asceticism, Diogenes on, ii, 180 (187); Epictetus on, 155 (101); pride in, 177 (176); Utopian idea of, xxxvi, 216

Ascham, Johnson on, xxxix, 236

Asciburgium, founded by Ulysses, xxxiii, 96

Asclapo, Roman physician, ix, 160

Asclepius (see Æsculapius)

Ascolano, Aurelio, xxxi, 61

Ascoli, Eurialo d', xxxi, 61 note

Ascot, Duke of, xxxviii, 54, 56, 58, 60

Asdente, Dante on, xx, 86

Ashburton, Alexander Lord, xliii, 300

Ashley, Lord, and Locke, xxxvii, 3

Ashtaroth (see Astarte)

Asia, cause of barbarism of, x, 28; wealth of ancient, ix, 399 note 1

Asinius, friend of Pliny, ix, 268

Asinius, Pollio (see Pollio)

Ask Me No More, xl, 361

Askew, in Shoemaker's Holiday, xlvii, 449, 450, 452, 453, 470

Asmach, Herodotus on the, xxxiii, 18-19

Asmadai, Asmodai, or Asmodeus, reference to story of, iv, 161; in the battle, 216; lustfulness of, 379

Aspasia, of Miletus, accused of impiety, xii, 70, 71; and the Megarians, 69; Plutarch on, xii, 62-3

Aspasia, concubine of Cyrus, xii, 63

Aspatia's Song, xl, 330

Asphalax, blindness of the, xxix, 62

Asphalion, squire of Menelaus, xxii, 53-4

Aspirations, worldliness and, xix, 30-1; inborn in man, 45

Ass, descent of the, as traced by stripes, xi, 171-4; why not improved, 55

Ass, Job's description of the wild, xxiv, 58-9

Ass and Bull, story of, xvi, 12-13

Ass and Horse, fable of, xvii, 44

Ass and Lapdog, fable of, xvii, 13

Ass in Lion's Skin, fable of, xvii, 30

Ass's Brains, fable of the, xvii, 42

Assaracus, in Hades, xiii, 233

Assattha, tree of, xlv, 601

Assent, Dante on haste in giving, xx, 344; Harvey on, xxxviii, 101; Penn on, to please, i, 353 (149)

Assertorial principles, xxxii, 345

Assignats, Burke on the, xxiv, 269-71, 338-44, 383-90

Assimilation, Freeman on, xxviii, 257

Assistance, asking, is honoring, xxxiv, 378; Confucius on, xliv, 54 (15); only to be given by superiors, xviii, 6; willingness to accept, ii, 246 (7)

Associates (see Company)

Association, Burke on effects of, xxiv, 109-10; Emerson on principle of, v, 270-1; Locke on, as means of education, xxxvii, 38 (49), 42 (58); Mill on education by, xxv, 90-1

Association of ideas, Hume on, xxxvii, 322-3, 345-50

Assurance in children, xxxvii, 55, 56

Assyria, Milton on ancient, iv, 395; Raleigh on history of, xxxix, 117-18

Astarte, Ashtaroth, or Astoreth, Milton on, iv, 13-14, 101; crescent of, xlii, 1282

Astarte, in Manfred, xviii, 428-30; Manfred on, 420-1; further references to, 415, 423, 438

Astolfo, in Life a Dream, with Estrella, xxvi, 18-19; his claim to throne, 19-20; agrees to king's plan to try Segismund, 25-6; Segismund with, 38-9, 40-1; Rosaura and, 61; in the battle, 64-5; reunited with Rosaura, 67

Astonishment, Burke on, xxiv, 51, 52, 135

Astoreth (see Astarte)

Astræa, footsteps of, xxv, 360

Astrologers, in Dante's Hell, xx, 86

Astrology, Augustine, St., on, vii, 108-10; Don Quixote on, xiv, 93; Hobbes on, xxxiv, 377; interest in, reason of, v, 307; unknown in Utopia, xxxvi, 207

Astronomy, Augustine, St., on ancient, vii, 67; Dante's, xx, 294-5,

326-7; Emerson on our ignorance of, v, 85; Helmholtz on science of, xxx, 182; Hobbes on, xxxiv, 377; Hume on, xxxvii, 444; Huxley on Greek, xxviii, 227; Locke on study of, xxxvii, 147, 157, 165-6; Marlowe's, xix, 218-19; modern foundation of, xxxix, 55 note; Montaigne on study of, xxxii, 49-50; Prometheus, originator of, viii, 172

Astur, ally of Æneas, xiii, 332-3

Astyanax, son of Hector, xiii, 119, 147

Astyochus, Greek admiral, xii, 135

Aswattha, the banyan tree, xlv, 867

Asychis, king of Egypt, xxxiii, 69-70

Asylas, in the ÆNEID, xiii, 316, 332, 383

Asyniur, goddesses, xlix, 321 note

Atabalipa, Milton on, iv, 333; Raleigh on, xxxiii, 313, 327, 329, 331, 341

Atalanta, reference to apple of, xxxix, 144

ATALANTA, chorus from, xlii, 1247-9

Atarbechis, city of, xxxiii, 25

Atè, Æschylus on, viii, 32, 73, 90, 193; Virgil on, xiii, 353

Athamas, in sack of Troy, xiii, 112; Dante on, xx, 125

Athanasian Creed, Bagehot on, xxviii, 203

Athanasius, St., Pascal on, xlviii, 308 (868); on psalm-singing, vii, 195; on the Trinity, xxxiv, 84

ATHEISM, ESSAY ON, Bacon's, iii, 44-7

Atheism, Berkeley on, xxxvii, 247; Browne on, iii, 285; Browning on, xli, 958; Burke on, xxiv, 239; Burns on, vi, 214; Hume on, xxxvii, 431; Mill on, xxv, 31; Milton on, iv, 426; Molière on charges of, xxvi, 203; Pascal on, xlviii, 69 (190), 80 (221), 81 (225), 82 (228); of physicians, iii, 265 note; preferable to superstition, 47

Atheist, in PILGRIM'S PROGRESS, xv, 139-40

Atheists, as witnesses, xxv, 232-3; Pascal on, xlviii, 69 (190)

Athena, birth of, iii, 141; holder of key to thunderbolts, viii, 147; wardress of Delphi, 116; Egyptian worship of, xxxiii, 33, 34, 42, 88, 91; Ruskin on, xxviii, 147 (see also Minerva)

Athena, in THE FURIES, with Orestes and the Furies, viii, 130-4; at trial of Orestes, 136, 137, 141; ordains court of Areopagus, 142; casts vote for Orestes, 144, 145; appeases the Furies, 146-55

Athenæus, and Cicero, ix, 141-2

Athenais, Queen, ix, 142

Athene, in THE ODYSSEY, friend of Ulysses, xxii, 10-11

Athenians, prayer of the, ii, 226 (7); Taine on the, xxxix, 435-6

Athenodorus, the ghost and, ix, 328-9

Athenodotus, Marcus Aurelius on, ii, 195 (13)

Athens, Æschylus on, viii, 151-5; Aristophanes on decline of manhood at, 453-4; and on politics of, 439-41, 463-4; beautifying of, by Pericles, xii, 49-53; books in ancient, xxviii, 57; bounty of ancient, xii, 109; Burke on Areopagus of, xxiv, 355; capital causes in, ii, 24; capital executions in, 45-6; Collins on music in, xli, 491; Dante on, xx, 171-2; economic resources of, xxviii, 44; houses and streets of ancient, xxviii, 56-7; liberty of press in, iii, 203-4; military spirit of, decline of, xxvii, 392; Milton on learning of, iv, 405-8; named for Minerva, xx, 208 note 3; Newman on intellectual supremacy of, xxviii, 40-3; population under Pericles, xii, 77; religious liberty in, xxxvii, 416; sacred galleys of, xii, 43 note 5; St. Paul in, xliv, 469 (16-34); Schiller on art and liberty in, xxxii, 250-1; Shelley on golden age of, xxvii, 354-5; on the drama in, 355, 357; Spartan policy toward, xxxvi, 19; teachers in, rewards of, x, 142-3; the Thirty at, xii, 149-50 (for various portions of Athenian history, see PLUTARCH'S LIVES OF THEMISTOCLES, PERICLES, ARISTIDES, ALCIBIADES, DEMOSTHENES)

Athens, Duke of, constable of France, xxxv, 47, 48, 49

ATHENS, MAID OF, xli, 815-16

ATHENS, UNIVERSITY LIFE AT, xxviii, 52-62

Athlete, life of an, Epictetus on, ii, 155 (104)

Athole, Earl of, James I and, xlii, 1208

Atilius, Lucius, called the wise, ix, 9

Atinas, in the ÆNEID, xiii, 414, 418

Atlantic Sisters, Pleiades called, iv, 311

Atlantis, Bacon on, iii, 165-7

ATLANTIS, NEW (see NEW ATLANTIS)

Atlas, Æschylus on, viii, 168 and note 21, 171; Homer on, xxii, 10; Virgil on, xiii, 165, 238, 276, 277

ATLI, THE SONG OF, xlix, 433-43; remarks on, 268

Atli, in the VOLSUNG TALE, xlix, 331; his future foretold, 333, 350,

358; Brunhild and, 356; wedded to Gudrun, 362-3; his dreams, 363; sends for Gunnar, 364-5; in the battle, 369, 370, 371; Gunnar and, 372; his end, 373-5

Atli, in the EDDA, his future foretold, xlix, 403, 408-9, 418; Brunhild and, 404; wedded to Gudrun, 428-30; his dreams, 430-2; sends for Gunnar, 433-4; with Gunnar, 439-40; Oddrun and, 461-3; his eating of his children, 441-2; death, 443

Atmosphere, composition of the, xxx, 150-1; pressure of the, 152-5; resistance of the, 18-19; a blanket for the earth, 222; temperature dependent on altitude, 223

Atolls, Darwin on, xxix, 491-4; formed from barrier reefs, 499-503; causes of destruction of, 504-5; absence of, in West Indies, 506; in the Pacific, 425, 477-91

Atom, the universe in the, xlviii, 26

Atonement, commencement of, xviii, 434

ATREUS, HOUSE OF, viii, 5-155

Atreus, Thyestes and, viii, 65-6; Sidney on, xxvii, 20

Atropos, "the blind Fury," iv, 76

Attachments, Pascal on human, xlviii, 159 (471), 161 (479)

Attagis, species of, in South America, xxix, 106

Attainder, bills of, in U. S., xliii, 198 (3, 10)

Attentions, Yu-tzu on, xliv, 6 (13), 25 (2)

Attia, mother of Octavius, xii, 264

Attic Boy, Cephalus called the, iv, 38

Attic comedy, coarseness of, viii, 418

Attica, Newman on, xxviii, 41-2; Rousseau on, xxxiv, 181

Atticus, Titus Pomponius, character of, ix, 82; Cicero's letters to, 83, 85, 87, 97, 104, 138, 147, 176, 178, 179; essays dedicated to, 7-8, 45

Atticus, Herodes, xxviii, 61-2

Attila, in Dante's HELL, xx, 54

Attilio, Count, in THE BETROTHED, at Don Rodrigo's, xxi, 76-84; 108-9, 188-90; goes to Milan, 303-4; procures Cristoforo's removal, 312-17; dies in plague, 557

Attinghausen, Baron, in WILHELM TELL, xxvi, 394-400, 442-7

Attius, Tullus, xii, 225

Attorney, Hobbes on power of, xxxiv, 430-1

Atys, in the ÆNEID, xiii, 201

Aubignac, D', Corneille and, xxxix, 379; Hugo on, 383

Aubigny, Lord d', xxxv, 24, 30

Aubrecicourt, Eustace d', xxxv, 35, 36, 43, 44, 47

Aubrey, on Milton, xxviii, 180-1

Auburn, the deserted village, xli, 521

Auckland Islands, ferns in, xxix, 260-1

Audacity, Hippocrates on, xxxviii, 5

Audley, James, at Poitiers, xxxv, 43-4, 45, 48-9; honored by Prince Edward, 54-5; his gift to squires, 56-7; new gift from Prince, 58-9

Audley, Lord Chancellor, xxxvi, 117, 122, 125, 126, 128, 129, 131, 135, 136, 137

Audrehem, Arnold d', xxxv, 45

Audubon, on the frigate bird, xi, 189; on birds' nests, 266; on transportation of seeds, 431

Auerbach's wine cellar, xix, 79-94

Aufidius, death of, xxxii, 14

Aufidius, Tullus, Coriolanus and, xii, 173-5, 177-9, 181, 190-1; death of, 191

AUGURIES OF INNOCENCE, xli, 601-4

Augurs, College of, ix, 222 note 4; duties of, 263 note 1; Pliny on, 263; seniority among, 69

Augury, defined, xxxiv, 397; among the Germans, xxxiii, 100-1

AUGUST, SONG COMPOSED IN, vi, 48-9

AUGUSTA, EPISTLE TO, xli, 812-15

AUGUSTA, To, xli, 810-12

Augustan Age, Macaulay on, xxvii, 410

Augustin, Donna, xxiii, 249-50, 404, 406

Augustine, St., Bishop of Hippo, vii, 3-4; Alypius and Nebridius friends of, 90-5; astrology rejected by, 108-10; baptism of, 152-3; books "on the fair and fit," 58-62; Carthage, in, 33-5; Caxton on teachings of, xxxix, 14-15; Chaucer on, xl, 16, 46; on Christ, vii, 119-20, 205-6; on Christ and Church, xxxix, 41 note; communistic household of, vii, 99; concubine of, 48, 100; CONFESSIONS, 5-206; CONFESSIONS, remarks on, xxxi, 1; CONFESSIONS, object in writing, vii, 23, 25, 168-70; conversion of, 80-1, 85-8, 123-43; in Dante's PARADISE, xx, 421 note 4; De Saci on, 399-400; on the dead, xxxix, 96; on death, xlviii, 343; death, his fear of, vii, 100; on deception, xlviii, 106 note; Descartes and, 414; disappointments of, vii, 89-90; on distribution of animals, 287 note 49; diviners and, 48-50; Donatists and, xxxix, 37; on doubtful points, 40 note 31; evil, on question of, vii, 105-7, 110-11; Faustus and, 70-3;

friend, loss of, 50-4; on God, 5-8, 29-30, 40, 62-3, 78, 102-4, 120, 171-3, 182-9; on goodness of all things, 115-16; on happiness, 183-6; Hugo on, xxxix, 362; infancy and boyhood, vii, 8-21; learning, on his, 62-4; Luther on, xxxvi, 280, 315; on man, xlviii, 31 note; Manichæans, among, vii, 37-47, 66-70, 77-9; marriage, his wish for, 97-9; memory, on the, 173-83; Milan, in, 79-80; on miracles, 365; xlviii, 286 (812); on monks, xxxix, 39 note 25; mother's death, 158-66; Orosius and, xx, 330; Platonists partly convert, vii, 112-18; Pascal on, xlviii, 87, 309 (869); on praise, xxxix, 70; on righteousness, xlviii, 170; Rome, in, vii, 73-7; Scriptures, attitude toward, 37, 119-22; studies of, 36-7; rhetoric, teacher of, 48, 79, 145-8; trials and temptations of, 189-204; truth, his search for, 96-7; Walton on, xv, 341, 346, 357-8; wills, on two, in man, 136-9

Augustine of Canterbury, Roper on, xxxvi, 136; See of London, changed by, xxxv, 264; Stamford University, suppressed by, 391

Augustus, Æneas, compared with, xiii, 20-5, 38; ÆNEID saved by, xiv, 107; Agrippa and, iii, 71; *Ajax* of, iv, 416; arts of, iii, 18; beauty of, 112; Britain's tribute to, xxxv, 332; calm nature of, iii, 110; censorship of books under, 205; Dante on victories of, xx, 309-10; death of, iii, 10; decree of, in LUKE, xliv, 362 (1); diet of, xxxvii, 18; favorites of, xii, 403; Horace and, xxvii, 73; xxxix, 171; Herod's son on, xlviii, 66 (179); Rome, liberator of, iii, 136; M. Aurelius on, ii, 261 (31); motto of, xix, 379; Ovid and, 38, 57; Pascal on, xlviii, 51 (132); on pets, xii, 36; pleasure in small children, 382 note 11; postal service of, ix, 387 note; Scribonia, his divorce of, xiii, 38; times of, iii, 47; vestal virgins and, ix, 265 note; Virgil and, xiii, 3, 17-19, 57, 85, 238; xxxix, 171 (see also Octavius)

Auld, William, lines on, vi, 374 note 16; reference to, 239

AULD FARMER'S NEW YEAR SALUTATION, vi, 155-8

AULD HOUSE, THE, xli, 574-5

AULD LANG SYNE, vi, 335; Whittier on air of, xlii, 1439

Auld Lichts, Burns on, party of, vi, 16, 67-70, 96-7, 110-12, 192-4

AULD ROB MORRIS, vi, 473

AULD ROBIN GRAY, xli, 570-1

Aulestes, death of, xiii, 405

Auletes, Æneas, ally of, xiii, **333**

Aunus, death of, xiii, 386-7

Aurelia, Regulus and, ix, 239

Aurelia, Cæsar's mother, xii, 279, 281, 282

Aurelian, Bacon on, iii, 136

Aurelius, King, v, 388

Aurelius, Marcus, sketch of life and work, ii, 192; Alexander the prophet and, xxxvii, 406; Arnold on, xlii, 1185; Machiavelli on, xxxvi, 66, 71; MEDITATIONS of, ii, 193-306; Pope on, xl, 447

Aurelius, Scaurus, xxxiii, 117

Auret, Marquis d', xxxviii, 54-61

Auricles, of the heart, xxxviii, 86-91, 142, 143

Aurinia, worship of, xxxiii, 100

Aurochs, deterioration of the, xi, 140

Aurora, Cephalus, the Attic Boy, and, iv, 38; Orion and, xxii, 74; Tithonus and, v, 96; xxii, 71; Zephyr and, iv, 31

AURORA, TO, xl, 322-3

Aurora Borealis, Kelvin on, xxx, 277

Austerity, Bagehot on, xxviii, 177-9; not agreeable to women, 189; party spirit and, 193; strength of, lies in itself, 197

Austin, St., Augustine called, xxxix, 14-15; xl, 16

Austin, Adam, FOR LACK OF GOLD, xli, 545

Austin, Charles, edits *Parliamentary Review*, xxv, 79; in debating society, xxv, 82-3, 84; Mill on, 53-5, 66; in Utilitarian movement, 70

Austin, John, Mill on, xxv, 52-3; his friendship with Mill, 46, 51; paper for *Westminster Review*, 65; for *Parliamentary Review*, 79; later years of, 115-7, 167

Australia, Darwin on, xxix, 455-76; European species in, xi, 90, 420; fossil mammals of, 388; glaciers in, 418; marsupials of, 126; native species reduced, 141; productions of, reason of inferiority, 118; useful plants, absence of, in, 51-2

Australians, Darwin on the, xxix, 246, 457-9; dances of the, 475-6; dogs not domesticated by, xi, 269

Austria-Hungary, Freeman on, xxviii, 272-3, 279

Authorities, Bacon on, in philosophy, xxxix, 128-9; Emerson on quoting, v, 75-6; Hugo on citing, xxxix, 408; Raleigh on, 105

Authority, Bacon on vices of, iii, 31, 51; Channing on, in religion, xxviii, 354-5; Hobbes on legal, xxxiv, 430; Kempis on obedience to, vii, 221; knowledge on, xxxii,

37-9; Lowell on decline of, reverence for, xxviii, 480; Luther on, xxxvi, 287; Mill on limits of, xxv, 212-17, 281-301; Pascal on, and reason, xlviii, 445-51; Pascal on, in religion, 95 (260); Paul on, xxxvi, 287-8; Pliny's remarks on, ix, 349-50; truths on, xxv, 238-49

Authors, in law, xxxiv, 430, 431, 433-4; Pascal on egotism of, xlviii, 20 (43); relation of, to public, xxxix, 266-7

Autobiographies, preeminent, xxxi, 1

Autobiography, Cellini on, xxxi, 5; Cicero on, ix, 108; James on influence of, i, 71; Vaughan on, 73-4

Autolycus, xxii, 277-8

Automata, Descartes on, xxxiv, 45-6; Hobbes on, 319

Automedon, in sack of Troy, xiii, 119

Autonoë, in THE BACCHÆ, viii, 379, 400, 406

Autonomy of the Will, explained by concept of freedom, xxxii, 377-8; Kant on, xxxii, 362-4, 367; the supreme principle of morality, 363, 371, 376

Autumn, Ode to, xli, 903-4

Autumn, Burns on, vi, 242-3; Campbell on, xli, 791; Collins on, 493; Longfellow on, xlii, 1360; Shakespeare on, xl, 284; Shelley on the, xli, 856

Auxerre, battle of, xxxix, 86

Auxiliary troops, Machiavelli on, xxxvi, 47-50

Ava, plant, xxix, 433

Avalanches, cause of, xxx, 224-5

Avalos, Alfonson d', xxxi, 191 note

Avan, province of, xliii, 26

Avarice, Æsop's Fable on, xvii, 32

Avarice, Arabian proverb on, xvi, 211; Arabian verses on, 316; Browne on, iii, 344; Cicero on, in old age, ix, 70; Dante's punishment of, xx, 29-31, 224-6; instances of, 230-1; Dante on, 227 note 1; Epictetus on growth of, ii, 144-5; Krishna on, xlv, 872; miserliness contrasted with, xxxvi, 53; Mohammed on, xlv, 894; Pascal on, xlviii, 167 (502); Penn on, i, 347-8; Shakespeare on, xlvi, 358

Avaricious and Envious, fable of, xvii, 32

Avenant, Sir William d', Dawn Song, xl, 364

Aventinus, son of Hercules, xiii, 266

Avernus, Lake, xiii, 220

Averroes, Dante on, xx, 21 note

Aversion, Hobbes on, xxxiv, 350-3; language of, 358

Avianius, Cicero and, ix, 109

Aviaries, Bacon on, iii, 123

Avicenna, in Dante's Limbo, xx, 21; on tumefaction, xxxviii, 121

Avila, Don Louis de, works of, xiv, 59

Avilion, island-valley of, xlii, 1026

Aviones, Tacitus on the, xxxiii, 118

Avitus, letter to, ix, 225

Avoidance, Aurelius on, ii, 238 (20)

Awa', Whigs, Awa', vi, 381

Awe, Confucius on, xliv, 30 (22), 57 (8)

Awood, John, More and, xxxvi, 127

Ax, speckled, story of, i, 88-9

Axioms, Montaigne on, xlviii, 397; Pascal's rules for, 411

Aye My Wife She Dang Me, vi, 551

Ayeshah, wife of Mohammed, xlv, 1006 note 1

Ayr, The Brigs of, vi, 242-8

Ayr, Farewell Song to Banks of, vi, 250

Ayrton, William, in Hazlitt's discussion, xxvii, 281-92

Aytoun, Sir William, Refusal of Charon, xli, 943-4

Azara, Don Felix, on carrion-hawks, xxix, 67, 69; on cattle in Paraguay, xi, 86; on hydrophobia, xxix, 374; on ostrich eggs, 103; on Pampas Indians, 117 note; on plants along new tracks, 131; on wild horses in droughts, 146; on wasps and spiders, 46 note 9; on S. American rainfall, 57 note

Azazel, standard bearer of Satan, iv, 103

Azores, stocked by glaciers, xi, 410

Azotos, siege of, xxxiii, 81

Azpetia, Don Sancho de, the Biscaine, xiv, 76

Azura, Phineas Ibn, xlv, 977 note 24

Azzecca-Garbugli, in The Betrothed, xxi, 41, 43-9, 77, 80, 81, 84, 424, 662

Azzolino, Dante on, xx, 53 and note 8

Baalim, Milton on, iv, 101

Baal-peor, xliv, 284 (28)

Baba Mustafa, in Ali-Baba, xvi, 448-9, 450-1

Babel, Tower of, Browne on, iii, 288; Hobbes on, xxxiv, 336; Milton on, iv, 107, 346-7; its builders in Limbo, 149

Babie, The, by Miller, xli, 944-5

Babieca, horse of the Cid, xiv, 17-18; saddle of, 515

Babington, Rev. Dr., lines on, vi, 533

Babrius, Valerius, Æsop and, xvii, 3

Baby, by MacDonald, xlii, 1164-5

Babylon, Milton on, iv, 395; Milton on captivity in, 354; psalm on

captivity in, xliv, 323; Raleigh on, xxxix, 74

BABYLON: or BONNIE BANKS O' FORDIE, xl, 58-9

Baçan, Alvaro de, xiv, 405

Baccalaos, Newfoundland called, xxxiii, 290

BACCHÆ, THE, of Euripides, viii, 349-415

Bacchic mysteries, Herodotus on, xxxiii, 41-2

Bacchus, Amalthea's son, iv, 164; Circe and, 47; Dryden on, xl, 402; Euripides on, viii, 352-3, 363, 364-5

Bacchus, India, return from, xiii, 238; mirth, father of, iv, 31; mother of, xii, 281; Pentheus and, viii, 116; Sophocles on, 278-9

Bacchus, Thebes, guardian of, viii, 203-4; worship of, described, 379-82; worship of, various forms of, xii, 351 note (see also Dionysus Iacchus)

Bachelors, ancient penalty on, ix, 424 note 3

Bachiacca, the embroiderer, xxxi, 58 note 2, 369 note 5

Bachiacca, the painter, xxxi, 58 note 2, 67, 68-9

Bachman, on carrion vultures, xxix, 199

Backbite, Sir Benjamin, in SCHOOL FOR SCANDAL, xviii; epigram of, 128; Maria's lover, 115; Sneerwell's, at, 118-22, 129-30, 131-3; Lady Teazle's, at, after the scandal, 179-84

Backsliding, in religion, xv, 156-8

Bacon, Francis, Emerson on, v, 453-4, 456, 458; ESSAYS, iii, 7-149; remarks on ESSAYS, 4; Hazlitt on, xxvii, 291 note 14; Herbert, George, and, xv, 387; Hobbes and, xxxiv, 318; inquiry on, xi, 1; INSTAURATIO MAGNA, PREFACE TO, xxxix, 122-49; INSTAURATIO MAGNA, remarks on preface to, 3; Jonson on, xxvii, 60-1; Jonson on times of, v, 455; language of, xxxix, 206; LIFE, xl, 358-9; life and works, iii, 3-4, 152; Montaigne and, xxxii, 3; NEW ATLANTIS, iii, 151-91; NOVUM ORGANUM, preface to, xxxix, 150-4; Pope on, xl, 448; on prodigies, xxxvii, 413-14; Raleigh on, xxxix, 118; on reform, v, 385; on Rome, 376; Shakespeare not mentioned by, xxxix, 334; Shelley on, xxvii, 350-1; on similitudes, 347; Voltaire on, xxxiv, 99-103

Bacon, Sir Nicholas, iii, 3; Jonson on, xxvii, 60

Bacon, Roger, Emerson on, v, 410; Newman on, xxvii, 48

Bacteria, absorption of oxygen by, xxxviii, 343; air and, 351-2; animal nature of, 359; Lister on, 271

Badow, Richard, founder of Clare Hall, xxxv, 401

Baer, Von, on embryos, xi, 479; on standard of organization, 135; on the bee, 386

Badgemagus, King, xxxv, 121-3; tomb of, 216

Bagehot, Walter, ON MILTON, xxviii, 171-214; life and works of, 170

Baglioni, Malatesta, xxxi, 73 note 5

Baglioni, Orazio, xxxi, 73 note 5, 76-8, 84 and note

Bagot, Charles, correspondence with Mr. Rush, xliii, 283-5

Bahamas, Raleigh on the, xxxiii, 390

Bahia, Darwin on, xxix, 22, 521-2

Bahia Blanca, Darwin on, xxix, 85-117

Bahrám, reference to, xli, 973

Bail, excessive, forbidden, xliii, 208 (8); right of, in Massachusetts, 73 (18)

Bailiff, Chaucer's, xl, 27-8

Baillie, Lady Grisel, WERENA MY HEART, xl, 409-10

Baillie, Joanna, Constantine of, xxv, 16 note

Bailly, M., as mayor of Paris, xxiv, 391-2; on October Sixth, 222 note; Burke on death of, 227 note

Bain, Alexander, Mill and, xxv, 157 note 2, 167, 196

Baird, Dr., on Franklin, i, 61

Báithis, sons of, xlix, 257

Bajazet, Raleigh on, xxxix, 103; Selymus and, iii, 53

Bakbak, story of, xvi, 180-4

Baker, Henry Williams, HYMN, xlv, 548

Baker, Sir Samuel, on the giraffe, xi, 231

Bakewell, the agriculturist, v, 376

Balaam, death of, xxix, 99; Milton on, iv, 375; prophecy of Rome, xxxvi, 344

Balaam's Ass, Luther on, xxxvi, 285

Balaguet, Emir of, xlix, 128-9, 141

Balan, Balin and, xxxv, 115

Balance, Penn on, i, 365-6

Balance of Power, Bacon on, iii, 52

Balance of Produce and Consumption, x, 387

Balance of Trade, doctrine of, x, 329-46; methods used to make favorable, 346-7; absurdity of whole doctrine, 377-87; criterions of, 372-6

Balbo, Girolamo, xxxi, 66 note
Balbus, Cornelius, Cæsar and, xii, 324; Cicero and, ix, 118, 119
Bald Head, Australia, xxix, 474-5
BALD MAN AND FLY, fable of, xvii, 17
Baldini, Bernardone, and the diamond, xxxi, 367-8, 376, 377; and the necklace, 408; relations with Cellini, 376, 415-16, 419, 438
Baldock, in EDWARD II, xlvi, 26-8, 35, 51, 58, 59, 60, 62-3
Balducci, Giacopo, xxxi, 113-14
Baldwin, and the Genovese, iii, 293
Baldwin, son of Ganelon, xlix, 107, 109
Baleen, of whales, xi, 236-40
Baligant, Emir of Babylon, xlix, 196 note
Balin le Savage, xxxv, 115
Baliol, John, Dante on, xx, 369 note 8
Baliol, the devil, in FAUSTUS, xix, 211
Ball, John, Froissart on, xxxv, 62-3; in Wat Tyler's Rebellion, 65, 70, 73, 74, 77; death of, 82
BALLADS, TRADITIONAL, xl, 51-189
Ballantine, John, inscription to, vi, 242; reference to, 372 note 3
Ballantyne, James, and Scott, xxv, 446-8
Ballemar, Chili, xxix, 369
Balliol, John, founder of Balliol College, xxxv, 402
Ballmer, George, loss of, xxiii, 39, 42
BALLOCHMYLE, FAREWELL TO, vi, 115
BALLOCHMYLE, LASS OF, vi, 230
Ballot, Burke on the, xxiv, 355; Mill on the, xxv, 165
Balmerino, Burns on, vi, 306
BALOW, xl, 189-90
Balsam of Fierebras, xiv, 80-1; prepared by Don Quixote, 138
Balsham, Hugh, founder of Peter College, xxxv, 401
BALTIC, THE BATTLE OF THE, xli, 798-800
Balzac, Jean Louis de, Philarchus on, xiii, 63
Ban, King, xxxv, 159-60
Bancroft, George, and Emerson, v, 482
Band dog, Harrison on the, xxxv, 371-3; cross between bear and, 375
Banda Oriental, province of, xxix, 155-71
Bandaging, Harvey on, xxxviii, 116-21
Bande Nere, Giovanni delle, xxxi, 16 note 1
Bandinello, Baccio, xxxi, 14 note 1; Cellini, relations with, 99, 364, 374, 379, 380, 381, 383-7, 417, 418-19, 429; choir by, 430; Duke

Cosimo and, 360 note 4, 362, 409, 433-4; father of, 14-15; "Hercules" of, 384-5 note 1, 433-4; knight of St. James, 428 note; "Picta" of, 437-8
Bandini, Giovan, 110 note
Bandini, Don Juan, xxiii, 244-5, 248-9, 408
Bank failures, Ruskin on, xxviii, 118
BANK OF FLOWERS, ON A, vi, 361
Banking corporations, x, 482-4
BANKNOTE, LINES ON A, vi, 232
Bank-notes (see Paper Money)
Bankruptcy, Smith on, x, 282
Bankruptcy laws, Ruskin on, xxviii, 118; under control of Congress, xliii, 196 (4)
Banks, power of Congress to incorporate, xliii, 223-4, 226-30, 237-40
Banks and banking, Smith on, x, 240-69
BANKS OF AYR, FAREWELL TO, vi, 250-1
BANKS OF THE DEVON, vi, 303
BANKS O' DOON, vi, 422-4
BANKS OF NITH, vi, 362
Banks, Sir J., expedition of, xxix, 225
Bannerets, Harrison on, xxxv, 234
BANNOCKBURN, vi, 502-3
BANNOCKS O' BEAR MEAL, vi, 523
Banquets, Cicero on, ix, 62; skeletons at Egyptian, xxxii, 16, 19
Banquo (in MACBETH), captain of Duncan, xlvi, 307; with witches, 309-11; with king's messengers, 311, 312-13; received by king, 314; at Macbeth's castle, 317; with Fleance, 321; with Macbeth before the murder, 321-2; after murder, 329, 330; murder of, 339; ghost of, 341-2, 343, 351; soliloquy of, 332-3; with Macbeth as king, 333-4; plot to kill, 334-7
Banyan tree, xlv, 867
Baptism, Browne on, iii, 309-10; Calvin on, xxxix, 54; conversion by, story of, vii, 51; Dante on necessity of, xx, 18, 422; Luther on, xxxvi, 279, 280, 332, 336; Milton on, iv, 356-7; Pascal on, xlviii, 172 (520), 343; Pascal on, of children, xlviii, 380; Paul, St., on, xliv, 472-3; Quakers on, xxxiv, 66-7
Barabbas, xliv, 421 (18-19, 25)
Baraquan, Orinoco called, xxxiii, 328 note
Barateve, island of, xxxiii, 231-2
BARBARA, by Smith, xlii, 1192-4
BARBARA ALLAN, a ballad, xl, 69-70
BARBARA FRIETCHIE, xlii, 1439 41
Barbarians, Milton on invasion of the, iv, 99
Barbariccia, the demon, xx, 90, 92
Barbarossa, Frederick (see Frederick I)

Barbarossa, the pirate, xiv, 405
Barbauld, Anna Lætitia, LIFE, xli, 568; Burns on, vi, 434
Barberry, crosses of the, xi, 111
BARBER'S STORY, in ARABIAN NIGHTS, xvi, 171-200
Barbers, verses on, xvi, 165
Barca, Giacopino della, xxxi, 90-1, 92
Barce, nurse of Sichæus, xiii, 179
Barclay, Robert, *Apology* of, xxxiv, 74; on Quaker faith, 68
BARCLAY OF URY, xlii, 1424-7
BARD, THE, xl, 468-72
BARD'S EPITAPH, A, vi, 228-9
Bardi, Simone dei, husband of Beatrice, xx, 3
Barding, among the Germans, xxxiii, 96
Bardism, Renan on, xxxii, 175-7, 148
Bards, ancient title of, v, 183; Renan on Celtic, xxxii, 148, 175-7
Barebones, Hugo on, xxxix, 400
BAREFOOT BOY, THE, xlii, 1431-4
Barfleur, capture of, xxxv, 8, 9 note; importance of, 11 note 3
Bargaining, Bacon on, iii, 93
Bargello, the, xxxi, 103 note
Bar-Jesus, xliv, 458 (6-11); Pascal on, xlviii, 299
Barking-bird, Darwin on the, xxix, 306
Barlaam and Josaphat, xxvi, 4
Barlass, Kate, xlii, 1200-1, 1202, 1207, 1216-17
Barlow, Gen., at Gettysburg, xliii, 351
Barmekis Feast, xvi, 195-7
Barnabas, at Antioch, xliv, 455 (22-6), 464; Jerusalem, mission to, 455 (30), 457 (25), 463; Lystra, men of, and, xxxvi, 311-12; Paul and, xliv, 450 (27), 458 (2-7), 460-2, 465 (36-7)
Barnacle Geese, Harrison on, xxxv, 353
Barnave, on October sixth, xxiv, 222 note
Barnfield, Richard, THE NIGHTINGALE, xl, 290
Barnhelm, Minna von, and Bruchsal, xxvi, 364-5; Franzisca, scenes with, 301-3, 309-10, 311-13, 332-4, 338-40, 341; Just, scene with, 310-11; landlord, scene with, 303-8, 309; Riccaut de la Marlinière, scene with, 334-8; Tellheim, scenes with, 312-15, 341-8, 353-64
Barnwell, George, xxvii, 319 note, 324
BARON OF BRACKLEY, a ballad, xl, 120-3
Baron, origin of word, xxxiv, 383
Barontus, story of, xxxii, 184
Barrande, M., "colonies" of, xi, 365; discoveries of, 360; on palæozoic animals, 379; on silurian deposits, 377; on succession of species, 375

Barras, Comte de, xliii, 184
Barratry, in Massachusetts, xliii, 76 (34)
Barré, Burke on, xxiv, 417
Barrett, Elizabeth, and Browning, xviii, 356
Barrier-reefs, Darwin on, xxix, 494-503
Barriers, relation of, to species, xi, 396-7
Barry, the actor, xxvii, 289
Barsabbas, xliv, 430 (23), 464 (22)
Bartas, Du, *Creation* of, xxxix, 333
Barter, human propensity to, x, 19-20; inconveniences of, 29; in relation to division of labor, 21-4
Barterers, in Dante's HELL, xx, 87-8, 91-4
Bartholomew, the apostle, xliv, 373 (14), 430 (13); patron of New Atlantis, iii, 163
BARTHRAM'S DIRGE, xli, 788-9
Bartolini, Onofrio de, xxxi, 429 note
Barton, George, xxxiii, 237, 243, 246
Barzanes, in Utopia, xxxvi, 192
Basan and Basil, xlix, 104, 114
Bashan, mountain of, xliv, 228
Bashfulness, Emerson on, v, 114; Locke on, xxxvii, 54-5, 128; Basil and Basan, xlix, 104, 108, 114
Basil, Council of, xxxix, 45-6
Basil, St., at Athens, xxviii, 56, 62; on use of Homer, viii, 210
Basil, the smith (see Lajeunesse)
Basilio, in LIFE A DREAM, relates story of Segismund, xxvi, 20-3; his plan to try Segismund, 23-7; hears of Segismund from Clotaldo, 27-8; with Segismund, 41-7; in the battle, 64-5; resigns crown to Segismund, 66-7
Basilisk, the serpent, xlvii, 651 note
Baskerville, Sir Thomas, xxxiii, 235
Basket, Fuegia, xxix, 222-3, 237-8, 242, 244
Basoche, Hugo on the, xxxix, 369
Basset, Lord, at Crecy, xxxv, 23; at Poitiers, 42; at Poix castle, 17
Bassompierre, M. de, xxxviii, 54
Basstarnians, xxxiii, 122-3
Bassus, Aufidius, ix, 243 note 3
Bassus, Gabius, Pliny on, 389, 391
BAT, BIRDS, AND BEASTS, fable of, xvii, 20
Batalus, Plutarch on, xii, 200
Batavians, Tacitus on the, xxxiii, 111-12
Bateman, William, founder of Trinity Hall, xxxv, 401
Bates, Mr., on ants, xi, 294; on butterflies, 465, 466
Bath, Knights of the, xxxv, 232
Baths, health, in NEW ATLANTIS, iii, 183; Locke on cold, xxxvii, 13-14; origin of name, vii, 163
Bathsheba, Winthrop on, xliii, 100

Batrachians, absence of, from islands, xi, 435-6

Bats, Blake on, xli, 601; Collins on the, 492; range of, xi, 437; wings of, 186

Bats'-eyes, Mrs., in PILGRIM'S PROGRESS, xv, 189, 190

Battiferra, Laura, xxxi, 445 note

Battista, Giovan (Il Tasso), xxxi, 25-6, 28, 360 note 5, 409

Battle, eyes vanquished first in, xxxiii, 120; not too strong, xliv, 351 (11)

Batjan, island of, xxxiii, 231-2

Baubo, reference to, xix, 165-6

Baugé, M. de, at Metz, xxxviii, 26; prisoner to De Vaudeville, 44-5

Bauhin, Caspar, on the heart, xxxviii, 86

Baumgarten, Conrad, in WILHELM TELL, flight of, xxvi, 372-5; Hedwig and, 443; Rootli League, at, 491, 495, 414; Uri, at keep of, 462, 463; Wolfshot killed by, 387

Bavius, Shelley on, xxvii, 375-6

Bayle, Pierre, Carlyle on, xxv, 462-3

Bazeilles, the Moine of, xxxv, 24-5

Beagle Channel, xxix, 233

BE NOT DISMAYED, xlv, 572

Beacon, first, in Ireland, xlix, 229

BEAGLE, VOYAGE OF THE, xxix

Beales, Mr. Mill on, xxv, 185

BEAR AND TWO FELLOWS, fable of, xvii, 31

BEAR AND WILLOW WREN, story of, xvii, 201

Bearing, Brynhild on, and forbearing, xlix, 325; Epictetus on, and forbearing, ii, 179 (183); Jonson on, xl, 299-300; Kempis on, vii, 228; Penn on, i, 356, 364 (294); (see also Patience)

Bears, Darwin on black, xi, 188; in Egypt, xxxiii, 37

BEARSKIN, story of, xvii, 197

Bearwards, Harrison on, xxxv, 322

BEAT! BEAT! DRUMS! xlii, 1484

Beatitude, Raleigh on, xxxix, 94

Beatrice, Dante and, xx, 3-4

Beatrice, in DIVINE COMEDY, xx, 10-12, 270-7, 282-418, 420; Arnold on speech of, xxviii, 73; Hugo on, xxxix, 367; Ruskin on, xxviii, 145

Beattie, James, Minstrel of, xxxix, 314; references to, vi, 174, 185

Beatty, Mr., with Franklin, i, 148-9

Beauchamp, Philip, On Natural Religion, xxv, 49-50

Beauchamp, Richard, Earl of Warwick, v, 419; xxxv, 108

Beaujeu, Lord, xxxv, 24, 30, 38

Beaumarchais, Hugo on, xxxix, 375, 376, 403

Beaumont, in EDWARD II, xlvi, 24

Beaumont, Francis, sketch of life and works, xlvii, 638; LETTER TO

JONSON, xl, 328-30; PHILASTER, xlvii, 639-718; TOMBS IN WESTMINSTER ABBEY, xl, 327

Beaumont, Sir George, Wordsworth on picture, by, xli, 620-2

Beaumont and Fletcher, Dryden on, xxxix, 334; editorial remarks on plays of, xlvii, 638; Emerson on plays of, v, 125; Hazlitt on, xxvii, 291; PHILASTER, xlvii, 639-718

BEAUTIFUL, THE SUBLIME AND, xxiv, 7-148

BEAUTIFUL MISS ELIZA J—N, vi, 532

Beautiful Palace, in PILGRIM'S PROGRESS, xv, 49

BEAUTY, BACON'S ESSAY ON, iii, 111-12

BEAUTY, EMERSON'S ESSAY ON, v, 307-21

Beauty, Augustine, St., on, vii, 58, 60; Berkeley on, xxxvii, 242; Burke on, xxiv, 15, 39, 47, 77-109, 125-35; Burns on, vi, 501, 587; Channing on study of, xxviii, 339; Coleridge on, xxvii, 272, 277; Crashaw on, xl, 370; Daniel on, 225; Darley on, xli, 938-9; Darwin on, ii, 210-12, 511; xxix, 427; David on things of, xli, 509; Emerson on, v, 105, 140, 173, 174, 207, 229; Hugo on, xxxix, 366-8; 406; Hume on, xxvii, 218; xxxvii, 309, 444-5; Keats on, and melancholy, xli, 906; M. Aurelius on, ii, 206-7, 216 (20); Milton on, iv, 6, 57, 66, 169, 381, 444; More on, xxxvi, 215-16, 224; Nashe on, xl, 266; Pascal on, xlviii, 16 (32), 419-20; Plato on, ii, 95; Poe on sense of, xxviii, 388-90; Poe on, and sadness, 394; Raleigh on, xl, 209; Ruskin on, of woman, xxviii, 151-2; Schiller on influence and development of, xxxii, 221, 224, 248-84, 287-91, 298-313; Shakespeare on, xl, 270, 278, 280-1; xlvi, 136; Waller on, xl, 367; Whitman on, xxxix, 415, 417

Beauty and the Beast, Emerson on legend of, v, 361; Hugo on, xxxix, 369

BEAUTY BATHING, xl, 203-4

BEAUTY, GENIUS IN, xlii, 1226

BEAUTY, THE TRUE, xl, 360-1

BEAUTY, TIME, AND LOVE, xl, 223-6

Beaver, Harrison on the, xxxv, 360

Bebius, death of, xxxii, 14

Beccaria, Abbot, in Dante's HELL, xx, 136 and note 10

Béchamp, M., xxxviii, 367 note, 374

Becket, Thomas à, Bacon on, iii, 53; Chaucer on, xl, 11; Dryden on, xxxix, 172 note 21; Harrison on, xxxv, 266, 403

Bede, Venerable, sketch of life, xx, 330 note 27; first doctor of Cam-

bridge, xxxv, 398; in Dante's PARADISE, xx, 330; on Purgatory, xxxii, 187

Bedford, Duke of, Burke and, xxiv, 400; Burke's reply to attack of, 401-43; estates of, v, 420

Bedivere, Sir, xlii, 1019-26

Bedr, battle of, xlv, 956 note 4, 961 note 12, 962 note 2, 972

Bedr Basim, xvi, 349-50, 352-4.

Bedr-ed-Din, the Gardener, xvi, 131

Bedr-el-Budur, the Sultan's daughter, xvi, 380-443

Beds, in old England, xxxv, 313-14; Locke on, for children, xxxvii, 24

Bedsores, Paré on, xxxviii, 57.

Beelzebub, in PARADISE LOST, iv, 93-4, 97, 118-21

Beelzebub, in PILGRIM'S PROGRESS, xv, 30

BEELZEBUB, ADDRESS OF, vi, 215-16

Beer, Harrison on making of, xxxv, 298-300

Bees, Browne on wisdom of, iii, 278 (15); cell-making instinct of, xi, 279-88; clover and, 108; drones and queen, 214-15; as fertilizing agents, 87-8; Harrison on, xxxv, 365; mice and, xi, 88; Milton on, iv, 109, 242; parasitic, xi, 275; Pope on, xl, 438; sting of, xi, 214; Swift on, xxvii, 121; time-saving of, xi, 108; Virgil's description of, xiii, 90; Von Baer on, xi, 386; wax of, 266

Beethoven, his musical setting of EGMONT, xix, 246

Beetles, Brazilian, xxix, 44 and note 7; Collins on, xli, 492; dung-feeding, xxix, 516 note; at Port St. Julian, 184; at sea, xi, 429; xxix, 172-3; springing, xxix, 41; without anterior tarsi, xi, 148; wingless, 148-9

Beet-root sugar, Pasteur on, xxxviii, 320 note

Begbie, Ellison, vi, 29 note

BEGGARS, THE JOLLY, vi, 129-40

Beggars, Blake on, xli, 603; Luther on, xxxvi, 329-30; More on, 164

BEGGAR'S SONG, in FAUST, xix, 38

Beginnings, Æsop on, xvii, 14-15, 21; Goethe on, xix, 352; Hugo on, and ends, xxxix, 372; Machiavelli on, xxxvi, 12; merry, make sad endings, vii, 235 (7); most easy to check, 225

Behavior, Bacon on, iii, 132; Emerson on, v, 223; Epictetus on, ii, 175 (164)

Behemoth, references to, iv, 242; xliv, 139 (15)

Behmen, Jacob, Emerson on, v, 145, 184, 243

BEHOLD, MY LOVE, HOW GREEN THE GROVES, vi, 538-9

BEHOLD THE HOUR, THE BOAT, ARRIVE, vi, 456

BEHOLD THE HOUR, THE BOAT, ARRIVE, vi, 503-4.

Behring, the navigator, Emerson on, v, 86

Bekkluld, sister of Brynhild, xlix, 327

Belacqua, in Dante's PURGATORY, xx, 162-3

Belcher, the devil, in FAUSTUS, xix, 211

Belgians, eating custom of, xxxv, 303

Belial, in PARADISE LOST, iv, 102-3, 113-16, 222

Belial, in PARADISE REGAINED, iv, 379-81

Belianis, Don, Burke on romance of, xxiv, 20; Cervantes on romance of, xiv, 54-5; Don Quixote on, 20, 101; to Don Quixote, 15

Belief, Hobbes on, xxxiv, 361-2; Hume on, xxxvii, 342, 343-50, 351-3, 394, 397-9, 403; Pascal on, xlviii, 34 (81), 42 (99), 90-103, 174 (536); through understanding and will, 406-8

Belisarius, Dante on, xx, 308; Raleigh on, xxxix, 103

BELL, THE, story of, xvii, 378-83

Bell Mountain, Chili, xxix, 272-5

Bellario, in PHILASTER, as Philaster's boy, xlvii, 652-3; sent to princess, 655-7, 661; with Arethusa, 662-3; accused as Arethusa's lover, 668-9, 672; with Philaster, 674-8; Arethusa ordered to dismiss, 678-81; parting from Arethusa, 682-3; meets Philaster in woods, 686-7; with Arethusa in wood, 690-1; asleep on bank, 695; wounded by Philaster, 696; taken by Pharamond, 697-8; saved by Philaster, 698-9; with Philaster in prison, 700-2; announces to king marriage of Philaster, 703; denounced by Megra, 713; condemned to torture, 714; confesses, 714-18

Bellarmati, Girolamo, xxxi, 342 note 3

Bellarmine, Cardinal, xv, 329

Bellay, M. du, Montaigne on, xxxii, 64, 104-5

BELLE DAME SANS MERCI, xli, 917-19

Bellefontaine, Benedict, the farmer of Grand-Pré, xlii, 1356; on evening of Evangeline's betrothal, 1362-5, 1368-9; at betrothal feast, 1371; on day of exile, 1378, 1380; death, 1382

Bellegarde, Abbé, on ridicule, xxxix, 188

Bellerophon, reference to, iv, 230

Bellerus, reference to, iv, 78

BELLES OF MAUCHLINE, vi, 62

Belles Lettres, Hume on, xxxvii, 309

BELLING THE CAT, fable of, xvii, 39
Bellona, reference to, iv, 134
BELLS, THE, by Poe, xlii, 1283-6
BELLY AND THE MEMBERS, fable of,
xvii, 22; Menenius Agrippa on
fable of, xii, 157
Belper, Lord, Mill on, xxv, 54, 70
Belphœbe, Spenser's, xxxix, 66, 68;
Burke on Spenser's, xxiv, 144
Beltenebros, name assumed by Ama-
dis, xiv, 225
Belus, father of Dido, xiii, 97
Belus, the god, iv, 108
Belzoni, on inhabitants of Gournou,
v, 207
Bembo, Pietro, xxxi, 197-8
Bembus, Cardinal, patron of poets,
xxvii, 43, 54
Benchuca, Darwin on the, xxix, 349-
50
Bendelio, Alberto, xxxi, 54, 281,
283, 284-5
Bene, Albertaccio del, xxxi, 149,
150, 197, 453-4
Bene, Alessandro del, xxxi, 71-3
Bene, Ricciardo del, xxxi, 333
Benedetto, Ser, xxxi, 138-9, 145, 146
Benedict, St., Dante on, xx, 380
note 3, 421 note 6
Benedict, Emerson on, v, 301-3
Benedictines, Dante on corruption
of the, xx, 381-2
Benedictis, Jacobus de, hymn by,
xlv, 565
Benefaction, the rule of good men,
v, 199
Beneficence, Kant on moral worth
of, xxxii, 328-9; recompense of,
xvi, 348
Benefices, of Catholic Church,
xxxvi, 294-9, 301; Luther on,
303, 306
Benefits, Bacon on common and
peculiar, iii, 35; Cicero on, ix,
19-20, 26-7; Emerson on, v, 100,
230-1; Hobbes, of receiving, xxxiv,
386; Tacitus on, xlviii, 29 note
(see also Favors)
Benegridran, Welsh chief, quoted, v,
419
Benengeli, Cid Hamete, xiv, 75, 187
Benevento, battle of, xx, 68 note 1
Benevolence, Bacon on, iii, 34-6;
Burns on, vi, 263; Emerson on,
v, 28, 109, 199, 220-1, 226; Epictetus on, ii, 163 (128); Hobbes
on, xxxiv, 354; Kant on, xxxii,
361, 366, 372; Mill, James, on,
xxv, 36-7; More on, xxxvi, 210;
Pope on, xl, 450; universality of,
ix, 370 note
Benezet, Anthony, i, 107, 297
Bengal, cause of early civilization
of, x, 27
Benham, William, translator of
IMITATION OF CHRIST, vii
Benincasa of Arezzo, xx, 168 note 2

Benintendi, Niccolo, xxxi, 157-8
Ben-Manasseh, Israel, xxxix, 399
Bennett, Harry, xxiii, 423
Bensalem (see NEW ATLANTIS)
Bentham, Jeremy, Mill on, xxv,
40-1, 45, 46-8, 62-3, 68-9, 76-8,
132, 170; Review of his Book of
Fallacies, xxvii, 237-65
Bentham, Sir Samuel, Mill on, xxv,
41
Benthamism, Mill on, xxv, 46-8,
68-76, 141
Bentivoglio, Annibale, xxxvi, 64
Benvegnato, Messer, xxxi, 69-71
Benvenuti, Benvenuto, xliii, 30
Benvenuto (see Cellini)
Benzo of Milan, xxxviii, 34
Beowulf, Breca and, xlix, 19-20;
Daeghrefu and, 76; death of, 81-4,
85, 91; Dragon and, 71, 73, 76-
81; Eadgils and, 73; funeral of,
90, 92-4; Grendel and, 25-8, 64;
Grendel's mother and, 42-50, 65;
Hetwaras and, 72; Herthel and,
74; Hrothgar and, 11-24, 31-2, 34;
Hygelac and, 61-66, 67, 72, 75-6;
Hygelac's thane, 11; king, 67, 72;
Renan on, xxxii, 154; Scyld's
son, xlix, 5, 6; sea-adventures,
21-2
BEOWULF, epic of, xlix, 5-94; re-
marks on, 3-4
Béranger, Pierre Jean de, Poe on,
xxviii, 385
Bérard, J. F., on fruits, xxxviii,
321
Berengario, Giacomo (see Carpi)
Berenger, Raymond, daughters of,
xx, 176 note 14, 311 note 27;
and Romeo, his steward, 311 note
26
Berengier, in SONG OF ROLAND, xlix,
125, 142-3, 155, 178
Berenice, daughter of Ptolemy,
xlviii, 253
Bergamo, Bartolommeo of, xxxvi,
45
Berkeley, in EDWARD II, xlvi, 67-8,
69
Berkeley, George, sketch of life and
works, xxxvii, 198; DIALOGUES,
199-302; Emerson on anecdote of,
v, 275; Emerson on idealism of,
159-60; Hazlitt on, xxvii, 291;
Hume on philosophy of, xxxvii,
436 note
Berkeley, Lord Thomas, at Poitiers, xxxv, 50-1
Berkenshaw, Mr., and Pepys, xxviii,
309-10
Berlinghieri, Berlinghier, xxxi, 105
Bermuda, birds of, xi, 433, 434;
Raleigh on, xxxiii, 390
BERMUDA, SONG OF EMIGRANTS IN,
xl, 385-6
Bernabo of Milan, xxxvi, 76

Bernard, of Clairvaux, St., Anastasius and, xxxvi, 356; *Considerations* of, 361; in Dante's PARADISE, xx, 418-25; hymns by, xlv, 562, 563; on idleness, xxxix, 14; IMITATION OF CHRIST, attributed to, vii, 208; quotation from, v, 105; on the soul, xxxiv, 104-5

Bernard, of Morlaix, hymns by, xlv, 560, 561

Bernard, of Quintavalle, xx, 333 note 17

Bernard, son of Pepin, xxxix, 84, 87

Bernardi, Giovanni, xxxi, 137 note 2

Bernardo del Carpio (see Carpio)

Bernardo, in HAMLET xlvi, 87-92, 97-100

Bernardone, Pietro, xx, 334 note 21

Berners, Lord, translator of Froissart, xxxv, 1

Berni, Francesco, and the capitolo, xxxi, 247 note

Bernice, and Agrippa, xliv, 487 (13), 488 (23), 490 (30)

Bernoulli, on conservation of force, xxx, 183; on comets, xxxiv, 121; on integral calculus, 128-9

Beroe, wife of Doryclus, xiii, 202

Berreo, Antonio de, xxxiii, 313, 323, 324-5, 326, 330, 335-6, 338-47, 383

Berries, Locke on, xxxvii, 21

Bert, Paul, on ferments, xxxviii, 369

Bertha of Bruneck, in WILHELM TELL, xxvi, 384-5; with Fürst, 433-4; with Gessler, 429-30; Rudenz and, 399-400, 419-23, 433, 449, 461-2, 474

Berthelot, M., Pasteur on, xxxviii, 367

Berti, Bellincione, xx, 68 note 1, 351-2

Berti, Gualdrada, xx, 68 note 1

Bertoldi, Pierfrancesco, xxxi, 440

Bertrand de Born, in Dante's HELL, xx, 120 note

Bessel, on distance of stars, xxx, 330

Bessy, in FAUST, xix, 149-51

BESSY AND HER SPINNIN WHEEL, vi, 468

Beste, J. R., translator, xlv, 567

Bestia, the tribune, xii, 244; trial of, ix, 103

Bethsaida, Jesus on, xliv, 387 (13)

Betrayers, in Dante's HELL, xx, 142-6

BETROTHED, THE, by Manzoni, xxi

BETTER PART, THE, xlii, 1184-5

Bettini, Baccio, xxxi, 184-5

Beulah-Land, Bunyan on, xv, 158-9, 313

Beuve, Sir, xlix, 167

Beverages, universal use of, xxix, 314

Beverley, John of, xxxv, 398

Bevilacqua, xxxi, 48-9

BEWARE O' BONIE ANN, vi, 351

BEWICK AND GRAHAME: xl, 123-30

BEYOND THE VAIL, xl, 356-7

BE YOUR WORDS MADE, GOOD SIR, xl, 216-17

Beza, patron of poetry, xxvii, 43

Bhaddiya, xlv, 793

BHAGAVAD-GITA, THE, xlv, 801-84; remarks on, 800

Bhutas, evil spirits, xlv, 873 note 2

Bianchi, faction of, its origin, xx, 135 note 4; strife with the Neri, 27 notes, 103-4 notes

Biarni Heriulfsson, xliii, 5-8

Bias, one of Seven Sages, ix, 29

Bibbiena, Cardinal, Sidney on, xxvii, 43

BIBLE, BOOKS FROM THE, xliv, 71-495; xlv, 499-544

Bible, Apollinarii and the, iii, 209; Augustine, St., on the, vii, 37, 78-9, 87-8; Bagehot on the, xxviii, 210-11; Browne on, iii, 272-4, 284-9, 294; Bunyan on, xv, 232-3, 307; Calvin on, xxxix, 33, 41, 51; Dante on, xx, 390, 391, 410; Emerson on, v, 42; xlii, 1299; Hobbes on, xxxiv, 371, 362; Hugo on, xxxix, 370, 371, 372, 406; Hume on, xxxvii, 396, 414; Kempis on the, vii, 218, 368-9; Locke on, as reading for children, xxxvii, 142-3, 175; Luther on, xxxvi, 283-5, 341-3; Mill on, xxv, 252; Milton on, iii, 213, 252, 254; iv, 333-57; Mohammed on, xlv, 1013; Pascal on, xlviii, 140 (428), 174 (532), 178 (548), 189 (568), 192 (573), 194 (579), 199 (598), 200 (601), 218, 232 (684), 234, 100 (283), 315 (900), 355; Burke on pictures of God in the, xxiv, 61-2; Rousseau on belief in the, xxxiv, 303-8, 310-12; Ruskin on, xxviii, 106-7; Swift on, xxvii, 115, 116; Winthrop on examples of the, xliii, 101, 109-10; Woolman on influence of, i, 178 (see also Gospel, New and Old Testaments)

Bibulus, Calpurnius, consul with Cæsar, xii, 284, 285; Cicero on, ix, 114, 125, 142; edict of, 153; Lucceius and, 91; in Parthia, 153; in Parthian War, xii, 337; Pompey and, ix, 101, 102

BICHAM, YOUNG: a ballad, xl, 85-8

Biggs, Walter, DRAKE'S ARMADA, xxxiii, 236-68

Bigotry, in literature, xxvii, 233-4; and philosophy, xxxvii, 416-17

Bikki, in VOLSUNG TALE, xlix, 376, 377, 378, 410, 444

Bildad the Shuhite, xliv, 75, 84, 100, 112, 143; Walton on, xv, 341

Bill of Rights, in Constitution, xliii, 207-8

Bills of Credit, under Confederation, xliii, 175; forbidden to states under Constitution, 198 (10)

Bills of Exchange, x, 247, 254

Bimbisāra, King, xlv, 771-2

Bingham, editor, Mill on, xxv, 65, 66, 75, 77, 79

Bingham, the Kanaka, xxiii, 151-2

Biography, Bagehot on methods of, xxviii, 171-3; Carlyle on, xxv, 415-17, 413; history made up of, v, 72; Johnson on, xxvii, 186; poetry, compared with, xxxix, 294

Bion, Bacon on, iii, 45

Biorn, son of Karlsefni, xliii, 21

Birago, Francesco, Manzoni on, xxi, 468

Birderg, son of Ruan, xlix, 239-40

Birds, Burns on the haunts of, vi, 48; Darwin on color of, xi, 146; fears of, 266; xxix, 424; migratory, iv, 241; nests of, xi, 266; non-flying, 147-8, 186; of oceanic islands, 433-4; seeds distributed by, 407-10, 430-1; sexual selection among, 102; tame, instances of, xxix, 422-3

Birks, of Aberfeldy, The, vi, 292-3

Birnam Wood, xlvi, 350, 366, 368, 370

Birney, Gen., at Gettysburg, xliii, 371

Birth, Browne on life before, iii, 304 (39); Buddha on, xlv, 678-9; Burke on preference to, xxiv, 200; Hippolytus on, viii, 314; Pascal on accident of, xlviii, 383; on advantages of noble, 112 (322); on respect for, 113 (324), 117 (335, 337); Shakespeare on, xlvi, 105; "a sleep and a forgetting," xli, 611

Birtha, Dame, xx, 344 note 24

Birthday Ode for 31st December, 1787, vi, 306-7

Birthplaces, Plutarch on, xii, 197

Biscop, Benedict, xxxv, 310

Bishop Orders His Tomb, xlii, 1117

Bishops, Calvin on, xxxix, 44; in Catholic Church, xxxvi, 296, 308; confirmation of, 304; early elections of, 279-80; Luther on, 317-18; Ruskin on, xxviii, 111

Bithynia, Pliny's administration of, ix, 383-437

Bitias, in the Æneid, xiii, 101, 320, 321

Bitterness, as source of the sublime, xxiv, 75-6

Bixby, Mrs., Letter to, xliii, 446

Bizcacha, Darwin on the, xxix, 136-7, 398, 469

Black, "wisdom's hue," iv, 35

Black, John, Mill on, xxv, 61-2

Black-Eyed Susan, xl, 412-13

Black Islands, The Young King of the, xvi, 50-9

Black Prince, Audley and, xxxv, 54-5, 58-9; in campaign of Crecy, 5-6, 10-11, 12, 23, 26, 29, 31; Froissart and, 3; King John and, 55, 57-8, 59; in Poitiers campaign, 34-7, 40-7, 53, 58-60

Blacklock, the poet, Burke on, xxiv, 141

Blacklock, Dr., Epistle to, vi, 387

Blackmore, Sir Richard, xxxix, 181 note, 183 note

Blackness, Burke on effects of, xxiv, 121-5

Blacksmith, The Village, xlii, 1323

Blackwood's Magazine, Carlyle on, v, 334

Blæsus, Velleius, story of, ix, 238-9

Blair, Sir James, Elegy on, vi, 287-9

Blake, William, Poems, xlii, 597-606

Blame (see Censure)

Blamire, Susanna, poem by, xli, 593-4

Blanc, Mont, Byron on, xviii, 405; Coleridge on, xli, 724

Blancandrin, xlix, 98-9, 100, 101, 110-12, 114

Blanche-Taque, battle of, xxxv, 20-1

Blasphemers, in Dante's Hell, xx, 47, 59-61

Blasphemy, in early Massachusetts, xliii, 84 (3); penalized in Athens, iii, 203

Blastus, the chamberlain, xliv, 457 (20)

Blenheim, After, xli, 749-51

Blessed Damozel, The, xlii, 1196-1200

Blind animals, Darwin on, xi, 150-2; xxix, 62

Blind Boy, The, xl, 452-3

Blind man, parable of the, xliv, 375 (39)

Blind-man, Mr., in Pilgrim's Progress, xv, 101-2

Blindness, Milton on His, iv, 86

Blindness, Milton on, iv, 139, 420-2; Schiller on, xxvi, 389

Bliss, Hindu conception of perfect, xlv, 828; Hogg on the greatest, xli, 784

Blood, circulation of the (see Circulation of Blood)

Bloodhounds, Harrison on, xxxv, 369

Blood-poisoning, Harvey on, xxxviii, 132-3

Bloody-Man, the giant, xv, 224

Blossius, Caius, Gracchus and, ix, 21-2; Lelius and, xxxii, 81

Blossom, The, xl, 319-20

Blossoms, To, xl, 348

Blot in the 'Scutcheon, A, xviii, 356-400

BLOW, BUGLE, BLOW, xlii, 1003
Blundell, Dr., on puerperal fever, xxxviii, 235, 243
Bluntness, Shakespeare on, xlvi, 236
Blushing, Hobbes on, xxxiv, 356
BLYTHE HAE I BEEN ON YON HILL, vi, 493
BLYTHE WAS SHE, vi, 301-2
BOADICEA: AN ODE, xli, 551-3
Boastfulness, Bacon on, iii, 134-5; Kempis on folly of, vii, 219-20
BOAT SONG, by Burns, vi, 278-9
Boats, of the Britons, xxxv, 380; in ancient Egypt, xxxiii, 47; of the Germans, 121
Boatswain, in THE TEMPEST, xlvi, 379-81, 439
Bobadilla, Francesco de, Bishop of Salamanca, xxxi, 35 note 2, 40, 43-7
Bobolink, Bryant on the, xlii, 1264-6
Boccaccio, on Arthur, xxxix, 22; Chaucer and, 162, 167, 172, 175, 179-80 (2); Dryden on, 162; Hazlitt on, xxvii, 285-6; Hume on, 234; Johnson on language of, xxxix, 212; Macaulay on, xxvii, 389; Montaigne on, xxxii, 91; novels of, xiii, 66; Sainte-Beuve on, xxxii, 137; Sidney on, xxvii, 9
Bochartus, on Virgil, xiii, 36
Bodleian Library, Emerson on, v, 434-5
Body, Browne on the, iii, 302 (37); Descartes on the, xxxiv, 45-6; Epictetus on care of the, ii, 160 (118), 176 (173), 178 (178); Goethe on beauty of, xix, 393-4; Hindu doctrine of soul and, xlv, 862, 863, 864; M. Aurelius on the, ii, 200 (2), 207 (3), 212 (16), 253 (60), 259 (21); Montaigne on mind and, xxxii, 57; More on pleasures of the, xxxvi, 213-14, 215; Pascal on mind and, xlviii, 31; Pascal on, after death, 343; Paul, St., on the, xlv, 508 (15, 19-20); Penn on the, i, 337 (2); Socrates on the, ii, 55
BODY OF LIBERTIES, THE, xliii, 70-89
Boece (see Boëtius)
Boethius, Anicius (see Boëtius)
Boethius, Hector, on the Scotch, xxxv, 286
Boëtie, Stephen de la, Montaigne and, xxxii, 113, 115; Montaigne on, 74-5, 80-1, 86-8
Boëtius, Anicius Manlius, birth and death of, xl, 330 notes 24, 25; Chaucer on, xl, 46, 47; in Dante's PARADISE, xx, 330; Sidney on, xxvii, 26, 28
Bœotia, Newman on, xxviii, 42
Bohemia, blind king of (see John of Bohemia)
Boians, Tacitus on the, xxxiii, 111, 119

Boiardo, Dryden on, xiii, 13
Boileau, Addison and, xxvii, 167; on Christianity, xxxii, 167; encomiums and censures of, xxxiv, 148; on human reason, 145-6; on poetry, xxxix, 408; Sainte-Beuve on, xxxii, 128, 136
Boils (see Furuncles)
Bolabola, island of, xxix, 494, 499
Bolas, use of, in S. America, xxix, 55, 123
Boldness, Bacon on, iii, 33-4; Confucius on, xliv, 47 (5); Penn on, i, 351 (119); of saints and wicked men, vii, 234 (3)
Boleyn, Anne (see Bullen)
Bolingbroke, Lord, on Addison's Cato, xxvii, 177; on bishops, xxxiv, 81; Burke on, xxiv, 237, 274; lines to, xxvii, 288; on Marlborough, xxxiv, 100; Pope to, xl, 417-18, 450-1; Swift and, xxviii, 15; Voltaire on, xxxiv, 159
Bollandists, the, xxxii, 189 note
Bologna, Antonio, in DUCHESS OF MALFI (see Antonio)
Bologna, Giovan, xxxi, 438 note
Bologna, Il (see Primaticcio)
Bologna Phials, xxx, 29 note 10
Bombast, defined by Burke, xxiv, 139
Bona Dea, worship of, xii, 281
Bonaparte (see Napoleon)
Bonatti, Guido, xx, 86 note 7
Bonaventura, Father, in THE BETROTHED, xxi, 137
Bond, Thomas, Franklin on, i, 121-2, 143-4
Bones, used as fuel, xxix, 209
BONIE DUNDEE, vi, 268-9
BONIE JEAN, vi, 494-6
BONIE LAD THAT'S FAR AWA, vi, 320-1
BONIE LASS OF ALBANY, vi, 299-300
BONIE MOOR-HEN, THE, vi, 274
BONIE PEG-A-RAMSAY, vi, 549
BONIE PEGGY ALISON, vi, 31-2
BONIE WAS YON ROSY BRIER, vi, 576
BONIE WEE THING, vi, 428
Boniface, Archbishop, xx, 245 note 4
Boniface VIII, Pope, arrest and death of, xx, 230 note 15; Dante on, 80 note, 281 note 15, 365 note 11, 400 note 3, 411 note 6, 416 note 8; death of, xxxi, 144 note 2; Ghino di Tacco and, xx, 168 note 2; Montefeltro and, 114-15 notes
Bonnell, Captain, anecdote of Lord Loudoun, i, 160-1
BONNIE BANKS O' FORDIE, xl, 58-9
BONNIE GEORGE CAMPBELL, xl, 115-16
Bonnivard, Byron on, xli, 832
BONNY BARBARA ALLAN, xl, 69-70
BONNY DUNDEE, xli, 770-2
Booby, Darwin on the, xxix, 20

Book, custom of saving by the, xxxv, 387

Book-keeping (see Accounting)

BOOK-WORMS, THE, vi, 277

BOOKS, MONTAIGNE'S ESSAY ON, xxxii, 89-105

Books, Bacon on, iii, 58; Browne on, 285-6, 289 (24); Carlyle on, xxv, 379, 381, 389-90; censorship of (see Censorship); Channing on, xxviii, 349-51; Confucius on, xliv, 10 (9); Ecclesiastes on, 354 (12); Emerson on, v, 8-12, 97, 122, 183-4; Epictetus on, ii, 170 (145); Goethe on, xix, 28, 45-6; Heminge on fate of, xxxix, 155; Hobbes on, xxxiv 339-40; Hume on use of, xxxvii, 395 (9); Locke on, for children, 140-3; Milton on, iii, 202-3, 210-12, 214; Newman on education by, xxviii, 31-8; Pascal on, xlviii, 123 note 9, 417; Pliny on, ix, 244; prefaces of, xxxix, 3; Rousseau on, xxxiv, 303-4; Ruskin on, xxviii, 99-117, 120-1, 130-1, 141; Ruskin on, for girls, 155-7; tested by durability, xxxix, 218-19; transcripts of their times, 433-40, 460-1 (see also Reading)

Boorde, Andrew, verses from, xxxv, 304 note

Boötes, constellation, xx, 417 note 5; mentioned by Homer, xxii, 78

Booth, M. L., translator of Pascal, xlviii

BORDER BALLAD, by Scott, xli, 764

Boreas, Orithea and, xxvii, 284; Virgil on, xiii, 79, 140

Borghild, wife of Sigmund, xlix, 291, 295-6

Borgia, Cæsar, son of Pope Alexander, xxxvi, 15; cruelty of, 56; Countess of Forli and, 75; Guido Ubaldo and, 74; Macaulay on, xxvii, 408-9; Machiavelli on, xxxvi, 24-30; Oliverotto and, 33; troops of, 48

BORGIA, LUCRETIA, LINES ON HAIR OF, xlii, 929

Borgny, wife of Sigmund (see Borghild)

Borgny, wife of Vilmund, xlix, 457-9

Borgoignon, Nicolas, xxxiii, 263 note

Borgoo, the negroes of, v, 207-8

Boric Acid, as antiseptic, xxxviii, 400-1

Born, Bertrand de, in Dante's HELL, xx, 120 note

Borneil, Giraud de, xx, 255 note 3

Bornoos, language of, v, 208

Boron, Robert de, xxxv, 108

Borromeo, Federigo, in THE BETROTHED, xxi, 367-76; Abbondio and, 433-44; Lucia and, 413-18, 432; in Milan famine, 477-9, 486;
in plague, 526, 548-9, 552, 554-5; unnamed and, 377-88

Borrow, George, and the Gypsies, v, 448

Borrowing, Emerson on, v, 99-100; Shakespeare on, xlvi, 102

Bors, Sir, in THE HOLY GRAIL, at the abbey, xxxv, 181-2; birds, omen of, 172, 181-2; at Carbonek Castle, 218-21; at Carteloise Castle, 200-2; chastity of, 168, 172; Galahad and, 110, 114, 190-1, 218, 225; gentlewoman and, 176-7; hermit and, 171-2; lady's champion, 172-5; Lancelot and, 226; Lionel and, 176, 183-7; Percivale and, 187-8, 225-6; at Sarras, 223-4; in ship of Faith, 192, 200; temptation of, 178-81; visions of, 173-4, 182; wounded knight rescued by, 207

Borsiere, Guglielmo, xx, 69 and note 4

Bortolo, in THE BETROTHED (see Castagneri), xxi

Bos, Abbé du, on painting and poetry, xxiv, 54

Bosanquet, F. C. T., reviser of Pliny, ix

Bosola, Daniel de, in DUCHESS OF MALFI, Antonio and, xlvii, 740, 746-8, 810-11; Cardinal and, 722-3, 799-800, 805-6, 812-14; Castruccio and, 737-8; death of, 815; Delio and, 769; Duchess and, 727-8, 739, 741-2, 744, 762-3, 764-7, 773-4, 775-6, 777-80, 785-9, 792-3; Ferdinand and, 728-30, 756-7, 769, 776-7, 780-1, 789-92, 797-8, 814; Julia and, 800-2; old lady and, 738-9, 743-4

Bosquet, M., on cirripedes, xi, 357

Bossu, Le, epic code of, xxxix, 405; on heroes of poetry, xiii, 24

Bossuet, on Cromwell, xxxix, 396; Sainte-Beuve, History of, xxxii, 131-2; Taine on, xxxix, 452

Bostock, Mr., Walton on, xv, 414, 422-3

BOSTON HYMN, xlii, 1313-16

Boston News-Letter, Franklin on, i, 20

Boswell, James, remarks on Life of Johnson, by, xxvii, 164; Burns on, vi, 327 note 1; Thackeray on, xxviii, 7

Boswell, Robert Bruce, translator of PHÆDRA, xxvi, 123

Botallus, on circulation of blood, xxxviii, 98

Botany, Emerson on science of, v, 307; Locke on study of, xxxvii, 157

Botany Bay, morality of children of, v, 255

Botero, Giovanni, xxi, 467

Botofogó Bay, Darwin on, xxix, 36-7

BOTTLE, A, AND FRIEND, vi, 277

Bouchardat, M., on fermentation, xxxviii, 368

Bougainville, on the Fuegians, xxix, 244

Boulders, in the Azores, xi, 410; erratic, Darwin on, xxix, 201, 264; Helmholtz on, xxx, 237-41

Boullogne, Jean, xxxi, 438 note

Bouncer, Bet, in SHE STOOPS TO CONQUER, xviii, 211, 231

Bounties, Smith, Adam, on, x, 347, 392-406, 426-9, 444

Bountiful, in PILGRIM'S PROGRESS, xv, 235

Bounty, and frugality, i, 344; St. Paul on, xlv, 538 (6-7)

Bourbon, Cardinal de, brother of Charles IX, xxxviii, 50

Bourbon, Constable of, his attack on Rome, xxxi, 71-2; death, 72-3 note 4

Bourbon, Francis de, xxxi, 347 note; and Cellini, 347-8

Bourdeaux, Smith on situation of, x, 276

Bourdillon, M. de, xxxviii, 46

Bourges, surrender of, xxxviii, 48-9

Bourne, Richard, xliii, 148

Boutron, M., on fermentation, xxxviii, 369-70

Bowie, Alexander, reviser of Harvey, xxxviii, 63

Bowles, William Lisle, DOVER CLIFFS, xli, 697-8

Bowring, Sir John, xxv, 62-3, 64, 86-7

Bowyer, Sir William, and Dryden, xiii, 431

Boyardo, Matthew, Cervantes on, xiv, 53

Boyd, Rev. Wm., Burns on, vi, 173 note 8

Boyhood, Augustine, St., on, vii, 13; Emerson on, v, 65; Wordsworth on, xli, 611

Boyle, Robert Johnson on, xxxix, 242

Boynton, Sir Edward, house of, v, 414

Braccio, Fortebracci, Machiavelli on, xxxvi, 44, 46

Brachs, defined, xx, 429

Brackenburg, in EGMONT, xix, 260-1, 264, 285, 311-15, 318-21

Brackley, Lord, in COMUS, iv, 46

BRACKLEY, THE BARON OF, xl, 120-123

Bracy, the bard in CHRISTABEL, xli, 736, 739-41, 744

Bradamant, xxxii, 52 note 44

Braddock, Gen., Franklin on, i, 134-42

Braddock's defeat, i, 141

Bradford, Andrew, Franklin with,

i, 23, 27, 28; paper of, 62, 63; as postmaster, 67, 102

Bradford, William, i, 23, 27-8

Bradlaugh, Charles, and Mill, xxv, 198

Bradley, James, astronomer, xxx, 333-4

Bradshaw, John, Milton on, v, 202

Bradwardine, Bishop, Chaucer on, xl, 46; Newman on, xxviii, 48

BRAES O' KILLIECRANKIE, vi, 381

BRAES OF YARROW, by Hamilton, xli, 586-9

BRAES OF YARROW, by Logan, xli, 512-13

Brage, Norse god, v, 404

Bragging, Emerson on, v, 405

Brahma, Hindu god, xlv, 814, 833, 835-56, 881-3

BRAHMA, Emerson's, xlii, 1294

Brahma Sahampati, xlv, 737-9

Brahman, Buddha on qualities of a, xlv, 641; virtues of a, 880

Brahmins, Emerson on the, v, 185

Brain, Berkeley on the, xxxvii, 243-4; in birds, xxxviii, 141-2; Harvey on the, 105; Pascal on the, xlviii, 25 (70)

Bramador, hill of, xxix, 382

Bramber, Nicholas, xxxv, 80 and note

Bramimonde, Queen, xlix, 119, 195, 196, 197, 207

Bran Galed, horn of, xxxii, 152

Branchiæ, Darwin on, xi, 196-7

Brand, Bishop, xliii, 21

Brandabarbaray, of Boliche, xiv, 147

Brandan, St., Renan on legend of, xxxii, 149, 183-5; and Judas, 154

Brandebourg, Marquis of, at Metz, xxxviii, 32

Brander, in FAUST, xix, 80-94

Brandini, Giovanbattista, xxxi, 427

Branstock, xlix, 278, 279

Brasidas, quoted, xxxiv, 220

Bratius, on hounds, xxxv, 369

Brava Island, xxxiii, 211

Bravery, Confucius on exterior, xliv, 61 (12); fable of, at a distance, xvii, 16-17

BRAVING ANGRY WINTER'S STORMS, vi, 304

Bravoes, in Lombardy, xxi, 10-13

BRAW LADS O' GALLA WATER, vi, 481

BRAW WOOER, THE, vi, 574

Brawn, Harrison on, xxxv, 349-51

Braxfield, Lord, story of, xxv, 445-6

Brazil, Darwin on, xxix, 22-4, 29-48, 521-6; Francis Pretty on, xxxiii, 211-13

Bread, Locke on eating of, xxxvii, 17-18, 19; price of, compared with meat, x, 157-8, 160-1; wheat and oatmeal, compared, 171

Breadalbane, Burns on district of, vi, 291-2

Breadalbane, Earl of, vi, 215 note

BREAK, BREAK, BREAK, xlii, 1006
Breathing (see Respiration)
Breca, and Beowulf, xlix, 19-20
Bredi, the thrall, xlix, 275-6
Breeding, close, diminishes vigor, xi,
110, 140, 318; cross (see Inter-
crosses)
Brefeld, Oscar, on fermentation,
xxxviii, 329-31, 361-2
Breintnal, Joseph, i, 60, 61, 62, 66
BREMEN TOWN MUSICIANS, THE,
xvii, 120-3
Brennus, reference to, xx, 308
Breton, Nicholas, PHILLIDA AND
CORIDON, xl, 199
Bretons (see Celtic Races)
Breuer, Thomas, cow of, xxxv, 343
Brevity, "the soul of wit," xlvi,
119; in speech and writing, xxxii,
45-6
Brewing, in old England, xxxv, 298-
300
Briareus, in Dante's HELL, xx, 131-2,
193; Jupiter and, iii, 42; Milton
on, iv, 95; Virgil on, xiii, 221
(see also Ægæon)
BRIAR-ROSE, LITTLE, story of, xvii,
146-9
Bribery, in elections, Plutarch on,
xii, 165; a ground of impeach-
ment, xliii, 202 (4); Penn on, i,
371 (384)
BRIDGE, THE, xlii, 1328-9
BRIDGE OF SIGHS, by Hood, xli, 932-
5; Poe on, xxviii, 400-1
Bridges, expense of maintaining, x,
474-7; made of hide, xxix, 279-80
Bridgewater, Earl of, president of
Wales, iv, 47
Bright, John, on American Civil
War, xxv, 172; on woman suffrage, 194
Bright, Mynors, Stevenson on,
xxviii, 295
BRIGS OF AYR, THE, vi, 242-8
Brisk, Mr., in PILGRIM'S PROGRESS,
xv, 233-4
Brissac, M. de, at Perpignan,
xxxviii, 15-16
Brissot, Jean Pierre, Burke on, xxiv,
401
Britain, Cæsar in, xii, 294-5; plant-
ed by descendant of Æneas, xiii,
20
British Constitution, Burke on the,
xxiv, 395-6; Lowell on the, xxviii,
470; James Mill on, xxv, 63-4;
representation under, xxiv, 335-
6; Ruskin on, xxviii, 135
Britomartis, Spenser's, xxxix, 66, 68
Britons, agriculture of the, xxxv,
324; boats of the, 380, food of
the, 285; houses of the, 308; mirrors among, 340; productions of
the, 332; use of woad by the, 331
Brittany, Arthurian legends in,
xxxii, 169-70; Christianity in,

178, 179, 180-2, 183 note 26, 189;
English descent on, xxxviii, 13-
14; Machiavelli on, xxxvi, 9-10;
Paré on pastimes in, xxxviii, 14-
15; Renan on, xxxii, 143, 147
Broca, Paul, objections to natural
selection, xi, 222
Brockden, the scrivener, i, 69, 78
Brocket, defined, xxxv, 361
Brodie, Sir Benjamin, on puerperal
fever, xxxviii, 260
Brome, Alexander, THE RESOLVE, xl,
378
Bromios, Bacchus called, viii, 116,
352, 353
Bronn, Heinrich, on geological for-
mations, xi, 347, 364; objections
to natural selection, 220-2
Brontë, Emily, poems by, xlii, 1156-7
Bronze-casting, Cellini's method of,
xxxi, 369 note 1, 392-7
Bronzino, Il (see Allori)
Brooke, Christopher, and Dr. Donne,
xv, 332
Brooke, Lord, Emerson on, v, 427;
Hazlitt on, xxvii, 291; Milton on,
iii, 238-9; tombstone of, v, 477
Brooke, Samuel, xv, 332, 362
Brosse, Peter de la, xx, 168 note 7
Brothels, Luther on, xxxvi, 350
Brotherliness, Burns on, vi, 88, 263,
389, 547; Bacon on emulation be-
tween, iii, 21
Brothers, Browning on, and sisters,
xviii, 380
Brothers, Montaigne on, xxxii, 76
Brothers of Death, xxi, 281 note
Brougham, Lord, and Edinburgh
Review, xxvii, 236; in Edinburgh
society, xxv, 84; on English
clergy, v, 447; Mill and, xxv, 62;
on Milton's Satan, xxviii, 208;
and the Times, v, 466
Broughton, Hugh, xlvii, 555 note,
602 note 2
Brouncker, Lord, Voltaire on,
xxxiv, 127
Broune, Adam, almoner to Edward
Second, xxxv, 402
Brown, Dr., and Franklin, i, 24-25
Brown, John, Mill on, xxv, 171 and
note
Brown, Lieut., at Gettysburg, xliii,
359, 373, 374
Brown, Richard, xxiii, mate of the
"Alert," 422
Brown, Robert, on classification, xi,
453-4
Brown, Thomas Edward, MY GAR-
DEN, xlii, 1195
Browne, Maurice, xxxiii, 282, 295,
299
Browne, Sir Thomas, on the Bible,
iii, 288 (23); Catholic Church,
attitude toward, 266 (3), 268 (5);
charity of, 325-6, 328-31, 345;
Christianity of, 265 (1); on

Church of England, 268 (5); contentment, dreams, 341-3; on death, 303-4, 308; on death and burial, his own, 305-6; desires of, 347; disease hated by, 338-9; Emerson on, v, 450; on faith and reason, iii, 284-7; on the future life, 310-18; on God, 274-7, 293; heresies of, 269-71; Lamb on, xxvii, 282-3; learning and lack of pride, iii, 336; on length of life, 306-8; sketch of life and works, 262; love of the beautiful and harmonious, 338; love of mysteries and miracles, 272 (9, 10); on the medical profession, 339; his prayers, 333-4, 343-4; a Protestant, 265 (2); on providence, 279; RELIGIO MEDICI, 263-347; on religious disputes, 269; on salvation, 319-23; on spirits, 294-8, 302-3; on study of nature, 277-9; sympathy of, with all things, 324; tenderness and love of friends, 332-3; toleration of, 268 (6); at variance only with himself, 334-5, 339-40

Browne, William, ON COUNTESS OF PEMBROKE, xl, 343

Brownell, George, i, 10

BROWNHILL INN, EPIGRAM AT, vi, 437

Browning, Robert, sketch of life and works, xviii, 356; A BLOT IN THE 'SCUTCHEON 357-400; short Poems by, xlii, 1106-55; SONNET ON, by Landor, xli, 926

Browning, Elizabeth Barrett, lines to, by Robert Browning, xlii, 1137-43; poems by, xli, 948-70

Brown-Séquard, on mutilations, xi, 148

BRUAR WATER, PETITION OF, vi, 293-5

Bruce, Michael, TO THE CUCKOO, xli, 583-4

Bruce, Robert, Burns on, vi, 396, 502-3, 117 note 4

Bruchsal, Count von, in MINNA VON BARNHELM, xxvi, 306, 342, 364-5

Bructerians, Tacitus on the, xxxlii, 114

Brummel, simplicity of, v, 386

Brunelleschi, Agnello, xx, 106 and note

Brunet, Gustave, xxxii, 111

Brunetto Latini, xxviii, 76

Brunetto, Ser, in Dante's HELL, xx, 64-6

Brunswick, House of, Burke on title of, xxiv, 171-3

Bruttius, Cicero the Younger on, ix, 182

Brutus, Decimus (Albinus), xii, 327-8, 329, 342; Bacon on, iii, 70-1; Cicero on, ix, 9, 186, 187

Brutus, Lucius Junius, first Roman tribune, xii, 157, 163, 325; Cor-

neille on sons of, xxvi, 118; Dante on, xx, 20; death of, ix, 73; Virgil on, xiii, 239

Brutus, Marcus, Cæsar and, xii, 314, 321, 325-6, 330-1, 343-4; ix, 170, 178; after Cæsar's death, xii, 262, 331, 344; Cæsar's ghost and, 332-3; iii, 96; Cicero and, xii, 264, 272; xxxii, 99; Cicero on his relations with, ix, 148-50; letter to, 184-9; in Dante's HELL, xx, 144 and note 1; death and burial, xii, 350; descent of, 325; Hobbes on vision of, xxxiv, 328-9; Lepidus and, xii, 344; loans of, x, 99-100; at Marseilles, xx, 221 note 7; Montaigne on, xxxii, 98; at Philippi, xii, 349-50; on virtue, v, 130-1

Bruyère, La, Burke on, xxiv, 383 note; Hume on, xxxvii, 307; on Manners, xxvii, 173, 174; Sainte-Beuve on, xxxii, 136

Bryant, William Cullen, poems by, xlii, 1262-73; JUNE of, Poe on, xxviii, 393-4

Brydone, Patrick, vi, 184 note 9

Brynhild, ending of, xlix, 357-9, 405-12, 420-1; grief of, 342-7, 397-8, 404-5; Gudrun and, 332-3, 339-42; Gunnar and, 339, 403-4; at Hindfell, 317, 318; Morris on, 273; name of, reason of, 327; Oddrun on, 460-1; Sigurd and, 319-26, 328-30, 347-8, 350, 351-2, 398, 402-3, 418-19; wooing of, 336-9, 396-7, 415-16, 421; remarks on story of, 267

BRYNHILD, FRAGMENTS OF LAY OF, xlix, 417-21; remarks on, 267-8

BRYNHILD, THE HELL-RIDE OF, xlix, 413-16; remarks on, 268

Bryso, Dante on, xx, 344

Bubastis, the Egyptian Artemis, xxxiii, 81

Bubastis, city of, xxxiii, 33-4, 37; temple of Artemis at, 70-1

Bubble, Madam, in PILGRIM'S PROGRESS, xv, 310-13

Bubonax, death of, xxvii, 55

Buch, Captal de, xxxv, 36, 42, 48, 51, 60

Buchanan, George, and Montaigne, xxxii, 3, 68; Sidney on tragedies of, xxvii, 49

Buchanan, Robert W., LIZ by, xlii, 1247

Buchheim, C. A., translator of Luther, xxxvi, 2

Buck, defined, xxxv, 361

Buckingham, Dukes of (see Stafford, Villiers)

Buckingham, Earl of, in Tyler's Rebellion, xxxv, 68

BUCKWHEAT, THE, story of, xvii, 377-8

Bucolic poets, Shelley on, xxvii, 359

Buddha, on animals, xlv, 722-5; attainment of Buddhaship, 627-38; birth of, 617-26; daily habits, 643-6; death, 647-61; first resolutions to strive for Buddhaship, 591 note 1; on indifference, 728; life of the, 588; Malunkyaputta sermon of, 662-7; on mendicant ideal, 764-6; Middle Doctrine of, 677-81; Noble-craving Sermon, 729-46; Pasenadi and, 691-2; story of Hare-Mark on Moon, 712-16; story of Husband-honorer, 708-11; on the truth, 673; Visākhā and, 770-1, 786-8, 791, 793-4, 796-8; on way of purity, 717

Buddha uproar, xlv, 617

Buddhism, Taine on, xxxix, 449, 457

Buddhist priests, ordination of, xlv, 756-63

BUDDHIST WRITINGS, xlv, 587-798

Budli, King, xlix, 331, 336, 339, 342

Budlungs, names of the, xlix, 270-1

Buenos Ayres, Darwin on, xxix, 133-4; revolution in, 153-4

Buffon, George Louis, on classics, xxxii, 131-2; on creative force of America, xxix, 187-8; on evolution, xi, 6, 9; Franklin and, i, 154; Sainte-Beuve on, xxxii, 128

Buford, Gen., at Gettysburg, xliii, 351

BUFFOON AND COUNTRYMAN, fable of, xvii, 45

Bugiardini, Giuliano, xxxi, 89 note

Bubel, Burkhart am, in WILHELM TELL, xxvi, 401, 410

BUILDING, Bacon's ESSAY ON, iii, 114-7

Building materials, demand for, x, 174-5, 186; supply of, does not limit population, 174; value of, 173-4

BUILDING OF THE SHIP, xlii, 133-43

Building rent, by what determined, x, 510-11

Buildings, as capital, x, 228

Bujamonti, Giovanni, xx, 73 note 7

Bulgarians, Freeman on the, xxviii, 241-2, 278

Bulimus, Darwin on the, xxix, 368

Bull, why more sublime than ox, xxiv, 58

Bull, Bishop, on angels, xx, 407 note 5

BULL AND ASS, story of, xvi, 12-13

Bull feasts, xlix, 214-15

Bullen, Anne, Henry VIII and, xxxvi, 107, 116, 119; Thomas More and, 127, 128

Buller, Charles, Carlyle and, xxv, 329; Mill on, 70, 85, 140, 126, 128

Bullies, Burns on, vi, 234

Bullion, movements of, x, 341

Bullock, J. C., editor of Adam Smith, x

Bulls, Papal, Luther on, xxxvi, 328-9

Bulwer Lytton, Emerson on, v, 457

Bumper, Sir Harry, in SCHOOL FOR SCANDAL, xviii, 147-9

Bunau-Varilla, Philippe, xliii, 479

BUNDLE OF STICKS, fable of, xvii, 41

Bunyan, John, sketch of life and works of, i, 14, 23; Franklin on, i, 14, 23; Hazlitt on, xxvii, 289; PILGRIM'S PROGRESS, xv, 5-324; Thoreau on, xxviii, 433

Buonaccorti, Giuliano, xxxi, 205 note 3, 366

Buonacossi, Pinamonte, xx, 85 note 5

Buonaparte, Lucien, on Macpherson, xxxix, 345

Buonaparte, Napoleon (see Napoleon)

Buonarroti (see Michelangelo)

Buonaventura, St., in Dante's PARADISE, xx, 336-40; sketch of, 336 note 4

Buondelmonte, Dante on, xx, 357; murder of, 119 note 11, 357 note 31

Buoso of Cremona, xx, 136 note 9

Burchell, on size of animals and vegetation, xxix, 99-100; on ostriches, 103; on S. African implement, 284-5

Bürger, Gottfried August, on Percy's Reliques, xxxix, 342, 343-4; Wordsworth on, 343

Burgh, Benet, xxxix, 16

Burghers, in FAUST, xix, 37-8

Burghersh, Bartholomew de, xxxv, 23, 36, 42, 52, 56

Burgoyne, Gen., Burns on, vi, 55

Burgundy, Machiavelli on, xxxvi, 9-10

Burgundy, Duke of, in LEAR, xlvi, 204-5, 209, 210

Burials, in ancient Egypt, xxxiii, 42-4; in NEW ATLANTIS, iii, 182

Burians, Tacitus on the, xxxiii, 120

Burke, Edmund, aims and character of, xxiv, 396-7, 423-5; Bagehot on party spirit of, xxviii, 193; Burns on, vi, 55; conservatism of, xxiv, 396; on English lawyers, v, 431; Fox and, 219-20; author of war with France, xxiv, 442-3; ON FRENCH REVOLUTION, 149-397; generalizations of, v, 456, 458; Goldsmith on, xli, 518; Keppel and, xxiv, 437-8; LETTER TO A NOBLE LORD, 399-443; on liberty, 156-7; life and works, sketch of, 5-6, 28, 150, 400; love of order, 150; on the nobility, 418-19; Pay-Office and Establishment Acts, 406-14; pension of, 400, 403-4, 422-5; on pensions, 416-18; on his services, 415-16; ON THE SUBLIME AND BEAUTIFUL, 7-148; ON TASTE, 11-26

Burke, Gen., Mill and, xxv, 186

Burke, Richard, death of, xxiv, 400; Edmund Burke on, 426-7

Burlador, to Sancho Panza, xiv, 541

Burleigh, Lord, to his son on expenses, v, 409

Burlesque, Fielding on the, xxxix, 185-7

Burn, Dr., on settlement laws, x, 146, 148-9; on wages, 150

Burnel, the Asse, xl, 48

Burnes, William, father of Robert Burns, vi, 15; epitaph on, 54

Burnet, Bishop, *History of Own Time*, xxv, 11; on French clergy, xxiv, 297-8

Burnet, Gov., and Franklin, i, 34, 62

BURNET, MISS, ELEGY ON, vi, 419

Burney, Martin, in Hazlitt's discussion, xxvii, 286, 292

BURNING BABE, THE, xl, 222

Burns, John, of Gettysburg, xliii, 352

BURNS, MISS, LINES ON, vi, 278

Burns, Robert, POEMS AND SONGS, vi, 1-609; Arnold on, xxviii, 77, 79, 84-90; daughter of, vi, 59-60; death, lines on his own, 64; first book of, 232; elegy on himself, 99; Emerson on, v, 22, 127, 315; Hazlitt on, xxvii, 292-3; Jacobitism of, vi, 296 note; life and works, sketch of, 15-18; possessions, inventory of, 194-6; wife of (*see* Armour, Jean)

Burton, Sir Richard F., on ARABIAN NIGHTS, xvi, 3; on deserts, xxviii, 424

Burton, Robert, death of, v, 396

Busbacca, the courier, xxxi, 199-203

BUSHBY, JOHN, LINES ON, vi, 520

Bushby, Mr. of New Zealand, xxix, 445-6

Business, character in, v, 193-4; Confucius on, xliv, 5 (5); Emerson on the ways of, v, 47-8; honesty in, iii, 8-9; love and, 29; xl, 319; method in, i, 372-3 (403); Penn on qualities for, 358 (210-12); suspicion bad in, iii, 86; three parts of, 67; time the measure of, 66; Woolman on, i, 188, 204 and note, 206, 245, 285, 311, 312, 318-19; youth and age in, iii, 110-11

Busirane, Spenser's, xxxix, 68

Busiris, city of, xxxiii, 33, 34

Busiris and his Memphian cavalry, iv, 98

Busk, Mr., on avicularia, xi, 248

Buslidius, Hieronymus, xxxvi, 255

Busy-bodies, commonly envious, iii, 24

Butcher, S. H., translator of Homer, xxii

Butchers, excluded from juries, xxxvii, 108

Butes, and Dares, xiii, 194; death of, 385-6, 407

Buthrescas, in Utopia, xxxvi, 244

Buti, Cecchino, xxxi, 443, 444

Butler, Joseph, Bishop, Hazlitt on, xxvii, 291; on meaning of "natural," xi, 1; Mill on *Analogy of Religion* of, xxv, 30

Butler, Samuel, Emerson on *Hudibras* of, v, 450; Voltaire on *Hudibras* of, xxxiv, 150-1

Buto, city of, xxxiii, 33, 37; oracle of, 42, 80

Butterflies, in Brazil, xxix, 43-4; dimorphism of, xi, 61; flocks of, at sea, xxix, 172; imitation by, xi, 465-7

Butterfly, symbol of the soul, xx, 188 note

Button, coffee-house of, xxvii, 190

Button, Jemmy, xxix, 222-4, 233, 234, 235-8, 241-2, 244-5

Butyric acid, production of, xxxviii, 344

Butyric fermentation, xxxviii, 345-56, 358

Butyric vibrios, xxxviii, 343-4

Buyck, in EGMONT, xix, 247-53

Buys, M., Dutch envoy, xxvii, 108

Buzareingues, Giron de, on fertilization, xi, 325

By-employments, Smith on, x, 124-6

By-ends, in PILGRIM'S PROGRESS, xv, 103-11, 113, 281, 288

Byron, Admiral John, on brutality of Fuegians, xxix, 231; on wolves in Falkland Islands, 208

Byron, George Gordon, Lord, sketch of life and works, xviii, 402; Arnold on, xlii, 1181-2; Carlyle on, xxv, 360-1, 437, 442; Emerson on, v, 275, 450, 462; Goethe on, xxxii, 134; Hugo on, xxxix, 380; MANFRED of, xviii, 403-44; Mill on, xxv, 96-7, 99; and Newstead Abbey, v, 414; Poe on lines by, xxviii, 401-2; poems by, xli, 803-37

BYRON AND GOETHE, by Mazzini, xxxii, 399-419

Byzantium, Pliny on expenses of, ix, 402; Trajan on, 418

CA' THE YOWES TO THE KNOWES, by Burns, vi, 376-7, 530

CA' THE YOWES TO THE KNOWES, by Pagan, xli, 569

Cabbage, fertilization of the, xi, 112

Cabot, John, account of life, xliii, 47 note; account of discoveries, 47-50; Hayes on, xxxiii, 272, 273

Cabot, Sebastian, Hayes on, xxxiii, 272, 273

Caccia of Asciano, xx, 124 and note 7

Cacciaguida, in Dante's PARADISE. xx, 350-362

Caccianimico, Venedico, xx, 76 and note 2

Cactornis, Darwin on species of, xxix, 401, 418

Cactus, Darwin on, xxix, 179 note 9, 278

Cacus, the robber, xiii, 278-9; Burke on, xxiv, 133; Cervantes on, xiv, 11, 29, 53; Dante on, xx, 105; Hercules and, xiii, 279-81

Cadmus, founder of Thebes, viii, 355; Dante on, xx, 106; letters invented by, xxxiv, 335, xli, 834; Milton on, iv, 276; sower of the giant's sod, viii, 359

Cadmus, in the BACCHÆ, viii, 356-7, 361-2, 406-14

Cadwallader, John, Woolman on, i, 280

Cadwallo, Gray on, xl, 469

Cadytis, city of Syria, xxxiii, 82

Cæcilius, C., Pliny on, ix, 268

Cæcilius, Statius, on old age, ix, 54, 58; in Dante's Limbo, xx, 238

Cæcilius, the freedman, and Verres, xii, 230

Cæcilius, the orator, and Cicero, xii, 256-7; ix, 84-5; on orators, xii, 198

Cæcina, Aulus, letter to, ix, 167

Cæculus, and Æneas, xiii, 345

Cæcus, name of, xii, 162

Cædicus, and Remulus, xiii, 309

Cælianus, Sempronius, ix, 393

Cælius, Marcus Rufus, and Cicero, xii, 256 note, 270; ix, 155, 156; Pliny on, 214 note 4

Caen, city of, xxxv, 11; defence against Edward the Third, 7, 11-12; capture of, 12-14; importance of, 11 note 3

Cæneus, in the ÆNEID xiii, 226, 316

Cæpio, Servilius, and Cæsar's daughter, xii, 285; in Germany, xxxiii, 117

Caerleon, ancient see of, xxxv, 264; university of, 391

Cæsar, Caius Julius, reputed ancestor of Æneas, xiii, 19; in African War, xii, 317-19; Alexander and, xiii, 28; xxxvi, 52; ambitiousness of, xii, 283; Analogy of, xxvii, 61; Anti-Cato of, xii, 259, 276, 319; Antony's funeral oration on, 344; Atticus and, ix, 156-7; Bacon on, iii, 110, 136; Blake on laurel crown of, xli, 603; brevity of, xii, 317; on British tides, xxx, 293; Browne on valor of, iii, 291; Brutus on, ix, 178; Brutus and ghost of, xii, 332-3; Brutus, Decimus, and, iii, 70-1; Burke on, xxiv, 95; Cæcina and, ix, 169-70; calendar reformed by, xii, 323; Calpurnia, wife of, 285; in Catiline conspiracy, 279-81, 242-3; on

Cato, ix, 251; Cervantes on, xiv, 11, 513; Cicero, relations with, xii, 244, 251, 257, 259, 260, 276-7, 279-80, 286; Cicero on his relations with, ix, 117, 118, 119, 120-1, 122, 124, 125, 126, 127-8, 131, 132, 133, 134, 162-3, 168-9, 171, 176, 177, 178, 187; Cicero on character of, 169, 176; Cicero on consulship of, 84, 85; clemency of, xii, 321-2; Cleopatra and, 315-16; xviii, 44, 46; Clodius and, ix, 118; conspiracy against, xii, 325-6, 343-4; consulship, first, of, 247, 284-6; consulship, third, 341; consulship, fifth, 342; Curio and, xx, 119 note 10; Dante on, 221 note 2, 254, 309; death, prodigies preceding, xii, 326-7; xlvi, 91; death of, xii, 327-30; death, state of affairs after, ix, 178, 185; death, signs following, xii, 332; death of, Webster on, xlvii, 814; dictatorship of, xii, 301; Dryden on, xiii, 16-17; early offices, xii, 277; Egypt, war in, 315, 316; Egyptian priest and, v, 275-6; Emerson on, 72, 211, 275; extravagance of, xii, 277-8; Fiorino of Cellino and, xxxi, 6; funeral orations on aunt and wife, xii, 277; in Gaul, 286, 289-98; generalship of, 286-9; generosity to the Republicans, 170; as High Priest, 279; Hugo on, xxxix, 375; kingship desired by, xii, 323-4; Lucceius and, ix, 91; at the Lupercalia, xii, 324-5, 343; Machiavelli on liberality of, xxxvi, 55; Marian party revived by, xii, 278-9; Milton on, iv, 389; Montaigne on history of, xxxi, 100, 102; Octavius, heir of, xii, 264; one of nine worthies, xxxix, 21; Pascal on, xlviii, 51 (132); Pharnaces and, xii, 317; Pharsalia, magnanimity after, 314-15, 259; the pilot and, iii, 106; pirates and, xii, 274-5; plans of, 322-3; Pliny on, ix, 214; Plutarch's LIFE OF, xii, 274-333; Pompeia, wife of, 277, 281-2, 249, 250; Pompey, early relations with, 284, 285-6, 293, 295, 296; Pompey, final contest with, 298-314, 257-8, 337-8, 339-40; and Pompey's statues, 260; Pompey and, Bacon on, iii, 83, 130, 148; Pompey and, Cicero on, ix, 4-5, 127-8, 168-9, 170; Pompey's sons and, xii, 320-1; Pope on, xl, 445; as prætor, xii, 281, 244; Revelius and, 322; Suetonius on, xxxii, 65; Senate, relations with, ix, 129; Shakespeare on portents before death of, xlvi, 21; sick soldier and, xxvii, 21; Sidney on, xxvii, 24; in Spain, xii, 283-4; story of the storm,

307; studies at Rhodes, 275-6; Sylla and, 274; iii, 43; Tacitus on, xxxiii, 111; triumphs of, xii, 320, 321; Virgil on, xiii, 238; will of, xii, 331; worshipped as a god, 331

Cæsar, Lucius, saved by sister, xii, 348

Cæsarion, son of Cæsar, xii, 316; death of, 398-9; made king by Antony, 378

Cæsonius, Cicero on, ix, 83

Cæstius, Cicero and the younger, xxxii, 99

Cagli, Benedetto da, xxxi, 213, 241-2

Cagnano, Angelo da, xx, 118 note 8

Cagnazzo, the demon, xx, 90, 94

Cahors, reference to, xx, 47

Caiaphas, the high priest, xliv, 365 (2), 436 (6); in Dante's HELL, xx, 99

Cain, and Abel, xlvi, 181 note 7; Bacon on, iii, 25; author of BEOWULF on, xlix, 8, 41; Cowley on, xxvii, 68; Milton on, iv, 333-4; Mohammed on, xlv, 1011-12; tree of Eve and, xxxv, 196

Caina, first round of Hell, xx, 133-7

Cairns, in old Ireland, xlix, 229

Cairo, Arabian idea of, xvi, 152

Caithness, in MACBETH, xlvi, 365-6

Cajeta, nurse of Æneas, xiii, 243

Cajetan, Cardinal, xxxvi, 358

Calaber, Quintus, Shelley on, xxvii, 366

Calamities, Emerson on compensation of, v, 106-7; limitation of, 135; human delight in, xxiv, 42-4; Montaigne on consolation in, xxxii, 46-7; Woolman on, i, 246-7

Calandrino, Boccaccio's, xxvii, 404

Calasirians, district of the, xxxiii, 84-5

Calatinus, Atilius, epitaph of, ix, 68

Calboli, Fulcieri da, xx, 203 and note 13

Calboli, Rinieri da, in Dante's PURGATORY, xx, 201-3

Calc Spar, crystallization of, xxx, 31, 251; effect of, on polarized light, 34-5

Calcabrina, the demon, xx, 90, 94

Calchas, the seer, Æschylus on, viii, 11; Landor on, xli, 927; Simon and, xiii, 107-8; in Trojan War, 109

Calculus, integral and differential, xxxiv, 128

Calderon, de la Barca, Pedro, sketch of life and works, xxvi, 3-4; LIFE IS A DREAM, 5-68; Shelley on, xxvii, 356

Caldwell, Gen., at Gettysburg, xliii, 368, 371, 417

CALEDONIA: A BALLAD, vi, 349

Calendar, Cæsar, reforms, xii, 323

Calendar, Egyptian, xxxiii, 7; Lateran Council, revision of, xxxix, 60

Calentura, Biggs on the, xxxiii, 256

CALF, THE, vi, 235-6

Caliban, in THE TEMPEST, xlvi, son of Sycorax, 390; Prospero and, 391-3, 407, 416-19, 430-2, 440-1; Stephano and, 409-12, 415-16; Trinculo and, 408, 409; Hugo on, xxxix, 372; Hunt on, xxvii, 309; Johnson on, xxxix, 239

California, admission of, xliii, 327 note; Dana on history of, xxiii, 173-4; Dana in (1835), 59-265, 395-6; Dana in (1859), 396-417; Drake in, xxxiii, 222-6; southern boundary of, xliii, 313-14

California, Gulf of, navigation of, xliii, 314

California Rangers, xxiii, 256-8

Caligula (Caius Germanicus), his descent, xii, 403; Germans and, xxxiii, 117; wish of, iii, 330 note

Callao, Darwin on, xxix, 386, 388; ruins of old, 389-90

Callias, Alcibiades and, xii, 116; Aristides and, 106-7; Aristophanes on, viii, 431; birth of, xii, 62; at Marathon, 85; Socrates and, ii, 6

Callicles, son of Arrhenidas, xii, 219

CALLICLES, THE SONG OF, xlii, 1172-4

Callicrates, builder of Parthenon, xii, 51; of Athenian wall, 52

Callicrates, the soldier, xii, 98

Callidromus, the slave, ix, 388

Callimedon, called the Crab, xii, 220

Callinicus, meaning of, xii, 162 note

Calliope, mother of Orpheus, iv, 75, 231

Callippides, the tragedian, xii, 143

Callisthenes, Alexander and, xxvii, 39; xxxii, 59; on the Phocian War, ix, 105

Callisto, Diana and, xx, 252; changed to constellation, 417 note 5

Callistratus, the orator, influence on Demosthenes, xii, 200; Melanopus and, 207

Callixtus, Bishop, xx, 401 note 5

Callot, Hugo on, xxxix, 365

Calodera Maculata, xxix, 137

Calonne, M. de, on reign of Louis XVI, xxiv, 280 note; on France under the Revolution, 281 notes, 334-5, 387 note

Calosoma, instance of, at sea, xxix, 172

Calpurnia, wife of Cæsar, xii, 285; her dream, 327; and Antony, 344-5

Calpurnia, wife of Pliny, ix, 260

note 1; Pliny on, 270; letters to, 293, 294, 313

Calumniators, punishment of, in Rome, ix, 310 note 8

Calumny, Shakespeare on, xlvi, 137 (see also Detraction)

Calvary, Mount, xliv, 422 note 4

Calventius, Cicero on, ix, 118

Calvin, John, DEDICATION OF THE INSTITUTES, xxxix, 29-54; Knox and, 61 note; life and works, sketch of, 29 note; Pope on, xl, 445; Voltaire on, xxxiv, 85; Wyclif and, iii, 234

Calvinism, doctrines of, xxxix, 51-4; in France, 29-50; Mill on, xxv, 266-7

Calvinists, debt of, to St. Augustine, vii, 4; in France, xxxix, 87-8; low ideas of human nature, xxviii, 318; Pascal on, xlviii, 275 (777), 306

Calvinus, Domitius, at Pharsalia, xii, 312

Calvisius, correspondent of Pliny, letters to, ix, 238, 240, 285, 332, 351

Calvisius, dependent of Cæsar, xii, 381

Calypso, Dido and, xxxix, 165; Odysseus and, xxii, 9, 10, 62-3, 72-8, 100

Cambalu, seat of Cathaian Can, iv, 332

Cambray, peace of, More at, xxxvi, 109-10

Cambrian Period, antiquity of the, xi, 359-60; absence of deposits before, 360-3

Cambridge University, Emerson on, v, 432-3; Harrison on, xxxv, 391-400, 401

Cambuscan, reference to, iv, 38

Cambyses, expedition against Egypt, xxxiii, 5; Ladike and, 91; prophecy of, xlviii, 252

Camden, the antiquary, and Ben Jonson, xlvii, 518

Camera Apostolica, xxxi, 42 note 3

Camerinus, Sulpicius, ix, 197 note 5

Camers, son of Volsceus, xiii, 346

Camertus, in the ÆNEID, xiii, 402

Camiccione de Pazzi, xx, 135 and note 6

Camilla, in the ÆNEID, xiii, 270-1, 379-82, 384-90; Dante on, xx, 8, 20

Camilla, in story of CURIOUS IMPERTINENT, xiv, 323-63, 368-73

Camillo, Cardinal, in THE CENCI, at banquet, xviii, 290, 292; Beatrice and, 350, 352-3; Bernardo and, 348-9; Count Cenci and, 281-5; with Giacomo, 299-300; at the trial, 339-44

Camillus, Cicero on, ix, 167; Virgil on, xiii, 239

Camino, Gaïa da, xx, 214 note 10

Camino, Gherardo da, xx, 213 note 7, 214

Camino, Riccardo da, death of, xx, 323 note 13; Lombardo and, 211 note; wife of, 179 note 4

Camoëns, Wordsworth on sonnets of, xli, 697

Campana, mountain, xxix, 272-5

Campanella, the physiognomist, xxiv, 111-12

CAMPASPE AND CUPID, xl, 212

CAMPBELL, BONNIE GEORGE, a ballad, xl, 115-16

Campbell, J., FREEDOM AND LOVE, xli, 801-2

Campbell, Thomas, poems by, xli, 789-801; Mill on poems of, xxv, 17; on English nobility, v, 429

Campegines, Cardinal, xxxvi, 108, 109

Campion, Thomas, poems by, xl, 290-4

Campistron, Hugo on, xxxix, 378, 383

CAN YE LABOUR LEA, vi, 465

Canace, reference to story of, iv, 38

Canada, invited into the Confederation, xliii, 176

CANADIAN BOAT-SONG, by Moore, xli, 840-1

CANADIAN BOAT-SONG, by Wilson, xlii, 1105-6

Canals, expense of, x, 474-7; Smith on, 156-7

Canary Islands, Drake in the, xxxiii, 241; Vespucci on, xli, 31

Candace, queen of Ethiopia, xliv, 447 (27)

CANDLE, CHEMICAL HISTORY OF A, xxx, 89-178

Candle-wood, xxx, 90

Candolle, A. de, on alpine species, xi, 180-1; on Australian species, 423; on insular plants, 432; on naturalization of plants, 125; on oaks, 66-7; on plants with large seed, 407; on struggle for life, 77; on wide-ranging plants, 69-70, 140, 446; on winged seeds, 158

Candor, Whitman on, xxxix, 424-5

Candour, Mrs., in SCHOOL FOR SCANDAL, xviii, 116-21, 129-33, 179-83

Candy, Locke on, xxxvii, 22

Canidia, Sidney on, xxvii, 22

Canidius, lieutenant of Antony, xii, 361; in Parthian war, 368-9; in war of Antony and Octavius, 379, 385, 386, 388, 389, 391

Caninius, letter to, ix, 368

Canneschi, Machiavelli on the, xxxvi, 64

Canning, George, and free trade, xxv, 67; on reform, v, 385

Cannon, known to ancients, iii, 146

Canôbos, city of, viii, 185

Canoes, Columbus on Indian, xliii, 25; Vespucci on, 38

Canon law, Luther on, xxxvi, 321, 323, 339-40

Canonization of saints, Mill on, xxv, 223-4

CANST THOU LEAVE ME THUS, MY KATIE, vi, 544

Canterbury, Harrison on the See of, xxxv, 264; archbishops of, 265-6, 268

Canterbury, Archbishop of, in EDWARD II, xlvi, 12, 13, 14-16, 76

Canterbury Tales, Dryden on, xxviii, 77-8; xxxix, 172, 173-5; proem to, 19-21; sources of, 167-8, 180

CANTERBURY TALES, PROLOGUE TO, xl, 11-34; Dryden on, xxxix, 168, 173; editorial remarks on, xl, 10

Cantillon, on wages, x, 72

Cantiron, John de, xxxv, 99

Cantyman, the cacique, xxxiii, 323

Canuri, Raleigh on the, xxxiii, 387

Canute, buried in Winchester, v, 480; Knighton Guild and, xxxv, 330; laws against adultery, 385; suppers of, 302

Capaneus, in Dante's HELL, xx, 60-1

Cape de Verd Islands, Darwin on, xxix, 11-16; Pretty on, xxxiii, 209-11; productions of, xi, 440

Capernaum, Jesus on, xliv, 387(15)

Capet, Hugh, Dante on, xx, 228-9; Raleigh on, xxxix, 87

Capillary Attraction, Faraday on, xxx, 96-7

Capilupus, Montaigne on, xxxii, 32

Capital, accumulation of, x, 277-90; circulating and fixed, 224-6 (see also Circulating Capital, Fixed Capital); combinations of, to fix wages, 151; defined, 224; distribution of, in agriculture, manufactures, and trade, 321-4; employments of, 301-18; importance of increase of, 283-4; increase of, effect on profits, wages, and interest, 294-5; investment of, 231; labor and, relations of, 6, 69-71, 221-2, 272, 349; loans as, 291; naturally seeks domestic industries, 349-51; naturally seeks most profitable industries, 351; profits in relation to, 93, 99, 100; revenue and, as determining industry, 275-7; taxes on, 528-34; wages in relation to increase of, 73-7

Capital Causes, in ancient Athens, ii, 24; Bacon on mercy in, iii, 138

Capital Cities, industry in, x, 276-7; virtual universities, xxviii, 37, 38-9

Capital Punishment, in old Massachusetts, xliii, 77 (44, 47), 84-6; More on, xxxvi, 158-9

Capitalists, combinations of, x, 70-1; Smith on interests of, 218-20

Capitation taxes, Smith on, x, 538-40; in U. S., xliii, 198 (4), 204 (5)

Capitolo, the, xxxi, 247 note

Capocchio, in Dante's HELL, xx, 124-5, 126

Capons, Harrison on, xxxv, 354

Caprara, Cardinal, and Napoleon, v, 216

CAPRICE, MONODY ON, vi, 516-7

Caprichioso, on Rozinante, xiv, 541

Caprona, surrender of, xx, 89 note

CAPTAIN CAR, a ballad, xl, 105-8

CAPTAIN! MY CAPTAIN, xlii, 1496-7

CAPTAIN'S LADY, THE, vi, 364-5

Captiousness, Locke on, xxxvii, 131

CAPTIVE RIBBAND, THE, vi, 383

Captive, story of the, xiv, 401-44

Captivity in Babylon, Pascal on, xlviii, 216 (637, 639)

Capuchins, Manzoni on the, xxi, 52-3

Capulets, Dante on the, xx, 171

Capuri, Raleigh on the, xxxiii, 352

Capybara, Darwin on the, xxix, 60

Capys, author of the Capuan name, xiii, 331; Privernus and, 316-17; Trojan horse and, 104

CAR, CAPTAIN, a ballad, xl, 105-8

Caracalla, as a charioteer, iii, 51; Machiavelli on, xxxvi, 67, 68-9, 71

Caracaras, Darwin on, xxix, 66

Caradoc, mantle of, xxxix, 22

Caradosso, Messer, xxxi, 50 note, 64

Carapana, district of, xxxiii, 336 note 23, 382, 383-4

Carapana, king of Emeria, xxxiii, 342-3, 345

Caratach, on valor, v, 81

Carbo, Caius, Africanus and, ix, 102; Gracchus and, 22, 23

Carbolic Acid, as an antiseptic, xxxviii, 271-80, 400

Carbon, Faraday on combustion of, xxx, 165-6, 168-70, 176-7; Helmholtz on combustion of, 210-11; tests of presence of, 168

Carbonek Castle, xxxv, 218-19

Carbonic Acid, as gas, liquid, and solid, xxx, 13 note; composition of, 165-6; method of decomposing, 166-8; heat generated by formation of, 210-11; made by burning candles, 157-9; natural sources of, 159-60; produced in respiration, 172, 175; used by plants, 175-6; properties and weight, 160-2; tested by lime-water, 158-9, 160-1

Carbonic Acid Gas, fermentation in, xxxviii, 317-28

Cardan, Emerson on, v, 183; on dogs, xxxv, 375; on pigeons, 355;

on rogues in England, 388-9; on sheep, 348

Cardenio, in DON QUIXOTE, xiv, 213-18, 250-65, 278-9, 283-4, 374-84

CARDIN O'T, THE SPINNIN O'T, vi, 563

Cardinals, Luther on, xxxvi, 290-1

Cardoness, lines on, vi, 533

Cardoon, Darwin on the, xxix, 131-2, 161

Cards, Locke on playing, xxxvii, 188-9

Care, Burns on, vi, 322; Cicero on freedom from, ix, 25; Cowper on, xli, 555; David on uses of, 503; Goethe on, xix, 31; Milton on, iv, 87; pays not debt, xlvii, 480

Careless, in SCHOOL FOR SCANDAL, xviii, 147-51, 154-9

Carelessness in children, xxxvii, 51, 114-17

Carentan, Edward III at, xxxv, 8-9; importance of, 11 note

Carew, Thomas, poems by, xl, 360-2

Carey, Dr., Bishop of Exeter, xv, 351

Carey, Henry, SALLY IN OUR ALLEY, xl, 414

Carians in Egypt, xxxiii, 79-80, 84

Caribbean Savages, lack of foresight in, xxxiv, 182; love among, 197

Caricatures, Fielding on, xxxix, 186-7

Cariola, in DUCHESS OF MALFI, xlvii, 727, 732, 736, 737, 745, 758-9, 761-2, 767, 775, 781-2, 786, 787, 789

Carlandrea, in THE BETROTHED, xxi, 133

CARLE AN THE KING COME, vi, 367

Carlile, Cristopher, with Drake, xxxiii, 235, 237, 238, 239, 240, 242-6; at St. Domingo, 249; at Cartagena, 253, 254-5, 259; at St. Augustine, 263-4; remarks on his services, 262

Carlile, Richard, prosecution of, xxv, 60

Carlo, San, body of, in Milan plague, xxi, 543-4; plague named after, 523

Carlo Emanuele I, of Savoy, xxi, 454-6, 487

Carloman, son of The Bald, xxxix, 86

Carloto, and Valdovinos, xiv, 46

Carlovingian Poetry, Renan on, xxxii, 165, 167

Carlovingians, Raleigh on the, xxxix, 84-7

Carlyle, Thomas, on America and Americans, v, 472; xxviii, 477; on art, v, 472; CHARACTERISTICS, xxv, 333-71; first entry into Edinburgh, 375; Emerson and, v, 3; Emerson on, 22, 327, 333-5, 459;

Essay on Scott, xxv, 409-68; French Revolution, 140; heroism in, v, 126-7; INAUGURAL ADDRESS, xxv, 375-406; remarks on INAUGURAL ADDRESS, 332; life and works, 329-32; Life of Cromwell, xxxix, 439; London Review and, xxv, 133; Mill and, 87, 114-15; Mill on, 94, 106; reading of, v, 475; on unbelief, xxv, 108; Wordsworth on, v, 337

Carmagnola, and the Venetians, xxxvi, 45

Carmenta, the prophetess, xiii, 283

Carnal Policy, town of, xv, 21

Carnal Sinners, in Dante's HELL, xx, 22-5, 48

Carneades, an African, xxviii, 60; in Athens, x, 143; Manzoni on, xxi, 119; Montaigne on, xxxii, 56; in Rome, iii, 204-5

Carnesecchi, Piero, xxxi, 146 note 6

Carnot, Sadi, on heat, xxx, 204-5

Caro, Annibale, xxxi, 101 note 5; Cellini and, 170, 173; Giovanni Gaddi and, 101 note 4, 139; language of, xxxix, 212; translator of Virgil, xiii, 57-8

Caroli River, xxxiii, 368, 370

Caroline, Queen, and the Times, v, 466

Carpathian Wizard, Proteus called, iv, 69

Carpenter, Chaucer's, xl, 21

Carpentry, as recreation, xxxvii, 186-7

Carpi, Giacomo da, xxxi, 53 and note, 284

Carpigna, Guido di, xx, 204 note 16

Carpino, Plano, x, 326-7

Carpio, Bernardo del, Cervantes on romance of, xiv, 54, 516; Orlando and, 21, 238

Carr, Sir Robert, Hugo on, xxxix, 400

Carranchas, Darwin on, xxix, 66-7

Carrero, Don Pedro de Puerto, xiv, 407

Carrion Hawks, of South America, xxix, 66-70; smelling-power of, 198-200

CARRON IRON WORKS, IMPROMPTU ON, vi, 289

Carrying Trade, capital used in, x, 313-4, 349-50; encouragement of the, 389-90; limits of, 317; a sign of wealth, 316

Cartagena, Drake at, xxxiii, 148-50, 161-6, 253-61, 268

Carthage, Cato on, ix, 52; city of Dido, xiii, 88, 90; loved by Juno, 76, 91; Machiavelli on destruction of, xxxvi, 19; mercenaries of, 44; More on mercenaries of, 154; Raleigh on, xxxix, 74, 119; Rome

and, xiii, 78-9, 326; schools of, vii, 73-4

Carthagena (see Cartagena)

Carthusian Monks, Pascal on, xlviii, 175 (539)

Carus, Metius, Regulus and, ix, 197; Fannia and, 323

Cartwright, William, ON THE QUEEN'S RETURN, xl, 368

Cary, Henry F., translator of Dante, xx

Casa, Cecchino della, xxxi, 72

Casa, Giovanni della, "book on manners" (*Galateo*), reference to, xvii, 172, 174

Casalodi, Alberto da, xx, 85 note 5

Casarita, Darwin on the, xxix, 107-8

Casati, Father Felice, xxi, 532, 614-17

Casaubon, Isaac, at Oxford, v, 433; on changes, xxxix, 77

Casca, and Cæsar, xii, 329

Cascades, in glaciers, xxx, 232-3, 246

Casella, Dante and, xx, 153 and note 5; Milton on, iv, 83

Cash Credits, in Scotland, x, 247-9, 255-7

Casion, Mount, xxxiii, 81

Casnero River, xxxiii, 373

Caspians, Harrison on the, xxxv, 372

Cassada, Darwin on, xxix, 33

Cassandane, wife of Cyrus, xxxiii, 5

Cassander, Demades and, xii, 224

Cassandra, in AGAMEMNON, viii, 43-55; Apollo and, 49; Corœbus and, xiii, 115, 117; death of, viii, 60; Homer on death of, xxii, 162-3; prophecy of settlement of Italy, xiii, 137; Ruskin on, xxviii, 146; Trojan horse and, xiii, 111

Cassavi, a kind of bread, xxxiii, 157, 247-8

Cassero, Giacopo del, xx, 165 and note 5

Cassero, Guido del, xx, 118 note 8

Cassiodorus, John, on idleness, xxxix, 14

Cassiopeia, reference to, iv, 35

Cassipa, Lake, xxxiii, 371

Cassipagotos, Raleigh on the, xxxiii, 367, 369, 371

Cassius, the consul, in Germany, xxxiii, 117

Cassius, Quintus, xii, 338

Cassius, Roman jurist, ii, 169 (144); ix, 325 note 2

Cassius Longinus, Cæsar and, xii, 321, 326, 329, 342; ix, 170; Cicero on, 153; conduct after Cæsar's death, xii, 262, 344; in Dante's HELL, xx, 144 and note 1; xiii, 17; flight of, xii, 331-2; at Philippi, 349-50, 332

Castagneri, Bortolo, in THE BE-

TROTHED, xxi, 298-301, 452, 563-6, 665

Castalio, Locke on, xxxvii, 75

CASTARA, ROSES IN BOSOM OF, xl, 257-8

CASTAWAY, THE, xli, 553-5

Castello, Guido da, xx, 213 and note 9

Castes, Channing on, xxviii, 355-8; the four Hindu, xlv, 880

Castiglione, Baldassare, the *Courtier* of, xxvii, 172

Castiglione, Valeriano, xxi, 467-8

CASTLE GORDON, vi, 297-8

Castlemaine, Lady, xxviii, 306, 307

Castor and Pollux, Homer on, xxii, 159; in Rome, xii, 154; seamen's term, xxxiii, 305; Virgil on, xiii, 215-16; worshipped in Germany, xxxiii, 120

Castor-berry, cultivated in Egypt, xxxiii, 47

Castoro, Francesco, xxxi, 16-17

Castracani, Castruccio, xxvii, 418

Castration, Harvey on, xxxviii, 116-17

Castriota, John, xlvii, 468 note 9

Castro, Chili, Darwin on, xxix, 295

Castruccio, in DUCHESS OF MALFI, xlvii, 724-5, 737-8, 739, 748, 750, 806

Casualties, of feudal law, x, 529-30

Caswell, E., translator of hymns, xlv, 562, 568

Cat, "turning of the," iii, 62

CAT, ON A FAVOURITE, xl, 473-5

CAT AND Fox, fable of, xvii, 26

CAT-MAIDEN, fable of the, xvii, 44; Bacon on fable of, iii, 102

Catabaptists, Calvin on, xxxix, 47

Cataclysms, Darwin on, xi, 87, 109; Lyell on, xxxviii, 429, 439

Catalano, in Dante's HELL, xx, 98-9

Catamarans, described, xxiii, 26-7

Catastrophes, Pope on, xl, 421-2; require a comic element, xxviii, 183-4

Catastrophism (see Cataclysms)

Catechising, Herbert on, xv, 411

Catechumens, Pascal on, xlviii, 381

Categorical Imperative, Kant on the, xxxii, 345, 350-63, 384-6, 392-3, 395

Categories (see Predicaments)

Caterina, mistress of Cellini, xxxi, 318-22, 326-30, 332

Caterpillars, instincts of, xi, 263

Cates, Thomas, xxxiii, 236, 237

Catesby, and Hastings, xxxix, 79

Cathedrals, Burke on grandeur of old, xxiv, 66; Hugo on mediæval, xxxix, 368; origin of, xxxv, 269

Catherine of Aragon, queen of Henry VIII, xxxvi, 107-10, 119; xxxix, 90

Catholic Church, Roman (see Roman Catholic Church)

Catiline, Lucius, Augustine, St., on, vii, 28; Cicero on, ix, 83, 86; xxvii, 51; conspiracy of, xii, 233-44, 279-80; ix, 3; Pope on, xl, 422; Virgil on, xiii, 294

Catillus, in the ÆNEID, xiii, 266, 378, 384

Cato, Addison's drama of, xxvii, 169, 176-9, 189-90; Dennis on, 196-208; Johnson on, 196-7; Shelley on, 357-8; Voltaire on, xxxiv, 138; xxxix, 238

Cato, Gaius, Cicero on, ix, 100, 102

Cato, Dionysius, alleged author of Caton, xxxix, 16

Cato the Censor, on agriculture, ix, 64-6; x, 358; on Carthage, ix, 52; in Cicero's essay on OLD AGE, 8, 46-77; as club member, 62, 251; conciseness of, 214; on dreams, xl, 38, 39; on enemies and friends, ix, 39; Fabius Maximus and, 48-9; on feeding, x, 159-60; on friendships, ix, 34; Greek literature studied late by, 55; Greek philosophers and, iii, 205; knowledge of herbs, xxxv, 252; Livy on, iii, 105; Locke on, xxxvii, 187; Lucius Flaminus and, ix, 61; old age of, 46, 51, 52, 57, 59, 62-3; on orators, 262; Origins of, 59, 73; quæstorship of, 49; Sidney on, xxvii, 14, 39-40; son of, ix, 10, 77, 175; Virgil on, xiii, 240; the wise, ix, 9, 10; on yeomen, xxxv, 241

Cato of Utica, Burke on, xxiv, 42, 95; Cæsar and, xii, 280-1, 284, 285, 286, 293, 294, 319, 338; Cæsar on, ix, 251; during Catiline conspiracy, xii, 242-3, 280; Cicero and, 244-5, 255, 257, 258-9, 270; Cicero's correspondence with, ix, 140, 158, 159; Cicero on, xxiv, 319; on Cicero, xxxii, 63; in Civil War, xii, 257, 258-9, 310, 317; Dante on, xx, 59, 148-50; death of, xii, 319; ix, 165; indictment for extortion, 120; Pompey and, 101-2; xii, 299; Rousseau on, xxxiv, 232; as a senator, ix, 90, 102; Sidney on, xxvii, 24; Virgil on, xiii, 18, 294

CATON, PROLOGUE TO, xxxix, 15-17

Catorthóseis, defined, ii, 229 (14)

Cats, breeds of, why impossible to improve, xi, 55; correlated variation in, 29, 156; in Egypt, xxxiii, 36-7; flowers dependent on, xi, 88; fruit trees injured by, xxix, 148; inherited mental qualities in, xi, 267; Jenner on, xxxviii, 153; in S. America, xxix, 132

Cattans, Tacitus on the, xxxiii, 112-14, 116

Cattinaro (see Gattinara)

Cattle, color of, its importance, xi, 209; crosses between Indian and common, 305; descent of, 35-6, 44; in old Egypt, xxxiii, 25; in Falkland Islands, xxix, 205-7; forests and, x, 176-7; grass-growth and, xxix, 131; importation of foreign, x, 355-6, 358-9; insects and, xi, 86; as medium of exchange, x, 30; new breeds of, xi, 121; Niata, 230; xxix, 158-60; price of, in relation to agriculture, x, 191-3; recognition among, xxix, 158; trees and, xi, 86; as wealth, x, 327

Catullus, Gaius Valerius, Montaigne on, xxxii, 92; pet-bird of mistress of, xii, 382 note

Catulus, Quintus Lutatius, Cæsar and, xii, 279; in Catiline conspiracy, 280; Clodius and, 250

Catulus, teacher of Aurelius, ii, 195 (13)

Caulfield, Capt., xxxiii, 325, 347, 348, 349, 354, 357, 363, 369, 377, 382, 386

Cauquenes, mineral springs of, xxix, 280-1

Cause and effect, Berkeley on, xxxvii, 205; in divine matters, xxxix, 110-11; Emerson on, v, 88, 94, 294-5; in human affairs, xxxvii, 373-83; Hume on, 325-36, 338-41, 349, 350, 352-3, 356-62, 365-70, 384-5 and note, 392-4, 419-20, 427 note, 429-30, 439-40; Hume's doctrine, Emerson on, v, 456; in ideas, xxxvii, 323, 346, 348; Lowell on, xxviii, 459; Marcus Aurelius on, ii, 221 (45); in matter, xxxvii, 372-3; Raleigh on, xxxix, 105; Shelley on, xxvii, 355

Causes, Berkeley on, xxxvii, 251-2, 273; Browne on, iii, 277 (14); Burke on, xxiv, 108-9; definitions of, xxxvii, 368, 384-5 note; Emerson on, v, 137-8; Hobbes on, xxxiv, 389-92; Hume on ignorance of, xxxvii, 351; Hume on ultimate, 328-9; Hunt on, xxvii, 305; identity of ancient and modern, xxxviii, 405-6, 439-40; as immediate volitions of God, xxxvii, 362-5; Lyell on uniformity of secondary, xxxviii, 406; Socrates on, ii, 90-6; Taine on moral, xxxix, 441; Whewell on, xi, 1

CAUTERETZ, THE VALLEY OF, xlii, 1006

Caution, Confucius on, xliv, 22 (10); Machiavelli on, xxxvi, 86; mountain of, in PILGRIM'S PROGRESS, xv, 126; Penn on, i, 351

Cautions, Penn's personal, i, 364-5

Cava, burial-place of, xiv, 436

Cavalcanti, Cavalcante, Dante on, xx, 42-3

Cavalcanti, Guido, xx, 43 notes 6 and 7, 191 note 5

CAVALIER, SONG OF THE, xxviii, 404

Cavalletti, Scipione, xxxi, 17

Cave, Edward, *Gentleman's Magazine* of, i, 154

Cave-animals, blindness of, xi, 150-2

Cavendish, Henry, on gravitation, xxx, 294-5

Caves, use of, in NEW ATLANTIS, iii, 181-2

Caviare, to the general, xlvi, 128

Cawdor, Thane of, xlvi, 307, 308, 311, 313

Caxton, William, life and works of, xxxix, 5 note; PREFACES AND EPILOGUES, 5-28; remarks on prologues of, 3

Caylen, Darwin on, xxix, 297

Cebes, friend of Socrates, ii, 33; book on virtue, iii, 252 and note; with Socrates in prison (see PHÆDO, Plato's)

Cecidomyia, Darwin on the, xi, 478

Cecil, Sir Robert, dedication to, xxxiii, 311-15

Cecil, William, xxxiii, 237, 256, 267

Cecilia, St., Dryden on, xl, 400, 405-6

CECILIA'S, ST., DAY, SONG FOR, xl, 398-406

Celæno, the Harpy, and Æneas, xiii, 139

Celandine, Wordsworth on the, xli, 629-30

Celano, Thomas à, DIES IRÆ, xlv, 563

Celer, Asinius, surmullet of, x, 190

Celer, friend of Pliny, ix, 320

Celer, Metellus, origin of name, xii, 162; wife of, 250

Celer, Roman knight, ix, 266

Celestial city, in PILGRIM'S PROGRESS, xv, 159

CELESTIAL SURGEON, THE, xlii, 1261

Celestine V, Dante on, xx, 14-15 note 3, 115 note 14

CELIA, by Sedley, xl, 393

CELIA, To, by Jonson, xl, 298-9

Celibacy, Calvin on, xxxix, 40; Luther on, xxxvi, 318-21; vows of, 317 note

Cellini, Andrea, xxxi, 8-9, 10

Cellini, Benvenuto, accident to eye, xxxi, 388-9; Alessandro de' Medici and, 155, 156, 163-67, 179, 181; Altoviti, bust of, 399-400, 401; Angelica, the Sicilian, and, 132-3, 134, 141-2, 143-4; Anguillara, Count, and, 56-7; "Apollo and Hyacinth" of, 387-8; arabesques of, 62-3; arms of, 108; in artists' club, 57-62; Ascanio, servant of, 193-6, 197, 222-3, 269, 273, 276, 289, 290, 291, 317, 341, 350, 351, 363, 366; AUTOBIOGRAPHY of, 5-454; AUTOBIOGRAPHY of, remarks

on, 1-2; Baldini and, 415-16; Bandinello and, 380, 381, 383-7; banishment of, 16-17; Benedetto and, 138-9; Benintendi and, 157-60; birth and family, 6-10; bronze statues, first, 301-3; brother of, 16, 20; brother's death, 102-10; CAPITOLO ON THE PRISON, 263-8; Caterina and, 318-22, 326-30, 332; Charles V and, 186, 188-9; childhood of, 10-11; "Christ" of, 435, 437, 452 and note; Clement, Pope, early relations with, 17, 42, 46-7, 76, 79-80, 81-3; Clement, in service of, 90-100, 102, 108, 110-22, 124-32, 139, 141, 146-8; coin designs by, 98-9, 102, 152, 163, 323, 326; Comte de Saint Paul and, 347-8; Cosimo de' Medici and, 356-65, 369-70, 372-83, 387-94, 395-9, 402-9, 412-15, 416-21, 423-5, 427-39, 447-9, 452-4; country-house at Trespiano, 441 note; daughter by Jeanne Scorzone, 332-3; dog of, 111, 115, 183, 239-40; escape from prison, 225-32; Étampes, Mme. d', and, 305, 306, 309-11, 313-14, 323, 336-7, 339-40, 343-4; Farnese, Pier, and, 354-5; Faustina's maid and, 54-5; in Ferrara, 280-5; Ferrara, Cardinal, and, 210-11, 269-74, 287-8; fever in Florence, 393-5; Fontainebleau, work at, 301, 307, 308-9, 314, 332; France, journey to, 196-204; in France, 204-6, 286-7, 291-4, 312-13, 315-17, 337-8, 340, 349-52; France, queen of, and, 453-4; Francis First and, 205, 210-11, 217, 222, 260, 272, 281, 286-7, 290-309, 312, 323, 326, 330-1, 333-49, 363, 365-7, 390; Giovanni Gaddi and, 101, 116, 139-40, 167, 171-3, 175; Galluzzi and, 261-2; Gambetta and, 370-1; Giacomo da Carpi and, 53-4; Guasconti and, 29-34; Guidi and, 311-12; halo of, 262; Holy Land, intentions to visit, 289-90; Il Bologna and, 323-6, 327-8; imprisonment of, 212-32; imprisonment, second, 237-61; at the inn, 161-3; Jeanne Scorzone and, 332; Julius III and, 401; "Jupiter" of, 291, 294, 301, 339-40; pedestal for "Jupiter," 305, 338, 346; "Jupiter," exhibition of, 338-40; life after 1562, 2; Lippi, Francesco, and, 25, 29; Lo Sbietta and, 440-6, 447-8, 449-51; Lucagnolo and, 37-9; Luigi Pulci and, 65-71; "Mars" of, 308, 323 note 2, 340-2, 346; medals by, 47, 50, 64, 88-90, 132, 145-6, 164, 181-2, 197-8, 280; Medici, Cardinal de, and, 145; Michael Angelo and, 25, 88-9, 400, 402; minor works, 25, 27-8, 29, 35, 36, 43-4, 53, 63-4, 94-8,

108, 117, 124-5, 187, 189-91, 269-72, 291, 301; mistress in Rome, 111; monument to brother, 107-8; Moro's daughter and, 100-2; musical training, 11, 12, 13, 15, 18, 22-3, 40-1; musician to the Pope, 41-3; "Narcissus" of, 388; necromancy, practised by, 133-7; "Neptune" of, 432-9, 441, 445, 446, 452-3; Pantasilea and, 58; Pascucci and, 209-10; Paul, Pope, and, 151-3, 165, 170-1, 186-8, 191-3, 211-12, 216-18, 222, 223, 232-3, 235-6, 237-8, 242, 249-50, 254, 255-6, 260-1; Paulino, boy of, 41, 43-4; "Perseus" of, 357 notes 3 and 4, 363-4, 369-70, 373-4, 389, 390-4, 395-9, 414, 416-20, 423-6, 427-30; pilgrimage of thanksgiving, 421-2; Pompeo and, 126, 131, 139, 141, 148-50; Pompeo's daughter and, 153-5; Porzia Chigi and, 35-7, 38, 40, 47; prophecies of, 183-5, 262; pulpit for S. Maria del Fiore, 431; reliquary for Mantua, 86; restorations by, 382-3, 388, 389-90, 412-14; robbery of, attempted, 298-300; in Rome, 25-9, 34-5, 181-3, 399-402; among Roman ruins, 51, 52; in sack of Rome, 71-83, 215-16; Salamanca, Bishop of, and, 35, 40, 43-7; in Siena, trouble with postmaster, 274-8; in Siennese war, 409-11, 422-3; sick with plague, 55-6; sister of, 85, 278, 355-6; soldier of Ceri and, 48-9; son of, 380-1; SONNET ON HIS LIFE, 3; SONNET TO CASTELLAN, 255; Taine on memoirs of, xxxix, 460; Torrigiani, relations with, xxxi, 23-5; Vasari and, 179-81; in Venice, 155-60, 371-2

Cellini, Cecchino, brother of Benvenuto, xxxi, 15-16, 20, 87-8, 92 note 1; Dargello guard and, 102-5; death of, 106-7, duel and exile, 16, 17; monument, 107-8

Cellini, Cosa, xxxi, 85

Cellini, Cristofano, xxxi, 8

Cellini, Giovanfrancesco (see Cellini, Cecchino)

Cellini, Giovanni, father of Benvenuto, xxxi, 8-14, 15, 17, 19, 20, 21, 22-3, 33-4, 40-1, 43, 84-5; death of, 87; the Eight and, 40, 84; the Medici and, 92 note; Pierino and, 18-20

Cellini, Liperata, xxxi, 87-8, 174, 355-6, 364

Cellini, Luca, xxxi, 7

Cellino, Fiorino da, xxxi, 6

Celsus, Aulus Cornelius, Bacon on, iii, 86; Milton on, 253 note 33; on care of stomach, ix, 371 note

Celsus, governor of Cilicia, xxviii, 62

Celsus, the philosopher, Pascal on, xlviii, 198 (597), 274 (770)

Celtchar, the Luin of, xlix, 253

CELTIC RACES, POETRY OF THE, xxxii, 141-191

Celtic Races, Christianity and, xxxii, 178-90; Emerson on the, v, 351, 355; future of, xxxii, 190-1; Herodotus on the, xxxiii, 21; literature of the, xxxii, 148-78; mythology of, 160-2; Renan on character of the, 143-50

Cemetery Ridge, at Gettysburg, xliii, 358

CENCI, THE, by Shelley, xviii, 281-353; editorial remarks on, 272; story of the, 275-6

Cenci, Beatrice, arrest of, xviii, 332-5; assassins and, 324-8; at banquet, 289-93; Bernardo and, 352-3; Camillo and, 282; Count Cenci and, 285, 296-7, 307-11, 319-23; condemned to death, 350-3; Giacomo and, 314-15; Lucretia and, 294-6, 329-31; madness of, 303-7; Orsino and, 285-7, 307-11; portrait of, by Guido, 279; in prison, 344-8; Shelley on character of, 279; trial of, 338-43

Cenci, Bernardo, Beatrice and, xviii, 294-6, 344-7, 352-3; Count Cenci and, 297, 320, 330-1; Lucretia and, 293-6; Pope and, 349

Cenci, Cristofano, sent to Salamanca, xviii, 285; death announced, 289-90

Cenci, Count Francesco, banquet of, xviii, 288-93; Beatrice and, 285, 295, 296-7, 318-24; Cardinal Camillo and, 281-4; chapel built by, 278; Lucretia and, 297-8, 318-20; murdered, 326-8; plots against, 310-14, 317-18

Cenci, Giacomo, accused by Marzio, xviii, 338; Beatrice and, 314-15, 343-8, 351; Camillo and, 299-300, Orsino and, 300-2, 312-18, 335-7

Cenci, Lucretia, accused by Marzio, xviii, 338; arrest of, 332-4; at the banquet, 289; Beatrice and, 294-6, 303-11, 324-8, 329-31, 345-8, 351; Bernardo and, 293-4; Count Cenci and, 297-8, 318-23; remarks on religion of, 278

Cenci, Rocco, son of Francesco, xviii, 285, 289-90

Cenci Palace, Shelley on, xviii, 279-80

Cennini, Bastiano, xxxi, 165

Censorinus, Plutarch on, xii, 152

CENSORIOUS CRITIC, BURNS'S REPLY TO A, vi, 290

Censoriousness, Burns on, vi, 192-4; Kempis on, vii, 253 (1, 2); Jesus on, xliv, 375 (41-2); Locke on, xxxvii, 130; M. Aurelius on, ii, 294, 301 (12); Molière on, xxvi, 204-5; Penn on, i, 342-3,

363 (274), 414; Raleigh on, xxxix, 72; Sidney on, xxvii, 33-4
Censors, duties of Roman, ix, 419 note 2
Censorship, Milton on government, iii, 217-21
Censorship of Press, Milton on, iii, 202-44; Pascal on, xlviii, 319-20
Censure, Browne on, iii, 331; Heminge and Condell on, xxxix, 155; man's dislike of, ii, 141 (67); Marcus Aurelius on endurance of, 195 (13), 273 (27), 275 (34); Pascal on human dislike of, xlviii, 44-5
Census (U. S.), provisions for taking, xliii, 193 (3)
Centano, Andrea, xxxi, 237, 238
Centaurs, beginning of their feud with men, xxii, 303; in Dante's HELL, xx, 51-2; Theseus and, 247 note
Centralization, Mill on, xxv, 125-6, 320-5
Cephalos, the Attic boy, iv, 38
Cephas, Peter called, xx, 378 note 16; Christ's appearance to, xlv, 522 (4)
Cephisophon, in THE FROGS, viii, 464
Cerbaia, Orso da, xx, 168 note 6
Cerbellon, Gabriel, xiv, 407
Cerberus, Æneas and, xiii, 225; in Dante's HELL, xx, 25-6; Hercules and, 39 and note
Cerchi, Veri de', head of Bianchi faction, xx, 27 note 4
Cerealis, letter to, ix, 236
Ceremonies, Browne on religious, iii, 267 (3); Confucius on, xliv, 9 (4), 11 (15); Hume on religious, xxxvii, 346-7; Locke on excess of, 132-3; Luther on religious, xxxvi, 392-7; Montaigne on, xviii, 12-13; Pascal on religious, xlviii, 92 (250-2); Penn on religious, i, 380-1 (507), 405 (175); Rousseau on religions, xxxiv, 291-2, 312-13; Shakespeare on, xlvi, 193 note 35, 341; lead to superstition, iii, 48; Swift on, xxvii, 107-8
CEREMONIES, ESSAY ON, Bacon's, iii, 131-2
Ceres, daughter of (see Proserpine); Proserpine and, iv, 164; in THE TEMPEST, xlvi, 426
Ceri, Rienzo da, xxxi, 48 note 2, 73
Ceroxylus Laceratus, xi, 236
Certainty, Descartes on, xxxiv, 29; impossibility of, xlviii, 29, 129 (387), 150 (437); Pascal on, 87 (234)
Certus, Publicius, ix, 357-60
Cervantes, Miguel de, author of DON QUIXOTE, xiv; captivity of, 413; Galatea of, 57; Hugo on, xxxix, 369; life and works of,

xiv, 3-4; Sainte-Beuve on, xxxii, 137
Cervolles, Arnaud de, xxxv, 39 note 4, 48, 49
Cesano, Gabriel, 270 note 3, xxxi, 271, 272
Ceserino, Gabbriello, xxxi, 47
Cessation, the trance of, xlv, 747-53
Cethegus, Caius, in Catiline conspiracy, xii, 279-80, 238, 240; executed, 243, 251
Cethegus, Marcus, old age of, ix, 64
Ceylon, slavery not practised in, xxxv, 239 note
Chacao, Chili, xxix, 292
Chachidiablo, on Don Quixote, xiv, 542
Chærephon, Plato on, ii, 7
Chæronea, Demosthenes at battle of, xii, 213; iv, 81
Chafing Gear, defined, xxiii, 19
Chagos Islands, xxix, 504
Chagres, river, xxxiii, 148
Chalk Formations, Darwin on, xi, 373
Chalmers, on the public, xxviii, 130
CHALMERS, WILLIE: a song, vi, 238-9
Chalybe, priestess of Juno, xiii, 258
Chalybes, the, viii, 180 and note 43
Cham, Amalthea and, iv, 164
Chama, shells of the, xxix, 485
Chamavians, Tacitus on, xxxiii, 114
CHAMBERED NAUTILUS, THE, xlii, 1442
Chamberland, THE GERM THEORY, xxxviii, 283, 382-9
Chamisso, on coral islands, xxix, 492; on seeds, 480; on transported stones, 487
Chamois Hunter, in MANFRED, xviii, 412-17
Chamois Hunter, song of, in WILHELM TELL, xxvi, 370-1
Chamouni, glacier of, xxx, 227-30, 232-3
CHAMOUNI, HYMN IN THE VALE OF, xli, 724-6
Champlain, Lake, naval forces on, xliii, 284
Chance, in Chaos, iv, 133-5; Emerson on, v, 88; Hume on, xxxvii, 351, 384; Pope on, xl, 425; providence in, iii, 281-3; Sophocles on, viii, 279; in thoughts, xxxix, 125
Chancellorsville, Haskell on, xliii, 348
Chandos, Sir John, in French invasion, xxxv, 178; Lord Clermont and, 41; at Crecy, 23; at Poitiers, 43, 46, 53
Ch'ang-chü, Confucius on, xliv, 63 (6)
Change, Carlyle on, xxv, 366-8; Confucius on, xliv, 55 (36), 59 (3); dread of, v, 99; Emerson on,

xliii, 1312; Goethe on, xxxix, 272;
Hooker on, 195; the law of the
universe, ii, 220 (36), 221 (42,
43), 248 (18, 19, 23), 249 (25),
251 (47), 257 (6), 272 (19),
280 (7), 282 (11), 283 (18), vi,
537; xxix, 521; Lowell on, xlii,
1465-6; Lyell on uniformity of,
xxxviii, 419-40; Marcus Aurelius
on, ii, 201 (3), 214 (3); Pascal
on, pleasure of, xlviii, 122 (355);
Shakespeare on, xl, 280; tendency
to, xi, 257-8, 317; Tennyson on,
xlii, 1025 (see also Innovation,
Vicissitude)
Changelings, legerdemain of, iii,
295
Channa, charioteer of Buddha, xlv,
659
Channing, Dr., on puerperal fever,
xxxviii, 264
Channing, Edward T., cousin of R.
H. Dana, xxiii, 420-1
Channing, William Ellery, Coleridge
on, v, 331; life and character of,
xxviii, 318; ON THE LABORING
CLASSES, 319-80
CHANSON DE ROLAND, xlix, 95-208;
Arnold on, xxviii, 71-2
Chanticleer, in NUN'S PRIEST'S TALE,
xl, 35-51
Chao, Duke, xliv, 24 (30) note 8
Chao of Sung, xliv, 20 (14)
Chaos, Descartes on, under natural
laws, xxxiv, 36-7; Milton's description of, iv, 133-5
Chapelain, Jean, Corneille and,
xxxix, 381; Dryden on, xiii, 13
Chapman, George, Arnold on, xxviii,
82; Dryden on, xiii, 64; on man,
v, 182
CHAPMAN'S HOMER, ON FIRST LOOK-
ING INTO, xli, 919-20
Character, beauty and, v, 320;
Browne on outward signs of, iii,
326-7; circumstances and, xxv,
110-11; concealment of, impossible, v, 295-6; consistency of, 70-
1; culture and, xxxii, 250-1, 269;
discernment of, v, 147-8; education and natural, xxxvii, 47-8;
force of, cumulative, v, 71; influence of, in our civilization, 259;
Locke on the native, xxxvii, 89-
90; maker of its own forms, v,
214; M. Aurelius on, ii, 218 (28),
292 (15); Mill on, xxv, 265; the
supreme end, v, 258; talent and,
contrasted, 165-6
CHARACTER, ESSAY ON, Emerson's, v,
191-205
CHARACTERISTICS, Carlyle's, xxv, 333-
71; remarks on, 332
Charaxos, and Rhodopis, xxxiii, 68,
69
Charcoal, combustion of, xxx, 165-6
Charesha, island of, xxxiii, 149, 161

CHARGE OF THE LIGHT BRIGADE,
Tennyson's, xlii, 1039
Charity, Bacon on, iii, 34-5, 95;
xxxix, 135; Browne on, iii, 324,
326, 328, 345; Dante on, xx, 207-
8, 396-8; Dante's allegory of, 268
note 11; Dante's star of, 179 note
9; David on, xliv, 196-7; Emerson
on popular, v, 67; Emerson on
relating our, 134; Herbert on, xv,
413; Hobbes's definition of, xxxiv,
354; Kempis on works of, vii,
227; Luther on, xxxvi, 262, 268;
method of, iii, 268; Milton on,
iv, 360; More on, xxxvi, 210;
offences against, iii, 329-31; Pascal on, xlviii, 191, 224 (663, 665),
279 (793), 280-1; Paul, St., on,
xlv, 519 (1-13); Penn on, i, 343-
4, 377 (469-70), 415-16; pleasure
from, xix, 38; Pope on, xl, 441,
450; pure and sentimental, xviii,
178
Charity, in PILGRIM'S PROGRESS, xv,
55-6
Charity, Mount, xv, 295
Charixenus, and Endamidas, xxxii,
83
Charlatanism, Arnold on, xxviii, 66
Charlemagne, and the Church, xx,
310; in Dante's PARADISE, 363;
division of empire of, iii, 146;
extinction of race of, xxxix, 84;
at Fontarabbia, iv, 105; HYMN
attributed to, xlv, 559; one of
nine worthies, xxxix, 22; the
Northmen and, v, 355; in Spain,
xlix, 96
Charlemagne, in SONG OF ROLAND,
xlix, 96
Charles I, of Anjou, abilities of, xx,
175 note 11; Conradine and, 117
note 3, 229 note 10; Machiavelli
on success of, xxxvi, 43; Nicholas, Pope, and, xx, 82 note 9;
Thomas Aquinas and, 229 note
11; victories in Italy, 68 note 1,
117 notes; wife of, 176 note 14
Charles I, of England ("martyr"),
controversy over, iv, 5; Drake to,
xxxiii, 129; on English law, v,
439; execution of, place of, xxxix,
377-8; fondness for plays, xxxiv,
156; Harvey and, xxxviii, 64;
Marvell on death of, xl, 382-3;
Milton on, xxviii, 194; Swift on
reign of, xxvii, 104; Vane on,
xliii, 129-30, 134; Voltaire on,
xxxiv, 88
Charles II, of England, Emerson
on, v, 418; Hobbes and, xxxiv,
318; Milton on restoration of, iv,
5; Presbyterians and, xxxiv, 82;
Puritans and, xxvii, 146-7;
Quakers and, xxxiv, 74; Shelley
on drama under, xxvii, 358; Waller and, xxxiv, 149

CHARLES II, EPITAPH ON, xl, 392
Charles II of Naples, Dante on, xx, 176 note 13, 229 note 14, 311 note 24, 369 note 11
Charles V, Emperor, Adrian, Pope, and, xxxvi, 106; Clement VII and, xxxi, 119 note 5; on Eraso, xv, 331; France, passage of, through, xxxi, 335 and note; at Landresy, xxxviii, 17; Luther on, xxxvi, 260, 276; melancholy of, iii, 51; at Metz, xxxviii, 24, 27, 29-30, 32; More, Thomas, on, xxxvi, 140-1; the Netherlands and, xix, 246; Raleigh on, xxxix, 90-1; Rome, visit of, to, xxxi, 186-9; Ruysum in EGMONT on, xix, 249; Seldius and, xxxix, 95-6; at Therouenne, xxxviii, 35, 45; in triumvirate of kings, iii, 52; Valdesso and, xv, 418-19; war with Francis I, xxxi, 71 note, 342 note 1, 348 note 1; wealth of, xxxiii, 318
Charles V, in DR. FAUSTUS, xix, 226, 229-32
Charles VI of France, Duke of Gueldres and, xxxv, 104-5; Voltaire on wars under, xxxiv, 88
Charles VII, organizes national army, xxxvi, 49
Charles IX of France, in Bayonne, xxxviii, 52; at Bourges, 48; at Havre de Grace, 51; Navarre, King of, and, 50; Paré and, 51, 52, 53-4, 55; Raleigh on, xxxix, 87; Voltaire on reign of, xxxiv, 88
Charles, Duke of Alençon, xxxv, 26, 28, 30
Charles of Almaine, in Crecy campaign, xxxv, 10, 28
Charles the Bald, son of Debonnaire, xxxix, 86
Charles of Burgundy, secrecy of, iii, 72
Charles the Fat, xxxix, 86
Charles of Lorraine, xx, 228 note 7
Charles of Luxembourg, at Crecy, xxxv, 27-8
Charles Martel, king of Hungary, xx, 317-21
Charles the Simple, xxxix, 86-7
Charles of Valois, and the empire, xx, 311 note 24; in Florentine troubles, 27 note 8, 229 note 12
Charles, Elizabeth, translator, xlv, 572
Charles, Mr., agent of Pennsylvania, i, 166, 169
Charles Island, Galapagos group, xxix, 397-8
Charles's Wain (see Wain)
CHARLES, KING, HERE'S A HEALTH TO, xli, 773
CHARLIE, HE'S MY DARLING, vi, 522
CHARLIE IS MY DARLING, xli, 579-80

CHARMING MONTH OF MAY, vi, 539
Charmion, maid of Cleopatra, xii, 382; death of, 402
Charmion, in ALL FOR LOVE, xviii, 37-8, 68, 70, 84, 85, 95, 96-9
Charms, Burns on immortal, vi, 305; origin of term, xxvii, 11
Charny, Sir Geoffrey, xxxv, 52
CHARON, THE REFUSAL OF, xli, 943-4
Charon, Æneas and, xiii, 224-5; Dante on, xx, 15-16; description of, xiii, 221-2; Dirce and, xli, 924; reference to, viii, 423
Charon, in THE FROGS, viii, 424-5, 427
Charondas, iii, 255 note 46
Charron, Montaigne and, xxxii, 109; Pascal on, xlviii, 23 (62); on reason, xxxix, 104; on religious creeds, xxxiv, 293 note
Chartel, Capt., xxxviii, 19
Chartism, and the Times, v, 466
Chartist Day, nobility on, v, 424
Charybdis, and Circe's song, iv, 53; description of, xiii, 144-5; Ulysses at, xxii, 175, 180
Chase, Mohammed on the, xlv, 1008, 1018; Pascal on the, xlviii, 53; value of the, to princes, xxxvi, 51
Chassoygnet, the tree, xxxix, 13
Chaste women, often forward, iii, 23
Chastillon, M. de, xxxviii, 19
Chastisement of children, xxxvii, 36, 37-9, 40-1, 42, 43, 59, 64-6, 69-71, 99-100
Chastisements of heaven, Woolman on, i, 246-7
Chastity, beauty and, xlvi, 136; Franklin's rule of, i, 84; Jonson on, xl, 303; Pascal on, xlviii, 129 (385); Paul, St., on, xlv, 510 (25-6); "she that has," iv, 57-8; spirit of, in NEW ATLANTIS, iii, 177; sun-clad power of, iv, 67; "unblemished form of," 52
Chasuarians, Tacitus on the, xxxiii, 114
Château le Comte, xxxviii, 22-3
Chateaubriand, Carlyle on, xxv, 442; on criticism, xxxix, 405-6; Taine on, 437
Chateauneuf, John of, xxxv, 99, 103
Chatelet, court of, Burke on, xxiv, 357
Chatham Island, Darwin on, xxix, 395-7
Chatham, Lord, better than his speeches, v, 191; on confidence, 385; and the dictionary, 175; reference to, 71
Chatterton, Hazlitt on, xxvii, 292; SAXON POEMS of, xxxix, 346; Shelley on, xli, 890; SONG FROM ÆLLA, xli, 571-2; Wordsworth on, 675
Chaucer, Geoffrey, Arnold, Matthew,

on, xxviii, 77-81; Boccaccio and, xxxix, 179-80; CANTERBURY TALES, PROLOGUE TO, xl, 11-34; Caxton on, xxxix, 19-21; Dido, his picture of, v, 287; Dryden on, xxxix, 161, 162, 167-80; Emerson on, v, 149, 188, 450; Froissart and, xxxv, 4, on good blood, v, 182-3; Hazlitt on, xxvii, 285-6; NUN'S PRIEST'S TALE, xl, 35-51; Ovid, compared with, xxxix, 161, 167-9; reference to, iv, 37-8; Ruskin on, xxviii, 146; Shakespeare and, xxxix, 241; Shelley on, xxvii, 367; Sidney on, 9, 45; sources of his tales, xxxix, 167-8, 180; Thoreau on, xxviii, 426; Wordsworth on, xxxix, 347; Wordsworth on language of, 286 note

Chaucians, Tacitus on the, xxxiii, 115

Chaumber, Christopher, xlii, 1208

Chaurias, ii, 262

Chaussier, on puerperal fever, xxxviii, 260

Cheagle, John, i, 190

Cheating, impossibility of, v, 103

Chebar, Milton on, iv, 25 (6)

Checks and Balances, Washington on, xliii, 259-60

Check, Sir John, Milton on, iv, 82

CHEER UP, MY MATES, xl, 375

Cheerfulness, in music, xli, 490; Penn on, i, 351 (119); in prosperity, no credit, vii, 258 (1)

Cheiron, and Prometheus, viii, 191 note 69

Chemical affinity, capacity of, to do work, xxx, 210-14; converted to heat and light, 59, 211, 212; correlation with electricity, 76-84, 212-14; defined, 47; illustrations of, 47-59; measurement of, 218

CHEMICAL HISTORY OF A CANDLE, xxx, 89-178

Chemistry, Huxley on study of, xxviii, 230

Chemmis, island of, xxxiii, 80-1; worship of Perseus in, 44-5

Chemos, description of, iv, 100

Ch'en Ch'eng, xliv, 49 (22)

Ch'en Wen, xliv, 17

Chenab, sediment of the, xxxviii, 424

Chénier, Marie-Joseph, on reason, xxxii, 130

Cheops, king of Egypt, xxxiii, 64-5

Chephren, king of Egypt, xxxiii, 65-6

Cherbourg, taking of, by Edward III, xxxv, 8, 9 note

Chernubles, in SONG OF ROLAND, xlix, 131, 143

Cherries, Locke on eating of, xxxvii, 21

CHERRY-RIPE, by Campion, xl, 290-1

CHERRY-RIPE, by Herrick, xl, 243

Cherubim, the, in Heaven, iv, 41, 11 (11)

Cherubino, Mæstro, xxxi, 273, 276, 277, 278

Cheruscans, Tacitus on the, xxxiii, 116

Chess, among Mohammedans, xlv, 1018 note 12

Chesterfield, Lord, Johnson's letter to, xxxix, 216-17, 191 note; lines ascribed to, 324; on truth in gentlemen, v, 389

Cheucau, Darwin on the, xxix, 305-6, 296

CHEVALIER'S LAMENT, THE, vi, 322

CHEVY CHASE, xl, 94-102; Johnson on, xxvii, 210

Chi, Confucius on the, xliv, 9 (1, 6), 21 (22), 36 (16), 56 (1)

Chi Huan, xliv, 63 (4)

Chi K'ang, xliv, 8 (20), 19 (6), 34 (6), 41 (17) note (18, 19), 49 (20)

Ch'i-tiao K'ai, xliv, 15 (5)

Chi Tzu-ch'eng, xliv, 39 (8)

Chi Tzu-jan, xliv, 36 (23)

Chi Wen, xliv, 17 (19)

Chiana, river, xx, 122 note 2, 341

Chicheley, Henry, xxxv, 402

Chicken-pox, and smallpox, xxxviii, 182

Chicken Cholera, Pasteur on, xxxviii, 393

Chickens, counting, before they're hatched, xvii, 43; Harvey on incubation of, xxxviii, 88-9; 90-1; incubation of, 135; instinctive fears of, xi, 269-70

Chiding of children, Locke on, xxxvii, 43, 44-5, 51, 63-4, 67, 96, 100

Chidley, Mr., on Dr. Donne, xv, 347-8

Chief Justice, presides at impeachment of president, xliii, 194 (6)

Chieh-yü, xliv, 63 (5)

Chieh-ni, xliv, 63 (6)

Chien, Duke, xliv, 49 (22) note

Chigi, Agostino, xxxi, 35 note 4

Chigi, Porzia, and Cellini, xxxi, 35-40, 47

Chih, music-master, xliv, 27 (15)

Chilaway, Job, i, 275

Child, is father to the man, xli, 615

CHILD, ON A NEW-BORN, xli, 593

CHILD OF QUALITY, TO A, xl, 406-7

CHILD'S GRACE, A, xl, 343

Childbirth, Browne on curse of, iii, 273 (10); Holmes on, xxxviii, 255-6, 264-6; Pasteur on, 400-1

Childeric III, xx, 228 note 7

Childhood, intimations of immortality in, xli, 609-15; shows the man, iv, 405; wisdom sends us to, xlviii, 98 (271)

Children, Arabian proverb on, xvi, 359; Bacon on, iii, 22; xl, 359; confidence of, v, 65; Confucius on, xliv, 5 (6); Dante on, and parents, xx, 319-20; De Quincey on griefs of, xxvii, 336; fable on training of, xvii, 28-9; Goethe on fashioning of, xix, 360; ingratitude of, Lear on, xlvi, 225, 226, 254; Jesus on, 407 (15-17); liberties of, in Massachusetts, xliii, 82; Locke on training of, xxxvii, 9-195; memory's voices, viii, 92; Mill on control of, xxv, 314; misfortune made harder by, vi, 234; Montaigne on, and parents, xxxii, 75-7; Penn on training of, i, 402-3; the Psalmist on, xliv, 315 (3-5); in Utopia, xxxvi, 194, 195, 197-8, 203

CHILDREN, by Longfellow, xlii, 1331-2

CHILDREN, DEATHS OF LITTLE, xxvii, 299-303

CHILDREN, INSTITUTION AND EDUCATION OF, xxxii, 29-73

CHILDREN AND PARENTS, Bacon's ESSAY ON, iii, 20-1

CHILDREN'S HOUR, THE, xlii, 1347-8

Chile, climate of, xxix, 261; Darwin on, 269-383; horses in, 166-7; Lyell on earthquakes in, xxxviii, 410; Pretty on coast of, xxxiii, 216-17

Chileus the Arcadian, xii, 10

Chillingworth, Locke on, xxxvii, 170

CHILLON, ON THE CASTLE OF, xli, 832

CHILLON, THE PRISONER OF, xli, 821-31

Chiloe, climate and productions of, xxix, 260; Darwin on, 290-8, 309-15; orchard-making in, 316

Chimæra, reference to, xiii, 221

Chimæra, statue called, xxxi, 412

Chimango, Darwin on the, xxix, 66-8

Chimborazo, Emerson on, v, 170-1

Chimneys, in Elizabethan England, xxxv, 313

China, ancient government of, xliv, 68 note 1; ancient ordnance in, iii, 146; ancient, selection in, xi, 48; ancient shipping of, iii, 165; cause of early civilization of, x, 27-8; inoculation in, xxxiv, 99; law against visitors in, iii, 169, 170; Mill on unprogressiveness of, xxv, 277-8; Pascal on history of, xlviii, 197-8; Smith on conditions in, x, 75-6; state of wealth of, 100-1, 309; women of, xxxvii, 16

CHINESE SACRED WRITINGS, xliv, 5-69

Ching, Duke, xliv, 40 (11), 44 (8), 58 (12), 63 (3)

Chioccia, Bartolommeo, xxxi, 317, 326

Chionis Alba, xxix, 106-7

Chiostra, Ulivieri della, xxxi, 21-2

Chiromancy, Browne on, iii, 327; Jonson on, xlvii, 537

Chiron, iii, 320; with the Argonauts, xxxiv, 132; the Centaur, xxxvi, 60; in Dante's HELL, xx, 52; his refusal of immortality, xxxii, 27

Chironomus, asexual reproduction of, xi, 478-9

Chiu, Duke, xliv, 48 (17) note

Chivalry, Burke on age of, xxiv, 224-5; Cervantes on books of, xiv, 498-503, 507, 512-14; Don Quixote's defence of, 514-21; examples of romances of, 51-8; order of, for girls and boys, xxviii, 162 note; Renan on origin of, xxxii, 166-7; romances of, parodied by Cervantes, xiv, 3, 12; Ruskin on, xxviii, 147-8 (see also Knight-errantry)

Chlorate of potash, experiments with, xxx, 53-4

Chloreus, the priest, xiii, 388-9

Chloride of calcium, experiment with, xxx, 54 note 18

Chloris, in Hades, xxii, 159

Chloris, sonnets to, xiv, 348-9

CHLORIS, ON, vi, 532

CHLORIS BEING ILL, vi, 569

CHLORIS, INSCRIPTION TO, vi, 579

CHLORIS, Sedley's, xl, 392

Choaspes, river, iv, 395

Chochilaicus, Danish king, xlix, 3

CHŒPHORÆ (see LIBATION-BEARERS)

Choiseul, Duke de, Burke on estate of, xxiv, 262

Choler, Bacon on, iii, 98

Chonos Archipelago, Darwin on, xxix, 298-308

Chorazin, Jesus on, xliv, 387 (13)

Chorus, the, in tragedy, iv, 417

Chorus of Captive Women (see LIBATION-BEARERS, viii)

Chorus, of Danites (see SAMSON AGONISTES, iv)

Chorus of Frogs (see FROGS, THE, viii)

Chorus of Trozenian Women (see HIPPOLYTUS, viii)

Chorus of Furies (see FURIES, THE, viii)

Chorus of Huntsmen (see HIPPOLYTUS, viii)

Chorus of Initiated Persons (see FROGS, THE, viii)

Chorus of Inspired Damsels (see BACCHÆ, THE, viii)

Chorus of Old Men (see AGAMEMNON, viii)

Chorus of Priests and Suppliants (see ŒDIPUS THE KING, viii)

Chorus of Theban Elders (see AN-TIGONE, viii)

Chou, Chinese dynasty, xliv, 9 note 9, 11 (14)

Chou, Duke of, xliv, 22 (5) note, 26 (11), 65 (10, 11)

Chou, Emperor, xliv, 63 note 1, 67 (20), 68 (1) note, 69 note

Chriemhild (see Grimhild)

Christ, Arnold on, xlii, 1184-5; Augustine, St., on, vii, 57-8, 78, 113, 119-20, 205-6; Bacon on prophecy of, iii, 96; Bunyan on, xv, 56-7, 215-19, 289; Calvin on, xxxix, 52-3; Church doctrine of, xlviii, 333; Clement, St., on, xlv, 553-4; the "Counsellor," iii, 55; Dante on, xx, 313-15, 341 note 6; in Dante's PARADISE, 384-7; as David's son, xliv, 414 (41-4); genealogies of, 193-4; Greek Hymn on, xlv, 553; Hell visited by, xx, 36 note, 51 note; Herbert on, xv, 406; Hugo on, xxxix, 360; Jewish rejection of, xlviii, 271 (760-2); Jews in NEW ATLANTIS on, iii, 176; John the Baptist on, xliv, 366 (15-17); Keble on, xlv, 579; the kingdom of, xxxvi, 290; Lessing on, xxxii, 207-9, 212; Luther on, xxxvi, 363, 365, 376-7; Luther on belief in, 364-6, 368, 370-2, 373-5, 377; Moses's prophecy of, xliv, 444 (37); Niceta of Remisiana on, xlv, 558; Pascal on, 158 (466), 163 (483), 169 (512), 173 (526-8), 176 (543, 545-54), 185, 186, 198 (596), 199 (599-600), 201 (607, 609), 224 (665), 225 (666, 668), 226 (670), 230-1, 272 (764-74), 275 (776), 276 (780, 781-5), 281 (794-7), 282 (800), 289 (822), 301 (846), 337-9, 354-5; Paul, St., on, xxxvi, 386; Penn on, i, 376 (456), Platonists on, vii, 112-13; proofs of, 265-83; prophecies of, xlviii, 189-92, 205, 206 (616-17), 208-9, 218, 219 (644), 222 (656), 223 (659), 224 (662), 226 (670), 236, 239 (701, 706), 240 (707-12), 248 (715), 249 (720), 252, 256-64, 265-6, 267 (744), 268 (749), 269 (751-8, 761), 292, 298; Quakers on, i, 198; second coming of, xliv, 394 (35-59), 406 (22-37), 407 (8), 415 (8-11), 416 (25-36); second coming of, Browne on, iii, 290; "unconscious prophecies" of, viii, 185 note 59, 191 note 69; Vane on, xliii, 130 (see also Jesus)

Christ, in PARADISE LOST, iv, 139-48, 198-9, 202, 224-9, 234-46, 296-300, 323; Bagehot on Milton's, xxviii, 202-4

Christ, in PARADISE REGAINED, iv, 363-415

CHRIST, IMITATION OF, Kempis's vii, 209-379

CHRIST'S NATIVITY, ON THE MORNING OF, iv, 7-15

CHRISTABEL, by Coleridge, xli, 726-44

Christian, in PILGRIM'S PROGRESS, xv; ancestors of, 267-8; Apollyon and, 60-5; Atheist and, 139-40; at Beautiful Palace, 49-51, 57-9; in Beulah-land, 158-60; burden of, 13, 42; By-ends and, 103-5; charity and, 55-6; death of, 161-2; in Delectable Mountains, 124-7; at Difficulty Hill, 45-6; in Enchanted Ground, 140-1; Evangelist and, 14-15, 24-9, 90-3; Faithful and, 71-9; Flatterer and, 137-8; Formalist and Hypocrisy with, 43-5; Giant Despair and, 118-23; Good-Will and, 30-2; on Guilt, Mistrust, and Faint-Heart, 134-6; Hold-the-world and, 110-11; Ignorance and, 128-9, 149-53; at Interpreter's House, 32-41; on Little-Faith, 130-4; on Lot's wife, 113-15; at Lucre Hill, 111-13; at Mount Sinai, 24; Obstinate and, 15-16; Piety and, 52-3; Pliable and, 15-18; Prudence and, 54-5; at River of Life, 115-16; Simple and Sloth with, 43; in Slough of Despond, 18-19; Talkative and, 82-5, 90; Timorous and Mistrust with, 47; in valley of Humiliation, 60, 244; in valley of the Shadow of Death, 65-70; at Vanity Fair, 94-8; Worldly Wiseman and, 21-4

Christian of Troyes, xxxv, 108; on the Bretons, xxxii, 189; on France, xxviii, 76-7; Renan on, xxxii, 154

CHRISTIAN BROKER, STORY OF THE, xvi, 127-41

Christian Church, Calvin on, xxxix, 43-6, 54; schools of early, xxxv, 282-3

CHRISTIAN CHURCH, HYMNS OF, xlv, 545-86

Christian Holy Days, xv, 408-9

CHRISTIAN LIBERTY, Luther on, xxxvi, 362-97; remarks on Luther's, 260

Christian Morality, Mill on, xxv, 252-5

CHRISTIAN SACRED LITERATURE, xliv, 355-495; xlv

Christiana, in PILGRIM'S PROGRESS, xv; at Beautiful Palace, 226-30, 240-2; death of, 314-17; at Difficulty Hill, 220-3; dream of, 202; in Enchanted Ground, 305; Great-Heart and, 214-20; Honest and, 255; ill-favored ones and, 199-202; in Immanuel's Land, 289;

at the Inn, 266-7; at Interpreter's
House, 203-14; lions and, 225;
Mercy and, 188-92, 196-7; at
Mnason's Inn, 283; pilgrimage of,
182-6; in Slough of Despond,
192-3; song of, 198-9; Timorus
and, 187-9; in valley of Humiliation, 243-7; in valley of Shadow
of Death, 248-50; at wicket-gate,
193-4
Christianity, Bacon on, iii, 35; bardism and, xxxii, 176-8; Browne on,
iii, 265 (2), 272 (9), 273 (10),
291, 319; Carlyle on modern, xxv,
353; Celtic Races and, xxxii, 178-
90; Channing on influence of,
xxviii, 373-4; Dante on, and salvation, xx, 368-9; Emerson on, v,
30-8, 86, 161-2; and freedom of
conscience, xliii, 130; Goethe on,
xxv, 398; heathenisms in modern,
v, 288; Hobbes on belief in,
xxxiv, 361-2, 394; Hugo on,
xxxix, 359-62; Hume on, xxxvii,
396, 414-15; Lessing on, xxxii,
207-12; Luther on, xxxvi, 388,
391; Manzoni on, xxi, 177-8;
Marcus Aurelius and, xxv, 228-
30; James Mill on, 30, 32; J. S.
Mill on, 244-6, 252-5; paganism
in, v, 286; Pascal on, xlviii, 69
(194), 84, 89 (241), 91 (245), 92
(251), 97 (269), 149, 150 (441),
151 (444), 153 (450), 158 (468),
164 (491), 167 (503), 175 (537-8),
176 (542, 544), 184-96, 197 (589),
200 (601, 606), 201, 206 (615),
237 (693), 277 (783), 342-3, 376;
Pascal on fundamentals of, 184-
96; Pascal's proofs of, 102 (289),
265; Penn on, i, 377 (468), 416 (296-
99); perpetuity of, 204-9; poetry
and, xxxix, 362-3, 373; porches
of, xli, 503; Renan on marvelous
element of, xxxii, 167; Rousseau
on belief in, xxxiv, 303-9, 310-12;
Rousseau on miracles of, 297
note; Ruskin on modern, xxviii,
127-8; rapid spread of, xxxiv,
401; Shelley on, xxvii, 362-3;
spread without books, iii, 220;
Taine on, xxxix, 448-9, 457; in
Utopia, xxxvi, 238-9; Vanity Fair
opposed to, xv, 99; Wordsworth
on, xxxix, 330
Christians, Browne on instability of,
iii, 290; disciples first called, xliv,
455 (26); early, forbidden to
teach, vii, 130; forbidden to read
by Julian, iii, 209; and heathen
taxes, i, 226 note; Marcus Aurelius on, ii, 289 (3) Mohammed
on, xlv, 1010, 1014, 1016, 1017;
Pascal on, xlviii, 94 (256), 118,
175 (540), 176 (541), 227 (671),
316 (903); Pascal on early and
later, 378-82; persecutions of,

foretold by Jesus, xliv, 415 (12-
19); persecution of, in Jerusalem,
446 (1), 456 (1); persecution
of, by Marcus Aurelius, ii, 192;
Pliny's letter on the, ix, 425-7;
attitude towards poetry, xxxix,
330; Trajan on the, 428 and note;
Woolman on oppression by, i,
320-1
Christina, Queen, Pascal to, xlviii,
366-8
Christmas, celebration of, xv, 408;
spirits at, xlvi, 92
CHRISTMAS HYMN, xlv, 574-5
Chronology, Hakluyt on, xxx, 339;
Hume on, xxxvii, 444; Locke on
study of, 147, 164, 167-8; Newton's system of, xxxiv, 129-33
Chryseis, Agamemnon's slave, viii,
60
Chrysippus, ii, 177 (177)
Chrysogonus, Alcibiades and, xii,
143; freedman of Sylla, 226-7
Chrysostom, St., and Aristophanes,
iii, 204; in Dante's PARADISE, xx,
340 note 35; Olympias and, xv,
381; Walton on eloquence of, 399
Chrysostom, in DON QUIXOTE, burial
of, xiv, 105-8, 116-17; canzone of,
109-12; Marcella and, 92-8, 112-
16
Chryssipus, citations of, xxxii, 31;
on logic, 64-5
Ch'ü Po-yü, xliv, 49 (26), 53 (6)
Chung-kung, disciple of Confucius,
xliv, 15 note 2, 18 note 1, 19 (4),
34 (2), 38 (2), 42 (2)
Church, Burke on an established,
xxiv, 239-47; civil authority in
the, xliii, 78-9; Emerson on decline of the, v, 34-8, 285; Emerson
on the future of the, 305; Emerson
on revivification of, 42; liberty
and the, xliii, 70; liberties of the,
in Massachusetts, 86-8; Mill on
an established, xxv, 72; Pascal on
early idea of the, xlviii, 379; politics and the, xxiv, 160; Raleigh
on, xl, 208; Ruskin on the true,
xxviii, 128; Tennyson on the, xlii,
1093; in Utopia, xxxvi, 246-9
CHURCH, FUTURE PEACE AND GLORY
OF THE, xlv, 576
Church Councils (see Councils)
Church Fathers, Calvin on the,
xxxix, 37-41; Kempis on the, vii,
229-31
Church Music, Augustine, St., on,
vii, 194-5; Dr. Donne on, xv,
357-8
Church Services, Herbert on, xv,
405-7; Paul, St., on, xlv, 521 (26-
35)
Church of England (see England,
Church of)
Churchman, John, i, 209, 237, 238
Churchmen, best single, iii, 22;

kings and, 53; remuneration of, x, 139-40

Churchyards, Montaigne on, xxxii, 19

Chyle, Harvey on, xxxviii, 133-4

Ci-Devant Genius, in FAUST, xix, 180

Ciacco, the glutton, in Dante's HELL, xx, 26-8

Ciampolo, in Dante's HELL, xx, 92-4

Cianghella, Dante on, xx, 352 note 12

Ciawani, Raleigh on the, xxxiii, 351

Cibber, Colley, THE BLIND BOY, xl, 452-3; Voltaire on, xxxiv, 142

Cibo, Cardinal, xxxi, 47

Cicero, Marcus, Tullius, the orator, Antony and, xii, 262-3, 265, 268, 334, 346, 348; at Athens, xxviii, 53; Atticus and, ix, 89-90, 97-8; made Augur, 256; Augustine, St., on Hortenses of, vii, 36-7; Bestia, case of, and, ix, 103; birth and parentage, 225; brother, his love for, 93-5; building ideas, 115; Cæsar and, 117, 118, 119, 120-1, 122, 124, 125, 126, 127-8, 131, 132, 133, 134, 162-3, 168, 171, 176, 177, 178, 187, 259, 260, 276-7, 280, 319, 321, 323; conspiracy against Cæsar, 261-2; after Cæsar's death, 185-8, 262-3; Catiline and, 279-80, 335-44; xxvii, 51; Cato and, ix, 140, 144, 146, 158-60, 319; xxxii, 63; character, 81-2, 105-9, 144-6, 230, 245, 255, 270; xii, 231; iii, 135; in Cilicia, ix, 140-55, 256-7; in Civil War, 169, 257-9, 301; Clodius and, 249-54, 254-5; consulship, 83-5, 86, 233; Crassus and, 133; in Dante's Limbo, xx, 20; on death of daughter, ix, 175-6, 261; death, 267-8; at Delphi, 228; Demosthenes compared with, xii, 198-9, 269-73; xxxix, 166; on divination, ix, 168-9; divorce, 261; stories of miraculous dreams, xl, 39-42 note 66; eloquence of, xxxii, 98-9; exile, ix, 91-3, 95-7, 128-9, 252-4; called father of his country, 244-5; on fear as a critic, 322; flight, 266-7; on FRIENDSHIP, 7-44; on public games, 111-12; on gestures in speaking, 236 note; Greek epistles, 246; on right of heirs to prosecute, 180-1; design for a history, 261; Hume on, xxxvii, 307; on husbandry, xxvii, 65-6; impeachment, ix, 250-2; Jonson on, xxvii, 60; as a lawyer, xxvii, 237; ix, 89, 113; Lentulus and, 123-4; LETTERS, 81-189; on his library, 104, 109-10; life and works, 3-6; on living over again, 307; Locke on study of, xxxvii, 168, 170, 172; Lucretius and, iii, 205; on

study of lyric poets, xxxii, 54; defence of Milo, ix, 255-6; Montaigne on works of, xxxii, 96-8; Octavius and, ix, 263-5, 268, 347; xlvi, 25; ON OLD AGE, ix, 45-77; us an orator, 229; on orators, iii, 115; Pascal on, xlviii, 16 (31); on philosophers, xxxiv, 346; on philosophy, ix, 259-60; xxxii, 9; on physical knowledge, xxiv, 9; Pliny on, ix, 193, 214, 215, 263-4, 365; Plutarch's LIFE OF, xii, 225-68; as a poet, ix, 226; iii, 338; Pompey and, ix, 90-1, 97, 99, 117, 120, 125, 126, 127-8, 133, 168-9; as prætor, 232-3; on his public services, 87; quotations from, i, 86; xlviii, 123 notes 4, 5, 7, 14; in retirement, ix, 165-7; return from exile, 97-100, 124-5, 130, 254; on Roman success, iii, 46-7; case of Roscius, ix, 227; instances of sarcasm, 246-9, 322, 323; case of Satyrus, 84-5; at school, 226; his school, 163; Senate thanks, 158-60; as Senator, 90, 99, 101, 114; case of Sestius, 102, 103; Shelley on, xxvii, 350; in Sicily, ix, 229; iii, 226; Sidney on, xxvii, 30; principles of statesmanship, ix, 134; with Sylla, 226; travels, 227-8; case of Vatinius, 132; case of Verres, 230-1; on his writings, 118-19, 135-6, 151

Cicero, Marcus Tullius, 2d (son of the above), birth, ix, 85; Cæstius and, xxxii, 98-9; Cicero on, ix, 94; as consul, xii, 268; letter to, ix, 91-3; at school, 152, 179, 180, 181-3

Cicero, Quintus, Atticus and, ix, 87-8; Cæsar and, 117, 118, 122, 131, 134; in Clodian troubles, xii, 254; death of, 266; in Gallic wars, 295 note; letters to, ix, 93, 100, 114; in Parthian War, 143; with Pompey, 126; Pomponia and, 139; letter of, to Tiro, 183

Cichuli, in DA DERGA'S HOSTEL, xlix, 221, 257

Cicones, Ulysses and the, xxii, 121

Cid, The, Cervantes on, xiv, 516; Emerson on, v, 211, 222; excommunication of, xiv, 160

Cieza, Pedro de, xxxiii, 327

Cimabue, Giovanni, Dante on, xx, 191; Hazlitt on, xxvii, 293, 295

Cimaroons, of Central America, xxxiii, 138; Drake and the, 157-60, 171-90, 194-5, 197, 199, 201; houses of, 174; king's residence, 176; religion of, 175; Spaniards and, 172, 176; town of, 175; weapons of, 173

Cimber, Tullius, and Cæsar, xii, 329

Cimbrians, Tacitus on the, xxxiii, 156

Cimmeria, Homer on, xxii, 152
Cimon, builder of porticoes at Athens, xxviii, 40-1; commissioner to Greek confederacy, xii, 104; death of, 48; Emerson on, v, 275; military successes of, xii, 34; Montaigne on, xxxii, 34; at Olympic games, xii, 9; ostracism of, 46-7; Pericles and, 42-3, 47; Plato on, 107; political arts of, 45; sons of, 67; Spartans favor, 24
Cincinnatus, Cicero on, ix, 66; Dante on, xx, 309 note 12; Locke on, xxxvii, 187
CINDERELLA, story of, xvii, 104-11
Cinna, Caius Helvius, death of, xii, 331
Cinna, Lucius Cornelius, Cæsar, relationship to, xii, 274; Cicero on supremacy of, ix, 127; Dryden on, xiii, 16
Cioli, Francesco, xxxi, 438 note
Cioli, Simone, xxxi, 438 note
Cipango, Cabot in, xliii, 49
Circassia, inoculation in, xxxiv, 95-6
Circe, daughter of Helios, xxii, 140; Bacchus and, iv, 47; goddess of speech, xxii, 152; Jove, horses of, and, xiii, 253; Picus and, 249-50; songs of, iv, 53; Ulysses and, xxii, 144-51, 169-73; Ulysses's companions and, 142; Virgil on, xiii, 243-4
Circensian Games, Pliny on, ix, 351-2
CIRCLES, ESSAY ON, v, 155-166
Circulating Capital, defined, x, 225-6; four kinds of, 228-9; maintenance of, in regard to neat revenue, 236; necessity of, 229-30; sources of, 230
Circulation of the Blood, Descartes on, xxxiv, 40-5; Harvey on, xxxviii, 64, 65, 87, 91-147; Pascal on, xlviii, 41 (96)
Circumcision, ancient practice of, xxxiii, 51; the apostles on, xliv, 463-4; Dante on, xx, 422; in Egypt, xxxiii, 22, 23; Emerson on, v, 175; Pascal on, xlviii, 202-3, 226-7, 227 (672); Paul, St., on, xlv, 510 (18-19); the Quakers on, xxxiv, 66-7
CIRCUMCISION, UPON THE, iv, 42
Circumcision of Christ, feast of the, xv, 408
Circumstances, Emerson on indifferency of, v, 93; independence of (see Independence of C.); Johnson on, xxxix, 236; Lowell on consideration of, xxviii, 449, 454; Mill on doctrine of, xxv, 110-11; Penn on importance of, i, 363 (278), 364 (293); political institutions, the result of, xxiv, 156; Pope on, xl, 443

Ciriatto, the demon, xx, 90, 92
Cirongilio, of Thracia, xiv, 320
Cirripedes, crosses of, xi, 113; development of branchiæ of, 196-7; first appearance of, 357, 341; larvæ of, 481; parasitic, 159
Cisseus, death of, xiii, 337, 414
Citations, Cervantes on, xiv, 11-12; Emerson on, v, 75-6; Hugo on, xxxix, 407-8; Montaigne on, xxxii, 31
Cities, Bacon on, iii, 69; xl, 358; country and, relations of, i, 359; v, 212-13; x, 319-22; Cowley on life in, xxvii, 67-8; Emerson on, v, 234; Goldsmith on, xli, 529-30; Newman on, xxviii, 38-9; pleasures of, iv, 34; poetry and, xxvii, 70; power of inhabitants of, 387; Thoreau on life in, xxviii, 409-10; in Utopia, xxxvi, 186; Whitman on life in, xlii, 1495-6; Wordsworth on life in, xxxix, 287
Citizens, Confucius on pattern, xliv, 61 (13)
Citizenship, American, xliii, 210
Citizenship, M. Aurelius on, ii, 230 (22), 245 (54), 279 (6), 287 (33)
Cittern, defined, xx, 429
CITY OF BRASS, story of, xvi, 310-39
City of Destruction, xv, 15, 180
City of God, St. Augustine's, vii, 4
Civil Law, Locke on study of, xxxvii, 169
Civil Wars, Pascal on, xlviii, 110 (313)
Civilis, on the gods in war, v, 371
Civility, in children, xxxvii, 50, 110; Locke on, 131, 132; Manzoni on, xxi, 510-11
Civility, Mr., in PILGRIM'S PROGRESS, xv, 23, 28
Civilization, Carlyle on our, xxv, 351; Channing on modern, xxviii, 373-4, 378-9; dependent on power of navigation, x, 26-28; disease and, xxxviii, 153; due to wants of men, xxxiv, 181-2; Emerson on our, v, 85-6, 259; fire-arms and, x, 471; Hugo on progress of, xxxix, 356-62; morality and, xxxiv, 164, 191; Pope on growth of, xl, 437-41; progress of, in relation to poetry, xxxix, 356-71; Rousseau on beginnings of, xxxiv, 202-13, 232-3; Rousseau on cost of, 173-8; Woolman on, i, 223
Clackitt, Mrs., in SCHOOL FOR SCANDAL, xviii, 112, 117-8
Clara, in EGMONT, Brackenburg and, xix, 260-2, 287-8, 311-15, 317-21; Egmont and, 262-4, 288-92, 328-9
Clara, Donna, in DON QUIXOTE, xiv, 452-7, 466, 469-70

Clare, Saint, xx, 298 note 5
Claribel, daughter of Alonso, xlvi, 399, 404
Claridiane, Alphebo and, xiv, 16
Clarin of Balaguet, xlix, 99
CLARINDA, MISTRESS OF MY SOUL, vi, 311
CLARINDA, VERSES TO, vi, 321
Clark, Dr., on Unitarianism, xxxiv, 84-5
Clarke, Bishop of Bath, xxxvi, 107-8, 114, 119
Clarke, Edward, Locke to, xxxvii, 5
Clarus, Septitius, letter to, ix, 211
CLASSIC, WHAT IS A, xxxii, 126-139
Classics, Arnold on, xxviii, 69, 70; Héricault on, 68-9
Classical Literature, Augustine on, vii, 18-19; Browne on, iii, 285-6; the grotesque in, xxxix, 368; Hugo on, 363; Hume on, xxvii, 232-3; Huxley on study of, xxviii, 221-9; Locke on, xxxvii, 81-2; Milton on study of, iii, 209-10; Shelley on immorality in, xxvii, 352-3; Swift on study of, 118-19
Classification, Darwin on, xi, 142-3, 450-62; Darwin's theory, effect of, on, 524-6; embryos in, 488-9; Emerson on, v, 7-8; Häckel on, xi, 472; rudimentary organs in, 496
Claudian, the poet, Shelley on, xxvii, 366; Taine on, xxxix, 450
Claudine, Claudas's son, xxxv, 222
Claudius, name of, xii, 162
Claudius I, Emperor, descent of, xii, 403; famine in reign of, xliv, 455 (28); and the Jews, 471 (2); Nonianus and, ix, 208
Claudius, Appius (Cæcus), old age of, ix, 59; Pyrrhus and, 51-2
Claudius, Appius, the decemvir, iii, 28; Plutarch on, xii, 170
Claudius, King, in HAMLET, xlvi, 87-199; death of, 197; Gertrude and, 93, 159-60; Hamlet and, 94-6, 132-3, 137-8, 162-4, 194-6; Hamlet on, 155, 156; Hamlet's father murdered by, 108-9; Hamlet's friends and, 116-17, 133-4, 150; Laertes and, 94, 169-70, 172, 174-8, 186-8, 194-6; marriage of, 93; Norway and, 93-4, 118-19; Ophelia and, 167-8; Polonius and, 119-21; remorse of, 151-2
Claudius, Publius (see Clodius)
Clauserus, on poets, xxvii, 54
Clausius, on freezing-point, xxx, 243
Clausus, in ÆNEIS, xiii, 267-8, 338
Claveret, and Corneille, xxxix, 379
Claverhouse (see BONNY DUNDEE)
Clay, Henry, in Treaty of 1814, xliii, 273
Clean Beasts, texts on, interpreted, xv, 85

Cleandrides, and Pericles, xii, 61
Cleanliness, Franklin on, i, 84; Woolman on, 323-4
Cleante, in TARTUFFE, Damis and, xxvi, 260-7; Orgon and, 198-205, 254, 266-8, 280, 281-2; Mme. Pernelle and, 191, 193-4, 195-6; Tartuffe and, 250-2, 284; on Valère's marriage, 205-7
Cleanthes, Newman on, xxviii, 52-3; on philosophy, ii, 169 (142); remark of, xii, 115; verses on acquiescence, ii, 179 (184); on the voice, xxxii, 30
CLEANTHES, HYMN OF, ii, 185-6
Clearness, less affecting than obscurity, xxiv, 53-7
Cleigenes, Aristophanes on, viii, 440
Cleisthenes, reference to, viii, 431
Cleitophon, pupil of Euripides, viii, 448
Cleitus, son of Mantius, xxii, 214-15
Clemency, in commanders, xxxvi, 58-9; More on, 196; pity and, xxxiv, 193; Pliny on, ix, 361; in princes, xxxvi, 56-7
Clemens, Attius, letter to, ix, 203, 260
Clement, St., of Alexandria, hymn by, xlv, 553-4
Clement, Friar, Bacon on, iii, 103
Clement V, Pope, Dante on, xx, 81 and note 4, 401 note 8, 416 note 7
Clement VII, Pope, bastard son of Medici, xxxi, 88 note; Cellini and, 42, 46-7, 76, 79-80, 81, 82, 83, 90-1, 92-4, 95-100, 102, 108, 110, 112-14, 116-22, 124-32, 139, 141, 146-8; Charles V and, 119 note 5; the Colonnesi and, 72 note; death of, 148; election of, 35; events of life, 17 note; Foiano and, 248 note; Machiavelli and, xxvii, 384, 419; reputed father of Alessandro de' Medici, xxxi, 182; in sack of Rome, 71, 73, 74, 76, 79-80, 81, 82-3, 215, 216; war with Florence, 90
Clement VIII, in THE CENCI, xviii, 275, 281-2, 299-300, 348-9
Clemenza, Queen, xx, 321 note 1
Cleobuline, Pascal on, xlviii, 12 (13)
Cleocritus, the Corinthian, xii, 89, 101
Cleombrotus, in Limbo, iv, 150; not with Socrates in prison, ii, 47
Cleomenes, Emerson on, v, 191; and the Samians, xxxii, 63
Cleon, the Athenian, Aristophanes on, viii, 435, 436; dream of, iii, 97; Pericles and, xii, 72-3, 75
Cleon, in POLYEUCTE, xxvi, 87, 100-1
Cleonice, called Byzantine Maid, xviii, 423
Cleopas, xliv, 424 (18); and Jesus, xv, 412
Cleopatra, at Actium, xii, 387-8;

Antony and, 352-7, 362-3, 375-82, 390, 395, 396; Antony's soldier and, 394; burial and statues of, 402; Cæsar and, 315-16; Cæsar and, Dryden on, xviii, 44, 46; Dante on death of, xx, 310, in Dante's HELL, 23; daughter of, xii, 403; death of, 400-2; death, plans for, 392; monument of, 394; Octavius and, 392-3, 394, 397-8, 399-400; Octavius and, Dryden on, xviii, 47-8; Pascal on nose of, xlviii, 63 (162); revels in Alexandria, xii, 392; Seleucus and, 394; Virgil on, xiii, 295-6

Cleopatra, in ALL FOR LOVE, xviii, 11; Alexas and, 84-8; Antony, her love for, 23, 25-6, 35-9; Antony, message to, 40-2; Antony, scenes with, 43-9, 50-1, 79-83, 95-6; death of, 96-9; Dolabella and, 54-5, 67-72; Octavia and, 12, 62-5; suicide attempted by, 84; Ventidius on, 72-3

Cleopatra, statue called, xxxi, 332 note 1

Cleophantus, son of Themistocles, xii, 34

Cleophon, Aristophanes on, viii, 439, 465-6

Cleremont, in PHILASTER, xlvii, 639-716

Clergy, Dryden on satires on the, xxxix, 172-3; Emerson on the, v, 12, 34-41, 309; Herbert on duties of the, xv, 411-12; Luther on the, xxxvi, 376; Luther on marriage of the, 317-21; maintenance of the, x, 486; More on idleness of the, xxxvi, 191; paid, remarks on a, v, 446; scandal of the, breeds atheism, iii, 46

Clergymen, as examples, xv, 400

Clerk, Chaucer's, xl, 19

Clerk, John, manœuvre of breaking the line, v, 372

Clermont, Lord, and Chandos, xxxv, 41; death of, 45

Cletus, Bishop, xx, 401 note 4

Cleveland, Grover, and Hawaii, xliii, 464 note 5

CLEVER ELSIE, story of, xvii, 129

Clifford, Lord Thomas, xxxv, 23

Clifton, John, and street-lamps, i, 125

Climate, adaptation to (see Acclimatization); æsthetic disposition and, xxxii, 300; compensations of, v, 91; enjoyment of life and, xxix, 270; influence of, in struggle for existence, xi, 83-4, 91; industry and, xxxiv, 181; jurisprudence and, xlviii, 105; martial disposition and, iii, 146; of northern and southern hemispheres, xxix, 265; reacts on man, xxviii, 420; relation of, to productions, ii,

395-6; Taine on effects of, xxxix, 448; variations due to, ii, 146

Climbing Plants, development of, xi, 252-5; various methods of, 195

Climorin, xlix, 118, 152

Cline, Henry, on inoculation, xxxviii, 208-9

Clinias, father of Alcibiades, xii, 110

Clinton, Sir Henry, Burns on, vi, 55

Clinton, Gov., story of, i, 111

Clisthenes, Aristides and, xii, 81; Plutarch on, 38

Clitandre, Molière on, xxvi, 204-5

Clitumnus River, Pliny on the, ix, 334-5

CLOAK, THE OLD, xl, 190-2

Cloanthus, in the ÆNEID, xiii, 93, 97, 186-90

Clocks, gravity, xxx, 186-7

Clodia, and Cicero, xii, 249-50; called Quadrantia, 250

Clodius, Publius, Antony and, xii, 335; Cæsar and, 286; ix, 118; Cæsar's wife and, 249, 281-2; Cicero and, xii, 250-4; ix, 4, 99, 129; death of, xii, 255; Pompey and, ix, 101, 102; trial of, xii, 249-50; widow of, 341; the soldier, and Antony, 347

CLOE, by Prior, xl, 407-8

Clœlia, reference to, xiii, 294

Clonius, in the ÆNEID, xiii, 316, 352

Clotaldo, in LIFE IS A DREAM, in battle, xxvi, 64; escape and recapture, 56, 62-3; Rosaura and, 15-18, 61-2; Segismund and, 27-8, 33-7, 47-51, 67

Cloth, defects of garments of, xlv, 595 note 9

Clothing, demand for materials of, x, 174-5, 186; Locke on, xxxvii 10-11, 15-16, 31; materials of, do not limit population, x, 174; price of, 212-16; price of materials of, 172-3

Clothing (see also Apparel, Dress)

Clotho, Dante on, xx, 232

CLOUD, THE, by Shelley, xli, 875-7

Clouds, on the Corcovado, xxix, 39; lesson from the, xv, 238

Clough, Arthur Hugh, Poems by, xlii, 1165-8; reviser of Plutarch's Lives, xii, 4

Clover, and bees, xi, 87-8, 108-9

Clubs, established by Cato, ix, 62

Clusius, Charles, xxxv, 253

Clymene, in Hades, xxii, 160; mother of Phaëton, xx, 358 note 1; reference to, vii, 380

Clytemnestra, in HOUSE OF ATREUS, viii, 14-18, 26-7; Ægisthus and, 69, 70; Agamemnon and, 35-40, 57-65, 92-3; Cassandra and, 41-3; dream of, 93-4; ghost of, 119-20;

Homer on, xxii, 41, 163; Orestes and, viii, 98-100, 106-11; Voltaire on, xxxix, 382

Clytius, Cydon and, xiii, 337; death of, 323

Clytoneus, in the ODYSSEY, xxii, 107

Cnossus, Governor of, and Epictetus, ii, 151 (93)

Coadjutors, Luther on, xxxvi, 297, 303

Coal, heat from burning of, xxx, 210-11; price of, x, 176-9

Coal-gas, cause of brightness of, xxx, 114; carbon in, 168

Coal-mines, rent of, x, 175-6, 178

Coan, Hippocrates called, xx, 268 note 15

Coati, Dana on the, xxiii, 160

Coats of Arms, Hobbes on, xxxiv, 382

Cobbett, William, Carlyle on, xxv, 424-5, 462

Cobham, Raynold, in Crecy campaign, xxxv, 6, 9, 17, 23, 29, 32; at Poitiers, 42, 52, 53, 55

Cobites, alimentary canal of, xi, 194

Cock, lesson on the, xv, 239

Cock, Thoreau on the, xxviii, 437

COCK AND FOX, fable of, xvii, 35

COCK AND HORSES, fable of, xxvii, 143

COCK AND PEARL, fable of, xvii, 9; Bacon on, iii, 35

Cock-Fights, Blake on, xli, 601

Cockatrix, fabulous serpent, xlvii, 798 note 3

Cockburn, Alexander, in Jamaica case, xxv, 190

Cockburn, Alison R., FLOWERS OF THE FOREST, xli, 494

COCKPEN, THE LAIRD O', xli, 576-7

Cocles, Horatius, Virgil on, xiii, 294

Cocoanut Trees, Francis Pretty on, xxxiii, 210

Cocoanuts, Biggs on, xxxiii, 244

Cocytus, Dante on the, xx, 62; Homer on, xxii, 150; Milton on, iv, 125; Plato on, ii, 110; Virgil on, xiii, 216

Codes, the conscience of nations, v, 256

Codfish, Hayes on the, xxxiii, 284

Coelius, at Actium, xii, 386

Coffee, Burke on the taste for, xxiv, 16

Cog-wheels, considered as levers, xxx, 192-3

Cohesion, Faraday on, xxx, 24-42

Cohn, naturalist, on bacteria, xxxviii, 342 note

Coila, Burns on, vi, 93-4, 251

Coilus, king of Picts, vi, 183 note 6

Coinage, expense of, x, 375, 475; origin of, 32-3; regulation of, by Congress, xliii, 174, 175, 196 (5)

Coke, Sir Edward, Burke on, xxiv, 180

Colbert, Jean Baptiste, administration of, x, 446-7; policy of, 364

Colchians, Herodotus on the, xxxiii, 51

Cold, Locke on endurance of, xxxvii, 10, 11, 14

COLD'S THE WIND, xl, 326

Coleman, Mr., EPILOGUE by, xviii, 195-6

Coleman, William, i, 60, 63-4, 65

Coleridge, Hartley, SHE IS NOT FAIR, xli, 937

Coleridge, Samuel Taylor, Arnold on, xxviii, 82; Bagehot on, 210; Emerson on, v, 331-3, 458-9; on fancy, xxxix, 322; on French Language, v, 403; life and works of, xxvii, 268; Mill on, xxv, 53, 106-7; on Milton's Satan, xxviii, 206; Poems by, xli, 698-749; ON POESY OR ART, xxvii, 269-77; Wordsworth on, v, 337

Colewort, only medicine in Rome, xxxv, 252

Colgrevance, Sir, xxxv, 185-6

Coligni, Burke on, xxiv, 196

Coliseum, Byron's lines on the, xviii, 439-40

COLLAR, THE, xl, 353

Colleagues, Confucius on sordid, xliv, 61 (15)

College Men, Franklin on, i, 16

College of the Six Days' Works (see Solomon's House), iii

Colleges, Carlyle on use of, xxv, 380; genius and, v, 439-40; office of, 12; study of dead matter in, 267

Collier, Jeremy, xxxix, 164 note 6, 182-3

Collingwood, Admiral, Emerson on, v, 362, 372, 391

Collins, Anthony, Burke on, xxiv, 237

Collins, John, friend of Franklin, i, 15-16, 22, 29, 32, 33-5, 38

Collins, John, the poet, TO-MORROW, xli, 607

Collins, Michael, case of, xxviii, 125-7

Collins, William, Poems by, xli, 487-93; Wordsworth on poems of, xxxix, 342

Collinson, Peter, Franklin on, i, 153, 154, 166

Colnett, on discolored sea, xxix, 27; on lizards, 408-9; on Galapagos Islands, 415-16

Colonia del Sacramento, xxix, 157

Colonies, Bacon on, iii, 89-92; motive of establishing, x, 414-23; in subject states, xxxvi, 10-11; wages and profits in, x, 97-8

Colonna, Fabrizio, xxvii, 412
Colonna, House of, and Clement VII, xxxi, 72 note
Colonna, Stefano, xxxi, 382 note
Colonna Infame, story of, xi, 4-6
Colonnades, Burke on, xxiv, 67, 118-19
Colonnesi, Alexander VI and the, xxxvi, 25; Orsini and, 40, 41; Valentino and, 25-6
Color, beauty and, xxiv, 100, 134; Berkeley on, xxxvii, 214-19, 282; cause of, xxxiv, 125; climate and, xi, 146; constitutional peculiarities and, 29-30; Goethe on operation of, xxxix, 270; Hume on, xxxvii, 319; importance of, to animals, xi, 98, 209; nature of, illustrated, xxx, 274; as source of the sublime, xxiv, 72
Colpoda, Pasteur on, xxxviii, 353, 359
Columba, Renan on, xxxii, 180, 182
Columbus, Christopher, Emerson on, v, 86; Smith on, x, 417-20; Voltaire on, xxxiv, 101
COLUMBUS, LETTER OF, xliii, 22-8
COLUMBUS, PRAYER OF, xlii, 1506-8
Columbus, Realdus, on the circulation, xxxviii, 102; on the heart, 74; on the lungs, 70
Columella, on agriculture, xxvii, 68-9; on country life, 65; on enclosures, x, 163; on flowers, xxxv, 250; on vineyards, x, 163-4
Combe, George, xxviii, 218 note
Combination, of capitalists, x, 70-1; Mill on liberty of, xxv, 215; to fix wages, x, 151; of workmen, 71
Combustion, of carbon and other substances compared, xxx, 168-70, 176-7; chemical affinity, the cause of, 57; with and without flame, 108-9; heat generated by, 210-11; oxygen necessary to, 57-9, 107-8; illustrations of, in oxygen, 48-9, 55-6, 143-4; water produced by, 117-19
COME, LET ME TAKE THEE TO MY BREAST, vi, 501
COME UNDER MY PLAIDIE, xli, 591-2
Comedy, burlesque and, xxxix, 185-7; Cervantes on, xiv, 502-7; Dryden on origin of, xxxix, 224; Fielding on epic, 184; Hugo on, 363-9, 374; Hume on standards of, xxvii, 231-2; Johnson on, xxxix, 234; Macaulay on wit in, xxvii, 402-3; M. Aurelius on, ii, 290 (6); popular notions of, xxxix, 225; Sidney on, xxvii, 29-30, 48-9; Voltaire on translations of, xxxiv, 143
Comenius, John Amos, iii, 248 note
Comestor, Petrus, xx, 339 note 33
Comets, Bacon on effects of, iii, 144; nature and motion of, xxxiv, 120-1
Comfort, Confucius on, xliv, 46 (3); Kempis on, vii, 246 (9), 249 (4), 257-60, 280-9
COMIC EPIC IN PROSE, Fielding's, xxxix, 184-90
Comines, Philip de, on England, v, 369; Montaigne on, xxxii, 104
Cominius, Roman consul, xii, 158, 159; names Coriolanus, 161
Comitatus, institution of the, xlix, 79 note 2
Commandments, The Ten, Locke on, xxxvii, 141; Milton on giving of, iv, 351; More on, xxxvi, 158-9
Commendams, Luther on, xxxvi, 297, 303
Commendation, St. Augustine on, vii, 59
Commentators, Johnson on, xxxix, 253-61; Locke on, xxxvii, 180-1; Montaigne on, xxxii, 111; Voltaire on, xxxiv, 135
Commerce, in agricultural system, x, 451-6, 459-63; Bacon on, in ancient times, iii, 165, 168; capital used in, x, 304, 306-7, 310-17; domestic, sacrificed to foreign, 331-2; favored above agriculture, 6; foreign (see Foreign Commerce); Harrison on, xxxv, 236-7, 237-8; honor and, xli, 535; interferences with, by landed nations, x, 456-7; internal, 319-20, 465; language and, xxxix, 212; military spirit and, xxvii, 391-2; necessity of, x, 26-8, 302; regulation of (U. S.), xliii, 196 (3), 198 (6); Wordsworth on, xli, 693; works and institutions for facilitating, x, 474-85 (see also Trade)
Commercial Policy, Washington on our, xliii, 264-5
Commercial Pursuits, Emerson on, v, 47-8
Commercial System, x, 326-47; Channing on the, xxviii, 373-4; Emerson on the, v, 47-9; false relations under, 266; Harrison on, xxxv, 237-8; More on, xxxvi, 191-2; origin of, x, 29; producers and consumers under, 444-5; results of, v, 416; Ruskin on the, xxviii, 119-20; Tennyson on the, xlii, 1053-5; ways of trade under, v, 47-8
Commercial Treaties, Smith on, x, 407-13
COMMISSARY GOLDIE'S BRAINS, vi, 488
Commissions, Bacon on standing, iii, 58
Commodus, Machiavelli on, xxxvi, 67, 69, 71; statue called, xxxi, 332 note 1

Common, Dorothy (see Dol Common)

Common Law, suits at, in U. S., xliii, 208 (7); Winthrop on the, 111

Common Sense, Dryden on, xxxix, 170-1; Epictetus on, ii, 150 (90); limitations of, xxviii, 428; Montaigne on, xlviii, 397, 401; in morals, Kant on, xxxii, 334-5

Common Things, Emerson on, v, 21-2; Penn on, i, 345 (68)

Commons, House of, Voltaire on, xxxiv, 90-2

Commonwealth, English (see Instrument of Government)

Commonwealths, More on, xxxvi, 250

Commotions, Calvin on, xxxix, 46-9

Communion, holy, Bunyan on, xv, 236-7; Calvin on, xxxix, 40; Kempis on, vii, 349-79; St. Paul on, xlv, 514 (16-17); Quakers on, xxxiv, 67; Rousseau on, 313

Communism, Emerson on, v, 270-1; instituted by Christ, xxxvi, 239; Lowell on, xxviii, 483; More on, xxxvi, 177, 178-9, 195-6, 197, 200-1, 250, 252, 253, 254

Commutative Justice, Hobbes on, xxxiv, 422-3

Como, Lake, Manzoni on, xxi, 7

Compacts, Mohammed on, xlv, 927

Companies, regulated and joint-stock, x, 480

Company, Confucius on, xliv, 30 (29), 55 (39); determines manners, xxxvii, 132-3; Epictetus on choice of, ii, 166 (137); Epictetus on vulgar, 154 (99), 157 (107), 175 (167); Kempis on, vii, 220; Locke on importance of, xxxvii, 53, 135-6; Massinger on, xlvii, 829; Pascal on choice of, xlviii, 10 (6); St. Paul on, with evil-doers, xlv, 507 (9-13); Penn on, i, 352 (128); of strong and weak, xvii, 31

Comparison, necessary to criticism, xxxix, 218-19

Comparisons, Goethe on, xxxix, 269; Hume on, xxvii, 225-6; Wordsworth on, xxxix, 329

Compass, of the Phœnicians, v, 476

Compass-flower, xlii, 1407

Compassion, Augustine, St., on, vii, 34-5; Bacon on, iii, 36; Hobbes on, xxxiv, 356; Pliny on, ix, 370 note (see also Pity, Sympathy)

Compensation, Darwin on growth of, xi, 158-60; Epictetus on, ii, 126 (27); Gray on, xl, 473; Pope on, in nature, 422-3; of pleasure and pain, Socrates on, ii, 48; Whitman on, xxxix, 426-8

COMPENSATION, ESSAY ON. Emerson's, v, 89-107

Competition, as cause of quarrels, xxxiv, 403, 404; excessive, generates fraud, xxviii, 327; Hobbes on, xxxiv, 385; of labor, restraints on, x, 126-38, 143-52; of labor, unnaturally encouraged, 138-43; Mazzini on, xxxii, 403; necessary to good management, x, 157; in professions, 138-43; as regulator of prices, 60; results of, v, 416

Competitive Prices, tendency to minimum, x, 65

Competitive System, Ruskin on the, xxviii, 136

Complacency, Penn on, i, 353-4

COMPLAINT OF THE ABSENCE OF HER LOVER, xl, 196

Complaints, of children, xxxvii, 96; Kempis on, vii, 237 (6)

Complaisance, Hobbes on, xxxiv, 423-4

Compleat Angler, Walton's, xv, 326

Compliance, Cicero on, ix, 39-40; Locke on, xxxvii, 110

Compliments, Bacon on, iii, 132

Compositæ, Darwin on, xi, 157, 225, 491

Composition, Hume on rules of, xxvii, 219

Compositions, Luther on papal, xxxvi, 300

Compound Animals, Darwin on, xxix, 217-18

Compound Fractures, Lister on, xxxviii, 272-4, 276-7

Compound Words, Johnson on, xxxix, 198, 199-200

Comprehension, Raleigh on, xxxix, 108 note

Compromise of 1850, xliii, 327 note

Compromises, Lowell on, xxviii, 476; Mill on, xxv, 59; with sin, xlii, 1449

Compulsion, Locke on, in education, xxxvii, 61, 186

Comte, Auguste, Mill on, xxv, 108-9, 135-8, 157 note 2, 216

COMUS: A MASK, iv, 46-74; Bagehot on, xxviii, 213; at Ludlow Castle, v, 427

Conaire, story of, xlix, 214-62

Conall Cernach, xlix, 240-1, 246, 259, 260, 263-4

Conceit, Æsop's fable of, xvii, 19; Epictetus on, ii, 143 (72); results of, xxxiv, 367; Smith on, of mankind, x, 113

Conceit, country of, in PILGRIM'S PROGRESS, xv, 128

Concentration, Buddha on, xlv, 717-19, 720-1, 745

Concepcion, Chili, earthquake at, xxix, 322-7

Conception, Point, Dana on, xxiii, 72; gale off, 223-30

Conceptions, Berkeley on, xxxvii, 233; Descartes on reality of, xxxiv, 29, 34; Hobbes on impossible, 335; Taine on various kinds of, xxxix, 443-4

Conchenn, the giant, xlix, 255

Concini, wife of, v, 194

Concino, Bartolommeo, xxxi, 449 note

Conciseness, Pliny on, ix, 214-7; Pope on, xl, 417

Concord, even among devils, iv, 123

CONCORD HYMN, xlii, 1296-7

Concrete Qualities, due to participation in abstracts, ii, 95-7

Concy, Raoul of, xxxv, 35, 36

Condé, Prince of (Louis I of Bourbon), constable at Bourges, xxxviii, 49; at Danvilliers, 20-1; in Germany, 19; at Metz, 24; at Turin, 9; wounded at St. Denis, 52-3; wounded at St. Quentin, 46

Condé, "the Great," before Rocroi, xxi, 25; at Seneffee, xxxix, 183

Condell, Henry, PREFACE TO SHAKESPEARE, xxxix, 155-6

Condillac, Abbé de, on languages, xxxiv, 184; Mill on, xxv, 45, 49

Condiments, Locke on, xxxvii, 17

Conditions of Life, direct and indirect effects of, xi, 26-9, 145-7; effect of changed, on fertility, 316; law of, 218; slight changes in, beneficial, 317; Taine on, xxxix, 447-9

Condolence, Sulpicius on, ix, 172; Pliny on, 287

Condor, Darwin on the, xxix, 196-201

Condorcet, Burke on, xxiv, 442; death of, alluded to, 227 note; Life of Turgot by, xxv, 76

Conduct, Buddha on, xlv, 717-19; not motives, to be judged, xxv, 37; Penn's rules of, i, 351

Confectionery, Locke on xxxvii, 22

CONFEDERATION, THE ARTICLES OF, xliii, 168-79

Conference, maketh a ready man, iii, 128

Confervæ, Darwin on, xxix, 24-8

Confession, Augustine, St., on, vii, 65; Dante on, xx, 274 (note 2); Herbert on, xv, 404-5; Kempis on, vii, 292 (1); Luther on, xxxvi, 321-2, 383-4; Pascal on, xlviii, 43-4

CONFESSIONS OF ST. AUGUSTINE, vii, 5-206

Confidence, between parents and children, xxxvii, 86-7; daughter of fortune, iii, 105; Hobbes on, xxxiv, 353, 355, 380; Kempis on over-, vii, 234 (4); in self, Emerson on, v, 63-7; 72-3; Epictetus on, ii, 120 (9)

Confiscations, Burke on, xxiv, 303, 304; Machiavelli on, xxxvi, 58, 62

Conformity, Burke on, xxiv, 45; Emerson on, v, 66, 68-9; Mill on, xxv, 163, 261, 263, 266, 275-6; Milton on, in religion, iii, 240; Penn on, i, 411-12

Confucius, the basket-bearer on, xliv, 51 (42); Chi Huan and, 63 (4) note 3; Chieh-yü and, 63 (5); Duke Ching and, 63 (3); the gate-keeper on, 51 (41); habits and character of, 6 (10), 22 (4, 9, 12, 13), 23 (17, 20), 24 (26, 31), 25 (37), 28 (4, 9), 31-3; on himself, 7 (4), 18 (25, 27), 21 (1), 22 (2, 3, 5, 7, 8, 10, 11), 23 (16, 18, 19, 21, 22, 23), 24 (27, 29, 32), 25 (33), 28 (2), 28 (6, 7, 8), 29 (15), 34 (1), 44 (10), 50 (30, 37), 52 (2), 65 (8); in K'nang, 28 note, 36 (22); life and works, 3; Sainte-Beuve on, xxxii, 136; story of, v, 472; on his teachings, xliv, 13 (15), 16 (12), 23 (23), 24 (24), 27 (1); on tiger-skins, xxviii, 429; Tzu-kung on, xliv, 67 (22) note 6, 67 (23), 68 (24, 25); the warden of Yi on, 12 (24); wanderings of, 63-4

CONFUCIUS, SAYINGS OF, xliv, 5-69; remarks on SAYINGS, 3

Confusion, and grandeur, xxiv, 68-9; worse confounded, iv, 136

Congregation Day, Mohammedan, xlv, 954 note 2

Congress, power to propose amendments, xliii, 204; power to incorporate banks, 223-4, 226-30, 237-40; under the Confederation, 169-70, 172-6; under the Constitution, 192-9; power to establish courts, 202 (1); powers forbidden to, 207 (1); implied powers of, 227-37; relations with President, 201-2; power to prescribe proofs of state records, 203; power to admit new states, 203-4; power over territories, 204; power to punish treason, 203

Congress of 1774, xliii, 219-20

Congreve, William, comedies of, xxxix, 245; Dryden and, xiii, 70; Macaulay on, xxvii, 402-3; Voltaire on, xxxiv, 142; Wordsworth on, xxxix, 347

Conio, Alberigo of, xxxvi, 46

Conjectural Criticism, Johnson on, xxxix, 258, 260

Connate Ones, the seven, xlv, 626

CONNECTICUT, FUNDAMENTAL ORDERS OF, xliii, 63-9

Conon, at Ægospotami, xii, 149

Conquered States, arms in, xxxvi, 72; factions in, 72-3; Machiavelli on, 8-12, 18-19

Conquerors, Jesus on, iv, 390

Conquerors, Locke on, xxxvii, 109

Conquest, Hobbes on right of, xxxiv, 403; More on foreign, xxxvi, 168-9; Rousseau on right of, xxxiv, 218; vanity of, xl, 258-9

Conrad III. and Cacciaguida, xx, 352 note 15

Conradino, of Naples, xx, 229 note 10

Conrayer, Father, xxxiv, 81, 97

Conscience, Bacon on matters of, iii, 14-15; Beaumont on, xlvii, 644; Carlyle on, xxv, 339; Cenci on, xviii, 324; Dante on, xx, 120, 155; Emerson on, v, 66; Epictetus on power of good, ii, 161 (119); Goethe on persistency of, xix, 19; Hobbes on, xxxiv, 360-1; intellect and, xxviii, 334; Kempis on good, vii, 254-5; liberty and, v, 256; liberty of, Vane on, xliii, 130-2; Mill on liberty of, xxv, 218-59; Milton on liberty of, iii, 232-8; Pascal on rest and security of, xlviii, 317 (908); Raleigh on, xxxix, 73; Rousseau on, xxxiv, 245-6, 276-83; Webster on guilty, xlvii, 792-3, 812

Consciousness, Carlyle on, xxv, 347; in death and rebirth, xlv, 697-8; of modern society, xxv, 348-9; origin of, xxxii, 278-9

Consecration, Luther on, xxxvi, 279

CONSERVATION OF FORCE, Helmholtz on, xxx, 181-220; discovery of the law, $1^2$3-4; statement of the law, 184, 218-19

Conservatism, Burke on, xxiv, 305, 396; Emerson on, v, 274; Lowell on, xxviii, 484

Conservatism, false, Smith on, xxvii, 237-65

Consideration, Penn on, want of, i, 341, 362 (263)

Considius, the Senator, Cæsar and, xii, 286

Consigne, Queen, and the mastiff, xxxv, 373

Consistency, Confucius on, xliv, 55 (36); Emerson on, v, 70-2

Consolation, fallacy of false, xxvii, 254-5; for death, God alone can give, vi, 287; Kempis on, vii, 262 (3), 288-9; Kempis on inward, 268-348; Pascal on, xlviii, 336, 343-4; Pliny on, ix, 287; in public calamities, xxxii, 121-2; Sulpicius on, ix, 172

Conspicuousness, human love of, xxviii, 96-7; why honorable, xxxiv, 381

Conspiracies, Machiavelli on, xxxvi, 63-4

Constable, Henry, DIAPHENIA, xl, 233

Constable, Thomas, translator of Corneille, xxvi, 69

Constance, Council of, xxxvi, 333, 334

Constance, wife of Henry VI, xx, 298 note 7

Constancy, hyacinth, the flower of, vi, 431; Penn on, i, 351 (119)

CONSTANT LOVER, THE, xl, 363

CONSTANT TIN SOLDIER, THE, xvii, 312-16

Constantine the Great, and Council of Nicæa, xxxvi, 286; Dante on, xx, 82 note 10; 280 note 11, 307 note 1, 372 note 7, 8; the Donation of, xxxvi, 310 note; and the nails of the cross, iii, 293; sons of, 53; Sylvester and, xx, 82 note 10, 115

Constitution, first written, xliii, 63 note; Lowell on an unwritten, xxviii, 482

Constitution, Holmes on the frigate, xlii, 1443 note

CONSTITUTION OF UNITED STATES, xliii, 192-211; the act of the people, not of States, 224-6; defended in Federalist, 212-17; Hamilton on the, 212-16; implied powers under the, 227-8, 229, 230-37; Lincoln on the, 337, 339, 342; Lowell on framers of the, xxviii, 474-5; powers of nation and state under, xliii, 222-3, 224-6, 229-30, 239; Washington on the, 256-7

Constitutional Convention, Jay on, xliii, 219, 220; suggested by Vane, 141-2

"Constitutional Society," Burke on the, xxiv, 153

Consulates, expense of, x, 479

Consumers, sacrificed in Commercial System, x, 444-5

Consumption, annual, dependent on annual labor, x, 5; the end of production, 444; immediate and durable, 287-90; productive and unproductive, 271-2, 278-83; taxes on, 541-73; unproductive, More on, xxxvi, 191-2; unproductive, Smith on, x, 243

Contagious Diseases, Holmes on, xxxviii, 238 (3); Jenner on, 172-3

Contemplation, activity and, ii, 125 (24); Buddha on, xlv, 720, 745; Burke on, xxiv, 40, 48; Epictetus on duty of, ii, 121 (13, 14), 141 (68); Hindu ideal of, xlv, 827-8; Kempis on, vii, 260 (3), 307 (3), 333 (1); Mill on, xxv, 98; Mon-

taigne on, xxxii, 9; More on, xxxvi, 218-19, 243; Pascal on, xlviii, 59 (146); Plutarch on proper objects of, xii, 36-7; Rousseau on, xxxiv, 288; Schiller on, xxxii, 297; two ways of, xxxix, 123

Contempt, Bacon on, iii, 142; Hobbes on, xxxiv, 351, 378; Kempis on self, vii, 285 (1); Locke on, xxxvii, 129; Rousseau on beginnings of, xxxiv, 209

CONTENT, BY GREENE, xl, 289
CONTENT AND RESOLUTE, xl, 338
CONTENT, O SWEET, xl, 326-7
CONTENTED WI' LITTLE AND CANTIE WI' MAIR, vi, 542

Contentment, Epictetus on, ii, 118 (6), 121 (14), 127 (31), 159 (114), 163 (127), 165 (133), 178 (182), 183 (17)

CONTENTMENT, by Holmes, xlii, 1445-7

Contentment, Kempis on, vii, 219 (2), 297 (5); Marcus Aurelius on, ii, 201 (5), 204 (13), 212 (16), 213 (3), 217 (23), 218 (25), 235 (11), 244 (49, 50), 249 (27), 257 (7), 260 (26), 278 (1), 287 (35), 290 (7), 296 (20); Rousseau on, xxxiv, 268; Shelley on, xli, 849; wealth and, 535; Woolman on, i, 222; work necessary to, 147-8 (see also Acquiescence, Independence of Circumstances, Tranquillity)

Contiguity of ideas, xxxvii, 323, 346, 347

Continental Congress, xliii, 160 note, 168 note

CONTINENTAL DRAMA, xxvi

Continents, Darwin on, xi, 362; Geikie on evolution of, xxx, 342-67; are rising areas, xxix, 506; species, affinity of, in same, xi, 397-8

Continuity, Pascal on, xlviii, 122 (355)

Contracts, Descartes on, xxxiv, 22; Hobbes on, 410-17, 431; known only to man, x, 19; laws impairing, forbidden in U. S., xliii, 199; Mill on freedom of, xxv, 311-13

Contradiction, Locke on, xxxvii, 130-1, 133, 134; Montaigne on, xxxii, 42; Pascal on, xlviii, 128 (384); Penn on, i, 353-4 (149)

Contraries, the life of each other, iii, 330; in temper and distemper, 51

Contrast of ideas, xxxvii, 323 note 4

Contrite, Mr., in PILGRIM'S PROGRESS, xv, 283-4, 287

Contrition, Dante on, xx, 274 note 2; Kempis on, vii, 335; Luther

on, xxxvi, 268; Pascal on, xlviii, 322 (923)

Controversies, Bacon on, iii, 13; Browne on religious, 269; Franklin on habit of, i, 15-16, 132; Penn on, 356 (184); truth and, xxxiv, 55; uncertainty indicated by, xlviii, 315 (902); unsettled, iii, 329

Contumely, Hobbes on, xxxiv, 425

Conveniences, Rousseau on, xxxiv, 206-7

Convention, society loves, v, 218

Conventionalities, Lowell on, xxviii, 452

Convents, Luther on, xxxvi, 316-17, 321-2, 342

Convergence of Character, xi, 138-9

Conversation, attention to, ii, 246 (4), 250 (30); Bacon on, iii, 87-9; Emerson on, v, 160; Epictetus's rules of, ii, 175 (164), 176 (171), 177 (175); Franklin on the ends of, i, 19; Goethe on, xxxix, 266; Kempis on, vii, 222; one to one, v, 117-18; Penn on, i, 352 (see also Intercourse)

CONVERSATION, ESSAY ON, Swift's, xxvii, 97-105

Conversini, Benedetto, governor of Rome, xxxi, 212-14, 234

Conversion, joy in, of men, vii, 127; Pascal on, xlviii, 388-91; true, Emerson on, v, 32

Conveyances, in Massachusetts, xliii, 72

Conviction, Epictetus on, ii, 154 (99); is genius, v, 63; necessary to persuasion, xix, 27-8

Convicts, children of, moral sentiment of, v, 255; More on, xxxvi, 160-3

Conway, Gen., i, 142

Cook, Chaucer's, xl, 21-2; Dryden on Chaucer's, xxxix, 174

Cook, Capt., on kelp, xxix, 255

Cook, Lady (see Danvers, Jane), xv (424)

Cook, Sir Robert, xv, 423-4

Cookery, Penn on, i, 345 (61)

Cooper, Fenimore, Carlyle on, xxv, 409, 413-14

Cooper, Joseph, i, 56

COOPER O' CUDDY, vi, 564

Cooperation, conscious and unconscious, ii, 242 (42); of labor (see Division of Labor); man made for, ii, 200 (1); in nature, 221 (40, 45), 241 (38), 242 (43), 246 (9)

Cope, Prof., on reproduction period, xi, 197

Copenhagen, battle of, v, 358-9; industries of, x, 276-7

Copernicus, Nicolaus, life and works, xxxix, 55 note; misunderstood, v, 70; Pascal on opinion

of, xlviii, 80 (218); REVOLUTIONS
OF HEAVENLY BODIES, xxxix, 55-
60
Copiapo, town of, xxix, 375; valley
of, 370-1
Copiers, Horace on, xiii, 40
Copland, on puerperal fever,
xxxviii, 268
Copley Medal, given to Franklin, i,
156
Copper, action of nitric acid on,
xxx, 133-4
Copulation, unnatural, in Massachu-
setts law, xliii, 85
Copyrights, provision for, xliii, 197
(8)
Coquimbo, earthquake at, xxix, 362-
3; terraces at, 363-4; town of,
362
Coral Formations, Darwin on, xxix,
425, 477-508; Lyell on, xxxviii,
428, 431
Corallines, Darwin on, xxix, 216
Corals, fish feeding on, xxix, 490;
stinging, 489; unable to live out
of water, 486
Coras, ally of Turnus, xiii, 266
Corbet, Richard, FAREWELL, RE-
WARDS, AND FAIRIES, xl, 323-4
CORBIES, THE TWA, xl, 75
Corcovado, Mount, Brazil, xxix, 39;
Chiloe, 292, 309
Cord, proverb of the, iii, 41
Cordelia, in KING LEAR, xlvi, 205;
disowned by father, 206-7, 210;
rejected by Burgundy, 210; grief
for father's misfortunes, 272-3;
her suitors, 204-5, 209-10; letter
to Kent, 238; ordered to be
hanged, 300; remarks on char-
acter of, 202; taken by France,
211; taken prisoner, 291-2; with
doctor in French camp, 274-5;
with Kent, 285; with father at
his awakening, 286-8
Cordilleras (see Andes)
Cordova, Gonzalo Fernandez de, in
Mantuan contest, xxi, 454-6, 487-9
Corellia, Pliny and, ix, 268-9, 318-
20
Corellius, Pliny on, ix, 268-9, 273,
356
Corfinius, in Civil War, xii, 311;
house of, 317.
Cori, Smith on the, x, 419
CORIDON AND PHILLIDA, xl, 199-200
CORINNA SINGS, xl, 291-2
CORINNA'S MAYING, xl, 348-50
CORINNA TO TANAGRA, xli, 924-5
Corinth, Christian Church of, xlv,
499
CORINTHIANS, EPISTLES TO THE, xlv,
499-544
Corinthians, crafts most respected
among, xxxiii, 85
Coriolanus, accusations against, xii,

168-9; Alcibiades, compared with,
192-6; Antiates, inroad of, into,
164; banishment of, 171-3; character of, 152-3; consulship, defeat
of, for, 164-5; Johnson on, xxxix,
251; love of, for mother, xii, 155;
on the multitude, 166-7; name,
origin of, 161; reprieved, 169-71;
Rome, in war against, 177-83;
seditions of the poor and, 156,
157-8, 164; training of, to arms,
153; trial and death of, 190-1;
among the Volscians, 173-5; in
Volscian War, 158-61; war, first
experience in, 153-4
CORIOLANUS, PLUTARCH'S LIFE OF,
xii, 152-91
Cormac Condlongas, xlix, 231-2, 260
Cormac, King of Ulaid, xlix, 213
Cormorant, Harrison on the, xxxv,
358
Cormorants, habits of, xxix, 213-14
Corn, Cicero on growth of, ix, 65;
duties on importation of, x,
546, 357-8; as measure of value,
41-3, 44-5; parable of the, xv,
208; price of, as affected by
bounties, x, 393-6, 401-3; prices
of, 12; real value of, 403; Rousseau on, xxxiv, 210
Cornaro, Francesco, xxxi, 150 note,
151, 177-8, 222, 231-2, 237-8
Cornaro, Marco, xxxi, 47 note
Cornaro, Pietro, xxxi, 116 note 4
Cornbury, Lord, lines to, xxvii, 287
Corneille, and his critics, xxxix,
379-81; Hugo on, 391, 392; Hugo
on Athalie of, 371-2; Hume on
POLYEUCTE of, xxvii, 234; on
length of the drama, xiii, 7; life
and works, xxvi, 70; on love,
xlviii, 62 (162); Macaulay on,
xxvii, 402; POLYEUCTE, xxvi, 71-
121; Sainte-Beuve on, xxxii, 129;
Shakespeare and, xxxix, 376;
Voltaire and, 450; Voltaire on
Pompey of, xxxiv, 138
Cornelia, vestal virgin, ix, 265-6
Cornelia, in Dante's Limbo, xx, 20;
Cornelia, wife of Cæsar, xii, 274,
277
Cornelianus, letter to, ix, 308
Cornelius, Caius, prophecy of Phar-
salia, xii, 314
Cornelius, the centurion, xliv, 451
(1-48)
Cornelius, in DR. FAUSTUS, xix,
203-5
Cornelius, in HAMLET, xlvi, 93-4,
118-19
Corners, of corn, in Elizabethan
England, xxxv, 257-60, 262.
Cornhill Magazine, xxviii, 4
Cornificius, in Civil War, xii, 311

note; fellow candidate of Cicero, ix, 83

Cornwall, tin-mines of, x, 179-81

Cornwall, Duke of, in LEAR, xlvi, given part of kingdom, 203, 205, 207; at Gloucester's, 232-3; with Kent and Oswald, 234-7; death of, reported, 271, 288; Edmund and, with Gloucester's letter, 259; reported war with Albany, 229, 249; with Gloucester, 263-6; with LEAR, 242, 244, 245, 248

Cornwall, in SHOEMAKER'S HOLIDAY, xlvii, 510

Cornwallis, Burns on, vi, 55; surrender of, xliii, 180-4

Corœbus, builder of Eleusis, xii, 51; death of, xiii, 117; in sack of Troy, 115, 116, 117

CORONACH, by Scott, xli, 765

Coroner's Juries, in Massachusetts, xliii, 78 (57)

Corporal Punishment, of children, xxxii, 57-8; xxxvii, 37-9, 40-1, 42, 43, 59, 64-6, 69-70, 71-2, 99-100; in Massachusetts, xliii, 77 (46)

Corporations, Burke on punishment of, xxiv, 288-9; Hobbes on, xxxiv, 432-3; power of Congress to create, xliii, 226-30, 237-8; Smith on, x, 482-5; trade, 126-38

Corpre, son of Conaire, xlix, 237-8

Corpse, in THE FROGS, viii, 424

Corpuscularians, xxxvii, 177

Correcting, Pascal on, xlviii, 11 (9)

Correction, acceptance of, ii, 238 (21); advantages of, xlviii, 174 (535); in anger, i, 363 (271), 364 (289-90); of children, xxxvii, 110; Marcus Aurelius on, of others, ii, 195 (10), 279 (4), 295; reason of anger under, xlviii, 34 (80) (see also Punishment)

Corrections, Locke on, xxxvii, 134

Correggio, Hazlitt on, xxvii, 293

Correlated Variation, xi, 29-30, 155-8; instances of, 209

CORRELATION OF PHYSICAL FORCES, Faraday on, xxx, 75-87

Corruption, implies goodness, vii, 115; Locke on, xxxvii, 57; in public affairs, iii, 31

Corsablis, King, xlix, 128, 140

Corsets, Locke on, xxxvii, 15-16

Corsica, Freeman on, xxviii, 265

Corso Donati (see Donati)

Cortese, Tommaso, xxxi, 98 note, 112 note

Cortez, Keats on, xli, 920; Raleigh on, xxxiii, 327, 341

Coruncanius, Tiberius, ix, 14, 22, 61

Coruncanius, Titus, ix, 55

Corvées, defined, x, 478

Corvus, M. Valerius, old age of, ix, 68

Cory, William Johnson, poems by, xlii, 1159-60

Corybantes, reference to the, viii, 354

Corycian Rock, the, viii, 116

Corydon, and Thyrsis, iv, 33

Corynæus, xiii, 219, 405

Coseguina, eruption of, xxix, 309-10

Cosimo, St., xxxi, 163 note 1

Cosington, Sir Thomas, xxxv, 66

Cosmography, Hobbes on, xxxiv, 377

Cosmos, the, ii, 239 (25); Milton's ideas of, iv, 248-50 (see also Universe)

Cosmus, Duke of Florence, on faithless friends, iii, 16; calm nature of, iii, 110

Cossus, Virgil on, xiii, 240

Cost of Living (see Food-supply)

Costanza, Queen of Arragon, xx, 158 note 5, 176 note 14

Costiveness, Locke on, xxxvii, 24-7

Costume (see Dress)

Cotta, Lucius, Cicero on, xii, 248

Cotta, Publius, Cicero on, xii, 247-248

Cottage, and palace, vi, 147

Cotters, life of, Burns on, vi, 160-2; Scotch, x, 124

COTTER'S SATURDAY NIGHT, THE, vi, 142-7; an idyllic poem, xxxix, 314; remark on, vi, 17

Cottius (see Spurinna)

Cotton, Charles, and Walton, xv, 326; Wordsworth on Winter of, xxxix, 324-6

Cotytto, goddess of nocturnal sport, iv, 49

Coulson, Walter, xxv, 60, 79

Councillors, of kings, iii, 56-7; of kings, More on, xxxvi, 150; Penn on, i, 369 (360); Webster on duty of, xlvii, 722

Councils, Church, Luther on, xxxvi, 278; Pascal on, xlviii, 309 (871)

Councils, Ecclesiastical, Luther on, xxxvi, 286-8, 304

Counsel, boldness in, iii, 34; of friends, 73-4, 126; good, excels wealth, viii, 275; right of legal, in U. S., xliii, 208 (6); safer to receive than to give, 221 (3)

COUNSEL, ESSAY ON, Bacon's, iii, 55-59

Counsellors, Confucius on, xliv, 57 (6); evil, in Dante's HELL, xx, 108-16; of kings, xxxvi, 166-7; Machiavelli on, 80-2

Count, meaning of, xxxiv, 383

Countenance, expressions of the, xxviii, 290-1

Counterfeiters, in Dante's HELL, xx, 126-7

Counterfeiting, punishable by Congress, xliii, 197

Country, pleasures of the, iv, 32-4; and town, relations of, x, 132-7, 319-22

COUNTRY GLEE, xl, 325-6

COUNTRY LAIRD, EPIGRAM ON A, vi, 533

COUNTRY LASS, THE, vi, 467

Country Life, Bacon on, iii, 93; Cicero on, ix, 64-8; Cowley on, xxvii, 65-74; Emerson on, v, 52; Locke on, xxxvii, 186-7; Penn on, i, 359; Smith on, x, 134-6; Smith on attractiveness of, 321; Wordsworth on, xxxix, 285-6

COUNTRY LIFE, ESSAY ON, Cowley's, xxvii, 65-74

COUNTRY SEAT, ON A BEAUTIFUL, vi, 533

Country Workmen, Smith on, x, 24-5

Courage, Buddha on, xlv, 609-10; Confucius on, xliv, 46 (27), 50 (30), 60 (8), 62 (23, 24); Hobbes on, xxxiv, 353, 380; in Latin the same as virtue, xii, 153; Locke on, xxxvii, 102-8; and oppression, iii, 40; not roughness, xxxvii, 54; without courtesy, xliv, 25 (2), 62 (24); without good breeding, xxxvii, 76; worldly, Socrates on, ii, 57-8

Court, fees of, x, 472-3

Court Mantle, trial by, xxxii, 152 note

Court Records, in Massachusetts, xliii, 77 (48), 79 (64)

COURT OF SESSION, EXTEMPORE IN, vi, 269

Courtesy, Bacon on, iii, 36; benevolence of, v, 220-1, 226; first point of, is truth, 216; intellectual quality in, 218; oft found in lowly sheds, iv, 55; Yu-tzu on, xliv, 6 (12, 13); Confucius on, 6 (15), 7 (3), 10 (8), 11 (18), 12 (22), 13 (13), 21 (45), 25 (2), 26 (8), 38 (1), 40 (15), 43 (3), 51 (44), 55 (32), 58 (13), 61 (11), 69 (3)

Courtiers, Burns on, vi, 233; Confucius on, xliv, 57 (2); Montaigne on, xxxii, 43; Simon Eyre on, xlvii, 481

COURTIN', THE, xlii, 1455-7

Courts, Bacon on, xl, 358; congressional regulation of, xliii, 197 (9); pleasures of, iv, 34; Raleigh on, xl, 208; United States, xliii, 202; Webster on princes', xlvii, 721-2 (see Judicature)

Courtship, naturally done by men, xlviii, 425

Couthony, Mr., on coral-reefs, xxix, 500 note

Covenants, Hobbes on, xxxiv, 410-17, 431; the keeping of, 417-23

Coventry, Sir William, and Pepys, xxviii, 313

Coventry, Bishop of, in EDWARD II, xlvi, 10-11

Coventry, Countess of, beauty of, v, 315

Covered, chapter of the, xlv, 889-91

Coverley, Sir Roger de, xxvii, 89-90; Addison's and Steele's parts in, 88, 174-5

Covetousness, Buddha on, xlv, 685; freedom from, 686-7; the cause of war, xxviii, 134-5; Epicurus on, ii, 153 (95); Hobbes on, xxxiv, 354, 381; Jesus on, xliv, 393 (15); Locke on, xxxvii, 97; Mohammed on, xlv, 984; More on cause of, xxxvi, 196; Pascal on, xlviii, 191, 224 (663); Penn on, i, 347-8, 391 (4); Paul, St., on, xlv, 507 (11), 508 (10); the sin of, in FAUSTUS, xix, 220-1 (see Avarice)

Cowardice, Locke on, xxxvii, 102; how developed, 104

Cowards, insult dying majesty, xvii, 13

Cowley, Abraham, OF AGRICULTURE, xxvii, 65-74; on Chaucer, xxviii, 81; xxxix, 175-6; Dryden on, xiii, 64-5, 432; Dryden on, xxxix, 170 note 13; life and works, xxvii, 64; Poems by, xl, 374-8 Pindaric Odes of, xxxix, 336; popularity of works of, 337

Cowper, William, Hymns by, xlv, 575, 576; Poems by, xli, 546-67; Emerson on, v, 22; Mill on works of, xxv, 16; Verses of Selkirk, xxxix, 310-11; The Task of, 314

Cowpox, first appearance of, xxxviii, 176-7; inoculation for, 177-9, 200-1, 209-13, 214-26, 228-9, 231; Jenner on, 150, 151-231; not fatal or infectious, 177-8, 188, 201, 207 8; origin and symptoms of, 154-5, 164-9, 170-1; 179, 190-2, 194-200, 209-13, 215-16, 220, 223, 228-9; return of, 160-1, 171-2; scarlatina and, 226-7; and measles, 226 note; smallpox and, 155-62, 165, 169-70, 181, 183, 195 note, 197, 203, 206-9, 211, 213-14, 216 note, 220, 221, 223-6, 227, 231; sources of spurious, 181-93; treatment of, 196, 197-9, 211, 219-20, 223, 229

Cows, held sacred in Egypt, xxxiii, 25

Cox, William, xxxiii, 282, 297, 298

COXCOMB, EPITAPH ON A NOTED, vi, 520

Coya (see Peru)

Crabs, at St. Paul's, xxix, 20; hermit, 482 and note; notopod, 175

23

Crabs, giant, of Keeling Islands, xxix, 488-9

CRABS, FABLE OF THE, xvii, 30

Crabtree, in SCHOOL FOR SCANDAL, uncle of Backbite, xviii, 115; at Lady Sneerwell's, 118-22; on Backbite's epigram, 128; in gossip at Sneerwell's, 129-30, 131-2; at Teazle's, after the scandal, 181-3

Crabwinch, the, xxx, 193

Craft, Hobbes on, xxxiv, 366, 381; revenge's scheming child, viii, 110

Craftiness, Eliphaz on, xliv, 79 (12-14); Locke on, xxxvii, 127 (see Cunning) iii

Craigdarroch, Burns on, vi, 385-6, 404

CRAIGIEBURN WOOD, vi, 427, 547

Crane, in FAUST, xix, 181; the prudent, iv, 241

CRANE AND WOLF, fable of the, xvii, 11

Cranes, war with dwarfs alluded to, iv, 104

Cranmer, Archbishop of Canterbury, xxxvi, 119, 122, 126

Craon, Lord, xxxv, 35

Crashaw, Richard, WISHES FOR MISTRESS, xl, 369-71; ON SAINT TERESA, 372

Crassipes, son-in-law of Cicero, ix, 133

Crassus, Gaius Licinius, law of, ix, 40-1

Crassus, Lucius, the orator, Sidney on, xxvii, 51-2

Crassus, Marcus Licinius, Asia contract, ix, 90; Catiline's Conspiracy and, xii, 237; Cicero and, ix, 126, 133; xii, 246-7, 251, 254; death of, 298; Dryden on, xiii, 16-17; influence of, xii, 232; Milo and, ix, 101; and the Parthians, xxxiii, 116-17; Pompey and, ix, 102; reference to, xx, 231 note 20

Crassus, Publius, Roman jurisconsult, ix, 55, 64, 69; son of Marcus, admirer of Cicero, xii, 254; killed in Parthia, 256

Crassus, brother of Piso Galba's adopted son, victim of Nero, ix, 197 note 4

Crassinius, Caius, at Pharsalia, xii, 312-3

Cratais, mother of Scylla, xxii, 172

Craters, of Galapagos Islands, xxix, 394; of elevation, 511

Cratinus, reference to, viii, 429

Cratinus, on Aspasia, xii, 63; on Pericles, 38-9, 52

Cratippus, Cicero and, xii, 245; Cicero the Younger, and, ix, 181-2

Craving, Buddha on noble and ignoble, xlv, 731

Cravings, of children, xxxvii, 91-4

Creation, Bacon on the, iii, 8; Berkeley on the, xxxvii, 289-96; Calvin on the, xxxix, 51-2; centres of, xi, 400-3; Dante on manner of, xx, 315-16 note 9; Descartes on, xxxiv, 38-9; Dryden on the, xl, 398-9; Emerson on the, xlii, 1311-12; greater than destruction, iv, 245; Hume on, of matter, xxxvii, 444 note; Job, description of, in, xliv, 134 (4-11); March, date of, xl, 44; Mill on problem of, xxv, 33; Mohammed on the, xlv, 898-9, 910; Mohammed on, of man, 889, 895, 900, 901, 910; music on morning of, iv, 11 (12); Owen on, xi, 14; Pascal on the, xlviii, 82-3, 211 (625); prophecy of, iv, 106, 119; Raleigh on the, xxxix, 104, 106-11, 113-15; reason of the, iii, 300; of the soul, 301-2; special, objections to, xi, 417, 432-3, 436, 437, 438, 446, 473-4, 475, 493-4, 510, 512, 513, 514, 516, 517, 518, 522; special, of species, objections to, 72, 109, 143, 150, 151, 162, 165, 168, 174-5, 189, 202, 206, 258-61, 309-10, 330; special, Owen on, 14; Raphael relates story of, iv, 235-246; Uriel describes the, 156

Creative Genius, Aristophanes on, viii, 422

Creator, Addison on the, xlv, 547

Crecy, battle of, xxxv, 26-30; losses at, 32 and note; order of the English at, 23-4; order of French, 24-6

CRECY, THE CAMPAIGN OF, xxxv, 5-33

Credit, Bacon on assuming, iii, 106; Franklin on assuming, i, 79; Luther on, xxxvi, 348-9 (see also Loans) x

Credits, cash, in Scotland, x, 247-9, 255-7

Credulity, Hobbes on, xxxiv, 389; reason of, human, xxiv, 18

CREECH, WILLIAM, LAMENT FOR, vi, 281-3

Creeds, best when clearest, xxxiv, 298; Bronte on, xlii, 1156; decline of, reason of, xxv, 242-6; xxxiv, 399-402; determined by accident of birth, 293 note; Emerson on modern, v, 82; Hobbes on belief in, xxxiv, 362; Locke on, xxxvii, 135-6; origin of, xxxiv, 390; Pope on religious, xl, 441; Rousseau on usefulness of, xxxiv, 312; truth of, impossibility to finding, 301-8; of Utopia, xxxvi, 237-50

Creeper, the, in Tierra del Fuego, xxix, 253-4

Creighton, Robert, Bishop of Wells, xv, 396

Cremona, reference to, iv, 24 (4)

Creon, brother of Jocasta, sent to Delphi by Œdipus, viii, 199; returns, 199-201; suspected by Œdipus, 209; disclaims guilt, 212-6; last scene with Œdipus, 239-42; King of Thebes, forbids burial of Polynices, 244, 248-50; hears of burial, 251-3; condemns Antigone, 255-261; with Hæmon, 263-7 warned against his crimes, 274-7; sees death of son, 281; of wife, 283

Cresceus, Attilius, Pliny on, ix, 294-5

Crespino, the Bargello, xxxi, 212

Cressy, Drayton on, xl, 228 (see Crecy)

Cretaceous Era, in Europe, xxx, 362

Crete, Anchises on, xiii, 135; Homer on, xxii, 272

Creteus, death of, xiii, 323

Cretheus, son of Æolus, xxii, 158

Creüsa, ghost appears to Æneas, xiii, 129-30; in sack of Troy, 126, 128

Crevasses, formation of, xxx, 237, 248; in glaciers, 225, 230-2

Crewe, Mrs., lines addressed to, xviii, 105-8

Crichton, Admirable, Hazlitt on, xxvii, 291

CRICKET AND GRASSHOPPER, by Keats, xli, 919

Crifford, John, xxxv, 402

Crime, reasons of, Augustine, St., on, vii, 28-32; Confucius on causes of, xliv, 26 (10); and law, xlviii, 105 note 2; made by distrust, v, 58-9; nature hostile to, 101-2; prevention of, laws for, xxv, 304; and punishment, inseparable, v, 94; retribution of, 104-5; retribution of (see Retribution); Stoic doctrine of, ix, 333 note 1; trials of, in U. S., xliii, 207 (5), 208 (6) (see also Penology)

Crimes, great, never single, xxvi, 166

Criminal Codes, sanguinary, Emerson on, v, 93

Criminals, equality of, v, 120; public and private, 289; proper treatment of, ii, 150 (88); real punishment of, 120 (12)

Crinisus, father of Acestes, xiii, 183

Crises, Lowell on, xlii, 1449

Crisis, the, shows the man, ii, 173 (157)

Crispinus, and Horace, xviii, 16

Crispus, xliv, 471 (8); baptism of,

xlv, 502 (14); destruction of, iii, 53

Cristoforo, Father, Attilio and, xxi, 188; death, 646; life and character, 55-69; Lucia and, 39-40, 52, 127, 135-8, 632-4, 627-31; Renzo and, 605-13, 632-4; Rodrigo and, 86-90

Critias, and Alcibiades, xii, 144,150

Critical Periods, xxv, 107-8

Criticism, of art, xxiv, 28; of art, Goethe on, xxxix, 275-6, 277-8; Bagehot on, xxviii, 201; comparison necessary to, xxvii, 225-6; xxviii, 72-4; xxxix, 218-19; delicacy requisite to just, xxvii, 221-4; false method of, xxxix, 304-5; fallacies of poetic, xxviii, 67-72; Hugo on, xxxix, 404-6; Hume on, xxxvii, 314, 379-80, 444-5; Johnson's ideas of, xxxix, 254-60; Johnson on conjectural, 257, 258, 259-60; of manners, morals, and religion, xxvii, 232-4; Mazzini on mission of, xxxii, 419; Montaigne on, xlviii, 396; need of negative, xxv, 248; of others (see Censoriousness); Pascal's method of, xlviii, 16-17; physical organs in relation to, xxvii, 221; practice necessary to, 224-5; prejudice fatal to, 226-7; of poetry, xxxix, 327-33; possibility of fixing standard of, xxvii, 229-32; reason in, 227-8 (see also Taste)

Critics, Burke on mistake of, xxiv, 49; Burns on, vi, 339; Dryden on, xviii, 14-15, 19; Johnson on, xxxix, 251; knowledge requisite to, xxiv, 19-21; qualifications of, xxvii, 221-8; xxxix, 331-2

Crito, friend of Socrates, ii, 20, 25, 47, 51-2, 111-14

CRITO, Plato's, ii, 31-44

Critobulos, of Cyrene, xxxiii, 91

Critobulus, and Socrates, ii, 20, 25, 47

Critolaus, in Rome, iii, 204-5

Crobylus, the orator, xii, 211

Croce, Baccino della, xxxi, 103, 132

Crocodile, in Book of Job, xliv, 140 note 1; the, creation of, iv, 242; Herodotus on the, xxxiii, 37-8

Crocker, Mrs., and More, xxxvi, 121-2

Crocus, David on the, xli, 506

Crœsus, Chaucer on dream of, xl, 43; death of, xxxii, 5; and Solon, iii, 78

Croghan, George, and Braddock, i, 140

Croll, on age of earth, xi, 359; on geological time, 339; on glacial period, 418-19

Cromwell, Burke on, xxiv, 196; Carlyle on, xxv, 383, 384-7; Car-

lyle's Life of, xxxix, 439; Defoe
on, xxvii, 145; Emerson on, v,
249; his fast proclamation, xliii,
126 note; Hazlitt on, xxvii, 289;
Hugo on, xxxix, 374-5, 396-9; as
Lord Protector, xliii, 113 note,
123 (33); Milton on, xxviii, 195;
Pascal on, xlviii, 65 (176); Pope
on, xl, 448; and the Quakers,
xxxiv, 73, 74; quotation from, v,
166; Swift on, xxvii, 102; Waller's elegy on, xxxiv, 148-9
Cromwell, preface to Hugo's, xxxix,
354-408
CROMWELL, ODE ON, xl, 381-4
CROMWELL, SONNET TO, iv, 85
CROMWELL'S RETURN, ODE ON, xl,
381-4
Cromwell, Sir Richard, xxxvi,
127
Cromwell, Sir Thomas, and More,
xxxvi, 119, 122, 125, 126
Cronion, father of Venus, xxii, 111;
name of Zeus, 168; references to,
36, 37, 53
Cronos, his curse on Zeus, viii, 187-
8; overthrown by Zeus, reference
to, 140; the war against, 163-4
Crosfield, George, i, 320
Crosfield, Jane, i, 323
Cross, the, in architecture, xxiv,
66-7
Cross, of Jesus, exhortation to bear
the, vii, 342; few bearers of, 262-
3; royal way of the, 263-7; spell
of the, xix, 52
Cross Breeding (see Intercrosses)
Cross Lies, iii, 134
Cross, Robert, xxxiii, 238, 253
Crossbow, Helmholtz on the, xxx,
197-8
Crossing (see Intercrossing)
CROSSING THE BAR, xlii, 1098
Crossley, Hastings, translator of
Epictetus, ii, 115
Crossness, founded in Vinland, xliii,
13
CROW AND FOX, fable of, xvii, 12-13
CROW AND PITCHER, fable of, xvii,
33
CROWDIE EVER MAIR, vi, 581
Crowds, not company, iii, 69
Crown Servants, Confucius on, xliv,
45 (20); Tzu-hsia on, 66 (13)
Crowns, Hippolytus on usurped, viii,
329-30; Jesus on, iv, 387
Crucifixion, The, xliv, 422-3
Cruelty, in children, xxxvii, 108-9;
in commanders, xxxvi, 58-9;
Hobbes on, xxxiv, 356, 424; in
princes, xxxvi, 56-7; of single and
married men, iii, 23; well and
ill employed, xxxvi, 33
Cruelty, Mr., juryman in PILGRIM'S
PROGRESS, xv, 101-2
Crüger, Dr., on orchids, xi, 203-4
CRUIKSHANK, MISS, TO, vi, 350-1

CRUIKSHANK, MR., EPITAPH FOR, vi,
303
Crusaders, in Dante's PARADISE, xx,
363
Crustacea, South American, xxix,
175-6
Crying, of children, Locke on,
xxxvii, 98-100
Crystallization, different forms of,
xxx, 30-1, 36
Crystals, perforated, xxix, 162-3
Ctesius, son of Ormenus, xxii, 219
Ctesiphon, Emerson on, v, 236; in-
dictment of, xii, 217
Ctesippus, xxii, 314; death of, 315;
and Demosthenes, xii, 209; with
Socrates, ii, 47; and Ulysses, xxii,
292
Ctimene, daughter of Anticleia, xxii,
217-18
Cuba, Independence of, xliii, 467-8,
470 (1), 476 (16); slavery in, v,
48
Cucao, Chiloe Islands, xxix, 313
Cuccagua, land of the, xxi, 200 note
Cúchulainn, xlix, 254
Cuckoo, habits of the, xxix, 63-4;
instincts of, xi, 270-5; Words-
worth on the, xxxix, 318-19
CUCKOO, TO THE, by Michael Bruce,
xli, 583-4
CUCKOO, TO THE, by Wordsworth,
xli, 656-7
Cudworth, Dr., xiii, 31; xxxvii, 177
Cudworth's Risk, v, 283
Cuentas, Sierra de las, xxix, 162
Cuevas, Luis Gonzaga, xliii, 309
Culan, Baron de, xxxviii, 39
Cultivated Classes, rage of the, v, 69
Culture, Arnold on, xxviii, 222;
Confucius on, xliv, 16 (14); Hux-
ley on, xxviii, 222; and morality,
Rousseau on, xxxiv, 164; neces-
sity of valor in our, v, 127-8;
Rousseau on progress of, xxxiv,
181; proper aim of, xxxii, 293;
in relation to freedom and virtue,
232, 250-1, 269-70, 282-3, 287-91;
Schiller on office of, 258-9; Thoreau
on, xxviii, 431; timidity of our,
v, 99
CULTURE AND SCIENCE, Huxley's,
xxviii, 215-32
Cumberland, Goldsmith on, xli, 518-
19
Cuming, on sheels, xxix, 414, 516
Cunizza, xx, 322 note 6
Cunning, Bacon on, iii, 60-3; fable
on, xvii, 35; Locke on, xxxvii,
127; Penn on, i, 354 (150-1);
Webster on, xlvii, 731
CUNNINGHAM, ALEX., TO, vi, 326
CUNNINGHAM, ALEXANDER, song to,
vi, 576-7
Cunningham, Allan, poems by, xli,
802-3
Cupavo, son of Cycnus, xiii, 333

Cupentus, death of, xiii, 414
Cupid, assumes form of Ascanius, xiii, 99-100; blindness of, v, 311; Dante on worship of, xx, 316; and Psyche, iv, 73
CUPID AND CAMPASPE, xl, 212
Cupidity (see Covetousness)
Curan, in KING LEAR, xlvi, 229-30
Curianus, Assidius, ix, 272-4
Curiatii, reference to the, xx, 308 note 9
Curio, Gaius Scribonius, xx, 119 note 10; and Antony, xii, 334-5, 337; and Cæsar, 286, 300, 301-2; and Memmius, ix, 156; and Pompey, 101, 102
Curiosity, Augustine, St., on, vii, 29, 197-9; Burke on, xxiv, 29-30; in children, xxxvii, 111-14; folly of, vii, 215 (1); Goethe on, xix, 17, 338, 339; Hobbes on, xxxiv, 354, 389-90; Kempis on, vii, 272 (4), 299 (1); Locke on, in children, xxxvii, 94; Marcus Aurelius on, ii, 207 (4); Montaigne on, xxxii, 44; noble and mean, xxviii, 117; Pascal on, xlviii, 13 (18), 60 (152); Penn on, i, 402 (135); Tzu-kung on, xliv, 62 (24)
Curious-Impertinent, history of the, xiv, 322-63, 368-73
Curious Persons, envious, iii, 24
Curius, Manius, Cicero on, ix, 14, 18, 84; and Coruncanius, 22; old age of, 66-7; reference to, iv, 387; in war with Pyrrhus, ix, 61
Curle, Dr., xv, 398
Curnach, xlix, 233
Currency, debasement of the, x, 34; depreciation of the 589-90; effect of debasement on rents, 40 (see Money)
Curricle, Lady Betty, epigram on, xviii, 128
Curse, of Faust, xix, 62-3
Curses, Chaucer on, xl, 29
Curtius, Quintus, on Alexander, xxxvii, 374-5; Cicero and, ix, 118
Curtis, John, i, 276
Curule-chair, defined, xx, 429
Curves, more beautiful than angles, xxiv, 98-9, 103
Cusco, Milton on, iv, 333
Cuscrad, son of Conchobar, xlix, 248
Cush, the Benjamite, Psalm concerning words of, xliv, 152
Cushing's Battery, at Gettysburg, xliii, 359, 373, 398, 405, 406
Custom, Calvin on, xxxix, 41-2; Descartes on ease of following, xxxiv, 14; Emerson on defiance of, v, 73; Harvey on, xxxviii, 106; "honored in breach," xlvi, 104-5; Hume on, xxxvii, 327, 339-41, 349, 394; and innovations, iii, 65;

and justice, xlviii, 105, 107 (297), 110 (309, 312); and manners, xxxvii, 376; Mill on, xxv, 208, 276-7; in modes of living, v, 54; and nature, iii, 101; obedience to, xlviii, 113-14; obedience to, a result of ignorance, xxxiv, 388; overcome by custom, vii, 236 (2); Pascal on, xlviii, 39 (89), 40 (90, 92, 93), 41 (97); in religion, 91 (245), 93 (252); not resisted, becomes necessity, vii, 130; Shakespeare on, xlvi, 157-8; Winthrop on, xliii, 90-1 (see also Conformity, Habit, Precedent)
CUSTOM, Bacon's ESSAY ON, iii, 103-4
Customs, Augustine, St., on, vii, 42; Burke on, xxiv, 88, 304-5; Goethe on, xix, 75; Woolman on, i, 201 (see Duties)
Customary Conjunction, xxxvii, 342, 349, 366-7, 439-40
Cuttle-fish, Darwin on habits of, xxix, 17-18; eyes of, xi, 200-1; supposed to have no heart, xii, 16 note
Cuvier, on conditions of life, xi, 218; on the Diodon, xxix, 24; on monkeys, xi, 356; reference to, v, 18
Cybele, mother of the Gods, iv, 43; viii, 352; ix, 405 note; xiii, 135; and the ships of Æneas, 299-300
Cyclades, the, described, xiii, 135
Cyclic-Uproar, xlv, 617
Cycloid, invention of the, xxxiv, 129
Cyclops, the, in the ÆNEID, xiii, 151-3; and the Phæacians, xxii, 85; of Sindbad, xvi, 264-7; and Ulysses, xxii, 122-34; at Vulcan's forge, xiii, 286
Cycnus, and Phaeton, xiii, 333
Cydon, and Clytius, xiii, 337
Cyllene, hoar, iv, 45
Cyllenius, messenger of Jove, xiii, 85 (see also Mercury)
Cymodoce, the nymph, xiii, 334
Cymothoe, reference to, xiii, 80
Cynemernes, in Utopia, xxxvi, 246
Cynesians, Herodotus on the, xxxiii, 21
Cynicism, Comus on, iv, 65; Epictetus on true, ii, 158-9, 160-1; tolerated in Athens, iii, 204
Cynics (see Diogenes, Demetrius, Antisthenes)
Cynosarges, at Athens, xii, 5
Cynthia, and the boar of Calydon, xiii, 253-4; and the Latmian shepherd, xl, 248; the moon called, 237, 248, 253; name of Diana, xxxix, 66; reference to, iv, 36
Cyprian Epic, Herodotus on, xxxiii, 57

Cyprian, St., xxxix, 40 note 30; xxxvi, 140; Luther on, 280; on sin, xxxix, 42

Cypris (see Aphrodite)

Cyprus, conquered first by Amasis, xxxiii, 91

Cyrene, Amasis and, xxxiii, 90-1; School of, iii, 204

Cyrus, the Elder, Bacon on, iii, 136; and Cassandane, xxxiii, 5; the cities of, iv, 395; first post ascribed to, ix, 387 note; gardening of, xxxvii, 187; on immortality, ix, 75; and the Jews, xxxii, 204; xlviii, 215 (633); liberality of, xxxvi, 56; Machiavelli on, 20-1, 22, 87; on his old age, ix, 56; Pascal on, xlviii, 239 (701); prophecy of, 245; and Scipio, xxxvi, 52; Sidney on, xxvii, 13, 20; and Tomyris, xx, 194; the young soldier of, xxxii, 85

Cyrus, the Younger, and Aspasia, xii, 63; park of, ix, 68; Xenophon on, 68

Cytheris, and Antony, xii, 341

DA DERGA'S HOSTEL, DESTRUCTION OF, xlix, 209-64

Dacia, Freeman on, xxviii, 275

Dacier, Dryden on, xiii, 12

Dædalus, Dante on, xx, 320 note 15; Virgil on, xiii, 211-12

Dæghrefn, death of, xlix, 76

DAER, LORD, LINES ON MEETING, vi, 252-3

DAFFODILS, THE, xli, 654-5

DAFFODILS, TO, xl, 347

Dag, son of Hogni, xlix, 385-7

Dagon, god of the Philistines, iv, 102, 419, 429-30

Dahish, the Efrit, xvi, 320-4

Daigne, the apothecary, xxxviii, 24

DAINTY DAVIE, vi, 502

Dairy Products, price of, x, 198-9

Daisies, Shelley on, xli, 865; for simplicity, vi, 431, 500

DAISY, STORY OF THE, xvii, 316-20

DAISY, TO THE, xli, 655-6

Dalibard, M., i, 154, 155

Dalila, wife of Samson, iv, 424, 428-9, 432, 437-43

Dalmatia, Freeman on, xxviii, 265

Dalrymple, Dr., reference to, vi, 372

Damaris, xliv, 470 (34)

Damiano, Pietro, xx, 378 and note 13

Damiano, St., xxxi, 163 note 1

Damien, reference to, xli, 544

Damis, in TARTUFFE, disinherited, xxvi, 247; Dorine and, 198, 233-4; Loyal and, 275, 276, 277; Pernelle and, 190, 191-2; Tartuffe and, 237, 241-2, 243-6, 268

Damœtas, reference to, iv, 75

Damon, ostracism of, xii, 81;

Pythias and, Browne on, iii, 332; teacher of Pericles, xii, 39

DAMON AND SYLVIA, vi, 439

Damonides, of Œa, xii, 45

Dampier, on gold countries, xiii, 62

Dana, Francis, xxiii, 3

Dana, Richard Henry, Jr., life and works, xxiii, 3-4; TWO YEARS BEFORE THE MAST, 5-391; TWENTY-FOUR YEARS AFTER, 395-426

Danae, founder of Ardua, xiii, 257; Jove and, vii, 19; xlvi, 51; xlvii, 586, 588; Marlowe on, xlvi, 29; Sophocles on, viii, 272; Suckling on, xl, 362; Tennyson on, xlii, 1004

Danaos, an Egyptian, xxxiii, 45; daughters of, viii, 185-6; xiii, 343; xxxiii, 86-7, 91

Danby, Earl of, Dedication to, xviii, 5-10; George Herbert and, xv, 396

Dancer, in FAUST, xix, 181

Dancing, Confucius on, xliv, 9 (1); Cowley on, xxvii, 69; Emerson on beauty of, v, 313; among the Germans, xxxiii, 109; Locke on, xxxvii, 50, 182

Dancing-Master, in FAUST, xix, 181

Dandini, on Socrates, etc., v, 279

Danger, admiration excited by, ix, 364; Bacon on, iii, 59; Goethe on, xix, 340; Locke on insensibility to, xxxvii, 102; of others, pleasure in, xxiv, 43-4; passions excited by, 36; way of, in PILGRIM'S PROGRESS, xv, 46, 221

Daniel, the prophet, Dante on, xx, 240 and note 12; on dreams, xl, 43; on God, xxxvi, 345; learning of, iii, 209; Luther on, xxxvi, 346; Milton on, iv, 384; Nebuchadnezzar and, xx, 299 note 1; Pascal on, xlviii, 236; prophecies of, 249 (722-3), 259

Daniel, Arnault, Dante on, xx, 255 and note 2

Daniel, Samuel, sonnets by, xl, 223-6

Daniel, the Saxon, xxxiii, 294, 299

Dante Alighieri, ancestry of, xx, 350 notes 1 and 2; Arnold on selections from, xxviii, 73, 80; banishment of, xx, 180 and note 10, 229 note 12; banishment predicted, 43, 64-6, 357-61; Beatrice and (see Beatrice); Browning on the painting of, xlii, 1138-9; at Campaldino, xx, 166 note 8; Carlyle on, xxv, 461; Casella and, iv, 83; Cavalcanti and, xx, 43 note 6; Cellini on line of, xxxi, 316; date of descent into Hell, xx, 90 note; DIVINE COMEDY; Dryden on, xxxix, 162; Emerson on, v, 186; English love of, 450; father of, xx, 351 note 2; as a Franciscan, 70 note 9; Goethe on, xxxii, 412;

Hazlitt on, xxvii, 286; Hugo on, xxxix, 367, 372-3; Huxley on, xxviii, 225; life and works, xx, 3-4; Macaulay on, xxvii, 389; Milton on, xxviii, 180; on the ocean, xliii, 31; on St. Peter's keys, xxviii, 112-13; in poet's band, xx, 19; religious belief of, 391, 397; rescue of child from drowning, 79 note; Ruskin on creed of, xxviii, 115; Sainte-Beuve on, xxxii, 127, 133, 137; Shelley on, xxvii, 348, 351, 364, 365, 366, 367; Sidney on, 9; Thoreau on, xxviii, 433; Wordsworth on sonnets of, xli, 697

Danti, Vincenzo, xxxi, 438 note

Danube, Herodotus on the (Ister), xxxiii, 21; Tacitus on the, 95

Danvers, Charles, and George Herbert, xv, 397

Danvers, Jane, wife of George Herbert, xv, 397, 401, 402, 413, 423-4

Danvilliers, siege of, xxxviii, 20-2

Daphne, and Apollo, xl, 386; iv, 64; grove of, iv, 164; Webster on, xlvii, 758

Daphne, in Tartuffe, xxvi, 194

Dapper, in The Alchemist, xlvii, 528-35, 576-7, 579, 581-5, 621-2, 623-5

Darby, Earl of, and Dryden, xiii, 430

Dardanus, born in Italy, xiii, 137; Electra's son, 276; founder of Troy, xx, 20 note 5; Virgil on, xiii, 250

Dare-not-lye, Mr., xv, 285, 287

Dares, death of, xiii, 407; and Entellus, 194-8; xxxix, 182

Dares, Trojan priest, Caxton on, xxxix, 9

Daring, Graham on, xl, 369; Locke on, xxxvii, 102; Shakespeare on, xlvi, 320

Darius, prophecy of, xlviii, 252

Darius III, Dryden on, xl, 403; empire of, xxxvi, 17-18; Greek cities and, 23; Raleigh on, xxxix, 103

Dark Ages, Shelley on the, xxvii, 362-3

Dark-land, in Pilgrim's Progress, xv, 301

Darkness, in architecture, xxiv, 71; children's fear of, xxxvii, 126; sublimity and, xxiv, 70-1; sublimity of, 120-5; terror in idea of, 63; usefulness of, xxviii, 431; "visible," iv, 92

Darkness, Byron's poem, xli, 816

Darkness, Our Lady of, xxvii, 340

Darley, George, Loveliness of Love, xli, 938-9

Darning-Needle, The, xvii, 334

Darwin, Charles Robert, Origin of Species, xi; sketch of life and works, 5-8; Voyage of Beagle, xxix

Darwin, Erasmus, xi, 5, 10 note

Darwin, George, on lunar disturbances, xxx, 296-7; on long period tides, 313

Darwin, Horace, on lunar disturbances, xxx, 296-7

Darwinism, Lowell on, xxviii, 475 note

Datarius, Papal, xxxvi, 298 note, 300

Dathan, reference to, xliv, 283 (17)

Datis, general of Darius, xii, 84

Dativo, the pedagogue, xxxviii, 14-15

Datur Hora Quieti, xli, 772-3

Daunton Me, To, vi, 319-20

Dauphin, heir-apparent of France, xxxv, 229

Davaine, Dr., xxxviii, 382

Davenant, Dr., Bishop of Salisbury, xv, 399

D'Avenant, Sir William, Dawn Song, xl, 364; Swift on, xxvii, 117

David, and the Amorites, xliii, 110; Bagehot on, xxviii, 175-6; Burns on, vi, 240; on Christ, xliv, 432 (25-31); Dante on, xx, 186-7; in Dante's Paradise, 372; faults of, xv, 263; God's covenant with, xliv, 259 (3-4), 260 (20-51); Goliath and, xxxvi, 49; Kempis on, vii, 351 (8); Locke on stories of, xxxvii, 142-3; Mephibosheth and, xliii, 110; Milton on, iv, 353, 398; Mohammed on, xlv, 928; Nathan and, xxvii, 27; one of nine worthies, xxxix, 21; Pascal on, xlviii, 91 (243), 235 (690), 236, 269 (752); Paul on, xliv, 459 (22); on the Sabbath, xliv, 373 (3-4); sword of, xxxv, 198; and the tabernacle, xliv, 318; and the temple, 445 (46); in valley of death, xv, 67, 136; water, story of, i, 297-8; v, 130; Winthrop on, xliii, 100

David, Psalms of, xliv, 148-97, 209-35, 256-7, 273, 276-7, 288-92, 312, 313, 317, 319, 323-36; remarks on, 146; Sidney on, xxvii, 11, 14

David, Song to, xli, 496-510

David, King, of Britain, xxxv, 264

Davie, Epistle to, vi, 70-4

Davie, Second Epistle to, vi, 113-114

Davies, Charms of Lovely, vi, 429-30

Davies, Miss, Epigram on, vi, 429

Davies, Mr., on puerperal fever, xxxviii, 241

Davies, Tom, Lamb on, xxvii, 314 note

Davy, Sir Humphry, and conservation, law of, xxx, 183; Faraday and, 3; on frictional heat, 205-6; potassium, discovered by, 124 note

Dawn Song, by D'Avenant, xl, 364

Dawn Song, by Shakespeare, xl, 274

Day, Is Coming, The, xlii, 1242

Day, Is Done, The, xlii, 1326-7

Day is Past and Over, The, xlv, 554-5

Day Returns, vi, 331

Days, by Emerson, xlii, 1294-5

Days that Were, xlii, 1245

Dead, Brynhild on the, xlix, 395; Calvin on masses for the, xxxix, 39; grief for, xxvii, 300; knowledge of the, xxxix, 96-7; Luther on masses for, xxxvi, 322-3; Pascal on prayers for the, xlviii, 344-5

Dead Man's Lane, in Pilgrim's Progress, xv, 130

Dean of Faculty, The, vi, 584

Death, Adam's first view of, iv, 334; Addison on contemplation of, xxvii, 84-5; Æschylus on, viii, 75; Arabian inscriptions on, xvi, 315-19, 326-7, 331-2, 334-6, 443, 460; Aristophanes on, viii, 462; Aristotle on, xxxviii, 89; Barbauld on, xli, 568; Beaumont on, xlvii, 677; Beowulf on, xlix, 45; Browne on, iii, 263, 303-4, 305, 309, 339; Browning, Robert, on, xlii, 1106-7; Browning, Elizabeth B., on, xli, 968-70; Bryant on, xlii, 1262-4; Buddhist ideas of, xlv, 678, 697, 700, 752; Bunyan's allegory of, xv, 161-2, 314-22; Burke on idea of, xxiv, 36; Burns on, vi, 67, 313; Byron on fear of, xviii, 422; Calderon on, xxvi, 65; children mitigate, iii, 20; Cicero on, ix, 70-4; Clough on, xlii, 1166; comes to all alike, xxvii, 82 note 2; Confucius on, xliv, 35 (11); Diogenes on, ii, 180 (187); Drummond on, xl, 335; Dryden on, xviii, 93, 94; Ecclesiastes on, xliv, 347 (1), 350 (5-6); Emerson on, v, 135, 304-5; Epictetus on, ii, 131 (44, 45), 135 (55), 158 (112), 164 (130, 131), 165 (132, 134, 135), 167 (139), 174 (161), 181 (188); Euripides on, in misery, viii, 331; Faust on, xix, 61-2; fear of, disposes to peace, xxxiv, 385; "felicity of wretched men," xlvi, 67; Fitzgerald on, xli, 973-5, 978, 981; friends lessen fear of, iii, 75; friendship takes sting from, ix, 16; Goethe on, xix, 419; Gray on, xl, 457-8, 466; Grenville on, xlii, 1045; Hamlet's soliloquy on, xlvi, 135; xxxiv, 135-6; the happiest, ii, 181 (189);

Harvey on cause of, xxxviii, 129; Harvey on two kinds of, 115; Henley's wish for, xlii, 1258; Herbert on, xl, 351-2; Hindu conception of, xlv, 806-7; Job on, xliv, 76-7, 94 (10-12), 106 (23-6); Kempis on meditations of, vii, 239-41; knowledge of world after, xxxix, 96-7; Longfellow on, xlii, 1330; love and, 1076; Marcus Aurelius on, ii, 202 (11), 203 (12), 204 (14), 205 (17), 207 (3), 210 (7), 215 (5, 6), 216 (14), 222 (47, 48), 223 (50), 224 (4), 232 (29), 234 (2), 238 (24), 239 (28), 244 (47), 247 (10), 248 (19), 250 (33), 252 (50), 259 (18), 260 (25), 261 (31), 267 (58), 268 (3), 272 (21), 274 (33), 285 (29), 288 (36), 289 (3), 300 (5), 303 (23), 305 (31, 34, 35), 306 (36); Milton on, iv, 168, 324, 335, 360, 459; Mohammed on, xlv, 989; Montaigne on, xxxii, 7-8, 9-28; Montaigne's conceptions, Pascal on, xlviii, 24, 401; More on, xxxvi, 126; Nashe on, xl, 265-6; to be overcome by Christ, iv, 144; Pascal on, xlviii, 63 (166, 168), 64 (169), 65 (175), 71, 79 (210), 80 (215-16), 153 (447), 335-43; Penn on, i, 380 (500-5); Pope on knowledge of, xl, 435; Raleigh on, xxxix, 99, 103; Raleigh on thoughts of, xl, 207; Roman expression for, xii, 243; Rossetti, C. G., on, xlii, 1228, 1229; Rousseau on, xxxiv, 268-9; Schiller on, xxvi, 459; scholar's dread of, xix, 28; Shakespeare on, xl, 275; Shakespeare on fear of, xlvi, 297; Shelley on, xviii, 307, 308, 350-1; xli, 855, 892; Shirley on, xl, 359, 360; Socrates on, ii, 15-16, 24, 26, 27-8, 50-9, 61; Sophocles on, v, 126; viii, 259; Swinburne on, xlii, 1253; terror of, in animals, xxxiv, 181; Utopian ideas of, xxxvi, 241-2; Valley of Shadow of, xv, 65-70, 248-52; Vaughan on, xl, 356; "where is thy victory," xlv, 525 (55); White on, xli, 938; Whitman on, xlii, 1503-4, 1508; "who kings and tars dispatches," xli, 515; Woolman on nearness to, i, 206-7

Death, in Paradise Lost, iv, 127-30, 136, 300-5, 309-10; Burke on, xxiv, 53

Death, Essay on, Bacon's, iii, 9-11

Death Bed, The, xli, 935

Death and Doctor Hornbook, vi, 79-84

Death, by Donne, xl, 313

Death of a Fair Infant, On the, iv, 18-21

DEATH AND THE OLD MAN, a fable, xvii, 40

DEATH OF POOR MAILIE, vi, 43-5

DEATH, PRAYER IN PROSPECT OF, vi, 36

DEATH, SONG OF, vi, 452

DEATH STANDS ABOVE ME, xli, 930

DEATH, THE TERROR OF, xli, 921-2

DEATH'S MESSENGERS, xlv, 701-7

DEATHS OF LITTLE CHILDREN, Hunt's, xxvii, 299-303

Debasement, of currency, x, 34; effect on money rents, 40

Debates, Penn on, i, 352 (133-6)

Debauchery, Burns on, vi, 193; courage and, xxxvii, 57

De Bouillon, Cardinal Retz on, v, 317

Debt, Emerson on, v, 100; Franklin on, i, 95; imprisonment for, in Massachusetts, xliii, 75 (33); Penn on collecting, i, 343 (48); in Utopia, xxxvi, 201

Decebalus, King of Dacia, ix, 388 notes 2, 4

Deceit, Pascal on sources of, xlviii, 37-8; punishment of, in Hell, xx, 47; Whitman on, xxxix, 425

DECEMBER, THOU GLOOMY, vi, 456

Decemviri, Roman, ix, 290 note 2

Decency, Mill on offences against, xxv, 307

Decii, deaths of the, ix, 73

Decius, Publius, Cicero on, ix, 61

Decius, Roman Emperor, persecutions under, xxxviii, 412

Decker (see Dekker)

DECLARATION OF INDEPENDENCE, xliii, 160; Lincoln on, 337

DECLARATION, THE MECKLENBURG, xliii, 166-7

Declaration of Right, Burke on, xxiv, 164-5, 180-1

DECLARATION OF RIGHTS, xliii, 157-9

Deeow, Isaac, i, 56-7

Decurii, Roman, ix, 203 note

DEDICATION, A, by Burns, vi, 221-4

Dee, Dr., the magician, xlvii, 564 note 4

Deer, ages, various of the, xxxv, 361; in Brazil, xxix, 59-60

Defects, compensation for, v, 102; Hugo on, xxxix, 406; Shakespeare on single, xlvi, 105

Defence, national, expense of, x, 468-71

Deference, Emerson on, v, 217; Pascal on, xlviii, 111 (317)

Definitions, Burke on, xxiv, 12; Goethe on, xix, 126-7; Hobbes on, xxxiv, 339-40, 346; Hume on, xxxvii, 371-2; Johnson on, xxxix, 200-4; Pascal on, xlviii, 410, 411, 429-30, 431-5, 440-1

Defoe, Daniel, EDUCATION OF WOMEN, xxvii, 158-61; Emerson on, v, 450; on Englishmen, 353; Essay on Projects, i, 14; Franklin on, i, 23-4; life and works, xxvii, 142; SHORTEST WAY WITH DISSENTERS, xxvii, 143-57

DEFORMITY, BACON'S ESSAY ON, iii, 112-13

Deformity, Browne on, iii, 280; Burke on, xxiv, 87; envy and, iii, 24

Degerando, Landor on, v, 329-30

Deglutition, Harvey on, xxxviii, 92

Degradation, geological (see Denudation)

Deïanira, and Nessus, xx, 52 and note

Deïdamia, Dante on, xx, 110, 239

DEIL, ADDRESS TO THE, vi, 147-51

DEIL'S AWA WI' THE EXCISEMAN, vi, 467

Deiotarus, Cicero on, ix, 141, 142, 146, 149, 153, 156; in war of Antony and Octavius, xii, 384

Deïphile, in Limbo, xx, 339

Deïphobe, the Sibyl, and Æneas, xiii, 212-42

Deïphobus, in Hades, xiii, 228-9; at Trojan horse, xxii, 55

Deism, Franklin on, i, 57; Mill on, xxv, 35, 50; Pascal on, xlviii, 184, 186; Rousseau on, xxxiv, 289, 290-1, 293, 298, 309-10

Dejection, Coleridge on, xxv, 89; defined by Hobbes, xxxiv, 355; results of, 367

DEJECTION: AN ODE, xli, 745-9

DEJECTION, STANZAS WRITTEN IN, xli, 848-9

Dekker, Thomas, Hazlitt on, xxvii, 291; life and works, xlvii, 445; POEMS BY, xl, 325-7; SHOEMAKER'S HOLIDAY, xlvii, 447-515

Delaware, Lord, at Crecy, xxxv, 23; at Poitiers, 42

Delay, Bacon on, iii, 59 60; Penn on, i, 372 (390); Shakespeare on, xl, 268

Delectable Mountains, in PILGRIM'S PROGRESS, xv, 59, 124

DELIA: AN ODE, vi, 359-60

Deliberation, Hobbes on, xxxiv, 356-7; language of, 358

Delicacy, as cause of beauty, xxiv, 99-100; of imagination, Hume on, xxvii, 221-24

Delight, Burke on, xxiv, 33-4; Hobbes on, xxxiv, 352-3; how caused by pain, xxiv, 113-14; Shelley on, xli, 847-8

Delilah (see Dalila)

Delille, Hugo on, xxxix, 388-9

Delio, in DUCHESS OF MALFI, xlvii, 721, 723; in presence chamber scene, 724, 726-7; learns Antonio's marriage, 740; advises An-

tonio, 742-3; despatched to Rome, 745; with Antonio, after interval, 754-5; on Malatesti, 768; on Bosola, 769; with Julia in Rome, 750-1; on Antonio's betrayal, 751; with Antonio in Milan, 793-6, 807-9; in final scene, 816

Delius, and Cleopatra, xii, 352-3, 382

Delos, island of, xiii, 133-4

Delphi, navel of earth, v, 347; building of temple of, xxxiii, 90

Delphian Oracle, Æschylus on ambiguity of, viii, 51; Emerson on, xlii, 1299; prophets of, viii, 115-16

Delphos, King, viii, 116

Delrio, Manzoni on, xxi, 553

Deltas, Lyell on, xxxviii, 423

DELUDED SWAIN, THE PLEASURE, vi, 506

Deluge, Calvin on the, xxxix, 42; Locke on, xxxvii, 176; Milton on, iv, 340-3; Pascal on, xlviii, 211 (625), 220 (644)

Deluges, Bacon on, iii, 143

Demades, Alexander and, xii, 217; death of, 224; Demosthenes and, 203, 206, 221; fickleness of, 207

Demagogues, Hamilton on, xliii, 215

Demand, effectual and absolute, x, 59

Demand and Supply, equalization of, x, 60-1; of laborers in regard to population, 84-5; as regulators of price, 59-60

Demaratus, the Spartan, xii, 32

Demas, in PILGRIM'S PROGRESS, xv, 111-13, 313

Demeter, functions of, viii, 359-60; Hades, ruler of, xxxiii, 63; hymn to, viii, 430; Iasion and, xxii, 74; the Isis of Egyptians, xxxiii, 33, 81; mystic rites of, 86-7; Rhampsinitos and, 63

Demetrius, the Cynic, and Nero, ii, 132 (45)

Demetrius, the Grammarian, and the philosophers, xxxii, 51

Demetrius, of Phaleron, and Æsop, xvii, 2; on Aristides, xii, 80, 81

Demetrius, son of Philip II, iii, 53

Demetrius, the silversmith, xliv, 474-5

Democracy, Aristotle on, xxiv, 273 note; Burke on, 241-2, 272-3; education and, xxv, 112; Emerson on, v, 254; justified by example of Lincoln, xxviii, 461; Machiavelli on, xxv, 384; Mill on, 111, 124, 149, 204-6, 272; James Mill on, 71-2; nobility and, iii, 36-7; Rousseau on, xxxiv, 226; supposed shortcomings of, xxviii, 443

DEMOCRACY, ESSAY ON, Lowell's, xxviii, 464-85

Democracy in America, Mill on, xxv, 124-5; James Mill on, 131

Democritus, Browne on, iii, 330; death of, ii, 207 (3); Huxley on, xxviii, 227; on kitchen gardens, x, 163; in Limbo, xx, 20 note 9

Demodocus, the minstrel, xxii, 105-6, 111, 117; Milton on, iv, 22

Demogorgon, xlvii, 543 note 14; Milton on, iv, 135

Demoleüs, and Æneas, xiii, 191

Demons, Hobbes on possession by, xxxiv, 370-2; Milton on, iv, 37

Demonstration, Hume on, xxxvii, 351 note, 443-4; judgment and fancy in, xxxiv, 364-5; Pascal's method of, xlviii, 410-13, 428-44

Demophon, steward of Alexander, xxxii, 58

Demophoon, Dante on, xx, 324

Demosthenes, on action, iii, 33; Æschines on, ix, 224-5; Alexander demands, xii, 216-17; early ambition, 200; opposes Antipater, 220; compared with other Athenian orators, 203; Athens honors, 223-4; birth and education, 199; Carlyle on, xxv, 394-5; Cicero compared with, xii, 198-9, 267-73; xxxix, 166; Cicero on, xii, 245; condemnation and banishment, 219-20; courage in resisting populace, 209; on the Crown, 217; death of, 221-3, 273; iv, 81; determined disposition, xii, 207-8; fiery eloquence of, ix, 365-6; not an extempore speaker, xii, 203; faults, 208; flight from battle, 213; pronounces funeral oration, 214; suit against guardians, 201; Harpalus and, 218; forms new league, 216; Midias and, 207; Mill on, xxv, 19; nicknames, xii, 199-200; old woman and, ix, 363; orations, xii, 208-10; Philip of Macedon and, 207, 210-13, 215; Pliny on, ix, 195, 214; Plutarch's LIFE OF, xii, 197-224; first entry on public business, 201-2, 206; on public speaking, ix, 262-3; recalled to Athens, xii, 320-1; Sainte-Beuve on, xxxii, 137; urged to new studies, xii, 202; style, 206; teachers, 200-1; methods of training himself, 205-6

Dempster, George, Burns on, vi, 167, 175, 185

Denham, Sir John, Dryden on, xxxix, 171; on Henry VIII, xxiv, 265

Denham, Mr., and Franklin, 41, 42, 49, 50-2

Denial, not scepticism, xxxvii, 203-4

Denman (see Denham)

Dennis, John, on Addison's Cato, xxvii, 176-7, 178, 179, 197-208; on Shakespeare, xxxix, 223, 243

Denny, Gov., Franklin on, i, 133, 152, 156-7, 168, 170
Dente, Vitaliano del, xx, 73 note 6
Denudation, Darwin on geological, xi, 336-7, 339, 345; xxix, 335-6; Geikie on, xxx, 355-6; Lyell on, xxxviii, 421-2, 436
DEPARTURE, by Patmore, xlii, 1158
Dependencies, Machiavelli on, xxxvi, 8-12, 18-19; arms in, 72; factions in, 72-3
Dependent Origination, xlv, 639, 680-1
Deposition, Rousseau on right of, xxxiv, 225, 231
Depravity, Dante on human, xx, 211-13; Emerson on doctrine of, v, 278
Depth, grander than other dimensions, xxiv, 63-4
De Quincey, Thomas, life and works, xxvii, 334; LEVANA AND LADIES OF SORROW, 335-41
Dercennus, in ÆNEID, xiii, 391
Dercetæus, and Antony, xii, 397
Descartes, René, on comets, xxxiv, 120; geometry, work in, 114, 127; on God, xxxvii, 365 note; life and works of, xxxiv, 3; on light, 124; Locke on system of, xxxvii, 177; ON THE METHOD, xxxiv, 5-62; reasons for and against publishing METHOD, 49-62; remarks on METHOD, 5-6; provisory code of morals, 21-5; compared with Newton, 110-15; Pascal on, xlviii, 33-4, 414-15; beginning of new philosophy, xxxiv, 28-34; physical investigations, 35-48, 51-3; idea of planetary motions, 116; on rainbow, 124; Rousseau on, 255-6; scepticism of, xxxvii, 431-2; on the soul, xxxiv, 105; on telescopes, 126; travels, 10-11, 25-7; Voltaire on, 110-15
Descent, in classification, xi, 460-2
Description, Burke on verbal, xxiv, 53-7; Wordsworth on powers of, xxxix, 312
Desdemona, Lamb on, xxvii, 326-7
DESERTED VILLAGE, THE, xli, 521-32; an idyllic poem, xxxix, 314
Deserters, article of, in Spanish Treaty, xliii, 293-4
Deserters, the Egyptian, xxxiii, 18-19
Deserts, Burton on, xxviii, 424; Shakespeare on, xlvi, 131
DESIDERIA, xli, 690
Desire, defined by Hobbes, xxxiv, 350; love contrasted with, 351; xxiv, 77; Milton on, iv, 170; offences through, ii, 202 (10)
Desires, Augustine, St., on worldly, vii, 191-203; Bacon on, and fears, iii, 50; Buddha on noble and ignoble, xlv, 731; Dante on, xx,

217-20; Descartes on limitation of, xxxiv, 23-4; Emerson on unbridled, v, 96; Epictetus on, ii, 169 (145); Hindu reward of righteous, xlv, 829-30; Hobbes on, xxxiv, 350-4, 366-7, 384, 385-6; Kempis on, vii, 219, 282-3, 287, 302-3, 327 (6); language of, xxxiv, 358; Locke on, xxxvii, 116, 117; Locke on, of children, 91-6; Marcus Aurelius on, ii, 212 (16); Mill on, xxv, 264-5
Despair, defined by Hobbes, xxxiv, 353; Epictetus on, ii, 173 (156); in music, Collins on, xli, 489
Despair, the giant, in PILGRIM'S PROGRESS, xv, 118-23, 291-3
Despoblado, valley of, xxix, 375-6
DESPONDENCY: AN ODE, vi, 206-8
Despondency, Mr., in PILGRIM'S PROGRESS, xv, 291-2, 294, 306, 316, 318-19
Despotism, legitimate with barbarians, xxv, 213; origin of, xxxiv, 220-4; Rousseau on, 230-1; secrecy surrounding, xxiv, 52
De Staël, Madame, and the Emperor, xxvii, 248; on herself, v, 450
Destinies, in MANFRED, xviii, 423-8
DESTRUCTION OF DA DERGA'S HOSTEL, xlix, 209-64
Destruction, Way of, in PILGRIM'S PROGRESS, xv, 46, 221-2
Determination, why honorable, xxxiv, 380; Pliny on, ix, 262
Determinism (see Free Will)
Detraction, Jesus on, xliv, 374 (22); Kempis on, vii, 303-4, 322 (5), 323-4; Penn on, i, 362-3, 398-9 (85-89); Socrates on, ii, 15; superiority to, ii, 119 (7)
DETRACTION, ON THE, WHICH FOLLOWED CERTAIN TREATISES, iv, 81, 82
Detritus (see Denudation)
Detroit, River, navigation of, xliii, 306
Deucalion, son of Minos, xxii, 272
DEUKS, DANG O'ER MY DADDIE, vi, 466
DEUS, EGO AMO TE, xlv, 568-9
De Vere, Sir Aubrey, GLENGARIFF, xli, 936-7
De Vere, Edward, A RENUNCIATION, xl, 296
De Vere, house of, its motto, v, 388-9
Devereux, Col., at Gettysburg, xliii, 409, 411
Devereux, Penelope, and Sidney, xxvii, 5-6
Devereux, Robert, A PASSION, xl, 294
Devil, Bacon on, enviousness of the,

iii, 27; Bunyan on, xv, 197-8; Dante on, xx, 166 note 12; Goethe on, xix, 19; Kempis on, vii, 276 (7); More on, xxxvi, 105; Penn on, i, 362 (267)

DEVON, BANKS OF THE, vi, 303

Devonshire, Duke of, Emerson on, v, 429

DEVOTED WIFE, THE, xlv, 708-11

Devotion, false, Kempis on, vii, 273 (5); Molière on false, xxvi, 203, 204

Dexter, Afranius, case of, ix, 337-40

Dexter, H. M., translator of hymn, xlv, 553

Dexterity, favored by division of labor, x, 13

Dextro-Tartrate of Lime, fermentation of, xxxviii, 332-40

Dhanañjaya, xlv, 770, 771-2, 776-81

Dhritirashtra, xlv, 801

Diadematus, surname of Metellus, xii, 162

Dialects, Johnson on, xxxix, 193

Dialogue, Franklin on, i, 23

DIALOGUE SONG: PHILLY AND WILLY, vi, 541

DIALOGUES OF HYLAS AND PHILONOUS, xxxvii, 199-302; remarks on, 198

DIALOGUES OF PLATO, ii, 3-114

Diamonds, same as charcoal, xxx, 28; pounded, as means of death, xxxi, 257

Diana, Camilla and, xiii, 380-2; chastity of, iv, 58; goddess of childbirth, xl, 248; Latmian Shepherd and, 248; worship of, at Ephesus, xliv, 474-5 (see also Artemis)

DIANA, HYMN TO, xl, 306-7

Diana of Foix, Montaigne to, xxxii, 29

DIANEME, To, xl, 345

DIAPHENIA, xl, 233

Diaries, in travel, iii, 49

Diastole (see Systole and Diastole)

Diaz, Ruy (see Cid)

Dibdin, Charles, TOM BOWLING, xli, 514

Dicearcus, Montaigne on, xxxii, 20

Dicers, More on, xxxvi, 212

Dichogamous Plants, xi, 112

Dickens, Charles, Emerson on, v, 457, 491; THE IVY GREEN, xlii, 1194

Dickie of Dryhope, xl, 112-13

Dickson, J. F., paper by, xlv, 756

Dicomes, king of the Getæ, xii, 385

Dictes, Caxton on, xxxix, 9

DICTES AND SAYINGS OF THE PHILOSOPHERS, xxxix, 10-13, 5 note

DICTIONARY, PREFACE TO JOHNSON'S, xxxix, 191-216

Didactic Art, Schiller on, xxxii, 287

Didactic Poetry, Poe on, xxviii, 387-8; Wordsworth on, xxxix, 314

Diderot, Carlyle on, xxv, 369; Hobbes and, xxxiv, 318

Didias, Julianus (see Julianus)

Dido, Æneas and, xiii, 85-179; Calypso and, xxxix, 165; Carthage founded by, xiii, 87-8; Chaucer's picture of, v, 287; death of, xiii, 179-81; Dryden on, 30-9; harshness of her reign, xxxvi, 57; in Hell, xx, 23; in the Mournful Fields, xiii, 226-7

Didymus, Newman on, xxviii, 38

Diego, the negro, with Drake, xxxiii, 143-4, 147-8, 153, 157

DIES IRÆ, DIES ILLA, xlv, 563-5

Diet, Bacon on changes of, iii, 85; of children, Locke on, xxxvii, 16-22

Difficulty, Burke on, xxiv, 315; Channing on value of, xxviii, 325; source of the sublime, xxiv, 68

Difficulty, hill of, in PILGRIM'S PROGRESS, xv, 45, 220-1

Diffidence, Browning on, xviii, 362; Hobbes on, xxxiv, 353, 380; Pliny on, ix, 288; quarrels caused by, xxxiv, 403, 404

Diffidence, wife of Despair, in PILGRIM'S PROGRESS, xv, 119, 122, 291

Digby, Sir Kenelm, v, 368; Pope on, xl, 444

Diggory, in SHE STOOPS TO CONQUER, xviii, 214-15, 251-2

Dignity, Confucius on, xliv, 55 (32); Emerson on, v, 217; Hobbes on, xxxiv, 378; Kant on, xxxii, 365; morality alone possesses, 366

Digressions, Raleigh on, xxxix, 118

Dilettantes, Emerson on, v, 167

Diligence, Carlyle on, xxv, 377-8; Penn on, i, 360 (234)

Dimorphism, Darwin on, xi, 61; reciprocal, 319-22

Dinas Bren, eagles of, xxxv, 356

Dinmont, Dandie, Ruskin on, xxviii, 144

Dinomache, mother of Alcibiades, xii, 110

Diocles, son of Orsilochus, xxii, 47, 213

Diocletian, Bacon on, iii, 51; miracles under, xlviii, 293 (832)

Dioclides, accuser of Alcibiades, xii, 128-9

Diodon Antennatus, habits of, xxix, 23-4

Diodorus, on Themistocles, xii, 35

Diogenes of Apollonia, on the soul, xxxiv, 104

Diogenes, the Cynic, Browne on, iii, 320; on comedies, ii, 290 (6);

Dandini on, v, 279; Emerson on, 211; Epictetus on, ii, 163 (128); freedom of, 168 (141); on friends, xxxii, 83; health of, ii, 161 (118); Hegesias and, xxxii, 60; on indifference of circumstances, ii, 180 (187); in Limbo, xx, 20; lines on, xxv, 455; Marcus Aurelius on, ii, 257 (3); mission of, 157 (108); Philip and, 159 (113); on philosophy, xxxii, 60; on recommendations, ii, 136 (57); Rome, Ambassador to, x, 143; in Rome, iii, 204-5; ix, 54; Rousseau on, xxxiv, 232; and the statues, ii, 177 note; on strength of soul, 138 (62); tub of, referred to, vi, 198; Voltaire on, xxxiv, 104; will of, iii, 306 note

Diognetus, Aurelius's debt to, ii, 193 (6)

Diogoras, iii, 45

Diomede, in Hell, xx, 110; Minerva and, xiii, 108-9; reference to, 92; return of, from Troy, xxii, 38, 39

Diomedes, Dryden on, xiii, 26; in Italy, 272-3; refuses aid to Latinus, 369-71

Diomedes, friend of Alcibiades, xii, 119

Dion, Cocceianus, ix, 420 a

Dion, in PHILASTER, xlvii, in presence chamber scene, 639-49; before Pharamond's house, 663-9; scene with Philaster, 669-73; at the hunt, 684-5, 687-9, 690, 694, 697-700; on Philaster, 702; on Arethusa, 704; in the sedition, 705, 706-7; in final scene, 712, 714-16

Dion Prusœus, and the Rhodians, iii, 201

Dion, of Syracuse, and Plato, xii, 80

Dione, mother of Venus, xx, 316 note 1, 383 note 13

Dionysius, the Elder, in Hell, xx, 53; and tragedy, iv, 416

Dionysius, the Younger, Plato and, iii, 204, 216; xxvii, 41; xxxvi, 167; as a poet, xviii, 15-16

Dionysius, St., of Alexandria, xx, 330 note 22; on God, xxxix, 108-9; quoted, xxxv, 347; vision of, iii, 210

Dionysius, the Areopagite, xx, 407 notes 3 and 5; xliv, 470 (34)

Dionysius, king of Portugal, xx, 370 note 15

Dionysius, school of, ix, 165

Dionysius, surnamed Thrax, Cicero on, ix, 152

Dionysus, in the BACCHÆ, viii, 349-415; Dryas's son and, 272-3; Euripides on, 358, 360, 371-2; festivals of, 418; in the FROGS, 419-66; Hades, ruler of, xxxiii, 63; Osiris and, identified by Herodotus, 25, 29-30, 74-5, 81 (see also Bacchus)

Diophantus, at Athens, xxviii, 60

Diopithes, decree of, xii, 70

Diores, death of, xiii, 412; in the foot-race, 192-3

Dioscorides, Dante on, xx, 20

Dioscuroi, unknown in Egypt, xxxiii, 26 (see Castor and Pollux)

Diotimus, ii, 260 (25), 262 (37)

Dipamkara, xlv, 596-8; Buddha and, 599-601, 613-14

Diphilides, and Themistocles, xii, 9

Diphilus, Cicero on, ix, 115; xxvii, 405 note 8

Diræ, the, xiii, 425

Dirce, daughter of Achelous, viii, 371

Dirce, river, Bacchus bathed in, viii, 371

DIRCE, by Landor, xli, 924

Direct Taxes, apportionment of, xliii, 193 (3), 198 (4), 204 (5); under the Confederation, 172

DIRGE, by Sidney, xl, 214-15

DIRGE, Fidele's, xl, 275

DIRGE OF LOVE, Shakespeare's, xl, 274-5

DIRGE, A SEA, xl, 275

Dis, in Scandinavian mythology, xlix, 311 note; Proserpine and, iv, 164

Dis, Pluto called, xlvi, 426

Dis, city of, xx, 35 et seq.

Disappointment, defined by Burke, xxiv, 34; Penn on, i, 342 (32), 403 (152)

Disasters, bring out leaders, xix, 385

Disciples, chorus of, in FAUST, xix, 35; Pascal on, xlviii, 172 (519); Woolman on, i, 209

Discipline, Kempis on, vii, 246 (7); Penn on, i, 344; Plutarch on lack of, xii, 152; self, Epictetus on, ii, 154 (100)

Discontent, cause of, xxviii, 470; Emerson on, v, 81; Penn on, i, 342 (38-40)

Discontent, in PILGRIM'S PROGRESS, xv, 76

Discontentment, Epictetus on, ii, 123 (20), 127 (31, 32), 128 (35); Epictetus on, 133 (49); Epictetus on, 167 (140); Marcus Aurelius on, 213 (3), 227 (8), 235 (11), 259 (17), 262 (34), 284 (25), 285 (28), 296 (20), 303 (26); public, iii, 27, 38, 40, 42-3

Discord, Burke on Homer's figure of, xxiv, 57; in chaos, iv, 135; daughter of sin, 312; Pope on, xl, 425; proclaims itself, xxv, 333

Discouragement, easy, Emerson on, v, 80

Discourse, absurdities of, xxxiv, 372-3; discretion and fancy in, 365; excessive length or brevity of, xlviii, 29; Hobbes on ends of, xxxiv, 359-62; Kempis on proper, vii, 220; Pascal on natural, xlviii, 12 (14) (see also Conversation, Inquiry, Reasoning)

DISCOURSE, ESSAY ON, Bacon's, iii, 87-9

Discretion, better than daring pride, xlix, 162; defined by Hobbes, xxxiv, 363; in discourse, 365

Discretion, damsel in PILGRIM'S PROGRESS, xv, 51

Discriminating Duties, x, 370-88

Discussion, liberty of, James Mill on, xxv, 71, 218-19, 260

Disease, Browne on, iii, 309; carried by Europeans, xxix, 459-60; cause of, Rousseau on, xxxiv, 175-6; caused by animals, xxxviii, 153; contagious, Jenner on, 172-3; death's messenger, xlv, 702; Emerson on, v, 127; germ theory of, xxxviii, 382-402; Herodotus on cause of, xxxiii, 40; inheritance of, Pliny on, ix, 206; sign of sanitary neglect, xxviii, 470; source of error, xlviii, 38

Diseases, Adam's vision of, iv, 334-5; cure of desperate, xlvi, 162; effects of, different, xxix, 458 note; incurable, in Utopia, xxxvi, 220-1

Disgrace, fear of, in children, xxxvii, 41-4; Locke on fear of, 103

Dishonesty, for gain, i, 406 (184)

Disinterestedness, Hume on, xxxvii, 375

Dislike (see Aversion)

Disobedience, Locke on, xxxvii, 64-6

Disorder, and grandeur, xxiv, 68-9

DISORDER, A SWEET, xl, 345-6

Dispatch, Bacon on, iii, 66-7; in public business, i, 371-2

Dispensations, Luther on, xxxvi, 325, 331-2

Dispersal, means of, of plants and animals, xi, 403-11; during glacial period, 411-17, 422-6; of freshwater species, 427-31

Despondency, Mr., in PILGRIM'S PROGRESS, xv, 291-2, 294, 306; parts with Christiana, 316; death, 318-9

Disposition, Locke on, xxxvii, 60-1; not inherited, xx, 319-21

Dispositions, of children, xxxvii, 47, 89-90, 96

Disputes, passion in, iii, 328-9

Disputing, Franklin on, i, 15-16, 132; Locke on habit of, xxxvii, 133, 135, 170-1; Mon-

taigne on, xxxii, 42-3, 44; Penn on, i, 352 (133-6), 356 (184)

Disrespect, Locke on, xxxvii, 128

Dissatisfaction, Pascal on human, xlviii, 47 (109)

Dissections. Harvey on, xxxviii, 112, 147

Dissent, dishonoring, a way of, xxxiv, 379; Locke on, xxxvii, 134

Dissenters, Mill on duty of, xxv, 34; Milton on value of, iii, 235-6, 241-2; Price on duty of, xxiv, 160 note 3 (see Non-conformity)

DISSENTERS, SHORTEST WAY WITH, Defoe's, xxvii, 143-57

Dissertation on Liberty and Necessity, i, 43-4, 57-8

Dissimulation, Bacon on, iii, 17-20 (see also Hypocrisy); in Hell, xx, 47; Pascal on, xlviii, 43; Penn on, i, 392 (15-16), 394 (37-46); Raleigh on, xxxix, 71-2; Stevenson on, xxviii, 291

Distance, Berkeley on idea of, xxxvii, 234-6

DISTANT FRIEND, TO A, xli, 689-90

Distinction, Carlyle on love of, xxv, 409-11; human thirst for, xxviii, 96-7; Rousseau on love of, xxxiv, 229

Distinctions, Locke on, xxxvii, 181-2; nice, Bacon on, iii, 68

Distress, goods taken in, xliii, 76 (35)

Distresses, of others, pleasure in, xxiv, 41-4

Distribution, Hobbes on, xxxiv, 426; importance of just, xxviii, 363; in agricultural systems, x, 457-8; in Utopia, xxxvi, 195-6, 200-1; Mill on laws of, xxv, 158; progress of wealth dependent on, x, 57; of produce (see Wages, Rent, Profits)

Distributive Justice, Hobbes on, xxxiv, 422-3, 426; Hume on, xxxvii, 424

District of Columbia, slave-trade in, xliii, 327 note; under Congress, 197 (17)

Distrust, Emerson on, v, 289; expensiveness of, 58-9; opponent of reform, xxvii, 251-2; Webster on, xlvii, 729

Disturbances, charges of creating, xxxix, 46-9

Disuse, of parts, effects of, xi, 147-52

DITTY, by Sidney, xl, 215-16

DITTY IN PRAISE OF ELIZA, xl, 250-2

Divergence of Character, xi, 122-6; how it leads to formation of species, etc., 126-9; limits to, 139-41

Diversification, of structure and habits, xi, 123-6; limits to, 139-41

Diversion, Pascal on, xlviii, 52-8, 63
(167-8), 64 (170-1), 113 (324)
Diversity, Mill on need of, xxv,
277-8
Dives, and Lazarus, xv, 36; xliv,
404 (19-31)
Divination, Augustine, St., on, vii,
110; in Egypt, xxxiii, 42; among
the Germans, 100-1; pagan methods of, xxxiv, 396-7; Pascal
on, xlviii, 287-8; Prometheus first
teacher of, viii, 173 and note 35;
Vindicianus on, vii, 50, 108
DIVINE COMEDY, Dante's, xx; Arnold on selections from, xxviii,
73; Carlyle on, xxv, 461; Cellini
on line of, xxxi, 316; its relation
to Celtic myths, xxxii, 188; Dante
on, xx, 361-2, 392; Hugo on,
xxxix, 367, 372; Macaulay on the,
xxvii, 389; remarks on, xx, 4;
Shelley on, xxvii, 364, 366
DIVINE IMAGE, THE, xli, 605-6
Divine Laws, Emerson on, v,
26-8
Divine Men, Emerson on, v, 201
Divine Mercy, in DIVINE COMEDY,
xx, 11 note 5
Divine Nature, attributed to only
one or two, v, 29
Divine Right, Rousseau on, xxxiv,
225
DIVINE SERVICE AT LAMINGTON, vi,
453
Divine Spirit (see Over-soul)
Divine Things, judged by human,
iii, 48; iv, 198
Divine Truths, Pascal on, xlviii,
406-7
Diviners, punishment of, in Hell,
xx, 83-6
Divinity, Emerson on, in man, v,
74-7; study of, Faustus on, xix,
201-2, 203
DIVINITY STUDENTS, ADDRESS TO, v,
25-43
Divisibility, infinite, Hume on,
xxxvii, 437-8 note; Pascal on,
xlviii, 437-44
Division of Labor, advantages of, x,
9-18, 22-3; dependent on amount
of capital, 222; Kant on, xxxii,
318; limits to, x, 24-8; mischief
of, v, 415; in nature, xi, 107;
origin of, x, 19-22
Divisions, fable on, xvii, 32
Divorce, among Arabs, xlv, 999
note; Bagehot on, xxviii, 190;
Jesus on marriage after, xliv, 404
(18); Mill on, xxv, 312-13; Milton on, xxviii, 189-92; Paul, St.,
on, xlv, 509 (10-11); in Utopia,
xxxvi, 222-3
DO YOU REMEMBER ME, xli, 929
Dobell, Sydney, BALLAD by, xlii,
1160

Dobrizhoffen, on hail-stones, xxix,
128; on ostriches, 105-6
Dobson, story of, xlv, 705-7
Docility, Pascal on, xlviii, 94 (254)
Doctor, Chaucer's, xl, 22-3
Doctors (see Physicians)
Doctrinaires, Low 'l on, xxviii, 449
Doctrines, Confucius on strange,
xliv, 8 (16); traditional, absence
of vitality in, xxv, 246
Dodger, in SHOEMAKER'S HOLIDAY,
xlvii, 453, 469-71, 474, 504
Dodington, George Bubb, SHORTEN
SAIL, xl, 475
Dodona, Oracle of, Æschylus on,
viii, 185; Herodotus on, xxxiii,
31; origin of, 32-3
DOE, ONE-EYED, fable of, xvii, 38
Doeg, the Edomite, xliv, 210-11
DOES HAUGHTY GAUL INVASION
THREAT, vi, 567-8
DOG IN THE MANGER, fable of, xvii,
27
DOG AND SHADOW, fable of, xvii, 10
DOG AND WOLF, fable of, xvii, 21
Dog Watches, explained, xxiii, 18
Dogmas, Dunkers' attitude towards,
i, 115-16; Emerson on, v, 36;
Goethe on, xix, 126-7
Dogmatism, Franklin on, in speech,
i, 19; Hume on, xxxvii, 441; Pas-
cal on, xlviii, 131 (395), 146;
Rousseau on, xxxiv, 298-301
Dogmatist, in FAUST, xix, 181
Dogs, associative instinct in, xxix,
164; Burke on our contempt for,
xxiv, 59; Darwin on instincts of,
xi, 267, 268; held sacred in Egypt,
xxxiii, 36-7; Harrison on, xxxv,
369-75; Hunter on descent of,
xxxviii, 153 note; man, love of,
in, iii, 46; xi, 269; origin of, 34,
35, 36-7, 49
Dol Common, in THE ALCHEMIST,
Dapper and, xlvii, 576, 583, 624-
5; Face and, 521, 524-8, 539-40,
627-9; Mammon and, 554, 559,
584, 586, 587-91, 602-9; Spanish
don and, 574, 575, 576; Subtle
and, 521, 524-8, 539-40, 626-7
Dolabella, Cornelius, accusation of,
xii, 276; Antony and, 340, 342;
Cæsar and, 341; Cicero and, ix,
164; Cleopatra and, xii, 400; extravagance of, 317
Dolabella, in ALL FOR LOVE, Antony
and, xviii, 23, 52-3, 56, 57-61, 65,
66, 79-83; Cleopatra and, 53, 54-5,
67, 72
Dolben, Gilbert, and Dryden, xiii,
431
Dolcino, the friar, xx, 118 note 5
Dolius, in the ODYSSEY, xxii, 67,
337, 341, 344
Dolphin, Dana on the, xxiii, 22;
of Hippo, Pliny's story of, ix,
368-70

Domat, Burke on, xxiv, 300 note

Domestic Animals, adaptability of, to climate, xi, 153; breeding of, 46-7; descent of, 34-45; diseases from, xxxviii, 153-4; fertility of, xi, 304-5, 323-4; mental qualities of, 267-70

Domestic Industries, capital naturally seeks, x, 349-51; protection of (see Protective Duties)

Domestic Races, improvement not limited, xi, 55-6; adapted to use of man, 52; origin of, 34-5, 44, 45-6, 53-4, 56-7

Domestic Trade, capital used in, x, 310-11; limit of, 316-17

Domestication, improves fertility, xi, 305; eliminates sterility of species, 42; variation under, 25-57

Dominant, technical definition of, xi, 70

Dominic, St., Dante on, xx, 332 note 8, 337-8; Luther on, xxxvi, 315

Dominica, Drake at, xxxiii, 235, 247-8

Dominicans, Dante on the, xx, 335 note 30; Milton on the, iv, 150

Dominis, Antonio de, on the rainbow, xxxiv, 124

Domitian, as an archer, iii, 51; dream of, 96; Helvidius and, ix, 354 note; philosophers and, ii, 116; ix, 250 note; Pliny on, 265-7, 274 note, 329, 335, 336-7; spiders, toys of, xxxv, 366-7; Tiberius and, xxxvi, 3; the turbot of, xxxix, 374

Domitius, and Antony, xii, 384; Cicero on, ix, 120; xii, 258; in Civil War, 304, 311, 312; Pharnaces and, 316-17

Donalbain, in MACBETH, xlvi, 306, 317, 324, 329, 330-1, 332, 365

DONALD THE BLACK, GATHERING SONG OF, xli, 762-3

Donatello, his "Judith," xxxi, 357 note 3; Cellini on, 358, 373, 374-5 note

Donati, Corso, enemy of Dante, xx, 241 note 3; death of, 246 and note 6; head of Neri faction, 27 note 5; Piccarda and, 298 note 6

Donati, Simon, and Schicchi, xx, 126 note

Donatists, Calvin on the, xxxix, 37; Pascal on the, xlviii, 289 (822)

Don Galaor, Cervantes on, xiv, 21, 103-4

Don John of Austria, xiv, 404, 405, 406; Raleigh on, xxxix, 92

Donkey (see Ass)

DONKEY, MAN, AND BOY, fable of, xvii, 36-7

Donn Désa, xlix, 214; sons of, 214, 217, 223, 225, 229, 247

Donne, John, advowsons presented to, xv, 348; appearance and character, 374; benefice declined by, 334-6; birth and education, 327-9; Book of Devotions by, 355; burial of, 373; charity in life of, 363-4; conduct of Deanery, 364-6; Dean of St. Paul's, 351-2; death of, 371-2; domestic sorrows, 337-9; Ellesmere, Lord, and, 330, 331; embassy to Bohemia, 351; in France, 339-40; friends of, 358; Hazlitt on, xxvii, 283-4; Herbert and, xv, 359-60, 388; Mrs. Herbert and, 380-83; HYMN TO GOD, 360; James the First and, 343-4, 347, 353; King, Dr., and, 354-5; last sickness of, 355-6, 366-9; lecturer of Lincoln's Inn, 350; LINES TO GEORGE HERBERT, 359; LINES ON HIS MISTRESS, xxvii, 284; lines from Epithalamion of, 283-4; marriage of, xv, 330-2, 356; monument of, 370, 373-4; More, Sir George, and, 332-3; mother of, 364; ordination of, 346; Poems by, 342, 359, 360; xxvii, 284; xl, 310-21; as a poet, xv, 356-7; preaching of, 347-8; Prolocutor of the Convocation, 352; Pseudo-Martyr of, 344; studies and writings, 361-2; travels of, 329-30; VALEDICTION by, 342; vision of, 340-2; Walton and, 326; Walton's LIFE OF, 327-74; wife's death, 348-9; will of, 362-3; Wolly, Francis, and, 333

Don Quixote, Amadis of Gaul imitated by, xiv, 238-40; on arms and learning, 393-9; balsam prepared by, 138; Biscaine squire and, 71-2, 75-8; calling and manner of life of, 19; at Chrysostom's funeral, 116-17; countryman and his boy and, 39-42; disciplinants and, 533-5; Dorothea and, 285-93, 296-300, 387-9, 483; dream of triumph of, 180-3; Dulcinea and, 104, 105, 224-31, 234; encaged, 488-96, 507-12; epitaphs on, 540, 542; Eugenio the goatherd and, 531-2; first sally, 25; friars and, 69-70; galley slaves and, 187-97; goatherds and, 85-98; hearse, adventure of, 155-9; Holy Brotherhood and, 479-81; home returning of, 536-9; at the inn, 27-31, 127-9, 135-7, 139-41, 451; innkeeper and, 468-9; knighting of, 32-8; on knight errantry, 100-4; knightly tales read by, 20-1; "Knight of the Ill-favored Face," 159-60; library burnt, 51-8; Mambrino's helmet and, 175-7, 472-4; Maritornes and, 130-2, 457-63; merchants of Toledo and, 43-5; on romances, 514-21; Sancho Panza and, 62-4, 79-84, 300-3, etc.; sheep and, 146-50; sickness of, 59; sonnets in praise

of, 15-17; windmills, adventure of, with, 65-6; wine-bags and, 364-8; Yanguesian carriers and, 119-26

DON QUIXOTE OF THE MANCHA, Cervantes's, xiv; Lowell on, xxviii, 450-1

DOON, THE BANKS O', vi, 422-4

Doria, Branca, xx, 142 note 6

Dorian Music, described, iv, 104

Dorigen, and Sophocles, v, 125-6

Dorine, in TARTUFFE, Cleante and, xxvi, 196-7; 253; Damis and, 198, 233-4; Elmire and, 256-7; Loyal and, 273, 276, 277; Mariane and, 217-22; 228-32; Orgon and, 199-200; 208-17, 269, 272, 278; Mme. Pernelle and, 190, 192-3, 194-5; Tartuffe and, 234-6, 281

Doris, eggs of the, xxix, 215 note

Dorothea, in DON QUIXOTE, xiv, 266-93, 296-300, 374-84, 387-9

Dorothea, in HERMANN AND DOROTHEA, with the fugitives, xix, 346-8; described by Hermann, 383; in the French invasion, 391-2; found by the doctor, 392-4; the magistrate on, 395; with Hermann at the fountain, 402-6; returns to bid farewell to companions, 407-11; goes home with Hermann, 412-16; presented to his parents, 420 1; reproved in play by the pastor, 422-3; resolves to return to companions, 423-5; Hermann tells her his love, 426-7; begs father's forgiveness, 427-8; betrothed to Hermann, 428; tells of her first lover, 429-30

Dorset, Earl of, Raleigh on, xxxix, 78; Voltaire on, xxxiv, 150

Doson, name of, xii, 162 note

Dotage, Rousseau on, xxxiv, 179-80

Doubleday, Gen., at Gettysburg, xliii, 351, 373, 388, 408

Doubt, Blake on, xli, 603; Carlyle on, xxiv, 362; Dante on, xx, 303; Descartes on state of, xxxiv, 15, 21-4, 28, 32-3; Hobbes's definition of, 360; Krishna on, xlv, 821-2 (see also Scepticism)

Doubting Castle, xv, 118, 291-3

Doughty, Master, with Drake, xxxiii, 209, 211, 212, 213, 214

Douglas, Burns on family of, vi, 397; family and arms of, xxxv, 103

Douglas, Sir Archambault, xxxv, 95-6, 103

Douglas, Earl James, burial of, xxxv, 102; at Otterburn, 89, 91, 92-3; Percy and, 85, 86; raid of, 83-4 (see also ballads of OTTERBURN and CHEVY CHASE)

Douglas, John, the author, Goldsmith on, xli, 518, 519-20; with Raleigh, xxxiii, 345-6, 347, 348

Douglas, Katherine (see Barlass)

Douglas, Lord, at Poitiers, xxxv, 48

Douglas, Lady Margaret (see DOUGLAS TRAGEDY)

Douglas, Stephen A., Lowell on, xxviii, 452-3

DOUGLAS TRAGEDY, THE, xl, 51-4

DOVE, JOHN, EPITAPH ON, vi, 126

Dove-house, Blake on a, xli, 601

DOVER BEACH, xlii, 1183-4

DOVER CLIFFS, by Bowles, xli, 697-8

DOWN THE BURN, DAVIE, vi, 504

DOWY HOUMS O YARROW, xl, 116-18

Draghinazzo, the demon, xx, 90, 93

DRAKE, SIR FRANCIS, REVIVED, xxxiii, 125-203

DRAKE'S FAMOUS VOYAGE ROUND THE WORLD, xxxiii, 207-33

DRAKE'S GREAT ARMADA, xxxiii, 237-68

Drake, Sir Francis, armadas of, xxxiii, 234-5; on Barbary Coasts, 208; at Cape Blanco, 208-9; Cafuego pursuit, 219-20; in Canaries, 241; at Canno, 221; at Cape Verde Islands, 209-10, 242-7; Cartagena, expeditions against, 148-50, 160-6, 253-61; Chagres Fleet and, 192; Chili, on coast of, 217-19; Cimaroons and, 157-60; in Cuba, 262; death of, 235; DEDICATORY EPISTLE TO ELIZABETH, 130-1; at Dominica, 247-8; at Ferro and Cape Blanco, 242; fleet of, and commanders of, 237-8; at Fogo and Brava Islands, 211; French captain and, 192-4; Garret, John, and, 136; at Guatulco, 220-1; Harrison on, xxxv, 338; at Isle of Pinos, xxxiii, 138-9, 148; at Isle of Victuals, 146; at La Mocha, 217; life of, chief events, 126, 132; at Lima, 219; in Malay Islands, 227-33; in New Albion, 222-6; at Nombre de Dios, 139-44; 171-2; in Pacific Ocean, 177, 216, 226; in Panama, 172-84; at Port Pheasant, 135-8; at Port St. Julian, 213-15; Prizes and losses of, 267-8; Raleigh's colony and, 265-7; Resolution of Land-Captains, 257-9; Rio Grande expedition, 154-6; at St. Augustine, 262-5, 267; at St. Christopher's, 248; at St. Domingo, 248-53; 267-8; at St. Helena, 265; at Santiago, 210-11; at Santa Marta, 167; in Sound of Darien, 153-4; on coast of S. America, 211-13; on coast of Spain, 238-41; Spanish prize, 168-9; Spanish treasure train taken by, 194-6; stores of, 157, 166; in Strait of Magellan, 215-16; at Venta Cruz, 184-6; plan against

Veragua, 188-92; wound of, 145;
wrongs and purpose to avenge,
133-4

Drake, Sir Francis (nephew) xxxiii,
127; DEDICATION TO CHARLES I,
129; DEDICATION TO THE READER,
132

Drake, Dr., James, xxxix, 173

Drake, John, brother of Sir Francis,
xxxiii, 134, 141, 142, 144, 148,
151-2, 157, 160; death of, 170

Drake, Joseph, brother of Francis,
xxxiii, 171

Drake, Thomas, brother of Francis,
xxxiii, 214, 238

Drama, in Athens, xxvii, 355, 357;
Burns on imported, vi, 396; Dryden on, xiii, 7-11, 14; Goethe on,
xxxix, 274; Hugo on, 370-94;
Hugo on Greek, 358-9, 364-5; language in, correctness of, xxxix,
393-4; length of, 402-4; love as
basis of, 221; Macaulay on, xxvii,
402; influence of, on morals, 356;
narrations in, xxxix, 229; originality in, 382-5; pleasure in, reason of, 233-4; popular and poetical ideas of, xix, 9-15; reading
of, xxxix, 234; reality in, 385-8;
refinement in false, 389-90; Shelley on, xviii, 277, 278; xxvii, 355-
6; Sidney on place and time in,
46-7; society, state of, and, 356-8;
tragedy and comedy in, mingled,
xxxix, 223-4; unities of, 231-5,
376-82; verse in, 388, 390-3

DRAMAS, CONTINENTAL, xxvi

DRAMAS, ELIZABETHAN, xlvi, xlvii

DRAMAS, GREEK, viii

DRAMAS, MODERN ENGLISH, xviii

Dramatic Poetry, Wordsworth on,
xxxix, 313

Dramatists, Aristophanes on duty
of, viii, 450, 452

Drances, and Æneas, xiii, 365; denounces Turnus, 368, 373-4

Drawbacks, Smith on, x, 346-7;
called bounties, 406; on exports,
389-91

Drawing, Locke on knowledge of,
xxxvii, 144-5

Drayton, Michael, poems by, xl, 226-
32

DREAM, A, by Burns, vi, 217-20

DREAM, A, OF THE UNKNOWN, xli,
865-6

Dreams, Adam on, iv, 186; Augustine, St., on, vii, 190; Bunyan on,
xv, 229-30; Calderon on, xxvi, 48-
50, 52, 62; Chaucer on, xl, 37-8
note 34, 39-43; Descartes on,
xxxiv, 33-4; Elihu on, xliv, 125
(15-17); Hobbes on, xxxiv, 327-9;
Homer on, xxii, 282; Hume on,
xxxvii, 322; Pascal on, xlviii, 129

(386); Pliny on, ix, 212; **Tenny-**
son on, xlii, 1038

Dress, in ancient Egypt, xxxiii, 41-
2; in Elizabethan England, xxxv,
304-7; of the Germans, xxxiii,
105; Herrick on disorder in, xl,
345-6; Locke on, xxxvii, 10-11,
15-16, 31; Luther on luxury in,
xxxvi, 348; Pascal on, xlviii, 36-7,
111 (315-16); Shakespeare on,
xlvi, 102; in Utopia, xxxvi, 189,
193, 205 211 (see also **Apparel**)

Dreux, battle of, xxxviii, 51

Dreux, Earl of, xxxv, 15

Drewry, Sir Robert, and Dr. Donne,
xv, 339, 358

Drinking, Burns on, vi, 106, 193;
Brynhild on, xlix, 394; of children, xxxvii, 19-21, 32; Cotton
on, xxxix, 324-5; Dryden on, xl,
402; Johnson on, xxvii, 190;
Locke on, xxxvii, 15, 188-9; More
on, xxxvi, 215; Omar Khayyam
on, xli, 971, 973, 976-7, 979-81,
983-4, 986, 987; Penn on, i, 345
(65-7); Shakespeare on, xlvi,
326-7

DRINKING, by Cowley, xl, 375-6

Drinking Song, by Jordan, xl, 373

DRINKING SONG, by Sheridan, xli,
567

Drinking Song (16th century), xl,
192-4

Drinking Song, of Tony Lumpkin,
xviii, 209-10

Dris, fosterer of Conaire, xlix, 243-4

Drought, Bacon on, iii, 143; Darwin on effects of, xxix, 145-7

Drugger, in THE ALCHEMIST, xlvii,
535-9, 564-6, 577, 580-1, 610-11,
612, 625-6, 627, 634

Druids, Burke on, xxiv, 53; Milton
on, iv, 75; Voltaire on, xxxiv, 90

DRUMLANRIG, ON DESTRUCTION OF
WOODS OF, vi, 435

Drummond, William, poems by, xl,
335-40

Drunkenness, as a crime, xxv, 306;
Hobbes on, xxxiv, 368-9; St. Paul
on, xlv, 507 (11), 508 (10); Penn
on, i, 346 (72); price of wine and,
x, 381-2; Woolman on, i, 204-5

Drusilla, wife of Felix, xliv, 486
(24)

Drusus, in Germany, xxxiii, 117;
marriage of, xii, 403; Pillars of
Hercules and, xxxiii, 115

Dryden, John, translation of ÆNEIS
and DEDICATION, xiii; ALL FOR
LOVE, xviii, 5, 101; Arnold on,
xxviii, 82-4; CHARLEMAGNE, HYMN
OF, translation of, xlv, 559; on
Chaucer, xxviii, 77-8, 81; as a
critic, xxvii, 209; on his critics,
xxxix, 180-3; Gray on, xl, 467;
Hazlitt on, xxvii, 288, **life and**

works, xxxix, 160 note; xviii, 3-4;
Locke and, xxxvii, 3; Macaulay
on, xxvii, 402; Mill on, xxv, 16;
on Milton, xxviii, 210; Pepys and,
316; PREFACE TO FABLES, xxxix,
160-83; remarks on his work, xiii,
429; l, 55; on Shakespeare, xxxix,
262, 334; SHORT POEMS by, xl,
394-406; Taine on, xxxix, 452;
Voltaire on, xxxiv, 137; Words-
worth on *Indian Emperor* of,
xxxix, 340 and note
Dryops, death of, xiii, 338
Duad, of St. Augustine, vii, 60
Dualism, in nature (see Polarity)
Duan, meaning of, vi, 180 note
Duban, the Sage, story of, xvi, 33-
43
Dubartas, *The Creation* of, xxxix,
333
Dubthach Chafer, xlix, 253, 261
Duca, Guido del, in Purgatory, xx,
201-3, 207 note
Ducato, value of the, xxxi, 39 note 1
DUCHESS, MY LAST, xlii, 1115
DUCHESS OF MALFI, xlvii, 721-816;
remarks on, 720
DUCKLING, THE UGLY, xvii, 237-46
Ducks, descent of, xi, 36; non-
flying, 147; shoveller, 237-8;
steamer, xxix, 215; wild and do-
mestic, compared, xi, 29
Duclaux, M., Pasteur and, xxxviii,
287
DUDDON RIVER, VALEDICTORY SON-
NET TO, xli, 694-5
Duelling, Hobbes on, xxxiv, 381-2;
Locke on, xxxvii, 184; Swift on,
xxvii, 107
Duera, family of, xx, 136 note 9
Dufferin, Lady, LAMENT by, xli,
945-7
Dugong, Darwin on the, xi, 378
Du Gueuelin, saying of, v, 317
Duilius, Gaius, Cato on, ix, 62
Duke, meaning of, xxxiv, 383
Dulcinea del Toboso, mistress of
Don Quixote, xiv, 24, 75; Don
Quixote and, 104-5, 233-4; epi-
taph on, 542; Oriana to, 17;
Sancho Panza and, 231-2, 306-8;
Solis Dan on, 16-17; Sonnet on,
540
Dull, in PILGRIM'S PROGRESS, xv, 220
Dumas, M., on fermentation, xxxviii,
368
Dumont, Pierre Etienne, on Ben-
tham's works, xxv, 46, 47;
Traité des Judicaires, xxv, 77
DUMOURIER, GENERAL, IMPROMPTU ON
DESERTION OF, vi, 491
Dunbar, Col., Franklin on, i, 138,
141, 143, 152
Dunbar, William, lines to, vi, 268
note

Duncan, in MACBETH, in camp near
Forres, xlvi, 306-8; horses of, 331;
Lady Macbeth and, 316, 317-18,
322; Macbeth and, 313-15, 317-18,
338; murder of, 320-31
Duncan, Edmund, xv, 414-15, 419
DUNCAN DAVISON, vi, 317-18
DUNCAN GRAY, vi, 476
DUNDAS, ROBERT, ON THE DEATH
OF, vi, 307-8
Dundee, Burns on, vi, 306
DUNDEE, BONIE, by Burns, vi, 268-9
DUNDEE, BONNY, by Scott, xli, 770-2
Dunkers, beliefs of the, i, 115-16
Dunlop, John, poem by, xli, 595
Dunning, Mr., Burke on, xxiv, 417
Dunstan, St., Harrison on, xxxv,
265
Dunyzad, in ARABIAN NIGHTS, xvi,
11
Duport, Dr., Dean of Peterborough,
xv, 387
Duppa, Dr., Walton on, xv, 358
Duquesne, Fort, attack on, i, 140-1,
143-4
Duranti, Durante, xxxi, 188 note,
256
Duras, Robert of, xxxv, 46
Durer, Albert, method of, iii, 112
Duress, in Massachusetts, xliii, 77
(40)
Durham, Bishop of, at Otterburn,
xxxv, 87-8, 96-7, 98-9, 100-1
Durham, John George Lambton,
Lord, xxv, 139-40
Durindana, sword of Roland, xlix,
124, 134, 136, 143, 153, 182-3
Duris, the Samian, on Alcibiades,
xii, 143; Cicero on, ix, 155; on
Pericles, xii, 66
Dust, infusorial, in St. Jago, xxix,
15
Dutch, Goldsmith on the, xli, 540-1
Duties, Customs, administration of,
best, x, 552-5; discriminating, 370-
88; excise and customs, 548; ex-
emption from, 407, 425-6; high,
effect of, 551-2; historically considered, 548-50; on importation of
necessities, 546; name, origin of,
548; origin of, 479; of passage,
558-9; protective, on foreign
goods, 348-59; removal of, 365-9;
retaliatory, 363-5; for revenue,
369, 390; to equal taxes, 361-3;
under U. S. Constitution, xliii,
196 (8), 198 (5, 6), 199 (2, 3);
for war purposes, x, 359-61
Duty, Channing on, xxviii, 347;
Confucius on, xliv, 54 (23); defined, xxxii, 365, 370; Emerson
on, v, 26, 43, 79-80, 300-1; Epictetus on, ii, 118 (2), 151 (91),
163 (124), 165 (132), 176 (170),
176 (172), 184 (22); Hindu doc-

trine of, xlv, 814; Hobbes on natural, xxxiv, 407-8, 417-29; imperatives of, xxxii, 352-65, 384-6; Kant on, 327-35, 335-6, 337-43, 356-7; Kempis on, vii, 232 (5); Lælius on, ix, 10; Locke on, xxxvii, 60, 62, 137; M. Aurelius on, ii, 201 (5), 218 (24), 220 (33), 223 (1), 225 (6), 234 (2), 238 (22), 239 (26), 251 (45); Mill on compulsion to, xxv, 213-14; Pascal on reminders of, xlviii, 46 (104); perfect and imperfect, xxxii, 352 note; Poe on sense of, xxviii, 388; poetry, as the subject of, 388, 391; principles of, xxxii, 371-5, 363-4; Ruskin on, xxviii, 98, 162; Vishnu Purana on, 433; Woolman on, i, 197; worth of, intrinsic, xxxii, 366, 370-1

DUTY, ODE TO, by Wordsworth, xli, 665-7

Dyer, Chaucer's, xl, 21

Dyer, Sir Edward, MY MIND TO ME, xl, 211-12

Dyes, Woolman on, i, 324

DYING MAN IN HIS GARDEN, xli, 493-4

Dymas, in ÆNEID, xiii, 115, 116, 118

Dyslogistic Fallacies, xxvii, 258-9

Eadgils, xlix, 72 note 3, 73 note

Eagerness, Confucius on, xliv, 27 (16)

EAGLE AND ARROW, fable of, xvii, 43

Eagle(s), in old England, xxxv, 356; Job's description of, xliv, 138; Manfred on, xviii, 412

Eanmund, xlix, 72 note 3, 79

Earle, John, letter of, xxxviii, 185-7

EARLY PIETY, xlv, 577

Early Rising, Locke on, xxxvii, 22, 23

EARNEST CRY AND PRAYER, vi, 165-71

Earnestness, Confucius on, xliv, 60 (6); Kempis on, vii, 246 (7)

Ears, drooping, cause of, xi, 29

Earth, age of, xi, 335-9, 359-60, 407-13; ancient opinions of its motion, xxxix, 58; changes in, xi, 360-2, 404-5; xxxviii, 405-40; Copernicus on motion of the, xxxix, 55-60; Descartes on the, xxxiv, 37; Faraday on, xxx, 7-8; Geikie on past history of, 353-4; interior of the, 313-14, 319-21; Lactantius on the, xxxix, 60; Milton on, iv, 172, 108, 248-50, 266, 311; motion of poles of, xxxiv, 131-2; palpitation of, xxx, 297; Raleigh on changes in the, xxxix, 112; rigidity of the, xxx, 313-14, 319-21; Socrates's idea of the, ii, 105-10; temperature of, changes in, xxxviii, 416

Earth-Spirit, in FAUST, xix, 24-6

EARTHLY PARADISE, PROLOGUE OF THE, xlii, 1240-1

Earthquakes, Darwin on, xxix, 320-31, 531; effect of, on the weather, 372-3; Lyell on, xxxviii, 428; oblivion in, iii, 143; rain and, xxix, 372-3; Woolman on, as judgments of God, i, 246

Ease, after pain, iv, 65; Confucius on, xliv, 6 (14); deliciousness of, due to toil, xxviii, 324-5; Hobbes on desire for, xxxiv, 385; Tennyson on, xlii, 1028-9, 1030-1; Yu-tzu on, xliv, 6 (12)

Ease, Plain of, in PILGRIM'S PROGRESS, xv, 111

East India Company, end of, xxv, 160; forts of, x, 478-9; Mill on, xxv, 22; mismanagement of, x, 491

Eastburn, Samuel, i, 243, 248, 256, 259

Easter, celebration of, xv, 408

EASTER, Spenser's, xl, 254

Easter Choruses, in FAUST, xix, 33-5

EASTER SONG, by Herbert, xl, 355

Eating, Augustine, St., on continency in, vii, 191-3; Confucius on excessive, xliv, 62 (22); Locke on children's, xxxvii, 16-22, 32-3; Luther on freedom of, xxxvi, 325; More on pleasure of, 215; Penn on, i, 345 (59)

Ebusus, and Corynæus, xiii, 405

Ecbatan, reference to, iv, 332

Eccentricity, Mill on, xxv, 272-3

Eccentrics, defined, iii, 48 note

Eccius, John, xxxvi, 357, 358-9

ECCLESIASTES, BOOK OF, Buddha, resemblances of, to, xlv, 588; xliv, 339-54; remarks on, 338; l, 31

Ecclesiastical Princedoms, xxxvi, 39-42

Ecgtheow, xlix, 13, 16, 18 note 3

Echecrates of Phlius, ii, 45-7, 81-2, 96-7

Echeneus, in the ODYSSEY, xxii, 98, 160-1

Echephron, son of Nestor, xxii, 45

Echetus, the king, xxii, 257, 303

Echinades, Herodotus on the, xxxiii, 9

Echion, father of Pentheus, viii, 371, 372; husband of Agave, 408

Echo, the nymph, Dante on, xx, 335 note 3; Milton on, iv, 52; Shelley on, xli, 883

ECHOES, by Moore, xli, 842-3

Eclipses, foretold by ancient philosophers, vii, 67; Pericles on, xii, 74; signs of ill, xlviii, 65 (173)

Economical Table, of Quesnai, x, 458, 465

Economists, of France, x, 464-5; on land taxes, 503

Economy, beauty in, v, 314; Burke on true, xxiv, 418; Emerson on, v, 55; of nature, xi, 159-60

ECSTASY, AN, xl, 350-1

Ector, Sir, in the HOLY GRAIL, xxxv, 164-6, 167-8, 169-70, 171, 189, 215, 216

Ed-Dejjal, Muslim Antichrist, xvi, 251 note

Ed-Dimiryat, king of the Jinn, xvi, 322, 323, 324

EDDA, ELDER, SONGS FROM THE, xlix, 383-464; remarks on, 266-8

Edelfla, the tree, xxxix, 12

Eden, Burns on, vi, 150; Dante in, xx, 260-86; Milton on, iv, 160-1, 162-4

Edgar, king of England, navy of, xxxv, 380; and the wolves, 359

Edgar, in KING LEAR, Edmund and, xlvi, 213-15, 216-17, 295-8; flight of, 230, 238-9; Gloucester and, 267-9, 276-9, 282-5, 291; Goneril's letter found by, 284, 290; Lear and, 260-3; as madman, 255-9; madness of, remarks on, 202; soliloquy of, 266-7

Edh-Dhubyani, Arab poet, xvi, 312 note 1

Edinborough, Franklin on men of, i, 16

Edinburgh, built of foreign timber, x, 177; industries of, 277

EDINBURGH, ADDRESS TO, vi, 264-6

Edinburgh Review, Emerson on the, v, 327; establishment of, xxvii, 236; Mill on, xxv, 63-4, 142; Whig organ, xxvii, 380; Wordsworth on, v, 483

Editors, Carlyle on, xxv, 463; Johnson on, xxxix, 247, 254-60; Stevenson on duty of, xxviii, 295

Edmund, in KING LEAR, bastard son of Gloucester, xlvi, 204; Albany and, 290-1, 293-4; before battle, 290-1; character of, 202; confession of, 297, 299-300; Curan and, 229-30; death of, 301; Edgar and, 212-17, 230-1, 296; Gloucester and, 253, 259; Goneril and, 263, 269-70, 284; Lear and Cordelia with, 291-2; Regan and, 276, 288-9

Education, Channing on, xxviii, 370-2; Confucius on, xliv, 46 (28), 55 (38); Emerson on, v, 7-15, 50-3, 200-1, 266-7, 272-3; Epictetus on lack of, ii, 156 (105); Franklin on female, i, 16, 97-8; Goethe on, xxv, 398-9; Goethe on, of artists, xxxix, 265, 268-70, 278-9; Hippocrates on, xxxviii, 4; Hume on importance of, xxxvii, 376; Huxley on, xxviii, 218-31; Kant on moral, xxxii, 341 note 2; Luther on, xxxvi, 338-43; Marcus Aurelius on, ii, 193 (4); Mill on, xxv, 9, 29, 30, 39, 73, 90-1, 112, 116, 119, 314-17; Newman on, xxviii, 31-38; Pascal on, xlviii, 17 (34), 37-8, 41 (95); Penn on, i, 337-9; Pliny on, ix, 316-18, 336; Ruskin on, xxviii, 96, 105, 114, 139, 140, 151-61; Schiller on, xxxii, 219-313; Smith on, x, 138-43, 228, 485-6; in Utopia, xxxvi, 244-5; Vaughan on, i, 73; Washington on need of public, xliii, 260; Wordsworth on, v, 336

EDUCATION, ESSAY ON, Bacon's, iii, 103-4

EDUCATION, LOCKE'S THOUGHTS CONCERNING, xxxvii, 5-195; remarks on, 3, 4

EDUCATION, MILTON'S TRACTATE ON, iii, 247-259; remarks on, 246

EDUCATION OF CHILDREN, Montaigne's, xxxii, 29-73

EDUCATION OF THE HUMAN RACE, xxxii, 193-217; remarks on, l, 35, 42

EDUCATION OF WOMEN, by Defoe, xxvii, 158-61; remarks on, l, 42

EDWARD, a ballad, xl, 56-8

Edward I, of England, Dante on, xx, 176 note 16, 369, note 8

Edward II, of England, in abbey, xlvi, 60-1; at Berkeley, 67-8, 77-8; at Boroughbridge, 48-9; capture of, 61-3; crown yielded by, 65-7; delights of, 7; death of, 79-80; flight of, 57-9; Gaveston and, xlvi, 5, 7-18, 23-4, 28-30, 34-5, 40, 46-7; Gurney and Matrevis with, 70, 72-4; Isabella, Queen, and, 18-19, 22-3, 34; iii, 53; in Kenilworth Castle, xlvi, 64-5; nobles' quarrel with, 32-4, 50-1, 55-6; Normandy lost by, 45; Raleigh on murder of, xxxix, 75; Spencer and, xlvi, 43-4, 47-8; at Tynemouth, 37

EDWARD THE SECOND, xlvi, 5-84; remarks on, 3; Lamb on, 4

Edward III, in EDWARD THE SECOND, xlvi, 45, 52-4, 58, 71, 76-7, 81, 82-4; in France (see Crecy); St. Patrick's Purgatory and, xxxii, 187; Raleigh on, xxxix, 75-6; victories over kings, xxxv, 233

Edward IV, beauty of, iii, 112; census of England under, xxv, 243; founder of King's College, 401; licence to sheep exporters, 347; Raleigh on, xxxix. 78-9

Edward V, murder of, xxxix, 79

Edward the Confessor, miracles of, xlvi, 359-60

Edward, the Black Prince (see Black Prince)

Edwardes, Richard, AMANTIUM IRÆ, xl, 204-6

Edwards, Jonathan, Hazlitt on, xxvii, 291

Fdwards, Milne, on organization, xi, 135; on physiological division of labor, 126; on types, 471

Eels, in Egypt, xxxiii, 38

Effects, Pascal on reason of, xlviii, 111 (315)

Effiat, Marquis d', and Bacon, xxxiv, 100

Effort, Channing on value of, xxviii, 324; Confucius on, xliv, 21 (20); ECCLESIASTES on uselessness of, xliv, 339-42, 345 (15-16); Johnson on high, xxxix, 208

Efrits, species of genii, xvi, 9 note

Egbert, the navy of, xxxv, 380

Egerton, Lady Alice, in COMUS, iv, 46

Egerton, Lord, Jonson on, xxvii, 61

Egerton, Thomas, in COMUS, iv, 46

Eggs, number of, as securing against destruction, xi, 81

Egidio, in THE BETROTHED, xxi, 180, 336, 338-9

Egidius, the disciple, xx, 333 note 18

Egil, Emerson on, v, 357

Eglemore, Sir, xiv, 101

Eglentyne, Madame, in CANTERBURY TALES, xl, 14

EGMONT, Goethe's, xix, 247-331; remarks on, 246

Egmont, Count, Alva and, xix, 294, 299, 301-2, 303-10; arrested, 310-11; Clara and, 262-4, 288-92, 311-15; Ferdinand and, 301, 323-9; historically, 242; Margaret and, 257-9; Netherlanders' love of, 248, 249-50; with Orange, 278-84; in prison, 315-17; Raleigh on, xxxix, 91; rashness of, xix, 277; rioters and, 271-2; on way to scaffold, 330-1; with secretary, 273-8; hears his sentence, 322-3; sleep and vision, 329-30

Ego, Berkeley on the, xxxvii, 269-71; Buddhist denial of the, xlv, 668-75; Pascal on, xlviii, 112 (323), 158 (469); Schiller on, xxxii, 252-5

Egotism, Emerson on value of, v, 243-4; Kant on, xxxii, 354, 361; Pascal on, xlviii, 155 (457)

Egremont, Earl of, i, 51

Egypt, agriculture of, xxxiii, 11; artificial lake in, 76-7; canals of, 53-4, 81; civilization of, why early, x, 27; "Deserters" of, xxxiii, 18-19; fathers and sons in, x, 66; freedom in ancient, v, 93; gods in, xxxiii, 74; xxxviii, 407; history of, xxxiii, 48-91; Israel in, xliv, 442-4; kings of, xxxiii, 7, 48-91; labyrinth of, 75-6; land of, nature

and extent, 7-14; pigeons in ancient, xi, 43; plagues of, iv, 350; xliv, 246 (43-51), 281 (27-36); pyramids of, xxxiii, 64-6, 68, 70; Rousseau on arts of, xxxiv, 181; shipping in ancient, iii, 165; species in, unchanged, xi, 220; wealth of ancient, x, 309; wonders of, xxxiii, 21

EGYPT, ACCOUNT OF, Herodotus's, xxxiii, 5-91; remarks on, 3; l, 18

Egyptian Feasts, skeleton at, xxxii, 16, 20

Egyptians, anointing among, xxxiii, 47; antiquity of the, 5-6, 12; athletics among, 44-5; boats and navigation of, 47-8; calendar of the, 7; chronology of the, xxxiv, 130; circumcision among, xxxiii, 51; classes among the, 84-5; costumes, 41-2; diet and feasts of, 40-1, 45-6; divination among, 42; of the fens, 45-7; gnats, manner of protection from, 47; gods of the, 7, 26-31, 74-5, 80-1; health, care of, 40; hero-worship not practised by, 30; lotos and papyrus eaters, 45-6; manners and customs of the, 21-2; medical skill of, Homer on, xxii, 54; medicine among, xxxiii, 42; memory of, 40; mode of greeting, 41; monogamy practised by, 45; mourning and burial customs, 42-4; old age, respect for, 41; oracles of, 33, 42, 80; Perseus worshipped by, 44-5; religious celebrations of, 33-5; religious customs, 22-3; sacred animals of, 23-9, 35-40; sanctity of temples, 35; song of, 41; transmigration believed in by, 63

Ehrenberg, on infusoria, xxix, 15; on phosphorescence of sea, 177

Eichthal, Gustave d', xxv, 109

Eidothëe, daughter of Proteus, xxii, 57-9

Eimeo, island of, xxix, 429

Ekphantus, on motion of earth, xxxix, 58

Elaine, mother of Galahad, xxxv, 214 (see Galahad, birth of); Renan on, xxxii, 160-1

Eland, Cumming on the, xxviii, 422

Elasticity, force of, xxx, 197-202

Elater, Darwin on the, xxix, 41

Elatreus, in the games, xxii, 107

El-Bakbuk, story of, xvi, 173-7

Elbe, Tacitus on the, xxxiii, 119

Elbo, island of Anysis, xxxiii, 72

ELDER EDDA, SONGS FROM THE, xlix, 383-464

Eldon, Lord, and the cartoons, v, 434; Holdship and, 384-5; on impressment, 378; never "ratted," 391

El Dorado, city of, xxxiii, 313, 328,

330, 331-3; Milton on, iv, 333;
Smith on, x, 422
Elect, Pascal on the, xlviii, 192
(575), 193 (577)
Election, doctrine of eternal, xxxix,
53
ELECTION BALLAD, vi, 402-6
ELECTION BALLAD FOR WESTERHA',
vi, 392-3
Election Expenses, Mill on, xxv, 179
Elective Franchise, Emerson on the,
v, 251-2; Mill on the, xxv, 165;
in U. S., xliii, 211 (15) (see also
Suffrage)
Electoral College, first provision for,
xliii, 199-200; amended provision,
209-10, 211
Electra, daughter of Atlas, xiii, 276;
Dante on, xx, 20 and note 5; in
THE LIBATION-BEARERS, viii, 74-
95; Voltaire on, xxxix, 383
Electric Fish, xi, 198-200
Electricity, and the ether, xxx, 276,
277; Franklin on, i, 153-5; mag-
netism and, xxx, 84-7, 215; mo-
tive force of, 214-17; production
of, 62-6, 76-84, 214, 215; trans-
ferability of, 69-74
Electro-magnetism, xxx, 86, 215
Elegance, born, not bred, v, 223;
Burke on, xxiv, 102-3; true, in
few wants, v, 56
Elegiac Poets, Milton on, xxviii,
179-80
Elegy, Sidney on the, xxvii, 29;
Wordsworth on the, xxxix, 313
ELEGY, by Byron, xli, 810
ELEGY IN A COUNTRY CHURCHYARD,
Gray's, xl, 455-9
Eleians, in Egypt, xxxiii, 82-3
Elements, creation of the, xx, 315-
16
Elephantine, Herodotus on, xxxiii, 9
Elephants, habits of, xxix, 96; in-
crease of, xi, 79 80; insects and,
370; seldom destroyed by beasts
of prey, 83; weight of, xxix, 99
ELEU LORO, xli, 759-60
Eleusis, chapel of, at Athens, xli, 51
Eleutheria, establishment of the, xii,
102
Elevation, coral reefs and land,
xxix, 505-6; Lyell on, of land,
xxxviii, 423, 428, 431, 433
El-Fadl, the vizier, xvi, 203-10
El-Feshsharf, story of, xvi, 187-94
ELFIN MOUND, THE, xvii, 276-83
Elfmounds, champions of the, xlix,
256
Elgin, song of, Burns on, vi, 145
Elgin, Lord, and the Greek remains,
v, 374
El-Heddar, story of, xvi, 177-80
Eli, name of Chief Good, xx, 399;
sons of, iv, 102
Elian le Blank, xxxv, 172

Elias, Calvin on, xxxix, 43, 47; St.
James on, xlviii, 308 (868)
Eliazar, and Argusus, xxxv, 162;
son of Pelies, 218, 219, 220
Eligius, St., xl, 14 note 68
Elihu, son of Barachel, xliv, 123-34;
remarks on speech of, 72
Elijah, Augustine on, vii, 193;
Bunyan on, xv, 161; Jesus and,
xliv, 384 (30); Milton on, iv, 372,
376, 382; Zarephath and, xliv,
369 (25-6)
Eliot, John, BRIEF NARRATIVE, xliii,
147-56; life and works of, 147
note; on wine, v, 130
Eliott, Sir Thomas, xxxvi, 140-1
Eliphaz, the Temanite, xliv, 75, 77,
95, 107, 142-3
Elisabat, the barber, xiv, 219, 222
Elisabeth, mother of John, xliv, 357
(5-7), 358 (13, 24-5), 359 (36, 41-
5), 360 (57-60)
Elisha, and Naaman, xliv, 369 (27)
Eliwlod, xxxii, 176-7
Elixir, Sir Mammon on the, xlvii,
542
ELIXIR, THE, xl, 352
ELIZA, FAREWELL TO, vi, 228
ELIZA, QUEEN OF THE SHEPHERDS,
xl, 250-2
ELIZABETH, L. H., EPITAPH ON, xl,
304
Elizabeth, of Bohemia, Walton on,
xv, 350, 351
ELIZABETH OF BOHEMIA, xl, 294-5
Elizabeth, Queen of England, Drake
and, xxxiii, 126, 130-1; in The
Faerie Queene, xxxix, 66; Harrison on progresses of, xxxv, 345;
Hugo on, xxxix, 374; Johnson on
times of, 229; literary age of,
xviii, 3; Mary Queen of Scots
on, vi, 421; the navy of, xxxv,
376-78; Philip II and, xxxiii,
234; pictures of, xxxix, 84; Raleigh and, 70 note 1; xxxiii, 310;
secretaries of, stories of, iii, 60,
62; Sidney and, xv, 388; stockings
first worn by, x, 214
Elizabethan Age, Emerson on the,
v, 452-5
ELIZABETHAN DRAMAS, xlvi, xlvii
Elizabethan England, ale-drinking
in, xxxv, 300-1; ale-houses in,
257; apparel and attire, 304-7;
the church in, 264, 268-84; cities,
towns, bishoprics, parishes, and
estates of, 242-7; climate, soil,
and products, 323-34; commerce
of, 236-8; customs of, 349;
degrees of people in, 229-41;
dishes of, 314, 339; dogs in, 369-
75; fairs and markets, 256-63,
346; food and diet in, 285-303;
fowls, wild and tame, 352-8; gar-

dens and orchards of, 248-55;
holidays in, 279; houses and
furniture in, 308-14, 325-6; interest in, 315-16; laws and licences
in, 331-2; learning in, xxxix, 236-
7, 240; live stock of, xxxv, 343-51;
luxuries of life in, 313-15, 339;
manners in, 235-6, 239-40, 244,
287-89, 292-4, 301-3; minerals and
metals, 335-42; navy and shipping
of, 376-81; poor relief, beggars,
vagabonds, and jugglers, 317-22;
punishment of vagabonds, 321-2;
punishments of crime in, 382-90;
rents and tenures, 314-15, 316;
universities of, 391-404; wealth
of, 314-15, 316; wild beasts, ver-
min, and insects, 359-68; woolen
manufactures in, 347
ELIZABETHAN ENGLAND, DESCRIPTION
OF, xxxv, 227-404
Elizabethan Language, Johnson on,
xxxix, 206
El-Kuz el Aswani, story of, xvi,
184-7
Ellesmere, Lord, relations with
John Donne, xv, 330, 331, 332-3
Elliot, Sir Gilbert, xl, 111
Elliot, Jane, LAMENT FOR FLODDEN,
xli, 495-6
Elliot of Lariston, xli, 787
Elliott, Willie, and Scott, xxv, 451
Ellis, Sarah, wife of Woolman, i,
195
Ellis, William, xxv, 56, 66, 81, 83
El-Mihraj, the king, xvi, 250
Elmire, in TARTUFFE, Cleante and,
xxvi, 197-8; Orgon and, 254-8;
265-6; Pernelle and, 189-90, 196;
Tartuffe and, 236-43, 258-64, 272,
278, 281, 283
El-Móin, the vizier, xvi, 203-20,
236-8, 241
El-Muntasir bi-llah, Caliph, xvi, 171-
172
Eloquence, Augustine, St., on, vii,
71; Burke on, xxiv, 136-48, 314;
Carlyle on, xxv, 394-6; Descartes
on study of, xxxiv, 8, 9; Hobbes
on, 375, 387; Hume on, xxxvii,
403-4; Milton on, iv, 125; Mon-
taigne on, xxxii, 63, 66; Pascal
on, xlviii, 10, 12-13, 15 (25-6);
Penn on, i, 352-3; Pliny on, ix,
364-67; Woolman on, i, 326
Elpenor, and Artemidora, xli, 927;
Homer on, xxii, 151, 153-4, 169
ELPHINSTONE'S TRANSLATIONS, ON,
vi, 277
Elpinice, sister of Cimon, xii, 47;
Pericles and, 66-7
ELSIE, CLEVER, story of, xvii, 129
Elspeth, in WILHELM TELL, xxvi,
424-5, 427-8
Ely, Island of, xxxv, 331, 334

Elymas, the sorcerer, xliv, 458 (8-11)
Elysian Fields, Æneas's visit to, xiii,
233; Britain reputed locality of,
xxxv, 323; Homer on the, xxii,
63
Elysium, Socrates on, ii, 107-8, 110
Emancipation, Lincoln and, xxviii,
455-60
EMANCIPATION PROCLAMATION, xliii,
344-6; Emerson on the, xlii, 1313
note
Emathian Conqueror, Alexander
called the, iv, 80
Embalming, in ancient Egypt, xxxiii,
42-4
Embassies, origin of, x, 479
Embellishment, is deformity, v, 312
Emblems, use of, v, 174-5, 182
Embryo Spirit, in FAUST, xix, 178
Embryological Characters, in classification, xi, 456
Embryological Resemblances, xi, 261
Embryology, Darwin on, xi, 478-90
Embryos, early death of, xi, 314-15;
in Milton's Limbo, iv, 150; pic-
tures of past, xi, 388
Emendation, Johnson on, xxxix,
255-60
Emeria, country of, xxxiii, 336 note
23, 342
Emerson, Ralph Waldo, Carlyle and,
xxv, 331; ENGLISH TRAITS, v, 327-
493; ESSAYS OF, 5-321; life and
work of, 3-4; Lowell on, xxviii,
481; personal acquaintances in
England, v, 481-5; POEMS by,
xlii, 1292-1316; remarks on, l, 36;
SPEECH AT MANCHESTER, v, 490-
3; visit to Stonehenge, 471-81
EMIGRANTS IN BERMUDA, xl, 385-6
Emilius, Paulus (see Æmilius)
Eminence, Confucius on, xliv, 41
(20); verses on, xvi, 246
Emlen, Samuel, i, 302-4, 314
Emmet, Æsop's fable of the, xxxiii,
133
Emmets (see Ants)
Emonides, death of, xiii, 345
Emotions, Emerson on the, v, 70,
74; Mill on the, xxv, 37; Steven-
son on display of, xxviii, 290-1
Empedocles, Bacon on, iii, 69; in
Dante's Limbo, xx, 20; on evolu-
tion, xi, 6; in Milton's Limbo,
iv, 150; Sainte-Beuve on, xxxii,
121; Sidney on, xxvii, 9; sphere
of, ii, 299 (3); on the world,
xxxix, 109-10
EMPEROR'S NEW CLOTHES, THE, xvii,
251
EMPIRE, ESSAY ON, Bacon's, iii, 50-
55
Employers (see Capitalists)
Employment, necessary to contentment, i, 147-8; Woolman on, 245
Employments, Johnson on the lower,

xxxix, 191; Smith on, x, 65-6, 106-52

Empty Sack, proverb of the, i, 96

Emulation, Bacon on, between brothers, iii, 21; envy and, xl, 430; defined by Hobbes, xxxiv, 356

Enceladus, and Ætna, xiii, 150

Enchanted Ground, in PILGRIM'S PROGRESS, xv, 140-1, 305-8

Enclos, Ninon de l', xxvii, 294

Enclosures, advantage of, x, 160; Democritus and Columella on, 163; effect of, xi, 85-6

Encolpius, reader to Pliny, ix, 332

Encyclopædists, Burke on the, xxiv, 259; Carlyle on the, xxv, 350

END OF THE PLAY, xlii, 1099

Endicott, Gov., xliii, 93

Endor, Witch of, iii, 95; xviii, 423

Endowments, Carlyle on, xxv, 391-2; Mill on, 119

Ends, Kant's kingdom of, xxxii, 364, 367 note, 369-70

Endurance, Locke on, xxxvii, 100-1, 106-8

Endymion, called Latmian shepherd, xl, 248

Enemies, fable of despicable, xvii, 17; fable on promises of, 29-30; Jesus on loving, xliv, 374 (27, 35)

Energy, Hume on idea of, xxxvii, 355-70; ill-temper and, xxviii, 181-2 (see also Force)

Engagements, Mill on liberty of, xxv, 311-13

En-gedi, reference to, xli, 497

Engelier, the Gascon, xlix, 125, 142, 145, 152, 178

Enghien, Duc d', xxxviii, 24

Engines, Helmholtz on, xxx, 199-202; improvement in, due to boy, x, 15

England, Alfieri, on, v, 343; in American Civil War, xxv, 172-3; xxviii, 118; apprenticeships in, x, 127-9; artificiality of, v, 376-7; Carlyle on history of, xxv, 382-3; Catholic Church in, xxxv, 264-8, 279, 280; climate and situation, v, 343-9; coasts of, action of sea on, xxxv, 336-7; commercial laws of, x, 425-45; country of contradictions, v, 376; Elizabethan (see Elizabethan England); estates of, 422-3; first book in, xxxix, 5 note; food in, xxxv, 249, 257, 349-51, 353, 354, 365-6; foreign policy, v, 486; France and, in trade, x, 385-6; France and, in war, iii, 79; free trade movement in, xxv, 67; Goldsmith on, xli, 541-3; influence of, v, 344-5; interest, rates of, in, x, 94-5; liberalism in, xxv, 67-8; liberty, ideas of, in, 210-11;

luxury and rioting in, xxxvi, 156-7; Milton on, iii, 226, 233-5, 237; minerals and metals, xxxv, 336-42; money of, x, 45-6; More on causes of theft in, xxxvi, 151-7; names of places in, v, 421; Norman, navy of, xxxv, 380; pauperism in, v, 486; peerage of, Carlyle on, xxv, 388-9; penalties in, xliii, 97-8; poor laws of, x, 145-50; post-office established in, ix, 388 note; press of, v, 465-71; prices in, i, 318; x, 203-5, 213-4; xxxv, 236-7, 240-1, 259-61; progress of wealth of, x, 285-7; races of, v, 365-6; Raleigh on, xxxix, 75-84; Royal Society and Academies of, xxxiv, 158-62; Saxon, x, 32, 202; xxxv, 380; sea-power of, iii, 84; serving men in, xxxvi, 152-4; sheep-raising in, 154-6; stages in (1772), i, 318-9; state of (1782), xxiv, 407-8; Tennyson on, xlii, 1032; Thomson on, xl, 453-4; trade treaty with Portugal, x, 408-13; universities of, v, 432-40; wages in, i, 318; x, 80-1, 150-1; weights and measures in, xxxv, 261-2; Winthrop on government of, xliii, 97; Wordsworth on, xli, 690-691, 693; workmanship in, xxxv, 240, 339

ENGLAND AND SWITZERLAND, xli, 691

England, Bank of, operations of, x, 252, 253; power of, v, 412; privileges of, x, 483; profits of, 490

England, Church of, Browne on, iii, 268; Burke on, xxiv, 247-52; Defoe on establishment of, xxvii, 143-57; under Elizabeth, xxxv, 264, 268-84; Emerson on, v, 441-8; Voltaire on, xxxiv, 79-82

ENGLAND, MY ENGLAND, xlii, 1259-60

ENGLAND, YE MARINERS OF, xli, 797-8

English, ability of the, v, 375; American interest in the, 52; aristocracy, 417-32; Austin on the, xxv, 116; belles lettres among the, xxxiv, 143-58; brutality among the, v, 359-60; Burke on the, xxiv, 234-5; character of the, v, 395-6, 397-8; character summarized, 485-90; close union of the, 379-80; cockayne, 402-3; constitutional force, 396; courage and tenderness of, 361-2; diet of, 362-3; dinner among the, 386-7; domestic life of the, 383-4; dulness of the, 392-3; freedom of, 369-70; Goldsmith on the, xli, 541-2; government of the, xxxiv, 86, 93; hatred of pretension, v, 386; horsemanship of, 364; industry

and machinery, 410-12; literature of, 449-64; love of custom, 384-5; love of home, 383; love of private independence, 401-2; machinery, results of, on, 415-16; maritime inclinations of the, 360; mechanical tendencies of the, 381; Mill on the, xxv, 42, 43, 99-100, 153-4; Mirabeau on the, xxviii, 482; moroseness, v, 393-5; narrow patriotism of, 403-4; natural sincerity of the, 387-92; patience of the, 373; pertinacity of the, 374; physique of, 360-1; plain-dealing of the, 367-8; pluck of the, 380; practicalness of, 368-9; pride in wealth, 407-9; propriety of the, 385-6; prosperity, love of, 372; the race, 349-59, 365-6; religion of, 440-9; xxiv, 238-9; religious sects among the, xxxiv, 65-85; respect for property, 413-14; Ruskin on the, xxviii, 118-30; sea supremacy of the, v, 343; self-esteem, 404-5; social system, artificiality of, 377-8; sports of, 363; stoutness of mind of the, 396; Taine on the, xxxix, 440, 444, 449; testiness of the, v, 399; thoroughness of the, 373; trade of the, xxxiv, 93-4; travelers, 396-7; underlying strength, 401; universities, 432-40; utility, love of, 370-1, 460-2; vigor of the, 381-2; in war, 371-2; wars of the, xxxiv, 86-8; wealth of the, v, 411-12, 413; wealth, use of, 416-17; Wordsworth on the, xli, 692-3

ENGLISH, LETTERS ON THE, Voltaire's, xxxiv, 65-162

English Channel, tides of, xxx, 301-2

English Civil War, Marvell on, xl, 379; Vane on, xliii, 129-30

English Comedy, Voltaire on, xxxiv, 139-43

English Commonwealth, Milton on the, xxviii, 194-5; discussion under the, 196 (see also INSTRUMENT OF GOVERNMENT)

English Drama, blank verse in, xix, 198; gentility in, v, 125; Shakespeare and, xxxix, 240-1, 243-4; Shakespearized, v, 10; in Shakespeare's time, xxxix, 240-1; (16th century) Sidney on, xxvii, 46-9; Voltaire on, xxxiv, 133-43

ENGLISH DRAMAS, MODERN, xviii
ENGLISH ESSAYS, xxvii

English Language, Caxton on old, xxxix, 26-7; Dryden on, xiii, 56; Johnson on, xxxix, 191-206; Locke on study of, xxxvii, 173-4; Milton on, iii, 208; iv, 21; Sidney on, xxvii, 52-3; Whitman on the, xxxix, 430

English Law, Mill on, xxv, 46

English Literature, Bagehot on, xxviii, 183; Emerson on, v, 449-64; in 17th century, xxxix, 452; Taine on, 461-2; Thoreau on, xxviii, 426

ENGLISH LITERATURE, INTRODUCTION TO TAINE'S, xxxix, 433-62

English Money, Smith on, x, 33-4

ENGLISH PHILOSOPHERS, xxxiv, 317-434; xxxvii

English Poetry, Arnold's review of, xxviii, 75-90; Eliot on, l, 9; Emerson on, v, 186; Wordsworth's retrospect of, xxxix, 333-47

ENGLISH POETRY, xl, xli, xlii

English Revolution, Burke on principles of, xxiv, 164-81; Price on the, 164

English Tragedy, Voltaire on, xxxiv, 133-8

ENGLISH TRAITS, Emerson's, v, 327-493; remarks on, l, 52

ENID'S SONG, xlii, 1007

Enipeus, and Tyro, xxii, 158

Enis-el-Jelis, story of, xvi, 203-41

Enjoyment, of the present, xliv, 342 (12-13, 24), 346 (18-19), 350 (15); social, ii, 118 (3); temperance in, 198

Enlightenment, Kempis's prayer for, vii, 298-9

Enna, field of, iv, 164

En-Nabighah, Arab poet, xvi, 312 note 1

Ennius, on death, ix, 72-3; Dryden on, xxxix, 171; on Fabius, ix, 49; old age of, 50-1; on principles of nature, xxvii, 65; quoted, ix, 15-31; Shelley on, xxvii, 361; Sidney on, 9, 40

Enoch, Bunyan on, xv, 161; identified with Idris, xlv, 922 note 5; Pascal on, xlviii, 205; book of, 214

Enoch's Pillars, iii, 289 note 53

Ens, father of the Predicaments, iv, 22

Entellus, character of, xiii, 62; Dares and, 195-8

Enteritis, Holmes on, xxxviii, 260

Enthusiasm, Emerson on, v, 58, 166; method of divination, xxxiv, 397

ENVIER AND ENVIED, story of, xvi, 84-7

ENVIOUS WEZIR, story of, xvi, 39-40

Environment, Taine on, xxxix, 447-9

ENVY, ESSAY ON, Bacon's, iii, 23-8

Envy, Æschylus on, viii, 34; Augustine, St., on, vii, 30; Bacon on extinguishing of, iii, 136; beginnings of, xxxiv, 209; Blake on, xli, 602; Burns on, vi, 94; Dante on, xx, 203; in Dante's PURGATORY, 198; death and, iii, 11; defined by Hobbes, xxxiv, 356;

Emerson on, v, 64; emulation and, xl, 430; fable on, xvii, 32-3; Molière on, xxvi, 270; physical effects of, xxxviii, 131; Penn on, i, 362 (267-9), 398-9; public, Penn on, 370 (367); sin of, in FAUSTUS, xix, 221; Socrates on, ii, 15; the vice of republics, xlii, 1355

Envy, in PILGRIM'S PROGRESS, xv, 98-9

Eocene Period, in Europe, xxx, 362-3

Eocene Strata, Lyell on, xxxviii, 425-6

Eochaid Feidlech, xlix, 211-13

Eofor, xlix, 75 note 1, 88, 89

Eomer, in BEOWULF, xlix, 60

Eos, and Kephalos, viii, 307

Eotens, sword of, xlix, 49, 51, 52-3, 79

Eozoon, Darwin on the, xi, 360

Epaminondas, Bacon on, iii, 106; Cicero on death of, ix, 106; on death, xxxii, 7; Emerson on, v, 132, 211; Pascal on, xlviii, 121 (353); Plutarch on, xii, 155, 195-6; poverty of, 80; Sidney on, xxvii, 44

Epaphos, child of Zeus and Io, viii, 185; the same as Apis, xxxiii, 79

Epaphroditus, freedman of Octavius, xii, 398

Epaphroditus, master of Epictetus, ii, 116; and the shoemaker, 130 (40)

Epeius, and the horse of Troy, xviii, 112; xxii, 117

Ephesian Books, burning of the, iii, 212

Ephesians, on examples of virtue, ii, 297 (26)

Ephesus, Herodotus on plains about, xxxiii, 9

Ephialtes, the Athenian, xii, 43, 46; murder of, 47-8

Ephialtes, the giant, in Dante's HELL, xx, 131, 132; Homer on, xxii, 160 (see also Alœan Twins)

Ephorus, and Theopompus, ix, 152

Ephraim, children of, xliv, 244 (9); Milton on, iv, 425-6; son of Jacob, xlviii, 241

EPIC AND SAGA, xlix

Epic Poetry, Dryden on, xiii, 5-11, 14; xxxix, 165-6; Fielding on, 184; Hugo on, 357-9, 370, 371, 372; Milton on, v, 181; Poe on, xxviii, 384; Sidney on, xxvii, 31-2; Wordsworth on, xxxix, 313

Epic Poetry, Dryden on, xiii, 5-11, Shelley's, xxvii, 366

Epicaste, in Hades, xxii, 159

Epicharmus, rule of, ix, 122; on the understanding, xxxii, 39

Epicles, of Hermione, xii, 9

Epicrates of Acharnæ, xii, 27; Cicero the Younger on, ix, 182

Epics, prose, xxxix, 184-5

Epictetus, on anger, xlviii, 34 (80); banishment of, ix, 250 note; on changes, ii, 298 (35); on consistency, xlviii, 121; corn-superintendent and, ii, 125 (24); on desire and avoidance, 298 (37); on free will, 298 (36); GOLDEN SAYINGS OF, 117-86; Governor of Cnossus and, 151 (93); on himself, 159 (114); Hume on philosophy of, xxxvii, 337; on impossibilities, ii, 297 (33); life and teachings of, 116; Marcus Aurelius's acquaintance with, 194 (7); Pascal on, xlviii, 13 (18), 144 (431), 157 (466-7), 392-5, 402-6; priest of Augustus and, ii, 131 (43); the rich man and, 126 (25); on soul and body, 221 (41); the thief and, 120 (11); on words of bad omen, 297 (34); the young man and, 140 (65)

Epicureans, Bacon on, iii, 8

Epicurism, Locke on, xxxvii, 32

Epicurus, Aristophanes on, xxxii, 66; in Athens, iii, 204; xxviii, 59; xxxvii, 416; Augustine, St., on, vii, 100; Chaucer on, xl, 20; Dante on, xx, 41; freedom from citations, xxxii, 31; on God, iii, 45; Hugo on, xxxix, 360; on man as proper study of self, iii, 28; Mill on, xxv, 36; not an atheist, iii, 285; on pain, ii, 254 (64); on philosophy, xxxii, 55; property of, xxviii, 61; quotation from, xxxix, 120; religious principles of, xxxvii, 417-25; on sickness, ii, 276 (41); on the soul, xxxiv, 104

Epicycles, defined, iii, 48 note

Epicydes, and Themistocles, xii, 10

Epidaurian Giant, xxvi, 128

Epidaurus (see Æsculapius)

Epidemics, as a check to increase, xi, 84

Epigenes, with Socrates, ii, 21, 47

EPIGRAM, by Prior, xl, 408

EPILOGUE, by Browning, xlii, 1155

Epimenides, iii, 69; viii, 173 note 34

Epimetheus, fable of, iii, 42; Pandora and, iv, 175

Epiphanius, leader of Arabic school, xxviii, 60; Milton on, iii, 213

EPIPHANY, xlv, 578-9

Epirot, Pyrrhus called the, iv, 85

Epitaphs, Wordsworth on poetic, xxxix, 314

EPITHALAMIUM, Spenser's, xl, 238-50

Epitomes, Shelley on, xxvii, 351

Epixyes, and Themistocles, xii, 32

Epoch, Taine on importance of, xxxix, 446, 450-1

EPODE, by Jonson, xl, 301-4

Epuremei, Raleigh on the, xxxiii, 367, 371, 378; religion of, 388

Equability, is piety, xlv, 810

Equality, among low races, xxix, 245; ants pattern of, iv, 242; Ball, John, on, xxxv, 62; Burke on, xxiv, 185, 197; envy of, iii, 25; of fortune, 35; v, 92; of goods, Milton on, iv, 67; Hobbes on, xxxiv, 402-3, 425-6; Jefferson on, xliii, 160; Lowell on, xxviii, 483; Montaigne on, xxxii, 25; More on, xxxvi, 177, 178-9; natural, of men, v, 279; x, 22; Pascal on, xlviii, 107 (299), 382-4; Paul, St., on, xlv, 537 (14); principle of, discovered by Plato, xxvii, 363; realized in æsthetics, xxxii, 312; of rights, v, 250-1; sedition bred by, iii, 38; Spartan principle of, v, 252; of trades, x, 121-6

Equanimity, Hindu doctrine of, xlv, 866; Marcus Aurelius on the term, ii, 281 (8)

Equestrian Order, of Rome, ix, 213 note 2

Equipage, demand for, x, 174-5

Equity, Hobbes on, xxxiv, 426; Mohammed on, xlv, 1009

Equivocation, Penn on, i, 353 (144)

Erasistratus, xxxviii, 70, 93, 94

Erasmus, on the English universities, xxxv, 394-5; on folly, xxvii, 33; More on, xxxvi, 93; at Oxford, v, 433

Eraso, secretary of Charles V, xv, 331

Erastus, the disciple, xliv, 474 (22)

Erato, reference to, xiii, 244

Ercilla, Alonso de, Cervantes on, xiv, 57

Ercoco, reference to, iv, 332

Erechtheus, Athens the city of, viii, 333; references to, 148; xxvi, 144

Eric the Red, xliii, 5, 6, 8, 12, 13

Ericetes, death of, xiii, 352

Erichtho, Dante on, xx, 37

Erichthonius, reference to, xiii, 72

Erinnyes, reference to the, viii, 276

Eriphyle, Homer on, xxii, 160; in the Mournful Fields, xiii, 226; slain by son, xx, 302 note 12, 194

Erisichthon, Dante on, xx, 241

Eristics, Socrates on the, ii, 96

Ermine, hunting of the, xiv, 332-3; Smart on the, xli, 506

Ernst, H. C., translator of Pasteur, xxxviii, 283

Eros, and Anteros, xii, 113 note 3; xviii, 420; song to, viii, 310

Eros, servant of Antony, xii, 395

Erosion, Darwin on, xxix, 335-6; Geikie on, xxx, 356 (see also Denudation)

Erotic Poetry, Shelley on, xxvii, 359-60

Erp, son of Gudrun, xlix, 376, 379, 380, 444, 452-3, 456

Erpingham, at Agincourt, xl, 228

Error, Augustine, St., on origin of vii, 61; Berkeley on, xxxvii, 242; Emerson on, v, 18; Euripides on, viii, 308-9; hill of, in PILGRIM'S PROGRESS, xv, 125; Hobbes on, xxxiv, 345; knowledge of, necessary to truth, iii, 212-13; Milton on, iv, 405; Pascal on sources of, xlviii, 37-8; Sophocles on correction of, viii, 275

Erskine, Thomas, Lord, Burns on, vi, 167, 269, 478

Ertanax, the fish, xxxv, 192

Erymanthus, and Hercules, xiii, 238

Erynnis, references to the, xx, 38; xxii, 214

Erysipelas, and puerperal fever, xxxviii, 249, 253 note, 255, 262, 265, 266, 267

Erythrabolos, city of, xxxiii, 54

Erythræan Sea, Herodotus on, xxxiii, 8, 9-10; Milton on, iv, 17

Esau, Augustine, St., on, vii, 193; Bunyan on, xv, 127, 132-33; Woolman on, i, 311

Eschilus (see Æschylus)

Escobar, Pascal on, xlviii, 318 (915)

Escovedo, Raleigh on, xxxix, 92-3

Escremis, xlix, 129-30, 142

Escurial, Bacon on the, iii, 115

Esdras, Pascal on, xlviii, 214-15; Raleigh on, xxxix, 105

ESOPUS TO MARIA, vi, 517-20

Espanola, Drake at, xxxiii, 235

Esquife, friend of Don Quixote, xiv, 49

Esquimaux, Darwin on the, xxix, 246

ESSAY ON MAN, Pope's, xl, 417-51; l, 35

Essays, founded by Montaigne, xxxii, 3

ESSAYS, AMERICAN, xxviii, 317-485

ESSAYS, Bacon's, iii, 7-149

ESSAYS, Emerson's, v, 5-321

ESSAYS, ENGLISH, xxvii, xxviii

ESSAYS, FRENCH, GERMAN, etc., xxxii

Essence, defined, ii, 70; knowledge of, 64-6 (see also Real Existence)

Essex, Earl of, and Bacon, iii, 3; Emerson on, v, 191; Jonson on, xxvii, 60; A PASSION, xl, 294

ES-SINDIBAD OF THE SEA, xvi, 242-309

Es-Sindibad, the Porter, xvi, 242-5, 309

Establishment, misuse of word, xxvii, 258

Estampes, M. d', governor of Brittany, xxxviii, 13, 14, 15

Este, Azzo da, and Del Cassero, xx, 165 note 5

Este, Ippolito d', Cardinal of Ferrara, xxxi, 206 note 5, 210-11, 260-1, 269-72, 273, 279, 286-8, 290, 294-5, 297, 306, 333-4, 349

Este, Obizzo da, and Ghisola, xx, 76 note 2; murder of, 53 note 9

Esteem, love of, in children, xxxvii, 41-4; Pascal on, xlviii, 60 (148-9, 153), 117 (333), 132 (400, 404); Penn on, i, 365 (313); for rank, Pascal on, xlviii, 386

ESTEEM FOR CHLORIS, vi, 535

Esther, reference to, xx, 215

Estorause, King, xxxv, 223, 224

Estorgan, in SONG OF ROLAND, xlix, 130, 142

Estouteville, Jean d', xxxi, 292 note

Estramarin, xlix, 99, 130, 142-3

Estrella, in LIFE A DREAM, with Astolfo, xxvi, 18-19; her claim to throne, 19-20; agrees to king's plan, 25-6; with Segismund, 39-40; chosen queen of Segismund, 67

Estrés, M. d', Paré on, xxxviii, 26, 45

Etáin, daughter of Eochaid, xlix, 213-14

Etáin, daughter of Etar, xlix, 212-13

Etampes, Madame d', mistress of Francis I, xxxi, 295 note, 343 note; Cellini and, 305, 306, 309-11, 313-14, 323, 336-7, 339-40, 343-4, 348

Etearchos, king of Ammonians, xxxiii, 19-20

Eteocles, and Polynices, xx, 109 note; viii, 243, 247-8, 249; sung by Statius, xx, 237 note 3

Eteoneus, squire of Menelaus, xxii, 48-9, 210

ETERNAL GOODNESS, THE, xlii, 1414-16

Eternal Life, Kempis on desire of, vii, 328

Eternity, Browne on, iii, 274-5; Burke on idea of, xxiv, 55; Hindu doctrine of, xlv, 806-7; in an hour, xli, 601; human life and, ii, 274 (32); ocean of, in MIRZA, xxvii, 78, 80-1; Pascal on, xlviii, 30; shadows of, xl, 357-8; time and, iv, 40-1

Eterscél, King, xlix, 213, 214

Ethan the Ezrahite, Maschil of, xliv, 259-62

Ethelred, navy of, xxxv, 380

Ethelwald, at Winborne, v, 367

Ether, luminiferous, Kelvin on, xxx, 268, 276-9, 285-6

Ethics, common rational basis of, xxxii, 323-35; empirical and metaphysical bases of, 337-76; Hobbes on, xxxiv, 377; Hume on standard of, xxvii, 216-17; Kant on science of, xxxii, 317, 318; Mill

on Christian, xxv, 252-5; need of metaphysic of, xxxii, 318-21; need of philosophical basis, 335-6; Pascal on, xlviii, 24 (67); 318 (912); Pope on study of, xl, 417 (see also Morals)

Ethiopia, Herodotus on, xxxiii, 15, 18-19

ETHIOPIA SALUTING THE COLORS, xlii, 1490-1

Ethiopian Eunuch, xliv, 447 (27-40)

Ethiopians, circumcision among, xxxiii, 51; Homer on the, xxii, 9-10

Ethnology, importance of, xxviii, 238-43; a physical science, 244 (see also Race)

Etna (see Ætna)

ETON COLLEGE, ON A DISTANT PROSPECT OF, xl, 459

Ettrick Forest, men of, at Flodden, xli, 494 note

Etymology, Johnson on English, xxxix, 195-7

Eu, Comte d', at Dreux, xxxviii, 51

Eu, Earl of, in English wars, xxxv, 11, 51

Eucharist, Calvin on the, xxxix, 39-40, 54; institution of the, xliv, 417 (19-20); Kempis on the, vii, 349-79; Luther on the, xxxvi, 336-7; Newman on doctrine of the, xxviii, 38; Pascal on the, xlviii, 81 (224), 222 (654), 225 (666), 227 (670), 278 (789), 306-7, 340-1, 354-5; St. Paul on the, xlv, 516 (23-9)

Euchidas, the Platæan, xii, 102

Euclia, the goddess, xii, 102

Euclid, the mathematician, Huxley on, xxviii, 227; in Limbo, xx, 20; on unity, xlviii, 441-2

Euclid, friend of Socrates, ii, 47

Eudæmon, name of, xii, 162 note

Eudamidas, will of, xxxii, 83, 84

Eudes, Mayor of Palace, xxxix, 87

Euergetes, name of, xii, 162 note

EUGANEAN HILLS, LINES WRITTEN AMONG, xli, 858-64

Eugene, Prince, xli, 751; and the English merchants, xxxiv, 93-4; story of, xxvii, 109

Eugenio, the goatherd, in DON QUIXOTE, xiv, 525-32

Eugenius, Calvin on, xxxix, 45, 46

Eulogies, fancy and judgment in, xxxiv, 364

Eulogistic Fallacies, xxvii, 258-9

Eumæus, swineherd of Odysseus, xxii, 193-207, 216-21, 224-8, 238, 243-6, 247, 251-4, 300-1, 304-5, 310-20; Cowley on, xxvii, 72

Eumedes, death of, xiii, 407

Eumenides, Hugo on the, xxxix, 366; name of, xxvii, 341
Eumenius, death of, xiii, 385
Eumolpus, Pliny on, ix, 420-1
Eunapius, at Athens, xxviii, 54-5
Eunoë, river, xx, 264
Eunomus, and Demosthenes, xii, 201-2
Eunuchs, envy of, iii, 24; king's favor for, 113
Euodius, conversion of, vii, 154; at funeral of Monnica, 162
Eupeithes, father of Antinous, xxii, 342; death of, 345
Euphelia, and Cloe, xl, 407-8
Euphrantides, the Prophet, xii, 18
Euphrasia, in PHILASTER (see Bellario)
Euphrates, the philosopher, ix, 204-5; quoted, ii, 172 (154)
Euphrosyne, reference to, iv, 31
Eupolis, and Alcibiades, ix, 154; on Pericles, ix, 217 note; xii, 39
Euripides, and Æschylus, xxxix, 450; Aristophanes on, viii, 418, 421; BACCHÆ of, 349-415; defeats of, xxxix, 334; dispute with Æschylus in THE FROGS, viii, 441-465; domestic relations of, 452; on hiding wickedness, xxxix, 73; HIPPOLYTUS of, viii, 287-348; Hugo on, xxxix, 365; Hugo on Suppliants of, 359; Johnson on, 220; on liberty of speech, iii, 193; life and works, viii, 286; in Limbo, xx, 238 note 6; Milton on, iv, 417; Shelley on, xxvii, 354; Sophocles, compared with, 196; on the Spartans, iii, 204; verses of, in Syracuse, xxvii, 41
Euripus, the flux of, xxxviii, 79, 103, 104
Europa, reference to, xx, 402
Europe, American policy toward, xliii, 297-8; "better fifty years of," xlii, 1019; civilization of, cause of, xxxiv, 210; eastern, Freeman on, xxviii, 272-81; growth of continent of, xxx, 357-67; races of, xxviii, 266-81
Europeans, contact of, with native races, xxix, 459-60
Eurus, reference to, xiii, 79
Euryades, death of, xxii, 314
Euryalus, and Nisus, xiii, 192-3, 303-312
Euryalus, in the ODYSSEY, xxii, 107, 108, 114-15
Eurybates, henchman of Ulysses, xxii, 273-4
Eurybiades, Admiral of Greeks, xii, 11; given rewards for valor, 21; at Salamis, 88-9; Themistocles and, 15-16
Eurycleia, nurse of Telemachus,

xxii, 20-1, 31-2, 67-8, 239, 276-80, 317-18, 321-3
Eurycles, and Antony, xii, 388
Eurydamas, in the ODYSSEY, xxii, 263, 315
Eurydice, wife of Creon, vii, 280-1, 283-4
Eurydice, wife of Nestor, xxii, 46
Eurydice, wife of Orpheus, iv, 35
Eurylochus, in Circe's isle, xxii, 141-3, 147-8; at island of Helios, 176, 177-8
Eurymachus, suitor of Penelope, xxii, 19-20, 27, 64, 208, 222, 261-3; death of, 308-9; Melantho and, 263; Telemachus and, 235-6; Theoclymenus and, 293-4; Ulysses and, 264-6, 300-4
Eurymanthus, death of, xiii, 321
Eurymedon, in the ODYSSEY, xxii, 95
Eurymedusa, Homer on, xxii, 94
Eurynome, in ODYSSEY, xxii, 251, 259-60, 270, 309, 325
Eurynomus, wooer of Penelope, xxii, 22, 313
Eurypilus, Dante on, xx, 86
Euryptolemus, and Pericles, xii, 43
Eurypylus, in ÆNEID, xiii, 107, 165
Eurystheus, Epictetus on, ii, 143 (71)
Eurythmus, freedman of Trajan, ix, 309-10
Eurytion, in ÆNEID, xiii, 199, 200
Eurytion, the Centaur, xxii, 303
Eurytus, Homer on, xxii, 110
Eusebius, at Athens, xxviii, 62; on the Creation, xxxix, 107; Milton on, iii, 213
Eustochium, vision of, iii, 210
Euterpe, mother of Themistocles, xii, 5
Eutyches, on Christ, xx, 308 note 5
Eutychus, and Octavius, xii, 386 note
Eutychus, and St. Paul, xliv, 476 (9-12)
Evadne, and Laodamia, xiii, 226
Evandale, Lord, character of, v, 126
Evander, and Æneas, xiii, 276-84, 287-91; Cowley on Virgil's, xxvii, 72-3; in Italy, xiii, 274; lament over Pallas, 366-7
EVANGELINE, Longfellow's, xlii, 1353-1413; its debt to HERMANN AND DOROTHEA, xix, 334
Evangeline, daughter of Benedict Bellefontaine, xlii, 1356-7; her suitors, 1358; her love for Gabriel, 1358-60; her heifer, 1361; on evening of betrothal, 1362-3, 1365, 1368, 1369-70; at feast of betrothal, 1371, 1372; waiting for father's return, 1375-6; on day of expulsion, 1378, 1380, 1382;

in exile, 1384; her search for Gabriel, 1385-1408; in Philadelphia, as Sister of Mercy, 1408-9; in the plague, 1410-11; with Gabriel at last, 1411-13

Evangelist, in PILGRIM'S PROGRESS, xv, 14-15, 24-9, 91-3

Evangelus, servant of Pericles, xii, 56

Evans, mate of the "Alert," xxiii, 422

Eve, Adam accuses, iv, 290-3; Adam, first meeting with, 168-9, 258-60; Adam, her dependence on, 173-4; Adam, evening meal with, 165-6; Adam denounces, 316-17; Adam's love besought by, 317-18; Adam tempted by, 284-90; appearance of, at the feast, 193, 194-5; Bagehot on Milton's, xxviii, 198, 209-10; beauty of, v, 315; Browne on creation of, iii, 286; Bunyan on apple of, xv, 240; creation of, iv, 258-9; Dante on, in PARADISE, xx, 420 note 1; death suggested by, iv, 319; departs from Eden, 361-2; description of, 164-5; dream of, 184-6; feast prepared by, for Raphael, 191-2; hides from God, 297; judged, 298-9; labors of, 189; lamentation of, at loss of Eden, 329; prayer of, 187-9; temptation of, 276-83; tree of, xxxv, 196-7, 198

EVE OF ST. AGNES, xli, 907-17

Evelake, King, xxxv, 124, 125, 144-5, 159, 219, 222

EVELYN HOPE, xlii, 1120

Evening, Goethe on influence of, xix, 48, 49; Milton's description of, iv, 172

EVENING, To, xli, 491-3

EVENING STAR, To THE, xli, 790, 795-6

Events, cause of, Whewell on, xi, 1; Emerson on origin of, v, 138; relation of, to causes, xxxvii, 373-7; tests of worth of, v, 195-6

Evenus, the Parian, ii, 6, 48, 49

Everett, Edward, oration at Gettysburg, xliii, 441 note

Evil, Augustine, St., on, vii, 40, 60-1, 78, 105-7, 115-16; Buddha on, xlv, 677; Carlyle on, xxv, 358; Dante on cause of, xx, 211-12; Emerson on, v, 28; Epictetus on, ii, 174 (162); Hobbes on, xxxiv, 351-2; Hume on problem of, xxxvii, 389-91, 421-2; knowledge of, Mrs. Herbert on, xv, 380; knowledge of, Milton on, iii, 212-13; iv, 281; last infirmity of, xviii, 412; made by thought, xlvi, 123; Marcus Aurelius on, ii, 203 (11), 205 (17), 215 (7, 8), 220 (39), 234 (1), 271 (13), 275 (35);

Omar Khayyam on, xli, 984-5; Pascal on, xlviii, 133 (408), 337; Pope on, xl, 419-25, 444; Rousseau on, xxxiv, 267-9, 286-7; seeds of, fable on, xvii, 15; Socrates on, ii, 38; speaking and believing, vii, 217 (1); Woolman on, i, 266

Evils, as benefactors, v, 103; choose less of two, vii, 284; Goethe on imagined, xix, 31; Milton on imagined, iv, 56

Evolution, antiquity of idea of, xi, 6; Descartes on growth by, xxxiv, 12-13; generally accepted, xi, 257; growth of idea of, ii, 9-24

EVOLUTION, GEOGRAPHICAL, xxx, 342-67

Ewaipanoma, the, xxxiii, 372-3

Ewell, Gen., at Gettysburg, xliii, 365, 366, 378-9, 385-6

Exaggeration, Emerson on, v, 242

Example, best precept, xvii, 30; Chaucer on, and precept, xl, 25; Confucius on guiding by, xliv, 7 (3); education by, ix, 336; Epictetus on, and precept, ii, 177 (175); Epictetus on teaching by, 155 (102); Locke on teaching by, xxxvii, 59, 62, 68-9, 73-4; Spenser on teaching by, xxxix, 65

Examples, Bacon on use of, xxxix, 147; great men as, xlviii, 45 (103); Machiavelli on high, xxxvi, 20; Pascal on effect of, xlviii, 49 (117); Raleigh on historical, xxxix, 73-5, 93; true and feigned, xxvii, 23; use of good and evil, iii, 31

Excalibur, sword of Arthur, xli, 1020-3

Excess, causes defect, v, 92; Confucius on, xliv, 35 (15); Epictetus on, ii, 183 (12); Pascal on, xlviii, 29

Exchange, advantages of, x, 22-3; ancient media of, 30-1; effects of high price of, 330; medium of (see Money); power of, limits division of labor, 24; propensity to, 19-20; rates of, as criterion of balance of trade, 372-6; rates of international, 329-30

Excise Duties, vexation of, x, 564

Excises under U. S. Constitution, xliii, 196 (8)

EXCISEMEN, KIRK AND STATE, vi, 489-90

Excitement, man's sphere, xix, 68; Pascal on quest of, xlviii, 54, 55; Wordsworth on thirst for, xxxix, 287-8

Exclusionists, Emerson on, v, 98-9

Excommunication, Chaucer on, xl, 29 note 330; Dante on, xx, 365 note 10; Luther on, xxxvi, 289, 305, 306, 323; in Utopia, 244

Excuses, Confucius on, xliv, 56 (1);

fable of, xvii, 9-10; Locke on, xxxvii, 122, 126; Marcus Aurelius on, ii, 195 (12); Pascal on, xlviii, 22 (58); Penn on, i, 354 (150); Thackeray on, xxviii, 9; Tzu-hsia on, xliv, 66 (8)

Executive Power (U. S.), xliii, 199-202

Exercise, Burke on necessity of, xxiv, 113-14; Cicero on, ix, 58

Existence, annihilation of, heresy of, xlv, 672-3, 681; definition of, impossible, xlviii, 432; Hindu doctrine of persistent, xlv, 806-7; persistent, heresy of, 672-3, 680; struggle for (see Struggle for Existence) (see also Real Existence)

Exorcism, Pascal on, xlviii, 289 (820)

Expectation, Manzoni on, xxi, 664; never satisfied, v, 243-4

Expediency, St. Paul on, xlv, 508 (12), 515 (23)

Expenditure (see Consumption)

Expense, Bacon on, iii, 75-6; educational, xxxvii, 74-5; immediate and durable, x, 287-90

Experience, in animals, xxxvii, 392-3; Bacon on analysis of, xxxix, 140, 143-6; Bunyan on, xv, 297; Descartes on value of, xxxiv, 10-11, 13; education by actual, v, 12-15; faith superior to, 137; Hobbes on, xxxiv, 326, 333; Hume on, xxxvii, 317-20, 326-30, 375, 397, 424; Hume on conclusions from, 330-6, 338, 339-41, 349; mother of sciences, xiv, 175; necessity of moral, xxviii, 178; of others, i, 74; Raleigh on, xxix, 105; reason and, 134; xxxvii, 340 note; teacher of wisdom, best, xxviii, 351; thought and, Thoreau on, 411

Experience, the shepherd, in PILGRIM'S PROGRESS, xv, 125-8

Experiment, Bacon on necessity of, xxxix, 131, 134, 140, 141-2; Descartes on truth by, xxxiv, 12-13, 51

Explanations, actions the only true, v, 198-9

Expletives, Johnson on, xxxix, 201

Exports, and Exportation, bounties on, x, 392-406, 546; drawbacks on, 389-91; encouragement of, 346-7; of materials, discouraged, 424, 429-42; taxes on, from U. S., xliii, 198 (5)

Ex Post Facto Laws, xliii, 198 (3, 10)

Expression, Locke on correct, xxxvii, 171-4; means of, other than words, xxviii, 290-1; necessary to beauty, v, 317, 318

EXTEMPORANEOUS EFFUSION, vi, 375

EXTEMPORE IN COURT OF SESSION, vi, 269

Extempore Speaking, Locke on, xxxvii, 158-9

Extempore Writing, Carlyle on, xxv, 460-4

Extension, Berkeley on, xxxvii, 220-2, 224-6, 230-1, 282; Hume on idea of, 435-6; infinite divisibility of, xlviii, 437-44; as source of grandeur, xxiv, 63-70

External Circumstances, independence of (see Independence of C.)

Extinction of Species, Darwin on, xi, 120-1, 130-1, 140-1, 368-73; xxix, 189-90; Lyell on causes of, xxxviii, 425, 427

Extortioners, St. Paul on, xlv, 507 (11), 508 (10)

Extradition, between U. S. and Great Britain, xliii, 300, 307; under Confederation, 169

Extravagance, economically considered, x, 279-81; public, 282-3

Extremes, Molière on man's tendency to, xxvi, 203; Pascal on, xlviii, 29; Plutarch on, xii, 153

Eye, beauty of the, xxiv, 101; development of the, xi, 190-4; Helmholtz on the, 214; interpreter of the heart, xlviii, 421

Eyes, temptation of, St. Augustine on, vii, 196-7

Eylimi, King, xlix, 297, 298, 299

Eyre, Gov., prosecution of, xxv, 189-90

Eyre, Margery, in SHOEMAKER'S HOLIDAY, xlvii, 451-3, 458-61, 466-9, 475-82, 498-9, 508

Eyre, Simon, in SHOEMAKER'S HOLIDAY, character of, xlvii, 445; king and, 509-10, 513-14; Leadenhall built by, 513 note; Lord Mayor and, 473-4, 479-82; Mayor, 491, 499, 506-9; Ralph and, 451-4; Rowland and, 460-1, 498, 504; sheriff, 478-9; ship bought by, 467-9; at his shop, 457-61, 466-7

Eyre's Sound, glaciers in, xxix, 262

Eystein, and Sigurd, v, 357

Eyvind, and Olaf, v, 286

Ezekiel, and Æschylus, viii, 4; Pascal on, xlviii, 312 (886); vision of, iv, 101

Ezra, and the ass, xvi, 123 note

Ezzelin, reference to, xviii, 300

Fa, Jacques de la, xxxi, 323 note 1

Fabatus, letters to, ix, 260, 308, 318

Faber, Frederick William, HYMN BY, xlv, 584

Fabian, in POLYEUCTE, xxvi, 80-3, 109

Fabius Maximus, Cicero on, ix, 48-50; Pericles and, compared, xii, 38; Scipio and, xxxvi, 59; Virgil on, xiii, 240

FABLES AND FOLK-LORE, xvii
FABLES, PREFACE TO, Dryden's, xxxix,
160-83
Fables, law of compensation in, v,
96; remarks on, xvii, 2, 3
Fabricius, Gaius, Cicero on, ix, 18;
Dante on, xx, 227; on Epicurus,
ix, 61; Milton on, iv, 387; More
on, xxxvi, 172; Virgil on, xiii,
240
Fabricius, Hieronymus, Harvey on,
xxxviii, 80; on lungs, 68, 75; on
veins, 124
Face, Burke on beauty of the, xxiv,
101; character in the, iii, 326;
expressions of the, xxviii, 290-1;
ideal, rare, v, 316-17; sign of
mind, as, Shakespeare on, xlvi,
313
Face, in THE ALCHEMIST, confederates betrayed by, xlvii, 627-
9; Dame Pliant and, 566-7, 591-2,
593-4, 598-602; Dapper with, 528-
35, 576-7, 581-5, 623-4, 625;
Drugger and, 536-9, 564-6, 577-81;
as Jeremy the servant, 617-22;
Lovewit and, 622-3; Mammon
and, 541, 544-6, 548, 549-51, 554-
9, 585-6, 587-8, 591, 603-4, 605-6;
Subtle and, 521-8, 594 5; Surly
and, 557, 559, 574-6, 595-8, 608-
10
Facing-both-ways, Mr., in PILGRIM'S
PROGRESS, xv, 104
Fact, Hume on matters of, xxxvii,
324-36, 339-42, 349, 350, 439, 443-4
FACTION, ESSAY ON, Bacon's, iii,
129-131
Factions, Bacon on, iii, 39, 41;
Franklin on, i, 93
Facts, Burns on, vi, 218; Emerson
on, v, 191; worship of, 195-6
Fadl-ed-Din, the vizier, xvi, 203-10
Faerie Queene, LEAR, story of, in,
xlvi, 202; Shelley on, xxvii, 366
FAERIE QUEENE, PREFATORY LETTER
ON, xxxix, 64-8
Fafnir, xlix, 303, 304, 306, 312-15;
the heart of, 316-17
Failure, M. Aurelius on, ii, 227
(9), 244 (50)
Faint-Heart, in PILGRIM'S PROGRESS,
xv, 130, 134-5
Fainting, Harvey on cause of,
xxxviii, 119
FAIR ANNET, LORD THOMAS AND, xl,
61-5
FAIR INES, xli, 930-1; Poe on,
xxviii, 397-8
FAIR IS MY LOVE, xl, 255
FAIR YOUNG LADY, SONG TO A, xl,
397-8
FAIREST MAID ON DEVON BANKS, vi,
592
Fairfax, motto of house of, v, 388

Fairfax, Edward, Dryden on, xxxix,
161, 171
FAIRFAX, LORD GENERAL, AT SIEGE
OF COLCHESTER, iv, 84
FAIRIES, THE, by Allingham, xlii,
1162
Fairness, and fitness, Augustine, St.,
on, vii, 60
Fair-speech, Lord, in PILGRIM'S
PROGRESS, xv, 104
Fair-speech, town of, in PILGRIM'S
PROGRESS, xv, 103-4
Faith, American lack of, v, 57; Arnold on decline of, xlii, 1184;
Augustine, St., on, in Scripture,
vii, 87-8; Bacon on, and suspicion, iii, 87; Blake on children's,
xli, 603; Browne on, iii, 272 (9,
10), 284, 323; Bunyan's allegory
of, xv, 34-5; Calvin on, xxxix,
33, 53; Carlyle on, xxv, 358;
Dante on, xx, 389-90; Dante's
allegory of, 268 note 11; Dante's
star of, 179 note 9; decline of,
modern, v, 38, 287; xxv, 358-61;
Emerson on, v, 137-8, 152, 284,
292, 308; Hindu doctrine of, xlv,
857, 859, 873, 875; Hobbes on,
xxxiv, 361-2; Hume on Christian,
xxxvii, 415; Isidore on, xxxix, 116;
Jesus on, xliv, 403 (5-6); justification by, xxxvi, 364-77, 378, 381-
2, 382-3, 386-8, 395; justification
by, Hindu idea of, xlv, 809;
Kempis on necessity of, vii, 378
(2), 379 (5); Longfellow on, xlii,
1407; Luther on Christian, xxxvi,
362, 369-75, 391-2; Milton on, iii,
228-31; iv, 52, 356; More on,
under difficulties, xxxvi, 105;
Pascal on, xlviii, 92 (248), 97
(265-7), 99 (278-9), 138, 167
(504), 171 (516), 306; Paul, St.,
on, xlv, 519 (2, 13); Penn on, i,
376 (454); Pope on modes of, xl,
441; Rousseau on, articles of,
xxxiv, 298; Tzu-chang on, xliv,
65 (2); Voltaire on, and reason,
xxxiv, 109; Whitman on, xxxix,
414; Wordsworth on, 330-1; of
youth, xix, 34-5 (see also Fidelity,
Promises)
Faithful, in PILGRIM'S PROGRESS, xv,
59-60, 71, 73-89, 94-102
FAITHFUL JOHN, tale of, xvii,
61-8
Faithfulness, Confucius on, xliv, 6
(8), 14 (15), 30 (24), 40 (10),
47 (8), 53 (5); Jesus on, 403
(10-12)
Falada, the speaking horse, xvii,
184-8
Falconer, Hugh, on crocodiles, xi,
364-5; on elephants, 370; on
periods of modification, 351

Falconer, the Jesuit, xxix, 119

Falkland Islands, climate and productions of, xxix, 258-9; Darwin on, 58, 202-18; peat in, 304; tameness of birds in, 423

Falkland, Lord, on ceremony, v, 210; Pope on, xl, 444

FALL OF FYERS, LINES ON THE, vi, 296

FALL OF THE LEAF, vi, 333

FALLACIES OF ANTI-REFORMERS, Smith's, xxvii, 237-65

Fallen Angels, in PARADISE LOST, muster of, iv, 103-105; names on earth of, 99; number of, 98-99; in Pandemonium, 109-10; pastimes of the, 124-6; punishment of, yearly, 307-9; rebellion of, 201, 209, 212-29

Falling Bodies, law of, xxx, 18-20

Falloppio, system of, xxxviii, 408

Falsaron, xlix, 128, 139-40

False accusers, branded in Rome, ix, 310 note 8

False Opinions, injuriousness of, ii, 245 (57)

False Prosecutions, in Massachusetts, xliii, 76 (37)

False Witness, punished by death, xliii, 85 (11)

Falsehood, Bacon on, iii, 7, 8, 134; Dante places, in Hell, xx, 47; Emerson on, v, 27, 104; Hobbes on, xxxiv, 339; Kant on, xxxii, 332-3, 350, 353, 372; Locke on early training in, xxxvii, 31; Marcus Aurelius on, ii, 267 (1); Montaigne on, iii, 9; Penn on, i, 353 (144); semblance of, to be avoided, xx, 70-1; Spanish proverb on, iii, 20; Whitman on, xxxix, 425

Fame, Augustine, St., on, vii, 59; Bacon on, iii, 38, 132; Burns on, vi, 273, 325; Byron on, xli, 810; Carlyle on, xxv, 436; Confucius on, xliv, 5 (1), 6 (16), 13 (14), 41 (20), 50 (32); Dante on, xx, 101, 191-2, 311 note 25; death and, iii, 11; Diogenes on, ii, 180 (187); Epictetus on, 131 (43); Huxley on, xxviii, 217; "infirmity of noble minds," last, iv, 76; Marcus Aurelius on, ii, 203 (12), 205 (17), 210 (10), 214 (3), 216 (19), 220 (33, 35), 237 (16, 18), 244 (51), 246 (6), 250 (34), 263 (44); Milton on, iv, 76, 340, 389-91; Pascal on love of, xlviii, 60 (148), 61 (153, 158); Pliny on, ix, 305, 351; Pope on, xl, 447, 448; results of desire for, xxxiv, 386; Seneca on, xxxix, 70; Virgil's figure of, xiii, 162-3; Virgil's figure of, Burke on, xxiv, 57

FAME, ESSAY ON, Bacon's, iii, 147-9

Familiarity, Bacon on, iii, 131-2; breeds contempt, xvii, 24; defeats dignity, xii, 43; Emerson on, v, 217; in friendship, 119-20; Kempis on, vii, 220; Locke on, of children, xxxvii, 85-8; Marcus Aurelius on, ii, 221 (44), 245 (1), 257 (6); Penn on, i, 351 (119); Shakespeare on, xlvi, 102; wonder destroyed by, xlviii, 40 (90)

Familiars, defined, xlvii, 729

Family, Feast of, in NEW ATLANTIS, iii, 172-6; founders of a, indulgent, 21, 37; origin of the, xxxiv, 206; Taine on the, xxxix, 454; in Utopia, xxxvi, 194, 195

Famine, Woolman on, as a judgment, i, 246

Fan Ch'ih, disciple of Confucius, xliv, 7 (5), 20 (20), 41 (21, 22), 43 (4), 45 (19)

Fanaticism, Burke on, xxiv, 301

Fancy, feeling and, xlviii, 98 (274-5); imagination and, xxxix, 316, 322-5; Hobbes on, xxxiv, 325, 363-5; Milton on, iv, 186; Pascal on, xlviii, 39 (86, 87); Wordsworth on, xxxix, 316-17, 322-5 (see also Imagination)

FANCY, by Shakespeare, xl, 268

FANCY, THE REALM OF, xli, 894-6

Fannia, mother-in-law of Helvidius, ix, 355, 358

Fannia, wife of Helvidius, ix, 322-324

Fannius, contemporary of Pliny, ix, 276-7

Fannius, Gaius, in Cicero's essay on FRIENDSHIP, ix, 8-9

Fano, Ludovico da, xxxi, 101 note 5, 169, 173

Faraday, Michael, CHEMICAL HISTORY OF A CANDLE, xxx, 89-178; FORCES OF MATTER, 5-88; life and work of, 3-4; on regelation of ice, 244, 254, 256

FARE THEE WELL, by Byron, xli, 819-21

FAREWELL, THE, by Burns, vi, 225-6, 234-5

FAREWELL, LOVE'S, xl, 232

FAREWELL, REWARDS, AND FAIRIES, xl, 323-4

FAREWELL THOU STREAM, vi, 543

FAREWELL TO ELIZA, vi, 228

FAREWELL TO THE WORLD, xl, 299

Farfarello, the demon, xx, 90, 93

Farinata degli Uberti, Dante on, xx, 42-5

FARMER, IN THE CHARACTER OF A RUINED, by Burns, vi, 22-3

Farmers, in agricultural system, x, 448-9, 461-2; capital of, 225-6; indolence of, reason for, 14; monopoly unknown among, 358;

pleasures of, ix, 64-7; studies for, xxviii, 339

Farming (see Agriculture)

Farnese, Alessandro, xxxi, 77 note, 78, 260 note (see also Paul III)

Farnese, Pier Luigi, xxxi, 153 note 2, 354 note 2; Cellini and, 155, 211-12, 216, 235-6, 256, 267 note 11, 354-5; prevision of his murder, 262, 267 note 8; wife of, 242 note

Farrel, Capt., at Gettysburg, xliii, 393-4, 409

Farrer, Nicholas, xv, 415-17; George Herbert and, 392, 414, 418, 419-20; letter from Herbert to, 425-6

Farrington, Abraham, i, 187, 192

Fashion, Channing on, xxviii, 328; classes of, v, 212-14, 218-21; Emerson on, 209, 212, 220, 226-7; Goldsmith on pleasures of, xli, 528

Fastidiousness, in love, xlviii, 421-2; Penn on, i, 402 (135-46)

Fasts, Calvin on, xxxix, 40; Luther on, xxxvi, 325

Fatalism (see Necessity)

Fata Morgana, references to, xvii, 291; xlii, 1402

Fate, Academics, the, on, xxxix, 114; Calderon on, xxvi, 66; Chaucer on, xl, 46, 48; fable on, xvii, 38-9; Herodotus's belief in, xxxiii, 4; irremovable, by prescience, xiii, 308; lines on, v, 283; Machiavelli on, xxxvi, 83-4; Marcus Aurelius on, ii, 201 (3), 215 (6, 9), 218 (26), 226 (8), 256 (75), 279 (5); Omar Khayyam on, xli, 982-3; ordained of old, viii, 90; superior to gods, 41; unavoidable rather than unexpected, xii, 326 (see also Necessity)

Fates, the, iv, 44-5; xiii, 181; Æschylus on the, viii, 152; De Quincey on the, xxvii, 336; guides of necessity, viii, 174; of Norse mythology, xlix, 291 note (see also Destinies)

Father, loss of a, Plutarch on, xii, 152

Father Abraham's Sermon, i, 3, 96

Fathers, honored in NEW ATLANTIS, iii, 174; tyrannical, Shelley on, xviii, 301 (see also Parents)

Fathers of the Church, Calvin on, xxxix, 37-41; Milton on, iv, 213

Fatimah, in story of Ala ed Din, xvi, 436-8

Fattore, Il, xxxi, 35 note 3, 40, 57

Faucon, Capt., xxiii, 169, 171, 195; (in 1859), 404; in Boston, 421-2

Faulkner, F., translator of Pasteur, xxxviii, 283

Fault-finding (see Censoriousness)

Faults, compensation for, v, 102; Confucius on, xliv, 13 (7), 54

(29); man's dislike to hear own, ii, 141 (67); Pascal on hiding of, xlviii, 43-4; Penn on, i, 351 (123); pointing out of, xlviii, 174 (535); Shakespeare on single, xlvi, 105; uncorrected, become habits, ii, 144 (75)

Faults, geological, xi, 338

Fauns, referred to, iv, 75

Faunus, Latin god, xiii, 422; father of Latinus, 245

Faust, Doctor, historical character, original of Goethe's tragedy, xix, 4

Faust, in Goethe's FAUST, at Auerbach's wine-cellar, xix, 84, 91; in witches' kitchen, 95-7; vision of Helena, 99-100; restored to youth, 103-6; before Margaret's door, 153-4; kills Valentine, 156; compact with Mephistopheles, 60-70; curse of, 62-3; starts out, 78-9; dissatisfied, calls on spirits, 21-7; interrupted by Wagner, 27-29; first sight of Margaret, 107; demands her from Mephistopheles, 107-10; in Margaret's chamber, 110-13; his corruption undertaken by Mephistopheles, 18-19; in despair, attempts suicide, 30-5; in forest cavern, 136-9; urged by Mephistopheles to return to Margaret, 139-41; in study, Mephistopheles appears, 48-60; learns appointment with Margaret, 125-8; with Margaret in garden, 128-34; in summer-house, 135-6; learns casket given to church, 116-17; on Walpurgis'-Night, 161-74; vision of Margaret, 175; learns her imprisonment and determines to free her, 184-6; on way to prison, 186-7; in dungeon with Margaret, 187-95; with Margaret, on his religion, 143-5; on Mephistopheles, 146; plans secret meeting with Margaret, 147-8; with Mephistopheles, 148-9; with Wagner before the gate, 40-5; his aspirations, 46; with the dog, 47-8

Faust, tragedy of, Goethe's, xix, 7-195; remarks on, 4-6

Faustina, wife of Marcus Aurelius, ii, 200 (17)

Faustus, in Marlowe's FAUSTUS, and the horse-courser, xix, 232-4; at court of Vanholt, 235; recalls spirit of Helen of Troy, 236; birth, education, and practise of magic, 199-200; dissatisfied with human learning, takes to magic, 200-203; half repents, 217-18; discusses astronomy, 218-19; calls on Christ, 219; with Lucifer, 220; with Seven Sins, 220-2; promised

to see Hell, 222; studies astronomy on Olympus, 222; remarks on dying utterance of, 198; remarks on speech to Helen, 198; renounces God for Belzebub, 212; compact with Mephistophilis, 213-17; travels of, 222-3; in Rome, at Pope's feast, 223-5; returns home, his fame, 226; at Emperor's court, 229-32; urged to repent, 237; renews compact, 238; wins Helen of Troy for paramour, 238-9; last hours, 239-42; taken by devils, 242-3; with Valdes and Cornelius, 203-5; conjures Mephistophilis, 206-9

FAUSTUS, DR., Marlowe's, xix, 199-243; remarks on, 198

Faustus, Bishop of Manichees, vii, 66; St. Augustine on, 70-73

Favonius, iv, 87; ix, 99; Cæsar, opposed by, xii, 293; Pompey and, 303-4, 310

Favorinus, ii, 179 note

FAVORITE CAT, ON A, xl, 473-5

Favorites, Marlowe on, xlvi, 25; royal, Bacon on, iii, 70, 99

Favors, apt to be repeated, i, 102; Cicero on, ix, 33; claim returns, xix, 126; Emerson on receiving, v, 100; Hobbes on, xxxiv, 386; Marcus Aurelius on, ii, 194 (8); Mohammed on, xlv, 890, 894; Socrates on, ii, 297 (25); Woolman on, i, 255

FAVOUR, ON RECEIVING A, vi, 375

Fawcett, Mr., xxv, 191

Fawkener, Everard, postmaster-general, i, 151

Fawkes, Guy, Hazlitt on, xxvii, 294-295

Fawn, defined, xxxv, 361

Fay, Godemar du, xxxv, 20-1

Fazio, Friar, in THE BETROTHED, xxi, 136

Fear, Augustine, St., on, vii, 29; Burke on, xxiv, 51-2; cause of, 110-12; critic, the most rigid, ix, 322; darkness, cause of, xxiv, 70, 120-3; David on use of, xli, 503; delight caused by, xxiv, 114; dishonorableness of, 380; Emerson on, v, 99; Epictetus on, ii, 135 (55); eyes of, to see under the ground, xiv, 164; of God, Bunyan on, xv, 154-5; of God, necessary to grace, 262; guide to duty, v, 133; Hobbes's definition of, xxxiv, 353; honoring, a way of, 378; hope and, iv, 57; ignorance, cause of, v, 17; instinctive, xi, 266; judge of souls, viii, 135; Locke on, xxxvii, 102, 105; loudness, cause of, xxiv, 72; love and, xxxvi, 57-9; Marcus Aurelius on,

ii, 284 (25), 287 (34); music and, xli, 489; obscurity cause of, xxiv, 52-3; Pascal on religious, xlviii, 96 (262); power, idea of, cause of, xxiv, 57-62; in privation, 63; sounds, intermitting, cause of, 73-4; suddenness, cause of, 73; vastness, in idea of, 63-4, 115 (see also Sublime)

Fearing, in PILGRIM'S PROGRESS, xv, 176, 256-62, 276-7

Fearlessness, Confucius on, xliv, 47 (4), 49 (21)

Fears, and desires, iii, 50; make us traitors, xlvi, 353; may be liars, xlii, 1165

Feasts, in New Atlantis, iii, 175

FEATHERS, THE THREE, xvii, 166-169

Feathers, fine, and fine birds, xvii, 18

Febo, Cavalier del, xiv, 123

Federal Government, and state governments, xliii, 222-3; 224-7, 229-30, 239; Jay's argument for a, 217-21

FEDERALIST, THE, (NOS. I and II), xliii, 212-21

Federigo, Cardinal, in THE BETROTHED, xxi, 367-76; with the Unnamed, 377-88; visits Lucia, 413-18; visits Lucia's village, 424-7; advises Lucia, 432; reprimands Abbondio, 433-44; in Milan famine, 477-9, 486; in plague, 526, 548-9; 552, 554-5

Feeble-mind, in PILGRIM'S PROGRESS, xv, 176-7, 274-7, 278-9, 285, 288, 292, 295, 306; parts with Christiana, 316; death, 318

Feejee Islanders, cannibalism of, v, 207

Feeling, beautiful in, the, xxiv, 103-4; fancy and, xlviii, 98 (274-5); Longfellow on, xlii, 1391; Mill, James, on, xxv, 74; necessary to persuasion, xix, 27-8; reason and, xlviii, 98 (276-8), 99 (282); reason and, Schiller on, xxxii, 257-63; reasoning and, xlviii, 9-10; virtue, basis of, xxxii, 373; Ruskin on, xxviii, 116-18; sense of, as source of sublime, xxiv, 76; Wordsworth on need of developing, xxxix, 287-8

Feelings, Mill on the, xxv, 37, 95, 264-5; thoughts and, xxxix, 286-7; undermined by analysis, xxv, 91

Fees, in New Atlantis, not permitted, iii, 156, 158

Feet, Locke on care of the, xxxvii, 11-13

Feigning, Lady, in PILGRIM'S PROGRESS, xv, 104

Felice, Father (see Casati Felice), xxi

Felice, partner of Cellini, xxxi, 138, 172-4, 176-7, 178, 180

Felician, Father, in EVANGELINE, xlii, 1358-9; in the church, 1374; on day of exile, 1380, 1382; with Evangeline in wanderings, 1385, 1387, 1390-1, 1395; at Basil's, 1397, 1400

Felician of Silva, books of xiv, 20

Felicion, the shoemaker, ii, 130 (40)

Felicity, Hobbes on, xxxiv, 359; lies in progress, 384

Felix, Roman governor, xliv, with Paul, 484 (24-35), 486 (22-7)

Felix, governor of Armenia, in POLYEUCTE, tells Pauline of Severus's approach, xxvi, 78-80; his wrath at Polyeucte, 95-8; his dilemma, 99-100; determines not to pardon Polyeucte, 111-12; with Polyeucte, 112-14, 116; condemns Polyeucte to death, 117-18; becomes a convert, 120-1

Felix V, Pope (see Amadeus, Cardinal)

Felixmarte of Hircania, xiv, 101, 320

Fellowes, Sir Charles, researches of, v, 374

Fellow-feeling, Confucius on, xliv, 54 (23)

Fellowship, in pain, divides not smart, iv, 373

Felon, origin of word, xxxv, 383

Felons, children of, v, 359

Felony, crimes included under, xxxv, 383-4

Feltro, Bishop of, xx, 323 note 15

Fencing, Locke on, xxxvii, 183-4; Milton on, iii, 257

Fenelon, Hume on ethics of, xxvii, 216

Fennians, Tacitus on the, xxxiii, 122-3

Feoblas, balsam of (see Balsam of Fierebras)

Fer Caille, xlix, 221, 226, 247, 257

Fer Gair, xlix, 214, 223, 230, 247

Fer le, xlix, 214, 223, 247

Fer Rogain, xlix, 214, 223, 225, 228, 230-1 ct scq.

Ferdinand II, in THE BETROTHED, in Mantuan contest, xxi, 81

Ferdinand IV, Dante on, xx, 369 note 9

Ferdinand V, of Spain, Machiavelli on, xxxvi, 75-6; Pope Julius and, 47; Raleigh on, xxxix, 89-90

Ferdinand, son of Alva, in EGMONT, xix, 298-9, 300-2, 310; final scene with Egmont, 323-9

Ferdinand of Naples, iii, 52

Ferdinand, in DUCHESS OF MALFI, in presence chamber scene, xlvii;

724-6; hires Bosola to watch Duchess, 727-30; Antonio on, 726-7; at court of Malfi, 755; with Duchess, 755-6; with Bosola, 756-7; in Milan, his frenzy, 795, 796-8, 810; death, 814; learns flight of Duchess, 769-70; letter to Duchess, 773; on Malatesti, 768; parting counsel to Duchess, 730-2; learns her fault, 751-4; with Bosola after murder, 789-92; with Bosola at Malfi, 776-7; with Duchess in prison, 777-8; his purposes of vengeance, 780-1; with Duchess in chamber, 759-61; his return to Rome, 762

Ferdinand, in THE TEMPEST, in shipwreck, xlvi, 380, 388; led by Ariel's song, 393-4; meeting with Miranda and Prospero, 394-7; at his task, 412; with Miranda, 413-15; betrothed to Miranda, 423-9; at chess with Miranda, 437; reunion with father, 437-8

Ferguson, Sir Adam, vi, 167; Carlyle on, xxv, 382

Ferguson, Sir Samuel, FAIR HILLS OF IRELAND, xli, 947-8

Ferguson, Robert, vi, 16; Burns on, 87, 92, 93; INSCRIPTION FOR HEADSTONE OF, 269-70; INSCRIPTION UNDER PORTRAIT OF, 270; LINES ON THE POET, 458

Fermentation, Pasteur's Theory of, xxxviii, 289-381

Fermo, Oliverotto of, xxxvi, 31-3

Fernando Noronha, Darwin on, xxix, 21

Fernondo, in Cardenio's story, xiv, 215-18, 253-61

Fernando, and Dorothea, xiv, 271-277

Fernando, and Lucinda, xiv, 278-9

Fernando, Don, reunion with Dorothea, xiv, 374-84

Ferragosto, the, xxxi, 42 note 2

Ferrante, Don, in THE BETROTHED, xxi, 428, 431; learning of, 464-9; in the plague, 647-9

Ferrara, Cardinal (see Este, Ippolito d')

Ferrara, Duke of, xxxvi, 8; and Cellini, xxxi, 208-9, 280, 282-3, 285; and Louis, xxxvi, 13; and Paul III, xxxi, 280

Ferrara, Marquis of, xx, 53 note 9

Ferrer, Antonio, at Milan, xxi, 205-6, 207, 223-34

FERRIER, MISS, To, vi, 289-90

Ferro, Drake at, xxxiii, 242

Fertility, as distinction between varieties and species, xi, 326 (see also Sterility)

Fertilization, methods of, xi, 203-5; remarks on, 109-14

Fesque, defined, xxvii, 113

Festino, Mrs., xviii, 117

Festus, Porcius, xliv, 486 (27); and Paul, 486 (1-27), 490 (24, 30-1)
FETE CHAMPETRE, THE, vi, 327-8
Feudal Laws, of succession, x, 529-30
Feure, Raoul le, xxxix, 5
Fevers, Indian treatment of, xliii, 36
Fèvre, le, Dryden on, xiii, 15
"Few sometimes may know when thousands err," iv, 210
Fewster, Mr., xxxviii, 193, 204, 224
Fiad sceme, the giant, xlix, 255
Fiaschino, the chamberlain, xxxi, 282, 285
Fichte, Mazzini on, xxxii, 402; patriotism of, 409; on silent work, xxv, 433-4
Ficinus, on nature, xxxix, 114
FICKLE FORTUNE: A FRAGMENT, vi, 37
Fickleness of man, vii, 309 (1)
Fiddler, in FAUST, xix, 181
FIDDLER, A, IN THE NORTH, vi, 511
Fiddler's Song, from JOLLY BEGGARS, vi, 134-5
FIDELE, by Collins, xli, 487
FIDELE'S DIRGE, xl, 275
Fidelity, Penn on, i, 357; of princes, xxxvi, 59-60; worth of, intrinsic, xxxii, 366
Field, Barron, in Hazlitt's discussion, xxvii, 289
Field, parable of the, xv, 208
Fielding, Henry, Hazlitt on, xxvii, 289; HUNTING SONG, xli, 513-14; his Joseph Andrews, xiv, 3; PREFACE TO JOSEPH ANDREWS, xxxix, 184-90; sketch of life and works, 184 note; religion of, xxviii, 16; Thackeray on, 7, 18
Fiennes, house of, motto of, v, 388
Fierabras, xiv, 514-15
Fierebras, Balsam of, xiv, 80-1
Fieschi, Bonifazio de', xx, 245 note 4
FIESOLE, EPITAPH AT, xli, 929
Fife, in LIFE A DREAM, with Rosaura, arrival in Poland, xxvi, 5-10; with Segismund, 11-14; arrested, 15-17; in the tower, 52-3; found by soldiers, 54-6; with Rosaura again, 61; in the battle, 63-4; death, 64-5
Fig-tree, Indian, iv, 291; parable of, xliv, 396 (6-9); proverb of the, v, 11
Figulus, C. Marcius, mention of, ix, 85
Figures, Berkeley on, xxxvii, 220-2; Plato's definition of, v, 182
FILE AND SERPENT, fable of, xvii, 21
Filippo Argenti, Dante on, xx, 34
Filippo, Francesco di (see Lippi Francesco)
Final Causes (see First Cause)
Finance, Burke on science of, xxiv, 376

Finches, in Galapagos Islands, xxix, 401-2
Findlater, Andrew, xxv, 196
Findlay, song on, vi, 51-2
Fineness, defined by Burke, xxiv, 103, 132
Fines, excessive, forbidden, xliii, 208 (8); More on, xxxvi, 170, 173
Fingers, in story of DARNING-NEEDLE, xvii, 336
Finite, the, a manifestation of the infinite, xxviii, 353
Finitude, Kelvin on, xxx, 270
Finn, story of, xlix, 35 note 5, 36, 37, 38
Finnbogi, the Norseman, xliii, 17-19
Finns, sailors' notion of, xxiii, 43
Fiorentino, Giuliano, xxxi, 73
Fiorino of Cellino, xxxi, 6
Firdonsi, Sainte-Beuve on, xxxii, 136
Fire, lesson of the, xv, 238; Marcus Aurelius on, ii, 270 (9); methods of producing, xxx, 59-60; methods of producing, by friction, xxix, 432-3
Fire-arms, and civilization, x, 471
Fire Bells, Poe on, xlii, 1284-5
Fire-engines, ancient, ix, 396 note
Fireflies, Darwin on, xxix, 40
Firenzuola, Giovanni of, xxxi, 27-9
Fireside, to make a happy, vi, 389
Firk, in SHOEMAKER'S HOLIDAY, at Ralph's departure, xlvii, 451-4; at Eyre's, 458-61, 465-9, 475; announces Eyre's appointment, 478-9; at Old Ford, 481-2; before shop, 487-9; with Ralph, 490-1; at Lord Mayor's, 494-7; at Hammon's wedding, 499-506; at Eyre's dinner, 506-7, 509, 513
Firmament, Addison on the, xl, 410; xlv, 547; Habington on the, xl, 258
Firminus, and his astrology, vii, 108-10
Firmus, Romanus, letter to, ix, 213, 271
First Cause, Hume on the, xxxvii, 328-9; ideas of different, xxxix, 106, 108; Marcus Aurelius on the, ii, 256 (75), 268 (1), 273 (28); Pascal on knowledge of, xlviii, 27, 28, 336; Rousseau on, xxxiv, 255-6
First Fruits (see Annates)
First Principles, Pascal on, xlviii, 99 (282)
Fish, creation of, iv, 240; electric organs of, xi, 198-200; flying, 186-7; flying, Pretty on, xxxii, 211; fresh-water, distribution of, xi, 427-8; heart in, xxxviii, 73, 95, 138, 140; Herodotus on breeding of, xxxiii, 46-7; Mohammed on eating of, xlv, 1018; price of, by what determined, x, 54, 208; price

of, rent as element in, 154; respiration of, xxx, 175; teleostean, xi, 357-8

Fisher, Bishop of Rochester, xxxvi, 120, 122

FISHER, THE, fable of, xvii, 27

FISHER AND LITTLE FISH, fable of, xvii, 32

Fisher Boy, song of, in WILHELM TELL, xxvi, 370

Fisheries, produce of, source of capital, x, 230-1

FISHERMAN, THE, AND HIS WIFE, xvii, 89-96

FISHERMAN, THE, story of, xvi, 28-59

Fishes, hearts in, xxxviii, 81-2, 88; Smart on, xli, 500

Fishing, Franklin's early ideas of, i, 36

Fistinghound, the, xxxv, 370

Fitch, the shop-keeper, xxiii, 410

Fitela, and Sigemund, xlix, 30

Fitness, Augustine, St., on, vii, 60; beauty and, v, 312; cause of beauty, xxiv, 89-91; in works of art, 91-3; Penn on, i, 355 (161)

Fitzgerald, Edward, RUBAIYAT OF OMAR KHAYYAM, xli, 970-88

Fitz-James, Lord, xxxvi, 137

Fitz Roy, Capt., Darwin on, xxix, 9

Five, Nature's love of number, xlii, 1301

FIVE CARLINS, THE, vi, 389-92

Fixed Capital, defined, x, 225-6; depends on circulating capital, 229; expense of maintaining, 234-6, 240; kinds of, four, 227-8; resemblance to money, 236-7, 240

Fjolnir, xlix, 309-11, 367, 435

Flaccus, Gaius Valerius, Dante on, xx, 19

Flaccus, M. Lænius, Cicero on, ix, 91-2

Flame, direction of, xxx, 101; Faraday on, 99; forms of, 101-3; illumination from, cause of, 110-14, 164; structure of, in candles, 104-7

Flamens, Roman, ix, 228 note 1

Flamingoes, Darwin on, xxix, 78

Flamininus, Lucius, expelled from Senate, ix, 61

Flat-fish, peculiarities of, xi, 240-43

Flatterer, in PILGRIM'S PROGRESS, xv, 137-8

Flatterers, Epictetus on, ii, 182 (4), 183 (13); fable of, xvii, 12-13; in Hell, xx, 47, 78

Flatteries, the four, xii, 356 note

Flattery, Bacon on, iii, 133; Burke on, xxiv, 46, 157; Chaucer on, xl, 48; Cicero on, ix, 39-42; Confucius on, xliv, 5 (3), 18 (24), 61 (17); Hobbes on, xxxiv, 387; Kempis on avoiding, vii, 303 (5); love of, reason for, v, 229;

Machiavelli on, xxxvi, 80; parasite of Luxury, vi, 262; Shakespeare on, xlvi, 140; a way of honoring, xxxiv, 378

Flavius, the tribune, and Cæsar, xii, 325; Cicero on, ix, 151, 154

Fleance, in MACBETH, xlvi, 321-2, 337, 339-40, 346

Fleetness, limits of, xi, 56

Fleetwood, Dr., and the Spectator, xxvii, 172

Fletcher, John, ASPATIA'S SONG, xl, 330; Custom of the Country, xxxix, 182-3; life and works, xlvii, 638; Massinger and, 818; MELANCHOLY, xl, 330-1 (see also Beaumont and Fletcher)

Fletcher, Master, with Drake, xxxiii, 214, 218

Flibbertigibbet, xlvi, 257

Flies, Harrison on, and spiders, xxxv, 366-7; Pascal on, xlviii, 124 (367)

Flipotte, in TARTUFFE, xxvi, 189, 196

FLODDEN, LAMENT FOR, xli, 495-6

Flodden, men of Ettrick Forest at, xli, 494 note

Flogging, Dana on, xxiii, 379-81; in England, v, 359-60

Florence, arms of commune of, xxxi, 13 note 3; auxiliaries employed by, xxxvi, 47; built in imitation of Rome, xxxi, 6; Dante on, xx, 44 note 12, 108 note, 119 note 11, 171-2, 351-8; dress in (16th century), xxxi, 30 note 2; the "Eight" of, 16 note 2; factions in, xx, 27, 103-4 and notes; Guelfi and Ghibellini in, 68 notes 1, 2; guilds of, xxxi, 12 note 2; Macaulay on, xxvii, 390; mercenaries of, xxxvi, 44; name, origin of, xxxi, 6-7; patrons of, xx, 58 note 5; Pistoja and, xxxvi, 56-7; the plague in, xxxi, 87 note 6; policy towards Pisa and Pistoja, xxxvi, 72; republican party of, xxxi, 31 note 1, 33 note 1; subjugation of, xxvii, 411, 420; wealth of (14th century), 388

Florida, cession of, xliii, 286-95

Florimell, Spenser's, xxxix, 68

Florio, John, translator of Montaigne, xxxii, 3

Floripes, Princess, xiv, 514

Florismarte of Hircania, xiv, 53

Florus, and Agrippinus, ii, 119 (8)

Flower, Prof., on conformity of type, xi, 473

FLOWER IN THE CRANNIED WALL, xlii, 1039

FLOWER, THE, by Herbert, xl, 354

Flowers, Bacon on, v, 118-19; beauty of, Burke on, xxiv, 80; beauty of, Darwin on, xi, 211; Columella on, xxxv, 250; correlation in, xi, 156-

8; Emerson on, as gifts, v, 229, 240; insects and, relations of, xi, 106-7, 108-9, 110-11; parable of the, xv, 207-8

FLOWERS OF THE FOREST, xli, 494

FLOWERS, LITTLE IDA'S, xvii, 355-62

FLOWERY BANKS OF CREE, vi, 515-16

Flue, Klaus von der, in WILHELM TELL, xxvi, 401, 411

Flute, Alcibiades on the, xii, 111-12; Dryden on the, xl, 399

Fluxions, invented by Newton, xxxiv, 128-9

Fly, on the chariot-wheel, iii, 134

FLY AND BALD MAN, fable of, xvii, 17

Flycatchers, tyrant, Darwin on, xi, 187-8

Flying-fish, Darwin on, xi, 186-7; Pretty on, xxxiii, 211

FLYING TRUNK, THE, xvii, 364-70

Focaccia of Cancellieri, xx, 135 note 4

Fœtus, blood in the, xxxviii, 77; circulation in the, 96-9; Harvey on formation of the, 135; heart in the, 89, 139, 143-4; liver in the, 134-5

Fogliani, Giovanni, xxxvi, 31, 32

Fogo, Island of, xxxiii, 211

Foiano, Benedetto da, xxxi, 248 note

Foix, Diana of, Montaigne to, xxxii, 29

Foix, Gaston de, xlvii, 723

Folco, of Genoa, xx, 322 note 8, 324

Folger, Peter, i, 9

FOLK-LORE AND FABLE, xvii

FOLLOW THY FAIR SUN, xl, 292

FOLLOWERS, ESSAY ON, Bacon's, iii, 125-6

Folly, Burns on, vi, 192-3; ECCLESIASTES on, xliv, 351 (1-3), 352 (12-15)

FOLLY, HUMAN, xl, 336

FOLLY, RAPTURES OF, vi, 489

Folques, of Marseilles, xx, 322 note 8, 324

Fonblanque, Mill on, xxv, 61, 66, 70, 84, 113, 128

Fondness, Confucius on, xliv, 60 (8)

Fontaine, M. de, xxxviii, 52

Fontainebleau, Cellini's work on, xxxi, 307

Fontana, Domenico, xxxi, 142

Fontanes, Sainte-Beuve on, xxxii, 135

Fontenelle, M., on affectation in nature, v, 348; on Newton, xxxiv, 111, 122

Fontenelle, Miss, addresses spoken by, vi, 474, 508-10; EPIGRAM ON, 475

Food, in ancient Egypt, xxxiii, 40, 45-6; animal, Darwin on, xxix, 129-30; as circulating capital, x, 228-9; labor in relation to, 155-6;

Locke on, of children, xxxvii, 16-22; materials and, comparative values of, x, 186-8; Mohammed on lawful, xlv, 1008-9, 1018; necessity of, iv, 1945 Penn on selection of, i, 345 (59-62); rent of land used for, x, 155-71; of rich and poor, 174; variability due to excess of, xi, 25

Food-supply, industry and, x, 86, 87, 88-9; population and, 83-4, 174; wages and, 78-9, 87-8, 90-1

Fool, in KING LEAR, xlvi, 221-4, 227, 228-9, 239-42, 259-7, 260-2; remarks on character of, 202

Fool, in PILGRIM'S PROGRESS, xv, 295

Fool, song of, from JOLLY BEGGARS, vi, 132

Fool-hardiness, Locke on, xxxvii, 102

Fools, disclosed by words, xvii, 31; Browne on, iii, 282 (18); Paradise of, iv, 149-50; Pascal on, xlviii, 34 (80); "rush in where angels fear," xxiv, 193; Solomon on, xxxvi, 165; test of, iii, 60; in Utopia, xxxvi, 224; wise men and, 274-5

Foot-pound, defined, xxx, 188

FOOTSTEPS OF ANGELS, xlii, 1319

Foppa, Ambrogio, xxxi, 50 note

FOR A' THAT, vi, 140

Forbearance, Brynhild on, xlix, 325; Epictetus on, ii, 179 (183); Locke on habit of, xxxvii, 20

Forbes, Edward, on Atlantic Islands, xi, 404; on distribution, 412, 417; on fossils, 340; on glaciers, xxx, 235, 239, 241; on shells, xi, 146; on species, 242

Force, Bacon on, iii, 101; Emerson on, v, 257; Hume on idea of, xxxvii, 355-70; Milton on, iv, 106, 449; Pascal on, xlviii, 117 (334)

Force, in PROMETHEUS BOUND, viii, 156

FORCE, CONSERVATION OF, xxx, 181-220

FORCES, CORRELATION OF, xxx, 75-87; Helmholtz on, 197, 215, 218

FORCES OF MATTER, Faraday on, xxx, 5-88

Foreign Commerce, advantages of, x, 342-3, 377-80; of agricultural states, 456; capital least attracted by, 323; capital used in, 310-14; disadvantages of, 321; gains in, 377-80; government interferences with, 346-406; Luther on, xxxvi, 348, 349; Mun on, x, 328; necessity of, 315-16

Foreign Competition, Emerson on, v, 296

Foreign Conquests, More on, xxxvi, 168-9

Foreign Dominions, Bacon on, iii, 80-1; Machiavelli on, xxxvi, 8-12, 18-19; arms in, 72; factions in, 72-3

Foreign Missions, "pious editors," view of, xlii, 1452

Foreign Nations, Washington on relations with, xliii, 261-5

Foreign Things, Emerson on love of, v, 84; Harrison on love of, xxxv, 248-9, 251-2; Holinshed on love of, 335

Foreigners, liberty of, in Massachusetts, xliii, 83-4

Foreknowledge, Chaucer on, xl, 46 note 147; is fore-sorrow, viii, 14; Milton on, iv, 141; not necessity, xx, 359 note 7

Forel, on tides, xxx, 297

Forese, in Purgatory, xx, 241-3

Foresight, Hobbes on, xxxiv, 333, 358-9; Machiavelli on, xxxvi, 49; may be vain, vi, 126

Foresters, Emerson on, xlii, 1305, 1306-7

Forests, Darwin on sublimity of, xxix, 530; Emerson on beauty of, v, 233-4; Geikie on destruction of, xxx, 366-7; growth of, checked by cattle, x, 176-7; rent of, 176-7; Thoreau on, xxviii, 424-5

Forges, in Dante's HELL, xx, 122-3

Forgetful Green, in PILGRIM'S PROGRESS, xv, 246

Forgetfulness, Augustine, St., on, vii, 180-1; Keats on, xli, 898-9; Pascal on, xlviii, 125 (372)

Forgiveness, Bacon on, iii, 15, 16, 36; Jesus on, xliv, 405 (3-4); Marcus Aurelius on, ii, 194 (7); Pittacus on, 153 (96)

Forli, Countess of, xxxvi, 13, 75

FORLORN, MY LOVE, NO COMFORT NEAR, vi, 572-3

Formal, and material, ii, 217 (21), 228 (13), 249 (29), 247 (10)

Formal Instinct, Schiller on the, xxxii, 256-63

Formalist, in PILGRIM'S PROGRESS, xv, 43-6

Formality, Bacon on, iii, 131-2; Pascal on, xlviii, 92 (249-52); Penn on, i, 351 (119), 405; as source of power, xxxiv, 375; Swift on, xxvii, 110-11

Fornication, Mohammed on, xlv, 927; Mohammedan punishment of, 982 note 6, 984; Paul, St., on, 506-7, 508 (13-18); punishment of, in old England, xxxv, 384-5; punishment of, in Utopia, xxxvi, 221; Spirit of, iii, 177

FORSAKEN GARDEN, A, xlii, 1255

FORSAKEN MERMAN, THE, xlii, 1168-72

Fort George, massacre of, i, 160

Fort William Henry, attack on, i, 228, 229

Fortebraccio (see Braccio)

Fortescue, George, xxxiii, 238, 267

Fortinbras, in HAMLET, xlvi, 90, 93, 118-19, 164, 198-9; not in original story, 86

Fortitude, Dante's star of, xx, 148 note 5; defined by Hobbes, xxxiv, 354; Locke on, xxxvii, 102-4, 104-8; the virtue of adversity, iii, 17

Fortresses, Machiavelli in, xxxvi, 74-5

Fortunatus, xlv, 526 (17)

FORTUNE, ESSAY ON, Bacon's, iii, 104-6

Fortune, Browne on, iii, 281-3; Burns on fading, vi, 178; changes of, xxxix, 100-1, 103; Chaucer on, xl, 50; Cicero on, ix, 27, 106-7; Cockburn on, xli, 494-5; Dante on, xx, 31; Descartes on, xxxiv, 23; Emerson on, v, 88, 92; favors the brave, ix, 300; good, honorable, xxxiv, 380; inequality of, verses on, xvi, 243; injustice of, lines on, vi, 458; life entangled with, ii, 182 (1); love and, xlvi, 144; Machiavelli on, xxxvi, 83-6; Marcus Aurelius on good, ii, 234 (36); Montaigne on changes of, xxxii, 5-6; More's lines on, xxxvi, 130; Mortimer on, xlvi, 83; Pope on gifts of, xl, 443-8; Raleigh on, xxxix, 96, 100-2; Shakespeare on, xlvi, 123, 130; Tennyson on, xlii, 1007; Vespucci on, xliii, 31; virtue and, xxxi, 13

FORTUNE, FICKLE, a fragment, vi, 37

FORTUNE, RAGING, a fragment, vi, 38

FORTUNE, TO, by Thomson, xl, 454

Foscea, Bernardin di, xx, 204 note 18

Fosians, Tacitus on the, xxxiii, 116

Fossiliferous Strata, Lyell on formation of, xxxviii, 421-4, 429-31, 433-4, 434-7

Fossils, Falloppio on, xxxviii, 408; old ideas of, xi, 175; xxxviii, 417 (see Palæontological Collections)

Fothergill, Dr., i, 126, 154, 166, 167

Fouche's Police, v, 468

Foulk, Samuel, i, 266, 268, 280

Foundations, Pascal on, xlviii, 115 (330)

Founders of States, Bacon on, iii, 136; Machiavelli on, xxxvi, 20-3

FOUNTAIN, THE, xli, 617-19

Fountains, Bacon on, iii, 121-2

Fourier, Mill on, xxv, 110

Fowl, descent of, xi, 36

Fox, Bishop, and More, xxxvi, 95; quoted, xxxv, 398

Fox, Charles J., and Burke, xxiv, 6; v, 219-20; Burns on, vi, 55, 168-9, 357; the debt of honor, v, 220; Emerson on, 275; Napoleon on, 220

Fox, Dr., and John Donne, xv, 369-70

Fox, George, Emerson on, v, 145, 243; Penn and, xxxiv, 76; on slavery, i, 176; Voltaire on, xxxiv, 72-3

Fox and Cat, fable of, xvii, 26
Fox and Crow, fable of, xvii, 12
Fox and Goat, fable of, xvii, 46
Fox and Grapes, fable of, xvii, 23
Fox and Lion, fable of, xvii, 24
Fox and Mask, fable of, xvii, 18
Fox and Mosquitoes, fable of, xvii, 37
Fox and Stork, fable of, xvii, 17
Fox and Wolf, Grimm's story of, xvii, 177-9
Fox, Cock, and Dog, fable of, xvii, 35
Fox Without a Tail, fable of, xvii, 38

Foxes, in San Pedro Island, xxix, 297

Fox-goose, the, in Egypt, xxxiii, 38
Fracastorius, on the heart, xxxviii, 79
Fragment of Song, vi, 249, 471
Frailty, Burns on, vi, 193
Framms, of the Germans, xxxiii, 98
France, apprenticeships in, x, 129; armies of, xxxvi, 49; belles lettres in (18th century), xxxiv, 143; Burke on old régime in, xxiv, 274-80; Calvinism in, xxxix, 29-50; church property, confiscation of, in, xxiv, 253-69; clergy of, under the old régime, 287-95; departments, communes, and cantons in, 321, 330-1; economists of, x, 464-5; England and, trade of, 385-6; England and, in war, iii, 79; Goldsmith on, xli, 539-40; interest, rates of, in, x, 95-6; Machiavelli on, xxxvi, 9-10, 16-17, 64-5; More on kingdom of, 168; nobility of, under the old régime, xxiv, 282-7; parliaments, abolition of, 270; parliaments, old, of, 354-6; poetry, early, of, xxviii, 75-7; Raleigh on kings of, xxxix, 84-8; revenue laws of, x, 566-7; Swiss mercenaries in, xxxvi, 49; Taine on, xxxix, 454-5; taxation in (18th century), x, 570-2; theatre in (18th century), xxxiv, 157-8; treaty with U. S., xliii, 267-72; Voltaire on civil wars of, xxxiv, 88

France, King of, in Lear, in love with Cordelia, xlvi, 204-5, 209-11; notified of Lear's misfortunes, 249-50; his invasion of England, 272, 275

Francesca di Rimini, in Hell, xx, 23-5

Francesco, Gian (see Penni)

Franchise, qualifications for the, v, 251-2

Francis, Mr., Attorney-General of Pennsylvania, i, 117

Francis I, Andrea del Sarto and, xlii, 1134, 1136; Calvin to, xxxix, 29, 49-50; at Camp Marolle, xxxviii, 13; Charles V and, xxxi, 71 note, 335, 342 note 1, 348 note 1; Cellini and, 95, 205, 210, 217, 222, 260, 272, 281, 286-7, 290-3, 294-8, 302, 303, 304, 305-9, 312, 313, 314, 323, 326, 330-1, 333-6, 337-8, 339-40, 342, 343-9, 363, 365-7, 390; Clement and, vii, 124; expedition against Turin, xxxviii, 9; Guido Guidi and, xxxi, 311 note 1; at Landresy, xxxviii, 17; Piero Strozzi and, xxxi, 343-4; and poets, xxvii, 43; Raleigh on, xxxix, 87; in triumvirate of kings, iii, 52; war with England, xxxi, 348 and note 1

Francis II, Raleigh on, xxxix, 87

Francis, St., Dante on, xx, 332-4; Luther on, xxxvi, 315; in Paradise, xx, 421; quoted, vii, 333

Francis, St., Xavier, hymn attributed to, xlv, 568-9

Franciscans, Dante on the, xx, 339 note 28; in limbo, iv, 150

Francisco, in Hamlet, xlvi, 87-8
Francisco, in The Tempest, xlvi, 400, 421

Franco of Bologna, xx, 191 note 3
Franklin, Chaucer's, xl, 20-1
Franklin, Abiah, mother of Benjamin, i, 9, 12-13

Franklin, Benjamin, ability to write, advantages gained by, i, 62-3, 65; aids his workmen to start in business, 97, 108-9; ancestry and family of, 6-10; anecdote of fish, 36; anecdote of wharf, 11; Art of Virtue, 90-1; as Assembly's commissioner to England, 157-70, 174; assists Braddock, 134-40, 142-3; Autobiography of, 5-170; becomes printer, 14; becomes vegetarian, 17; birth of, 3, 9, 171; Bond, the Doctors, and, 143-4; Boston, departure from, 22-3; Boston, first return to, 30-1; Bradford, work for, 23, 27; in business with Meredith, 55-6, 58-9, 61, 62-4; in business for self, 64-6; in charge of frontier defences, 145-9; city-watch, suggests reform of, 103; clerk of Assembly, 101-2, 111-12, 119-20; colonel of militia, 150-2;

commissioner to the Indians, 120-1; daily program of, 87; death of, 173; degrees conferred on, 129, 173; *Dialogue* advocating a militia, 145, 150; disputatious turn of, 15-16; *Dissertation on Liberty and Necessity*, 43-4, 57-8; domestic life of, 69, 80; Dunham, Mr., work for, 50-2; early occupations of, 3, 10-11, 13-14; education of, 3, 10, 12, 18; felicity of his life, 5, 89; "fire" engine, 115; five kings and, 79-80; food, indifference to, 12; Hemphill and, 98-9; hospital, 121-3; industry of, 47, 51, 61, 66, 79; influence of, 121-2; influence of Abel James on, 71-2; intrigues of, 68; Journal of, 51 note; journalist, 96-7; Junto formed by, 59-61; at Keimer's, 27-9, 36-7, 52-6, 58; Keimer's new religion and, 37; Keith, Sir William, relations with, 29-32, 35-6, 40-3, 51; languages studied by, 99; letters of, as Busy Body, 62; library, founds first public, 69-70, 77-9; life of, 3-4; life of, chief events in, 171-4; in London, 42-51; on London streets, 126-8; marriage of, 69; match for, projected by Mrs. Godfrey, 67-8; member Royal Society, 156; moderation of, 91, 19; moral living, plan of, 82-90; *New England Courant*, connection of, with, 3, 20-2; open stove invented by, 116; organizes fire company, 103-4; organizes militia, 109-11; paper money discussion, 65; parents of, 11-13; Party for Virtue projected by, 93-5; *Pennsylvania Gazette* established by, 62, 108; Philadelphia, arrival at, 3, 26-7; Philadelphia, second trip to, 32-4; Philosophical Society founded by, 109; *Plain Truth*, 110; *Plan of Union*, 129-31; poetry of, juvenile, 15; *Poor Richard's Almanac*, 95-6; postmaster, 102; postmaster-general, 128-9, 151, 154, 173; prayers used by, 81-2, 87; Presbyterian Church and, 80-2; proprietary quarrels, 132-4, 151-2, 156-8; prose writing, practise in, 15-17; public offices, 3-4, 119-20; public printer, 63, 65-6, 101-2; Read, Miss, and, 26, 29, 37-8, 40, 43, 51, 69; reading, love of, 14, 15, 16, 17, 18, 44, 79; James, relations with brother, 3, 14-15, 17, 20-2, 31, 100; religious belief of, 6, 18, 43-4, 57-8, 80, 86-7, 94; Revolution, share in, 4, 173-4; scientist, 3, 119, 152-6; settlement of claims, 162-3; son, death of, 100; street-lamps improved by, 125; streets, moves improvement

of, 124-8; Socratic method adopted by, 18, 36-7; success, reason of, 92; surname, origin of, 7; swimming abilities of, 49, 50-1; temperance of, 46-7; tyranny, hatred of, 21; University of Pennsylvania founded by, 109, 117-19; Vaughan on character and influence of, 72-7; *Way to Wealth*, 173; Whitefield and, 106-8; Woolman's book on slavery published by, 197 note

Franklin, Benjamin, uncle of the preceding, i, 8, 9, 10

Franklin, Benjamin, Mrs. (see Read, Miss)

Franklin, James, establishes *New England Courant*, i, 20-1; relations of, with Benjamin, 3, 14-15, 17, 20-2, 31, 100

Franklin, John, brother of Benjamin, i, 13, 32

Franklin, John, uncle of Benjamin, i, 7, 8

Franklin, Josiah, brother of Benjamin, i, 13

Franklin, Josiah, father of Benjamin, i, 3, 9, 10-11, 11-13

Franklin, Matthew, i, 202

Franklin, Samuel, i, 8, 14

Franklin, Sir John, equipment of, v, 86; Parry on, 362; search for, 374

Franklin, Thomas, grandfather of Benjamin, i, 7

Franklin, Thomas, uncle of Benjamin, i, 7-8

Franklin, William, son of Benjamin, i, 120, 135, 136, 139, 145, 165

Frankness, Bacon on, iii, 8, 18; Cicero on, ix, 39-41; Confucius on, xliv, 36 (20); Emerson on, v, 67

Franzesi, Matio, xxxi, 172-3

Franziska, in MINNA VON BARNHELM, with Minna, xxvi, 301-3; with landlord, 303-7; with Minna on finding Tellheim's ring, 307-10; with Just, 310-11; prepares Minna to receive Tellheim, 311-12; drags off landlord, 312-13; with Just, agrees to meet Tellheim, 316-19; with the landlord, 319-20; warned to beware of the landlord, 320-1; with Werner, talk of Tellheim, 322-3; with Tellheim, 329-32; with Werner again, 332; with Minna, the plot to win Tellheim, 332-4; in scene with Riccaut, 334, 337, 338-9; growing interest in Werner, 340, 341; tells her mistress's misfortunes, 348-9; with Tellheim, in the plot, 351-2; at interview of Minna and Tell-

heim, 354, 356, 361, 364; tries to explain to Werner, 362; reconciliation with Werner, 366

Fraser, on Berkeley's DIALOGUES, xxxvii, 198

Fraser, General, reference to, vi, 55

Fraser's Magazine, Carlyle on, v, 334

Fraternities, ancient, ix, 424 note 2

Fraud, Dante on, xx, 71 note; punishment of, in Hell, 47, 75-146

Freawaru, xlix, 62 and note, 63 note

Frederick I, Luther on, xxxvi, 277; and Milan, xx, 221-2 note 8

Frederick II, birth of, xx, 298 note 7; in Hell, 45 note; Luther on, xxxvi, 277; Parma, defeat at, xx, 213 note 6; Pierro delle Vigne and, 56; treason punished by, 97 note 3

Frederick of Sicily, Dante on, xx, 370 note 12

Frederick the Great, Mill's interest in, xxv, 11; and Voltaire, xxxiv, 64

Free Trade, Emerson on, v, 265

Freedom, Æschylus on uncontrolled, viii, 135; from care, Cicero on, ix, 25; definition of perfect, v, 17; Emerson on, xlii, 1313; Epictetus on, ii, 183 (10, 15), 149 (83), 166 (136), 168 (141, 142); fable on, xvii, 21-2; Goethe on, xix, 390; insolence and, vi, 274; inward slaves, impossible to, iv, 403; of labor, Smith on, x, 129-30; law of nature, xxvi, 12; necessary to true allegiance, iv, 140; Penn on use of, i, 412 (253); from worldly things, vii, 301-2

FREEDOM AND LOVE, xli, 801-2

Freeman, Edward A., life and works, xxviii, 234; RACE AND LANGUAGE, 233-83; l, 18

Freeport, Sir Andrew, xxvii, 91; Johnson on, 175

Freethinkers, Burke on, xxiv, 237; Carlyle on, xxv, 369

Free Trade, Bacon on, iii, 91; Mill on, xxv, 67, 303-4; Smith on, x, 4, 348-69, 386-7, 454-7

Free-Will, Adam's, iv, 189; beauty and, xxxii, 282-3; Berkeley on, xxxvii, 274; cause of evil, vii, 105; Channing on, xxviii, 343-4; Confucius on, xliv, 30 (25); Dante on, xx, 212, 220, 304 and note; distinguishes man from beasts, xxxiv, 178-9; Epictetus on, ii, 124 (20, 22), 127 (29), 149 (83); given to man, iv, 140-1; human, 295; Hume on, xxxvii, 371-2, 384-5, 387, 390-4; Kant on, xxxii, 377-90; Machiavelli on, xxxvi, 84, 88; Mill on doctrine of,

xxv, 111; Raphael on, iv, 196-7; Rousseau on, xxxiv, 266-8; Schiller on, xxxii, 278 (see also Autonomy of the Will)

Freezing-point, of water, xxx, 242-4

Freke, Dr., on origin of species, xi, 16

Fremont, John C., Dana on, xxiii, 412

Fremy, M., xxxviii, 322-4, 369-70

Frenada, counselor of Philip II, xix, 285

French, Colonel, i, 30, 41

French, in American Revolution, i, 142; Burke on the, xxiv, 235-6; descent from Hector, claimed for, xiii, 20; Dryden on the, 24; Goldsmith on the, xli, 539-40; influence of the, v, 393; military abilities of the, xxv, 322; polite rather than true, v, 389; sentiments of the, xxv, 43; sociability of the, 43; Taine on the, xxxix, 440, 449, 454-5; wiser than they seem, iii, 67

French Academy, Voltaire on, xxxiv, 158-62

French Civil War, Burke on the, xxiv, 196-7

French Classical Drama, Pellison on, xxviii, 68

French Classics, xxxii, 127-8, 129-32, 134

FRENCH DRAMAS, xxvi; Dryden on, xviii, 13

FRENCH ESSAYS, xxxii, 3-191

French Language, Burke on the, xxiv, 147; Dryden on, xiii, 56; Hugo on changes in, xxxix, 394; Huxley on study of, xxviii, 229; Johnson on changes in, xxxix, 212; Locke on study of, xxxvii, 145, 164; Sainte-Beuve on, xxxii, 123-4; Sidney on, xxvii, 53

French Literature, Hugo on, xxxix, 404; Taine on, 452

French and Indian War, in America, i, 133-49; Woolman on, 228-30, 241-2, 272-3, 275

French Money, Smith on, x, 33-4

French Nation, Freeman on the, xxviii, 264-5, 266

FRENCH PHILOSOPHERS, xxxiv, 1-315

French Revolution, aristocrats in, xxiv, 431-2; army under, 358-71; assignats of, 269-71, 338-44, 383-90; church-lands sale, 271, 339-41; church property confiscated in, 253-69, 295-311; clergy in, 287-9; clergy, civil constitution of the, 296-7; completeness of, 402; population and wealth, decline of, under, 280-2; executive power, **constitution of, 347-54; fanati-**

cism and proselytism of, 301-2;
finances of, 375-93; Goethe on, xix,
334, 387-91; good of the, xxiv,
395; gunpowder, making of, in,
435 note; inconsistencies of, 371-
4; invasion of Holland, 441;
judicial power, constitution of,
354-8; leaders of, 314-15; letters,
men of, in, xxiv, 258-60, 433-4;
Lowell on, xxviii, 447; Mill on,
xxv, 45-6, 87, 205-6; mistakes of,
xxiv, 183-8; monied interest in,
257-8; municipal guards, 374-5;
Napoleon on, xxviii, 482; National Assembly in, xxiv, 188-98,
216-19, 312-14, 346-7, 371-4; nobility in, 282-7, 440; October sixth
and, 219-29; paper currency of,
338-44, 383-90; Paris, preeminence
of, in, 345-6; parliaments abolished by, 270; public debts, care
of, 321-38; representation under,
255-63; revenue system of, 375-
93; Sheridan on, xviii, 104;
spread of principles of, xxiv, 411-
12; sympathy of English clubs
with, 152-9; Washington's policy
toward, xliii, 265
FRENCH REVOLUTION, REFLECTIONS
ON THE, Burke's, xxiv, 149-397
Frenzy, first of ills, viii, 13
Fresh-water Productions, Darwin
on, xi, 118-19; distribution of,
427-31
Frestron, the enchanter, xiv, 61, 66
Fretting, David on, xliv, 190 (8)
Freydis, daughter of Eric the Red,
xliii, 6; in Vinland, 17-20
Freyia, the goddess, xlix, 277
Freyr, Germanic god, xlix, 14 note 2
Friar, Chaucer's, xl, 17-18; Dryden
on Chaucer's, xxxix, 172
Friars, in Milton's Limbo, iv, 150;
More on, xxxvi, 165
FRIARS' CARSE HERMITAGE, INSCRIP-
TION AT, vi, 550
FRIARS' CARSE HERMITAGE, VERSES
IN, vi, 325
FRIARS' CARSE HERMITAGE, WRITTEN
IN, vi, 337
Friction, chemical effects of, xxx,
206-7; heat generated by, 59-60,
205-6
FRIEND, To A DISTANT, xli, 689-90
Friends, Confucius on, xliv, 57 (4);
Confucius on choice of, 6; Emer-
son on love of, v, 158; faithful,
rare, vii, 321 (2); falling out of
faithful, xl, 204-6; forgiveness of,
iii, 16; little, may prove great,
xvii, 14; many, equal to none,
41; no whit worse than brothers,
xxii, 119; Pascal on advantage of,
xlviii, 61 (155); Ruskin on impossibility of choosing, xxviii, 99;
Samson on, iv, 423; Shakespeare

on, xlvi, 102; Shelley on false,
xviii, 301; single men best, iii, 22
Friends, Society of (see Quakers)
FRIENDS, FOLLOWERS AND, ESSAY ON,
Bacon's, iii, 125-6
FRIENDS AND LAND I LOVE, FRAE
THE, vi, 445
Friendship, Augustine, St., on false
and true, vii, 55; Blair on, vi,
175; Browne on, iii, 332-3; Burns
on, vi, 189; Coleridge on, xli,
720; Confucius on, xliv, 42 (23);
Confucius on false, 18 (24); Emerson on, v, 203-4; Epictetus on
true, ii, 148 (82); excess in, ix,
330 and note; Goethe on, xxxix,
265-6; xix, 394; Hume on, xxxvii,
423; immortality of, i, 402 (127-
34); Kempis on true, vii, 318-19;
Locke on, xxxvii, 7; Lothario on,
xiv, 328-9; Machiavelli on, xxxvi,
57; Manzoni on, xxi, 193; Marcus
Aurelius on false, ii, 293 (15);
of parents and children, xxxvii,
86-7; Pascal on, xlviii, 44, 45
(101); Penn on, i, 350-1; pity
and, xxxiv, 193; seldom between
equals, iii, 126; Shakespeare on,
xlvi, 102; Swift on, xxvii, 97;
toast to, xli, 595; Tzu-chang on,
xliv, 65 (3)
FRIENDSHIP, ESSAY ON, Bacon's, iii,
69-75
FRIENDSHIP, ESSAY ON, Emerson's,
v, 109-23
FRIENDSHIP, ESSAY ON, Montaigne's,
xxxii, 74-88; remarks on, 3
FRIENDSHIP, SONNET ON, xiv, 251
FRIENDSHIP, TREATISE ON, Cicero's,
ix, 7-44
Friesshardt, in WILHELM TELL,
xxvi, 424-8, 454-5
Frigate-bird, Darwin on the, xi, 189,
190
Frights, Locke on, xxxvii, 104, 124-6
Fringing-reefs, Darwin on, xxix,
497-503
Frisians, Tacitus on the, xxxiii, 115
Frivolousness, Confucius on, xliv,
5 (8)
Frobisher, John, Harrison on, xxxv,
338
Frobisher, Martin, death of, xxxiii,
235; with Drake, 234, 237, 248,
253-4, 264; northwest passage and,
270
Froda, xlix, 62 note, 63 note
Frog, story of, who became a god,
xlv, 722-3
Frog and Mouse, fable of, xx, 95
note
FROG AND Ox, fable of, xvii, 19
FROG-KING, tale of the, xvii, 51-4
Frogs, in Brazil, xxix, 39-40; hearts
in, xxxviii, 88; in oceanic islands,
xi, 435-6; snakes and, xxxv, 364;
on volcanic islands, xxix, 404-5

FROGS, THE, of Aristophanes, viii,
419-66; remarks on, 418
FROGS AND HARES, fable of, xvii, 16
FROGS DESIRING A KING, fable of,
xvii, 15
Froissart, Jean, BATTLE OF OTTER-
BURN, xxxv, 3-4; BATTLE OF POI-
TIERS, 34-60; CAMPAIGN OF CRECY,
5-33; CHRONICLES of, remarks on,
l, 22; on the English, v, 394; life
and works, xxxv, 3-4; Montaigne
on, xxxii, 100-1; in Scotland, xxxv,
89-90; WAT TYLER'S REBELLION,
61-82
Fronde, Pascal on the, xlviii, 311
(878)
Frondeurs, the, xxxiv, 88 note
Frontinus, Roman lawyer, ix, 273
Fronto, teacher of Marcus Aurelius,
ii, 192, 195 (11)
Frosch, in FAUST, xix, 79-94
Froth, in NEW WAY TO PAY OLD
DEBTS, xlvii, 819-23, 876-9
Frothingham, Ellen, translator of
Goethe, xix, 333
Frugal, Master, in NEW WAY TO
PAY OLD DEBTS, xlvii, 836
Frugality, Bacon on, iii, 75-6; economically considered, x, 278-9;
Franklin on, i, 89, 95-6; Franklin's rule of, 83, 85; Hobbes on,
xxxiv, 387; motives of, x, 282,
283; Penn on, i, 344
Fruits, beauty of, reason for, xi,
211-12; cultivation of, in Elizabethan England, xxxv, 254; fer-
mentation of, xxxviii, 289, 325;
fermentation of, in carbonic acid
gas, 317-28; as gifts, v, 229-30;
importance of down and color of,
xi, 98; Locke on eating of, xxxvii,
21-2; ripening of, xxxviii, 321
FRUITS OF SOLITUDE, Penn's, i, 331-
416
Fucci, Vanni, in Hell, xx, 103-4
Fuegians, Darwin on the, xi, 50;
xxix, 219-24, 227-32, 234-9, 241-6,
250
Fuentes, Darwin on, xxix, 13-14
Fugger, commercial house of, xxxvi,
301 note, 349
FUGITIVE SLAVE ACT, xliii, 327-33
Fugitive Slaves, constitutional provision for, xliii, 203; Lincoln on,
335-6, 341; Whittier on, xlii,
1421-4
Fugitives, usually single men, iii, 22
Fulgentio, and Dr. Donne, xv, 362
Fullarton, Col., vi, 184 note 9, 185,
190
Fuller's Teazel, xi, 45
Fulvia, wife of Antony, xviii, 45;
xii, 341-2; Cicero and, 238; death
of, 357; Octavius and, 354, 357;
son of, 403
Fulvius, and Ennius, xxvii, 39-40
Functions, conversion of, xi, 195-7

FUNDAMENTAL ORDERS OF CONNEC-
TICUT, xliii, 63-9
Fundanus, daughter of, ix, 286-7
FUNDEVOGEL, story of, xvii, 149-51
Funding, system of, x, 580, 584-5
(see National Debt)
FUNERAL, THE, xl, 310-11
Funerals, in ancient Egypt, xxxiii,
42-4; German, 110; Indian, xliii,
36; in Utopia, xxxvi, 242
Fungi, Pasteur on, xxxviii, 310, 313
and note
Fungus, edible, in Tierra del Fuego,
xxix, 252
Fur, thickness of, to what due, xi,
146
Furies, Æschylus on the, viii, 117,
127-9, 152; Dante on the, xx, 38;
De Quincey on the, xxvii, 336-7;
Emerson on, v, 97; Virgil on the,
xiii, 425
FURIES, THE, of Æschylus, viii, 115-
55; Voltaire on, xxxix, 382
Furnace, in NEW WAY TO PAY OLD
DEBTS, xlvii, 825-8, 830-1, 832,
834, 835, 840-1, 842, 844-6, 880,
897
Furnius, and Antony, xii, 381
Furnivall, Dr., xxxv, 228
Fürst, Walter, in WILHELM TELL,
friend of Stauffacher, xxvi, 380;
Melchthal and, 385-6, 390; with
Stauffacher, 386-8; begins revolt,
391-4; at the rendezvous, 405-14;
with Tell at Altdorf, 427-35; at
death of Attinghausen, 442-7; with
Rudenz, 448-50; at destruction of
Keep, 460-3; hears death of Emperor, 463-7; in final scene, 474
Furuncles, Pasteur on, xxxviii, 390-4
Fusconi, Francesco, xxxi, 171 note,
173-5, 177
Fuscus, letter to, ix, 370, 373
Fusella, Ambrogio, in THE BE-
TROTHED, xxi, 246-7, 256-7
Future, Confucius on knowledge of
the, xliv, 9 (23); Hobbes on the,
xxxiv, 333; Kempis on care of
the, vii, 305 (2, 3); Milton on foreknowledge of the, iv, 342; Pascal
on the, xlviii, 362; Pascal on our
care for, 64 (172); past to, rea-
sonings from, xxxvii, 335; Pope
on blindness to, xl, 420; uncertainty of the, xxxix, 101, 102;
veil of the, v, 146-7; worry over
the, ii, 123 (19), 246 (8)
Future Life (see Immortality, Hereafter)
FUTURE PEACE AND GLORY OF THE
CHURCH, xlv, 576
FYERS, FALL OF, LINES ON THE, vi,
296

Gabinia, Lex, Cicero on, ix, 23
Gabinius, Aulus, campaigns of, xii,
335-6; Cicero and, 252; in Civil
War, 339; Crassus and, ix, 133;

return to Rome, 122; suit against, 119-20; Syria given to, xii, 251
Gabriel, Archangel, song of, in FAUST, xix, 16; in Luke's gospel, xliv, 358 (19, 26-38); Mohammed and, xlv, 908 note; Gabriel in PARADISE LOST, iv, 171, 172, 177, 179-83, 208, 216, 295; in PARADISE REGAINED, iv, 366
Gabriel, in EVANGELINE (see Lajeunesse)
Gadarenes, xliv, 380 note 5
Gaddi, Agnolino, xxxi, 134, 135
Gaddi, Cardinal de', xxxi, 210-11
Gaddi, Giovanni, xxxi, 101 note 4, 116, 139-40, 167, 171-3, 175
Gaddi, Niccolo, xxxi, 76 note
Gaia, daughter of Gherardo, xx, 214 note 10
Gain, Confucius on pursuit of, xliv, 12, 58 (10); Penn on thirst for, i, 351 (127), 361 (252); Smith on hope of, x, 113-14; Tennyson on lust of, xlii, 1053
Gaius, friend of Paul, xliv, 474 (29), 475 (4); baptism of, xlv, 502 (14)
Gaius, in PILGRIM'S PROGRESS, xv, 266-78
Galahad, Sir, in HOLY GRAIL, at Abblasoure, xxxv, 130; Arthur and, 115, 120, 222; bed of, 196-9; birth of, 114-15, 117, 120, 160; Bors and, 218; buried at Sarras, 207; adventure of burning tomb, 217-18; at castle of Carbonek, 218-19; at castle of Carteloise, 200-3; at court, 113; death, 224-5; Gawaine and, 164, 188-9; at abbey of Gore, 217; Guenever and, 119-20; sees hart and four lions, 203-4; Holy Grail and, 108, 219-21; made king, 224; knighting of, 110-11; Launcelot and, 134-5, 209-11; at castle of Maidens, 130-2, 134; Sir Melias and, 126-7, 128-9; Mordrains and, 216-17; at Mortaise, 151; at parting of the roads, 127; Percival and, 134-5, 145, 208, 218; prayer for death, 222-3; thrown into prison, 223-4; at Sarras, 223; shield of, 122-5; led to ship of Faith, 190-2; Siege Perilous and, 114; at castle of strange custom, 204-8; sword of, 192-6, 199-200; adventure of the tomb, 125-6; at tourney, 117; at hermitage of Ulfin, 189-90; virginity of, 168, 217; and queen of Waste Lands, 142; at the well, 217; at the White Abbey, 121
GALAHAD, SIR, by Tennyson, xlii, 1036-8
Galaor, Don, mistress of, xiv, 103-4
Galapagos Archipelago, Darwin on, xxix, 394-424; health conditions in, 387; species of, xi, 433, 439-44

Galatea, in PHILASTER, xlvii, 640-1; Arethusa and, 661-2; at the hunt, 684, 686, 687-90; Pharamond and, 657-9, 660-1, 663-4; on Philaster, 646, 647
Galaxy, Milton on, iv, 244 (see also Milky Way)
Galba, Emperor, death of, iii, 10; empire foretold to, 96; speech of, 43; Tacitus on, 32
Galdino, Father, in I PROMESSI SPOSI, xxi, 50-2, 310-12
Galeazzo, de' Visconti, xx, 179 notes 5 and 7
Gale-Jones, Mill and, xxv, 83
Galen, on the arteries, xxxviii, 69, 70, 71-2, 85, 94; on the blood, 93-4; Browne on, iii, 278 (14); on the circulation, xxxviii, 102-5; on the heart, 87, 144; Huxley on, xxviii, 227; immortality doubted by, iii, 285-6; ostentation of, 134; on the pulse, xxxviii, 68, 73
Galesus, in ÆNEID, xiii, 262
Galfridus, on Arthur, xxxix, 22
Galileo, Emerson on, v, 70, 86; heliocentric theory and, xxxix, 55 note; the Inquisition and, xxxiv, 113; Milton on, iii, 226; on tides, xxx, 294; "Tuscan artist," iv, 97
Galitta, case of, ix, 399
GALLA WATER, BRAW LADS O', vi, 481
Galland, Antoine, translator of ARABIAN NIGHTS, xvi, 3
GALLANT WEAVER, THE, vi, 437
Gallatin, Albert, in Treaty of 1814, xliii, 273
Galleotti, Pietro Pagolo, xxxi, 164 note 7, 167, 181, 273, 277, 278, 279, 289, 291, 317, 350, 363, 366
Galleys, of the Germans, xxxiii, 121
Gallinazo, Darwin on the, xxix, 69-70
Gallio, proconsul of Achaia, xliv, 471 (12-17)
Gallipoli, description of, xxviii, 56
GALLOWAY, EARL OF, EPIGRAMS ON, vi, 496-7
Gallura, Nino di, in Purgatory, xx, 178-9; Ugolino and, 138 note
Gallus, Cornelius, Cicero on, ix, 64; death of, xxxii, 14; Lælius on, ix, 10
Gallus, Flavius, xii, 368, 369
Gallus, M. Fadius, letter to, ix, 109
Gallus, friend of Pliny, letters to, ix, 231, 345
Galluzzi, Bernardo, xxxi, 261-2
GALUPPI'S, A TOCCATA OF, xlii, 1122
Galvanic Batteries, xxx, 214
Gama, Vasco de, x, 417
Gamaliel, xliv, 440 (34-9); Paul and, 480 (3)
Gambier, James, Lord, xliii, 273
Gambling, Blake on, xli, 604; Locke

on, xxxvii, 188; Pascal on pleasure of, xlviii, 55-6
Gambling Laws, Mill on, xxv, 308-9
Games, five, of skill, xii, 75 note; in Utopia, xxxvi, 190-1
Gandaline, squire of Amadis, xiv, 173; sonnet to Sancho Panza, 17
Ganelon, in Charlemagne's Council, xlix, 103, 104; sent to King Marsil, 106-9; death of, 206-7, 146; embassy and crime, 110-23, 125, 127; in Hell, xx, 136 note 12; Marsil and, xlix, 106-9; Roland and, 133, 137, 150, 163-4; trial of, 198, 199-202
Ganges, Harrison on, xxxv, 246
Ganymede, and Jove, xiii, 190; xx, 182
Garba, Pedro, xiv, 515
Garcia, Diego, xiv, 319
GARDEN, A, by Marvell, xl, 379
Garden of Delight, Harun Er-Rashid's, xvi, 220-2
GARDEN, THE DYING MAN IN HIS, xli, 493-4
GARDEN, A FORSAKEN, xlii, 1255-7
GARDEN, MY, by Brown, xlii, 1195
Garden, parable of the, xv, 207-8
GARDEN OF PARADISE, THE, xvii, 298-312
GARDEN OF PROSERPINE, xlii, 1251-3
GARDEN, THOUGHTS IN A, xl, 386-8
Gardening, Locke on, xxxvii, 186-7
GARDENS, ESSAY ON, Bacon's, iii, 117-23, 4
Gardens, kitchen, Smith on, x, 162-3; proportion in, xxiv, 86; in Utopia, xxxvi, 186-7
GARD'NER WI' HIS PAIDLE, vi, 360
Gareth, Sir, xxxv, 132, 133; xxxix, 24-5
Garget, superstition of the, xxxv, 328
Garland, Hugo on, xxxix, 400
Garnett, on THE PRINCE, xxxvi, 3-4
Garret, John, and Drake, xxxiii, 136
Garrick, David, epitaph on, xxvii, 313; Goldsmith on, xli, 518, 520; as Hamlet, xxvii, 318; Hazlitt on, 289-90; Lamb on, 322-3; PRO-LOGUES by, xviii, 109-10, 201-2
Garrison, William Lloyd, Mill on, xxv, 171
Garter, Order of the, xxxv, 233-4
Gärtner, Joseph, on sterility of hybrids, xi, 300-1; on mongrels and hybrids, 327, 328; on prepotency, 111; on reciprocal crosses, 308; on sterility of species, 299, 314, 322; on varieties, 325-26
Gas, cause of brightness of illuminating, xxx, 114
Gasabel, squire of Don Galaor, xiv, 173
Gascoigne, George, LOVER'S LULLABY, xl, 198

Gascony, Machiavelli on, xxxvi, 9-10
Gases, expansion of, Joule on, xxx, 208-9; expansion of, measurement of, 198-9; transparency of, 43; vapors and, difference of, 105; volume of, 42; weighing, method of, 151-2
GATHERING SONG OF DONALD THE BLACK, xli, 762-3
Gatta, Il, Cellini on, xxxi, 317
Gattinara, Giovanni Bartolommeo di, xxxi, 215 note, 216
Gauchos, character of, xxix, 169-70; riding skill of, 166
Gaudry, M., on fossils, xi, 378
Gaufred, and Richard, xl, 48-9
Gaul, Cæsar's campaigns in, xii, 289-98
Gauls, risings of, repeated, xxxvi, 18; in Rome, xiii, 294; Tacitus on, xxxiii, 111
Gautama, Siddhartha, xlv, 588
Gaveston, in EDWARD II, banishment, xlvi, 14-18; conspiracies against, 11-13, 31; Coventry and, 10-11; Edward and, 9-11, 14, 15, 17-19, 29, 30, 35, 37; flight and capture, 39-42; historically, 3; preparations for marriage, 35; Mortimer and, 25, 35; nobles and, 7-9, 14; return, 29-30; Spencer and, 26; in Tynemouth, 36, 37; Warwick and, 42-3
Gawaine, Sir, in HOLY GRAIL, meets Aglovale, xxxv, 134; nephew of Arthur, 115; Bagdemagus and, 216; dream of, 164-5, 168; Galahad and, 132-3, 189; Guenevere and, xlii, 1230, 1232, 1235-6, 1239; at hermitage, xxxv, 133-4; Holy Grail and, 118, 120, 164, 166; mother of, xlii, 1235; at Nacien, 167-71; return home, 216; meets Seven Knights, 133; skull of, xxxix, 22; and the sword, xxxv, 112-13; Uwaine and, 166-7
Gay, John, Addison and, xxvii, 186-7; Eclogues of, xxxix, 339; Hazlitt on, xxvii, 292; POEMS by, xl, 412-13; Swift and, xxviii, 15
GAY GOSS-HAWK, THE, xl, 70-3
Gay-Lussac, on fermentation, xxxviii, 314
Gazehounds, Harrison on, xxxv, 369
GAZELLE, THE SHEYKH AND THE, xvi, 20-3
Geary, General, at Gettysburg, xliii, 385
Geese, of Falkland Islands, xxix, 214-15; Harrison on, xxxv, 354
Gehenna, Hinnom called, iv, 100
Geikie, Sir Archibald, GEOGRAPHI-CAL EVOLUTION, xxx, 339-67; life and works, 338

Gellius, Aulus, on classics, xxxii, 126

Gellius, Lucius, xii, 247

Gellius, Marcus, Cicero on, xii, 248-9

Gelon, gift of, xii, 166; Macaulay on, xxvii, 418

Gemellinus, Virdius, ix, 393

Gemini, sign of, Dante on, xx, 382 note 8

Geminius, and Antony, xii, 381-2

Geminius, friend of Pliny, ix, 324, 353, 385

Genera, formation of, illustrated, xi, 127, 132; in geological record, 367-8, 354-9; large, vary most, 71-2; species in, resemble each other, 73-4

General Principles, Hume on, xxxvii, 314

Generalization, Bacon on, xxxix, 140; Bentham on, xxvii, 257-9; Emerson on, v, 157-9; Hume on, xxxvii, 395 (6), 438 note

Generation, alternate, xi, 478; artificial, in New Atlantis, iii, 184; death and, xxxviii, 89; economic aspect of, x, 83; Heraclitus on, ii, 221 (46); Marcus Aurelius on, 215 (4, 5), 228 (13); passions of, xxiv, 37, 38-9; Socrates on, ii, 60-1; spontaneous, Harrison on, xxxv, 368

Genesis, Bagehot on, xxviii, 211; Browne on, iii, 299; Hugo on, xxxix, 357; Milton on events of, iv, 333 et seq.; selection, principle of, in, xi, 48

Geneva, Lake, sedimentary deposits in, xxxviii, 422-3

Genii, ancient belief in, v, 310; species of different, xvi, 9 note

Genitor, Julius, letters to, ix, 249, 360

Genius, Carlyle on, xxv, 336-7; colleges and, v, 439-40; Emerson on, 10, 63, 139, 148-51, 178, 274, 292; excesses and, 181; freedom requisite to, xxv, 270; Hugo on, xxxix, 384, 388, 406; Pascal on, xlviii, 279 (793); penalty of, v, 92-3; Poe on, xxviii, 385; recognition of, v, 205; Sainte-Beuve on, xxxii, 130; Schiller on, 250; talent and, v, 172; Thoreau on, xxviii, 426; trade and, v, 47, 193; tragedy of, 54; Wordsworth on, xxxix, 350

GENIUS IN BEAUTY, xlii, 1226

Gens, nature of the, xxviii, 255

Gentilesse, Chaucer on, v, 182-3; Emerson on word, 209

Gentility, Emerson on word, v, 209; in English drama, 125

Gentillis, Albericus, at Oxford, v, 433

GENTLEMAN, LINES TO A, vi, 397

Gentlemen, Chi Tzu-ch'eng on, xliv, 39 (8); Confucius on, 5 (1), 8 (12, 13, 14), 10 (7), 13 (5, 10, 11), 14 (16, 24), 16 (15), 19 (3), 20 (16), 21 (24), 24 (25), 25 (36), 28 (6), 29 (13), 39 (4, 11), 14 (16, 24), 16 (15), 19 26), 47 (7), 49 (24), 50 (29), 51 (45), 52 (1), 54 (17-22), 55 (31, 33, 36), 57 (7, 8), 58 (10), 62 (23, 24), 69 (2, 3); Emerson on, v, 208-11, 218-19, 220-1; Locke on making of, xxxvii, 76, 82; Newman on education of, xxviii, 34; Pascal on, xlviii, 18 (35), 25 (68); Ruskin on production of, xxviii, 137-8; Tseng-tzu on, xliv, 26 (4, 6), 42 (24), 50 (28); Tzu-hsia on, 66 (9, 10, 12); Yu-tzu on, 5 (2)

Gentleness, ECCLESIASTES on, xliv, 352 (4); manliness of, ii, 295

Gentry, Burns on the, vi, 160-4, 247; Confucius on example of, xliv, 25 (2); Hobbes on, xxxiv, 382

Gentucca, Dante on, xx, 245, 274 note 3

Genus (see Genera)

Geoffrey of Anjou, in SONG OF ROLAND, xlix, 100, 191, 193-4

Geoffrey of Monmouth, on Arthur, xxxii, 163; chronicle of, 168; legend of Lear in, xlvi, 202

Geographical Changes, Darwin on, xi, 404-5

Geographical Distribution, xi, 395-449; in classification, 457

GEOGRAPHICAL EVOLUTION, by Geikie, xxx, 337-67

Geography, Geikie on study of, xxx, 339-41; geology, relations to, 341-2; Hobbes on, xxxiv, 377; Hume on, xxxvii, 444; Locke on study of, 147, 157, 164-5, 166-7; Milton on study of, iii, 253

Geological Evolution, Geikie on, xxx, 338, 342-67

Geological Formations, age of, xxx, 350-1; Darwin on, xi, 347-9; Lyell on, xxxviii, 419-37

Geological Record, Darwin on the, xi, 333-94; Lyell on imperfections in, xxxviii, 420-37

Geology, Emerson on, v, 239, 307; Geikie on importance of, xxx, 341-2; Lyell on, xi, 109; xxxviii, 404, 440; papers on, 403-40; species, theory of, in relation to, xi, 526-7

GEOLOGY, PROGRESS OF, Lyell's, xxxviii, 405-18

Geometrical Spirit, Pascal on the, xlviii, 427-44

Geometry, beginning of, xxxiii, 53; Descartes on, xxxiv, 16, 17, 19, 31; Descartes's work on, 3, 114,

127; Hobbes on, 339, 377; Hume on, xxxvii, 324, 329, 437-8 note; Locke on study of, 148, 164, 166; Newton on, xxxix, 157-8; Pascal on, xlviii, 27-8, 416, 428, 429 note, 431, 434-8

George, St., Carlyle on, xxv, 438; Emerson on, v, 407

George II, and Pitt, xxiv, 349

George III, and American Colonies, xliii, 161-3, 185; Burns to, vi, 217-220

George IV, debauchery of, v, 428; picture ships of, 312

George, Henry, Lowell on, xxviii, 483

GEORGE CAMPBELL, BONNIE, xl, 115-16

Georgia, island of, vegetation in, xxix, 265

Georgia, State of, settlement of, i, 105

Geraint, saint of Brittany, xxxii, 169

Geraldine, in CHRISTABEL, xli, 728-44

Gerard, in A BLOT IN THE 'SCUTCHEON, xviii, 357-8, 360, 374-7

Gerard of Roussillon, xlix, 125, 167, 178

Gerard, Balthazar, murderer of William of Orange, iii, 103

Gereia, in ROLAND, xlix, 100, 103, 125, 141, 145, 155, 178

Gergonne, M., Mill on, xxv, 42

Geri of Bello, in Hell, xx, 121 and note

Gerier, in SONG OF ROLAND, xlix, 100, 103, 125, 141, 145, 155, 178

GERM THEORY, Pasteur's, xxxviii, 382-402

German Empire, Freeman on the, xxviii, 268-9; language as factor in forming of, 265

GERMAN ESSAYS, xxxii, 195-395

GERMAN NOBILITY, ADDRESS TO, Luther's, xxxvi, 274-352; remarks on, 260

German Language, Huxley on study of, xxviii, 229

German Literature, established by Luther, xxxvi, 260; in 19th century, xxxix, 452; Taine on, 461

German Philosophy, Carlyle on, xxv, 369

Germanic Peoples, works dealing with early, l, 20-1, 27

Germanic Races, Taine on, xxxix, 444, 448, 455

Germanicus, Cæsar, hatred of cocks, xxxii, 59; descent and children of, xii, 403; in Germany, xxxiii, 117

Germanicus, Caius (see Caligula)

Germans, agriculture of, xxxiii, 103-4, 110, 122, 123; arms and prac-
tices of war, 98, 99 101, 102, 103, 112-13, 117, 120, 121, 122; assemblies of, 101-2; bathing of ancient, cold, xxxvii, 13-14; boats of, xxxiii, 121; Cæsar's campaign against the, xii, 290-1, 293-4; chastity of, xxxiii, 106; children of, 106-7; coats of arms among, xxxiv, 382-3; crimes, penalties of, xxxiii, 102, 107; dances and games, 109; divination among, 100-1; dress of, 105, 117; Emerson on, v, 351, 355, 387-8; family ties and hospitality, xxxiii, 107-8; feasts, broils, and reconciliations, 108; food and drink, 109; funerals among, 110; gifts, their delight in, 104, 108; habitations of, 104-5; heroes and battle-songs, 96; inheritance, laws of, 107; kings and generals, 98-9, 121; lands, herds, and use of metals, 97-8, 110, 122; life, daily, 108; marriage among, 105-6; origin of, 95; physical character of, 97; priesthood, power of, among, 98-9; princes among the, 102-4; purity of race, 97; queen among, only, 122; religion of the, 100, 118-19, 120, 121-2; Romans and, 116-17; seasons of, 110; slavery among, 109-10; slavery among, Harrison on, xxxv, 239; Taine on, xxxix, 440, 444, 448; time, reckoning of, xxxiii, 101; tribes and name of, 95-6, 111-23; usury unknown to, 110; village chiefs, 102; women, 99-100, 105

Germany, classes in, v, 379; Emerson on science of, 456, 461; geography of, xxxiii, 95, 97; Luther on temporal state of, xxxvi, 348-51; Machiavelli on cities of, 38; monasteries in, 331; papal power in, 290-6, 303, 308-11, 332-3, 343-7; pilgrimages in, 325-6; Romans in, xxxiii, 116-17

GERMANY, by Tacitus, xxxiii, 95-123; remarks on, 94

Germs, defined by Pasteur, xxxviii, 359-60

Gerson, Jean de, as author of IMITATION OF CHRIST, vii, 208

Gertrude, the Signora, in THE BETROTHED, xxi, 144-82, 308-9, 339-40, 646

Gertrude, Queen, in HAMLET, Claudius and, xlvi, 93, 96-7; death, 197; Hamlet and, 94-5, 96, 153-9; Laertes and, 169-70; Ophelia and, 134, 166-7; at Ophelia's funeral, 185, 186, 187; at the play, 141, 145, 146; with Polonius, 119-21

Gertrude, in WILHELM TELL, xxvi, 377-80

Gertrude of Wyoming, Mill on, xxv, 17

Gervase, in THE BETROTHED, xxi,

97, 113-15, 118, 120, 122, 124, 130, 191
Gervais of Tilbury, xxxii, 160 note 8
Gervasius, the martyr, vii, 153
Geryon, monster, Dante on, xx, 71-2, 74; Virgil on, xiii, 221, 266
Gessler, in WILHELM TELL, Armgart and, xxvi, 455-7; cap of, 383, 462; death of, 458-9; Rudenz and, 432-3; Stauffacher and, 378-9, 414; Tell and, 418-9, 428-36, 438, 440, 450-3, 457; tyranny of, 379
GET UP AND BAR THE DOOR, a ballad, xl, 88-9
GETTYSBURG, BATTLE OF, xliii, 347-440
GETTYSBURG ADDRESS, Lincoln's, xliii, 441
GHENT, TREATY OF, xliii, 273-82
Gherardeschi, Ugolino de', xx, 138-40
Ghibellines, Dante on, xx, 310 note 23; in Florence, 68 note 1; friends of Papacy, 308 note 7; Guelfs and (see numerous notes to DIVINE COMEDY)
Ghirlandajo, Hazlitt on, xxvii, 293, 295
Ghosts, Browne on, iii, 303; Burke on fear of, xxiv, 52; Hobbes on, xxxiv, 329, 392; Locke on, xxxvii, 124-6, 175; Milton on, iv, 58-9; Pliny on, ix, 326-9; Socrates on, ii, 74
GHULEH, THE PRINCE AND THE, xvi, 39-40
Gianciotto, Lord of Rimini, xx, 24 note 3
Giangiacomo of Cesena, xxxi, 41-2
Gianotti, Gianotto, xxxi, 27
Giants, Burke on, xxiv, 133; in Dante's HELL, xx, 130-3; in Milton's Limbo, iv, 149
Gibbon, Edward, Carlyle on, v, 334; on changes in human affairs, xxxviii, 413; style of, v, 22; on Tacitus, xxxiii, 94; Wordsworth on, v, 483
Gibbon, General John, at Gettysburg, xliii, 347 note, 353, 357, 358, 367, 371, 372, 375, 381, 382, 384, 391, 393, 394, 395, 399, 400-1, 403, 404, 405, 415, 428, 431-2
Gibeah, the Levite woman in, iv, 103
Giberti, Gianmatteo, xxxi, 102 note
Giddiness, defined, xxxiv, 367
Gideon, Locke on, xxxvii, 187; Milton on, iv, 387, 425; Pascal on, xlviii, 289 (822), 393
Giese, Tidemann, xxxix, 56
Gifford, George, with Raleigh, xxxiii, 325, 347, 349, 354, 357, 363, 369, 377, 382, 386
Gifts, Burns on, vi, 200; among the Germans, xxxiii, 108; Hobbes on, xxxiv, 378, 410, 411, 412; Kempis

on, vii, 275 (4); Krishna on, xiv, 875; in law, xxxiv, 410, 411, 412; Penn on, i, 340 (20); Plutarch on accepting, xii, 80-1; Shakespeare on, xlvi, 136; Stella's definition of, xxvii, 137; Woolman on, i, 209; worth of, lies in giver, xlv, 821
GIFTS, by Thomson, xlii, 1195-6
GIFTS, EMERSON'S ESSAY ON, v, 229 32
GIFTS, HER, by Rossetti, xlii, 1227-8
Gila River, navigation of, xliii, 315
Gilbert, Sir Humphrey, life of, xxxiii, 270; Spaniards, expeditions against, 310; VOYAGE TO NEWFOUNDLAND, 271-308; remarks on voyage of, 234
Gilbert, Sir John, xxxiii, 306, 349, 363, 369
Gildas, and the bards, xxxii, 176
Giles, St., on Archbishop Turpin, xlix, 175
Giles, Peter, on More's UTOPIA, xxxvi, 144, 255-7
Giliolo, Girolamo; xxxi, 280, 282
Gill, Mr., on changes of drainage, xxix, 379-80
GILPIN, JOHN, DIVERTING HISTORY OF, xli, 559-67
Gines, of Passamonte, xiv, 192-3, 195, 196, 199-200, 303
Ginn, Mohammed on the, xlv, 910
Ginori, Federigo, xxxi, 89-90, 95
Giotto, Dante on, xx, 191 note 4; Hazlitt on, xxvii, 293, 295
Giovanna, Queen of Naples, xxxvi, 44
Giovanni, Pier, xxxi, 127
Gipsies, Browne on, iii, 327
Giraffe, development of, xi, 230-3; tail of, 206
Giraldus Cambrensis, narratives of, xxxii, 186
GIRDLE, ON A, xl, 366-7
GIRL WITHOUT HANDS, THE, xvii, 123-8
Girls, Confucius on, xliv, 62 (25); Locke on training of, xxxvii, 11, 14-15, 54; Ruskin on education of, xxviii, 151-61
Giuki, King, xlix, 331, 334, 335; daughter of, 318, 331
Giukings (see Niblungs)
Giulio, value of the, xxxi, 163 note 3
GIVE ALL TO LOVE, xlii, 1205-6
GIVE ME MORE LOVE, xl, 362
GIVE ME THE SPLENDID SILENT SUN, xlii, 1494-6
Giver, "God loveth a cheerful," xlv, 538 (7)
Glacial Period, Darwin on, xi, 417-19; distribution of life, effect of, on, 411-17, 422-6; in Europe, xxx, 365; species, effect of, on, xxxviii, 427
Glaciers, of the Alps, xxx, 224; ap-

pearance of, 225-33; bending and bursting of, explained, 241-50; boulders, distribution of, by, 237-9, 240-1; cause of, 224-5; crevasses in (see Crevasses); Darwin on, xxix, 262-4; dirt-bands of, xxx, 239; extent of former, 240-1; longitudinal rifts explained, 249; movement of, 233-7; origin of name, 225; purity of waters from, 252; effect of, on rocks, 240; structure of ice of, 251-2; temperature of, 243; utility of, 252-3

Gladstone, and free trade, xxv, 67; on King of Naples, v, 288

Glass, discovery of, xxxv, 310-11

Glaucus, Dante on, xx, 289; death of, xiii, 407; in Hades, 227;

Glaumoor, wife of Gunnar, xlix, 365, 367, 368

Gleichen, Baron de, xxv, 232 note 4

GLENCAIRN, EARL OF, LAMENT FOR, vi, 424

Glendowyn, Simon, at Otterburn, xxxv, 95, 102

GLENGARIFF, by De Vere, xli, 936-7

GLENRIDDELL'S FOX, ON, vi, 432

Glibness, Confucius on, xliv, 15 (4), 37 (24), 50 (34), 53 (10), 57 (4)

GLOOMY WINTER'S NOW AWA', xli, 608-9

GLORIA IN EXCELSIS, xlv, 553

GLORIES OF OUR BLOOD AND STATE, xl, 359-60

Glory, Byron on, xli, 809-10; Hobbes on desire for, xxxiv, 404; Kempis on, vii, 254 (2), 317 (5); Milton on, iv, 381, 389-92; Pascal on love of, xlviii, 60 (150-1), 113 (324), 132 (404); "paths of," xl, 456; Pliny on, ix, 203; Plutarch on desire for, xii, 253; Tennyson on, xlii, 1039; Walton on, xv, 369; Webster on, xlvii, 786

Glosses, Luther on, xxxvi, 298

Gloucester, Earl of, in KING LEAR, blinded, xlvi, 264; Cornwall and, 263-4; 265-6; Edgar and, 204, 258, 267-9, 276-9, 283-5, 291, 298; Edmund and, 203-4; 213-15, 230-3; 253, 259; Kent and, 234, 235, 237-8; Lear and, 241-2, 248, 253, 257-8, 259, 262, 279-81; Oswald and, 283-4

Glub, Charles, xxxiii, 169

Gluttony, Dante's punishment of, xx, 25-6, 240-2; examples of, 247; Kempis on punishment of, vii, 242 (3); sin of, in FAUSTUS, xix, 221

Glycerin, production of, xxx, 91

GLYNN, THE MARSHES OF, xlii, 1470-3

Gmelin, on independent creations, xi, 412

Gnadenhut, Franklin fortifies, i, 146-8; massacre at, 145

Gnatho, Sidney on, xxvii, 20, 29

Gnomon, learned from Babylon, xxxiii, 53

GO, LOVELY ROSE, xl, 367

GO ON, SWEET BIRD, AND SOOTH MY CARE, vi, 310

GOAT AND FOX, fable of, xvii, 46

Goatherd, in DON QUIXOTE, xiv, 525-30

Goats, sacred to Mendesians, xxxiii, 28

GOBLET, INSCRIPTION ON A, vi, 548

Goblins, Burke on fear of, xxiv, 52; Locke on, xxxvii, 124-6, 175

God, Aristotle on, xxxix, 110; Augustine, St., on, vii, 5-10, 40, 62-3, 78, 102-4, 120, 171-3, 182-9; v, 155; Bacon on unworthy ideas of, iii, 45, 47; Berkeley on existence and nature of, xxxvii, 246-50, 267-9, 273-4, 276-9, 281, 293, 296; Browne on, iii, 274, 275, 278-9, 294; Burke on, xxiv, 39, 60-2; Calvin on knowledge of, xxxix, 51; Channing on study of, xxviii, 340, 342-3; Cowper on ways of, xlv, 575-6; Dante on, xx, 300, 391; Descartes on existence and nature of, xxxiv, 29-33; "dice of, always loaded," v, 94; Emerson on, 151, 152; Emerson on ideas of, 285-6; Emerson on knowledge of, 75; Epictetus on, ii, 137 (59-61), 141 (68); "helps those who help themselves," xvii, 36; Hobbes on, xxxiv, 390; Hume on, xxxvii, 318, 362-5, 388-91, 419-28; Locke on, 123-4, 126; Marcus Aurelius on existence of, ii, 304 (28); Mill on common notions of, xxv, 31-2; Mill on worship of, 176; Milton on, iv, 147, 234, 256-7; 426; Montaigne on existence of, xlviii, 396-7; morality and idea of, xxxii, 374; Pascal on existence and nature of, xlviii, 82, 84-7, 90-1, 163-4, 194 (580); Pascal on misery of man without, 23-67, 130 (389); Penn on low ideas of, i, 405-6; Pope on knowledge of, xl, 418-19; Raleigh on, xxxix, 115-17; Raleigh on, as the Creator, 107, 108-9, 110-11, 113-14; Rousseau on, xxxiv, 256, 258-62, 274-6, 298, 392 (see also Providence, Sacred Books)

God, in FAUST, xix, 17-20

God, in PARADISE LOST, iv, 140-3, 145-6, 198-9, 201-2, 224-5, 234, 310, 324-5; Bagehot on Milton's, xxviii, 207

GOD, A MIGHTY FORTRESS IS OUR, xlv, 570-1

GOD, NOW THANK WE ALL OUR, xlv, 571

GOD THE FATHER, HYMN TO, xl, 311-12

Godfrey de Bouillon, in Dante's PARADISE, xx, 363 note 5; "one of nine worthies," xxxix, 22

Godfrey, Thomas, i, 58, 60, 67

Godlyman, Mr., in PILGRIM'S PROGRESS, xv, 295

Godolphin, Lord, and Addison, xxvii, 169-70

Gods, date of, on earth, xxxiii, 73, 74; first named in Egypt, 7, 26-7, 30-1; Herodotus on the, 6-7; Plutarch on, xii, 78-9; Roman and Greek, Dryden on, xiii, 48

Godwin, Mary, second wife of Shelley, xviii, 272

Goethe, Johann Wolfgang von, Arnold on, xlii, 1181, 1182; on the beautiful, v, 311; Byron compared with, xxxii, 411-14; Carlyle and, xxv, 329, 330; Carlyle on, v, 472; xxv, 338, 404, 441, 461; characteristics of, xxxii, 402, 407-11; charities of, v, 199; on classics, xxxii, 132; on compensation of growth, xi, 158; as a critic, xxxii, 129; device of, xxv, 107; EGMONT, xix, 247-331; Emerson on, v, 22; on evolution, xi, 6, 10 note; FAUST, xix, 7-195; HERMANN AND DOROTHEA, 335-431; on himself, xxv, 424; honor due to, xxxii, 416; the Iphigenia of, xxxix, 438; life and works, xix, 3-6; loneliness of, xxviii, 17; MAHOMET'S SONG, xxx, 253; on Manzoni's drama, xxi, 3; Mazzini on, xxxii, 399-400; PROPYLAEN, INTRODUCTION TO, xxxix, 264-80; remarks on PROPYLAEN, l, 55; reaction against, xxxii, 400; Schiller and, xxvi, 368; on self-development, xxv, 164; Taine on, xxxix, 452; Wilhelm Meister, xxv, 396-9; on the will, v, 300-1

GOETHE AND BYRON, ESSAY ON, Mazzini's, xxxii, 399-419

Goeze, J. M., and Lessing, xxxii, 194

Goguier, M. de, and Paré, xxxviii, 23, 45

Gold, "all not, that glitters," xviii, 201; "all that glitters is not," xl, 475; all doth lure, xix, 114; found generally virgin, x, 182; Harrison on, xxxv, 338; good to buy gold, v, 249; man's god, i, 347 (87); More on, xxxvi, 202-3, 205-6; "sacred hunger of pernicious," xiii, 133; type of wisdom, xxviii, 104 (see also Precious Metals)

GOLD, FOR LACK OF, xli, 545

Gold-mining, in Chili, xxix, 283-284

Golden Age, Don Quixote on the, xiv, 86-7; Hume on, xxxvii, 421; Milton on, iv, 11

Golden Calf, xliv, 283 (19), 444 (41); Milton on, iv, 102

Golden Fleece, Stukeley on, v, 476-7

GOLDEN GOOSE, story of the, xvii, 169-72

Golden Hind, Drake's ship, xxxiii, 215 note 5; in Gilbert's voyage 270, 282, 305

Golden Legend, iii, 44 note; PROLOGUE TO, xxxix, 14-15

Golden Rule, of Confucius, xliv, 38 (2), 54 (23); of Jesus, 374 (31); Kant on the, xxxii, 361 note; of Tzu-kung, xliv, 16 (11)

GOLDEN SAYINGS OF EPICTETUS, ii, 117-186

Golden Years, Luther on, xxxvi, 314 note

GOLDIE, JOHN, EPISTLE TO, vi, 100-101

GOLDIE'S BRAINS, ON COMMISSARY, vi, 488

Goldsmith, Oliver, DESERTED VILLAGE, xli, 521-32; Emerson on, v, 22; to Johnson, xviii, 199; life and works, 198; RETALIATION, xli, 517-21; Sainte-Beuve on, xxxii, 133; SHE STOOPS TO CONQUER, xviii, 197-269; Thackeray on, xxviii, 7, 10, 18; THE TRAVELLER, xli, 532-44; WHEN LOVELY WOMAN, 517

Goleta, loss of, xiv, 406-7; sonnet on, 410

Goliath, Cervantes on, xiv, 11; Mohammed on, xlv, 925 note

Gomez, in EGMONT, xix, 297-9

Gomita, the friar, in Hell, xx, 93 and note 4

Gomorrah, Browne on, iii, 284

Goneril, in KING LEAR, Albany and, xlvi, 270-1, 294, 295-6; before battle, 289; Cordelia and, 211; death of, 299; Edmund and, 269-70, 275-6, 284, 290, 296; Lear and, 205, 212, 217-18, 223-8, 243-4; Regan and, 227, 240, 245-8, 271-2, 293-4; Ruskin on, xxviii, 143

Gonzaga, Carlo, xxi, 454

Gonzaga, Ercole, xxxi, 86 note 3

Gonzaga, Ippolito, xxxi, 350, 354

Gonzaga, Ludovic, death of, xxxii, 14

Gonzaga, Vincenzo, xxi, 454

Gonzago, Federigo, xxxi, 86 note 2

Gonzales, Mariano, companion of Darwin, xxix, 333, 383

Gonzalo, in THE TEMPEST, Ariel and, xlvi, 406-7; at banquet, 420-1, 423; in island after wreck,

397-402, 419-20; Prospero and, 386, 434-6, 438; in shipwreck, 380, 381
Gonzalo, Don, xxi, 454-6, 487-9
Gooch, Dr., on puerperal fever, xxxviii, 241-2
Good, Arabian verse on sowing, xvi, 26; Browning on, xlii, 1147; Confucius on, xliv, 14 (25), 53 (12), 58 (11); for evil, ii, 153; xliv, 50 (36), 374 (27-35); for good's sake, ii, 163 (126); i, 375 (441); nature of, ii, 137 (59, 60); Pascal on search for, xlviii, 139, 156 (462); unlimited, xx, 207-8
Good and evil, Augustine, St., on, vii, 60; Emerson on, v, 227; Euripides on, viii, 334; Hobbes on, xxxiv, 351-2, 429; Marcus Aurelius on, ii, 220 (39), 242 (41), 256 (1), 283 (20), 293 (16); Milton on, iii, 212; Pope on, xl, 419-25; Shakespeare on, xlvi, 123
Good Breeding, Locke on, xxxvii, 76-7, 82, 83, 84-5, 128, 129, 132; Swift on, xxvii, 106-11 (see also Manners)
GOOD-BYE, by Emerson, xlii, 1292-3
Good-conscience, in PILGRIM'S PROGRESS, xv, 319
Good Friday, Walton on, xv, 408
Good Hope, Cape of, xxxiii, 233
GOOD MANNERS AND GOOD BREEDING, ESSAY ON, xxvii, 106-11
GOOD MORROW, THE, xl, 320-1
Good Nature, Emerson on, v, 219; Hobbes's definition of, xxxiv, 354; Locke on, xxxvii, 76, 126
Goodness, Cicero on, ix, 14, 15; Emerson on, v, 67; Pliny on, ix, 275; sensuous and ascetic, xxviii, 175-9; "thinks no ill," iv, 155; Tzu-chang on, xliv, 65 (2)
GOODNESS AND GOODNESS OF NATURE, iii, 34-6
Good Sense, Descartes on, xxxiv, 5
Good-Will, Buddha on, xlv, 612; Hobbes on, xxxiv, 354; Kant on, xxxii, 323-4, 344, 368, 370
Good-Will, in PILGRIM'S PROGRESS, xv, 29-32
Goody Blake, tale of, xxxix, 282
Gookins, Capt., xliii, 152, 154, 155
GOOSE WITH GOLDEN EGGS, fable of, xvii, 34
GOOSE-GIRL, THE, xvii, 184
Gorboduc, Sidney on, xxvii, 46
GORDON CASTLE, vi, 297-8
Gordon, Dr., on puerperal fever, xxxviii, 239-40
Gordon, Lord George, in Newgate, xxiv, 232
Gordon, Thomas, translator of Tacitus, xxxiii, 93
Gorges, Butshead, xxxiii, 349, 363, 369

Gorgias, Cicero on, xii, 245-6; native of Sicily, xxviii, 60; old age of, ix, 50; Plato on, ii, 5; riches of, x, 142
Gorgons, Æschylus on the, viii, 183
Goring, John, xxxiii, 237, 244, 245, 256, 259
Gorini, Lattanzio, xxxi, 360, 361, 379, 409
Gorner Glacier, xxx, 230, 237
Gosan, fertility of, xxxv, 328
Gospel, Bunyan's parable of the, xv, 34; Calvin on the, xxxix, 52; Jesus on the, xliv, 403 (16); Luther on the, xxxvi, 269, 270, 342-3, 364-5; Mohammed on the, xlv, 1013; Pascal on the, xlviii, 189 (568), 222 (658), 267 (742), 281 (798-800), 403, 404; Paul, St., on the, xxxix, 49
GOSPEL ACCORDING TO LUKE, xliv, 355-426
GOSS-HAWK, THE GAY, xl, 70-3
Gosson, Stephen, and Sidney, xxvii, 6
Gothel, Dame, the enchantress, xvii, 73-4
Gothinians, Tacitus on the, xxxiii, 120
Gothones, Tacitus on the, xxxiii, 120-1
Goths, learning despised by, xxxv, 404; on poetry, xxvii, 38-9
Gouast, Capt., xxxviii, 47-8
Goulburn, Henry, xliii, 273
Goujon, Jean, Hugo on, xxxix, 367
Gould, John, on cuckoos, xi, 273; on color of birds, 146
Gournay, Mlle. de, xlviii, 24 note; Montaigne and, xxxii, 109
Gournou, husbandry of, v, 207
Goveanus, Andreas, xxxii, 72
Government, Bacon on, iii, 14, 39-40; Bentham on criticism of, xxvii, 252-4, 257-8; better no, than cruel, xvii, 15; Burke on, xxiv, 208, 209-10, 413; Calvin on civil, xxxix, 54; checks to evil, v, 93; Confucius on, xliv, 7 (1), 8 (19), 44 (11), 69 (2); dangers of money-power in, xxv, 112; by discussion, xxviii, 478; duties of, x, 466-7; Emerson on, v, 250-4, 257-8, 260-1, 265; expenses of, x, 468-88; expenses of, unproductive, 283; Goldsmith on, and human happiness, xli, 544; Hamilton on efficiency of, xliii, 214-15; importance of, overrated, xxviii, 331; Jay on necessity of, xliii, 217; Jefferson on, 160; Lincoln on perpetuity of, 336-7; Lowell on forms of, xxviii, 477-8; Machiavelli on kinds of, xxxvi, 227-8, 229; Mill on powers of, xliii, 227-8, 229; Mill on form of, xxv, 111-12; Mill on science of, 103-6; Milton's plan

of, xxviii, 196; not an end, i, 365 (311); "of, by, and for the people," xliii, 441; Pascal on foundations of, xlviii, 108 (304), 110 (311); Penn on, i, 367-70; Pope on, xl, 440, 441; revenue of, x, 489-590; Rousseau on origin and forms of, xxxiv, 219-27; Ruskin on visible, xxviii, 132; self-defence first duty of, 446; superstition on, iii, 47; Swift on perfect form of, xxvii, 97; Vane on, xliii, 129; Washington on duty to, 257; Washington on, and liberty, 258

GOVERNMENT, ARBITRARY, by Winthrop, xliii, 90-112

Government Intervention, with capital, x, 351-2; with education, xxv, 315-17; with equality of employments, x, 126-52; with foreign commerce, 346-413; with freedom of contract, xxv, 311-13; with individual liberty, 211-17, 281-301; with industry, x, 466; with marriage, xxv, 317-18; with movements of precious metals, x, 328-34, 398-401; objections to, xxv, 318-25; with rates of interest, x, 101, 298-9; De Tocqueville on, xxv, 125; with trade, 303-11 with wages, x, 82, 150-1

Government Ownership, Mill on, xxv, 320-3; Smith on, x, 489-97

GOWDEN LOCKS OF ANNA, vi, 399

Gower, John, Dryden on, xxxix, 170; Johnson on, xxviii, 78; Sidney on, xxvii, 9

Gracchi, conciseness of the, ix, 214; Emerson on the, v, 191; Machiavelli on the, xxxvi, 36

Gracchus, Caius, with Tiberius, ix, 22; his tribuneship, 23

Gracchus, Tiberius, Blosius and, xxxii, 81; friends of, ix, 21, 22; revolution of, 23

Grace, Bunyan on, xv, 36-7, 66-8, 219; Dante on reception of, xx, 409; Kempis on, vii, 260, 336-41, 274-5; Milton on, iv, 141-2, 144; misinterpretations of doctrine of, xxxix, 48; Pascal on, xlviii, 142, 148, 168 (508), 171 (517), 172 (520-2), 219 (643), 333, 372; Penn on, i, 382 (528)

GRACE, A CHILD'S, xl, 343

GRACE AFTER DINNER, vi, 454

GRACE AFTER MEAT, vi, 490

GRACE BEFORE AND AFTER MEAT, vi, 490

GRACE BEFORE DINNER, vi, 454

Grace, in PILGRIM'S PROGRESS, xv, 283, 286

GRACE, JAMES, EPIGRAM ON, vi, 549

Grace, Robert, i, 60, 63-4, 65, 116

Gracefulness, beauty without, v, 317; Burke on, xxiv, 102

Graceless, Christian first named, xv, 50

Graces, De Quincey on the, xxvii, 336

Gradation, necessity of, in change, v, 313-14

Graeme, Sir John, and Barbara Allan, xl, 69

Graeme, Sir Robert, xlii, 1203-4, 1215, 1220, 1221-2, 1224

Graffiacan, the demon, xx, 90, 92

Grafting, xi, 310-11; Cicero on, ix, 66; in Elizabethan England, xxxv, 254; Webster on, xlvii, 742

Graham, George, xxv, 56-7, 66, 81

Graham, Marquis of, Burns on, vi, 167

GRAHAM, MISS, INSCRIPTION TO, vi, 528

Graham, James, MY DEAR AND ONLY LOVE, xl, 368-9

Graham, Robert, of Gartmore, IF DOUGHTY DEEDS, xli, 544-5

GRAHAM, ROBERT, of Fintry, EPISTLE TO, vi, 329-31

GRAHAM, ROBERT, SECOND EPISTLE TO, vi, 449

GRAHAM, ROBERT, BURNS TO, vi, 375

GRAHAM, WILLIAM, LINES ON, vi, 520

GRAHAME AND BEWICK, a ballad, xl, 123-30

Gram, the sword, xlix, 299, 307-8, 311, 327, 338, 349

Gramimond, horse of Valdabrun, xlix, 153

Grammar, Augustine, St., on rules of, vii, 20-1; of foreign languages, xxxvii, 147, 149, 153-6; Locke on study of, 153-6; Montaigne on study of, xxxii, 61-2; Penn on teaching, i, 338 (6, 8)

GRAMMARIAN'S FUNERAL, THE, xlii, 1126

Granacci, Elisabetta, mother of Cellini, xxxi, 8-10

Granacci, Stefano, xxxi, 8-9

Grand, M. le, xxxviii, 12

Grand-Pré, village of, xlii, 1353, 1354-5; burning of, 1381-2

Grand Jury, in U. S., xliii, 207 (5)

Grandeur (see Sublime)

Grandgent, Prof., on Dante, xx, 4

Grandison, Sir Charles, xxvii, 289

Grandonie, xlix, 151, 154-56

Grani, Sigurd's horse, xlix, 303, 319, 336-7, 360, 423

Granite, Darwin on, xxix, 301

Granmar, King, xlix, 292

GRANT, DAVID, LINES ON, vi, 373

Grant, Prof., on origin of species, xi, 12

Grant, Sir Robert, Hymn by, xlv, 552

Grant, U. S., terms of surrender at Appomattox, xliii, 447-8

Granulations, Lister on, xxxviii, 274-5

Granville, Lord, Burns on, vi, 56; on America, i, 166-7

Granville, Cardinal, xxxix, 91

Grape, Cicero on the, ix, 65-6

Grapes, Locke on, xxxvii, 21

GRAPES, SOUR, fable of, xvii, 23

Grasse, Count de, xliii, 180

GRASSHOPPER AND ANT, fable of, xvii, 25

GRASSHOPPER AND CRICKET, by Keats, xli, 919

Grasshoppers, Harrison on, xxxv, 367-8

Grassuccio, Il, xxxi, 34

Gratian, the monk, xx, 329 note 17

Gratilla, wife of Rusticus, ix, 274 note

Gratitude, Burns on emotions of, vi, 300 note; benefits, for small, iii, 36; to God, Kempis on, vii, 260; greed, go not together, and, xvii, 11; Hobbes on, xxxiv, 386, 423; Milton on, vi, 159; no, in the wicked, xvii, 17; rich, the tribute of, vi, 528; sign of noble souls, xvii, 20; Wordsworth on, xli, 665

Grave, Bryant's choice of a, xlii, 1268-9

Grave-digger, riddle of the, xlvi, 180-1

Gravelines, battle of, xix, 250

Gravitation, Bacon on, xxxiv, 102-3; Cartesian idea of, 116; Faraday on, xxx, 9-23; Helmholtz on law of, 182; illustrations of, 9, 10-11; universality of, 12-14, 18-20; illustration of laws of, 21-3; Kelvin on, 315-17, 295; Leibnitz on theory of, xi, 520; Locke on, xxxvii, 176; Newton's discovery of universal, xxxiv, 117-23; Newton on, xxxvii, 365 note; Newton's *Principia*, expounded in, xxxix, 157 note (see also Gravity)

Gravity, centre of, xxx, 14-18; moving force, 186-90, 197; old view of, xxxiv, 325

Gravity, the quality, Cicero on, in age, ix, 70; Hobbes on, xxxiv, 380; Penn on, i, 351 (119)

Gray, Asa, on holly, xi, 107; *Manual of Flora*, 125; on plants of New and Old Worlds, 416; on sexes in trees, 113; on spores, 524

Gray, Farquhar, vi, 190

Gray, Thomas, Arnold on, xxviii, 84; Bagehot on, 199, 200; THE BARD of, James Mill on, xxv, 16; Burns on, vi, 187; Hazlitt on, xxvii, 292; poems by, xxxix, 290; poems by, xl, 455-75; quoted, vi,

142; Wordsworth on, xxxix, 290, 309

Grease, and cow-pox, xxxviii, 153-5 and note, 190-2; disease of horses, 153, 155 note 3; and smallpox, 162-4, 193, 207-8

Great Acts, require great means, iv, 386

Great Britain, Burke on crown of, xxiv, 162-82; Freeman on, xxviii, 266-7; naval forces on Great Lakes, xliii, 283-5; realm of, iv, 47; Treaty of 1783 with, xliii, 185-91; Treaty of 1814 with, 273-82; Treaty of 1842 with, 299-308; wages in, x, 77-82; cost of living in, 82

Great-grace, in PILGRIM'S PROGRESS, xv, 130-1, 134-5

Great Harry, Longfellow on the, xlii, 1333

Great-Heart, in PILGRIM'S PROGRESS, xv, 176; at Mnason's house, 282, 284-5; fight with Monster, 286-7; kills Giant Despair, 290-2; encounter with Slay-good, 274-5; with Feeble-mind, 278-9; on Christian and Faithful, 280-1; experience with Mr. Fearing, 256-61; on Self-will, 263-5; with Gaius, 267-8; his riddle, 272; in Delectable Mountains, 293-4; meets Valiant, 299-305; in the Enchanted Ground, 305-8; on Madam Bubble, 312; parts with Christiana, 315; in PILGRIM'S PROGRESS, conducts the women, 214-24; fights with Grim the giant, 225; leaves the pilgrims, 226-7; returns to pilgrims, 241; in valley of Humiliation, 243-7; in valley of Death, 248-53; with Mr. Honest, 254-5

Great Lakes, naval forces on, xliii, 283-5

Great Men, acquiescence of, v, 64; Aristotle on, 398; belief in, natural, 202; Confucius on, xliv, 10 (9); illustrate their places, v, 132; independence of, 68; love and, iii, 28; love of, xlviii, 426; make great things, v, 18; obligations of, i, 412-14; Pascal on vices of, xlviii, 45 (103); past and present, v, 86; smiles of, vi, 197; worship of, Carlyle on, xxv, 410-11; worship of, meaning of, v, 19

Great Place, Bacon on, iii, 29-32 (see also Ambition); Confucius on, xliv, 13 (14); Dyer on, xl, 211; Epictetus on, ii, 131 (43); Penn on, i, 399-400; penalty of, v, 92-3

Great Riches, Luther on, xxxvi, 349

Great Sacrifice, Confucius on the, xliv, 10 (10, yi)

GREAT SPIRITS NOW ON EARTH SOJOURNING, xli, 921

Great works, from childless men, iii, 20, 22

Greatness, appeals to future, v, 71; Burns on, vi, 91; domesticity and, i, 73; essence of, v, 131; known by accident, xxv, 425-6; latent, 433-4; Mammon on, iv, 117; original, always, v, 201; pleasure of, xlviii, 110 (310); Pascal on, 66 (180), 121 (353), 127 (378), 131 (397), 279 (793), 382-8, 418; Pope on, xl, 447; Seneca on, iii, 16; Shakespeare on, xlvi 165; transitoriness of, xvi, 315-9, 326-7, 331-2, 334-6; true, Kempis on, vii, 217 (6); unconsciousness of, xxv, 422; unpopularity of, 419-21; Webster's fable of, xlvii, 776; quest of, 811; worldly price of, xviii, 435

GREATNESS, TRUE, by Watts, xl, 408

GRECIAN URN, ODE ON A, xli, 901-3

Greco, Giovanni, xxxi, 101 note 5

Greece, Ancient, works dealing with, l, 19, 26; Caxton on women of, xxxix, 11; Collins on music in, xli, 401; colonies of, x, 414; decline of military spirit in, xxvii, 392; decline of morality in, 397; freedom of speech in ancient, iii, 201, 203-4; history of, Carlyle on, xxv, 381-2 (see also Plutarch's Lives of Themistocles, Pericles, Aristides, Alcibiades, and Demosthenes); languages, study of in, xxxvii, 156, 174; letters and arts of, v, 155-6; literature of, later, xxvii, 359-60; literature of, Jesus on, iv, 408; patriotism in, strength of, xxvii, 415-16; Pliny on, ix, 349; religion, philosophy and art of, xxxix, 455-6; Roman dominion in, xxxvi, 18; Romans in, 11, 12, 13, 19, 77; Rousseau on cause of arts of, xxxiv, 181; Schiller on culture of, xxxii, 232-3, 237-8, 248; the Turkish dominion in, xxxvi, 10; Turkish power in, beginning of, 47 (see also Hellas)

GREECE, THE ISLES OF, xli, 833-5; remarks on, l, 25, 29

Greed, Confucius on, xliv, 57 (7); FABLE OF, xvii, 34; "goes not with gratitude," 11 (see also Covetousness)

Greedy, Justice, in NEW WAY TO PAY OLD DEBTS, xlvii, Furnace on, 827; at Lady Allworth's 830-2; Marrall and Overreach on, 835-6; at Overreach's, 854-5, 856, 857, 860, 861-2, 863, 864, 865; with Tapwell, 878-9

Greek Church, Freeman on, xxviii, 241; Luther on, xxxvi, 318

Greek Classics, xxxii, 127

Greek Comedy, Hugo on, xxxix, 364-5

Greek Drama, debt of, to Homer, xiii, 7; Hugo on, xxxix, 358-9, 364-5, 377, 403; Voltaire on, 382

Greek Dramas, l, 19, 32

Greek Hymns, xlv, 553-7

Greek Language, Carlyle on, xxv, 381; Emerson on, v, 267; Huxley on, xxviii, 221-9; Locke on, xxxvii, 71-2, 81-2, 136, 155, 174, 178-81; Mill on, xxv, 25; Montaigne on, xxxii, 67, 68; Milton on, iii, 249, 253-4; More on, xxxvi, 145; study of, Augustine, St., on, vii, 17

Greek Learning, study of, iii, 209-10

Greek Literature, Hugo on, xxxix, 357-9, 364-5

Greek Names, xii, 161-2

Greek Philosophers, Cudworth on, xxxvii, 177

Greek Philosophy, divisions of, xxxii, 317

Greek Science, Huxley on, xxviii, 227

Greek Tragic Dance, Coleridge on, xxvii, 272

Greek Tragedy, decay of, viii, 418 (see THE FROGS)

Greeks, and barbarians, xxxvii, 156, 174; calendar of the, xxxiii, 7; chronology of the, xxxiv, 130; in Egypt, xxxiii, 90; Freeman on the modern, xxviii, 273, 281, 275-6; Goethe on culture of the, xxxix, 264-5; poetry among the, xxvii, 11-12; Schiller on art of the, xxxii, 267; Taine on the, xxxix, 435-6, 448

GREEN GROW THE RASHES, vi, 50-1

GREEN LINNET, THE, xli, 657-8

Greene, Robert, CONTENT, xl, 289

Greenhead Ghyll, xli, 630, 642

Greenland, Christianity in, xliii, 13, 14; colonized by Eric the Red, 5, 6; subsidence in, xxxviii, 428

Greenough, Horatio, Emerson on, v, 328-9

Greenvile, John, xxxiii, 349, 363, 369

Greenville, Sir Richard, xxxiii, 234

GREENWOOD TREE, UNDER THE, xl, 268-9

Gregory I, St., the Great, on angels, xx, 407; and the Angles, v, 361, xxviii, 48; and England, xxxvi, 136; heathen antiquities destroyed by, iii, 144; on sin, xxxvi, 283

Gregory, St., Nazianzen, Basil, St., and, students at Athens, xxviii, 53-4, 56-62; *Christ Suffering*, iv, 416

Gregory VII, and Henry IV, xxxvi, 308 note 25

Gregory Bay, the climate at, xxix, 247

Gregson, Mr., on puerperal fever, xxxviii, 240-1

Grendel, in BEOWULF, ravages of, xlix, 8-10, 13, 19; and Beowulf, 17-18, 22, 24, 25-9, 32, 41, 61-2, 64; hand of, 28, 32-3, 42; head of, 50, 51, 52; mother of, 41-50, 65

Grenville, Lord, and Burke, xxiv, 402

Grenville, Sir Richard, xlii, 1041-6

Gresham, Mr., and More, xxxvi, 122

Gretchen, in FAUST (see Margaret)

GRETHEL, HANSEL AND, xvii, 82-9

Greville, Fulke, Hazlitt on, xxvii, 282-3

Grey, half brother to Richard III, xxxix, 79, 80

Grey, Dr., on Shakespeare, xxxix, 252

Greyhounds, Harrison on, xxxv, 369-70

Grief, alone and with mates, xlvi, 262; Augustine, St., on, vii, 30, 52; beauty's canker, xlvi, 394; Browning, E. B., on, xli, 964; Burke on, xxiv, 34-5; Coleridge on, xli, 745; desires to be alone, xlvii, 486; Hobbes on, xxxiv, 353; instructs the wise, xviii, 403; Marcus Aurelius on, ii, 284 (25), 285 (28), 287 (34); physical effects of, xxxviii, 131; Shakespeare on, and joy, xlvi, 144; Shakespeare on silent, 362; and tears, xxvii, 299; "what need a man forestall his," iv, 56

Griefs, reduced by sympathy, iii, 72

Griego, John, xxxiii, 218

Grieve, James, Epitaph on, vi, 53

Griffith, John, i, 192

Grifir, prophecy of, xlix, 308; in the Edda, 267

Griflet, Sir, xxxv, 134

Grifolino, of Arezzo, in Hell, xx, 124 and note

Grignapoco, the bravo, xxi, 126

Grignon, R. S., translator of Luther, xxxvi, 2

Grim, the giant, xv, 224-5

Grimes, Sir Thos., and Dr. Donne, xv, 362

Grimhild, wife of Giuki, xlix, 331; and Sigurd, 333, 334, 335; and Brynhild, 336, 339, 341, 343; and Gudrun, 360, 361, 362, 425-6, 427,

429; remarks on magic potion of, 267

Grimm, Baron, on Shakespeare, xxxix, 335

Grimm, Hermann, Emerson and, v, 4

Grimm, Jakob, xvii, 48

Grimm, Wilhelm, xvii, 48

Grimms' HOUSEHOLD TALES, xvii, 47-232; remarks on, 2

Gripe-man, the schoolmaster, xv, 106

Gripir, the prophecy of, xlix, 267

Grisi, Julia, in England, v, 430

Griso, in THE BETROTHED, xxi, 110-12, 125-8, 186-7, 190, 193; despatched to Monza, 194-6; finds Lucia, 304; with Rodrigo in the plague, 557-8, 560-2; his death, 563

Grisolan, in DUCHESS OF MALFI, xlvii, 725, 726, 744, 809, 813

Grocyn, Doctor, xxxvi, 94

Grolier, Jean, xxxi, 337 note 1

Grose, Francis, Capt., epigram on, vi, 371; lines on, 369, 411

Grote, George, xxv, 80, 81; Mill on, 51-2, 196; in Parliament, 126; and *Westminster Review*, 65-6

Grotesque, Hugo on the, xxxix, 363-70, 374-5; origin of word, xxxi, 63

Ground-rent, how determined, x, 511; taxes on, 514-16

Groups, of organic beings, xi, 142-3; sudden appearance of specific, 354-9

Grout, Sir Jenken, epitaph of, v, 221-2

Grove's Battery, xxx, 78

Growth, compensation of, xi, 158-60; laws of, defined, 222; laws of, effects of, 225-7; law of nature, v, 106-7

Grub Street, Swift on, xxvii, 126

Gryphon, symbol of Christ, xx, 267 note 10

Gryphons, Æschylus on the, viii, 183-4 and note 55

Grypus, name of, xii, 162 note

Guachos, compared with Guasos, xxix, 275-6

Guadagni, Felice, xxxi, 182-3, 196, 209

GUADALUPE HIDALGO, TREATY OF, xliii, 309-26

Gualdrada, Dante on, xx, 68 note 1

Guam, cession of, xliii, 470 (2), 471 (5), 473

Guanaco, Darwin on the, xxix, 179-82

Guardian Angels (see Tutelary A.)

Guardians, Hobbes on power of, xxxiv, 432; Mohammed on duties of, xlv, 980-1

Guascar, xxxiii, 313, 327, 331, 341

Guasconti, and Cellini, xxxi, 29-33

Guasos, of Chili, xxix, 275-6

Guayatecas, Darwin on, xxix, 298-308

Guayna-capac, xxxiii, 313, 327, 328-9

GUDE ALE KEEPS THE HEART ABOON, vi, 551

GUDEWIFE, COUNT THE LAWIN, vi, 401

Gudrid, the Norsewoman, xliii, 11, 14, 15, 16, 21

Gudrun, at Alfscourt, xlix, 360, 425-6; Atli and, 362-3, 373-5, 428-32, 441-3, 451-2; Brynhild, quarrel with, 339-42, 344; daughter by Sigurd, 358; death of, 379, 446-9; dream of, 331-3; drink of, 361, 427; future foretold, 358-9, 408-10; Gunnar and, 372, 440; married to Jonaker, 376, 444; Morris on, 273; Renan on, xxxii, 149; runes to brethren, xlix, 364-5, 435-7; Sigurd, her marriage to, 335-6, 396-422; at Sigurd's death, 349-57, 401-2, 418, 419, 423-4; story of, remarks on, 267, 268; Swanhild avenged by, 378, 446, 450-2

GUDRUN, FIRST LAY OF, xlix, 351-7; remarks on, 268

GUDRUN, SECOND LAY OF, xlix, 422-32

GUDRUN, THE WHETTING OF, xlix, 444-9; remarks on, 268

Guelfs, and Ghibellines in Italy (see numerous notes to Dante); opposed to papacy, xx, 308 note 8, 310 note 21

Guenevere (see Guinevere)

GUENEVERE, THE DEFENCE OF, xlii, 1230-40

Guerra, Pablo de la, xxiii, 406, 415

Guest, Lady Charlotte, xxxii, 145, 154-5

Guevarra, Fernando de, xiv, 516

GUIANA, DISCOVERY OF, Raleigh's, xxxiii, 311-94

Guiana, advantages of, xxxiii, 390-2; drunkenness in, 332-3; extent of, 366; first knowledge of, 313; French attempts on, 336-7; gold of, 316-18, 370-1, 379-80; Milton on, iv, 333; productions and climate of, xxxiii, 389-90; Raleigh's exploration of, 346-86; religions and customs of, 388; riches of, 327, 328, 332, 335, 337, 371; settled from Peru, 327-8, 330; slave and other trades to, 345-6; Spanish attempts to conquer, 330-6, 338-46; tribes of, 386-7; wealth of, 313, 388-9

Guicciardine, Montaigne on, xxxii, 103-4

Guicciardini, Francesco, xxxi, 425 note

Guid-guid, Darwin on the, xxix, 306

Guidi, Giacopo, xxxi, 423-4

Guidi, Guido, xxxi, 311-12, 333, 350-1, 363

Guido, Da Vinci and, xxxix, 450; Hazlitt on, xxvii, 293; portrait of Beatrice Cenci, xviii, 279

Guidoguerra, in Hell, xx, 68 and note 1

Guildenstern, in HAMLET, xlvi, 116-17, 123-7, 131, 133-4, 140, 147-9, 150, 160, 161, 173, 189, 198

Guilds, labor, x, 126-38

Guillotine, in Elizabethan England, xxxv, 386

Guilt, Manzoni on, xxi, 339; Shakespeare on, xlvi, 166; what quick eyes has, xviii, 72

Guilt, in PILGRIM'S PROGRESS, xv, 130, 134-6

Guines, Earl of, Constable of France, at Caen, xxxv, 7, 11-14

Guinevere, and Launcelot, xiv, 100, 515; xx, 353 note 2; xxxv, 110, 121, 139 (see also GUENEVERE, DEFENCE OF); in HOLY GRAIL, xxxv, 114, 119, 120, 121; Renan on, xxxii, 149

Guinicelli, Guido, xx, 191 note 5, 254-5

Guion, type of temperance, iii, 213

Guiscard, Robert, xx, 116 note; in Paradise, 363

Guise, Duke of, at Boulogne, xxxvii, 18; at Danvilliers, 20-1; at Metz, 24, 25, 26, 27, 28 9, 30, 32, 33, 34, 35; at Moncontour, 54; murder of, xxxix, 377

Guittone, Dante on, xx, 255

Guizot, M., in England, v, 390-1

Gulf Stream, Dana on the, xxiii, 361

Gulliver's Travels, Thackeray on, xxviii, 19-21

Gulike, country of, xxxvi, 145, 146

Gumila, the Jesuit, x, 422

Gummere, Francis B., translator of BEOWULF, xlix, 3-4

Gun-cotton, xxx, 58 note

Gunnar, son of Giuki, xlix, 331; Atli and, 364, 365, 367, 433-6; Brynhild and, 336-7, 339, 341, 342-4, 345, 357-9, 403-11, 419-21; editor's remarks on story of, 267; Gudrun and, 360, 361, 408, 426; imprisoned, 370-1, 438, 439-40; Oddrun and, 358, 457, 460, 461-4; Sigurd and, 334, 335, 347-9, 350, 355-6, 398-400, 402-3, 417-18, 451; in the worm-close, 372, 440, 463-4

Gunning, Elizabeth and Maria, v, 315-16

Gunpowder, combustibility of, compared with iron, xxx, 76; force of, 198; invention of, Don Quixote on, xiv, 398-9; invention of, effect on civilization, x, 471

Gunpowder Plot, attributed to Machi-

avelli, xxvii, 381; discovery of, iii, 281 note

Gunshot Wounds, Lister on, xxxviii, 280; Paré on, 11-12, 40, 55

Günther, Dr., authority on fishes, xi, 242; on fish, 427-8

Gurney, in EDWARD II, xlvi, 70, 72-4, 77-8, 80-1

Gusman, Felix, father of St. Dominic, xx, 338 note 18

Gustavus Adolphus, hymn attributed to, xlv, 572

Guthlaf, xlix, 35 note 5, 38

Gutters, Franklin on, i, 127

Guttorm, son of Giuki, xlix, 331, 348, 349, 359, 400-1, 418; on royalty of truth, v, 388

Guy of Warwick, xiv, 101

Guyard, the groom, xxxviii, 21-2

Guyon, Sir, xxxix, 66, 68

Guyot, quoted, xxviii, 418-19

Gwendolen, chess-board of, xxxii, 152

Gwrhyr Gwalstawd Ieithoedd, xxxii, 157-9

Gyara, ii, 132 (45) note

Gyas, the Latin, xiii, 337

Gyas, the Trojan, xiii, 83, 97, 186-91

Gyges, death of, xiii, 323

Gylippus, Plutarch on, xii, 61, 131

Gylippus, sons of, in the ÆNEID, xiii, 404

Gynæcea, goddess, xii, 281

Habbab, xlv, 923 note 8

Habeas Corpus, Johnson on writ of, xliii, 457; privilege of, 198 (2)

Haberdasher, Chaucer's, xl, 21

Habington, William, Poems by, xl, 257-9

Habit(s), Bacon on, formation of, iii, 102; Burke on, xxiv, 88; changed, exhibited by insects, xi. 187; changed without change of structure, 189-90; diversification of, 123-5, 187-89; in eating, xxxvii, 18, 19, 20; endurance of cold and heat as a, 10-11; Epictetus on evil, ii, 144 (75); errors due to, xlviii, 37; Goethe on, xix, 72; hereditary, in plants, xi, 152; Hume on, xxxvii, 339-41, 349, 394; inherited, effect of, xi, 29, 267-70; instinct, compared with, 262-3; Kempis on, vii, 284 (5); Locke on importance of, xxxvii, 4, 15, 20, 45-6, 93-4, 97-8, 98, 119-20; perfects qualities of mind, xlviii, 422; Shakespeare on, xlvi, 158; of sleeping, xxxvii, 22-3; teaching of, 46-7; ten times nature, v, 385; transitional, xi, 184-7; variation due to, 10

HAD I A CAVE, vi, 498

HAD I THE WYTE, SHE BADE ME, vi, 566-7

Hades, Æneas's visit to, xiii, 220-33; Rhampsinitos in, xxxiii, 63; Socrates's description of, ii, 110; Ulysses's visit to, xxii, 152-68

'Hadigah, wife of Mohammed, xlv, 886

Hadley's Quadrant, inventor of, i, 60

Hadrian, Emperor, enviousness of, iii, 25; Marcus Aurelius on, ii, 260 (25), 262 (37)

Haeckel, Prof., on phylogeny, xi, 472

Haemmerlein, Thomas (see Kempis, Thomas à)

Hæmon, in ÆNEID, xiii, 320, 331; in ANTIGONE, viii, 260-1, 263-7, 279, 281

Hæthcyn, in BEOWULF, xlix, 74, 75, 87

Hafiz, quotation from, v, 301, 463

Hafsah, wife of Mohammed, xlv, 1006 note 1

Haggai, prophecies of, xlviii, 259-60

HAGGIS, ADDRESS TO A, vi, 266-7

Haidinger's, Brushes, xxx, 279-80

Hail-storms, Darwin on, xxix, 127-8

Hainault, John of, in Crecy campaign, xxxv, 10, 15, 21, 28, 30; in EDWARD II, xlvi, 53-5, 56, 57, 60

HAIR, TO A LOCK OF, xli, 757-8

Hair, St. Paul on long, xlv, 516 (14-15); teeth and, relation of, xi, 30, 156

Hake, King, death of, v, 357

Hakewill, Wordsworth on, xxxix, 334 note

Hakluyt, Richard, Drayton on, xl, 232; on geography and chronology, xxx, 339

Haldeman, Prof., on species, xi, 13

Halden, Henry of the, xxvi, 388-9

Haldor, character of, v, 400-1

Haldudo, John, in DON QUIXOTE, xiv, 41

Hales, Chief Justice, on cost of living, x, 81

Hales, the irrefragable, xxviii, 48

Halesus, in ÆNEID, xiii, 268, 338, 340-1

Halifax, punishment of theft in, xxxv, 386

Halifax, Lord, and Addison, xxvii, 169-70; Voltaire on, xxxiv, 150

Halitherium, Darwin on, xi, 378

Halitherses, in ODYSSEY, xxii, 26-7, 240, 343

Halius, son of Alcinous, xxii, 107; dance of, 114

Halket, George, LOGIE O' BUCHAN, xli, 585

Hall, Bishop, Encomium of, iii, 200 and note; Walton on, xv, 358

Hall, David, partner of Franklin, i, 119

Hall, Jim, in Two Years Before the Mast, xxiii, 26, 419

Hall, Sir John, xlii, 1220

Hallam, Henry, Emerson on, v, 456-7

Halley, Edmund, on comets, xxxiv, 120; Newton on, xxxix, 159

Halloween, vi, 116-125

Halonesus, speech on, xii, 204 note

Ham, son of Noah, Burns on, vi, 172; Milton on, iv, 348

Haman, minister of Pharaoh, xvi, 335 note 9; Mohammed on, xlv, 944, 945

Hamburgh, taxation at, x, 522; trading enterprises of, 490, 492

Hamdir, in the Volsung Tale, xlix, 376, 378, 380; in the Edda, 444, 445, 446

Hamdir, The Lay of, xlix, 450-6; remarks on, 268

Hame, Hame, Hame, xli, 802

Hamilcar, and Agathocles, xxxvi, 30

Hamilton, Alexander, article in the Federalist, xliii, 213-16; and Washington's Farewell Address, 250 note

Hamilton, Andrew, i, 41, 42, 63, 66

Hamilton, Duchess of, beauty of, v, 315-6

Hamilton, Gavin, Burns on, vi, 75, 77, 111; Epitaph for, 230; dedication to, 221-4; extempore epistle to, 233-4; farewell to, 235

Hamilton, Gavin, vi, 208-9

Hamilton, Mary: a ballad, xl, 118-20

Hamilton, William, The Braes of Yarrow, xlii, 586-9

Hamilton, Sir William, Mill on philosophy of, xxv, 173-7

Hamish, The Revenge of, xlii, 1474-9

Hamlet, Prince of Denmark, Arnold on, xxviii, 73; Bagehot on, 198-9; in churchyard, xlvi, 181-7; Claudius and, 152, 162-3, 175-8, 192-4, 197; death of, 197-8; scene with Gertrude, 153-9; the ghost and, 105-8; Guildenstern's report on, 133-4; Horatio and, 104-5, 140-1, 173, 188-90; Laertes, duel with, 194-6; pretended madness, 115-16; Ophelia and, 100-1, 103-4, 120, 135-7; at Ophelia's funeral, 186-7; in the original story, 86; Osric and, 190-3; at the play, 141-3, 144, 145-7; players and, 128-31, 138-9; Polonius and, 121-3, 127-8, 153; with Rosencrantz and Guildenstern, 123-7; Ruskin on, xxviii, 142; soliloquy of, xlvi, 135; soliloquy, Lamb on, xxvii, 315-16; soliloquy translated by Voltaire, xxxiv, 135-6

Hamlet, Tragedy of, xlvi, 87-199; editorial remarks on, 86; Johnson on, xxxix, 225, 237; Lamb on stage representation of, xxvii, 317-19, 320-2, 330; Thoreau on, xxviii, 426; Voltaire on, xxxiv, 134

Hammon, Master, in Shoemaker's Holiday, xlvii, 461-2, 463-4, 471-3, 483-6, 490, 500-2

Hammon, the god, iv, 14 (22)

Hamor, and Jacob, xv, 110

Hananiah, death of, xlviii, 291 (827)

Hancock, Gen., at Gettysburg, xliii, 353, 355, 356, 361, 367, 372, 375, 380, 381, 384, 387, 390, 392, 393, 415, 431-2; Haskell on, 381-2, 428

Hancock, John, signer of Declaration, xliii, 164

Handsome Nell, vi, 19-20

Hanmer, Sir Thomas, xxxix, 249

Hannibal, Cervantes on, xiv, 513; Cicero on, ix, 18; Fabius and, 49; Machiavelli on, xxxvi, 58; story of, before Rome, iii, 237

Hans in Luck, story of, xvii, 179

Hansel and Grethel, xvii, 82-9

Happiness, Augustine, St., on, vii, 184-6; Bacon on highest, iii, 8; Browne on, 346-7; Burns on, vi, 325; Dante's allegory of, xx, 223; Epictetus on, ii, 118 (3), 152 (94), 162 (122), 164 (129), 170 (147), 171 (151); Franklin on, i, 58, 91, 128; Goldsmith on, xli, 528, 534, 544; Kant on, xxxii, 323, 325-6, 329, 346, 348-9, 373; Kempis on, vii, 288-9; Locke on, xxxvii, 9; Marcus Aurelius on, ii, 202 (8), 211 (12), 223 (51), 233 (34); Mill's theory of, xxv, 94; More on, xxxvi, 207-16; Pascal on, xlviii, 54, 58, 63 (165), 64 (170), 138, 150 (437), 157, 418; Penn on, i, 360-1; Pliny on greatest, ix, 351; Pope on, xl, 415-16, 441-50; Rousseau on search for, xxxiv, 287; Shakespeare on, xlvi, 123; Surrey on, xl, 197-8; Washington on, and virtue, xliii, 243; Wotton on, xl, 295-6

Happiness, That We Should Not Judge of Our, Until After Our Death, xxxii, 5-8

Happy Insensibility, xli, 898-9

Happy Life, Character of a, xl, 295-6

Happy Life, Means to Attain, xl, 197-8

Happy Warrior, Character of the, xli, 672-4

Hardiness, Locke on, xxxvii, 100-1, 106-8

Haquin, king of Norway, xx, 370 note 16

Harapha, of Gath, with Samson, iv, 445-50

Harbors, expense of maintaining, x, 475

Harcourt, Godfrey of, in French invasion, xxxv, 5-9, 12-14, 16, 18, 23, 29

Hardcastle, in SHE STOOPS TO CONQUER, with Mrs. Hardcastle and Tony, xviii, 203-6; with Kate, 206-7; trains his servants, 214-15; receives Marlow and Hastings, 218-22; discusses Marlow with Kate, 232-4, 242-3; catches Marlow with Kate, 242-3; with Marlow and his servants, 246-8; with Sir Charles Marlow, 256-9; with Tony and wife in the garden, 262-4; sees Kate and Marlow, 265-6; reconciled to Marlow, 267; to Hastings, 267-8; gives Kate to Marlow, 269

Hardcastle, Kate, in SHE STOOPS TO CONQUER, with father, hears of young Marlow, xviii, 206-8; with Miss Neville, 208-9; meets Marlow, 225-7; discusses him with her father, 232-4; pretends to be barmaid, 238-9; with Marlow as barmaid, 240-2; caught by her father, 242-3; undeceives Marlow and tries to detain him, 248-50; tells of Marlow's love for her, 259; besought by Marlow, 265-6; makes herself known, 267; united to Marlow, 269

Hardcastle, Mrs., in SHE STOOPS TO CONQUER, at home with Hardcastle and Tony, xviii, 203-6; Miss Neville and, 208-9; with Hastings, 228-9; with Tony and Miss Neville, 229-31, 250-1; and Miss Neville's jewels, 235-8; recovers jewels, 244-5; Tony's letter and, 252-3; orders Constance to aunt's, 253, 255-6; fooled by Tony, 261-4; plans finally upset, 267-9

Hardness, Berkeley on, xxxvii, 223

Hardships, Channing on value of, xxviii, 324-5

Hardwicke, Dr., xxxviii, 175

Hare, Mr., system of personal representation, xxv, 165-6

HARE AND TORTOISE, fable of, xvii, 39

HARE WITH MANY FRIENDS, fable of, xvii, 40

HARE-MARK IN MOON, story of, xlv, 712-16

HARES AND FROGS, fable of, xvii, 16

Hargreaves, James, inventor of spinning-jenny, v, 410

Harleian Miscellanies, Emerson on, v, 127

Harlequin, Thackeray on, xxviii, 5

Harley, Burns on, vi, 274

Harm, Marcus Aurelius on, ii, 215 (7), 230 (22)

Harmonia, wife of Cadmus, viii, 412

Harmony, Confucius on, xliv, 61 (11); Dryden on, xl, 398

HARP OF THE NORTH, FAREWELL, xli, 773-4

HARP THAT ONCE THROUGH TARA'S HALLS, xli, 840

Harpalus, Demosthenes and, xii, 218

Harpalyce, in ÆNEID, xiii, 86

Harpies, Æneas and the, xiii, 138-9; in Dante's HELL, xx, 55

Harpocras, physician, ix, 377, 378

Harras, Rudolph der, in WILHELM TELL, xxvi, 428-34, 454-9

Harriers, Harrison on, xxxv, 369

Harris, John, with Drake, xxxiii, 184

Harris, Tom, friend of Dana, xxiii, 190, 199-204, 272, 279, 418

Harrison, Benjamin, and Hawaii, xliii, 464 note

Harrison, William, collaborator of Holinshed, xxxv, 228; DESCRIPTION OF ELIZABETHAN ENGLAND, 227-404

Harrowing, origin of word, ix, 65

Harry, David, i, 53, 6t 7

Harsnett, Dr., and Dr. Donne, xv, 348

Hart, Christ typified by a, xxxv, 204; defined, 361

HART AND HUNTER, fable of, xvii, 20

HART IN THE OX-STALL, fable of, xvii, 22-3

Hart, Sir Robert, at Otterburn, xxxv, 93, 102

Harte, Bret, THE REVEILLE, xlii, 1482

Hartley, David, Hazlitt on, xxvii, 291; Mill on philosophy of, xxv, 49

Hartlib, Samuel, iii, 246; Cowley on, xxvii, 70; Milton on, iii, 247

Hartsocher, Voltaire on, xxxiv, 129

Harun Er-Rashid, in ARABIAN NIGHTS, xvi, 65-71, 107, 120-1, 220-1, 225-36, 240-1, 302-5

Harut, the fallen angel, xvi, 62 note

HARVARD CLASSICS, Editor's Introduction, l, 3-14; Reader's Guide to, 17-72

HARVARD COMMEMORATION ODE, xlii, 1458-69

Harvey, William, discoverer of circulation of blood, xxxiv, 129; Descartes on, 42 note; life and works of, xxxviii, 64; ON MOTIONS OF HEART AND BLOOD, 65-147

Hasdrubal, Chaucer on wife of, xl, 49

Hasiy Ibn Wâil, xlv, 923 note

Haskell, Frank A., ACCOUNT OF

GETTYSBURG, xliii, 347-440; life of, 347 note

Haste, half-sister of delay, xlii, 1035; "from the Devil," xvi, 165; "make, slowly," xix, 379; Penn on excessive, i, 365 (300), 398 (76-8); "that mars all decency," xx, 155

Hastings, in SHE STOOPS TO CONQUER, admirer of Miss Neville, xviii, 208-9, 217-18; at the alehouse, 211-14; arrival at Hardcastle's, 216-18; with Mr. Hardcastle, 218-22; with Miss Neville, 222-3; carries on jest with Marlow, 224; presents Marlow to Kate, 225-6; with Mrs. Hardcastle, 228-9; with Tony, 230-2, 235; plans to elope with Constance, 243; learns loss of jewels, 245; his letter to Tony, 253-4; denounces Tony, 254; and Marlow, 255; hears Miss Neville gone, 256; recovers Constance through Tony, 260-1; with Miss Neville, 264; wins consent to marriage, 268-9

Hastings, Lord, Raleigh on, xxxix, 78, 79, 80

Hastings, Warren, Burke on, xxiv, 6; on Oriental literature, v, 464; Sheridan and, xviii, 104

Hatch, mate on "Alert," xxiii, 422

Hate-good, Lord, in PILGRIM'S PROGRESS, xv, 97-101

Hate-light, Mr., in PILGRIM'S PROGRESS, xv, 101-2

Haterius, Augustus on, xxvii, 59

Hatred, Buddha on, xlv, 685, 686-7; Confucius on, xliv, 62 (24); Hume on, xxxvii, 342; Marcus Aurelius on, ii, 291 (8); Pascal on, xlviii, 154 (451); Penn on, i, 363 (269)

Hats, Locke on, xxxvii, 11, 14

HAUNTED PALACE, THE, xlii, 1274

Hauteclere, sword of Oliver, xlix, 144, 150, 160

Hauter, axiom of, xxxviii, 217 note 2

Havre de Grace, siege of, xxxviii, 51-2

Hawaiian Islands, Annexation of, xliii, 464-6

Hawker, Robert Stephen, poem by, xlii, 1157

Hawkins, Sir John Drake and, xxxiii, 126, 133, 235; Melendez and, 265; at San Juan, 334

Hawkins, William, in Cape Verde Islands, xxxiii, 246

Hawks, carrion, xxix, 66-70; guided to prey by sight, xi, 98; sacred in Egypt, xxxiii, 36, 37

Hay, John, Convention with Panama, xliii, 479

Hay, Lord, ambassador of King James, xv, 339, 351

Hays, Gen. Alex., at Gettysburg, xliii, 358, 365, 408

Hayes, Edward, captain of "Golden Hind," xxxiii, 270, 282, 301, 306; VOYAGE TO NEWFOUNDLAND, 271, 308

Hazard, Capt., at Gettysburg, xliii, 396

Hazing, on board ship, xxiii, 56 note

Hazlitt, William, Carlyle on, xxv, 361; life and writings, xxvii, 280; PERSONS ONE WOULD WISH TO HAVE SEEN, 281-95; Stevenson on, xxviii, 299-300

Head, and limbs, related, xi, 29; Locke on coverings for the, xxxvii, 11, 14

Head, Sir Francis, on America, xxviii, 419

Heady, Mr., in PILGRIM'S PROGRESS, xv, 101-2

Healfdene, xlix, 6

HEALING QUESTION, A, xlii, 126-46

Health, Antoninus's care of, ii, 197; Burke on pleasure in idea of, xxiv, 36, 38; Carlyle on, xxv, 423-4, 435-6; Carlyle on care of, 402-3; Channing on, xxviii, 366-7; Descartes on, xxxiv, 50; Epictetus on, care of, ii, 160 (118); Hunt on, xxvii, 307; More on, xxxvi, 213-14, 215; Locke on importance of, xxxvii, 9, 10; Pascal on use and misuse of, xlviii, 374; Pope on, xl, 443; rules of, xxxvii, 10-28; unconsciousness of, xxv, 333-48; Woolman on, care of, i, 244-5

HEALTH, by Pinkney, xxviii, 394-5

HEALTH, TO ANE I LOE DEAR, vi, 590

HEALTH, HERE'S HIS, IN WATER, vi, 191

HEALTH, HERE'S TO THY, vi, 28-9

HEALTH, REGIMEN OF, Bacon's, iii, 85-6

HEALTH TO THEM THAT'S AWA, vi, 477

Heardred, xlix, 67, 72 and note 3

Hearing, art of, ii, 147 (81); speaking and, 182 (6)

Heart, Descartes on motion of the, xxxiv, 39-45; in the fœtus, xxxviii, 135, 139, 143-4; Harvey on motions and uses of the, 64-147; Harvey on structure of the, 138-45, 147; importance of the, 145; in lower animals, 137-8, 140; lungs and, 68, 73-6, 93, 94, 95-9, 105, 138-9; nourishment of the, 106; the seat of life, 89

HEART'S COMPASS, xlii, 1227

HEART'S HOPE, xlii, 1225

Hearth-money, x, 517

Heat, Berkeley on real existence of, xxxvii, 205-10, 211; chemical action of, xxx, 218; dependent on expansion and compression, 222-3; Descartes on, xxxiv, 37-8; effect of, on cohesion, xxx, 38-40, 42; evolved from chemical affinity, 81-2; Faraday on, 59-61; generated by friction and impact, 205-6; Locke on endurance of, xxxvii, 10-11, 14; mechanical equivalent of, xxx, 207-9; mechanical power produced by, 198-202, 204-5; mechanical theory of, 209-10, 242; from moonlight, 273; as motion, theory of, 209-10; old theory of, 202-4; Pascal on, xlviii, 125 (368); produced by combustion of carbon, xxx, 210-11; produced by combustion of hydrogen, 212, 213-14; produced by electrical currents, 215; production of, in New Atlantis, iii, 186; radiant, xxx, 271-2; transference and conduction of, 70-2

Heaven, Augustine, St., on, vii, 158-9; Bernard of Morlaix on, xlv, 560-1; Browne on, iii, 314-15; Browne on hope of, 312-13, 317-18; Browning on, xlii, 1114; Bunyan on, xv, 18, 163-4, 232; Burns on, vi, 146; compared to mustard seed, iii, 77; Darwin on, xxix, 301; Fitzgerald on, xli, 982; gate of, Milton on, iv, 150-1; Hobbes on, xxxiv, 359; Kempis on, vii, 325 (3, 4), 326, 330; Luther on, xxxvi, 266; Milton on, iv, 198, 199, 200, 207; Rousseau on, xxxiv, 272; saints in, vii, 346-7

HEAVENLY BODIES, REVOLUTIONS OF THE, xxxix, 55-60

Heavens, Dante's ten, xx, 294 note 3

Hebe, and Heracles, xxii, 167; Keats on, xli, 896; references to, iv, 22, 32; xl, 249

Heber, Reginald, Hymns by, xlv, 577-9

Hebrew Literature, Milton on, iv, 408; Wordsworth on, xxxix, 321

Hebrew Prophets, piety and grossness of the, v, 175

HEBREW SACRED WRITINGS, xliv, 71-354

Hebrews, Raleigh on history of, xxxix, 118 (see also Israelites, Jews)

Hebron, seat of giants, iv, 422

Hecataios, the historian, xxxiii, 73

Hecate, in MACBETH, xlvi, 345, 348; Virgil on, xiii, 220

Hectic Fever, Machiavelli on, xxxvi, 12

Hector, and Ajax, v, 97; Burke on, xxiv, 134; Caxton on, xxxix, 21; Chaucer on, xl, 43; in Dante's HELL, xx, 20; Dares Phrygius on, xiii, 34; ghost of, appears to Æneas, 112-13; Shelley on Homer's, xxvii, 352-3

Hecuba, at death of Priam, xlvi, 130; madness of, xx, 125; in sack of Troy, xiii, 121

Hedge, F. H., translator of Luther's Hymn, xlv, 570

Hedwig, in WILHELM TELL, xxvi, 416-19, 442-3, 444, 467-70, 473

Heedless, in PILGRIM'S PROGRESS, xv, 251, 307-8

Hegel, on civil history, v, 455; on planetary motions, xxx, 294; Taine on, xxxix, 452

Hegesias, and Diogenes, xxxii, 60

Height, less grand than depth, xxiv, 63-4

Heimer of Hlymdale, xlix, 327, 336

Heimskringla, Emerson on the, v, 356-7

Heine, Taine on, xxxix, 435

Heineccius, on Roman Law, xxv, 46

Heinsius, on Horace, xiii, 12

HELEN, To, xlii, 1275-6

HELEN OF KIRCONNELL, xl, 333-4

Helen of Troy, Æschylus on, viii, 7, 19-20, 30-2; Burke on Homer's description of, xxiv, 143-4; Dante on, xx, 23; Darley on, xli, 939; Deiphobus and, xiii, 228-9; in FAUSTUS, xix, 236-7, 238-9; Herodotus on, xxxiii, 54-9; in the ODYSSEY, xiii, 51-6, 211, 212-13; Proteus and, xxxiii, 54-7; Theseus and, xxvi, 128; in siege of Troy, xiii, 122-3; xxii, 54, 55; vest of, xiii, 98; wife of Thone and, iv, 64

Helena, Jove-born, iv, 64 (see Helen of Troy)

Helenor, the Trojan, death of, xiii, 315-16

Helenus, in ÆNEID, xiii, 141, 142, 143-6; Dryden on, 21

Helgi Hunding's-Bane, in the VOLSUNG TALE, xlix, 291-3, 294-5; SECOND LAY OF, 385-92; remarks on LAY of, 266-7

Helgi, the Norseman, xliii, 17-19

Helice, reference to, xx, 417 note 5

Heliocentric Theory, xxxix, 55 note

Heliodorus, Dante on, xx, 231 and note 18; Sidney on, xxvii, 15

Heliogabalus, Machiavelli on, xxxvi, 70

Heliometer, Newcomb on the, xxx, 330

Heliopolis, city of, xxxiii, 8, 33, 34

Helios, giver of light, xxii, 140; herds of, 155; kine of, 172, 177-8;

wrath of, at the Greeks, 178-9; worshipped in Egypt, xxxiii, 33

Helios le Grose, xxxv, 159

Helizeus, More on, xxxvi, 165

Hell, Æneas's visit to, xiii, 220-32; Browne on, iii, 315-17; Browne on, fear of, 312-13, 317-18; Buddhist ideas of, xv, 232; Burke on paintings of, xxiv, 56; Burke on Virgil's picture of, 64; Burns on the fear of, vi, 213; Burns on, orthodox ideas of, 107; Dante's, xx, 5-146; Kempis on, vii, 242 (3, 4); Kempis on fear of, 244 (7); Luther on, xxxvi, 266; Marlowe on, xix, 215; Mill on notion of, xxv, 32; Milton's description of, iv, 91-2, 96, 125-6, 127, 133, 228-9; Milton's, Burke on, xxiv, 146; Mohammed on, xlv, 890-1, 894, 897, 899, 902, 903, 906-8, 911, 923, 946, 958, 987; Omar Khayyam on, xli, 982, 986; Pascal on belief in, xlviii, 88-9; Raleigh on thoughts of, xl, 207; Rousseau on, xxxiv, 273-4

HELL, HOW LOVE LOOKED FOR, xlii, 1479-82

HELLAS, by Shelley, xli, 846-7

Hellenes, John de, xxxv, 50

Hellenion, in Egypt, xxxiii, 90

Hellenora, Spenser's, xxxix, 68

Hellespont, Dante on the, xx, 262

Hellusians, Tacitus on the, xxxiii, 123

Helm Gunnar, xlix, 321, 415

Helmholtz, ON CONSERVATION OF FORCE, xxx, 181-220; on the eye, xi, 214; ICE AND GLACIERS, xxx, 221-59; life and works, 180

Help, in PILGRIM'S PROGRESS, xv, 19

Help, must come from self, v, 23; to those who help themselves, xvii, 36

Helper, yonder aids the helper here, xix, 43

Helpidius, vii, 79

Helvetians, Tacitus on the, xxxiii, 111

Helvetius, Mill's abstract of, xxv, 48

Helvia, mother of Cicero, xii, 225

Helvicus, tables of, xxxvii, 168

Helvidius, death of, ix, 250; Life, by Senecio, 323; Pliny on, 354-5

Hely, Mrs., and Pepys, xxviii, 299

Helymus, in the ÆNEID, xiii, 184, 192-3

Heman the Ezrahite, maschil of, xliv, 258

Hemi-organism, xxxviii, 322-4, 370

Heminge, John, PREFACE TO SHAKESPEARE, xxxix, 155-6

Hemionus, descent of the, xi, 171-4

Hemistichs, Dryden on, xiii, 65-6

Hemorrhages, Harvey on, xxxviii, 113

Hempe in prophecy indicating sovereigns of England, iii 96

Hemphill, Franklin on, i, 98-99

Hen, and chickens, parable of the, xv, 207

Henchman, Humphrey, on George Herbert, xv, 403

HENDERSON, MATTHEW, ELEGY ON, vi, 406

Hengest, the Dane, xlix, 35 note 5, 36, 37-8; Vortizern weds daughter of, v, 286

Henley, William Ernest, Poems by, xlii, 1257-60

Hennings, in FAUST, xix, 180

HENPECKED COUNTRY SQUIRE, EPIGRAMS ON A, vi, 62-3

HENPECKED HUSBAND, THE, vi, 343

Henriquez, Don Martin, xxxiii, 134

Henry I, Raleigh on, xxxix, 75

Henry II, of England, and Becket, xxxix, 172 note 21; sons of, iii, 53

Henry II, of France, Cellini on, xxxi, 295 note, 313; death foretold, iii, 96; expedition against Hesdin, xxxviii, 22; expedition to Germany, 19; Montgomery and, xxxiii, 193; Paré and, xxxviii, 23-4, 35, 45-6; siege of Danvilliers, 20-2

Henry III, of England, Dante on, xx, 176 and note 15; and the Jews, v, 360; Oxford students and, xxxv, 394

Henry III, of France, Bacon on, iii, 39; Montaigne on régime of, xxxii, 121; Raleigh on, xxxix, 77, 87; Voltaire on, xxxiv, 88

Henry IV, Emperor, and Gregory VII, xxxvi, 308 note 25

Henry IV, of England, and Chaucer, xxxix, 171; Raleigh on, 76-77

Henry IV, of France, and Acevedo, xxi, 12; Burke on, xxiv, 196, 284; compared with Lincoln, xxviii, 450-1; on manly exercises, v, 363; murder of, xxxix, 377; plots against, xxxiv, 88-9

Henry V, at Agincourt, xl, 227-8, 229, 230; Falstaff and, vi, 219; Macaulay on, xxvii, 395-6; Raleigh on, xxxix, 77

Henry VI, of England, Cambridge, founder of colleges at, xxxv, 401; death of, xxxix, 77, 79; Raleigh on, 77-8

Henry VI, of France, iii, 136

Henry VII, of Cyprus, xx, 370 note 21

Henry VII, Emperor, Dante on, xx, 415 note 6; death of, xxxiv, 88;

married to Constance, xx, 298 note 7

Henry VII, of England, and John Cabot, xliii, 47 note, 48, 50; chapel of, xxxv, 394; councillors of, iii, 57; greatness of, foretold, 96; King's College founded by, xxxv, 401; law of farmers, iii, 79; liberator, 136; mastiff and falcon of, xxxv, 372; Sir Thomas More and, xxxvi, 95; nobility and, iii, 54; Perkin Warbeck and, xxxiv, 103; Raleigh on, xxxix, 80-1; suspiciousness of, iii, 86; Voltaire on, xxxiv, 91-2

Henry VIII, and the abbeys, xxiv, 264-5; Anne Bullen and, xxxvi, 107, 116, 119; Bentham on times of, xxvii, 240; Burke on, xxiv, 422-5; Canterbury nun and, xxxvi, 120; Catherine, legality of marriage with, 107-9, 110; Christ's College founded by, xxxv, 402; Latimer and, v, 390; Sir Thomas More and, xxxvi, 96, 97-100, 102, 103, 111, 117, 119, 120, 122-4 125, 127, 130, 134, 139; More on, 143; More on marriage of, 104, 107-8, 110, 115-16, 119; More on Supremacy Act of, 128-9, 135-6; Protestantism in England not founded by, iii, 268; Raleigh on, xxxix, 81-2; Sacraments, his book on the, xxxvi, 123-4; severity of, xxxv, 389; studdery of, 346; on subversion of colleges, 403-4; on supremacy of the Pope, xxxvi, 124; Trinity College founded by, xxxv, 401; in triumvirate of kings, iii, 52; Wolsey and, xxxvi, 110-11

Henry of the Halden, xxvi, 388-9

Henry of Luxemburg, xx, 170 note 11

Henry of Navarre, Dante on, xx, 175

Henry, son of Richard of Almaine, xx, 53 note 10

Henslowe, Philip, Dekker and, xlvii, 445; Massinger and, 818; Webster and, 445

Heorogar, xlix, 7, 18, 66

Heorot, the hall of Hrothgar, xlix, 7 note 1

Hephæstion, and Proæresius, xxviii, 55; proctor of Oriental school, 60

Hephæstos, Prometheus and, viii, 158 note; in PROMETHEUS BOUND, 157-9; the snare of, xxii, 111-13; temple of, in Memphis, xxxiii, 49, 53, 59, 69, 72, 79 (see also Vulcan)

Hephestion, and Alexander, xlvi, 25

HER FLOWING LOCKS, vi, 116

HER GIFTS, xlii, 1227-8

Hera, guardian of marriage-bed, viii, 123; the peacock sacred to, 176 note 37 (see also Juno)

Heracleon, the Megarian, xxxii, 51

Heracles (see Hercules)

Heracles, in THE FROGS, viii, 420-4

Heraclides Ponticus, philosopher, xxxii, 60; on motion of earth, xxxix, 58

Heraclitus, death of, ii, 207 (3); Democritus and, iii, 330; on generation, ii, 221 (46); on incredulity, xii, 190; to judges, ii, 135 (54); in Limbo, xx, 20; Marcus Aurelius on, ii, 257 (3); on the sleepers, 242 (42)

Heraclitus, by Cory, xlii, 1159

Heraldry, the boast of, xl, 456; remarks on, xxviii, 428

Herbert, George, birth and family of, xv, 377-8; charity of, 413; childhood and education, 379; church at Layton Ecclesia, 391-2; church services by, 405-7, 409; clerk of Bemerton, 398-9; college career, 384-5; consumption of, 395-6, 414-15, 419-21; deacon, 391; death of, 421-3; Emerson on, v, 148; Farrer, Nicholas, letter to, xv, 425-6; friendships with Bacon, Andrews, Wotton, and Donne, 387-8; health, infirmity of, 389; on Holy Days, 407-9; LIFE OF, by Walton, 377-426; life, sanctity of his, 399-400; marriage, 396-8; mother, letter to his, 393-5; music, love of, 410; parson, rules as, 403-4; Poems by, 382, 383, 389, 402, 421; xl, 351-6; poor woman and, xv, 401-2; prayer, habits of, 409-10; *Sacred Poems,* 358-9, 400-1, 419-20; Salisbury walks, incidents of, 411-12; sermons, 404; sinecure given by James, 388; successor, lines to his, 402; as university orator, 385-7; wife of (see Danvers, Jane)

Herbert, Henry, xv, 378, 392, 395

Herbert, Magdalen, mother of George, xv, 377-8, 379-80; death of, 396; Donne, friendship with, 380-3; letter to, 393-5; son, relations with her, 389, 391-2

Herbert, Thomas, xv, 378-9

Herbert, Rev. W., on hybrids, xi, 301-2; on origin of species, 12; on struggle among plants, 77

Herborg, Queen, xlix, 352-3

Herbs, Harrison on, xxxv, 251-2

Hercules, Alcestis and, xli, 680; amours of, xii, 363; Antæus and, iv, 413; xiv, 21; xx, 132 note 6; birth of, xxii, 159; Cacus and, xiii, 279-81; Cerberus and, xx, 39 note; viii, 422, 433; character of, v, 192; compass, and the, 476; date of, xxxiii, 74-5; as Egyptian

god, xxxiii, 26-8, 42; as king of
Egypt, xxxviii, 407; envenomed
robe of, iv, 124; Epictetus on, ii,
143 (71); faith of, 162 (125);
genealogy of, viii, 182 note 50,
186; as a German god, xxxiii, 100;
in Germany, 96; in Hades, xxii,
167-8; Hylas and, xlvi, 9, 25;
Iole and, xx, 324; Iphitus and,
xxii, 295-6; the Mænad and, viii,
310; Nessus and, xx, 52 note;
parentage of, xii, 5; the pigmies
and, xxxix, 365; Pillars of, Tacitus on, xxxiii, 115; Prometheus
and, iii, 17; viii, 182, 186 note
63; Rhea and, xiii, 266; Virgil on,
238, 281-2; Waller on death of,
xxxiv, 149; Zeus and, xxxiii,
26
HERCULES, AND THE WAGGONER; a
fable, xvii, 36
Herder, quotation from, xxxii, 409
Herdsman's Song, from WILHELM
TELL, xxvi, 370
Hereafter, Arnold on doubt of the,
xlii, 1185; Buddha on questions
of the, xlv, 662-7, 675-6; Emerson on popular views of the, v,
89-90; Epictetus on the, ii, 158
(112), 181 (188); Epicurus on
the, xxxvii, 423-4; Euripides on
the, viii, 294-5; Goethe on the,
xix, 64-5; Hindu idea of, xlv,
835-7, 840, 865; hope of the, xl,
420; Kempis on the, vii, 325;
242-4; Mohammed on, xlv, 892,
893, 896, 926; Montaigne on the,
xxxii, 25; Omar Khayyam on the,
xli, 972, 976, 979, 981, 982, 983,
984, 985, 987; Pascal on question
of, xlviii, 70-2, 76, 77 (200), 79
(213), 80 (217); the philosopher's,
ii, 76-7; Pope on the, xl, 445-6;
Raleigh on the, xxxix, 97; Rousseau on the, xxxiv, 271-4, 285-6;
sailors' idea of, xxiii, 40-1; Shakespeare on the, xl, 268; xlvi, 135,
167; Shelley on, xviii, 350-1;
Socrates on, ii, 28, 51, 58, 104-5,
110-11; Vaughan on the, xl, 356-7
(see also Heaven, Hell, Paradise,
Purgatory, Hades)
Hereditary Princedoms, Machiavelli
on, xxxvi, 7-8; Pascal on, xlviii,
112 (320)
Heredity, Darwin on laws of, xi,
31-2; in habit and instinct, 267-
70; in individual differences, 59;
in mutilations, 148; in variations,
30-1
Heremod, xlix, 30, 53-4
Herennius, and Cicero, xii, 267
HERE'S A HEALTH TO KING CHARLES,
xli, 773
HERE'S A HEALTH TO THEM THAT'S
AWA, vi, 477

HERE'S HIS HEALTH IN WATER, vi,
191
HERE'S TO THY HEALTH, vi, 28-9
Heresies, Augustine, St., on, vii,
120; Bacon on, iii, 11-12; Browne
on, 269-72; Hobbes on, xxxiv,
388; Mill on, xxv, 249-52; Pascal
on, xlviii, 306, 307; speculative,
iii, 145
Heretics, Burns on, vi, 223; in
Dante's HELL, xx, 40, 117-18;
Hobbes on covenants with, xxxiv,
421; Luther on, xxxvi, 335;
Pascal on, xlviii, 296 (841), 300
(845), 303, 306, 307
Héricault, Charles d', on classics,
xxviii, 68-9
Herilus, and Evander, xiii, 291
Heriulf, the Norseman, xliii, 5, 6
Herman, in MANFRED, xviii, 431,
436, 437-9
HERMANN AND DOROTHEA, Goethe's,
xix, 335-431; remarks on, 334; l,
25
Hermaphrodites, Darwin on, xi,
109-10, 113
Hermes, guard of the dead, viii,
96, 100; herald of heaven, 23,
76; Herodotus on worship of,
xxxiii, 30-1; in the ODYSSEY, xxii,
10, 72-5, 113, 143-4, 331; in PRO-
METHEUS BOUND, viii, 189-93;
rod of, ii, 156 (106); iv, 326;
slayer of Argos, xxii, 11; Ulysses
and, iv, 63
Hermes Trismegistus (see Trisme-
gistus)
Herminius, death of, xiii, 384
Hermione, Homer on, xxii, 48;
Milton on, vi, 276
Herminones, Tacitus on the, xxxiii,
95-6
Hermippus, accuser of Aspasia, xii,
70
Hermits, Burns on life of, vi, 207;
in Milton's limbo, iv, 150
Hermodius, and Aristogiton, xxxii,
79
Hermogenes, precocity of, iii, 111;
with Socrates, ii, 47
Hermondurians, Tacitus on the,
xxxiii, 119
Hernandez, Gonzalo, xiv, 319, 513
Hernon, murderer of Phrynichus,
xii, 136
Hernox, Earl, xxxv, 202-3
Hero-worship, Carlyle on, xxv, 410-
11
Herod, the king, xliv, 456 (1), 457
(19-23); believed to be Messiah,
xlviii, 269 (753); gold raised, iv,
386; Pascal on, xlviii, 238 (700),
239 (701); persecution of, xliv,
456 (1); son of, xlviii, 66 (179);
in war of Antony and Octavius,
xii, 383, 391, 393

Herod, tetrarch of Galilee, xliv, 365 (1), 366 (19), 383 (7-9); Jesus and, 398 (31-2), 421 (7-11); Pilate and, 421 (12)

Herodes Atticus, xxviii, 61-2

Herodias, and John the Baptist, xliv, 366 (19)

Herodicus, and Hippocrates, xxxviii, 2

Herodotus, AN ACCOUNT OF EGYPT, xxxiii, 5-91; editorial remarks on ACCOUNT of, 1, 18; Hugo on, xxxix, 358; life and histories, xxxiii, 3-4; Shelley on, xxvii, 352; Sidney on, 9; Themistocles and, ix, 107-8

Heroes, Emerson on our love of, v, 19; Lowell on, xlii, 1450, 1451; of poems, Dryden on, xviii, 11; Pope on, xl, 447; Thoreau on, xxviii, 421; Yu-tzu on, xliv, 6 (13)

Heroic Poetry, Sidney on, xxvii, 31-2

HEROISM, ESSAY ON, v, 125-35

Heron, Mr., son-in-law of More, xxxvi, 112

HERON ELECTION BALLADS, vi, 556-63, 587

Herrick, Robert, Poems by, xl, 343-50

Herschel, Sir John, work of, v, 374

Herthum, German goddess, xxxiii, 118-19

HERVEY, WILLIAM, ON THE DEATH OF, xl, 376-8

HE'S OWER THE HILLS THAT I LO'E WEEL, xli, 573-4

Hesdin, siege of, xxxviii, 35-9; destruction of, 45

Hesiod, Cicero on, ix, 66; Clauserus on, xxvii, 54; on his estate, 71; Greek theogony due to, xxxiii, 31; Herodotus on time of, 31; quoted, ii, 297 (32); Sainte-Beuve on, xxxii, 136; Sidney on, xxvii, 8; Socrates on, ii, 28; teachings of, viii, 451

Hesione, wife of Prometheus, viii, 167 note 20, 175

Hesperian Tree, Milton on the, iv, 57

Hesperus, gardens of, iv, 73, 152

Hesperus, the star, iv, 172, 265

HESPERUS, THE WRECK OF THE, xlii, 1321

HESTER, by Lamb, xli, 753

Heteronomy of the Will, xxxii, 364; spurious principles of morality due to, 363-4, 371-5

Hetwaras, xlix, 72 note 2, 87

Heuer, Sir Roger, xl, 101

Heusinger, on effects of color, xi, 30

HEY, CA' THRO', boat song, vi, 278-9

Heyne, Carlyle on, xxv, 392-3

Heywood, Thomas, Hazlitt on, xxvii,

291; PACK, CLOUDS, AWAY, xl, 324-5

Hezekiah, Bunyan on, xv, 135; in Dante's PARADISE, xx, 372; Walton on, xv, 361

Hibernation, Darwin on, xxix, 110-11; Harvey on, xxxviii, 90, 138

HIC BREVE VIVITUR, xlv, 560-1

Hickey, Goldsmith on, xli, 518, 521

Hickson, Mr., Mill on, xxv, 142

Hide-curing, Dana on, xxiii, 156-7

Hides, price of, x, 201-7

Hiera, and Alcanor, xiii, 320

Hierius, Augustine, St., on, vii, 58-9

Hiero of Syracuse, Machiavelli on, xxxvi, 22-3; the poets and, xxvii, 41; Themistocles and, xii, 27; troops of, xxxvi, 48

Hierocles, the pedant in, xxxix, 221

Hierome, St., and Paula, xv, 381

Hieronymus Fabricius, xxxviii, 68, 75

HIGHLAND BALOU, THE, vi, 523

HIGHLAND GIRL, TO THE, xlii, 668-70

HIGHLAND HARRY BACK AGAIN, vi, 378

HIGHLAND MARY, vi, 472

HIGHLAND WIDOW'S LAMENT, vi, 524-5

HIGHLANDS, IN THE, xlii, 1260-1

High-mind, Mr., in PILGRIM'S PROGRESS, xv, 101-2

Highways (see Roads)

Hilarity, of heroism, v, 131

Hilarius, a Bithynian, xxviii, 60

Hilary, on the true church, xxxix, 44

Hildeburh, xlix, 35-6 note 5, 37, 38

Hildegard, in WILHELM TELL, xxvi, 424, 427-8

Hill, Gen. A. P., at Gettysburg, xliii, 365, 366, 370

Hilton, Walter, as author of IMITATION OF CHRIST, vii, 208

Himeræus, death of, xii, 221

HIND HORN, a ballad, xl, 59-61

Hindoos, Freeman on name of, xxviii, 281; idea of world, 428; Taine on the, xxxix, 444

Hinduism, xlv, 800 (see also Bhagavad-Gita)

Hinny, origin of the, xi, 329

Hipparchus, Huxley on, xxviii, 227; Marcus Aurelius on, ii, 244 (47); on precession of equinoxes, xxxiv, 131

Hipparchus, freedman of Antony, xii, 389

Hipparete, wife of Alcibiades, xii, 116-17

Hipparion, Darwin on the, xi, 378

Hippias, the comedian, xii, 341

Hippias of Elis, ii, 5; wealth of, x, 142

Hippo, the dolphin of, ix, 368-70

Hippocoön, in the ÆNEID, xiii, 198-9

Hippocrates, Dante on, xx, 268 note
15; editor's remarks on writings
of, l, 44; first aphorism of,
xxxviii, 2, 38; on the heart, 144;
LAW of, 4-5; life and works, 2;
in Limbo, xx, 20; Marcus Aurelius on, ii, 207 (3); OATH of,
xxxviii, 3; remarks on OATH, 2

Hippodamus, Cicero on, ix, 117-18,
121

Hippolytus, Virgil on, xiii, 269-70

HIPPOLYTUS, of Euripides, viii, 287-
348

Hippolytus, in Tragedy of HIPPOLY-
TUS, Aphrodite's hatred of, viii,
287-9; Artemis and, 289-90; death
of, 336-9, 343-8; huntsman and,
290-2; innocence told by Artemis, 341-2; Phædra and, 312-15;
Theseus and, 325-34; Voltaire on,
xxxix, 382

Hippolytus, in PHÆDRA, Aricia and,
xxvi, 127-9, 141-2, 143-7, 174-6;
death of, related by Theramenes,
180-2; denounced by Œnone, 163-
4; Dryden on, xviii, 13-14; Phædra
and, xxvi, 126-7, 135-7, 147-51;
Theramenes, scenes with, 125-30,
152-3, 162; Theseus and, 160-1,
164-8

Hipponicus, and Alcibiades, xii, 116

Hippopotamus, described in JOB,
xliv, 139-40; Herodotus on the,
xxxiii, 38

Hippotades, Æolus called, iv, 76

Hircania, dogs of, xxxv, 375

Hire, Confucius on, xliv, 46 (1)

Hirtius, and Cicero, xii, 164, 262;
death of, 264-5

Hisbon, death of, xiii, 339

Hispaniola, Columbus on, xliii, 23-
4, 26; Drake in, xxxiii, 248-53;
sheep in, x, 202

Hispulla, letter to, ix, 270

Historians, Dryden on, xviii, 5;
Montaigne on, xxxii, 99-102; as
teachers of virtue, xxvii, 17-18,
19, 21-4

History, Bacon on study of, iii, 129;
Burke on use and misuse of, xxiv,
289; Carlyle on reading of, xxv,
381; Cervantes on, xiv, 76; Channing on study of, xxviii, 340, 347-
8, 372; Comte's ages of, xxv, 108;
Descartes on study of, xxxiv, 7-
9; Emerson on, v, 12, 72, 73, 75,
77, 97; Franklin's observations on,
i, 93, 131; Freeman on science
of, xxviii, 253; Goethe on study
of, xix, 28-9; Hume on, xxxvii,
373-4, 379, 444; judgment and
fancy in, xxxiv, 364; lessons of,
xvi, 5; Locke on study of, xxxvii,
147, 164, 167, 168, 181; Montaigne on study of, xxxii, 44-8,
99-100; natural and civil, xxxiv,
373; organic and critical periods

of, xxv, 107-8; Pliny on, ix,
320, 332; poetry and, compared,
xxviii, 74; xxxix, 294; politics
and, xxi, 467; Raleigh on, xxxix,
72-4, 119-20; repetitions of, ii,
251 (49), 271 (14), 285 (27); iii,
269-70; right reading of, xxvii,
398; Rousseau on business of,
xxxiv, 201; Ruskin on study of,
xxviii, 153; Taine on study of,
xxxix, 433-62

History of civilization, reading
course in, l, 18-30

HISTORY OF THE WORLD, PREFACE
TO, Raleigh's, xxxix, 69-121

Hive-Bees, instincts of, xi, 279-88

Hixom, Ellis, with Drake, xxxiii,
127, 148, 168, 172, 187

Hjalli, the thrall, xlix, 371, 372,
438

Hjalprek, King, xlix, 300, 301-2

Hjordis, wife of Sigmund, xlix, 297,
298, 299, 300-1; wife of Alf, 302;
remarks on story of, 267

Hnaef the Scylding, xlix, 35 note 5,
37 note 9

Hnikar, xlix, 309-11

Hobart Town, Darwin on, xxix, 471

Hobbes, Thomas, Berkeley on,
xxxvii, 247; Hazlitt on, xxvii,
291; Iliad, translation of, by,
xxxix, 165; Leviathan burned at
Oxford, v, 433; life and works,
xxxiv, 318; Logic of, Mill on,
xxv, 17; OF MAN, xxxiv, 319-
434; on natural viciousness of
man, 191-2; style of, v, 450

Hodbrod, King, xlix, 292, 294-5

Hodge, in SHOEMAKER'S HOLIDAY, at
Ralph's departure, xlvii, 451-4; at
Eyre's, 458-61, 465-9, 475-9; at Old
Ford, 481; before shop, 487-9; at
Hammon's wedding, 499-506; at
Eyre's dinner, 506-7, 513

Hoel, Renan on, xxxii, 170

Hofe, Jorg im, in WILHELM TELL,
xxvi, 406, 409

Hoffman, M., xxvii, 109

Hogarth, on beauty, xxiv, 98-9;
Fielding on, xxxix, 187

Hogg, James, poems by, xli, 774-
88

Hogni, King, xlix, 292, 294, 385
note 2

Hogni, son of Giuki, xlix, 331; Atli
and, 364-8, 434-6; in battle, 369,
370, 371, 437; Brynhild and, 343,
344, 358, 405-6; death of, 372,
438-9; Sigurd and, 334, 348, 350,
399-400, 417-18, 423-4, 445, 451

Hogs, price of, x, 197

HOHENLINDEN, xli, 800-1

Hold-the-world, Mr., in PILGRIM'S
PROGRESS, xv, 106-10, 113

Holidays, Herbert on sacred, xv,
407-9; Luther on, xxxvi, 324;

Mill on, xxv, 28; in Utopia, xxxvi, 246

Holinshed, Raphael, his *Chronicles,* xxxv, 228; selection from *Chronicles,* 229-404

Holland, Burke on French invasion of, xxiv, 441-2; Burke on nobility of, 441; Goldsmith on, xli, 540-1; interest in, x, 96-7; republican government, importance of, to, 573; taxation in, 523; trade, attitude toward, in, 102

Holland, Lord, anecdote of, v, 198

Holland, Sir John, xxxv, 74

Holland, Sir Thomas, xxxv, 9, 13, 14, 17, 23

Holly-trees, and bees, xi, 107

Holmes, ·Oliver Wendell, life and works, xxxviii, 234; Poems by, xlii, 1442-7; ON PUERPERAL FEVER, xxxiii, 235-68; editor's remarks on PUERPERAL FEVER of, l, 45; SUNDAY HYMN, xlv, 584

Holmes, Robert, i, 29, 52

Holy Cross, royal way of the, vii, 263-7

Holy Communion, Kempis on the, vii, 349-79

HOLY FAIR, THE, vi, 101-8

Holy Ghost, Calvin on the, xxxix, 53; Charlemagne on, xlv, 559-60; Hobbes on the, xxxiv, 432

HOLY GRAIL, THE, by Malory, xxxv, 107-226; Caxton on, xxxix, 25

Holy Grail, Don Quixote on quest of, xiv, 515; legends of the, xxxii, 171-4

Holy-man, Mr., in PILGRIM'S PROGRESS, xv, 285, 287

Holy Roman Empire, Luther on, xxxvi, 343-7

HOLY THING, THAT, xlii, 1163-4

Holy Things, Tsai Wo on, xliv, 11 (21)

Holy Thursday, Walton on, xv, 408

HOLY THURSDAY, xli, 605

HOLY TULYIE, THE, vi, 67-70

HOLY WILLIE, EPITAPH ON, vi, 78;

HOLY WILLIE'S PRAYER, vi, 75-78

Holyoake, George Jacob, xxv, 232 note 3

Holystones, described, xxiii, 186

Homage, Pascal on, xlviii, 386

Home, Locke on education at, xxxvii, 53-8; prized first at evening, xix, 47; Ruskin on, xxviii, 150

HOME THEY BROUGHT HER WARRIOR DEAD, xlii, 1004

HOME-THOUGHTS, FROM ABROAD, xlii, 1110

HOME-THOUGHTS, FROM THE SEA, xlii, 1110

Homer, accused of drunkenness, xxvii, 374; on agriculture, ix, 66; Aristophanes on, viii, 451; Arnold on, xxviii, 72-3, 80; Augustine,

St., on, vii, 17, 18; Bacon on, iii, 106; Burke on, xxiv, 133-4; Burke on similes of, 18; Caxton on, xxxix, 9; claimed by seven cities, xxvii, 40; Clauserus on, 54; on country life, 71-2; Dante on, xxxix, 370; the dramatists and, xiii, 6-7; Dryden on, 15, 25, 27, 34, 44; xl, 406; Emerson on, v, 149, 186, 188; Greek theogony due to, xxxiii, 31; Fielding on, xxxix, 184; the fisherman and, iii, 336; Greek tragedies and, xxxix, 359, 365; Herodotus on time of, xxxiii, 31; heroes of, xxxix, 360; Hugo on, 357, 370, 371, 406; Hume on ethics of, xxvii, 216; intelligibleness of, xxxix, 260; Johnson on, 219; Keats on Chapman's translation of, xli, 919-20; Lang on, xxii, 347; life of, 3; in Limbo, xx, 19; the *Margites* of, iii, 210; Milton on, iv, 406; THE ODYSSEY of, xxii; oldest ballad singer, vi, 137 note; on Paris, xxxiii, 56-7; Pascal on, xlviii, 212 (628); Pliny on, ix, 284, 364-5; Sainte-Beuve on, xxxii, 132, 136; Shelley on, xxvii, 352-3, 359; Sidney on, 8, 14, 39; Spenser on, xxxix, 65; Socrates on, ii, 28; universal admiration of, xxvii, 220; Virgil and, xiii, 6, 40-2, 48; xxxix, 164-7

Homologies, serial, xi, 474-6

Homologous Parts, xi, 156

Honest, in PILGRIM'S PROGRESS, xv, 176, 254-66, 271, 280-1, 283-4, 290-1, 309-11, 316, 319

Honest Man, "Burns on the, vi, 111, 546; "the noblest work of God," 147, 254; xl, 447

Honesty, Bacon on, iii, 8; forced, i, 406; fortune and, iii, 105; Hamlet on, xlvi, 122, 123; instruction in, xxxvii, 98; Kant on pure, xxxii, 327-8; Mohammed on, xlv, 927; want and, i, 96

Honeycomb, Will, xxvii, 92-3

HONOR, ESSAY ON, Bacon's, iii, 135-7

Honor, Burns on, vi, 214; commerce and, xli, 535; Dante on love of, xx, 311 note 25; Dryden on, xl, 403-4; Hobbes on, xxxiv, 378-83; Kempis on temporal, vii, 318; Lessing on, xxvi, 347; Pascal on, xlviii, 59 (147); Pliny on loss of, ix, 350; venerableness of, v, 71-2

Honors, Confucius on, xliv, 13 (5), 23 (15), 27 (13); desire for, the strongest of motives, xxviii, 97; More on worldly, xxxvi, 211; Pope on, xl, 446, 448; Raleigh on, xxxix, 96, 97-8, 101

Hood, Thomas, BRIDGE OF SIGHS

by, xxviii, 398-400; Poe on FAIR
INEZ of, 397-8; Poe on *The
Haunted House* of, 398; Poems
by, xli, 930-6
HOOD, WILLIAM, EPITAPH ON, vi, 53
Hooke, saying of, v, 317
Hooker, General, xliii, 348, 439
Hooker, Thomas, on change, xxxix,
195; Jonson on, xxvii, 60; language of, xxxix, 206
Hooker, Sir William J., on Australian species, xi, 141; on correlation in flowers, 157; Darwin
and, 22; on descent of species,
19; on Galapagos species, 440;
xxix, 419, 420; on glacial period,
xi, 417, 420; on ovules, 224; on
sexes in trees, 113
Hope, allegory of, xx, 268 note 11;
American lack of, v, 57; Burns
on, vi, 455; Coleridge on, xxv,
93; Dante on, xx, 394; Dante's
star of, 179 note 9; Dryden on,
xxxiv, 137; fear and, iv, 57;
eternal fort of, xli, 503; Hobbes
on, xxxiv, 353, 380; life on a
single, ii, 183 (16); in music, xli,
489; "never comes that comes to
all," iv, 92; never satisfied, v,
243-4; Penn on, i, 360 (235);
Pope on, xl, 420, 433; Shelley's
Beatrice on, xviii, 351; sweetness
of, viii, 174; white-handed, iv, 52
Hope, Thomas, xxv, 333 note 1,
356; Carlyle on *Essay on Man* of,
362-5
Hopeful, in PILGRIM'S PROGRESS, xv,
103, 112, 114-27, 129, 131-5, 137-
8, 140-8, 158-67
Horace, accused of cowardice, xxvii,
374; on affecting the passions,
xxiv, 54; on art of poetry, xxvii,
116; an astrologer, xxxix, 167;
Augustus and, 171; on changes,
xlviii, 121 note; cold baths of,
xxxvii, 13; Dryden on, xiii, 53;
Dryden on, epistles of, 12; Dryden on translators of, xviii, 16-
17; Greek examples followed by,
18; on happiness, xlviii, 32 note
7; on himself, xxvii, 194-5; on
instruction in taste, xxiv, 22;
Locke on, xxxvii, 168; love of
country life, xxvii, 73; Montaigne
on, xxxii, 92; Newman on, xxviii,
54; on poetry, xxxii, 64; Sainte-
Beuve on, 136; as a soldier, 116;
on terror caused by wonders of
nature, xxiv, 61; Voltaire on,
xxxii, 138-9
Horace, Duke, at Metz, xxxviii, 26;
at Hesdin, 35, 37
Horatii, Dante on the, xx, 308
note 9
Horatio, in HAMLET, xlvi, on watch
at Elsinore, 88-92; tells Hamlet

of ghost, 97-100; on watch with
Hamlet, 104-7; sworn to secrecy,
110-12; with Hamlet, told to
watch king, 140-1; with Hamlet
after play, 146-7; on Ophelia,
166; letter from Hamlet, 173;
with Hamlet in grave-yard, 181-
5; at Ophelia's funeral, 187; with
Hamlet, hears of king's plot, 188-
90; with Osric, 191, 192, 193; on
the wager, 193; at the duel, 196,
197-8; with Fortinbras, 198-9; in
the original story, 86
Horatius, called Cocles, xiii, 294
Horn, Cape, Darwin on, xxix, 226-7
Horn, Count, xix, 246
Hornbills, instinct of, xi, 296
HORNBOOK, DOCTOR, DEATH AND, vi,
79-84
Horner, Francis, and *Edinburgh
Review*, xxvii, 236
Hornets, Harrison on, xxxv, 365
Horoscopy, defined, xxxiv, 397
HORSE AND ASS, fable of, xvii, 44
HORSE, HUNTER, AND STAG, fable of,
xvii, 23
Horse(s), descent of, xi, 171-4; described in Job, xliv, 138; of England, Harrison on, xxxv, 344-5;
in Falkland Islands, xxix, 206;
used by Germans in augury,
xxxiii, 100-1; grease disease of,
xxxviii, 153, 155 note 3; Pugliano
on, xxvii, 7; races of, xi, 36; remains of, in S. America, xxix, 142-
3; S. American, how broken, 164-
8; among the Tencterians, xxxiii,
114; swimming power of, xxix,
156; why not sublime, xxiv, 58
Horsemanship, Locke on, xxxvii,
183; Pugliano on, xxvii, 7; Webster on, xlvii, 725
HORSES AND COCK, fable of, xxvii,
143
Hortensius, and Cæsar, xii, 302;
and Caius Antonius, brother of
Mark Antony, 350; Cicero on, ix,
96; iii, 111; at trial of Murena,
xii, 255; Verres and, 231
Hosea, prophecy of, xlviii, 233
Hoskins, Jane, i, 192, 202
Hospitality, Emerson on modern,
v, 54; of heroism, 129-30; Homer
on, xxii, 210; obligations from, i,
209, 255; Penn on, 344 (54);
Socrates on, ii, 178 (181)
Hospitals, antiseptic treatment in,
xxxviii, 281-2; in Utopia, xxxvi,
196-7
Host, Chaucer's, xl, 32
HOST, EPIGRAM ON A KIND, vi, 296
Hottentots, food of, xxviii, 422;
sight of, xxxiv, 178
Houghton, Lord, SONNET, xlii, 1098
Hounds, Harrison on, xxxv, 369-70;
HOUSE OF ATREUS, Æschylus's, viii,

5-155; only extant tragic trilogy, 3; remarks on, 3-4

House-rent, taxes on, **x**, 510-18

House, George, i, 58-59

House of Commons, Burke on, xxiv, 192, 193, 200

House of Lords, Burke on, xxiv, 199

House of Representatives, xliii, 192-3, 194-5, 210-11; election of president by, 200, 209

Houses, Buddha on defects of, xlv, 595 note 11; taxes, on transfer of, **x**, 528, 532; in Utopia, xxxvi, 186-7, 193

How Cruel Are the Parents, **vi**, 570

How Lang and Dreary Is the Night, **vi**, 536

How Long and Dreary Is the Night, **vi**, 316

How Love Looked for Hell, xlii, 1479-82

How They Brought the Good News, xlii, 1107

Howard, Charles, dedication to, xxxiii, 311-15

Howard, Elizabeth, wife of Dryden, xviii, 3

Howard, Gen., at Fredericksburg, xliii, 428; at Gettysburg, 351, 355, 358, 379, 380, 422; Haskell on, 381, 382, 439

Howard, Henrietta, Countess of Suffolk, xvi, 416

Howard, Henry, poems by, xl, 196-8

Howard, Sir Robert, xiii, 30

Howard, Lord Thomas, xlii, 1041-2

Howe, William, Burns on, **vi**, 54-5

Hreidmar, xlix, 304, 305, 306

Hrethel, the king, xlix, 74-5

Hrethric, son of Hrothgar, xlix, 39, 57

Hrimnir, the giant, xlix, 277, 278

Hrodland (see Roland)

Hrothgar, xlix, 7-8; banquet of, 33-40; Beowulf and, 13, 15-19, 23-4, 31-2, 33-4, 53-8, 62; daughter of, 62 and note; Grendel and, 9-11; Grendel's mother and, 42-7

Hrothglod, xlix, 454-5

Hrothmund, son of Hrothgar, xlix, 39

Hrunting, the sword, xlix, 46-7, 48 note, 52, 56

Hsien, xliv, 49 (19)

Huan of Chí, xliv, 48 (16, 17, 18) note 4

Huan Túi, xliv, 23 note 6

Huber, Pierre, on ants, xi, 275, 276; on bees, 284; on caterpillars, 263; on Oxford, xxviii, 49

Huckster-Witch, in Faust, xix, 171

Hudibras, Voltaire on, xxxiv, 150-1

Hudson, Hendrik, Emerson on, **v**, 86

Hugh, St., patron of shoemakers, xlvii, 459 note

Hugh of Lincoln: a ballad, xl, 83-5

Hughes, Mr., and Addison's *Cato*, xxvii, 176

Hugo, Victor, Preface to Cromwell, xxxix, 354-408; Taine on, 435; work of, 354 note

Huguenots, in France, xxxix, 87-8; Pascal on the, xlviii, 275 (775), 310 (874)

Hugues, of St. Victor, **xx**, 339 note 32

Hui (see Yen Yüan)

Human Body, in art, xxxix, 268-9, 271; beauty of the, **v**, 315, 318; cause of beauty of, xxiv, 82-3; Whitman on the, xlii, 1483; Whitman on the, in art, xxxix, 424

Human Folly, xl, 336

Human Nature, Austin on pliability of, xxv, 116; benevolence in, i, 178; iii, 29; best studied in the family, xxviii, 353; Burke on study of, xxiv, 9, 47-9; Channing on, xxviii, 378; Channing on study of, 343; corruption of, vii, 339-40; education and, xxxvii, 90; Epictetus on, ii, 150 (86); goodness in, iii, 34-5; Hume on science of, xxxvii, 305-6; in laws, **v**, 256; love of appreciation in, ii, 225 (6); love of mankind in, 208 (4); malignity in, iii, 36; more foolish than wise, 33; Pascal on, xlviii, 40 (92, 93), 41 (94, 97), 50 (125-7); Pope on science of, xl, 417; represented by Prometheus, iii, 17; Schiller on, xxxii, 252-63; is social, ix, 38; three ideas of, xxviii, 318; truth the sovereign good of, iii, 8; uniformity of, xxxvii, 373-81; most virtuous when uncultivated, **v**, 291 (see also Nature in Men)

Human Seasons, The, xli, 920-1

Human Understanding, Hume on the, xxxvii, 303-445

Humanists, Huxley on the, xxviii, 225-6

Humanity, Locke on development of, xxxvii, 110

Humble-Bee, The, xlii, 1297-8

Humble-mind, the damsel, xv, 227

Humble Petition of Bruar Water, **vi**, 293-5

Humboldt, Alexander von, Darwin on *Narrative* of, xxix, 529-30; on earthquakes and the weather, 372, 373; on granitic regions, xi, 345; on marshes, xxix, 387; Thoreau on, xxviii, 418

Humboldt, Wilhelm von, on individuality, xxv, 262; on liberty,

163-4; on marriage, 312-13; on public degrees, 317

Hume, David, Carlyle on philosophy of, xxv, 369; Emerson on, v, 456; ENQUIRY CONCERNING THE UNDERSTANDING, xxxvii, 303-445; Franklin and, i, 142; Hazlitt on, xxvii, 291; life and works, 214; xxxvii, 304; Locke and, 4; Mill on, xxv, 40; in Parliament, 67; on rate of interest, x, 295; ON STANDARD OF TASTE, xxvii, 215-34; Wordsworth on, xxxix, 338 note

Humiliation, Valley of, xv, 60, 243-7

Humility, Bunyan on, xv, 76; Franklin's rule of, i, 84, 91; Goethe on, xix, 129; Jesus on, xliv, 399 (11), 407 (14); Kempis on, vii, 215 (4), 219 (7), 251 (2), 261 (4), 262-3, 272, 277-9, 285; Pascal on discourses of, xlviii, 127 (377); Penn on, i, 351 (119), 365 (307), 401 (116), 411 (247); song on, xv, 245; Woolman on, i, 207

Humming-birds, in Chili, xxix, 288-9

Humor, Bagehot on, xxviii, 183, 184; has only fancy value, xxxii, 366

Humorists, Thackeray on, xxviii, 5-6

Humors, the four, xl, 37 note 38; iii, 98 note

Humpback, story of the, xvi, 100-7, 201-2

Hunding, King, xlix, 291; sons of, 311, 312

Hundred, the, of the Germans, xxxiii, 98

Hungarians, and Turks, xxviii, 235-237

Hungary, Freeman on, xxviii, 280

Hunger, Homer on, xxii, 245; rebellions caused by, iii, 40; thirst and, powerful persuaders, iv, 278

Hunn, Conrad, in WILHELM TELL, xxvi, 404, 405, 411-12

Hunt, Gen., at Gettysburg, xliii, 403

Hunt, James Henry Leigh, DEATHS OF LITTLE CHILDREN, xxvii, 299-303; dedication to, xviii, 273; in Hazlitt's discussion, xxvii, 291, 293-4; life and writings, 298; POEMS by, xli, 893-4; REALITIES OF IMAGINATION, xxvii, 304-10

Hunt, William, Woolman on, i, 323

Hunter, Anne, poem by, xli, 594-5

Hunter's Song, from WILHELM TELL, xxvi, 370-1

Hunting, Harrison on, xxxv, 361-2; Locke on, xxxvii, 187; More on, xxxvi, 212-13; Pascal on, xlviii, 54

HUNTING SONG, by Fielding, xli, 513-14

HUNTING SONG, by Scott, xli, 768

Hunting Song, from WILHELM TELL, xxvi, 416

Huntingdon, Earl of, in Crecy campaign, xxxv, 8, 12

Hurlame, King, xxxv, 193

HUSBAND, THE, AND THE PARROT, xvi, 37-8

Husband-honorer, story of, xlv, 708-11

Husbandry (see Agriculture)

Husbands and wives, Oberon's counsel to, xix, 177; Paul, St., on, xlv, 508; Ruskin on, xxviii, 149-50; Tennyson on, xlii, 1011; understanding of, 293-4

Huskisson, and free trade, xxv, 67

Huss, John, Browne on, iii, 291-2; Luther on, xxxvi, 333, 334; rise of, iii, 206; Woolman on, i, 230-1; Wyclif and, iii, 234

Hussites, Luther on the, xxxvi, 336-7

Hutcheson, Francis, and Adam Smith, x, 3; on moral sense, 373 note

Hutchinson, Mrs., Hazlitt on, xxvii, 294

Hutchison, W. G., translator of Renan, xxxii, 141

Huxley, Thomas Henry, life and works of, xxviii, 216; SCIENCE AND CULTURE, 215-32; on species, xi, 18

Huygens, and Hartsocher, xxxiv, 179

Hyacinth, and Apollo, iv, 19 (4); reference to, xli, 883

Hyacinth, flower, for constancy, vi, 431; Milton on the, iv, 77

Hyades, the rainy, xlii, 1008; Virgil on the, xiii, 148

Hyarba, and Dido, xiii, 163-4

Hybernation (see Hibernation)

Hybreas, and Antony, xii, 351-2

Hybridism, xi, 298-332

Hyde Park Affair, Mill in, xxv, 184-6

Hydra, digestion of the, xi, 194-5; reference to, iv, 84

Hydrogen, its affinity for oxygen, xxx, 145; Faraday on, 47-8, 50-3; Helmholtz on, 212-14; production of, 124-9, 140; water produced by combustion of, 131; weight of, 129-30, 142

Hydrophobia, Darwin on, xxix, 374-375

Hydrostatic Paradox, the, v, 278-9

Hydrostatics, Pascal on, xlviii, 9

Hygd, Queen, xlix, 59-60, 61, 66, 72, 94 note

Hygelac, in BEOWULF, xlix, 59, 61, 66, 67; death of, 67 note 3, 72, 87; historical basis of, 3; kinsman of Beowulf, 17, 47; Ongentheow and, 88, 89; the ring of, 39-40

Hylas, and Hercules, xlvi, 9, 25; reference to, xlvii, 711

HYLAS, NYMPH'S SONG TO, xlii, 1241-2

HYLAS AND PHILONOUS, DIALOGUES OF, xxxvii, 199-302; remarks on, 198

Hyllus, death of, xiii, 413-14

Hymen, references to, iv, 34, 337

Hymettus, reference to, iv, 405

HYMN, by Addison, xl, 410

HYMN BEFORE SUNRISE, xli, 724-6

HYMN OF CLEANTHES, ii, 185-6

HYMN TO DIANA, xl, 306-7

HYMN TO GOD THE FATHER, xl, 311-12

HYMN ON THE MORNING OF THE NATIVITY, iv, 7-15

Hymns, of Christian Church, xlv, 545-86; Augustine, St., on, vii, 153; Herbert on, xv, 405-6

Hypaius, Virgil on, xiii, 115, 118

Hyperbolus, Aristophanes on, viii, 435; banishment of, xii, 87; ostracism of, 119-20

Hyperides, the orator, ix, 214 note 2; death of, xii, 221; Demosthenes and, 207

Hyperion, reference to, xx, 383

Hypermnæstra, and Lynceus, viii, 186 note

Hypocrisy, in Burns's HOLY FAIR, vi, 102-3; Fielding on, xxxix, 188; Jesus on, xliv, 391 (37-44), 392 (1-3); Marcus Aurelius on, ii, 209 (7); Milton on, iv, 155; Mohammed on, xlv, 995; in PILGRIM'S PROGRESS, xv, 43-6; in religion, vi, 101; Webster on, xlvii, 731

HYPOCRITE, THE, by Molière, xxvi, 189-284

Hypocrites, in Dante's HELL, xi, 97-9; Molière on, xxvi, 203, 204, 268

Hypotheses, Rousseau on, xxxiv, 201

Hypsipyle, and Jason, xx, 77; in Limbo, 239 note 8; Lycurgus and, 254 note

Hythloday, Raphael, xxxvi, 92, 143, 145 et seq.; Peter Giles on, 255, 257

I DO CONFESS THOU ART SAE FAIR, vi, 457

I DREAMED A LAY, vi, 21-2

I FEAR THY KISSES, xli, 849-50

I GAED A WAEFU' GATE YESTREFN, vi, 377

I HAE A WIFE O' MY AIN, vi, 324

I HAE BEEN AT CROOKIEDEN, vi, 447

I LO'ED NE'ER A LADDIE BUT ANE, xli, 590-1

I LOVE MY LOVE IN SECRET, vi, 363-4

I LOVED A LASS, xl, 340-1

I MURDER HATE, vi, 400

I PROMESSI SPOSI, Manzoni's, xxi

I REIGN IN JEANIE'S BOSOM, vi, 334

Iacchus, hymn to, viii, 431; song to, in THE FROGS, 428-9

Iadmon, master of Æsop and Rhodope, xxxiii, 68

Iago, Macaulay on, xxvii, 396-7

Iambic Poetry, Sidney on, xxvii, 29

Iapis, in the ÆNEID, xiii, 408-9

Iasion, and Demeter, xxii, 74

Iasius, born in Italy, xiii, 137

Ibis, sacred in Egypt, xxxiii, 36, 37, 39-40; described, 40

Iblis, name of Satan, xvi, 9 note; xlv, 929

Ibn-Abbas, companion of Mohammed, xvi, 162 note

Ibn Hankal, on Sogd, v, 129-30

Ibn Roschd, xx, 21 note

Ibn-Sina (see Avicenna)

Ibrahim, the sheykh, xvi, 221-36

Icarius, father of Penelope, xxii, 18, 69

Ice, structure of compressed, xxx, 250-1, 258-9; expansive power of, 120-3; pliability of, 247-50, 257-8; regelation of, 244, 254-6; snow transformed to, 245-6; temperature of, affected by pressure, 242-3

ICE AND GLACIERS, by Helmholtz, xxx, 221-59

Icebergs, Dana's description of, xxiii, 310-11, 326; action of, on rocks, xxix, 268 note; use of, in disseminating seeds, xi, 410

Iceland, birds of, xxix, 265; Christianity in, xxxii, 179, 183; poets in, xxvii, 10

Iceland Spar, crystallization of, xxx, 31; effect of, on polarized light, 34-5

Ictinus, builder of Parthenon, xii, 51

Idæus, in Hades, xiii, 227

Idealism, Berkeley's xxxvii, 202-302; Emerson on, v, 46, 159-60, 453

Idealist, in FAUST, xix, 182

Ideals, Lowell on, xlii, 1459, 1464; xxxviii, 474

Ideas, abstract (see Abstract Ideas); association of, xxxvii, 322-3, 345-8, 349, 350; Berkeley on reality of, 201-302; Channing on, xxviii, 345-7; defined by Hume, xxxvii, 317; defined by Locke, 320 note; Descartes on reality of, xxxiv, 29, 34; Goethe on exchange of, xxxix, 265-6; Hume on origin of, xxxvii, 318-20, 355-6, 369; Innate, Hume on, 320 note; Plato on, ii, 94-6; power of originating, xxxvii, 360-1, 363; Relations of, 324; Rousseau on general, xxxiv, 187-8, 257; test of, xxxvii, 320, 356

Ides, of March, xii, 327
Idiots, in Limbo, iv, 150; Mohammed on care of, xlv, 981 note 4
Idleness, Caxton on, xxxix, 6, 14;
as a crime, xxv, 306; discontent-
ment and, i, 147-8; More on,
xxxvi, 191; Penn on, i, 344 (57);
Smith on, x, 275-7
Idol, fable of the, xvii, 27
Idolatry, David on, xliv, 160 (4);
Lessing on, xxxii, 196; Milton
on, iv, 348; Mohammed on, xlv,
926, 927, 928, 929; Pascal on,
xlviii, 330; Paul, St., on, xlv,
511 (4-5)
Idomeneus, in the ÆNEID, xiii, 135,
144, 370
Idomeneus, historian, on Pericles,
xii, 47
Idris, Mohammed on, xlv, 922
Idyllic Poetry, Wordsworth on,
xxxix, 313-14
IF DOUGHTY DEEDS, xli, 544-5
Ignatius, and the lions, xv, 268
Igneous Rocks, production of,
xxxviii, 414, 416, 440
Ignis Fatuus, in FAUST, xix, 162-3;
Milton on, iv, 279-80
Ignorance, Augustine, St., on, vii,
29; is bliss, xl, 462; Epictetus
on, ii, 139 (64); Hindu Krishna
on, xlv, 864-5, 874, 878, 879;
Hobbes on, xxxiv, 388-9; karma
depends on, xlv, 639, 677-8, 683-
4; Pascal on, xlviii, 114-15; Penn
on, i, 337; Socrates's three kinds
of, xxxix, 12
Ignorance, in PILGRIM'S PROGRESS,
xv, 128-9, 149-53, 167
Iguana, Vespucci on the, xliii, 40
note
IL PENSEROSO, iv, 35-9; Wordsworth on, xxxix, 314
Ilia, mother of Romulus and Remus, xiii, 84
Iliad, Arnold on selections from
the, xxviii, 72-3; Burke on heroes
of the, xxiv, 133-4; Dryden on,
xiii, 15; editorial remarks on,
xxii, 3-4, 6; Mill on the, xxv, 12-
13; Pascal on, xlviii, 212 (628);
Poe on, xxviii, 384; Thoreau on,
426
Ilioneus, in the ÆNEID, xiii, 79,
93-5, 97, 250-1, 316
I'LL AYE CA' IN BY YON TOWN, vi,
554
I'LL GO AND BE A SODGER, vi, 38
I'LL MEET THEE ON THE LEA RIG,
vi, 471
Illumination, cause of, from flame,
xxx, 110-14, 164
Illuminato, Dante on, xx, 339 note
31
Ill-will, in PILGRIM'S PROGRESS, xv,
295

Illyria, the modern Albania, xxviii,
273
Ilus, son of Mermerus, xxii, 16; in
Hades, xiii, 233
I'M O'ER YOUNG TO MARRY YET, vi, 311
Imagery, Burke on, xxiv, 53-4
Images, Calvin on, xxxix, 39; Jamblichus on, v, 173; Pascal on,
xlviii, 329-30; not allowed in
Utopia, xxxvi, 247
Imagination, Bagehot on the, xxviii,
184; Berkeley on, xxxvii, 272,
285; Burke on, xxiv, 9, 17-22;
Descartes on train of, xxxiv, 330-
4; Emerson on, v, 180, 184, 319-
20; fancy and, xxxix, 316;
Hobbes on, xxxiv, 325-30; Hume
on, xxxvii, 316, 317, 343, 442;
Kant on, xxxii, 366; Marcus
Aurelius on, ii, 248 (17), 249
(29); Mill on, xxv, 100; Pascal
on, xlviii, 34-7, 39; reason and,
xxvii, 368, 370; Renan on, xxxii,
149, 190; Schiller on, 307-8; Shelley on, xxvii, 345; Wordsworth
on, xxxix, 316-24, 349
IMAGINATION, REALITIES OF, xxvii,
304-10
Imitation, Bacon on, iii, 31; Burke
on passion of, xxiv, 44-5; Coleridge on, xxvii, 271; Emerson on,
v, 39, 64, 84; fable of, xvii, 45;
Hobbes on, xxxiv, 379; Jonson
on, xxvii, 60; in nature, xi, 235,
465-7; pleasure and pain from,
xxxix, 234; power of, among savages, xxix, 221
IMITATION OF CHRIST, vii, 209-379;
remarks on, 208; l, 32-3
Immanuel's Land, xv, 59, 124
Immaterialism, advantages of, xxxvii,
296-8; possible objections to, 299-
300
Immodesty, Epictetus on, ii, 125
(23), 164 (130)
Immorality, commentaries on, xxxix,
182
Immortality, Arnold on unbelief in,
xlii, 1185; Browne on, iii, 270 (7),
302-3, 304-5; Browning on, xlii,
1124; Buddha on question of, xlv,
662-7, 675-6; Burns on, vi, 334,
395; Carlyle on, v, 335; Cicero
on, ix, 12, 74-6; Dante on certainty of, xx, 316; Descartes on,
xxxiv, 48; Egyptian belief in,
xxxiii, 63; Emerson on, v, 248,
304, 314; Franklin on, i, 80,
94; Hindu idea of, xlv, 806-
7; Hume on, xxxvii, 423-4; Lessing on belief in, xxxii, 199-202,
205-6, 208-9, 211; Marcus Aurelius on possibility of, ii, 217 (21),
252 (50); More on, xxxvi, 208,
240-1; Omar Khayyam on, xli,
981, 985; Pascal on question of,

xlviii, 70-1, 80 (218-20); Paul, St., on, xlv, 523 (12-55); Penn on, i, 379-80 (487-502); Rousseau on, xxxiv, 270-2; Shelley on, xli, 884; Socrates on, ii, 28, 59-63, 68-73, 78-81, 85-104; Voltaire on, xxxiv, 107; Xenophon on, ix, 75

IMMORTALITY, ODE ON INTIMATIONS OF, xli, 609-15

Impact, heat produced by, xxx, 206; mechanical effects of inelastic, 206-7

Impartiality, Penn on, i, 373-4

Impeachments, in United States, xliii, 193 (5), 194 (6, 7), 202 (4)

Imperatives, defined, xxxii, 344; hypothetical and categorical, 345; of skill, prudence, and morality, 345-70; possibility of categorical, 384-6, 392-3, 395

Imperfection, Pope on, xl, 420, 421, 423, 425

Impetuosity, Machiavelli on, xxxvi, 86

Implacable, Mr., in PILGRIM'S PROGRESS, xv, 102

Importation, of instruments and materials encouraged, x, 424-9; restraints on, 346, 348-69, 370-88, 444

Impossibilities, Marcus Aurelius on, ii, 230 (17)

Impostors, in Dante's HELL, xx, 125-8

Imposts, under U. S. Constitution, xliii, 196 (8), 199 (2)

Impressions, of childhood, xlviii, 37; defined by Hume, xxxvii, 317; the basis of ideas, 318-20, 355-6, 369

Imprisonment, Pascal on, xlviii, 53

Improvement, Goethe on spirit of, xix, 358, 361, 376-7; Penn on, i, 360 (227-32); Rousseau on faculty of, xxxiv, 179-80; Woolman on, 1, 223

Impudence, defined by Hobbes, xxxiv, 356

Impulses, Mill on, xxv, 264-5

Imran's Family, chapter of, xlv, 962-79

In Cæna Domini, papal bull, xxxvi, 307 note 21

Ina, and Peter's Pence, xxxiv, 90

Inachus, river-god, viii, 71, 178 note

Incas Bridge, in the Andes, xxix, 354

Incarnation, Pascal on the, xlviii, 173 (526)

Incivility, Locke on, xxxvii, 129-31

Inclination (s), of children, xxxvii, 60-2, 89-90, 93-4, 96; Goethe on following, xxxix, 278; defined by Kant, xxxii, 344 note; distinguished from propensities, xxxii, 356 note

Income (see Revenue)

Incomprehensible Truths, Pascal on, xlviii, 142, 438-9

Inconsiderate, in PILGRIM'S PROGRESS, xv, 299

Inconsiderate, Mrs., in PILGRIM'S PROGRESS, xv, 189-90

Inconsistency, Emerson on, v, 65-6, 70-1; Lowell on, xxviii, 454 (see also Consistency)

Inconstancy, Pascal on, xlviii, 47 (110), 48 (112)

INCONSTANCY IN LOVE, vi, 536-7

Incontinence, in Dante's HELL, xx, 22-5; in PURGATORY, 251-2

Incorporatio, defined, xxxvi, 298

Increase, of organic beings, xi, 79-82; checks to, 82-5

Incredulity, Heraclitus on, xii, 190

Incrustations, Darwin on, xxix, 19-20

Incubators, in Utopia, xxxvi, 184

Incubus, invoked by Faust, xix, 52

Incurables, in Utopia, xxxvi, 221

Independence, Emerson on, v, 68, 69, 72, 73, 78-9; of heroism, 134; verses on, by Burns, vi, 324

INDEPENDENCE, INSCRIPTION FOR ALTAR OF, vi, 563

INDEPENDENCE AND RESOLUTION, xli, 674-8

Independence of Circumstances, Epictetus on, ii, 121 (14), 123 (19), 124 (20), 126 (25), 127 (31), 130 (38), 133 (49), 168 (141), 169 (144), 169 (145), 171 (148), 172 (151), 180 (187, 188); Kempis on, vii, 222-3, 250, 253-4, 254-5, 307, 320-1, 335-6; Marcus Aurelius on, ii, 202 (7, 9), 209 (6), 212 (16), 213 (3), 224 (2), 230 (18, 19, 20), 232 (29), 233 (35, 36), 237 (16); 247 (16), 250 (29), 252 (55), 254 (67), 255 (68), 261 (32), 262 (35), 263 (41), 264 (45, 47) 265 (51), 271 (13, 15), 274 (31, 32), 282 (13), 286 (32, 33), 292 (11), 298 (1, 2), 299 (3)

Index, of Roman Church, iii, 206

Indexing, Swift on, xxvii, 119

India, British rule in, v, 488; cause of early civilization of, x, 27-8; rates of interest in, 99; under the mercantile company, 77; religion, philosophy, and art of, xxxix, 455, 457; shells as money in, x, 30; wealth of, ancient, 309

INDIAN AIR, LINES TO AN, xli, 850

Indian Mutiny, incident of, xlii, 1229-30

Indian Summer, description of, v, 233

Indians, Bacon on barbarism of, iii, 143; Chilian, xxix, 293, 296, 317-19; civility of, xxxvii, 135; Columbus on, xliii, 23, 24-5, 26-7; under control of Congress, 174, 196 (3);

drunkenness among, 153; Eliot on Christianity among, 147-56; fires, method of making, among, i, 148; houses of ancient, xxix, 377-8; medicines of, xxxv, 252; myths of, xvii, 1; Norsemen and (see Skrellings); Peruvian, xxix, 379, 389; poets of, xxvii, 10; religion of, iii, 45; v, 286; xl, 420-1; rum among, i, 121, 268-9; on servants, 413 (268); S. American, xxix, 75-6, 79-80, 83-4, 113-17, 183-4, 378-9, 392; Vespucci on, xliii, 32-45; Woolman's visit to, i, 265-81

Indictments, in U. S., xliii, 207 (5)

Indifference, Buddha on, xlv, 612-13, 673, 728, 745; Burke on, xxiv, 34; in Dante's HELL, xx, 14-15, 221-2; Epictetus on, ii, 119 (8), 133 (51); Hindu teaching of, xlv, 806, 810-11, 825, 858, 866; Marcus Aurelius on, ii, 203 (11, 12), 204 (14), 213 (1), 215 (8), 216 (15), 220 (39), 222 (49), 230 (20), 231 (23), 240 (32), 242 (41), 244 (52), 246 (3), 247 (14), 249 (27), 250 (31), 257 (4), 259 (20), 264 (46), 271 (17), 273 (28), 283 (15), 284 (22, 23), 287 (34), 293 (16); Pascal on, xlviii, 75-7, 77 (200), 80 (217); Penn on, i, 374; Tennyson on, xlii, 1059; Whitman on, xxxix, 416-17

Indignation, Drake on, xxxiii, 133; defined by Hobbes, xxxiv, 354; language of, 358

Individual, Franklin on power of the, i, 95; state and, ii, 230 (22), 245 (54); v, 258

Individual Differences, Darwin on, xi, 59-62, 93-6, 104-5

Individuality, Channing on, xxviii, 344-5; Cicero on, xlviii, 123 note 7; democracy and, xxviii, 480-1; Emerson on, v, 22-4, 118-19, 122, 132-3, 195; Epictetus on, ii, 119 (8), 120 (9); Marcus Aurelius on, ii, 222 (49), 224 (3), 247 (15); Mazzini on, xxxii, 402-3; Mill on, xxv, 163-4, 212-17, 261-301; Schiller on need of, xxxii, 236 (see also Self-reliance)

Induction, Bacon on, xxxix, 139, 140, 143; Mill on, xxv, 104

Indulgence, Locke on, xxxvii, 28-30, 33-4

Indulgences, sale of, xxxvi, 295 note, 301 note 16, 314 note; Dante on sale of, xx, 411 note 7; Luther on, xxxvi, 261-2, 265-73, 331-2

Industrial Problems, Smith on solution of, x, 4

Industrial Schools, proposed by Ticknor, xxviii, 380

Industries, domestic, capital naturally seeks, x, 349-51; infant, protection of, 353-4

Industry, climate and, xxxiv, 181; food-supply in relation to, x, 86-9; Franklin on, i, 61, 79, 89, 95-6; Franklin's rule of, 83, 85; Huxley on, xxviii, 230; paper money in relation to, x, 245, 258-9, 262-3; Penn on, i, 344-5, 360; quantity of, on what dependent, x, 244, 275-7, 349; wages in relation to, 86

INEQUALITY, ON THE, AMONG MANKIND, xxxiv, 167-234

Inequality, Emerson on, v, 106; Hobbes on, xxxiv, 425; immortality and, xxxii, 201; More on, xxxvi, 177-8, 250-1; Pascal on, xlviii, 127 (380); Penn on, i, 412 (255-8); Pope on, xl, 442-3

Inertia, of matter, Hobbes on, xxxiv, 325; Hume on, xxxvii, 365 note; Kelvin on, xxx, 315, 316

INES, FAIR, xli, 930-1

Inexperience, Hippocrates on, xxxviii, 5

Infallibility, Pascal on, xlviii, 310 (876), 311 (880)

Infancy, Augustine, St., on, vii, 9-11; Locke on impressions of, xxxviii, 9, 28-9, 34-5; nonconformity of, v, 65; Pope on, xl, 436; Wordsworth on, xli, 611

INFANT, ON AN, DYING AS SOON AS BORN, xli, 754-5

Infatuation, Buddha on, xlv, 685; freedom from, 686-7

INFERNO, Dante's, xx, 5-146

Infinite Divisibility, Hume on, xxxvii, 437-8 note

Infinities, in geometry, xxxiv, 127-8; Hume on, xxxvii, 437-8 note

Infinity, artificial, xxiv, 65; Burke on, 55, 67-8; Burke on sublimity of, 64-5, 117-20; Hobbes on, xxxiv, 334; Kelvin on, xxx, 270; Pascal on, xlviii, 28-8, 49 (121), 78 (206), 83 (231-3), 436-44

Infusoria, in air of St. Jago, xxix, 15; on surface of ocean, 24-8

Inga, emperor of Guiana, xxxiii, 331-2

Ingævones, Tacitus on the, xxxiii, 95

Ingcél, the One-eyed, xlix, 217, 222-6, 228-9, 230-62

Ingeld, and Freawaru, xlix, 62 note, 63 note

Ingenhousz, Dr., xxxviii, 181

Ingenuity, Penn on, i, 360 (229)

Ingenuousness, Locke on, xxxvii, 122

Ingolf, the Norseman, xliii, 5

Ingratitude, Cervantes on, xiv, 195; Hobbes on, xxxiv, 423; Shake-

speare on, xl, 273-4; Shakespeare on, of children, xlvi, 225, 226, 254; Sheridan on, xviii, 166

Inheritance, Bacon on riches by, iii, 93, 94; Burke on principle of, xxiv, 181; Emerson on, v, 51-2, 251; freedom of, in BODY OF LIBERTIES, xliii, 72 (10); in Massachusetts, 82 (81, 82); Mill on, xxv, 149; Mohammedan laws of, xlv, 981-2, 984, 998; Pascal on, xlviii, 383 (see also Heredity)

Inheritance Taxes, Smith on, x, 529, 532

Injuries, Browne on, iii, 334; Epictetus on repaying, ii, 153; Franklin on resenting, i, 83; Hobbes on, xxxiv, 386, 409; Machiavelli on, xxxvi, 11; Marcus Aurelius on, ii, 231 (25), 238 (20), 293 (18); Penn's maxim on, i, 364 (298); Socrates on, ii, 38

Injustice, Hobbes on, xxxiv, 409, 417-22, 426; Marcus Aurelius on, ii, 267 (1); Pascal on, xlviii, 79 (214), 154 (454); Socrates on, ii, 38

Innate Ideas, Hume on, xxxvii 320 note; Voltaire on, xxxiv, 106

Inner Life, admonitions concerning the, vii, 248-67

Inner Light, Kempis on the, vii, 269-70; Woolman on, i, 182, 184, 203, 222, 233, 258-9

INNER VISION, THE, xli, 688

Innis, anecdote of, i, 159-60

INNKEEPER, NICKNAMED "THE MARQUIS," vi, 534

Innocence, Goethe on, xix, 129; Marvell on, xl, 386; Sheridan on consciousness of, xviii, 163; virtue and, i, 375 (443-4)

INNOCENCE, AUGURIES OF, xli, 601-4

Innocent VI, and King John, xxxv, 34

Innocent, in PILGRIM'S PROGRESS, xv, 203-4

Innocent, Mount, xv, 295

Innovation, Bacon on, iii, 65-6; Berkeley on, xxxvii, 281; Burke on spirit of, xxiv, 181; Gallus on, xxxv, 332 note; Machiavelli on, xxxvi, 8, 21-2; Penn on, i, 360 (230-1); reform contrasted with, xxiv, 411; Smith on, xxvii, 251; Washington on, xliii, 257-8

Inns of the Court, xxxv, 400

Ino, in the BACCHÆ, viii, 379, 400; in the ODYSSEY, xxii, 80

Inoculation, Franklin on, i, 100; extended by Pasteur, xxxviii, 284; Voltaire on, xxxiv, 95-9; Woolman on, i, 247 (see also Vaccination)

Inquiry, Bacon on, xi, 1; Bacon's method of, xxxix, 138-47, 150-3;

Browne on, iii, 277; Burke on, xxiv, 7-8, 9, 48, 49; Buddha on useless subjects of, xlv, 662-7; Carlyle on, xxv, 334, 362; Channing on, xxviii, 336; Emerson on, v, 21; Hobbes on ends of, xxxiv, 359-62, 389-90; judgment and fancy in, 364-5; Hume on limits of, xxxvii, 442-5; Kempis on, vii, 272 (4), 378 (1, 2); 379 (5); Marcus Aurelius on, ii, 210 (11), 234 (3), 246 (4), 250 (30), 258 (11), 288 (37), 304 (29); Penn on, i, 354, 404 (164); Plutarch on improper love of, xii, 36

Inquisition, censorship of press by the, iii, 203, 206, 208; Galileo and, xxxiv, 113; in the Netherlands, xix, 251-2; Pascal on the, xlviii, 320

Inquisitiveness, of children, xxxvii, 111-14; Horace on, xxvii, 35 note 33

Insects, color of, xi, 146; flowers and, 106-7, 108-9, 110-11; Harrison on, xxxv, 365; hearts in, xxxviii, 89-90, 137; imitation among, xi, 235-6, 467; luminous, 199-200; neuter and sterile, 290-5; phosphorescent, xxix, 40-1; respiration in, xxxviii, 142; at sea, xxix, 173; wings of, developed from tracheæ, xi, 196

Insensibility, Pascal on, xlviii, 77 (197-8)

INSENSIBILITY, HAPPY, xli, 898-9

Insight, Confucius on, xliv, 39 (6)

Insincerity, Marcus Aurelius on, ii, 205 (16)

Inspiration, Emerson on, v, 28, 29, 45, 63, 74; Epictetus on, ii, 134 (53); Hobbes on, xxxiv, 368; Pascal on, xlviii, 91 (245); Plutarch on, xii, 183-4; Quaker doctrine of, xxxiv, 70-1

Instævones, Tacitus on the, xxxiii, 96

INSTAURATIO MAGNA, PREFACES TO, xxxix, 122-49; editorial remarks on, 3

Instigation, Mill on liberty of, xxv, 260, 307-9

Instinct, Burke on, xxiv, 428; Darwin on, xi, 262-97; Emerson on, v, 74-5; of giant crab, xxix, 488; Hume on, xxxvii, 395; Pascal on, xlviii, 119 (344), 131 (396), 448-9; Pope on, xl, 423-4, 435-6; Rousseau on, xxxiv, 276 note

INSTITUTES, DEDICATION OF CALVIN'S, xxxix, 29-54

Institutions, Burke on sudden changes in, xxiv, 304-5; Emerson on, v, 10, 72, 198

Institutions, Public, expense of, x, 473-88

Instruction, Emerson on, v, 248; Epictetus on need of, ii, 156 (105); expense of public, x, 485-486

Instructions, in Slough of Dispond, xv, 20

INSTRUMENT OF GOVERNMENT, THE, xliii, 113-25

Instruments, Berkeley on, xxxvii, 253-4; Smith on, x, 227-8, 424-442

Insurance, Smith on, x, 114-15

Insurance Corporations, x, 483, 484

Insurrections, congressional control of, xliii, 197 (15)

INTEGER VITÆ, xl, 293-4

Integrity, Franklin on, i, 91

Intellect, Archytas on, ix, 60; beauty and, xxxii, 282, 288; Carlyle on unconsciousness of high, xxv, 336; Channing on the, xxviii, 334, 337; Emerson on the, v, 139, 140, 198, 292-3; good, marred, and evil, xlv, 879; Hobbes on, xxxiv, 362-73; love and, xlviii, 421, 422; Marcus Aurelius on, ii, 215 (4); as measure of organization, xi, 135; Pascal on, xlviii, 9, 10 (7), 127 (378), 280; Rousseau on, xxxiv, 251-3

Intellectual Growth, Emerson on, v, 142

Intelligence, three scales of, xxxvi, 79

Intemperance, taught to children, xxxvii, 31-2; fruits of, iv, 334; Luther on, xxxvi, 349-50; a tyranny, xlvi, 357; Woolman on, i, 204-5 (see also Drunkenness)

Intention(s), Kant on, xxxii, 323-31; Kempis on purity of, vii, 310 (2); Locke on, xxxvii, 110; James Mill on, xxv, 37

Interbreeding, Darwin on close, xi, 110, 140, 318

INTERCOURSE, TRUTH OF, by Stevenson, xxviii, 287-94

Intercrossing, compared with change of conditions, xi, 317-18; importance of, 57; necessity of, 109-14; reciprocal, 308; between species, 298-318; species kept true by, 115-16; varieties, how affected by, 105, 114-15

Interdicts, Luther on, xxxvi, 282 note 323

Interest (ethical), as source of errors, xlviii, 38; as basis of friendship, ix, 26-7; Hobbes on, xxxiv, 277, 389; Kant on, xxxii, 344 note, 380 note, 391 note.

Interest (monetary), defined, x, 55; in Elizabethan England, xxxv, 315-16; unknown among ancient Germans, xxxiii, 110; legal regula-

tion of, x, 298-9; Luther on, xxxvi, 348-9; in early Massachusetts, xliii, 74 (23); Penn on, 1, 354; price of land dependent on rate of, x, 299; rates of, historically considered, x, 94-7, 99-100; rate of, on what dependent, 294-7; rate of, affected by taxes on profits, 527-8; rate of, due to insecurity, 101; rate of, determines building rent, 510-11; rates of, as index of profits, 102-3; taxes on, 519-22 (see also Usury)

Intermediate Varieties, absence of, xi, 179-84; in geological formations, 346-54

Intermitting, Burke on, xxiv, 73-4, 117-18

International Law, offences against, xliii, 197 (10)

International Relations, Washington on, xliii, 261-2

Interpreter, in PILGRIM'S PROGRESS, xv, 33-41, 204-14

Interruptions, Bacon on, iii, 66-7; Locke on, xxxvii, 133-4, 135

Interstate Commerce, xliii, 196 (3), 198 (6)

INTIMATIONS OF IMMORTALITY, xli, 609-15; Mill on, xxv, 98

Intolerance, Mill on, xxv, 38, 234-7; in politics, xliii, 214

Introspection, Burke on value of, xxiv, 9

Introversion, Emerson on, v, 20-1

Intuition, Emerson on, v, 63, 66, 74; Mill on doctrine of, xxv, 174-5; Mill on knowledge by, 146; Pascal on, xlviii, 41 (95), 99-100, 145 (434)

Intuitive Mind, Pascal on the, xlviii, 7-10

Invective(s), Browne on religious, iii, 268; Hobbes on, xxxiv, 364; Luther on, xxxvi, 354; Swift on, xxvii, 124

Inventions, monopolies of, in BODY OF LIBERTIES, xliii, 72 (9); Emerson on, v, 86; Franklin on patenting, i, 116-17; Penn on, 360 (230-2); profits of, x, 64; Voltaire on, xxxiv, 101-2; Woolman on, i, 223

Inventors, honors for, Channing on, xxviii, 370; in New Atlantis, iii, 190

INVENTORY, THE, vi, 194-6

INVERARY, THE BARD AT, vi, 286

Inverey, in THE BARON OF BRACKLEY, xl, 120-3

Investigation (see Inquiry)

Investitures, Luther on, xxxvi, 308-309

Investments, Smith on imprudent, x, 281

INVITATION, THE, by Shelley, xli, 866-7

INVITATION, APOLOGY FOR DECLIN-
ING AN, vi, 549
INVITATION, EXTEMPORE REPLY TO
AN, vi, 490
INVITATION, VERSIFIED REPLY TO AN,
vi, 210
Invocation, by Shelley, xli, 847-8
Inward Consolation, Kempis on,
vii, 268-348
Io, in PROMETHEUS BOUND, viii,
175-86
Iodine, vapor of, xxx, 42-3
Iolas, in the ÆNEID, xiii, 384, 414
Iole, Dante on, xx, 324; on Hercu-
les, v, 192
Ion, on Pericles, xii, 41
Ionian Sea, named from Io, viii,
185
Ionians, in Egypt, xxxiii, 79-80, 84
Iopas, in the ÆNEID, xiii, 101
Iophon, son of Sophocles, viii, 196,
287, 421
Iphicles, the kine of, xxii, 159
IPHIGENEIA, by Landor, xli, 927-8
Iphigenia, Æschylus on sacrifice of,
viii, 12-14; Dante on, xx, 305;
Landor on, xli, 927-8; Lucretius
on, iii, 14; Ruskin on, xxviii, 146
Iphimedeia, in Hades, xxii, 160
Iphitus, son of Eurytus, xxii, 295-
6; in sack of Troy, xiii, 114, 118
Iquique, town of, xxix, 383-4
Iras, Cleopatra and, xii, 382, 402;
in ALL FOR LOVE, xviii, 36-7, 68,
70, 84, 86, 96-99
Ireland, candle-eating in, xxxv, 374;
Christianity in, xxxii, 178, 179,
180-1, 182-90; Emerson on, v,
354; epic literature of, xlix, 210;
Freeman on, xxviii, 267, 276;
Mill on, xxv, 151-2, 187-8; New-
man on, xxviii, 50-1; poetry in,
xxvii, 125-30; Renan on, xxxii,
143, 146; woollen manufactures of,
x, 204
IRELAND, THE FAIR HILLS OF, xli,
947-8
Irenæus, St., on early converts,
xxviii, 38; Milton on, iii, 213
IRESON'S RIDE, xlii, 1434-7
Iris, Juno and, xiii, 48, 181; Milton
on, iv, 48, 73, 328; in THE TEM-
PEST, xlvi, 425-6, 427-8
Irish, cold baths among the, xxxvii,
13-14; Thackeray on the, xxviii,
15 (see also Celtic Races)
Irish Channel, tides in, xxx, 302
IRISH EMIGRANT, LAMENT OF THE,
xli, 945-7
Irish Rebel, story of the, iii, 103-4
Iron, beginnings of use of, xxxiv,
210-11; More on, xxxvi, 202;
combustion of, in oxygen, xxx,
144; action of, on water, 124-7
Iron Brigade, at Gettysburg, xliii,
347 note, 352
IRON HENRY, tale of, xvii, 51-4

IROQUOIS INDIANS, TREATY WITH,
xliii, 246-9
Irresolution, Hobbes on, xxxiv, 380,
387
Irrevocable Laws, fallacy of, xxvii,
241-7
Irus, the beggar, Ulysses and, xxii,
255-8
Irving, Edward, Carlyle and, xxv,
329
Isaac, son of Abraham, xliv, 442
(8); Augustine, St., on, vii, 196;
Mohammed on, xlv, 922; Pascal
on, xlviii, 205
Isabella, Queen, of Castile, on
forms, iii, 131; Raleigh on, xxxix,
89, 90
Isabella, Queen of Edward II, her
griefs, xlvi, 12-13, 18-19; sues for
Gaveston's recall, 19-22; reconciled to king, 23-4; at Gaveston's
return, 28-30; accused by king,
34; in Tynemouth, 37-9; sent to
France, 45, 51, 52-5; return with
Mortimer, 56-60; Edward on, 64,
66, 67; her triumph with Morti-
mer, 68-9; her part in king's
death, 69-70; with Prince Ed-
ward, 71, 76; at death of Kent,
77; accused of king's murder, 81-
3; committed to Tower, 83-4
Isæus, Demosthenes and, xii, 200;
Pliny on, ix, 223-5
Isaiah, Augustine, St., on, vii, 152;
Burns on, vi, 145; prophecy of
Eucharist, xlviii, 355; murder of,
xlv, 925 note
Isauricus, Servilius, xii, 306
Iscantinaro, Cesare, xxxi, 215, 216
Iselastic Games, ix, 436 note
Iseult, Renan on, xxxii, 149
Ishmael, xlii, 1370; Mohammed on,
xlv, 922
Isidore, Archbishop of Seville, xx,
330 note 26
Isis, the Egyptian Demeter, xxxiii,
81; Herodotus on, 25, 33, 34;
temple of, at Memphis, 89; Mil-
ton on, iv, 14, 102; as Suevian
goddess, xxxiii, 100
Islam, xlv, 963, 969 (see also Mo-
hammedanism)
Islands, species of oceanic, xi, 431-
44
Isle of France, Darwin on, xxix,
509-12
ISLES OF GREECE, xli, 833-5
Ismael the Sophy, beauty of, iii, 112
Ismarus, in the ÆNEID, xiii, 331
Ismene, in ANTIGONE, viii, 244-6,
257-60; in Dante's Limbo, xx,
239; in ŒDIPUS THE KING, viii,
240-1; in PHÆDRA, xxvi, 139-42
Ismenias, Plutarch on, xii, 37
Isocrates, Demosthenes and, xii,
200; Logos Arepagiticos of, iii,
194, 201; old age of, ix, 50; oration

for son of Alcibiades, xii, 119; on oratory at feasts, xxxii, 56; school of, iii, 256-7; on teachers, x, 142

Isodorus, C., slaves of, ix, 393 note 2

Isolation, Cicero on, ix, 38; Emerson on, v, 78, 217; Kempis on need of, vii, 335-6; qualities of mind due to, xxviii, 177-9, 193, 197; species in regard to, xi, 116-17

Israelites (see Jews)

Ister, Herodotus on the, xxxiii, 21

IT WAS A' FOR OUR RIGHTFU' KING, vi, 525

Italian Classics, xxxii, 127

ITALIAN ESSAYS, xxxii, 399-419

Italian Language, change in, xxxix, 212; Milton on study of, iii, 254; Sidney on, xxvii, 53

Italian Literature, Arnold on, xxviii, 76; Taine on, xxxix, 461

Italicus, Silius, Pliny on, ix, 246-248

Italy, Alfieri on, v, 343, 359; two civilizations of, xxxix, 448; Dante on distractions of, xx, 170-1; Goethe on art of, xxxix, 273, 279; Goldsmith on, xli, 535-7; Harrison on, xxxv, 235-6, 327; named Hesperia of old, xiii, 94, 137; language as factor in re-uniting, xxviii, 265-6; Louis XII in, xxxvi, 13-15, 25; Macaulay on mediæval, xxxvii, 384-95, 401; Machiavelli on princes of, xxxvi, 82-3; Machiavelli's plea for freedom of, 86-90; mercenaries in, 45-6; papal power in, 290; politics of, after Charles VIII, xxvii, 406-7, 409-10; Renaissance in, l, 23; Taine on mediæval, xxxix, 448; Turner on travels in, xxxv, 399; Virgil on ancient, iii, 79

Ithaca, Homer on, xxii, 64, 120

Ithacus (see Ulysses)

Ithuriel, in PARADISE LOST, iv, 177-8

Itinerant Preachers, Franklin on, i, 108; Penn on, 377 (461)

Itylus, and Philomela, xx, 215 note; Homer on, xxii, 281

ITYLUS, by Swinburne, xlii, 1249

Iülus (see Ascanius)

Ivon, and Ivor, xlix, 167, 178, 185

IVY GREEN, THE, xlii, 1194-5

Ixion, Æschylus on, viii, 132, 143; Virgil on, xiii, 231-2

Iwarawaqueri, the, xxxiii, 367, 369, 371

Jackson, Lidian, second wife of Emerson, v, 3

Jackson, Stonewall, and Barbara Frietchie, xlii, 1440-1

Jacob, and the angel, xlii, 1360; Augustine, St., on, vii, 196; Bunyan on dissimulation of, xv, 264;

Milton on, iv, 151, 328, 349; Mohammed on, xlv, 922, 934, 938-41; Pascal on, xlviii, 205, 207, 241; the Psalmist on, xliv, 280 (10), 281 (23); Stephen on, 442 (8), 443 (12, 14-16)

Jacob's Ladder, Bunyan on, xv, 240

JACOBITE'S EPITAPH, A, xli, 943

JACOBITES, YE, BY NAME, vi, 446-7

Jacobs, Joseph, compiler of Æsop's Fables, xvii, 3

Jacobus de Benedictis, hymn by, xlv, 565

Jael, Sisira and, iv, 443; xv, 58

Ja'far, vizier of Harun Er-Rashid, xvi, 66, 107, 226-31, 239-41

Jaguar, flesh of the, xxix, 129; habits of, 147-9

Jairus, the daughter of, xliv, 381 (41-2), 382 (49-56)

Jamaica, disturbance in, xxv, 188-90

Jamblichus, xxxiii, 412-13

James, St., the Great, xliv, 370 (10-11), 373 (14), 382 (51), 384 (28), 386 (54), 430 (13), 456 (2); in Dante's PARADISE, xx, 392-4

James, St., son of Alphaeus, xliv, 373 (15), 430 (13), 463 (13 21)

James II, of Aragon, xx, 370 note 14

James I, King of England, Bacon to, xxxix, 125-6; Bentham on, xxvii, 241; Bohemia and, xv, 350-1; Dr. Donne and, 343-45, 347, 348, 351-2, 353; Harvey and, xxxviii, 64; George Herbert and, xv, 385, 387, 388, 390; marriage bed of, x, 288; Andrew Melvin and, xv, 386; Puritans and, xxvii, 145-6; Raleigh on, xxxix, 82-4; charter to Virginia, xliii, 51-61

James II, Bentham on abdication of, xxvii, 247; Burke on, xxiv, 171, 175-6; Dissenters and, xxvii, 147; William Penn and, xxxiv, 78

James I, of Scotland, xlii, 1200-25; his imprisonment in England, xxxv, 286

James, king of Majorca, xx, 370 note 13

James, in PILGRIM'S PROGRESS, xv, 222, 226-7, 230-1, 248, 256, 262, 277-8, 290

James, Abel, letter of, to Franklin, i, 71-72

James Island, Darwin on, xxix, 398-9

JAMIE, COME TRY ME, vi, 363

Jan Yu, xliv, 10 note 4, 15 note 5, 19 (6) note 10, 20 (10), 23 (14), 34 (2), 35 (12), 36 (16, 21, 23), 37 (25), 44 (9, 14), 56 (1)

Jane, in SHOEMAKER'S HOLIDAY,

xlvii, 451, 453-4, 477, 483-6, 490, 500-3
Janizaries, Bacon on, iii, 54 and note
Jann, species of genii, xvi, 9 note
Jansenists, xlviii, 5; Pascal on the, 307 (865), 312 (887)
Jansenius, Cornelius, xlviii, 5, 293 (834)
Janus, Milton on, iv, 326; Virgil on, xiii, 85, 249, 264
Jarjaris, the Efrit, xvi, 80
Jason, son of Æson, in Dante's HELL, xx, 77
Jason, brother of Onias, xx, 81 note 5
Jason, the Christian, xliv, 468 (5-9)
Java, Drake at, xxxiii, 232-3
Jaws, and limbs, related, xi, 155
JAY AND PEACOCK, fable of, xvii, 18
Jay, John, article in the FEDERALIST, xliii, 216-21
Jealousy, Æschylus on, viii, 34; Bacon on, of husbands, iii, 23; Campion on, xl, 293; defined by Hobbes, xxxiv, 354; Dryden on, xviii, 67; Eliphaz on, xliv, 79 (2); music and, xli, 490; Pascal on, xlviii, 167 (502); Penn on, i, 358, 407; rage and, xxxiv, 367
JEAN, THY BONIE FACE, IT IS NA, vi, 334
Jefferson, Thomas, author of DECLARATION OF INDEPENDENCE, xliii, 160 note; the Mecklenburg Declaration and, 166 note
Jeffrey, Francis, Carlyle and, xxv, 330; Edinburgh Review and, xxvii, 236
Jehoshaphat, Last Judgment in, xx, 41 note 1
Jehovah, name of God (see JOB, BOOK OF, and PSALMS)
Jellaladeen, parable of, xxviii, 473-4
Jemimah, daughter of Job, xliv, 143
Jenner, Edward, life and works, xxxviii, 150; ON VACCINATION, 151-231
Jenner, Henry, xxxviii, 162, 169, 213, 222, 228
Jenner, Rev. G. C., xxxviii, 225-6
JENNY KISS'D ME, xli, 893
Jephthah, Dante on, xx, 305; daughter of, xlvi, 127; Milton on, iv, 387, 426
Jeremiah, Burns's paraphrase of, vi, 25; Calvin on, xxxix, 45; worshipped in Egypt, 37; imprisonment of, xlv, 925 note; Pascal on, xlviii, 214; Woolman on, i, 203
Jeremy, in SHE STOOPS TO CONQUER, xviii, 246-7
Jeroboam, Bunyan on, xv, 313
Jerome, St., apparition of, iii, 210; on angels, xx, 409 note 1; on idleness, xxxix, 14
Jerome of Prague, xxxvi, 333, 334

Jerusalem, Dante on destruction of, xx, 234 note 5, 313 note 6; Jesus on, xliv, 398 (34-5), 411 (41-4); Jews on situation of, v, 347; lament over destruction of, xliv, 248; Paré on destruction of, xxxviii, 32; Pascal on ruin of, xlviii, 222 (654); prayer for peace of, 312; prophecy of destruction of, xliv, 415 (20-4); temple of, washed with alum, xxxv, 336; Woolman on wickedness of, i, 215
JERUSALEM, THE GOLDEN, xlv, 561
JESSIE, THE FLOWER O' DUNBLANE, xli, 608
Jester's Song, from JOLLY BEGGARS, vi, 132
Jesting, Bacon on limits of, iii, 88; clumsy, no joke, xvii, 14; with malice, Sheridan on, xviii, 116
JESU, DULCEDO CORDIUM, xlv, 563
JESU, DULCIS MEMORIA, xlv, 562
Jesuits, Bacon on cunning of, iii, 60; miracles performed by, 292 (27); Pascal on, xlviii, 5, 303, 304 (854), 307 (865), 311 (882), 314 (891), 315 (902), 319 (919), 320
Jesus, apostles of, xliv, 373 (13-16); baptism of, 366 (21-2); birth of, 362 (7); birth of, hymns on, xlv, 567-8, 578-9; birth of, Milton on, iv, 354-5, 369; blind man restored by, xliv, 409 (35-43); Burns on, vi, 145; Browne on eclipse at death of, iii, 294 (29); Bunyan on, xv, 145; Calderon on death of, xxvi, 22; centurion and, xliv, 376 (2-10); Chaucer on language of, xl, 31; circumcision of, xliv, 363 (21); circumcision of, Milton on, iv, 42; coming of the Lord, 394 (35-59), 406 (22-37), 407 (8), 415 (8-11), 416 (25-36); Dante on darkness at death of, xx, 410-11; cures demoniacs, xliv, 385 (38-43), 390 (14-26); heals dropsy, 398 (1-6); Emerson on, v, 29, 30, 70, 72, 146, 148, 153, 160, 205; feasts in commemoration of, xv, 408-9; feeds five thousand, xliv, 383 (11-17); the fig-tree and, xxxv, 140; Francis, St., on love of, xlv, 568-9; Franklin on, i, 84; Gadarene miracle, xliv, 380 (27-39); genealogy of, 366 (23-38); Herod and, 383 (7-9); Hume on miracles of, xxxvii, 396; infirm woman cured by, xliv, 396 (11-17); Jairus's daughter raised by, 381 (41-2); Jerusalem, entry into, 411 (28-44); Jerusalem, foretells destruction of, 415 (20-4); John the Baptist and, 377; Kempis on cross of, vii, 262-3; Kempis on loving, 255-7; Lamb on, xxvii, 295; last supper, xliv, 417 (14-

37); lepers healed by, 405 (11-19), 371 (12-15); lullaby for infant, xl, 261-5; MacDonald on, xlii, 1163-4; Martha and Mary with, xliv, 388 (38-42); Mary Magdalene and, 378 (37-50); Mill on persecution of, xxv, 227-8; Mill on teachings of, 254; miraculous draught of fishes, xliv, 370 (4-11); Mohammed on, xlv, 921, 965-7, 979, 996-8, 1013, 1016, 1020-1; More on teachings of, xxxvi, 175; palsied man healed by, xliv, 371 (18-26); parable of fig-tree, 396 (6-9); parable of Good Samaritan, 388 (25-37); parable of great supper, 399 (15-24); parable of the importunate widow, 407 (1-5); parable of Lazarus, 404 (19-31); parable of lost sheep, 401 (3-7); parable of marriage feast, 399 (8-11); parable of old and new garments and wines, 372 (36-9); parable of the Pharisee and publican, 407 (9-14); parable of piece of silver, 401 (8-10); parable of prodigal son, 401 (11-32); parable of rich man, 393 (16-21); parable of sower, 379 (4-15); parable of ten servants, 410 (11-26); parable of unjust steward, 402 (1-13); parable of vineyard, 412 (9-18); in PARADISE REGAINED, iv, 363 et seq.; Pascal on, xlviii, 81 (222-3), 178-80, 182 (554), 267 (744), 278 (786-92), 280; Pascal on miracles of, 285 (808-13), 290 (826), 291 (829), 293 (834), 294 (838, 839), 298, 299; passion and death, xliv, 419-23; passion of, Milton on, iv, 24-5; Paul, St., on resurrection of, xlv, 522 (3-11); Peter and, xliv, 419 (55-62); Peter on, 432 (22-36), 435, 436 (10-12); Pharisees and, 391 (37-44), 403 (14-17); Plato and, xxvii, 363; teaches prayer, xliv, 389 (1-13); public ministry, 368-416; resurrection of, 423-4; Rousseau on, xxxiv, 310-11; on the Sabbath, xliv, 372 (1-11), 397 (14-16), 398 (1-6); Sadducees and, 413 (27-40); casts sellers out of temple, 411 (45-6); sermon on the mount, 374 (20-49); sends out seventy disciples, 386 (1-24); Shelley on, xxvii, 362; Sidney on parables of, 21; storm stilled by, xliv, 380 (22-5); temptation of, 367 (1-13); transfiguration of, 384 (29-36); on tribute money, 413 (22-6); xxxvi, 389; Watts on, xlv, 549-50; Wesley on, 572-3; widow of Nain and, xliv, 376 (11-17); on the widow's mite, 414 (1-4); women and, 379

(2-3); xv, 269); Woolman on, i, 291; Zacchaeus and, xliv, 409 (1-10) (see also Christ)

Jethro, daughter of, xlii, 1140

Jetter, in EGMONT, xix, 247-53, 266-72, 292-7, 312-13

Jevons, on Herodotus, xxxiii, 4

JEWISH PHYSICIAN, story of the, xvi, 150-8

Jews, Browne on the, iii, 290 (25); in England, v, 360; German, cold baths of, xxxvii, 13; Justine on the, in Egypt, iii, 294; Lessing on the, xxxii, 196-207; Lowell on the, xxviii, 472; Luther on the, xxxvi, 316, 327, 333, 348, 350; Milton on history of the, iv, 349-54; Mohammed on the, xlv, 913-15, 924-5, 932, 954, 966, 970, 996-7, 1010, 1013, 1014, 1015, 1016-17; in New Atlantis, iii, 176; orange-tawny worn by, 106 note; permanence of the, v, 351; Pascal on the, xlviii, 190, 197 (592), 207 (618), 208-13, 215 (633), 216-17, 220 (645-6), 224 (662-4), 226 (670-1), 229, 238 (701), 239 (702-4), 240-1, 242 (713), 248 (714), 261-2, 263 (735), 265, 267 (745-50), 271 (759-63), 274 (774), 285 (808), 289 (822), 292 (829), 355; Winthrop on commonwealth of the, xliii, 96

Jezebel, Raleigh on, xxxix, 74

JHANSI, IN THE ROUND TOWER OF, xlii, 1229-30

Jinni, defined, xvi, 9 note

Joab, Edomites and, xliv, 219; Winthrop on, xliii, 100

Joabin, merchant of New Atlantis, iii, 176

Joachim, Abbot of Flora, xx, 340 note 38

Joan of Arc, burning of, xxxix, 377; education of, xxviii, 158-9; Renan on, xxxii, 161-2

Joanna, wife of Chuzas, xliv, 379 (3), 424 (10)

Job, Browne on, iii, 308 (44), 332; Burke on, xxiv, 427; Milton on, iv, 367, 372, 390; Pascal on, xlviii, 65 (174)

JOB, THE BOOK OF, xliv, 73-143; compared with Æschylus, viii, 3; Burke on passages from, xxiv, 58-9, 60; editorial remarks on, xliv, 72; l, 18-19, 31; Hugo on, xxxix, 371; Lessing on, xxxii, 202; Pascal on, xlviii, 266 (741); Shelley on, xxvii, 348

Jocasta, in ŒDIPUS THE KING, viii, 218-19, 223-4, 228, 234-5; called Epicaste, xxii, 159

JOCK OF HAZELDEAN, xli, 758-9

JOCKEY'S TAEN THE PARTING KISS, vi, 582

Joel, prophecy of, xliv, 432

Johannes Parricida (see John of Suabia)

John, St., disciple of Jesus, xliv, 371 (10-11), 373 (14), 382 (51), 384 (28), 385 (49), 386 (54), 417 (8-13), 430 (13), 434 (1), 436-7; apocalypse of, iv, 157; v, 183; vi, 146; on the Eucharist, xlviii, 354-5; Gospel of, translated by Faust, xix, 50; Milton on, iii, 243; in Paradise, xx, 395-7, 423; in Samaria, xliv, 446 (14-25)

John, St., of Damascus, hymn by, xlv, 555

John, called Mark, xliv, 456 (12), 457 (25), 458 (5, 13), 465 (37-9)

JOHN BAPTIST, SAINT, by Drummond, xl, 335

John the Baptist, birth prophesied, xliv, 358 (13-17); birth of, 360 (57-63); childhood in desert, 361 (80); Dante on, xv, 240, 366 note 12, 421; Herod and, xliv, 366 (19-20), 383 (9); Jesus and, 377 (18-28); Kempis on, vii, 377 (3); Milton on, iv, 363-4, 370; Mohammed on, xlv, 919, 920, 925 note; Pascal on, xlviii, 269 (752), 277 (784); Paul, St., on, xlv, 459 (24-5); preaching of, 365 (2-18)

John XXI, Pope, xx, 340 note 34

John XXII, Pope, xx, 401 note 8; annates established by, xxxvi, 292 note

John of Austria, xxxix, 92

John, King of Bohemia, in Crecy campaign, xxxv, 10, 15, 21, 27-8

John of Burgogne, xxxix, 89

John, King of England, Bertrand and, xx, 120 note; Cistertians and, xxxv, 267-8; fowling laws of, 352; Voltaire on, xxxiv, 90

John, King of France, Black Prince and, xxxv, 55, 57-8, 59; capture of, 52-4, 59-60; cardinal of Perigord and, 39-42; at Poitiers, 34-7, 47-8, 49-51; prisoner in England, 233

John of Gaunt, and Chaucer, xxxix, 171

John of Hainault, in EDWARD II, xlvi, 53-5, 57

John, King of Portugal, xxxix, 90

John, Duke of Suabia, xxvi, 412 and note; murders Emperor, 464; as monk in WILHELM TELL, 468-73

John the Swede, in TWO YEARS BEFORE THE MAST, xxiii, 34, 43, 105, 106-9, 112, 132, 418

JOHN ANDERSON, MY JO, vi, 365

JOHN BARLEYCORN: A BALLAD, vi, 41-3

JOHN GILPIN, THE DIVERTING HISTORY OF, xli, 559-67

JOHNIE ARMSTRONG, xl, 102-4

JOHNIE LAD, COCK UP YOUR BEAVER, vi, 439

Johnson, Andrew, PROCLAMATION OF 1866, xliii, 453-8

JOHNSON, ESTHER, ON DEATH OF, xxvii, 131-40

Johnson, Esther, and Swift, xxviii, 6, 13, 22-5, 26; xxvii, 96; Thackeray on, xxviii, 22; on Vanessa, 26

Johnson, Samuel, LIFE OF ADDISON, xxvii, 165-211; Carlyle on, xxv, 426; LETTER TO CHESTERFIELD, xxxix, 216-17; PREFACE TO DICTIONARY, 191-216; editorial remarks on works of, 191 note; l, 55; Emerson on, v, 368, 456; Goldsmith to, xviii, 199; on Gower, xxviii, 78; Hazlitt on, xxvii, 283, 287; ON ROBERT LEVET, xli, 515; life and works of, xxvii, 164; on Milton, xxviii, 213; xxxix, 336, 337; on PARADISE LOST, xxviii, 210; parody by, xxxix, 303-4; on persecution, xxv, 230; on *Percy's Reliques,* xxxix, 342; on Pope, 339; on primogeniture, v, 430; paraphrase of Proverbs, xxxix, 309-10; A SATIRE, xli, 516; PREFACE TO SHAKESPEARE, xxxix, 218-63; style of, v, 22; as biographer of Swift, xxviii, 7; Thackeray on, 7; Wordsworth on *Prefatory Lives* of, xxxix, 346-7

Johnson, Sir William, treaty with Senecas, xliii, 247

Joint-stock Companies, x, 482-5

JOLLY BEGGARS, THE, vi, 129-40; Arnold on, xxviii, 89; editorial remarks on, vi, 17

JOLLY GOOD ALE AND OLD, xl, 192-4

Jonadab, son of Rechab, xliii, 101

Jonah, Ninevites and, xliv, 391 (30, 32)

Jonakr, King, xlix, 358, 376, 377, 410, 444

Jonas, ancestor of Launcelot, xxxv, 159

Jonathan, David and, xli, 498; Saul and, xliii, 110

Jones, Owen, Renan on, xxxii, 144

Jones, Paul, and Franklin, i, 173

Jones, Sir William, poems by, xli, 592-3

Jonson, Ben, THE ALCHEMIST, xlvii, 519-635; ON BACON, xxvii, 60-1; BEAUMONT'S LETTER TO, xl, 328-30; on beauty, xxviii, 423; *Devil is an Ass,* by, xxvii, 406; *Explorata* of, 58; Fielding on, xxxix, 189; Hazlitt on, xxvii, 291; life and works, 58; xlvii, 518; poems

by, xl, 297-310; ON SHAKE-
SPEARE, xxvii, 59

Jordan, Thomas, LET US DRINK, xl,
373

Jorge, Alvaro, xxxiii, 325 note

Jormunrek, King, xlix, 358-9, 376,
377-8, 380, 410, 444, 454, 455

Josaphat, Last Judgment in, xx, 41
note

Joseph of Arimathæa, xliv, 423 (50-
3); in Holy Grail legend, xxxv,
123-5, 144, 159, 217, 225

Joseph, husband of Mary, xliv, 358
(27), 362 (4), 366 (23); xl, 265

Joseph, Kaiser, as Count Lorraine,
xxv, 444

Joseph, in PILGRIM'S PROGRESS, xv,
231, 248, 250, 286, 290

Joseph, son of Jacob, Chaucer on
dreams of, xl, 43; the harlot and,
v, 70; xv, 73, 86; Locke on story
of, xxxvii, 142; Mohammed on,
xlv, 933-42, 945; Pascal on, xlviii,
211 (623), 238 (698), 241, 242,
273 (768); the Psalmist on, xliv,
280 (17-22); Stephen on, 442 (9-
15)

JOSEPH ANDREWS, PREFACE TO, xxxix,
184-90

Josephus, silence of, on Christ,
xlviii, 278 (787); on Jewish Law,
209, 210, 214, 215; Pascal on, 213
(629); on spirits, xli, 702 note

Joshua, Gibeonites and, vii, 315
(2); Milton on, iv, 352, 353; one
of nine worthies, xxxix, 21; in
Paradise, xx, 363; Pascal on,
xlviii, 212 (627)

Joule, James Prescott, law of conservation and, xxx, 183-4; on mechanical equivalent of heat, xxx,
207-8; on expansion of gases,
208-9

Jourbert, THE GERM THEORY, xxxviii,
283, 382-9

JOURNAL OF JOHN WOOLMAN, i, 177-
326

Journalism, Franklin's ideas of, i,
96-7

JOURNEY ONWARDS, THE, xli, 841-2

JOURNEYS IN DIVERSE PLACES,
xxxviii, 9-61; remarks on, 8

Jousts, Bacon on, iii, 101

Jove, in the ÆNEID, xiii, 84-5, 124,
164-5, 205, 326, 330, 347, 423-4;
Alcmena and, xl, 247; Amalthea
and, iv, 164; Augustine, St., on,
vii, 18; bird of, iv, 327; Danæ
and, xlvi, 51; Leda and, xl, 234;
Maia and, 246; Milton on, iv,
68, 276 (see also Jupiter)

Jowett, Benjamin, translator of
Plato, ii

Joy, Augustine, St., on, vii, 128,
185; Blake on, and grief, xli, 602;
Chaucer on, xl, 45; of Christians,

Pascal on, xlviii, 360-1; Confucius on, xliv, 57 (5); contrasted
with relief from pain, xxiv, 35;

Joy, Goethe on, xix, 120; Hobbes
on, xxxiv, 353; Jonson on un-
shared, xl, 300; in music, xli, 490-
1; Shakespeare on, and grief, xlvi,
144; son of Cupid and Psyche, iv,
73

Joyeuse, sword of Charlemagne,
xlix, 188

Joyous Friars, the, xx, 98 note 4

Ju Pei, Confucius and, xliv, 61
(20)

Juan Fernandez, Dana on, xxiii, 45-
52; earthquake at, xxix, 329

Juba, Plutarch on, xii, 317-19; 403

Juba, in Cato, xxvii, 198, 200-1,
205, 206-7; son of, xii, 320

Jubal, Dryden on, xl, 399

Jubilees, Papal, xxxvi, 314 note

Judæa, Christian Church in, xliv,
450 (31)

Judah, Tamar and, xviii, 100; tribe
of, xliv, 247 (68)

Judaism, Hobbes on, xxxiv, 398-9;
Lessing on, xxxii, 196-207; Pascal on, xlviii, 200 (601-3), 201-4,
228 (673), 229 (675), 375; Rousseau on, xxxiv, 303-5

Judas, called Barsabbas, xliv, 464
(22, 27), 465 (32)

Judas, son of James, xliv, 373 (16),
430 (13)

Judas of Galilee, xliv, 440 (37)

Judas Iscariot, xliv, 373 (16), 417
(3-6), 419 (47-8), 430 (16-20); St.
Brandan and, xxxii, 154; Bun-
yan on, xv, 110, 313; in Dante's
HELL, xx, 144; death of, iii, 288;
Hazlitt on, xxvii, 295; Pascal on,
xlviii, 276 (780); tilting with
Jesus, xx, 229 note 13

Judges, Bacon on, iii, 137-41; Burke
on elective, xxiv, 355; Epictetus
on, ii, 183 (8); Heraclitus on,
135 (54); marriage of, iii, 22;
in Massachusetts, xliii, 73 (20);
righteous, in Paradise, xx, 364-
7; Pascal on, xlviii, 109 (307);
pay of, x, 472-3; Pliny on, ix,
292-3; Shelley on false, xviii, 301;
Socrates on, ii, 22; Tseng-tzu on,
xliv, 67 (19); United States, xliii,
202; Winthrop on discretionary
power of, 96-106, 107-8, 109, 111

Judgment, Burke on standards of,
xxiv, 11; Dante on hasty, xx,
344; intellect and, xlviii, 10;
Hobbes on, xxxiv, 360, 363, 364-
7; human and divine, vii, 308
(5), 323-4; Kempis on rash, 226-
7; Massinger on, xlvii, 886;
Penn's rule of, i, 404-5; necessary to poets, xxxix, 312-13; Pas-

cal on, xlviii, 128 (381, 383);
Rousseau on the, xxxiv, 251-3;
sentiment compared with, xxvii,
217-18, 229; taste and, xxiv, 23-
6; wit compared with, i, 355
(171-3); xxiv, 17-18
Judgment Day (see Last Judgment)
JUDICATURE, ESSAY ON, Bacon's, iii,
137-41
Judicature, expenses of, x, 471-3,
487; Hobbes on, xxxiv, 427; in
U. S., xliii, 207 (5), 208 (6, 7,
8); in Utopia, xxxvi, 225
Judicial Penalties, Winthrop on,
xliii, 96-106, 107-8, 110-11
Judicial Power, of U. S., xliii, 202-
3, 209 (11)
Judicial Proceedings, in Massachusetts, xliii, 73-8, 81 (76)
Judith, the Jewess, in Paradise, xx,
420
Judith, wife of Louis Debonnaire,
xxxix, 86
Jugglery, Woolman on, i, 282-3
Julia, mother of Antony, xii, 334,
348
Julia, daughter of Cæsar, 285, 295;
in Dante's Limbo, xx, 20
Julia, wife of Marius, xii, 277
Julia, in DUCHESS OF MALFI, wife
of Castruccio, her jests, xlvii,
724, 725; with Cardinal, 748-50;
with Delio, 750-1; with Pescara,
794; on Bosola, 799; with Bosola,
800-2; last scene with Cardinal,
803-5
Julian, St., patron saint of hospitality, xl, 20 note 178
Julian, Emperor, at Athens, xxviii,
62; laws against Christians, vii,
130; iii, 209
Julianus, death of, xxxvi, 67;
Machiavelli on, 70
Julienne, name of Bramimonde,
xlix, 207
Juliers, Duke of, xxxv, 104-5
Julius II, Pope, his aggrandizement
of the papacy, xxxvi, 41; auxiliaries of, 47; Cæsar Borgia and,
29-30; economy of, 55; Ferrara
and, 8; impetuosity of, 85-6;
Luther and, 277, 353
Julius III, Pope, Cellini and, xxxi,
401; election of, 399 note 1
Julius, Caius, the physician, xxxii,
14
Julius, the centurion, xliv, 490 (1),
491 (3)
JULLANAR OF THE SEA, story of, xvi,
340-54
JUNE, Bryant's, xlii, 1268-9; Poe on,
xxviii, 393-4
Junior, letter to, ix, 354
Junius, author of Letters, Hazlitt
on, xxvii, 289
Junius, etymologist, Johnson on,
xxxix, 196-7

Junius, Franciscus, xxvii, 14
Junius, governor of Asia, xii, 275
Juno, in the ÆNEID, xiii, 77-8, 91,
124, 159-60, 202-3, 208, 253-5, 327-
30, 348-9, 399-400, 423-4; Hercules and, iii, 208 and note; Iris
attendant of, xiii, 48; goddess of
marriage, 158; xl, 249; in the
TEMPEST, xlvi, 427
Juno Ludovici, Schiller on the,
xxxii, 267
JUNO AND THE PEACOCK, fable of,
xvii, 24
Junto, Franklin's, i, 59-61, 100-1
Jupiter, adulteries of, xxxiv, 381;
attendants of, xiii, 48; Briareus
and, iii, 4½; Emerson on fable of,
v, 96; infancy of, viii, 354; Juno
and, iv, 170; Metis and, iii, 55
(see also Jove)
Jupiter, Dante's sixth Heaven, xx,
364-5
Jupiter Ammon, worship of, xxxiii,
26
Jurassic Period, in Europe, xxx,
362
Jurfalez, son of Marsil, xlix, 114,
167
Juries, arbitrary damages of, xliii,
97; Pliny on, ix, 216
Jurisprudence, Burke on science of,
xxiv, 243; Descartes on, xxxiv, 8;
Goethe on, xix, 75; Marlowe on,
201, 203; Milton on study of, iii,
255; Pascal on, xlviii, 105
Jurors, in Massachusetts, xliii, 77
(49, 50); private offences of, 79
(61)
Jury Trial, in Massachusetts, xliii,
75 (29, 30, 31), 81 (76); right
of, 158; in U. S., 202-3, 208
(6, 7)
Just, in MINNA VON BARNHELM,
xxvi, 287-93, 295-301, 310-11, 315-
19, 361, 365
Justice, Æschylus on, viii, 135, 142;
Burke on, xxiv, 231, 304; among
children, xxxvii, 97-8; Dante on
divine, xx, 367-8; Dante's star of,
148 note 5; Dennis on poetical,
xxvii, 198; distributive and commutative, iii, 344; Emerson on, v,
163, 194-5; expense of administration of, x, 471-3, 487; Franklin's
rule of, i, 83; Hobbes on, xxxiv,
417-23, 426; human and divine,
xlviii, 83 (233); Manzoni on, xxi,
54; Marcus Aurelius on, ii, 292
(10); More on, xxxvi, 226; of
nature, v, 27, 94; Pascal on, xlviii,
38, 104 (294), 107 (297-9), 110
(309, 312), 126 (375), 310 (878);
Penn on benefit of, i, 406; Penn
on delays of, 372 (390-4); Penn's
maxim of, 353; Plutarch on, xii,
86; Pope on origin of, xl, 440;
Shakespeare on human, xlvi, 281;

story of statue of, xlii, 1367-8;
Winthrop on, xliii, 98, 102
Justification, Bunyan on, xv, 28,
215-17; Calvin on, xxxix, 53;
Ignorance's idea of, xv, 151-2;
Luther on, xxxvi, 363-97
Justin of Val Ferrée, xlix, 144-5
Justina and St. Ambrose, vii, 153-4
Justinian, Dante on, xx, 170, 308;
Marlowe on *Institutes* of, xix,
201
Justus, Fabius, letter to, ix, 205
Justus, Titus, xliv, 471 (7)
Juturna, in the ÆNEID, xiii, 399-
400, 402-4, 410, 411, 422, 425-6
Juvenal, on death, iii, 10; the gro-
tesque in, xxxix, 368
Juvenale, Latino (see Manetti)
Kaabah, the, xlv, 886, 903 note,
1019
Kalm, Peter, on American colonies,
x, 194-5
Kamaduk, xlv, 814, 844
Kanakas, the, xxiii, 146-7, 150-5,
253-5
Kangaroo, young of the, xi, 245-
246
Kant, Immanuel, Emerson on, v,
148; life and works, xxxii, 316;
METAPHYSIC OF MORALS, 317-95;
Schiller on system of, 222
Kao Ch'ai, xliv, 36 note 12
Kao-tsung, xliv, 51 (43)
Kao-yao, xliv, 42
Kara, daughter of Halfdan, xlix,
392
Karen, in THE RED SHOES, xvii, 349-
54
Karlsefni, Thorfinn, xliii, 15-17, 18,
20-1
Karma, cessation of, xlv, 747; fruit-
ful and barren, 685-90; good and
bad, 691-2; kinds of, 682-4; meri-
torious and bodily, 682-4; on ig-
norance depends, 639, 677-8, 683-
4; proximate, 669 note
Karmabandh, xlv, 841
Knaim, brother of Ali Baba, xvi,
443, 445-7
Kassapa, xlv, 764, 765
Kastrill, in THE ALCHEMIST, xlvii,
577-81, 592-4, 598-602, 609-12, 620-
1, 629-31, 634-5
Kastriota, John, xlvii, 468 note 9
Katherine (see Catherine)
Kauri Pines, Darwin on, xxix, 451
Kay, Sir, steward of Arthur, xxxv,
112, 113
Keats, John, Arnold on, xxviii, 78,
79; Browning on, xlii, 1142;
buried in Rome, xxiii, 4; elegy
on death of, xli, 879; poems by,
xli, 894-922
Keble, John, hymn by, xlv, 579
KEEKIN-GLASS, THE, vi, 453
Keeling Islands, Darwin on, xxix,
477-90

Keightley, Thomas, remarks on his
Life of Milton, xxviii, 174
Keimer, friend of Franklin, i, 27-9,
36-7, 52-6, 58; goes to Barbadoes,
i, 66-7; paper of, 62
KEITH OF RAVELSTON, BALLAD OF,
xlii, 1160
Keith, George, i, 23
Keith, Sir William, character of, i,
42-3, 57; Franklin and, 29-32, 35-
6, 40-3, 51
KELLY BURN BRAES, vi, 463
Kelp, Darwin on, xxix, 255-7; Smith
on, x, 154
Kelvin (see Thomson, Sir William)
KEMBLE, MRS., ON SEEING, IN
YARICO, vi, 532
Kempenfelt, Cowper on, xli, 546,
547
Kempis, Thomas à, IMITATION OF
CHRIST, vii, 209-379; life of, 208;
Woolman on, i, 230, 231
Kenelm, St., xl, 42-3
KENMURE'S ON AND AWA, WILLIE,
vi, 447-8
KENNEDY, JOHN, LINES TO, vi, 232
KENNEDY, JOHN, DUMFRIES HOUSE,
vi, 196-7
Kennet, Bishop, on Swift, xxviii, 14
Kent, Earl of, in EDWARD II, in
quarrels of king and nobles, xlvi,
8, 10, 15, 30, 31, 32; quarrel with
king, 34; joins nobles, 36; a captive, 50; banished to France, 52,
53-4; return with Mortimer, 56,
57; his relenting, 58-9; suspected
by Mortimer, 70-1; attempts rescue of king, 72, 73-4; death, 76-7
Kent, in KING LEAR, with Gloucester and his son, xlvi, 203-4;
banished by Lear, 207-9; with
Lear in disguise, 218-19; with
Oswald, 220; and Fool, 221,
222; sent to Gloucester, 228; at
Gloucester's, quarrel with Oswald,
233-6; in stocks, 237-8, 239-41;
set at liberty, 242; in the storm,
248-50; finds Lear, 251-2; at the
hovel, 254-6, 257, 258; with Lear
in his madness, 259-62; flight with
Lear, 262; with gentleman in
French camp, 272-4; with Cordelia, 285; at Lear's awakening,
286, 287; Edgar on, 298; final
scene with Lear, 299, 300-1, 302;
editor's remarks on character of,
202; Ruskin on character of,
xxviii, 142
Kephalos, and Eos, viii, 307
Kepler, Johann, Emerson on, v,
183; heliocentric theory of, xxxix,
55 note; on tides, xxx, 294
Keppel, Lord, Burke on, xxiv, 438-
42
Kerguelen Land, species of, xi, 441
Kerim, the fisherman, xvi, 230-1
Kethe, William, hymn by, xlv, 551

Kevin, St., and the birds, xxxii, 159-60

Keymis, Capt., xxxiii, 325, 349, 381, 382, 385

Keyserling, Count, on origin of species, xi, 17

Keziah, daughter of Job, xliv, 143

Khemā, disciple of Buddha, xlv, 600

Khoja Hoseyn, in ALI BABA, xvi, 457-9

KID AND WOLF, fable of, xvii, 16-17

Kidron, reference to, xli, 498

Kilhwch and Olwen, tale of, xxxii, 153, 156-9

Kilissa, in THE LIBATION-BEARERS, viii, 100-2

KILLED AT THE FORD, xlii, 1352-3

KILLIECRANKIE, THE BRAES OF, vi, 381

KILLIGREW, MRS. ANNE, ODE TO, xl, 394-7

KILMENY, by Hogg, xli, 774-83

Kin, are less than kind, viii, 81; strange the power of, 158

Kindness, apt to be repeated, i, 102; Burns on, vi, 88, 264; Confucius on, xliv, 60 (6); defined by Hobbes, xxxiv, 354; the power of, v, 60; reward of, ii, 133 (59); stronger than severity, xvii, 36

King, Archbishop, and Swift, xxviii, 21

King, Dr., Bishop of London, xv, 346; relations with Dr. Donne, 354-5, 362; Walton on, 358

King, Gregory, on laborers' income, x, 81

KING LEAR, TRAGEDY OF, xlvi, 201-302; Ruskin on, xxviii, 142; Shelley on, xviii, 276, 356; stage representation of, xxvii, 325-6

KING THRUSHBEARD, story of, xvii, 151-5

Kingcraft, Confucius on, xliv, 39 (7), 40 (11, 14), 41 (19), 44 (15), 45 (16)

Kingdom of Ends, Kant's, xxxii, 364-5, 367 note, 369-70

KINGDOMS, TRUE GREATNESS OF, iii, 76-84

Kingdoms, all have graves, xl, 259; Raleigh on ruin of, xxxix, 74 (see also Princedoms)

Kingfishers, in Cape Verd Islands, xxix, 12; S. American, 151

Kings, councillors of, iii, 55-8; Burke on, xxiv, 174-5, 177-9; Confucius on, xliv, 44 (12); ECCLESIASTES on, 344 (13-16); Emerson on, v, 73; friendships of, iii, 70; More on enrichment of, xxxvi, 170-3; Penn on government of, i, 367-70; Raleigh on, xl, 208; Ruskin on false and true, xxviii, 132-3; such divinity doth hedge, xlvi, 169-70 (see also Princes, Rulers)

KINGS' CHILDREN, THE TWO, xvii, 208

KING'S COLLEGE CHAPEL, CAMBRIDGE, xli, 694

King's Evil, reference to, xlvi, 359-60

KING'S TRAGEDY, THE, xlii, 1200-25; remarks on, l, 23, 28

Kingship, Calvin on true, xxxix, 32; Milton on, iv, 387; Pascal on, xlviii, 52-3, 57-8, 109 (307-8), 110 (310), 115 (330); Pope on beginning of, xl, 438; Rousseau on origin of, xxxiv, 220-6; Shakespeare on, xlvi, 150

Kingsley, Charles, poems by, xlii, 1101-5

Kingston, Sir William, xxxvi, 137-8

KINMONT WILLIE, a ballad, xl, 109-15

Kinnersley, Mr., i, 153

KIRK AND STATE EXCISEMEN, vi, 489

KIRK OF SCOTLAND'S ALARM, THE, vi, 371-5

KISS, THE PARTING, vi, 336

Kisses, E. B. Browning on, xli, 965; Burns on, vi, 466; of love, Goethe on, xix, 427

Kitchen God, xliv, 10 note 6

Klopstock, on Bürger, xxxix, 343

Knavery, origin of, xxxiv, 213

Knight, Chaucer's, xl, 12-13, 34

Knight of the Redcrosse, Spenser's, xxxix, 66, 67

Knight, Andrew, on bees, xi, 266; on hermaphrodites, 109; on cause of variability, 25

Knight-errantry, Cervantes on tales of, xiv, 498-502, 506-7, 512-21; Don Quixote on, 100-4; expenses of, 140-1; literature of, 3, 12, 52-8; Manzoni on, xxi, 567; Sancho Panza on, xiv, 128-9

Knighthood, in Elizabethan England, xxxv, 231-4

Knolles, Francis, xxxiii, 237

Knolles, Sir Robert, xxxv, 72, 80, 81

KNOW, CELIA, xl, 361-2

Knowing Ones, in FAUST, xix, 182

Knowledge, action and, xxxii, 60-1; Augustine, St., on, vii, 68-9, 197-8; on authority, xxv, 238-49; xxxii, 37-9; xxxix, 130; Bacon on, 135, 148, 150; beauty and, xxxii, 282, 283, 288; Berkeley on reality of, xxxvii, 263-7, 284-5, 296-8; Browne on, iii, 328, 336-7; Browne on, of self, 276, 279; Bunyan on two kinds of, xv, 87; Carlyle on, xxv, 334; Channing on little, xxviii, 353; Comte's three ages of, xxv, 108; always conditional, xxxiv, 360; Confucius on, xliv, 20 (18), 60 (8); Dante on, xx, 304; desire of, inclines to peace, xxxiv, 385; ECCLESIASTES on, xliv, 340 (18),

347 (12); Epictetus on acquisition of, ii, 132 (46), 140 (65), 143 (72); of evil, Mrs. Herbert on, xv, 380; of evil, Milton on, iii, 212-13; iv, 281; is not happiness, xviii, 428; Harvey on advance of, xxxviii, 80; Harvey on pursuit of, 66; Hindu doctrine of, xlv, 821-2, 860; Hippocrates on requisites of, xxxviii, 4; Hobbes on attainment of, xxxiv, 360; intuitive and rational, xlviii, 99-100; Kempis on worldly and spiritual, vii, 307 (2), 319-20; Locke on, xxxvii, 111; Marcus Aurelius on, ii, 233 (32); Mill on à priori view of, xxv, 145-6; Milton on, iv, 170, 405; Pascal on impossibility of certain, xlviii, 29-31; Pascal on universality in, 18 (37); Paul, St., on, xlv, 511 (1-2); Penn on, i, 355, 365 (307); pleasure the basis of, xxxix, 295; Pope on human, xl, 420; power from, xxxiv, 375; xxxix, 148; pride in, ii, 177 (177); xlviii, 156 (460); progress of, due to passions and wants, xxxiv, 180-2; progress of, requires liberty, iii, 232-3, 241-2; quantity and quality of, xxviii, 341-2; as recollection, ii, 63-8; Ruskin on impossibility of, xxviii, 114; of self, Shelley on, xviii, 277; of sense and understanding, xxxii, 382-3; Sidney on object of, xxvii, 16-17; Socrates on, ii, 7-8; is sorrow, xviii, 403; taste dependent on, xxiv, 19-21, 26; temperance in, iv, 233; timidity of, xix, 29; Tennyson on, and wisdom, xli, 1016-17; Thoreau on, xxviii, 432-3; true and false, xlv, 878; two kinds of, xxxiv, 373; vanity of human, vii, 213 (3), 214-15, 216-17; xix, 22, 44, 69-70; xlviii, 114-15; Washington on diffusion of, xliii, 260; of the world, Locke on, xxxvii, 54-5, 79-82, 83-4 (see also Learning)
Knowledge, the shepherd, in PILGRIM'S PROGRESS, xv, 125-8
Know-nothing, Mrs., in PILGRIM'S PROGRESS, xv, 189
Knox, John, Carlyle on, xxv, 383-4, 403, 427-8; life and works, xxxix, 61 note; PREFACE TO REFORMATION IN SCOTLAND, 61-3
Kolita, disciple of Buddha, xlv, 600
Kölreuter, on the barberry, xi, 111; on fertility of varieties, 326; on hermaphrodites, 109; on reciprocal crosses, 308; on sterility of species, 299, 314
Konghelle, town of, v, 359
Korah, Psalms of sons of, xliv, 198-207, 254-5, 257-9

Koran, Bacon on the, iii, 44 note; Browne on the, 289; editor's remarks on, l, 21; Hume on morals of the, xxvii, 217; on duty of governors, xxv, 254; legend of Seven Sleepers in, xxxviii, 413; Pascal on the, xlviii, 198 (597)
KORAN, CHAPTERS FROM THE, xlv, 885-1021
Kostbera, wife of Hogni, xlix, 365-7, 368
Kotzebue, August, Carlyle on, xxv, 420-1; on Tahiti, xxix, 437
Krishna (see BHAGAVAD-GITA)
Kuan Chung, xliv, 12 note, 47 (10), 48 (17, 18) note
KUBLA KHAN, xli, 718-19
Kung-hsi Hua, xliv, 15 note 6, 18 note 3, 19 note 4, 36 (21), 37 (25) note 25
Kung-ming Chia, xliv, 48 (14)
Kung-shan Fu-jao, xliv, 59 (5)
Kung-shu Wen, xliv, 48 (14), 49 (19)
Kung-sun Ch'ao, xliv, 67 (22)
K'ung Wen, xliv, 16 (14)
Kung-yeh Ch'ang, xliv, 14 (1)
Kunz of Gersau, in WILHELM TELL, xxvi, 436-7
Kuoni, in WILHELM TELL, xxvi, 371-6, 394-5
Kush, son of Sheddad, inscription of, xvi, 317-18
Kusinārā, city of, xlv, 652-3
Kuteyt, the jailer, xvi, 237
Kypris, reference to, viii, 186
LA BELLE DAME SANS MERCI, xli, 917-19
Labdacus, father of Laius, viii, 204
Laberius, quoted, xxxii, 6
Labienus, lieutenant of Cæsar, xii, 289; death of, 359; in eastern campaign, 354, 357; goes over to Pompey, 304; story of, 258
Labor, Burke on necessity of, xxiv, 113; capital and, x, 6, 69-71, 221-2, 284, 303-18, 349; Channing on value of, xxviii, 324-5, 327; children sweeten, iii, 20; competition of, restraints on, x, 126-38, 143-52; competition of, unnaturally increased, 138-43; demand for (see Wages); division of (see Division of Labor); division of, dwarfs the mind, xxviii, 326; ECCLESIASTES on vanity of, xliv, 339 (3), 341 (11, 18-23), 344 (4-5), 345 (15-16), 346 (7); Emerson on, v, 49-53; 100-1, 297; excessive, results of, i, 205-6, 261-3; x, 87; xxviii, 326; exchange value of, x, 50; finished products of, 229; free and slave, cost of, 85; Hindu doctrine of, xlv, 813-15, 819-20, 826; independent and wage, x, 88-9;

Luther on, xxxvi, 330; Marcus Aurelius on, ii, 208 (5), 223 (1), 240 (33), 271 (12); More on condition of, xxxvi, 191-2, 192-3; original state of, x, 68-9; Penn on, i, 344-5; prices of, real and nominal, x, 39-40; productive and unproductive, 270-7; productive and unproductive in agricultural system, 449-53; productive power of, 9-28; products of, its natural recompense, 68-9; real ends of, v, 101; the real measure of value, x, 36-7, 39, 43, 53; real recompense of, 82; as recreation, xxxvii, 185-90; remuneration of (see Wages); respect due to, xxviii, 368-9; rest and, iv, 173; skilled and common, x, 107-8; talents of, fixed capital, 228; Tennyson on, xlii, 1028-9; Thoreau on value of, xxviii, 411; thought needed in, 339; in Utopia, xxxvi, 189-90, 192-4, 200; value of, how determined, x, 37; value of, to the scholar, v, 15; wages of (see Wages)

Labor, King, xxxv, 193

LABORER AND NIGHTINGALE, fable of, xvii, 34

Laborers, combinations of, x, 71

LABORING CLASSES, ELEVATION OF THE, Channing's, xxviii, 317-80; editorial remarks on, l, 42

Labyrinth, of Egypt, xxxiii, 75-6

Lacedæmonians, hospitality of the, ii, 297 (24)

Lacedæmonius, son of Cimon, xii, 67

Lacey, Father, Wood on, v, 363

Lachares, and Antony, xii, 388

Lachesis, reference to, xx, 232 note 4

LACK OF GOLD, xli, 545

Lactate of Lime, fermentation of, xxxviii, 340

Lactantius, Copernicus on, xxxix, 60; on doers, 114; on following authorities, 105; on Providence, 106-7

Lacy, Sir Hugh, in SHOEMAKER'S HOLIDAY, with Mayor, xlvii, 447-9; with Rowland, 449-50; with Dodger, learns Rowland not in France, 469-71, 474; seeks nephew at Lord Mayor's, 493; hears flight of Rose. 494; with Firk, 495-6; plans to stop wedding, 497; mistakes Ralph for Rowland, 502-4; learns of wedding, 504; with the king, 510-12

Lacy, Rowland, in SHOEMAKER'S HOLIDAY, in love with Rose Oateley, xlvii, 447-8; his travels, 448; appointed colonel, 448-9; with Sir Hugh, 449-50; delays departure for France, 450; Ralph and, 451, 452; summoned by Dodger, 453;

Sybil on, 455-6; as Dutch shoemaker, 456-7; takes service with Eyre, 459-61; the skipper and, 465, 468-9; plot discovered by uncle, 470-1, 474; with Margery, as Hans, 475, 476, 477; with Eyre as sheriff, 478, 479; at Mayor's, as Hans, 481-2; at Hodge's, 487; goes to Rose with Sybil, 488-9; with Rose, as Hans, 491-3; flight with Rose, 494; with Rose at Eyre's, 498-9; marriage, 504; pardoned by king, 508, 509; denounced by uncle, 510-11; marriage confirmed, 512; knighted, 512; on the shoemakers, 513

LAD THEY CA' JUMPIN JOHN, vi, 318

LADDIE'S DEAR SEL', vi, 368

LADIES OF BAGHDAD, stories of the, xvi, 60-71, 107-20

Ladike, wife of Amasis, xxxiii, 91

Ladislaus V, King, xxxvi, 333

Lady, Ruskin on title of, xxviii, 162-3

LADY, To A, WITH A GUITAR, xli, 870-3

LADY MARY ANN, vi, 462

LADY ONLIE, HONEST LUCKY, vi, 298

LADY OF SHALOTT, THE, xlii, 997-1002

LADY'S POCKET ALMANAC, LINES IN A, vi, 488

Lælius, called the wise, ix, 9; in Cicero's FRIENDSHIP, 7-9; in Cicero's OLD AGE, 46; Scipio and, 8, 10-13, 19, 43; Sidney on, xxvii, 42

Laertes, in Hamlet, gets leave to go to France, xlvi, 94; farewell to Ophelia, 100-3; and Polonius, 102; Reynaldo sent to watch, 113-15; return of, 168-72; with king, plans vengeance on Hamlet, 174-8; learns Ophelia's death, 178-9; at Ophelia's funeral, 185-7; Osric on, 191-2; duel with Hamlet, 194-6; confesses and dies, 197; not in original story, 86

Laertes, in the ODYSSEY, xxii, 14, 156-7, 217, 227-8, 336-42, 345; Cowley on, xxvii, 72; Plutarch on, xii, 260 note

Laertius, Diogenes, iii, 254 note 39; Montaigne on, xxxii, 100

Laestrygons, and Ulysses, xxii, 138-139

Lafayette, Burke on, xxiv, 440, 442

La Fontaine, Sainte-Beuve on, xxxii, 128, 135, 137

LAGGAN, LAIRD OF, EPIGRAM ON, vi, 497

Lagoon Islands, Darwin on, xxix, 484-5, 491-4; gradually formed from fringing-reefs, 498-503

Lagus, death of, xiii, 339

La Harpe, Hugo on, xxxix, 382, 385

Laing, Malcolm, on Macpherson, xxxix, 345
LAIRD O' COCKPEN, xli, 576-7
LAIRD OF LAGGAN, EPIGRAM ON, vi, 497
Lais, daughter of Timandra, xii, 151
Laius, death of, viii, 200-1, 218-19; Œdipus accused of killing, 210-11; prophecy of death of, 218
Lajeunesse, Basil, in EVANGELINE, xlii, 1358, 1359; at Benedict's house, 1363-5, 1366-7, 1368-9; denounces the English, 1373; in exile, 1379, 1385; as herdsman, 1394-8; with Evangeline, 1400, 1402, 1406
Lajeunesse, Gabriel, lover of Evangeline, xlii, 1358-60; at feast of betrothal, 1372; on day of expulsion, 1378, 1379; his wanderings in exile, 1385, 1388, 1390, 1394-5, 1400, 1402, 1405-6, 1407; found by Evangeline in plague, 1411-13
Lake, Dr., Walton on, xv, 412
Lake-dwellers, domestic plants and animals of, xi, 35
L'ALLEGRO, iv, 31-5; Bagehot on, xxviii, 186; an idyllic poem, xxxix, 314
Lalli, Gianstefano, xxxi, 439 note 4
Lally, letter on October Sixth, xxiv, 222 note
Lamachus, general in Sicilian expedition, xii, 126, 128, 130
Lamachus, the Myrinæan, xii, 203-204
Lamarck, on adaptive resemblances, xi, 462; on blind animals, xxix, 62; on evolution, xi, 6; on innate tendency to perfection, 136; objection to his theory of inherited habit, 295; on origin of species, 10
Lamartine, Taine on, xxxix, 435
Lamb, Charles, Hazlitt on, xxvii, 281; in Hazlitt's discussion, 281-95; on imagination, xxxix, 321 note; life and writings, xxvii, 312; poems by, xli, 752-5; ON TRAGEDIES OF SHAKESPEARE, xxvii, 313-31
LAMB AND WOLF, fable of, xvii, 9
Lambert, Hugo on, xxxix, 399
Lambertaccio, xx, 204 note 17
Lamberti, Mosca de' (see Uberti)
Lambwell, Sir David, xl, 101
Lamech, Pascal on, xlviii, 205
LAMENT, A, by Shelley, xli, 864-5
LAMENT, THE, by Burns, vi, 204-6
LAMENT FOR JAMES, EARL OF GLENCAIRN, vi, 424
LAMENT OF MARY QUEEN OF SCOTS, vi, 420-1
LAMENT, BURLESQUE, FOR WILLIAM CREECH, vi, 281-3
Lamentone, Il, xxxi, 156, 159

Lamias, in story of WILD SWANS, xvii, 295
Lampedo, queen of Amazons, xxxiii, 338
Lampetie, the nymph, xxii, 172, 178
Lampon, the diviner, xii, 41-2
Lampus, steed of the sun, xxii, 327
Lancaster, in EDWARD II, his opposition to Gaveston, xlvi, 7-9, 11-13; in exiling of Gaveston, 14-16; consents to his return, 19-23; on Gaveston's return, 28-31; quarrel with king, 31-4; in attack on Tynemouth, 36, 37-8; at capture of Gaveston, 39-41; in battle, 49; capture and death, 50-1
Lancaster, Capt., explanation of story of, xxix, 112-13
Lancaster, Duke of, in Tyler's Rebellion, xxxv, 69
Lancelet, simplicity of the, xi, 137
Lancelot, Sir, the best knight next to Galahad, xxxv, 116; Bors and, 226; at castle of the Grail, 211-15; at chapel of the dead man, 155-7; Chaucer on story of, xl, 45; departure on quest of Grail, xxxv, 119, 120, 121; Ector's vision of, 165, 169; at the forest chapel, 135; Galahad's father, 114-15, 120, 160; Galahad and, 110-11, 134-5, 209-11; Gawaine on, 164; Guinever and, xiv, 100; xx, 24 note 4, 353 note 2; xxxv, 139; xlii, 1232-5, 1238-40; at the hermitage, xxxv, 138-40; horse of, smitten, 163; loses horse and arms, 137; Lady of Shalott and, xlii, 999-1000, 1002; lineage of, xxxv, 117, 159; the marvelous sword and, 112; Mellyagraunce and, xlii, 1236-7; Nacien on, xxxv, 170; Renan on, xxxii, 170-1; returns home, xxxv, 215-16; robber knight and, 158-9; the Siege Perilous and, 111; sorrow of, 137-8; sword of, xxxix, 22; at the tourney, xxxv, 117; vision of, 158, 159-60; white knights and, 161-3
Land, building of the, xxx, 259-7; elevation and subsidence of (see Elevation, Subsidence); final source of all capital, x, 231; has existed in all ages, xxxviii, 422; improvements in, constitute fixed capital, x, 228; Lowell on ownership of, xxviii, 483; made of river silt, xxxiii, 7, 9-10; materials of, xxx, 342-50; price of, dependent on rate of interest, x, 299; price of, and usury, iii, 107, 109; produce of, source of capital, x, 230-1; as property, effect on wages, 69; rent of (see Rent); returns of, greater than labor,

x, 156; Rousseau on property in, xxxiv, 202; Ruskin on ownership of, xxviii, 136; taxes on, proportioned to produce, x, 508-10; proportioned to rent, 501-8; taxes on transfer of, 528-532

LAND O' THE LEAL, xli, 573

Landas, John of, at Poitiers, xxxv, 37-8, 39, 47, 48, 49

Landenberg, Berenger von, xxvi, 386 note 6; Henry of Halden and, 388; flight of, 462

Landi, Antonio, xxxi, 367-8, 377

Landi, Pierro di Giovanni, xxxi, 34, 88, 91, 178

Landino, on poets, xxvii, 54

Landlord, in MINNA VON BARN-HELM, xxvi, 287-91, 303-9, 310-11, 312-13, 319-22, 356

Landlords, interest of, x, 217-18

Landor, Walter Savage, Emerson on, v, 329-30; poems by, xli, 922-30

Landresy, Francis I at, xxxviii, 17

Landscape Gardens, poetic sentiment in, xxviii, 389

Lane, Edw. William, translator of ARABIAN NIGHTS, xvi, 4

Lane-Poole, Stanley, reviser of ARABIAN NIGHTS, xvi, 4

Lane, Ralph, governor of Virginia, xxxiii, 266-7

Lang, A., translator of Homer, xxii; LINES ON THE ODYSSEY by, 7; SONNET ON HOMER, 347

Langland, Bishop of Lincoln, xxxvi, 107

Langley, Samuel Pierpont, on heat from the moon, xxx, 273; on radiant heat, 272

Langobards, Tacitus on the, xxxiii, 118

Language, anomalies and absurdities of, xxxix, 192; Augustine, St., on acquisition of, vii, 12; command of, its importance, xxviii, 288-9; custom and, xxxix, 177 note; Emerson on, v, 177; Hobbes on, xxxiv, 335-43; Johnson on uses of, xxxix, 195; a means, not an end, iii, 246; natural, xxxix, 226-7; Pascal on, xlviii, 318 (912); Pascal's rules of, 15-16, 20-2; of the passions, xxxiv, 358; poets the authors of, xxvii, 347-8; race test, xxviii, 244-54, 261-82; Rousseau on origin of, xxxiv, 183-9, 205, 207; Shelley on use of familiar, xviii, 278-9; Stevenson on, xxviii, 288-90; superiority of, xxvii, 349; in various civilizations, xxxix, 443, 444 (see also Words)

LANGUAGE, AND RACE, xxviii, 235-83

Languages, classification of, xi, 459; continual change of, xxxix, 211-

14; dead, study of, v, 267; Descartes on study of ancient, xxxiv, 7; Franklin on study of, i, 99-100; Hugo on change in, xxxix, 394; Huxley on study of, xxviii, 229; Locke on study of, xxxvii, 145-64, 173-4, 179-81, 192; Milton on study of, iii, 249; Montaigne on study of, xxxii, 67-8; Pascal on, xlviii, 20 (45); Penn on teaching, i, 338, 339; Taine on, xxxix, 434

Langue d'oc and d'oil, xxviii, 75-6

Languet, Hubert, and Philip Sidney, xxvii, 5

Lanier, Sidney, poems by, xlii, 1470-82

Lankester, E. Ray, on homogeneity, xi, 476-7; on longevity, 220

Lannoy, reference to, xlvii, 767-8

Lano, Dante on, xx, 58 and note 3

Laocoön, death of, xiii, 110-11; statue of, xxxi, 332; the Trojan horse and, xiii, 104-5

Laodamas, in the ODYSSEY, xxii, 98, 107, 108, 114

Laodamia, and Evadne, xiii, 226

LAODAMIA, xli, 678-83; Emerson on, v, 126

Laodiceans, Bacon on, iii, 12

Laomedon, the Orchomenian, xii, 201; Emerson on, v, 286

LAP-DOG, EPITAPH ON A, vi, 496

LAPDOG AND ASS, fable of, xvii, 13

Laplace, on tides, xxx, 297, 302

LAPRAIK, J., EPISTLES TO, vi, 84-91, 108-10

Lares, Hobbes on, xxxiv, 395

Largeness (see Vastness)

Largus, Julius, ix, 417

Laris, and Thymbrus, xiii, 340

Lark, Milton on the, iv, 32, 383

La Rochefoucauld, Sainte-Beuve on, xxxii, 136

Lartius, Titus, xii, 158

Las Vargas, counsellor of Philip II, xix, 285

LASCELLES, CAPTAIN, LINES ON, vi, 520

LASS O' BALLOCHMYLE, vi, 230

LASS OF CESSNOCK BANKS, vi, 29-31

LASS OF ECCLEFECHAN, vi, 552-3

LASS THAT MADE THE BED TO ME, vi, 564

LASS WI' A TOCHER, vi, 586

LASSIE WI' THE LINT-WHITE LOCKS, vi, 540

LAST CONQUEROR, THE, xl, 360

LAST DUCHESS, THE, xlii, 1115

LAST INVOCATION, THE, xlii, 1508

Last Judgment, à Celano on, xlv, 563-5; Browne on the, iii, 310-12; Bunyan on, xv, 40, 84-5; Dante on kings at, xx, 369-70; Emerson on doctrine of, v, 89-90; Kempis on the, vii, 242, 319-20; location

of, belief concerning, xx, 41 note
1; Milton on the, iv, 12, 146,
357; Mohammed on, xlv, 890,
891-2, 896-908, 911, 923
LAST LEAF, THE, xlii, 1444-5
LAST LINES, xlii, 1156
LAST RIDE TOGETHER, THE, xlii,
1112
LAST ROSE OF SUMMER, xli, 839-40
Last Supper, xliv, 417 (14-37);
Pascal on, xlviii, 182 (554)
LAST TIME I CAME O'ER THE MOOR,
vi, 491
LAST WISH, THE, xlii, 1165
LAST WORD, THE, xlii, 1185-6
Latagus, death of, xiii, 351
Lateran, the, given to Sylvester,
xx, 82 note 10
Latimer, and Henry VIII, v, 390
Latin, Augustine, St., on study of,
vii, 16-19; Carlyle on, xxv, 381;
Emerson on study of, v, 267;
Franklin on study of, i, 99-100;
Huxley on study of, xxviii, 221-
9; Locke on study of, xxxvii,
71-2, 81-2, 136, 145-64, 168, 173-
4, 179-81; Mill on study of, xxv,
25; Milton on way to study, iii,
251-3; Montaigne on study of,
xxxii, 67-8; Penn on study of, i,
339 (15); wrong way to study,
iii, 249
Latin Classics, xxxii, 127
LATIN HYMNS, xlv, 558-69
Latin Literature, More on, xxxvi,
217; Taine on, xxxix, 461
Latin Philosophers, xxxvi, 145
Latini, Brunetto, Arnold on, xxviii,
76; in Dante's HELL, xx, 64-6
Latinus, in the ÆNEID, xiii, 245-7,
250-2, 364, 372-3, 395-6, 400-2;
in Dante's Limbo, xx, 20; Dryden on, xiii, 21-2
Latinus, Titus, dream of, xii, 175
Latitudinarian, Penn's, i, 411-12
Latmian Shepherd, Endymion called,
xl, 248
Latona, and the frogs, iv, 82; refer-
ences to, xiii, 93; xx, 231
Laud, and George Herbert, xv,
398-9; and the Star Chamber, iii,
194
Laudatory Personalities, Bentham
on, xxvii, 248-9
Lauderdale, Earl of, and Burke,
xxiv, 400; translator of Virgil,
xiii, 69-70
Laughter, ECCLESIASTES on, xliv, 340
(2); Epictetus on, ii, 175 (165);
Hobbes on, xxxiv, 355
Launcelot (see Lancelot)
Laurence, the martyr, vii, 258 (2);
Dante on, xx, 301 note 10
Laurentia, honors of, ix, 186
Laurentius, Andreas, xxxviii, 77;
on the heart, 79

Lausus, in the ÆNEID, xiii, 265-6,
341, 351, 354, 355
Lautizio, xxxi, 49, 270
Laval, M. de, xxxviii, 13, 15; xlviii,
352 note 2
Laval, Pyrard de, on atolls, xxix,
491
Lavinia, in the ÆNEID, xiii, 245,
252, 396-7; in Dante's Limbo, xx,
20
Law(s), Bentham on opposition to
reform of, xxvii, 237-65; correction the purpose of, ii, 150 (88);
defined in Hindoo Scriptures, v,
294; Goethe on human, xix, 75;
highest, is welfare of people, iii,
140; Hume on foundation of,
xxxvii, 386; inadequacy of, and
revenge, iii, 16; the intention of
lawgiver is the, xliii, 335; Jones,
Sir William, on, xli, 593; language of the, how corrupted, x,
473; Locke on study of, xxxvii,
169; Luther on, xxxvi, 340;
Machiavelli on good, 42; Marlowe on study of, xix, 201, 203;
Milton on study of, iii, 255; Montaigne on multiplicity of, xlviii,
395-6; More on, xxxvi, 225-6;
More on antiquated, 170, 173;
natural, superior to statutes, v,
252-3, 256; necessity of, to control officials, xxvii, 247-8; need-
less where not eluded, xxxiv, 227;
numerous, effect of, xxxv, 331-2;
Pascal on, xlviii, 105-6, 114 (325-
6), 209, 210; Pliny on spirit and
letter of, ix, 264, 285; Pope on
origin of, xl, 440; Raleigh on,
209; Rousseau on origin of, xxxiv,
216-19; Ruskin on, xxviii, 137;
Schiller on substitution of, for
force, xxxii, 226-30; Smith on,
and men, xxvii, 248-9; Socrates
on obedience to, ii, 39-41; Winthrop on penal, xliii, 96-111 (see
also Government Intervention)
Law, John, Burke on, xxiv, 390
LAWES, MR. H., TO, ON HIS AIRS,
iv, 83
Lawgivers, great, iii, 136
Lawmakers, Winthrop on, xliii, 104
Lawrence, St., on the Church, xxxvi,
270
LAWRENCE, TO MR., iv, 87
Lawsuits, Confucius on, xliv, 40
(13); St. Paul on, xlv, 507 (1-7)
Lawyer, Chaucer's, xl, 19-20
Lawyers, excluded from Utopia,
xxxvi, 225; Franklin on, i, 16;
Jesus on, xliv, 392 (45-52);
judges and, iii, 138-9; Milton on
mercenary, 250; remuneration of
(see Professions); Sidney on,
xxvii, 18
Laxness, Confucius on, xliv, 18 (1)
Lay, nautical term, xxiii, 28 note

LAY THY LOOF IN MINE, LASS, vi,
589
Lazarus, xliv, 404 (20-5); Browne
on, iii, 286; Dives and, xv, 36;
the Jews and, vii, 310 (2); Pas-
cal on, xlviii, 223 (658), 270
(754)
Laziness, Locke on, xxxvii, 114-17,
189-90
Lazo, Darwin on the, xxix, 54-5
Lazzaretto, in Milan plague, xxi,
600-3
Lead Pyrophorus, xxx, 56 note;
combustion of, 169, 176-7; how
made, 176 note
Lead-trees, xxx, 84 note
LEADER, THE LOST, xlii, 1109
Leaders, developed by disaster, xix,
385; of sedition, iii, 43
Leagues, More on, xxxvi, 226-8
Leah, type of active life, xx, 259
note 4
Leander, reference to, xx, 262
Leandra, in the goatherd's story,
xiv, 526-30
LEAR, KING, TRAGEDY OF, xlvi, 203-
302; editorial remarks on, 202;
Ruskin on, xxviii, 142; Shelley
on, xviii, 276, 356; stage representations of, xxvii, 325-6
Lear, in KING LEAR, divides kingdom between daughters, xlvi, 204-
6; disowns Cordelia, 206-7; resigns power, 207; quarrel with
Kent, 207-8; with France and
Burgundy, 209-11; coldly treated
by Goneril, 217-18, 219-20; with
Kent in disguise, 218-19; with Oswald, 220; and the Fool, 221-3;
scene with Goneril, 223-6; departure for Gloucester, 228-9; arrival at Gloucester's, 239-41; with
Gloucester, 241-2; with Regan and
Cornwall, 242-4; refused hospitality by both daughters, 245-7; goes
out into storm, 248-9; in the
storm, 250-2; at Edgar's hovel,
254-8; his madness, 260-2; warned
to fly, 262; conveyed to Dover,
263; refuses to see Cordelia, 273;
in fields near Dover, mad, 279-
82; taken by Cordelia's messengers, 282; awakening from sleep,
with Cordelia, 286-8; taken prisoner, 291-2; ordered to be killed
by Edmund, 299; with body of
Cordelia, 300-1; with Kent, 301;
death, 301-2
Lear, Bagehot on character of,
xxviii, 198-9; editorial remarks
on character of, xlvi, 202
Learchus, Dante on, xx, 125
Learning, and actions, xxxii, 60-1;
arms compared with, xiv, 393-8;
Confucius on, xliv, 5 (1), 6 (14),
26 (13), 49 (25); end of, iii, 248;
four ages of, 147; Hume on,

xxxvii, 310; Locke on, 76, 82-3,
136-63; Montaigne on, xxxii, 34;
Sidney on object of, xxvii, 16-17;
Tzu-hsia on, xliv, 5 (7), 66 (5)
(6); (see also Knowledge)
Leaves of Grass, PREFACE TO, xxxix,
409-32; remarks on, 3
Leblanc, Baptiste, xlii, 1385
Leblanc, René, the notary in EVAN-
GELINE, xlii, 1365-8, 1408
Lechartier, M., xxxviii, 321-2 notes
Lechery, the sin, in FAUSTUS, xix,
222
Lechery, Mr., in PILGRIM'S PROG-
RESS, xv, 190
Leda, mother of Castor and Pollux,
xx, 403 note 14; in Homer's
Hades, xxii, 159
Lee, E., translator of Sainte-Beuve,
xxxii, 107
Lee, Fitzhugh, at Gettysburg, xliii,
365
Lee, Richard Henry, xliii, 160 note
Lee, Gen. Robert E., FAREWELL TO
HIS ARMY, xliii, 449; at Gettys-
burg, 402, 425; terms of surren-
der at Appomattox, 447-8
LEEZIE LINDSAY, vi, 580
Lé fri flaith, xlix, 220, 245, 260,
263
Legacy-taxes, x, 529, 532
Legal Language, corruption of, x,
473
Legal Penalties, Winthrop on, xliii,
96-106, 107-8, 110-11
Legal Pleading, Pliny on, ix, 214-8,
236-7
Legal Tender, in England, x, 46;
in United States, xliii, 198 (10)
Legal Technicalities, More on, xxxvi,
225-6
Legality, Mr., in PILGRIM'S PROG-
RESS, xv, 23, 27-8
Legislation, Burke on methods of,
xxiv, 317-18; does not make the
state, v, 249-50; by experience
and fiat, xxxiv, 13; Lowell on,
xxviii, 454; in Utopia, xxxvi, 188
Legislative Commissions, Mill on,
xxv, 169-70
Legislative Powers, in United States,
xliii, 192-9
Legislators, Burke on qualities of,
xxiv, 317; fame of, compared with
poets, xxvii, 349
Legouvé, M., xxxix, 390
Leibnitz, Hazlitt on, xxvii, 291;
Hobbes and, xxxiv, 318; supposed
inventor of fluxions, 128-9; on
theory of gravitation, xi, 520
Leicester, in EDWARD II, xlvi, 61-2,
64-8
Leicester, Earl of, on Chaucer,
xxxix, 175, 177
Leif the Lucky, his baptism, xliii,
5; his expedition of discovery, 8-

12; Gudrid, and 14, 15; his house in Vinland, 15, 18; Freydis and, 20

Leiodes, and the bow of Ulysses, xxii, 299; death of, 315-16

Leisure, Milton on, iv, 36; Penn on, employment of, i, 344-5; Rufus on, ii, 118 (v)

Lela Zoraida, xiv, 392

Leland, on copper mines, xxxv, 341; on England, 243, 245

Lelius, and Blosius, xxxii, 81

Lemnos, crime of, viii, 97

Lemovians, Tacitus on the, xxxiii, 121

Lemur, Darwin on the flying, xi, 185-6

Lemures, mentioned, iv, 13 (21)

Lending, Penn on, i, 343 (47)

Length, less striking than depth, xxiv, 63

Lennox, in MACBETH, xlvi, in camp with Duncan, 307; at Macbeth's, 327-8, 329; at the banquet, 340, 341, 344; conversation with lord, 346-7; with Macbeth, 352; in war against Macbeth, 365, 366

LENORE, by Poe, xlii, 1273-4

Lent, Calvin on meat in, xxxix, 39; Herbert on, xv, 408

Lentulus Spinther, the consul, consulship of, xii, 254; letter to, ix, 123; property of, 156; recall of, 100, 102

Lentulus Sura, the consul, Antony and, xii, 334, 338; Cæsar and, 299-300, 301; in Catiline conspiracy, 238-40, 279-80; Cicero on death of, ix, 165; executed, 243, 251

Leo X, Pope, xxvii, 409; Cellini and, xxxi, 14; Luther to, xxxvi, 353-62; Machiavelli on, 42

Leo, Valerius, and Cæsar, xii, 289

Leocritus, in the ODYSSEY, xxii, 28-9, 315

Lcolin, imprisonment of, xxxii, 151

Leoline, Sir, (see CHRISTABEL)

Leon, St., on God, xlviii, 358

Leon of Salamis, ii, 19; Socrates and, 254 (66)

Leonardo da Vinci (see Vinci)

Leonela, in story of CURIOUS-IMPERTINENT, xiv, 341-362; 368-71

Leoni, Leone, xxxi, 257 note 3

Leosthenes, xii, 220

Leotychides, son of Alcibiades, xii, 132-3

Lepanto, battle of, iii, 83; Cervantes at, xiv, 3; Cervantes on, 404-5

Lepidotos, Herodotus on the, xxxiii, 38

Lepidus, Catius, letter to, ix, 262

Lepidus, Marcus Æmilius, xii, 327, 330; Africa allotted to, 257; Antony and, 347; Brutus and, 344; Cicero on, ix, 69, 185, 187, 188;

consul with Cæsar, xii, 341; death of, xxxii, 14; left in Rome by Cæsar, xii, 338; put out of government, 378; in the triumvirate, 265, 348-9

Lerna, Lake, viii, 179 note 40

Leroux, Paul, his article on God, v, 288

Lessing, Gotthold Ephraim, and Burke, xxiv, 28; EDUCATION OF THE HUMAN RACE, xxxii, 193-217; life and works, xxvi, 286; MINNA VON BARNHELM, 287-366; Taine on, xxxix, 437

LESSON, A, xli, 629-30

LET ME IN THIS AE NIGHT, vi, 553

LET THERE BE LIGHT, xlv, 586

LET US DRINK AND BE MERRY, xl, 373

Lethe, Dante on, xx, 62, 264; Milton on, iv, 125, 126

Létiche, story of, xlii, 1366

Leto, in Egyptian mythology, xxxiii, 80-1; Jove and, xl, 234; oracle of, xxxiii, 42, 80; Tityos and, xxii, 167; worshipped in Egypt, xxxii, 33

Letters, Hobbes on invention of, xxxiv, 335; invented by Prometheus, viii, 172

Letters, men of, why so called, xxviii, 104

Letters, Bacon on business, iii, 123; Goethe on, xxxix, 266; Locke on writing of, xxxvii, 172-3; Pliny on unsatisfactoriness of, ix, 286; Stevenson on, xxviii, 290

LETTERS OF CICERO, ix, 83-189; remarks on, 5, 81-2

LETTERS OF PLINY, ix, 195-438; remarks on, 193-4

LETTERS ON ÆSTHETIC EDUCATION, xxxii, 219-313

LETTERS ON THE ENGLISH, Voltaire's, xxxiv, 65-162

LETTY'S GLOBE, xli, 947

Leucaspis, in Hades, xiii, 222

Leucippus, school of, iii, 44

Leucothea, Milton on, iv, 70, 326; in the ODYSSEY, xxii, 80

Leuthold, in WILHELM TELL, xxvi, 424-7, 434, 436

Leuwenhoek, Voltaire on, xxxiv, 129

LEVANA AND OUR LADIES OF SORROW, xxvii, 335-41

Level, Lyell on changes of, xxxviii, 428-31, 433-4 (see also Elevation, Subsidence)

Leveridge, Mr., xliii, 148

Levers, velocity and power in, xxx, 192

LEVET, DR. ROBERT, ON THE DEATH OF, xli, 515-16

Levi, and Jesus, xliv, 372 (27-9)

Leviathan, in BOOK OF JOB, xliv, 140 (1-34); Job's description of, Burke on, xxiv, 59; old Irish idea of, xlix, 225; references to, iv, 95, 240; xv, 135, 136; xliv, 239 (14), 279 (26)

LEVIATHAN, FIRST PART OF, Hobbes's, xxxiv, 317-434

Levune, in EDWARD II, xlvi, 45, 51, 56

Lexicographers, Johnson on, xxxix, 191

Lexington, battle of, xliii, 166; Longfellow on battle of, xlii, 1351

LEWARS, JESSIE, COMPLIMENTARY VERSICLES TO, vi, 588-9

LEWARS, JESSY, INSCRIPTION TO, vi, 591

Lewes, G. H., on Egyptian races, xi, 220

LEY, LADY MARGARET, TO THE, iv, 81

Li, son of Confucius, xliv, 34 (7)

Liandola, Loderingo di, xx, 98 note 4

Lianour, Duke, xxxv, 131-2

Liar, Mr., in PILGRIM'S PROGRESS, xv, 101-2

Liars, fable on, xvii, 28

LIBATION-BEARERS, Æschylus's, viii, 71-114; Voltaire on, xxxix, 382

LIBELLER'S SELF-REPROOF, vi, 291

Libels, in Athens, iii, 203-4; in Rome, 205; Franklin on, i, 96-7

Liberality, in children, xxxvii, 97, 98; Hobbes on, xxxiv, 354, 380; Penn on, i, 344; of princes, xxxvi, 54-6; proverb on, xvi, 212

Liberators, great, iii, 136

LIBERTIES, THE BODY OF, xliii, 70-89

Liberty, art and, xxxii, 223, 224; Burke on, xxiv, 156-7, 208-11, 394; Byron on, xli, 832; contentment and, 535; duty of respecting others', xxxii, 360-1; Emerson on, v, 256, 260; extreme ideas of, iii, 22; Goldsmith on ills of, xli, 541-2; government and, xliii, 214-15, 258; Hamilton on jealousy of, 214; history of doctrine of, xxv, 163-4; Hume on religious, xxxvii, 429; inequality not inconsistent with, iv, 203; intellectual growth and, xxviii, 373; Kempis on, vii, 236 (2), 297-8, 308 (1); of labor, Smith on, x, 129-30; licence and, iv, 82; love of, in children, xxxvii, 60-1, 90, 117-18; Lovelace on, xl, 365-6; Milton on, iii, 199, 232-8; iv, 4, 117, 347-8; natural, Hobbes on, xxxiv, 407; natural, Smith's theory of, x, 4, 263; necessity and, Hume on, xxxvii, 371-91; Pascal on

excessive, xlviii, 127 (379); philosophy and, xxxvii, 416, 429; "pious editor's" creed of, xlii, 1452; refinement and, xxxii, 250-1, 269; Rousseau on love of, xxxiv, 220-1; Rousseau on renunciation of, 222-3; Schiller on, xxxii, 279-80; Smith on, x, 466; social, xxxiv, 408-10, 425-6; of speech and press in U. S., xliii, 207 (1); standing armies and, x, 469-70; Tennyson on, xlii, 1032; on trial in America, xliii, 243-4; Vane, Sir Henry, on, 128-9, 130-2; Ward, Nathaniel, on, 70; Washington on love of, 252-3; of the will (see Free Will); Whitman on, xxxix, 422-3; Woolman on, i, 211; works on, xxv, 6

LIBERTY, ESSAY ON, Mill's, xxv, 203-325; remarks on, 160-64

LIBERTY, CHRISTIAN, Luther on, xxxvi, 362-97

Liberty of the Press, Franklin on, i, 96-7; James Mill on, xxv, 71; John Stuart Mill on, 218-59; Milton on (see AREOPAGITICA); in U. S., xliii, 207 (1)

Libicocco, the demon, xx, 90, 93

Libo, and Antony, xii, 339

Libra, the constellation, referred to, xx, 151 note 2

Libraries, Hunt on, xxvii, 310; invention of, xxviii, 57; Ruskin on public, 135; subscription, proposed by Franklin, i, 69-70

Libya, Herodotus on, xxxiii, 12, 20

Licences, Smith on, x, 524-5

Lichas, in the ÆNEID, xiii, 337

Lichas, servant of Alcides, iv, 124

Licinianus, Valerius, Pliny on, ix, 264-7

Licinus, Largius, and professional applauders, ix, 230-1

Lidgate, Dan John, xxxix, 8

LIE, THE, xl, 207-10

Liebig, on fermentation, xxxviii, 362-75

Liemer, Harrison on the, xxxv, 370

Lies, cross, iii, 134; some, never penned, vi, 79; Stevenson on, xxviii, 287, 292-3 (see also Falsehood)

Life, advancement in, Ruskin on, xxviii, 96-7, 131-2; Arabian proverb on, xvi, 18; Bacon on monotony of, iii, 10; beginning of, on the earth, xi, 360-1; the best teacher, xxviii, 351; bridge of, in MIRZA, xxvii, 78-80; Browne on length of, 306 (42), 307 (43); Buddha on, xlv, 592, 673, 709-10; Burke on pleasure in idea of, xxiv, 36, 38; Burns on, vi, 152, 177-8, 204, 325, 334, 507, 585; Carlyle on, xxv, 334-6; Cicero on, ix, 76-

7; Cicero on various ages of, 57-8; Cory on, xlii, 1159-60; Dante on, xx, 5 note 1; Darwin's tree of, xi, 143-4; Dryden's lines on, xxxiv, 137; ECCLESIASTES on vanity of, xliv, 339-42, 345 (15-17), 346 (3-6); Emerson on, v, 26, 30, 67-8, 76-7; Epictetus on, ii, 141 (68), 163 (124), 174 (159), 181 (189), 182 (1), 183 (9), 184 (20); Goethe on false study of, xix, 74; Gray on, xl, 464; Greek dramatists on, viii, 279, 294-5, 390; Harvey on cause of, xxxviii, 89, 90, 91, 107; Herrick on, xl, 347, 348, 350; Hindu conception of, xlv, 806, 860, 862; Job on, xliv, 93-4; Jonson on worth of, xl, 298; Keats's seasons of, xli, 920-1; Kempis on, vii, 293 (3-4), 326-7; Kempis on the inward, 248-50; Longfellow on, xlii, 1330, 1341; Lowell on, 1460; Marcus Aurelius on, ii, 205 (17), 210 (10), 214 (3), 223 (50), 231 (24), 233 (33), 237 (16), 243 (46), 250 (40), 253 (61), 260 (24), 274 (30), 275, 305 (31); Mill on, xxv, 36; Milton on, iv, 84, 336; Montaigne on, xxxii, 24, 26, 27; not the result of chance, xxxiv, 259-60; Omar Khayyam on, xli, 971, 972, 981, 982; Pascal on, xlviii, 61 (156), 71, 79 (213), 129 (386); Penn on, i, 399; Plato on, ii, 251 (48); Pliny on, ix, 248; Poe on, xlii, 1291-2; Pope on, xl, 418; preservation of, as a duty, xxxii, 328; Psalm on vanity of, xliv, 193-4; Pythagoras on, xxxii, 47-8; Rossetti, C. G., on, xlii, 1229; Scott on, xli, 766; Shakespeare on, xlvi, 135, 370; Shelley on, xli, 892; Socrates on value of, ii, 37; Spencer on principle of, xi, 318; struggle for (see Struggle for Existence); Thackeray on, xlii, 1100; universal interest in, xix, 13; Webster on, xlvii, 811; without air (see Anærobian Life); without light, xxxviii, 380-1 (see also Organic Beings)
LIFE, by Bacon, xl, 358-9
LIFE, by Barbauld, xli, 568
LIFE, by Drummond, xl, 335-6
LIFE, A PSALM OF, xlii, 1316
LIFE, THE RIVER OF, xli, 794-5
LIFE, THE STREAM OF, xlii, 1165-6
LIFE, WHAT IS OUR, xl, 210
LIFE IS A DREAM, Calderon's, xxvi, 5-68; remarks on, 4
Ligarius, Quintus, trial of, xii, 259
Ligatures, Harvey on, xxxviii, 116-21; Lister on, 281
Ligea, reference to, iv, 70
Liger, in the ÆNEID, xiii, 316, 346-7
Light, in architecture, xxiv, 71;

Berkeley on, xxxvii, 218-19; composition of white, xxx, 274-5; Descartes on, xxxiv, 36, 37; diffraction of, xxx, 281; effects of various waves of, 273-4; frequency of vibration, 283; from flame, its cause, 110-14, 164; heat from, 273; intermitting, effects of, xxiv, 74; invisible, xxx, 271; knowledge of, 272-3; Milton on, iv, 138; Newton's discoveries in, xxxiv, 124-7; Noël's definition of, xlviii, 432 note; Pascal on, 125 (368); photographer's or actinic, xxx, 272; polarization of, 277-9; produced by chemical affinity, 81; refraction of, Faraday on, 31-5; sublimity of, xxiv, 70-1; velocity of, xxx, 283; vibrations of, 268-71, 275-6; wave lengths of, 280-3
LIGHT, THE WAVE THEORY OF, xxx, 263-86
LIGHT BRIGADE, CHARGE OF THE, xlii, 1039
LIGHT OF OTHER DAYS, xli, 837-8
LIGHT OF STARS, THE, xlii, 1317-18
LIGHT SHINING OUT OF DARKNESS, xlv, 575
Lighthorn, in EDWARD II, xlvi, 74-5, 78-81
Lighthouses, Franklin on, i, 165
Light-mind, Mrs., in PILGRIM'S PROGRESS, xv, 189-190
Lightning, Burke on grandeur of, xxiv, 70; Darwin on effects of, xxix, 72-3; Franklin on, i, 153-5; tubes formed by, xxix, 70-2
Like, buys like, v, 249; cures like, iv, 416
LIKE AS THE CULVER, xl, 257
Likeness, of all things, v, 240-1; attracts likeness, ii, 270 (9); ix, 26; in unlikeness, xxxix, 301
Lilies, Jesus on the, xliv, 394 (27)
LILIES OF QUEENS' GARDENS, xxviii, 139-68
Lilinau, story of, xlii, 1403
Lilith, Adam's wife, xix, 172
Liliuokalani, Queen, xliii, 464 note
Lilla, Hafiz on, v, 225
Lilly, Johnson on, xxxix, 236
Lima, Darwin on, xxix, 389
Limbo, Dante's, xx, 17-21; Milton's, iv, 149-50; spirits in, xx, 10 note 3
Limbs, and jaws, related, xi, 155
Lime Light, Faraday on, xxx, 111-12
Limestone, composition of, xxx, 343-4
Lime-water, composition of, xxx, 158
Limitations, Emerson on, v, 158-9
Linacer, Johnson on, xxxix, 236
LINCOLN, ABRAHAM, by Lowell, xxviii, 441-63
Lincoln, Abraham, absence of demagogism, xxviii, 462; his Americanism, 451-2; AMNESTY PROCLAMATION, xliii, 442-5; difficulties of,

xxviii, 446-8; EMANCIPATION PROC-
LAMATION, xliii, 344-6; FIRST IN-
AUGURAL ADDRESS, 334-43; GETTYS-
BURG ADDRESS, 441; Henry IV
compared with, xxviii, 450-1;
LETTER TO MRS. BIXBY, xliii, 446;
Lowell's lines on, xlii, 1462-3; not
a ready-made ruler, xxviii, 452-3;
power and fame at death, 463;
SECOND INAUGURAL ADDRESS, xliii,
450-2; self-unconsciousness, xxviii,
462; slavery problem and, 454-60
(see also EMANCIPATION PROC-
LAMATION); statesmanlike quali-
ties of, 445-6; tentative policy,
448-50, 453-4; trustfulness in the
people, 461-2; Whitman on death
of, xlii, 1496-7
LINCOLN, DEATH OF, by Bryant, xlii,
1272-3
Lincoln, Earl of (see Lacy, Sir
Hugh)
Lindsay, Lady Anne, AULD ROBIN
GRAY, xli, 570-1
Lindsay, Sir James, and Bishop of
Durham, xxxv, 98-9; and Matthew
Redman, 97-8, 100; at Otterburn,
93
Lindsey, Earl of, Dryden on, xviii, 9
Lineage, Don Quixote's two man-
ners of, xiv, 184
Ling, Duke of Wei, xliv, 49 (20),
52 (1)
Lingende, on miracles, xlviii, 300
(846)
Linnæus, on American plants, xxviii,
419; Emerson on, v, 18; on genus,
xi, 452; on increase of plants, 79;
mistake of, 463
LINNET, THE GREEN, xli, 657-8
Linos, song of, xxxiii, 41
Linus, in Dante's Limbo, xx, 20;
Sidney on, xxvii, 8
Lion, flesh of the, xxix, 129
LION AND FOUR OXEN, fable of,
xvii, 32
LION AND FOX, fable of, xvii, 24
LION AND MOUSE, fable of, xvii,
14
LION AND STATUE, fable of, xvii, 24
LION, FOX, AND OTHER BEASTS,
fable of, xvii, 42
LION IN LOVE, fable of, xvii, 41
LION, THE SICK, xvii, 13
LION'S SHARE, THE, fable of, xvii,
10
Lion-ant, of Australia, xxix, 466
note
Lionel, Sir, at the Abbey, xxxv,
110; at court, 111; in captivity,
176; believed to be dead, 178;
his character, 182; attempts to
slay Sir Bors, 183-5; combat with
Sir Colgrevance, 185-6; combat
with Bors prevented by miracle,
186-7; his return home, 216

Lippi, Filippino, xxxi, 24 note, 25
note 3
Lippi, Francesco, and Cellini, xxxi,
25, 29
Lipsius, on criticism, xxxix, 260;
Montaigne on, xxxii, 32
Liquefaction, cold caused by, xxx,
38-9
Liquids, cohesion of, xxx, 40-1
Liquor Trade, Mill on regulation of,
xxv, 309-10
Liquors, duties on, x, 381-2
Liris, death of, xiii, 385
Listening, the art of, ii, 147
(81)
Lister, Joseph, ON ANTISEPTIC PRIN-
CIPLE, xxxviii, 271-82; life and
work, 270; Pasteur on, 389
Lister, William, in Tyler's Rebellion,
xxxv, 75
Listlessness, Locke on, xxxvii, 114-
17, 189-90
LITERARY AND PHILOSOPHICAL ES-
SAYS, xxxii
Literature, Arnold on good, xxviii,
91; Carlyle on, xxv, 458, 464;
Carlyle on modern, 353-5; classical and romantic, xxxix, 363;
criticism of manners, morals, and
religion in, xxvii, 232-4; effeminacy
of our, v, 53; Emerson on, 161;
Huxley on ancient, xxviii, 221-9;
Ruskin on encouragement of,
134; Seneca on, xlviii, 123 note
6; for subsistence, remarks on,
xxv, 57-8; Taine on study of,
xxxix, 433-40, 460-1; Taine on,
as transcript of its times, 433-40,
460-1; tested by time, 218-19;
Thoreau on nature in, xxviii, 426-
7; Whitman on simplicity in,
xxxix, 418; why so called, xxviii,
104
Litigation, enemy of right and
wrong, vi, 308
LITTLE BRIAR-ROSE, story of, xvii,
146-9
Little-Faith, in PILGRIM'S PROGRESS,
xv, 130-37
LITTLE IDA'S FLOWERS, xvii, 355-62
Little John, in ROBYN HODE, in adventure with sorrowful knight, xl,
131, 132-3, 135-6, 138, 139, 140,
141; with sheriff of Nottingham,
149-55; in adventure with monks,
157-60, 162; at archery contest,
168; saved by ROBYN HODE, 169-
70; returns to green wood, 172,
182; with Robyn at court, 186
LITTLE RED CAP, xvii, 116-20
Little Round Top, at Gettysburg,
xliii, 357
LITTLE SEA-MAID, THE, xvii, 255-
76
LITTLE SNOW-WHITE, xvii, 155-64
Littleness, as cause of beauty, xxiv,

96-7, 131-4; infinite, is sublime, 64

Littlewit, John, xxxix, 169

Liu-hsia Hui, xliv, 53 note, 63 (2), 65 (8)

Live-loose, Mr., in PILGRIM'S PROGRESS, xv, 101-2

Liver, Harvey on the, xxxviii, 101-2, 134-5

Livermore, Thomas L., xliii, 347 note

Livia, Augustus and, iii, 52-3; the sons of, xii, 403; Tacitus on, iii, 18; Tiberius and, 148

LIVING TOO LONG, ON, xli, 930

Livingston, Robert R., in Louisiana Purchase, xliii, 267 note

Livre, French coin, x, 33

Livy, citizen of Cadiz and, ix, 224; on fall of the great, xxxix, 74 note; Macaulay on, xxvii, 414; Mill's delight in, xxv, 13; on prophecy of Pharsalia, xii, 314; Shelley on, xxvii, 352, 361; the Spaniard and, xxviii, 59

Liwarc'h Hên, Celtic bard, xxxii, 174

LIZ, by Buchanan, xlii, 1247

Lizards, of Galapagos Islands, xxix, 408-13; S. American, 110

Ljod, daughter of Hrimnir, xlix, 277, 278

Llama, Darwin on the wild, xxix, 179-82; Francis Pretty on, xxxiii, 218

Lloyd, Captain, in Mauritius, xxix, 511-12

Loadstones, Faraday on, xxx, 66

Loans, bank, x, 254-8; in Scotland, 247-9; Shakespeare on, xlvi, 102; Smith on, x, 291-4; by states, 491-2

Lobineau, Dom, *Saints of Brittany*, xxxii, 182

Local Administration, abuses of, x, 478

Local Expenses, x, 487-8

LOCHINVAR, xli, 769-70

LOCK OF HAIR, TO A, xli, 757-8

LOCK THE DOOR, LARISTON, xli, 786-788

Locke, John, on arguments, xxxvii, 351 note; Berkeley and, 198; on darkness, xxiv, 120-1; Emerson on, v, 148, 453, 455; on general words, xxiv, 138; Hazlitt on, xxvii, 281-2; *On Human Understanding*, i, 18; Hume on, xxxvii, 307, 320-1; on innate ideas, 320-1; life and works, 3-4; on matter, 365 note; Mill on, xxv, 49; Mill's abstract of, 48; on money, x, 327; on pleasure and pain, xxiv, 32 note; on power, xxxvii, 357 note; on property, xxxiv, 209; THOUGHTS CONCERNING EDU-

CATION, xxxvii, 5-195; Unitarianism and, xxxiv, 85; Voltaire on, 103-10; on wit and judgment, xxiv, 17

Lockhart, *Life of Scott*, Carlyle on, xxv, 412-19

LOCKSLEY HALL, xlii, 1009-19

Locrians, legislation of the, xxv, 231

Locrine, son of Brutus, iv, 68

Locusts, Darwin on, xxix, 348-9; Harrison on, xxxv, 367-8; the plague of, iv, 99; swarms of, blown by winds, xi, 408-9

Loderingo, in Dante's HELL, xx, 98

Lodge, Thomas, Poems by, xl, 218-21

Lodging, materials of, Smith on, x, 173-5, 186

Loe, Thomas, and William Penn, xxxiv, 75 note

Lofraso, Anthony, Cervantes on, xiv, 56

Logan, James, anecdote of, i, 113-14

Logan, John, BRAES OF YARROW, xli, 512

LOGAN, MAJOR, EPISTLE TO, vi, 257-60

LOGAN, MISS, TO, vi, 267-8

Logan, Sir W., on Canadian strata, xi, 360

LOGAN BRAES, vi, 492-3

Logic, Bacon on, xxxix, 132, 139, 141, 151, 152; Bacon on study of, iii, 129; Carlyle on, xxv, 337-8; Descartes on, xxxiv, 16-17; Goethe on, xix, 73-4; Hobbes on, xxxiv, 377; Hume on, xxxvii, 314; Kant on, xxxii, 317, 318; Locke on study of, xxxvii, 147-8, 169-71; Marlowe on, xix, 200 and note 10; Mill on study of, xxv, 18-19; Mill's work in, 104-5, 117-18, 134-6, 143-6; Milton on study of, iii, 250, 255; Montaigne on, xxxii, 64; Pascal on, xlviii, 415, 416

Logicians, Pascal on, xlviii, 131 (393)

LOGIE O' BUCHAN, xli, 585

Logris, realm of, xxxv, 193

Lokabynhas, xlv, 617

Loki, in STORY OF VOLSUNGS AND NIBLUNGS, xlix, 305, 306

Lombardi, commentator of Dante, xx, 147 note 2

Lombardo, Marco, xx, 311 note

Lombardo, Pietro, xx, 329 note 19

Lomna Drúth, xlix, 230, 232, 234, 237, 240, 244, 245, 247, 254, 255-6, 257, 259

LONDON, MDCCCII, xli, 692-3

London, Carlyle on, v, 335; Emerson on, 375, 485; Franklin on streets of, i, 126-8; Harrison on

Lord Mayors of, xxxv, 293; Herschel on, v, 347; industries of, x, 276-7; rent and lodging in, 125-6

London *Punch*, Emerson on, v, 470

London Review, The, xxv, 4, 129-30, 133-4, 138-42

LONDON SQUARE, IN A, xlii, 1166

London *Times, The*, Emerson on, v, 466-71

London University, Harrison on, xxxv, 391-2, 400, 403

Long, George, translator of Marcus Aurelius, ii, 191

Long Parliament, free printing suppressed by, iii, 194, 195-7; Milton on the, 200-2, 238, 243; xxviii, 194-5; theatres closed by, xviii, 3

LONG PARLIAMENT, NEW FORCERS OF CONSCIENCE UNDER THE, iv, 82-3

Longevity, Browne on, iii, 307 (43); Cicero on, ix, 71; Darwin on, xi, 219-20; its effect on traditions, xlviii, 211-12

Longfellow, Henry Wadsworth, poems by, xlii, 1316-1413; Poe on *Waif* of, xxviii, 391-2

LONGING, xli, 818-19

Longinus, Hugo on, xxxix, 362; quoted, xxiv, 46

Longstreet, Gen., at Gettysburg, xliii, 365, 366, 370

Lope Ruyz, tale of, xiv, 166-8

Lope de Vega, quoted, xxxix, 384

Lopez, Dr., xix, 233 note 1

Lopez, Francisco, xxxiii, 327, 328-9

LORD GREGORY, vi, 483

LORD THOMAS AND FAIR ANNET, xl, 61-5

LORD ULLIN'S DAUGHTER, xli, 792-4

Lord's Prayer, The, xliv, 389 (2-4); Dante on, xx, 189; Herbert on the, xv, 407; Locke on the, xxxvii, 141

Lords of Articles (Scotland), xxiv, 267 note

Lords of Trade, and Albany Convention, i, 129

Lorenzo the Magnificent, age of, xxvii, 389-90

LORIMER, MISS, INSCRIPTION TO, vi, 579

Lorraine, Cardinal of, Cellini on, xxxi, 295 note, 296, 310, 311; in FAUSTUS, xix, 224-5

Lorraine, François de, at Boulogne, xxxviii, 18

Los Angeles (in 1859), xxiii, 408

Losses, and crosses, lessons from, vi, 73; Epictetus on, ii, 120 (11), 126 (27); Smith on fear of, x, 114-15

LOST LEADER, THE, xlii, 1109

LOST MISTRESS, THE, xlii, 1111

LOST YOUTH, MY, xlii, 1343-5

Lot, Jesus on, xliv, 406 (28-9); Jesus on wife of, 406 (32); Mo-

hammed on, xlv, 917, 1007; wife of, xv, 113-14

Lothair, son of Louis Debonnaire. xxxix, 85-6

Lothario, and Anselmo, xiv, 323-63, 368-73

Lothario, gay, reference to, xix, 108

Lotos-Eaters, in Egypt, xxxiii, 45; Ulysses and the, xxii, 122

LOTOS-EATERS, THE, xlii, 1026-31; editor's remarks on, l, 19

Lotteries, Smith on, x, 113-14; Woolman on, i, 253

Lotto, Pier Maria di, xxxi, 84 note

Lotus-Eaters (see Lotos-Eaters)

Loudness, as source of the sublime, xxiv, 72

Loudoun, Lord, administration of, i, 161-2; attack on Louisburg, 160; death of, vi, 315 note; indecision of, i, 159-61; in proprietary quarrels, 158

Louis, of Bavaria, son of Debonnaire; xxxix, 86

Louis le Bègue, xxxix, 86

Louis, the Debonnaire, Raleigh on, xxxix, 84-6

Louis, son of Charles the Simple, xxxix, 87

Louis, Saint, wife of, xx, 176 note 14

Louis XI, barber of, xxxix, 374; Henry VII and, 80-1; leaden god of, 100; mercenaries of, xxxvi, 49; postal service established by, ix, 388 note; secrecy of, iii, 72

Louis XII, Macaulay on, xxvii, 407; Machiavelli on, xxxvi, 9, 13-15, 25

Louis XIII, Richelieu and, xxiv, 349

Louis XIV, Burke on reign of, xxiv, 258; Dryden on, xiii, 57; on duties of sovereign, xxxiv, 222; Emerson on, v, 405; English dislike of, xxxiv, 87; literature under, xxxix, 452; Mazarin and, xxiv, 349; Scarron and, xxxix, 368-9; Voltaire on, xxxiv, 154

Louis XVI, Burke on, xxiv, 213-16, 219-23, 230-2, 280, 284, 295; as king under the Constitution, 348-51; on October Sixth, 219-23; place of execution of, xxxix, 377-8

Louis, Don, in DON QUIXOTE, xiv, 453-7, 465-70

LOUISIANA, CESSION OF, xliii, 267-72

LOUSE, TO A, vi, 198-9

Louvain, Lipsius on, xxviii, 46-7

Louviers, town of, xxxv, 15

Louvois, and Louis, xiv, xxiv, 349

Love, Alcibiades on, xii, 113 note 2; among angels, iv, 262; Beaumont on, xlvii, 662-3; beginnings of conjugal and paternal, xxxiv, 206; Blake on, xli, 605, 606; Brome on, xl, 378; Browning,

E. B., on, xli, 953-4, 955, 958, 961, 966, 967-8; Browning, Robert on, xlii, 1143, 1154; Browning, Robert, on fraternal, xviii, 380; Burke on, xxiv, 37, 38, 39; Burns on, vi, 144, 189, 213, 507; business and, xl, 319; Byron on, xli, 820; Campbell on, 801-2; "can tame the wildest," xvii, 41; comfort in strength of, xli, 641; Confucius on, xliv, 9 (3), 13 (1-7), 17 (18), 21 (20, 21, 28), 22 (6), 24 (29), 30 (28), 38-9, 41 (22), 45 (19), 46 (2), 47 (5, 7, 8), 48 (17), 50 (30), 53 (8, 9), 55 (34, 35), 60 (6, 8); Corneille on causes and effects of, xlviii, 62-3; a cureless sorrow, xl, 253; death and, iii, 10; xlii, 1076; Hobbes's definition of, xxxiv, 354; desire contrasted with, xxiv, 77; Donne on, xl, 321; echoes of, xli, 843; Emerson on blindness of, v, 311; Envy compared with, iii, 23, 27; Euripides on, viii, 297, 306, 310-11, 314, 340; excited by theatre, xlviii, 11 (11); fear and, xxxvi, 57-9; xlvi, 143; friendship and, ix, 42; xxxii, 77-8; Goethe on, xix, 62, 127, 133-4; 287, 379; Greek epigram on, v, 317; Hume on, xxxvii, 342; inspired by virtue, ix, 18; is love forever, xlii, 1013; jealousy and, xl, 293; Jonson on, 302-4; Kant on practical, xxxii, 330; Kempis on, vii, 257 (4), 273-5; Longfellow on, xlii, 1335-6; Marcus Aurelius on the universal, ii, 284 (21); mathematically just, v, 102; Milton on, iv, 261, 269; Milton on misfortunes of, 317; Milton on wedded, 176; of misanthropes, ii, 184 (23); Moore on, xxviii, 396; More on, xxxvi, 224; music and, xli, 491; the panacea, v, 58-60; Pascal on decay of, xlviii, 50 (123); Pascal on passion of, 417-27; Paul, St., on, xlv, 519 (1-13), 526 (14); Penn on, i, 347 (82-3), 383-4 (545-56); physical cause of, xxiv, 125-6; physical effects of, xxxviii, 131; pity and, xl, 340; Poe on, xxviii, 403, 404; poets of, xxvii, 364-5; Raleigh on, xl, 208; refined by sense of beauty, xxxii, 310; remedy of all blunders, v, 293; Scott on, xli, 761, 769; Shakespeare on, xl, 268, 287 134), 289; xlvi, 116, 144, 210; Shelley on, xli, 848, 873; "short word that says much," xviii, 386-7; Sidney on, xxvii, 37; Sophocles on, viii, 267-8; in state of nature, xxxiv, 195-8; Stevenson on, xxviii, 294; Stoic definition

of, xxxii, 80; Swinburne on, xlii, 1256-7; Tennyson on, 1011, 1060, 1068; Tennyson on faith in, 1006-7; Thomson on, 1196; time and, xlvi, 177; Tzu-hsia on, xliv, 66 (6); unlawful, punished in Hell, xx, 22-5; unrequited, impossibility of, v, 123; Walton on, xv, 330; Webster on, xlvii, 761; Wordsworth on, xli, 681, 682; in young men, xiv, 216; Yu-tzu on roots of, xliv, 5 (2)

LOVE, ESSAY ON, Bacon's, iii, 28-9.

LOVE, by Coleridge, xli, 721-3

LOVE, by Herbert, xl, 351

LOVE, ALL FOR, xli, 809-10

LOVE, DIRGE FOR, by Sidney, xl, 214-15

LOVE, DIRGE OF, by Shakespeare, xl, 274-5

LOVE, THE FLIGHT OF, xli, 874

LOVE, GIVE ALL TO, xlii, 1295-6

LOVE, GIVE ME MORE, xl, 362

LOVE, SUMMONS TO, xl, 339-40

LOVE FOR LOVE, vi, 469

LOVE GREGOR: a ballad, xl, 65-9

LOVE IN HER EYES SITS PLAYING, xl, 412

LOVE IN THE GUISE OF FRIENDSHIP, vi, 310

LOVE IN THE VALLEY, xlii, 1186-92

LOVE LIES A-BLEEDING, xlvii, 637-718

LOVE LOOKED FOR HELL, How, xlii, 1479-82

LOVE NOT ME, xl, 334

LOVE THOU THY LAND, xlii, 1033-5

LOVE WILL FIND OUT THE WAY, xl, 388

LOVE-BEGOTTEN DAUGHTER, TO A, vi, 59-60

Love-gain, town of, xv, 106

Love-lust, Mr., in PILGRIM'S PROGRESS, xv, 101-2

Love-Potions, Webster on, xlvii, 756-7

Love-saint, Mr., in PILGRIM'S PROGRESS, xv, 285

LOVE-SWEETNESS, xlii, 1227

Love-the-flesh, Mrs, in PILGRIM'S PROGRESS, xv, 190

LOVE'S DEITY, xl, 317-18

LOVE'S FAREWELL, xl, 232

LOVE'S OMNIPRESENCE, xl, 322

LOVE'S PERJURIES, xl, 272

LOVE'S PHILOSOPHY, xli, 854

Lovejoy, Emerson on, v, 134

Lovelace, Richard, poems by, xl, 364-6

LOVELINESS OF LOVE, THE, xli, 938-9

Lovell, in SHOEMAKER'S HOLIDAY, xlvii, 449

Lovell, Lord, in NEW WAY TO PAY OLD DEBTS, xlvii, master of Allworth, 828; Overreach's plan to win, 837, 850, 858-9; with All-

worth on way to Overreach's, 851-4; Overreach on, 856-7; arrival at Overreach's, 859-60; with Margaret, 860-2; 867; with Lady Allworth at Overreach's, 863, 864; departure, 867; discharges Allworth, 869; with Overreach at Allworth's, 869-73; with Lady Allworth, 873-6; reconciliation with Lady Allworth, 885-7; with Wellborn, 888; in final scene, 893, 895-6, 897, 898-9

LOVELY LASS OF INVERNESS, vi, 521
LOVELY POLLY STEWART, vi, 438
LOVELY YOUNG JESSIE, vi, 484
LOVER, THE CONSTANT, xl, 363
LOVER AND HIS LASS, xl, 269
LOVER'S APPEAL, xl, 195-6
LOVER'S INFINITENESS, xl, 316-17
LOVER'S LULLABY, A, xl, 198
LOVER'S MORNING SALUTE TO HIS MISTRESS, vi, 537
LOVER'S RESOLUTION, THE, xl, 341-2
LOVESIGHT, by Rossetti, xlii, 1225
Lovewit, in THE ALCHEMIST, xlvii, 615-23, 629-35
LOVING IN TRUTH, xl, 216
Low Archipelago, Darwin on, xxix, 425
Lowell, James Russell, ABRAHAM LINCOLN, xxviii, 441-63; DEMOCRACY, 464-85; life and works, 440; poems by, xlii, 1447-69
Loxias, Apollo called, viii, 94, 113, 116
Loyal, Mr., in TARTUFFE, xxvi, 273-7
Lubbock, Sir John, on linking species, xi, 352; on sexual characters, 167; on variability in Coccus, 60
Lucagnolo, xxxi, 35, 37-9, 40, 43-4
Lucagus, death of, xiii, 346-7
Lucan, Browne on, iii, 308 (44); in Dante's HELL, xx, 19; Montaigne on, xxxii, 92; Nero and, xviii, 16; Shelley on, xxvii, 354, 366; xli, 890; Sidney on, xxvii, 14
Lucanus, Domitius, ix, 343-4
Lucas, Prosper, on inheritance, xi, 30; on resemblances, 329-30
LUCASTA, TO, GOING BEYOND THE SEAS, xl, 366
LUCASTA, TO, ON GOING TO THE WARS, xl, 364-5
Lucceius, Cicero on, ix, 91, 156; letter to, 104
Lucchesini, Girolamo, xxxi, 436 note
Lucetius, death of, xiii, 316
Luchdonn, the satirist, xlix, 225
Lucia, Dante on, xx, 11 note 6 182, 423
Lucia, in THE BETROTHED (see Mondella, Lucia)
Lucia, Sainte, xxxi, 389 note

Lucian, Alexander the prophet and, xxxvii, 406; atheism of, iii, 45; dispute of S. and T. in, 329; on love of lies, 7
Lucianus, in HAMLET, xlvi, 145, 146
Lucifer, in Dante's HELL, xx, 143-4; in FAUSTUS, xix, 220, 222; Marlowe on fall of, 208; pictured in Purgatory, xx, 193; Satan called, iv, 305; called the worm, xx, 26 note 1
Lucilius, and Brutus, xii, 390
Lucinda, in DON QUIXOTE, xiv, 213-18, 253-61, 278-9, 374-84
Lucius of Cyrene, xliv, 457 (1)
Luck, Hobbes on, xxxiv, 374; Gudrun on the trust in, xlix, 377; shallow men believe in, v, 294
LUCKNOW, THE PIPES AT, xlii, 1437-9
Lucre Hill, in PILGRIM'S PROGRESS, xv, 111, 288
Lucretia, in Dante's Limbo, xx, 20; reference to, 308
Lucretius, Cicero on, ix, 114; Claudian and, xxxix, 450; Montaigne on, xxxii, 92, 93; on pleasure of truth, iii, 8; on religion, 14; xxiv, 144; xxv, 31; in Rome, iii, 205; Sainte-Beuve on, xxxii, 137; Shelley on, xxvii, 361; Sidney on, 14; Swift on, 114; on terror caused by wonders of nature, xxiv, 61; Wordsworth on, v, 337-8
Lucullus, Cicero and, xii, 252; Clodius and, 250; faction of, iii, 130; Pompey and, 114
LUCY: by Wordsworth, xli, 685-8
LUCY ASHTON'S SONG, xli, 765-6
LUCY, COUNTESS OF BEDFORD, xl, 304-5
Ludlow, Hugo on, xxxix, 400
Luisens, Duke de, and Edw. Herbert, xv, 378
Luke, St., Dante on, xx, 268 and note 14; vocation and nationality of, xliv, 356
LUKE, GOSPEL ACCORDING TO, xliv, 355-426; Pascal on, xlviii, 194 (578)
Luke Dosa, iron crown of, xli, 544
LULLABY, by Shakespeare, xl, 270-1
LULLABY, A LOVER'S, xl, 198-9
LULLABY, A SWEET, xl, 200-1
LULLABY, OUR BLESSED LADY'S, xl, 261-5
Lully, Raymond, iii, 209 note; xlvii, 561 note
Lumpkin, Tony, in SHE STOOPS TO CONQUER, son of Mrs. Hardcastle, 204; his pranks, xviii, 204-5; Miss Neville and, 208-9; goes to ale-house, 205-6; at the ale-house, 209-11; with Marlow and Hastings, 211-14; with Constance Neville, 228, 229-30; with his mother,

230; with Hastings, 231-2; steals Miss Neville's jewels for her, 234-5; 236-8; with Miss Neville in the plot, 250-1; and the letter from Hastings, 251-4; denounced by all, 254; takes leave, 256; as driver in elopement plot, 260-4; finally releases Miss Neville, 268-9

Luned, in Arthurian legends, xxxii, 173 note

Lungs, developed from swimbladder, xi, 196; Fabricius on the, xxxviii, 68; Harvey on, 146, 147; heart and, relations of, 68, 73-6, 93, 94, 95-9, 105, 138-9; passage of blood through, 99-102, 104-5

Lupercalia, feast of, xii, 324-5

Luperci, Virgil on the, xiii, 294

Lupercus, letter to, ix, 364

Lupus, Nymphidius, Pliny on, ix, 389-90

Luscinius, Gaius, and Æmilius, ix, 22

Lust, Dante on, xx, 51; in Dante's HELL, 22-5; defined by Hobbes, xxxiv, 354; of the eyes, vii, 197; Hindu Krishna on, xlv, 872; love and, i, 347 (82-3); xl, 430; Milton on, iv, 58-9; Pascal on three kinds of, xlviii, 155 (458), 156 (460-1); Shakespeare on, xl, 288 (135); xlvi, 109, Webster on, xlvii, 748

Lutatius, Catulus, xii, 242; Cæsar and, 278-9

LUTE, To His, William Drummond's, xl, 337

Luther, Martin, ADDRESS TO GERMAN NOBILITY, xxxvi, 276-352; Browne on, iii, 266 (2); Carlyle on, xxv, 338; CHRISTIAN LIBERTY, xxxvi, 362-97; Emerson on, v, 70; hymn by, xlv, 570-1; letter to Archbishop Albert, xxxvi, 261; letter to Leo X, 353-62; letter to Nicholas Amsdorff, 274-5; life and works, 260; NINETY-FIVE THESES, 265-73; Taine on table-talk of, xxxix, 460; Voltaire on, xxxiv, 85; on wise men, v, 243; Wyclif and, iii, 234

Luxuries, defined by Smith, x, 541-2; Emerson on, v, 54-5; Milton on, iv, 65, 67; taxes on, Penn on, i, 344, 409-10; taxes on, Smith on, x, 542-5, 559-64; taxes on, when best paid, 499 (3)

Luxury, Burns on, vi, 147, 262; defined by Hobbes, xxxiv, 354; of doing good, xli, 533; Epictetus on, ii, 175 (168); generation and, x, 83; Goldsmith on, xli, 529, 531; Jonson on, xl, 303; Penn on, i, 341, 346; Pliny on, ix, 226; Woolman on, i, 204-6, 303-4

Luynes, Duke de, xlviii, 352 note, 2

Lycas, in the ÆNEID, xiii, 345-6

Lyceian King, Apollo called, viii, 203, 224

Lychnocaia, religious festival, xxxiii, 34

LYCIDAS, Milton's, iv, 74-79; Ruskin on, xxviii, 108-13

Lycis, reference to, viii, 419-20

Lycomedes, and Neoptolemus, ix, 34; at Salamis, xii, 19

Lycon, accuser of Socrates, ii, 10

Lycopodium, xxx, 109 note

Lycurgus, Aristides and, xii, 81; Bacon on, iii, 136; learning of, 204; young law-breaker and, ii, 150 (88)

Lycurgus, and Hypsipile, xx, 254 note

Lycus, in the ÆNEID, xiii, 83, 316

Lydgate, Dryden on, xxxix, 170

Lydia, the Christian, xliv, 466 (14-15)

Lyell, Sir Charles, on colonies of Barrande, xi, 365; Darwin to, xxix, 7; editor's remarks on papers of, l, 45; on geology, xi, 109; geology, works on, 335-6; life and works of, xxxviii, 404; on means of dispersal, xi, 403; on origin of species and geological record, 363; PROGRESS OF GEOLOGY, xxxviii, 405-18; on struggle for life, xi, 77; on subsidence of Pacific, xxix, 104 note; on succession of species, xi, 364; UNIFORMITY OF CHANGE, xxxviii, 419-40

Lygians, Tacitus on the, xxxiii, 120

Lying, Locke on, xxxvii, 121-2, 126

Lying-in Hospitals, Lee on, xxxviii, 261

Lyly, John, CUPID AND CAMPASPE, xl, 212; SPRING'S WELCOME, 213; Jonson on, 309

Lyncæus, eyes of, v, 177

Lynceus, in the ÆNEID, xiii, 323

Lynceus, and Hypermnæstra, viii, 186 note

Lyngi, King, xlix, 297, 298, 299, 311, 312

Lyon, Richard, and Wat Tyler, xxxv, 71

Lyric Poetry, Hugo on age of, xxxix, 356-7, 370, 371, 372; Milton on, v, 181; Sidney on, xxvii, 30-1; Wordsworth on, xxxix, 313

Lysander, admiral of Sparta, xii, 147, 149; Alcibiades and, 150; Cyrus and, ix, 68; on Spartan respect for age, 69

Lysanias of Sphettus, ii, 20

Lysanias, tetrarch of Abilene, xliv, 365 (1)

Lysias, Claudius, xliv, 484 (26), 486 (22)

Lysias, the orator, ix, 214 note 1

Lysicles, and Aspasia, xii, 62

Lysimachus, son of Aristides, xii, 108

Lysippus, and Alexander, ix, 107

Lyso, Cicero on, ix, 160

Lyte, Henry Francis, ABIDE WITH ME, xlv, 580

Lytton, Edward Earl, THE LAST WISH, xlii, 1165

Mab, fairy, Milton on, iv, 33

Mabinogion, The, xxxii, 145 note, 151-73

Mabon, son of Modron, xxxii, 156-9

M'ADAM, TO MR., vi, 197-8

Macariens, law of the, xxxvi, 173

Macario, Father, miracle of, xxi, 51-2

Macarius, the monk, xx, 380 note 4

Macaroni, Pagolo, xxxi, 317, 321

Macaulay, G. C., Editor of Froissart, xxxv, i; translator of Herodotus, xxxiii, 1

Macaulay, Thomas Babington, Emerson on, v, 457-8; life and works, xxvii, 380; ON MACHIAVELLI, 381-421; Mill on, xxv, 54, 84, 103-4, 105; poems by, xli, 940-3; in Union Debating Society, xxv, 54

Macaulay, Zachary, xxvii, 380

MACBETH, TRAGEDY OF, xlvi, 303-75; Hugo on witches in, xxxix, 366; Lamb on staging of, xxvii, 324-5, 327-8, 330, 331

Macbeth, general of Duncan, xlvi, 306, 307; made Thane of Cawdor, 308; with the witches, 309-11; with king's messengers, 311-13; received by king, 313-14; hatred of Malcolm, Prince of Cumberland, 314-15; letter to wife, 315; Lady Macbeth on, 315; return home, 316-17; hesitates to kill Duncan, 318-19; urged on by Lady Macbeth, 319-21; with Banquo before murder, 321-2; vision of dagger, 322-3; goes to murder, 323; with Lady Macbeth after murder, 324-6; with Macduff and Lennox, 327-8; on discovery of murder, 328, 329-30; chosen king, 332; with Banquo, 333-4; plots to kill Banquo, 334-7; tells Lady Macbeth, 337-9; at the banquet, 340-4; Lennox on, 346; with witches, shown apparitions, 349-51; learns Macduff's flight, 352; Macduff on, 357; in Dunsinane Castle, 366-8, 369; hears death of wife, 369-70; learns forest moving, 370; fights with young Siward, 371-2; and Macduff, 372-3; death, 374

Macbeth, Lady, letter from husband, xlvi, 315; plans to kill king, 316; receives husband, 316-17; welcomes king to castle, 318; urges husband to murder, 319-21; Dun-

can's gift to, 322; during murder, 323; with husband after murder, 324-6; on discovery of murder, 328-9, 330; with Banquo, 333; with husband, concerning Banquo's murder, 337-9; at banquet, 340, 341, 342-4; walks in sleep, 363-5; doctor on, 367; her death, 369-70, 375; Ruskin on, xxviii, 143

Maccabæus, Judas, Dante on, xx, 363 note 3; Milton on, iv, 392; one of nine worthies, xxxix, 21

Maccabees, Pascal on the, xlviii, 213 (630)

MacCarthy, D. F., translator of STABAT MATER, xlv, 565

Maccecht, son of Snade, xlix, 218, 219, 225, 226, 235-7, 238, 259, 260, 261-2, 263

M'Culloch, Mill on, xxv, 65, 67, 84

McCULLOCH VS. MARYLAND, xliii, 222-40

MacDonald, George, poems by, xlii, 1163-5

M'Dougal, Sir George, xxv, 429-30

Macduff, in MACBETH, xlvi, 317; with the porter, 326-7; discovers king's murder, 327-30; with Ross, 332; his flight to England, 346-7, 352; at English court, with Malcolm, 355-9; with Ross, learns death of family, 360-3; in war on Macbeth, 365, 369, 371; fight with Macbeth, 372-3; his victory, 374

Macduff, Lady, xlvi, 352-5

Macedo, Largius, and his slaves, ix, 251-3

Macedonia, Raleigh on, xxxix, 74, 119

Macer, Baebius, letters to, ix, 242, 305

Macer, Calpurnius, ix, 402, 412

Macer, Licinius, death of, xii, 232

M'Gill, Dr. William, vi, 357 note, 372

Machabeus (see Maccabæus)

Macherone, Cesare, xxxi, 114, 115

Machiavel, in EGMONT, xix, 254-60, 284-7

Machiavelli, *Art of War,* xxvii, 412-13; Bacon on, iii, 103; *Belphegor,* xxvii, 436; Cæsar Borgia and, 408-9; on Christianity, iii, 35; *Clizia* of, xxvii, 405; on democracy, xxv, 384; deserts of, xxvii, 420-1; *Discourses on Livy,* 414-15; efforts to relieve Italy, 409-12; life and works of, xxxvi, 3-4; *Mandragola* of, xxvii, 401-5; obloquy following death, 420; odiousness of, 381-3; political correspondence of, 406-7; THE PRINCE, xxxvi, 5-90; THE PRINCE, Macaulay on xxvii, 381-3, 413, 415; representative of Italian Renaissance, l, 23; his times, xxvii,

384-401; works of, Macaulay on, 401-6, 417-20

MACHIAVELLI, ESSAY ON, xxvii, 381-421

Machinery, advantages of, x, 235; fixed capital, 228; division of labor and, 14-15; Emerson on, v, 86, 415; power and velocity in, xxx, 190-3; in woollen manufactures, x, 214-15; work of, xxx, 184-5

MACKENZIE, DR., NOTE TO, vi, 224-5

M'Kenzie, Mr., of Applecross, vi, 215

Mackinlay, Rev. James, Burns on, vi, 171, 174, 254, 372

McKinley, William, Cuba and, xliii, 467 note; Hawaii and, 464 note

Mackintosh, Sir James, Emerson on, v, 148, 457

Maclean of Lochbuy, xlii, 1474-9

M'Lehose, Mrs., Burns and, vi, 309, 311

M'Leod, Isabella, verses on, vi, 315

M'LEOD, JOHN, ON THE DEATH OF, vi, 286-7

M'MATH, JOHN, EPISTLE TO, vi, 110-13

M'MURDO, JOHN, LINES ON, vi, 496

M'MURDO, JOHN, LINES TO, vi, 348

MacNeil, Hector, poems by, xli, 590-2

Maçon, Antoine de, xxxi, 304 note 2

Macpherson, James, Goldsmith on, xli, 520; Wordsworth on, xxxix, 344-6

M'PHERSON'S FAREWELL, vi, 313

Macrauchenia Patachonica, xxix, 186-7

Macready, and Browning, xviii, 356

Macrinius, letters to, ix, 226, 313

Macrinus, Emperor, Machiavelli on, xxxvi, 70

Macrinus, Minutius, letter to, ix, 342; Pliny on, 210

Macrobeus, on dreams, xl, 43; on Virgil, xiii, 14-15

Macrocosmus, sign of, xix, 23-4

Macronians, circumcision among, xxxiii, 51

Macureguarai, town of, xxxiii, 367, 376

MAD MAID'S SONG, xl, 344

Madasinia, Queen, xiv, 219, 222-3

Madeira, flora of, xi, 118; species of, 434, 443

Madeline, and Porphyro, xli, 908-17

Madison, James, papers for FEDERALIST, xliii, 212 note

Madness, cause of, xxiv, 37; Hobbes on, xxxiv, 367-72; Pascal on, xlviii, 135 (414); Shakespeare on, xlvi, 119, 122

MADRIGAL, by Drummond, xl, 335

MADRIGAL, by Shakespeare, xl, 273

Mæcenas, Antony and, xviii, 23; Dryden on, 16; Pliny and, xliii,

30; Plutarch on, xii, 361; Virgil and, xiii, 3; xxxix, 171

Maël, and Lancelot, xxxii, 171

Mælius, Spurius, death of, ix, 66

Mænads, Bacchus and the, viii, 204; Pentheus and the, 116; son of Dryas and, 273

Mæon, death of, xiii, 338

Mæonides, Homer called, iv, 139

Mævius, Dryden on, xiii, 13; Shelley on, xxvii, 375-6

Magæus, and Alcibiades, xii, 150-1

Magalotti, Gregorio, xxxi, 128 note

Magdalena, Drake at, xxxiii, 154-5

Magdalene, Mary, xliv, 378 (37-50), 379 (2), 424 (10); John Donne on, xv, 382; Kempis on, vii, 256 (1)

MAGDALENE, FOR THE, xl, 337-8

Magdolos, battle of, xxxiii, 82

Magellan, first to circumnavigate globe, xxxiii, 126; at Port St. Julian, 213

Magellan Clouds, described, xxiii, 30

Magellan, Straits of, Darwin on, xxix, 247; Pretty on, xxxiii, 215-16

Magic, Browne on, iii, 295 (31); Faust on, xix, 22; Faustus on, 202

Magicians, in Dante's HELL, xx, 86

Magistrates, expenses of, x, 486-7; marriage of, iii, 22; Vane on duties of, xliii, 130-1

Magna Charta, Burke on, xxiv, 179-80; Voltaire on, xxxiv, 91; Winthrop on, xliii, 102

MAGNA, INSTAURATIO (see INSTAURATIO MAGNA)

Magnane, M. de, xxxviii, 25

Magnanimity, friendship requires, v, 119; Hobbes on, xxxiv, 354, 380; Marcus Aurelius on term, ii, 281 (8); Ruskin on, xxviii, 131

Magnetism, Faraday on, xxx, 66-9; illustrated, 24; produced by electricity, 84-7, 215

Magneto-electrical Machines, xxx, 215

Magneto-electricity, discovered by Faraday, xxx, 3

Magnificence, a source of the sublime, xxiv, 68-9

Magnitude, in architecture, xxiv, 67; Pliny on, ix, 214-15; sublimity of, xxiv, 63-4, 115-16

Magnússon, Eirikr, xlix, 265

Magus, death of, xiii, 344-5

Magyars, Freeman on the, xxviii, 278; Turks and, 235-7

Maha Bharata, The, remarks on, xlv, 800

Maha-Brahma, xlv, 628, 632, 633

Maha-Maya, mother of Buddha, xlv, 620-4

Mahatmas, xlv, 836, 839

Mahew, Mr., among the Indians, xliii, 147, 149

Mahmúd, Omar Khayyam on, xli, 980

Mahomet (see Mohammed)

Maia, daughter of Atlas, xiii, 277; Jove and, xl, 246; mother of Mercury, xx, 383 note 13

Maiander, River, Herodotus on, xxxiii, 9

MAID OF ATHENS, xli, 815-16

Maimonides, Moses, on prophets, xlviii, 218 (2)

Mairet, and Corneille, xxxix, 379

Mâisar, game of, xlv, 1008 note 3

Majority, Burke on tyranny of the, xxiv, 273; Lincoln on rule of the, xliii, 340; Lowell on government by, xxviii, 478; Mill on tyranny of the, xxv, 206; Pascal on rule of, xlviii, 108 (301), 310 (878)

Mál, son of Telband, xlix, 239-40

Malacoda, in Dante's HELL, xx, 89

Malaspina, Alagia, xx, 226 note

Malaspina, Archbishop of Genoa, xxxi, 47 note 1

Malaspina, Conrad, in Purgatory, xx, 180

Malaspina, Marcello, and Dante, xx, 226 note

Malaspina, Morello, Dante and, xx, 104 note 5, 180 note 10

Malatesti, Count, in DUCHESS OF MALFI, xlvii, 755, 767-8, 797, 809, 812, 813, 815, 816

Malavolti, Catalano de', xx, 98 note 4

Malay Archipelago, Darwin on, xi, 352-3, 437

Malays, superstition of the, xxix, 483

Malaysia, Drake in, xxxiii, 227-33

Malchus, and St. Peter, xlviii, 267 (744)

Malcolm, in MACBETH, with Duncan in camp, xlvi, 306, 307; reports death of Cawdor, 313; made Prince of Cumberland, 314; after father's murder, 329, 330-1; suspected of murder, 332; at English court, 346; with Macduff, 355-9; and Ross, 360, 361; comforts Macduff, 362-3; in war on Macbeth, 365, 368, 371, 372; with Siward, 374; hailed as king, 374-5

Maldiva Archipelago, Darwin on, xxix, 503-4

Maldonado, town, Darwin on, xxix, 50-1

Maldonado, Lopez, Cervantes on, xiv, 57

Malebolge, in Hell, xx, 75

Malebranche, Nicholas, Berkeley on, xxxvii, 249; on God, 365 note; xxxiv, 105; Hume on, xxxvii, 307; Montesquieu on, xxxii, 123; Voltaire on, xxxiv, 71

Malfi, Duchess of, in DUCHESS OF MALFI, Antonio on, xlvii, 727; in presence chamber scene, 727-8; Bosola hired to watch, 729-30; with brothers, advised against marriage, 730-2; scene with Antonio, 733-7; Bosola on condition of, 739, 743; with Bosola, 741-2; plans to hide her condition, 742-3; birth of son, 745, 748; her unchastity believed by brothers, 751-4; with Ferdinand after interval, 755-6; plan to force confession, 757; with Antonio in chamber, 757-9; with Ferdinand, 759-62; with Bosola, 762-3; covers flight of Antonio, 762-5; confesses marriage to Bosola, 766; plans for flight, 766-7; betrayed by Bosola, 767, 769; banished from Ancona, 770-1; with Antonio near Loretto, 772; letter from brother, 773; parting from Antonio, 774-5; arrested by Bosola, 775-6; in imprisonment, 776-81; with Cariola, 781-2; with madmen, 783-5; with Bosola as old man, 785-7; death, 788, 792

Malice, Burns on, vi, 111; Emerson on limits of, v, 135; Martial on, xlviii, 19 (41); More on, xxxvi, 134; Woolman on, i, 285

Malice, Mr., in PILGRIM'S PROGRESS, xv, 101-2

Malignity, Bacon on, iii, 35-6

Malin, Admiral, at Gravelines, xix, 250

Mallon, Col., at Gettysburg, xliii, 409, 411

MALLY'S MEEK, MALLY'S SWEET, vi, 581

Malory, Sir Thomas, THE HOLY GRAIL, xxxv, 109-226; life and book, 108; PROLOGUE TO KING ARTHUR of, xxxix, 21-5

Malprimis, in SONG OF ROLAND, xlix, 128, 141

Malquiant, son of Malcus, xlix, 154

Malseron, in SONG OF ROLAND, xlix, 144

Malt, Harrison on making of, xxxv, 297

Malta, Coleridge on government of, v, 333; heat of, xxxvii, 10-11; Knights of, Mill on, xxv, 11

Malthus, debt of Darwin to, xi, 7; Emerson on, v, 259, 408; Mill on, xxv, 71

Maluco Islands, Drake in, xxxiii, 227-30

Malunkyaputta, xlv, 662-7

Mambrino's Helmet, xiv, 82, 175-7, 472-4

Mammals, first appearance of, xi, 356; in oceanic islands, 436-7

Mammary Glands, development of the, xi, 244-5

Mammon, Burns on followers of, vi, 91, 344; Jesus on, xliv, 403 (13); in PARADISE LOST, iv, 107, 116-18

Mammon, Sir Epicure, in THE ALCHEMIST, Subtle on, xlvii, 539-40; visit to Subtle's, 540-59; plot against, 559-60; his return, 584, 585-6; with Dol, 587-91, 602-4; with Subtle, 604-5; hears loss of Subtle's works, 605-6; returns with Surly, 619-20; with officers, 629-32

MAN, OF, by Hobbes, xxxiv, 317-434

Man, animals and, difference between, xxxiv, 178-80; antiquity of, xi, 35; xxxviii, 407-9, 426, 427; Augustine, St., on, vii, 59, 85-6; Bacon on, and God, iii, 46; Bildad on, xliv, 112 (4-6); Browne on, iii, 299, 340-1; Burns on, vi, 35, 243, 261-2, 301, 325, 358, 543; Byron on, xviii, 412; Channing on study of, xxviii, 343-4; Confucius on, xliv, 20 (17); David on, 153 (4-8), 330 (3-4); defined by Plato, xlviii, 432; Descartes on creation of, xxxiv, 38-9; Emerson on, v, 26, 74-7, 139, 238, 275, 278, 284-5, 299, 308; Epictetus on, ii, 120 (9), 122 (16), 137 (60-1), 162 (125), 166; "folly's microcosm," xix, 54; Franklin on, i, 76; God's ways to, iv, 435-6; Goethe on state of, xix, 17; Homer on littleness of, xxii, 258-9; Kant on, xxxii, 359-62; Kempis on, vii, 316-17; littleness of, xliv, 134 (3-41), 137 (1-30), 139 (1-14), 140 (1-11); Marcus Aurelius on, ii, 246 (3), 257 (7), 260 (27), 262 (34), 279 (6), 292 (14), 305 (32); Minerva on, v, 227; Mohammed on creation of, xliv, 889, 895, 900, 901, 910, 947; natural state of, xxxiv, 168, 171-200, 208-9, 402-6; Pascal on state of, xlviii, 25-31, 47 (111), 50 (125-7), 52-3, 57 (140), 63 (165), 77 (199), 78 (205-8), 122 (358), 130 (389-90), 131 (397), 132 (398-404), 133 (409), 134 (411-23), 139 (427), 147, 148, 150, 151, 163 (486), 168 (510-11), 195 (584), 223 (660), 402-3, 444; Pascal on study of, 58-9; Penn on, i, 339-41, 359 (220-2); Poe's tragedy of, xlii, 1292; proper study of himself, i, 80, 94; iii, 28, 276, 279; "proposeth, God disposeth," vii, 232; Rousseau on, xxxiv, 262-3; Rousseau on early, 171; Schiller on person and condition of, xxxii, 252-5; Schiller on what constitutes, 224-5; self-torture is the lot of, xix, 31; Shakespeare on, xlvi, 125, 165, 256-7; a social

being, ii, 128 (34), 136 (56), 162 (123), 230 (16), 246 (5), 247 (13), 252 (55), 267 (59), 270 (9), 291 (8); ix, 38; xxiv, 40; xxv, 341-3; Socrates on mediocrity of, ii, 83; supreme in strangeness, viii, 253-4; the temple of God, xlv, 505 (16-17), 534 (16); Tennyson on, xlii, 1058-9; thought requisite to, xlviii, 119 (339), 120 346-8); Timæus on, v, 182; transitoriness of, xliv, 262-3, 276 (15-16); twofold nature of, xxxvi, 363; universal and particular, v, 6; Zophar on, xliv, 90 (12)

MAN AND SATYR, fable of, xvii, 33

MAN AND SERPENT, fable of, xvii, 11

MAN AND TWO WIVES, fable of, xvii, 29

MAN AND THE WOOD, fable of, xvii, 21

MAN AND WOODEN GOD, fable of, xvii, 27

MAN, BOY, AND DONKEY, fable of, xvii, 36

MAN, ESSAY ON, by Pope, xl, 417-51

MAN THE REFORMER, Emerson's, v, 45-61

MAN WAS MADE TO MOURN, vi, 64-7

MAN'S A MAN FOR A' THAT, vi, 546; Arnold on, xxviii, 86

Manardi, Arrigo, xx, 204 note 16

Manasseh, Pascal on, xlviii, 241

Manchet, a kind of bread, xxxv, 295

Mandeville, Bernard, Addison and, xxvii, 190; on pity, xxxiv, 193

Mandeville, Sir John, on headless men, xxxiii, 372

Mandioca, Darwin on, xxix, 33

Mandrake, superstition of the, xlvii, 751 note 2

Maneros, song of, xxxiii, 41

Manetho, on Egypt, xxxviii, 407

Manetti, Latino Giovenale de, xxxi, 152 note, 186-7, 192

MANFRED: A DRAMATIC POEM, xviii, 403-44; remarks on, 402

Manfred, in MANFRED, with the spirits, xviii, 403-9; spell pronounced on, 409-11; on the mountain, 411-14; saved by chamois-hunter, 414; in hunter's cottage, 415-17; with Witch, relates his life, 418-22; determines to learn what death is, 422-3; in Hall of Arimanes, 427-8; calls up Astarte, 428-31; in castle, his calmness, 431-2; with Abbot of St. Maurice, 432-6; address to the sun, 436-7; Herman on, 437; Astarte and, 438; on beauties of night and the Coliseum, 439-40; summoned by spirits, 441-3; death, 444

Manfredi, Alberigo de', xx, 141 and note 4

Manfredi, King of Naples, Dante on, xx, 158-9 and note 3

Manfredi, Tribaldello de', xx, 136 note 13

Mangiadore, Pietro, xx, 339 note 33

Mangona, Alberto da, xx, 168 note 6

Manhood, Channing on true, xxviii, 343; Emerson on, v, 19-20, 87; Lowell on, xxviii, 451-2; xlii, 1466; Pascal on, xlviii, 18

Manichæans, vii, 3; Augustine, St., on the, 37-44, 66-72, 77-8, 78-9; Mill on, xxv, 31; Nebridius's argument against, vii, 104

Manilius, case of, xii, 232-3

Mankind, uniformity of, xxxvii, 373-81; unity of, v, 19-20

Manlius, Capitolinus, Virgil on, xiii, 294

Manlius, Marcus, in Catiline's conspiracy, xii, 236, 237; defeat of, xxxiii, 117

Manlius, Titus, Corneille on, xxvi, 118

Manna, Browne on, iii, 284-5

Mannellini, Bernardino, xxxi, 364-5, 394

Manners, in authors, criticism of, xxvii, 232; Hobbes on, xxxiv, 384-90; Hume on, of different ages, xxxvii, 376; Locke on, 50-2, 76-8, 128-35

MANNERS, ESSAY ON, by Emerson, v, 207-27

MANNERS, TREATISE ON GOOD, by Swift, xxvii, 106-11

Mannus, god of the Germans, xxxiii, 95

Manoa, city of, xxxiii, 313, 328, 330, 331-2, 332

Manoa, in SAMSON AGONISTES, iv, 427-8, 430-1, 433-4, 455-6, 457, 458-63

Mansfield, Count, xxxviii, 53-4

Mansfield, Lord, Pope on, xxvii, 287; on the press, v, 465

Mantius, son of Melampus, xxii, 214

Manto, Dante on, xx, 84-5; in Limbo, 239 note 9

Mantrap, Mrs., in SHE STOOPS TO CONQUER, xviii, 241, 267

Mantua, contest over Duchy of, xxi, 81, 454-6, 486-92; origin of, xx, 85-6; Virgil on, xiii, 333

Mantua, Marquis of, in DON QUIXOTE, xiv, 46, 81

Manual Labor, Emerson on, v, 49-53; Locke on, xxxvii, 185-90

Manuel, in MANFRED, xviii, 437-9

Manufacturers, interests of, x, 219-20

Manufactures, agriculture and, x, 11-12, 230-1, 319-22; in agricultural system, 450-6, 459-63;

capital used in, 304, 306, 307; commerce compared with, 323; division of labor in, 9-10; foreign competition keenest in, 355; favored by laws, 134-6; materials of, importation and exportation of, 424-42; military spirit and, iii, 81; xxvii, 391-2; monopolies in, x, 358; necessity of, 302, 465-6; prices of, 54, 211-16; protection of new, 353-4

Manzoni, Alessandro, I PROMESSI SPOSI, xxi; life and works, 3-6

Mära, the god, xlv, 632-6, 745

Maranon, river, xxxiii, 328 note, 330

Marat, Burke on, xxiv, 442

Marathon, battle of, xii, 85; Byron on, xli, 833

Marble, composition of, xxx, 159 note; crystallization of, 251; experiments with, 12-14

Marbois, Francis Barbé, xliii, 268

Marcela, and Chrysostom, xiv, 92-8, 112-16

Marcellinus, Pliny to, ix, 286

Marcellus, brother-in-law of Octavius, xii, 263

Marcellus, Caius, first husband of Octavia, xii, 358, 403

Marcellus, Marcus Claudius (d. 208 B. C.), Virgil on, xiii, 240-1

Marcellus, Marcus Claudius (d. 46 B. C.), Antony and, xii, 337; Cæsar and, ix, 170; xii, 299-300; Catiline and, 237; death of, ix, 73; Milo and, 100

Marcellus, Marcus Claudius (d. 23 B. C.), son of Octavia, xii, 403; Virgil on, xiii, 33, 241-2

Marcellus, in HAMLET, xlvi, 88-92, 97-100, 104, 106-7, 110-11

March, month of Creation, xl, 44; twenty-fifth of, xv, 408

MARCH, WRITTEN IN, xli, 619-20

March, George, Earl of, his raid into England, xxxv, 83-4; at Otterburn, 91, 93; Ralph Percy and, 101

Marcia, wife of Cato, in CATO, xxvii, 205-7; in Dante's Limbo, xx, 20, 149

Marcii, house of the, xii, 152

Marcius, and Cicero, xii, 238, 258

Marcius, Caius (see Coriolanus)

Marco, and Sejanus, iii, 98-9

Marco Polo on China, v, 75

Marco of the Serbs, xxxii, 164 note 12

Marcomanians, Tacitus on the, xxxiii, 119-20

Marcone, the goldsmith, xxxi, 15, 22

Marcus Aurelius (see Aurelius)

Mardion, the eunuch, xii, 382

Mardonius, general of Xerxes, xii,

9, 90, 91, 94, 95, 97, 98; death of, 100; at Platæa, 21

MARE, SALUTATION TO AN AULD, vi, 155-8

Margano, Pietro, xxxi, 103 note 1

Margaret, in FAUST, first meeting with Faust, xix, 107; wonders who he is, 110; in chamber, finds casket, 113-14; grieves for loss of casket, 116; finds second casket, 116-17; meets Mephistopheles at Martha's, 119-25; with Faust in garden, 128-34; in summer-house, 135-6; song of, 142-3; with Faust, on his religion, 143-5; dislike of Mephistopheles, 146; plans meeting with Faust, 147-8; with Bessy at the well, 149-51; prayer of, 151-2; Valentine on, 153; with Valentine, 156-8; in the cathedral, 159-61; vision of, seen by Faust, 175; imprisoned and doomed to death, 184; in the dungeon, with Faust, 187-95; remarks on story of, 5

MARGARET, THE AFFLICTION OF, xli, 660-2

Margaret d'Alençon, xxxi, 348 note 2

Margaret of Anjou, Raleigh on, xxxix, 77, 78

Margaret of Austria, xxxi, 164 note 6, 230 note

Margaret of Burgundy, xxxix, 5, 6-7, 9; Warbeck and, xxxiv, 103

Margaret of Parma, xix, 246; Raleigh on, xxxix, 91

Margaret of Parma, in EGMONT, regent of Netherlands, xix, 250-1; on the iconoclasts, 254; with Machiavel, on state of Netherlands, 254-6; suspects Egmont and Orange, 257-9; Egmont and Orange on, 278-9, 290-1; determines to abdicate, 284-7; her departure, 293

Margaris, in SONG OF ROLAND, xlix, 130-1, 143, 149

MARGARITAE SORORI, xlii, 1257-8

Marginal Notes, Cervantes on, xiv, 8-11

Margites, of Homer, iii, 210; xii, 216 note

MARGUERITE, To, xlii, 1174

Marguerite de Valois, xxxi, 295 note, 313

Maria, in SCHOOL FOR SCANDAL, in love with Charles Surface, xviii, 113, 114, 123; at Lady Sneerwell's, 115-21, 129; with Joseph Surface, 129, 133-4; Sir Peter and, 142; toasted by Charles, 148; reconciled to Charles, 191-3

Maria, the widow, in I PROMESSI SPOSI, xxi, 409, 500

Mariane, in TARTUFFE, and Mme.

Pernelle, xxvi, 190; in love with Valère, 198, 218; marriage put off by father, 205-7; with her father, ordered to marry Tartuffe, 207-17; with Dorine, 217-22; with Valère, 222-32; protests against marriage with Tartuffe, 253-4; in final scene, 281, 283; promised to Valère, 284

Marids, a kind of genii, xvi, 9 note

Marie Antoinette, Burke on, xxiv, 223-4; on October Sixth, 219-20

Marine Currents, Lyell on, xxxviii, 423, 424

Marine Species, the simultaneous changes in, xi, 374

MARINERS OF ENGLAND YE, Thomas Campbell's, xli, 797-8

Marini, Dryden on, xiii, 62

Mario, in England, v, 430

MARION'S MEN, SONG OF, xlii, 1266-8

Maritornes, the Asturian wench, xiv, 128, 129-33, 142-3; on knightly tales, 318; plot of, against Quixote, 457-61

Marius, Caius, Burke on confiscations of, xxiv, 263-4; Cæsar and, xii, 274, 277, 278; death of, xxvii, 24; Dryden on, xiii, 16

Marius, M., letter to, ix, 111

Marjaneh, in story of ALI-BABA, xvi, 448-9, 451, 454-6, 458-60

Mark, John surnamed, xliv, 456 (12), 457 (25), 465 (37-9)

Mark, St., Pascal on 13th chapter of, xlviii, 364-5

MARK YONDER POMP OF COSTLY FASHION, vi, 570-1

Market, extent of, limits division of labor, x, 24

Market Price, defined, x, 59; as determined by demand and supply, 59-61; effect of fluctuations on rent, wages, and profits, 62-3; natural price compared with, 61-6

Markets, in Utopia, xxxvi, 195-6

Markland, Leif Ericsson's, xliii, 9

Marl, Harrison on, xxxv, 324-5

Marlborough, Duke of, Addison on, xxvii, 194; Bolingbroke on, xxxiv, 100

MARLBOROUGH ROAD, THE OLD, xxviii, 414-15

Marliniere, Riccant de la, xxvi, 334-8

Marloff, Madame, in MINNA VON BARNHELM, xxvi, 293-5

Marlow, Sir Charles, in SHE STOOPS TO CONQUER, xviii, 256-9 264-9

Marlow, Young, in SHE STOOPS TO CONQUER, selected as husband for Kate Hardcastle, xviii, 206-7; Miss Neville on, 208; at the ale-house, 211-14; arrival at Hardcastle's, 216-18; with Mr. Hardcastle, 218-22, 224; meets Miss Hardcastle,

225-7; discussed by Kate and her father, 232-4, 242-3; with Kate as the barmaid, 239-42; with Miss Neville's jewels, 244-5; with Hardcastle and his servants, 246-7; ordered to leave house, 247-8; learns inn is Mr. Hardcastle's, 248-9; parting with Kate, 249-50; denounces Tony and Hastings, 254-5; protests against loving Kate, 257-8; love scene with Kate, 265-6; learns who she is, 267; united to Kate, 269

Marlowe, Christopher, EDWARD THE SECOND, xlvi, 3-84; DOCTOR FAUSTUS, xix, 199-243; influence on Goethe, 4; Hazlitt on, xxvii, 290-1; Jonson on, xl, 309; life and works, xix, 198; THE PASSIONATE SHEPHERD, xl, 259-60

Marmagne, Seigneur de, xxxi, 293 note

Marmontel, Mill on *Memoirs* of, xxv, 93

Maron, son of Euanthes, xxii, 125

Marque and Reprisal, Letters of, xliii, 171, 172, 197 (11), 198 (10)

Marquis, meaning of, xxxiv, 383

Marrall, in NEW WAY TO PAY OLD DEBTS, xlvii, 830-1; scene with Overreach, 835-8; with Wellborn, 838-40; with Wellborn at Allworth's, 841-4, 845-6; with Wellborn after dinner, 847-8; reports to Overreach, 849-51; at Overreach's, 854, 859, 863, 864, 865, 866; at Allworth's, 869-70; with Wellborn on way to Lady Allworth's, 878, 880-1; with Overreach, 888, 890, 891, 892-3; in final scene, 896-7

Marriage, Augustine, St., on, vii, 24, 48; Browne on, iii, 337-8; Cervantes on, xiv, 335; dispensations, xxxvi, 325; of divorced persons, Jesus on, xliv, 404 (18); from economic standpoint, x, 74-5, 83-4; Epictetus on, ii, 160 (116); equality in, viii, 187 and note; Euripides on, 314; among Germans, xxxiii, 105; Goethe on, xix, 349; Locke on, xxxvii, 194-5; Luther on, xxxvi, 350; Massinger on, xlvii, 875; Mill on, contracts of, xxv, 312-13; Milton on, iv, 176, 317; xxviii, 190; Mohammed on, xlv, 981, 983-4, 994; Moliere on, without love, xxvi, 212; Montaigne on, xxxii, 78; among Moravians, i, 150; in New Atlantis, iii, 177-9; Pascal on, xlviii, 129 (385), 347; Paul, St., on, xlv, 509, 510 (27-8, 33-40); Penn on, i, 346-7, 348-49 (92-105); Pliny on, for wealth, ix, 210-11;

of priests, Calvin on, xxxix, 40; of priests, Luther on, xxxvi, 317-21; prostitution and, iii, 177-8; Rousseau on effect of indissoluble, xxxiv, 198; Ruskin on, xxviii, 149; sanctity of, Æschylus on, viii, 123; sanctity of, Emerson on, v, 256; Shakespeare on xlvi, 137; Shakespeare on second, 144; state control of, xxv, 318; Stevenson on, xxviii, 293-4; Swift on, xxvii, 97; in Utopia, xxxvi, 221-3; Walton on, xv, 331; Webster's Antonio on, xlvii, 733, 734

MARRIAGE AND SINGLE LIFE, Bacon on, iii, 22-3

Marriott, John, hymn by, xlv, 586

Mars, as German god, xxxiii, 100 (see also Ares)

Mars, the planet, xlii, 1317-18; Dante's fifth heaven, xx, 347

Marsh, George, on the "Alert," xxiii, 209-12, 263-4; (in 1859), 404

Marshall, John, OPINION IN CASE OF McCULLOCH, 222-40

Marshall, Mr., of Leeds, xxv, 79

MARSHES OF GLYNN, xlii, 1470-3

Marsians, Tacitus on the, xxxiii, 96

Marsignians, Tacitus on the, xxxiii, 120

Marsil, King, in SONG OF ROLAND, xlix, 97-100, 103-5, 111-19, 149-51, 156, 157, 159, 168, 194-5, 196

Marsyas, Apollo and, xx, 287

Martel, Charles, king of Hungary, xx, 317-21

Martha, and Jesus, xliv, 388-9

Martha, in FAUST, with Margaret, xix, 117-18; learns husband's death, 119-25; with Mephistopheles in garden, 128-9, 131-2, 134; with Valentine, 156-8

Martha, in PILGRIM'S PROGRESS, xv, 286

Marthesia, Queen of the Amazons, xxxiii, 338

Martial, Elphinstone's translation of, vi, 277; Montaigne on, xxxii, 94; Pascal on epigrams of, xlviii, 19; Pliny on, ix, 258-9; on the ugly man, v, 316

Martigues, M. de, at Metz, xxxviii, 26; at Hesdin, 37, 38, 39-42

Martin IV, in Purgatory, xx, 244 and note 2

Martin V, Milton on, iii, 206

Martin, Sir, xx, 344 note 24

Martin, Theodore, translator of Schiller, xxvi, 367

Martineau, Harriet, Emerson and, v, 483

Martinez, Juan, xxxiii, 330, 331-2

Martini, Luca, xxxi, 180 note; Capitolo addressed to, 263

Martius, and Sophocles, v, 125-6

Martyrs, Bacon on, iii, 145; Browne on, 291 (25, 26); Bunyan on Christian, xv, 268; Emerson on, v, 104; Goethe on, of truth, xix, 29; Lowell on, xlii, 1450; Pascal on the, xlviii, 161 (481), 300 (844)

Marullus, the tribune, Cæsar and, xii, 325

Marut, the fallen angel, xvi, 62 note

Marvel, Mount, xv, 294

Marvell, Andrew, poems by, xl, 379-88

Marvellous, human love of the, xxxvii, 402-4

Mary, mother of Jesus, xliv, 358-60, 362 (5-7), 363 (19), 364 (48-51), 380 (19-21), 424 (10), 430 (14); at the cross (see STABAT MATER); Dante on, xx, 186, 227, 339; in Dante's PARADISE, 386-7, 419-20, 424; LULLABY for, xl, 261-5; Luther on, xxxvi, 388; Milton on, iv, 193, 366, 369, 377-8; Mohammed on, xlv, 920-1, 964 note, 965-6, 996, 1008, 1016, 1021; Pascal on virginity of, xlviii, 81 (222-3), 267 (742)

Mary, mother of John, xliv, 456 (12)

Mary, sister of Martha, xliv, 388-9

Mary of Brabant, and Biosse, xx, 168 note 7

Mary, Queen of Scots, Burns on, vi, 396

MARY, QUEEN OF SCOTS, LAMENT OF, vi, 420-1

Mary Tudor, Queen, Raleigh on, xxxix, 90

Mary, the Coptic girl, xlv, 1006 note 1

MARY, TO, IN HEAVEN, vi, 386-7

MARY HAMILTON, a ballad, xl, 118-20

Mary Magdalene (see Magdalene)

MARY MORISON, vi, 39

MARY UNWIN, TO, xli, 549-51

Maryland, Quakers in, i, 288

MARYLAND vs. McCULLOCH, xliii, 222-40

Marzio, in THE CENCI, xviii, 317, 325-6, 326-7, 328, 331, 338-43

Masaccio, frescoes of, xxxi, 24 note 1

Mascheroni, Sassol, xx, 135 note 5

Masinissa, old age of, ix, 58

Masistius, Plutarch on, xii, 94-5

MASK AND FOX, fable of, xvii, 18

Mason, Sir Josiah, xxviii, 218, 219-20

MASONIC SONG, vi, 254

Masons, Burns on, vi, 39

Masorah, Pascal on the, xlviii, 213 (630)

MASQUES, ESSAY ON, Bacon's, iii, 100-1

Mass (in physics), measured by inertia, xxx, 315-16

Mass (in Roman Church), Calvin on, xxxix, 40; Luther on, xxxvi, 330-1; Luther on, for the dead, 322-3; Rousseau on, xxxiv, 313

Massa, Boebius, impeachment of, ix, 331

Massachusetts, Folger on persecutions in, i, 9; Winthrop on government of, xliii, 90-112

MASSACHUSETTS BODY OF LIBERTIES, xliii, 70-89

MASSACHUSETTS TO VIRGINIA, xlii, 1419-24

Massena, Napoleon on, v, 41

Massicus, ally of Æneas, xiii, 332

Massinger, Philip, life and works, xlvii, 818; NEW WAY TO PAY OLD DEBTS, 819-99

Massive Ones, in FAUST, xix, 183

Masson, David, Bagehot on Life of Milton by, xxviii, 171-4

Masters, Epictetus's advice to, ii, 178 (180); Penn's counsel to, i, 357; single men best, iii, 22

Master's Eye, fable of the, xvii, 23

Mastic, Columbus on, xliii, 27

Mastication, Locke on, xxxvii, 17

Mastiff, Harrison on the, xxxv, 371-3, 374; cross between bear and, 375

Masurius, Epictetus on, ii, 169 (144)

MATCH, A, xlii, 1254

Matches, story of the, xvii, 366-9

Materialism, Berkeley on, xxxvii, 265, 286-7, 295-8; Channing on, xxviii, 332; Rousseau on, xxxiv, 257-61, 265-6; Schiller on, xxxii, 235-6; Voltaire on, xxxiv, 106-9

Materials, as circulating capital, x, 229; of manufacture, importation, and exportation of, 424-42; rent of land used to produce, 171-85; value of, compared with food, 186-8

Mathematical Mind, Pascal on the, xlviii, 7-10

Mathematicians, Franklin on, i, 60

Mathematics, ancient, xxviii, 227; Bacon on study of, iii, 129; Berkeley on the, xxxvii, 297; Burke on, xxiv, 21, 78; Descartes on study of, xxxiv, 8, 9, 18-19; Hobbes on, 377; Hume on the, xxxvii, 324, 329; Mill on, compared with logic, xxv, 18; Mill on indisputableness of, 239; Milton on study of, iii, 252, 253; moral sciences compared with, xxxvii, 354-5; Newton on, xxxix, 157-8; Pascal on, xlviii, 9, 10

Mather, Cotton, church history of, i, 9; Essays to do Good, 14

Matilda, in Dante's PURGATORY, xx, 261 note; Ruskin on, xxviii, 167

Matius, Caius, xii, 317 note

Matrevis, in EDWARD II, xlvi, 70, 72-4, 77-8, 80-1

Matter, Berkeley on existence of, xxxvii, 202-3, 206-7, 227-40, 250-62, 265-6, 268-71, 274-7, 279-81, 284, 286-7, 290, 294-6, 299-300; cause and effect in, 372-3; defined by Faraday, xxx, 8; idea of eternity of, xxxix, 107-8; Hume on creation of, xxxvii, 444 note; Hume on energy in, 357; Hume on inertia of, 365 note; Hume on reality of, 433-6; Locke on, 176; mind and, Channing on, xxviii, 332; not endowed with motion, xxxiv, 254-6, 257-8; qualities of, Bacon on, xxxix, 145; qualities of, Berkeley on, xxxvii, 205-27, 369 note; qualities of, Hume on, 435-6; as self-created, xxxix, 108; spirit and, Hindu doctrine of, xlv, 862, 863, 864

MATTER, FORCES OF, Faraday's, xxx, 5-88

Matters of Fact, Hume on, xxxvii, 324-36, 339-42, 349, 350, 439, 443-4; Raleigh on, xxxix, 105

Matthew, the apostle, xliv, 373 (15), 430 (13); Mahomet on, xlviii, 198 (597)

Matthew, in PILGRIM'S PROGRESS, xv, 232-3, 235-7, 238-9, 253, 255, 262, 269, 270-1, 272, 290

Matthews, Fuegian missionary, xxix, 222, 237, 239, 241

Matthias, the disciple, xliv, 430 (23-6)

Mattiacians, Tacitus on the, xxxiii, 112

MAUCHLINE, THE BELLES OF, vi, 62

MAUCHLINE LADY, THE, vi, 61

MAUD, Tennyson's, xlii, 1052-97

Maud, Queen, and the Pope, xxxv, 266

MAUD MULLER, xlii, 1427-31

Mauer, Hans auf der, in WILHELM TELL, xxvi, 405, 406, 408, 410, 412

Maugridge, William, i, 60

Maul, the giant, xv, 251-2

Maunciple, Chaucer's, xl, 27

Maupertius, axiom of least action, xi, 522

Maurice, F. D., Carlyle and, xxv, 331; in London Club, 85; Mill and, 4, 100-1

Maurice of Saxony, Machiavelli and, xxvii, 381

Mauricus, Junius, ix, 198 note; letter to, 209; Pliny on, 199

Mauritius, Darwin on, xxix, 509-12

Maurizio, Ser, xxxi, 156 note 4

Maurus, Rabanus, xx, 340 note 37

Maxim, defined by Kant, xxxii, 331 note 2, 351 note 7

Maximilian, Emperor, Macaulay on,

xxvii, 407; Machiavelli on, xxxvi, 81

Maximilla, Antonia, ix, 377

Maximinus, Machiavelli on, xxxvi, 69-70, 71

Maxims, Macaulay on general, xxvii, 415

Maximus, Fabius (see Fabius)

Maximus, freedman of Trajan, ix, 388-9, 392-3

Maximus, Nonius, letters to, ix, 229, 276, 296, 311, 326, 349, 362

Maximus, Q., and his son, ix, 175

Maximus, teacher of Aurelius, ii, 196 (15), 199

MAXWELL, DR., To, vi, 532

MAXWELL, JOHN, EPISTLE TO, vi, 448-9

Maxwell, Sir John, at Otterburn, xxxv, 92

Maxwell, Lord, xl, 101

MAY MOON, THE YOUNG, xli, 842

MAY MORNING, SONG ON, iv, 40

MAY, THE CHARMING MONTH OF, vi, 539

MAY, THY MORN, vi, 454

Maya, mother of Buddha, xlv, 600

Mayer, Julius Robert, on law of conservation, xxx, 183

Mayflower, Lowell on the, xlii, 1451

MAYFLOWER COMPACT, THE, xliii, 62

Mazarin, Louis XIV and, xxiv, 349; motto of, xxviii, 448; Pascal on, xlviii, 21 (56)

Mazzaroth, xliv, 136 note 15

Mazzini, Giuseppe, BYRON AND GOETHE, xxxii, 399-419; editorial remarks on paper of, l, 56; life of, xxxii, 398

Mead, Harrison on, xxxv, 301

Meade, General, seizes Gettysburg, xliii, 351; in battle of Gettysburg, 353, 354, 355, 356-7, 361-2, 367, 380, 385, 387, 389-90, 393, 394, 405, 415-17, 420, 421-2, 424; Haskell on, 350, 381, 382

Meals, Locke on, xxxvii, 18; of children, 19

Meanness, Confucius on, xliv, 25 (35), 26 (11); punishment of, v, 27

Means, and ends, Emerson on, v, 94; Penn on, i, 365 (310-19)

Measles, cowpox and, xxxviii, 226 note; Jenner on, 172; small-pox and, 213

Measure, Emerson on love of, v, 218

Measures, English and metric system of, xxx, 265

Meat, Augustine, St., on eating of, vii, 193; Darwin on eating of, xxix, 129-30; Locke on eating of, xxxvii, 16-17, 19; Mohammed on eating of, xlv, 1008, 1018; price of, Smith on, x, 157-8, 160-1, 191, 195-6, 197, 206-7

Mecca, the House of, xlv, 970 note
14

Mecca Suras, in Koran, xlv, 889-
953

Mechanic Arts Schools, proposed
by Ticknor, xxviii, 380

Mechanical Arts, Bacon on, xxxix,
128; poetry and, compared in
usefulness, xxvii, 367-70

Mechanics, compensation in, v, 91;
Hobbes on, xxxiv, 377; Newton
on science of, xxxix, 157-8; Penn
on, i, 339 (16)

Mechthild, in WILHELM TELL, xxvi,
425, 427-8

MECKLENBURG DECLARATION, xliii,
166-7

Meddling, Kempis on, vii, 236 (3),
252 (2), 299 (1); Marcus Aurelius
on, ii, 204 (13); Penn on, i, 375
(435)

Medea and Æson, xli, 680

Medes, Raleigh on history of, xxxix,
119

Mediæval Architecture, Hugo on,
xxxix, 368

Medici, Alessandro de, xxxi, 88
note, 102, 106, 109; Cellini and,
155, 156, 163-67, 179, 181; reputed son of Pope Clement, 182;
murder of, 165 note 9, 184

Medici, Bernardo de, xxxi, 151
note 2

Medici, Catherine de, xxxi, 295
note; cupbearer to, 429 note;
Count Mansfeld and, xxxviii, 53;
King of Navarre and, 50

Medici, Cosimo de, xxxi, 16 note 1,
185 note 4; Almeni and, 381
note; Cellini and, 356-9, 362-3,
365, 369-70, 372-3, 374-8, 379,
381-8, 389-90, 399, 403, 404-9,
409-10, 412-15, 416-19, 421-2, 423-
4; 427-37, 439, 447-9, 452-3, 454;
diamond of, 367-9, 376-7; Michael
Angelo and, 400-1, 402, 403;
mother of, 425 note; in Siennese
war, 409-10, 423; Tasso and, 25
note 4

Medici Family, arms of, xxxi, 13
note 3; banishment and return
of, 13-14; xxvii, 411

Medici, Francesco de, xxxi, 446

Medici, Giovanni de, xxxi, 71, 87
note 4

Medici, Giovannino de, xxxi, 16

Medici, Giuliano de, xxxi, 17 note,
88 note

Medici, Giulio de, xxxi, 17 note,
90 note 4 (see also Clement VII)

Medici, Ippolito de, xxxi, 88 note,
139 note; Cellini and, 143, 145,
146, 151

Medici, Isabella de, xxxi, 210 note

Medici, Lorenzino de, xxxi, 88
note, 165 note 9, 166-7, 182, 184,
372 and note

Medici, Lorenzo de, Bacon on, iii,
52; Cellini and, xxxi, 12; de-
scendants of, 88 note; mercantile
enterprises of, x, 491

Medici, Lorenzo Di Piero de,
Machiavelli to, xxxvi, 5-6, 87-90

Medici, Mary of, the wife of Concini and, v, 194

Medici, Ottaviano de, xxxi, 165
note 1, 179-80, 181

Medici, Pallone de, xxxi, 73

Medici, Piero de, father-in-law of
Strozzi, xxxi, 81 note 1; monument of, 140 note 4

Medici, Pietro de, xxxi, 12 note 1,
13

Medicina, Piero de, xx, 118-19

Medicine(s), for children, Locke on,
xxxvii, 27-8; Descartes on science
of, xxxiv, 50-1; Descartes on
study of, 8; in ancient Egypt,
xxxiii, 42; external, xxxviii, 133;
the germ theory in, 382; Goethe
on profession of, xix, 77; in
Greece, xxxviii, 2, 3, 4; Harrison
on, xxxv, 251-2; Hippocrates on
practise and study of, xxxviii,
2, 3, 4-5; Marlowe on study of,
xix, 201, 203; practise of, among
Indians, xliii, 36-7; Milton on
study of, iii, 253; More on study
of, xxxvi, 218; in New Atlantis,
iii, 185-6; papers on, xxxviii, 3-5;
153-231, 235-68, 382-402; Prometheus inventor of, viii, 173; Rousseau on, xxxiv, 176

Medina, origin of name, xlv, 1000
note 7; siege of, 998 note, 999
note 6

Medina Suras, in Koran, xlv, 954-
1021

Mediocrity, abhorred by the sublime, xxiv, 71

Meditation, Carlyle on, xxv, 336;
Hindu doctrine of, xlv, 810, 813,
857; Kempis on, vii, 233 (1);
Pascal on, xlviii, 63 (168); Plutarch on proper objects of, xii,
36-7; Rousseau on, xxxiv, 175

MEDITATIONS OF MARCUS AURELIUS,
ii, 193-306; remarks on, 192

Mediterranean Sea, countries about,
earliest in civilization, x, 26-7;
Shelley on the, xli, 856-7; Taine
on the, xxxix, 436

Medon, in ODYSSEY, xxii, 66-7, 230,
242, 316-17, 342-3

Medoro, and Angelica, xiv, 225,
238

Medusa, Dante on, xx, 38; Milton
on, iv, 126

Medusa, queen of amazons, xxxiii,
338

Medwin, story from, v, 359

Meekness, Confucius on, xliv, 46
(27); Goethe on, xix, 129; Woolman on, i, 182

MEETING OF THE WATERS, xli, 838-9
MEG O' THE MILL, vi, 485-6
Megænetus, pupil of Æschylus, viii, 448
Megæra, Dante on, xx, 38; Milton on, iv, 308
Megapenthes, son of Menelaus, xxii, 48, 210, 211
Megara, in Homer's Hades, xxii, 159
Megara, city of, xii, 68-9
Megatheroid Animals, habits of, xxix, 95-7
Megra, in PHILASTER, xlvii, 640-1; on Pharamond, 646, 647; with Pharamond, 659-61; before Pharamond's house, 663-4; caught with Pharamond, 665-8; accuses Arethusa, 668-9; at the hunt, 684-5, 686, 690; denounces Arethusa, 713; arrested, 716; freed, 718
Meinrad, of Hohenzollern, xxvi, 386 note 7
Melampus, Dionysus and, xxxiii, 29-30; Iphicles and, xxii, 159 note; story of, 214
Melancholy, Christianity and, xxxix, 361; Hobbes on, xxxiv, 367; in music, xli, 490; pleasures of, iv, 35-9
MELANCHOLY, by Fletcher, xl, 330-331
MELANCHOLY, ODE TO, xli, 906
Melancthon, on poetry, xxvii, 43
Melanopus, Callistratus and, xii, 207
Melanthius, in the ODYSSEY, xxii, 243-5, 248, 288-9, 299-300, 310-11, 312, 320
Melantho, daughter of Dolius, xxii, 263-4, 269
Melchthal, Arnold von, in WILHELM TELL, at house of Fürst, xxvi, 385-6; hears father's blinding, 388-90; enters league with Fürst and Stauffacher, 391-4; at the rendezvous, 400-14; with Tell at Altdorf, 427, 430, 431; at death of Attinghausen, 445; with Rudenz, 448-50; reports progress of revolt, 461-2; hears death of Emperor, 463-7
Melcombe, Lord, SHORTEN SAIL, xl, 475-6
Meleager, son of Althea, viii, 96; Dante on, xx, 249 and note 2
Melendez, Pedro, governor of Florida, xxxiii, 265
Melesigenes, Homer called, iv, 406
Meletus, accuser of Socrates, ii, 5, 10-15, 21, 23, 26
Melias, Sir, knighting of, xxxv, 126-7; adventures of, 127-9; promises to follow Galahad, 130
Melibœus, Milton on, iv, 68; Sidney on, xxvii, 28
Melissus, of Samos, xii, 64, 65; Dante on, xx, 344 note 20; The-

mistocles and, xii, 6; on the world, xxxix, 109-10
Mellus, Henry, xxiii, 408, 419-20
Mellyagraunce, and Launcelot, xlii, 1236-7
Melmoth, William, translator of Pliny, ix, 191
Melo, John de, Don Quixote on, xiv, 515
Melvin, Andrew, xv, 386, 423
Memmius, C., Gabinius and, ix, 120
Memnon, reference to, xiii, 92
MEMORABILIA, xlii, 1124-5
MEMORIAL VERSES, by Arnold, xlii, 1181-3
Memories, Homer on, of griefs, xxii, 218; Moore on, xli, 837; of pleasures, xvii, 45; Tennyson on, xlii, 1013
Memorizing, Confucius on, xliv, 43 (5); Locke on, xxxvii, 160-3; of poetry, Eliot on, l, 10
Memory, Augustine, St., on the, vii, 173-82; Calderon on persistency of, xxxiv, 326; Hobbes on, 326; Hume on the, xxxvii, 316, 341-2; Locke on exercising the, 161-3; in old age, ix, 53-4; Pascal on, xlviii, 41 (95), 125 (369); Raleigh on, xxxix, 101; reliance on the, v, 70; verse and, xxvii, 34-5
Memphis, statues of Amasis at, xxxiii, 89; embankments at, 49; temple of Isis at, 89; founded by Min, 49; camp of Tyrians in, 54
Men, Confucius on study of, xliv, 6 (16), 8 (10); constitute states, xli, 593; divine and undivine, xlv, 870-2; two kinds of, xlviii, 174 (534); women and, Ruskin on, xxviii, 149-50
Ménage, Abbé, on Le Bailleul, v, 317
Menalippus, reference to, xx, 137
Menander, on his comedy, xxxii, 64; on friendship, 86
Menas, the pirate, xii, 358, 359
Mendesians, sacred animals of, xxxiii, 25, 28
Mendicant Ideal, of Buddhism, xlv, 764-6
MENDICANTS, THE ROYAL, xvi, 71-106
Mendoza, city of, xxix, 350
Menelaus, Æschylus on, viii, 20, 27-9; Burke on grief of, xxiv, 35; in Egypt, Herodotus on, xxxiii, 58; in Egypt, Virgil on, xiii, 370; in ODYSSEY, xxii, 16-17, 37-8, 41-2, 48-64, 209-12; Pliny on, ix, 218 note 10; in Trojan horse, xiii, 112
Menenius, the senator, xxxix, 223
Menes (see Min)
Menexenus, with Socrates, ii, 47
Meng Chih-fan, xliv, 20 (13)
Meng Ching, xliv, 26 (4) note 3
Meng Chuang. xliv, 67 (18)

Meng Kung-Ch'o, xliv, 47 (12)

Meng Wu, Confucius and, xliv, 7 (6), 15 (7)

Meng Yi, disciple of Confucius, xliv, 7 (5)

Menico, in THE BETROTHED, xxi, 105, 127-8, 130, 134-5, 191

Menippus, Plutarch on, xii, 53

Menjot, M., Pascal on, xlviii, 348

Mennonists, on slavery, i, 224

Menœkeus, son of (see Creon)

Menœtes, in the ÆNEID, xiii, 187-8, 413

Menon, and Phidias, xii, 70

Mental Discourse, Hobbes on, xxxiv, 330-4; ends of, 359-60

Mental Powers, of animals, xi, 234-5

Mental Sciences, Helmholtz on, xxx, 181-2

Menteith, in MACBETH, xlvi, 365-6, 368

Mentes, form assumed by Pallas, xxii, 12, 14

Mentor, in ODYSSEY, xxii, 28, 240

Mephibosheth, and David, xli, 498; xliii, 110

Mephistopheles, in Goethe's FAUST, undertakes Faust's downfall, xix, 17-20; appears in Faust in shape of dog, 47-8; in Faust's study, appears as scholar, 49-59; as youth of high degree, 60; compact with Faust, 61-71; with the student, 71-8; starts with Faust, 78-9; at the wine-cellar, 83-93; in Witches' Kitchen, 95-107; promises Margaret to Faust, 107-10; in Margaret's chamber, 110-13; learns casket given to church, 115-17; visit to Martha's, 119-25; tells Faust of appointment, 125-8; with Martha in garden, 128-9, 131-2, 134-5; with Faust in cavern, 137-9; urges return to Margaret, 139-42; disliked by Margaret, 146-7; taunts Faust, 148-9; before Margaret's door, 154-5; with Valentine, 155-6; on Walpurgis-Night, 161-76; with Faust in the Plain, 184-6; in Open Country, 186-7; in dungeon, takes Faust, 195; Hugo on, xxxix, 365, 375

Mephostophilis, in Marlowe's FAUSTUS, conjured by Faustus, xix, 207-9; compact with Faustus, 213-17; with Faustus, on Heaven, astrology, etc., 217-19; with Faustus in Rome, 223-5; with Robin and Ralph, 228-9; with horse-courser, 232-4; renews compact with Faustus, 238

Mer de Glace, of Chamouni, xxx, 227-30, 232-3; movement of, 234-6, 239

Mercantile System, effect of, on revenue of the state, x, 550-1; principle of the, 326-47; producers and consumers under, 444-5

Mercator, work of, in mathematics, xxxiv, 128

Mercenary Soldiers, Bacon on, iii, 78; Machiavelli on, xxxvi, 47-8; More on, 232

Merchant, Chaucer's, xl, 18-19; the natural, v, 193

MERCHANT AND THE JINNI, story of, xvi, 17-20

MERCHANT AND HIS WIFE, story of, xvi, 13-14

Merchantman, duties on a, xxiii, 16-21

Merchants, in agricultural system, x, 451-5, 459-63; Bacon on, iii, 54; Harrison on, xxxv, 236-7; interests of, x, 219-20; in war (agreement with Mexico), xliii, 324

Mercurius, the spirit in the battle, xvii, 195

Mercurius Aulicus, royalist paper, iii, 219 note

Mercury, in the ÆNEID, xiii, 35, 85, 165-6, 176-7; frauds of, xxxiv, 381; as German god, xxxiii, 100; son of Maia, xiii, 276-7

Mercury (the metal), supposed parent of metals, xlvii, 552-3

Mercury (the planet), Dante's second Heaven, xx, 306-7

Mercy, Blake on, xli, 605, 606; Bunyan on name and practice of, xv, 234-5; Cowper on, xli, 549; Dryden on, xviii, 82; Hobbes on, xxxiv, 424; Jesus on, xliv, 374 (36); Luther on acts of, xxxvi, 268; Milton on, iv, 20 (8); in princes, xxxvi, 56; Shakespeare on, xlvi, 151; Solomon on, xliii, 100; Mercy, in PILGRIM'S PROGRESS, xv, 176; neighbor of Christiana, 188-9, 190-2; in Slough of Dispond, 192-3; admitted at the gate, 195; conversation with Christiana, 196-7; asks about the Dog, 197-8; her innocency, 201; at the Interpreter's House, 206; why she went on pilgrimage, 211-12; on Difficulty Hill, 222; in Beautiful Palace, 228; her dream, 229; her suitor, Mr. Brisk, 233-4; in Valley of Humiliation, 246-7; in Valley of Death, 249-50; and Mr. Honest and, 256; on Mr. Fearing, 262; married to Matthew, 269, 272; in Vanity Fair, 286; at By-way to Hell, 296; the looking-glass and, 296-7

Meredith, George, LOVE IN THE VALLEY, xlii, 1186-92

Meredith, Hugh, i, 52-3, 60; Franklin in business with, 55-6, 58-9, 61, 62-4; goes south, 64

Merit, contrasted with worthiness, xxxiv, 384; Hobbes on, 412; not envied, iii, 25; Pascal on word, xlviii, 170

Merlin, on Arthur, xlii, 1020; converted by St. Columba, xxxii, 178; Keats on, xli, 911; legend of, xxxii, 160; Renan on, 176; the Round Table and, xxxv, 142-3

MERMAID TAVERN, THE, xli, 898

Mermaid's, Chaucer on, xl, 46-7

MERMAN, THE FORSAKEN, xlii, 1168-72

Meroe, Herodotus on city of, xxxiii, 18

Merriman, Dr., xxxviii, 259-60

MERRY ANDREW'S SONG, vi, 132

MERRY HAE I BEEN TEETHIN A HECKLE, vi, 141

Merryman, in FAUST, xix, 10-14

Merton, Walter, xxxv, 402

Mertoun, Earl, in A BLOT IN THE 'SCUTCHEON, suitor of Mildred Tresham, xviii, 357-8; described by retainers, 359; arrival at Tresham's, 361; his love for Mildred, 362-4; secret visit to Mildred, 369-74; discovered, unknown, by Gerard, 375-7; under Mildred's window the last time, 389-90; killed by Tresham, 390-4

Mesaulius, Homer on, xxii, 205

Mescidius, Cicero on, ix, 114

Mesrur, the executioner, xvi, 66

Messalla, and Cicero, ix, 120; Cicero on, 96-7, 184

Messapus, in the ÆNEID, Æneas and, xiii, 412; ally of Turnus, 267, 272, 298, 302, 314, 352, 378, 380, 414, 418; Aulestes and, 405

Messiah, Milton on prophecies of the, iv, 351, 353-4; Mohammed on the, xlv, 997-8, 1010, 1016; Pascal on prophecies of the, xlviii, 190-2, 205, 206 (616-17), 208-9, 218, 224 (662), 240 (707)

Metabus, father of Camilla, xiii, 380-1

Metagenes, of Xypete, xii, 51

Metallurgy, beginnings of, xxxiv, 210-11

Metals, artificial, in New Atlantis, iii, 182; Harrison on source of, xxxv, 337-8; as medium of exchange, x, 30-1; prices of, 178-83, 186, 209-10

Metamorphic Rocks, xxx, 349

Metaphors, Bunyan on, xv, 7-8; Burke on pleasure from, xxiv, 18; Hobbes on, xxxiv, 364-5; Lowell on, xxviii, 471; Pliny on, ix, 365-7; Wordsworth on, xxxix, 317-19

Metamorphoses, of insects, xi, 478

Metamorphosis, Browne on, iii, 302, 305

Metaphysic of Morals, necessity of a, xxxii, 318-21, 338-43

Metaphysical Reasoning, Franklin on, i, 58

Metaphysicians, Burke on, xxiv, 433

Metaphysics, Aryan and Semitic, xxxix, 444; Bacon's attitude toward, iii, 152; Berkeley on, xxxvii, 297; Carlyle on, xxv, 355-7; Carlyle on German, 369; Channing on study of, xxviii, 340; Cowley on, xxvii, 69; defined by Kant, xxxii, 318; Goethe on, xix, 74-5; Hume on, xxxvii, 309-15, 355, 445; Locke on study of, 147-8; Milton on study of, iii, 250; Rousseau on, xxxiv, 257

Metelli, names of the, xii, 162

Metellus, the tribune, xii, 305

Metellus Quintus, Cicero on, ix, 130; free from resentment, xii, 195-6

Metempsychosis, Browne on, iii, 302 (37); Lessing on, xxxii, 216-17; of opinions, iii, 270; Socrates on, ii, 59-63, 74 (see also Transmigration)

Meteorology, Hobbes on, xxxiv, 377; origin of term, xii, 70 note; in Utopia, xxxvi, 207

Metheglin, Welsh drink, xxxv, 301

Method, in business, i, 372-3 (403); Goethe on, xix, 73; Locke on, xxxvii, 181

Methon, observations of, xxxiv, 132

Methuen, treaty drawn by, x, 408

Methusalem, Browne on, iii, 288

Metius, the traitor, xiii, 293

Meton, the astrologer, xii, 125-6

Metoposcopy, xlvii, 567 note 11; defined by Hobbes, xxxiv, 397

Metras, restored by Cicero, ix, 141-2

Metre, Shelley on, xxvii, 350; Whitman on, xxxix, 415; Wordsworth on, 298, 299-301, 302, 308, 311

Metric System, Kelvin on the, xxx, 265

Metrical Novels, Wordsworth on, xxxix, 313

Metrodorus, xii, 351

Metropolis, every, a university, xxviii, 37, 38-9

Metz, Paré on expedition against, xxxviii, 19; siege of, 24-35

Mexican War, cause of, xliii, 309 note

Mexico, ancient, iii, 166; Johnson on palaces of, xxxix, 236; Raleigh on conquest of, xxxiii, 341; seat of Montezume, iv, 333; TREATY WITH U. S., xliii, 309-26

Meyer, Heinrich, xxxix, 264 note

Meyer von Sarnen, in WILHELM TELL, xxvi, 400-13

Meymum, the son of Demdem, xvi, 85

Mezentius, ally of Turnus, xiii, 265, 272; in attack on Trojan town, 314; in the battle, 350-3; wounded by Æneas, 353-4; his death, 356-9; Dryden on, 21, 34

Miasma, source of, xxix, 386

Miaulina, xiv, 148

Mica, crystallization of, xxx, 30; effect on polarized light, 34

Micaiah, Calvin on, xxxix, 45; Milton on, iii, 240

Micceri, Pagolo, xxxi, 317-18, 319-20, 326-7, 328, 332

Mice, bees and, xi, 88; country and town, ii, 297 (22); country and town, fable of, xvii, 12; Darwin on, xxix, 380; in Galapagos Islands, 400-1; range of, xi, 153-4; use of ears of, 223

Michael, Archangel, in FAUST, xix, 16-17; in PARADISE LOST, iv, 208, 213-15, 325-6, 328-9, 331-59, 361

Michael, the fiddler in ÉVANGELINE, xlii, 1371, 1395

MICHAEL: A PASTORAL POEM, xli, 630-42

Michal, references to, xli, 499, 501

Michaux, on American trees, xxviii, 418

Michelangelo, Andrea del Sarto and, xlii, 1135; on Baccio d'Agnolo's cupola, xxxi, 430 note 3; on beauty, v, 314; Bugiardini and, xxxi, 89 note; cartoon on taking of Pisa, 24 and note 2; Cellini and, 2, 25, 88-9, 400; Cellini on, 358, 375, 436; Cosimo de' Medici and, 400-1, 402; "David" of, 357 note 3; "David" of, Bandinello on, 418-19; "The Fair" of, xxxix, 210; Hazlitt on, xxvii, 293; Hugo on "Last Judgment" of, xxxix, 369; Luigi Pulci and, xxxi, 65; Rossetti on, xlii, 1226; model for a "Samson," xxxi, 434; Torrigiani and, 24-5; work in S. Lorenzo Sacristy, 384 note 2; his man Urbino, 402 note

Michelet, Taine on, xxxix, 437

Micheletto, the engraver, xxxi, 95-6

MICHIE, WILLIAM, EPITAPH FOR, vi, 278

Michol, reference to, xx, 187

Mickle, Samuel, i, 59

Micocolembo, xiv, 147

Micomicona, Princess, xiv, 296-300

Microbe, origin of term, xxxviii, 382

Microscopic Organisms, Pasteur on, xxxviii, 360

Midas, Dante on, xx, 230; ears of, iv, 83

Midias, and Demosthenes, xii, 207

Middle Ages, classics of, xxxii, 127; the grotesque in the, xxxix, 368-9; Hugo on architecture of, 368; philosophy of, xxviii, 223-4; poetry of the, xxvii, 363-5; Taine on, xxxix, 450, 457; works dealing with, l, 22-3, 27-8

Middle Doctrine of Buddha, xlv, 677-81

Middleton, Newman on, xxviii, 48

Midian, reference to, xliv, 253 (9)

Midianites, Mohammed on the, xlv, 917 note

Midwifery, Holmes on, xxxviii, 265-6

Mien, the music-master, xliv, 55 (41)

Migāra, the treasurer, xlv, 772, 776-7, 781, 782-9

Might, and justice, xlviii, 107 (298-300), 310 (878); opinion and, 108 (303), 110 (311)

MIGHTY FORTRESS IS OUR GOD, xlv, 570-1

Migratory Birds, Milton on, iv, 241

Milan, Cathedral of, the eighth wonder, xxi, 198; corn scarcity in (1628), 204-7; fall of, xxxvi, 82; famine in, xxi, 470-86; insurrection of, 207-36, 278-82; Lazzaretto of, 482-3; Louis XII at, xxxvi, 7; Machiavelli on princedom of, 7; plague of, xxi, 488-9, 521-56, 578-92, 635; power of, before French invasion, xxxvi, 40; Sforza at, 44

Milbanke, Miss, wife of Byron, xviii, 402

Milbourne, Luke, xxxix, 180 note 34, 181

Mildmay, Sir Walter, xxxv, 401

Milinda, the king, xlv, 668-72

Military Affairs, Machiavelli on, xxxvi, 42-52, 71-2, 74-5

Military Service, in BODY OF LIBERTIES, xliii, 71

Military Spirit, in different states of society, xxvii, 391-2

Military Training, in Milton's Academy, iii, 257-8

Militia, Bacon on a, iii, 54; congressional control of, xliii, 197 (15, 16); provision for, under Confederation, 171; standing army and, x, 468-9; in United States, xliii, 207 (2)

Mill, Burke on composition of, xxiv, 130; Harrison on, xxxv, 349

MILKMAID AND PAIL, fable of, xvii, 43

Milky Way, ancient idea of, xlviii, 450; Bacon on the, iii, 105; Newcomb on the, xxx, 327, 333, 334; reference to the, iv, 244

Mill, James, xxv, 3; Analysis of Human Mind, 49, 195-6; death of, 131-2; early life of, 8; Elements of Political Economy, 23-4, 45; English law, abhorrence of, 46; ethics and psychology of, 72-3; examiner of Indian correspondence, 22-3; on feeling, 74; friendships, 39-40, 51-2; History of India, 9, 21-2; influence of, 62; influence among Benthamites, 68-71; criticized by Macaulay, 103-4; on Mackintosh and Tocqueville, 131; moral convictions, 35-8; on poetry and poets, 15-16; political belief,

71-2; political philosophy mistaken, 105; religious belief of, 30-3; son's education, 9-29; later relations with son, 117; tenderness lacking, 38; unpublished dialogue on government, 46; *Westminster Review*, connection with, 62-5, 86-7; work, estimation of, 132-3; writings for *London Review*, 129-30

Mill, John Stuart, address at St. Andrews, xxv, 195; on American Civil War, 170-3; AUTOBIOGRAPHY of, 7-199; AUTOBIOGRAPHY, reasons for writing, 7-8; a Benthamite, 46-8, 68-76; birth of, 8; Carlyle and, 114-15, 330; *Comte and Positivism*, 177; correspondence with Comte, 136-8; Council, offered seat in, 160; on Demosthenes and Plato, 19-20; dissatisfaction with present aims, 89-93, 96; *Dissertations*, 167-8; early essays, 50-1; early ideas of the poets, 16-17; early wish to be a reformer, 88; edits Bentham's work on evidence, 76-8; edits father's *Analysis*, 195-6; edits *London Review*, 129-30, 133-4, 138-42; education, 9-14, 16-17; education in political economy, 23-4; his education, remarks on, 25-9; elocution studied by, 20-1; *Examination of Hamilton's Philosophy*, 173-7; the *Examiner*, writings in, 113; as examiner in India House, 160; on fatalism, 110-11; father's relations with, 38-9, 117; father's friends, relations with, 39-40; feelings cultivated, 95; first newspaper articles, 60-1; France, visit to, 41-4; on French Revolution, 45-6, 87; friendship with Grote and the Austins, 51-5, 115; friendship with Maurice and Sterling, 100-3; happiness, new theory of, 94; his *History of Roman Government*, 14-15; hopes of human improvement, 153-4; in Hyde Park affair, 184-5; improvement club, 80-2; India Company, with, 57-9; in Jamaica Committee, 188-90; law read by, 46; ON LIBERTY, 203-325; remarks on, 160-4; life and works, 3-6; logic studied by, 17-19; logic, his work on, 104-5, 117-18, 134-6, 143-6, 157 note 2; London club formed, 84-6; love of the heroic, 76; marginal notes made for father, 45; marriage to Mrs. Taylor, 154-5; music, pleasure in, 95-6; Owenites debated with, 82-3; in Parliament, 178-99; *Parliamentary Reform*, pamphlet on, 164-5; *Parliamentary Review*, writings in, 79-80; philosophical studies, 48-50; on poetry, 75-6; his *Political Economy*, 151-3, 157-9; political philosophy of, 103-10, 111-12, 124-6,

148-51, 169-70; popular editions of works, 178; private reading, 14; religious and moral influences, 30-8; *Representative Government*, 169-70; Roebuck and, 98-100; his *Spirit of the Age*, 113-14; on his step-daughter, 169; *Subjection of Women*, 170; Taylor, Mrs., and, 120-4, 148, 154-9, 161-2; *Utilitarianism*, 170; Utilitarian Society formed by, 55-7; on verse writing, 15-16; *Westminster Review*, connection with, 63, 64 note, 66, 86-7; woman suffrage and, 70-1, 157 note 1; Wordsworth, acquaintance with, 96-8; writing, his method of, 143-4; writings (1830-2), 117-19; writings (1833-4), 128-9; on his writings, 156-7

Millar's *Historical View of English Government*, xxv, 11

Miller, Chaucer's, xl, 26-7; Dryden on Chaucer's, xxxix, 174

MILLER, HEY THE DUSTY, vi, 317

Miller, Rev. Alex., Burns on, vi, 106

Miller, Hugh, THE BABIE, xli, 944-5

Mills, wind and water, introduction of, x, 215

Milnes, Richard Monckton, SONNET, xlii, 1098

Milo, Titus Annius, Clodius and, xii, 254, 255; defence of, by Cicero, ix, 4; trial of, 100-1; xii, 255-6

Milo of Croton, Cicero on, ix, 55; his feat at Olympia, 57

Miltiades, Aristides and, xii, 84-5; Byron on, xli, 835; in fetters, xxvii, 24; Themistocles and, xii, 8

Miltitz, Charles, xxxvi, 358, 359

Milto, concubine of Cyrus, xii, 63

Milton, John, father of the poet, iv, 3

Milton, John, the poet, AREOPAGITICA, iii, 199-244; Arnold on, xxviii, 78, 81; Arnold on lines from, 73-4; Arnold on prose of, 82; austere goodness of, 179-80; Bagehot on COMUS, 213; Bagehot on PARADISE LOST, 201-12; Bagehot on SAMSON AGONISTES of, 184-5; blindness of, iv, 3, 5, 86, 88, 138-9; books of, burned at Oxford, v, 433; Browning on, xlii, 1109; Burke on, xxiv, 53, 55, 70-1, 104-5; Burke on his picture of Hell, 146; Carlyle on, xxv, 336-7, 461; on Charles II, xxvii, 182; daughters of, iv, 5-6; on divorce, xxviii, 190-2; Dryden on, xiii, 13, 51, 60; xxxix, 161; xl, 406; early desires to write a great epic, iv, 21-22; Eliot on Poems of, l, 9; Emerson on, v, 132, 149, 186, 450, 456; Gray on, xl, 467; Hazlitt on, xxvii, 282; highest merit of, v, 63; Hugo on, xxxix, 372-3; Hugo on Paradise of, 367; humor and

knowledge of ordinary life lacking in, xxviii, 183-6; Johnson on, 213; Keightley's *Life* of, remarks on, 174; liberty, his passion for, iv, 4, 194; life and works, 3-6; marriage to Mary Powell, xxviii, 187-90, 192; Masson's *Life* of, review of, 171-4; mention of, in *Cromwell*, xxxix, 400; James Mill on, xxv, 16; outline of life, xxviii, 174-5; Pascal on, xlviii, 69 (192), 153 (448), 154 (455); personal beauty, xxviii, 180-1; Poems of, iv; poetry of, remarks on, xxviii, 198-201; on poets, v, 181; political relations, xxviii, 193-6; political writings, 196-7; Ruskin on, 109, 114-15; Sainte-Beuve on, xxxii, 133; sensibility of, xxviii, 186; Severity, 182; Shelley on, xxvii, 351, 358, 365-7; xli, 880; Shelley on Paradise Lost of, xxvii, 372; strength of his nature, xxviii, 181; his studiousness, 182; Swift on, xxvii, 120; Thoreau on, xxviii, 426; Tractate on Education, iii, 247-59; at twenty-three, iv, 30; on his wife, deceased, iv, 88; Wordsworth on, xxxix, 321, 336-8; xli, 691, 692-3; Wordsworth on sonnets of, xli, 697; Wright on, xxviii, 198

Milton, Essay on, Bagehot's, xxviii, 171-214

Mimas, death of, xiii, 351

Mimnermus in Church, xlii, 1159-60

Mimosa, Longfellow on the, xlii, 1388

Min, first king of Egypt, xxxiii, 7, 48-9

Min Tzu-ch'ien, xliv, 19 (7), 34 (2, 4), 35 (12, 13)

Mincius, smooth-sliding, iv, 76

Mincius, the Triton, xiii, 333-4

Mind, anticipation of the, xxxix, 153; Bacon on operations of the, 141, 142-3, 151; Berkeley on the, xxxvii, 268, 269-71, 288; body and, connection between, xxiv, 113; body and, Pascal on, xlviii, 31; Burke on study of the, xxiv, 47-9; Byron on the, xviii, 443; xxxii, 405; Channing on improvement of the, xxviii, 340-8; Channing on power of, 362; Descartes on reality of the, xxxiv, 29; diffusion of, ii, 267 (57, 60); diseases of the, 144 (75); as the first cause, 92; geometrical and imaginative, xlviii, 419; heart and, relations of, v, 292; its hell, xlii, 1481; Helmholtz on sciences of, xxx, 181-2; Hume on perceptions of the, xxxvii, 316-17; Hume on study of the, 312-15; Locke on a

sound, 9; Locke on training the, 28 et seq., 74-5; Marvell on the, xl, 387; materialistic ideas of, xxxiv, 106-9; Marcus Aurelius on the, ii, 264 (48); mathematical and intuitive, compared, xlviii, 7-10; memory and, St. Augustine on, vii, 178-9; More on pleasures of, xxxvi, 213, 214-15; native propensities of the, xxxvii, 90; Penn on pleasures of the, i, 348-9 (96-98); perturbations of the, vii, 179; Pope on study of the, xl, 417; religiousness of, xlv, 875; Rousseau on the, xxxiv, 265-6; Schiller on nature of the, xxxii, 276-8; Shakespeare on diseases of, xlvi, 367; Shelley on the, xli, 879; troubled, no medicine for, xlvii, 678; virtues and defects of, xxxiv, 362-73; Watts on the, xl, 408 (see also Understanding)

Mind, My, to Me a Kingdom Is, xl, 211

Mindarus, xii, 137, 139

Mineralogy, Locke on study of, xxxvii, 157; in New Atlantis, iii, 187

Minerva, Jove's keys and, v, 96; on mankind, 227; the shield of, iv, 58 (see also Athena)

Mines, discovery of, in Chili, xxix, 336-7; fertility of, x, 175; produce of, a source of capital, 230-1; rent of, 176, 178-84

Minicianus, Cornelius, letter to, ix, 264

Mining, in Chili, xxix, 277, 282-4, 359-61, 366-7; Smith on projects of, x, 421-2

Minister, in Faust, xix, 170

Ministers, Burns on "whigs" of, vi, 79; Chaucer on, xl, 25; Penn on, i, 376-7 (457-467); who change to better their income, xv, 108-9; Woolman on true, 1, 184, 255; Woolman's counsel to, 324-6

Ministers (of state), Bacon on, iii, 99-100; Confucius on, xliv, 11 (19); Henry VII's policy toward, xxxix, 81; Machiavelli on, xxxvi, 79-80; Penn on, i, 369

Ministry, Emerson on the, v, 33-41; Sidney on the, xxvii, 18; Walton on the, xv, 345

Minna von Barnhelm, Lessing's, xxvi, 287-366; remarks on, 286

Minnesingers, Poe on the, xxviii, 390

Minorities, Lincoln on duty of, xliii, 339-40

Minority Representation, Mill on, xxv, 165-6

Minos, in Crete, xxii, 272; Dante on, xx, 21; Homer on, xxii, 166; judge of the dead, xiii, 225-6;

judge in Hades, xxvi, 172; Scylla and, viii, 96

Minotaur, Dante on the, xx, 50-1; reference to the, xxvi, 128

Minshull, Elizabeth, wife of Milton, iv, 6

MINSTREL, THE, AT LINCLUDEN, vi, 512

Minstrels, Homer on, xxii, 117

Minutius Æmilianus, ix, 209-11

Miocene, Upper, Lyell on the, xxxviii, 434

Mirabeau, Carlyle's estimate of, v, 191; Emerson on, 275; on the French aristocracy, 422; on October Sixth, xxiv, 222 note, on political societies, x, 464-5; ugliness of, v, 316

Miracles, Bacon on, iii, 162; of Bible, Browne on, 272-4, 284-7, 292 (27); Calvin on, xxxix, 36-7; Dante on Christian, xx, 390; Emerson on, v, 31, 32, 303; Hobbes on, xxxiv, 400; Hume on, xxxvii, 396-415; Marcus Aurelius on, ii, 193 (6); of Old Testament, Lessing on, xxxii, 199; only in ancient history, v, 30; Pascal on, xlviii, 284-304, 354, 365; Plutarch on, xii, 189-90; Rousseau on, xxxiv, 295-7; in Utopia, xxxvi, 242-3; Walton on, xv, 341-2; Whitman on, xxxix, 421

Miranda, in THE TEMPEST, with Prospero on island, xlvi, 381-7, 391; first meeting with Ferdinand, 394-7; with Ferdinand, at his task, 413-15; betrothed to Ferdinand, 423-9; discovered to Alonso, etc., 437-8; Hunt on, xxvii, 309; Shelley on, and Ariel, xli, 871

Miranda, Francesco, expedition of, xliii, 291

Mirandola, Galeotto della, xxxi, 353-4

Mirandola, Pico della, xlviii, 28 note

Mirandola, Picus, xv, 327

Mirrors, ancient, xxxv, 339-40

Mirth, ECCLESIASTES on, xliv, 340 (2), 347 (4), 350 (15); in music, xli, 491; parentage of, iv, 31; pleasures of, 31-5; religion and, Herbert on, xv, 410

MIRZA, VISION OF, by Addison, xxvii, 77-81

Misael, Luther on, xxxvi, 346

Misanthropy, Bacon on, iii, 36; Socrates on, ii, 82-3

Misbelievers, Mohammed on, xlv, 893, 943, 958, 960, 962, 969, 971-2, 991-2, 995, 997, 1013

Miscelin, a kind of bread, xxxv, 296, 328

Misenus, death and burial of, xiii, 217, 219; the Harpies and, 139

Miserliness, Blake on, xli, 602; contrasted with avarice, xxxvi, 53; More on, 212; in princes, 55-6

Misers, Burns on, vi, 233; fable of, xvii, 37; Penn on the, 1, 343 (45), 347 (88-91)

Misery, "acquaints with strange bedfellows," xlvi, 408; contemplation of, vii, 237-9; death's harbinger, iv, 264; islands in sea of, xli, 858-9; Kempis on bearing of, vii, 290; miracles and, xlvi, 238; origin and cessation of, xlv, 639-40, 677-8, 690; Pascal on human, xlviii, 131-2, 133 (405); truth and, iv, 375

Misfortune(s), Arabian verses on, xvi, 18; Burns on, vi, 73; children and, iii, 20; compensation for, v, 102-3, 106-7; envy bred by, iii, 24-5; indifference of, ii, 136 (56); Marcus Aurelius on bearing, 222 (49), 226 (8), 230 (18); of others, pleasure in, xxiv, 41-4; Penn on use of, i, 403 (150); profit from, ii, 156 (106); Woolman on, i, 266 (see also Adversity)

Misology, Kant on, xxxii, 325; Socrates on, ii, 82-4

Mississippi River, provision for navigation of, xliii, 190; sediment of, xxxviii, 424; Thoreau on the, xxviii, 421

MISTAKES OF A NIGHT (see SHE STOOPS TO CONQUER)

Mistletoe, origin of the, xi, 22-3

MISTRESS, HIS SUPPOSED, xl, 307-8

MISTRESS, LINES TO HIS, xxvii, 284

MISTRESS, THE LOST, xlii, 1111

MISTRESS MINE, xl, 267-8

MISTRESS, WISHES FOR THE SUPPOSED, xl, 369-71

Mistrust, in PILGRIM'S PROGRESS, xv, 47, 130; Christian on, 134-6; punishment of, 224

Misunderstanding, Emerson on, v, 70

Misuse, of good things, iv, 162; is loss, i, 346 (70); Sidney on, xxvii, 38

Mitchel, Dr., i, 153-4

MITCHELL, COLLECTOR, VERSES TO, vi, 582-3

Mites, Pascal on, xlviii, 26

Mitford, exposed by Grote, xxv, 66; Mill on history of, 14

Mithra, Utopian name of God, xxxvi, 238, 247

Mithridates, and Antony, xii, 371-2, 373

Mithridates, Chrysippus, ix, 379

Mithridates of Pontus, water-wheel of, xxx, 190

Mithropaustes, and Demaratus, xii, 32

Mitscherlich, on fermentation, xxxviii, 362, 367 and note

Mivart, St. George, objections to Natural Selection, xi, 229-61

Mlithe, the jester, xlix, 258

Mnason of Cyprus, xliv, 478 (16)

Mnason, Mr., in PILGRIM'S PROG-
RESS, xv, 281-2
Mnesicles, Athenian architect, xii, 52
Mnesiphilus and Themistocles, xii, 6
Mnesiptolema, daughter of Themis-
tocles, xii, 33, 34
Mnesitheus, of Athens, xxxv, 289
Mnestheus, in the ÆNEID, in arch-
ery contest, xiii, 199, 200; in bat-
tle, 414; at the combat, 399; in
defence of town, 323-4, 331; in
Trojan camp, 302, 307; in Trojan
games, 186-91
Mobs, Emerson on, v, 103, 256; Man-
zoni on, xxi, 224-5; Ruskin on,
xxviii, 118
Mocking-birds, in Brazil, xxix, 65;
Longfellow on, xlii, 1392
Moderation, Confucius on, xliv, 21
(27); Descartes on, xxxiv, 22;
Franklin on, i, 83; Hamilton on,
xliii, 214; Hume on, xxxvii, 423;
Kant on, xxxii, 324; Penn on, i,
363
MODERN ENGLISH DRAMA, xviii
Modern Europe, works dealing with,
l, 29
Modern Man, Whitman on the, xlii,
1484
Modestus, Metius, Pliny on, ix, 197,
264; Regulus and, 199
Modesty, Burke on amiability of,
xxiv, 94; Confucius on, xliv, 60
(6); Dryden on excessive, xviii,
12; Epictetus on, ii, 158 (111);
Hobbes on, xxxiv, 426; impudence
and, xviii, 217; resides with other
virtues, 207; in speech, Franklin
on, i, 19, 91; Steele on, xxvii,
188; violets for, vi, 431; virtue
and, ix, 262
Modification (see Variation)
Modred, Gray on, xl, 469
Mogador, island of, xxxiii, 208
Moggallāna, xlv, 716, 726, 727, 791
Mohammad, son of Suleyman Ez-
Zeyni, xvi, 203, 234-5, 236, 241
Mohammed, the prophet, Abu Ghal
and, xlv, 889 note 3; the believers
and, 919 note; the blind man and,
895 note; the caravan and, 955
notes 2, 3; Dante on, xx, 280 note
12; in Dante's HELL, 117; the hill
and, iii, 33; on himself, xlv, 1003;
Hobbes on, xxxiv, 398; Hume on
ethics of, xxvii, 217; Jews and,
xlv, 977 notes; on learning and
folly, v, 305; liaison with Mary,
xlv, 1006 note 1; life, 886; the
Meccans and, 956 note 5; at Ohod,
972 note; Pascal on, xlviii, 198
(595-601); the Quráish and, xlv,
1008 note 1; at siege of Medina,
999 note 6; on the spoils, 1006
note 32; the sun and, xvi, 34
note; supposed prophecy of, in the
Bible, xlv, 979 note 2; Thoreau

on, xxviii, 433; Voltaire on, xxxiv,
85; wives of, xlv, 999 note 2,
1001 note 16, 1003 note; on his
wives, 1001-2, 1004, 1005, 1006-7
Mohammed Aben Alhamar, xxxix, 88
Mohammedan Literature, l, 21-2, 27
Mohammedanism, xlv, 866; Bacon
on rise of, iii, 145; Browne on,
291; Rousseau on, xxxiv, 303;
Taine on, xxxix, 457 (see also
Koran)
Mohun, at Crecy, xxxv, 23
Moine, Le, Dryden on, xiii, 13
Moiris, king of Egypt, xxxiii, 10,
50
Moiris, Lake, built by Moiris the
king, xxxiii, 50; Herodotus on,
7, 76-7
Molecular Forces, Newton on, xxxix,
159
Moles, eyes of, xi, 149; xxix, 62
Molesworth, Sir William, xxv, 126,
128, 129, 134
Molière, Jean Baptiste Poquelin,
English dramatists and, xxxiv,
142; Goethe on, xxxii, 129-30;
Hazlitt on, xxvii, 294; Hugo on,
xxxix, 375, 376, 391, 392; life
and works, xxvi, 188; as Orgon
in TARTUFFE, 189; Sainte-Beuve
on, xxxii, 129-30, 135, 137; TAR-
TUFFE, xxvi, 189-284; Voltaire on
Misanthrope of, xxxiv, 139
Molinera, Lady, in DON QUIXOTE,
xiv, 38
Moloch, in PARADISE LOST, iv, 100,
112-13, 216; reference to, 14 (23)
Molothrus, Darwin on the, xxix, 62-
3; instincts of, xi, 273-4
Moluccas, Drake in the, xxxiii, 227-
30
Momemphis, battle of, xxxiii, 85-6
Moment, the, alone is decisive, xix,
378
Monad, Augustine, St., on the, vii,
60
Monaeses, and Antony, xii, 363,
372
Monaldi, Sandrino, xxxi, 245 note,
248-9
Monarchy, Burke on, xxiv, 274;
Emerson on, v, 254; Pope on, xl,
439; republics compared with, v,
256; Rousseau on origin of, xxxiv,
220-6 (see also Princedoms)
Monasteries, Harrison on, xxxv,
244; Luther on, xxxvi, 315-17,
321-2, 331, 342
Monatunkanet, xliii, 152, 156
Moncontour, battle of, xxxviii, 53
Mondella, Agnese, in I PROMESSI
SPOSI, mother of Lucia, xxi, 37-8;
advises Renzo, 41; with Father
Galdino, 50-3; advised by Father
Cristoforo, 71-4; plans marriage
of Lucia, 92-5, 98-9; with Menico,

105; at Abbondio's, 118, 120, 128-
30; goes to convent, 134-8; to
Monza, 138-49; 183-4; reunion
with Lucia, 410-12; with Cardinal
Federigo, 414-15; at the tailor's,
427-9; receives gift from the Unnamed, 445-6; learns Lucia's vow,
446-50; tries to find Renzo, 450-1;
corresponds with Renzo; 457-61;
flight to castle of Unnamed, 495-
502, 508-13; at the castle, 515-17;
learns Lucia's safety from Renzo,
641-2; returns home, 643-5; with
her grandchildren, 667

Mondella, Lucia, in I PROMESSI
SPOSI, marriage of, forbidden, xxi,
14; with Renzo, 36-7; confesses
Rodrigo's persecution, 39-42; sends
for Father Cristoforo, 49-53; advised by Father Cristoforo, 71-4;
plans for marriage with Renzo,
92-5, 98-9; consents to plan, 103-
4; plot to carry off, 110-11; at
Abbondio's with Renzo, 117-18,
121, 123, 130; goes to convent,
134-8; flight to Monza, 138-43; at
the convent, 144-9, 182-4; discovered by Rodrigo, 304; learns
of Renzo's mishaps, 306-9; ab-
duction of, 339-49; in castle of the
Unnamed, 351-8; release planned,
383-6; taken to village, 396-409;
reunion with mother, 410-12;
visited by Cardinal, 414-16; life
at the tailor's, 427-8; Donna Prassede and, 429-31; return home,
431-3; goes with Donna Prassede,
445; confesses vow to mother,
446-50; at Prassede's, unable to
forget Renzo, 461-3; taken with
plague, 592-3; found by Renzo,
620-6; absolved from vow, 629-33;
returns home, 645-6, 650-1; married to Renzo, 661-2; her daughter, 667; lesson of her life, 667-8

Mondrames, xxxv, 124

Money, Bacon on need of spreading,
iii, 42; Burns on, thirst for, vi,
88; in Chiloe, xxix, 291; as circulating capital, x, 228; congressional right of borrowing, xliii,
196 (2); Emerson on, strife for,
v, 19; evils from use of, 266; of
ancient Germans, xxxiii, 97; increase of, in relation to wages
and profits, x, 296-7; justice and,
Shakespeare on, xlvi, 281; makes
money, x, 98; as measure of value,
38-9, 43-4, 49; Milton on power
of, iv, 386; Mirabeau on, x, 465;
More on wrongs due to, xxxvi,
252; need of continual supply of,
x, 230; origin and use of, 29-35;
paper (see Paper Money); Penn
on love of, i, 408-9, 351 (127);
Plutarch on use of, xii, 161;

prolific nature of, i, 108; its proportion to produce circulated by
its means, x, 245; quantity of,
dependent on consumable goods,
280-1; quantity of, in relation to
industry, 244-5; regulation of, under Confederation, xliii, 174, 175;
regulation of, by Congress, 196
(5); revenue and, x, 237-40; as
reward for services, xxiv, 405;
Ruskin on love of, xxviii, 119;
scarcity of, x, 334-5; Sophocles on
power of, viii, 252; standards of,
x, 45-8; states forbidden to coin,
xliii, 198 (10); Tennyson on
power of, xlii, 1014, 1015; Tennyson on strife for, 1053-5; trade
does not require, x, 334; variation in value of, 38-9, 48; as
wealth, 237-40, 326-47; Woolman
on, pursuit of, i, 311, 312, 318-19

Money-love, Mr., in PILGRIM'S PROG-
RESS, xv, 106-11, 113

Money Prices, remark on, x, 49

Mongrels, compared with hybrids,
xi, 327-30

Monicongo, epitaph by, on DON
QUIXOTE, xiv, 540

Monied Interest, defined, x, 293;
increase of, 294; remarks on the,
xxiv, 258

Monimus, the Cynic, ii, 204 (15)

Monk, Chaucer's, xl, 15-17; Dryden
on Chaucer's, xxxix, 172

Monkeys, first appearance of, xi,
356; tails of, 243-4

Monkeys, in FAUST, xix, 94-100

Monks, Calvin on, xxxix, 39; Dante
on corruption of the, xx, 381-2;
Harrison on the, xxxv, 246; irregular, xxxvi, 321 note; Luther
on, 315-17, 329, 350-1; Luther on
confession of, 321-2; in Milton's
Limbo, iv, 159; Pascal on corrup-
tions of, xlviii, 313 (889); proverb on, xxxvi, 274

Monnica, mother of St. Augustine,
vii, 3; cares for son, 25-7, 73-6,
99, 142-3, 148; funeral of, 162-3;
last sickness and death of, 154,
158-61; life and character of, 154-
8; in Milan, 82-3; in the Milan
troubles, 153; offerings to the
churches, 83-4; piety of, 14-15;
prayer for, 164-6; vision of, 44-6;
Walton on visions of, xv, 341

MONODY, by Burns, vi, 516

Monogamy, among the Germans,
xxxiii, 105; of Greeks and Egyptians, 45

Monolith of Amasis, xxxiii, 88-9

Monopoly, enemy of good management, x, 157; forbidden, in BODY
OF LIBERTIES, xliii, 72 (9); in
manufactures and agriculture, x,
358; as means to riches, iii, 94

Monopoly Prices, x, 65
Monotony, of life, Bacon on, iii, 10;
  Marcus Aurelius on, ii, 243 (46)
Monroe, James, in Louisiana Pur-
  chase, xliii, 267 note
MONROE DOCTRINE, THE, xliii, 296-
  8; Russia and the, 459 note
Monstrosities, beauty in, iii, 280;
  Darwin on, xi, 27, 258; defini-
  tion of, 58; under nature and do-
  mestication, 58-9
Montagu, Earl of Huntingdon, xxxix,
  76
Montague, and Addison, xxvii, 168
Montague, Bishop, xv, 343-4
Montague, Lady Wortley, xxxiv, 97
Montague, picture-dealer, v, 333
Montagues and Capulets, xx, 171
  note 13
Montaigne, Michel Eyguem de, Art
  of Conversation, xlviii, 414; OF
  BOOKES, xxxii, 89-105; on Castalio, xxxvii, 75; on ceremony, xviii,
  12-13; character of, xxxii, 112;
  on his character, 71-2; in the civil
  wars, 119-22; commentators of,
  111-12; devotees of, 109; Dryden
  on, xxxix, 167; on his education,
  xxxii, 67-71; on his essays, 4, 74,
  89-90; OF FRIENDSHIP, 74-88; Hazlitt on, xxvii, 294; Hugo on lan
  guage of, xxxix, 394; INSTITUTION
  AND EDUCATION OF CHILDREN, xxxii,
  29-73; ON JUDGMENT OF HAPPI-
  NESS, 5-8; on his learning, 29-30;
  on lies, iii, 9; his life, résumé of,
  xxxii, 113; life and works, 3; literary style of, 122-4; as mayor
  of Bordeaux, 116-19; men of his
  time, 115; Pascal on, xlviii, 13
  (18), 23-4, 33 (74), 80 (220), 87-
  8, 111 (315), 113 (325), 286 (813),
  395-406; TO PHILOSOPHIZE IS TO
  LEARN HOW TO DIE, xxxii, 9-28;
  on his reading, 91-105; recovered
  letters of, 110; Rousseau on, xxxiv,
  280-1; Sainte-Beuve on, xxxii, 109-
  25, 134, 136-7; Steven de la Boetie,
  and, 74-5, 80-1, 86-8; on Tacitus,
  xxxiii, 94; times of, xxxii, 114;
  travels in Italy, iv, 216-7; Voltaire
  on Essays of, xxxiv, 103
MONTAIGNE, ESSAY ON, Sainte-
  Beuve's, xxxii, 109-25
Montanarolo, in THE BETROTHED,
  xxi, 334
Montanus, Calvin on, xxxix, 40
Montaperto, battle of, xx, 135 note 8
Montefeltro, Buonconte da, xx, 166
  and note 8
Montefeltro, Guido da, xx, 113 note
  4; in Dante's HELL, 112-16
Montejan, M. de, xxxviii, 9, 12, 13
Montelupo, Raffaello da, xxxi, 73
  note 7, 216
Monterey, Dana on, xxiii, 75, 85-8,
  239, 404

Montesquieu, on classification of
  citizens, xxiv, 333; inventor of
  national workshops, xxviii, 469;
  Le Temple de Gnide, xxxix, 404;
  Sainte-Beuve on, xxxii, 128;
  Sainte-Beuve on Spirit of Laws,
  131; Taine on, xxxix, 459
Montevideo, Darwin on, xxix, 155
Montevarchi, Francesco da, xxxi,
  445-6
Montferrat, William, Marquis of,
  Dante on, xx, 176 and note 17
Montgomerie, James, Burns on, vi,
  189 note
MONTGOMERIE'S PEGGY, vi, 25
Montgomery, M., and Henry II,
  xxxiii, 193
Montgomery, Sir Hugh, in CHEVY
  CHASE, xl, 99-100, 101; at Otter-
  burn, xxxv, 94; xl, 92, 93, 94
Montgomery, Richard, Burns on, vi,
  54
Montjoie, origin of cry of, xlix, 188
Montluc, Jean de, xxxi, 217 note 1,
  260
Montmorency, Maréchal de, xxxviii,
  53
Montone, Andrea de (see Braccio)
Montone, river, Dante on, xx, 70
  and notes
Montorsoli, Giovanni Angelo, xxxi,
  420 note
Montrose, Marquis of, MY DEAR
  AND ONLY LOVE, xl, 368-9
Moodie, Rev. Alexander, Burns on,
  vi, 104-5, 372-3 (see also TWA
  HERDS)
Moods, Pascal on, xlviii, 46 (107)
Moon, Addison on the, xlv, 547;
  Browning on the, xlii, 1142; Dante
  on the, xx, 292-7; Dryden on the,
  xl, 410; as Egyptian goddess,
  xxxiii, 29; Faust's apostrophe to
  the, xix, 22; heat from the, xxx,
  273; Milton on the, iv, 239, 250,
  311; motions and distance of, xxx,
  317-18; motion of, Copernicus on,
  xxxix, 57; motion of, Voltaire on,
  xxxiv, 118-19, 120; Pascal on su-
  perstitions concerning, xlviii, 13
  (18); Raleigh on the, xxxix, 113;
  Shelley on the, xli, 876, 879; tides
  and, xxx, 294-6, 305-6, 317-19;
  tides and, Descartes on, xxxiv, 37;
  tides and, Voltaire on, 110, 120;
  weather influenced by, xxx, 313
MOON, TO THE, by Shelley, xli, 870
MOON, TO THE, by Sidney, xl, 217
Moone, Thomas, with Drake, xxxiii,
  151, 217, 221, 238, 259, 267
MOOR-HEN, THE BONIE, vi, 274-5
MOORE, SIR JOHN, BURIAL OF, xli,
  843-4
Moore, Thomas, Poe on, xxviii, 390,
  396; poems by, xli, 837-43
Mora, Giangiacomo, the barber, xxi,
  5, 587

Moraines, lateral, central, and terminal, xxx, 226-7, 238-9

Moral, meaning of word, v, 291

Moral Causes, Taine on, xxxix, 441

Moral Education, Locke on, xxxvii, 28-59, 63-71, 82-126, 143, 168; Mill on, xxv, 36; Milton on, iii, 252, 254

Moral Instruction, Kant on, xxxii, 341 note 2

Moral Life, Buddhist precepts of, xlv, 759

Moral Perfection, Franklin on, i, 82, 89

Moral Philosophy, Hobbes on, xxxiv, 429; Hume on, xxxvii, 305-6, 314, 354-5, 444-5 (see also Ethics)

Moral Progress, Emerson on, v, 141-2

Moral Sciences, Channing on study of, xxviii, 340; Helmholtz on, xxx, 182; Taine on, xxxix, 451

Moral Sense, Bentham on term, xxv, 46; Emerson on the, v, 26-9, 294; Kant on, xxxii, 373, 392; Poe on the, xxviii, 388

Moralists, Sidney on, xxvii, 17-21, 24-5

Morality, autonomy the supreme principle of, xxxii, 363-4, 370-1, 375-6; Bacon on, and atheism, iii, 47; Bagehot on positive, xxviii, 212; beauty and, v, 320; belief in Providence and, xxxvii, 423, 428-9; in books, criticism of, xxvii, 232-3; Burke on beauty as basis of, xxiv, 95-6; Burns on, vi, 222; censorship of, iii, 217-19; charge of danger to, xxxvii, 385; common rational notions of, xxxii, 323-35; criticism of defects in, xxvii, 257; culture and, Rousseau on, xxxiv, 164; Descartes's code of, 21-4; Descartes on study of, 8, 9; defined, xxxii, 370; empirical and metaphysical bases of, 337-43, 356-7; empirical and rational bases of, 372-5; equalizes all, v, 301; esthetics and, xxxii, 282, 283, 287-91; first manifestations of, 295-6; Franklin's plan of, i, 82-90; free will and, xxxii, 378, 379-84, 386; Hume on standard of, xxvii, 216-17; immaterialism and, xxxvii, 297; immortality and, xlviii, 80 (219); imperatives of, xxxii, 347, 349-70, 384-6 (see also Categorical Imperative); interest attaching to ideas of, 380-1, 391-2; intrinsic worth of, 366, 370; Locke on popular, xxxvii, 135-6; love the secret of, xxvii, 354; Marcus Aurelius on the highest, ii, 255 (69); Mill on Christian, xxv, 252-5; Mill on standards of, 208-9; natural to man, xxxiv, 277-82; necessity and liberty in regard to, xxxvii, 385-

91; need of metaphysic of, xxxii, 318-21; refinement and, 250, 269; Pascal on standard of, xlviii, 128 (383); Pascal on true, 10; Penn on true, i, 391-2; philosophical basis of, need of, xxxii, 335-6; pleasure inseparable from, v, 95; poetry as teacher of, xxvii, 353-4, 356-7; religion and, Mill on, xxv, 31-2; revelation and, Dryden on, xiii, 32; of rugged countries, xli, 538-9; among savages, xxxiv, 190-5; spurious principles of, due to Heteronomy of Will, xxxii, 363-4, 371-2; unconscious of itself, xxv, 339-41; of youth and age, iii, 111; Washington on, xliii, 260

MORALS, FUNDAMENTAL PRINCIPLES OF, Kant's, xxxii, 317-95

Morangis, Abbé, Burke on, xxiv, 294

Moravians, attitude of, toward war, i, 146; marriage among, 150; practices of, 149-50

Moray, Earl John, his raid into England, xxxv, 83-4; at Otterburn, 91, 92, 93

Morbeke, Sir Denis, xxxv, 52, 59-60

Mordecai, Dante on, xx, 215; honors of, xxxiv, 379

Mordrains, King, xxxv, 195; Galahad and, 217

Mordred, son of Arthur, xx, 135 note 3

More and Less, tragedy of, v, 106

More, Sir George, and Dr. Donne, xv, 330-3, 336, 352

MORE, HANNAH, ON A WORK OF, vi, 200

More, Sir Thomas, accused of taking bribes, xxxvi, 121-2; accused of treason, 122-6; affection for his father, 113; ambassador to Cambray, 109-10; ambassador for merchants, 96; Anne Boleyn and, 119-20; ascetic practices, 115; on Augustine, St., 94; barrister, 94; burgess in Parliament, 95; the Canterbury nun and, 120; chancellor of Lancaster, 102; Charles V on, 140-1; at Charterhouse, 94; conviction of, 137-8; counsel for Pope, 96-7; Cromwell advised by, 119; daughters of, 95, 105-6; education and youthful wit, 93-4; embassies to Flanders and France, 103; on his embassy to Flanders, 143; embassy to Spain offered to, 101-2; on English Church, 109; freedom from anger, 109; Furnival's Inn and, 94; gentleness toward opponents, 102-3; Peter Giles on, 255; Henry VII, troubles with, 95; Henry VIII and, 96-7, 102, 103, 104, 107-8, 110, 115-16, 119, 123-4; heroism of, v, 131; imprisoned in tower, xxxvi, 127-31; indictment and trial, 132-7;

Jonson on, xxvii, 60; Johnson on, xxxix, 236; justice of, xxxvi, 112; on king's marriage and supremacy, 119, 123; lands of, 129; last days and death, 138-40; lawyer, 96; learning and power of speaking, 103; LIFE by Roper, 93-141; Lord Chancellor, 110, 111-14, 116-18, 121-2; manner of dress, 115; marriage, 94; patience with slanders of merchants, 103; piety of, 104-5, 114, 116-17, 118-19, 126, 127; poverty, 118; reader at Furnival's Inn, 94; religious writings and present from clergy, 114-15; Lord Rich with, 131-2; Sidney on, xxvii, 20; speaker of Parliament, xxxvi, 97-100; three wishes of, 104; under-sheriff of London, 96; unselfishness of his aims, 104; UTOPIA, 143-257; remarks on UTOPIA of, 92; virtues and wisdom of, 93; Walton on, xv, 327; Wolsey and, xxxvi, 100-1

Morelli, Dr., Dryden on, xiii, 58
Morequito, King, of Aromaia, xxxiii, 343-4, 368
Morgan, chariot of, xxxii, 152
Morgan, Col., at Gettysburg, xliii, 417-18
Morgan, Matthew, xxxiii, 237, 256, 263
Morgan, Miles, xxxiii, 276
Morgant, the giant, xiv, 21
Morley, his work on liberty, xxv, 6
Morluc (see Montluc)
Mormons, Mill on persecution of, xxv, 299-301
Morning, Berkeley on, xxxvii, 201; Gray on, xxxix, 290; Milton on, iv, 38, 173
Moro, Raffaello del, xxxi, 92, 100-2, 190-1
Morone, Macaulay on, xxvii, 409
Morpheus, reference to, iv, 35
Morphology, Darwin on, xl, 472-7
Morrell, Sir Charles, xl, 101
MORRIS, AULD ROB, vi, 473
Morris, Captain, i, 158
Morris, Gov., and Franklin, i, 132-3, 152; love of dispute, 131-2; quarrel with Assembly, 133, 144; retirement of, 133, 152
Morris, James, i, 112, 113
Morris, William, Poems by, xlii, 1230-45; PROLOGUE TO NIBLUNGS AND VOLSUNGS, xlix, 272-3; translator of songs from the EDDA, 384; translator of VOLSUNGA SAGA, 265
Mershead, E. D. A., translator of HOUSE OF ATREUS, viii, 1
Morsimus, reference to, viii, 423
Mortality (see Death)
Morte d'Arthur, favorite in old England, xxxix, 237; Holy Grail, story of, from Malory's, xxxv,

108-226; PROLOGUE to Malory's, xxxix, 21-5
MORTE D'ARTHUR, Tennyson's, xlii, 1019-26
Mortification, Ruskin on, xxviii, 97
Mortimer, the elder, in EDWARD II, xlvi, 7-9, 11-13, 14-16, 19-25, 31
Mortimer, the younger, in EDWARD II, in opposition to Gaveston, xlvi, 7-9, 11-13, 14-16; consents to his return, 19-22; made Marshal, 23-4; on Gaveston, 25; at Gaveston's return, 28-31; quarrel with king, 31-3; Edward on, 34-5; in attack on Tynemouth, 36, 37-8; at capture of Gaveston, 39-42; in battle, 49; captured, 50-1; escapes to France, 52, 53-5; his return in arms, 57, 59-60; the Queen and, 58, 61, 64; his triumph, 68-9; plots king's death, 69-70; with Kent, 70-1; new plots against king, 74-5; made Protector, 75-6; puts Kent to death, 76-7; suspected of king's death, 81; condemned to death, 82-3; Edward Third on, 84
Morton, Bishop of Durham, relations with Dr. Donne, xv, 334; Walton on, 334
Morton, Cardinal, xxxvi, 94
Morton, John, More on, xxxvi, 150-1
Mosca degli Uberti, in Hell, xx, 27-8, 119-20
Mosca, Il, xxxi, 438 note
Moschino, Il, xxxi, 438 note
Moses, Browning on, xlii, 1142-3; Bunyan on, xv, 75, 136; on clean beasts, 85; in Dante's PARADISE, xx, 423; on his own death, iii, 294 (29); Defoe on, xxvii, 156; Jesus and, xliv, 384 (30); Jesus on, xlvii, 277 (782); learning of, iii, 209; Lessing on, xxxii, 200; Machiavelli on, xxxvi, 20-1, 22, 87; meekness of, xv, 345; Milton on, iv, 90, 350-1, 353; on miracles, xlviii, 284 (803); Mohammed on, xlv, 898, 913-15, 922, 924, 932, 944, 979, 996, 997, 1006 note 32, 1011; More on law of, xxxvi, 159; Pascal on, xlviii, 193-4, 205, 207, 211 (622, 624), 213 (629, 631), 222, (657), 235 (690), 236, 242, 248 (714), 266 (741), 269 (752), 274 (774); Paul, St., on, xlv, 530 (13); prayers of, vii, 315 (2); his prophecy of Christ, xliv, 290 (826), 435 (22-3); the Psalmist on, 272 (6-8), 281 (26), 283 (16, 23), 284 (32); Psalms attributed to, 146, 262-4; on resurrection, 414 (37-8); Stephen on, 443 (20-40); taken from Limbo, xx, 18; wish of, iii, 236
Moses, in SCHOOL FOR SCANDAL, xviii, 139-41, 146-7, 150-57, 160-1

Mosquitoes and Fox, fable of, xvii, 37

Mosquitos, Drake on, xxxiii, 155

Mother, I Cannot Mind My Wheel, xli, 925

Mother, To My, by Poe, xlii, 1286-7

Mother Holle, story of, xvii, 111-14

Mother's Lament, A, vi, 333

Mother's Picture, On His, by Cowper, xli, 556-9

Motherhood, Holmes on, xxxviii, 264-5

Mothers (see Parents)

Motherwell, Song of the Cavalier, xxviii, 404

Motion, Berkeley on, xxxvii, 222-3, 224-6, 252, 282; first law of nature, v, 239, 241-2; Pascal on, xlviii, 435-7; Rousseau on, xxxiv, 254-5, 257-8

Motives, and actions, xxxvii, 373-81, 383 note, 386-7; James Mill on, xxv, 37; Ruskin on human, xxviii, 96-8

Motte, Andrew, translator of Newton, xxxix, 2

Motto to Burns's First Book, vi, 232

Moulds, bacteria and, xxxviii, 359; Pasteur on, 310, 312, 313 and note

Mounier, on October Sixth, xxiv, 222 note

Mountain-chains, formation of, xxix, 330-1; Geikie on, xxx, 353-4

Mountain Daisy, To A, vi, 201-3

Mountain of the Congregation, iv, 203

Mountain-torrents, Darwin on, xxix, 335-6

Mountains, as barriers of species, xxix, 346; difficulty of judging distances on, 345; Helmholtz on low temperature of, xxx, 222-3; resemblance of species of, xi, 411-14

Mountains in Labor, fable of, xvii, 16

Mountjoy, Lord, Harrison on, xxxv, 336 note

Mourning, in ancient Egypt, xxxiii, 42; Bacon on, iii, 9; Byron on, xli, 810; Confucius on, xliv, 12 (26), 62 (21), 67 (17); Dekker on, xlvii, 486; Ecclesiastes on, xliv, 347 (2, 4); Ennius on, ix, 73; Hamlet on, xlvi, 95; Pascal on, xlviii, 343, 344; Rossetti, C. G., on, xlii, 1228, 1229; Shakespeare on, xl, 281-2; Tzu-yu on, xliv, 67 (14)

Mourning, Valediction Forbidding, xl, 312-13

Mouse, To A, vi, 125-6; remarks on, 17

Mouse and Lion, fable of, xvii, 14

Mouse, The Town, and the Country Mouse, xvii, 12

Movement, definitions of, xlviii, 434

Moving Pictures, in New Atlantis, iii, 188

Mowis, tale of the, xlii, 1403

Mozzi, Andrea de', xx, 66 and note 5

Mozzi, Rocco di, xx, 59 note

Mucalinda, xlv, 641-2

Much, the miller's son, in adventure with knight, xl, 131, 132, 138, 139, 140; with monks, 157, 158, 159; at archery contest, 168, 169

Much-afraid, in Pilgrim's Progress, xv, 177; daughter of Dispondency, 291-2, 294; parts with Christiana, 316; death of, 318-19

Mucianus, Tacitus on, iii, 135; on Vitellius, 18, 148

Mucii, Plutarch on the, xii, 226

Muck-rake, man with, in Pilgrim's Progress, xv, 205

Muggins, Dick, in She Stoops to Conquer, xviii, 205, 210

Muhagerin, xlv, 961 note 14

Muir, William, Epitaph on, vi, 53

Muirkirk, John Shepherd, Burns on, vi, 374

Mulciber, his fall from Heaven, iv, 109; architect of Pandemonium, 108 (see also Vulcan)

Mule, Darwin on the, xxix, 334

Mule, The Sheykh and the, xvi, 26-7

Muley, Hameda, xiv, 406

Mulius, Homer on, xxii, 266

Müller, Fritz, on air-breathing crustaceans, xi, 201-2; on classification, 456; on crustaceans, 295; on dimorphism, 61; on larval stage, 486; on twining plants, 253

Müller, John, Browne on, iii, 278 (note)

Müller, Max, quoted, xxviii, 249

Multiple Organs, variable, xi, 160

Multitudes, effect of shouting of, xxiv, 72-3

Multrie, Rev. John, Burns on, vi, 173

Mummius, at Corinth, xiii, 240

Mun, Mr., book of, x, 331; on foreign trade, 328

Munatius, and Cicero, xii, 246

Munday, Anthony, Beauty Bathing, xl, 203-4

Munificence, proverb on, xvi, 211

Munremar, son of Gerrchenn, xlix, 239-40

Muralt, M. de, xxxiv, 139

Murder, Chaucer on, xl, 41; in Massachusetts law, xliii, 84-5; Mohammed on, xlv, 927, 990; punishment of, in old England, xxxv, 383, 384; Shakespeare on, xlvi, 132; Webster on, xlvii, 790

Murderers, in Dante's Hell, xx, 47;
53

Murena Licinius, defence of, xii, 270; trial of, 255
Muret, Mark Antony, xxxii, 68
Murillo, Hugo on, xxxix, 369
Murmuring, Penn on, i, 342
Murranus, death of, xiii, 413, 417
MURRAY, BONNY EARL OF, xl, 109
MURRAY, MISS EUPHEMIA, LINES ON, vi, 301-2
Murray, Gilbert, translator of Euripides, viii, 1
Musa, Arab general, xvi, 312 note 3 in story of CITY OF BRASS, 312-339
Musæus, Aristophanes on, viii, 451; Marlowe on, xix, 204; Milton on, iv, 37; Sidney on, xxvii, 8; Socrates on, ii, 28; in Virgil's Hades, xiii, 234
Musaget, in FAUST, xix, 180
Muses, Aristophanes on the, viii, 445; De Quincey on the, xxvii, 337; Milton on the, iv, 36, 74
Mushroom, Emerson on the, v, 60
Mushtari, reference to, xli, 983
Music, beauty in, xxiv, 105; Browne on, iii, 338; Browning on, xlii, 1114, 1146; Coleridge on, xxvii, 269, 276; Collins on, xli, 191; Confucius on, xliv, 12 (23), 26 (8), 43 (3); Dorian, Milton on, iv, 104; Dryden on power of, xl, 399, 400; Herbert on, xv, 384; Hobbes on, xxxiv, 377; instrumental, power of, xxiv, 54; Locke on study of, xxxvii, 182; Mill on effects of, xxv, 95; Mill on limitations of, 96; Milton on, iv, 41, 45; as recreation, iii, 257; the passions and, xli, 488-91; Poe on, xxviii, 389, 390; Ruskin on best, xxviii, 157; Schiller on, xxxii, 285-6
MUSIC, FOR, by Byron, xli, 808-9
MUSIC, THE POWER OF, xl, 400-6
MUSIC, WHEN SOFT VOICES DIE, xli, 878
MUSICAL INSTRUMENT, A, xli, 948-9
Musical Notes, rates of vibration of, xxx, 264-6
Musicians, Browning on, xlii, 1147
Musing, a deadly happiness, viii, 304
Mussato, Albertino, xx, 53 note 8
Mussels, no heart in, xxxviii, 137
Musset, De, Taine on, xxxix, 435
Mustapha, and Roxalana, iii, 53
Mustard-seed, parable of the, xliv, 397 (18-19)
Mutilations, inheritance of, xi, 148
Mutual Aid Societies, ancient, ix, 424 note 2
MY BONIE BELL, vi, 442
MY BONIE MARY, vi, 336
MY COLLIER LADDIE, vi, 460-1
MY DEAR AND ONLY LOVE, xl, 368-9

MY EPPIE ADAIR, vi, 369
MY EPPIE MACNAB, vi, 439
MY FAITH LOOKS UP TO THEE, xlv, 583
MY FATHER WAS A FARMER, vi, 39-41
MY GIRL SHE'S AIRY, vi, 62
MY HEART LEAPS UP, xli, 615
MY HEART'S IN THE HIGHLANDS, vi, 384
MY HIGHLAND LASSIE, O, vi, 211-12
MY HOGGIE, vi, 314
MY LAST DUCHESS, xlii, 1115
MY LORD A-HUNTING, vi, 275-6
MY LOVE IN HER ATTIRE, xl, 334
MY LOVE, SHE'S BUT A LASSIE YET, vi, 365
MY MOTHER BIDS ME BIND MY HAIR, xli, 594-5
MY NANIE O, vi, 49-50
MY NANIE'S AWA, vi, 544
MY NATIVE LAND SAE FAR AWA, vi, 457
MY PEGGY'S CHARMS, vi, 304-5
MY SPOUSE NANCY, vi, 507-8
MY TOCHER'S THE JEWEL, vi, 440
MY WIFE'S A WINSOME WEE THING, vi, 472
Mycene, reference to, xxii, 25
Mykerinos, king of Egypt, xxxiii, 66-68
Mylodon, Darwin on the, xxix, 96
Myopotamus, Darwin on the, xxix, 305
Myris, in ALL FOR LOVE, xviii, 22-3
Myrmex, Aristophanes on, viii, 465-6
Myrmidons, return of, from Troy, xxii 39
Myrrha, in Dante's HELL, xx, 126
Myrtle, David on the, xli, 506
Myrto, granddaughter of Aristides, xii, 108
Mysteries, Egyptian, xxxiii, 86-7; in religion, Browne on, iii, 272 (9) 273 (10)
Mystery, Carlyle on, xxv, 347-8; many shapes of, viii, 415
Mysticism, Emerson on, v, 184-5
Mystics, songs of, in THE FROGS, viii, 429-32
Mythology, Celtic, xxxii, 160-2; Descartes on study of, xxxiv, 7, 8; Renan on Classical, xxxii, 167; Taine on, xxxix; 434; Thoreau on, xxviii, 427
Myths, law of compensation in, v, 96; remarks of, xvii, 1
Naaman, the Syrian, xliv, 369 (27)
Nabal, Winthrop on, xliii, 99
Nabis, Prince of Sparta, xxxvi, 36, 63
Nachoran, Abraham's son, iii, 176
Nacien, the hermit, xxxv, 116, 119; 125, 159, 166, 167-70, 194-5
Nadab, Browning on, xlii, 1143
Naegling, the sword, xlix, 81

NAETHING, STANZAS ON, vi, 233-4
Naevius, Roman poet, iii, 205;
　quoted, ix, 53; old age of, 64
Nāga, the Great, xlv, 749
Nägeli, on plants, xi, 222
Naharvalians, Tacitus on the, xxxiii,
　120
Naiads, Homer on the, xxii, 183;
　Milton on the, iv, 53
Nails, as money in Scotland, x, 30;
　making of, 13
Naimes, Duke, xlix, 104-5, 120, 124,
　126, 163, 164, 185, 186, 191, 193
Nain, widow of, xliv, 376 (12-15)
Nairne, Lady, poems by, xli, 573-
　80
Name, good, a precious ointment,
　iii, 5
Names, among the Bornoos, v, 208;
　Epictetus on, ii, 172 (154); Goethe
　on, xix, 53; Hobbes on, xxxiv,
　337-43; independence of, v, 132;
　Thoreau on, xxviii, 429-30
Namur, William of, xxxv, 10
Nan Jung, Confucius on, xliv, 14
　(1), 34 (5)
Nan-kung Kuo, xliv, 47 (6)
Nantucket, Praying Indians of, xliii,
　149; Woolman's description of, i,
　256-8
Nan-tzu, xliv, 21 (26), 23 note 3
Naphtha, Browne on, iii, 284
Naples, betrayed by Ferdinand,
　xxxix, 89; conquest of, xxxvi, 14,
　15, 28; described by Marlowe,
　xix, 223; in 16th century, xxvii,
　411; Machiavelli on kingdom of,
　xxxvi, 7; papal authority in, 310-
　11; power of, before French inva-
　sion, 40; reasons of fall of, 82
NAPLES, STANZAS WRITTEN NEAR, by
　Shelley, xli, 848-9
Napoleon, aristocracy courted by, v,
　212; art of war of, 356; Bagehot
　on, xxviii, 206; Carlyle on, xxv,
　338, 422-3; on charlatanism, xxviii,
　66; compared with Milton's Satan,
　206; Emerson on, v, 275; Empire
　of, 390; English hated by, 389-90;
　etiquette of, 216; on French Revo-
　lution, xxviii, 482; on the heaviest
　battalions, v, 371; Hugo on, xxxix,
　397; Louisiana sold by, xliii, 267
　note; Mazzini on, xxxii, 404, 412;
　method of, v, 86; at the pest
　house, 300-1; the royal armies
　and, 102; on sublime and ridicu-
　lous, xxxix, 375; the wounded offi-
　cer and, xxv, 350
Napoleon III, Mill on, xxv, 153
Nar, the squinter, xlix, 258
Narahs, evil genii, xvi, 9 note
Naraka, xlv, 871, 872
Narcissus, cunning of, iii, 61; Dante
　on, xx, 295 note 2; Milton on,
　iv, 52; Shelley on, xli, 883
Nardi, Jacopo, xxxi, 157 note 5

Nariscans, Tacitus on the, xxxiii,
　119
Narrative Poetry, forms of, xxxix,
　313
Narrowness, of mind, Confucius on,
　xliv, 58 (9)
Narses, Bacon on, iii, 24
Narvaez, Roderick, and the Moor,
　xiv, 47
Nasagena, and Milinda, xlv, 668-72,
　693-7
Nashe, Thomas, poems by, xl, 265-
　267
Nashope, Indian town, xliii, 153-4
Nasidius, reference to, xx, 106
Naso, banished by Augustus, iii,
　205; Dante on, xx, 19
Nasomonians, Herodotus on the,
　xxxiii, 19-20
Nassaro, Matteo del, xxxi, 318 note
Nathan, and David, xliv, 209; Lu-
　ther on, xxxvi, 347; Sidney on,
　xxvii, 27
Natick, Eliot on, xliii, 151
National Antipathies, Browne on,
　iii, 330; Pascal on, xlviii, 104,
　105; Washington on, xliii, 261-2
National Armies, Machiavelli on
　need of, xxxvi, 50
National Banks, Marshall on, xliii,
　223-4, 226-30, 238-40 (see also
　United States Bank)
National Debt, congressional right to
　contract a, xliii, 196 (2); validity
　of, 211; Washington on, 260-1
National Debts, Smith on, x, 574-90
National Property, regulation of,
　xliii, 197 (17)
National Wealth, Bacon on sources
　and distribution of, iii, 41-2
Nationality, Freeman on sentiment
　of, xxviii, 239-40
Nations, amorousness of different,
　xlviii, 426; as determined by lan-
　guage, xxviii, 261-82; origin of,
　254-58; Pascal on division of world
　into, xlviii, 104-5; Rousseau on
　division of mankind into, xxxiv,
　218; Rousseau on origin of, 207;
　splendor of, how judged, v, 452;
　Taine on differences of, xxxix,
　446-56; Washington on relations
　with foreign, xliii, 261-5; Wool-
　man on prosperity of, i, 240-1 (see
　also Races)
NATIONS, WEALTH OF, Smith's, x
NATIVITY, HYMN ON THE, iv, 7-15
Naturæ Encheiresis, xix, 74
Natural, and artificial, xxv, 344;
　definition of word, xi, 1
Natural History, Bacon on, xxxix,
　143-6; Darwin's theory, its effect
　on, xi, 524-6; defined by Hobbes,
　xxxiv, 373
Natural Laws, Descartes on, xxxiv,
　36-7; suppose an Intelligent Agent,
　xi, 1; Whewell on, 1

Natural Liberty, Hobbes on, xxxiv, 407 (see also Natural State)

Natural Objects, Burke on effects of, xxiv, 136

Natural Philosophy, Bacon on study of, iii, 129; Berkeley on, xxxvii, 296-7; Hobbes on, xxxiv, 376; Hume on limits of, xxxvii, 329, 355, 444; Huxley on study of, xxviii, 230; Kant on, xxxii, 317, 318; Locke on, xxxvii, 174-8; Milton on study of, iii, 253; Newton on, xxxix, 158-9; Socrates on, ii, 5, 90

Natural Price, defined, x, 58-9; market rice tends to equal, 61-2; tends to minimum, 65

Natural Principles, Pascal on, xlviii, 40 (92), 41 (94)

Natural Rectitude, Bentham on term, xxv, 46

Natural Religion (see Religion)

Natural Rights, Hobbes on, xxxiv, 407-8, 417-29

Natural Science, Bacon on, xxxix, 135; Helmholtz on, xxx, 181-3

Natural Selection, xi, 93-144; Aristotle's idea of, 9 note; difficulties of theory, 178-261, 289-95, 312-14, 333-4; meaning of, 77; progress of idea of, 11-24; recapitulation of theory, 499-509; theory of, briefly stated, 23

Natural State, advancement of man from, xxxii, 301, 309-10; Hobbes on, xxxiv, 402-6; Pope on the, xl, 437; Rousseau on man in, xxxiv, 168, 171-200, 208-9; Schiller on, xxxii, 291-3

Natural Style, Pascal on, xlviii, 16 (29)

Naturalization, Bacon on, iii, 80; Freeman on, xxviii, 256-7; of plants, xi, 125; under control of Congress, xliii, 196 (4); of words, Johnson on, xxxix, 198

Naturalness, Locke on, xxxvii, 48, 49

Nature, adaptations in, xi, 76-7, 90-1; art and, xxvii, 12; art and, Confucius on, xliv, 20 (16), 39 (8); art and, Goethe on, xxxix, 268-71, 274; art and, Hugo on, 385-6; art and, Whitman on, 424; Bacon on observation of, 148; Bacon on interpretation of, 139-46, 150-3; Berkeley on beauties of, xxxvii, 244-5; Berkeley on laws of, 267; Browne on, iii, 275 (12), 279 (16), 278 (15), 280; Browne on study of, 276-7, 278-80; Bryant on, xlii, 1262; Burke on study of, xxiv, 7-8; Burns on, vi, 72, 94, 338-9, 537, 539; Channing on study of, xxviii, 339-40; Channing on unity of, 335-6; Cicero on accordance with, ix, 72; Cicero on rebellion against, 47; Coleridge on

wisdom in, xxvii, 273; complexity of, xi, 85-92; contemners of, in Dante's HELL, xx, 47, 63-6; Darwin on, xi, 95, 213-15, 219; Descartes's method of studying, xxxiv, 51-3; economy of, xi, 159-60; education by, v, 7-8, 63, 200-1; xxviii, 158-9; Emerson on, v, 25, 26-7, 56, 93-4, 106-7, 174, 178, 179, 197-8, 200, 201, 250, 285, 312; xlii, 1301, 1304, 1309; Epictetus on, ii, 164 (130); God and, St. Augustine on, vii, 171-2; God and, Hume on, xxxvii, 419-28; God and, Pascal on, xlviii, 82 (229), 90-1, 140 (428), 194 (580), 330; God and, Raleigh on, xxxix, 109, 114-16; God and, Rousseau on, xxxiv, 260-1; God and, Tennyson on, xlii, 1038-9; Goethe on study of, xxxix, 264; Goethe on unity of, xix, 24; Goldsmith on gifts of, xli, 534; Hindu doctrine of, xlv, 862; Hume on knowledge of, xxxvii, 327-9, 330-1; Hunt on love of, xxvii, 308; institutions influenced by, v, 352; interdependence of, xxx, 176; lessons of, xlii, 1293-4; living according to, ii, 256 (74), 278 (2); xxxvi, 208, 209; Locke on works of, xxxvii, 174, 177; Lyell on laws of, xxxviii, 406; Marcus Aurelius on study of, ii, 266 (2); Milton on gifts of, iv, 65-7; Milton on unity and degrees of, 195; "never betrayed the heart that loved her," xli, 653; Newton on phenomena of, xxxix, 158-9; "non facit saltum," xi, 205-6, 217; offences against, vii, 41-2; opposition in, ii, 60-1; Pascal on, xlviii, 25-7, 40 (91), 49 (119-21); Penn on life next to, i, 359; Penn on study of, 337 (3), 338-9; pleasure the plan of, xli, 659; Pope on, xl, 425, 433-4, 436, 441; proverb on, v, 95; Raleigh on, xxxix, 114-16; Ruskin on our carelessness of, xxviii, 123-4; Shelley on love of, xli, 848; Thoreau on attractions and benefits of, xxviii, 407-38; Whitman on life with, xlii, 1494; "will out," xvii, 44; Wordsworth on love of, xli, 614-15, 652-3, 694

Nature, Essay on, Emerson's, v, 233-48

Nature, Goodness of, essay on, iii, 34-6

Nature, Hymn to the Spirit of, xli, 864

Nature in Men, Bacon's essay, iii, 101-3

Nature, The Influences of, xli, 622-9

Nature and the Poet, xli, 620-2

Nature's Law: A Poem, vi, 236-8

Naturlangsamkeit, v, 114

Naucratis, city of, xxxiii, 90

Naudin, M., on origin of species, xi, 16-17; on reversion, 328

Naunton, Sir Robert, xv, 385

Nausicaa, daughter of Alcinous, xxii, 85-93; farewell to Ulysses, 116; Ruskin on, xxviii, 146

Nausithous, son of Poseidon, xxii, 95; reference to, 85

Nautes, in the ÆNEID, xiii, 205-6

Navagero, Bernardo, quoted, xxviii, 468-9

Navarre, King of, at Hesdin, xxxviii, 22; at Rouen, 49-50

Navidad, city of, xliii, 26

Navigation, ancient, iii, 165, 168; Emerson on, v, 352; Hobbes on, xxxiv, 377; power of, necessary to civilization, x, 26-8

Navigation Act of Great Britain, x, 359-61

Navy, Harrison on need of a, xxxv, 379

Navy, United States commander-in-chief of, xliii, 201 (1); under the Confederation, 171, 174, 175; under Constitution, 197 (13, 14)

Naxos, famed for vintage, xiii, 135

Naylor, James, Woolman on, i, 305; worshipped as Christ, v, 243

Neaera, and Helios, xxii, 172; reference to, iv, 76

Nealces, Virgil on, xiii, 353

Neale, Dr., Dean of Westminster, xv, 379

Neale, J. M., translator of hymns, xlv, 554, 555, 556, 560

Nearchus, in POLYEUCTE, urges Polyeucte to be baptised, xxvi, 71-4; persuaded to go to temple with Polyeucte, 88-90; blamed by Pauline, 93; doomed by Felix, 95; his death, 98

Nearchus of Tarentum, ix, 60

NEARER, MY GOD, TO THEE, xlv, 582

Nebaioth, in the Wilderness, iv, 383

Nebridius, friend of St. Augustine, vii, 50, 95, 104, 131-2; conversion of, 147; on divination, 108

Nebuchadnezzar, Bunyan on, xv, 101; Daniel and, xx, 299 note 1; dream of, xlviii, 249-50; image of, iii, 14; the Jews and, xlviii, 217; reference to, xlv, 925 note

Nebulæ, composition of, xxx, 328

Necessaries, of life, defined, x, 541; Kempis on, vii, 302 (4); Shakespeare on, xlvi, 247; taxes on, x, 542, 544-7, 572-3 (see also Food-Supply)

Necessary, Marshall on word, xliii, 232

Necessary Connection, Idea of, xxxvii, 355-70, 373

Necessity, Burns on, vi, 388; Chaucer on, xl, 46; Dante on, xx, 212; defined by Kant, xxxii, 377, 386;

foreknowledge not, xx, 359 note 7; Goethe on, xix, 391; Hume on doctrine of, xxxvii, 371-91; makes vile things precious, xlvi, 252; Mill on doctrine of, xxv, 110-11; Pascal on belief in, xlviii, 40 (91), 83 (233); Sophocles on, viii, 277; the spur of knowledge, xxxiv, 181-2; the tyrant's plea, iv, 167

Necker, M., on assignats, xxiv, 389; Burke on, 353-4; on French finances, 266; on population of France, 276; on wealth of France, 277-8

Necos, king of Egypt, xxxiii, 81-2

Necromancy, Cellini on, xxxi, 133-6, 142; Hobbes on, xxxiv, 397

Neglect, excuses for, ii, 195 (12); a way of dishonoring, xxxiv, 378

NEGOTIATING, ESSAY ON, Bacon's, iii, 123-4

Negus, empire of, iv, 332

Nehemiah, and the Sabbath-breakers, xliii, 99-100, 100

NEIDPATH, THE MAID OF, by Campbell, xli, 796

NEIDPATH, THE MAID OF, by Scott, xli, 761-2

NEIDPATH CASTLE, LINES COMPOSED AT, xli, 695

Neighbors, Confucius on love of, xliv, 46 (24); Jesus on, 388 (29-37)

Neleus, birth of, xxii, 158; Chloris and, 159; Homer on, 45; Melampus and, 214

Nelson, in the Baltic, v, 372; xli, 798-9; courage of his sailors, v, 396; death of, 362; Emerson on, 380; expecting duty, 401; feat of doubling, 372; at Trafalgar, 431; want of fortune, 408

Nemesianus, on hounds, xxxv, 370

Nemesis, Emerson on doctrine of, v, 97; Herodotus's belief in, xxxiii, 4; in MANFRED, xviii, 425-6, 428-9; Pliny on, ix, 285 note

Nemetes, Tacitus on the, xxxiii, 111

Némglan, and Conaire, xlix, 215

Nemours, Duc de, at Metz, xxxviii, 24

Nennius, on Arthur, xxxii, 162-3

Neocles, father of Themistocles, xii, 5

Neo-Druidism, xxxii, 176

Neoptolemus, and Lycomedes, ix, 34

Neoptolemus, son of Achilles (see Pyrrhus)

Nepenthes, reference to, iv, 64

Nephelogetes, and Alaopolitanes, xxxvi, 229

Nepoios, Raleigh on the, xxxiii, 361-2

Nepos, Licinius, Pliny on, ix, 271

Nepos, Metellus, Cicero on, xii, 247-8

Nepos, friend of Pliny, ix, 223, 253

Nepos, the prætor, decree of, ix, 290-1

Nepos, Proconsul of Spain, and Cæsar, xii, 293

Neptune, in the ÆNEID, xiii, 79-81, 208-9; Milton on, iv, 22, 47, 69; in sack of Troy, xiii, 124

Neptune, the planet, discovery of, xxx, 22

Nereids, reference to the, xiii, 81

Nereus, references to, iv, 68, 69; xiii, 117

Neri, beginning of party, xx, 135 note 4; faction in Florence, 27 note 3, 103-4 and notes

Neri, St. Philip, and the nun, v, 298

Nerius, Cn., informer, ix, 102

Nero, Drusus, ix, 242 note 2

Nero, Emperor, Apollonius on, iii, 51; Carlyle on death of, v, 334; Demetrius and, ii, 132 (45); descent of, xii, 403; harp of, iii, 51; Marcus Aurelius on, ii, 212 (16); Pliny on reign of, ix, 335, 336-7; as a poet, xviii, 15-16; Rome burned by, xl, 49; Spintrian recreations of, iii, 335

Nero, Francesco del, xxxi, 113 note 2

Nero, Tiberius, and Gabinius, ix, 120

Nerva, edict of, ix, 410; Pliny on, 221, 331; Trajan and, 374 note 2

Nervians, Tacitus on the, xxxiii, 111

Nervii, Cæsar's campaign against the, xii, 292

Nesle, Castle of, xxxi, 341 note 2

Nessus, Dante on, xx, 52 and note

Nestor, Achilles and, xxii, 332; birth of, 159; Cicero on, ix, 56-7; in the ODYSSEY, xii, 35-47

Netherlands, Bacon on government of, iii, 37; Browne on success of the, 281-2; under Charles V, xix, 246; manufactures of the, iii, 42; under Margaret of Parma, xix, 251-2; periodic returns in, iii, 144; Philip II and the, minin, 91-3; revolt of the, Mill on, xxv, 11

Nethersole, Sir Francis, xv, 385

Neufville, Nicholas de, xxxi, 293 note

Neuri, Herodotus on the, xlix, 287 note

Neuter Insects, Darwin on, xi, 290-5; sterility of, how developed, 313

Neutrality, Machiavelli on, xxxvi, 76-78; Pascal on, xlviii, 315 (899); Penn on, i, 374-5; Washington on policy of, xliii, 263-4, 265-6

NEVER THE TIME AND THE PLACE, xlii, 1154

Nevers, Duke of, and Mantua, xxi, 81, 454-5, 487

Nevil, Dr., and George Herbert, xv, 379, 384

Nevill, Sir Robert, xxxv, 23

Neville, Constance, in SHE STOOPS TO CONQUER, with Kate Hardcastle, xviii, 208-9; with Hastings at Hardcastle's, 222-3; carries on joke with Marlow, 224; with Tony Lumpkin, 228, 229-30; Tony's description of, 231; tries to get her jewels, 235-7; plans to elope, 243; with Tony in elopement plot, 250-1; Tony's letter and, 252-3; denounces Tony, 254; ordered to aunt's by Mrs. Hardcastle, 253, 255-6; refuses to elope, 264; wins consent to marry Hastings, 268-9

New Academy, xii, 227 note

New Albion, Drake's, xxxiii, 222-6

NEW ATLANTIS, Bacon's, iii, 153-91; editorial remarks on, 152; 1, 48

New Atlantis, acoustics in, iii, 187; air and water machines, 188; ancient commerce of, 165-6, 168-9; ancient expeditions against, 166-7; arrival at, 153-7; Christianity in, 161-3; dress in, 155, 159, 174, 179-80, 181; Feast of Family in, 172-6; food in, 158, 185; health, care of, in, 156, 183; instruments of warfare in, 188; Jews in, 176; jugglery in, 188-9; machines and engines in, 188; manufactures in, 186; marriage in, 177-9; medicine in, 183-6; mineralogy in, 187; optics in, 186-7; production of heat in, 186; production of odors and tastes, 187-8; scientific expeditions from, 171; self-sufficiency of, 168-9; Solomon's House in, 170 (see further Solomon's House); Stranger's House in, 157-8; treatment of visitors in, 159-60, 169-70; why unknown, 164 et seq.

NEW-BORN CHILD, ON PARENT KNEES A, xli, 593

New Caledonia, barrier-reef of, xxix, 499, 503

New England, historical documents of early, xliii, 62-112, 147-56

New England Courant, i, 3, 20, 21-22

NEW ENGLAND REFORMERS, v, 263-81

NEW FORCERS OF CONSCIENCE UNDER LONG PARLIAMENT, iv, 82-3

Newfoundland, American rights in fisheries of, xliii, 188; colonization of, xxxiii, 270; description of, 290-5; exploration of coast, 296-7; Hayes on banks of, 284

NEWFOUNDLAND, GILBERT'S VOYAGE TO, xxxiii, 271-308

New Jersey, settlement of, i, 288; slaves in, 186 note

New Lights, party of, vi, 16; Burns on, 95-6

New South Wales, Darwin on, xxix, 457-70

NEW TESTAMENT, SELECTED BOOKS
FROM, xliv, 355-495, xlv
New Testament, adversity the blessing of, iii, 17; corruption of, St.
Augustine on, vii, 79; Goethe on,
xix, 49-50; Lessing on the, xxxii,
209-11; Luther on, xxxvi, 368;
Mill on, xxv, 252; Pascal on,
xlviii, 218, 225 (666), 266 (740),
293 (835), 304 (852); Rousseau
on the, xxxiv, 310-12 (see also
Gospel)
NEW WAY TO PAY OLD DEBTS, xlvii,
819-99; remarks on, 818
New Year's Day, why celebrated,
xv, 408
NEW YEAR'S DAY: A SKETCH, vi,
394-6
New Zealand, Darwin on, xxix, 440-
54; fauna and flora of, xi, 387;
ferns in, xxix, 260; as an oceanic
island, xi, 434; species of, 421,
432, 441
New Zealanders, health of the, v, 85
Newby, Samuel, i, 222
Newcomb, Simon, sketch of life and
works, xxx, 324; EXTENT OF THE
UNIVERSE, 325-36
Newlights, American society called,
i, 215
Newman, Col., on humble-bees, xi,
88
Newman, John Henry, Call of David
quoted, xxviii, 176; HYMN by,
xlv, 581; IDEA OF A UNIVERSITY,
xxviii, 31-62; sketch of life and
works, 30
Newport, Magdalen, mother of George
Herbert, xv, 377-8, 379-83, 389,
391-2; letter to, 393-5; death, 396
News, Arabian proverb on, xvi, 167;
evil and good, iv, 457; suspense
in, 458
NEWS, LASSIES, NEWS, vi, 580
Newspapers, American, i, 20; Bentham on power of, xxvii, 241;
Carlyle on writing for, xxv, 463;
Ruskin on, xxviii, 101; Wordsworth on taxation of, v, 336
Newton, Sir Isaac, Burke on, xxiv,
108; Cartesian vortices disproved
by, xxxiv, 116-17; chronology of,
129-33; Emerson on, v, 70; gravitation, universal, discovered by,
xxxiv, 117-23; on gravitation, v,
321; xxx, 315-18; xxxvii, 365
note; Hazlitt on, xxvii, 281-2; the
heliocentric theory and, xxxix, 55
note; honors paid him, xxxiv, 155;
law of conservation and, xxx, 183;
Leibnitz on, xi, 520; life and
works, xxxix, 157 note; Locke on,
xxxvii, 178; mathematical discoveries of, xxxiv, 127-9; optics, discoveries in, 124-7; Pepys and,
xxviii, 316; on polarity in nature, v, 15; PREFACE TO Principia,

xxxix, 157-9; remarks on, l, 45;
Rousseau on, xxxiv, 256; spec-
trum discovered by, xxx, 274; on
tides, 294-5; Unitarianism and,
xxxiv, 84, 85; Voltaire on, 99,
110-15; Warden of Mint, 155;
Wordsworth on theory of, v, 338
Newton, Gen. John, at Gettysburg,
xliii, 358, 380, 393; Haskell on,
382
Newton, Sir John, xxxv, 66, 67-8,
69
New York, Whitman on, xlii, 1495-
1496
Nia, the waiter, xlix, 252
Niata Cattle, xxix, 158-60
Nibbio, in THE BETROTHED, xxi, 338
341-4, 348-50
Niblung, son of Hogni, xlix, 374
Niblungs, names of the, xlix, 270
NIBLUNGS AND VOLSUNGS, story of,
xlix, 265-381
Nicæa, Council of, xxxvi, 286, 304
Nicagoras, xii, 14
Nicandra, priestess of Dodona,
xxxiii, 32
Nicanor, xliv, 441 (5)
Nicely, Miss, marriage of, xviii, 119-
20
Nicephorius, steward of Q. Cicero,
ix, 116
Niceta, on motion of the earth,
xxxix, 58
Niceta of Remisiana, TE DEUM, xlv,
558
Nicety, is depraved modesty, xviii,
12
Nicholas, the gift of, xx, 227 note 3
Nicholas III, in Dante's HELL, xx,
81-2
Nicholas, in TWO YEARS BEFORE THE
MAST, xxiii, 148-9
Nicholas, the barber, in DON QUIX-
OTE, xiv, 48, 51-8, 241-9, 291-2,
316-17
Nicholas, Harry, xlvii, 634 note 10
Nichols, Joseph, i, 287
Nichols, Philip, editor of DRAKE
REVIVED, xxxiii, 127
Nichomedes, the mastiff of, xxxv,
373
Nicias, Alcibiades and, xii, 87, 119-
22; Cicero on, ix, 110; Hyper-
bolus and, xii, 120; peace of, 121;
power of, 119; in Sicilian expedi-
tion, 125, 126, 128, 130
Nicias, in Mandragola, xxvii, 403-4
Nicodemus, the Jew, on Jesus, xlviii,
285 (808), 292 (829)
Nicodemus, the Messenian, fickleness
of, xii, 207-8
Nicogenes, and Themistocles, xii,
28-9
NICOL, WILLIAM, EPITAPH FOR, vi,
278
Nicol Prism, the, xxx, 278
Nicolaüs of Antioch, xliv, 441 (5)

Nicomachus, Aristophanes on, viii, 465-6
Nicomedia, aqueduct of, ix, 397-8; fire at, 396; lake near, 401, 411-12; temple at, 405
Nicopolis, school of Epictetus at, ii, 116
Nicors, xlix, 17 note 1, 46
Nicostratus, Plato on, ii, 21
Nidau, Earl, at Poitiers, xxxv, 47
Niépce, discoverer of actinism, xxviii, 431
Nieuwentheit, Rousseau on, xxxiv, 260
Niger, name of, xii, 162
Niger, rival of Severus, xxxvi, 67-8
Night, Byron on beauties of, xviii, 439; Carlyle on, xxv, 347; Dryden's description of, xxxix, 340 note; Habington on, xl, 258; Milton on, iv, 133, 135, 173, 184, 315-16; Mohammed on the, xlv, 891; patroness of grief, iv, 25 (5); Shakespeare on, xl, 282; xlvi, 149; terrors, why greater at, xxiv, 52
Night, by Blake, xli, 599-601
Night, To the, by Shelley, xli, 854-5
Night, To, by White, xli, 938
Night, At the Mid Hour of, xli, 843
Night, Hymn to the, xlii, 1318-19
Night-hag, Milton on the, iv, 127
Nightingale, Æschylus on the, viii, 46-7; Homer on the, xxii, 281; Milton on the, iv, 36, 52, 172, 241; Swinburne on the, xlii, 1250
Nightingale and Laborer, fable of, xvii, 34
Nightingale, Ode to a, by Keats, xli, 899
Nightingale, Sonnet to the, Milton's, iv, 39-40
Nightingale, The, by Barnfield, xl, 290
Nightingale, The, story of, xvii, 320-9
Night-Watchers, Psalm of, xliv, 319
Nigidius, Publius, friend of Cicero, xii, 241-2
Nigrinus, counsel against Varenus, ix, 314
Nihilism, philosophy of, xix, 53; philosophical, Buddha, on, xlv, 681
Nile, Æschylus on the, viii, 184; breezes, why without, xxxiii, 17; delta of the, 12; Egypt a gift of the, 7, 9-11; Egyptian civilization due to, x, 27; embankments of, made by Min, xxxiii, 49; fish of the, 46-7; Lang on the, 347; Milton on the, iv, 349; mouths of the, xxxiii, 13; overflows of the, 14, 48; rise of the, cause of, 14-

16; sacred animals of the, 38; sources of the, 17-21
Nimeguen, Peace of, x, 364
Nimrod, Burns on, vi, 433; in Dante's Hell, xx, 131; the mighty hunter, iv, 346; pictured in Purgatory, xx, 194
Nine Worthies, the, xxxix, 21-2
Ninety-Five Theses, Luther's, xxxvi, 261-73; remarks on, 260
Ninevah, Milton on kingdom of, iv, 395
Ning Wu, xliv, 17 note 9
Nino di Gallura, (see Gallura, Nino di)
Ninus, Raleigh on, xxxix, 118
Niobe, Dante on, xx, 194; daughter of Tantalus, viii, 269
Niphæus, death of, xiii, 346
Niphates, Satan alights first on, iv, 156
Nirvana, attainment of, xlv, 754-5; Buddha on, 736-7; Buddha's passage into, 660-1; Buddha's search for, 592-4; the craving for, 731; Hindu doctrine of, 827
Nisroch, in Paradise Lost, iv, 218
Nisus, in the Æneid, xiii, 192-4; Dante on, xx, 8; Euryalis and, xiii, 302-12; Euryalis and, Sidney on, xxvii, 20
Nisus of Dulichmin, xxii, 258
Nith, The Banks of, vi, 362
Nithsdale's Welcome Hame, vi, 444
Nitocris, queen of Egypt, xxxiii, 49-50
Nitrate of Silver, under voltaic current, xxx, 134 note
Nitrogen, in air, xxx, 149-50; binoxide of, 43 note; weight of, 151
Niuthones, Tacitus on the, xxxiii, 118
No Churchman Am I, vi, 38-9
No, My Own Love, xlii, 926
Noah, Adam's vision of, iv, 339-45; Browne on story of, iii, 287; Jesus on days of, xliv, 406 (26-7); Kempis on, vii, 350 (4); Mohammed on, xlv, 916, 925; Pascal on, xlviii, 205, 220 (644); progeny of, iv, 346; taken from Limbo by Christ, xx, 18; wife of, xlv, 1007
Noailles, Count of, Burke on, xxiv, 440
Noailles, family of, xxiv, 262
Nobili, Antonio de', xxxi, 426 note
Nobility, Bacon on the, iii, 36-7, 53-4; Browne on the true, 325; Burke on a, xxiv, 287; Burns on, vi, 547, 557; Goldsmith on, xli, 522-3; Hobbes on, xxxiv, 375; Keppel on a, xxiv, 439-40; Machiavelli on a, xxxvi, 17, 34-6; More on, 211; origin of hereditary, xxxiv, 226-7; Pascal on, xlviii,

384, 385, 386-8; titles of, forbidden in United States, xliii, 170, 198 (8, 10); of Vanity Fair, xv, 100

Noble, C., on rhododendrons, xi, 303

NOBLE EARL'S PICTURE, VERSES FOR A, vi, 272-3

NOBLE LORD, LETTER TO A, xxiv, 399-443

NOBLE NATURE, THE, xl, 298

Noddy, Darwin on the, xxix, 20

Nodier, on school of Alexandria, xxxix, 385

Noël, Father, on light, xlviii, 432 note

Noëmon, son of Phronius, in the ODYSSEY, xxii, 32, 64-5

No-good, Mr., in PILGRIM'S PROGRESS, xv, 101-2

No-heart, in PILGRIM'S PROGRESS, xv, 220

Noise, much, little outcome, xvii, 16

NOISY POLEMIC, EPITAPH ON A, vi, 62

Nollet, Abbe, theory of electricity, i, 154-5

Nombre de Dios, account of expedition against, xxxiii, 126-7, 134-46; taking of, 235

Nominalism, Buddha on, xlv, 681

Nominations, in early Connecticut, xliii, 65

Nomphon, the sachem, xliii, 154

Non-combatants, agreement with Mexico concerning, xliii, 324-5

Non-conformists, called atheists, iii, 46

Non-conformity, of heroism, v, 133; of infancy, 65; Mill on, xxv, 148-9, 249-52, 272-3; Milton on, iii, 235-6; Montaigne on, xxxii, 42; necessary to manhood, v, 66-7; penalty of, 69-70; popular ideas of, 79; power of, 197; source of sanctity, 200; Whitman on, xxxix, 419; (see also Individuality)

Non-existence, Buddha on, xlv, 592, 677

Nonianus, and Claudius, ix, 208

Nonius, story of, xii, 258

Non-resistance, Emerson on, v, 479

Nonsuits, in Massachusetts, xliii, 74-75

NOON, SILENT, xlii, 1226

Norcia, Francesco da (see Fusconi)

Norfolk, 3d Duke of, imprisonment of, xxxix, 81; Thomas More and, xxxvi, 116-17, 122, 125-6, 131

Norfolk, Dukedom of, v, 421

Noriego, Senor, xxiii, 247, 404

Norman Conquest, Vane on the, xliii, 129

Norman Islands, Freeman on, xxviii, 263-4

Normanby, Marquis of, dedication to, xiii, 5-73

Normandy, Edward III's invasion of, xxxv, 6-10, 10-14; Machiavelli on, xxxvi, 9-10

Normandy, Duke of, at Poitiers, xxxv, 47

Normans, eating of the, xxxv, 302; Emerson on the, v, 358-9; Renan on the, xxxii, 168

Nornir, northern fates, xlix, 291 note, 314

Norris, Mr., speaker of Penn. Assembly, i, 120, 129

Norris of Bemerton, xxxix, 337

North, Goethe on the, xix, 69; Tennyson on the, xlii, 1005

North, Lord, Burke and, xxiv, 6; Burke on, 408

North America, Asia formerly united to, xxix, 144-5; glacial period in, xi, 418; productions of, related to European, 416-17, 419; zoology of, 143-4, 188; zoology of, changes in, xxix, 188; zoology of, compared with South America, 143-4

NORTH-EAST WIND, ODE TO THE, xlii, 1103

Northampton, Earl of, xxxv, 23, 26

Northburgh, Michael of, xxxv, 9 note, 11 note

Northern Hemisphere, climate of, xxix, 265

Northmen, Charlemagne and the, v, 355; government and people, 356-7

Northumberland, Earl of, xl, 95 (see Percy)

Norway, early depopulation of, v, 358; Freeman on, xxviii, 268

Nostradamus, reference to, xix, 23

Notes (see Annotations)

NOTHING, STANZAS ON, vi, 233-4

Not-right, Mr., in PILGRIM'S PROGRESS, xv, 277

Nottingham, Samuel, i, 192

Nourishment, Pascal on, xlviii, 122 (356)

Novello, Alessandro, xx, 323 note 18

Novello, Frederic, xx, 168 note 4

Novello, Guido, xx, 44 note 12

Novels, Burns on, vi, 61; Fielding on, xxxix, 184-90; Ruskin on, xxviii, 155-6

Novelty, Bacon on, iii, 143; human thirst for, xxiv, 29-30; Pascal on, xlviii, 37; wonder and, xlviii, 40 (90)

Novum Organum, Bacon's, iii, 4

NOVUM ORGANUM, PREFACE TO, xxxix, 150-4

NOW SLEEPS THE CRIMSON PETAL, xlii, 1004

NOW THANK WE ALL OUR GOD, xlv, 571

Nowell, Master, xxxv, 400

NOX NOCTI INDICAT SCIENTIAM, xl, 258-9

Numa, Bacon on, iii, 69; Hobbes on, xxxiv, 397; intercalary month of, xii, 323; on religious processions, 176; Virgil on, xiii, 239

Numa, in the ÆNEID, xiii, 346

Numantia, destruction of, xxxvi, 19

Numanus, death of, xiii, 317-19

Numbers, in battle, iii, 78; xliii, 364; effect of, in struggle for existence, xi, 84-5; Emerson on our respect for, v, 87; grandeur in, xxiv, 68; Hobbes on, xxxiv, 338-9; Pascal on, xlviii, 435-7; Prometheus as inventor of, viii, 172

Numitor, and Maeon, xiii, 338

Nun, Chaucer's, xl, 14-15

NUN'S PRIEST'S TALE, xl, 35-51; remarks on, 10; source of, xxxix, 168 note

NUR-ED-DIN, STORY OF, xvi, 203-41

NURSE AND WOLF, fable of, xvii, 29

NURSE'S SONG, xli, 604-5

NYMPH'S SONG TO HYLAS, xlii, 1241, 1242

NYMPH'S PASSION, A, xl, 300-1

Nymphs, references to, iv, 13 (20), 38

Nyseian Isle, iv, 164

Oak, Plutarch on the, xii, 154; species of, xi, 66-7

Oateley, Sir Roger, in SHOEMAKER'S HOLIDAY, with Lincoln, xlvii, 447-9; with Rowland Lacy, 449; with Hammon and daughter, 464, 471, 472-3; with Eyre, 473-4; learns Rowland Lacy is in London, 474; with Eyre at Old Ford, 479-82; finds Hans with Rose, 492; visited by Lincoln, 493-4; learns flight of Rose, 494; with Firk, 494-6; plans to stop wedding, 497; mistakes wedding, 502-4; hears daughter married, 504; with the king, 511-12

Oateley, Rose, in SHOEMAKER'S HOLIDAY, in love with Rowland Lacy, xlvii, 447-8; in the garden, her lament, 454-5; with Sybil, 455-6; the hunters and, 462-4; Hammon and, 471-3; with Eyre and wife, 481; discovers Rowland as Hans, 481-2; with Rowland, as Hans, 491-3; her flight, 494; with Rowland at Eyre's, 498-9, her marriage, 504; pardoned by king, 509; marriage confirmed, 511-12

Oaths, are but tools to deceive, xxvi, 111; Brynhild on, xlix, 325, 393; continuity of law by, xxvii, 245-7; Epictetus on, ii, 175 (166); Hobbes on, xxxiv, 416-17; Luther on sanctity of, xxxvi, 332-3; Mohammed on, xlv, 1018; Quaker attitude toward, xxxiv, 68-9; shall not enforce the wrong, viii, 132

Oaths of Office, Marshall on, xliii, 233-4

Oball, son of Conaire, xlix, 237-8

Obedience, Confucius on, xliv, 7 (5); is honor, xxxiv, 7; Kempis on, vii, 221, 285; Locke on, in children, xxxvii, 34-6, 64-6; Milton on, of subjects, iv, 211; Penn on, to parents, i, 355-6; Taine on sentiments of, xxxix, 454-5

Oberon, in FAUST, xix, 177

Obizzo of Este, Dante on, xx, 53 and note 9, 76 note 2

Object, and sensation, xxxvii, 236

Objects, two kinds of, xxxvii, 236

Obligation, defined by Kant, xxxii, 343, 370; epigram on, xl, 408; Franklin on, from favors, i, 102; Hobbes on, xxxiv, 386; Machiavelli on, xxxvi, 39; Pliny on, ix, 209; Woolman on, from gifts, i, 209

Oblin, son of Conaire, xlix, 237-8

Oblivion, Lowell on, xlii, 1465; Marcus Aurelius on, ii, 219 (33), 248 (21)

Obscenity, Shelley on, xxvii, 358

Obscurity, brings safety, xvii, 26; Confucius on, xliv, 6 (16), 50 (32); Greene on, xl, 289; Hobbes on, why dishonorable, xxxiv, 381; Hume on, xxxvii, 310; more affecting than clearness, xxiv, 53-7; terror caused by, 50-3

Observation, Confucius on, xliv, 8 (18), 24 (27); Goethe on, xxxix, 265, 269; misuse of, xii, 36; necessary to poets, xxxix, 312; unhonored task of, v, 16

Obsolete Words, Johnson on, xxxix, 199, 213-14

Obstacles, Channing on value of, xxviii, 325; Marcus Aurelius on, ii, 263 (41), 264 (47)

Obstinacy, constancy and, iii, 290; Epictetus on, in opinion, ii, 124 (23), 132 (47), 142 (69); Locke on, xxxvii, 64, 65, 66, 67, 70, 72; Penn on, in opinion, i, 404 (155-8)

Obstinate, in PILGRIM'S PROGRESS, xv, 15-17

Occam, Newman on, xxviii, 48

Occasion, Arabian verse on, iii, 59; Milton on awaiting, iv, 392-3

Occupation, Kempis on, vii, 232 (4); necessary to happiness, xlviii, 143

Occupations, Plutarch on mean, xii, 37

Ocean, currents of the, due to wind, xxx, 291; Darwin on the, xi, 362; xxix, 528-9; Geikie on floor of the, xxx, 345-7; organic discoloration of the, xxix, 25-8; Socrates's idea of, ii, 109; a sinking area, xxix, 506

Ocean Nymphs, Chorus of (see PROMETHEUS BOUND)

Oceanus, Herodotus on river, xxxiii,

15; Homer on, xxii, 152; Milton
on, iv, 69 (see also Okeanos)
Ochre, Widow, in SCHOOL FOR
SCANDAL, xviii, 129-30
Ockley, Simon, *History of Saracens,*
v, 127
Ocnus, ally of Æneas, xiii, 333
Octavia, Antony's wife, xii, 357-8,
359, 361, 362, 376, 377, 380; children of, 403; Virgil and, xiii, 33
Octavia, in ALL FOR LOVE, xviii,
11-12; scene with Antony, 57-61;
with Cleopatra, 63-4; discovers
Dolabella with Cleopatra, 72-3;
tells Antony, 74-5; farewell to
Antony, 77-8
Octavius, at Actium, xii, 386; xiii,
294-5; Actium, triumph after,
296; Antony and, xii, 263, 265,
345-6, 359, 361-2, 378; Antony,
war with, 380-9, 393, 394-5, 397;
Cæsar's heir, 264; Cæsarion killed
by, 399; Cicero and, 263-5, 268;
xlvi, 25; Cicero on, ix, 186; clemency to Alexandria, xii, 398;
Cleopatra and, 392-3, 397, 399-
400; xviii, 47-8; Dolabella and,
52; Dryden on, 39-40, 56; Empire
of, xii, 357; prophecy of his greatness, 263-4; in Rome, 351; in
second triumvirate, 347-9; in war
with republicans, 349-50 (see also
Augustus)
Octavius, the African, xii, 247
Octavius, Caius at Cæsar's death, xii,
330
Octavius, Cnæus, ix, 137-8
Octavius, Marcus, at Actium, xii,
386
October Sixth, Burke on, xxiv, 219-
29
Octopus, habits of the, xxix, 17-18
Oddrun, and Gunnar, xlix, 358,
408-9
ODDRUN, THE LAMENT OF, xlix, 457-
64; remarks on LAMENT, 268
Ode, Hugo on the, xxxix, 357, 370,
371, 372
ODE, by O'Shaughnessy, xlii, 1246
ODE IN IMITATION OF ALCÆUS, xli,
592-3
ODE ON INTIMATIONS OF IMMORTAL-
ITY, xli, 609; Emerson on, v, 485
ODE, WRITTEN IN MDCXLVI, xli,
488
Oderigi, in Dante's PURGATORY, xx,
191 and note 2
Odeum, of Athens, xii, 52
O DEUS, EGO AMO TE, xlv, 568-9
Odin, in the EDDA, xlix, 385, 388,
455 note; Emerson on, v, 357;
in the VOLSUNGA SAGA, xlix, 275;
276, 277, 279 note, 296 note, 298
note, 303, 305, 306, 321, 380
note 1
Odiousness, contrasted with sublimity, xxiv, 76

Odors, Berkeley on, xxxvii, 212, 219
Odysseus (Ulysses), Achilles and,
xxii, 106; Æneas and, xxxix, 165;
Æolus and, xxii, 136-8; Agamemnon on, viii, 35; Aias and, xxii,
166; Alcinous and, 94-107, 114-16,
118-20; Amphinomus and, 258-9;
Antinous and, 248-51; Athene and,
40, 187-92; as beggar, 238, 243-4,
247-8; the boar and, 278-9; bow
of, 295-6, 302-6; in Calypso's isle,
9, 10, 62-3, 75-8; Charybdis and,
174-5, 180; Charybdis and, Milton on, iv, 136; the Cicones and,
xxii, 121; in Circe's island, 140-9,
180; Circe's prophecy for, 169-72;
Ctesippus and, 292; the Cyclops
and, 122-35; Cyclops and, Virgil
on, xiii, 152; Dante on, xx, 110-
12 and note 7; Demodocus and,
xxii, 117; dog of, 246; dog of,
Pliny on, ix, 370 note; Don Quixote on, xiv, 224; Eumæus, swineherd of, xxii, 193-207, 216-21, 288-
90, 300-1; Eurycleia recognizes,
276-80; Eurymachus and, 264-6;
faithful servants received by, 320;
in the games, 108-10; in Germany,
xxxiii, 96; on God, ii, 126 (28);
Hades, his visit to, xxii, 149-68;
in island of Helios, 175-9; Hermes
and, iv, 63; Iphitus and, xxii,
295-6; Irus and, 255-8; Ithaca,
arrival in, 184, 186-7; Laertes and,
336-42; at Læstrygonia, 138-9;
Lotus-eaters and, 122 (see Lotos-
eaters); the mantle and, 206; Melantho and, 263-4; Milton on, iv,
22, 264; Minerva and, xiii, 109;
named by Autolycus, xxii, 278;
Nausicaa and, 88-93; Nestor on,
37, 38; omens of his success, 286-
7; Palamedes and, xiii, 106; Penelope and, xxii, 253-4, 268-76,
281-2, 323-30; Penelope and, Bacon
on, iii, 23; in Phæacia, xxii, 82-
4; Phæacia, departure from, 181-
3; Philomeleides and, 57; Pliny
on, ix, 218 note 9; Poseidon and,
xxii, 11; return home decreed by
Zeus, 72-4; righteousness of, 66;
at Scylla and Charybdis, 174-5;
Shelley on Homer's, xxvii, 352-3;
Sidney on, 20; the Sirens and,
xxii, 173-4; the siren and, Dante
on, xx, 223 note 4; Socrates on,
ii, 28; Spenser on, xxxix, 65; in
the storm, xxii, 78-81; Telemachus
and, 224-32, 291; in Troy, 118; in
Troy as a beggar, 54-5; in Trojan
horse, xiii, 112; xxii, 55; Virgil
on wanderings of, xiii, 370; the
wooers and, xxii, 284-5, 307-
17; wooers' friends and, 344-6;
wrecked, 179-80 (see also Ulysses)
ODYSSEY, Homer's, xxii; ÆNEID compared with, xiii, 40; xxxix, 165;

Burke on, xxiv, 35; editor's remarks on, l, 19; lines on, by Lang, xxii, 7; reference to the, iv, 264
Œbalus, ally of Turnus, xiii, 268-9
ŒDIPUS THE KING, viii, 197-242; Æschylus's supposed criticism of, 456; Shelley on, xviii, 276
Œdipus, birth of, viii, 231-2; blinds himself, 235; Creon and, 213-16; daughters of, 240-1; elected king of Corinth, 224; exile of, 241; exposed to death by father, 218; father's death learned by, 218-19; grief of, 223-4; Homer on, xxii, 159; Laius's murderer sought by, viii, 201, 204-5; life related by, 220-1; marriage to wife of Laius, 205; called Œdipodes, xxii, 159; in plague of the city, viii, 197-9; Polybus and, 225-9; Prynne on tragedies on, xxxiv, 157; remorse of, viii, 236-8; Sidney on example of, xxvii, 20; the sphinx and, iv, 414; viii, 209, 212; Teiresias denounces, 206-11; Voltaire on, xxxix, 382
Œnone, in PHÆDRA, with Phædra, learns her love, xxvi, 130-6; urges Phædra to live, 138-9, 147; prevents Phædra's death, 151; urges Phædra to assume throne, 153-5; announces Theseus's return, 156; urges Phædra to accuse Hippolytus, 158-9; accuses Hippolytus, 162-4; hears Hippolytus in love with Aricia, 170-2; denounced by Phædra, 173-4; kills herself, 179
ŒNONE AND PARIS, xl, 221
Offa, reference to, xlix, 60
Offences, against nature and custom, vii, 41-2; Jesus on, xliv, 404 (1-2)
Offenders, patience toward, ii, 293 (18)
Office (see Public Office)
Office Work, for literary workers, xxv, 578
Officials, Bacon's advice to, iii, 31; Bentham on criticism of, xxvii, 252-54; corruption of, inevitable under property system, xxxvi, 178; expences of, x, 486-7; legal responsibility of, xxvii, 247-8; private offences of, xliii, 79 (61); Penn on public, i, 370-4 (see also Public Office)
Offspring, universal love of, xl, 436
Og, king of Bashan, xliv, 320 (11); Milton on, iv, 17
Ogier, the Dane, xlix, 123, 125, 203
Ogle, Mrs., in SCHOOL FOR SCANDAL, xviii, 131-2
Ogygia, isle of Calypso, xxii, 100
O'Hagan, J., translator of DIES IRÆ, xlv, 563; translator of ROLAND, xlix, 95
O'Higgins, family of, in Chili, xxix, 369

Ohlenschlager, on Danish readers, v, 379
Ohod, battle of, xlv, 972 note, 976 note
Ohtere, son of Ongentheow, xlix, 87; sons of, 72, 73
Oicles, son of Antiphates, xxii, 214
Oil, as vehicle of taste, xxiv, 128
Okeanos, Æschylus on, viii, 161; in PROMETHEUS BOUND, 166-9
O'Kearney, Nicholas, xlix, 210
Oken, Emerson on, v, 183
Olaf, and Eyvind, v, 286
Olaf Tryggvason, and Leif Ericsson, xliii, 5
OLD AGE, ON, by Cicero, ix, 45-77; remarks on treatise, 6, 8
Old Age, Æschylus on, viii, 8; Aristophanes on, 407; beauty of, iii, 112; Browne on, 306-7; Browning on, xlii, 1148, 1151; Buddha on, xlv, 678; Burns on, vi, 177, 538; childishness of, xix, 14; Coleridge on, xli, 719-20; Collins's wish for, 607; comeliness of, ii, 207 (2); envy of, iii, 24; Goldsmith on best, xli, 524; Kingsley on, xlii, 1103; messenger of death, xlv, 701; Mill on happiness in, xxv, 36-7; Milton on, iv, 336; Pliny on order in, ix, 240; Rousseau on, xxxiv, 226; Shakespeare on, xl, 273; talkativeness of, i, 6; Wordsworth on, xli, 630
OLD AGE AND YOUTH, ESSAY ON, Bacon's, iii, 110-11
OLD CLOAK, THE, xl, 190-2
OLD FAMILIAR FACES, xli, 752
OLD IRONSIDES, xlii, 1443; remarks on, xxxviii, 234
OLD MAN AND DEATH, fable of, xvii, 40
Old Man of the Sea, the, xvi, 289-92
OLD MARLBOROUGH ROAD, xxviii, 414-15
OLD STOIC, THE, xlii, 1157
OLD SWEETHEART, LINES TO AN, vi, 231
OLD TESTAMENT, BOOKS FROM, xliv, 71-354
Old Testament, Calvin on the, xxxix, 52; Jesus on, xliv, 403 (16); Lessing on, xxxii, 199-207; Luther on, xxxvi, 367; Mill on, xxv, 252; miracles of, xlviii, 291 (827), 293 (835), 304 (852); Mohammed on, xlv, 1013; Pascal on, xlviii, 210, 211, 213 (631), 214-15, 218-23, 225 (666), 226 (670), 230, 231, 232-3, 235 (691), 236, 248 (714-36), 266 (740); Pascal on prophecies of, 190-2, 193 (576, 578); prosperity the blessing of, iii, 17
OLD WOMAN AND WINE-JAR, fable of, xvii, 45

Oldfield, Mrs., the actress, xxxiv, 156

Oldmixon, on the exiled princes, xxvii, 182

Oley, Barnabas, xv, 404

Olimpio, in THE CENCI, xviii, 317, 325, 326-7, 328, 331

Oliphant, Carolina, peoms by, xli, 573-80

Oliphant, Rev. James, Burns on, vi, 171

Oliva, Count, Egmont on, xix, 275-6

Olivares, Count D', xxi, 81

Oliver, friend of Roland, xlix, 96 (see also Olivier)

Oliver, Andrew, Franklin and, i, 4

Oliverotto of Fermo, xxxvi, 31-3

Olivier, in SONG OF ROLAND, xlix, 100, 103, 105; Ganelon on, 115, 116, 117; with Roland in return, 125, 132; at Roncesvalles, 133-6, 138, 140, 141, 143, 144-5, 147, 150, 152-3, 158, 160, 161-2, 166; his death, 168-72; blessed by Archbishop, 178; found by Charlemagne, 194; burial, 198

Olwen and Kilhwch, tale of, xxxii, 153, 156-9

Olympias, and Jove, iv, 276; xl, 401

Olympias, and St. Chrysostom, xv, 381

Olympic Games, Egyptians on the, xxxiii, 82

Olympiodorus, Plutarch on, xii, 94

Olympus, Mount, Homer on, xxii, 86

Olympus, physician of Cleopatra, xii, 399

Om, Hindu sacred syllable, xlv, 844

Omar, the Caliph, simplicity of, v, 58

OMAR KHAYYAM, RUBAIYAT OF, xli, 970-88; editorial remarks on, l, 22

Omberto, Count, in Dante's PURGATORY, xx, 190-1

Omens, Browne on, iii, 296; Hobbes on, xxxiv, 397; reading of, taught by Prometheus, viii, 173 and note 35

Omnipresence, Emerson on doctrine of, v, 94

ONE DAY I WROTE HER NAME, xl, 256

ONE-EYE, TWO-EYES, AND THREE-EYES, xvii, 219

ONE-EYED DOE, fable of the, xvii, 38

ONE NIGHT AS I DID WANDER, vi, 97

ONE WORD IS TOO OFTEN PROFANED, xli, 873

ONE WORD MORE, xlii, 1137-43

ONE'S SELF I SING, xlii, 1483-4

Onela, xlix, 72 note 3, 73 note, 79, 87

Onesti, Pietro degli, xx, 378 note 14

Ongentheow, xlix, 75 and note 1,

87-9; offspring of, 75; son of, 72 note 3

Onis, Don Luis de, xliii, 286-7

Ontario, Lake, naval forces on, xliii, 283

Onund, King, referred to, v, 357

Onythes, death of, xiii, 413

Opaqueness, cause of, xxxiv, 125

Open Air, Locke on the, xxxvii, 14-15

Open Sesame, xvi, 443

OPEN THE DOOR TO ME, OH, vi, 484

Opera, Wordsworth on the, xxxix, 313

Ophelia, in HAMLET, farewell to Laertes, xlvi, 100-3; advised by Polonius against Hamlet, 103-4; relates Hamlet's madness, 115-16; letter from Hamlet, 119-20; in plot to test Hamlet, 134; meeting with Hamlet, 135-7; at the play, 141-3, 145-6; her madness, 166-8, 171-2; death, 178-9; funeral, 185-6; Lamb on acting of, xxvii, 321-2; in the original story, xlvi, 86; Ruskin on, xxviii, 143

OPHELIA'S SONG, xl, 271

Ophion, Milton on fable of, iv, 309

Ophir, Milton on, iv, 332

Ophiuchus, constellation, mentioned, iv, 128

Ophiusa, alluded to, iv, 307

Opinion, all is, ii, 204 (15), 302 (22), 303 (25); Bacon on change of, iii, 31-2; Berkeley on, xxxvii, 248-9; bondage to, of others, iii, 35; confirmation of, 269; current, generally false, xx, 344; defined by Hobbes, xxxiv, 360, 361; Descartes on grounds of, 16; diversity of, reason for, 5; earnestness of, not intolerance, xxv, 37-8; fable of yielding to others', xvii, 36-7; Hume on differences of, xxvii, 215-16; knowledge and, xxxviii, 5; is knowledge in the making, iii, 235; liberty of, Mill on, xxv, 218-59, 260; life is, ii, 214 (3); Lowell on confidence of, xxviii, 464; Marcus Aurelius on change of, ii, 216 (12), 238 (21), 259 (16); Marcus Aurelius on freedom from, 244 (52), 246 (2), 263 (40), 265 (49), 293 (16); metempsychosis of, iii, 270; might and, xlviii, 108 (303), 110 (311); Milton on formation of, iv, 186; Milton on variety of, iii, 235-6; Montaigne on willingness to change, xxxii, 44; of others, may be best, vii, 221 (2, 3); prevailing, not necessarily true, xxxiv, 16; "queen of world," xlviii, 37 note; spoken, reacts on speaker, v, 98; Ruskin on, xxviii, 114; Seneca on slanderous, xxxix, 70

note; Socrates on, ii, 35-7; Tennyson on liberty of, xlii, 1032 (see also Public Opinion)

Opis, reference to, xiii, 380

Opium, Burke on taste for, xxiv, 16

Opium Trade, Ruskin on, xxviii, 118

Oppius, Atticus and, ix, 138; Cæsar and, xii, 289; Cicero on, ix, 178; Publius and, 120

Opportunities, Bacon on, iii, 59; finding and making, 132; Penn on, i, 365 (303)

Opposites, in nature (see Polarity); Socrates on, ii, 60-1, 98-101

Opposition, attitude toward, ii, 291 (9); some men's strength is in, iii, 130

Oppression, daunts courage, iii, 40; ECCLESIASTES on, xliv, 343 (1), 345 (8); Hobbes on fear of, xxxiv, 386; impossible in state of nature, 199-200; Penn on, i, 370 (365)

Oppressors, Job on, xliv, 110 (1-12)

Ops, mother of the gods, ix, 405 note

Ops, son of Peisenor, xxii, 20

Optics, Hobbes on, xxxiv, 377; in New Atlantis, iii, 186-7; Newton's discoveries in, xxxiv, 124-7

Oracles, Browne on, iii, 294 (29); Herodotus on founding of, xxxiii, 32-3; Hobbes on pagan, xxxiv, 396; Milton on, iv, 13; Pascal on, xlviii, 199 (601); Satan as giver of, iv, 374

Oral Teaching, Newman on, xxviii, 32-8

Orange, Prince of, in sack of Rome, xxxi, 82

Orange, William of (see William of O.)

Orante, in TARTUFFE, xxvi, 194-5

Orators, Penn on qualities of, i, 355 (173)

Oratory, action in, iii, 33; Cicero's book on, ix, 135; judgment and fancy in, xxxiv, 364; old age and, ix, 55-6; Pliny on, 214-18, 236-7, 364-5; rhetoric contrasted with, xxv, 338

Orbec, Vicomte d', xxxi, 294 note, 298

Orchard-making, in Chiloe, xxix, 316

Orchids, fertilization of, xi, 203-5; origin of, 250-2

Orco, Remiro d', xxxvi, 26-7

Ordas, Diego, xxxiii, 330-1

Order, as cloak for misgovernment, xxvii, 257-8; Franklin's rule of, i, 83, 84, 87-9; Heaven's first law, xl, 442; Pascal on, xlviii, 126 (373); Penn on, in homes, i, 344 (55-6); Pliny on, ix, 240

Order, in NEW WAY TO PAY OLD

Debts, xlvii, 825-8, 830, 832, 834, 835, 841, 843, 844-6, 880, 897

Ordination, Catholic doctrine of, xxxvi, 280 note; Luther on, 279; of Buddhist priests, xlv, 756-63

ORDINATION, THE, by Burns, vi, 171-4

Ordnance, antiquity of, iii, 146; Don Quixote on, xiv, 398-9

Oreb, references to, iv, 90; xliv, 253 (11)

O'Reilly, John Boyle, A WHITE ROSE, xlii, 1246

Orejones, Raleigh on the, xxxiii, 367

Orellana, Raleigh on, xxxiii, 330, 333

Orenoqueponi, Raleigh on the, xxxiii, 332 note, 387, 388

Orestes, in THE FURIES, viii, 117-18, 124-33, 137-46; Homer on, xxii, 10, 17, 39, 42, 62

Orestes, in THE LIBATION-BEARERS, viii, 71-2, 80-95, 97-100, 106-14; Mnesitheus and, xxxv, 289; Pylades and, vii, 53; ix, 17; Pyrrhus and, xiii, 142; Virgil on, 173

Organ, antiquity of the, xx, 185 note; Dryden on the, xl, 399-400

Organic Beings, affinities of, xi, 450-98; animal or vegetable, xxxviii, 356-9; classification of, xi, 450-62; increase of, 79-82; increase of, checks on, 82-5; complex relations among, 85-92; geographical distribution of, 395-449; geographical distribution of, Browne on, iii, 287-8; geological succession of, xi, 364-94 (see also Species)

Organic Periods, of history, xxv, 107-8

Organization, advance of, xi, 134-8; degree of, of ancient and living beings, 384-8; low, highly variable, 160; not the result of chance, xxxiv, 259-60; repetition a sign of low, xi, 160; standard of, defined, 229, 384, 386

Organs, with distinct functions, xi, 194-5; of extreme perfection, how developed, 190-206; highly developed, are variable, 161-4; incipient stages of useful, 229-55; of little importance, 206-9; multiple, variable, 160; rudimentary, atrophied, and aborted, 490-6; rudimentary, are variable, 160; with simultaneous functions, 195; specific and generic, compared, 164-8; use or beauty of, 209-15

Orgon, in TARTUFFE, relations with Tartuffe, xxvi, 196-7; returns home, 198-200; with Cleante, on Tartuffe, 201-5; on daughter's marriage, 205-7; Mariane with, 207-17; with Tartuffe after latter denounced, 243-50; prepares for

marriage of Tartuffe and Mariane, 253-4; refuses to believe Tartuffe false, 255-6; at meeting of Tartuffe and Elmire, 257, 263-4; orders Tartuffe away, 265; repents gifts to Tartuffe, 265-6; with Cleante, 266-8; with Madame Pernelle, 269-71; advised to pretend peace with Tartuffe, 272; ordered to vacate house, 274-8; warned to fly, 279-80; stopped by Tartuffe, 280-1; his property restored, 283-4

Oria, Pagan de, death of, xiv, 407-8

Oriana, Lady, Amadis and, xiv, 125, 225, 239; to Dulcinea, 17

Orient, Tennyson on the, xlii, 1017-18

Oriental Languages, Burke on, xxiv, 147

Oriental Literature, Hastings on, v, 464

Oriental States, Taine on, xxxix, 454

Origen, heresy of, iii, 270

ORIGIN OF SPECIES, Darwin's, xi

Original Sin, Bunyan's parable of, xv, 34; Burns on, vi, 75; Calvin on, xxxix, 52; Kempis on, vii, 339 (2); Lessing on doctrine of, xxxii, 212; Milton on, iv, 145, 333; Pascal on, xlviii, 83 (230) 147-8, 151 (445-7), 269 (752)

Originality, Bacon on, iii, 135-6; Emerson on, v, 63, 64, 84-5; Hugo on, xxxix, 406; Johnson on, 243; Mill on, xxv, 269-71; Pascal on perception of, xlviii, 10 (7), 108 (302); in poetry, Hugo on, xxxix, 383-5; in poetry, Wordsworth on, 348-51; Whitman on, 419 (see also Individuality)

Orinda, reference to, xl, 396

Orinoco, Raleigh on the, xxxiii, 338, 339, 341, 351, 362, 374-5; tributaries of the, 384

Orion, Aurora and, xxii, 74; Homer on, 160, 166; mentioned in JOB, xliv, 86, 136; Milton on, iv, 98; Virgil on, xiii, 47-8, 148, 353

Orithea, and Boreas, xxvii, 284

Orlando, Dante on, xx, 129 and note; in Dante's PARADISE, 363; Don Quixote on, xiv, 225, 238, 515; to Don Quixote, 16; Sidney on, xxvii, 13 (see also Roland)

Orlando Furioso, composition of, xxvii, 372; Montaigne on, xxxii, 95; Shelley on, xxvii, 366

Orleans, Duke of, at Poitiers, xxxv, 37, 47

Orleans, Duke of, (Egalité) Burke on, xxiv, 401, 440

Orme, Captain, on Braddock, i, 142

Ormond, Hugo on, xxxix, 399

Ornaments, Whitman on, xxxix, 424

Ornithology, Emerson on science of, v, 307

Ornithorhynchus Paradoxus, xxix, 466

Ornithus, death of, xiii, 385-6

Orodes, death of, xiii, 352

Oronte, Molière on, xxvi, 204-5

Orontes, in the ÆNEID, xiii, 79, 96

Oropus, case of, xii, 200

Oros, as king of Egypt, xxxiii, 74

Orosius, Paulus, xx, 330 note 23

Orphan House, Whitefield's, i, 105-6 107

Orphans in Massachusetts, xliii, 82 (84); Mohammed on, xlv, 892, 895, 927, 980-1

Orpheus, Æschylus on, viii, 67; Aristophanes on, 451; in Dante's Limbo, xx, 20; Dryden on, xl, 400; Euripides on, viii, 373; on hoariness, v, 182; Milton on, iv, 34-5, 37, 75, 231; Sidney on, xxvii, 8, 14; Socrates on, ii, 28; Virgil on, xiii, 215; in Virgil's Hades, 233

Orphic Mysteries, Herodotus on the, xxxiii, 41-2

Orses, death of, xiii, 352

Orsilochus, in the ÆNEID, xiii, 384, 385; in the ODYSSEY, xxii, 47, 188, 213

Orsini, Alexander VI and the, xxxvi, 25; Burke on, xxiv, 282; Colonnesi and, xxxvi, 40, 41; Duke Valentine and, 25-6, 28, 33, 48

Orsini, Franciotto, xxxi, 83 note 3

Orsino, Gierolimo, xxxi, 210 note

Orsino, in THE CENCI, with Beatrice, xviii, 285-7; plots against Beatrice, 287-8; returns petition, 294; with Giacomo, 300-2; 316-18; plans to win Beatrice, 302-3; learns Beatrice's wrong, 307-8; in plot to kill Cenci, 308-14; letter to Beatrice found, 332; with Giacomo after murder, 335-7; flight of, 337-8; accused by Marzio, 338

Orso, Count da Cerbaia, xx, 168 note 6

Orsono, volcano of, xxix, 292, 309

Orsua, Pedro de, xxxiii, 333, 374

Ortal, Jeronimo, xxxiii, 334

Orthodox, in FAUST, xix, 178

Orthodoxy, Burns on, vi, 222; Copernicus on, xxxix, 55; Penn on, i, 377 (472)

Orthography, Johnson on English, xxxix, 192-5

Ortolans, in France, x, 195

Ortygius, Virgil on, xiii, 316

Orus, the god, Milton on, iv, 14, 102

Osborne, Chas., friend of Franklin, i, 38-40

Osbrit Longhand, xlix, 249
O'Shaughnessy, Arthur, ODE by, xlii, 1246
Osians, Tacitus on the, xxxiii, 111, 120
Osiris, Dionysus and, xxxiii, 25, 74; Milton on, iv, 14 (24), 102; story of, iii, 232
Oslaf, xlix, 35, note 5, 38
Osman, humanity of, v, 226
Osprey, Harrison on the, xxxv, 358
Osric, in HAMLET, xlvi, 190-3, 195, 196
Ossa, and Pelion, Homer on, xxii, 160
Ossa, Jacques d' (see John XXII)
Ossar, Conaire's dog, xlix, 242
Ossian, and St. Patrick, xxxii, 177-8; Wordsworth on Books of, xxxix, 344-6
Ostenta, defined, xxxiv, 397
Ostentation, Bacon on, iii, 26; Penn on, i, 375; of virtue, ii, 177 (176) (see also Vainglory)
Osteomyelitis, Pasteur on, xxxviii, 394
Ostracism, at Athens, xii, 25-6; directed against persons of reputation, 81, 87; manner of, 87; remarks on, 120
Ostrich, Darwin on the, xi, 148; described in JOB, xliv, 137-8; eggs of the, xi, 274-5; xxix, 125; parasitical habits of the, 64; the S. American, 101-6
Oswald, in DA DERGA'S HOSTEL, xlix, 249
Oswald, in KING LEAR, xlvi, 217, 219, 220, 227, 233-6, 244, 263, 269-70, 275-6, 283-4
OSWALD, MRS., ODE TO, vi, 344
Othello, and Desdemona, Lamb on, xxvii, 317, 326-7; Macaulay on, 396; Ruskin on, xxviii, 142; Voltaire on, xxxiv, 134
Otho, Count, in SONG OF ROLAND, xlix, 125, 142, 178
Otho, Emperor, death of, xviii, 434; followers of, iii, 10
Otho IV, and Gualdrada, xx, 68 note 1
Otho, Marcus, xii, 235-6
Otos (see Otus)
Otter, son of Hreidmar, xlix, 304-5
OTTERBURN, THE BATTLE OF, xxxv, 83-105
OTTERBURN: A BALLAD, xl, 89-94
Ottergild, gold called, xlix, 306
Otters, in Chonos Islands, xxix, 305; in the Nile, xxxiii, 38; sanctity of, xlix, 305 note
Ottocar, King of Bohemia, Dante on, xx, 175 and note 6
Ottoman, Bacon on, iii, 136
Ottomans (see Turks)

Otus, Homer on, xxii, 160
Otway, Sylvester, Burns on, vi, 359
Otway, Thomas, Hazlitt on, xxvii, 292; Venice Preserved of, xxxiv, 134
OUR BLESSED LADY'S LULLABY, xl, 261-5
OUR LADY'S CHILD, tale of, xvii, 54-8
OUT OVER THE FORTH, vi, 422
Outcry, much, little outcome, xvii, 16
Outdoor Life, and love of beauty, xxxix, 415; Locke on, xxxvii, 14-15
OUTLAW, THE, xli, 755-7
Oven-bird, Darwin on the, xxix, 107
Over-population, leads to wars, iii, 146
Overreach, Sir Giles, in NEW WAY TO PAY OLD DEBTS, character of, xlvii, 818; uncle of Wellborn, 821; Wellborn on, 824; at Allworth's, 830-1; with Wellborn, 831; scene with Marrall, 835-8; Furnace on, 844-5; with Marrall after the dinner, 849-51; preparations for Lord Lovell, 854-5; with Margaret, 855-9; with Lovell, 859-60; at meeting of Lovell and Margaret, 860, 861-3 867; receives Lady Allworth and Wellborn, 863-4; believes Lady Allworth in love with Wellborn, 866; conference with Wellborn, 867-8; with Lovell at Allworth's, 869-73; his plot against Wellborn, 880-1, 885; with Allworth and Margaret, 882-5; at Allworth's in search of daughter, 888-9; with Wellborn, 889-93; learns daughter's marriage, 894-5; with Lovell, 895-6; crazed, 897-8
Overreach, Margaret, in NEW WAY TO PAY OLD DEBTS, Allworth and, xlvii, 824; intended for Lord Lovell, 837-8, 850; Lovell and Allworth on, 851-4; scene with father, 855-9; with Lovell, 860-2; with Allworth, 863; parting with Lovell, 867; Lady Allworth on, 875; scene with Allworth, 881-5; announces marriage to Allworth, 894-5; in final scene, 898
Overshot Wheels, xxx, 188-9
OVER-SOUL, ESSAY ON THE, v, 137-54
Over-soul, Aristotle's idea of an, xxxiv, 104; exhibited in laws of compensation, v, 89; Hindu doctrine of, xlv, 817, 828-9, 831-53, 862-3, 868-9; Pythagorean doctrine of the, ix, 74; relations of man to the, v, 75, 76; Virgil on the, xiii, 235-6
Overton, Hugo on, xxxix, 400

Over-trading, cause of scarcity of money, x, 334-5

Overwork, More on causes of, xxxvi, 191-2; Smith on results of, x, 87; Woolman on, i, 205-6, 261-2

Ovid, Chaucer compared with, xxxix, 161, 167-9; Dante on, xx, 106; Dryden on, xiii, 36, 37, 38, 53-4, 57; Dryden on Metamorphoses of, xxxix, 160; on himself in love, xxiv, 25; Montaigne on Metamorphoses of, xxxii, 70, 92

Ovieda, Gonzalo de, xxxiii, 333 note 18

Ovules, position of, xi, 224

Owannamug, the Indian, xliii, 153

Owen, Aneurin, xxxii, 145

Owen, Knight, in Purgatory, xxxii, 186; Renan on, 149

Owen, Prof. Richard, on cuttle-fish, xi, 482; on disadvantages of size, 370; on the dugong, 453; Emerson on, v, 461; on fossils, xi, 388; on generalized forms, 378; on highly developed parts, 161; on limbs, 473; on Megatheroid animals, xxix, 95-6; Mill on, xxv, 110; on non-flying birds, xi, 147; on origin of species, 14-15; the Solenhofen fossils and, xxviii, 122; on turkey-buzzards, xxix, 199

Owl, Darwin on the little, xxix, 138

Ox and Frog, fable of, xvii, 19

Oxen, English, Harrison on, xxxv, 344; German, Tacitus on, xxxiii, 97; More on, xxxvi, 184; sacred in Egypt, xxxiii, 23-5; why not grand, xxiv, 58

Oxen and Lion, fable of, xvii, 32

Oxenham, John, with Drake, xxxiii, 141, 144, 164, 177, 180, 190, 199

Oxford, Earl of, A Renunciation, xl, 296

Oxford, Earldom of, v, 421

Oxford University, Emerson on, v, 433-5; Harrison on, xxxv, 391-400, 402-3; Huber on, xxviii, 49-50; Newman on, 47-51

Oxidrakes, cannon of, iii, 146

Oxiones, Tacitus on the, xxxiii, 123

Oxnam, John (see Oxenham)

Oxygen, absorbed by bacteria, xxxviii, 343; absorbed by fruits, 321; in air, xxx, 147-51; breathing requires, 171-2; combustion in, 142-4; combustion requires, 57-9; Faraday on, 47-9; Helmholtz on, 213; hydrogen and, 53, 145; produced from water, 140; production of, easy method, 141-2; tested by nitrous oxide, 148; weight of, 142, 151; yeast and, xxxviii, 289-317, 329-32

Oysters, no heart in, xxxviii, 137; Raleigh on, xxxiii, 322

Ozeyr, and the ass, xvi, 123 note

Ozymandias of Egypt, xlii, 873-4

Paches, death of, xii, 108

Pacific Islanders, Pretty on, xxxiii, 226

Pacific Ocean, Darwin on, xxix, 425, 440; Drake and the, xxxiii, 126, 177

Pack, Clouds, Away, xl, 324-5

Pack of Ragamuffins, The, xvii, 69-70

Pacorus, death of, xii, 360

Pacuvius, play of, ix, 16-17; works of, lost, xxvii, 361

Padarn, coat of, xxxii, 152

Padilla, story of, xxi, 5

Padumuttara, xlv, 796-7

Pæëon, in Odyssey, xxii, 54

Pætus, Cæcinna, Arria and, ix, 253-5

Pætus, L. Papirius, letters to, ix, 161, 165, 166

Pagan, in Pilgrim's Progress, xv, 70

Pagan, Isobel, Ca' the Yowes, xli, 569

Pagan Learning, Milton on study of, iii, 209-10

Pagan Philosophy, Hugo on, xxxix, 360

Pagan Poets, Wordsworth on the, xxxix, 321

Pagani, Dante on the, xx, 205 note 27

Paganism, Bacon on, iii, 11; Hobbes on, xxxiv, 394-8; Hugo on, xxxix, 360; Pascal on, xlviii, 199 (601)

Pagano, Machinardo, xx, 114 note 8

Pagans, in Hell, Browne on, iii, 319; Dante on, xx, 18-21

Pagasus, death of, xiii, 385

Page, Curtis Hidden, translator of Molière, xxvi, 187

Paget, Stephen, translator of Paré, xxxviii, 7, 9 note

Pagno, Zanobi di, xxxi, 373

Pagolo, Pietro (see Galleotti)

Pain, Berkeley on idea of, xxxvii, 207, 211; Burke on standards of, xxiv, 11-12; cause of, 110-12; darkness as cause of, 122-5; of death, iii, 9; delight caused by, xxiv, 113-14; endurance of, xxxvii, 100-1, 106-8; Epictetus on, ii, 135 (55); fear of, xxxvii, 103, 105; Hunt on, xxvii, 301-2; of the imagination, xxiv, 16-22; from imitations, xxxix, 234; infinity as cause of, xxiv, 117-18; of the judgment, 22-4; Locke on, xxxvii, 92; Marcus Aurelius on, ii, 231 (26), 250 (33), 254 (64), 261 (28), 263 (42), 264 (47), 268 (1); of others, pleasure in, xxiv, 41-4; Pascal on yielding to, xlviii,

62 (160); passions excited by, xxiv, 36; philosophic attitude toward, ii, 75-6; pleasure in relation to, xxiv, 30-1, 36; removal of, not positive pleasure, 31-4, 35; Rousseau on, xxxiv, 268; of the senses, xxiv, 13-16; sensibility to, 24-5; Socrates on, and pleasure, ii, 48; sublimity always produced by, xxiv, 76; vastness as cause of, 115-16; Webster on, xlvii, 814

Paine, Thomas, Burke on, xxiv, 442; Franklin and, i, 173

Painting, Burke on effects of, xxiv, 136; Coleridge on, xxvii, 275; color in, xxxix, 270; color in historical, xxiv, 72; defined as mute poesy, xxvii, 271; Locke on study of, xxxvii, 186; knowledge of minerals needed in, xxxix, 270; Pascal on, xlviii, 51 (134); plastic art strives toward, xxxix, 274; poetry compared with, xxiv, 55-7, 146; reason of power of, 41, 45

Palace, Bacon's idea of a, iii, 115-17

Palæontological Collections, poorness of, xi, 340-6

Palamedes, Trojan War and, xiii, 106

Palamon and Arcite, story of, xxxix, 167, 169, 180

Palazzo, Conrado da, xx, 213 note 8

Pales, Milton on, iv, 273

Palgrave, Francis T., *Golden Treasury* of, xl, 10

Palinurus, in ÆNEID, xiii, 138, 148, 149, 183, 209-10, 222-4

Pallas Athene, in the ÆNEID, xiii, 124; in Trojan war, 77, 109 (see also Athene)

Pallas, son of Evander, in the ÆNEID, xiii, 276, 289, 291, 339-40, 341, 342-3, 361-4, 365-7, 428

Pallavicini, Cellini on, xxxi, 218 note, 219-21

Pallium, the, xxxvi, 296 note

Palmer, F. H., translator of KORAN, xlv, 885

Palmer, Ray, hymn by, xlv, 583; translator of hymn, 563

Palmer, London printer, i, 43, 44

Palmerin of England, xiv, 54

Palmerin de Oliva, xiv, 54

Palmerston, Lord, on English troops, v, 371

Palmus, death of, xiii, 351

Pampas, S. American, Darwin on, xxix, 86-147; changes of animals and plants in, 132; geology of, 141-3; view of the, from the Andes, 347; formation of the, 348

Pan, Browning on, xli, 948-9; date of, xxxiii, 74-5; as Egyptian god, 28; Emerson on, v, 238; Milton on, iv, 10 (8), 380; Syrinx and, xl, 386

Pan, HYMN OF, xli, 845-6

Panætius, on Aristides, xii, 81; Plutarch on, 17

PANAMA, CONVENTION OF U. S. WITH, xliii, 478-91

Panama Canal, xliii, 478 note

Panama, Isthmus of, Drake at, xxxiii, 179; formerly open, xi, 396-7

Panatuket, Eliot on, xliii, 155

Pandafilando, the giant, xiv, 297

Pandar, Chaucer's, xxvii, 20

Pandarus, in the ÆNEID, xiii, 320, 321-2; in the ODYSSEY, xxii, 281, 286

Pandemonium, palace of Satan, iv, 108; council in, 111-23

Pandora, Milton on, iv, 175

Panegyric, Pliny on, ix, 201; Swift on, xxvii, 124

Paniagando on Dulcinea del Toboso, xiv, 540

Panic, Hobbes on, xxxiv, 355

Panope, Milton on, iv, 76; in PHÆDRA, xxvi, 137-8, 179

Panopea, in the ÆNEID, xiii, 190, 192-3

Pansa, Cicero and, xii, 262; death of, 264-5

Pantasilea, mistress of Cellini, xxxi, 58, 65-71

PANTHEISM, THE HIGHER, xlii, 1038-9

Pantheus, priest of Apollo, xiii, 114; death of, 118

Panthers, said to be marked with constellations, xxvi, 12 and note

Paoli, of Corsica, Mill on, xxv, 11

Paolo, Padre, iii, 206; Dr. Donne and, xv, 362

Paolo of Rimini, xx, 24 note 3

Papacy, Dante's allegory of, xx, 267-9, 277-8, 280-1, 283; Dante on temporal authority of the, 213, 400-2; Henry VIII on the, xxxvi, 124; Luther on corruption of the, 355-7, 359; Machiavelli on temporal power of the, 40-2; Milton on the, iv, 358-9; More on supremacy of the, xxxvi, 135; Pascal on the, xlviii, 309 (871-7), 311 (880) (see also Popes)

Papal Pardons (see Indulgences)

Papamene River, xxxiii, 330 note, 335

Paper Money, advantages of, x, 240-9; limits to circulation of, 249-50; dangers of, 259-60; Franklin on, i, 65; effect on value of gold and silver, x, 268; effect on industry, 258-9; effect of increase on prices, 263-4

Paphlagonia, Pliny on, ix, 393 note 1

Paphos, island of Venus, viii, 364; xiii, 89-90; Emerson on, v, 236

Papian Law, the, ix, 430 note

Papin, Pierres, xiv, 148

Papirius, Gaius, flatteries of, ix, 40

Pappus, historian, xii, 222-3

Papremis, worship at, xxxiii, 33, 34-5, 38

Papunehang, the Indian, i, 277, 278

Papyrus, eaten in Egypt, xxxiii, 46

Parables, Bunyan on, xv, 8-9

Paracelsus, on creation of man, iii, 301; Emerson on, v, 183

Paraclete, Holy Ghost called, xlv, 559, 560

PARADISE, Dante's, xx, 287-427

Paradise, Marvell on, xl, 387; Mohammedan, xlv, 899, 902, 903-4, 905-6, 911-12, 922, 952, 963, 973

PARADISE, THE GARDEN OF, xvii, 298-312

Paradise of Fools, iv, 149-50

PARADISE LOST, Milton's, iv, 89-362; Arnold on selections from, xxviii, 73-4; Bagehot on, 201-12; composition of, iv, 5; Dryden on, xiii, 13; Hugo on, xxxix, 372; Poe on, xxviii, 383-4; Shelley on, xxvii, 365-6; subject compared with other great epics, iv, 264; Wordsworth on, xxxix, 336-8

PARADISE REGAINED, Milton's, iv, 362-415; date of, 5

Paradoxes, Berkeley on, xxxvii, 202; Goethe on, xix, 105

Paræus, on *Revelations*, iv, 416

Parallax, of stars, xxx, 329-30

Paralus, Plato on, ii, 21

Parana River, Darwin on the, xxix, 138-9, 147, 151-2; sediment of, xxxviii, 424

Parasitic Insects, xi, 275

Parceval, romance of, xxxii, 172-4

Parcitati, Montagna de', xx, 113 note 6

Pardon, right of, in early Massachusetts, xliii, 80-1

Pardoner, Chaucer's, xl, 29-31

Pardoning Power, of President, xliii, 201 (1)

Pardons, Hobbes on, xxxiv, 424

Pardoning, the honorablest revenge, xlvii, 778; proverb on, xvi, 70

Paré, Ambroise, JOURNEYS IN DIVERSE PLACES, xxxviii, 9-61; remarks on JOURNEYS of, i, 24, 44; life and works, xxxviii, 8

Paredes, Garcia de, xiv, 513

Parents, and children, intercourse between, xxviii, 293; and children, Locke on, xxxvii, 28-33, 34-48, 52 note, 52-3, 58-9, 63-71, 85-7, 88-96, 111-18; and children, Montaigne on, xxxii, 75-7; Confucius on duty to, xliv, 6 (10), 7, (5, 6, 7, 8), 14 (18-21), 45 (18); Mohammed on inheritances of, xlv, 981-2; Mohammed on kindness to, 926; Montaigne on education by, xxxii, 40; Penn on obedience to,

i, 355-6; Tzu-hsia on duty to, 5 (7); Yu-tzu on duty to, xliv, 5 (2)

PARENTS AND CHILDREN, ESSAY ON, Bacon's, iii, 20-1

Parigi, Piera de Salvadore, wife of Cellini, xxxi, 2

Paris, son of Priam, in Dante's HELL, xx, 23; Dares and, xiii, 194; Helen and, viii, 19-20; Mimas and, xiii, 351; King Proteus and, xxxiii, 55-6; punishment of, viii, 24; Webster on judgment of, xlvii, 758

Paris (city), industries of, x, 276; preëminence of, in French Revolution, xxiv, 345-6

Paris, Parliament of, on National Assembly, xxiv, 186

Paris, University of, site of, xxviii, 45-6

PARIS, TREATY OF, xliii, 185-91

Paris, Abbé, miracles of, xxxvii, 409

Paris, Ferdinand John, i, 167-9

PARIS AND ŒNONE, xl, 221

Park, Mungo, on desire for salt, xxix, 123

PARKER, HUGH, EPISTLE TO, vi, 322

Parker, Theodore, on democracy, xxviii, 473

Parliament, burgesses in, xxxv, 236; under the Commonwealth, xliii, 114-20; More's plea for freedom of, xxxvi, 99-100; Voltaire on, xxxiv, 86-90, 92

Parliament of Man, xlii, 1016

Parma, Duchess of (see Margaret of Parma)

Parma, Prince of, xix, 203 note 26

Parmenas, the deacon, xliv, 441 (5)

Parmenides, Dante on, xx, 344; Sidney on, xxvii, 9

Parmenius, Stephen, xxxiii, 299 note

PARNASSUS HILL, O WERE I ON, vi, 332

Parnell, More and, xxxvi, 121

Paros, marbles of, xiii, 135

Parrot, South American, xxix, 151

PARROT AND THE HUSBAND, story of, xvi, 37-8

Parry, C. H., Jenner to, xxxviii, 151

Parsees, of Bombay, xxv, 293 note; Freeman on the, xxviii, 281

Parsifal, legend of, xxxii, 173

Parsimony, Bacon on, iii, 93; Burke on, xxiv, 418; defined by Hobbes, xxxiv, 354; why dishonorable, 380; economically considered, x, 278-9; motives of, 282, 283

Parson, Chaucer's, xl, 24-6; Dryden on Chaucer's, xxxix, 172

Parson, Goldsmith's, xli, 525-6

Parsons, William, i, 60

Parthenon, built by Ictinus and Callicrates, xii, 51; Emerson on the, xlii, 1299

Parthenope, Milton on, iv, 70

Parthia, Antony's war with, xii, 363-75; Cicero in, ix, 141-3, 153; Milton on, iv, 395-6
Parthians, Tacitus on the, xxxiii, 116-17
Partiality, Penn on, i, 373-4
Participles, Johnson on, xxxix, 199
Particles, Johnson on, xxxix, 202
Parties, political, Emerson on, v, 254-5; Franklin's observations on, i, 93; Washington on, xliii, 255, 257, 258-9
PARTING AT MORNING, xlii, 1111
PARTING KISS, THE, vi, 336
Partisanship, of principle, i, 374-5 (432-8); of rulers, iii, 39
Partnerships, Franklin on, i, 109
Partridges, in Brazil, xxix, 56
Parvenu, in FAUST, xix, 170-1
Parvenus, envy of, iii, 24
Parvin, Benj., Woolman's companion to Indians, i, 268-80
Parwin, Omar Khayyam on, xli, 983
Pascal, Blaise, language of, xxxix, 394; LETTERS, xlviii, 325-68; life and works, 5-6; MINOR WORKS, 369-451; M. de Saci on, 392; THOUGHTS, 7-322; remarks on THOUGHTS, 6; l, 34
Pascal, Jacqueline, sister of Blaise, xlviii, 325-35, 346; letters of, 378-35; letter to, 325-7; profession of, 346
Pascal, pere, epitaph on, xlviii, 369; letter on death of, 335-46
"Pascha, The," Drake's flagship, xxxiii, 134
Paschal, St., Luther on, xxxvi, 267 (29)
Pascucci, Girolamo, the Perugian, xxxi, 196-7, 209-10, 211, 223
Pasenadi, the Kosalan, xlv, 691, 771-772
Pasiphaë, Dante on, xx, 50 note 3, 253; Massinger on, xlvii, 866; in the Mournful Fields, xiii, 226
Pasqualigo, Lorenzo, letter of, xliii, 47-8
Passion, Blake on, xli, 604; Bunyan's allegory of, xv, 35-6; Confucius on, xliv, 16 (10); in Dante's HELL, xx, 32, 48; Hindu Krishna on, xlv, 816, 864-5, 874, 878, 879; Kempis on, vii, 251 (1); nature seen in moments of, iii, 102; Penn on, i, 363-4; Poe on, xxviii, 403; reason and, iii, 284; in religion, i, 383 (533-40); simulation of, xlviii, 426-7 (see also Anger)
PASSION, THE, Milton, iv, 24-5
Passions, Burke on study of the, xxiv, 47-9; Burke on taste in the, 22; clearness not necessary to affect the, 53-4; David on the, xli,

503; Epictetus on correction of, ii, 183 (14); Harvey on physical effects of the, xxxviii, 131; Hobbes on the, xxxiv, 350-9; Hume on the, xxxvii, 373-4; infinity, its effect on the, xxiv, 64-5; intellectual differences caused by, xxxiv, 366-7; of love, xxiv, 37, 38-9; Pascal on the, xlviii, 134 (412-13), 418, 167 (502); physical causes of the, xxiv, 108-35; poetry, its effect on the, 53-7; Pope on the, xl, 428-31; power, its effect on the, xxiv, 57-62; privation, its effect on the, 63; Rousseau on the, xxxiv, 180-1; Ruskin on the, xxviii, 116-18; reason and, xxiv, 41; of self-preservation, 35-6; 38; of society, 37-46; strong, most creditable to conquer, vii, 245 (4); sublimity, its effect on the, xxiv, 51-76; thoughts and, xxxvii, 316, 319; vastness, its effect on the, xxiv, 63-4; words, their power over the, 136-48; Wordsworth on, xxxix, 350
PASSIONS, THE, by Collins, xli, 488-91
PASSIONATE SHEPHERD, Marlowe's, xl, 259
Passivity, and activity, ii, 271 (16)
Passover, feast of the, xliv, 416 (1)
Past, America's attitude toward the, xxxix, 409; Bacon on the, iii, 15, 65; Bentham on veneration of the, xxvii, 238-44; Byron on, xxviii, 402-3; Carlyle on, xxv, 367; Confucius on, xliv, 11 (21); Descartes on rejection of the, xxxiv, 15; ECCLESIASTES on the, xliv, 347 (10); Emerson on the, v, 8, 75-6, 107; Goethe on study of, xix, 28-9; Hobbes on the, xxxiv, 333; Lowell on worship of the, xlii, 1451; Pascal on the, xlviii, 362; Raleigh on the, xxxix, 101-2, 105; reasoning from, to future, xxxvii, 335; Tennyson on the, xlii, 1002-3 (see also Antiquity)
PAST, THE, by Bryant, xlii, 1269-71
PAST AND PRESENT, by Hood, xli, 935-6
Pasteur, Louis, on bacteria, xxxviii, 271; editorial remarks on papers of, l, 45; to his father, xxxviii, 285; GERM THEORY, 382-402; life and works, 284; THEORY OF FERMENTATION, 287-381
Pastimes, Locke on, xxxvii, 188
Pastoral Poetry, Sidney on, xxvii, 28
PASTORAL POETRY, by Burns, vi, 434
Pastoureaux, the, xxxv, 64 note
Pasture, rent of, x, 157-9, 160

Patagonia, Darwin on, xxix, 178-87, 193-202, 530

Patagonians, Darwin on the, xxix, 248

Patarbemis, and Amasis, xxxiii, 83-84

Patents, under control of Congress, xliii, 197 (8); Franklin on, i, 116-17

Paternus, Pliny to, ix, 219, 341

Pathos, Wordsworth on, in poetry, xxxix, 350-1

Patience, Bacon on lack of, iii, 141; better than pride, xliv, 347 (8); Buddha on, xlv, 610; Bunyan's allegory of, xv, 35-6; Byron's Manfred on, xviii, 416; Epictetus on, ii, 128 (34), 130 (39), 176 (170), 177 (174); Ferdinand's lesson in, xlvii, 797; Goethe on, xix, 377; Goethe's apothecary's lesson in, 418-19; instances of, given by Dante, xx, 208-9; Kempis on, vii, 228, 259 (6), 283-4, 290-2, 343; Manzoni on, xxi, 101; Marcus Aurelius, ii, 200 (1), 213 (3), 254 (63), 255 (70), 258 (14), 267 (59), 271 (11), 273 (27), 276 (42), 278 (3), 293 (18), 285 (30), 291 (9), 293 (18); Penn on, i, 351 (119), 356, 360 (234), 364 (294); in public office, 372-3; Rousseau on reason for, xxxiv, 285-6 (see also Bearing)

Patmore, Coventry, DEPARTURE, xlii, 1158; Ruskin on, xxviii, 148 note

Patriarchal Age, Hugo on, xxxix, 356-7; Pope on the, xl, 438

Patriarchs, Pascal on the, xlviii, 211-12; the twelve, xliv, 442 (8-9)

Patricians, Roman, ix, 306 note; Marcus Aurelius on, ii, 195 (11)

Patricius, father of St. Augustine, vii, 3, 156-7; St. Augustine and, 25; conversion of, 158; death of, 36; an unbeliever, 14

Patrick, St., on Gaelic heroes, xxxii, 144; Ossian and, 177-8; *Purgatory* of, 185-7

PATRIOT, THE, by Browning, xlii, 1125

Patriotism, Burke on, xxiv, 345; extreme, not fortunate, iii, 105; superior to friendship, ix, 23-4; Locke on, xxxvii, 5; Lowell on mock, xlii, 1452; Socrates on, ii, 40; universality of, xl, 534

Patroclus, and Achilles, Æschylus on, xxxii, 79; Homer on, xxii, 37, 164, 333; Marlowe on, xlvi, 25

Patron, in the ÆNEID, xiii, 192

Patronage, Johnson on, xxxix, 217

Paul, St., before Agrippa, xliv, 487-90; at Athens, 469 (15-34); in Antioch, 455 (25-6, 30), 457 (25), 457 (1); at Antioch of Pisidia, 458 (14-52); Augustine, St., on, vii, 121, 129; Bacon on, iii, 13, 36; Barnabas and, xliv, 458, 465; at Berœa, 469 (10-14); conversion of, v, 145; vii, 129; xliv, 448 (3-19); at Corinth, 470; Dante on, xx, 268 note 14; editorial remarks on teachings of, xliv, 428; Emerson on, v, 249; at Ephesus, xliv, 472; EPISTLES TO CORINTHIANS, xlv, 499-544; Euripides quoted by, iv, 416; Felix and, xliv, 486 (24-27); before Festus, 486-90; accused before Gallio, 471 (12-17); on himself, xlv, 503 (1-5), 512 (1-27), 522 (9-10), 527 (8-9), 531-4, 535 (5), 539-43; in Iconium, xliv, 461 (1-5); at Jerusalem, 478-490; at council of Jerusalem, 463; Kempis on, vii, 313; learning of, iii, 209; visit to Limbo, xx, 10 note 2; Luke and, xliv, 356; at Lystra, 461-2; in Macedonia, 475 (1-5); in Melita, 493-4; at Miletus, 476 (17-36); Mill on, xxv, 228, 252-3; misinterpretations of, xxxix, 48; missionary journeys, xliv, 458-78; Pascal on, xlviii, 100 (283), 196 (588), 226 (670), 228 (673, 674), 232 (683), 302 (851), 304 (853), 357; in persecution of Christians, xliv, 446 (3), 448 (1-2); at Philippi, 466-8; in Rome, 494-5; Taine on epistles of, xxxix, 460; at Thessalonica, xliv, 468 (1-9); at Troas, 475 (6-12)

Paul III, Pope, Cellini and, xxxi, 151-3, 165, 170-1, 186-8, 191-3, 211-12, 216-18, 222, 223, 232-3, 235-6, 237-8, 242, 249-50, 254, 255-6, 260, 260-1; Charles V and, 186-9; children of, 153 note 2, 193 note; Copernicus to, xxxix, 55, 59-60; election of, xxxi, 151 note 3; escape from early imprisonment, 233-4; Duke of Ferrara and, 280; in sack of Rome, 77 note

PAUL REVERE'S RIDE, xlii, 1348

Paula, St. Hierome and, xv, 381

Paulet, Sir Amyas, iii, 3

Pauline, in POLYEUCTE, her dream referred to, xxvi, 71; begs Polyeucte to stay, 74-5; with Stratonice, tells her old love for Severus, 75-6; her marriage to Polyeucte, 76-7; her dream, 77-8; learns Severus's approach, 78-80; with Severus, 83-6; with Polyeucte on his return, 87-8; her fears for Polveucte, 90-1; learns Polyeucte a Christian, 92-4; pleads for Polyeucte with father, 95-8; with Polyeucte in prison, 103-7; asks Severus to save Polyeucte, 108; last

appeal for Polyeucte, 114-16; follows him to death, 117; announces herself a Christian, 118-19; St. Victor on character of, 70

Paulino, Cellini's boy, xxxi, 41, 43-4

Paulinus, Valerius, letters to, ix, 267, 288, 351, 372

Paullus, Lucius, and his sons, ix, 175

Paulus, Lucius, Æmilius (d. 216 B. C.), death of, ix, 73

Paulus, Lucius, Æmilius (d. 160 B. C.), xxxii, 16

Paulus, Passienus, Priscus and, ix, 297-8

Paulus, Sergius, xliv, 458 (7, 12)

Paulus, the consul, and Cæsar, xii, 300

Pausanias, the Spartan monarch, Cleonice and, xviii, 423; haughtiness of, xii, 104-5; at Platæa, 91, 94, 96, 97, 98, 99; treason of, 26

Pavia, Bishop of (see Rossi, Girolamo de')

Pavy, Salathiel, xl, 307

Paxton Affair, Franklin in, i, 4

Payen, Dr., on Montaigne, xxxii, 109-11

Pazzi, Carlino de, xx, 135 note 7

Pazzi, Comiccione de', xx, 135 and note 6

Pazzo, in Dante's HELL, xx, 34 and note 12

Peace, Blake on, xli, 605, 606; Burns on, vi, 325; chamber of, in PILGRIM'S PROGRESS, xv, 57; "hath her victories," iv, 85; Hobbes on, xxxiv, 385, 406, 408; Milton on descent of, iv, 8-9; oversecurity in times of, vii, 278 (4); Pope on, xl, 443; the sovereign good, xlviii, 107 (299); temporal and eternal, vii, 312 (2); Tennyson on, xli, 1053-5, 1096-7; the true end of war, xiv, 394; Washington on, xliii, 260-1

Peaceableness, Kempis on, vii, 251-2

Peacock, Milton on the, iv, 241; sacred to Hera, viii, 176 note 37

PEACOCK AND JAY, fable of, xvii, 18

PEACOCK AND JUNO, fable of, xvii, 24

Pearcy (see Percy)

PEARL AND COCK, fable of, xvii, 9

Pears, Darwin on improvement of, xi, 51; Locke on eating of, xxxvii, 22

Pearson, Dr. G., xxxviii, 180, 209

Peasantry, Goldsmith on the, xli, 523

Peasants, and lords, xlii, 1305

Peasants' Song, in FAUST, xix, 41-2

PEASANT'S WISE DAUGHTER, THE, xvii, 190

Peat, formation of, xxix, 304-5

Pébrine, Pasteur on, xxxviii, 284

Pecci, Pier Antonio, xxxi, 145 note

Peckham, Sir George, xxxiii, 277

Pectoralis Reservatio, xxxvi, 299, 307

Peculators, in Dante's HELL, xx, 87-8, 91-4

Pedantry, Confucius on, xliv, 20 (16); Hobbes on, xxxiv, 349; Locke on, xxxvii, 161; Swift on, xxvii, 100, 108

Pediculi, Harvey on, xxxviii, 137

Pedro of Castile, xxxix, 88

Peebles, Rev. William, Burns on, vi, 105, 373 note

Peel, Sir Robert, blue books and, v, 374; law reform and, xxv, 67-8; model Englishman, v, 410

Peele, George, PARIS AND ŒNONE, xl, 221-2

Peele Castle, Wordsworth on, xli, 620

Peerage, English, Carlyle on the, xxv, 388-9

Peewit, habits of the, xxix, 127

PEG-A-RAMSAY, BONIE, vi, 549

PEGASUS AT WAULOCKHEAD, vi, 345

PEGGY, by Ramsay, xl, 411-12

PEGGY ALISON, BONIE, vi, 31-2

Peiræus, and Theoclymenus, xxii, 294

Peirson, Dr., on puerperal fever, xxxviii, 245

Peisander, in ODYSSEY, xxii, 263, 313, 314

Peisenor, the herald, xxii, 23

Peisistratus, in ODYSSEY, xxii, 35, 44, 47, 52, 53, 209, 211-14

Pelagianism, Pascal on, xlviii, 172 (521), 275 (777); Renan on, xxxii, 180

Pelagius, the monk, xxxv, 391

Pelasgians, gods of the, xxxiii, 30-1

Pelasgos, king of the Apian land, viii, 186 note 61

Peleus, father of Achilles, xxii, 164-5

Pelias, birth of, xxii, 158; in sack of Troy, xiii, 118

Pelican, habits of the, xlvi, 256 note 6; lesson of the, xv, 239; Shakespeare on the, xlvi, 170

Pelides (see Achilles)

Pelion, and Ossa, xxii, 160

Pella, studdery of, xxxv, 346

Pellean Conqueror, Alexander called, iv, 380

Pelles, King, Balin and, xxxv, 115-16; Sir Ector and, 215; at feast of Grail, 219, 220; grandsire of Galahad, 114; Launcelot and, 214; the sword and, 195-6

Pellinore, father of Percivale, xxxv, 191

Pellisson, on French classical poetry, xxviii, 68

Pelmus, death of, xiii, 351
Pelopidas, and Epaminondas, xii, 80
Peloponnesian War, xii, 67-9, 71-5
Pelops, Cicero's letter to, xii, 246
Pelorus, references to, iv, 96; xx, 202 note 5
Pembroke, in EDWARD II, xlvi, 14, 19-23, 30-1, 36, 41-2, 46, 49
Pembroke, Countess of, epitaph on, xl, 343
Pembroke, Earl of, George Herbert and, xv, 385, 392
Penagwog Indians, xliii, 155
Penal Code, Marshall on, xliii, 234-5
Penalties, Winthrop on prescribed, xliii, 96-106, 107-8, 110-11
Penance, Krishna on, xlv, 873, 876; Luther on, xxxvi, 265, 266; Pascal on, xlviii, 238 (698)
Penarius, T., Cicero and, ix, 121-2
PENCIL, VERSES WRITTEN WITH A, vi, 291-2
Pendulum, Faraday on the, xxx, 11; Helmholtz on the, 195-6
Penelope, in the ODYSSEY, the minstrel and, xxii, 18; web of, 24-5, 271; learns plot against Telemachus, 66-8; her dream, 69-70; grief of, 156; told of Telemachus's return, 233; rebukes the suitors, 235-6; with Telemachus on his return, 239, 240-2; sends for Ulysses, 251-4; goes among the wooers, 259-60; draws gifts from wooers, 261-3; talks with Ulysses as a beggar, 268-76; relates her dream, 280-1; prepares contest for the suitors, 282; longs to die, 285-6; at feast of the suitors, 294; brings forth bow of Ulysses, 295-7; wishes Ulysses to shoot, 303-4; told of Ulysses's return, 321-3; reûnion with Ulysses, 323-30; fame of, 336; Bacon on, iii, 23; Ruskin on, xxviii, 146
P'eng, xliv, 21 note 1
Penguin, habits of the, xxix, 214; Hayes on, xxxiii, 284; wings of, xi, 355-6
Penitence, David's prayer in, xliv, 192-3; Luther on, xxxvi, 265, 266, 383-4; Pascal on, xlviii, 223 (661); Webster on, xlvii, 807
Penitent, Mr., in PILGRIM'S PROGRESS, xv, 285-6, 287
Penn, Thomas, i, 129, 167
Penn, Vice-Admiral, xxxiv, 75, 76
Penn, William, anecdote of, i, 113-14; FRUITS OF SOLITUDE, 331-416; editor's remarks on FRUITS OF SOLITUDE, l, 34; Helmholtz descended from, xxx, 180; life of, i, 330; Pepys and, xxviii, 311; Voltaire on, xxxiv, 75-9
Penni, Gian Francesco, xxxi, 35 note 3, 40, 57

Pennsylvania, in French and Indian War, i, 133-49; land conveyed to, by United States, xliii, 247; loans of, x, 492-3; paper money in colonial, 266-7; Penn and, i, 330; quarrels between Assembly and governors of, 132-4, 137, 144-5, 156-8, 167-70, 174; settlement of, 288; Voltaire on, xxxiv, 77
Pennsylvania Assembly, on Franklin's plan of union, i, 131; in French War, 133-4, 139, 144-5; Philadelphia hospital and, 122-3; votes powder as "other grain," 114-15
Pennsylvania Gazette, i, 62, 96, 108
Penology, correction the purpose of, ii, 150 (88); in Elizabethan England, xxxv, 321-2, 382-90; Hobbes on, xxxiv, 424; More on, xxxvi, 151-2, 158-63, 223-4
Pensions, Burke on, xxiv, 416-17; Ruskin on, xxviii, 127
Pentapolin, and Alifamfaron, xiv, 146-7
Pentateuch, Hume on miracles of the, xxxvii, 414
Pentheus, in the BACCHÆ, opposes Dionysus, viii, 351; hears of bacchanals, 358-9; orders arrest of Dionysus, 362; with Dionysus, 366-71; house destroyed, 376; determines to go to bacchanals, 382-8; led by Dionysus, 390-4; death, 397-400; Cadmus on, 411; Mænads and, Æschylus on, 116; Virgil on distraction of, xiii, 173
Penthiselea, in ÆNEID, xiii, 92, 384
People, Confucius on the, xliv, 5 (5), 8 (19, 20), 26 (9); Lincoln on government by the, xliii, 441; Lincoln on justice of the, 342; Pascal on opinions of the, xlviii, 113 (324), 114 (327), 115 (328-30), 117 (335); Vane on sovereignty of the, xliii, 138-40 (see also Populace, Public Opinion)
Peor, Milton on, iv, 13 (22), 100
Pepin, son of Charlemagne, xxxix, 84, 85
Pepin, son of Louis Debonair, xxxix, 85-6
Pepin, of Aquitaine, xxxix, 86
Pepper-plant, Sindbad on the, xvi, 295
Pepys, Samuel, as a critic, xxviii, 310; Diary of, 297-303; editorial remarks on Diary of, 286; xxxi, 1; domestic troubles, xxviii, 314-15; Emerson on stories from, v, 428; musical compositions, xxviii, 309; old age of, 315-16; portrait by Hales, 303; on praise of God, v, 445-6; public services of, xxviii, 296-7, 313; respectability of, 310-13; his unique position, 295-6;

versatility of his desires and pleasures, 303-8; as a writer, 308-9
PEPYS, SAMUEL, ESSAY ON, Stevenson's, xxviii, 295-316
Perception(s), Augustine, St., on inward, vii, 176-7; Berkeley on, xxxvii, 204-38, 242-4, 247, 249, 250, 260, 263-7, 271-2, 275-6, 281, 282-7, 300; Buddha on, xlv, 747; Hume on, xxxvii, 316-17, 434-6; involuntary, Emerson on, v, 74-5; belongs to judgment, xlviii, 10; mediate and immediate, xxxvii, 204-5, 236-7, 238; reality of, 206
Perceval, Spencer, popularity of, v, 384
Percivale, Sir, in the HOLY GRAIL, the sword and, xxxv, 113; at the tourney, 117; meeting with Galahad, 134-5; at the hermitage, 135; with his aunt, 141-3; follows Galahad, 143; at monastery at King Evelake, 143-5; encounter with men at arms, rescued by Galahad, 145-6; the robber knight and, 146-7; how he got a horse, 147; how he helped the lion, 148; his dream, 148-50; tempted by devil in woman's shape, 151-5; Gawaine on, 164; virginity of, 168; meeting with Sir Bors, 188; meeting with Galahad, 190-1; meeting with Sister, 191; in ship of Faith, 191-2, 199; at castle Carteloise, 200-2; sees hart and lions, 203-4; at castle of strange custom, 204-8; meets Galahad and Bors, 218; comes to castle of Carbonek, 218-19; fed of Holy Grail, 219-21; commanded to go to Sarras, 221; goes to Sarras, 222-3; in prison, 223-4; farewell to Galahad, 225; becomes hermit, 225; death and burial, 226; Renan on, xxxii, 165; sister of, xxxv, 190-200, 204-7, 209, 210, 223
Percy, Lord Henry, in Scots' raid, xxxv, 84; loses pennon to Douglas, 85; follows Douglas, 86-8; in battle of Otterburn, 89, 94 (see also ballads of OTTERBURN and CHEVY CHASE)
Percy, Sir Ralph, in Scots' raid, xxxv, 84, 86; at battle of Otterburn, 89, 92; Earl March and, 101
Percy's Reliques, Wordsworth on, xxxix, 342-4, 346
Perdiccas, Socrates and, ii, 297 (25)
Peredur, legend of, xxxii, 171-2, 173; Renan on, 149, 154
Perez, Anthony, xxxix, 92
Perez, John, of Viedma, xiv, 447
Perez, Pero, the curate in DON QUIXOTE, xiv, 48, 51-8, 241-9, 252, 292-3

Perez, Ruy, of Viedma, the Captive in DON QUIXOTE, xiv, 401-44
Perfection, as cause of beauty, xxiv, 93-4; Descartes on attainment of, xxxiv, 12-13; degree of, in nature, xi, 213-15, 219; Franklin on moral, i, 82, 89; doctrine of innate tendency to (see Progressive Development); Kant on conceptions of, xxxii, 373-4; Pascal on, xlviii, 330-1; Rousseau on attainment of, xxxiv, 219
Perfections, of Buddhism, xlv, 607-13, 633, 635
Périandre, Molière on, xxvi, 204-5
Peribœa, daughter of Eurymedon, xxii, 95; reference to, xxvi, 128
PERICLES, LIFE OF, Plutarch's, xii, 36-79
Pericles, Alcibiades and, xii, 110, 112, 115; Anatagoras and, 56-7; v, 454; Aspasia and, xii, 62-3; Athens beautified by, 49-54; birth of, 38; character of, 78-9, 40-1; charges against, 53; Cimon and, 46-7; convention of Greeks proposed by, 57-8; death, 77-8; domestic economy of, 56; domestic troubles, 75-6; education of, 40-1; Ephialtes and, 47; government of, 45 6, 48-9; his large head, 38-9; marriage of, 62-3; military conduct of, 58-62, 63-7; Mill on, xxv, 268; Newman on, xxviii, 41, 58; as an orator, ix, 217; in Peloponnesian War, xii, 67-75; in public life, 42-3; removed from command, 75; sayings of, 44-5; his supremacy, 54-6
Pericles, the younger, xii, 77
Periclymenus, Homer on, xxii, 159
Pericoli, Niccolo de', xxxi, 155 note
Perier, Madame, letters to, xlviii, 328, 331, 335, 347, 350, 351
Perier, M., country house of, xlviii, 334 note; letters to, 335, 346, 348
Perigord, Bertrand, Cardinal of, xxxv, 34-5, 39-42, 46, 60
PERIGOT AND WILLIE'S ROUNDELAY, xl, 252-4
Perillus, and the Sicilian bull, xx, 112 note 1
Periodicals, Mill on, xxv, 63
Peripatetics, Locke on the, xxxvii, 177
Periphantes, tutor of Ascanius, xiii, 200
Periphas, in sack of Troy, xiii, 119
Peris, good jinn, xiv, 9 note
Perithoüs, in Tartarus, xiii, 231-2
Perjury, punishment of, in old England, xxxv, 384
Permanence, a word of degrees, v, 155-6
Pernambuco, Darwin on, xxix, 523-5
Pernelle, Madame, in TARTUFFE,

leaves Orgon's house, xxvi, 189-96; refuses to credit Tartuffe's falseness, 269-71; convinced, 278, 283

Pero, Homer on, xxii, 159

Perpendiculars, grander than inclines, xxiv, 64

Perpetua, in THE BETROTHED, with Abbondio, xxi, 21-4; with Renzo, 30-1; on night of Renzo's intended marriage, 118-20, 128-30; her anger, 190-1; in German invasion, 494-502, 508-13; at castle of Unnamed, 515-17; returns home, 517-20; dies in plague, 571

Perpetual Motion, Helmholtz on, xxx, 219-20

Perpignan, camp of, xxxviii, 15-17

Perrault, discoverer of circulation of sap, xxxiv, 129

Perry, English drink, xxxv, 301

Perse, mother of Circe, xxii, 140

Persecutions, Bacon on, iii, 14-15; Browne on, 291; Emerson on folly of, v, 103-4; examples of religious, xxv, 227-30; Hume on, xxxvii, 417; Johnson on, xxv, 230; Mill on, 230-4; Rousseau on, xxxiv, 313 note; Voltaire on, 73

Persephone, Ceres's daughter, xli, 896; hymn to, viii, 430; maidservant of, 434

Perseus, king of Macedon, xlviii, 134 (409, 410)

Perseus, son of Danae, worship of, in Chemmis, xxxiii, 44-5

"Perseus," Cellini's statue of, xxxi, 357 notes 3, 4; 369-70, 389, 390-4, 395-9, 414, 416-19

Perseverance, not genius, xxviii, 385; proverb on, xv, 209; Zoroaster on, v, 82

Persia, cities of, shown to Jesus, iv, 395; Raleigh on, xxxix, 74, 118-19

Persistency, Epictetus on, ii, 173 (156); of heroism, v, 133

Personal Cautions, Penn's, i, 364-365

Personal Force, Emerson on, v, 209-10

Personal Instruction, Newman on, xxviii, 32-8

Personal Representation, Hare's, xxv, 165-6

Personal Rights, equality of, v, 250-1

Personalities, defamatory, xxvii, 249-51; laudatory, 248-9

Personality, and condition, Schiller on, xxxii, 252-5; extinction of (see Nirvana); reality of (see Ego)

Personifications, Wordsworth on, xxxix, 288

Persons, natural and artificial, xxxiv,

430-4; as the object of government, v, 250-3

PERSONS ONE WOULD WISH TO HAVE SEEN, xxvii, 281-95

Persuasion, Æschylus on, viii, 153; Franklin on methods of, i, 19; Pascal on, xlviii, 11 (10), 406-17

Pertelote, in NUN'S PRIEST'S TALE, xl, 36-49

Pertinax, Machiavelli on, xxxvi, 66, 71; slain by Prætorian Guards, 67

Pertness, Locke on, xxxvii, 113-14

Peru, ancient, iii, 166-7; conquest of, xxxiii, 341; Darwin in, xxix, 383-93; empire of, xxxiii, 327; Johnson on palaces of, xxxix, 236; Lopez on, xxxiii, 328-9; mines of, x, 180-1; religion of the Incas, xxxiii, 388; riches of, 314, 388

Pescara, Macaulay on, xxvii, 409

Pescara, Marquis, in DUCHESS OF MALFI, xlvii, 769, 793, 794-5, 796-9, 809, 813, 815

Pescennius, Cicero and, ix, 93

Pestalozzi, on help, v, 23; Mill on work of, xxv, 163

Pestilence, as a judgment of God, i, 246

PESTILENCE, IN TIME OF, xl, 265-6

Petar, "hoist with own," xlvi, 159

Peter, St., Æneas healed by, xliv, 450 (32-5); with Ananias and Sapphira, 438-9; angel of, xv, 341-2; Bunyan on, 135, 136; chosen apostle, xliv, 373 (14); on circumcision, 463 (7-11); Cornelius and 451 (5-48); his defence, 454 (1-18); his denial of Jesus, 418 (34), 419 54-62); editorial remarks on teachings of, 428; imprisoned, 436 (1-12), 456 (3-4); with Jesus, 382 (45, 51), 384 (20, 28, 32-6), 395 (41), 408 (28), 417 (8-13), 418 (31-4); at Jesus's tomb, 424 (12); keys of, xx, 184 note 7; lame man cured by, xliv, 434 (1-16); Luther on keys of, xxxvi, 284-5; Malchus and, xlviii, 267 (744); miracles done by, xliv, 439 (15); in Paradise, xx, 387-91, 400-2, 423; Paul, St., and, xxxvi, 286; on day of Pentecost, xliv, 431-3; in Samaria, 446 (14-25); Tabitha and, 450 (36-43); Tansillo on, xiv, 331

Peter, Prince, of Arragon, Dante on, xx, 176 and note 12

Peter III, of Arragon, Dante on, xx, 175 and note 10

Peter the Great, standing army of, x, 469

Peter Lombard, Sentences of, xxxvi, 341 note

Peter of Provence, Don Quixote on, xiv, 515, 516-17

Peterborough, Lord, Berkeley and, xxxvii, 198; Dryden and, xiii, 430

Petermann, the sacristan in WIL-
HELM TELL, xxvi, 405, 406, 413,
424, 427, 466
Peters, Rev. Hugh, Burke on, xxiv,
159-60, 214
Peters, Secretary, i, 129
Petition, right of, in United States,
xliii, 207 (1)
Petition of Right (English), Burke
on, xxiv, 180
Petrarch, Chaucer and, xxxix, 167;
Hume on, xxvii, 234; on spirit of
Italy, xxxvi, 90; Macaulay on,
xxvii, 389; Milton on, xxviii, 180;
Shelley on, xxvii, 364; Sidney on,
9; Wordsworth on sonnets of, xli,
697
Petrella, Castle of, xviii, 280, 310
Petrels, Darwin on, xxix, 307-8;
habits of, xi, 189
Petro, Granius, xii, 288
Petronius, arbiter of revels to Nero,
iii, 213; on poetry, xxvii, 114,
117-18
Petrucci, Pandolfo, xxxvi, 73; min-
ister of, 79
Pets, animal, Augustus on, xii, 36;
Harrison on, xxxv, 370-1
Pettinagno, Piero, xx, 200 note 6
Peucinians, Tacitus on the, xxxiii,
122-3
PEYSTER, COLONEL DE, EPISTLE TO,
vi, 585
Pezoro, Signior, xxxiii, 189, 191
Pfeiffer, in WILHELM TELL, xxvi,
376-7
Phæax, and Alcibiades, xii, 119, 120
Phædimus, king of Sidon, xxii, 64
PHÆDO, Plato's, ii, 45-114
Phædondes, ii, 47
PHÆDRA, Racine's, xxvi, 125-85; Dryden on, xviii, 13-14; editorial re-
marks on, xxvi, 124
Phædra, in HIPPOLYTUS, daughter of
Minos, her love for Hippolytus,
viii, 288; song of her woes, 292-
3; her illness, 294-303; tells her
shame, 304-6; urged to love on,
307-9; hears Hippolytus tempted,
311-12; anger at nurse, 316; determines to die, 317-18; death of,
319-20; her innocence told by
Artemis, 341
Phædra, in PHÆDRA, apparent hatred
of Hippolytus, xxvi, 126-7, 136-7;
her malady, 130-4; confesses love
for Hippolytus, 135-7; hears of
Theseus's death, 137-8; urged to
live for son, 138-9; interview with
Hippolytus, 147-51; her grief, 153-4;
her son chosen king, 152; her grief, 153-4; sends
to offer Hippolytus the crown,
155; her prayer to Venus, 156;
learns Theseus's return, 156-8;
urged to accuse Hippolytus, 158-
9; tells Theseus his wrong, 159-

60; begs Theseus to spare Hippolytus, 168-9; learns love of Hip-
polytus for Aricia, 169-73; denounces Œnone, 173-4; Panope
tells despair of, 179; confesses to
Theseus, 183-4
Phædra, in Homer's Hades, xxii,
160; Virgil on, xiii, 226, 269
Phædrus, translator of Æsop, xvii, 2
Phaëthon, steed of the sun, xxii, 327
Phæthusa, the nymph, xxii, 172
Phaeton, references to, xx, 74, 358
note 1; xlvi, 14
Phalaris, in ÆNEID, death of, xiii,
323
Phalaris, the tyrant, bull of, iii, 320;
xx, 112 note 1; Marcus Aurelius
on, ii, 212 (16)
Phanias the Lesbian xii, 18
Pharamond, in PHILASTER, suitor
of Arethusa, xlvii, 639-40; with
the King and Arethusa, 641-3;
denounced by Philaster, 644-7;
with Arethusa and Philaster, 654-
5; with Galatea, 657-9; and Megra, 659-61; his fault reported to
Arethusa, 661-2; before his lodging, 663-4; caught with Megra,
664-7; at the hunt, 684, 685, 689-
90; finding of Arethusa, 694-5;
finds Bellario wounded, 697-8;
arrests Philaster, 698-9; taken
prisoner by citizens, 705, 707, 708-
10; rescued by Philaster, 711-12;
sent home, 718
Pharaoh (of Exodus), Mohammed
on, xlv, 892, 898, 902, 913-14,
932, 944-6
Pharaoh (time of Joseph), dreams
of, xl, 43; Joseph and, xliv, 442
(10)
Pharaoh, wife of, Mohammed on,
xlv, 1008
Pharisaism, leads to superstition, iii,
48
Pharisees, beliefs of the, xliv, 483
(8); Bunyan on, xv, 110; Jesus
on the, xliv, 377 (30-5), 391 (37-
44), 403 (14-17), 407 (10-14);
Pascal on the, xlviii, 292 (829),
295 (839), 298, 299
Pharnabazus, Alcibiades and, xii,
149, 150; Plutarch on, 138, 139,
140, 142
Pharnaces, and Cæsar, xii, 317
Pharnapates, Plutarch on, xii, 360
Pharos, death of, xiii, 337
Pharsalia, battle of, xii, 310-14;
Antony at, 340
Phebe, daughter of Gaius, xv, 277-8,
286
Phegeus, death of, xiii, 408
Phelps, Oliver, xliii, 247
Phemius, in ODYSSEY, xxii, 13, 18,
245, 316-17

Pheræus, Alexander, xxvii, 30

Pheres, birth of, xxii, 158; death of, xiii, 340

Pheros, king of Egypt, xxxiii, 53-4

Phidias, accusation and death of, xii, 69-70; beautifies Athens, 51; Epictetus on, works of, ii, 138 (61); the "Jove" of, xlii, 1299; statue of Minerva, xii, 52-3

Philadelphia, city-watch of, i, 103; fire company formed by Franklin, 103-4; Library, founded by Franklin, 69-70, 77-79; Longfellow on, xlii, 1408; public hospital established, i, 121-3; situation of, v, 347; streets of, improved by Franklin, i, 124-5; University of (see University of Pennsylvania)

Philadelphia Catechism, xxiii, 21

Philadelphia Experiment, the, i, 155

Philadelphus, name of, xii, 162 note

Philagrus, tutor of Nepos, xii, 248

Philanthropy, Bacon on, iii, 34-6; Emerson on false, v, 67; Epictetus on true, ii, 183 (18); Marcus Aurelius on, 211 (11); moral worth of, xxxii, 328-9

Philarch, officer of Utopia, xxxvi, 187

PHILASTER, Beaumont and Fletcher's, xlvii, 639-718; remarks on, 638

Philaster, in PHILASTER, heir to Sicily, xlvii, 640; with king and Pharamond, 643-7; with the courtiers, 647-8; sent for by princess, 648-9; Arethusa on, 649-50; scene with Arethusa, 650-3; with Pharamond, 653-5; Bellario and, 655-7; with courtiers, hears Arethusa faithless, 670-4; questions Bellario, 674-8; with Arethusa, concerning Bellario, 680-2; in the woods, 686; meeting with Bellario, 686-7; finds Bellario with Arethusa, 691-2; attempts to kill Arethusa, 693-4; his regrets, 695; wounds Bellario, 696; saves Bellario, 698-9; in arrest, 699; summoned to death, 700; in prison 700-2; married to Arethusa, 703; condemned by king, 704-5; sent to quiet rebels, 707-8; rescues Pharamond, 710-12; in final scene, 712-14, 716-18

Philip, the apostle, xliv, 373 (14), 430 (13)

Philip, the deacon, xliv, 441 (5), 446 (5-13), 447 (26-40), 478 (8)

Philip, tetrarch of Ituræa, xliv, 365 (1)

Philip II, King of Macedon, Alexander and, xii, 37; v, 329; Demetrius and, iii, 53; Demosthenes and, xii, 207, 210-14; death of, 214-15; dream of, iii, 95-6; forces of, xxxvi, 50; love of

horseraces, xxvii, 31; Marcus Aurelius on, ii, 274 (29); the poor woman and, v, 273; Thebes and, xxxvi, 44

Philip II, King of Spain, Drake and, xxxiii, 133; Elizabeth and, 234; the Netherlands and, xix, 249-255-6; Raleigh on, xxxix, 91-3; wealth of, xxxiii, 319, 329-30

Philip III, King of France, Dante on, xx, 175 and note 7

Philip IV, King of France, beauty of, iii, 112; Pope Clement and, xx, 81 note 6, 369 note 7, 175 and note 9, 228 notes 4 and 5, 230 notes 15 and 16, 281 note 15

Philip IV, King of Spain, Calderon and, xxvi, 3

Philip V, King of Macedon, Machiavelli on, xxxvi, 83; the Romans and, 12, 13

Philip VI, King of France, in Crecy campaign, xxxv, 10, 15-16, 18-30

Philip of Burgundy, xix, 246

Philippa, Queen, Froissart and, xxxv, 3

Philippi, battle of, xii, 333; Antony at, xviii, 35

Philippi, Dr. A., xxxviii, 426-7

Philippine Islands, cession of, xliii, 470-7

Philippus, stepfather of Octavius, xii, 263

Philips, Ambrose, To CHARLOTTE PULTENEY, xl, 451-2

Philiscus, at Athens, xxviii, 60

Philistines, festival of, iv, 429-30; Samson and, 425

Philitis, the shepherd, xxxiii, 66

PHILLADA FLOUTS ME, xl, 389

PHILLIDA AND CORIDON, xl, 199

Phillips, Erasmus, in Hazlitt's discussion, xxvii, 289

Phillips, Wendell, Mill on, xxv, 171

Phillis, Milton on, iv, 33

PHILLIS, by Lodge, xl, 220

PHILLIS THE FAIR, by Burns, vi, 497

PHILLIS THE QUEEN OF THE FAIR, vi, 500

PHILLY AND WILLY, vi, 541

Philo, the Academic, xii, 226

Philo, the Jew, xlviii, 210

Philoctetes, in ODYSSEY, xxii, 39, 110, 289-90, 300-1, 305, 310-20

Philolaus, on motion of earth, xxxix, 58; Plato on, ii, 49

Philologus, Cicero and, xii, 267; death of, 268

Philology, an historical science, xxviii, 245-6; important results of, 238 (see also Language)

Philomeleides, and Ulysses, xxii, 57

Philomela, Milton on, iv, 36; story of, xx, 215 note 1

Philon, the shepherd, xl, 202-3

PHILONOUS AND HYLAS, DIALOGUES OF, xxxvii, 199-302

Philopœmon, Prince of Achaia, xxxvi, 51-2

Philosophers, Augustine, St., on, vii, 67-9; Burns on, vi, 354; charges against, ii, 9-10; Cicero on, xlviii, 123 note 4; Comte's rule of, xxv, 137-8; Dante on unskilful, xx, 344; death and, ii, 53-7; Epictetus on, 142, 143, 152, 156, 158-62; French, Burke on, xxiv, 259-60; Harvey on true, xxxviii, 66; the hereafter desired by, ii, 76-7; Marcus Aurelius on true, 219 (30); moral, Sidney on, xxvii, 17-21, 24-5; Pascal on, xlviii, 10, 140 (430), 142, 167 (503), 172-3; attitude toward pleasure and pain, ii, 75-6; poets compared with in usefulness, xxvii, 367-70; Rousseau on, xxxiv, 248-9; sacred and literary, v, 148; Sidney on, xxvii, 16; statesmen and, Plutarch on, xii, 56

PHILOSOPHERS, ENGLISH, xxxvii

PHILOSOPHERS, FRENCH AND ENGLISH, xxxiv

Philosopher's Candles, xxx, 128-9

Philosopher's Stone, Sir Epicure Mammon on the, xlvii, 543; Milton on, iv, 153

Philosophia Prima, xxxiv, 377

Philosophic Radicalism, Mill on, xxv, 71-3

Philosophic Radicals, in Parliament, xxv, 126-8, 138-9

PHILOSOPHICAL ESSAYS, xxxii

PHILOSOPHISE, THAT TO, IS TO LEARNE HOW TO DIE, xxxii, 9-28

Philosophy, Arnold on our, xxviii, 66; Athenian, Milton on, iv, 406-7; authority and, xxxix, 105, 128-9; Berkeley on innovations in, xxxvii, 281; Browne on righteousness of, iii, 276-7; Byron on, xviii, 431-2; Carlyle on, xxv, 355; Cicero on, ix, 46; Cowley on, xxvii, 65; Dante's allegory on, xx, 223; Descartes on study of, xxxiv, 8, 10; empirical and pure, xxxii, 317-18; as an employment, x, 15-16; Epictetus on, ii, 132 (56), 143 (72); need of, in ethics, xxxii, 335-6, 338-40; extreme limits of practical, 389-90, 394; Faustus on, xix, 200, 203; Hume on different species of, xxxvii, 305-15, 329, 330, 337-8; irreligion and, iii, 44; Kant on divisions of, xxxii, 317; knowledge of consequences, xxxiv, 376; liberty needed by, xxxvii, 416-17, 429; magic and, iii, 296; Marcus Aurelius on, ii, 205 (17), 227 (9), 235 (12); Montaigne on study of, xxxii, 50-2, 54-6; "more things than dreamt of in," xlvi, 112;

Plato on true, xxxii, 39; practical, best, ix, 205; Raleigh on, xxxix, 115; reading course in, l, 31-40; religion and, Voltaire on, xxxiv, 109-10; school and practical, xxxvi, 173-6; several branches of, xxxiv, 376-7; Socrates on, ii, 48, 73, 75-6; Taine on, xxxix, 453, 454, 455-6; Tasso on, xxxii, 34-5; transcendental, 320; of various races, xxxix, 443, 444

Philostratus, and Octavius, xii, 398

Philotas, on Antony, xii, 355-6

Philotimus, Cicero on, ix, 117, 155

Phineas, Burns on, vi, 172

Phinehas, xliv, 284 (30)

Phlebotomy, Harvey on, xxxviii, 121, 122, 123

Phlegethon, river, xiii, 229; source of the, xx, 62

Phlegyas, Dante on, xx, 33; in Tartarus, xiii, 232

Phocion, Carlyle on, xxv, 394-5; courage and honesty of, xii, 208; death of, xxvii, 24; on the event of the battle, v, 134; Landor on, 330; Marcus Aurelius on, ii, 292 (13); as orator, xii, 205

Phocylides, Sidney on, xxvii, 9, 14

Phœbe, name of Diana, viii, 115; xxxix, 66

Phœbe, the deaconess, ix, 427 note

Phœbus, Milton on, iv, 24 (4), 48, 76; wain of, 51 (see also Apollo)

Phœnicians, circumcision among, xxxiii, 51

Phœnix, Æsop on the, xvii, 304; Dante on, xx, 102; Herodotus on, xxxiii, 38-9; Milton on, iv, 190, 462; Virgil on the Greek, xiii, 129, 191

Pholus, Dante on, xx, 52; death of, 407

Phorcys, Homer on, xxii, 11

Phorkides, the, viii, 183

Phormisius, pupil of Æschylus, viii, 448

Phosphorescent Insects, Darwin on, xxix, 40-1

Phosphoresence, of the sea, xxix, 176-8

Phosphorus, combustion of, in oxygen, xxx, 144; flame of, 112

Phosphorus (youth), statue of, v, 179

Photographic Light, xxx, 272

Phraates, king of Parthia, in war with Antony, xii, 363, 364, 366, 370; in war with Media, 376

Phrontis, the pilot, xxii, 41

Phrygians, antiquity of the, xxxiii, 5-6

Phrynichus, accuser of Alcibiades, xii, 128-9, 135-6

Phyllis, Dante on, xx, 324 note 30

Phylogeny, defined, xi, 472
Physcon, name of, xii, 162 note
Physic (see Medicine)
Physical Science, Channing on study of, xxviii, 338-40; Descartes on, xxxiv, 50; Faraday on, xxx, 88; Huxley on, xxviii, 218-30; Pascal on, xlviii, 24 (67), 446-8
Physical Training, of children, xxxvii, 10-28; Milton on, iii, 256-9; Montaigne on, xxxii, 41, 57, 59; for women, xxviii, 151-2
Physicians, atheism of, iii, 265 note; Bacon on best, 86; early guilds of, xxxviii, 2, 3; Hippocrates on, 2, 3, 4-5; Pascal on costumes of, xlviii, 36
Physics (see Natural Philosophy)
Physiognomy, beauty of the, xxiv, 101; Browne on, iii, 326-7; of religious sects, v, 351; science of, 299; Webster on, xlvii, 728
Physiology, papers on, xxxviii, 79-147
Phytophagic Species, xi, 64-5
Pia, of Sienna, xx, 167 and note
Piazza, the anointer of Milan, xxi, 4-5
Picard, M., xxxiv, 118
Piccarda, in Paradise, xx, 296-8 and note
Piccolomini, Alfonso, xxxi, 278 note 1
Pickering, Timothy, xliii, 246
Pickett's Charge at Gettysburg, xliii, 403-15, 427
Pickthank, in Pilgrim's Progress, xv, 99-100
Pico, Don Andres, xxiii, 415
Pico, Galeotto, xxxi, 305 note 1
Pictet, Prof., on birds, xi, 355; on chalk formations, 383-4; palæontology, work on, 356
Picture-books, Locke on, xxxvii, 141
Picture of Little T. C., xl, 379-81
Pictures, less affecting than words, xxiv, 53-7; moving, in New Atlantis, iii, 188
Picus, son of Saturn, xiii, 245; Circe and, 249-50
Picus Mirandola, xv, 327
Piedmont, Prince of, xxxviii, 37
Piemont, Sonnet on Massacre of, iv, 86
Pienne, M. de, xxxviii, 26
Pierce, Mr., on wolves, xi, 103
Piercy (see Percy)
Pierino, and Cellini, xxxi, 17-20
Pierres, Mosen, xiv, 515
Pierus, daughters of, xx, 147 note 1
Pietra, Nello della, xx, 167 note
Piety, of act, speech and mind, xlv, 874-5; Carlyle on, xxv, 403; Dryden on, xiii, 25; Epictetus on true, ii, 174 (163); false, a double sin, xlviii, 321; Herbert on decay of,

xv, 411-12; Hindu conception of, xlv, 809-10, 827; Pascal on, xlviii, 94 (255), 165 (496), 361; Penn on, i, 377 (470); Segrais on, xiii, 25
Piety, in Pilgrim's Progress, xv, 52-3, 242-3
Piety, Early, xlv, 577
Piffero, Ercole del, xxxi, 17
Pigeons, analogous variations of, xi, 168; breeds of domestic, 37-9; circumstances favorable to breeding of, 55; correlation in, 30, 156; descent of, 39, 43, 52-3; in Elizabethan England, xxxv, 353-4; in history, xi, 43; instincts of tumblers, 268; reversion of, 169-70
Pigray, the surgeon, xxxviii, 51, 53
Pigs, held abominable in Egypt, xxxiii, 28-9
Pi Hsi, xliv, 60 (7)
Pilate, Pontius, governor of Judæa, xliv, 365 (1); and the Galilæans, 396 (1); and Jesus, 420 (1-7), 421 (11-25); Pascal on, xlviii, 267 (744), 278 (791)
Pilgrimage, Raleigh's, xl, 206-7
Pilgrimages, Luther on, xxxvi, 313-15, 325-6; Milton on, iv, 150
Pilgrim's Progress, Bunyan's, xv, 5-324; authorship of, 323-4; Franklin on, i, 14, 23; remarks on, xv, 4; 1, 34; widespread influence of, 173-4
Pilgrims, Lowell on the, xlii, 1451
Pilgrims of the Night, xlv, 584-5
Pillar of Cloud, xlv, 581
Pilli, Raffaello, de', xxxi, 388, 445-6
Pillows, in old England, xxxv, 314
Piloto, Cellini on, xxxi, 65 note, 150
Pin, M. du, Burke on, xxiv, 359; on French army, 359-62
Pinabel of Sorrence, xlix, 109, 201, 202-5
Pincheira, Darwin on, xxix, 281-2
Pindar, Alexander and, iv, 80; Browning on, xli, 957; the English, xiii, 65; Hiero and, xxvii, 41; Horace on, 194; house of, spared, iv, 80; Hugo on, xxxix, 358; Sidney on, xxvii, 31
Pindaric Line, Dryden on the, xiii, 56
Pindarus, freedman of Cassius, xii, 350
Pindenissus, siege of, ix, 143
Pineda, Juan de, iii, 289 note
Pine-tree, Emerson on the, xlii, 1305-13
Pinkney, Edward C., Health by, xxviii, 394-5
Pins, manufacture of, x, 10-11
Piombo, Sebastian del, xxxi, 101 note 6, 118 note 2
Pioneers! O Pioneers! xlii, 1486-90
Pious Editor's Creed, xlii, 1452-4

PIPES AT LUCKNOW, xlii, 1437
PIPPA'S SONG, xlii, 1115
Piracy, punishment of, in old England, xxxv, 387; under control of Congress, xliii, 172, 197 (10)
Piræus, companion of Telemachus, xxii, 222, 240
Piræus, port of, established by Themistocles, xii, 23
Pirithoüs, Racine on, xxvi, 161
Pisa, and Florence, xxxvi, 19
Pisistratus, and his daughter's lover, xx, 208 note 4; Emerson on, v, 249; Macaulay on, xxvii, 418; Newman on, xxviii, 40; Solon and, ix, 72
Piso, Calpurnius, Pliny on, ix, 287-8
Piso, Julius, ix, 432
Piso, Cæsonius, Lucius Calpurnius, Cicero on, iii, 68; Cicero and, xii, 252; Clodius and, 250-1; made consul, 285
Piso, son-in-law of Cicero, xii, 252
Pissuthnes, the Persian, xii, 63-4
PITCHER AND CROW, fable of, xvii, 33
Pitigliano, Count of, xxxvi, 45; Cellini on, xxxi, 305 note 1
Pitt, William, Earl of Chatham, George II and, xxiv, 349
Pitt, William, and Burke, xxiv, 400; Burns on, vi, 55-6, 169, 218, 433; Mazzini on, xxxii, 404
Pittacos, maxim of marriage, viii, 187 note
Pittacus, on forgiveness, ii, 153 (96)
Pittheus, and Hippolytus, xxvi, 166, 287
Pity, Bacon on, iii, 10, 36; Blake on, xli, 605, 606; Burke on passion of, xxiv, 42; envy and, iii, 26; Hobbes on, xxxiv, 356; language of, 358; love and, xl, 403; a natural feeling, xxxiv, 192-5; Pascal on, xlviii, 154 (452); without power to relieve, xviii, 177
Pizarro, Francisco, xxxiii, 313, 329; Raleigh on, 327, 341
Place, independence of, v, 132; no sanctity in, iv, 343; showeth the man, iii, 32; virtue indifferent to, xii, 197
Plagiarism, Montaigne on, xxxii, 32
Plagues, of Egypt, Milton on, iv, 350
Plain Truth, Franklin's pamphlet, i, 110
Planariæ, Darwin on, xxix, 37-8
Plancus, Munatius, xii, 347, 380
Planets, Bacon on motion of, iii, 39; Berkeley on the, xxxvii, 245; cause of movements of, xxxiv, 115-20, 122-3; Copernicus on motions of the, xxxix, 57-60; Dante on the, xx, 383; Dante on motions

of, 326 and note 3; Locke on motion of, xxxvii, 166; Marlowe on movements of, xix, 218-19; Milton on motion of the, iv, 249, 311; Raleigh on the, xxxix, 113; Rousseau on movement of the, xxxiv, 255-6
Plans, road long from, to acts, xxvi, 233
Planta, Pompeius, governor of Egypt, ix, 378
Plantain, Biggs on the, xxxiii, 244
PLANTATIONS, ESSAY ON, Bacon's, iii, 89-92
Plants, advantages of diversity of character, xi, 124; of all seasons, iii, 118-19; breeding of, xi, 47-8; checks on increase of, 82-5; complex relations with animals, 85-92; distribution of, 405-11; divided into groups, 142-3; domestic, descent of, 34-5, 44; experiments on, in New Atlantis, iii, 183-4; fertilization of, xi, 110-13; most fragrant, iii, 119; fresh-water, distribution of, xi, 429-31; habits of, hereditary, 152; rate of increase of, 79-82; insects and, relations of, 106-7, 108-9, 110-11; live on carbonic acid, xxx, 175-6; sexes in, separation of, xi, 107; the young of the world, v, 240
Plastering, in Elizabethan England, xxxv, 309
Plastic Arts, Goethe on, xxxix, 268-9, 271, 273, 274, 275, 278-9
Plata River, Darwin on the, xxix, 155; Drake at, xxxiii, 212
Platæa, annual sacrifice at, xii, 102-3; battle of, 21; campaign of, 91-101
Plathane, in THE FROGS, viii, 435-6
Platinum, weight of, xxx, 9 note 1, 52
Plato, Academy of (see Academy of Plato); APOLOGY OF, ii, 3-29; on censorship of books, iii, 216-17; on children, xxxii, 54; on children of the gods, v, 202; Christianity and, xxvii, 363; Cicero on, xii, 245; CRITO of, ii, 31-44; in Dante's Limbo, xx, 20; DIALOGUES of, remarks on, l, 31-2; Dionysius and, iii, 204, 216; xxvii, 41; on disease, xxxiv, 176; ideas of education, xxxii, 58; Emerson on, v, 249; on principle of equality, xxvii, 363; on faith and sincerity, xxxii, 39; four flatteries of, xii, 356 note; on freedom of the will, ii, 169 (142); on happiest state, xii, 271 and note; on indifference of places, ii, 284 (23); influence of, on English thought, v, 452-3; on kings and philosophers, xxxvi, 166, 167; on life and death, ii,

250 (35), 251 (44, 45); life and
works, 1-2; Lowell on, xxviii, 465;
man defined by, xlviii, 432; Mill
on, xxv, 19-20, 35; Montaigne
on *Commonwealth* of, xxxii, 34;
Montaigne on DIALOGUES of, 97-8;
Montesquieu on, 123; More on
Republic of, xxxvi, 175; Newman
on, xxviii, 58-9; old age of, ix,
50; Pascal on, xlviii, 14, 80 (219),
116, 273 (769); PHÆDO of, ii, 45-
114; on pleasure, ix, 62; on the
poets, xiii, 33, 40-2; preferences
of, xxxix, 98; Sainte-Beuve on,
xxxii, 137; school of, xxviii, 60-1;
Shelley on, xxvii, 350; shows of,
xii, 80; Sidney on, xxvii, 9, 26;
on socialism, xxxvi, 177; at Socrates's trial, ii, 21, 25; on the
soul, xxxiv, 104; on souls in the
stars, xx, 300 note 3; on speculation, v, 454; Spenser on, xxxix,
65; spirits, belief in, iii, 297 (33);
on training of body and mind,
xxxii, 57; two horses of the soul,
xii, 362 note; on the universe,
v, 321; on viewing life, ii, 251
(48); wealth of, xxviii, 60, 142;
on wise men and the public,
xxxvi, 176; on words and deeds,
xl, 31; on the world, xxxix, 110
Plato's Year, iii, 144 note, 270 note
Platonism, Emerson on, v, 453
Platonists, on Christ, vii, 112-13;
Mill on title of, xxv, 20
Plautianus, and Severus, iii, 71
Plautus, the *Casina*, of, xxvii, 405;
Dryden on, xxxix, 182; Hugo on,
365; in Limbo, xx, 238; *Menæchmi*
of, xxxix, 239; Montaigne on,
xxxii, 93; Sidney on, xxvii, 47, 48
Play, of adults, xxxvii, 188; of chil-
dren, 95, 118-19, 121; instinct of,
Schiller on, xxxii, 262-6, 307-9;
out-door, xxxvii, 15
PLAY, THE END OF THE, xlii, 1099
Playhouses, Swift on, xxvii, 128
Playthings, Locke on, xxxvii, 119-
21, 138-9
Pleading, Pliny on conciseness in
legal, ix, 214; Shelley on, xviii,
351-2
Pleasanton, Gen., at Gettysburg,
xliii, 380-1, 383, 393, 422; Haskell
on, 382
Pleasing, Pascal on art of, xlviii, 409
Pleasure, analysis of, ii, 289 (2);
Archytas on sensual, ix, 60;
Berkeley on idea of, xxxvii, 207,
211; Burke on standards of, xxiv,
11-12; Cicero on, ix, 60-1; Confucius on, xliv, 5 (1); Cowper on,
xli, 548; effects of cessation of,
xxiv, 34-5; as the end of life,
xliv, 340 (1), 342 (12-13, 24), 346
(18), 350 (15), 351 (7-10); xlv,

871; Epictetus on indifference to,
ii, 118 (2); Epictetus on use of,
150 (86); of farmers, ix, 64-7;
Goldsmith on lowly, vi, 116; highest, after danger or pain, vii, 127-
8; Hobbes on, xxxiv, 353; of the
imagination, xxiv, 16-22; in imitations, xxxix, 234; inseparable
from morality, v, 95; of the judgment, xxiv, 22-4; Keats on, xli,
894, 896; Kempis on worldly, vii,
284 (4); Krishna on, xlv, 879-80;
of love, xxiv, 37, 38-9; Marcus
Aurelius on, ii, 203 (12), 205
(16), 231 (26), 241 (34), 258
(10); may be spared, iv, 218; of
melancholy, 35-9; Mill on, xxv,
36; of mirth, iv, 31-5; Montaigne
on, xxxii, 9-10; More on, xxxvi,
207, 208-16; not the end of man,
ii, 259 (19); of old age, ix, 61-
4; in one thing, ii, 234 (7); the
order of nature, xli, 659; pain in
relation to, xxiv, 30-1; pain and,
Shelley on, xxvii, 369; pain and,
Socrates on, ii, 48; Pascal on,
xlviii, 66 (181), 376, 420-1; Pascal on principles of, 409; Pascal
on yielding to, 62 (160); philosophic attitude toward, ii, 75-6;
physical action of, xxiv, 126; physical causes of, 127-35; Pope on,
xl, 428, 429; power and, xxiv, 57;
rare, ii, 183 (11); removal of, not
like positive pain, xxiv, 31-5, 37;
of the senses, 13-16; sensibility to,
24-5; of society, 37-46; two kinds
of, xxvii, 368; Utopian idea of,
xxxvi, 199; Vaughan on innocent,
i, 77; wants and, Goldsmith on,
xli, 538; a weaker idea than pain,
xxiv, 36; Wordsworth on principle
of, xxxix, 294-5
PLEASURE ARISING FROM VICISSITUDE,
xl, 472-3
Pleiad, Taine on the, xxxix, 452
Pleiades, called Atlantic Sisters, iv,
311; mentioned in Job, xliv, 86,
136; Milton on the, iv, 239; Tennyson on the, xlii, 1010
Pliable, in PILGRIM'S PROGRESS, xv,
15-21, 72-3
Pliant, Dame, in THE ALCHEMIST,
xlvii, 592-4, 598-601, 607-8, 626,
631, 634-5
Pliny the Elder, on bees, xxxv, 365;
on breeding among savages, xi,
48; death of, ix, 194, 298-301;
habits of, 243-5; on lead mines of
Wales, xxxv, 340; Mæcenas and,
xliii, 30; on marl of Britain, xxxv,
324; on pears, xi, 51; on pigeons
in Rome, 43; Sainte-Beuve on,
xxxii, 121; on sugar, xxxv, 290;
Tacitus and, xxxiii, 94; on torrid
zone, xxxix, 112; on the viper,

xxxv, 362 note, 364 note; works of, ix, 242-3

Pliny, the Younger, on his abstemiousness in sickness, ix, 312-13; attends recitations, 209; as augur, 263; as counsel for Bætica, 331-2; on boldness in writings, 364-7; on the Christians, ix, 425-7; clemency of, 361-2; Corellius on, 269; his dealings with merchants, 332-4; description of inundation, 342; dream of, 212; equal hospitality of, 225-6; fame of, during his life, 362-3; on his friendships, 330; his belief in ghosts, 326-9; on giving library to his town, 201-3; as governor of Bithynia, 383 et seq.; grief for Corellius Rufus, 208; humanity of, 370 note; in the Hundred Court, 229-31, 267-8, 362; indulgence of others' levity, 360-1; on interpretation of a will, 264, 285; as lawyer and judge, 216-17, 237, 264, 268-9, 271, 290, 292-3, 296-7, 314-15, 362, 376-7; legacy from Curianus, 272-4; LETTERS OF, 195-438; LETTERS, editor's remarks on, l, 20; life and works, ix, 193-4; life in Laurentum, 373; life in Tuscum villa, 370-2; occupations of, 205; made a privileged citizen, 375; prosecution of Certus, 355-60; on purchasing a new property, 257-8; on reason for reciting his works, 320-2; on reciting his writings, 348; Regulus, relations with, 197-9; seeks office of augur or septemvir, 381; on selling an estate, 318-19; as a senator, 335-40; slaves and servants, relations with, 219, 288-9, 332, 341; on the spring, 271-2; statue purchased by, 245-6; method of study, 200; a supper of, 211; the temple of, 379-80; with his tenants, 372; town under his patronage, 260; correspondence with Trajan, 374-438; speech on Trajan, 255-7, 307; to Trajan, on princes, xxxiv, 220; made treasurer of Saturn, ix, 376, 380 note 1; vanity of, iii, 135; verses by, ix, 317; verses on, 259; during eruption of Vesuvius, 302-5; villa of, 231-6; villa in Tuscany, 278-85; villas on Larian Lake, 352-3; wealth of, 380 note 2; wife of (see Calpurnia); wish to live in history, 330-2; on his works, 353-4; on his writings and lectures, 275-6; Zosimus, servant of, 288-9

Pliocene Strata, Lyell on, xxxviii, 426

Plistoanax, king of Sparta, xii, 60-1

Plodding, wins the race, xvii, 40

Plotinus, Emerson on, v, 129; the "union" of 146

Ploughman's Life, The, vi, 26

Plover, long-legged, xxix, 126-7

Plowman, Chaucer's, xl, 26

Plumptre, E. H., translator of Greek Dramas, viii, 1

Plums, Locke on, xxxvii, 21

Pluralities, Harrison on, xxxv, 273-4; Luther on, xxxvi, 331; Milton on, iv, 82; iii, 221

Plutarch, on dissimulation, xxxix, 72; on Elysian Fields, xxxv, 323; Emerson on heroes of, v, 191; historian of Heroism, 127; Irish myths and, xxxii, 188; on his knowledge of Latin, xii, 198; life and works of, 3-4; Montaigne on, xxxii, 30, 45-6; 95-6; on motion of the earth, xxxix, 58; on poets, xxvii, 42; on Saturn, iii, 47; Shelley on, xxvii, 352; study of advised, iii, 252; on victors of the games, xxxiv, 270

Plutarch's Lives, xii; editor's remarks on, l, 19, 48; Franklin on, i, 14; Mill on influence of, xxv, 76; Shakespeare and, xxxix, 237

Pluto, in The Frogs, viii, 463-66; helmet of, iii, 59; Hugo on, xxxix, 366

Plutocracy, Mill on dangers of, xxv, 112

Plutus, Dante on, xx, 29; fable of, iii, 93; Webster on, xlvii, 765

Plymouth, settlement of (see also Mayflower Compact)

Plymouth Rock, Lowell on, xlii, 1451

Plynteria, feast of, xii, 145

Po-niu, disciple of Confucius, xliv, 19 (8)

Po-yi, xliv, 17 note 10, 23 (14), 58 (12), 64 (8)

Po-yü, son of Confucius, xliv, 58 (13), 60 (10)

Podalirius, and Alsus, xiii, 405-6

Podesta, in I Promessi Sposi, xxi, 77-84, 302, 423-4, 575

Podolia, honey of, xxxv, 365

Poe, Edgar Allan, life and works of, xxviii, 382; poems by, xlii, 1273-92; The Poetic Principle, xxviii, 381-404

Poems, Poe on length of, xxviii, 383-7

Poesy or Art, Coleridge on, xxvii, 269-77

Poesy, Defense of, by Sidney, xxvii, 7-55

Poesy, The Progress of, xl, 465-8

Poet, The, by Emerson, v, 167-189

Poet, Advice to a Young, xxvii, 112-30

Poetic Diction, Wordsworth on, xxxix, 298, 307-11

Poetic Principle, The, by Poe, xxviii, 381-404

Poetical Beauty, Pascal on, xlviii, 17 (33)

Poetical Justice, Dennis on, xxvii, 198

Poetry, advantages of, over prose, xxxix, 300-2; in America, Whitman on, 409-32; Aristotle on, xiii, 36-7; xxvii, 21-2; Arnold on study of, xxviii, 65-91; the aspiration for supernal beauty, 389-91; Bentham on, xxv, 75; Burke on cause of power of, xxiv, 136-48; Byron's definition of, xxxii, 417; characteristics of high, xxviii, 74-5; classes of readers of, xxxix, 327-32; Coleridge on, xxvii, 269-70; comic, 29-30; common life in, xxxix, 285-6; compared with history and biography, 294; compared with painting in effect on the passions, xxiv, 53-7; compared with reason in usefulness, xxvii, 367-70; Confucius on, xliv, 26 (8), 58 (13), 60 (9); contemptible subjects in, xxxix, 304; criticism of, 327-33; defined, xxvii, 345; Descartes on study of, xxxiv, 8, 9; didactic, xxviii, 387-8; Dryden on, epic and dramatic, xiii, 5-11, 14; Dryden on virtues of, xxxix, 165-6; earliest form of teaching, xxvii, 8-10; effects of, on society, 352-67; elegiac, 29; Eliot on reading of, I, 9-10; Eliot on translations of, 4; Emerson on power of, v, 161; enervating, xxvii, 38-40; English (16th century), 43-53; English, retrospect of, xxxix, 333-47; English, review of, xxviii, 75-90; estimate of, by comparison, xxviii, 72-4; exhortation to honor, xxvii, 54-5; expression of high delights, 346; false criticism of, xxxix, 304-5; fancy and imagination in, 316-26; fancy and judgment in, xxxiv, 364; favored by eminent men, xxvii, 112; Franklin on usefulness of writing, i, 17; future of, xxviii, 65-6; Goldsmith on, xli, 531-2; habits of order produced by, xxvii, 375; heroic, 31-2; high standards necessary in, xxviii, 66-7; hints for encouragement of, xxvii, 125-30; historic and personal estimates of, xxviii, 67-72; Hobbes on, xxxiv, 377; honored by great men, xxvii, 42-3; Hugo on taste in, xxxix, 404-5; Hugo on originality in, 383-5; Hugo on rules in, 382-5, 407-8; Hume on rules of, xxvii, 219; iambic, 29; inspiration of, 371-2; lack of appreciation of high, xxxix, 332-47; language of, 281-2, 283, 285-6, 288-94, 297-9, 303-4, 307-11, 417-19; learning unnecessary to, xxvii, 116-18; Locke on, xxxii, 159-60; of love, xxvii, 364-5; lyric, 30-1; Mazzini on, xxxii, 401-2; Mazzini on Goethe's conception of, 410-11; measure in, xxvii, 349-51; merit of, as measured by length, xxviii, 383-7; James Mill on, xxv, 15; Milton on study of, iii, 255-6; Montaigne on, xxxii, 30, 63-4; music and, xxxix, 315-16; national awakening influenced by, xxvii, 376-7; nature and, xxxix, 423-4; its need of giving immediate pleasure, 294-5; need of, in periods of wealth, xxvii, 371; not an imitative art, xxiv, 144-5; observation of order and relations in, xxvii, 347; originality in, xxxix, 348-51, 419; pastoral, xxvii, 28; Plato on, 42; Plato's banishment of, 40-2; Pliny on, as method of study, ix, 317-18; popularity as test of, xxxix, 351-3; reason of power of, xxiv, 41, 45; powers requisite for producing, xxxix, 312; primitive, ancient, and modern, 356-73; profitableness of, xxvii, 35-6; prose and, xxxix, 290-1 note; purpose in, 286; record of best moments, xxvii, 372-3; relation of feeling and action in, xxxix, 287-8; relation of substance and style in, xxviii, 75; religion and, xxvii, 113-16; xxxix, 329-31; requirements of, 415-17; restricted meaning of, xxvii, 349; rhyme in, 120; rhythm in, xxvii, 390; Romans and, xxvii, 10-11; romantic and classical, xxxix, 362-3; rural life and, xxvii, 70-1; Sainte-Beuve on reason in, xxxii, 130-1; satiric, xxvii, 29; Schiller on, xxxii, 285-6; science compared with, xxxix, 295-6; science related to, 296-7; similes in, xxvii, 121; source of all knowledge and virtue, 371; sources of, xxviii, 403-4; stories compared with, xxvii, 351; superiority of, to other arts, 349; taste in, xxxix, 282; Thoreau on nature in, xxviii, 426-7; three classes of readers of, xiii, 60-2; three general kinds of, xxvii, 14-15; tragic, 30; truth and, xxxix, 424-5; truth and duty may be introduced incidentally, xxviii, 391, 403; truth its object, xxxix, 294, 296; turns all things to loveliness, xxvii, 373; universality of, 348-351; xxxix, 296-7; as untruth, xxvii, 36-7; various kinds of, 28-32; xxxix, 313-14; of various races, 443, 444; verse and rhyme in, xxvii, 34-5, 52; as teacher of virtue, 16-

28; as promoting wantonness, 37-8; Whitman on future, xxxix, 409-32; word from the Greek, xxvii, 12-13; Wordsworth on, xxxix, 281-2, 283-306, 307-11, 312-26, 327-53; Wordsworth on materials of, 281; world created anew by, xxvii, 373-4

POETRY OF THE CELTIC RACES, xxxii, 141-91

POETRY, ENGLISH, xl, xli, xlii

POETRY, SHELLEY'S DEFENCE OF, xxvii, 343-77

Poets, Aristophanes on duty of, viii, 450, 452; authors of language, xxvii, 347-8; banished by Plato, 40-2; Browning on, xlii, 1113-14; Burke on narrowness of, xxiv, 49; Burns on, xi, 86-7, 91, 114, 329-30, 339, 450-1; called vates, xxvii, 10-11; defined in universal sense, 347; Dryden on, xviii, 5; Emerson on great, v, 149; fame of, xxvii, 349; happiest and best of men, 374-5; historians as, 352; Jonson on, xl, 310; to be judged only by time, xxvii, 352; as legislators and prophets, xxvii, 348; Manzoni on advice of, xxi, 487; meaning a maker, xxvii, 12, 32; O'Shaughnessy on, xlii, 1246-7; Pascal on, xlviii, 17 (34), 19 (39); philosophers as, xxvii, 350-1; philosophers, compared with, 367-70; qualifications requisite to, xxxix, 312; shoemakers and, xxvii, 121; Socrates on wisdom of, ii, 8; Tasso on, xxvii, 374 note; unacknowledged legislators of the world, 377; Whitman on, xxxix, 413-30, 432; Wordsworth on, 292-3, 296, 297-8, 316-17; xli, 675

POET'S DREAM, THE, xli, 878-9

POET'S PROGRESS, THE, vi, 338-41

POET'S WELCOME TO HIS LOVE-BEGOTTEN DAUGHTER, vi, 59-60

POETS, ODE ON THE, xli, 896-7

Poggini, Domenico, xxxi, 365, 375, 377

Poggini, Gianpagolo, xxxi, 365 note, 375, 377

Pogius of Florence, xxxix, 17

Pointers, instincts of, xi, 267, 268

Poisoning, Harvey on, xxxviii, 132-3; punishment of, in old England, xxxv, 384

Poisons, regulation of sale of, xxv, 304-6

POITIERS, THE BATTLE OF, xxxv, 34-60

Poix, Edward III at, xxxv, 17

Polarity, in affairs of government, v, 256; in nature, 14-15, 91-3

Polarization of Light, xxx, 277-9

Pole, Cardinal, and Machiavelli, xxvii, 384

POLEMIC, EPITAPH ON A NOISY, vi, 62

Polemo, the sophist, xxviii, 61

Polemon, King, capture of, xii, 364

Polenta, Guido da, xx, 113 note 3

Policy, and justice, xxiv, 304; Penn on, i, 354 (152-4)

Polite Letters, Hume on, xxxvii, 309

Politeness, Character and, xxxii, 250, 269; Locke on, xxxvii, 50, 132-3; origin of, xxxiv, 208; the ritual of society, v, 425-6; Swift on ceremonial, xxvii, 107-8 (see also Manners)

Polites, and Circe, xxii, 142; death of, xiii, 121

Politian, mentioned, xxvii, 390

Political Economy, Burke on beginnings of, xxiv, 415; effects of a mistaken, x, 458-9; human nature in, xxviii, 483; Mill on, xxv, 152-3; need of imagination in, xxvii, 368, 370; objects of, x, 325; systems of (see Commercial S., Agricultural S.)

Political Institutions, dependent on circumstances, xxiv, 156; Hamilton on, xliii, 212; Mill on choice of, xxv, 111-12

Political Parties, Washington on, xliii, 255, 257, 258-9

Politicians, Smith on, x, 365; Socrates on, ii, 7-8; Webster on, xlvii, 767

POLITICS, ESSAY ON, Emerson's, v, 249-261

POLITICS, ON, by Burns, vi, 480.

Politics, Burke on science of, xxiv, 209-10; Channing on, xxviii, 329-30; corruption in, under property system, xxxvi, 178; friendship in, ix, 22-4, 30-1; Hamilton on intolerance in xliii, 214; Hobbes on science of, xxxiv, 376; Hume on science of, xxxvii, 314, 379, 444; Lowell on science of, xxviii, 452; Mill on science of, xxv, 103-6; Milton on study of, iii, 254; reading course in, l, 48-51; Thoreau on, xxviii, 413

Poll-taxes, Smith on, x, 526-7, 538-40

Pollio, Asinius, orator, ix, 214 note 3; in African War, xii, 318; Cæsar, and, 303; on Cæsar, xxxii, 102

Polonius, in HAMLET, the prototype of, xlvi, 86; Laertes, and, 94; farewell advice to Laertes, 102; counsels Ophelia against Hamlet, 103-4; sends Reynaldo to Laertes, 113-15; hears Hamlet's madness, 115-16; reports to king, 118, 119-21; scene with Hamlet, 121-3; announces players, 127, 129, 130-1;

asks king to play, 133, 139-40;
plan to test Hamlet's madness,
134, 138; at the play, 141, 146;
summons Hamlet to queen, 149;
in hiding at Hamlet's meeting
with mother, 151, 153; death,
153; Hamlet on, 154, 159, 162-3
Polus, the actor, xii, 197 note, 221
Polyalces, Plutarch on, xii, 68
Polybus, in the ODYSSEY, xxii, 51,
313; death of, 315
Polycarp, Bunyan on, xv, 268
Polycaste, daughter of Nestor, xxii,
46
Polycrates, tyrant of Samos, xii, 65;
Anacreon and, xli, 834; death of,
prophesied, iii, 95; Emerson on,
v, 99
Polydamna, wife of Thon, xxii, 54;
Helen and, xxxiii, 57
Polydeuces, and Castor, xxii, 159
Polydore, Molière on, xxvi, 204-5;
murder of, xiii, 133
POLYEUCTE, Corneille's, xxvi, 71-
121; remarks on, 70
Polyeucte, in POLYEUCTE, goes to be
baptized, xxvi, 71-5; Pauline on,
76-7; Severus on, 82; returns to
Pauline, 86-7; determines to go
to temple, 88-90; his deeds in
temple, 93-4; his conduct at death
of Nearchus, 97, 98; in prison,
100-3; with Pauline in prison, 103-
7; with Felix, 112-14; last scene
with Pauline, 114-15; refuses to
yield and condemned, 116-17
Polygamy, Browne on, iii, 337; Mill
on, xxv, 299-300
Polylerites, More on the, xxxvi, 160
Polymnestor, Dante on, xx, 231 note
19
Polymorphic Genera, xi, 60-1
Polynices, and Eteocles, xx, 109
note; references to, in ANTIGONE,
viii, 243, 247-8, 250-1, 280
Polypheides, son of Mantius, xxii,
214, 215
Polypheme, the Cyclops, xiii, 152-3;
reference to, xli, 966
Polyphemus, Burke on, xxiv, 133;
remarks on story of, xxii, 3;
Ulysses and, 11, 125-34
Polytheism, Lessing on, xxxii, 196
Pomarre, Queen, of Tahiti, xxix,
439-40
Pomham, the Indian, xliii, 155
Pommiers, Aymenion of, xxxv, 36,
42, 48
Pomona, reference to, iv, 193; Ver-
tumnus and, 273
Pomp, Milton on, iv, 192; Penn on,
i, 407
Pompeia, wife of Cæsar, xii, 277;
Clodius and, 249-50, 281-2
Pompeius, Quintus, quarrel with
Sulpicius, ix, 7

Pompeius Saturninus, letter to, ix,
200
Pompeius, Sextus, xii, 358-9 (see
Pompey, Sextus)
Pompeo, xxxi, 95-6, 126, 131, 139,
141, 148-50, 153
Pompey, accusations against, ix, 101-
2; Cæsar and, iii, 130, 148; ix,
4-5; xii, 257-8, 260, 284, 285-6,
291, 293, 295, 296; Cæsar and,
Cicero on, ix, 168-9; 170; Cæsar,
final contest with, xii, 298-313;
Cæsar killed beside statue of, 330;
Cæsar presented with head of,
315; Cicero and, ix, 90-1, 117, 120,
125, 126, 127-8, 168-9; xii, 232,
251, 252, 254, 257-8; Cicero on,
ix, 84, 97, 127; Cicero on death
of, 165; Clodius and, xii, 254;
Crassus and, 284; Dryden on, xiii,
16-17; in Egypt, xxxii, 6; as man-
ager of corn supplies, ix, 99; marries Cæsar's daughter, xii, 277,
285; at Milo's trial, ix, 100-1;
xii, 255; Milton on, iv, 389; in
Parthian war, ix, 153; Pascal on,
xlviii, 239 (701); preparations of,
ix, 102; provincial laws of, 418
note 2; sea-power of, iii, 83; sons
of, xii, 320; temperate life of,
349; Sylla and, iii, 70; Webster
on death of, xlvii, 814
Pompey, Sextus, Erichtho and, xx,
37 note 2; refuses to break word,
xii, 358-9; in Sicily, 358; war on,
362
Pomponia, and Q. Cicero, ix, 139;
Philologus and, xii, 268
Ponkipog, Eliot on, xliii, 151
Pontanus, Sidney on, xxvii, 14
Pontitianus, and St. Augustine, vii,
132-5
Pontonous, in the ODYSSEY, xxii, 98
Pontormo, Jacopo Carrucci da, xxxi,
418 note
Pooley, Thomas, persecution of, xxv,
232 note 2
Poor, Burns on life of the (see
TWA DOGS); Luther on care of
the, xxxvi, 329-30; Montaigne on
the, xxxii, 122
Poor Laws, in Elizabethan England,
xxxv, 317-19; of England, x, 145-
50; Ruskin on, xxviii, 127 and
note 17
POOR MAILIE, DEATH OF, vi, 43-5
POOR MAILIE'S ELEGY, vi, 45-7; re-
marks on, 17
Poor Richard's Almanac, i, 3, 95-6,
172
POORTITH CAULD AND RESTLESS LOVE,
vi, 479-80
Pope, Alexander, on Addison, xxvii,
183, 184, 188, 189; Addison's
Cato and, 177, 178; Arnold on,
xxviii, 82-4; Burns on, vi, 358;
Byron on, xxxii, 133-4; as editor

of Shakespeare, xxxix, 246-8, 334;
Emerson on, v, 462; ESSAY ON
MAN, xl, 417-51; Hazlitt on, xxvii,
287-9; ON A LADY AT COURT, xl,
416; lines by, on friends, xxvii,
287-8; Milton and, xxxix, 336;
on Milton's God, xxviii, 207; on
modesty in speech, i, 19; Ralph
and, 40, 157; Sainte-Beuve on,
xxxii, 133, 136; on Shakespeare,
xxxix, 222, 228, 240; SOLITUDE
by, xl, 415; Swift and, xxviii, 15,
27; Swift on, 14; on Swift, 13;
on Thomson, xxxix, 341; Voltaire
on, xxxiv, 152-3, 155; Wordsworth on, xxxix, 338-9; Wordsworth on *Iliad* of, 340; Wordsworth on *Windsor Forest* of, 340
Pope, Sir Thomas, xxxvi, 139-40
Pope, in PILGRIM'S PROGRESS, xv,
70
Pope's Months, xxxvi, 294, 303
Popery, Milton on, iii, 241
Popes, benefices and the, xxxvi, 294-
9; bishoprics and, 295-6, 303-4,
308; bulls of the, 328-9; Calvin
on the, xxxix, 44-5; court of the,
xxxvi, 292, 308; custom of kiss-
ing their feet, 311; Dante on covetousness of the, xx, 400-2; Dante
on temporal authority of the, 213;
Datarius of the, xxxvi, 298 note,
300; encroachments in Germany,
290-4, 303, 308-9; England and,
xxxiv, 90; how regarded in Italy,
xxvii, 386; jubilees of the, xxxvi,
314 note; legates of, 332; attitude
toward liberty of press, iii, 206-7;
Luther on pomp of the, xxxvi,
289-90, 295, 308, 312; Luther on
powers of the, 265-6, 267, 270,
271, 325; Luther on right of pun-
ishing, 283, 286; Luther on vices
and encroachments of the, 289-
313, 332-3, 337, 339-40; monasti-
cism encouraged by, 315; Pascal
on the, xlviii, 309 (871-7), 311
(880, 882); their relation with
temporal power, xxxvi, 278-83, 305,
309-11; relations with empire, 309-
11, 343-7; their right to interpret
Bible, 283-5; their rights over
councils, 286-8; saints and, 327;
as vicars of Christ, 361 (see also
Papacy)
Popillius, and Cicero, xii, 267
POPLAR FIELD, THE, xli, 547-8
Poplicola, Plutarch on, xii, 184
Poppy-water, Locke on, xxxvii, 27
Populace, Bacon on movements of
the, iii, 42; Browne on the, 325;
disapproval of the, v, 69-70; kings
and, iii, 54; nobility and, xxxvi,
34; praises of the, iii, 132; in
princedoms, xxxvi, 34-7; Shakespeare on likes of the, xlvi, 162;
superstition of, iii, 47

Popular Science, Freeman on, xxviii,
243
Popularity, Carlyle on, xxv, 419-20;
Hobbes on, xxxiv, 374; Milton on,
iv, 389; Penn on, i, 366; as test
of poetry, xxxix, 351-3
Population, Bacon on need of limit-
ing, iii, 41; laws of, in Utopia,
xxxvi, 194-5; limited only by food
supply, x, 174; Mill on restriction
of, xxv, 71; regulated by demand
for labor, x, 84; relation of, to
poverty, 83-4
Poquelin (see Molière)
Porphyro, and Madeline, xli, 909-17
Porphyry, the vision of, v, 145
Porpoises, Darwin on, xxix, 49
Porsena, reference to, xiii, 293
Port Famine, Darwin on, xxix, 247,
249
Port Pheasant, xxxiii, 135-6
Port Plenty, Drake at, xxxiii, 148,
157
Port Royal, Pascal on nuns of,
xlviii, 296 (841)
Portail, Antoine, xxxviii, 48
Portents, defined, xxxiv, 397; study
of, in Egypt, xxxiii, 42
Porter, in MACBETH, xlvi, 326-7
PORTER, THE, AND THE LADIES OF
BAGHDAD, xvi, 60-71
Porter, Edward, xxxiii, 349, 363, 385
Portia, death of, xlvii, 779 note
Portillo Pass, Darwin on, xxix, 333;
origin of name, 344
Portinari, Folco, father of Beatrice,
xx, 3
Porto Praya, Darwin on, xxix, 11-
12
Porto Rico, cession of, xliii, 470
(2), 473, 475
PORTRAIT, A, Sheridan's, xviii, 105-8
Portraits, Coleridge on, xxvii, 274-5
Portugal, discoveries of, x, 417;
reading and writing in, xxxvii,
137; taxes on precious metals in,
x, 398-401; trade treaty with Eng-
land, 408-13
PORTUGUESE, SONNETS FROM THE,
xli, 950-68
PORTUGUESE CHAPEL HYMN, xlv,
567-8
Portunus, reference to, xiii, 190
Porzia, Madonna (see Chigi, Porzia)
Poseidon, among the Ethiopians,
xxii, 9-10; origin of name of,
xxxiii, 30; in the ODYSSEY, xxii,
9-10, 11, 78-81, 113, 184-5; Tyro
and, 158
Posidonius, on tides, xxx, 294
POSIE, THE, vi, 431
Positiveness, Franklin on, i, 19
Possession, better than prospect, xvii,
32; use the only, xix, 32
Possibilities, Aurelius on, ii, 238
(19)
Post-office, expense of maintaining,

x, 475; government ownership of, 490

Post-offices, under Confederation, xliii, 174; under Constitution, 197 (7)

Postal Service, Marshall on, xliii, 234; progress of, ix, 387 note

Posterity, Bacon on care of, iii, 20, 22; Penn on care of, i, 358-9; Raleigh on greatening, xxxix, 96-8; Woolman on care of, i, 242-3

POSTHUMOUS CHILD, ON A, vi, 418

Postponement, Marcus Aurelius on, ii, 206 (1), 212 (14), 216 (17)

Postumus, name of, xii, 162

Potassium, tester of water, xxx, 118, 124 note; why it decomposes water, 145-6

Potatoes, cultivation of, x, 170; introduced into England by Drake, xxxiii, 126; nourishment in, x, 171; wild, in Chonos Islands, xxix, 302-3

Potentates, Raleigh on, xl, 208

Pothinus, the eunuch, xix, 315, 316

Potiphar's wife, in Dante's HELL, xx, 127 note 6

Pots, fable of the, xvii, 31

Potts, Stephen, i, 52-53, 60

Poultry, price of, x, 196-7; in Utopia, xxxvi, 184

Pourceaugnac, Hugo on, xxxix, 374

Poverty, Arabian verses on, xvi, 136; Browne on, iii, 345; Burns on, vi, 546; Carlyle on, xxv, 350-1; Confucius on, xliv, 6 (15), 47 (11), 56; and crime, Confucius on, 26 (10); and crime, Shakespeare on, xlvi, 281; Goldsmith on, xli, 529; Hobbes on, xxxiv, 380; Jesus on, xliv, 374 (20); Kempis on, vii, 297 (4); Lear on hardships of, xlvi, 254-5; Lucan on, xx, 333 note 16; money and, xxxvi, 252; More on fear of, 196; old age and, ix, 48; Penn on, i, 344 (52); relation of, to marriage and generation, x, 83-4; due to property system, xxxvi, 177-8; a cause of sedition, iii, 40, 41; in subjects, xxxvi, 171, 172; unmerited, makes proud, xix, 398

Powell, Anthony, with Drake, xxxiii, 237; in Drake's Armada, 235, 249, 256, 259, 265, 267

Powell, Mary, first wife of Milton, xxviii, 187-90, 192; iv, 4

Power, Burke on idea of, xxiv, 57-62; Confucius on, xliv, 8-9; the desire for, xxxiv, 385; different kinds of, xxx, 6-10; education confers the only true, xxviii, 139-40; Emerson on thirst for, v, 19; force is not, viii, 360; gives no true claim to obedience, xxviii, 204-5; Hobbes on sources of,

xxxiv, 374-5; honor in relation to, 378, 380-3; Hume on idea of, xxxvii, 355-70; love of, in children, 90-1, 96; Pascal on, xlviii, 110 (310); penalties of, v, 92-3; political, Washington on distribution of, xliii, 259-60; the pomp of, xl, 456; real and imaginary, xlviii, 109 (307, 308); resides in transition, v, 77; Ruskin on love of, xxviii, 162; Shelley on fear of, xviii, 334; thirst for, iii, 26-7, 34; velocity and, in machines, xxx, 190-3; worldly, price of, xviii, 435; worldly, transitoriness of, xvi, 315-19, 326-7, 331-2, 334-6

Pozzobonelli, Michele, xxi, 532, 547

Practicalness, More on, xxxvi, 174-6

Practice, Bacon on, iii, 101-2; early, makes the master, xxvi, 416; Locke on teaching by, xxxvii, 46, 47, 49-50; Marcus Aurelius on, ii, 300 (6)

Praed, Mill on, xxv, 84

Prætors, Roman, ix, 290 note 2

Pragmatic, defined by Kant, xxxii, 347 note

Pragmatick, in PILGRIM'S PROGRESS, xv, 299

PRAISE, ESSAY ON, Bacon's, iii, 132-3

Praise, Augustine, St., on, vii, 59, 70; Augustine, St., on desire of, 199-203; belongeth to God alone, 257 (4); children's love of, xxxvii, 41-4; 185; Cicero on, ix, 108, 159; danger from, v, 103; desire of, i, 366 (320-1); Emerson on the highest, v, 41; "foolish face of," 69; Goldsmith on love of, xli, 539; Hobbes on, xxxiv, 359; independence of, vii, 254 (2, 3); Jesus on, xliv, 374 (26); Jonson on, xl, 308-9; Kempis on danger of, vii, 322 (5); Kempis on love of, 317-318; Locke on, of children, xxxvii, 112; love of, the strongest motive, xxviii, 96-8; Marcus Aurelius on, ii, 216 (19, 20), 237 (16), 253 (62), 260 (21), 266 (53), 274 (34); as means of training, xxv, 90-1; Milton on, iii, 200; Milton on popular, iv, 389; Pascal on, xlviii, 123 note 10; Penn on, i, 400-1; Pliny on, iii, 135; Pliny on, ix, 259; Raleigh on, xxxix, 96; results of competition for, xxxiv, 385; results of desire of, 386; Rufus on leisure for, ii, 118 (5); of self, Pliny on, ix, 203; superiority to, v, 201

Praising, the delight of, xli, 926

Prassede, Donna, in I PROMESSI SPOSI, xxi, 428-31, 445, 462-4, 647

Prato, Giovanni of, xxxi, 226, 256, 259

Prayer, in affliction, vii, 305; allegory of, xv, 193-4; Browne's, iii, 343-4; Calvin on, xxxix, 53; for cleansing the heart, vii, 303; Coleridge on the best, xli, 717; by Dante, xx, 189; David on, xli, 507, 509; xliv, 182 (6); for the dead, Browne on, iii, 270-1; for the dead, Dante on, xx, 168-9; Emerson on, v, 36, 81; for enlightenment, vii, 298-9; Epictetus on, ii, 136 (58); against evil thoughts, vii, 298; Franklin's, i, 87; to do God's will, vii, 288; gratitude the most perfect, xxvi, 311; Jesus on, xliv, 389 (1-13), 407 (1-7); Kempis on proper, vii, 287; Luther on, xxxvi, 323; Marcus Aurelius on, ii, 226 (7), 275 (40); Milton on, iv, 323, 326; Mohammed on, xlv, 893, 930-1, 933, 985, 991-2, 1009; Pascal on, xlviii, 169 (513-14), 346; Penn on formal, i, 378 (478); Raleigh on dying, xxxix, 99-100; Rousseau on, xxxiv, 288; Shakespeare on, xlvi, 151, 152; in sickness, by Pascal, xlviii, 370-8; for the spirit of devotion, vii, 271; Tennyson on, xlii, 1026; Thomson's, i, 87; in times of doubt, vii, 315 (2); in Utopia, xxxvi, 247, 249; Woolman on, i, 183, 301

PRAYER, A, IN PROSPECT OF DEATH, vi, 36

PRAYER: O THOU DREAD POWER, vi, 249-250

PRAYER, A, UNDER PRESSURE OF VIOLENT ANGUISH, vi, 33-4

Preacher, Goldsmith's, xli, 525-6

Preaching, Emerson on, v, 34-37, 42; Luther on Christian, xxxvi, 376-7

Precedents, Hobbes on, xxxiv, 388; Lowell on, xxviii, 453

Precepts, the Buddhist, xlv, 759

Precious Metals, demand for, x, 182-3, 185; effect of increase and decrease of, 210-11; exportation and importation of, 280-1; in foreign trade, 312-3; movements of the, 280-1, 328-33; not indispensable to trade, 334; price of, 178-182, 209-10; steadiness of price of, 333-4; taxes on exportation of, 398, 401; in Utopia, xxxvi, 202-3; value of, compared with corn, x, 186-7; value of,

reason for, 422; variation in value of, 38-9, 48; effect of variation on rents, 40-1; as wealth, 335-46

Precious Stones, prices of, x, 183-4, 185, 186; reason for high prices of, iii, 92; in Utopia, xxxvi, 203, 205, 211-12

Precious Things, David on, xli, 509-10; for those that prize them, xvii, 9

Precision, excessive, v, 219

Precocity, Bacon on, iii, 111

Preconception, Seneca on, xlviii, 123 note 5

Predecessors, the memory of, iii, 32

Predestination, St. Augustine on, vii, 49; Browne on, iii, 274, 323; Calvin on, xxxix, 53; Dante on, xx, 374; Hume on doctrine of, xxxvii, 388-91; Jansenist doctrine of, xlviii, 5; Omar Khayyam on, xli, 983, 984

Predicaments, of Aristotle, St. Augustine on, vii, 62; sons of Ens, iv, 22

Predictions (see Prophecies)

Pre-existence, Augustine, St., on, vii, 9; Cicero on proofs of, ix, 75; Lessing on, xxxii, 216-17; Socrates on, ii, 63-8; Wordsworth on intimations of, xli, 609-15

Prefaces, Hugo on, xxxix, 354-5; remarks on, 3; to speeches, a waste of time, iii, 67

PREFACES TO FAMOUS BOOKS, xxxix

Prejudice, Burke on, xxiv, 235; fatal to a critic, xxvii, 226-7; Pascal on, xlviii, 42 (98); in PILGRIM'S PROGRESS, xv, 295; Tennyson on, xlii, 1033

Prelates, and kings, iii, 53

Premium, Mr., in SCHOOL FOR SCANDAL, xviii, 139; Sir Oliver Surface as, 146-7, 150-59

Premiums, for encouragement of industry, x, 406

Premunire, defined, xlvii, 836 note

PREPARATIONS, a poem, xl, 201-2

Prepotency, in animals, xi, 329; instances of, 319-20

Presage, defined, xxxiv, 397

Presbyter, is but priest writ large, iv, 83

Presbyterianism, Franklin on, i, 80; Voltaire on, xxxiv, 82-3

Prescott, Mill on, xxv, 80, 81

Prescription, rights by, Burke on, xxiv, 300

Present, the, alone can be lost. ii, 204 (14); Emerson on the, v, 21-2; Hobbes on the, xxxiv, 333; Longfellow on the, xlii, 1317; Omar Khayyam on enjoyment of

the, xli, 972, 973, 974, 983; Pascal on the, xlviii, 362; Pascal on neglect of the, 64 (172); a point in eternity, ii, 241 (36); Raleigh on the, xxxix, 93; represents all eternity, ii, 241 (37), 262 (36); Shakespeare on the, xl, 268, 269; Thoreau on the, xxviii, 436-7; use of the, ii, 206 (1), 212 (14), 216 (17), 218 (26)

PRESENT IN ABSENCE, xl, 321

PRESENT CRISIS, THE, xlii, 1447-51

Presents, defined by Stella, xxvii, 137 (see also Gifts)

Presidency, price of the, v, 92

Press, liberty and licentiousness of the, xxvii, 258-9; Franklin on liberty of, i, 96-7; Mill on liberty of the, xxv, 218-59; pious editor's idea of liberty of, xlii, 1453; liberty of, in U. S., xliii, 207 (1); Mill on writing for, xxv, 57-8

Pressure, effect of, on temperature, xxx, 243-4

Preston, Captain, xxxiii, 314, 321, 327, 335

Presumption, of mankind, Smith on, x, 113; Pascal on, xlviii, 79 (214)

Presumption, in PILGRIM'S PROGRESS, xv, 43, 219-20

Pretas, xlv, 873 note 2

Pretences, Cicero on, ix, 39-40; Raleigh on, xxxix, 73

Pretexts, Thackeray on, xxviii, 9

Pretino, Il, xxxi, 164 note 5

Pretty, Francis, DRAKE'S VOYAGE, xxxiii, 205-33

PRETTY PEG, vi, 534

Prevention, better than cure, i, 365 (304)

Priam, Burke on, xxiv, 134; character of, xiii, 21; death of, 122; in sack of Troy, 120-1; Shakespeare on death of, xlvi, 129-30; visit to Arcadia, xiii, 277

Priam, grandson of King Priam, xiii, 200-1

President of United States, xliii, 199-202; duties and powers, 201-2; election, early method, 199 2, 3); election, amended method of, 209-10; impeachment of, 194 (6), 202 (4); his part in legislation, 195-6; Lincoln on duty of, 342; oath, 201 (7); qualifications, 200 (4); removal or death of, 200 (5); salary, 200 (6); term of, 199 (1); veto power of, 195-6

Price, Dr. Richard, Burke on, xxiv, 159-80, 201-2, 203-4, 213-15

Price, Thomas, xxxii, 145

Price, everything has its, v, 101

Prices, of agricultural products, x, 12; of bread and meat, 157-9,

160-1; bounties, their effect on, 396-8, 401; of cattle, 191; of clothing, 212-16; of coal and wood, 176-8; of commodities made by employments, 124-5; comparative, of food and materials, 186-8; component parts of, 50-7; of dairy produce, 198-9; as dependent on wages and profits, 103-4; in England (1772), i, 318; of fish, x, 208; of hogs, 197; of limited or uncertain products, 200-11; of manufactures, as affected by progress, 211-16; of meat, as dependent on price of hides, 206-7; of metals, 178-83, 209-11; of metal manufactures, 211-12; natural and market, 58-67; of necessaries in relation to wages, 78-9, 87-8, 90-1; paper currency, its effect on, 263-4; of poultry, 196-7; of precious stones, 183-4; of produce determine progress of cultivation, 200; of produce, effect on rents, 216; of producible things, 190-200; progress of society, its effect on, 186-216; real and nominal, 36-49; regulated by corn, 397; regulation of, by law, 151-2; rent and, relations of, 155; scarcity, 188-9; taxes on consumption, in relation to, 544; variations in, 123; of venison, 195-6; of wool and hides, 201-7 (see also Values)

Pridam le Noire, xxxv, 173; his fight with Sir Bors, 174-5

Pride, Æschylus on, viii, 222; Augustine, St., on temptations of, vii, 200-3; Browne on, iii, 336; Burke on, v, 98; Confucius on, xliv, 26 (11); folly of, vii, 219-20; fosterer of inequality, xxxvi, 253; Franklin on, i, 92; Hunt on, xxvii, 306; instances of, given by Dante, xx, 193-4; Jesus on, xliv, 399 (11), 407 (14); Marcus Aurelius on, ii, 282 (10), 304 (27); Mohammed on, xlv, 927; Pascal on human, xlviii, 133 (405-7), 156 (460); Penn on human, i, 339-41; provokes envy, iii, 26; punishment of, in Purgatory, xx, 188-92; results of, xxxiv, 367; the sin, in FAUSTUS, xix, 220; Tennyson on, xlii, 1063; virtue and, xl, 430; in one's virtues, ii, 177 (176); womanly, xl, 256; Woolman on, i, 285

Pride of Life, daughter of Adam, xv, 74

PRIDE OF YOUTH, xli, 764-5

Priestley, Huxley on, xxviii, 217; Lowell on, 472

Priestman, Thomas, i, 327

Priests, actors and, xix, 27; Buddhist, ordination of, xlv, 756-63;

Caxton's tale of two, xxxix, 18-19; Chaucer on, xl, 25; Dryden on satires of, xxxix, 172-3; Emerson on, v, 33-41; false, Shelley on, xviii, 301; Kempis on qualities of, vii, 359-60; 369 (6, 7); Luther on, xxxvi, 279, 280, 282-3, 350-1, 373-4, 376; marriage of, Calvin on, xxxix, 40; marriage of, Luther on, xxxvi, 317-21; Pascal on, xlviii, 312 (885); punishments of, xxxvi, 323 note; Quaker attitude toward, xxxiv, 70; in Utopia, xxxvi, 244-6, 248; Whitman on, xxxix, 430

Primal Four, the, xix, 51

Primary Qualities, xxxvii, 219, 223-4

Primary Schools, origin of, xxviii, 379

Primaticcio, Francesco (Il Bologna), xxxi, 314 note, 323-6, 327-8, 332, 338

Prime, the, in Low Countries, iii, 144

Primogeniture, Hobbes on, xxxiv, 426; Johnson on, v, 430; Pascal on, xlviii, 104 (291), 112 (320)

Primum Mobile, iii, 39 note

Prince, etymology of word, xxxv, 229

PRINCE, THE, Machiavelli's, xxxvi, 5-90; editorial remarks on, 3; Garnett on, 3-4; influence of, xxvii, 381-2; Macaulay on, 383; 413-15

PRINCE AND THE GHULEH, THE, xvi, 39-40

Prince Rupert's Drops, xxx, 29 note 9

Prince of Wales, title of heir of England, xxxv, 229

Prince, need of adaptability in, xxxvi, 84-6; clemency and cruelty, 56-7, 58-9; counsellors of, 80-2; Duke Chon on, xliv, 65 (10); expedients of, for security, xxxvi, 71-5; faith of, 59-60; flatterers of, 80; Goldsmith on, xli, 522-3; liberality and miserliness in, xxxvi, 54-6; duty of, in military affairs, 50-2, 71-2, 74-5; More on, 149; Pliny on praise of, ix, 255; means of acquiring reputation, xxxvi, 75-9; secretaries of, 79-80; should avoid contempt and hatred, 62-71; should not depend on fortune, 84; should they excite love or fear, 57-9; Tzu-kung on, xliv, 67 (20, 21); virtues and vices of, xxxvi, 53-4, 60-1; Webster on, xlvii, 740 (see also Kings, Rulers)

Princedoms, absolute and limited by nobility, xxxvi, 16-17; acquired by crimes, 30-4; acquired by fortune,

23-30; advantages of new, 82; arms in new, 71-2; arms and factions in mixed, 72-3; best friends in new, 73-4; civil, 34-7, 74; ecclesiastical, 39-42; hereditary, 7-8; military affairs of, 42-52, 71-2, 74-5; mixed, 8-19; new, acquired by merit, 20-3; the several kinds of, 7; strength of, 37-9

Principal and Agent, Hobbes on, xxxiv, 430-1

Principia, Newton's, Locke on, xxxvii, 178

PRINCIPIA, PREFACE TO NEWTON'S, xxxix, 157-9

Principles, assertorial, problematical, and apodictic, xxxii, 345; Emerson on, v, 88; Epictetus on, ii, 127 (30); Marcus Aurelius on, 211 (13), 213 (3), 216 (16), 290 (5); Pascal on intuitive, xlviii, 100

Printing, Hobbes on invention of, xxxiv, 335

Printing-houses, Franklin on, i, 47 note

Prior, Matthew, poems by, xl, 406-8; Voltaire on, xxxiv, 150, 159

Prioress, Chaucer's, xl, 14-15; Dryden on, xxxix, 174

Priscian, in Dante's HELL, xx, 66

Priscilla, wife of Aquila, xliv, 471 (2-4, 18-19), 472 (26)

Priscus, Cornelius, letters to, ix, 227, 258, 294, 322

Priscus, Javolenus, anecdote of, ix, 297-8

Priscus, Vibius, xxxv, 367

PRISONER OF CHILLON, xli, 821-31

Prisoners of War, in agreement with Mexico, xliii, 325-6

Prisons, Cellini in praise of, xxxi, 263-5; Emerson on, v, 58-9

Pritchard, Mrs., Hazlitt on, xxvii, 390

Privacy, Penn on, i, 366-7, 370

Private Property (see Property)

Privation, Burke on terror in, xxiv, 63

Privernus, death of, xiii, 316-17

PRO PATRIA MORI, xli, 838

Proæresius, leader of Attic school, xxviii, 60; Hephæstion and, 55

Proairesis, Milton on, iii, 254 note

Probability, Hume on, xxxvii, 351-3, 397-9; Pascal on doctrine of, xlviii, 317 (908), 319 (917-18, 920), 321 (922)

Probity, Franklin on usefulness of, i, 91

PROBLEM, THE, by Drummond, xl, 336-7

PROBLEM, THE, by Emerson, xlii, 1299

Problematical Principles, xxxii, 345

Probus, the soldiers and, iii, 43

Prochorus, xliv, 441 (5)

Procula, Serrana, Pliny on, ix, 210

Proclus, on beauty, v, 319; on God and the world, xxxix, 111; on the universe, v, 173, 182

Procopius, xxxii, 188 note 30

Procrastination, Bentham on, xxvii, 256; Machiavelli on, xxxvi, 13

Procris, in Homer's Hades, xxii, 160; in the Mournful Fields, xiii, 226

Proctophantasmist, in FAUST, xix, 173-4

Proculeius, Cleopatra and, xii, 396-7

Proculus, meaning of name of, xii, 162

Proculus, Vettius, ix, 357

Procurators, Roman, ix, 310 note 5

Prodicus of Ceos, ii, 5

Prodigal Son, parable of the, xliv, 401 (11-32)

Prodigality, Augustine, St., on, vii, 29; economically considered, x, 279-81; liberality and, i, 344; motives of, x, 282; public, 282-3; punishment of, in Dante's HELL, xx, 29-30, 48

Prodigies, Plutarch on, xii, 42

Prodius, character of, iii, 68

Production, bounties on, x, 404-5; consumption the object of, 444; on what dependent, 5-6, 283-4; improvement in, causes of, 9-28; improvement in, dependent on capital, 222; improvements in, effect on prices, 186-216; improvements in, raise rents, 216-17; effects of increase in, on wages, profits, and interest, 297; less important than intellectual improvement, xxviii, 363; a means, not an end, 230; Mill on laws of, xxv, 158; taxes on, x, 508-10

Productive Labor, in agricultural system, x, 449-50; defined, 270; employment of capital is, 303-6; maintenance of, 271-2; proportion of, on what dependent, 273-7

Professions, competition in, unnaturally increased, x, 138-43; liberal, remuneration of, 106, 108, 111-13

Profitableness, Aurelius on, ii, 243 (45), 252 (53)

Profit(s), in by-employments, x, 125-6; capital and, 93, 99, 100; of city and country, 120; clear and gross, 101; as fixed by competition, 294; defined, 55; dependent on prices, 123; by what determined, 58; tendency of, to equality, 105; extraordinary, 63-4; effect of increase of commodities on, 297; effect of increase of money on rate of, 296-7; inequalities, natural, 107, 108-9, 111, 117; inequalities due to government interference, 126-52; as indicated by rate of interest, 94-9, 102-3; as affected by market fluctuations, 62-3; maximum of, 102; minimum of, 101; an element in natural price, 58-9; in new trades, 122; effect of high, on prices, 103-4; as affected by progress, 275; proportion in different employments, 67; of speculators, 120-1; of stock, as element in prices of commodities, 51-2, 54; taxes on, 518; wages and, 118-19; of wholesale and retail trade, 119-20

Profusion, a source of grandeur, xxiv, 68-9

Progne, changed to swallow, xx, 181 note 4

Prognostics, Browne on, iii, 296; Hobbes on, xxxiv, 394, 396-7

Progress, dependent on art, xxxii, 244 et seq.; Emerson on, v, 155-66; Goethe on, xix, 358, 361, 376-7; Pascal on, xlviii, 121 (354), 122 (355); effect of, on landlords, capitalists, and wage-earners, x, 216-20; effect on prices, 186-216; liberty necessary to, iii, 232 et seq.; Tennyson on, xlii, 1018-19; due to wants, xxxiv, 181-2; of wealth, x, 57, 319-24

Progressive Development, Darwin on, xi, 227, 228-9; objection to law of, 220

Progressive State, effect of, on profits, x, 93; effect of, on wages, 73-5, 85-6

Prohibition, Mill on, xxv, 296-7

Projects, Franklin on new, i, 131; imprudent, economically considered, x, 281; Penn on, i, 360

PROLOGUE, A, by Burns, vi, 273-4

PROLOGUE SPOKEN AT DUMFRIES, vi, 393

PROLOGUES TO FAMOUS BOOKS, xxxix

Promeneia, the priestess, xxx'ii, 32

Prometheus, crime and punishment of, viii, 156-9; fire stolen by, 157 note, 160 note; Heracles and, 182, 186 note 63; Hobbes on, xxxiv, 391; Io and, viii, 177-86; Jove and, v, 96; lament of, viii, 159-61; marriage with Hesione, 167, 175; Mazzini on, xxxii, 418; with ocean nymphs, viii, 161-6; with Okeanos, 166-9; his services to man, 164-5, 171-3; type of human nature, iii, 17; Zeus and, viii, 182, 187-94

PROMETHEUS BOUND, viii, 156-94; editorial remarks on, 3; Voltaire on, xxxix, 382

Promises, of captives, fable of, xvii, 34; Descartes on, xxxiv, 22; of enemies, fable on, xvii, 30; Goethe on written, xix, 66-7; Kant on, xxxii, 332-3, 350, 353, 360; in law,

xxxiv, 410-17; Marcus Aurelius on breaking, ii, 209 (7); Penn on, i, 356-7; of princes, xxxvi, 59-60; of princes, Beaumont on, xlvii, 641; Yu-tzu on, xliv, 6 (13)

Promissory Notes, as money, x, 264-5

Proofs, Hume on, xxxvii, 351 note, 397; Pascal on, xlviii, 19 (40)

Propagation (see Population)

Propensity, and inclination, xxxii, 356 note

Property, Burke on representation of, xxiv, 199-200; under democracy, xxviii, 466-7; denunciations of, their origin, 469; elective franchise based on, v, 251-2; xxviii, 466-7; Emerson on cares and uses of, v, 51, 52; Emerson on the institution of, 49, 252; Emerson on reforms of, 269; Emerson on wrongs of, 99; by gift or inheritance, 251; in labor, x, 129; in land, effect on wages, 69; Locke on, xxxiv, 209; Locke on love of, xxxvii, 91, 97; Lowell on rights of, xxviii, 477, 484; Mill on private, xxv, 149; More on system of, xxxvi, 176-8, 250-3; Pascal on private, xlviii, 106 (295); Pascal on rights of, 383-4; reliance on, is want of self-reliance; v, 87; Rousseau on, xxxiv, 202; Rousseau on origin of, 206, 212; Rousseau on effects of system, 214-15; secures private, U. S. Constitution, xliii, 207-8; weight of, in government, v, 253

Prophecies, Bacon on, iii, 95-8; Browne on, 311; Hume on, xxxvii, 414-15; not miracles, xlviii, 285-6; among pagans, xxxiv, 396-7; Pascal on, xlviii, 218-23, 230, 236, 237-64, 287-8; Rousseau on, xxxiv, 300-1

Prophesying, St. Paul on, xlv, 520 (1-6), 521 (22-5), 522 (37-9)

Prophets, armed and unarmed, xxxvi, 22; God's compact with the, xlv, 969 note; Lessing on Hebrew, xxxii, 199; Milton on Hebrew, iv, 408; not acceptable in own country, xliv, 369 (24)

Proportion, as cause of beauty, xxiv, 78-89; Emerson on love of, v, 218; in works of art, xxiv, 91-3

Proportional Representation, xxv, 165-6, 193

Proprietors, in agricultural system, x, 448

Propriety, Tzu-hsia on, xliv, 66 (11); works on, xxvii, 172-3

PROPYLAEN, INTRODUCTION TO THE, xxxix, 264-80

Prose, in the drama, xxxix, 393; poetry and, Wordsworth on, 290-1; qualities of fit, xxviii, 83

Proserpine, Dis and, iv, 164; the moon called, xx, 43 note 9 (see also Persephone)

PROSERPINE, THE GARDEN OF, xlii, 1251-3

Prosopitis, island of, xxxiii, 25

Prosper, on idleness, xxxix, 14

Prosperity, Arabian verses on, xvi, 213; Bacon on, iii, 17; its dependence on virtue, xliii, 243; dependent on God, xliv, 315; ECCLESIASTES on, 348 (14); excessive, punished by Nemesis, ix, 285 note; happiness and, i, 360, 361; Kempis on, vii, 237 (2), 278 (3, 4); love and, iii, 29; Machiavelli on blindness of, xxxvi, 83; Marcus Aurelius on, ii, 261 (33); Pascal on, xlviii, 46 (107), 361; Raleigh on, xxxix, 70, 100-1; religion and, iii, 46

Prospero, in THE TEMPEST, with Miranda, tells his story, xlvi, 381-7; with Ariel, 387-91; with Caliban, 391-3; with Ferdinand, 394-7; in scene of Ferdinand and Miranda, 413, 414, 415; plot against, 416-18; invisible at banquet, 420, 421, 422-3; betroths Miranda to Ferdinand, 423-5, 427; in the conspiracy of Caliban, 428-30, 431-2; in final scene, 432-42; epilogue spoken by, 442

PROSPICE, by Browning, xlii, 1106

Prostitution, Bacon on, iii, 177-8; Blake on, xli, 604; in ancient Germany, xxxiii, 106; Luther on houses of, xxxvi, 350; punishment of, in old England, xxxv, 384-5

Protagoras, banishment of, xxxvii, 416; books burned in Athens, iii, 203; wealth of, x, 142

Protasius, the martyr, vii, 153

Protean Genera, xi, 60-1

Protective Duties, Smith on, x, 348-65; removal of, 365-9

Protectorate, The English (see INSTRUMENT OF GOVERNMENT)

Proteic Matter, formation of, xxxviii, 379-80

Protesilaus and Laodamia, xli, 679-83

Protestant Church, music of, xxxix, 441-2

Protestantism, Catholicism and, iii, 266 (3), 268 (5); Shelley on, xviii, 277 (see also Reformation)

Proteus, king of Egypt, xxxiii, 54-6; called Carpathian Wizard, iv, 69; Menelaus and, xxii, 58-63; Milton on, iv, 153; iii, 240; representative of nature, v, 239

PROTHALAMION, Spenser's, xl, 233-8

PROUD WORD YOU NEVER SPOKE, xli, 923

Proudhon, not the first against property, xxviii, 469

Proverbs, Don Quixote on, xiv, 175; Emerson on, v, 97-8; law of compensation in, 98; Manzoni on, xxi, 78; the ready money of experience, xxviii, 451

Proverbs, Book of, paraphrase from, xxxix, 309-10

Providence, academics on, xxxix, 114; Browne on, iii, 278, 281-3; Calvin on, xxxix, 52; epic poetry requires belief in, xiii, 49; Epictetus on, ii, 126 (28), 129 (36), 134 (53), 158 (110), 162 (125), 184 (24); Franklin on, i, 6, 58, 80, 94; Hume on, xxxvii, 362-5, 422-3; Marcus Aurelius on, ii, 201 (3); More on, xxxvi, 240; Pascal on, xlviii, 336; Raleigh on, xxxix, 73-93, 103-9; Washington on, xliii, 242; Woolman on, i, 185

Provinces, Machiavelli on acquired, xxxvi, 8-12, 18-19; arms in acquired, 72; factions in, 72-3

Provisions (see Food-supply)

Proxenus, office of, xii, 120 note

Prudence, Burns on, in enjoyment, vi, 337; Dante's allegory of, xx, 268 note 13; Dante's star of, 148 note 5; Emerson on, v, 60-1, 129, 162; Hobbes on, xxxiv, 333-4, 349, 365-6, 375, 402; Kant on imperatives of, xxxii, 346, 348-9; Kempis on, vii, 217-18; Locke on, xxxvii, 82; of speech, Burke on, xxiv, 158; Whitman on, xxxix, 425-8; in youth, Sheridan on, xviii, 137

Prudence, in PILGRIM'S PROGRESS, xv, 54-5, 230-3, 238-9

Prudentius, Walton on, xv, 361

Prusa, baths at, ix, 415

Prynne, on the drama, xxxiv, 156-7

PSALM, FIRST, PARAPHRASED, vi, 34

PSALM, NINETEENTH, VERSIFIED, vi, 35

PSALM CXIV, PARAPHRASE OF, iv, 15

PSALM CXXXVI, PARAPHRASE OF, iv, 16-18

PSALM FOR THE CHAPEL OF KILMARNOCK, vi, 356-7

PSALM OF LIFE, xlii, 1316-17

Psalm-singing, origin of, vii, 153

PSALMS, THE BOOK OF, xliv, 147-336; Augustine, St., on, vii, 148-9; editorial remarks on, xliv, 146; l, 31; Esdras and, xlviii, 215; idea of God in, xxiv, 61; Herbert on, xv, 405; HYMNS based on, xlv, 547-52; Pascal on, xlviii, 198 (596); Sidney on, xxvii, 11; Smart on, xli, 499-510

Psammetichos, king of Egypt, xxxiii, 5-6, 17, 18-19, 78-81

Psammis, king of Egypt, xxxiii, 82-3

Psellus, Michael, xli, 702

Pseudo-Martyr, of Dr. Donne, xv, 328-344

Psyche, Cupid and, Milton on, iv, 73

PSYCHE, ODE TO, xli, 904-6

Psychology, future of, xi, 527

Ptolemy, and Gabinius, xii, 335, 336

Ptolemy Ceraunus, xii, 86 note

Ptolemy Epiphanes, xlviii, 254

Ptolemy Euergetes, xlviii, 253, 254

Ptolemy Philadelphus, xlviii, 253

Ptolemy Philopator, xlviii, 253

Ptolemy Soter, xlviii, 253

Ptolemy, son of Abubus, xx, 141 note 5

Ptolomea, round of, in Hell, xx, 141 note 5

Public Affairs, boldness in, iii, 33

Public Buildings, in war (agreement with Mexico), xliii, 325

Public, flattery of the, not equal to truth, ix, 40-1; ingratitude of, xix, 170; Mill on the, xxv, 223 (see also People, Populace)

Public Debts, Burke on, xxiv, 255-6, 261, 303; Smith on, x, 574-90

Public Duties, Christianity and, xxv, 253-4

Public Education, Mill on, xxv, 315-17

Public Hospitals, idea of Thomas Bond, i, 121

Public Institutions, expence of, x, 473-88

Public Interests, in relation to landlords, capitalists, and wage-earners, x, 217-20

Public Lands, as source of revenue, x, 493-7

Public Libraries, Carlyle on, xxv, 391; proposed by Franklin, i, 69-70

Public Life, character in, v, 192-3; Epictetus on, ii, 160 (117); Penn on, i, 370-1

Public Measures, Franklin on, i, 131

Public Men, complaints of, iii, 26; Franklin on, i, 93

Public Office, Bacon on, iii, 29-32; Channing on, xxviii, 329; Cicero on conduct of, ix, 134; Confucius on, xlv, 45 (20), 50 (27); often held in contempt, ix, 37; Emerson on corruption in, v, 289; Franklin on holding, i, 111-12; in New Atlantis, iii, 156, 158; qualifications for, i, 371-4; xxiv, 198-9; Tzu-lu on, xliv, 64 (see also Officials)

Public Opinion, Emerson on independence of, v, 68, 69; Epictetus on dread of, ii, 171 (150), 174 (158), 176 (172); government by,

xxviii, 482; improper field for,
xxv, 291-6; Kempis on independence of, vii, 254-5; Marcus Aurelius on, ii, 208 (4), 271 (18), 273
(27), 274 (34), 300 (4); Socrates
on, 297 (23); Mill on, xxv, 163,
271-2, 275, 279-80; Pliny on weight
of, ix, 321; Plutarch on desire of,
xii, 253 and note; proper field
of, xxv, 283-4, 290-1; Raleigh on,
xxxix, 70, 72; Socrates on, ii, 33-
4, 35-7; tyranny of, xxv, 207-10,
234-6; Wordsworth on, xxxix, 353
Public Ownership, objections to, xxv,
320-3
Public Peculators, in Dante's HELL,
xx, 87-8, 91-4
Public Revenges, Bacon on, iii, 16
Public Schools, Locke on, xxxvii,
53-7
Public Service, in BODY OF LIBER-
TIES, xliii, 71
Public Spiritedness, Mill on, xxv, 69
Public Works, expence of, x, 473-8
Public Worship, Franklin on, i, 81;
Penn on, 377-8 (473)
Publicans, xliv, 366 note 2
Publicola, at Actium, xii, 386, 387
Publilia, wife of Cicero, ix, 5, 82;
xii, 261
Publius, Paul and, xliv, 494 (7-8)
Pucci, Antonio, xxxi, 222 note
Pucci, Roberto, xxxi, 119 note 4,
232
Puck, in FAUST, xix, 177, 183
Pudens, Servilius, legate to Pliny,
ix, 385
PUERPERAL FEVER, CONTAGIOUSNESS
OF, xxxviii, 235-68
Puerperal Fever, relations with ery-
sipelas, xxxviii, 249, 253 note, 255,
262, 266, 267; with other fevers,
262-3; Pasteur on, 395-401
Puffendorf, on liberty, xxxiv, 223;
works of, xxxvii, 168-9
Pugliano, John Pietro, xxvii, 7
Pulci, Luigi, xxxi, 65-71; Dryden
on, xiii, 13; reference to, xxvii,
390
PULLEY, THE, by Herbert, xl, 355-6
Pulleys, power and velocity in, xxx,
190-2
Pulmonary Artery, Harvey on the,
xxxviii, 74, 75, 84, 85, 93, 96, 97,
102, 145, 146, 147
Pulmonary Veins, uses of, xxxviii,
75-6, 93, 96, 145, 147
Pulse, Galen on the, xxxviii, 68;
Harvey on the, 68-73, 81, 84-6, 92,
129, 135, 146
PULTENEY, CHARLOTTE, LINES TO, xl,
451-2
Puma, habits of the, xxix, 286-7;
meat of the, 129
Punch, Emerson on London, v, 470,
490-1
Punctuality, Swift on, xxvii, 110

Punishment, of children, xxxvii, 36,
37-9, 40-1, 42, 43-4, 44-5, 59, 64-6,
69-72, 99-100, 110; Confucius on,
xliv, 7 (3); judicial, in Massachusetts, xliii, 77 (46); Marshall
on power of, 234-5; as means of
association, xxv, 90-1; Montaigne
on corporal, xxxii, 57-8
Punishments, cruel, forbidden in
United States, xliii, 208 (8); prescribed, Winthrop on, 96-106, 107-
8, 110-11
Punna, the slave-girl, xlv, 628
Punnavaddhana, xlv, 772
Punta Alta, remains at, xxix, 93-5
Purana, Taine on the Indian, xxxix,
436
Purdie, Tom, description of, xxv,
448-9
Purgatory, Dante's visit to, xx, 147-
286; gate of, guarded by St.
Peter's angel, 9 note 11; Luther
on, xxxvi, 266, 267; Pascal on,
xlviii, 171 (518), 344; of St. Patrick, xxxii, 185-7; Shakespeare on,
xlvi, 107-8; Socrates's idea of, ii,
110
Purification, Dante on, xx, 233
Purist, in FAUST, xix, 179
Puritans, Defoe on the, xxvii, 145-
6; editorial remarks on the, iv, 6;
Emerson on the, v, 38; on secular
music, vi, 17
Purity, Kempis on, vii, 252
PURITY, THE WAY OF, xlv, 717-19
Purpose, Epictetus on, in life, ii,
118 (2); lack of, 202 (7), 205
(16), 207 (4); Marcus Aurelius
on, 212 (14), 213 (2); Shake-
speare on, xlvi, 144
Pursuits, Mohammed on ill-chosen,
xlv, 927
Pursy, Mrs., in SCHOOL FOR SCAN-
DAL, xviii, 130-1
Purusha, xlv, 862
Purushottama, xlv, 869
Pus, due to bacteria, xxxviii, 270;
Pasteur on microbe of, 387-8
(see also Suppuration)
Pusey, Edward B., translator of St.
Augustine, vii
Pusillanimity, defined by Hobbes,
xxxiv, 354; why dishonorable, 380;
irresolution and, 387
Putijma, the cacique, xxxiii, 381,
385
Putrefaction, cause of, xxxviii, 271
Putyma, lord of Aromaia, xxxiii,
363
Pygmalion, king of Tyre, xiii, 87;
Dante on, xx, 230
Pygmies, war of, with cranes, iv,
104
Pylades, in THE LIBATION-BEARERS,
viii, 107; Orestes and, vii, 53;
ix, 17; Sidney on, xxvii, 13

Pyramids, of Egypt, Herodotus on, xxxiii, 64-6, 68, 70; Emerson on, xlii, 1300; Milton on, iv, 107

Pyramis, and the mulberry, xx, 429

Pyramus, and Thisbe, xx, 257

Pyrgo, the nurse, xiii, 203

Pyrilampes, and Pericles, xii, 53

Pyriphlegethon, Homer on the, xxii, 150; Plato on, ii, 109, 110

Pyrrha, and Deucalion, iv, 323

Pyrrhic Dance, Byron on the, xli, 834

Pyrrhonism, Carlyle on, xxv, 356; Hume on, xxxvii, 439, 440-1; of Montaigne, xlviii, 395

Pyrrhus, king of Epirus, Appius's speech against, ix, 51; Cicero on, 18; in Dante's HELL, xx, 54; Decius on, ix, 61; called Epirot prince, xx, 308 note 11; Machiavelli on, xxxvi, 18; Pascal on, xlviii, 53; surnamed the Eagle, xii, 86 note

Pyrrhus, son of Achilles, Andromache and, xiii, 141-2; Chaucer on, xl, 49; Homer on (Neoptolemus), xxii, 165; Priam killed by, xiii, 121-2; Priam and, Shakespeare on, xlvi, 129-30; slain by Orestes, xiii, 142; in Trojan horse, 112; in sack of Troy, 119-20

Pythagoras, Dandini on, v, 279; Emerson on, 70, 183; Golden Verses of, i, 85; on guardian spirits, iii, 297 (33); Hugo on, xxxix, 360; on life, xxxii, 47; Marcus Aurelius on, ii, 243 (47); proverb of, iii, 72; school of, 256-7; Sidney on, xxvii, 9; on the soul, ix, 74; on suicide, 72

Pythagoreans, custom of the, xxxix, 56; alleged debt to British philosophy, iii, 233-4; on the stars, ii, 297 (27)

Pytheas, the orator, Antipater and, xii, 220; on Demosthenes, 203

Pythian Lord, Apollo called the viii, 23

Pythoclides, teacher of Pericles, xii, 39

Python, the Byzantine, xii, 203

Python, the serpent, Milton on, iv, 308

QUA CURSUM VENTUS, xlii, 1167

Quadians, Tacitus on the, xxxiii, 119-20

Quadratilla, Numidia, Pliny on, ix, 324-5

Quadratus, Numidius, Pliny on, ix, 296-7, 324-6

Quagga, descent of the, xi, 171-4

Quail, falling sickness of, xxxv, 352

Quakers, attitude of, toward lot-

teries, i, 112-13, 253; attitude of, toward war, 112-14, 116, 198-200, 225-8; duty toward unwise laws, 294; in England, 319; epistle of (1759), 239-43; Folger on persecution of, 9; in French and Indian War, 228-30; history of, xxxiv, 71-9; Lamb on, xli, 753; principles of, i, 236; settlements of, in America, 239-40; shifts to support their principles, 114-15; slavery and, 176, 215, 216-17, 221, 233-4, 238, 261, 284; Smith on decline of, 283; Voltaire on doctrines of, xxxiv, 65-71 (see also Woolman, Penn)

Qualities, of Hinduism, xlv, 864-6, 880; primary and secondary, xxxvii, 219, 223-4, 435-6

Quarles, Francis, AN ECSTASY, xl, 350-1

Quarrels, causes of, xxxiv, 404; Shakespeare on, xlvi, 102

Quasir, god of poetry, xlix, 427 note

Quatrefages, M., on hybrids, xi, 304

Queens, Bacon on, iii, 52-3; Confucius on, xliv, 58-9

QUEEN'S RETURN FROM LOW COUNTRIES, xl, 368

Queintanonina, Lady, Don Quixote on, xiv, 515

Quesnai, Mr., on agricultural system, x, 457-9, 464

Questions, Bacon on habit of asking, iii, 88; Buddha on useless, xlv, 662-7; of children, xxxvii, 111, 112-14; Stevenson on, xxviii, 292; sudden, iii, 62-3

Quiescence, Buddha on, xlv, 721

Quillota, Chili, Darwin on, xxix, 271

Quinault, Voltaire on, xxxiv, 148

Quintilian, on the body in speaking, ix, 236 note; Mill on, xxv, 19; teacher of Pliny, ix, 193

Quintius, Titus, conqueror of Macedon, xxxvi, 83; Milton on, iv, 387

Quirinius, governor of Syria, xliv, 362 (2)

Quiriquina, earthquake at, xxix, 321-7

Quixada, Guttierre, xiv, 515-16

Quotations, Cervantes on, xiv, 8-11; Locke on, xxxvii, 161; Montaigne on, xxxii, 31

Qurân, xlv, 944

R. T. H. B., To, xlii, 1258

Rabaud, M., on National Assembly, xxiv, 315 note

RABBI BEN EZRA, xlii, 1148-53

Rabbinism, chronology of, xlviii, 216

Rabbits, descent of, xi, 36; in Falkland Islands, xxix, 207-8

Rabelais, Hazlitt on, xxvii, 294; Hugo on, xxxix, 369; language of, 394; Montaigne on, xxxii, 91; Morris-Dance of Heretics, iii, 12;

Sainte-Beuve on, xxxii, 109, 134; Voltaire on, xxxiv, 151

Rabirius Posthumus, his desire for riches, iii, 92

Race, the, is not to the swift, xliv, 351 (II)

Race, blood relationship, as tested by, xxviii, 251-2, 254-61; counteracting forces to, v, 351-2; Emerson on influence of, 350-1; extension of ties of, xxviii, 282-3; language and, editor's remarks on, l, 18; language not a proof of, xxviii, 244-8; language a practical test of, 261-82; language as a presumption of, 248-54; meaning of word, 234; not a fixed thing, v, 352; sentiment of, its growing importance, xxviii, 235-43; Taine on, xxxix, 446-7 (see also Races)

RACE AND LANGUAGE, Freeman's, xxviii, 233-83

Race, Cape, Hayes on, xxxiii, 296

Races, Emerson on human, v, 349; origin of, xxviii, 254-8; political divisions and, 261-2; Taine on differences of, xxxix, 443-56

Rachel, in Dante's Limbo, xx, 12, 18; in Dante's PARADISE, 420; Milton on, iv, 29; references to, xxvii, 338; xlii, 1330; type of contemplative life, xx, 259 note 4

Racine, Jean Baptiste, Hugo on, xxxix, 381, 390-1; Hugo on Athalie of, 371-2; Hume on Athalia of, xxvii, 234; life and works, xxvi, 124; PHÆDRA, 125-85; Sainte-Beuve on Athalie of, xxxii, 131; Taine on, xxxix, 435

Radcliffe, Dr., on electric fish, xi, 198

Radicalism, Emerson on, v, 274

Raffael (see Raphael)

Rafinesque, on species, xi, 13

RAGAMUFFINS, THE PACK OF, xvii, 69-70

Rage, Hobbes on, xxxiv, 367

RAGING FORTUNE, a fragment, vi, 38

Rahab, in Dante's PARADISE, xx, 325; lies of, xv, 264

Raillery, in conversation, xviii, 116; Locke on, xxxvii, 130; Swift on, xxvii, 101

Raimbaud, Dante on, xx, 363 note 4

Rainbow, cause of the, xxxiv, 124; the first, iv, 344-5; lesson of the, xv, 238

RAINY DAY, THE, xlii, 1326

Rajas, xlv, 864, 873, 875, 878, 879, 880

Rakshasas, xlv, 873 note

Raleigh, Sir Walter, colony of, xxxiii, 234, 235, 266-7; DISCOVERY OF GUIANA, 311-94; dream of Eldorado, x, 422; Emerson on, v, 191; Gilbert and, xxxiii, 270, 282,

283; HIS PILGRIMAGE, xl, 206; Jonson on, xxvii, 60-1; language of, xxxix, 206; life and works, xxxiii, 310; xxxix, 69 note; THE LIE, xl, 207-10; PREFACE TO HISTORY OF WORLD, xxxix, 69-121; editor's remarks on PREFACE, 3; l, 24, 33; REPLY TO MARLOWE'S PASSIONATE SHEPHERD, xl, 260-1; St. Joseph captured by, xxxiii, 325; Spenser's letter to, xxxix, 64-8; Trinidad explored by, xxxiii, 321-3; VERSES, xl, 210; WHAT IS OUR LIFE, 210

Ralph, in FAUSTUS, xix, 226-9

Ralph, in SHOEMAKER'S HOLIDAY, sent to the wars, xlvii, 451-4; his return, 476-8; at Lord Mayor's, 481; reported dead, 485; at Hodge's shop, 487-9; with wife's shoe, 489-91; stops Hammon's wedding, 499-500; reunited to Jane, 500-2; mistaken for Rowland, 503; at Lord Mayor's dinner, 507, 513

Ralph, James, i, 38-40, 40-1, 43, 44-5, 51, 157

Rama, teachings of, xlv, 735

Ramath-lechi, Samson at, iv, 422

Ramayana, The, remarks on, xlv, 800

Ramazan, reference to, xli, 985

Rambler, Johnson's, xxvii, 164

Ram-Dass, Carlyle on, xxv, 422

Ramiel, in PARADISE LOST, iv, 216

Rammaka, monastery of, xlv, 730

Ramsay, Sir Andrew Crombie, on the cuckoo, xi, 272; on degradation, 336-7; on faults, 338

Ramsay, Allan, PEGGY, xl, 411-12; Burns on, vi, 16, 87, 92, 93, 435

Ramuzzini, on diseases of overwork, x, 86

Ran, the goddess, xlix, 305 note

Rand, and the adder, v, 286

RANDOLPH OF ROANOKE, xlii, 1416-19

Randver, son of Jormunrek, xlix, 376-8, 444, 453 note

Rank(s), Channing on, xxviii, 355-8; is but the guinea's stamp, vi, 546; not inconsistent with liberty, iv, 203; Pascal on, xlviii, 383, 384, 386; without bounty, xliv, 12 (26)

RANKINE, JOHN, EPISTLE TO, vi, 57-9

RANKINE, JOHN, EPITAPH ON, vi, 64

RANKINE, JOHN, REPLY TO ANNOUNCEMENT OF, vi, 56

RANTIN DOG, THE, vi, 191

RANTIN, ROVIN ROBIN, vi, 98-9

Ranulph, of Chester, xxxv, 243

Rapacity, Machiavelli on, xxxvi, 56, 62

Raphael, the archangel, in FAUST,

xix, 16; in PARADISE LOST, iv, 189-263

Raphael, the painter, accused of immorality, xxvii, 374; Agostino Chigi and, xxxi, 35 note 4; Andrea del Sarto and, xlii, 1135; Emerson on, v, 188; Hazlitt on, xxvii, 293; Il Fattore and, xxxi, 35 note 3; Madonnas of, xlii, 1138; sonnets of, 1137-8

Rapture, David on, xli, 503; so deep its ecstasy was pain, xix, 13

RAPUNZEL, story of, xvii, 71-4

Rare Things, Penn on, i, 345 (69)

Rarity, forerunner of extinction, xxix, 190

Rashness, belongs to youth, ix, 53; Emerson on, v, 114; Penn on, i, 351 (119)

RASSELAS, Johnson's, xxvii, 164

Rastall, Judge, Walton on, xv, 327

Rastelli, Giacomo, xxxi, 100 note 3

Rat, Brander's song of the, xix, 82-3

Rational, term, ii, 280 (8)

Rational Soul, Marcus Aurelius on the, ii, 289 (1)

Rationalism, Rousseau on, xxxiv, 299-301

Rats, range of, xi, 153-4

Ratsey, Gamaliel, xlvii, 524 note 19

Rattlesnakes, Dana on, xxiii, 161-2; Darwin on, xi, 213

RATTLIN ROARIN WILLIE, vi, 268

Raulin, Jules, xxxviii, 376 note

Rause, James, xxxiii, 138, 139, 148

RAVEN, THE, by Poe, xlii, 1276-80

Ravenna, battle of, Macaulay on, xvii, 412-3; Machiavelli on, xxxvi, 89

Ravens, Epictetus on, ii, 134 (53); Harrison on, xxxv, 357

RAVENS, THE THREE, xl, 74

RAVENS, THE SEVEN, xvii, 114-16

Ravillac, murderer of Henry IV, iii, 103

RAVING WINDS AROUND HER BLOWING, vi, 315

Ravishment, divine enchanting, iv, 53

Rawley, Dr., Bacon's literary executor, iii, 152

Reaction, in human affairs, v, 294-5 (see also Polarity)

Read, Rebecca, first marriage of, i, 51-52; Franklin and, 26, 29, 37-38, 40, 43, 69, 80

Readers, of poetry, three classes of, xiii, 60-2

Reading, Bacon on, iii, 128-9; Carlyle on, xxv, 380-1, 389-90; Channing on, xxviii, 349-50; for children, xxxvii, 140-3; choice of, xxviii, 102; Confucius on, xliv, 20 (11), 21 (25), 40 (15); Emerson

on our, v, 73; Emerson on right, 11-12; Epictetus on, ii, 170 (145); folly of trying to limit, iii, 209-15; for girls, xxviii, 155-7; Kempis on, vii, 218; Locke on instruction in, xxxvii, 137-40; Marcus Aurelius on, ii, 194 (7); Milton on, iv, 407; Newman on education by, xxviii, 31-2, 33-8; Pascal on, xlviii, 25 (69); Pliny on, ix, 318; power given by, xxviii, 139-40; preparation for, 102-3; proper method of, 103-17; true, impossible under modern conditions, 119 (see also Books)

Ready-to-halt, in PILGRIM'S PROGRESS, xv, 177, 279, 288, 292, 316, 317-18

Ready-writing, Carlyle on, xxv, 460-4; Dryden on, xxxix, 163

Real Existence, Berkeley on, xxxvii, 205-72, 281-5, 287-302; Buddhist denial of, xlv, 672-3, 677; Descartes on, xxxiv, 29; ECCLESIASTES on, xliv, 348 (24); Emerson on, v, 104; Hume on evidences of, xxxvii, 324-36, 342, 349, 350, 433, 439, 443-4; Montaigne on, xlviii, 398; Rousseau on, xxxiv, 250-1; Schiller on, xxxii, 253-4; Socrates on, ii, 90-6

Real Presence, Pascal on, xlviii, 306-7; Tillotson on, xxxvii, 396

Realist, in FAUST, xix, 182

REALITIES OF IMAGINATION, Hunt's, xxvii, 304-10

Reality, alone beautiful, v, 312; in art, Hugo on, xxxix, 385-6

REAPER, THE SOLITARY, xli, 670-1

Reason, in animals, Darwin on, xi, 262; in animals, Descartes on, xxxiv, 47-8; of animals, Hume on, xxxvii, 392-5; Bacon on the, iii, 8; Boileau on human, xxxiv, 145-6; Browne on the, iii, 269, 276-7, 320; Burke on standards of, xxiv, 11; Calderon on the, xxvi, 51; Carlyle on, xxv, 337-8; Chénier on, xxxii, 130; in criticism of art, xxvii, 227-8; Dante on, xx, 220; Descartes on conduct of the, xxxiv, 5, 17-20; Descartes on equal distribution of, 5-6; direct and indirect interests of, xxxii, 391 note; discursive and intuitive, iv, 196; Epictetus on, ii, 118 (4, 6), 128 (33), 129 (37), 137 (59), 169 (144); experience and, xxxvii, 340 note; xxxix, 134; faith and, Browne on, iii, 273-4, 284; faith and, Kempis on, vii, 379 (4, 5); faith and, Voltaire on, xxxiv, 109; Franklin on, i, 36; Goethe on, xix, 71; habit and, xxxvii, 98; happiness in obedience to, ii, 202 (8), 208 (4), 209 (6), 210 (7),

211 (12), 223 (51); Helmholtz on the, xxx, 183; Hobbes's saying on, xxv, 104; Hume on objects of, xxxvii, 324; imagination and, xxvii, 367-70; xlviii, 35-6; instinct and, Pascal on, 119 (344); instinct and, Pope on, xl, 435; Kant on faculty of, xxxii, 383; Kant on purposes of, 325-7; Kempis on natural, vii, 340 (2); limits of practical, xxxii, 389-90, 394-5; Locke on the, xxxvii, 114; love and, xlviii, 425; man's misuse of, xix, 17; Marcus Aurelius on the, ii, 212 (15), 213 (1), 216 (13, 16), 217 (22), 228 (10), 229 (14), 230 (16), 231 (27), 241 (35), 271 (10), 282 (12), 286 (33), 288 (38); Milton on, iv, 66, 272; Montaigne on the, xlviii, 398; morality from, xxxii, 335-6, 338-40, 342; More on the, xxxvi, 208; "our affections' king," xl, 301; Pascal on, xlviii, 32-3, 35, 120 (345); the passions and, xxiv, 41; xxxiv, 180-1; xlviii, 134 (142-3); Penn on, i, 404-5; pity and, xxxiv, 194; in poetry, Sainte-Beuve on, xxxii, 130-1; Pope on, xl, 427-8, 430-1; possibility of pure, practical, xxxii, 393-4; the province of, xlviii, 446-9; Raleigh on, xxxix, 104, 117 note; in religion, xxxii, 204, 212-14; in religion, Pascal on, xlviii, 81 (226), 84, 91 (245), 93 (252), 94 (253), 95 (259-60), 96 (263), 97 (267), 98 (270, 272-82), 188 (561, 563), 316 (903); in religion, Raleigh on, xxxix, 116-17; in religion, Renan on, xxxii, 190; Rochester on, xxxiv, 146-7; Schiller on the, xxxii, 293-4; Shelley on, xxvii, 345, 368; sensation and, Schiller on, xxxii, 257-63; the senses and, Pascal on, xlviii, 38 (83); senses do not limit, xxxiv, 32; sentiment and, xxxvii, 309; Shakespeare on, xlvi, 165; in sleep, St. Augustine on the, vii, 190; speech and, xxxiv, 340; "what a wretched aid," xviii, 88; will and, xxxii, 343

Reasoning, from analogy, xxxvii, 392, 395 (7); Bacon on, in matters of fact, xxxix, 136, 139-40, 142-3, 151-2; Buddha on, xlv, 747; with children, xxxvii, 67-8, 88, 95-6; difference in powers of, 394 note; different kinds of, 351 note; ends of, xxxiv, 359-62; feeling and, xlviii, 9-10; Hobbes on, xxxiv, 343-9; Hume on accurate, xxxvii, 309-11, 437-9; Hume on demonstrative, 324, 332, 437-8, 443; Hume on, in matters of fact, 324-36, 338-9, 340, 341-2, 350, 393-5,

397-9, 439, 443-4; Locke on, 170; Pascal on, xlviii, 410-13; Raleigh on, in matters of fact, xxxix, 105; Socrates on, ii, 83-4
Rebbye, Sir Ralph, xl, 100
Rebecca, in Dante's PARADISE, xx, 420
Rebellion, a capital crime in early Massachusetts, xliii, 85-6; Hobbes on, xxxiv, 419-20; Machiavelli on, xxxvi, 9; Penn on, i, 356 (178); punishment of, in United States, xliii, 211
Rebellions, Bacon on, iii, 38-44
Rebels, the vanquished only are, xxvi, 64
Rebirth, Buddhist doctrine of, xlv, 693-700, 754; Hindu doctrine of, 830, 836-7, 865, 872; old belief in, xlix, 392
Rebours, M., xlviii, 326
Recalcati, Ambrogio, xxxi, 152 note 5
Recklessness, Confucius on, xliv, 22 (10); Locke on, xxxvii, 102
Recollection, Augustine, St., on, vii, 173-82; Hobbes on, xxxiv, 332; knowledge as, ii, 63-8; of sorrow pleasant, ix, 106
RECOLLECTION, THE, by Shelley, xli, 867-70
Recombes, Louis de, xxxv, 44
Recommendations, Diogenes on, ii, 136 (57)
Recompense, Jesus on, xliv, 399 (12-14)
Reconstruction, Johnson's plan of, xliii, 456-8; Lincoln's plan of, 442 note
Recreation, labor as, xxxvii, 187-90 (see also Diversion)
Recreations, of children, xxxvii, 95-6, 118-19, 182-3
Rectitude, beauty and power from, v, 292; a perpetual victory, 196; Pliny on doubtful, ix, 213
RECUYELL OF HISTORIES OF TROY, xxxix, 5-9
RED, RED ROSE, vi, 514
Red River, sediment of, xxxviii, 424
Red Rowan, in KINMONT WILLIE, xl, 114
Red Sea, origin of name, xxix, 25; passage of the, xliv, 282 (9), 322 (13-15); Milton on passage of the, iv, 17, 99, 350-1; Mohammed on passage of, xlv, 915; Pascal on passage of, xlviii, 219, 229
RED SHOES, THE, xvii, 349-54
Redemption, Dante on human, xx, 313-15; Pascal on types of, xlviii, 276 (781); typified by Red Sea, 219, 229
Reding, Itel, in WILHELM TELL, xxvi, 401-14
Redman, Sir Matthew, at Otterburn, xxxv, 95; Lindsay and, 97-8, 100

Redman, Merey, i, 251, 255, 258
Redress, for every wrong, xviii, 309
REED AND TREE, fable of, xvii, 25
REEDS OF INNOCENCE, xli, 599
Reefs, coral, Darwin on, xxix, 491-505; as showing areas of subsidence, 505-6
Rees, William, xxxii, 145; on saints of Wales, 181
Reeve, Chaucer's, xl, 27-8; Dryden on Chaucer's, xxxix, 174
Refinement, Channing on, xxviii, 357-8 (see also Culture)
Reflection, Buddha on, xlv, 747; Epictetus on, ii, 159 (115); Goethe on, xxxix, 265; Locke on habit of, xxxvii, 163; Marcus Aurelius on, ii, 253 (59); necessary to poets, xxxix, 312; Rousseau on faculty of, xxxiv, 251-3; Schiller on, xxxii, 297
Reform, Bacon's advice on, iii, 31; Bacon on popular, 48; Burke on methods of, xxiv, 316-18; Descartes on political, xxxiv, 14-15; destruction and, Burke on, xxiv, 305; false methods of opposing, xxvii, 237-65; innovation contrasted with, xxiv, 411; Lowell on, xxviii, 484-5; Lowell on opposition to, 471-2; More on, xxxvi, 150, 174-6; Tennyson on, xlii, 1033-5
Reform Bill, English, Emerson on, v, 377; Wordsworth on, 336
Reformation, Browne on the, iii, 266 (2), 267 (4); early attempts at, xxv, 231; in England, iii, 234; Hobbes on causes of the, xxxiv, 401-2; Lowell on the, xxviii, 469; LUTHER'S ARTICLES OF, xxxvi, 302-52; Luther's part in the, 260; James Mill on the, xxv, 33; Taine on the, xxxix, 457; Woolman on the, i, 288; works concerning the, l, 24
REFORMATION IN SCOTLAND, PREFACE TO KNOX'S, xxxix, 61-3
REFORMER, MAN THE, v, 45-61
Reformers, Burke on, xxiv, 211-12; Emerson on, v, 268-9
REFORMERS, FALLACIES OF ANTI-, xxvii, 237-65
REFORMERS, NEW ENGLAND, v, 263-81
Regan, in KING LEAR, xlvi, 205; farewell to Cordelia, 211; plot against father, 212; at Gloucester's, 232-3, 234, 237; with father, 242-8; with Gloucester, 263-6; with Oswald, her love for Edmund, 275-6; with Edmund, before battle, 288-9; after battle, quarrel over Edmund, 293-4; her sickness, 294-5; poisoned by Goneril, 299; Ruskin on, xxviii, 143

Regelation of Ice, xxx, 244, 254-6
REGENCY BILL, ODE ON THE DEPARTED, vi, 351-3
REGIMEN OF HEALTH, ESSAY ON, Bacon's, iii, 85-6
Regin, the Lay of, xlix, 267; Sigurd and, 302, 303-8, 312-13; slaying of, 316-17
Regiomontanus, prophecy of, iii, 97 (see Müller, John)
Registration Duties, x, 528-34
Regnault, on mechanical equivalent of heat, xxx, 209
Regnault's Apparatus, xxx, 198-9
Regnier, Mathurin, Sainte-Beuve on, xxxii, 134
Regrets, Emerson on, v, 81
Regulus, Marcus, Aurelia and, ix, 239; Blæsus and, 239; Pliny on, 196-9, 216, 239-40, 261, 262, 291-2; his son, 260-1, 262; Verania and, 238
Regulus, Marcus Atilius, Bacon on, iii, 137; death of, ix, 73; Milton on, iv, 387
Rehoboam, Dante on, xx, 194
Reinauld, of Mount Alban, xiv, 21-2
Reincarnation, Lessing on, xxxii, 216-17
Relations, and friends, Cicero on, ix, 14
Relations of Ideas, xxxvii, 324
Relaxation, Amasis on need of, xxxiii, 87-8; Pascal on, xlviii, 15 (24), 127 (380); sudden, effect of, xxiv, 124
Relevancy, in writing, Pliny on, ix, 284
Relics, Browne on, iii, 293 (28); Hume on, xxxvii, 348; Pascal on, xlviii, 295 (839), 340, 365
Reliefs, feudal, x, 530
RELIGIO MEDICI, Browne's, iii, 263-347; editorial remarks on, l, 34
Religion, of ascetic natures, xxviii, 177, 178-9; on authority, Channing on, 354-5; on authority, Emerson on, v, 152-3; on authority, Lessing on, xxxii, 203; on authority, Mill on, xxv, 238-46; on authority, Milton on, iii, 229-31, 240-1; iv, 359; on authority, Pascal on, xlviii, 445-6, 446-7; on authority, Rousseau on, xxxiv, 294; in authors, criticism of, xxvii, 233-4; Bacon on, iii, 44-48; Bentham on criticism of faults in, xxvii, 257; Browne on doubts in, iii, 269; Buddha on useless questions of, xlv, 662-7; Bunyan on, xv, 77-78, 84, 108-11; Bunyan on backsliding in, 156-8; Burke on fear in, xxiv, 62; Burns on, vi, 146, 214; Carlyle on, xxv, 352-3, 382; changes in, iii, 144-5;

xxxiv, 399-402; Cowper on, xxxix, 310; decline of, v, 287-8, 290; determined by accident of birth, xxxiv, 293 note; duties of, 315; Emerson on, v, 28-9, 153-4, 205, 446; force in matters of, iii, 14-15; freedom of, in U. S., xliii, 207 (1); freedom of, Vane on, 130-2; of the future, Emerson on, v, 305; of ·the future, Lessing on, xxxii, 214-16; geography in, iii, 265 (2); Goethe on, xix, 144-5; Herbert on, mirth and, xv, 410-12; Hobbes on, xxxiv, 354-5, 390-402; Hume on revealed, xxxvii, 406-7; hypocrisy in, vi, 101; xxvi, 204; individualism and, v, 290-1; Mill on, xxv, 49-50, 154; Mill on dissenters in, 34-5; miracles in, xxxvii, 403, 406-7, 410, 411-12, 413; morality and, xiii, 32; xxv, 31-2; xxxvii, 423, 428-9; mysteries in, Browne on, iii, 272 (9), 273 (10); Newman on teaching of, xxviii, 37-8; origin of, xxxiv, 390; Pascal on, xlviii, 68, 91 (245), 93 (252), 95 (260), 97 (268), 98 (273-90), 158 (470), 184, 192 (574); Pascal on the true, 140 (430), 145 (433), 158 (468), 163 (487), 164 (489, 491-4), 189 (565), 195 (585), 197, 200 (605-6), 287-8, 300 (844); Penn on, i, 376-84, 365 (311); iii, 44; philosophy and, xxxiv, 109-10; poetry and, xxvii, 113-14; xxxix, 329-31; Raleigh on, 94, 116-17; reason and, xxxii, 212-14; xxxvii, 418-22; xlviii, 81 (226), 84; Rousseau on natural, xxxiv, 289, 290-2, 293, 298, 309-10; scepticism in, xlviii, 72-7, 82 (230); science and, iii, 284-6; xxx, 3; xxxix, 134-5; self-reliance in, v, 38-41; of sensuous natures, xxviii, 176-7; Shelley on, xxvii, 348; state, Burke on need of, xxiv, 240-7; Taine on, xxxix, 453-4, 455-6, 457-8; virtue the essence of, v, 26; wars of, xiii, 16; xxxiv, 86; Washington on, xliii, 260; Woolman on, i, 181-2; Woolman on unity in, 239

RELIGION, UNITY IN, ESSAY ON, Bacon's, iii, 11-15

Religion and Philosophy, reading course in, l, 31-40

Religions, come from imaginative men, v, 184; the four, iii, 290 note 58; national, remarks on, v, 440; original, allegorical, xxvii, 348; of Utopia, xxxvi, 237-50; represent culture of votaries, v, 285-7

Religious Errors, origin of, v, 185

Religious Exercises, Kempis on, vii, 231-3

Religious Instruction, expense of, x, 486, 488; Locke on, xxxvii, 123-6, 142-3

Religious Liberty, Mill on, xxv, 210, 226-46, 252-5

Religious Life, Buddha on the, xlv, 666, 678-9, 687, 690; Kempis on a, vii, 229; Pascal on the, xlviii, 317 (906)

Religious Sympathy, Freeman on, xxviii, 239

Religious Teachers, compared with poets, xxvii, 349

Religious Tests, forbidden in U. S., xliii, 205 (3); Mill on, xxv, 232-3

Religious Writings, base tone of, v, 90

Religiousness, of act, speech and mind, xlv, 874-5

Rembrandt, Hazlitt on, xxvii, 293

Remedies, fable on impossible, xvii, 39; Pascal on belief in, xlviii, 287

Remedy, things without, xlvi, 337

REMEMBER, by C. G. Rossetti, xlii, 1228-9

Remembrance, Hobbes on, xxxiv, 332; rosemary for, xlvi, 171

Remonstrances, Cicero on, ix, 38-9

Remorse, Byron on, xviii, 433; Shelley on, 335

REMORSE: A FRAGMENT, vi, 52-3

REMORSEFUL APOLOGY, vi, 510

Remulus, and Cædicus, xiii, 309; death of, 384

Remus, the Latian, killed by Nisus, xiii, 308

Remus, twin of Romulus, Virgil on, xiii, 84-5, 293

Renaissance, Huxley on the, xxviii, 225, 227; in Italy, xxvii, 388-90; Taine on the, xxxix, 451; works of and concerning the, l, 23-4, 28-9

Renan, Ernest, life and works, xxxii, 142; POETRY OF CELTIC RACES, 143-91

Rendu, Pere, on glaciers, xxx, 241

Renfusa, city of New Atlantis, iii, 161

Rengger, on cattle in Paraguay, xi, 86

Reni, Guido, Raphael's sonnets and, xlii, 1138 (see also Guido)

Renons, the German collector, xxix, 285

Rent(s), in agricultural system, x, 448, 449; building and ground, 510-11; Burke on, xxiv, 308; of coal mines, x, 175-6, 178; considered as produce of nature, 305; corn, 41-3; corn, in Elizabethan England, xxxv, 262; defined, x, 56; by what determined, 58; ex-

traordinary, 64; of forests, 176-7; gross and neat, 233-4; of houses, taxes on, 510-18; in kind, Pliny on, ix, 372; of land, by what determined in general, x, 153-5; of land cultivated for food, 155-71; 184-5; of land used to produce materials, 172-5; 184-5; of land, taxes on, 501-8; market prices, their effect on, 62; of metallic mines, 178-82; money, affected by variation of value of gold, 40-1; of precious stone mines, 183-4; prices and, relations between, 155; prices of commodities, as determined by, 52-3; profits and wages, confounded with, 56-7; progress of society in relation to, 216-17, 274-5; taxes on, 501-8, 510-18; taxes on, when best paid, 499 (3)

RENTON, MR., NOTE TO, vi, 283

Renty, Sir Oudart, at Poitiers, xxxv, 49-50

Renunciation, Buddha on, xlv, 608; Emerson on, v, 27; Hindu doctrine of, xlv, 813, 823, 826, 858, 876; Kempis on, vii, 308 (1); Pascal on, xlviii, 89 (240)

RENUNCIATION, A, by De Vere, xl, 296

Renzo Tramaglino (see Tramaglino)

Reparation, Penn on, i, 351

Repentance, Calvin on, xxxix, 53; Cenci on, xviii, 319; Jesus on, xliv, 401 (7, 10), 405 (3-4); Marcus Aurelius on, ii, 258 (10); Raleigh on, xxxix, 85; time for, xv, 265

Repetition, Burke on effects of, xxiv, 64-5, 73; Darwin on effects of, xxix, 336; Pascal on, xlviii, 20 (48); sublimity of, its cause, xxiv, 117-20

Rephan, xliv, 444 (43)

Replevin, in Massachusetts, xliii, 75 (32)

Repose, our foster-nurse of nature, xlvi, 274

Representation, Jefferson on right of, xliii, 161; of minorities, Mill on, xxv, 165-6; personal, Mill on, 165-6; principles of, adopted by French Revolution, xxiv, 321-38; of property, Burke on, 199-200

Representative Government, Mill on, xxv, 71-2

Representatives, Congressional, xliii, 192-3, 194 (1), 195 (6, 7), 205 (3), 210-11; qualities needed by, v, 192-3 (see also Agents)

Reproach, independence of, vii, 254 (2, 3); worse than violence, iv, 208

Reproduction, period of, change in, xi, 197

Reproductive System, affected by conditions of life, xi, 316; sensitiveness of, 27-8

Reproofs, in anger, i, 364 (289-92); Cicero on, ix, 38-9; usefulness of, xliii, 100; vain, i, 375 (446-7);

Reproval, our fear of, vii, 323-4

Republican Government, on trial in America, xliii, 243-4

Republics, Dryden on, xviii, 7-8; limitation of authority in, xxv, 204-6; Machiavelli on difficulty of conquering, xxxvi, 19; military affairs of, 43; monarchies compared with, v, 256

REPUTATION, ESSAY ON, Bacon's, iii, 135-7

Reputation, daughter of fortune, iii, 105; the desire for, ii, 256 (73); Locke on, xxxvii, 44, 83, 122; a matter of imagination, xlviii, 35; Pascal on desire of, 59 (147); Plutarch on desire of, xii, 253; as power, xxxiv, 374, 375; Rousseau on love of, 229; Webster on, xlvii, 761 (see also Fame)

Reputations, of great men, beyond their acts, v, 191

REQUIEM, by Stevenson, xlii, 1261-2

REQUIESCAT, by Arnold, xlii, 1175

Requisition, right of, under Confederation, xliii, 169; under Constitution, 203

Rerir, son of Sigi, xlix, 276-7

Resemblance of ideas, Hume on, xxxvii, 323, 346-7

Resemblances, analogical, xi, 462-7; Browne on, iii, 327; deformity and, 48; embryonic, xi, 479-81; family, iii, 21; in nature, xi, 472-7; Pascal on, xlviii, 51 (133); pleasure in finding, xxiv, 18-20

Resentment, Pascal on, xlviii, 113 (324); Penn on, i, 356 (182-5), 363 (270-1)

Reservation, in speech, Penn on, i, 401

Reservations, Papal, xxxvi, 299, 303, 306

Reserved Cases (Catholic Church), xxxvi, 307

Residences, Bacon on, iii, 114-17

RESIGNATION, by Longfellow, xlii, 1329-31

Resignation, Burns on, vi, 33; Penn on, i, 342 (see also Acquiescence)

Resolution, Buddha on, xlv, 611; from despair, iv, 95; Franklin's maxim on, i, 83, 84; why honorable, xxxiv, 380; Kempis on, vii, 231 (2)

RESOLUTION AND INDEPENDENCE, xli, 674-8

Resolutions, hasty, Penn on, i, 356-7

RESOLVE, THE, by Brome, xl, 378
Respect, ceremonious and natural,
xlviii, 385-6; Dryden on, xviii, 38;
friendship and, ix, 36; an inferior
degree of astonishment, xxiv, 51;
Kant on, xxxii, 331 note 3; Locke
on want of, xxxvii, 128-31; love
and, xlviii, 424, 426
Respectability, Penn on, i, 361-2;
religion of, xxviii, 312; Stevenson
on, 310-11; virtue and, 312-13
RESPECTS, CEREMONIES AND, ESSAY
ON, iii, 131-2
Respiration, compared with combustion of a candle, xxx, 170-8;
Descartes on use of, xxxiv, 44;
Galen on, xxxviii, 68; in high
altitudes, xxix, 341; pulse and,
xxxviii, 68, 72-3
Rest, Burke on state of, xxiv, 113;
complete, is death, xlviii, 50 (129);
Cowper on, xli, 555; after good
works, iii, 30; Herbert on, xl,
355-6; labor and, vii, 292 (4);
xxviii, 325-6; needed by man, iv,
173; Pascal on complete, xlviii, 50
(129), 51 (131); second law of
nature, v, 239, 247; temporal and
eternal, vii, 312 (2); Tennyson
on, xlii, 1028-9
Restitutus, letter to, ix, 312
Restlessness, Herbert on, xl, 355-6;
Pascal on, xlviii, 50 (130), 52-5
Restoration, English, drama of the,
xviii, 3; Milton on, iv, 5
Results, Arabian proverb on, xvi,
36; Machiavelli on, xxxvi, 61;
Webster on weighing, xlvii, 751;
Whitman on certainty of, xxxix,
426-8
Resurrection, Browne on the, iii,
313-14; Bunyan on, xv, 233; celebration of the, 408; Dante on certainty of, xx, 316; Jesus on, xliv,
413 (27-40); Milton on the, iv,
356; Mohammed on the, xlv, 960-
1, 923; Pascal on, xlviii, 80 (222-
3); Paul, St., on, xlv, 523 (12-
55); Sadducees on, xliv, 413 (27-
36); songs of the, xix, 33-5
RESURRECTION, THE DAY OF, xlv,
555-6
Retail Trade, profits in, why greater
than in wholesale, x, 119
Retailing, capital used in, x, 304,
306; necessity of, 302-3
RETALIATION, by Goldsmith, xli, 517-
21
Retaliation, Mohammed on law of,
xlv, 1013; Shelley on, xviii, 277;
Socrates on, ii, 38-9
Retaliatory Duties, x, 363-5
Retirement, Goldsmith on, xli, 524;
Kempis on, vii, 234 (5)
RETREAT, THE, xl, 357-8
Retribution, Æschylus on, viii, 18-

19, 21-2, 32, 64-5, 73, 84, 87, 88,
93, 97, 110, 125-6, 136, 151; Asaph
on, xliv, 237 (17-20); Bildad on,
100 (5-21); Buddhist doctrine of,
xlv, 685-6, 687-90, 691-2, 694-7;
Christ, the teacher of, xxxii, 209;
David on, xliv, 153 (12-16), 157
(5-6), 185 (16, 21), 189 (1, 2),
190 (9-38), 217 (6-11); doctrine
of, among the Jews, xxxii, 199-
202; ECCLESIASTES on, xliv, 349
(11-13); Elihu on, 128 (21-30);
Eliphaz on, 78 (8), 96 (20-35);
Emerson on, v, 94, 104-5; Franklin on, i, 80, 94; future need-
lessness of doctrine, xxxii, 214;
Hindu doctrine of, xlv, 871-2;
Jesus on, xliv, 374 (21-6), 375
(38), 404 (25); Hobbes on legal,
xxxiv, 424; Job on, xliv, 106 (17-
33), 111 (18-25), 114 (13-23), 120
(3); Kempis on, vii, 242-4; More
on doctrine of, xxxvi, 208, 240-1;
Omar Khayyam on, xli, 984, 986;
ORESTEIA deals with subject of,
viii, 3-4; popular ideas of, v, 89-
90; Whitman on, xxxix, 426-7; Zophar on, xliv, 103 (5-29)
Retz, Cardinal de, miracle related
by, xxxvii, 408-9; Voltaire on,
xxxiv, 88
Reuben, Winthrop on, xliii, 100
REVEILLE, THE, xlii, 1482-3
Revelation, Bunyan on, xv, 100,
153; Emerson on, v, 33, 144-6;
Franklin on, i, 57, 58; Lessing
on, xxxii, 195-213; Pascal on,
xlviii, 288 (818); Rousseau on,
xxxiv, 291-312; superior to morality, xiii, 32; yearning for, xix,
49
Revelation, Book of, Paræus on, iv,
416
REVENGE, ESSAY ON, Bacon's, iii,
15-16
Revenge, Burns on, vi, 111; contempt the best, iii, 334; Epictetus
on, ii, 169 (143); forgiveness and,
153 (96); Hobbes on desire of,
xxxiv, 367, 424; Marcus Aurelius
on best, ii, 234 (6); masters fear
of death, iii, 10; music and, xli,
489; Schiller on, xxvi, 465; Shelley on, xviii, 277; what will not,
descend to, iv, 268
REVENGE, THE, xlii, 1041-6
Revengefulness, defined by Hobbes,
xxxiv, 354; language of, 358
Revenue, capital and, as determining industry, x, 275-7; composed
of wages, profits, and rent, 233;
duties for, 369, 390; gross and
neat, 234-40; as measured by
money, 237-40; public, Burke on,
xxiv, 375-6; sources of, x, 55-6;
sources of public, 489-590

Revenue Bills, under Constitution, xliii, 195

REVERE, PAUL, RIDE OF, xlii, 1348

Reverence, Burke on, xxiv, 51; Goethe on, xxv, 397-8; Locke on, xxxvii, 89; Tennyson on, xlii, 1033

REVERIE OF POOR SUSAN, xli, 671

Reversion, Darwin on, xi, 169-70; instance of, among pigeons, 41; of mongrels and hybrids, 328, 329; remarks on, 42; tendency to, 31, 32; tendency to, does not prevail against selection, 114

Reviewers, Carlyle on, xxv, 354

Reviews, Smith on, xxvii, 237

Reviling, ECCLESIASTES on, xliv, 352 (20)

Revilius, Caninius, xii, 322

Revision, of writings, Pliny on, ix, 322

Revolution, ages of, Emerson on, v, 21; Burke on, xxiv, 179, 304-5; Franklin on, i, 93; Jefferson on right of, xliii, 160-1; Pascal on, xlviii, 106; reform contrasted with, xxiv, 411

Revolution Society, Burke on the, xxiv, 153-6, 215; answer to doctrines of, 164-81, 203-6

Revolutionists, Burke on, xxiv, 211-13, 312, 313

REVOLUTIONS OF HEAVENLY BODIES, DEDICATION OF, xxxix, 55-60

Rewards, as means of association, xxv, 90-1; for children, xxxvii, 39-41, 42, 44-5, 59, 94; Emerson on, v, 280, 300; Marcus Aurelius on, ii, 277 (42)

Reynald, in HAMLET, xlvi, 113-15

Reynard the Fox, Locke on, xxxvii, 141

Reynolds, Sir Joshua, Goldsmith on, xli, 518, 521; Hazlitt on, xxvii, 293; Sheridan on, xviii, 106; on taste, xxxix, 282, 305

Reynolds, General, at Gettysburg, xliii, 351, 353, 354; Haskell on, 354

Reynolds, Mr., More and, xxxvi, 130

Reynolds, Mrs., in Hazlitt's discussion, xxvii, 286, 289

Rhadamanthus, Homer on, xxii, 63, 102; Socrates on, ii, 28; Virgil on, xiii, 230

Rhamnes, death of, xiii, 308

Rhamnus, and Antony, xii, 373

Rhampsinitos, king of Egypt, xxxiii, 59-63

Rhapsodies, Montaigne on, xxxii, 32

Rhea, mother of the gods, ix, 405 note; Bacchus and, viii, 351; Hercules and, xiii, 266; Jove and, xx, 61-2

Rhesus, reference to, xiii, 92

Rhetoric, Burke on, xxiv, 144; Carlyle on, xxv, 393-6; Descartes on study of, xxxiv, 9; Goethe on, xix, 28; Hobbes on, xxxiv, 377; Locke on study of, xxxvii, 169-70, 171-2; Marcus Aurelius on, ii, 208 (5); Montaigne on study of, xxxii, 61-2; oratory contrasted with, xxv, 338; Penn on, i, 352 (137-41), 401 (126); Plutarch on, xii, 55; simplicity in, v, 314

Rhetoricians, Pliny on, ix, 224

Rhexenor, son of Nausithous, xxii, 95

Rhine, Byron on the, xli, 818-19; Cæsar's bridge over, xii, 294; Tacitus on the, xxxiii, 95; Thoreau on the, xxviii, 420-1

Rhinoceros, old Arabian idea of the, xvi, 261

Rhoda, the maid, xliv, 456 (13-15); St. Peter and, xv, 342

Rhodius, Apollonius, xxvii, 366

Rhodon, tutor of Cæsarion, xii, 399

Rhodopis, Herodotus on, xxxiii, 68-9

Rhœtus, in the ÆNEID, xiii, 309, 340

Rhone, sediment of the, xxxviii, 422-3

Rhorty's Battery, at Gettysburg, xliii, 359, 373, 406

Rhyme, Dryden on, xiii, 58; Hugo on, xxxix, 392; Milton on, iv, 89; Montaigne on, xxxii, 63; Pope on advantages of, xl, 417; Sidney on, xxvii, 34; Swift on, 120; Whitman on, xxxix, 415

Rhymer, on Shakespeare, xxxix, 223, 226

Rhythm, Poe on, xxviii, 390; Shelley on, xxvii, 350; Sidney on, 53; universal inclination to, iii, 338

Ribeira Grande, Darwin on, xxix, 12-13

Ribemont, Eustace, at Poitiers, xxxv, 37-9, 49

Ricardo, David, Emerson on, v, 259; as member of Parliament, xxv, 67; Mill and, 23, 39-40, 67

Ricardo, Duke, in Cardenio's story, xiv, 214-15

Riccaut, in MINNA VON BARNHELM, xxvi, 334-8

Ricci, Federigo de', xxxi, 447, 449-50

Riccio, Pier Francesco, xxxi, 359-60, 361-2, 370, 398, 402-3

Rice, cultivation of, x, 169-70

Rice ap Howell, in EDWARD II, xlvi, 59, 60, 61-3

Rice, Hugh ap, xxxv, 402

Rich, Lord, and More, xxxvi, 131-5

Richard I, accusations of God, v, 286

Richard II, Chaucer and, xxxix, 171; Raleigh on, 76; in Tyler's Rebellion, xxxv, 64-5, 67-8, 69-70, 71-5, 77-82

Richard III, Raleigh on, xxxix, 79-80; reference to, xl, 470

Richard the Third, stage presentation of, xxvii, 323-4

Richard, Archbishop of Canterbury, xxxv, 270

Richard of St. Victor, xx, 330 note 28

Richard of the Lea, the knight in ROBYN HODE, xl, 133-41, 142-8, 164-6, 170-1, 172-5, 176-7, 183, 185-6

RICHARDSON, GABRIEL, EPITAPH FOR, vi, 549

Richardson, Samuel, Franklin on style of, i, 24; Hazlitt on, xxvii, 289

Richelet, Hugo on, xxxix, 384

Richelieu, Burke on, xxiv, 196; Joseph the Capuchin and, xxxix, 374; Louis XIII and, xxiv, 349; in Mantua contest, xxi, 81, 455, 486-7

RICHES, ESSAY ON, Bacon's, iii, 92-5

Riches, advantage of, remains to maker, v, 50; Burns on, vi, 51, 91, 213, 344-5; Cicero on, ix, 37; compensation of, v, 92; Confucius on, xliv, 6 (15); Curius, Manlius, on, ix, 66; death and, xvi, 317-18, 327, 335-6; Dekker on, xl, 327; ECCLESIASTES on, xliv, 345 (10-14), 346 (1-2), 351 (11); Emerson on true, v, 226; Epictetus on true, ii, 178 (182); friendship and, ix, 27; good and evil, xlvii, 765; grow in Hell, iv, 107; happiness and, i, 360, 361; xix, 372; heirs to, v, 51-2; Herbert on, xv, 394; why honorable, xxxiv, 380; independence of, v, 571; Jesus on, xliv, 374 (24), 393 (16-21), 408 (24-5); Job on, xix, 122 (24-5, 28); Kempis on, vii, 284 (4); loss of, no misfortune, ii, 126 (25); Massinger on, xlvii, 874; Milton on, iv, 386-7; Morris on, xlii, 1243; Nashe on, xl, 265; Pascal on property of, xlviii, 110 (310); Penn on pursuit of, i, 408-9; poetical idea of, v, 236-7; Pope on, xl, 446, 448; as power, xxxiv, 374; Psalm on folly of trust in, xliv, 206-7; Raleigh on, xxxix, 95, 101; Raleigh on pursuit of, 95, 97-8; results of competition of, xxxiv, 385; Stoic dictum of, ix, 138; Thoreau's idea of, xxviii, 406; Utopian opinion of, xxxvi, 205-6, 212; virtue and, i, 359 (219); Walton on, xv, 333; Webster on, xlvii, 730; Woodnot on,

xv, 392; Woolman on, i, 204 note, 220, 243 (see also Wealth)

Richmond, Duke of, and George Herbert, xv, 390

RIDDELL, CAPTAIN, LINES TO, vi, 347

RIDDELL, CAPTAIN, RHYMING REPLY TO, vi, 348

RIDDELL, MARIA, EPIGRAM ON, vi, 510

RIDDELL, MRS., ON BIRTHDAY OF, vi, 507

RIDDELL, ROBERT, LINES TO MEMORY OF, vi, 550

RIDDELL, ROBERT, SONNET ON, vi, 521

RIDDELL, WALTER, EPITAPH FOR, vi, 517

RIDDELL, MRS. WALTER, ON THE CARRIAGE OF, vi, 517

Ridiculous, Fielding on the, xxxix, 187-9

Riding, Locke on, xxxvii, 183, 184

Ridolfi, Niccolo, xxxi, 47 note 2

Riemer, on Goethe, v, 199

Rigby, Dr., xxxviii, 235, 259, 261

Right, Augustine, St., on wrong and, vii, 40-1; Confucius on seeing and doing, xliv, 9 (24); disputes on wrong and, xxxiv, 389; "doth its own likeness breed," viii, 32; Emerson on, v, 66, 993; Franklin's early view of, i, 57-8; "gives way to delight," viii, 304; Kant on tests of, xxxii, 352-5; law and, xxxiv, 407; "makes room where weapons want," xlvi, 54; Manzoni on, xxi, 20; James Mill on, xxv, 37; Pope on, xl, 419-25; for right's sake, xlv, 809; Rousseau on, xxxiv, 276; success as the measure of, ix, 291; of the sword, Pascal on, xlviii, 311 (878)

Right Reason, Bentham on phrase, xxv, 46

Right-Timing, Penn on, i, 354-5

Righteousness, Æschylus on, viii, 32; Augustine, St., on, vii, 40-1; Burns on rigid, vi, 192; Confucius on, xliv, 54 (17), 56 (2); David on, 185 (15-22), 190, 191-2, 218 (10-11); ECCLESIASTES on, 348 (15-16), 348 (20), 349 (12, 14), 350 (2); Elihu on, 129 (2-8), 130 (6-7); Eliphaz on, 107 (3); of God, Elihu on, 130 (2-7); Justice, compared with, xxxiv, 421; Pascal on hunger after, xlviii, 96 (264); "the path of," xl, 78; the Psalmist on, xliv, 293 (4-9); reward of, 266 (12-15); reward of desire for, xlv, 829-30; wickedness, contrasted with, xliv, 147, 236-8, 241 (10); Woolman on, i, 197

Rights, Burke on, of man, xxiv, 207-11; Hobbes on, natural, xxxiv,

407-8; Jefferson on, xliii, 160; of persons and of property, v, 250-3; renunciation and transference of, xxxiv, 408-10; social, 408-10, 425-6

RIGHTS OF WOMAN, THE, vi, 474

Rigogli, Giovanni, xxxi, 56

Rigor, pushed too far, xxvi, 432

RIGS O' BARLEY, vi, 47-8

Rimini, Francesca da, xx, 24-5; Hugo on, xxxix, 367

Rimini, Malatestino da, xx, 113 note 5; Cassero and, 118 note 8

Rimmon, the god, iv, 102

Rimsky-Korsakoff, influence of ARABIAN NIGHTS on, xvi, 4

Rinaldo, Dante on, xx, 363 note 4; Spenser on, xxxix, 65

Rinaldo d'Este, Dryden on, xiii, 34

RING AND THE BOOK, DEDICATION OF, xlii, 1154-5

Ringrave, Captain, xxxviii, 19

Ringrave, Count, death of, xxxviii, 54

Rinkart, Martin, hymn by, xlv, 571

Rio Grande River, xliii, 313, 315

Rio Negro, Darwin on, xxix, 74-5

Rio Sauce, Darwin on the, xxix, 118-19

Riolan, John, on the heart, xxxviii, 86

Riolanus, on arteries, xxxviii, 72

Riou, reference to, xli, 800

Ripamonti, on plague of Milan, xxi, 521

Ripheus, in Dante's PARADISE, xx, 373-4; death of, xiii, 117-8; in sack of Troy, 114-16

Ripley, George, xlvii, 561 note

Riquet, and the Languedoc canal, x, 477

Risks, human contempt of, x, 114-15; Penn on, i, 362

Rites, Bacon on religious, iii, 48; Luther on religious, xxxvi, 392-7; Penn on religious, i, 380-1 (507), 405 (175)

Ritter, Karl, Geikie on, xxx, 339

Rituals, without reverence, xliv, 12 (26)

Rivalry, friendship and, ix, 20-21; fruits of, xxvi, 91; Pliny on, happy, ix, 248

RIVER OF LIFE, by Campbell, xli, 794-5

Rivers, second Earl of, xxxix, 10-11, 13; death of, 79, 80

Rivers, John, xxxiii, 238

Rivers, Pascal on, xlviii, 13 (17)

Riviere, Mercier de la, x, 464

RIZPAH, by Tennyson, xlii, 1046-1051

Rizzio, murder of, xxxix, 377

Roads, expence of maintaining, x, 474-7; Smith on good, 156-7

ROADS, ROUGH, EPIGRAM ON, vi, 249

Roannez, Charlotte Gouffier de, xlviii, 352 note 1; letters to, 352-65

Roannez, M. de, on reason, xlviii, 98 (276)

Roanoak, colony of, xxxiii, 234, 235, 266-7

ROB MORRIS, AULD, vi, 473

Robb, D. C., translator of Pasteur, xxxviii, 283

Robbers, in Dante's HELL, xx, 47, 54, 102-3; rich and poor, xlv, 689-90

Robert, of Normandy, Henry I and, xxxix, 75

Robert, king of Sicily, Dante on, xx, 319 note 11, 321 note 2; poets and, xxvii, 43

ROBERT OF LINCOLN, xlii, 1264-6

Roberton, Mr., on puerperal fever, xxxviii, 242-3, 257-8

Roberts, inventor of the mule, v, 411

Robertson, F. W., translator of Lessing, xxxii, 193

Robertson, Rev. John, Burns on, vi, 173, 254

Robertson, Joseph, of London Review, xxv, 134; Wordsworth on, v, 483

Robin, parable of the, xv, 208

Robin, M. Ch., xxxviii, 356-61

ROBIN GRAY, AULD, xli, 570-1

Robin Hood, Emerson on character of, v, 362; Maid Marian and, xli, 898 (see also Robyn Hode)

Robin the Ostler, in FAUSTUS, xix, 226-9

ROBIN-REDBREAST, CALL FOR THE, xl, 331

ROBIN SHURE IN HAIRST, vi, 342

Robinson, Mr. Alfred, marriage of, xxiii, 247-51; (in 1859), 406

Robinson, Gen., at Gettysburg, xliii, 351

Robinson, Henry Crabbe, and story of THE FISHERMAN, xvii, 89 note

Robinson, Ralph, translator of UTOPIA, xxxvi, 2

Robyn Hode, in ROBYN HODE, his friends and customs, xl, 130-3; the knight and, 134-40, 148, 164-6, 170-1; welcomes Little John, 153; with the Sheriff, 155-7; and the monk, 157, 159-63; at archery contest, 167-70, in knight's castle, 170-1; returns to greenwood, 172; rescues knight, 173-5; the king and, 176-85; at court, 186; returns to greenwood, 187-8; death, 188-9

ROBYN HODE, A GEST OF, xl, 130-89

Rochambeau, Count de, xliii, 180

Roche-sur-Yon, at Metz, xxxviii, 24, 25, 26; Navarre and, 49-50
Rochefoucauld, Duke de, Burke on, xxiv, 262-3, 440; Voltaire on *Maxims* of, xxxiv, 103
Rochester, Earl of, ON CHARLES II, xl, 392; Hugo on, xxxix, 399-400; Voltaire on, xxxiv, 145-7
Rockingham, Lord, Burns on, vi, 55; Burke and, xxiv, 5
Rocks, Geikie on, xxx, 343, 352-3; Lyell on volcanic, xxxvii, 417-18; metamorphic, xxx, 349-50; sedimentary, 344-5, 354-5; stratified and crystalline, xxxviii, 415-16
Rocks Wandering, the, xxii, 170-1
Roc's Egg, Aladdin and the, xvi, 440-1; story of the, 256-7, 287-8
RODDICK, WILLIAM, EPITAPH ON, vi, 520
Roderigo, in DUCHESS OF MALFI, xlvii, 725, 744, 809, 812, 813, 815
Roderigo, counsellor of Philip, xix, 285
Rodney, Emerson on character of, v, 362
RODNEY'S VICTORY, LINES ON, vi, 489
Rodolph, Emperor, Dante on, xx, 170 and note 12, 174-5
Rodrigo, Don, in I PROMESSI SPOSI, bravoes of, xxi, 15; relations with Abbondio, 21; Lucia and, 39; palace and friends of, 74-85; conference with Cristoforo, 86-90; plans of vengeance, 106-8; rallied by Attilio, 108-9; plans to carry off Lucia, 109-11; learns failure of plans, 185-7; advises with Attilio, 188-90; plans to have Renzo banished, 196-7; learns Lucia's whereabouts, 304-5; determines to seek aid of the Unnamed, 305-6, 327-32; conference with Unnamed, 333-6; goes to Milan, 423-4; takes the plague, 557-60; taken to the Lazzaretto, 561-3; in the Lazzaretto, 612-13; death of, 654
Roebuck, John Arthur, Mill on, xxv, 57, 81, 82, 83, 85, 99-100; in Parliament, 126-7; in *Westminster Review*, 66
Roger, in SHE STOOPS TO CONQUER, xviii, 214-15
Roger, in SHOEMAKER'S HOLIDAY (see Hodge)
Roger of Doncaster, xl, 188
Rogers, B. B., translator of Aristophanes, viii, 1
Rogers, Mr., first husband of Miss Read, i, 51-2, 69
Rogers, Samuel, poems by, xli, 596-7
Rohan, M. de, xxxviii, 13, 15, 19
Roland, in SONG OF ROLAND, with Charlemagne at Cordres, xlix, 100, 103; advises against Marsil,

103-4; offers to go to Marsil, 105; quarrel with Ganelon, 106-7, 108; Ganelon on, 110-11, 116; plot against, 111, 116-19; in return to France, 121; given rear guard, 122-5; prodigies preceding death of, 147-8; before battle of Roncesvalles, 132, 133, 134-6, 137-8; in the battle, 139, 142, 143-4, 145, 147, 150, 152, 153-4, 155-6, 158, 159, 160; the horn of, 161-4, 181, 197; renews fight, 166-7, 168-9; with Oliver, 170-2; with Walter, 172-3; last fight, 173-7; with Archbishop Turpin, 177-80; his death, 180-4; body of, found by Charlemagne, 191-4; his tomb, 198; Renan on, xxxii, 165 (see also Orlando)
ROLAND, SONG OF, xlix, 97-208; remarks on, 96; I, 22
Roland de Vaux of Tryermaine, xli, 737-8, 740
Roman Catholic Church, Augustine, St., on the, vii, 86, 87; Bacon on, iii, 137; Browne on, 266 (3), 268 (5); Calvin on, xxxix, 34-5, 38-41, 44-6; cardinals of, xxxvi, 290-1; Dante on, xx, 213, 378-9; in England, xxxv, 264-8, 279, 280; Hobbes on revolt from, xxxiv, 401-2; Hume on ceremonies of, xxxvii, 346-7; Knox on the, xxxix, 61; liberty of the press under, iii, 206-8; Luther on, xxxvi, 277-83; Machiavelli on temporal power of, 40-2; Mill on, xxv, 241-2; Pascal on, xlviii, 302 (849, 850), 305 (857-62), 308 (867), 309 (869-70), 311 (878, 881), 312 (885), 313 (889), 314 (890, 896), 316 (905), 319-20, 352-3, 354; services in, xxxv, 278; Shelley on, in Italy, xviii, 277-8 (see also Papacy)
Roman Classics, Sainte-Beuve on, xxxii, 177
Roman Empire, Bacon on fall of, iii, 146; decline of, xxxviii, 412; Hugo on fall of, xxxix, 361-2; liberty of press in, iii, 205-6; life in early (see Pliny, LETTERS); literary works of, l, 20, 27; Luther on, xxxvi, 344; Machiavelli on cause of overthrow of, 50; power of the soldiery in, 65-6
Roman Names, Plutarch on, xii, 161-2
Roman Provinces, ix, 416 note 2
Roman Time, ix, 243 note 4
ROMANCE AND CHRONICLE, xxxv
Romance-poetry, Arnold on the, xxviii, 76-7
Romances, Cervantes on, xiv, 498-502, 506-7, 512-14; defended by Don Quixote, 514-21; Fielding on, xxxix, 184-90; Whitman on, 424

Romanianus, friend of Augustine, vii, 99

Romano, Giulio, xxxi, 35 note 3, 57, 60, 62, 85-6

Romano, Ezzolino di, xx, 53 note 8

Romans, Caxton on the, xxxix, 16; eating customs of the, xxxv, 303; xxxvii, 18-19; education among the, 52 note; Emerson on the, v, 52; houses and public buildings of early, 55; poetry among the, xxvii, 10-11; swimming among, xxxvii, 14; Taine on the, xxxix, 444, 448

Romantic Literature, Hugo on, xxxix, 363

Romantic Movement, Hugo in, xxxix, 354 note; Wordsworth in, 281 note

Romanus, the martyr, xv, 268

Romanus, Voconius, Pliny on, ix, 228-9, 375-6; Pliny's letters to, 196, 221, 297, 334, 352

Rome, agrarian law of, x, 415; allies of, iii, 82; America and, ix, 5; assimilation of other nations by, xxviii, 257; Bacon on, v, 376; Bacon on triumphs of, iii, 84; bribery in, xii, 164-5; burning of, Chaucer on, xl, 49; custom of candidates in early, xii, 164; Carthage and, Virgil on, xiii, 178-9; Cicero on success of, iii, 46-7; civil war in, 40; xii, 303-5, 320; colonies of, x, 416; corn importations in, 160; England compared with, xxxiv, 86-7; of Evander's time, xiii, 283-4; foreign policy of, xxxvi, 19; freedom of, due to her arms, 43; freedom of press in, iii, 204-5; galleys of, xxxv, 376 note; the Germans and, xxxiii, 116-17; Goethe and Byron on, xxxii, 412 note; greatness of, prophesied, iii, 95; conquest of Greece, xxxvi, 11, 12, 13, 19; Grecian art in, xxxii, 251; history of, Carlyle on, xxv, 381-2; history of, Dante on, xx, 308-10; history of, Virgil on, xiii, 293-6; interest in, x, 99-100; kings of, Virgil on, xiii, 239; Luther on, xxxvi, 313; Marlowe on, xix, 223-4; medicine in, xxxv, 252; Milton on, iv, 400-3; money in, x, 31, 33, 34, 45; More on standing armies of, xxxvi, 154; naturalization policy of, iii, 80; penology in, xxxvi, 160; pigeons in ancient, xi, 43; poetry of, Shelley on, xxvii, 360-1; Prætorian emperors of, xxxvi, 23; present level of, xxx, 366; provincial policy of, xxxvi, 12, 18, 77; Raleigh on, xxxix, 74; religion and philosophy of, 456; religious matters in early, xii, 176-7; religious toleration in, xxxiv, 398; xxxvii,

416; republic of, Machiavelli on, xxv, 385; Republican, works dealing with, l, 19-20, 26; sack of, by Imperialists, xxxi, 71-83; seditions in early, xii, 155-7, 162-3; See of (see Papacy); selection known in, xi, 48; Shelley on, xli, 891; value of silver in, x, 189-90; slavery in early, xii, 176; study of language in, xxxvii, 156, 174; Taine on, xxxix, 448; turdi cultivated in, x, 195; of Virgil's time, Dryden on, xiii, 16-17; Volscian Wars of, xii, 158-9, 177-88

Romeo, steward of Raymond Berenger, xx, 311 note 26

Romeo and Juliet, Lamb on, xxvii, 316; Ruskin on, xxviii, 142

Romilly, Sir Samuel, apprentice bill of, v, 408; on buying seat in Parliament, 378 note; on chancery, 378; on English laws, 360; his love for his wife, 384; Mill and, xxv, 70; on public speaking, v, 373

Romilly, Edward, xxv, 126

Romilly, John, xxv, 126

Romoaldo, St., xx, 380 note 5

Romoli, Vincenzio, xxxi, 133, 134, 135, 168, 170, 176

Romulus, the asylum of, xiii, 283; Dryden on, 18; Machiavelli on, xxxvi, 20-1, 22; ordered Romans to live in arms, iii, 81; parentage of, xx, 320 note 16; prophecy of, xiii, 84-5; suckled by Wolf, 293; Virgil on, 237; Waller on, xxxiv, 149

RONALDS OF THE BENNALS, THE, vi, 26-8

Roncesvalles, battle of, xlix, 96, 133-84

Roncesvaux (see Roncesvalles)

Ronsard, on the ÆNEID, xiii, 45, 46; Montaigne on, xxxii, 64; Taine on, xxxix, 452

Roosevelt, Theodore, CONVENTION WITH PANAMA, xliii, 490-1

Roper, William, son-in-law of More, xxxvi, 92, 93; LIFE OF MORE, 93-141

Ropes, Henry, at Gettysburg, xliii, 390-1

Rosa, Vincent de la, in the goatherd's story, xiv, 526-8

ROSABELLE, xli, 766-7

ROSALIND'S MADRIGAL, xl, 218

ROSALINE, by Lodge, xl, 219

Rosas, General, xxix, 78, 82, 84-5, 115-16, 154

Rosaura, in LIFE A DREAM, arrival in Poland, xxvi, 5-10; with Segismund, 11-15; with Clotaldo, 15-18; at palace, with Segismund, 37-8; reason of coming to Poland, 61; returns to tower, with Segis-

mund, 61-2; reunited with As-
tolfo, 67
Roscius, case of, xii, 227
Roscommon, Lord, *Silenus* of, xiii,
59; Voltaire on, xxxiv, 150;
Wordsworth on, xxxix, 347
Rose, in SHOEMAKER'S HOLIDAY (see
Oateley)
ROSE, A WHITE, xlii, 1246
ROSE, THE RED, RED, vi, 514
Rose, Aquila, i, 23; elegy on, 28;
son of, 66
ROSE AYLMER, xli, 922
ROSE-BUD, A, BY MY EARLY WALK,
vi, 302
ROSE-RED AND SNOW-WHITE, xvii,
226
Rosegli, Mariano, xxxi, 442
Rosemary, flower of remembrance,
xli, 494; xlvi, 171
Rosencrantz, in HAMLET, xlvi, 116-
17, 123-7, 131, 133-4, 140, 141,
147-8, 150, 159, 160, 161, 162, 163,
165, 173, 189, 198
Roses, Harrison on, xxxv, 255;
Massinger on, xlvii, 824
ROSES IN THE BOSOM OF CASTARA,
xl, 257-8
Roses, Wars of the, Raleigh on,
xxxix, 83
ROSLIN INN, EPIGRAM AT, vi, 276
Ross, in MACBETH, reports victory
to Duncan, xlvi, 307-8; messenger
to Macbeth, 311; and the old man,
331; with Macduff, 332; at the
banquet, 340, 341, 342, 344; with
Lady Macduff, 352-3; at English
Court, 360-2; with Siward, 374
Ross, Alexander, WOOED AND MAR-
RIED, xli, 580-1
Ross, Captain, at Keeling Island,
xxix, 477, 482
Rösselmann, the priest in WILHELM
TELL, at Rootli league, xxvi, 405-
15; before Gessler's cap, 424; with
Tell at Altdorf, 426-35; reports
murder of emperor, 463
Rossetti, Christina Georgina, poems
by, xlii, 1228-30
Rossetti, Dante Gabriel, poems by,
xlii, 1196-1228
Rossi, Girolamo de', xxxi, 259 note
1, 312, 350-1
Rosso, Il, xxxi, 48 note 1, 56, 204-
5, 314 and note, 338
Rotund, the, in building, xxiv, 65-6
and note
Rouen, capture of, xxxviii, 49;
Smith on, x, 276
ROUGH ROADS, EPIGRAM ON, vi, 249
Roughness, of manners, xxxvii, 129;
more sublime than smoothness,
xxiv, 64; why not beautiful, 127
Roumania, Freeman on, xxviii, 274-6
Round Table, the, xxxv, 142; why
founded, 168; knights of the, xiv,

100; Renan on the, xxxii, 164;
Tennyson on the, xlii, 1025; seen
at Winchester, xxix, 22
Round Top, at Gettysburg, xliii, 354,
357
ROUND TOWER AT JHANSI, xlii, 1229-
30
Rous, Sir Francis, xxv, 386
Rousseau, Jean Jacques, his principles of composition, xxiv, 319;
remarks on *Confessions* of, xxxi,
1; editor's remarks on DISCOURSE
of, l, 35; Emerson on, v, 275;
Hume and, xxvii, 214; Hazlitt
on, 294; Hobbes and, xxxiv, 318;
ON INEQUALITY, 166-234; life and
works, 164-5; Mill on work of,
xxv, 250-1; SAVOYARD VICAR, xxxiv.
235-315; Sainte-Beuve on SAVO-
YARD VICAR of, xxxii, 128; Stevenson on, xxviii, 299-300
Roux, Maitre, xxxi, 48 note 1, 56
ROVER, THE, by Scott, xli, 761
Rovere, Francesco Maria della, xxxi,
76 note 1
ROWAN TREE, THE, xli, 577-8
Rowe, Nicholas, editor of Shake-
speare, xxxix, 246, 256; Johnson
on, 244; on Shakespeare, 241
Rowlands, Richard, OUR BLESSED
LADY'S LULLABY, xl, 261-5
Rowley, in SCHOOL FOR SCANDAL,
with Sir Peter, xviii, 123-5; with
Sir Oliver, 135-6; plans to try
Charles and Joseph Surface, 138-
9; with Charles Surface, 159-60;
with Sir Oliver, 160-1; in visit to
Joseph Surface, 175-6; announces
arrival of Sir Oliver, 178; with
Sir Peter after scandal, 184-6; at
Joseph Surface's, 189-93
Roxalana, Solyman's wife, iii, 53
Roxanes, and Themistocles, xii, 31
Roy, M. le, i, 155
ROYAL GEORGE, LOSS OF THE, xli, 546
Royal Society of England, Franklin
and, i, 153, 155-6
Royalty, Calvin on true, xxxix, 32
Roye, Lord, xxxv, 58
Royer-Collard, Rémusat on, xxxii,
130
Rozinante, horse of Don Quixote,
dialogue with Babieca, xiv, 17-18;
Don Quixote on, 228; the mares
and, 119-20; named, 23, 76; son-
net on, 541
Ruæus, commentator of Virgil, xiii,
44, 45, 52, 58-9
RUBAIYAT OF OMAR KHAYYAM, xli,
970-88
Rubens, Hazlitt on, xxvii, 293; Hugo
on, xxxix, 366, 370
Rubicant, the demon, xx, 90, 92
Rubicon, passage of the, xii, 302-3
Rucellai, Cosimo, xxvii, 412
Rucellai, Luigi, xxxi, 150

RUDELY THOU WRONGEST MY HEART'S DESIRE, xl, 256

Rudeness, grandeur and, xxiv, 68

Rudenz, Ulrich of, in WILHELM TELL, with Attinghausen, xxvi, 394-9; in love with Bertha, 399-400; with Bertha in the forest, 419-23; with Gessler in Altdorf, 428; defies Gessler, 432-3; joins the League, 447-50; takes Sarnen keep, 461; recovers Bertha, 461-2; in final scene, 474

Rudeyneh, xvi, 340 note

Rudimentary Organs, xi, 490-6; in classification, 454; highly variable, 160

Ruffo, John, Cervantes on, xiv, 57

Rufinus, letter to, ix, 343

Rufus, C. Musonius, ii, 116, 118 (5) and note

Rufus, Calvisius, letter to, ix, 257

Rufus, Caninius, letter to, ix, 246

Rufus, Corellius, Pliny on, ix, 206-8

Rufus, Curtius, story of ghost and, ix, 327

Rufus, Satrius, in Certus's case, ix, 358

Rufus, Verginius, Pliny on, ix, 221-3, 296

RUGBY CHAPEL, xlii, 1176-81

Ruggieri, Archbishop, xx, 138 note 1

Rugians, Tacitus on the, xxxiii, 121

RUIN, To, by Burns, vi, 203-4

RUINED FARMER, IN THE CHARACTER OF A, vi, 22-3

RUISSEAUX, ROBERT, ELEGY ON THE DEATH OF, vi, 99

Rukh's Egg, story of the, xvi, 256-7, 287-8; Aladdin and, 440-1

RULE, BRITANNIA, xl, 453

Rulers, Bacon on, iii, 50-55; Confucius's advice to, xliv, 5 (5), 7 (1, 3), 8 (19, 20, 21), 40 (9), 41 (17, 19), 42 (1, 2), 43 (3, 6), 44 (13, 15), 45 (17), 51 (44), 52 (4), 53 (10), 69 (2); Epictetus to, ii, 128 (34); Franklin on, i, 131; partisanship of, iii, 39; reverence for, 39 (see also Princes)

Rules, for children, xxxvii, 45-6; laying down, for others, ii, 397 (29)

Rum, Indians and, i, 121; Woolman on selling, 268-9

Ruminants, and pachyderms, xi, 378

Rumor, Æschylus on, viii, 15; Bacon on, iii, 147-9; false, a sign of sedition, 38; in Milton's Chaos, iv, 135; Raleigh on, xxxix, 70; Virgil on, xiii, 162-3

RUMPELSTILTSKIN, story of, xvii, 164

Ruodi, in WILHELM TELL, xxvi, 371-6, 460, 462, 463

Rupilius, Publius, made consul by Scipio, ix, 33

Rush, Richard, correspondence with Bagot, xliii, 283-5

Ruskin, John, Greenough and, v, 329; life and works of, xxviii, 94; SESAME AND LILIES, 95-168

Russel, the fox, xl, 48

Russell, first Baron, xxiv, 422-5

Russell, Lord John, pluck of, v, 380

Russell, Rev, John, Burns on, vi, 100, 107, 171, 174, 372

Russell, Jonathan, xliii, 273

Russell, Mr., in TWO YEARS BEFORE THE MAST, xxiii, 99, 104, 148, 256-7

Russell, W. Clark, on Dana's work, xxiii, 4

Russia, the bureaucracy of, xxv, 321-2; monks in, iii, 104; TREATY WITH UNITED STATES, xliii, 459-63

Rusticity, Burns on, vi, 260; Locke on, xxxvii, 76

Rusticucci, Giacopo, xx, 68 and note 3; in Hell, 27-8

Rusticus, teacher of Marcus Aurelius, ii, 194 (7), 199

Rusticus Arulenus, his death, ix, 196 note, 198 note; wife of, 274 note

Rustum, reference to, xli, 972

Ruth, Bunyan on, xv, 212; in Dante's PARADISE, xx, 420 note 2; Keats on, xli, 901; Milton on, iv, 81

RUTH: OR THE INFLUENCES OF NATURE, xli, 622-9

Rutherford, Milton on, iv, 83

Rütimeyer, on cattle, xi, 36

Ruysum, in EGMONT, xix, 248-53

Rymer, Dryden on, xxxix, 162

Saadi, on the ugly schoolmaster, v, 316

Saavedra, the captive, xiv, 413 (see Cervantes)

Sabacos, king of Egypt, xxxiii, 70-1, 78

Sabæans, Mohammed on, xlv, 1016

Sabbath, Emerson on the, v, 35, 42; Jesus on the, xliv, 372 (1-11), 397 (14-16), 398 (1-6); Pascal on the, xlviii, 202

Sabbath Laws, Mill on, xxv, 298-9

Sabellius, Dante on, xx, 344 note 21

Sabinian, and heathen antiquities, iii, 144

Sabinianus, letters to, ix, 361, 363

Sabines, rape of the, alluded to, xiii, 293

Sabinus, Statius, letter to, ix, 264

Sable, Marchioness de, letter to, xlviii, 347

Sabrina, in COMUS, iv, 68-71

Sachems, Indian, xliii, 151

Sacheverell, Henry, xxvii, 168

Saci, M. de, conversation with Pascal, xlviii, 392

Sackville, Lord, Burns on, vi, 55

Sacrament, of the Altar, Kempis on, vii, 349-79

Sacraments, Quakers on the, xxxiv, 67

Sacred Poetry, Sidney on, xxvii, 14

SACRED WRITINGS, xliv, xlv

Sacrifices, Confucius on, xliv, 10 (12), 11 (17); Hindu doctrine of, xlv, 814, 819-20, 874; Pascal on, xlviii, 338

Sacrilege, Dr. Donne on, xv, 354

Sadducees, xliv, 413 (27-40), 483 (8), 439 (17); Hobbes on the, xxxiv, 371

Sadness, connection of, with beauty, xxviii, 394

SAGA AND EPIC, xlix

Sagacity, Mr., in PILGRIM'S PROGRESS, xv, 180, 193

Sagas, Emerson on the, v, 356-7

Sages, in the ÆNEID, xiii, 417-18

Saibah, xlv, 1019 note

Sailing, Franklin on, i, 164

Sailors, Dana on life of, xxiii, 373-4; duties of, 19-21; how to improve their condition, 374-90; Woolman on hardships and depravity of, i, 305-8, 315

Sailor Songs, Dana on, xxiii, 270-1

ST. AGNES, THE EVE OF, xli, 907-17

St. André, Louis of, xxxviii, 21

St. Andrea, Giacomo da, xx, 58 note 4

St. Aubin, Capt., xxxviii, 48

St. Augustine (see Augustine)

St. Augustine, Drake at, xxxiii, 264-5, 267

St. Bartholomew, massacre of, Bacon on, iii, 14; Capt. Tetu on, xxxiii, 193

Sainte-Beuve, Charles Augustin, on charlatanism, xxviii, 66; as a critic, l, 56; life and writings, xxxii, 108; ON MONTAIGNE, 109-25; Port Royal of, xxxix, 439; Taine on, 440; WHAT IS A CLASSIC, xxxii, 126-39

ST. CECILIA'S DAY, SONG FOR, xl, 398

St. Clair, Sir John, i, 138

Saint-Cyran, letter of, xlviii, 328

St. Denis, battle of, xxxviii, 52-3

St. Domingo, Drake at, xxxiii, 235, 248-53, 267-8; productions of, x, 419-20; village of, xxix, 13-14

St. Elmo's Light, xxix, 49

St. Etienne, Raband de, on National Assembly, xxiv, 315 note

St. Helena, island of, xxix, 512-17; species of, xi, 432

Saint-Hilaire, Geoffroy, on compensation of growth, xi, 158; on homologous parts, 473; on origin of species, 10-11, 15-16

St. John, H. (see Bolingbroke)

St. John, Newfoundland, settlement of, xxxiii, 270, 288-9

St. John's River, navigation of, xliii, 303-4

St. Jago, Darwin on, xxix, 11-16; health conditions at, 387

St. Lawrence River, navigation of, xliii, 306

Saint-Lo, Edward III at, xxxv, 11; importance of, 11 note

Saint-Martin, Capt., xxxii, 14

St. Omer, the iconoclasts at, xix, 255

St. Paul's Rocks, Darwin on, xxix, 18-21

St. Peter's, the building of, xxxvi, 261, 269, 272

St. Quentin, the wounded of, xxxviii, 46-7

Saint-Simon, Mill on, xxv, 44; Mill on school of, 107-10

St. Winifred's Well, xxxvii, 13

SAINT, FOLLOW YOUR, xl, 291

Saintré, John of, xxxv, 47, 48, 52

Saints, Bunyan on the, xv, 58; canonization of, xxv, 223-4; disputes on the merits of, vii, 344-6; Hume on relics of, xxxvii, 348; Kempis on the, vii, 229-31; Luther on glorification of, xxxvi, 326-8; Pascal on, xlviii, 279-80, 308 (868), 365; patience of the, vii, 312 (3)

Saint's Days, Luther on, xxxvi, 324

Saïs, city of, xxxiii, 33, 34, 84, 86, 88

Sakelde, in KINMONT WILLIE, xl, 109-10, 112-13

Saki, reference to the, xli, 978

Sakka, the god, xlv, 625, 628, 632, 714-16

Saladin, Emerson on, v, 211; in Limbo, xx, 20 and note 7

Salamanca, Bishop of (see Bobadilla)

Salamander, Cellini and the, xxxi, 11; invoked by Faust, xix, 51

Salamis, Æschylus at, viii, 3; Aristides at, xii, 88-9; battle of, 17-20; Byron on, xli, 833; drama on, viii, 3

Salaries, of public officials, i, 371 (385-6); taxes on, x, 537-8

SALATHIEL PAVY, ON, xl, 307

Sale, Sir Robert, in Tyler's Rebellion, xxxv, 75-6

Salem, reference to, iv, 25 (6)

Salih, brother of Jullanar, xvi, 344-52

Salimbene, Francesco, xxxi, 25, 29

Salimbeni, Niccoli, xx, 124 and note

Salinator, and Fabius, ix, 49

Salinator, Fuscus, Pliny on, ix, 296-7, 306

Salius, death of, xiii, 353; in the foot-race, 192-4

Salisbury Cathedral, Emerson on, v, 478

Salisbury, Earl of, in Tyler's Rebellion, xxxv, 69, 70, 72, 81

Salisbury, university of, xxxv, 391

Sallust, on the viper, xxxv, 364 note

Sallust, on war, xxxvi, 153

Sallustius, Cicero on, ix, 114

Sallutio, Scipio, xii, 318

SALLY IN OUR ALLY, xl, 414-15

Salmanassar, reference to, iv, 395

Salmasius, defender of Charles the First, iv, 5

Salmon and Dog-fish, tale of, xlvii, 776

Salmoneus, in Tartarus, xiii, 231

Salmydessos, viii, 181 and note 46

Salomon's House (see. Solomon's House)

Salt, crystallization of common, xxx, 30 note 12; the desire of vegetarians for, xxix, 123; incrustations of, in Patagonia, 89-90; Locke on use of, xxxvii, 17; used to melt ice, xxx, 38-9

Salt-lakes, in South America, xxix, 76-8

Salterello, Lapo, xx, 352 note 12

Salutations, Mohammed on, xlv, 989

Salvani, Provenzano, xx, 192 and note

Salvation, Browne on, iii, 319-23; Bunyan on means of, xv, 230-1; Calvin on, xxxix, 35, 52-3, 54; Dante on requisites of, xx, 313-15, 368-9, 422; Jesus on, xliv, 388, 408 (18-30); Lessing on, xxxii, 212; Luther on, xxxvi, 262, 269, 272, 365, 366, 369, 370, 381-2; meaning of, xv, 231; of non-Christians, xx, 368-9, 373-4; Peter on, xliv, 436 (12); Ruskin on false ideas of, xxviii, 112; the wall of, in PILGRIM'S PROGRESS, xv, 41

Salviati, Alamanno, xxxi, 426 note

Salviati, Cardinal, xxxi, 119-20, 124, 285 note

Salviati, Giovanni, xxxi, 47 note 2

Salviati, Jacopo, xxxi, 14 note 4, 71, 77, 78

Salviati, Piero, xxxi, 431

Salzburg, Archbishop of, xix, 334

Sam, in TWO YEARS BEFORE THE MAST, xxiii, 104-6, 112, 132, 418

Sama-Ved, xlv, 844

Samarchand, Temir's throne, iv, 332

Samaria, founding of church in, xliv, 446 (5-8); the woman of, xx, 232

Samaritan, the good, xliv, 388 (33-5)

Samaritans, belief confined to Pentateuch, iii, 290 (25)

Samos, war with Athens, xii, 63-6

Sampson, John, xxxiii, 237, 239-40, 243, 246, 256, 259, 263

Samson, Browne on, iii, 286; Delilah and, iv, 290; slays with the jaw-bone of an ass, xv, 300

Samson, in SAMSON AGONISTES, lament of, iv, 418-21; his deeds sung by chorus, 422-3; his marriages, 424; his victory over Philistines, 425; Manoa's lament over, 427-8; reveals secret to Dalila, 428-9; hears of feast, 430; relates how shorn by Dalila, 432; his despair, 433-5; rejects reconcilement with Dalila, 437-43; with Harapha, 446-50; summoned to show feats of strength, 452; goes to temple, 454-5; his feat there, 458-62

Samson, Duke, in SONG OF ROLAND, xlix, 100, 125, 141, 153, 178

SAMSON AGONISTES, iv, 418-63; Bagehot on, xxviii, 184-5; date of, iv, 5; introduction to, 416-17

Samuel, Luther on, xxxvi, 347; the Psalmist on, xliv, 272 (6-8); Saul and, xv, 341

Samuel, in PILGRIM'S PROGRESS, xv, 232, 250, 255, 286, 290

San Carlo, plague of, xxi, 523

San Diego (1834), xxiii, 101; (in 1859), 409-11; Dana on, 126

San Francisco (1834), Dana on, xxiii, 231, 238; (in 1835), 395-6; (in 1859), 396-403; Drake in Bay of, xxxiii, 222; history of, xxiii, 413-14

San Gallo, Antonio da, xxxi, 204 note 1

San Gallo, Francesco da, xxxi, 409 and note

San Juan, Dana on, xxiii, 143-4

San Lorenzo, island of, xxix, 390

San Pedro (in 1859), xxiii, 407

San Pedro Island, Darwin on, xxix, 297-8

San Severino, Roberto of, xxxvi, 45

San Salvador, Columbus on, xliii, 22

Sanacharib, expedition against Egypt, xxxiii, 72

Sancho Panza, Cervantes on, xiv, 13; Gandaline to, 17; becomes squire to Don Quixote, 62-4; promises not to aid master against knights, 68-9; beaten by the lackeys, 70; asks for promised island, 79; reason of name, 76; conversation with Don Quixote, 79-84; prefers to eat without ceremony, 85-6; the carriers and, 119-21; his doubts, 121-6; relates the adventure, 128; his idea of knight-errantry, 128-9; adventure with Maritornes, 133-7; takes Don Quixote's balsam, 139; refuses to pay innkeeper and is tossed in blanket, 141-3; discouraged, 144-5; in adventure of hearse, 155-7; tries to dissuade Don Quixote from perilous adventure, 163-5;

his tale, 166-8; his distress, 168-70; rebuked for his merriment, 172-4; plans for his future earldom, 185-6; loses his ass, 200; finds wallet, 201; rebels, 221-3; despatched with letter to Dulcinea, 235-7, 304-9; his embassy, 241-5; returns with curate and barber, 248-9; does not wish to become a churchman, 286; nor a ruler of Moors, 289-90; becomes vassal of Micomicona, 299; quarrel with Quixote over Dulcinea, 300-3; recovers his ass, 303-4; in wine-bags adventure, 364-8; the barber and, 470-2; 474-7; enchanted, 486-7; promised his wages, 489; the curate and, 497; proves his master not enchanted, 508-10; plans for his earldom, 521-2; lament over Don Quixote, 536; his return home, 537-8; sonnet to, 541; epitaph on, 542; Lowell on, xxviii, 450-1; story of wine, xxvii, 222

Sanctuary, right of, among Romans, ix, 388 note 1
Sand Dunes, Darwin on, xxix, 86-7
Sandauce, children of, xii, 18, 89
Sanderson, Robert, Walton's life of, xv, 326
SANDS OF DEE, xlii, 1102
Sandwich Islanders, belief of, v, 103; Dana on, xxiii, 149-55, 253
Sandwich Islands, Dana on, xxiii, 253
Sandwich Land, sonw in, xxix, 265
Sandys, Sir Edwin, xxvii, 61
Sandys, George, Dryden on, xxxix, 161
Sanga, Battista, xxxi, 102 note 7
Sangreal (see Holy Grail)
Sanhedrin, Pascal on the, xlviii, 241
Sanjnya, xlv, 801, 805, 806, 847, 852, 856, 883-4
Sañjiva, xlv, 749
Sankara, xlv, 844
Sânkhya, xlv, 809, 813, 833
Sanna, in story of FUNDEVOGEL, xvii, 149-51
Sannayâs, xlv, 876
Sansovino, Giacopo del, xxxi, 156 note 2, 160, 371-2
Sant Angel, Luis de, xliii, 22
Santa Barbara, xxiii, 61-2; (in 1859), 405-6; fandango at, 248-51; funeral at, 135-7
Santa Croce, Paolo, referred to, xviii, 349
Santa Cruz River, Darwin on, xxix, 191-4
Santacroce, Antonio, xxxi, 74, 75, 82-3
Santi, the goldsmith, xxxi, 35

Santiago, Cape Verde Islands, Drake at, xxxiii, 234-5, 267
Santiago, Chili, Darwin on, xxix, 279; Drake at, xxxiii, 218
Santiago, island of, xxxiii, 210
Santiago de Tolon, xxxiii, 136; Drake at, 161
Santini, Giovan Battista, xxxi, 443
Sapia, of Sienna, xx, 199 and note 3
Sapor, and Valerian, xxxix, 103
Sapphira, wife of Ananias, xliv, 438 (1-10); Bunyan on, xv, 127; Dante on, xx, 230
Sappho, Byron on, xli, 833
SAPPHO REDIVIVUS, vi, 345-6
Saragossa, Charlemagne at, xlix, 97, 196-7
Sarah, and Abraham, xxxvi, 285; lies of, xv, 264; in Paradise, xx, 420
Sarandib, island of, xvi, 302
Sardanapalus, xx, 351 note 6; Calvin on, xxxix, 47; city-building of, xxxv, 378; stealing of treasures of, xxxiii, 77
Sarepta (see Zarephath)
Sâriputta, xlv, 716, 749; the Demons and, 726-8
Sark, battle of, vi, 183 note 5
Sarlabous, Captain, xxxviii, 52
Sarmatia, ix, 386 note 3
Sarmatians, Tacitus on the, xxxiii, 123
Sarmentus, Octavius's page, xii, 382
Sarmiento, Don Juan, xxxiii, 334, 342
Sarmiento, Mount, xxix, 257-8
Sarnen, Meyer von, in WILHELM TELL, xxvi, 400-13
Sarpedon, death of, xiii, 342; reference to, 79
Sarrebruck, Earl of, xxxv, 10, 37, 39, 47
SARTO, ANDREA DEL, xlii, 1130-7
Satan, in BOOK OF JOB, xliv, 73-5
Satan, in PARADISE LOST, seducer of mankind, iv, 91; his fall and awakening in Hell, 91-2; speech with Beelzebub, 92-5; rises and wakens the fallen angels, 95-8; raising of his standard, 103; speech to the angels, 106-7; proposes man's seduction, 106, 120; in council of fallen angels, 111; undertakes to find out man and his world, 121-2; issues from council, 123; wings to gates of Hell, 126-7; meets Sin and Death, 127-30; voyage through chaos to the world, 134-7; seen by God flying to earth, 140; on outer sphere of world, 148-9; beholds interior of world, 151-2; in the sun, 153; inquires way to earth, 154-5; first view of earth, 156; alights on Niphates, 156; his re-

morse, 158-60; decides against submission, 160; his perturbation betrays him, 160; arrives at Eden, 160-2; sees Adam and Eve, 164; resolves to work fall of man, 166-7, 170-1; found at Eve's ear, 177-8; before Gabriel, 179-83; stirs rebellion in Heaven, 200-1, 202-3; rebuked by Abdiel, 204; asserts self-existence of angels, 205; in the rebel forces, 209; combat with Abdiel, 209-12; encounter with Michael, 213-15; encourages his forces, 217-18; proposes infernal engines, 218-19; in second day's battle, 221, 222; returns to Eden, 265; assumes form of serpent, 266, 268; his spite, 266-8; tempts Eve, 274-83; returns to Hell, 302-6; announces his success, 306; changed to a serpent, 307; how overcome by Christ, 355-7

Satan, in PARADISE REGAINED, undertakes to ensnare Christ, iv, 364-6; tempts him in guise of old man, 371-5; appeals to fellows for aid, 379; undertakes to tempt Christ again, 381; tempts Jesus to eat, 383-6; tempts with riches, 386-8; tempts by glory, 388-92; tempts Jesus to assume his throne, 392-9; shows him kingdoms of earth, 394-7; shows Rome, 400-2; demands that Christ worship him, 403; tempts by offer of wisdom, 404-8; warns him of sorrows in store, 408-9; tempts by fear, 409-12; carries Jesus above Jerusalem, 413; his fall, 413-14; overcome by Christ, 415

Satan, Bagehot on Milton's, xxviii, 198, 204-9; Burke on Milton's portrait of, xxiv, 55; Calvin on, xxxix, 46-7; Goethe on name of, xix, 102; the grotesque in ideas of, xxxix, 365; Mohammedan (see Iblis); meaning of name of, iv, 304; Shelley on Milton's, xxvii, 365-6

Satiety, and fear of death, iii, 10
SATIRE, A, by Johnson, xli, 516-17
Satires, Sidney on, xxvii, 29; Swift on, 124-5; Wordsworth on, xxxix, 314
Satirists, Dryden on, xviii, 15-17
Satisfaction, Bacon on, xxxix, 127; Johnson on, 208; never attained, v, 243-4, 246
Sattwan, xlv, 864, 873, 875, 879
Saturn, Dante on reign of, xx, 376 note 5; in Italy, xiii, 283; Jove and, iv, 68; Milton on, 103; Plutarch on, iii, 47; Vesta and, iv, 35
Saturn, the planet, Dante's seventh Heaven, xx, 375

Saturnalia, feast of, ix, 235 note 3
Saturnia, Virgil on, xiii, 323
Saturninus, bequest of, ix, 285
SATYR AND MAN, fable of, xvii, 33
Satyric Drama, xii, 41 note
Satyrs, reference to the, iv, 75
Satyrus, the actor, and Demosthenes, xii, 202
Satyrus, A. Caninius, relations with Cicero, ix, 84-5
Saufeius, Cicero on, ix, 151-2
Saul, king of Israel, xliv, 459 (21); Dante on, xx, 194; David and, xli, 500; xliv, 218; Jonathan and, xliii, 104, 110; Psalms on David's deliverance from, xliv, 162-6, 216-17; his vision of Samuel, xv, 341; the witch of Endor and, iii, 95
SAUL, SONG OF, BEFORE HIS LAST BATTLE, xli, 832
Saul, the apostle (see Paul)
Saunderson, Mr., Burke on, xxiv, 141-2
Sauntering, origin of word, xxviii, 407
Saurophagus, Darwin on the, xxix, 64-5
Saussure, in the Alps, xxx, 235
Saut-perdu, horse of Malquiant, xlix, 154
Savage, James, Channing on, xxviii, 379
Savage State, progress of man from, xxxii, 301, 309-10; Rousseau on the, xxxiv, 171-200, 208-9
Savages, Darwin on, xxix, 530-1; poverty of, x, 5-6; power of imitation among, xxix, 221
Save-all, Mr., in PILGRIM'S PROGRESS, xv, 106-11, 113
Savella, in THE CENCI, comes to summon Cenci, xviii, 328-9; finds him dead, 330-1; finds Orsino's letter, 332; with Beatrice and Lucretia, 332-5
Savelli, Giovan Battista, xxxi, 140 note 3
Saveself, in PILGRIM'S PROGRESS, xv, 156
Savile, Sir Henry, xxvii, 61
Saving, economically considered, x, 278-9; motives of, 282, 283; not happiness, xix, 372
Savonarola, Machiavelli on, xxxvi, 22; the party of, xxxi, 31 note 1, 33 note 1
Savoyard, story of the, xxxii, 46
SAVOYARD VICAR, FAITH OF A, xxxiv, 235-315; editorial remarks on, 164, 165; Sainte-Beuve on, xxxii, 128
SAW YE BONIE LESLEY, vi, 470
SAW YE MY DEAR, MY PHILLY, vi, 535
Saxo Grammaticus, xlvi, 86
Saxon Race, Emerson on the, v, 491
Saxons, Celts and, v, 351; in England, 365-6

Saxony, breeding in, xi, 46
Say, M., Mill on, xxv, 44
SAY NOT THE STRUGGLE NAUGHT
    AVAILETH, xlii, 1165
Say-Well, in PILGRIM'S PROGRESS,
    xv, 82
Sayce, Mr., quoted, xxviii, 249, 251
Saying, and Doing, Bunyan on, xv,
    84
Sbietta, Lo, xxxi, 440-6, 447-8, 449-
    51
Scæva, Cassius, xii, 287
Scævola Pontifex, Cicero on, ix, 7
Scævola, Quintus Mucius, his part
    in Cicero's essay on Friendship,
    ix, 7-9; the publicani and, 137
Scala, Alberto della, xx, 222 note 9
Scala, Can Grande della, Dante on,
    xx, 360 note 14; leader of Ghibel-
    lines, 283 note 6; patron of Dante,
    3; reference to, 8 note 6
Scales (constellation), Milton on, iv,
    182
Scali, Giorgio, xxxvi, 36
Scaliger, on his emendations, xxxix,
    260; on poets, xxvii, 43; Sainte-
    Beuve on, xxxii, 130; on Virgil,
    xiii, 39; xxvii, 54
Scandal, Garrick on, xviii, 109-10;
    punishment of, in Dante's HELL,
    xx, 117-20; Sheridan's Maria on,
    xviii, 116
Scander Beg, xlvii, 468 note 9
Scaptius, M., ix, 149 50
Scacramouch, xlviii, 12 note 1
Scarborough, John, i, 202
SCARING SOME WATER FOWL, ON,
    vi, 300
Scarlatina, and cowpox, xxxviii,
    226-7
Scarlet Fever, Jenner on the,
    xxxviii, 172
Scarlok, in ROBYN HODE, in adven-
    ture with knight, xl, 131, 132,
    138, 139-40; with monk, 157; at
    archery contest, 168; at shoot in
    forest, 182; with Robyn at court,
    186
Scarmiglione, Dante on, xx, 89
Scarron, Goldsmith on feasts of,
    xli, 517; Hugo on, xxxix, 368-9
Scatheloke (see Scarlok)
Scelidotherium, Darwin on the, xxix,
    93-4
Sceptic, in FAUST, xix, 182
Sceptical Philosophy, Hume on,
    xxxvii, 337-8, 431-45
Scepticism, Bacon on, xxxix, 147-8,
    150; Bacon on contemporary, iii,
    7; Berkeley on, xxxvii, 202, 203-
    4, 245-6, 284, 287; Carlyle on,
    xxv, 368; defence of, xxxvii, 337-
    8; Descartes, xxxiv, 28; Emerson
    on, v, 284, 294; Hume on, xxxvii,
    324-38, 431-45; of Montaigne,
    xlviii, 395-8, 401; Pascal on, 71-7,

78 (202), 82 (230), 125-7, 129
    (387), 130 (390-2), 131 (395),
    145, (432, 434); Rousseau on,
    xxxiv, 247; Socrates on, ii, 83-4
Sceptics, Browne on the, iii, 320;
    Mill on, xxv, 34; Pascal on, xlviii,
    99 (282)
Sceva, sons of, xliv, 473 (14-16)
Schedo (see Schio)
Scheggia, Raffaellone, xxxi, 449-51
Schelling, philosophy of, v, 455
Schicchi, Gianni, xx, 126 note 1
Schiller, Carlyle on, xxv, 461;
    Emerson on, v, 191; Goethe
    and, xix, 3; Goethe on, xxv,
    102; LETTERS ON ÆSTHETIC
    EDUCATION, xxxii, 219-313; life
    and works, xxvi, 368; on truth,
    xxv, 367; WILHELM TELL, xxvi,
    369-474; work of, xxxii, 220
Schio, Girolamo, xxxi, 112 note
    117-20
Schismatics, in Dante's HELL, xx,
    117-20
Schisms, Bacon on, iii, 11-12; breed
    atheism, 46; Milton on, 233, 235-
    6, 241-2; Pascal on, xlviii, 301
    (846), 303; Paul, St., on, xlv, 501
    (10) (see also Heresies)
Schlegel, Friedrich, Carlyle on, xxv,
    361; Carlyle on Lectures of, 362-4
Schoine, Egyptian measure, xxxiii, 8
SCHOLAR, THE, by Southey, xli, 751
SCHOLAR, THE AMERICAN, v, 5-24
Scholars, Browne on power of, iii,
    329; Confucius on, xliv, 13 (9),
    41 (20), 46 (3); Goethe on closet,
    xix, 27; manual labor and, v, 53;
    soldiers and, Don Quixote on, xiv,
    393-8; Tseng-tzu on, xliv, 26 (7);
    Tzu-chang on, 65 (1); Tzu-hsia
    on, 66 (13); unteachable, ii, 146
    (80)
Scholarships, Smith on, x, 138-41
Scholasticism, attacks on, xxxvii, 4
Scholiasts, Johnson on, xxxix, 253
Schomberg, Nicolas, xxxi, 92 note
    2; xxxix, 56
School, Locke on going away to,
    xxxvii, 53-7
SCHOOL FOR SCANDAL, Sheridan's,
    xviii, 111-96; remarks on, 104
Schoolmaster, Goldsmith's, xli, 526-7
Schoolmen, Bacon on the, iii, 129;
    Carlyle on the, xxv, 337-8; debt
    of, to St. Augustine, vii, 4; Hobbes
    on the, xxxiv, 372-3; Hume on
    the, xxxvii, 321; Mill on, xxv,
    248; Reformation as caused by
    the, xxxiv, 401; subtlety of, iii,
    47-8; Voltaire on the, xxxiv, 105;
    on war, iii, 52
Schützenberger, M., xxxviii, 304-7
Schurz, Carl, at Gettysburg, xliii,
    351
Sciancato, in Dante's HELL, xx, 108
Science, another kind of ignorance,

xviii, 428; Augustine, St., on irreligious, vii, 67-8; on authority, xxxix, 128-31; Bacon on popular, 129-30; Carlyle on, xxv, 334; Channing on study of, xxviii, 338-40; defined by Hobbes, xxxiv, 348-9; Emerson on our, v, 307-8, 308-9; need of experiment in, xxxix, 131-2, 134; faith and, Browne on, iii, 284-6; Faraday on study of, xxx, 88; the finding of analogy, vi, 8; Helmholtz on study of, xxx, 181; Hobbes on, xxxiv, 348-9; Hume on, xxxvii, 308, 310; Huxley on applied, xxviii, 229-30; literary study compared with, 220-9; logical method in, xxxix, 132, 141; Montaigne on study of, xxxii, 48-9; natural and mental, compared, xxx, 181-3; Pascal on false, xlviii, 200 (604); Pasteur on, xxxviii, 289, 372; poetry and, xxviii, 65-6; xxxix, 420; Pope on, xl, 426-7; public attitude toward, xxviii, 121-3; reading course in, l, 44-7; reason and authority in, xlviii, 446-9; religion and, Bacon on, xxxix, 134-5; religion and, Faraday on, xxx, 3; sensuality of our, v, 173-4; several branches of, xxxiv, 376-7; teaching of, Emerson on, v, 267; as source of power, xxxiv, 375; value of, xxviii, 218-20

SCIENCE AND CULTURE, Huxley's, xxviii, 215-32; editorial remarks on, l, 43

Sciences, Bacon on divisions of the, xxxix, 138; deductive and experimental, xxv, 105; Locke on study of, xxxvii, 149; Montaigne on the, xlviii, 398; Pascal on the, 446; Pascal on infinity of the, 27-8; Sidney on object of, xxvii, 16

Scientific Congresses, Newman on, xxviii, 35-6

SCIENTIFIC PAPERS, xxx, xxxviii.

Scientists, Emerson on our, v, 309

Sciography, Hobbes on, xxxiv, 377

Sciorina, Giacopa della, xxxi, 90-1, 92

Scipio Africanus, Antiochus and, xlviii, 254; charged with peculation, v, 131; Cicero on, ix, 52; Cyrus and, xxxvi, 52; Ennius and, xxvii, 40; "the highth of Rome," iv, 276; the Iberian maid and, 381; leniency of, xxxvi, 58-9; Livy on, iii, 111; Milton on iv, 389, 390; statue of, ix, 154-5

Scipio Asiaticus, results of conquests of, ix, 360 note 1

Scipio, father-in-law of Pompey, xxxii, 7; xii, 301, 309, 311, 312; speech of, on tribune law, ix, 40; war against Cæsar, xii, 317-19

Scipio, Publius, argument for justice, ix, 17; in Cicero's essay on OLD AGE, 46; on friendship, 20-1, 29, 30; his friendships, 32; the Greek philosophers and, iii, 205; his belief in immortality, ix, 12; Lælius and, 8, 12-13, 19, 43; Lælius on, 10-11; made Pontifex Maximus, 64; Q. Pompeius and, 35

Scipios, Caxton on the, xxxix, 16; Virgil on, xiii, 240

Sciro, reference to, xxvi, 128

Scissor-beak, Darwin on the, xxix, 149-51

Scissor-tail, Darwin on the, xxix, 151

Scoffers, Goethe on, xix, 19; Sidney on, xxvii, 33-4

Scoffing, habit of, in discourse, iii, 80; at religion, 46

Scolds, punishment of, in old England, xxxv, 386

Scoresby, on color of water, xxix, 28

Scornigiani, Farinata de', xx, 168 note 5

Scorpion, Harrison on the, xxxv, 364

Scorzone, Jeanne, xxxi, 332-3

Scotch, Burns on the, vi, 170; Carlyle on character of the, xxv, 427-8; Harrison on diet of the, xxxv, 285-7, 303

SCOTCH BARD, ON A, vi, 226-8

SCOTCH DRINK, vi, 151-55

Scotland, agriculture of, xxxv, 326; apprenticeships in, x, 129; banking operations in, 245-9, 252, 255-7, 264-5; Burns on, vi, 169; Burns on learning of, 273-4; Burns's vision of, 182-4; Emerson on, v, 354; Harrison on eating in, xxxv, 285-6; Knox on Reformation in, xxxix, 61-3; quarries and mines, xxxv, 325; Raleigh on union with England, xxxix, 83; rate of interest in, x, 95; soil of, xxxv, 324, 325; union with England, economic effect of, x, 194, 207; wages in, 80-1; wolves and foxes in, xxxv, 359; Wordsworth on critics of, xxxix, 338 note (see also Caledonia)

SCOTS PROLOGUE FOR SUTHERLAND, vi, 396-7

Scott, Master, in SHOEMAKER'S HOLIDAY, xlvii, 471, 472, 473

Scott, Michael, Dante on, xx, 86 and note 6

SCOTT, MISS JEAN, EPIGRAM TO, vi, 286

SCOTT, MRS., EPISTLE TO, vi, 270-2

SCOTT, ESSAY ON, Carlyle's, xxv, 409-68; remarks on, 332

Scott, Sir Walter, ambition of, xxv, 454-5; babyhood, incidents of, 429-30; Ballantyne and, 446-7; as biographer of Swift, xxviii, 7; Byron

and, xxxii, 401; Carlyle on Lockhart's *Life* of, xxv, 412-19; death of wife, 466-7; dinner with the Regent, 445-6; Emerson on, v, 223, 462; fame, indifference to, xxv, 436; financial ruin and last writings, 464-5; a genuine, healthy man, 423-6; Goethe's influence on, 441-2; lameness, 427; last days, 468; letters of, 444; *Liddesdale Raids*, 430-3; life at Abbotsford, 448-54; life up to thirty, 426; life, middle period of, 435-6; *Life of Napoleon*, Mill on, 87; love of animals for, 452-3 and note; Mill on, 97; *Minstrelsy of Scottish Border*, 434; national influences, 427-8; not a great man, 419-23; poems by, xli, 755-74; poems criticized, xxv, 439-41; popularity of, 411-12; in printing business, 437-8; productive faculty of, 462; Ruskin on heroes and heroines of, xxviii, 144-5; success in literature, xxv, 434-5; Taine on, xxxix, 437; unconsciousness of, xxv, 438-9; *Waverley Novels*, 443-4, 455-9; Wordsworth on, xli, 648-50

Scotus, Duns, Hazlitt on, xxvii, 292; the subtle doctor, xxviii, 48

Scowling, Marcus Aurelius on, ii, 249 (24)

Scribes, Jesus on the, xliv, 414 (45-7)

Scribonia, and Augustus, xiii, 38

Scribonianus, and his wife, ix, 254

Scriptures (see Bible)

Scrofa, Cicero on, ix, 152

Scrofula, and inoculation, xxxviii, 178, 203, 231

SCROGGAM, MY DEARIE, vi, 460

Scroop, Lord, xl, 109-10, 115

Scrope, P., on earthquakes, xxix, 373

Scrovigni, arms of the, xx, 73 note 5

Scuda, value of the, xxxi, 39 note 1

Scudamour, Sir, xxxix, 68

Scudéri, Corneille and, xxxix, 379 81

Scudéry, Mlle. de, on Chaucer, xxxix, 178; Dryden on, xiii, 13; Pascal on *Artamène* of, xlviii, 12 note 2

Scull, Nicholas, i, 60

Sculpture, Browning on, xlii, 1114; Coleridge on, xxvii, 275-6; Emerson on, v, 202; Goethe on, xxxix, 268-9, 271, 273, 274, 275, 278-9; Schiller on, xxxii, 285-6; training for, xxxix, 271

Scurvy, Dana on, xxiii, 356-7

Scyld the Scefing, xlix, 5, 6

Scylla, Æschylus on, viii, 50; Bacon on fable of, xxxix, 128; Homer on, xxii, 171-2; Milton on, iv, 53, 127; slaying of her father, viii, 96; Ulysses at, xxii, 175; Virgil on, xiii, 144-5

Scythian, and the Athenian, xxxvii, 10

Sea, discoloration of the, xxix, 26-8; Emerson on the, v, 341-2; geological changes under the, xxxviii, 414, 415, 417; Longfellow on the, xlii, 1337; phosphorescent, xxix, 176-8; sunrise at, xxiii, 13 (see also Ocean)

SEA, BY THE, xli, 688-9

SEA DIRGE, xl, 275

Sea Stories, Dana on, xxiii, 5

Sea-captains, Dana on, xxiii, 374-6, 381-5; religious, 389 90

Sea-fire, Emerson on, v, 340-1

SEA-MAID, THE LITTLE, xvii, 255-76

Sea-pen, Darwin on the, xxix, 111-12

Sea-power, Bacon on, iii, 83-4; Emerson on, v, 355-6

Sea-sawdust, Darwin on, xxix, 25

Sea-slugs, Darwin on, xxix, 16-17

Sea-urchins, forceps of, xi, 246-8

Sea-weed, Darwin on, xxix, 255-7

Seals, Darwin on, xxix, 301-2; Francis Pretty on, xxxiii, 212

Seamen (see Sailors)

Search Warrants, in U. S., xliii, 207 (4)

SEAS, ON THE, AND FAR AWAY, vi, 528

Seasons, Burns on the, vi, 408-9; Campbell on, xli, 790-1

Seasons, Thomson's, Wordsworth on, xxxix, 339-42

SEASONS, THE HUMAN, xli, 920-1

Sebastian, in THE TEMPEST, xlvi, in shipwreck, 380-1; in island after wreck, 397-403; in plot with Antonio, 403-7, 420; at the banquet, 420, 421; denounced by Ariel, 421-3; imprisoned by Ariel, 432; before Prospero, 434, 436, 437; in final scene, 440, 441

Sebastian del Piombo, xxxi, 101 note 6, 118 note 2

Sebright, Sir J., on crossing, xi, 37

Secession, Johnson, on right of, xliii, 456; Lincoln on, 337, 339-40, 341, 343; Lowell on doctrine of, xxviii, 457

Second Sight, of Bards, vi, 244

Second Thought, the wiser, viii, 306

Secondary Qualities, Berkeley on, xxxvii, 219, 223-4; Hume on, 435

Secrecy, Bacon on habit of, iii, 18-19; Marcus Aurelius on, ii, 209 (7); Penn on, i, 353

Secret, in PILGRIM'S PROGRESS, xv, 184-5

Secrets, Manzoni on spread of, xxi, 193-4; never kept, vii, 322 (4);

Milton on, iv, 431; proverb on, xvi, 63; Webster on, xlvii, 803

Sects, Bacon on religious, iii, 11-12; Browne on new, 271; Franklin on positiveness of, i, 116; Milton on, iii, 233, 235-6, 241-2; physiognomy of, v, 351; rise of new, iii, 144-5; Ruskin on, xxviii, 112

Secundus, Gaius Plinius Cæcilius (see Pliny the Younger)

Secundus, Pomponius, ix, 242 note 1; on public opinion, 321

Security, Jonson on, xl, 305; Kempis on over-, vii, 278 (4); suburb of hell, xlvii, 806

Sedgwick, Gen., at Antietam, xliii, 428; at Gettysburg, 360, 380, 422; Haskell on, 381

Sedgwick, Prof., xxxviii, 434; Mill on, xxv, 130

Sedillot, M., xxxviii, 382, 388

Sedimentary Deposits, Lyell on, xxxviii, 421-4, 431, 433-4

Sedimentary Formations, rate of, xi, 338-9; manner of, 343-4

Sedimentary Rocks, Geikie on, xxx, 344-5, 354-5

Sedition, Calvin on charges of, xxxix, 47-9; Hobbes on, xxxiv, 387

SEDITIONS AND TROUBLES, ESSAY ON, Bacon's, iii, 38-44

Sedley, Sir Charles, poems by, xl, 392-3

Seducers, in Dante's HELL, xx, 47, 75-7

Seeds, Darwin on destruction of, xi, 82; dissemination of, 203, 405-11, 430-1; fable of, xvii, 14-15; plants without, Dante on, xx, 263 and note; plumed, xi, 90; transportation of, xxix, 479-80; use of nutriment in, xi, 91; winged, Darwin on, 158

Seeley, Thomas, xxxiii, 238

SEEMING WISE, ESSAY ON, Bacon's, iii, 67-9

Segismund, in LIFE A DREAM, as prisoner in chains, xxvi, 11-13; with Rosaura, 13-15; birth of, related by Basilio, 21-2; reason of imprisonment, 22-3; plan to try, 23-4; his awakening in palace, 27-30; with chamberlain, 31-3; with Clotaldo, 33-7; second sight of Rosaura, 37-8; with Astolfo, 38-9; with Estrella, 39-40; quarrels with Astolfo, 40-1; with the king, 42-7; in the tower again, 47-51; rescued by soldiers, 53-63; sends Clotaldo back, 62-3; in the battle, 64; on his father, 65-6; made king, 68

Segrais, on the ÆNEID, xiii, 23-33, 36, 37, 39, 45-8, 57; on readers of poetry, 60-1; Voltaire on, xxxiv, 148

Seiches of Forel, xxx, 297

Seius, nightingale of, x, 189-90

Sejanus, Tiberius and, iii, 71, 98-9

Selden, Burke on, xxiv, 180; Milton on work of, iii, 211

Seldius, Charles V and, xxxix, 95

Selection, by man, Darwin on, xi, 46-9, 54-7; by man, in Elizabethan England, xxxv, 254-5; by man and nature, compared, xi, 96-7; by man, in New Atlantis, iii, 183-4; Natural, xi, 93-144; Sexual, 101-3; unconscious, 49-54

Seleucus I, prophecy of, xlviii, 253

Seleucus Callinicus, xlviii, 253

Seleucus, Ceraunus, xlviii, 253

Seleucus Philopator, xlviii, 254

Self, Emerson on meaning of, v, 74; fear of, xlviii, 124 note 12; Pascal on, 154 (455); Shelley on principle of, xxvii, 370

Self-analyzing, Shelley on, xviii, 302

Self-assertion, Sterling on, xxv, 267 note

Self-conceit, fable on, xvii, 19

Self-condemnation, Byron on, xviii, 433

Self-confidence, Locke on, xxxvii, 128

Self-contempt, Kempis on, vii, 285 (1)

Self-control, Confucius on, xliv, 14 (23), 38 (1), 44 (13); Epictetus on, ii, 154 (100), 183 (15); Hindu teaching of, xlv, 811-12, 825, 826, 828, 289; Kant on, xxxii, 324; Kempis on, vii, 216 (3), 315 (1), 336; Locke on, xxxvii, 37, 62, 93, 184-5; Milton on, iv, 387; Pascal on, xlviii, 62 (160)

Self-defence, a natural right, xxxiv, 408; a social right, 409, 415

Self-denial, Epictetus on, ii, 154 (100), 155 (101), 174 (159); Franklin on, i, 96; Kempis on, vii, 283 (4), 308-9, 316 (4), 336 (3), 341 (1); Locke on, xxxvii, 28, 33, 37; training in, 33-4, 37, 93-4

Self-dependence, Confucius on, xliv, 54 (14); Pascal on, xlviii, 122 (359)

Self-education, Franklin's example of, i, 73

Self-esteem, Kempis on, vii, 253-4; Milton on, iv, 261

Self-examination, Bacon on, iii, 73; Burke on value of, xxiv, 9; Carlyle on, xxv, 339; Epictetus on, ii, 145 (76), 152 (93), 154 (98), 170, (146), 182 (7); Franklin's plan of, i, 85-88; Kempis on, vii,

232 (4); Marcus Aurelius on, ii, 228 (11), 232 (31), 288 (37)

Self-fertilization, preventives of, xi, 111-12

Self-help, Emerson on, v, 55-6

Self-importance, Emerson on, v, 243-4

Self-interest, Carlyle on doctrine of, xxv, 370; Franklin on, i, 93; God's providence, x, 4; as the mover of society, 20; Pascal on, xlviii, 38; Rousseau on, xxxiv, 277-8, 281

Self-knowledge, Pascal on, xlviii, 24 (66); Shelley on, xviii, 277

Self-love, Kempis on, vii, 302 (1); Pascal on, xlviii, 42-5, 159 (474-7), 162-3, 164 (492), 341, 421; Pope on, xl, 427-8, 433, 440, 441, 450; Raleigh on, xxxix, 117; reason of, ix, 36; Sidney on, xxvii, 7

Self-mastery (see Self-control)

Self-possession, Goethe on, xix, 79

Self-praise, Pliny on, ix, 203

Self-preservation, Kant on duty of, xxxii, 328, 352-3, 360; passions of, xxiv, 35-6; passions of, contrasted with those of sex, 38

Self-regarding Conduct, Mill on, xxv, 282-5

SELF-RELIANCE, ESSAY ON, Emerson's, v, 63-88

Self-reliance, in children, xxxvii, 55; Epictetus on, ii, 118 (4), 120 (9), 138 (61), 153 (98), 155 (103), 159 (115), 166 (137); of heroism, v, 132-3; Kempis on, vii, 221 (2), 321 (3); Luther on, xxxvi, 276-7; Marcus Aurelius on, ii, 202 (6, 8), 209 (5), 213 (3), 216 (18), 218 (29), 247 (12), 249 (28); necessity of religious, v, 29, 38-41

Self-respect, Channing on, xxviii, 345; Locke on, xxxvii, 128; Marcus Aurelius on, ii, 209 (7)

Self-restraint, Hindu doctrine of, xlv, 826

Self-reverence, the bridle of vice, iii, 178

Self-sacrifice, Bacon on, iii, 36

Self-satisfaction, Pascal on, xlviii, 166 (499); Pope on, xl, 432

Self-sufficingness, Emerson on, v, 197

Self-trumpeters, fallacy of, xxvii, 247-8

Self-trust, the essence of heroism, v, 129; of the scholar, 16-19

Self-truth, Shakespeare on, xlvi, 102

Self-will, Pascal on, xlviii, 159 (472), 160 (475-6), 162 (482); Plato on, xii, 166

Self-will, Mr., in PILGRIM'S PROGRESS, xv, 263-5

Selfishness, Bacon on, iii, 63-4; Kant on, xxxii, 354, 361; Mill on limiting, xxv, 268; Pascal on, xlviii,

155 (456-7), 160 (477), 162 (483); Rousseau on, xxxiv, 278, 281

Selina, Helen, LAMENT by, xli, 945-7

SELKIRK, ALEXANDER, SOLITUDE OF, xli, 548-9

Selkirk, Alexander, supposed lines by, xxxix, 310

Selwyn Correspondence, Emerson on the, v, 428

Selymus I, Bajazet and, iii, 53

Selymus II, Bacon on, iii, 53

Semele, mother of Bacchus, viii, 278, 310-11, 349-50

Seminary Ridge, at Gettysburg, xliii, 352

Semiramis, Burns on, vi, 433; Dante on, xx, 22

Semitic Races, Taine on the, xxxix, 444

Semnones, Tacitus on the, xxxiii, 117-18

Sempronius, in Cato, xxvii, 200, 201, 202-3, 204-5

Senate, Burke on necessity of a, xxiv, 346-7; origin of name, ix, 52

Senate, United States, xliii, 193-5; equal suffrage in, 204 (5); powers with the President, 201 (2); election of Vice-President by, 200, 210

Senators, oath and qualifications of, xliii, 205 (3), 211

Sencha, son of Ailill, xlix, 253, 261

Seneca, on adversity, iii, 16; cold baths of, xxxvii, 13; Dante on, xx, 20; on death, iii, 9, 10; xlviii, 337; diet of, xxxvii, 18; on education, 83-4; on evil opinions, xxxix, 70 note; on fame, 70; method of avoiding vice, iii, 312; Milton on tragedies of, iv, 416; Montaigne on, xxxii, 30, 95-6; quotations from, xlviii, 123 notes 2, 3, 6, 16; Tacitus on, iii, 94; vanity of, 135

Seneca Indians, xliii, 247

Senecio, Herennius, as counsel for Baetica, ix, 331; death of, 250; life of Helvidius by, 323; on Licinianus, 267; on orators, 262; Regulus on, 197

Senecio, Sempronius, accused of forgery, ix, 309-10

Senecio, Socius, letter to, ix, 208

Senjer, the chamberlain, xvi, 218-19

Sennacherib, Dante on, xx, 194; Mohammed on, xlv, 925 note (see also Sanacharib)

SENNACHERIB, DESTRUCTION OF, xli, 804-5

Sennet, defined, xix, 224 note

Sensation(s), Berkeley on, xxxvii, 204-38, 242-4, 247, 249, 250, 260, 263-7, 271-2, 275-6, 282-8, 300; Buddha on, xlv, 747; as the Ego, 673-5; Hobbes on, xxxiv, 323-5; Hume on, xxxvii, 316, 318-20,

341-2, 363; Rousseau on, xxxiv, 251-3; Ruskin on, xxviii, 116-18; same in all men, xxiv, 13-16

Sense(s), Bacon on, xxxix, 134, 135, 141-2, 151; as source of the beautiful, xxiv, 96-106; Calderon on, xxvi, 51; Descartes on uncertainty of, xxxiv, 28, 34; Goethe on, xix, 50; the Hell of, xlii, 1479-80; Hindu teachings on world of, xlv, 811; Hobbes on, xxxiv, 323-5; Hume on evidence of, xxxvii, 432-6, 439; Kant on knowledge through, xxxii, 382-3; More on pleasures of, xxxvi, 215-16; Petrarch on, xxxix, 103 note; pleasures of, xxxiv, 353; Pope on scale of, xl, 423; reason and, xxxiv, 32; xlviii, 38 (83); satisfactions of the, i, 348 (96); Socrates on the, ii, 53-55; as source of the sublime, xxiv, 70-6

Sensibility, Bagehot on, xxviii, 176-7; requisite to poets, xxxix, 312, 313 note; Schiller on education of, xxxii, 243-4; taste and, xxiv, 23, 24-5

SENSIBILITY, FRAGMENT ON, vi, 260

SENSIBILITY, POEM ON, vi, 452-3

Sensible Qualities, Berkeley on, xxxvii, 205-27, 232-3, 252, 263-4, 266; Hume on, 435-6

Sensible Things, Berkeley on xxxvii, 204-40, 242-4, 247, 260, 266-7, 271, 300

Sensitiveness, Cicero on, ix, 88; Ruskin on, xxviii, 116

Sensual Pleasure, Archytas on, ix, 60; Buddha on, xlv, 743-5

Sensuous Goodness, Bagehot on, xxviii, 175-7

Sensuous Instinct, Schiller on the, xxxii, 255-63

Sensuousness, Schiller on, xxxii, 291-3

Sentiment, Hume on standard of, xxvii, 217-21, 229-30; Lowell on dangers of misplaced, xxviii, 447; James Mill on, xxv, 74; reason and, xxxvii, 309; thought and, 316, 319

Sentimentality, Carlyle on, xxv, 340-1

Sentry, Captain, xxvii, 91-2

Senzeille, Thierry on, xxviii, 28

Seppi, in WILHELM TELL, xxvi, 371, 375, 376

Septemvirs, Roman, ix, 381 note 1

Septicemia, Pasteur on, xxxviii, 382-8

Septimus Severus (see Severus)

Septitius, letters to, ix, 195, 330, 332

Seraphim, Milton on the, iv, 41

Scrapion, in ALL FOR LOVE, xviii, 21-4, 25, 86-7, 98-100

Serbonian Marsh, xii, 335-6; Milton on the, iv, 125

SERENADE, by Scott, xli, 760-1

SERENADE, by Shelley, xxviii, 385-6

SERENADE, FROM THE SPANISH STUDENT, xlii, 1325

Sergeant of the Law, Chaucer's, xl, 19-20

Sergesthus, in ÆNEID, xviii, 93, 97, 186-91, 302, 323

Sergius, and Antony, xii, 341

Sermon on the Mount, xliv, 374 (20-49)

Sermons, Pascal on, xlviii, 11 (8)

Serpa, Pedro Hernandez de, xxxiii, 335, 364

SERPENT AND FILE, fable of, xvii, 21

SERPENT AND MAN, fable of, xvii, 11

SERPENT AND WOODMAN, fable of, xvii, 17

Serpents, winged, in Egypt, xxxiii, 39-40

Serranus, in the ÆNEID, xiii, 308

Serristori, Averardo, xxxi, 401 note, 447

Servants, children and, xxxvii, 42-3, 52-3, 73-4, 94, 110, 124; Confucius on, xliv, 62 (25); Epictetus on, ii, 178 (179, 180); Indians on, i, 413 (268); Job on, xliv, 121 (13-15); liberties of, in Massachusetts, xliii, 82-3; Penn on, i, 408; Penn's counsel to, 357-8; single men best, iii, 22; taxes on, x, 527; troubles with, v, 59; unproductive laborers, x, 270

Servianus, letter to, ix, 306

Servibilis, in FAUST, xix, 176

Service, Confucius on true, xliv, 49 (23), 54 (37); Emerson on honest, v, 103; Marcus Aurelius on, ii, 225 (6), 277

Services, Cicero on mentioning, ix, 33; Emerson on, v, 232

Servility, Penn on, i, 351 (119)

Servilius, Publius, ix, 121

Serving-men, More on, xxxvi, 152-3, 154

Servitude, impossible in state of nature, xxxiv, 199-200; involuntary, prohibited in United States, xliii, 210; Milton on, iv, 211

Servius Tullius, first coiner of money in Rome, x, 33

SESAME AND LILIES, Ruskin's, xxviii, 95-168; remarks on, 94

Sesostris, king of Egypt, xxxiii, 50-3

Sestius, Bestia and, ix, 103; charged with bribery, 102, 103; Pompey and, 125

Setebos, xlvi, 393

Sethos, king of Egypt, xxxiii, 72

Settala, Lodovico, xxi, 523, 529-30, 533

Settlement, Act of, Burke on the xxiv, 172-3

Settlement Laws, of England, x, 145-50
SEVEN RAVENS, THE, xvii, 114-16
Seven Sages, the, ix, 9
Seven Sleepers, legend of, xxxviii, 412-13
SEVEN SWABIANS, THE, xvii, 216
Seven Years' War, America in, i, 133-49
Severinus, St., xxxvi, 267 (29)
Severity, Bacon on, iii, 32; with children, xxxvii, 36, 39, 67, 85; kindness stronger than, xvii, 36
Severus, Alexander, Machiavelli on, xxxvi, 66, 67, 71
Severus, Annius, letters to, ix, 245, 272
Severus, brother of Marcus Aurelius, ii, 195 (14), 199
Severus, Catilius, letters to, ix, 219, 251, 255, 307
Severus, Septimus, Bacon on, iii, 110; death of, 10; Machiavelli on, xxxvi, 67-8, 71; Plautianus and, iii, 71; Sidney on, xxvii, 24
Severus, in POLYEUCTE, Pauline on, xxvi, 76-7; reported to be coming to Armenia, 78-9; his love for Pauline, 80-1; learns Pauline's marriage, 82-3; with Pauline, 83-6; with Pauline in Polyeucte's prison, 107-8; determines to save Polyeucte, 108-10; denounces Felix, 119-20; won by Christians, 120-1
Sewa, Arnold von, in WILHELM TELL, xxvi, 400-1, 411
Sewell, George, DYING MAN IN HIS GARDEN, xli, 493
Seward, William H., Alaska Purchase and, xliii, 459
Sexes, Hume on difference of the, xxxvii, 376; James Mill on relations between, xxv, 72-3; in plants, separation of, xi, 107
Sextius, Publius, Cicero and, xii, 247
Sextus, Bishop, xx, 401 note 5
Sextus, teacher of Marcus Aurelius, ii, 194 (9)
Sexual Characters, secondary, defined, xi, 161; their variability, 161, 166-7
Sexual Passion, Burke on the, xxiv, 37, 38-9; in state of nature, xxxiv, 195-8; Wordsworth on origin of, xxxix, 301
Sexual Selection, xi, 101-3; beauty and, 212
Seyton, in MACBETH, xlvi, 367, 369
Sforza, Ascanio, xxxi, 235 note
Sforza, Francesco, citadel of, xxxvi, 75; Macaulay on, xxvii, 396; Machiavelli on, xxxvi, 24, 46, 50; the Milanese and, 44
Sforza, Ludovico, Bacon on, iii, 52; at Milan, xxxvi, 9; Montaigne on, xxxii, 6
Sforza, Sforza, xxxi, 193 note

Sguazzella, the painter, xxxi, 205 note 2
SHADOW, THE, story of, xvii, 337-49
Shadow of Death, valley of, xv, 248-52; xliv, 171 (4)
Shadows, Celtic Isle of, xxxii, 188
Shadrach, the slave, Dana and, xxiii, 3
Shadwell, Dryden and, xviii, 3; Voltaire on, xxxiv, 139; Wordsworth on, xxxix, 334
Shaftesbury, Earl of, on burlesque, xxxix, 186; on English poetry, 338; Locke and, xxxvii, 3; Montesquieu on, xxxii, 123; satire on, xviii, 3
Shahrazad, xvi, 11-15
Shah-Zeman, king of Samarkand, xvi, 5-11; Jullanar and, 340-54
Shahriyar, King, xvi, 5-15
Shakalik, story of, xvi, 195-200
Shakers, Emerson on the, v, 284-5, 303
Shakespeare, Arnold on, xxviii, 78, 79, 80, 81; Arnold on selections from, 73; Bagehot on, 184; carelessness of future fame, xxxix, 244-5; Carlyle on, xxv, 336, 425, 438-9, 457, 460-1; the Celtic element in, xxxii, 168; Coleridge on, xxvii, 268; inclination to comedy, xxxix, 226; defects of, 227-30, 244; on his own defects, 323; Dryden on, xviii, 18; early editions of, xxxix, 337; Emerson on, v, 15, 149, 188, 223, 450, 451, 452, 455-6; English drama, indebted to, 10; Gray on, xl, 467; HAMLET, xlvi, 85-199; Hazlitt on, xxvii, 282; his debt to Holinshed's *Chronicles*, xxxv, 228; Hugo on, xxxix, 370, 372, 373, 375, 376, 393, 403, 406; KING LEAR, xlvi, 201-302; KING LEAR, Shelley on, xxvii, 356; lack of learning, xxxix, 239-40; Landor on, xli, 926; language of, xxxix, 206, 227; Macaulay on comedies of, xxvii, 403, 404; MACBETH, xlvi, 303-75; James Mill on, xxv, 16; Milton on, iv, 34; originality of his genius, xxxix, 240-4; as a player, 322; action in his plots, 237-8; the poet of nature, 220-3; publications of his works, 245-63; Ruskin on creed of, xxviii, 115; Ruskin on heroes and heroines of, 141-3; Sainte-Beuve on, xxxii, 133, 135; Shelley on, xxvii, 351; short poems by, xl, 267-89; the sonnet and, xli, 697; Swift on, xxvii, 117; THE TEMPEST, xlvi, 377-442; THE TEMPEST, Hunt on, xxvii, 309; Thackeray on, xxviii, 7-17; Thoreau on, 426; his times and sources, xxxix, 236-7; tragedy and comedy mixed, 223-5;

unities neglected by, 239, 230-6; Voltaire on, xxxiv, 133-5; Wordsworth on, xxxix, 300, 321, 333-6, 347; Wordsworth on *Sonnets*, 335-6 note

SHAKESPEARE, Arnold's sonnet on, xlii, 1175

SHAKESPEARE, ON, by Jonson, xxvii, 59

SHAKESPEARE, ON, by Milton, iv, 26

SHAKESPEARE, PREFACE TO, by Johnson, xxxix, 191 note, 218-63

SHAKESPEARE, PREFACE TO FIRST FOLIO OF, xxxix, 155-6

SHAKESPEARE, TO THE MEMORY OF, by Jonson, xl, 308-10

SHAKESPEARE, ON THE TRAGEDIES OF, by Lamb, xxvii, 313-31

Shakiriyeh, the, xvi, 250-1

Shallowness, Confucius on, xliv, 27 (16)

SHALOTT, THE LADY OF, xlii, 997-1002

Shame, Burke on, xxiv, 264; Confucius on, xliv, 46 (1); Dante on, xx, 73; defined by Hobbes, xxxiv, 356; Milton on, iv, 165, 291; sense of, in children, xxxvii, 41-4, 64, 71, 185; a slow poison, viii, 304; the only grief without redress, xxvi, 80; Pope on, xl, 446; virtue and, 430; Webster on, xlvii, 760

Shame, character in PILGRIM'S PROGRESS, xv, 77-9

Shamelessness, Epictetus on, ii, 125 (23)

Shamgar, the goad of, xv, 58

Shandy, Walter, xxv, 337

Shang, and Shih, xliv, 35 (15)

Shao, Confucius on, xliv, 22-3; music of, 12 (25)

Shao Hu, xliv, 48 (17) note

Shao-lien, xliv, 64-5

Shaving, Franklin on, at home, i, 128

She, Duke of, xliv, 45 (16, 18)

SHE IS NOT FAIR, xli, 937

SHE SAYS SHE LOES ME BEST OF A', vi, 531

SHE STOOPS TO CONQUER, Goldsmith's, xviii, 197-269

SHE WAS A PHANTOM OF DELIGHT, xli, 667

SHE WALKS IN BEAUTY, xli, 809

SHE'S FAIR AND FAUSE, vi, 347

Sheba, Queen of, reference to, xix, 216

Shechem, Bunyan on, xv, 110

Sheep, appeal of a, vi, 43-5; destruction of, for wool, x, 202; parable of the, xv, 207; sacred in Thebes, xxxiii, 26

Sheffield, the mercer, xxxix, 27

Shelburne, Burns on, vi, 55

Shelley, Percy Bysshe, Arnold on, xxviii, 89-90; Browning's debt to, xviii, 356; buried in Rome, xxiii, 4; Byron and, xxxii, 401; Carlyle on, xxv, 361; THE CENCI, xviii, 273-353; death of, xxvii, 298; DEFENCE OF POETRY, 343-77; remarks on DEFENCE of, l, 56; life and works, xviii, 272; Mazzini on, xxxii, 408; on Milton's Satan, xxviii, 205; poems by, xli, 845-93; SERENADE by, xxviii, 385-6; on his own works, xviii, 273

Shell-fish, the heart in, xxxviii, 137-138

Shells, color of, xi, 146; freshwater, distribution of, 428-9; Lyell on, xxxviii, 426, 427; Tennyson on, xlii, 1086-7; transportation of land, xi, 438-9

Shelton, Thos., translator of Cervantes, xiv, 3; dedication by, 5

Shem, Pascal on, xlviii, 211 (625)

Shemei, Winthrop on, xliii, 100

Shen Ch'ang, xliv, 16 (10)

Shenstone, Burns on, vi, 187; Wordsworth on *Schoolmistress* of, xxxix, 343 note

Sheol, references to, xliv, 83 (9), 89 (8), 94 (13), 100 (13), 106 (13), 111 (19), 113 (6), 151 (5), 161 (10), 179 (3), 181 (17), 207 (14), 258 (3), 262 (48), 296 (3), 327 (7), 351 (10)

Shepherd, in ŒDIPUS, viii, 230-2

SHEPHERD, THE PASSIONATE, xl, 259-60

SHEPHERD OF TENDER YOUTH, xlv, 553-4

SHEPHERD'S BOY, fable of the, xvii, 28

Shepherd's Calendar, Sidney on, xxvii, 45-6

Shepherd-dogs, S. American, xxix, 163-4

SHEPHERDESS, THE UNFAITHFUL, xl, 202-3

Sherbrooke, Lord, quoted, xxviii, 483

Sheridan, Richard B., DRINKING SONG, xli, 567; on easy writing, xxv, 462; Goldsmith on, xli, 518, 519; life and works, xviii, 104; Macaulay on, xxvii, 402-3; A PORTRAIT, xviii, 105-8; SCHOOL FOR SCANDAL, 111-96; Swift and, xxviii, 27

Sheridan, Thomas, xviii, 104

Sheriff of Nottingham, in ROBYN HODE, xl, 132; with Little John, 149-50; brought before Robyn Hode, 153-6; holds archery contest, 166-7, 168; attempts to capture Robyn Hode, 171-2; captures

knight, 172-3; killed by Robyn Hode, 174-5
Sherman, Roger, xliii, 160 note
Sherman, Wm. T., march of, to the sea, xlii, 1490
SHERRAMUIR, THE BATTLE OF, vi, 379
Sherwell, Thomas, xxxiii, 199
SHEYKH AND THE HOUNDS, story of the, xvi, 23-6
SHEYKH AND THE MULE, story of the, xvi, 26-7
SHEYKH AND THE GAZELLE, story of the, xvi, 20-3
Sheytans, species of genii, xvi, 9 note
Shiftiness, Hobbes on, xxxiv, 366, 381; lines on, viii, 434-5
Shifts, Penn on, i, 354
Shih, and Shang, xliv, 35 (15)
Shimei, reference to, xli, 497
SHIP, THE BUILDING OF THE, xlii, 1332-43
Ship-masters, Dana on, xxiii, 374-6, 381-5; religious, 389-90
Ship Money, case of, v, 360
Shipley, Jonathan, i, 5
Shipman, Chaucer's, xl, 22
Shippen, quoted, xxxiv, 86
Ships, Franklin on speed of, i, 163-4; invented by Prometheus, viii, 172
Shirley, Braddock's secretary, i, 141
Shirley, Gen., Franklin on, i, 143, 161-2
Shirley, James, poems by, xl, 359-60
Sho'hâib, xlv, 917-18
SHOEMAKER'S HOLIDAY, THE, xlvii, 447-515; remarks on, 445
Shoes, Locke on, xxxvii, 11
SHOES, THE RED, xvii, 349-54
Sholts, Harrison on, xxxv, 374
Shongi, Zealand chief, xxix, 443-4, 453
Shooting Star, in FAUST, xix, 183
SHORTEN SAIL, xl, 475-6
Short-hand, Franklin's, i, 8; Locke on, xxxvii, 145
Shortreed, Mr., and Scott, xxv, 430-2
Short-wind, in PILGRIM'S PROGRESS, xv, 220
Shovel, Sir Cloudesly, monument of, xxvii, 84
Show, a poor substitute for worth, xvii, 18
Shrewdness (see Cunning)
Shrewsbury, Duke of, Dryden on, xiii, 431-2
Shrimps, Harvey on, xxxviii, 90; the heart in, 137-8
SHROUD, THE, a story, xvii, 207-8
SHRUBBERY, THE, xli, 555
Shu-ch'i, xliv, 17 note 10, 23 (14), 58 (12), 64 (8)

Shu-sun Wu-shu, xliv, 67 (23), 68 (24)
Shuckburgh, E. S., translator of Cicero, ix
Shun, Emperor, xliv, 21 (28), 27 (18, 20, 21), 42 (22), 47 (6), 52 (4, 45), 68 (1) note
Shusy Pye, xl, 85
Shuter, Mr., the actor, xviii, 201
Siberia, remains in, xxix, 266-7
Sibyl, Virgil on the, xiii, 145-6 (see Deiphobe)
Sibylline Books, Bacon on the, iii, 59; Hobbes on, xxxiv, 396-7; Pascal on, xlviii, 212 (628)
SIC A WIFE AS WILLIE HAD, vi, 461
Sichæus, and Dido, xiii, 87, 157; in Virgil's Hades, 227
Sicilian Bull, the, xx, 112 note 1
Sicilian Vespers, reference to, xx, 318 note 10
Sicily, changes of species in, xxxviii, 426-7; Coleridge on government of, v, 332-3; geology of, xxxviii, 427; popes in, xxxvi, 310-11; Raleigh on history of, xxxix, 119
Sicinnus, Plutarch on, xii, 17
SICK LION, THE, fable of, xvii, 13
Sickles, Gen., at Gettysburg, xliii, 356, 359, 367-71, 425, 439; Haskell on, 350, 367
Sickness, Epicurus on, ii, 276 (41); lessens fear of death, xxxii, 20 11; Pascal on use of, xlviii, 370-8; Pliny on virtue in, ix, 326; Rousseau on causes of, xxxiv, 175-6; Woolman on, i, 207, 244-5
Siddhartha Gautama, xlv, 588
Sidney, Sir Philip, Arcadia of, xlvi, 202; Arcadia of, Johnson on, xxxix, 228; Arcadia, written at Wilton House, v, 427; DEFENSE OF POESY, xxvii, 7-55; Elizabeth and, xv, 388; Emerson on, v, 191; Johnson on language of, xxxix, 206; Jonson on, xxxvii, 60; life and works, 5-6; poems by, xl, 213-17; Pope on, 444; Pugliano and, xxvii, 7; Shelley on, xli, 890; ugliness of, v, 317; Wotton on, 386
Siebel, in FAUST, xix, 80-94
Siege Perilous, the, xxxv, 111-12, 114; made by Merlin, 143
Siegfried, mortality of, v, 96
Sienna, the Brigata Godereccia of, xx, 124 note 7
Siennese, Dante on the, xx, 124 note 6, 201 note 8
Sierra Leone, Pretty on, xxxiii, 233
Sieve, superstition of the, xix, 98
Sieyès, Burke on, xxiv, 434-5
Sigebert, the monk, xx, 331 note 29
SIGEDRIFA, THE LAY OF, xlix, 393-5; remarks on, 267
Sigemund, saga of, xlix, 29-30
Siggeir, king of Gothland, xlix, 278-

82; sons of, 284; with Sigmund and Sinfjotli, 288-9; his death, 290

Sighs, De Quincey's Lady of, xxvii, 339-40

Sight, Berkeley on realities of, xxxvii, 234-5; Burke on means of, xxiv, 115; Burke on pleasures of the, 15; Milton on sense of, iv, 421; Whitman on the, xxxix, 414-15

Sigi, son of Odin, xlix, 275-6

Sigismund, Emperor, and Huss, xxxvi, 333

Sigismund, father of Manfred, xviii, 438

Siglorel, the wizard, xlix, 145

Sigmund, in VOLSUNGA SAGA, xlix, 278; the sword of, 279-80; King Siggeir and, 280; the wolf and, 283; Signy's children and, 283-4; his son Sinfjotli, 284-8; his revenge on Siggeir, 288-90; marriage to Borghild, 291; at death of Sinfjotli, 295-6; last battle, 297-9; the avenging of, 308-12; remarks on story of, 267

SIGN-POSTS, VERSICLES ON, vi, 343

Signora, the, in I PROMESSI SPOSI (see Gertrude)

Signy, daughter of Volsung, xlix, 278-9, 280-5, 288, 289, 290

Sigrun, Queen, xlix, 292, 293, 294-5, 385-7, 389-92

Sigurd Fafnir's-Bane, birth and growth of, xlix, 301-4; his sword, 306-7; Grifir's prophecy, 308; avenges his father, 308-12; slays Fafnir, 312-15; Regin and, 316-17; hears of Brynhild, 317-18; takes gold of Fafnir, 319; meeting with Brynhild, 319-26; his semblance and array, 326-7; at Hlymdale, 327-8; renews troth to Brynhild, 328-30; Brynhild on, 332-3; his marriage to Gudrun, 333-6, 396, 422; his wooing of Brynhild for Gunnar, 337-9, 396-7, 415-16, 421; with Gudrun, 340; his visit to Brynhild in grief, 344-7; slaying of, 347-50, 398-402, 417-18, 421, 422-3; lament for, 351-7; his daughter, 358; burned beside Brynhild, 359, 410-11, 413; fame of, 359-60; Morris on, 273; remarks on story of, 267, 268

Sigurd, King, and Eystein, v, 357

SIGURD, SHORT LAY OF, xlix, 396-412; remarks on, 267

Sihon, king of Amorites, xliv, 320 (11)

Silanus, Julius, in Catiline conspiracy, xii, 240, 242; Cicero on, ix, 84

Silas, the disciple, xliv, 464 (22, 27), 465 (32); with Paul, 465 (40), 467-9, 471 (5)

Silence, Bacon on habits of, iii, 18-19; Carlyle on, xxv, 347-8, 394;

Confucius on, xliv, 8 (18), 53 (7), 61 (19); Emerson on, v, 160-1; Franklin's maxim of, i, 83, 84; Kempis on, vii, 233-5; in love, xlviii, 424; may be a lie, xxviii, 292; Montaigne on, xxxii, 42; Pascal on, xlviii, 20 (44); Penn on, i, 352 (129), 401 (118-20); Shakespeare on, xlvi, 102; sole cure of wrong, viii, 25; speech and, Carlyle on, xxv, 413; terror in, xxiv, 63

Silenus, Don Quixote on, xiv, 125; Hugo on, xxxix, 364, 365

Silicified Trees, Darwin on, xxix, 351-2, 373

Siloa, reference to, iv, 90

Siloam, tower in, xliv, 396 (4)

Silurian Period, in Europe, xxx, 358-9

Silva, Pedro de, xxxiii, 334-5

Silva, in EGMONT, xix, 297-300, 302, 322

Silvanus, xlv, 528 (19)

Silver, demand for, x, 182-3; as measure of value, 43; More on, xxxvi, 202-3; price of, x, 182; reason of value of, 422; seldom found pure, 182; value of, compared with corn, 186-7; variation in value of, 38-9, 42, 48; variation, effect of, on rents, 40-1 (see also Precious Metals)

Silvia, daughter of Tyrrheus, xiii, 260

SILVIA, by Shakespeare, xl, 269-70

Silvio, in DUCHESS OF MALFI, xlvii, 724, 725, 726, 728, 768, 769

Silvius Æneas, Virgil on, xiii, 237

Silvius, Jacobus, on veins, xxxviii, 124

Simeon, xliv, 363 (25-35); finds Jesus in the temple, iv, 369; Herbert on song of, xv, 405; prophecy of, iv, 378

Similes, Bunyan on, xv, 175; Burke on pleasure from, xxiv, 18; Dryden on use of, xiii, 242-3; Johnson on, xxvii, 194-5; Sidney on, 51; Swift on, 121

Similitudes, Bacon on, xxvii, 347

Simmias, with Socrates in prison (see PHÆDO, Plato's)

Simoisius, Burke on, xxiv, 133

Simon, Archbishop of Canterbury, xxxv, 73

Simon of Cyrene, xliv, 422 (26)

Simon, the Indian, xliii, 155

SIMON LEE, THE OLD HUNTSMAN, xli, 662-5

Simon Peter, chosen apostle, xliv, 373 (14); Jesus and, 370 (3-11), 378 (40); mother-in-law of, 369 (38-9); in PARADISE REGAINED, iv, 376-7

Simon, son of Onias, panegyric on, xxiv, 69-70

Simon, the sorcerer, xliv, 446 (9-
13), 447 (18-24); Bunyan on, xv,
110; Dante on, xx, 79
Simon, the tanner, xliv, 451 (43)
Simon of Tours, xx, 244 note 2
Simon, the Zealot, xliv, 373 (15),
430 (13)
Simonides, of Ceos, xii, 197 note;
Hiero and, xxvii, 41; Themistocles
and, xii, 9-10
Simony, defined, xxxvi, 299; punishment of, in Dante's HELL, xx, 47,
79-82
Simple, in PILGRIM'S PROGRESS, xv,
43; hanged, 219-20
SIMPLEX MUNDITIIS, xl, 297
Simplicianus, St. Augustine on, vii,
123-5, 129-30
Simplicity, Confucius on, xliv, 46
(27); Goethe on, xix, 129; Jonson on, xl, 297; Kempis on, vii,
252; necessary to friendship, ix,
31; reward of, vi, 243; Whitman
on, xxxix, 418
Sims, and Dana, xxiii, 3
SIMSON, WILLIAM, EPISTLE TO, vi,
92-7
Simulation, Bacon on, iii, 17-20; of
love, xlviii, 426-7 (see also Hypocrisy)
Sin, Augustine, St., on, vii, 27-32,
76-7, 105-7; Berkeley on, xxxvii,
274; Bunyan on living in, xv,
209; denouncing and abhorring, xv,
86; future punishment of, vii, 242-
4; in gold and in rags, xlvi, 281;
knowledge of, necessary to virtue,
iii, 212-13; man not compelled to
xxxiv, 287; Omar Khayyam on,
xli, 984-5; Pascal on, xlviii, 225-
6, 330; Pascal on source of, 341,
346, 358; problem of (see Evil);
retribution of (see Retribution)
Sin, in PARADISE LOST, at the gates
of Hell, iv, 127; announces herself to Satan, 129-30; opens gates,
132-3; paves road to world, 136;
journeys to earth, 300-5; arrives
in Paradise, 309-10
Sinai, Mount, cause of sounds on,
xxix, 382; references to, iv, 12
(17), 351; xv, 24
Sincere, the shepherd, in PILGRIM'S
PROGRESS, xv, 125-8, 297
Sincerity, Franklin on, i, 58, 83; in
friendship, v, 115-16
Sinclair, Sir John, at Otterburn,
xxxv, 93
Sindibad (see Es-Sindibad)
Sinfjotli, son of Sigmund, xlix, 285-
91, 293-4, 295-6
Singers, high reward of, x, 113
Single Life, St. Paul on, xlv, 510
(32, 34)
SINGLE LIFE AND MARRIAGE, ESSAY
ON, iii, 22-3
Single Men, greatest, iii, 20

Sinking Funds, misapplication of, x,
582
Sinnis, reference to, xxvi, 128
Sinon, betrays Troy, xiii, 105-11;
Chaucer on, xl, 45; in Dante's
HELL, xx, 127-8
Sinope, water supply of, ix, 423
Sins, the Seven Deadly, in FAUSTUS,
xix, 220-2
Sion (see Zion)
Siracides, on beggary, xxxix, 98;
on God, 109; quoted, 70
Sirens, the, xxii, 170; Dante on the,
xx, 223; Milton on the, iv, 70;
Ulysses and the, xxii, 173-4
Siret, the surgeon, xxxviii, 53
Sirius, distance of, xxx, 330; refer-
ences to, xiii, 136, 335; worshipped
by Arabs, xlv, 909 note 4
Sisera, and Jael, iv, 443; reference
to, xliv, 253 (9)
Sismondi, and Manzoni, xxi, 3
Sisters, and brothers, Browning on,
xviii, 380
SISTERS, THE TWA, xl, 54
Sisyphus, Homer on, xxii, 167; Jon-
son on, xlvii, 554; Socrates on, ii,
28
Sitones, Tacitus on the, xxxiii, 122
Siward, in MACBETH, in war against
Macbeth, xlvi, 361, 365, 368-9, 371,
373; on his son, 374
Siward, the younger, in MACBETH,
xlvi, 371, 374
SIX NATIONS, TREATY WITH THE,
xliii, 246-9
SIX SWANS, THE, xvii, 141-5
Sixtus, Laurence and, vii, 258 (2)
Skadi, xlix, 275-6
Skanda, xlv, 844
Skanderbeg, xlvii, 468 note 9
Skeletons, at Egyptian banquets,
xxxii, 16, 20
Skelton, John, xxxix, 27-8; Milton
on, iii, 214 and note
Skene, and his wife, xlii, 1230
Skepticism (see Scepticism)
SKETCH IN VERSE, vi, 357-8
Sketches, unfinished, why pleasing,
xxiv, 68
Skill, Kant on imperatives of, xxxii,
345-6, 347-8
Skill, Mr., in PILGRIM'S PROGRESS,
xv, 235-7
Skin-changers, xlix, 286 note
SKINNER, CYRIACK, SONNETS TO, iv,
87, 88
Skinner, John, Johnson on, xxxix,
196-7; TULLOCHGORUM, xli, 581-3
SKIPPER IRESON'S RIDE, xlii, 1434-7
Skrellings, the, xliii, 13, 15-17
Skunks, Darwin on, xxix, 92
Sky, Kelvin on color of the, xxx,
283-5; Omar Khayyam on the, xli,
983
SKYLARK, THE, by Hogg, xli, 785-6
SKYLARK, To A, by Shelley, xli, 851-4

SKYLARK, TO THE, by Wordsworth, xli, 659-60

Slander, Penn on, i, 353 (145); proper attitude toward, ii, 176 (169); Shakespeare on, xlvi, 160; superiority to, ii, 119 (7) (see also Detraction)

Slanderers, Sheridan on male, xviii, 116

Slang, Jack, in SHE STOOPS TO CONQUER, xviii, 205, 210

Slave Labor, compared with free, x, 85; Woolman on, products of, i, 298

Slave-making Ants, xi, 275-9

Slave Trade, in Treaty of Ghent, xliii, 282; in Webster-Ashburton Treaty, 300, 306-7; Woolman on, i, 250, 251-3, 309

Slavery, abolition of, in America, xxviii, 455-60; abolition of, in rebellious states, xliii, 344-6; attempted justification of, i, 211-13; congressional control of, xliii, 198 (1), 204 (5); Darwin on, xxix, 525-7; Darwin on instances of, 35; Emerson on, xlii, 1315; Epictetus on, ii, 131 (41); among the Germans, xxxiii, 109-10; in Greece and Rome, iii, 81; Homer on, xxii, 246; impossible in state of nature, xxxiv, 200; Lincoln on, xliii, 451; Lincoln's attitude toward, 334, 341; Lowell on, xlii, 1449-50; in Massachusetts, xliii, 83-4; in New Jersey, i, 186 note; origin of, xxxiv, 214-15; Pascal on, xlviii, 79 (209); the peace of, iv, 119; production and, i, 211; prohibited in U. S., xliii, 210; Quakers and, i, 176, 215-17, 221, 233-4; 238, 261, 284; in southern colonies, 215-16; in the territories, xliii, 339; Whittier on, xlii, 1421-4

Slavery Contracts, illegal, xxv, 311-12

SLAVE'S LAMENT, THE, vi, 465

Slavonic Race, Freeman on the, xxviii, 276-7

Slay-good, the giant, xv, 274-5

Sleep, Browne on, iii, 342-3; Burke on, xxiv, 124; of children, Locke on, xxxvii, 22-4; Coleridge on, xli, 707; Goethe's Egmont on, xix, 329; of impostors, Shelley on, xviii, 324; Milton on, iv, 38, 61; Shakespeare on, xlvi, 325, 344, 402-3; Shelley on, xli, 855

SLEEP, THE, by E. B. Browning, xli, 968-70

SLEEP, TO, by Daniel, xl, 226

SLEEP, TO, by Keats, xli, 920

SLEEP, TO, by Sidney, xl, 217

SLEEP, TO, by Wordsworth, xli, 696

SLEEPING BEAUTY, by Rogers, xli, 596-7

SLEEPING BEAUTY, story of, xvii, 146-9

Sleepy-head, in PILGRIM'S PROGRESS, xv, 220

Sleigh-bells, Poe on, xlii, 1283-4

Sloane, Sir Hans, i, 44

Sloane, Sir John, Museum of, v, 345-6

Slocum, Gen., at Gettysburg, xliii, 356, 358, 380, 422; Haskell on, 381

Sloth, the sin, in FAUSTUS, xix, 221-2

Sloth, in PILGRIM'S PROGRESS, xv, 43; hanged, 219-20

Slothfulness, ECCLESIASTES on, xliv, 352 (18)

Slough of Despond, xv, 18-20, 192

Slow-pace, in PILGRIM'S PROGRESS, xv, 220

Slow-worm, Harrison on the, xxxv, 364

Sluggishness, in children, xxxvii, 114-17; lines on, xxxix, 309-10

Smallness, as source of beauty, xxiv, 96-7, 131-4

Small-pox, chicken-pox and, xxxviii, 182; cow-pox and, 155-62, 169-70, 181, 183, 188, 195 note, 197, 203, 206-9, 211, 213-14, 214, 216 note 220, 221, 223-6, 227, 231; heel-disease of horses and, 162-4, 193, 207-8; inoculated, 178, 202-3; mortality from, 239; propagated by contagion, 238; cases of return of, 203-5, 229-30; scrofula and, 231; source of, 153, 172; spurious, 184-7; treatment of, 200, 225; varieties of, 173, 199

SMALLPOX, VACCINATION AGAINST, xxxviii, 153-231

Smart, Christopher, SONG TO DAVID, xli, 496-510

SMELLIE, WILLIAM: A SKETCH, vi, 268

Smells, beauty in, xxiv, 106; Berkeley on, xxxvii, 212, 219; as sources of the sublime, xxiv, 75-6

Smiles, of villainy, xlvi, 110

Smith, Adam, life and works, x, 3-4; Mazzini on, xxxii, 402; Mill on, xxv, 24; WEALTH OF NATIONS, x; Wordsworth on, xxxix, 338 note

Smith, Alexander, BARBARA, xlii, 1192-4

Smith, Dr., Andrew on African animals, xxix, 97-9

Smith, F., on ants, xi, 276, 293

Smith, Rev. George, Burns on, vi, 105

Smith, Goldwin, on Jamaica Committee, xxv, 190 note

SMITH, JAMES, EPITAPH ON, vi, 137; EPISTLE TO, 175-180

Smith, John, with Drake, xxxiii, 197

Smith, John, the Quaker, i, 283

Smith, Sydney, FALLACIES OF ANTI-REFORMERS, xxvii, 237-65; life and works, 236; quoted, v, 431

Smith, Sir Thomas, on the English, xxxv, 382

Smooth-man, Mr., in PILGRIM'S PROGRESS, xv, 104

Smoothness, as cause of beauty, xxiv, 97-8, 103, 127-30

Smugglers, Smith on, x, 563

Smyrdis, prophecy of, xlviii, 252

Snails, Harvey on, xxxviii, 90; the heart in, 137-8

Snake, in SCHOOL FOR SCANDAL, with Lady Sneerwell, xviii, 111-13; suspected of treason, 115; detected in forgery, 139; employed by Lady Sneerwell in plot, 187; confesses, 192-3

Snakes, Buddhist ideas of, xlv, 724; Darwin on, xi, 213; South American, xxix, 108-9

Sneerwell, Lady, in SCHOOL FOR SCANDAL, conversation with Snake, xviii, 111-13; with Joseph Surface, 114-15; on slander, 116; plots against Maria, 122; in gossip with friends, 129-33; at Lady Teazle's after the scandal, 179-81; with Joseph Surface, 186-7; accuses Charles, 191-2

Sneezing, Pascal on, xlviii, 62 (160)

Snorri, son of Karlsefni, xliii, 16, 21

Snow, Darwin on red, xxix, 342; effect of, on rocks, 337-8; height of perpetual, 261; structure of frozen, 344 note; transformation of, to ice, xxx, 245-6, 251

Snowdon, Ruskin on, xxviii, 160

Snow-line, Helmholtz on the, xxx, 223-4

SNOW-WHITE AND ROSE-RED, xvii, 226

SNOW-WHITE, LITTLE, xvii, 155-64

SO OFT AS I HER BEAUTY DO BEHOLD, xl, 255

Soap-bubbles, experiments with, xxx, 40-1, 51-2

Soaring, of birds, Darwin on, xxix, 200-1

Sociability, Hobbes on, xxxiv, 423-4

Social Acts, natural, ii, 225 (6), 290 (4), 296 (21), 302 (20)

Social Contract, Rousseau on the, xxxiv, 224-5

Social Improvement, dependent on art, xxxii, 244 et seq

Social Phenomena, Huxley on, xxviii, 231

Social Pleasures, Burns on, vi, 88; Epictetus on, ii, 118 (3)

Social Reform, Emerson on, v, 270-2; possibility of, 58; to come through love, 59-60

Social Relations, penalty of false, v, 99

Social Science, Comte's stages of, xxv, 108

Social Virtues, and self-love, xl, 440, 441, 450

Socialism, Austin on, xxv, 116; of early Christians, xliv, 433 (44-5), 438 (32-6); Emerson on, v, 270-1; Lowell on, xxviii, 483-4; Mill on, xxv, 149-51; of Moravians, i, 149-50; More on, xxxvi, 177, 178-9, 195-6, 197, 200-1, 250, 252, 253, 254; Morris on, xlii, 1242-5; St. Simonian, xxv, 109; Woolman on, i, 269

Society, aimlessness of, v, 245; Bacon on aversion to, iii, 69; Burke on civil, xxiv, 207-8; Carlyle on, xxv, 341-4; Carlyle on modern, 348-62; as a contract, Burke on, xxiv, 244-5; desires that dispose to, xxxiv, 385; Emerson on the state of, v, 6, 80; the end of man, ii, 230 (16), 232 (30), 236 (14); founded on mutual deceit, xlviii, 44; frivolousness of, v, 197; good, defined, 208-9; the individual and, xxv, 212-17, 281-301, 302-3; individuality and, v, 66; interests of, in relation to landlords, wage-earners, and capitalists, x, 217-20; man in relation to, xl, 433-41; Mill on so-called, xxv, 147; Mill on tyranny of, 206-10; natural and ideal, xxxii, 225-30; necessary to man, ix, 38; never advances, v, 85-6; Pascal on, xlviii, 79 (211); Pascal on ties of, 108 (304); passions which belong to, xxiv, 37-46; passions that incline to, xxxiv, 406; a perpetual disappointment, v, 113; rights and duties of man in, xxxiv, 408-10, 417-29; Rousseau on origin of, 168, 189-90, 202-25; Rousseau on spirit of, 232-3; Rousseau on state of, 264; state of, effect on profits, x, 93, 100; state of, effect on wages, 73-7, 85-6; state of, in relation to its poetry, xxxix, 356-71; worst, is some relief, xix, 63

SOCIETY, A PROSPECT OF, xli, 532-44

Sociology, Huxley on study of, xxviii, 231-2

Socinians, Voltaire on the, xxxiv, 84-5

SOCRATES, APOLOGY OF, ii, 3-29

Socrates, on absolutes, ii, 97-8; Alcibiades and, xii, 110, 112-13, 114-15, 116; xlvi, 25; Aristophanes on, viii, 465; ii, 5; Aspasia and, xii, 62; Browne on, iii, 292; calmness

of, ii, 139 (64), 149 (85); on
causes, 90-6; charges against, i, 4,
5, 10; Cicero on, ix, 9, 10, 12;
the cook and, xxxix, 374; as cor-
rupter of youth, ii, 20-1; Dandini
on, v, 279; in Dante's Limbo, xx,
20; on death, ii, 15-16, 24, 26, 27-
8, 50-9, 61; on death and the
Thirty, xxxii, 22; death of, why
delayed, ii, 45-6; deformity of, iii,
113; demands reward for his services, ii, 23-4; on discontents, 298
(39); dress of, 297 (28); on duty,
165 (132); idea of earth, 105-10;
eloquence of, 3; Emerson on, v,
70, 131, 145, 211; Epictetus on,
ii, 124 (21), 127 (32), 134 (52),
151 (91), 154 (99), 177 (175), 179
(184); on essential opposites, 98-
101; Euripides and, viii, 286; on
doing evil, ii, 38; on God, 126
(28); hatred against its origin, i,
4, 7-10; on the hereafter, 104-5,
110-11; on hospitality, 178 (181);
Hugo on, xxxix, 360; Hume on
death of, xxxvii, 416; as example
of humility, i, 84; on immortality,
ii, 59-63, 68-73, 85-104; on incan-
tations, v, 182; inward voice of,
ii, 18; on knowledge as recollection, 63-8; last hours of, 46-114;
life and philosophy, 1, 2; the lyre
of, ix, 55; Marcus Aurelius on, ii,
198, 207 (3), 209 (6), 254 (66),
257 (3); Meletus and, 10-15; Mill
on, xxv, 35; Mill on condemnation of, 227; Milton on, iv, 390,
406-7; on misology, ii, 82-4; mission of, 157 (108); on his mission, 18-20, 23; Myrto and, xii,
108; early studies in natural science, ii, 90-1; on obedience to
laws, 39-41; ostentation of, iii,
134; Pascal on, xlviii, 273 (769),
337; Penn on, i, 360 (227); Perdiccas and, ii, 297 (25); on pleasure and pain, 48; on his pleasure,
172 (153); as a poet, 48-9; xxvii,
42; Pope on, xl, 447; in prison,
ii, 179 (185); prophesy on accusers, 26-7; as public officer, 19;
on public opinion, 35-7, 297 (23);
on his readiness for trial, 133
(48); refuses to beg mercy, 21-2,
25-6; refuses to escape, 37-44; refuses to be silent, 25; religion of,
12-14, 23; Rousseau on, xxxiv,
311; against Sicilian expedition,
xii, 125; sons of, ii, 21, 29, 34, 43,
112; on the soul, xxxiv, 104; on
suicide, ii, 49-50; method of teaching, xxxii, 36; teachings of, ii, 1,
16-17; xxviii, 87; virtue's chief
favorite, xxxii, 53; vision of, ii,
32; wealth of, xii, 81; wisdom of,
ii, 6-9, 16; on women, xxxix, 11-

13; world-citizenship of, ii, 121
(15); xxxii, 46
Socrates, the historian, iii, 209
Socratic Method, Franklin and the,
i, 18-19, 36-7; Mill on the, xxv,
20, 247-8
Soderini, Francesco, xxxi, 181-2, 184
Soderini, Piero, xxxi, 13 note 1;
Vespucci's letter to, xliii, 29
Sodom, Browne on, iii, 284; Bunyan
on, xv, 115; Milton on wickedness
of, iv, 103; Mohammed on, xlv,
902 note, 910 note 5
SODGER, I'LL GO AND BE A, vi, 38
Soest, in EGMONT, xix, 247-53, 266-
72, 293-5, 313
Sofala, Milton on, iv, 332
Softness, beauty in, xxiv, 103
Sogd, hospitality of, v, 130
Sogdiana, mentioned, iv, 396
Soger, term applied to sailors, xxiii,
129 note
Sogliani, Giovanbattista, xxxi, 29
Soirées, Carlyle on, xxv, 409-10
Solace, God the true, vii, 288-9
Solamona, king of Atlantis, iii, 168-
169
Solar Spectrum, xxx, 274
Solar System, motion of the, xxx,
326
Soldanieri, Gianni, xx, 136 note 11
Soldiers, ambition of, iii, 98; love
of, 29; Machiavelli on different
kinds of, xxxvi, 42-50; marriage
of, iii, 22; Massinger on qualities
of, xlvii, 829; pay of, why low, x,
115; quartering of, in United
States, xliii, 207 (3); students
compared with, by Don Quixote,
xiv, 393-8
SOLDIER'S DREAM, xli, 789-90
SOLDIER'S FORTUNE, THE, xxvi, 287-
366
SOLDIER'S RETURN, THE, vi, 486-8
Soldiers' Song, in FAUST, xix, 39
Soldiers' Song, from JOLLY BEGGARS,
vi, 129-30
SOLEMN LEAGUE AND COVENANT, vi,
548
SOLEMN MUSIC, AT A, iv, 41-2
Solicitation, liberty of, xxv, 307-9
Solidification, heat evolved in, xxx,
38-9
Solidity, Berkeley on, xxxvii, 223
Solinus, Milton on, iii, 253 note
35
Solis Dan, to Don Quixote, xiv, 16-
17
SOLITARY REAPER, THE, xli, 670-1
SOLITUDE, by Pope, xl, 415-16
Solitude, Bacon on real, iii, 69;
Burke on, xxiv, 40; contrary to
human nature, ix, 38; delight in,
iii, 69; impossible, 340-1; Kempis
on, vii, 233-5; Marvell on, xl, 386,
387; Milton on, iv, 36-7, 38, 255,

270; Pascal on, xlviii, 53; Penn on, i, 333; Selkirk on, xli, 548; terror in idea of, xxiv, 63

Solomon, Arabian idea of power of, xvi, 310-12; in the Arthurian Legends, xxxv, 197-9; Browne on salvation of, iii, 322; Bunyan on, xv, 107; Burns on loves of, vi, 51; Burns on Proverbs of, 151; in story of CITY OF BRASS, xvi, 320-4; Cowley on, xxvii, 65; Dante on, xx, 329-30 and notes 20, 21; Dante on salvation of, 344 note 23; Dante on wisdom of, 343 and notes; as author of ECCLESIASTES, xliv, 338; on fools, xxxvi, 165; the genii and, xvi, 29 note; the harlots and, xliii, 99; idolatry of, iv, 101, 380; Kempis on, vii, 350 (4); his largeness of heart, xxxix, 83-4; lost book of, iii, 289 (24); magic palace of, xlii, 1144; on mercy, xliii, 100; Milton on, iv, 274, 354; mines of, xxxv, 338; Pascal on, xlvii, 65 (174), 221 (651), 273 (769); Psalms attributed to, xliv, 146, 235-6, 315; Sainte-Beuve on, xxxii, 136; Sidney on Songs of, xxvii, 14; temple of, iv, 100; xliv, 445 (47); versified, vi, 192; on violence, xxxix, 98; on wisdom and riches, 95; wives of, iv, 381; xv, 263-4; works of, in New Atlantis, iii, 170

Solomon's House, in New Atlantis, iii, 162, 170, 181-91; comment on, 152; a father of, 179-80

Solon, Crœsus and, iii, 78; on custom, xxxvii, 29; epitaph of, ix, 72; on happiness, xxxii, 5, 6; old age of, ix, 55; Pisistratus and, 72; on reward and punishment, 185; Sainte-Beuve on, xxxii, 136; Sidney on, xxvii, 9

Solosmeo, Antonio, xxxi, 140 note 4, 141, 144

SOMEBODY, FOR THE SAKE OF, vi, 545-6

Somerby, George, xxiii, 424

Somers, Lord, xxiv, 166-7; Addison and, xxvii, 168; on PARADISE LOST, xxxix, 337 note

Somerset, Duke of, on colleges, xxxv, 404

Somerset, Earl of, and Dr. Donne, xv, 344

Son of the Vine, in New Atlantis, iii, 173, 175

Soncino, Raimondo di, despatches of, xliii, 48-50

SONG, by Blake, xli, 606

SONG, by Donne, xl, 314-15

SONG, by C. G. Rossetti, xlii, 1228

SONG, by Sidney, xl, 213-14

Songs, Milton on, iv, 34, 36, 41, 125

SONNET, THE, by Wordsworth, xli, 696-7

Sonnets, Pascal on false, xlviii, 17; Taine on study of, xxxix, 435; Wordsworth on, 314

SONNETS FROM THE PORTUGUESE, xli, 950-68

Sons, Yu-tzu on duties of, xliv, 5 (2); Confucius on duty of, 6 (11), 7 (5, 6, 7, 8), 14 (20), 45 (18)

Soothfastness, xlv, 864-5, 873, 874, 879

Sopater of Berœa, xliv, 475 (4)

Sophia, Princess, title of, xxiv, 172

Sophists, the, xii, 6

Sophocles, the Ægæan and, xlii, 1184; Æschylus and, viii, 442; ANTIGONE, 243-84; Aristophanes on, 421, 466; Carlyle on tragedies of, xxv, 382; Hugo on, xxxix, 365; life and works, viii, 196; Milton on, iv, 417; ŒDIPUS THE KING, viii, 197-242; old age of, ix, 53-4; Pericles and, xii, 45; Sainte-Beuve on, xxxii, 137

Sophocles, duke of Athens, v, 125-6

Sophronius, and Basil, xxviii, 62

Sorcery, Pascal on, xlviii, 287-8

Sordello, in Dante's PURGATORY, xx, 170 and note 9

Sorli, son of Gudrun, xlix, 376, 380, 444, 452, 454, 455-6

SORROW, LEVANA AND OUR LADIES OF, xxvii, 337-41

Sorrow(s), Augustine, St., vii, 52; better than laughter, xliv, 347 (3); come in battalions, xlvi, 168; folly of, ii, 123 (19); godly and worldly, xlv, 535 (10); joy and, xix, 120; knowledge is, xviii, 403; Pascal on, xlviii, 375-6; past and future, xlvii, 767; pleasure of, xxvii, 369; Pliny on feeling and hearing, ix, 341; Raleigh on two sorts of, xxxix, 102; tears and, xxvii, 299

Sorrows of Werther, Goethe's, xix, 3; Carlyle on, xxv, 354

Sosicles, the Pedian, xii, 19

Sosthenes, xliv, 471 (17); xlv, 501

Sot, fable of the, v, 73

Sotthiya, the grass-cutter, xlv, 631

Soul, ancient ideas of the, xxxiv, 104-5; Arabian belief of the, iii, 270 (7); Augustine, St., on the, vii, 60-1; Berkeley on the, xxxvii, 268, 269-71; body and, Buddha on, xlv, 662-7, 678-9; body and, Epictetus on, ii, 178 (178), 120 (10); body and, Hume on, xxxvii, 358, 363; body and, Marcus Aurelius on, ii, 200 (2), 207 (3), 212 (16), 213 (3), 239 (29); Cicero

on the, ix, 74; creation and transmission of the, iii, 301-2; Dante on the, xx, 250; Descartes on creation of the, xxxiv, 48; Descartes on existence of the, 29, 32, 39; Emerson on the, v, 10, 139; Emerson on laws of the, 27; Epictetus on care of the, ii, 139 (64); as a harmony of the body, 78-9, 85-9; immortality of the (see Immortality); Hindu doctrine of the, xlv, 807, 860, 864; Locke on the, xxxiv, 105-6; Lowell on the, xlii, 1466; Montaigne on the, xlviii, 397; nature and, v, 8; Omar Khayyam on the, xli, 981, 982; Pascal on the, xlviii, 82 (230), 83 (233); Pascal on immateriality of the, 120 (349); Plato's two horses of the, xii, 362 note; pre-existence of the (see Pre-existence); Prior on the, xl, 408 (269); progressiveness of the, v, 77; Raleigh on the, xxxix, 106; reality of the, v, 104; relations of the, to the divine spirit, 75; Rousseau on the, xxxiv, 264-6, 270-1; Shakespeare on the, xl, 288 (136); spherical form of the, ii, 292 (12); strength of, Diogenes on, 138 (62); transmigration of (see Transmigration); Voltaire on the, xxxiv, 107-9; Whitman on the, xxxix, 418

Soul-sides, the two, xlii, 1143
Soul of the World (see Over-soul)
Sound, More on pleasures of, xxxvi, 215-16; as source of the sublime, xxiv, 72-4; velocity of, xxx, 265-6; vibrations of, compared with light, 268-70, 275; wave theory of, 263-7

Sounds, beauty in, xxiv, 104-5; Berkeley on, xxxvii, 212-14, 219, 282; Burke on intermitting, xxiv, 73-4; repetition of, cause of sublimity in, 117-19

South, Tennyson on the, xlii, 1005
South America, Darwin on, xxix, 22-393; Drake in, xxxiii, 211-21; geology of west coast, xi, 342-3; species of, 417, 419; zoology of, compared with North, xxix, 143-4; zoology, changes in, 188-9

South American Republics, Monroe on, xliii, 297-8

South Shetland Islands, vegetation of, xxix, 265

South Wind, Kingsley on the, xlii, 1104

Southampton, tides at, xxx, 288
Southern Cross, Dana on the, xxiii, 30; Darwin on the, xxix, 531
Southern Hemisphere, climate and productions of, xxix, 265-8; leaving in, 457

Southern, Henry, xxv, 64, 86

Southey, Robert, poems by, xli, 749-52; on romance-poetry, xxviii, 76

Southwell, Sir Richard, xxxvi, 131-2, 135

Southwell, Robert, THE BURNING BABE, xl, 222

Sovereignty, Hobbes on rights of, xxxiv, 413; Vane on popular, xliii, 138-40

Sower, parable of the, xliv, 379 (4-15)

Space, abolished by the soul, v, 140-1; Aristotle on, 182; Hume on idea of, xxxvii, 437; Pascal on, xlviii, 78 (206), 435-7; Pascal on infinite divisibility of, 437-44

Spain, Bacon on empire of, iii, 81; Freeman on, xxviii, 267-8; Goethe on, xix, 86; Monroe on affairs of, xliii, 297, 298; in New World, x, 421-3; Raleigh on kings of, xxxix, 88-93; Raleigh on wealth of, xxxiii, 318-20, 329-30; under Roman dominion, xxxvi, 18; Taine on history of, xxxix, 449; taxes on precious metals in, x, 398-401; TREATY OF U. S. WITH, (1819), xliii, 286-95; TREATY OF U. S. with (1898), 469-77

Spangenberg, Bishop, i, 146
Spaniards, Paré on cruelty of, xxxviii, 33-4, 39; slowness of, iii, 66; wisdom of, 67
Spaniels, Harrison on, xxxv, 369, 370-1
Spanish Armada, Drake and the, xxxiii, 126; Macaulay on the, xli, 940-3; prophesied, iii, 97; Providence in defeat of, 281
Spanish Infantry, Machiavelli on, xxxvi, 89
Spanish Language, Sidney on, xxvii, 53
Spanish Literature, Taine on, xxxix, 461
Spanish Student, Serenade from the, xlii, 1325
Spanish War, Treaty ending, xliii, 469-77
Sparhawk, Harrison on the, xxxv, 357
Sparks, Jared, ordination of, xxviii, 318
Sparrow, Francis, xxxiii, 379, 380
Sparta, age honored at, ix, 69; boys in, iii, 103; Dante on, xx, 171-2; Descartes on pre-eminence of, xxxiv, 13; education in, iii, 256; elders of, ix, 52; reason of freedom of, xxxvi, 43; iron money of, x, 31; a military state, iii, 81-2; military spirit of, xxvii, 392; Milton on, iii, 204; policy of, toward Athens and Thebes, xxxvi, 19; precious metals in, x, 333;

Rousseau on laws of, xxxiv, 227; warriors most honored in, xxxiii, 85

Spartans, Bacon on the, iii, 80; Emerson on the, v, 52; lyrics among the, xxvii, 31; respect for seniority, xxxiii, 41; Taine on the, xxxix, 445 (see also Lacedemonians)

Spay, defined, xxxv, 361

Speaking, Locke on good, xxxvii, 171-2; Manzoni on thinking before, xxi, 538; Pascal on, xlviii, 20 (47)

Species, aberrant, xi, 468; allied, struggle with each other, 90; ancient and modern compared in organization, 384-8; resemblance of ancient and modern, 388-90; centres of creation of, 400-3; connected by extinct links, 377-82; why distinct, 333-4; doubtful, 62-9; duration of, 347-8; geographical distribution of, 395-449; groups of, appearance and disappearance, 367-8; intercrossing between, 112, 115-16; of large genera, vary most frequently, 71-2; of large genera, resemble each other, 73-4; lost, do not reappear, 365, 366-7; Lyell on changes of, xxxviii, 424-7, 430-1, 434; Lyell on extinction of, 425, 427, 430-1; meaning of, xi, 58; new, appear gradually, 364, 365; favorable conditions for production of new, 114-20; production of new, in New Atlantis, iii, 183-4; number of, limits to, xi, 139-41; origin of, progress of opinion on, 9-24; past, present, and future, 134; evidence of their being permanent varieties, 72, 73-4, 165, 330; Rousseau on immutability of, xxxiv, 260; simultaneous changes of, xi, 373-7; special creation of, objections to doctrine, 72, 109, 143, 150, 151, 162, 165, 168, 174-5, 189, 202, 206, 258-61, 309-10, 330, 417, 432-3, 436, 437, 438, 446, 473-4, 475, 493-4, 510, 512, 513, 514, 516, 517, 518, 522; sterility between, 42, 298-318; sterility does not determine, 300, 321-2; succession of, in geological record, 364-94; sudden appearance of, in geological record, 354-9; varieties compared with, 322-3, 326, 349-50; how varieties become, 122-9; why well defined without intermediate forms, 179-84; wide-ranging, vary most, 69-70; also in wide-ranging genera, 444-5

Species, Origin of, Darwin's, xi

Specific Characters, more variable than generic, xi, 164-68

Speciousness, beauty contrasted with, xxiv, 103

Spectator, The, xxvii, 172, 174-6, 181; Addison and Steele's parts in, 88; Franklin's use of the, i, 16-17; selections from the, xxvii, 77-85, 89-94

Spectator Club, Steele's, xxvii, 89-94

Spectrum, the diffraction, xxx, 280-1; Faraday on the, 33; the prismatic, 274; solar, 274; Voltaire on the, xxxiv, 125

Speculation (financial), in Elizabethan England, xxxv, 257-60; profits of, x, 120-1

Speculation (philosophical), Bacon on, iii, 94; Browne on, 277; Buddha on useless, xlv, 662-7; Carlyle on, xxv, 355-7, 368; Hume on, xxxvii, 442; Kempis on, vii, 215 (1), 272 (4); Lessing on religious, xxxii, 212-13; Milton on, iv, 248; Rousseau on, xxxiv, 248, 249, 261; Scepticism and, xxxvii, 337; Adam Smith on, x, 15-16; Sydney Smith on, xxvii, 260-1

Speculative Men, Goethe on, xix, 70

Spedding, J., editor of Bacon, xxxix, 1

Speech, Bacon on, iii, 111; Burke on, xxiv, 53-7, 158; Carlyle on, xxv, 393-6, 413; Coleridge on, xxvii, 270; Confucius on, xliv, 47 (4), 49 (21), 53 (7), 55 (40), 57 (6); Epictetus on, ii, 147 (81), 175 (164), 182 (5, 6); Franklin on, i, 19, 83; Hobbes on, xxxiv, 335-43; liberty of, Mill on, xxv, 215, 218-59, 260; liberty of, in U. S., xliii, 207 (1); Marcus Aurelius's rule of, ii, 261 (30), 302 (17); Montaigne on, xxxii, 65-7; Pascal on freedom of, xlviii, 319-20; Penn's rules of, i, 352, 401-2; Quaker idea of, 193-4, 236; religiousness of, xlv, 874; rules of, vii, 222; Sidney on, xxvii, 34; Themistocles on, iii, 73

Speght, editor of Chaucer, xxxix, 170 note 16

Spelling, learned by play, xxxvii, 139

Spence, Dr., i, 152-3; apparatus purchased by Franklin, 119

Spence, William, on Blacklock, xxiv, 141; on England, v, 406

Spence, Sir Patrick: a ballad, xl, 75-7; Coleridge on, xli, 745

Spencer, Earl of Kent, xxxix, 76

Spencer, Herbert, on beginning of organization, xi, 138; idea of evolution and, 6; on origin of species, 16; on principle of life, 318; inventor of term "Survival of Fittest," 77

Spencer, the elder, in EDWARD II, xlvi, 44, 48-9, 59, 60

Spencer, the younger, in EDWARD II, xlvi, 26-8; presented to king, 35; advice to king, 43-4; on Gaveston's death, 46; adopted by king, 47, 48; in the battle, 48, 49; sends Levune to France, 51; with Edward after battle, 55-6; in Edward's flight, 57, 59; in the abbey, 60; captured, 62-3

Spenser, Edmund, Arnold on, xxviii, 78; Burke on Belphebe of, xxiv, 144; creed of, v, 454; A DITTY, xl, 250; Dryden on, xiii, 13, 27, 56, 57, 60, 61, 64, 65; Emerson on, v, 149, 450; EPITHALAMION, xl, 238-50; Hazlitt on, xxvii, 286; heroes and heroines of, xxviii. 146; Johnson on, xxxix, 244; language of, 206; life and works, 64 note; James Mill on, xxv, 16; Milton on, iii, 212-13; PERIGOT, xl, 252; PREFATORY LETTER ON FAERIE QUEENE, xxxix, 64-8; Prince Arthur of, xiii, 20; PROTHALAMION, xl, 233-8; Shelley on, xxvii, 354; SONNETS, xl, 254-7; Thoreau on, xxviii, 426; Wordsworth on, xxxix, 321, 333; Wordsworth on sonnets of, xli, 697

Spensippus, death of, xxxii, 14; school-house of, 58

Spermatozoa, nature of, xxxviii, 358

Sphinx, Œdipus and the, iv, 414

Spices, Locke on use of, xxxvii, 17

Spider, parable of the, xv, 206

Spiders, aëronautic, xxix, 173-5; Browne on, iii, 278 (15); in Brazil, xxix, 46-8; flies and, Harrison on, xxxv, 366-7; Pope on instinct of, xl, 436

SPINNERS, THE THREE, xvii, 80-2

Spinola, Ambrogio, xxi, 489, 525, 539

Spinoza, Berkeley on, xxxvii, 247; Emerson on, v, 148; Hobbes and, xxxiv, 318

Spinther, Lentulus, death of, xii, 330

Spiridion, Calvin on, xxxix, 39 note 24

Spirit, superior to intellect, v, 198

Spirit of the Times, Goethe on, xix, 29

SPIRIT, THE, IN THE BOTTLE, xvii, 193-7

Spirits, Browne on, iii, 294-8; Hobbes on possession by, xxxiv. 370-2; of the impure, ii, 73-4; Locke on, xxxvii, 124-6, 174-6; Milton on, iv, 101, 174, 195-6, 215-16; terror of, 51-2

Spiritual, true meaning of, v, 291

Spiritual Delights, Kempis on, vii, 260 (1)

Spiritual Enlightenment, prayer for, vii, 298-9

Spiritual Estate, Luther on the, xxxvi, 278-83

Spiritual Gifts, St. Paul on, xlv, 517 (1-31)

Spiritual Knowledge, Channing on, xxviii, 340-1

Spiritual Life, admonitions profitable for the, vii, 213-47

Spiritual Progress, Kempis on, vii, 222-3

Spiritualism, in Utopia, xxxvi, 242

Spite, repaid by spite, iv, 268

Spleen, Harvey on the, xxxviii, 136

Splendor, Goldsmith on, xli, 528, 529; happiness and, 528-9

Sponges, no heart in, xxxviii, 137

Spontaneity, Emerson on, v, 10, 74

Spontaneous Generation, Frémy on, xxxviii, 370; Lamarck on, xi, 10, 136; Pasteur on, xxxviii, 354, 382

Spontaneous Impressions, Emerson on, v, 64

Spontaneous Variation, Darwin on, xi, 223; instances of, 222-3

Sportfulness, of heroism, v, 131

Sporting Plants, xi, 28

Spotswood, Col., i, 102

Sprengel, on flowers, xi, 157; on hermaphrodites, 109; on fertilization, 111

Spring, Burke on pleasantness of, xxiv, 67-8; Campbell on, xli, 791; Collins on evenings in, 493; Goethe on, xix, 40; Milton on, iv, 73; Shelley on the, xli, 856; Shakespeare on, xl, 269; Tennyson on the, xlii, 1010; Swinburne on, 1247-9

SPRING, by Nashe, xl, 266-7

SPRING, by Shakespeare, xl, 270

SPRING, EARLY, by Wordsworth, xli, 659

SPRING, ODE ON, by Gray, xl, 463-4

SPRING, SONG COMPOSED IN, by Burns, vi, 200-1

SPRING, TO, by Blake, xli, 598

SPRING'S WELCOME, xl, 213

Springs, as motive force, xxx, 197

Spruceness, Pascal on, xlviii, 111 (316)

Spur-kites, xxxiii, 160

Spurinna, Cottius, Pliny on, ix, 226-7

Spurinna, Vestricius, Pliny on, ix, 226, 240-1; letters to, 248, 287

Squinternotto, bravo in THE BETROTHED, xxi, 335

Squire, Chaucer's, xl, 13-14

Squirrels, flying, origin of, xi, 185

Srubdaire, the giant, xlix, 255

Ssu-ma Niu, xliv, 39 (3, 4, 5)

STABAT MATER, xlv, 565-7

Staël, Mme. de, on English poets, xxxix, 345

Stafford, Edward, 3rd Duke (of

earlier creation), (1478-1521), xxxv, 401

Stafford, Humphrey, 1st Duke (earlier creation), (1402-1460), xxxix, 77-8, 79, 80

Stafford, Lord, at Crecy, xxxv, 23, 32

Stag, defined, xxxv, 361; fable of the, v, 102

Stagirite, reference to the, xx, 156

Staig, Jessie, lines on, vi, 532

Stamford, university of, xxxv, 391

Stamp Act, xliii, 157 note, 158; Franklin on the, i, 4, 173

Stamp-duties, x, 528-34; legal, 473

Stand-fast, in PILGRIM'S PROGRESS, xv, 309-13, 316, 320-2

Standing Armies, advantages of, iii, 83; danger of, 54; Johnson on, xliii, 457; Macaulay on, xxvii, 393; Machiavelli on, xxxvi, 42-50; More on, 153-4; need and dangers of, x, 469-70; Vane on a, xliii, 133-5; Washington on, 255

Standish, John, and Wat Tyler, xxxv, 79; made a knight, 80

Standley, William, i, 214, 223

Stanhope, Earl, on French Revolution, xxiv, 159

Stanley, Mr., in SCHOOL FOR SCANDAL, xviii, 138; Sir Oliver Surface as, 175-7

Stanley, Lord, Mill on, xxv, 296

Stanton, Daniel, i, 235, 236

Stanton, Richard, xxxiii, 237

STANZAS, by Shelley, xli, 877-8

Star-Chamber, on unlicensed printing, iii, 194

Star-fish, eyes of, xi, 191; forceps of, 246-8

Star-form, in nature, xlii, 1301

Stars, Addison on the, xl, 410-11; Berkeley on the, xxxvii, 245; Burke on grandeur of the, xxiv, 68; composition of, xxx, 328; dark, 335-6; distance of, 329-30, 333-4; distribution of, in space, 331, 332-3; Emerson on beauty of the, v, 25; the forget-me-nots of angels, xlii, 1369; Habington on the, xl, 258-9; influence of, Cellini on, xxxi, 241; influence of, Milton on, iv, 311; Marcus Aurelius on lesson of the, ii, 297 (27); Milton on the, iv, 49, 51, 174, 188, 247-50; Newcomb on contemplation of the, xxx, 326; number of, 334-5; proper motions of, 328, 332, 333-4; Raleigh on the, xxxix, 113; Shelley on the, xli, 879; Wotton on the, xl, 294-5;

STARS, THE LIGHT OF, xlii, 1317

State, Burke on the, xxiv, 244-5; church and, xliii, 78-9; duties and expenses of the, x, 446-88; education by the, xxv, 315-17;

Emerson on the, v, 249, 250, 261; Hobbes on the, xxxiv, 319; the individual and the, ii, 39-41, 230 (22), 245 (54), 287 (33); v, 258; natural and ideal, xxxii, 225-30; no, that hangs on one man's will, viii, 266; the perfect, lines on, v, 249; revenue of the, x, 489-590; Ruskin on meaning of, xxviii, 140; Taine on the, xxxix, 454; what constitutes a, xli, 592-3 (see also Society)

State Church, Burke on a, xxiv, 240-70

State Enterprises, Smith on, x, 489-93

State Rights, Lowell on doctrine of, xxviii, 457

Stateliness, preferable to fellowship, v, 217; Penn on, i, 407

Staten Land, Dana on, xxiii, 334

States, ages, three of, iii, 147; founders of, 136; Confucius on strength of, xliv, 39 (7); Goldsmith on barren, xli, 538; Goldsmith on strength of, 532; Machiavelli on foundations of, xxxvi, 42; Raleigh on ruins of, xxxix, 74; rise and fall of, iii, 282 (17); temporality of, xlviii, 206 (614); tributary, xxxvi, 8-12, 18-19, 72-3; Woolman on prosperity of, i, 240-1

STATES, TRUE GREATNESS OF, iii, 76-84

States, of U. S., admission of new, xliii, 203-4; commerce between, 196 (3); committee of, 174-5, 176; disputes between, 172-4, 202 (1, 2); Federal government and, 222-3, 224-7, 229-30, 239; Hamilton on union of, 216; Jay on union, 217-21; Johnson on rights of, 456; Lincoln on rights of, 333, 342; powers of, 208 (10); relations of the, under Confederation, 169; relations of, under the Constitution, 203; republican government secured to the, 204; rights and powers of, under the Confederation, 169-72, 174, 176-7; rights and powers of, under Constitution, 197 (16), 198 (6) (Sec. 10), 210; suits against, not allowed, 209-11

States-General, French, Burke on composition of, xxiv, 189-92

Statesmanship, ideal and practical, xxxvi, 174-6; Lowell on, xxviii, 445-6, 449, 452, 454, 460; Newman on, 35

Statesmen, Bacon on, iii, 77; Burke's standard of, xxiv, 305; Confucius on, xliv, 36-7; Goethe on, policy of, xix, ▲56; Plutarch

on, xii, 56; Raleigh on, xl, 208; Smith on, x, 365

Statianus, Plutarch on, xii, 364

Stationary State, effect of, on profits, x, 100; Smith on, 86; effect of, on wages, 75-6, 85-6

Statius, Dryden on, xiii, 6; in Purgatory, xx, 234-8; Shelley on, xxvii, 366

STATUE AND LION, fable of, xvii, 24

Statues, Mohammed on, xlv, 1018; public, Pliny on, ix, 227; speaking, Plutarch on, xii, 189

Statute Laws, Winthrop on, xliii, 110-11

Stauffacher, Gertrude, in WILHELM TELL, xxvi, 377-80

Stauffacher, Werner, in WILHELM TELL, with Pfeiffer, xxvi, 376-7; with Gertrude, stirred to action, 377-81; at building of keep, 382; conversation with Tell, 383-4; at Fürst's, 386-94; at the rendezvous, 401-15; with Tell at Altdorf, 427-36; at death of Attinghausen, 442-7; with Rudenz, 448-9; reports murder of Emperor, 463-7; in final scene, 474

STAY MY CHARMER, vi, 314

STAY, O SWEET, xl, 318-19

Steadfastness, Confucius on, xliv, 24 (25), 45 (22); Hindu doctrine of, xlv, 879

Steam, volume of, xxx, 120-3

Steam-engines, Helmholtz on, xxx, 199-202

Steele, Sir Richard, Addison and, xxvii, 166, 170, 176, 177, 180, 182, 184-6; on Addison, 188, 189, 190-1; the *Guardian* of, 177; life of, 88; on Peerage Bill, 185; religion of, xxviii, 16; the *Spectator* and, xxvii, 172, 174-5, 181; THE SPECTATOR CLUB, 89-94; the *Tatler* of, 171; Thackeray on, xxviii, 10, 18

STEER HER UP AN' HAUD HER GAUN, vi, 552

Steevens, George, editor of Shakespeare, xxxix, 335

Steeving, described, xxiii, 269-70

Stefano, in THE BETROTHED, xxi, 133

Stella, Swift on death of, xxvii, 131-40; Thackeray on, xxviii, 22 (see also Johnson, Esther)

STELLA, ELEGY ON, vi, 283-6

Stenches, Burke on, xxiv, 75

Stendhal, Taine on, xxxix, 459-60

Stephanas, household of, xlv, 502 (16), 526 (15)

Stephano, in THE TEMPEST, xlvi, 408-12, 415-19, 430-2, 440-1

Stephen, St., the Martyr, appointed deacon, xliv, 441 (5); editorial remarks on teachings of, 428; martyrdom of, 445 (54-60); mar-

tyrdom of, Dante on, xx, 208-9; Pascal on death of, xlviii, 282 (800); trial of, xliv, 441 (9-53)

Stephen, St., the Sabaite, HYMN by, xlv, 556

Stephen, King, and the Bishop of London, xxxv, 266-7; the tailor and, xl, 192

Stephen, Leslie, on Berkeley's Dialogues, xxxvii, 198; on Hume, xxvii, 214

Stepney, Wordsworth on, xxxix, 347

Stereo-chemistry, Pasteur on, xxxviii, 284

Sterility, cause of, xi, 309-12; in dimorphic plants, 319-22; of first crosses and hybrids, 298-305; laws of, 305-9; origin of, 312-18; in species, eliminated by domestication, 42, 305; among varieties, 325-6

Sterling, John, Carlyle and, xxv, 331; in London Club, 85; *London Review* and, 133; Mill and, 4; Mill on, 100-3

Sterne, on readers, xxv, 354

Stesilaus, of Ceos, xii, 7, 82

Stesimbrotus, on Pericles, xii, 53

Steven, Rev. James, poem to, vi, 235-6

Stevenson, Robert Louis, life and works, xxviii, 286; poems by, xlii, 1260-2; TRUTH OF INTERCOURSE, xxviii, 287-94; SAMUEL PEPYS, 295-316; remarks on PEPYS of, l, 57

Steward, Chaucer's, xl, 27

Stewart, Jack, Dana on, xxiii, 411

Stewarts (see Stuarts)

Stheneboeas, references to, viii, 451, 452

Sthenelus, in the ÆNEID, xiii, 112, 407

Stillingfleet, Bishop, Locke and, xxxiv, 107

Stimson, Ben, Dana on, xxiii, 420

Stinging, power of, in marine animals, xxix, 489-90

Stingo, the Landlord in SHE STOOPS TO CONQUER, xviii, 211, 212-14

Stirling, Earl of, To AURORA, xl, 322-3

Stobi, John of, ii, 184 note

Stock, divisions of, x, 224-32; investment of, 231-2; lent at interest, 291-300; taxes on, 528-34 (see also Capital)

Stock, custom of pulling the, vi, 117 note 5

Stock-dove, Wordsworth on the, xxxix, 318

Stockings, invention of, x, 214

Stoeckl, Edward de, xliii, 459

STOIC, THE OLD, xlii, 1157

Stoicism, Epictetus on true, ii, 145 (78); Milton's Comus on, iv, 65; Montaigne on, xlviii, 401-2; Socrates on, ii, 75-6

Stoics, Browne on the, iii, 320; on crimes, ix, 333 note; on death, iii, 10; Hume on the, xxxvii, 337; Hume on doctrine of the, 389-90; Milton on philosophy of, iv, 407; on necessity, iii, 285; Pascal on the, xlviii, 120-1, 122 (360), 157 (465); on riches, ix, 138; on suicide, 308 (44) (see also Aurelius, Marcus, and Epictetus)

Stokes, Whitley, translator of Da Derga's Hostel, xlix, 209

Stoksely, Bishop of London, xxxvi, 110-11

Stone Age, as pictured by Æschylus, viii, 171 note 29

Stonehenge, Burke on, xxiv, 68; Emerson on, v, 473-7

Stones, knowledge of, necessary to art, xxxix, 270; transportation of, by ice, xxx, 241; transported by trees across water, xxix, 486-7

Storer, John, i, 251, 254

Stories, compared with poems, xxvii, 351; practise of telling, xvii, 1

Stork and Fox, fable of, xvii, 17

Storks, Pope on, xl, 436

Storks, The, story of, xvii, 329-34

Storms, on land and at sea, xxix, 548-9

Storrs, Robert, on puerperal fever, xxxviii, 266, 267

Stoves, in Elizabethan England, xxxv, 310; open, invented by Franklin, i, 116

Strabo, on English tin, xxxv, 338; on hounds, 369; on prodigies preceding Cæsar's death, xii, 326; on studdery of Pella, xxxv, 346; on tides, xxx, 293-4; on torrid zone, xxxix, 112

Strafford, Bagehot on trial of, xxviii, 183-4; Charles I on, v, 400

Stranger's House, in New Atlantis, iii, 157

Strangers, Emerson on, v, 109-10; liberties of, in Massachusetts, xliii, 83-4

Strathallan's Lament, vi, 296-7

Stratified Rocks, Lyell on, xxxviii, 415-16

Stratius, Homer on, xxii, 45

Stratonice, in Polyeucte, xxvi, 75-8, 86, 91-5

Strauchius, Chronology of, xxxvii, 167-8

Straw, Jack, xxxv, 63, 65, 70, 73, 74, 77; Chaucer on, xl, 50; death of, xxxv, 82

Strawberry, cultivation of the, xi, 54-5

Stream, Confucius on the, xliv, 29 (16)

Stream of Life, The, xlii, 1165-6

Street-lamps, improved by Franklin, i, 125

Streets, expense of maintaining, x, 477; Franklin on cleanliness of, i, 124, 128

Strength, Cicero on, ix, 57; Confucius on, xliv, 11 (16), 20 (10), 46 (27), 50 (35), 60 (8); David on, xli, 508-9; from misfortunes, v, 102-3; Nashe on, xl, 266; as a cause of the sublime, xxiv, 57-9; what is, without wisdom, iv, 420

Strength, in Prometheus Bound, viii, 156 9

Strenuousness, Mohammed on, xlv, 991

Stricca, Dante on, xx, 124

Strong, the battle is not to the, xliv, 351 (11)

Strophades, abode of the Harpies, xiii, 138

Strophius of Phocis, Clytemnestra and, viii, 36; Orestes and, 98-9

Stroza, on hounds, xxxv, 369-70

Strozzi, Fra Alessio, xxxi, 33

Strozzi, Bernardo degli, xxxi, 103 note 2

Strozzi, Filippo, xxxi, 81 note 1, 118 note 3, 199 note 2

Strozzi, Leone, xxxi, 328 note

Strozzi, Piero, xxxi, 303-4 note 1, 348, 409 note 1

Strozzi, Prior degli, xxxi, 372

Struggle for Existence, xi, 76-92; Tennyson on, xlii, 1058

Struggle, alone pleases, xlviii, 51 (135)

Strutt, Mill on, xxv, 54, 79; in Parliament, 126

Struve, theory of, xxx, 335

Strymonius, Virgil on, xiii, 340

Stuart, Lady Arabella, xv, 386

Stuart, Charles Edward, Burns on birthday of, vi, 306; supposed lament of, 322 (see also He's Ower the Hills, Wha'll Be King but Charlie, Charlie Is My Darling)

Stuart, Lady Jane, xxv, 8

Stuart, Sir John, and James Mill, xxv, 8

Stuart, Robert, xlii, 1208, 1213, 1220

Stuarts, Burns on the, vi, 279, 290

Stubbornness, man's worst ill, viii, 281; Locke on, xxxvii, 64, 65, 89; Sophocles on, viii, 257, 265

Stucco, Lady, in School for Scandal, xviii, 131

Student, Chaucer's, xl, 19

Students, Carlyle's advice to, xxv, 377-9; in Faust, xix, 37; soldiers and, Don Quixote on, xiv, 393-8; in Utopia, xxxvi, 192, 194, 206

Studies, Essay on, Bacon's, iii, 128-9

Studiousness, Bagehot on, xxviii, 182

Study, Burke on methods of, xxiv, 7-8; Burke on object of, 48; of children, xxxvii, 83, 137-8, 149-52; Confucius on, xliv, 26 (12), 27 (17); Ecclesiastes on, 354 (12); Epictetus on, ii, 170 (145); hours for, iii, 102; Locke on listlessness in, xxxvii, 114-19; Milton's course of, iii, 251-6; Montaigne on, xxxii, 9; Montaigne on aim of, 38-9; Montaigne on exessive, 55-6; pleasures of, iv, 37, 39; Pliny's method of, ix, 200, 316-18; thought and, Confucius on, xliv, 8 (15), 55 (30); Tzu-hsia on, 66 (7)

Stufa, Pandolfo della, xxxi, 429 note

Stufa, Prinzivalle della, xxxi, 31 and note 3

Stukeley, on Stonehenge, v, 476-7

Stupidity, town of, in PILGRIM'S PROGRESS, xv, 254, 255

Stussi, in WILHELM TELL, xxvi, 453-5, 458-9

Stygian Lake, Dante on the, xx, 32

Style, Pascal's rules of, xlviii, 12-17, 20-2

Styx, Aristophanes on the, viii, 433; Dante on the, xx, 62; Milton on the, iv, 125; oaths by the, xiii, 424; xxii, 76; xxvi, 168; Socrates on, ii, 109-10; Virgil on the, xiii, 226, 300

Subhadda, xlv, 654-8

Subject States, arms in, xxxvi, 72; Bacon on, iii, 80-1; factions in, xxxvi, 72-3; Machiavelli on, 8-12, 18-19; More on, 168-9

Subjection, Kempis on, vii, 221

Subjects, single men not best, iii, 22

SUBLIME AND BEAUTIFUL, Burke's, xxiv, 7-148; remarks on, 28

Sublimity, in building, xxiv, 66-7; Burke on source of, 36, 76; Burke on tests of, 76; color as source of, 72; compared with the beautiful, 106-7; defined, 46; difficulty as a source of, 68; feeling as source of, 76; heightened by the grotesque, xxxix, 366-7; infinity a source of, xxiv, 64-5; light and darkness as sources of, 70-1, 120-5; littleness as cause of, 64; magnificence a source of, 68-70; passion caused by, 51; physical causes of, 108-25; pleasure in contemplating, 46; power a cause of, 57-62; privation a source of, 63; smells and tastes as sources of, 75-6; sound as source of, 72-4, 117-19; succession and uniformity causes of, 65-6, 117-20; terror the first principle of, 51-2; ugliness and,

102; vastness a cause of, 63-4, 115-16; Wordsworth on, xxxix, 351

Submarine Changes, Lyell on, xxxviii, 414, 415, 417

Submarines, in New Atlantis, iii, 188

Submission, Kempis on, vii, 250-1; Pascal on, xlviii, 97 (268-70)

Subscriptions, Franklin's advice on getting, i, 123-4

Subsidence, areas of, as shown by coral reefs, xxix, 505-6; Lyell on, xxxviii, 423, 428-9, 431, 433-4; rate of, xxix, 507

Subsidies (see Bounties)

Subsistence, relation of, to population, x, 84 (see Food-Supply)

Substance, son of Ens, iv, 22-23

Subterranean Changes, Lyell on, xxxviii, 414-18

Subterranean Movements, Lyell on, xxxviii, 428-30

Subtle, in the ALCHEMIST, with Face, xlvii, 521-8; with Dapper, 528, 529-35, 576-7; with Dapper as Priest of Fairy, 582-5, 622, 623-5; with Drugger, 535-9, 564-7; with Mammon, 539-40, 547-55; in plot against Mammon, 559; finds Mammon with Dol, 604-7; with Kastril and Dame Pliant, 591-4; quarrel with Face over Pliant, 594-5; dealings with Puritans, 560-3, 567-8, 568-73, 574-5, 576, 611, 612-13; plot against Surly as the Don, 595-602; on Surly and Pliant, 607; denounced by Surly, 608-9; promises coming of Count, 610; renews claims to Pliant, 613; hears Lovewit's return, 613-14; his plot with Dol, 626-7; betrayed by Face, 627-9

Subtlety, Raleigh on, xxxix, 78

Success, in business, price of, v, 47, 48-9; requires toil, ii, 173 (157); a source of power, xxxix, 375

Succession, effect of, on the imagination, xxiv, 65; physical cause of sublimity of, 117-20

Succession Act, Burke on the, xxiv, 172-3

Succession-taxes, x, 529

SUCH A PARCEL OF ROGUES IN A NATION, vi, 445

Suckling, Sir John, poems by, xl, 363-4

Sucro, death of, xiii, 412

Sudassana the Great, xlv, 652-3

Suddenness, disagreeable, xxiv, 103; as source of sublime, 73

Suddhodana, father of Buddha, xlv, 600, 620

Sudra, caste of, xlv, 880

Suevian Sea, Tacitus on the, xxxiii, 121

Suevians, origin of the, xxxiii, 96;

Tacitus on the, 117-22; worship of Isis by, 100

Suffering, alone and with others, xlvi, 262; Longfellow on, xlii, 1318; Shakespeare on, xlvi, 140; strength equal to, iv, 115-16

Suffolk, Duke of, xxxix, 77-8

Suffrage, Lowell on universal, xxviii, 466-7, 478-80; Mill on democratic, xxv, 71-2; woman (see Woman S.)

Sugar, in ancient times, xxxv, 290; cause of pleasantness of, xxiv, 128-9; composition of, xxx, 174; potash and, 54 note; profits of cultivation of, x, 166-7

Suicide, Browne on, iii, 308 (44); Bunyan on, xv, 120; Epictetus on, ii, 122 (17, 18); xlviii, 395; Goethe's Faust on, xix, 32-3; Hamlet on, xlvi, 96, 135; Kant on, xxxii, 352-3, 360; Milton on, iv, 320; Mohammed on, xlv, 984; punishment of, in old England, xxxv, 385; Shelley on, xviii, 307; Socrates on, ii, 49-50; in Utopia, xxxvi, 221

SUICIDE, ON A, vi, 533

Suicides, in Dante's HELL, xx, 55-9

Suiones, Tacitus on the, xxxiii, 121

SUITORS, ESSAY ON, Bacon's, iii, 126-8

Sujātā, story of, 627-9

Suleyman (see Solomon)

Sulivan, Capt., on Falkland Islands, xxix, 203, 205, 206, 207

Sully, Burke on, xxiv, 196

Sulphindigotic Acid, xxx, 83 note

Sulpicius, Caius, in Catiline conspiracy, xii, 240

Sulpicius, Publius, quarrel with Pompeius, ix, 7

Sulpicius, Servius, letter to Cicero, ix, 172; letter from Cicero, 175

Sultan, Pascal on the, xlviii, 37, 48 (113)

SULTAN'S STEWARD, STORY OF THE, xvi, 141-50

Sultans, death of, concealed, iii, 148

SUMEDHA, THE STORY OF, xlv, 591-616

Summer, beauties of, v, 25; Campbell on, xli, 791; evening in, 493; one swallow makes not a, xiv, 104

Summer, of All-Saints, xlii, 1360-1

Summers, William, xxxviii, 167, 169

Summoner, Chaucer's, xl, 28-9

Summons, judicial, in Massachusetts, xliii, 73 (21), 74 (25)

Summum Bonum, Buddhist, xlv, 729-46; Pascal on, xlviii, 123 (361); various ideas of, 32

Sumptuary Laws, Penn on, i, 409-410; Smith on, x, 287

Sun, Addison on the, xl, 410; xlv, 547; Bunyan's lesson from the, xv, 238; Burke on grandeur of the, xxiv, 70; Copernicus on motion of, xxxix, 57; Dante's fourth

Heaven, xx, 327; David on the, xliv, 166 (4-6); Goethe on the, xix, 16; Herodotus on the, xxxiii, 15-16, 73; human mind compared with, ii, 266 (57); Manfred on the, xviii, 436-7; Milton on the, iv, 16, 152-3, 158, 194, 249, 311; Pascal on the, xlviii, 25-6; Raleigh on the, xxxix, 113; Raleigh on changes in, 112; source of all forces, xxx, 220; started in Aries, xx, 6 note 5; Tacitus on the, xxxiii, 121; tides affected by, xxx, 289-92, 305

Sun-dial, invented in Babylon, xxxiii, 53

Sun-spots, Pascal on, xlviii, 40 (91)

SUN AND WIND, fable of, xvii, 35

SUN, FOLLOW THY, xl, 292

SUN OF MY SOUL, THOU SAVIOUR DEAR, xlv, 579

SUN-DAY HYMN, xlv, 584

SUN-FLOWER, AH, xli, 598

Sunday Laws, Mill on, xxv, 298-9

Sunderland, Earl of, Peerage Bill of, xxvii, 184-5

Sunrise, lines on, iv, 32; on land and sea, xxiii, 13

Sunset, Thoreau on, xxviii, 437-8; Thoreau's allegory of, 434-5

Superfluities, attitude of Quakers toward, i, 319; Kempis on, vii, 302 (4); Penn on taxing, i, 344 (53), 409-10; Woolman on, 263-4, 303-4

Superfluity, of words, vii, 221

Supernatural Agencies, belief in, xxxviii, 406, 410-11

Supernaturalist, in FAUST, xix, 182

SUPERSTITION, ESSAY ON, Bacon's, iii, 47-8

Superstition, Burke on, xxiv, 307; in Burns's HOLY FAIR, vi, 102-3; defined by Hobbes, xxxiv, 355; fable on, xvii, 27; in literature, xxvii, 234; origin of, xxxiv, 390; piety and, xlviii, 94 (255); Pope on, xl, 439-40

Superstition, in PILGRIM'S PROGRESS, xv, 99

Suplee, Capt., at Gettysburg, xliii, 411

Suppiyā, xlv, 791

SUPPLICATION, A, by Cowley, xl, 374

SUPPLICATION, A, by Wyatt, xl, 194-5

Supply, annual, on what dependent, x, 5-6

SUPPOSED MISTRESS, HIS, by Jonson, xl, 307-8

SUPPOSED MISTRESS, WISHES FOR THE, xl, 369-71

Suppuration, causes and prevention of, xxxviii, 271-81

Supremacy Act, More on, xxxvi, 135-6

Supreme Court, of United States, xliii, 202; appointment of judges,

201 (2); Lincoln on decisions of, 340-1; Marshall on duties of, 223, 239

Sura, Attius, Pliny on, ix, 384

Sura, Licinius, letters to, ix, 271, 326

Sureties, Hobbes on, xxxiv, 434

Surface, Charles, in SCHOOL FOR SCANDAL, in love with Maria, xviii, 113, 114; his bankruptcy, 117, 118, 121, 122; Rowley on, 123; Sir Peter on, 124; Sir Oliver on, 137; Sir Oliver plans to try, 138-41; Maria on, 142; at home, 147-9; with Sir Oliver as Premium, 150-5; in the picture room, 155-9; with Rowley, 159-60; suspected with Lady Teazle, 135-6, 139, 141-2, 166, 169-70, 186, 192; at Joseph's, 169-73; mistakes Sir Oliver for Premium, 188-9; reconciled with Sir Oliver, 190; reconciled to Maria, 191-4

Surface, Joseph, in SCHOOL FOR SCANDAL, relations with Lady Sneerwell, xviii, 113; calls on Lady Sneerwell, 114-22; Sir Peter on, 124; on Backbite's epigram, 128; with Maria at Sneerwell's, 129, 133-4; with Lady Teazle, 134-5; Sir Oliver on, 137; Sir Oliver plans to try, 138; Maria and, 142; with Lady Teazle, 161-4; with Sir Peter, 165-8; with Charles, 169-71; denounced by Lady Teazle, 173-4; visited by Sir Oliver as Stanley, 174-8; Lady Sneerwell and, 186-7; expels Sir Oliver as Stanley, 188-9; denounced by Sir Oliver, Peter, and Lady Teazle, 189-90; accuses Charles with Lady Sneerwell, 191; follows Sneerwell, 192

Surface, Sir Oliver, in SCHOOL FOR SCANDAL, reported to be coming home, xviii, 120-1; his return, 124; with Rowley, 135-6; with Sir Peter, 136-7; plans to try his nephews, 138-41; at Charles's house, 146-7, 150-5; in picture room, 155-9; after the sale, 160-1; visits Joseph as Stanley, 174-7; mistaken for physician, 182-3; with Sir Peter after scandal, 184-5; returns to Joseph's as himself, 188-9; denounces Joseph, 189; reconciled to Charles, 190-3

Surgery, antiseptic principle in, xxxviii, 271-82; the germ theory in, 382, 388-9; papers on, 9-61, 235-68, 271-82, 382-402; in 16th century, 43

Surly, Pertinax, in THE ALCHEMIST, with Mammon at Subtle's, xlvii, 540-3, 546-58; plot against, 559; fails to meet Face, 574; as Spanish don, 574; with Face and Subtle, 595-8; presented to Dame Pliant, 600-1; exposes fraud to her, 607-8; denounces Subtle and Face, 608-9; with Kastrill, 609-10; and Drugger, 610-11; quarrel with Kastrill, 611-12; returns with Mammon, 619-20; with officers, 629-32

Surprise, Marcus Aurelius on, ii, 259 (15), 301 (13)

Surrey, Earl of, death of, xxxix, 81; Jonson on, xxvii, 60; poems by, xl, 196-8; Sidney on, xxvii, 45

Surt, the giant, xlix, 315 note

Surtees, Robert, BARTHRAM'S DIRGE, xli, 788-9

Survival of the Fittest, term invented by Spencer, xi, 77 (see also Natural Selection)

Susagus, ix, 388 note 2

SUSAN, THE REVERIE OF POOR, xli, 671

Susanna, friend of Jesus, xliv, 379 (3)

SUSPICION, ESSAY ON, Bacon's, iii, 86-7

Suspicion, simplicity and, iv, 155; Webster on, xlvii, 729

Suspiciousness, Confucius on, xliv, 50 (33)

SUTHERLAND, MR., PROLOGUE FOR, vi, 396-7

Sutlej, sediment of the, xxxviii, 424

Suttee, practise of, iii, 103

SWABIANS, THE SEVEN, xvii, 216

Swaflod, the maid, xlix, 344

SWALLOW AND OTHER BIRDS, fable of, xvii, 14

SWALLOW, SWALLOW, O, xlii, 1005

Swallow, Swinburne on the, xlii, 1249-51

Swamps, Thoreau on, xxviii, 423-4

Swan, Milton on the, iv, 241; Socrates on death-song of the, ii, 77-8

SWANS, THE SIX, xvii, 141-5

SWANS, THE WILD, xvii, 283-98

Swanhild, daughter of Sigurd, xlix, 376, 444; wedding and slaying of, 376-8, 444, 447-8, 450; her future foretold, 358-9, 408, 410

Swanwick, Anna, translator of EGMONT, xix, 245

Swarga, xlv, 840, 872

Swearing, Hobbes on, xxxiv, 416-17

SWEARING COXCOMB, ON A, vi, 534

Sweden, Freeman on, xxviii, 268; geological elevation of, xxxviii, 428

Swedenborg, Emanuel, Emerson on, v, 22, 183, 185; on the English, 403; the illumination of, 145; on truth, 144

SWEET AFTON, vi, 443

SWEET DISORDER, xl, 345-6

SWEET AND LOW, xlii, 1002

Sweet-meats, Locke on, xxxvii, 22

SWEET TIBBIE DUNBAR, vi, 364

SWEET WILLIAM'S GHOST, xl, 79-81
SWEETEST LOVE, I DO NOT GO, xl, 315-16
Sweetness, Berkeley on, xxxvii, 211-12; nature of, xxiv, 127-9; relaxing, 129-30
Swift, nest of the, xi, 289-90
SWIFT, JONATHAN, ESSAY ON, xxviii, 5-27
Swift, Jonathan, academy planned by, xxiv, 159; Addison and, xxvii, 187, 191; ambition of, xxviii, 8-9; attitude toward inferiors and superiors, 7-8; benefactions of, 15; Berkeley and, xxxvii, 198; biographers of, xxviii, 7; his bitterness, 9-10; as a churchman, 15-17; ON CONVERSATION, xxvii, 97-105; at court, xxviii, 14; ON DEATH OF STELLA, xxvii, 131-40; Directions to Servants, xxxvi, 4; Drapier's Letters, xxviii, 17-18; Emerson on, v, 450; An Englishman by all but birth, xxviii, 10; Goldsmith on, xli, 518; ON GOOD MANNERS, xxvii, 106-11; Gulliver's Travels, xxviii, 19-21; Hazlitt on, xxvii, 292; life and writings of, xxviii, 6; literary style, 10; loneliness and greatness, 26-7; loneliness and suffering, 17; on marriage and children, 18-19; Modest Proposal, 18; morality of his times, 9; on new and obsolete words, xxxix, 213; religion of, xxviii, 15-17; Stella and, 22-5, 26; Temple and, 10-14; his unhappiness, 21-2; Vanessa and, 25-6; Voltaire on, xxxiv, 151-2, 155; TO A YOUNG POET, xxvii, 112-30; remarks on YOUNG POET, l, 55
Swimbladder, Darwin on the, xi, 195-6
Swimming, Locke on, xxxvii, 14
Swinburne, Algernon C., poems by, xlii, 1247-57
Swine, abominated in Egypt, xxxiii, 28-9
SWINEHERD, THE, story of, xvii, 246-50
Swine-pox, xxxviii, 207
Swiss, in France, xxxvi, 49; Goldsmith on the, xli, 537-8; in Italy, xxxvi, 47; Machiavelli on the, 43; Pascal on the, xlviii, 109 (305)
Swiss Cantons, ancient league of, xxvi, 391 note
Swiss Confederation, Freeman on, xxviii, 270-2
Swiss Republic, Bacon on, iii, 37
Swiss Soldiers, Machiavelli on, xxvi, 89
Switzerland, connection with the German Empire, xxvi, 408-9; first settlement of, 407-8; Goldsmith on, xli, 537-8; taxes in, x, 522-3
SWITZERLAND AND ENGLAND, xli, 691
Sybaris, death of, xiii, 407
Sybil, in SHOEMAKER'S HOLIDAY, xlvii, 455-6, 462-4, 482, 488-9, 492, 494, 496
Sycophants, bites of, xxxix, 59
Sycorax, the witch, xlvi, 389-90
Sydenham, Locke and, xxxvii, 4
Sydney, Australia, Darwin on, xxix, 455-6
Sykes, Gen., at Gettysburg, xliii, 359, 380, 383, 422; Haskell on, 382
Sykes, John, i, 194, 196, 198, 236
Sylla, Faustus, Cicero on, xii, 249
Sylla, Lucius Cornelius, Burke on confiscations of, xxiv, 263-4; Cæsar and, xii, 274, 277; Cæsar on, iii, 43; called Felix, 106; Dryden on, xiii, 16; ignorance of, xxvii, 24; name of, xii, 162; Pompey and, iii, 70; the tower of Archelaus and, xxxv, 336
Syllogism, Bacon on the, xxxix, 139-40; Hobbes on meaning of, xxxiv, 340; Mill's theory of the, xxv, 118; Montaigne on the, xxxii, 64
SYLVANDER TO CLARINDA, vi, 309
Sylvester, follower of St. Francis, xx, 333 note 19
Sylvester, Joshua, LOVE'S OMNIPRESENCE, xl, 322
Sylvester, Pope, and the Lateran, xx, 82 note 10
Symbols, Epictetus on, ii, 172 (154); expression by, v, 173; mistaken use of, 184-5; universal use of, 174-5, 182
SYME, JOHN, COMPLIMENTS OF, vi, 548
Symeon Niger, xliv, 457 (1), 463 (14)
Symmachus, prefect of Rome, vii, 80
Symmetry, Pascal on, xlviii, 15 (28)
Symonds, J. Addington, translator of Cellini, xxxi
Symonds, Thomas, xliii, 180
Sympathy, Bacon on, iii, 72; Browne on, 332; Burke on, xxiv, 40-4; Emerson on false, v, 81-2; excessive, Emerson on, 217; natural to man, xxxiv, 279; pleasure in, xxxix, 295
Synagogue, Pascal on the, xlviii, 302 (851), 304 (852)
Syncope, Paré on, xxxviii, 57
Syndercomb, Hugo on, xxxix, 400
Synods (see Councils)
Syphax, in Cato, xxvii, 198, 200, 201, 202-3
Syphogrants, officers in Utopia, xxxvi, 187, 189, 192, 196, 198
Syracuse, expedition against, xii, 125-8, 130, 131

Syria, Raleigh on, xxxix, 74; Sesostris in, xxxiii, 51
Syrians, circumcision among ancient, xxxiii, 51
Syrinx, and Pan, xl, 386; references to, iv, 46, 380; Webster on, xlvii, 758
Systematic Affinity, defined, xi, 307
Systems, Voltaire on, xxxix, 395
Systole and Diastole, of arteries, xxxviii, 68-9, 71, 84-5; of the heart, 79, 82-3, 84-5
Tabernacle, references to the, iv, 351-2; xliv, 444
Tabitha, xliv, 450 (36-42)
Table, Mohammed's chapter on the, xlv, 1008-21
Tabor, the, xx, 91 note
Tabus, xlix, 210
Tacca, Giovan Francesco della, xxxi, 236-7
Tacca, Giovan Piero della, xxxi, 40
Tacco, Ghino di, xx, 168 note 2
Tachompso, island of, xxxiii, 18
Tacitus, Cornelius, on benefits, xlviii, 29 note; celebrity of, ix, 362; his silence on Christ, xlviii, 278 (787); funeral orator of Verginius, ix, 222; GERMANY, xxxiii, 95-123; remarks on GERMANY of, I, 20; life and works, xxxiii, 94; on miracles of Vespasian, xxxvii, 407-8; Pliny's letters to, ix, 200, 214, 298, 302, 330
Tact, Ruskin on, xxviii, 116
Taddeo, Dante on, xx, 338 note 21
Tadino, Alessandro, xxi, 478, 488; in plague of San Carlo, 523-4, 529, 553-4
Tagarasikkhi, xlv, 691
Tāghūt, xlv, 986 note 16
Tagua-tagua, Lake, xxix, 282
Tagus, in the ÆNEID, xiii, 311, 413
Tahattawans, the sachem, xliii, 153-4
Tahiti, Darwin on, xxix, 426-40
Tahitians, Darwin on the, xxviii, 422
Tai-po, xliv, 25 (1) note
Taillefer, at Hastings, xxviii, 71
TAILOR, REPLY TO A, vi, 239-41
TAILOR, STORY TOLD BY THE, xvi, 158-71
TAILOR, THE VALIANT LITTLE, xvii, 97-104
Tails, use and development of, xi, 206-7
Taine, Hippolyte Adolphe, life and works, xxxix, 433 note; INTRODUCTION TO ENGLISH LITERATURE, 433-62; remarks on INTRODUCTION of, I, 56-7
Take-heed, in PILGRIM'S PROGRESS, xv, 251
TAKE, O TAKE, xl, 272-3
Tale-bearers, Mrs., Candour on, xviii, 117
Talent, character contrasted with, v,

165-6; differences of, due to division of labor, x, 21-2; duty of developing, xxxii, 353-4, 361; genius contrasted with, v, 149, 172; not good in itself, xxxii, 323; reason brilliantly expressed, 130
Tales, remarks on, xvii, 2
Talib, son of Sahl, xvi, 310-11, 312-37
Taliessin, Celtic bard, xxxii, 174; reference to, xl, 471
TALK OF HIM THAT'S FAR AWAY, vi, 319
Talkative, in PILGRIM'S PROGRESS, xv, 79-89
Talkativeness, excessive, ii, 182 (5); vii, 221-2; Shakespeare's advice against, xlvi, 102
Talkers, Bacon on, iii, 19; Confucius on, xliv, 47 (5)
Talleyrand, on necessity, v, 479
Talmud, the, iii, 44 note; Pascal on the, xlviii, 216
TAM THE CHAPMAN, LINES ON, vi, 63
TAM GLEN, vi, 366-7
TAM O' SHANTER, vi, 411-18
TAM SAMSON'S ELEGY, vi, 254-7
Tamahamaha, king of Sandwich Islands, xxiii, 151
Tamar, Pascal on story of, xlviii, 267 (743)
Tamas, xlv, 864, 873, 875, 878, 879, 880
Tamerlane, Bacon on, iii, 24; Bajazet and, xxxix, 103
Tanabuso, bravo in THE BETROTHED, xxi, 335
Tanais, death of, xiii, 413
Tanagra, Landor on, xli, 924
Tancarville, Earl of, at Caen, xxxv, 7, 11-14; at Poitiers, 37, 51, 57
Tang, xliv, 42 note 8, 68 (1) note
Tannahill, Robert, poems by, xli, 608-9
Tansillo, Luigi, quoted, xiv, 331
Tan-tai Mieh-ming, xliv, 20 (12)
Tantalus, Cervantes on, xiv, 112; Homer on, xxii, 167; Milton on, iv, 126; Webster on, xlvii, 723
Tanusius, xii, 293 note
Tapacolo, Darwin on the, xxix, 288
Tapalguen, Sierra, xxix, 128-9
Taprobane, Greek name of Ceylon, xxxv, 239 note
Tapwell, in NEW WAY TO PAY OLD DEBTS, xlvii, 819-23, 876-9
Tarantula, Harrison on the, xxxv, 364
Taratan, herald in New Atlantis, iii, 174
TARBOLTON LASSES, vi, 24
Tarchon, Tuscan chief, xiii, 289, 292; ally of Æneas, 331-2, 336; in battle, 387-8

Tarentum, Fabius at, ix, 49

Targhetta, Miliano, xxxi, 189

Tariff (see Duties)

Tarlatti, Ciacco de', xx, 168 note 3

Tarn, Mount, Darwin on, xxix, 250-1

Tarquin, on his friends, ix, 27; reference to, xlvi, 323

Tarquinius Superbus, attempts to return to Rome, xii, 153-4

Tarquins, Virgil on the, xiii, 239

Tarquitus, death of, xiii, 345

Tartars, raids of, iv, 305

Tartarus, Milton on, iv, 208; Socrates's description of, ii, 108-9, 110; Virgil on, xiii, 229, 230-2

Tartrate of Lime, fermentation of, xxxviii, 332-40

TARTUFFE, Molière's, xxvi, 189-284; editorial remarks on, 188; Goethe on, xxxii, 129-30; Hugo on, xxxix, 367, 374-5

Tartuffe, in TARTUFFE, discussed by Mme. Pernelle and others, xxvi, 191-3, 195; relations with Orgon, 197, 199-200; discussed by Orgon and Cleante, 201-5; chosen by Orgon for Mariane's husband, 208-17; sent for, by Elmire, 233; with Dorine, 234-5; with Elmire, 236-41; denounced by Damis, 243; with Orgon, 243-50; with Cleante, 250-2; led on by Elmire, 258-63; caught by Orgon, 264; refuses to leave house, 265; sends Mr. Loyal to claim property, 273-7; the box of Argas and, 266-7, 279; comes to arrest Orgon, 280-2; himself arrested, 282-3

Tar-water, Berkeley on, xxxvii, 198

Tasks, Locke on, xxxvii, 60

Tasmania, Darwin on, xxix, 471

Tasso, Battista del, xxxi, 25-6, 28, 360 note 5

Tasso, Torquato, Dryden on, xiii, 13, 24, 25, 27, 34, 44; a madman, xxvii, 374; on philosophy, xxxii, 34-5; on poets, xxvii, 374; Sainte-Beuve on, xxxii, 137; Scudéri on, xxxix, 380; Shelley on, xxvii, 354; the sonnet and, xli, 697; Spenser on, xxxix, 65

TASTE, ESSAY ON, Burke's, xxiv, 11-26

TASTE, THE STANDARD OF, Hume's, xxvii, 215-34

Taste, Burke on standards of, xxiv, 11-12; Burke on study of, 9; constituents of, 22-3; definition of, 12-13; delicacy of, xxvii, 221-4; differences of, due to organs, 221; differences of, due to particular humors, 230-1; differences due to age or country, 231-4; differences of, judged by degree of pleasure, xxiv, 21-2; reason of so-called differences of, 18-21; Emerson on

good, v, 218; habits affect sense of, xxiv, 15-16; of the imagination, 16-18; improved by practice, xxvii, 224-5; not a separate faculty, xxiv, 25-6; Poe on, xxviii, 388; in poetry, Hugo on, xxxix, 404-5; possibility of determining a standard of, xxvii, 229-30; prejudice and, 226-7; as matter of reason, 227-8; Reynolds on, xxxix, 282, 305; Schiller on cultivation of, xxxii, 248-52, 269-70, 282-3, 287-91, 312-13; sense of, Burke on, xxiv, 127-8; sense of, same in all men, 14-15; of the senses, 13-16; for sensible objects and in the passions, 22; as matter of the understanding, 23-6; variety of, xxvii, 215-16; want of, its cause, xxiv, 23; Wordsworth on, xxxix, 338, 348-51

Tastes, Berkeley on, xxxvii, 210-12, 219; as sources of the sublime, xxiv, 75-6

Taste-that-which-is-good, the cook, xv, 267

Tathāgata, a name of Buddha, xlv, 647 note

Tatti, Giocopo, xxxi, 156 note 2

Taulchinne, the juggler, xlix, 247

Taureas, and Alcibiades, xii, 124

Taurus, commander for Octavius, xii, 386

Taurus, the sign, reference to, iv, 109

Taxation, equality of, x, 498-9; general rules of, 498-501; heavy, unfits for empire, iii, 78-9; popular attitude toward, v, 258; without representation, xliii, 157 (3)

Taxes, on capital, x, 528-34; capitation, 538-40; on commerce, iii, 54; on consumption, x, 541-73; direct, apportionment of, xliii, 193 (3), 198 (4); duties and, x, 361; farming of, 568-9; on house rent, 510-18; on interest of money, 519-22; on luxuries, 542-5, 559-64; on luxuries, payment of, 499 (3); on luxuries, Penn on, i, 344 (53), 409-10; national, under the Confederation, xliii, 172; national, under Constitution, 196 (8), 198 (5); on necessaries, x, 542, 544-7, 572-3; on necessaries, as requiring duties on foreign goods, 361-3; on newspapers, Wordsworth on, v, 336; on produce of land, x, 508-10; on profits, 518; on rent of land, 501-8; on rent, payment of, 499 (3); source of, 56; on stimulants, Mill on, xxv, 309-10; on transfers of property, x, 528-34; on wages, 534-8; for war, Quakers on, i, 225-8

Taylor, Dr., of Norwich, vi, 100

Taylor, Father, Dana on, xxiii, 117

Taylor, Jeremy, Emerson on, xlii, 1300; Wordsworth on, xxxix, 323-4

Taylor, Thomas, Emerson on, v, 483

Taylor, Mrs., and J. S. Mill, xxv, 4; Mill on, 120-4, 148, 154-9; death of, 161

Taylor, P. A., Mill on, xxv, 190 note

Taylor, W., on fancy and imagination, xxxix, 316

TE DEUM LAUDAMUS, xlv, 558

Tea, Burke on taste for, xxiv, 16

Teachers, Channing on importance of, xxviii, 371, 372; Confucius on, xliv, 8 (11); Locke on, xxxvii, 73-85, 137, 149-52, 164, 179; Montaigne on, xxxii, 35-6; need of personal, xxviii, 32-8; paid, Socrates on, ii, 5-6; pay and consideration of, x, 141-3; qualities needed by, ii, 157 (108), 162 (121); sacred and literary, v, 148

Teaching, Burke on method of, xxiv, 12-13; Confucius on, xliv, 22 (8); Pope on methods of, i, 19 (see also Education)

TEAR-DROP, THE, vi, 545

Tears, Byron on, xli, 810; De Quincey's Lady of, xxvii, 338-9; false, true pity move, xiii, 108; Hunt on, xxvii, 299; Laertes on, xlvi, 179

TEARS, IDLE TEARS, xlii, 1002

Teazle, Lady, in SCHOOL FOR SCANDAL, marriage with Sir Peter, xviii, 122-3; scene with Sir Peter, 125-8; at Lady Sneerwell's, 129-33; Joseph Surface and, 134-5, 162-4, 169; suspected with Charles Surface, 135-6, 139, 141-2, 166, 169-70, 186, 192; reconcilement and new quarrel with Sir Peter, 143-5; caught behind screen, 172-4; at Joseph Surface's after reconcilement to husband, 189-93; epilogue spoken by, 195

Teazle, Sir Peter, in SCHOOL FOR SCANDAL, guardian of Surface brothers, xviii, 112; on Lady Teazle, 122-3; scene with Rowley, 123-5; scene with Lady Teazle, 125-8; at Sneerwell's, 130-3; with Sir Oliver, 136-7; his plan to make trial of Charles Surface, 139-41; with Maria, 142; reconcilement and new quarrel with Lady Teazle, 143-5; at Joseph Surface's house, 165-9, 171-4; at home after the scandal, 183-6; at Joseph Surface's, 189-93

Tedaldi, Lionardo, xxxi, 350, 352-3

Tedmur, inscription of, xvi, 334-5

Teeth, and hair, related, xi, 30, 156

Tegan, mantle of, xxxii, 152

Tegetmeier, on bees, xi, 287

Tegghiaio, in Dante's HELL, xx, 27-8

Teiresias, in ANTIGONE, viii, 273-7;
in the BACCHÆ, 355-7, 359-63; Homer on, xxii, 149, 154-5; in ŒDIPUS THE KING, viii, 207-11

Telauges, and Socrates, ii, 254 (66)

Teleclides, on Pericles, xii, 39, 55

Telegraph, Helmholtz on the, xxx, 215-17

Telemachus, in the ODYSSEY, roused to action by Pallas, xxii, 12-17; rebukes Penelope, 18; with the suitors, 19-20; complains of suitors in assembly, 23-6; asks for ship to go to Pylos, 27-8; counselled by Pallas, 29-30; prepares for sailing, 31-2; sails, 33; with Nestor at Pylos, 34-47; with Menelaus at Sparta, 48-64; plotted against by the suitors, 65-6, 68-9, 70; warned by Athene to return home, 208-9; departs with gifts, 209-13; takes ship at Pylos, 213-16; his landing in Ithaca, 221-3; at Eumæus's hut, 224-8; recognizes Ulysses, 229-30; in plan to destroy the suitors, 230-2; hears return of his enemies, 236-7; returns to mother, 238-9; relates what he had heard, 241-2; receives Eumæus and Ulysses, 246-7; rebukes Antinous, 248-9; the sneeze of, 252; warned by Eumæus, 254; protects Ulysses in fight with Irus, 256-7; rebuked by Penelope, 261; advises suitors to retire, 266; removes arms from hall, 267-8; goes to assembly-place, 287-8; protects Ulysses from the wooers, 291-2; replies to Agelaus, 293; advised to expel Ulysses, 294; with the bow of Ulysses, 297-8; orders Penelope away, 304; gives Ulysses the bow, 305; with Ulysses against the suitors, 309-17; hangs faithless servants, 319; in meeting of father and mother, 323-4; in final fight, 344-5; Tennyson on, xlii, 1008

Telemus, the soothsayer, xxii, 133

Teleology, Kant on, xxxii, 367 note

Telescopes, Newton on, xxxiv, 126-7

Tell, Walter, in WILHELM TELL, at home, goes to Altdorf with father, xxvi, 416, 419; at Altdorf, 425-36; reunion with mother, 442-3; at home again, 467-9

Tell, Wilhelm, in WILHELM TELL, residence of, xxvi, 374 note; son-in-law of Fürst, 387; takes Baumgarten across the lake, 374-5; arrival at Stauffacher's, 381; at home, starts for Altdorf, 416-19; at Altdorf with Walter, 425-6; neglects to bow to Gessler's cap, 426-8; at building of the Keep, 382; conversation with Stauffacher, 383-4; ordered to shoot apple from son's head, 428-34; arrested by

Gessler, 434-6; embarked at Flüelen, 436; escape of, 439-42; in wait for Gessler, 450-3; with Stussi, 453-4; kills Gessler, 457-8; returns home, 469; with Duke John, 469-73; in final scene, 474

Tellheim, Major von, in MINNA VON BARNHELM, changing of his room referred to, xxvi, 288-90; announces intention to leave inn, 291; with Just, 292-3; with Madame Marloff, 293-5; destroys note, 295; with Just, agrees to keep him, 295-7; pardon asked by Minna, 297-8; prepares to leave inn, 298; Minna on, 302-3; discovered by his ring, 307-8; with Minna, takes leave of her, 312-15; with Werner, 324-9; with Franziska, 329-32; scene with Minna, 341-8; hears her misfortunes, 348-9; borrows money of Werner, 349-51; determines to marry Minna, 350-1; returns to Minna, with Franziska, 351-2; seeks reconciliation, 353-5; letter from king, 355-7; offers himself to Minna, 357-61; accuses Minna of faithlessness, 361; refuses Werner's money, 362; final reconciliation, 363-4; with Minna's uncle, 364-5; reconciliation with Werner, 365

Tell-true, in PILGRIM'S PROGRESS, xv, 301

Tellus, reference to, xx, 267

Temminck, on classification, xi, 457

Temper, Penn on, i, 353

Temperance, Channing on, xxviii, 364; Cicero on, ix, 58; common notion of, ii, 57-8; Dante's star of, xx, 148 note 5; definitions of, i, 82; Epictetus on show of, ii, 177 (176); Franklin on, i, 18, 46, 89; Franklin's rule of, 83, 84; Greek idea of, xxv, 36; of heroism, v, 130; instances of, xx, 239-40; Manzoni on habits of, xxi, 248; Marcus Aurelius on, ii, 198, 263 (39), 301 (15); Milton on, iii, 311-13; iv, 65-6, 67, 336; necessity of, in pleasure, v, 92; Penn on, i, 345-6; philosopher's reason of, ii, 75-6; the virtue of prosperity, iii, 17

Temperance Ships, Dana on, xxiii, 314-15

Temperature, production of high, xxx, 111 note; why low, on mountains, 222-3

TEMPEST, THE, xlvi, 377-442; Hunt on, xxvii, 309; stage representation of the, 328-30

Temple, Sir William, Swift and, xxvii, 96; xxviii, 6, 10-14

Temples, pagan, Burke on grandeur of, xxiv, 66

Temporal Estate, Luther on the, xxxvi, 278-83

Temporal Happiness, Penn on, i, 360-1

Temporary, in PILGRIM'S PROGRESS, xv, 156

Temptation, Burns on, vi, 586; Kempis on, vii, 224-6, 259-60, 292-3, 311-12; More on, xxxvi, 105; necessary to virtue, iii, 212-13, 218; Pascal on, xlviii, 289 (821); Paul, St., on, xlv, 514 (13); Rousseau on reasons of, xxxiv, 286; seek not, iv, 273; supposes fallibility, 271; Winthrop on, xliii, 103; yielding to, Epictetus on, ii, 144 (75); yielding to, Kempis on, vii, 219 (2)

Temptation, In, xlv, 572-3

Temptations, of the flesh, vii, 191-7; of curiosity, 197-9; of pride, 199-203

Temsice, George, xxxvi, 143

Ten Thousand, Emerson on the, v, 198; retreat of the, xii, 371

Tencterians, Tacitus on the, xxxiii, 114

Tenderness, in friendship, v, 116-17

Tenedos, island of, xiii, 104

Tenements, Channing on, xxviii, 367

Teneriffe, identified as mountain of Atlas, viii, 168 note 21

TENNANT, JAMES, EPISTLE TO, vi, 353

Tennent, Gilbert, Franklin on, i, 123-4

Tennyson, Alfred Lord, ARABIAN NIGHTS' influence on, xvi, 16; Emerson on, v, 463; Poe on, xxviii, 402; poems by, xlii, 997-1098; Wordsworth on, v, 483

Terah, father of Abraham, iv, 15

Terence, Augustine, St., on, vii, 19; on compliance, ix, 39, 401 in Dante's Limbo, xx, 238; Montaigne on, xxxii, 92-94; quotations from, xlviii, 123 note 11; Scipio and, xiii, 70

Terentia, wife of Cicero, ix, 5; in Catiline conspiracy, xii, 241; Clodius and, 249-50; divorce of, ix, 82; xii, 261; letter to, ix, 91

TERESA, ST., ON THE BOOK AND PICTURE OF, xl, 372

Tereus, and Progne, xx, 181 note 4

Termagant, xlvi, 139 note 3

Tern, the snow-white, xxix, 482

Ternate, Drake at, xxxiii, 227-30

Terray, Abbé, interest under, x, 96

Terrier, Sir Tivy, xviii, 145

Terriers, Harrison on, xxxv, 369

Territories, under control of Congress, xliii, 204

Terror, as a means of authority,
ix, 349-50; Burke on, xxiv, 42,
51-2; cause of, 110-12; darkness,
as cause of, 70, 120-3; delight
caused by, 114; in idea of infinity, 64-5; intermitting sounds,
as cause of, 73-4; loudness as
cause of, 72; obscurity, as cause
of, 52-3; idea of power, as cause
of, 57-62; in privation, 63; suddenness as cause of, 73; in idea
of vastness, 63-4, 115 (see also
Sublimity)

Terry, Job, Dana on, xxiii, 37

Tertian Fever, Harvey on, xxxviii,
133

Tertiary Deposits, Lyell on, xxxviii,
425-6

Tertullian, on Christians, xlviii,
360; on the church, 314 (890);
on Esdras, 214

Tertullus, Cornutus, colleague of
Pliny, ix, 380 note 1; on Certus,
358

Tertullus, the orator, xliv, 484 1-8)

Teru-tero, Darwin on the, xxix, 127

Testa, C. Trebatius, letters to, ix,
137, 180

Testimony, Hobbes on, xxxiv, 415;
Hume on, xxxvii, 398-9; Mohammed on, xlv, 1019-20

Tethys, references to, iv, 69; viii,
161

Tetu, French captain, xxxiii, 192-4,
195, 196, 199, 201

Tetzel, xxxvi, 295 note 9

Teucer, accuser of Alcibiades, xii,
128-9

Teucer, and Belus, xiii, 97

Teucrus, Virgil on, xiii, 135

Teuthrania, Herodotus on plains of,
xxxiii, 9

Teutonic Literature, Renan on early,
xxxii, 154

Teutonic Races, Christianity and,
xxxii, 179

Teutons, compared with Slavs in,
situation, xxviii, 276-7

Texas, history of, xliii, 309 note

Thackeray, William Makepeace, Emerson on, v, 457; END OF THE
PLAY, xlii, 1099; life and works,
xxviii, 3-4; ESSAY ON SWIFT, 5-27;
remarks on ESSAY, l, 56

Thais, Alexander and, xl, 401, 404,
405; in Dante's HELL, xx, 78

Thalberg, and the Queen, v, 386

Thales, in Dante's Limbo, xx, 20;
on death, xxxii, 27; Lycurgus and,
iii, 204; Sidney on, xxvii, 9

Thames, importance of the, v, 348

Thammuz, Milton on, iv, 101

Thamûd, xlv, 902, 916, 929

Thamyris, blind, iv, 139; death of,
xiii, 407

THANATOPSIS, xlii, 1262-4

Thankfulness, human, ii, 131 (42);
for virtue, 170 (146)

THANKSGIVING, A PSALM OF, xliv,
154

THANKSGIVING FOR A NATIONAL VIC-
TORY, vi, 489

Thanksgivings, Roman, Cato on, ix,
158

Thaqif, tribe of, xlv, 930 note

Thargelia, the courtesan, xii, 62

THAT'S THE LASSIE O' MY HEART, vi,
578

Theagenes, Chariclea and, xxvii, 15;
Sidney on, 13

Theano, the priestess, xii, 131

Theatre, Hugo on the Greek, xxxix,
358-9; Hugo on the modern, 401-2;
Montaigne on the, xxxii, 72-3;
morality and the, xxvii, 356; Pascal on the, xlviii, 11 (11); Swift
on the, xxvii, 128; Voltaire on
the, xxxiv, 156-8

Theatrical Representations, Lamb
on, xxvii, 316-31

Thebes (Egypt), distance from sea,
xxxiii, 9; extent of, 12; sacred
animals of, 25-6

Thebes (Grecian), building of, xx,
133; founders of, xxii, 158;
Philip of Macedon and, xxxvi, 44;
Spartan policy toward, 19; the
war against, viii, 246-8

Thebez, the prophet of, iv, 383

Theft, Augustine, St., on, vii, 27-9;
Confucius on, xliv, 41 (18); Mohammed on, xlv, 1012; More on
causes and punishment of, xxxvi,
151-63; penalty of, by the Law,
xliii, 100, 104; punished in second
circle of Hell, xx, 47; punishment
of, in old England, xxxv, 385-6,
387, 389

THEIR GROVES O' SWEET MYRTLE, vi,
572

Themes, Locke on, xxxvii, 57-9, 173

Themis, Æschylus on, viii, 164 note,
186; goddess of assemblies, xxii,
24; mother of Prometheus, viii,
157 note; second prophet at
Delphi, 115

Themistocles, accused of treason, xii,
26; Aristides and, 81-3, 87, 88-9,
106, 107; rebuilds Athens, 22-3;
is banished, 25; birth and boyhood of, 5-7; character of, 7-8, 9-
10, 21-2; children of, 34-5; children of, ix, 188; Cicero on, 23-4,
106; death of, xii, 34; Emerson on,
v, 275; escapes death by dream,
xii, 32-3; Herodotus and, ix, 107;
honors conferred on, xii, 21;
honors to family, 35; loses favor
with confederates, 24; at Marathon, 85; memory of, ix, 53; Montaigne on, xxxii, 34; in Persian
war, xii, 10-20; proposes destruc-

tion of Greek fleet, 23; proposes ships, 8; prosperity, 32; public treasury and, 84; at Salamis, 88-90; the Seriphian and, ix, 48; the soldier and, iii, 343; incurs displeasure of Sparta, xii, 24; the statue and, 33; tomb of, 35; his wanderings, 27-9; Xerxes and, 29-31; iii, 148-9

THEMISTOCLES, LIFE OF, Plutarch's, xii, 5-35

THENIEL MENZIES' BONIE MARY, vi, 298-9

Theobald, Johnson on, xxxix, 248-249

Theoclymenus, in the ODYSSEY, xxii, 215, 221-2, 242, 293-4

Theocratic Society, Hugo on, xxxix, 357

Theocritus, on husbandry, xxvii, 72; an idyllic poet, xxxix, 314; reference to, xli, 950

Theodoric, Bacon on, iii, 136

Theodorus, death of, xii, 398; high priest of Athens, 144-5

Theodotus, with Pompey's head, xii, 315

Theogenes, the statue of, v, 97

Theogiton, the Megarian, xii, 101

Theognis, Sainte-Beuve on, xxxii, 136

Theology, Bagehot on modern, xxviii, 211-12; Carlyle on, xxv, 379-80; Channing on, xxviii, 341; Descartes on, xxxiv, 8, 9-10; Emerson on our, v, 39; false, cure for, 291; Goethe on, xix, 75-6; Hume on, xxxvii, 444, 445; Luther on study of, xxxvi, 341-3; Marlowe on, xix, 201-2, 203; of Middle Ages, xxviii, 224; Milton on study of, iii, 255; Milton on true, 233; Pascal on, xlviii, 48 (115), 404, 445; popular, Emerson on, v, 90-1; women and, xxviii, 154

Theomancy, defined, xxxiv, 397

Theophanes, the Lesbian, xii, 258

Theophilus, Antony's steward, xii, 388-9

Theophrastus, on anger and desire, ii, 202 (10); Cicero on, xii, 245; on Demades, 205; Huxley on, xxviii, 227; Milton on study of, iii, 253 note 29; on morals and sickness, xii, 77-8; Newman on, xxviii, 59; Plutarch on, xii, 118; Zaleucus and, ix, 155

Theopompus, Cæsar and, xii, 314-15; Ephorus and, ix, 152

Theoris, the priestess, xii, 209

Theory, Burke on, xxiv, 8-9, 48-9; Goethe on, xix, 77; practise and, Mill on, xxv, 26; practical man's distrust of, v, 57-8; Smith on, xxvii, 260-1; test of truth of, xi, 519

Theramenes, pupil of Euripides, viii, 448; Aristophanes on, 435

Theramenes, in PHÆDRA, xxvi, 125-9, 146, 152, 180-3

THERE WAS A BONIE LASS, vi, 550

THERE'LL NEVER BE PEACE TILL JAMIE COMES HAME, vi, 421

Theresa, St., Pascal on, xlviii, 166 (499), 308 (868), 319 (917)

Thermo-electric Batteries, xxx, 218

Thermodon, Plutarch on, xii, 212-213

Thermometers, freezing-point of, xxx, 242

Thermopylæ, Byron on, xli, 834

Thermus, Cicero on, ix, 84, 152

Theron, death of, xiii, 337

Thersites, Epictetus on, ii, 158 (110); Pliny on, ix, 218 note 8

Theseus, acts and loves of, xxvi, 128, 149; the Amazons and, viii, 142; Ariadne and, xxii, 160; the centaurs and, xx, 247 note 7; in Epirus, xxvi, 161; in Hades, xiii, 224; Hercules compared with, v, 192; Hippolyta and, xiii, 384; Machiavelli on, xxxvi, 20-1, 22, 87; the Minotaur and, xiii, 212; xx, 50 note 4; ship of, ii, 45-6; in Tartarus, xiii, 232

Theseus, in HIPPOLYTUS, plotted against by Aphrodite, viii, 288; returns to find wife dead, 320-4; dooms Hippolytus, 324-5; scene with Hippolytus, 326-33; hears accident of Hippolytus, 336-40; hears of his innocence, 341-2; at his death, 345-8

Theseus, in PHÆDRA, his absence referred to, xxvi, 125-6; reported dead, 137, 140; rumored still alive, 152; his return, 156, 159-62; hears dishonor of Hippolytus, 162-4; banishes Hippolytus, 164-8; tells Phædra, 168-9; with Aricia, 177-8; becomes suspicious of wrong, 178-9; learns death of Hippolytus, 180-2; learns his innocence, 183-5

Thesmophoria, the, xxxiii, 86

Thespis, reference to, xxxix, 369

Thessalus, accuser of Alcibiades, xii, 127, 131

Thestylis, reference to, iv, 33

Thetford, university of, xxxv, 391

Thetis, Achilles and, v, 96; her flight from Chiron, xx, 182; in Dante's Limbo, 239 note 10; Milton on, iv, 70; Virgil on, xiii, 244; Zeus and, viii, 182 note 49

Theudas, xliv, 440 (36)

Thevet, Andrew, xxxiii, 322, 330, 337

Thibault, king of Navarre, xx, 92 note 3

Thief, Epictetus on punishment of the, ii, 120 (12)

THIEF AND HIS MOTHER, fable of the, xvii, 28

Thierry, in SONG OF ROLAND, xlix, 201, 202-6

Thierry, Augustin, *History of the Conquest*, xxxii, 180 note; Taine on, xxxix, 437

THINE AM I, MY FAITHFUL FAIR, vi, 506

Thiodrek, the king, xlix, 422

Thirlwall, Mill on, xxv, 83, 84

THIS IS NO MY AIN LASSIE, vi, 575

Thisbe, and Pyramus, xx, 257

Thistles, South American, xxix, 136

THO' CRUEL FATE SHOULD BID US PART, vi, 98

Thoas, in the ÆNEID, xiii, 341

Thoas, and Hypsipyle, xx, 77 note 4

Thomas, the apostle, xliv, 373 (15), 430 (13)

Thomas, Gov., Franklin on, i, 109, 114-15, 116

THOMAS RYMER AND THE QUEEN OF ELFLAND, xl, 77-9

Thompson, Capt., at San Diego, xxiii, 114-15

Thompson, William, Mill on, xxv, 83

Thomson, C. P., Mill on, xxv, 84

THOMSON, CATHERINE, SONNET ON, iv, 84

Thomson, James (1700-48), Burns on, vi, 187; TO FORTUNE, xl, 454; Hazlitt on, xxvii, 292; prayer written by, i, 87; quotation from, vi, 234; RULE BRITANNIA, xl, 453; Wordsworth on his *Castle of Indolence*, xxxix, 342; Wordsworth on *Seasons* of, 339-42

THOMSON, ADDRESS TO SHADE OF, vi, 443

THOMSON, ON SOME COMMEMORATIONS OF, vi, 475-6

Thomson, James (1834-82), GIFTS, xlii, 1195

Thomson, Dr. James, on chemistry, xxv, 17; on freezing-point, xxx, 243; on regelation of ice, 254; on plasticity of ice, 257; on tides, 307

Thomson, N. H., translator of THE PRINCE, xxxvi, 1

Thomson, Sir William, on age of earth, xi, 359, 360; on freezing-point, xxx, 243, 244; life and work, 262; THE TIDES, 287-321; WAVE THEORY OF LIGHT, 263-86

Thone, and Helena, iv, 64

Thonis, the Egyptian, xxxiii, 55

Thoösa, daughter of Phorcys, xxii, 11

Thor, at Utgard, v, 373

Thora, daughter of Hakon, xlix, 360, 425

Thórdharson, Jón, xliii, 5

Thoreau, Henry David, sketch of life and works, xxviii, 406; on

the truth, 293; ON WALKING, 407-38

Thorfinn Karlsefni, xliii, 15-17, 18, 20-1

Thorgeir, son of Snorri, xliii, 21

Thori, the Norseman, xliii, 11, 12

Thorndike, Herbert, xv, 389

Thorold, Earl Tresham (see Tresham)

Thorough, is no word of peace, viii, 297

Thorstein, son of Eric the Red, xliii, 6, 14

Thorstein the Swarthy, xliii, 14

Thorvald, son of Eric the Red, xliii, 6; voyage to Vinland, 12-14

Thorvard the Norseman of Gardar marries Freydis, daughter of Eric the Red, xliii, 6; with Freydis makes voyage to Vinland, 17-20

Thorycion, Aristophanes on, viii, 429, 430

THOU FAIR ELIZA, vi, 441

THOU HAST LEFT ME EVER, JAMIE, vi, 504-5

Thought, aberrations of, four principal, ii, 295 (19); "act in fancy," xlv, 813; action and, Carlyle on, xxv, 355; Channing on, xxviii, 333-48, 352-55; Descartes on reality of, xxxiv, 29; duty of man, xlviii, 59 (146); Hobbes on, xxxiv, 325-30, 334, 359-62; Hume on limits of, xxxvii, 317-20, 322, 346; not wisdom, viii, 360; liberty of, Mill on, xxv, 218-59, 260; liberty of, Milton on, iii, 232-8; makes place, vii, 327 (5); man born for, xlviii, 417; Pascal on, 119 (339), 120 (346-8), 124 (365), 125 (370); preventing power of, 95 (259); as product of matter, xxxiv, 106-9; Rousseau on, 251-3; Schiller on courage of, xxxii, 243; sensation and, xxxvii, 316; Socrates on pure, ii, 54; study and, Confucius on, xliv, 8 (15), 55 (30); swifter than time, xviii, 324; Walton on sympathy of, xv, 341

Thoughtlessness, Buddhist idea of, xlv, 703

Thoughts, Bacon on good, iii, 30; Bunyan on good, xv, 150-1; chance in, xxxix, 125; character, determined by, ii, 229 (16); connection of, xxxix, 162; defined, xxxvii, 317; Emerson on, v, 148, 175, 435-6; Emerson on our rejected, 63-4; evil, a prayer against, vii, 298; feelings and, xxxix, 286-7; Goethe on exchange of, 265-6; Marcus Aurelius on purity of, ii, 207 (4), 210 (8); Penn on government of, i, 396-

8; Shakespeare on, xlvi, 102;
source of, outside of human will,
v, 138; two at same time impossible, xlviii, 59 (145); wandering
of, Byron on, xviii, 440; Browning on, 397; wandering, Dante
on, xx, 164; worldly and heavenly,
vii, 327 (5, 6)
THOUGHTS IN A GARDEN, xl, 386-8
THOUSAND AND ONE NIGHTS, xvi
Thrace, the modern Roumania,
xxviii, 274; Sesostris in, xxxiii,
50
Thrasea, Pætus, Stoic philosopher,
ix, 196 note; Pliny on, 323, 324
Thrasiline, in PHILASTER, xlvii, 639-
49, 663-4, 669-73, 684-5, 700, 702,
706
Thraso, Sidney on, xxvii, 29; Thaïs
and, xx, 78 note 6
Thrasybulus, of Stiria, xii, 137; ac-
cuses Alcibiades, 147
Thrasymedes, son of Nestor, xxii,
35, 45, 46
THREE FEATHERS, story of the, xvii,
166
THREE LITTLE MEN IN THE WOOD,
xvii, 74-9
THREE RAVENS, THE, xl, 74
THREE SPINNERS, THE, xvii, 80-2
THREE WARNINGS, THE, xlv, 705-7
Thrift, Confucius on, xliv, 25 (35)
Thrush, nests of the, xi, 296; Whit-
man on the, xlii, 1498
THRUSHBEARD KING, story of, xvii,
151-5
Thucydides, of Alopece, rival of
Pericles, xii, 48, 54; on Pericles,
44, 55
Thule, King of, song of, xix, 113-14
THUMBLING, story of, xvii, 132-7
THUMBLING AS JOURNEYMAN, xvii,
137-41
Thumomancy, defined, xxxiv, 397
Thunder, Beaumont on, xlvii, 653;
Longfellow on, xlii, 1376
Thunderstorms, Darwin on, xxix, 72
Thurloe, Hugo on, xxxix, 399
Thyestes, feast of, viii, 66
Thymbræan God, Apollo called, xx,
193 note
Thymbrus, and Laris, xiii, 340
Thymœtes, Virgil on, xiii, 104, 331
Thyn, Captain, xxxiii, 349, 357, 363,
369, 382
Thyrsis, and Corydon, iv, 33
Thyrsus, freedman of Octavius, xii,
393
Thyrsus, sacred wand of Bacchus,
viii, 351
THYRZA, ELEGY ON, xli, 805-7
TIBBIE, I HAE SEEN THE DAY, vi,
20-1
Tibboos, Emerson on rock, v, 208
Tiber, river, origin of name, xiii,
283

Tiberius, aided by mother, iii, 148;
caution of, 18; Dante on victories
of, xx, 310 note 19; death of, iii,
10; in Germany, xxxiii, 117; mentioned in LUKE, xliv, 365 (1);
Marcus Aurelius on, ii, 304 (27);
Marco and, iii, 98-9; Milton on,
iv, 401-2; memoirs of, xxxvi, 3;
the pictures and, xlvii, 545; Sejanus and, iii, 71
Ticino, Freeman on, xxviii, 265
Tickell, on Addison, xxvii, 187
Ticknor, Elisha, xxviii, 379-80
Tidal Waves, Kelvin on, xxx, 288-9
Tidal Harmonic Analyser, xxx, 307-
10
Tide Gauge, the, xxx, 303-4
Tide Predictors, xxx, 310-12
Tides, ancient knowledge of, xxx,
293-4; declinational, 305-6; defined, 287-90; Descartes on, xxxiv,
37; due to attraction of sun and
moon, xxx, 289-90, 294-6, 305-6,
317-19; dynamic action of, 301;
elastic, 313, 319; equilibrium
theory of, 298-300; harmonic
analysis of, 304-10; meteoro-
logical, 290-2; moon as cause of,
294-6, 305-6, 317-19; observation
of, 302-4; prediction of, 310-12;
spring and neap, 298-9; true solar
and lunar, how known, 292-3;
Voltaire on, xxxiv, 110, 120;
weather, influenced by, xxx, 313
TIDES, ESSAY ON, Kelvin's, xxx,
287-321
Tierny, Dr., xxxviii, 208, 222-3
Tierra del Fuego, boulders in, xxix,
264; climate and productions of,
258-9; Darwin on, 58, 219-46,
251-8; glaciers of, 262, 240; peat
in, 304; snow-line in, 261; trees
in, 303
Tigellinus, and Burrhus, iii, 62
TIGER, THE, a poem, xli, 597-8
Tigillinus, death of, xxxii, 14
Tignoso, Federigo, xx, 204 note 21
Tigranes, and the Romans, iii, 78
Tigris, river, in Eden, iv, 265
Tillotson, Dr., on the real presence,
xxxvii, 396
Timæa, Alcibiades and, xii, 132-3
Timæus, on plants and man, v, 182;
Plutarch on, xii, 129; on the
Pyrrhian War, ix, 105; Timoleon
and, 107
Timandra, and Alcibiades, xii, 150,
151
Timarete, the priestess, xxxiii, 32
Time, abolished by the soul, v, 140-
1; Bacon on, xxxix, 130; brings
evil and good, xxxvi, 13; cleanses
all, viii, 126; consists of two days,
xvi, 18; definitions of, xlviii, 432-
4; duration of past, xi, 335-9,
359-60; duration of past, Lyell on,

xxxviii, 406-13; element of, in
formation of species, xi, 117;
eternity and, iii, 274; Hume on
idea of, xxxvii, 437, 438; the
greatest innovator, iii, 65; lifter
of the veil, viii, 331; like a river,
ii. 221 (43); makes manifest the
righteous, viii, 215; the measure
of business, iii, 66; measures all
things, iv, 198; method and, xix,
73; Milton on, iv, 40-41; numbers motion; 27; Pascal on, xlviii,
49 (122); Penn on use of, i,
333-4; Raleigh on, xl, 208, 210;
among the Romans, ix, 243 note
4; Shakespeare on, xl, 280-1;
slower than thought, xviii, 324;
subtle thief of youth, iv, 30;
teaches many a lesson, viii, 190;
as the test of books, xxxix, 218-
19; unhasting stride of, viii, 389
Time-server, Lord, in PILGRIM'S
PROGRESS, xv, 104
Timeliness, Bacon on, iii, 67; Penn
on, i, 354
Timesileus, Plutarch on, xii, 59
Timidity, Hippocrates on, xxxviii,
5; of modern society, v, 80
Timocreon, on Themistocles, xii,
24-5
Timoleon, fortune of, iii, 106; Landor on, v, 330; Timæus and, ix,
107
Timon, of Athens, xii, 390-1; Alcibiades and, 124-5; misanthropy
of, ix, 38; tree of, iii, 36
Timon, the deacon, xliv, 441 (5)
Timon of Phlius, on Zeno, xii, 40
Timon, teacher of Arthur, xxxix,
66
Timorous, in PILGRIM'S PROGRESS,
xv, 47, 224
Timorous, Mrs., in PILGRIM'S PROG-
RESS, xv, 186-90
Timorousness, Locke on cure of,
xxxvii, 104-8
Timotheus, Athenian general, Apol-
lodorus and, xii, 209; Bacon on,
iii, 106
Timotheus, musician at Alexander's
feast, xl, 401-6
Timothy, at Berœa, xliv, 469 (14);
circumcision of, 465 (1-3); xxxvi,
388-9; at Corinth, xliv, 471 (5);
the Corinthians and, xlv, 506 (17),
527 (1), 528 (19); sent to Macedonia, xliv, 474 (22), 475 (4); St.
Paul on, xlv, 525 (10-11); Penn
on, i, 404 (163)
Timoxena, wife of Plutarch, xii, 3
TIN SOLDIER, THE CONSTANT, xvii,
312-16
TINDER-BOX, THE, story of, xvii, 370-6
Ting, Duke, xliv, 44 (15)
Tinker's Song, from JOLLY BEGGARS,
vi, 136

Tinochorus, Darwin on the, xxix, 106
TIPPLING BALLAD, A, vi, 479
Tiquitoc, on Dulcinea, xiv, 542
Tiradritto, bravo in THE BETROTHED,
xxi, 334
Tirante the White, xiv, 55, 101
Tiresias, in Dante's HELL, xx, 84;
Milton on, iv, 139
Tiro, freedman of Cicero, ix, 82,
118; Cicero's letter to, 160; letter
of Cicero the Younger to, 181;
letter of Q. Cicero to, 183
Tiro, Calestrius, letter to, ix, 206
Tiro, Julius, codicils of, ix, 309
Tirsan, father of family in New At-
lantis, iii, 172
Tirynthian Groom, Hercules called
the, xl, 247
Tisaphernes, and Alcibiades, xii, 133-
4, 138
Tisiphon, wreath of, xlvi, 65
Tisiphone, Dante on, xx, 38; in
Virgil's Hades, xiii, 230
Tisso, Prince, anecdote of, v, 309
Titania, in FAUST, xix, 177
Titans, Milton on the, iv, 95, 103;
sons of Okeanus and Earth, viii,
164 note 14; in Tartarus, xiii, 230-
1; war of, referred to, viii, 163-4
Tithes, David on, xli, 503; Harrison
on, xxxv, 274; Hindu doctrine of,
xlv, 814
Tithonus, Aurora and, v, 96; xxii,
71; xl, 240; reference to, xx, 181
Titian, Cellini and, xxxi, 371-2; Haz-
litt on, xxvii, 293; portraits by,
286
Titius, the quæstor, xii, 368, 380
Titles, Austin on, xli, 545; Hobbes
on, xxxiv, 383; Pope on, xl, 446
Titmouse, habits of the, xi, 188, 289
Titus, Paul, St., and, xxxvi, 389,
394; Paul, St., on, xlv, 529 (13),
535 (6-7), 536 (6, 13-15), 537 (16-
24), 543 (18)
Titus, the Emperor, beauty of, iii,
112; Jerusalem destroyed by, xx,
234 note 5, 310; xxxv, 336; xxxviii,
32; Pope on, xl, 445
Tityos (see Tityus)
Tityrus, Sidney on, xxvii, 28
Tityus, Homer on, xxii, 166-7; in
Tartarus, xiii, 231
Tivitivans, Raleigh on the, xxxiii.
351-2, 387
Tmolus, Euripides on, viii, 366; ref-
erence to, xli, 845
TOADEATER, THE, vi, 453
Toads, adders and, xxxv, 364; South
American, xxix, 109-10
Tobacco, Burke on taste for, xxiv,
16; Harrison on use of, xxxv,
251; introduced into England by
Drake, xxxiii, 126; profits of cul-
tivation of, x, 167-8
Tobbia, the goldsmith, xxxi, 124-5,
127, 130, 132

Tobias, Augustine, St., on, vii, 196;
Milton on, iv, 189,
TOCCATA OF GALUPPI'S, A, xlii, 1122
Tocqueville, M. de, Mill on his
Democracy, xxv, 124-5
Toledo, Eleanora di, xxxi, 356 note
1; Cellini and, 377, 378-9, 381-2,
399, 404-9, 413-15, 424-5, 426, 429-
30, 432-4, 435-6, 438, 445, 452-3
Toledo, Pietro Alvarez de, xxxi, 142
note
Toleration, in ancient Athens, iii,
204; in ancient nations, xxxvii,
416-17; Lord Brook on, iii, 239;
Burke on, without any belief, xxiv,
298; Hume on, xxxvii, 429; Mill
on, xxv, 38; Mill on popular ideas
of, 210; Milton on, iii, 240-1; Pascal on, xlviii, 348-50; in Utopia,
xxxvi, 239-40
Tolleme la Feintes, xxxv, 124
Tollendal, Lally, letter on October
Sixth, xxiv, 222 note
Tolls, Smith on, x, 475-7
Tolmides, Athenian general, xii, 58,
59
Tolosa, Lady, in DON QUIXOTE, xiv,
38
Tolumnius, in the ÆNEID, xiii, 376,
404, 411
TOM BOWLING, xli, 514-15
TOMB, THE BISHOP ORDERS HIS, xlii,
1117
TOMBS IN WESTMINSTER ABBEY, xl,
327-8
TO-MORROW, by Collins, xli, 607
To-morrow, Omar Khayyam on, xli,
973; sees undone what happens
not to-day, xix, 14; Shakespeare
on, xlvi, 370
Tomyris, Cyrus and, xx, 194
Tonio, in THE BETROTHED, xxi, 95-
8, 113-15, 118, 120-2, 130, 191, 568
Tonson, on Addison, xxvii, 184
Too-Bold, in PILGRIM'S PROGRESS,
xv, 307-8
Tooke, Horne, xxvii, 292
Tooke, William Eyton, xxv, 56; in
Utilitarian movement, 70; and
Westminster Review, 66
TOOTHACHE, ADDRESS TO A, vi, 251-2
Toparimaca, Raleigh on, xxxiii, 360-1
Tophet, Hinnom named, iv, 100
Topiawari, king of Aromaia, xxxiii,
345, 365-8, 375-9
Torello, Lelio, xxxi, 430 note
Torquatus, A., Cicero on, ix, 140:
Dante on, xx, 309; Virgil on, xiii,
239
Torralva, Lope Ruyz and, xiv, 166-8
Torrens, Col., Mill on, xxv, 60
Torrigiani, Piero, xxxi, 23-5
TORTOISE AND BIRDS, fable of, xvii,
30
TORTOISE AND HARE, fable of, xvii,
39

Tortoises, on Chatham Island, xxix,
397; Darwin on meat of, 399; of
Galapagos Islands, 417; habits of,
405-8
Torture, judicial, Harrison on,
xxxv, 382; Hobbes on, xxxiv,
415; in Massachusetts, xliii, 77
(45)
Tosa, Cianghella, xx, 352 note 12
Totems, in Ireland, xlix, 214 note
Touch, beauty to sense of, xxiv,
103-4
Touraine, Earl of, at Poitiers, xxxv,
47
Tourneys, Bacon on, iii, 101
Tournon, François de, xxxi, 273
note
TOUSSAINT L'OUVERTURE, xli, 671-2
Town, and country, relations of, x,
132-7, 319-22
TOWN MOUSE AND COUNTRY MOUSE,
fable of, xvii, 12
Town Meetings, disturbers of, xliii,
78 (56)
Towns, Goethe on life in, xix, 377;
in Massachusetts, xliii, 79-80, 81;
origin of, x, 321-2
Townshend, Goldsmith on, xli, 518,
520
Toxodon, Darwin on the, xxix, 94
Trade, advantages of, x, 22-3; Balance of (see Balance of T.); division of labor limited by facilities
of, 24-5; Emerson on the ways
of, v, 47-8; genius in, 193-4; Goldsmith on evils of, xli, 523, 532;
government interference with,
xxv, 303-11; home and foreign, x,
349-50; human propensity to, 19-
20; Locke on learning a, xxxvii,
185-90; necessity of, x, 29; Penn
on ways of, i, 406 (185-6); tyranny of, v, 416; "the vena porta of
wealth," iii, 107; Voltaire on,
xxxiv, 941 wholesale, three kinds
of, x, 310; Woolman on, i, 188,
204 and note, 206 (see also Commerce)
Trades, equality of, the requisites
to, x, 191-6; exclusive, profits and
wages in, 65, 66; government
interferences with equality of,
126-52; incorporated, 126-38; inequalities, natural, of various,
106-26; inequalities, political, 126-
52; Tzu-hsia on, xliv, 66 (4)
Trade-winds, effect of Andes Mountains on, xxix, 342-3
Trading Companies, x, 480-5
TRADITIONAL BALLADS, xl, 51-189
Traditions, over-reverence of, iii, 48
Tragedy, before Æschylus, viii, 3;
Athenian, iv, 406; Augustine, St.,
on, vii, 34; better read than seen,
xxxix, 234; Cervantes on, xiv,
503; Dennis on unity of place in,

xxvii, 204; Dryden on, compared with epic poetry, xiii, 7-11, 14; English, Voltaire on, xxxiv, 133-8; French classical, xxvi, 70; Greek, Hugo on, xxxix, 358-9, 364-5; Johnson on origin of, 224; Lamb on stage representation of, xxvii, 316-31; Macaulay on eloquence in, xxvii, 402; Marcus Aurelius on lessons of, ii, 290 (6); Milton on, iv, 416-17; in periods of decay, xxvii, 357; pleasure in, Burke on, xxiv, 41-3; pleasures of, Milton on, iv, 37; pleasure in, the reason of, xxvii, 369; xxxix, 234; popular notions of, 225; requires a comic element, xxviii, 183-4; Schiller on, xxxii, 286; Sidney on, xxvii, 30; Voltaire on translations of, xxxiv, 143 (see also Drama)

TRAGIC FRAGMENT, A, vi, 23-4

Traitors, Æschylus on, viii, 193; punishment of, in Dante's HELL, xx, 48, 133-44

Trajan, the Christians and, ix, 428 and note; Dante on, xx, 187 and note; in Dante's PARADISE, 372, 373-4; expedition against Decebalus, ix, 388 note 4; the forum of, 383 note 3; the government of, 374 note 1; justice of, 308-10; Pliny and, 193; Pliny on, 255, 307; Pliny's correspondence with, 374-438; success of empire of, 384 note 1; times of, ii, 219 (32)

Trajano, the chamberlain, xxxi, 126, 151, 153

Tramaglino, Renzo, in I PROMESSI SPOSI, marriage of, forbidden, xxi, 14, 20-1; put off by Abbondio, 26-30; learns of Don Rodrigo, 31-3; plans of vengeance, 34-5; with Lucia, 37; hears of Rodrigo's persecution, 39-41; with Azzecca-Garbugli, 42-9; returns, 53-4; promises not to attack Rodrigo, 72-4; plans for marriage with Lucia, 92-9; threatens to kill Rodrigo, 102-3; wins Lucia's consent, 103-4; at the inn, 113-16; at Abbondio's 117-18, 121, 123-4, 130-1; goes to convent, 134-8; to Monza, 138-43; in Milan, 197-203; in the insurrection, 213, 214-16; in attack on corn superintendents, 220, 222, 228, 230; proposes appeal to Ferrer, 236-8; at the inn, 239-53; arrested, 259-66; rescued, 267; flight to Bergamo, 268-301; disappearance of, 450-1; actual truth of disappearance, 451-3; demanded by Don Gonzalo, 452-3; corresponds with Agnese, 457-61; returns to Bergamo, 563-4; taken with plague, 564; determines to seek Lucia, 565-8; re-

turns to native village, 568-76; goes to Milan, 576-92; learns Lucia's sickness, 592-3; suspected of being a poisoner, 593-7; at the Lazzaretto, 598-603; meets Cristoforo, 604-13; search for Lucia, 614-20; finds Lucia, 620-6; leads Cristoforo to her, 627-9; reunited to Lucia, 631-4; returns to tell Agnese, 635-42; preparations for marriage, 643-5, 650; asks Abbondio to perform ceremony, 651-2; outlawry removed, 659-60; married to Lucia, 661-2; at Bergamo, 662-5; in business with Bortolo, 665-6; daughter born to, 667; lessons he had learned, 667

Trance of Cessation, xlv, 747-53

Tranibores, in Utopia, xxxvi, 187, 192

Tranquillity, Epictetus on, ii, 143 (71), 149 (85), 153 (94), 180 (188); Franklin on, i, 84; Marcus Aurelius on, ii, 213 (3), 224 (2), 240 (31), 250 (37), 251 (43)

Tranquillus, Suetonius, letters to, ix, 212, 424-5

Transcendentalists, belief of the, xxviii, 318

Transfers, taxes on, x, 528-34

Transfiguration, the, xliv, 384 (29-36)

Transformations, Browne on, iii, 295

Transition, beauty lies in, v, 313; Darwin on modes of, xi, 194-8

Transitional Habits, xi, 184-7

Transitional Structures, xi, 184-7

Transitional Varieties, absence of, xi, 179-84; in geological formations, 346-54

Transitoriness, of things, v, 155-6, 159

Translating, as a means of study, ix, 316

Translations, Dryden on, xiii, 67-8; Eliot on, l, 4; Johnson on, xxxix, 214; Shelley on vanity of, xxvii, 350; Voltaire on, xxxiv, 135, 136-7, 143

Transmigration, Egyptian belief in, xxxiii, 63; Lessing on, xxxii, 216-17; rebirth not, xlv, 693, 697-700; Socrates on, ii, 59-63, 74-5; Virgil on, xiii, 235-6

Transparency, cause of, xxxiv, 125-6

Transsilvania, Freeman on, xxviii, 278

Transubstantiation (see Real Presence)

Trapemernes, in Utopia, xxxvi, 246

Traube, Moritz, xxxviii, 331-2 note 1, 361

Travel, Bacon on, iii, 48-50; Confucius on, xliv, 14 (19); Darwin on, xxix, 527-33; Descartes on, xxxiv, 47; education by, iii. 259; xxxii, 40, 46-7; Emerson on, v,

83-4; Epictetus on thirst for, ii, 121 (14), 142 (70); Locke on, xxxvii, 191-4; Pliny on motives of, ix, 345-6

TRAVELLER, ADMONITION TO A, xli, 695-6

TRAVELLER, THE, by Goldsmith, xli, 532-44

TRAVELS AND VOYAGES, xxxiii

Traversaro, Pier, xx, 204 note 16

Treachery, punished in Hell, xx, 133-44

Treason, most horrid where trust is, xviii, 82; punishment of, in Dante's HELL, xx, 48, 133-44; punishment of, in old England, xxxv, 382-3; against United States, xliii, 203

Treasure-trove, Smith on, x, 231-2

Treaties (United States), under the Confederation, xliii, 172, 175; under Constitution, 198 (10), 201 (2); interpretation of, 202

Treaties of Commerce, Smith on, x, 497-13

Trebatius, Cicero on, ix, 118; Cicero and, xii, 257

Trebellius, Plutarch on, xii, 340

Trebonius, on Antony, xii, 343; Cicero on, ix, 118

Trebúat, son of Hua-Lonsce, xlix, 233

Tree, parable of the rotten, xv, 210

TREE AND REED, fable of, xvii, 25

Tree of Knowledge, Milton on, iv, 163, 185-6, 243, 254-5, 280, 281-3

Tree of Life, highest in Eden, iv, 162, 163

Trees, as abodes, Buddha on, xlv, 596 note 12; conditions favorable to, xxix, 57-8; experiments on, in New Atlantis, iii, 183-4; Darwin on, xxix, 319-20; imperfect men, v, 240; Locke on study of, xxxvii, 157; separated sexes in, xi, 113; silicified, xxix, 373; silhified, in the Andes, 351-2; Thoreau on climbing, xxviii, 436

TRELAWNY, AND SHALL, DIE, xlii, 1157-8

Tremellius, Emanuel, xxvii, 14

Trent, city of, Freeman on, xxviii, 265

Trent, Council of, on liberty of press, iii, 206, 208; schoolmen at, 47-8

Tresham, Austin, in A BLOT IN THE 'SCUTCHEON, betrothed to Guendolen, xviii, 361; on Mertoun's suit, 362, 364; in scene between Earl Tresham and Mildred, 382, 384-6; with brother after duel, 394-5; with Thorold at death, 399-400

Tresham, Earl, in A BLOT IN THE 'SCUTCHEON, described by retainers, xviii, 359-60; welcomes Mertoun and his suit, 361-6; Guendolen on, 367-8; hears Mildred's fault from Gerard, 374-7; with Guendolen, sends for Mildred, 378-9; with Mildred, 379-84; under Mildred's window, 388-9; meeting with Mertoun, 390-4; with Guendolen after duel, 394-5; with Mildred after Mertoun's death, 396-9; death of, 400

Tresham, Guendolen, in A BLOT IN THE 'SCUTCHEON, betrothed to Austin, xviii, 361; on Mertoun's suit, 362, 363, 364-6; with Mildred, 366-8; with Earl Tresham, 378-9; in scene between Tresham and Mildred, 382-3, 384-8; with Earl Tresham after duel, 394-5; with Thorold at death, 399-400

Tresham, Mildred, in A BLOT IN THE 'SCUTCHEON, sought by Mertoun, xviii, 358, 362-4; age of, 365; with Guendolen, 366-8; with Mertoun, 369-74; relations with Mertoun, 372-3; discovered by Gerard, 375-7; with Earl Tresham, 379-84; with Guendolen, confesses Mertoun her lover, 386-8; in chamber, waiting for Mertoun, 396; with Thorold after Mertoun's death, 396-9; dies, 399

Trespasses, in Massachusetts, xliii, 74 (24)

Tresvaux, Abbé, Renan on, xxxii, 182

Treverians, Tacitus on the, xxxiii, 111

Treves, Marlowe on, xix, 222-3

Trials, jury, xliii, 202-3; right of prompt, 77 (41); in United States, 202-3, 207 (5), 208 (6, 7); Winthrop on right of, 97

Triassic Period, in Europe, xxx, 361

Tribocians, Tacitus on the, xxxiii, 111

Tribulation, Kempis on, vii, 263 7, 291-2, 304-6, 324-5, 329-30; More on, xxxvi, 105; Pascal on, xlviii, 369

Tribunes, of Rome, xii, 157; power of Roman, ix, 359 note 9

Tributary States, Machiavelli on, xxxvi, 8-12, 18-19; 72-3; More on, 168-9

Trickery, Penn on, i, 363

Trieste, Freeman on, xxviii, 265

Trifles, Confucius on, xliv, 54 (26), 55 (33); Franklin on, i, 84; Marcus Aurelius on, ii, 219 (32); Pascal on, xlviii, 52 (136), 77 (198); Penn on, 365-6 (314); profiting in, iii, 51

Trifling, Locke on, xxxvii, 114

Trimorphism, Darwin on, xi, 61; reciprocal, 319-22

Trina, in WISE FOLKS, xvii, 204-207

Trinculo, in The Tempest, xlvi, 408, 409-12, 415-19, 430-2, 440-441

Trinidad, Raleigh on, xxxiii, 322-3

Trinity, Browne on the, iii, 275 (12); Coleridge on doctrine of the, v, 331-2; Dante on the, xx, 342 note 15, 391, 426-7; first taught by Moses, xlviii, 269 (752); Lessing on doctrine of the, xxxii, 211-12; Mohammed on the, xlv, 1016; Newman on doctrine of the, xxviii, 38; universal idea of a, v, 169

Trinity, The Holy, xlv, 577-8

Trip, in School for Scandal, xviii, 146-7, 161

Triptolemus, Socrates on, ii. 28

Trismegistus, Hermes, iii, 273 note; Milton on, iv, 37; Pascal on, xlviii, 212 (628)

Trist, Nicholas P., xliii, 309

Tristan, in Dante's Hell, xx, 23; Renan on, xxxii, 170, 171; Ysoude and, xiv, 515

Tristram, Sir, xxxix, 25

Triton, references to, xiii, 80; xli, 694

Triumph, The, xl, 297-8

Triumphs, Essay on, Bacon's, iii, 100-101

Triumphs, Cato on, ix, 158; Roman, Bacon on, iii, 84

Trivia, name of Diana, xx, 384 note 2; Hippolytus and, xiii, 269-70

Troilus, and Achilles, xiii, 92

Trochilus, and crocodile, xxxiii, 37

Trophimus the Ephesian, xliv, 479 (29)

Tropics, Darwin on scenery of the, xxix, 522-3, 529-30; More on the, xxxvi, 146; not always habitable, xxxix, 112

Trotti, Alfonso de', xxxi, 283-5

Troubadours, Arnold on the, xxviii, 75-6

Trouble, man born into, xliv, 79 (7); none free from, vii, 237 (1)

Trotter, W. F., translator of Pascal, xlviii

Troubles, Manzoni on. xxi, 668

Trouvères, Renan on the, xxxii, 168-9

Troy, Æschylus on siege of, viii, 25; Augustus planned to rebuild, xiii, 22; downfall caused by Helen, viii, 30-2; Herodotus on plains about, xxxiii, 9; Herodotus on story of, 57-9; the horse of Homer on, xxii, 117-18; the horse of Virgil on, xiii, 104-12; Recuyell of Histories of. xxxix, 5-9; remarks on siege of, xxii. 3; taking of, related by Æneas. xiii, 103-24; taking of, announced, viii, 6, 16-17

Troyes, ancient fair of, x, 33

True Loyal Natives, The, vi, 488

Truelove, Edward, xxv, 232 note 3

Trumball, Sir William, and Dryden, xiii, 430

Trumpeter Taken Prisoner, fable of, xvii, 44

Trumpets, Dryden on, xl, 399

Trunk, The Flying, xvii, 364-70

Trussel, in Edward II, xlvi, 66

Trusts, Penn on, i, 357 (191)

Truth, in art, v, 314; St. Augustine on, love of, vii, 186-7; on authority, Mill on, xxv, 238-49; Bacon on search for, xxxix, 135, 138-47, 150-3; beauty and, Keats on, xli, 903; Berkeley on, xxxvii, 242; Buddha on, xlv, 610-11; Bunyan on, xv, 8-9; Channing on, love of, xxviii, 337-8; with children, xxxvii, 112, 113; commotions due to spread of, xxxix, 46-7; Confucius on, xliv, 9 (22), 13 (8, 9), 30 (24), 53 (5), 54 (28), 55 (31); courtesy and, v, 216; Descartes on, xxxiv, 5, 16-20, 27; diversity of, iii, 240; eloquence and, i, 352-3; Emerson on, v, 27, 67, 78-9, 144-5, 194, 195, 299; exact difficulty of, xxviii, 287, 291-2; of fact and of sentiment, 287-8, 292-3; Franklin on, i, 58; friendship and, v, 115-16; historical, Montaigne on, xxxii, 102; Hindu Krishna on, xlv, 821, 864-5; Hume on, xxxvii, 338, 432; Kempis on, vii, 215-16, 272; liberty necessary to progress of, iii, 232-3, 241-2; Locke on inquiry of, xxxvii, 171; Lowell on, xlii, 1449, 1450, 1459, 1461-2; Milton on, iii, 229, 239-40; Montaigne on, xlviii, 398; men natural lovers of, v, 275, 278; in nature, 293, 388; opinions and, xxxiv, 13, 16; Pascal on, xlviii, 14 (21), 29, 38, 79 (211), 99 (282), 128-9, 194 (582), 305 (857), 427-8, 438; Penn on, i, 353, 354, 404 (164); persecution and, xxv, 230-2; Poe on inculcation of, xxviii, 388; poetry and, 388, 391, 403; xxxix, 294, 296; Quakers on, i, 200; Rousseau's method of seeking, xxxiv, 250-3; Schiller on, xxxii, 244; xxv, 367; search for, ii, 171 (149); Socrates's test of, 94; speaking and hearing, xxviii, 293-4; an attribute of speech, xxxiv, 339; suppressed, Milton on, iii, 203; told with bad intent, xli, 602; said to lie in a well, xxviii, 478; Whittier on, xlii, 1427

Truth, Essay on, Bacon's, iii, 7-9

Truth of Intercourse, Stevenson's, xxviii, 287-94

Truthfulness, Locke on, xxxvii, 126;
    Whitman on, xxxix, 424-5
Truttes, Bernard of, xxxv, 60
Tryon, vegetarian, i, 17, 36
Tsai Wo, disciple of Confucius, xliv,
    11 (21), 16 note, 21 (24), 34 (2),
    62 (21)
Tsai-Yü, xliv, 16 (9)
Tsang Wen, xliv, 16 (17, 18), 53
    (13)
Tsang Wu-chung, xliv, 47 (13), 48
    (15)
Tseng-Hsi, xliv, 37 (25)
Tseng-tzu, disciple of Confucius, xliv,
    13 note, 5 (4), 6 (9), 25 (3), 26
    (4-7), 36 (17) note 13, 42 (24),
    50 (28), 67 (16-19)
Tso Ch'in-ming, xliv, 18 (24)
Tubero, Quintus, T. Gracchus and,
    ix, 21
Tucker, Ellen, wife of Emerson, v, 3
Tucker, Lieut., with Drake, xxxiii,
    245, 267
Tucutuco, Darwin on the, xxix, 61-2
Tudwal, grindstone of, xxxii, 152
Tufton, Sir Louis, xxxv, 23
Tuidle of Ulaid, xlix, 235
Tuisto, god of the Germans, xxxiii,
    95
Tulchinne, the juggler, xlix, 246-7
Tullia, daughter of Cicero, ix, 82,
    151; death of, 17,6; Plutarch on,
    xii, 261 (see also Tulliola)
Tulliola, letter to, ix, 91; Cicero on,
    94
Tullius, M., Cicero on, ix, 102
TULLOCHGORUM, xli, 581-3
Tullus, Domitius, will of, ix, 343-5
Tullus, friend of Cicero, xii, 249
Tullus, the king, xiii, 239
Tultie, Salomon de, xlviii, 13 note
Tumefaction, Harvey on, xxxviii, 121
Tumors, Harvey on treatment of,
    xxxviii, 116-17
Tungrians, the original Germans,
    xxxiii, 96
Tunstall, Bishop of Durham, xxxvi,
    107-8, 109, 114, 119, 143
Tuppukkoowillin, xliii, 152, 156
Turco, Darwin on the, xxix, 287-8
Turdil, in ancient Rome, x, 195
Turenne, Pope on, xi, 441; Sainte-
    Beuve on, xxxii, 131
Turgis, Count of Tortosa, xlix, 129,
    142
Turgot, Mill on, xxv, 76
Turin, Paré on expedition against,
    xxxviii, 9-11
Turkey, Burke on, xxiv, 275; poets
    in, xxvii, 10; Smith on, 253
Turkey-buzzard, Darwin on the,
    xxix, 69, 199, 302
Turkey-cock, hair of the, xi, 103
Turkish Empire, Freeman on races
    in, xxviii, 273-9; Machiavelli on
    the, xxxvi, 16, 17; power of sol-
    diery in, 70

Turks, kindness of, to animals, iii,
    35; Magyars and, xxviii, 235-7;
    royalty of the, iii, 53
Turn-about, Lord, in PILGRIM'S
    PROGRESS, xv, 104
TURN ALL THY THOUGHTS TO EYES,
    xl, 293
Turnaway, in PILGRIM'S PROGRESS,
    xv, 129-30
Turn-back, in PILGRIM'S PROGRESS,
    xv, 156
TURNER, ANDREW, ON, vi, 534
Turner, Charles Tennyson, LETTY'S
    GLOBE, xli, 947
Turnspits, Harrison on, xxxv, 374
Turnus, in the ÆNEID, Lavinia and,
    xiii, 245; descent of, 261; stirred
    by Alecto against Æneas, 258-9;
    beginning of war, 263-5; his allies,
    265-71; shield of, 270; attacks Tro-
    jan fleet and town, 297-302, 314-
    25; renews battle, 336-7; kills
    Pallas, 341-3; drawn from battle
    by Juno, 349-50; challenged by
    Æneas, 364; denounced by Drances,
    368, 373-4; his reply, 375-6; agrees
    to fight Æneas, 377; in cavalry
    fight, 378-80, 392; determines to
    fight Æneas in single combat, 394-
    8; in Rutulian fight, 406-8, 410-
    14; final combat with Æneas, 418-
    28; remarks on duel with Æneas,
    50-2; Dante on, xx, 8; Milton on,
    iv, 264; Sidney on, xxvii, 26
Turpin, Archbishop, in SONG OF RO-
    LAND, xlix, 103, 106; with Roland
    in return to France, 125; at
    Roncesvalles, 137, 140-1, 144, 145,
    147, 149, 150-1, 154, 157-8, 162-3,
    167, 172, 173, 174-5, 176; last
    benediction, 177-80; found by
    Charlemagne, 194; his tomb, 198
Turpio, Ambivius, Cicero on, ix, 63
Turtles, catching of, in Keeling
    Island, xxix, 484
Tuscany, Pliny's description of, ix,
    278-9
Tuscus, Minutius, husband of Corel-
    lia, ix, 319; letter to, 316
Tutelary Angels, Browne on, iii,
    288, 297-8; Elihu on, xliv, 126
    (22); Walton on, xv, 341-2
Tutors, Locke on, xxxvii, 70-85, 88,
    137, 149-52, 164, 179
TWA CORBIES, THE, xl, 75
TWA DOGS, THE, vi, 158-65; editorial
    remarks on, 17; an idyllic poem,
    xxxix, 314
TWA HERDS, THE, vi, 67-70
TWA SISTERS, THE, xl, 54-6
'TWAS NA HER BONIE BLUE E'E, vi,
    571
Tweeddale, Marquis of, xxv, 8
Twelfth Day, celebration of, xv,
    408
Twelve Peers, Charlemagne's, xlix,
    185

Twelve Tables, Law of, xlviii, 209,
210
TWENTY YEARS HENCE, xli, 923
TWENTY-FOUR YEARS AFTER, Dana's,
xxiii, 395-426
TWENTY-THREE, ON BEING ARRIVED
AT THE AGE OF, iv, 30
Twist, Tom, in SHE STOOPS TO CON-
QUER, xviii, 205
TWO APRIL MORNINGS, xli, 615-17
TWO BLACK HOUNDS, story of the,
xvi, 23-6
TWO KINGS' CHILDREN, story of the,
xvii, 208
Two-tongues, Mr., in PILGRIM'S
PROGRESS, xv, 104
TWO YEARS BEFORE THE MAST, xxiii;
editorial remarks on, l, 52
Twrch Trwyth, Arthur and, xxxii,
153
Tyaga, xlv, 876
Tybris, reference to, xiii, 283
Tydeus, Athenian general, xii, 148;
and Menalippus, xx, 137; Virgil's
mention of, in Hades, xiii, 227
Tydides, bravest of the Grecian
train, xiii, 79
Tyler, Wat, leader of the rebellion,
xxxv, 63, 65, 70, 73, 74, 77, 78;
Richard Lyon and, 71; death, 78-9
Tyndall, John, on Faraday, xxx, 4;
on glaciers, 235, 237, 239, 242,
247, 251, 258
Tyndareus, Lede and, xxii, 159
Types, law of succession of, xi, 388-
90
Typhœus, Dante on, xx, 318 note 8;
Virgil on, xiii, 321
Typhon, the giant, viii, 168 and note
22; deposed by Apollo, xxxiii, 74;
Milton on, iv, 95
Typology, Pascal on, xlviii, 218-36
Typotherium, Darwin on the, xi, 378
Tyrannicide, Mill on, xxv, 218 note
Tyranny, adage on, xvi, 36; death
a gentler lord than, viii, 57; law-
lessness and, 135; of majorities,
xxv, 204-6; Milton on, iv, 348; of
opinion, xxv, 206-10; origin of,
xxxiv, 220-4, 230-1; Pascal on,
xlviii, 116 (332); Pope on, xl,
439; of rulers, xxv, 203-4
Tyrant Flycatchers, Darwin on, xxix,
64-5
Tyrants, Cicero on, ix, 27; in
Dante's HELL, xx, 53
Tyre, antiquity of, xxxiii, 27
Tyrian Cynosure, referred to, iv, 55
Tyrker, the German, xliii, 8, 10-11
Tyrnop, pot of, xxxii, 152
Tyro, Homer on, xxii, 25, 158
Tyrrhene Trump, Æschylus on the,
viii, 136
Tyrrhenus, in the ÆNEID, xiii, 383
Tyrrheus, in the ÆNEID, xiii, 260-2
Tyrtæus, Sidney on, xxvii, 9, 14
Tysander, in Trojan horse, xiii, 112

Tythes, Smith on, x, 508-10
TYTLER, WILLIAM, ADDRESS TO, vi,
279-80
Tzetzes, xxxii, 188 note 31
Tzu-ch'an, xliv, 16 (15), 47 (9, 10)
Tzu-chang, disciple of Confucius,
xliv, 8 (18), 9 (23), 16 (18), 36
(17) note 14 (19), 39 (6), 40 (10,
14), 41 (20), 51 (43), 52 (5), 55
(41), 60 (6), 65 (1, 2, 3), 67 (15,
16), 69 (2)
Tzu-ch'in, disciple of Confucius, xliv,
6 (10), 58 (13) note 8, 68 (25)
Tzu-chien, disciple of Confucius,
xliv, 15 (3)
Tzu-hsia, disciple of Confucius, xliv,
5 (7), 7 (8), 10 (8), 20 (11), 34
(2), 39 (5), 42 (22), 45 (17), 47
(10), 65 (3), 66 (4-13)
Tzu-kao, xliv, 35 note 7, 37 (24)
Tzu-kung, xliv, 6 (10, 15), 8 (13),
11 (17), 15 (3, 8), 16 (11, 12, 14),
19 (6) note 9, 21 (28), 23 (14),
28 (6), 29 (12), 34 (2), 35 (12,
15), 36 (18), 39 (7, 8), 42 (23),
45 (20), 46 (24), 48 (18), 50 (30,
31, 37), 52 (2), 53 (9), 54 (23),
61 (19), 62 (24), 67 (20-3), 68
(24-5)
Tzu-lu, disciple of Confucius, xliv,
8 note 5, 15 (6, 7), 16 (13), 18
(25), 19 (6) note 8, 21 (26), 22
(10), 23 (18), 25 (34), 29 (11),
30 (26), 35 (11, 12) note 7 (14),
36 (17) note 15 (21, 23), 37 (24,
25), 40 (12), 42 (1), 43 (3), 46
(28), 47 (13), 48 (17), 49 (23),
50 (38), 51 (41, 45), 52 (1, 3),
56 (1) note 2, 59 (5), 60 (7, 8),
62 (23), 63 (6), 64 (7)
Tzu-sang Po-tzu, xliv, 18 (1)
Tzu-Yu, disciple of Confucius, xliv,
7 (7), 14 (26), 20 (12), 34 (2),
47 (9), 59 (4), 66 (12), 67 (14,
15)

Ubaldini, Ottaviano, xx, 45 note
Ubaldini, Ruggieri degli, xx, 138
note 1
Ubaldini, Ugolina, xx, 205 note 28
Ubaldino degli Ubaldini, xx, 245
note 3
Ubaldo, Guido, fortresses of, xxxvi,
74
Ubbriachi, arms of the, xx, 73
note 4
Uberti, family of, xx, 98 note 5
Uberti, Farinata degli, xx, 42-5
Uberti, Mosca degli, in Hell, xx,
27-8, 119-20
Ubertini, Antonio, xxxi, 58 note 2,
369 note 5
Ubertini, Francesco, xxxi, 58 note 2
Ubians, Tacitus on the, xxxiii, 111
Uchali, king of Algiers, xiv, 404-5,
411
Uddaka, the disciple, xlv, 734-6,
739-40

Udders, developed by use, xi, 29
Ufeus, ally to Turnus, xiii, 269, 270, 272; death of, 411, 417
Ugliness, Browne on, iii, 280; Burke on, xxiv, 102; Emerson on, v, 176, 317
UGLY DUCKLING, THE, xvii, 237-46
Ugo, Marquis, xx, 357 note 25
Ugolina, of Azza, xx, 204 note 20
Ugolini, Antonio, xxxi, 256, 259, 261
Ugolino, Count, xx, 138 note 1, 205 note 28; Arnold on speech of, xxviii, 73; Hugo on, xxxix, 367
Uladislaus, Dante on, xx, 370 note 17
ULALUME, xlii, 1281-3
Ulfin, Sir, xxxv, 190
Uliades, the Samian, xii, 104
ULLIN'S DAUGHTER, xli, 792-4
Ulubræ, xxvii, 29 note 29
Ulrich of Rudenz (see Rudenz)
Ulrich, the smith in WILHELM TELL, xxvi, 406
Ulysses (see Odysseus)
ULYSSES, by Tennyson, xlii, 1007-9; editor's remarks on, l, 19
Umbro, the priest, in the ÆNEID, xiii, 269, 345
Umm Salmâ, xlv, 978 note
Unbelievers, Mill on, xxv, 34-5, 233; moral teachings of, 255; Pascal on, xlviii, 69 (189); salvation of, xx, 368-9, 373-4
Uncertain, town of, in PILGRIM'S PROGRESS, xv, 275
Uncertainty, Burke on terribleness of, xxiv, 73
Uncle Remus, remarks on stories of, xvii, 1
UNCO GUID, ADDRESS TO THE, vi, 192-4
Unconsciousness, as sign of health, xxv, 333-48
Unction, among the ancients, ix, 312 note; Luther on, xxxvi, 279
Undershot Wheels, xxx, 194
UNDERSTANDING, ENQUIRY CONCERNING HUMAN, xxxvii, 303-445
Understanding, Bacon on the, xxxix, 141, 142-3, 151-2; body and, xxiv, 113; Confucius on, xliv, 8 (17), 55 (32); feeling and, xlviii, 10 (6); friendship aids, iii, 72-3; Hobbes on the, xxxiv, 330; Job on, xliv, 116 (12-28); Kant on world of, xxxii, 394; knowledge through the, 382, 383; Marcus Aurelius on destruction of the, ii, 268 (2); Pascal on beliefs of the, xlviii, 406-7; petrifaction of, ii, 124 (23); reason compared with, xxxii, 383; taste and, xxiv, 23-6
Undine, invoked by Faust, xix, 51
Undulation, principle of, in nature, v, 14-15

UNFAITHFUL SHEPHERDESS, THE, xl, 202-3
Unferth, son of Ecglaf, xlix, 19-20, 22, 32, 38, 47, 56
Unicorn, Job on the, xxiv, 59
Uniformity, of human nature, xxxvii, 373-81; effect of, on the imagination, xxiv, 65; cause of sublimity of, 119
UNIFORMITY OF CHANGE, Lyell's, xxxviii, 419-40
Uniformity of Character, how maintained, xi, 115-16
Unio, defined, xxxvi, 298
Union, and division, fable on, xvii, 32; ECCLESIASTES on value of, xliv, 344 (9-12); strength in, xvii, 42
Union, American, Hamilton on, xliii, 216; Jay on, 217-21; Lincoln on, 336-7, 343; Longfellow on, xlii, 1342-3; Washington on, xliii, 253-6
Union Fire Company, formed by Franklin, i, 103-4
Unitarianism, Coleridge on, v, 331-2; formulation of, xxviii, 318; Voltaire on, xxxiv, 84-5
United States, ARTICLES OF CONFEDERATION, xliii, 168; boundaries of, 275-80, 287-8, 299-303, 305-6, 313-14; Carlyle on, v, 334; xxviii, 477; CONVENTION WITH PANAMA, xliii, 478-91; Cuba and, 467-8, 470 (1), 476 (16); DECLARATION OF INDEPENDENCE, 160; democracy in, xxviii, 466-70, 474-7; Emerson on political institutions in, v, 253-6; greatness of nature in, 480; annexation of Hawaii, xliii, 464-6; chances for heroism in, v, 134; remarks on history of, xliii, 3; Jay on, 217-18; Longfellow on, xlii, 1342-3; Lowell on, 1469; Marshall on government of, xliii, 225-6; names of places in, v, 421; natural superiority of, 473; naval forces on Great Lakes, xliii, 283-5; original documents in history of, 160-491; its attitude toward the past, xxxix, 409; opportunities for a poet in, v, 186; policy of, toward Europe and in America, xliii, 297-8; acquisition of Porto Rico, Guam and Philippines, 470-7; Rome and, comparable, ix, 5; 7; Russia and, xliii, 296; science in, xxx, 324; Taine on sects in, xxxix, 457; Thoreau on, xxviii, 418; TREATY WITH FRANCE (1803), xliii, 267-72; TREATY WITH GREAT BRITAIN (1783), 185; TREATY OF 1814 WITH GREAT BRITAIN, 273-82; TREATY OF 1842 WITH GREAT BRITAIN, 299-308; TREATY WITH MEXICO, 309-26; TREATY WITH RUSSIA, 459-63; TREATY WITH SIX NATIONS, 246-9; TREATY WITH

SPAIN (1819), 286-95; TREATY OF
1898 WITH SPAIN, 469-77; Whitman on poetry in, xxxix, 409-32;
Wordsworth on, v, 336
United States Bank, Marshall on
the, xliii, 222-4, 226-30, 238-9
UNITED STATES CONSTITUTION, xliii,
192-211
Unity, David on excellence of, xliv,
319; enforced, ends progress, iii,
232-6, 241; why excluded from
numbers, xlviii, 441; Mohammed's
chapter of, xlv, 893; of nature,
Emerson on, v, 240; of nature,
Epictetus on, ii, 129 (36); of
nature, Marcus Aurelius on, 221
(40, 45), 241 (37, 38), 246 (9),
304 (30); of nature, Pope on, xl,
433-4, 436; in religion, Pascal on,
xlviii, 309 (871); in religion, St.
Paul on, xlv, 501 (10)
UNITY IN RELIGION, ESSAY ON, Bacon's, iii, 11-15
Unity of Type, defined, xi, 472;
law of, 218
Universal-Monarch-Uproar, xlv, 618
Universe, Addison on wonders of, xlv,
547; arrangements of the, prove
God, xxxiv, 255-6, 258-61; Berkeley on wonders of the, xxxvii, 244-
6; Buddha on question of extent
of, xlv, 662-7; Channing on the,
xxxviii, 335-6; Descartes on growth
of the, xxxiv, 36-7; Emerson on,
v, 93-4, 173, 182, 323-36; Goethe
on the, xix, 24; Hindu idea of,
xlv, 864; Hume on man in regard
to, xxxvii, 389-90; man with respect to the, xl, 419-25; Marcus
Aurelius on, coöperation of the,
ii, 221 (40, 45), 235 (9), 241
(38), 242 (43), 246 (9), 265 (50);
Milton's ideas of, iv, 248-50;
nature of ii, 218 (27), 235 (10),
239 (25), 279 (6); Pascal on
greatness of the, xlviii, 25-6; Pope
on the, xl, 433-4; unity and symmetry of the, xxx, 327-8
Universities, defined, xxviii, 31;
courses at, originally apprenticeships, x, 127-8; Luther on, xxxvi,
338-43; necessity of, to highest
education, xxviii, 32-9; origin of,
xxv, 379; sites of, xxviii, 40-51;
trade corporations formerly called,
x, 127
UNIVERSITY, IDEA OF A, by Newman,
xxviii, 31-62
UNIVERSITY CARRIER, ON THE, iv,
26, 27
UNIVERSITY LIFE AT ATHENS, xxviii,
52-62
University of Paris, site of, xxviii,
45-6
University of Pennsylvania, founded
by Franklin, i, 109, 117-19, 172
Unnamed, the, in I PROMESSI SPOSI,

xxi, 327-31; castle of, 333-4; so-
licited by Rodrigo, 335-8; regrets
undertaking against Lucia, 345-7;
with Nibbio, 349-50; with Lucia,
351-4; further doubts and regrets,
358-63; visits Cardinal Federigo,
364-6, 377-88; returns to free Lucia, 393-5; takes her to village,
397-404; announces his reformation, 418-22; sends gift to Agnese,
445; his humility, 502-6; during
German invasion, 506-7, 511-14
Unproductive Labor, in agricultural
system, x, 450-3, 459-63; defined,
270-1; maintenance of, 272-3;
More on, xxxvi, 191-2; proportion of, on what dependent, x,
273-7
Unsocial Acts, Marcus Aurelius on,
ii, 218 (29), 272 (23)
Unteraar Glacier, xxx, 226-7; movement of, 235
UNWIN, MARY, TO, xli, 549-51
UP IN THE MORNING EARLY, vi, 316
UP-HILL, xlii, 1229
Upaka, the ascetic, xlv, 740-1
Upatissa, disciple of Buddha, xlv,
600
Upavāna, xlv, 648-9
Upholsterer, Chaucer's, xl, 21 note
192
Uppalavannā, disciple of Buddha,
xlv, 600
Uprightness, Confucius on, xliv, 20
(17); without courtesy, 25 (2);
with learning, 60 (8)
Uproars, of Buddhism, xlv, 617-18
Upton, critic of Shakespeare, xxxix,
252
Urania, Dante on, xx, 265; Milton
on, iv, 230-1
Urban VIII, in Mantuan contest,
xxi, 455
Urbiciani, Buonaggiunta, xx, 244
and note 1
Urbino, Duke of, xxxi, 76 note 1
Urbino, Gian di, xxxi, 81 note 4
URBS SION AUREA, xlv, 561-2
Urganda, in DON QUIXOTE, xiv, 49-
50
Urgel, Nicholas, Cardinal of, xxxv,
34
Uriah, reference to, xliii, 99
Uriel, in PARADISE LOST, iv, 153-4,
156, 160, 171-2, 216
Urien, a Breton saint, xxxii, 169
Urim, reference to, iv, 388
Uruguay River, Darwin on the,
xxix, 160; sediment of, xxxviii,
424
Use, Burke on effects of, xxiv, 88;
Darwin on, and disuse, xi, 29,
147-52; Keats on, xli, 896; neces-
sary to true possession, xix, 32;
Shakespeare on, xlvi, 158 (see
also Habit)
Usefulness, as source of beauty,

xxix, 427; Marcus Aurelius on, ii, 209 (6), 243 (44)

Usipians, Tacitus on the, xxxiii, 114

Uspallata Mountains, Darwin on the, xxix, 351

Usurers, in Dante's HELL, xx, 72-3; Sheridan on, xviii, 140-1

Usurpation, Machiavelli on, xxxvi, 33-4; Pascal on beginning of, xlviii, 106 (295); Washington on, xliii, 260

Usury, Dante on, xx, 48-9; in India and ancient Rome, x, 99-100; worst method of gain, iii, 94 (see also Interest)

USURY, ESSAY ON, Bacon's, iii, 106-9

Uther Pendragon, xxxix, 24

Utilitarian Doctrine, of structures, xi, 209-15; objections to, 222-3, 229-55

Utilitarian Society, The, xxv, 55-7

Utilitarianism, Carlyle on, xxv, 369-70; Mill on school of, 68-76; Mill's work in, 4-5; James Mill's, 37; origin of name, 55-6

Utility, beauty and, xxiv, 89-91; in ethics, xxv, 213; Locke on, xxxvii, 182-3; Schiller on, xxxii, 223; as end of science, xxxix, 144; Shelley on, xxvii, 368-9; in works of art, xxiv, 91-3

UTOPIA, More's, xxxvi, 143-257; editorial remarks on, 92; l, 48; Peter Giles on, xxxvi, 255-7; Sidney on, xxvii, 20

Utopia, agriculture and live stock in, xxxvi, 183-4, 188-9, 217; antiquity of, 179; bondmen in, 219-20, 223-4; its cities, 182-3, 184, 187, 194, 195; dining-halls, 196, 197-9; distribution in, 195-6, 200-1; dress in, 189; drinks of, 184; education and learning in, 206-7; 217-19, 244-5; families and distribution of population, 194-5; fools and deformed persons, 224; foreign trade, 201, 219; government and magistrates, 187-8, 225; health and prosperity of people, 216-17; hospitals in, 196-7; the island of, 181-2; language of, 217-18; laws and justice, 225; marriage institutions, 221-3; iii, 179 and note 57; occupations and amusements, xxxvi, 188-94, 200; philosophy, 207-16; use of precious metals and stones, 202-6; punishments in, 220, 223-4; readiness of people to learn from others, 179-80, 217, 219; relations with other states, 226-8; religions of, 237-50; sciences, crafts and occupations, 188-94, 200; care of the sick, 220-1; situation of,

256-7; socialism in, 177, 178-9, 186, 195-6, 197, 200-1, 250, 252, 253, 254; statues of good men, 224; strangers in, 197; travelling in, 199-200; wars of, 195, 201-2, 228-37

Utopus, king of Utopia, xxxvi, 182, 186-7, 239-40

Uwaine, Sir, death of, xxxv, 167; Galahad and, 123; Gawaine and, 133-166-7; Seven Knights and, 133; at the White Abbey, 121-2

Uzziel, on guard at Eden, iv, 177

VACATION EXERCISE, AT A, iv, 21-23

Vaccination, Franklin on, i, 100; history of, xxxviii, 150, 214; Woolman on, i, 247

VACCINATION AGAINST SMALLPOX, Jenner's, xxxviii, 153-231

Vacuity, Burke on idea of, xxiv, 63

Vacuum, Pascal on the, xlviii, 450-1

Vadimon, Lake, Pliny on, ix, 346-7

Vagabonds, More on, xxxvi, 163

Vagon, xxxv, 121

Vaila, battle of, xxxvi, 45

Vain-confidence, Mr., in PILGRIM'S PROGRESS, xv, 116-17

VAINGLORY, ESSAY ON, Bacon's, iii, 134-5

Vain-glory, Hobbes on, xxxiv, 355, 387; language of, 358

Vain-hope, in PILGRIM'S PROGRESS, xv, 167

Vaisya, task of a, xlv, 880

Vajirā, the priestess, xlv, 671

Val-holl, xlix, 293 note

Valdabrun, xlix, 118, 153-4

Valdes, in DR. FAUSTUS, xix, 203-5

Valdesso, John, xv, 418-19; Herbert on, 425-6

Valdimagra, Marquis of, xx, 104 note 5

Valdivia, Darwin on, xxix, 315-16; earthquake at, 320-1

Valdovinos, history of, xiv, 46

Vale, Earl de, xxxv, 156; families and distribution of population, 194-5; fools and deformed persons, 224; foreign trade, 201, 219; government and magistrates, 187-8, 225; health and prosperity of people, 216-17; hospitals in, 196-7; the island of, 181-2; language of, 217-18; laws and justice, 225; marriage institutions, 221-3; iii, 179 and note 57; occupations and amusements, xxxvi, 188-94, 200; philosophy, 207-16; use of precious metals and stones, 202-6; punishments in, 220, 223-4; readiness of people to learn from others, 179-80, 217, 219; relations with other states, 226-8; religions of, 237-50; sciences, crafts and occupations, 188-94, 200; care of the sick, 220-1; situation of,

VALEDICTION, by Donne, xv, 342-3

VALEDICTION, FORBIDDING MOURNING, xl, 312-13

Valentine, in FAUST, xix, 152-9

Valentino, Duke, Cæsar Borgia called, xxxvi, 15

Valère, in TARTUFFE, in love with Mariane, xxvi, 198; marriage put off by Orgon, 205-7; Orgon on, 212; with Mariane, on marriage with Tartuffe, 222-32; advises flight of Orgon, 279-80; promised Mariane, 284

Valeria, and Coriolanus, xii, 184-5

Valerian, and Sapor, xxxix, 103

Valerius, character in SOPHOCLES, v, 125-6

Valiant-for-the-Truth, in PILGRIM'S PROGRESS, xv, 177, 299-305, 315-16, 319-20

VALIANT LITTLE TAILOR, THE, xvii, 97-104

Valkyria, xlix, 293 note

Vallejo, Don Guadelope, xxiii, 415

VALLEY OF CAUTERETZ, IN THE, xlii, 1006

Valley of the Shadow of Death, xv, 65-70

Valmiki, Sainte-Beuve on, xxxii, 136

Valor, Browne on true, iii, 291; defined by Hobbes, xxxiv, 354; Emerson on, v, 159; Segrais on, xiii, 25

Valori, Bartolommeo, xxxi, 118 note 3

Valors, our, the best gods, v, 81

Valparaiso, Darwin on, xxix, 269

Value(s), comparative, of food and materials, x, 186-8; exchange, 36-7, 39, 43, 50, 53; in exchange and use, 34-5; labor as determining, 50, 53; of limited or uncertain products, 200-11; measured by corn, 41-3; measured by money, 38-9, 43-44, 49; profits as element in, 51-2; rent as element in, 52-3; scarcity, 188-9; standards of, 45-8; of unlimited productions, 190-200 (see also Prices)

Vampire-bats, in Chile, xxix, 32

Vanbrugh, Sir John, Voltaire on, xxxiv, 141-2

Vandals, learning despised by, xxxv, 404; origin of the, xxxiii, 96

Van Diemen's Land, climate of, xxix, 260; Darwin on, 470-3

Vandyke, Hazlitt on, xxvii, 293

Vane, Sir Henry, A HEALING QUESTION, xliii, 126-46; sonnet to, iv, 85

Vanessa (see Vanhomrigh)

Vangiones, Tacitus on the, xxxiii, 111

Vanholt, Duke of, in FAUSTUS, xix, 235

Vanhomrigh, Esther, Swift and, xxviii, 6, 24-6

Vanini, Berkeley on, xxxvii, 247

Vanities, worldly, vii, 214 (4)

Vanity, all is, xliv, 339-42, 354; Fielding on, xxxix, 189; folly of, vii, 219-20; Franklin on, i, 6; of life, xlviii, 62 (161-2), 63 (164); Pascal on human, 60 (150); Penn on, i, 410-11; in speech, 401 (119); the strongest human motive, xxviii, 96-8; Woolman on, i, 285

Vanity, Limbo of, iv, 149-50

Vanity Fair, in PILGRIM'S PROGRESS, xv, 93-4; altered after Faithful's death, 283-4

Vansen, in EGMONT, xix, 267-70, 294-7

Vapor, differs from gas in permanency, xxx, 105

Varchi, Benedetto da Monte, xxxi, 34 note; sonnet on Cellini, 173, 175

Varenus, and the Bithynians, ix, 313-15

Vargas, Diego Peres of, xiv, 66-7

Vargas, Garcia Perez de, xiv, 513

Variability, causes of, xi, 25-9, 56; due to changed conditions, 145-7; due to use and disuse, 147-52; hereditary, 127; of highly developed parts, 161-4; in important organs, 60; of mongrels and hybrids, 327-8; of multiple, rudimentary or low structures, 160; of secondary sexual characters, 166-7; of specific and generic organs, 164-8

Variation(s), analogous, xi, 168-71; Burke on beauty in, xxiv, 98, 130; climate not the cause of, xi, 395-6; correlated, 29-30, 155-8; Darwin on abrupt, 258-61; first appearance of, 483-4; inheritance of, 30-1; of instincts, 266; laws of, 145-77; St. Hilaire on cause of, 11; Spencer on cause of, 16; spontaneous (see Spontaneous Variation); technical meaning of, 58; under domestication, 25-57; under nature, 58-75; *Vestiges of Creation* in, 13

Varieties, classification of, xi, 460; compared with species, 62-9; evidence of their being incipient species, 72, 73, 74, 165, 330; extinct intermediate, 334-5; 346-54; fertility of, 322-6; how they become species, 122-9; intercrossing between, 112; intermediate, why absent or rare, 179-84; meaning of, 58; not clearly distinct from species, 349-50; of same species, struggle with each other, 90

Variety, of opinion, Milton on, iii, 235-7, 240; Pascal on, xlviii, 48 (114); source of pleasure in, xxvii, 277

Varro, M. Terentius, on country life, xxvii, 65; Pompey's lieutenant, xii, 306; works of, lost, xxvii, 361

Varus, and the Germans, xxxiii, 117

Vasari, Giorgio, Cellini and, xxxi, 179, 180-1, 439 note

Vasava, xlv, 844

Vassellario (see Vasari)

Vastness, in architecture, xxiv, 67; a cause of the sublime, 63-4; not lovable, 133-4; physical cause of sublimity of, 115-16

Vatable, xlviii, 288 note

Vatinius, Cicero and, ix, 124, 132; xii, 232; Cicero on, 247; Vaudeville, M. de, xxxviii, 42-5

Vaughan, Benj., letter of, to Franklin, i, 72-77
Vaughan, Henry, poems by, xl, 356-8
Vauvenargues, Sainte-Beuve on, xxxii, 137
Vedius, P., Cicero on, ix, 157
Vega, Lope de, xxvi, 3; Carlyle on, xxv, 420
Vegetable Kingdom, beauty in the, xxiv, 8; distinguished from animal, xxxviii, 356-9
Vegetarianism, Franklin's, i, 17, 36
VEIL, BEYOND THE, xl, 356-7
Veillantif, horse of Roland, xlix, 124, 137
Veins, arteries anciently called, xxxviii, 85; arteries and, 108, 116, 122, 145-6, 147; communication of, 120; Harvey on the, 124-8, 145
Vejento, in Certus case, ix, 359
Veleda, worshipped as divinity, xxxiii, 100
Velitræ, colony of, xii, 163-4
Vellutus, condemns Coriolanus, xii, 169, 170; protests against colony of Velitræ, 163; first of the tribunes, 157
Velocity, as a motive force, xxx, 194-6; measurement of working power of, 196-7; power and, in machines, 190-3
Vena Arteriosa, xxxviii, 91
Vena Cava, xxxviii, 96, 108
Venafro, Antonio of, xxxvi, 79
Vendosme, M. de, xxxviii, 22-3
Venedians, Tacitus on the, xxxiii, 122-3
Veneration, never dies out, v, 29
Venery, Franklin's rule of, i, 84
VENETIAN REPUBLIC, ON THE EXTINCTION OF THE, xli, 691-2
Veneziano, Bastiano, xxxi, 116, 118
Venezuela, cities of, xxxiii, 314
Vengeance, Drake on, xxxiii, 133; Raleigh on Divine, xxxix, 73-93 (see also Retribution)
VENI CREATOR SPIRITUS, xiv, 559
Venice, Browning on, xlii, 1122; growth and decline of, xxxvi, 45; land-tax of, x, 503-4; King Louis and, xxxvi, 13, 14, 15, 25, 78; mercenaries of, 45; overthrown by Pope Julius, 41; policy toward subject cities, 73; Pope on, xl, 448; power of, before French invasion, xxxvi, 40; Shelley on, xli, 860-1; situation of, v, 347; in 16th century, xxvii, 411; trade of, x, 417; Wordsworth on, xli, 691-2
Venison, price of, x, 195-6
Venner, Thomas, xxxiii, 237, 253
Venta Cruz, Drake at, xxxiii, 184-5

Ventana, Sierra de la, xxix, 119-22
Ventidius, xii, 359, 360, 361; in Parthia, xxxiii, 116-17
Ventidius, in ALL FOR LOVE, returns from East, xviii, 24-7; scene with Antony, 27-35; conversation with Antony on Octavius, 39-40; on Alexas, 40-1; on Cleopatra's gifts, 41-3; in meeting of Antony and Cleopatra, 44-9; advises Antony to seek terms, 51-3; on Antony's love, 55-6; brings Octavia to Antony, 57-61; in meeting of Dolabella and Cleopatra, 66-7, 69, 72; tells Antony of Dolabella's treachery, 73-8; with Antony after last defeat, 88-93; death, 94; Dryden on character of, 24
Ventilation, need of, xxx, 172
Ventricles, of the heart, xxxviii, 83, 84, 85, 86-91, 93, 105, 138-9, 140, 141, 142; right and left, 73-4, 76-7
Venulus, in the ÆNEID, xiii, 272, 369-71, 387-8
Venus, Adonis and, alluded to, iv, 73; born of the sea, xl, 373; Emerson on, fable of, v, 313; Mars's minion, xlvi, 426 note 15; mother of mirth, iv, 31; statue of, in Vatican, xxxi, 332; zone of, referred to, iv, 381 (see also Aphrodite)
Venus, in ÆNEID, seeks Jove in Trojan's behalf, xiii, 83-4; meeting with Æneas, 86-9; persuades Cupid to enter form of Ascanius, 98-9; warns Æneas to fly, 123-4; plans marriage of Æneas and Dido, 159-61; seeks Neptune in Æneas's behalf, 208; seeks aid of Vulcan for Æneas, 284-5; brings Æneas arms, 292; complains to Jove, 327-8; cures Æneas of his wound, 409
Venus, the planet, Dante on, xx, 148 note 3, 258; Dante's third Heaven, 316-17
"Venus de Medici's," Burke on the, xxiv, 102
Veracity, in art, v, 314
Veragua, town of, xxxiii, 188
Verania, wife of Piso, Regulus and, ix, 238
Verbal Nouns, Johnson on, xxxix, 199
Verbosity, Montaigne on, xxxii, 46
Vercingetorix, xii, 296, 298
Verdi, Francesco and Antonio, xxxi, 58 note
Verdicts, special, in Massachusetts, xliii, 75 (31)
Vere, Baron, character of, v, 400
Verecundus, grammarian of Milan, vii, 132; kindness and conversion of, 146-7

Vergentorix, xii, 296 and note, 298
Vergezio, Giovanni, xxxi, 101 note 5
Vergilia, wife of Coriolanus, xii, 185, 186
Vergilius, Caius, Cicero and, xii, 253
Verginius, Rufus, Pliny on, ix, 221-3
Vermilion, Miss, in SCHOOL FOR SCANDAL, xviii, 129
Verneuil, M. de, on changes of species, xi, 374-5
Vernon, Franklin and, i, 32, 34, 35, 54, 63
Veronese, Hugo on, xxxix, 369
Verres, Cicero and, ix, 3; prosecution of, xii, 230-1
Verrocchio, Andrea del, xxxi, 418
Verse, in the drama, Hugo on, xxxix, 388, 390-3; Pope on advantages of, xl, 417; Sidney on, xxvii, 15, 34-5; Voice and, sisters, iv, 41
Verses, Locke on making of, xxxvii, 159-60, 173; James Mill on making of, xxv, 15
Versification, Montaigne on, xxxii, 63-4; Shelley on, xxvii, 350
Versifying, Sidney on, xxvii, 52-3
Vertumnus, and Pomona, iv, 273
Verulam (see Bacon, Francis)
Vesalius, on the heart, xxxviii, 83
Vespasian, death of, iii, 10; empire foretold to, 96; Jerusalem and, xxxviii, 32; miracles of, xxxvii, 407-8; night business of, ix, 243; Pascal on miracles of, xlviii, 286 (816); Tacitus on, iii, 32; times of, ii, 219 (32)
Vesper, Keats on, xli, 904
Vespucci, Amerigo, ACCOUNT OF HIS FIRST VOYAGE, xliii, 29-46; Emerson on, v, 407; life of, xliii, 29 note
Vespucci, Giorgio Antonio, xliii, 30
Vesta, reference to, iv, 35
Vestal Virgins, office of, ix, 265 note
Vestiges of Creation, xi, 13-14
Vesuvius, Pliny on the eruption of, ix, 298-301, 303-5
Veto, presidential, xliii, 195-6
Vetus, and Cæsar, xii, 277
Vexation, Eliphaz on, xliv, 79 (2); Marcus Aurelius on, ii, 204 (16), 239 (27), 250 (38)
Vibius, and Cicero, xii, 252-3
Vibration, frequency of, defined, xxx, 264
Vibrios, xxxviii, 345-59, 385-5; butyric, 343-4; Pasteur on, 338-40
Vibullius, Cicero on, ix, 120-1
Vice, Augustine, St., on, vii, 60-1; beginnings of, xxxiv, 208; Burns on wretchedness of, vi, 338; degrees of, xxvi, 166; Emerson on, v, 71, 104; Epictetus on, ii, 182 (3), 183 (10); false arguments of, iv, 66; Franklin on, i, 91, 96; Hobbes on, xxxiv, 429; Jonson on

knowledge of, xl, 301; knowledge of, Mrs. Herbert on, xv, 380; knowledge of, necessary to virtue, iii, 212-13; Lessing on worldly retribution of, xxxii, 201-2; Locke on knowledge of, xxxvii, 80-1; not natural to man, xxxiv, 191-2, 277-82, 287; nature opposed to, v, 28, 101; necessary to virtue, iii, 330; Pascal on, xlviii, 45 (102); Pope on, xl, 431; Pope on supposed prosperity of, 443-9; prosperity and, Bacon on, iii, 17; its own punishment, xvii, 33; public opinion and, xxvii, 397-8; Rousseau on punishment of, xxxiv, 273; Scriptural warrant for, xv, 263-5; taught to children, xxxvii, 30-3; Taine on, xxxix, 441; Whitman on punishment of, 426-7
Vice-President (United States), amended method of election, xliii, 209-10; former manner of election, 199 (2, 3); impeachment, 202 (4); president of Senate, 194 (4); succession to presidency, 200 (5), 209 (12); qualifications, 210; term of office, 199 (1)
Vices and Virtues, game of, xxxvi, 190-1
Vich Ian Vohr, v, 215
Vicissitude, Arabian inscriptions on, xvi, 315-19, 326-7, 331-2, 334-6; Browne on, of states, iii, 282; Carlyle on, xxv, 366-7; Casaubon on, xxxix, 77; Emerson on, v, 155-6; Marcus Aurelius on, ii, 219 (33, 36), 231 (23), 234 (4), 236 (15); Montaigne on, xxxii, 5-6; Raleigh on, xxxix, 74, 100-1, 103
VICISSITUDE, ODE ON PLEASURES OF, xl, 472-3
VICISSITUDE OF THINGS, ESSAY ON THE, iii, 143-7
Vicorati, Francesco da, xxxi, 7
Victorinus, Augustine, St., on, vii, 125-7
Vicuna, Darwin on the, xxix, 380
Vides, governor of Cumana, xxxiii, 343, 344
VIGIL STRANGE I KEPT, xlii, 1485-6
Vigne, Pierro delle, in Dante's HELL, xx, 56 and note
Vigo, Drake at, xxxiii, 240-1
Vigo, John de, xxxviii, 11
Viguiere, Pauline de, v, 315
Vijayuttara, the conch, xlv, 632
VILLAGE BLACKSMITH, THE, xlii, 1323
Villagers, Thoreau on, xxviii, 413
Villars, Marquis de, xxxviii, 35, 39
Villemarqué, M. de la, xxxii, 145, 175
Villiers, Charles, Mill on, xxv, 54, 83, 84, 85
Villiers, George, Mill on, xxv, 84, 85
Villiers, George, 1st Duke of Buck-

ingham, iii, 5; Voltaire on, xxxiv, 150; Wotton on, v, 421

Villiers, George, 2nd Duke, Clarendon on, v, 362; his house at Cliefden, xxxix, 160 note 1; Voltaire on, xxxiv, 150

Villon, Arnold on, xxviii, 80-1

Vilmund, lover of Borgny, xlix, 457, 458

Vinci, Leonardo da, xxvii, 293; his cartoon of capture of Piso, xxxi, 24 and note; Cellini on, 374-5; Guido and, xxxix, 450

Vincula, San Pietro ad, xxxvi, 29, 30

Vindicianus, St. Augustine and, vii, 49-50, 108

Vindictiveness, Penn on, i, 356 (185) (see Revenge)

Vine, Cicero on culture of the, ix, 65-6

Vineyards, profits of, x, 165-6; value of, 163-4

Vingi, the messenger, xlix, 364, 365, 368

VINLAND, THE VOYAGES TO, xliii, 5-22; remarks on, l, 22

Vintner, in FAUSTUS, xix, 227-8

Violence, punishment of, in Hell, xx, 47, 51-73

Violets, for modesty, vi, 431; Wotton on, xl, 295

Violins, Dryden on, xl, 399

Viper, Harrison on the, xxxv, 362-3

Virbius, son of Hippolytus, xiii, 269-70

Virgil, ÆNEID of, xiii, 75-428; an astrologer, xxxix, 167; Augustine, St., on study of, vii, 16-17; Augustus and, xiii, 18-19; xxxix, 171; on generation of bees, xxxv, 365; birthplace of, xx, 220 note 4; body of, removed to Naples, 155 note; Burke on, xxiv, 75; Burke on his figure of Fame, 57; Burke on his picture of Hell, 63; Burke on his picture of Vulcan's forge, 143; Caxton on, xxxix, 26; Cowley on, xxvii, 65; Dante's guide to Hell and Purgatory, xx, 7-13; in Dante's Limbo, 173; Dryden on, xiii, 14-69; xl, 406; the Georgics of, xxxix, 314; Homer and, xiii, 6; xxxix, 164-6; Hugo on, 382; Italicus and, ix, 247; life and works, xiii, 3-4; Locke on, xxxvii, 168; machinery of, xiii, 48-52; reputed a magician in Middle Ages, xix, 223 note; Montaigne on, xxxii, 92; morals of his poem, xiii, 19-39; Raleigh on, xxxix, 119; a republican at heart, xiii, 17-18; on rustic life, xxvii, 72-3; Sainte-Beuve on, xxxii, 136; Scaliger on, xxvii, 54; Shelley on, 361; Sidney on Georgics of, 14; similes of, xiii, 42-4; Spenser

on, xxxix, 65; times of, xiii, 16-17; Wordsworth on figure of, xxxix, 317, 319

VIRGIL, To, by Tennyson, xlii, 1051-2; editor's remarks on, l, 20

Virgilianæ, Sortes, xxvii, 10-11

Virgilius, Browne on, iii, 292

Virginia, Drayton on, xl, 231; Quakers in, i, 288; Winthrop on patent of, xliii, 93

VIRGINIA, FIRST CHARTER OF, xliii, 51-61

VIRGINIA, MASSACHUSETTE TO, xlii, 1419-24

VIRGINIAN VOYAGE, TO THE, xl, 230-2

Virginity, Paul, St., on, xlv, 510 (25-6, 34), 511 (37); Milton on, iv, 58, 67

Virginius, Flavius, story of, ix, 236 note

VIRGINS, To THE, xl, 345

Virgoe, Thomas, xxxviii, 165-6

Virgularia Patagonica, Darwin on, xxix, 111-12

Virnes, Christopher de, Cervantes on, xiv, 57

Virtue, adversities help unto, vii, 312 (2); in ambition and in authority, iii, 32; Augustine, St., on, vii, 60; Bacon on, iii, 17, 104, 105-6; beauty and, 111-12; Browne on, 320, 340; Burke on beauty in, xxiv, 95-6; Burns on, vi, 338; cannot change at once, xxvi, 166; Channing on, xxviii, 334; Cicero on, ix, 25-6, 37, 41, 44, 48; the company of, ii, 182 (2); Confucius on highest, xlv, 21 (27), 36 (19); consists in comparison, xxxiv, 362; the chief aim in education, xxxvii, 57-8, 82, 83, 163, 184; Emerson on, v, 26-9, 71, 77, 139, 162-3, 289; an object of envy, ix, 201; Epictetus on, ii, 140 (66), 161 (119); Epicurus on, xxxvii, 423; examples of, ii, 297 (26); excessive, xlviii, 121 (353), 122 (357); fortune and, xxxi, 12; Franklin on, i, 83-4, 90 note 91; Franklin's Art of, 90-1; Franklin's party of, 93-5; alone is free, ii, 183 (10); iv, 73; friendship and, ix, 15, 18, 22, 26, 37, 42; happiness and, Pope on, xl, 443-50; the hereafter, belief in, and, iii, 312, 317-18; Hindu ideas of, xlv, 858, 870, 880, 881; Hobbes on, xxxiv, 429; Hume on standards of, xxvii, 216-17; Hume on teaching of, xxxvii, 305; immortality, belief in, and, xxxvi, 241, 242; intellectual, xxxiv, 362-3; intrinsic worth of, xxxii, 366; Jonson on, xl, 301; Kant on pure, xxxii, 357 note; knowledge of

world and, xxxvii, 54; in Latin equivalent to courage, xii, 153; learning and, xxxvii, 136; Locke on, 44, 123, 126; love of, natural to man, xxxiv, 277-82; loveableness of, xxiv, 94-5; Machiavelli on, xxxvi, 53; Machiavelli on appearance of, 60-1; Marcus Aurelius on, ii, 237 (17); measurement of, xlviii, 121 (352); Milnes on pleasures of, xlii, 1098-9; Milton on, iv, 56, 62, 123, 179, 375; Milton on study of, iii, 252, 254; modesty and, ix, 262; Montaigne on, xxxii, 9-10, 52-3; More on, xxxvi, 208, 209, 210, 215, 216; nature leagued with, v, 101-2; no penalty to, 105; not mere absence of vice, xxvii, 277; not virtue if she tumble, xviii, 202; ostentation of, ii, 177 (176); Pascal on maxims of, xlviii, 14 (20); passion and, xl, 430; Penn on complete, i, 375; pleasure in seeing, ii, 244 (48); Plutarch on, xii, 86; Plutarch on contemplation of, 37-8; Pope on vice and, xl, 431; popular idea of, v, 67; pure, tests of, xxxii, 327-34; quotations on, i, 86-7; "reason in practice," xxxii, 130; refinement and, 250, 269; reward of, xxxiv, 272; reward of, Emerson on, v, 27, 90; reward of, Jonson on, xl, 305; reward of, Lessing on, xxxii, 201-2; reward of, Pliny on, ix, 202-3; reward of, Rousseau on, xxxiv, 270; its own reward, ii, 163 (126), 256 (73); iii, 312; xxxix, 427-8; xlv, 809, 810; riches and, iii, 92; Rousseau on grounds of, xxxiv, 284-6; Rousseau on natural, 190-5; sensuous and ascetic, xxviii, 175-9; Shakespeare on, xlvi, 108; Sidney on teachers of, xxvii, 17-28; Socrates on, ii, 17, 58, 111; Taine on, xxxix, 441; Tennyson on wages of, xlii, 1039; through love and fear, xl, 303; trial necessary to, ii, 156 (106); iii, 212-13, 218-19; unconsciousness of true, xxv, 339-41; vice necessary to, iii, 330; Wordsworth on, xxxix, 333 (see also Morality)

VIRTUE, by Herbert, xl, 351-2

Virtues, the seven, xx, 173 notes 2 and 3

VIRTUOUS YOUNG LADY, TO A, iv, 80-1

Vis Inertiæ, Hume on, xxxvii, 365 note

Vis Viva, defined, xxx, 195; measure of, 197 note; transformed to weight, 197

Visakha, story of, xlv, 770-98

Visconti, Galeazzo de', xx, 179 notes 5 and 7

Vishnu, xlv, 844; in the BHAGAVAD-GITA, 800

Vishnu Sarma, quoted, v, 302

Vision, Burke on method of, xxiv, 115

VISION, A, by Burns, vi, 513-14

VISION, THE, by Burns, vi, 180-90

VISION OF MIRZA, Addison's, xxvii, 77-81

Visions, Hobbes on, xxxiv, 328-9; Walton on, xv, 341-2

Vitaliano del Dente, xx, 73 note 6

Vitelli, Burke on the, xxiv, 282; Cæsar Borgia and, xxxvi, 28, 33, 48

Vitelli, Niccolo, at Citta di Castello, xxxvi, 74

Vitelli, Paolo, xxxvi, 26, 31, 44

Vitellius, Mucianus and, iii, 148

Vitellozzo, Machiavelli on, xxxvi, 32, 33

Vitet, M., on CHANSON DE ROLAND, xxviii, 71

Vitruvius, on architecture, v, 182; xxxi, 8

Vittore, Father, in THE BETROTHED, xxi, 606

Vivian, Christian king, xlix, 208

Vivien, and Merlin, xxxii, 160

VIVIEN'S SONG, xlii, 1006-7

Vivisection, Harvey on, xxxviii, 79; in New Atlantis, iii, 184

Vocation, Bacon on choosing, for children, iii, 21; content in one's, ii, 219 (31); Epictetus on choice of, 155 (104); Pascal on choice of, xlviii, 41 (97), 48 (116), 49 (117)

Voconius, Cicero on, xii, 248

VOGLER, ABT, Browning's, xlii, 1144-8

Voice, power of human, i, 107-8; verse and, sisters, iv, 41

Voiture, Voltaire on, xxxiv, 148

Voland, the Devil called, xix, 168

Volcanic Bombs, xxix, 519-20

Volcanoes, as dependent on changes of surface, xxix, 506-7; earthquakes and, relations of, 329; Geikie on, xxx, 348; simultaneous eruption of, xxix, 309-10

Volition, Rousseau on, xxxiv, 256 (see also Will)

Volscians, Coriolanus with the, xii, 173-5; final defeat, 191; war of Rome against the, 158-9; second war with Rome, 177-88

Volsung, son of Rerir, xlix, 278-9, 280-2

VOLSUNGA SAGA, xlix, 275-381; PROLOGUE IN VERSE, 272-3; remarks on the, 266-9

Volsungs, names of, xlix, 270; songs dealing with, 383-464

VOLSUNGS AND NIBLUNGS, story of the, xlix, 265-381; editor's remarks on, l, 21

Voltaic Batteries, xxx, 78, 214; ex-

amples of action of, 134-5; power of, 131

Voltaire, Carlyle on, xxv, 438; on circumstances, xxviii, 454; Corneille and, xxxix, 450; on Greek drama, 382; Hazlitt on, xxvii, 294; on Horace, xxxii, 138-9; Lessing and, xxvi, 286; LETTERS ON THE ENGLISH, xxxiv, 65-162; remarks on LETTERS of, l, 25, 35; life and works, xxxiv, 64; Sainte-Beuve on, xxxii, 128, 137; on Shakespeare, xxxix, 223, 235, 238; on systems, 395; on taste, 404; *Le Temple du Goût*, 404

Volterra, Daniello da, xxxi, 453 note
Volterra, Niccolaio, xxxi, 19
Voltimand, in HAMLET, xlvi, 93-4, 118-19
Volumnia, mother of Coriolanus, xii, 155; begs him to desist from war, 185-8
Volusus, in the ÆNEID, xiii, 378
Von Baer, on bees, xi, 386; on embryos, 479; on organization, 135
Vopiscus, name of, xii, 162
Vortigern, Hengist and, v, 286
Voss, on Milton, xxxix, 336
Voters, qualifications of, v, 251-2
Voting, right of, in United States, xliii, 211 (see also Elective Franchise)
Vows, Dante on, xx, 303-6; ECCLESIASTES on, xliv, 345 (4-5); Hobbes on, xxxiv, 413-14; Shakespeare on, xlvi, 103, 104
VOYAGE OF THE BEAGLE, Darwin's, xxix; editor's remarks on, l, 46, 52
Voyages, Darwin on sea, xxix, 527-9
VOYAGES AND TRAVELS, xxxiii
Voyages and Travels, books dealing with, l, 52-3
Vulcan, in the ÆNEID, xiii, 285-7; forge of, 286; forge of, Burke on, xxiv, 143; lameness of, v, 311; sons of, iv, 64
Vulgarity, Confucius on, xliv, 8 (14), 13 (11), 14 (16), 25 (36), 41 (16), 46 (23, 25, 26), 47 (7), 49 (24), 54 (1), 51 (20), 55 (33), 57 (8); Ruskin on, xxviii, 116
Vulpius, Christiane, wife of Goethe, xix, 3
Vultures, Harrison on, xxxv, 357-8
Vyasa, Sainte-Beuve on, xxxii, 136
Wacarima, Mount, xxxiii, 383
Wace, Robert, xxxii, 168
Wadsworth, Gen., at Gettysburg, xliii, 351
Wage-earners, interest of, connected with general interests, x, 218
Wager, Pascal on necessity of the, xlviii, 84-7
Wages, affected by market fluctuations, x, 62-3; in by-employments, 124; relation to cost of living,

78-82, 87-8, 90-2; defined, 55; dependent on state of society, 72-7, 85-6; determination of, 58; determined by competition, 68-72, 295; determined by time, hardship and skill, 50; in England (1772), i, 318; tendency of, to equality, x, 105; in exclusive trades, 66; industry, relation of, to, 86-9; increase of money, effect of, on, 296; inequalities of, due to government interference, 126-50; natural inequalities of, 106-17; in novel trades, 121-2; population determined by, 83-5; price of commodities, an element in, 50; prices affected by high, 103-4; profits and, confounded, 56-7, 118-19; proportion of, between different employments, 67; real, 82-3; regulation of, by law, 150-1; relation of, to rates of interest, 94-6; scarcity, 122; taxes on, 534-8; effect of taxes on consumption and, 542-3

WAGES, by Tennyson, xlii, 1039
Waggoner, fable of the, xvii, 36
Wagner, in FAUST, xix, 27-9, 40-8
Wagner, in DR. FAUSTUS, xix, 202, 205-6, 210-12, 234, 236
Wagner, Moritz, on isolation of species, xi, 116
WAIF, PROEM TO LONGFELLOW'S, xxviii, 391-2
Wain, constellation of the, xx, 429; Homer on the, xxii, 78
Wainfleet, William, xxxv, 402
Wakan, xliii, 152
Wakes, Luther on, church, xxxvi, 324
Waking, Locke on method of, xxxvii, 23-4
Waldseemuller, Vespucci and, xliii, 29 note
Wales, agriculture of, xxxv, 326; bards of, xxvii, 10; Christianity in, xxxii, 181; education in (1848), xxviii, 160; lead mines of, xxxv, 340; literature of, xxxii, 144-5, 150-70; realm of, Milton on, iv, 17; Renan on, xxxii, 143; soil of, xxxv, 324, 377
Walid Ibn Mughairah, xlv, 890 note 2, 909 note
Walker, Mr., of the *Times*, v, 467
WALKING, ESSAY ON, Thoreau's, xxviii, 405-38
Wallace, A. R., Darwin and, xi, 5-6, 21; on origin of species, 402
Wallace, William, Burns on, vi, 93, 147, 527, 183
Walleechu, Indian god, xxix, 79-80
Wallenstein, quoted, xxi, 490
Waller, Edmund, Dryden on, xxxix, 161, 171; poems by, xl, 366-7; Voltaire on, xxxiv, 147-50

Walls, why less grand than colonnades, xxiv, 119-20

Walpurgis-Night, in FAUST, xix, 161 76; Dream, 176-84; remarks on, 6

Walsh, William, Dryden on, xiii, 431

Walter, Count, in SONG OF ROLAND, xlix, 125, 146-7, 172-4

Waltham, Thomas, at Otterburn, xxxv, 95

Walton, Izaak, LIFE OF DR. DONNE, xv, 327-74; LIFE OF HERBERT, 377-426; life and works, 326; LIVES, editorial remarks on, l, 33

Walworth, Nicholas, xxxv, 67, 71, 79, 80

WALY, WALY, O, xl, 331-3

Wamesut, town of, xliii, 154

WANDERING WILLIE, vi, 482-3

Wang-sun Chia, xliv, 10 note 6

Want-wit, in PILGRIM'S PROGRESS, xv, 295

Wanton, Madame, in PILGRIM'S PROGRESS, xv, 73, 190

Wants, and pleasures, xli, 538

Wanuretona, xxxiii, 368-9

War(s), ancient and modern, iii, 84, 147; Arjuna on, xlv, 803-4; benefit of, iii, 83; Blake on, xli, 603; causes of, iii, 82-3; expenses, x, 468-71; fall of empires always accompanied by, iii, 146; improvements in art of, v, 86; Goethe's Jetter on, xix, 252-3; Hindu teachings on, xlv, 808; Hobbes on causes and state of, xxxiv, 404; Hobbes on desires that lead to, 385; a horrid ruthless fiend, xxvi, 380; judgment of God, i, 246; justification of, iii, 52; Machiavelli on preparation for, xxxvi, 50-2; maintenance of, x, 338-42; Massinger on school of, xlvii, 829; Milton on, iv, 338-9, 398; More on, xxxvi, 228; More on preparation for, 153-4; over-population a cause of, iii, 146; pleasure in distant, 8; provisions for, under the Confederation, xliii, 171-2, 174, 175; provisions for, under Constitution, 197 (11-16), 199 (3); Quaker attitude toward, i, 112-15, 198-200, 222, 225-8; xxxiv, 69; readiness for, of different states of society, xxvii, 391-2; Rousseau on, xxxiv, 218; rules of, in treaty with Mexico, xliii, 324-6; Socrates on cause of, ii, 55; Tennyson on, xlii, 1054-5, 1067, 1096-7; true strength in, iii, 78; unjust, support of, xxviii, 134-5; Voltaire on religious, xxxiv, 86; Washington on preparation for, xliii, 260-1; Woolman on, i, 263

War of 1812, Treaty of Peace, xliii, 273-82

Warbeck, Perkin, Bacon on, xxxiv, 103

Warburton, William, Lessing on, xxxii, 200; Johnson on, xxxix, 250-1; on Shakespeare's plays, 246, 247

Ward, Nathaniel, xliii, 70 note

Wardlaw, Henry, on the Scotch, xxxv, 286

Ware, Rev. Henry, colleague of Emerson, v, 3

Warfare, in Utopia, xxxvi, 228-37

Wargny, Robert of, xxxv, 11

Warner, Master, in SHOEMAKER'S HOLIDAY, xlvii, 461-2, 463-4

Warrants, in Massachusetts, xliii, 73 (21); in U. S., 207 (4)

Warren, Henry Clarke, translator of Buddhist Writings, xlv, 587

Warrenites, Mill on the, xxv, 164

WARRIOR, THE HAPPY, xli, 672-4

Warton, on Thomson, xxxix, 341-2

Warwick, Earl of, in Crecy campaign, xxxv, 8, 9, 18, 23, 29; at Poitiers, 42, 47, 53, 55

Warwick, Earl of, in Edward IV's reign, v, 420

Warwick, Richard Beauchamp, Earl of, v, 419

Warwick, in EDWARD II, in quarrel with Gaveston, xlvi, 9, 11-13, 14-16; consents to his return, 19-22, 23, 24; on Gaveston's return, 30-2; in attack on Tynemouth, 36; capture of Gaveston, 39-43; in battle, 49; death, 50-1

Washington, George, Commander-in-Chief, xliii, 180; Emerson on, v, 132, 191, 222; FAREWELL ADDRESS, xliii, 250-66; FIRST INAUGURAL ADDRESS, 241-5; not a great reader, xxviii, 350; president of Constitutional Convention, xliii, 192 note; sweet in his grave, v, 135

WASHINGTON, ODE ON BIRTHDAY OF, vi, 526

Wasps, in Brazil, xxix, 45-6

Wastefulness, Confucius on, xliv, 25 (35); Locke on, xxxvii, 108, 109; Mohammed on, xlv, 926

WAT TYLER'S REBELLION, xxxv, 61-82; Chaucer in, xxxix, 171

WAT YE WHA'S IN YON TOWN, vi, 555

Watchall, in NEW WAY TO PAY OLD DEBTS, xlvii, 825-7, 832, 841

Watches, fall in price of, x, 212

Watches, ship's, xxiii, 17-18

Watchful, the porter, in PILGRIM'S PROGRESS, xv, 49-51, 227, 242

Watchful, the shepherd, in PILGRIM'S PROGRESS, xv, 125-8, 297

Water, action of iron on, xxx, 124-7; decomposition of, 43-8, 131 note, 136-40; different states of, 119-23; Faraday on properties of,

8-10; freezing-point of, 242-4;
Helmholtz on decomposition of,
212-14; presence of, tested by
potassium, 118, 124, 145-6; pro-
duced by combustion, 117-19, 131;
weight of, 52
Water of Paradise, in New Atlantis,
iii, 183
Water-carriage, Adam Smith on, x,
25-6
Water Companies, Smith on, x, 483,
484
WATER-FOWL, ON SCARING SOME, vi,
300
WATERFOWL, TO A, xlii, 1271-2
Water-hogs, Darwin on, xxix, 60-1
Water-power, Helmholtz on, xxx,
188-90, 194
Watson, Joseph, i, 38-40
Watts, Isaac, hymns by, xlv, 549,
550; TRUE GREATNESS, xl, 408
WAUKRIFE MINNIE, vi, 382
Waverley Novels, Carlyle on, xxv,
455-9
Waves, Kelvin on, xxx, 289
Wayland, Germanic Vulcan, xlix, 18
note 5
Wazilah, xlv, 1019 note
WE ARE SEVEN, xli, 683-5
WE MUST BE FREE OR DIE, xli,
690-1
Weak, to be, is miserable, iv, 94
Weakness, as cause of beauty, xxiv,
99; no excuse, iv, 439
Wealhtheow, Queen, xlix, 22-3, 38-
40, 66
Wealth, aristocracy and, v, 211;
Burns on, vi, 41; Channing on
distinctions of, xxviii, 356; Confucius on, xliv, 13 (5), 23 (15),
27 (13), 44 (9), 47 (11); contentment and, xli, 535; death and,
xvi, 317-18, 327, 335-6; Emerson
on hunger for, v, 245; Goldsmith
on accumulation of, xli, 522, 528;
growth of, not necessarily beneficial, xxviii, 375; ignorance of,
the best riches, xli, 523; land as
source of (see Agricultural System); Lowell on, xxviii, 477, 484;
Marcus Aurelius on, ii, 261 (33);
a means, not an end, xxviii, 900;
measurable by labor it can buy,
x, 36-7; Mill on production and
distribution of, xxv, 158; Milton
on, iv, 386-7; money as, x, 238-9,
326-47; Morris on real, xlii, 1243;
national, on what dependent, x,
5-6; natural progress of, 319-24;
obligations of, i, 412-14; old age
and, ix, 48; Pascal on private,
xlviii, 383; Pascal on pursuit of,
150 (436), 317 (906); Pascal on
respect for, 113 (324), 118; on
pride in, 156 (460); poverty and,
Carlyle on, xxv, 350-1; Penn on
private, i, 409 (221); production

and distribution of (see Production, Distribution); progress of,
dependent on distribution, x, 57;
proportioned to neat, not gross,
revenue, 234; public and private,
connected, 351-2; unused, fable
of, xvii, 37; Walton on, xv, 333;
Woolman on, i, 188 (see also
Capital, Riches)
WEALTH OF NATIONS, Adam Smith's,
x; remarks on, 3-4; l, 49
Weapons, change and return of,
iii, 146-7
Weariness, Pascal on, xlviii, 51
(131)
WEARY PUND O' TOW, vi, 458
Weather, influence of moon on, xxx,
313
Weathercock, in FAUST, xix, 179-80
Weaver, Chaucer's, xl, 21 note 191
WEAVERS, TO THE, GIN YE GO, vi,
312
Webb, Gen., at Gettysburg, xliii,
407, 408, 411
Webb, George, Franklin on, i, 53-4,
60, 62
Weber, Mill on Oberon of, xxv, 95
Webster, John, CALL FOR THE ROBIN,
xl, 331; DUCHESS OF MALFI, xlvii,
721-816; Hazlitt on, xxvii, 291;
life and works, xlvii, 720
WEBSTER-ASHBURTON TREATY, xliii,
299-308
Wedded Love, Milton on, iv, 176
Wedding Bells, Poe on, xlii, 1284
Weddings, Webster on secret, xlvii,
731
WEE JOHNIE, EPITAPH ON, vi, 230
WEE WILLIE GRAY, vi, 550
Weeping, Hobbes on, xxxiv, 356;
Hunt on, xxvii, 299
Weevil, Harrison on the, xxxv, 297
Wehaloosing, Indian town, i, 278-9
Wei, King of, xliv, 23 note 3,
43 (3)
Wei-sheng Kao, xliv, 17 (23)
Wei-sheng Mou, xliv, 59 (34)
Weight, measured by inertia, xxx,
315-16; as a motive force, 186-
90; transformed to ves viva, 197;
used to produce electricity, 218
Weights, English and metric system
of, xxx, 265; regulation of, viii,
174, 196 (5)
Weiler, Jost von, in WILHELM TELL,
xxvi, 401, 411, 412
WELL I REMEMBER, xli, 925
Wellborn, in NEW WAY TO PAY OLD
DEBTS, xlvii, at Tapwell's, 819-22;
with Allworth, 823-5; at Lady Allworth's, 831-5; Overreach's plot to
ruin, 837; at Overreach's, with Marrall, 838-40; with Marrall at Lady
Allworth's, 841-4, 846; with Marrall after dinner, 847-8; thought
to be engaged to Lady Allworth,
849-50; at Overreach's with Lady

Allworth, 863, 864, 866, 867; conference with Overreach, 867-8;
Tapwell and Froth on, 876-7;
creditors and, 877-80; advised by
Marrall, 880-1; Lady Allworth on,
885-6; with Lovell and Lady Allworth, 887-8; quarrel with Overreach, 889-93; in final scene, 894,
895, 896-9
Welfare, Michael, i, 115
Wellington, Duke of, on Briscoll, v,
444; Cintra affair and, 391; Emerson on, 390; fear of public creditors, 384; on the life-guards, 396;
weighed his soldiers, 371
Wellington, Mount, Darwin on,
xxix, 473
Wells, Darwin on ebbing, xxix, 483
Wells, Dr. W. C., and idea of nat-
ural selection, xi, 11-12
Welsh, Jane Baillie, wife of Car-
lyle, xxv, 329-30, 331-2
Welsh (see Celtic Races)
Wen, Duke, xliv, 48 (16)
Wen, King, xliv, 25 note, 27 note 8
Wenceslaus, king of Bohemia, Dante
on, xx, 175 and note 6, 369 note
10
Weohstan, xlix, 79
Wer-wolves, xlix, 287 note
WERE MY LOVE YON LILAC FAIR,
vi, 494
Were-gild, xlix, 295 note
WERENA MY HEART LICHT, xl, 409
Werner, of Attinghausen, in WIL-
HELM TELL (see Attinghausen)
Werner, Paul, in MINNA VON BARN-
HELM, lends money to Tellheim,
xxvi, 292-3; with Just at the inn,
298-301; the landlord and, 320-2;
with Franziska, 322-3; plots to
give Tellheim money, 324; with
Tellheim, 324-9; at meeting of
Franziska and Tellheim, 329, 330-
1, 332; with Franziska alone, 332;
announces Tellheim's coming, 340;
lends money to Tellheim, 349-51;
returns with money, 362; reconciliation with Tellheim, 365; with
Franziska, 366
Werni, in WILHELM TELL, xxvi,
371-6
WERT THOU IN THE CAULD BLAST,
vi, 591
Wesley, Charles, hymns by, xlv,
572-5
Wessels, Capt., at Gettysburg, xliii,
396, 403
West, Thoreau on the, xxviii, 416-
21
West Indies, absence of atolls in,
xxix, 506; Columbus on discovery
of, xliii, 22-8; origin of name of,
x, 418; Raleigh on disadvantages
of, xxxiii, 390, 392; zoology of
the, xxix, 144
WEST WIND, ODE TO THE, xli, 856-7

Westbrook, Harriet, wife of Shel-
ley, xviii, 272
WESTMINSTER ABBEY, Addison's,
xxvii, 82-5
WESTMINSTER ABBEY, ON THE TOMBS
IN, xl, 327-8
WESTMINSTER BRIDGE, UPON, xli, 689
Westminster Review, The, xxv, 62-8,
86-7; combined with London Re-
view, 129
Westwood, Darwin on insects, xi, 73
WET SHEET, A, AND A FLOWING SEA,
xli, 803
WHA IS THAT AT MY BOWER-DOOR,
vi, 51-2
Whales, Darwin on Greenland, xi,
236-40; jumping out of water,
xxix, 239 note
WHA'LL BE KING BUT CHARLIE, xli,
578-9
Whappet, Harrison on the, xxxv,
373-4
Wharton, Marquis of, Addison and,
xxvii, 170-1
WHAT CAN A YOUNG LASSIE DO, vi,
430
WHAT GUILE IS THIS, xl, 254
Whately, Mill on, xxv, 144
Wheat, parable of the, xv, 208
Wheatley, Mr., editor of Pepys,
xxviii, 295
Wheels, toothed, considered as levers,
xxx, 192-3
Whelks, the heart in, xxxviii, 137-8
WHEN THE ASSAULT WAS INTENDED
TO THE CITY, iv, 80
WHEN I HAVE BORNE, xli, 693
WHEN THE KYE COMES HAME, xli,
783-5
WHEN LILACS LAST IN THE DOOR-
YARD, xlii, 1497-1505
WHEN LOVELY WOMAN STOOPS, xli,
517
WHEN SHE CAM' BEN SHE BOBBED,
vi, 459
WHEN WE TWO PARTED, xli, 807-8
WHENAS IN SILKS, xl, 346
WHERE ARE THE JOYS I HAVE MET,
vi, 505
WHERE THE BEE SUCKS, xl, 272
WHERE LIES THE LAND, xlii, 1168
Whewell, William, controversy with
Mill, xxv, 145; on general laws,
xi, 1; Mill on, xxv, 134-5
Whiddon, Jacob, xxxiii, 313, 323,
326, 346, 347, 349, 370, 371
Whig Party, English, James Mill
on, xxv, 64
WHIGS, AWA', vi, 381
White, Henry, xxxiii, 238, 253
White, Joseph, Woolman on, i, 235,
244, 304
White, Joseph Blanco, TO NIGHT,
xli, 938
WHITE ROSE, A, xlii, 1246
Whitefield, Rev. George, i, 105-8;
building erected for, 105, 118

WHITEFOORD, SIR JOHN, LINES TO, vi, 427

Whitman, Walt, life of, xxxix, 409 note; poems by, xlii, 1483-1508; PREFACE TO LEAVES OF GRASS, xxxix, 409-32; PREFACE of, editorial remarks on, 3; l, 56

Whipping, in early Massachusetts, xliii, 77 (43); Locke on, of children, xxxvii, 38-9, 42, 43, 59, 64-6, 69-70, 71-3, 99-100

Whisky, Burns on, vi, 154, 170-1

WHISTLE, THE, vi, 384-6

WHISTLE AND I'LL COME TO YOU, MY LAD, vi, 499

WHISTLE O'ER THE LAVE O'T, vi, 368

Whiston, on comets, xxxiv, 121

Whitsunday, xv, 409

Whitsunday Island, xxix, 491

Whittier, John Greenleaf, poems by, xlii, 1414-41

Wholesale Trade, why smaller profits in, x, 119

Wholesaling, capital used in, x, 304, 306, 310

Wholesome, Tribulation, in the ALCHEMIST, his dealings with the Alchemist, xlvii, 562; scene with Ananias, 567-8; with Subtle, 568-73; returns with Ananias, 621, 630-1, 633

WHY SO PALE AND WAN, xl, 363-4

WHY, WHY TELL THE LOVER, vi, 573

Wickedness, Asaph on, xliv, 237 (3-12, 17-20); Bildad on, 100 (5-21); Buddha on expiation of, xlv, 687-90; David on, xliv, 4-6, 185 (16, 21), 189 (1, 2), 190 (9-38), 217 (1-11); ECCLESIASTES on, 348 (17), 349 (11-14), 350 (2); Eliphaz on, 96 (20-35); future punishment of, vii, 242-4; xxxiv, 272, 273; harms only the doer, ii, 266 (55); Job on, xliv, 86 (24), 91 (6), 105 (7-33), 110 (2-12), 114 (13-23), 120 (3); Kempis on, vii, 254 (1); not free, ii, 166 (136); "the path of," xl, 78; prayer for overthrow of, xliv, 155-7; Raleigh on punishment of, xxxix, 73-93; righteousness contrasted with, xliv, 147, 236-8, 241 (10); is weakness, iv, 439; Zophar on, xliv, 103 (5-29)

WIDOW BIRD, A, xli, 870

Widow's Mite, xliv, 414 (1-4)

Wife of Bath, in Canterbury Tales, xl, 23-4; Dryden on the, xxxix, 174; prologue of, 170

WIFE, THE DEVOTED, xlv, 708-11

WIFE OF USHER'S WELL, xl, 81-2

Wight, O. W., translator of Pascal, xlviii

Wiglaf, xlix, 78-86, 87, 92

Wikiri, Raleigh on the, xxxiii, 381, 387

Wilberforce, Samuel, xxv, 84

Wild Ass, in JOB, xliv, 137

Wild-head, in PILGRIM'S PROGRESS, xv, 299

WILD SWANS, THE, xvii, 283-98

Wildness, Thoreau on, xxviii, 421-9

Wilfrid, Bishop, and the slaves, v, 441

Wilfulness, Shakespeare on, xlvi, 248

Wilhelm Meister, Carlyle on, xxv, 396-9; Wordsworth on, v, 337

WILHELM TELL, Schiller's, xxvi, 369-474; remarks on, 368

Wilkinson, editor of Swedenborg, Emerson on, v, 459

Will, absolute and conditional, xx, 302; autonomy of the (see Autonomy of the Will); belief and, xlviii, 42 (99); beliefs of the, 406-7; Coleridge on the, v, 332; defined, xxxii, 377; freedom of the (see Free Will); Hobbes on the, xxxiv, 357-8; Hume on power of the, xxxvii, 357-61, 363, 365-6; inferior to the soul, v, 144; Kant on absolute value of the, xxxii, 323-34, 368, 370; Marcus Aurelius on the, ii, 235 (8); obligations of the, xxxii, 344-62; power of the, v, 301; reason and, xxxii, 343; Rousseau on the, xxxiv, 256; Woolman on human, i, 311-12, 313

Will o' the Wisps, in FAUST, xix, 183

WILL YE GO TO THE INDIES, MY MARY, vi, 210

Wills, as evidences of character, ix, 343; Mohammed on, xlv, 1020; Montaigne on men's dislike of, xxxii, 12

Willdo, Parson, xlvii, 884, 894, 895, 897, 898

William the Conqueror, census under, xxxv, 243; introduced money payments of taxes, x, 32; love of deer, v, 364; Vane on, xliii, 129; Voltaire on, xxxiv, 89

William III, king of England, Burke on election of, xxiv, 165-8; Dissenters and, xxvii, 147; Johnson on, 168

William and Mary, Burke on titles of, xxiv, 165-8

William I, of Orange (d. c. 808), xx, 363 note 4

William of Orange (the Silent), anecdote of, v, 301

William of Orange (the Silent), in EGMONT, love of Netherlanders for, xlvi, 233; suspected by Margaret, 257-8; sent for by Margaret, 259; visit to Egmont, 278-83; gone from Brussels, 294; summoned by Alva, 299; plan to arrest, 301-2; declines to come, 302-3

William II, of Sicily, in Paradise, xx, 372 note 9

William of North Berwick, xxxv, 93

William of Wykeham, Carlyle on, v, 481

WILLIE BREW'D A PECK O' MAUT, vi, 376

WILLIE NICOL'S MARE, ELEGY ON, vi, 399

Willis, Nathaniel P., Poe on lines by, xxviii, 386-7

Willoughby, Lord, xxxv, 23, 42, 56

WILLOW-WREN, THE, AND THE BEAR, xvii, 201

WILLY DROWNED IN YARROW, xli, 510-12

Wilson, Capt., (in 1859), xxiii, 403-4; in San Diego, 115-16

Wilson, J., BOAT SONG, xlii, 1105-6

WILT THOU BE MY DEARIE, vi, 511

Wilton Hall, Emerson on, v, 477-8

Winchester, Bishop of, in EDWARD II, xlvi, 65, 66, 67, 69

Winchester Cathedral, Emerson on, v, 480-1

WINCHESTER, MARCHIONESS OF, EPITAPH ON, iv, 28-30

Winckelmann, on the study of beauty, v, 309-10

Wind, Coleridge on the, xli, 748

WIND AND SUN, fable of, xvii, 35

Windmills, Helmholtz on, xxx, 194-195

Winds, Herodotus on cause of, xxxiii, 17; in GARDEN OF PARADISE, xvii, 299-303; names of the, iv, 312

WINDOW, WRITTEN ON A, vi, 290

Window-taxes, x, 517-18

Windows, ancient, ix, 234 note; in old England, xxxv, 310, 311; in Utopia, xxxvi, 187

Wine, desire of, which warriors overturns, iv, 432; of Egypt, xxxiii, 40; Eliot on, v, 130; Homer on effects of, xxii, 205, 303; invented by Bacchus, viii, 360; Mohammed on, xlv, 1018; Omar Khayyam on, xli, 971, 980, 986, 987; Pascal on, xlviii, 25 (71); price of, in regard to drunkenness, x, 381-2; sweet poison of, misused, iv, 47

Wine Manufacture, Pasteur on, xxxviii, 290, 318 note

Wines, Burns on, vi, 154

Winfield, Sir Richard, xxxvi, 102

Wings, of insects, developed from tracheæ, xi, 196; peculiar uses of, 186; used for other purposes than flight, xxix, 215; various kinds of, xi, 202

Winkelried, Arnold von, at Sempach, xxvi, 446 note

Winkelried, Struth von, in WILHELM TELL, xxvi, 400-14

Winter, Burns on, vi, 507; Collins

on, xli, 493; Goethe on departure of, xix, 40; Shelley on, xli, 857

WINTER, Shakespeare's, xl, 267

WINTER: A DIRGE, by Burns, vi, 32-3

WINTER, ODE TO, Campbell's, xli, 790-2

WINTER, ODE ON, Cotton's, xxxix, 324-6

WINTER, THE, IT IS PAST, vi, 320

WINTER NIGHT, A, vi, 260-3

WINTER OF LIFE, vi, 538

WINTER'S, GLOOMY, NOW AWA', xli, 608-9

Winter, Master, with Drake, xxxiii, 209, 216, 237, 238, 256

Winter, William, with Gilbert, xxxiii, 282, 295

Winterhie, Robert, xxxiii, 214

Winthrop, John, ON ARBITRARY GOVERNMENT, xliii, 90-112

Wisdom, Buddha on, xlv, 609, 717-19, 755; Carlyle on, xxv, 390; Confucius on, xliv, 20 (20), 21 (21), 30 (28), 42 (22), 50 (30), 58 (9); cunning and, i, 354 (151); iii, 60; defined, ii, 72; acquisition of, by discussion, xxv, 223; ECCLESIASTES on, xliv, 340 (17-18), 341 (12-16), 347 (11-12), 348 (16, 19), 349 (1), 351 (2, 13-18), 352 (10); Elihu on, 123 (9); Emerson on, v, 12-15, 105, 248; fear of God, the beginning of, xliv, 292 (10); necessary to friendship, ix, 22; highest, Kempis on, vii, 214 (3); highest, Penn on, i, 411 (244-8); Hindu conception of, xlv, 860-1; Job on, xliv, 116 (12-28); learning and, xxxvii, 137, 184; needs leisure, xxiv, 198 note 1; Locke on, xxxvii, 127; love and, iii, 28, 29; Marcus Aurelius on, ii, 227 (9); Massinger on, xlvii, 836; Milnes on delights of, xlii, 1098-9; Montaigne on aim of, xxxii, 9; ostentatious, ii, 177 (175); Pascal on pride in, xlviii, 156 (460); Paul, St., on, xlv, 505 (18-20); Pope on, xl, 448; profitless with God, vii, 286 (2); pleasures of, iii, 8; Raleigh on, xl, 209; Ruskin on, xxviii, 134; Schiller on love of, xxxii, 243; slow growth of, ii, 173 (155); Socrates on human, 9; Solomon on, xxxix, 95; spiritual, Kempis on, vii, 307 (2), 309 (4); Tennyson on, xlii, 1016-17; true, attained by death, ii, 54-7; true, Epictetus on, 177 (177); true, Kempis on, vii, 310-11; true, Montaigne on, xxxii, 51; virtue and, Cicero on, ix, 14; way to, vii, 218 (4); ii, 140 (66); Webster on opinion of, xlvii, 740;

what else is (song), viii, 389-90;
worldly, i, 392-5; only true meas-
ure of worth, ii, 58 (see also
Knowledge)
Wisdom, Robert, Beaumont on, xl,
328
Wisdom of Ages, Bentham on,
xxvii, 238-41
WISDOM FOR A MAN'S SELF, ESSAY
ON, iii, 63-4
WISE, SEEMING, ESSAY ON, iii, 67-9
WISE FOLKS, a story, xvii, 204
Wise Man, Penn's, i, 395-6, 355
(167)
WISH, A, by Rogers, xli, 596
WISH, THE LAST, xlii, 1165
Wishes, fable on, xvii, 40; oft hide
the object we wish for, xix, 379
WISHES FOR SUPPOSED MISTRESS, xl,
369-71
Wit, acquired, xxxiv, 366; Beaumont on, xl, 329; cause of differences of, xxxiv, 366; death and,
xl, 266; discretion and fancy in,
xxxiv, 365; good nature and,
Sheridan on, xviii, 132; has only
fancy value, xxxii, 366; Hobbes
on, xxxiv, 363; judgment compared with, xxiv, 17-18; malice
and, Sheridan on, xviii, 116;
natural, xxxiv, 363; Penn on, i,
355; piety and, Goldsmith on,
xviii, 199; puny, can work but
puny sin, viii, 314; Raleigh on,
xl, 209; without good breeding,
xxxvii, 76
Witch, in MANFRED, xviii, 418-22
Witch, in FAUST, xix, 101-6
Witch, young, in FAUST, xix, 179
Witchcraft, Browne on, iii, 294-6;
first English law against, xlvii,
525 note 22; Hobbes on, xxxiv,
397; punishment of, in Dante's
HELL, xx, 47, 83-6; punishment
of, in old England, xxxv, 308
Witches, Hobbes on, xxxiv, 329; in
early Massachusetts, xliii, 84 (2)
Witches, in MACBETH, xlvi, 305-6,
308-10, 347-51
Witford, Mr., Roper on, xxxvi, 95
Wither, George, poems by, xl, 340-2
Witherington, the squire, xl, 97,
100
Withington, Lothrop, xxxv, 228
Witnesses, Hume on evidence of,
xxxvii, 398-9; right of summon-
ing, in U. S., xliii, 208 (6)
Witticisms, Pascal on, xlviii, 20
(46)
Wives, husbands and, Goethe on,
xix, 420-1; husbands and, St. Paul
on, xlv, 508, 511 (39); husbands
and, Ruskin on, xxviii, 149-50;
impediments to great works, iii,
22; Massinger on choice of, xlvii,
875; Milton on, iv, 445; Milton
on false, 437-8; Penn on choice

of, i, 348 (92-3); Oberon's counsel to, xix, 177; "pearls of price,"
131; proverb of, i, 80
Wizards, in FAUST, XIX, 166-7
WOE IS ME, MY MOTHER DEAR, vi,
25
Woe, joy and, Blake on, xli, 602;
luxury of, Calderon on, xxvi, 7;
nothing unscathed by, viii, 262;
from too much prosperity, 32;
springs from wrong, 32, 64
Wolf, F. A., on Homeric question,
xxii, 3-4
Wolf, Johann Christian von, xxxii,
320 note
WOLF AND CRANE, fable of, xvii, 11
WOLF AND DOG, fable of, xvii, 21
WOLF AND FOX, Grimm's tale of,
xvii, 177
WOLF AND KID, fable of, xvii, 16
WOLF AND LAMB, fable of, xvii, 9
WOLF AND NURSE, fable of, xvii, 29
WOLF AND SEVEN KIDS, a tale, xvii,
59-61
WOLF IN SHEEP'S CLOTHING, fable
of, xvii, 26
Wolfe, Charles, BURIAL OF SIR JOHN
MOORE, xli, 843-4
Wolfe, Reginald, Cosmography of,
xxxv, 228
Wollenschieuuen, the, xxvi, 372 note,
387
Wolfram of Eschenbach, Renan on,
xxxii, 154
Wolly, Sir Francis, Dr. Donne and,
xv, 333, 336
Wolsey, ambition to be Pope, xxxvi,
106; as Chancellor, 111-12; removed from Chancellorship, 111;
Charles V and, 107; as commissioner, 108, 109; suggests divorce
of Queen Catherine, 107; More
and, 96, 100-1, 103; Bishop
Stoksely and, 110-11
Wolves, Darwin on development of,
xi, 103-4; dogs and, xxxv, 375;
why less despicable than dogs,
xxiv, 59; in Egypt, xxxiii, 37;
habits of, v, 388; men changed
to, xlix, 286 note
Woman (en), adroitness of, xli, 371;
Æschylus on insight of, viii, 22;
arguing with, xl, 192; Beaumont's
Philaster on, xlvii, 682; beauty
of, as caused by delicacy, xxiv,
99; beauty of, Emerson on, v,
315-16; beauty of, Pascal on,
xlviii, 420; beauty of, Ruskin on,
xxviii, 151-2; "brief as love of,"
xlvi, 143; Browne on, iii, 337
(9); Bunyan on, xv, 269; two
burdens of, viii, 293; Burns on,
vi, 140-1, 177, 231, 272, 347, 506;
Celtic ideal of, xxxii, 149;
Chaucer on, xl, 44; Chaucer on
counsel of, 46; counterfeit weakness in, xxiv, 94; creation of,

Milton on, iv, 258-9; De Vere on, xl, 296; DIVINE COMEDY, written in praise of, xx, 4; Donne on fickleness of, xl, 315; Don Quixote on affections of, xiv, 167; Dryden on, xviii, 49, 69; ECCLESIASTES on, xliv, 348 (26-8); education of, Defoe on, xxvii, 158-61; education of, Franklin on, i, 16, 97-8; education of, Ruskin on, xxviii, 140, 151-61; Emerson on, v, 224; Euripides on, viii, 314; "frailty thy name is," xlvi, 97; Goethe's Dorothea on duties of, xix, 407; happiest knowledge of, iv, 173; individuality of, Emerson on, v, 133; Lessing on, xxvi, 312; liberties of, in Massachusetts, xlii, 82; in literature, xxviii, 141-7; love of, by what won, iv, 444; love of, Poe on, xxviii, 402, 404; Mac-Neil on marriages of, xli, 592; Mephistopheles on creation of, xix, 99; Milton on, iv, 165, 260, 269, 293, 299, 338, 438, 441; man and, compared in evil, xix, 166-7; man and, relations of, xlviii, 425; in Mohammedan countries, xlv, 1005 note 30; Mohammedan verses on, xvi, 10-11; Montaigne on friendships of, xxxii, 78; More on idleness of, xxxvi, 191; Patmore on, xxviii, 148; Paul, St., on, xlv, 516 (7-12); as the subject of poetry, xxviii, 404; public duties of, 161-8; Raleigh on, xxxix, 94; Ruskin on sphere of, xxviii, 140-51; to be shielded, not tempted, xiv, 332-3; Socrates on, xxxix, 11-13; Shakespeare on, xlvi, 137; Tennyson on, xlii, 1017; in Utopia, xxxvi, 189, 194, 195, 197, 228, 234, 245; Virgil on, xiii, 177; Webster on inconstancy of, xlvii, 749; Webster's Bosola on, 743; Wither on, xl, 341-2

Woman Suffrage, Mill on, xxv, 70-1, 157 note 1, 193-4; movement started by Mill, 180

WOMAN, THE RIGHTS OF, vi, 474

Woman's Rights, Emerson on, v, 314; Mill on, xxv, 5

WOMEN, EDUCATION OF, by Defoe, xxvii, 158-61

Wonder, mean and noble, xxviii, 117; caused by novelty, xlviii, 40 (90); Wordsworth on, xxxix, 341

Wood, price of, x, 176-7

Wood, Antony, on universities, xxviii, 47

Woodcock, Katherine, wife of Milton, iv, 5; Milton on, 88

WOODEN GOD, fable of the, xvii, 27

WOODLARK, TO THE, vi, 569

WOODMAN AND SERPENT, fable of, xvii, 17

Woodnot, Arthur, xv, 392-3, 398, 399, 420, 422-3

WOODNOTES, xlii, 1301-13

Woodpeckers, color of, xi, 207-8; habits of, 188-9

Woodruff's Battery, at Gettysburg, xliii, 359, 373, 397, 405, 406

Woods, Emerson on beauty of, v, 233-4

Woods, Mr., Prologue written for, vi, 273-4

Woodville, Dr., xxxviii, 209, 214-15, 216, 220

Woodward, Hezekiah, on Lord's Prayer, v, 396

Woodward, Samuel, on cirripedes, xi, 357; on geological formations, 347

WOOED AND MARRIED AND A', xli, 580-1

WOOER, THE BRAW, vi, 574

Wool, price of, x, 201-7

Woolen Manufactures, improvements in, x, 214-15

Woolman, Elizabeth, i, 192

Woolman, John, birth and education of, i, 177-8, 182, 195; business attitude of, 188, 203-4, 245, 285; creed of, 181-2, 238-9; death of, 327-8; Delaware, journey to, 194; doubts of, 197-8; manner of dress, 263-5, 317 note; duty, incidents of his sense of, 185, 188, 202-3, 244, 250, 260, 264; on dyes, 323-4; early occupation, 182-3, 188; East Jersey, journeys to, 187, 191-2; English journey, 302-23; epistle to Friends in N. Carolina, 218-220; exhortation to follow inner light, 285-6; first speeches in meeting, 183-4; in the French war, 229-30; on Huss and à Kempis, 230-1; Indian visit of, 265-81; journey to back settlements, 189-91; letter on affliction, 206-7; letter to wife, 249; life and character, 176; in London, 316 and note; Long Island visit of, 202-3; marriage of, 195; Maryland visited by, 286-92; miraculous appearance of Divine Truth, 208; misunderstanding with a friend, 237; New England journeys of, 192-4, 248-59; parents, his relations with 178-9, 180; Pennsylvania visit of, 231-2; pleurisy of, 300; robins, incident of killing the, 178; Scotch servant and, 184-5; simplicity of life, 188, 203; on slavery, 211-13, 215-16; slavery, his book on, 195-6, 197, 260-1; slavery, his first opposition to, 186; slavery among Quakers op-

posed by, 216-17, 219, 233-4, 284;
slaves, education of, moved by,
217; slave-owners visited by,
235-7, 243-4, 254-5, 260; slave-
owners' wills, refuses to write,
196-7, 200-2; slave-sale, restitu-
tion for assisting in, 293, 296;
slave-states, uneasiness in, 191, 209-
11; slave-trade, petition against,
251-3; on the small-pox, 244-7;
southern journey, 208-24; spiritual awakening, 177-82; as a
tailor, 188-9, 203, 204; trade with
Barbadoes, 296-7; vision of death
and the slaves, 320-1; West Indian visit, desires and scruples
about, 296-9; youthful faults,
179-81

WOOLMAN, JOHN, JOURNAL OF, i,
177-326; editorial remarks on, l,
34

Woolman, Samuel, i, 195-6

Words, acts and, Bunyan on, xv,
84; acts and, Confucius on, xliv,
8 (13), 50 (29); 14 (22, 24), 16
(9); acts and, Epictetus on, ii,
177 (175); acts and, Goethe on,
xix, 14; acts and, Marcus
Aurelius on, ii, 283 (16), 292
(18); aggregate, simple abstract,
and compound abstract, xxiv,
136-7; Berkeley on, xxxvii, 284,
285, 288-9, 251, 261; Burke on,
xxiv, 53-7, 136-45, 145-8; Confucius on, xliv, 43 (3), 54 (22),
69 (3); Dryden on antiquated,
xxxix, 177; Emerson on, v, 170;
Goethe on, xix, 28, 76, 105;
Hobbes on use of, xxxiv, 336-9;
Johnson on, xxxix, 195; Kempis
on, vii, 221, 323 (1); meaning
of, xxxiv, 339-40, 342-3, 346;
Montaigne on, xxxii, 62-7; Pascal
on arrangement of, xlviii, 15
(23); Pascal on meanings of, 21
(50); Penn on, i, 401-2 (123-6);
Ruskin on importance of, xxviii,
104-8; Stevenson on, 288-9, 290;
Swift on, xxvii, 123; Tzu-kung
on, xliv, 68 (23); wise men's
counters, money of fools, xxxiv,
340

Wordsworth, William, Arnold on,
xlii, 1181, 1182-3; xxviii, 82; his
modernization of Chaucer, 79;
Emerson on, v, 22, 335-8, 463;
Emerson's second visit to, 483-5;
Mazzini on, xxxii, 408; Mill on,
xxv, 96-9; poems by, xli, 609-97;
on poetry, xxviii, 66; PREFACES
to poems, xxxix, 281-353; the Romantic Movement and, 281 note;
the study of, xxviii, 410

Work, Carlyle on, xxv, 380-1; Emerson on, v, 297; Goethe on, xxv,
404; Hindu doctrine of, xlv, 813-

15, 819-20, 823-4, 826, 876-7, 880-
1; without hope, Coleridge on,
xxv, 93

Work (mechanical), amount of, defined, 184-6; amount of, not increased by machines, xxx, 190-3;
capacity for, exhausted by per-
formance, 185-7, 189-90, 195, 197,
198, 211, 212, 214, 217-18; performed by gravity, 186-90; changed
to heat, 205-7; measurement of,
187-8; produced by chemical forces,
210-14; produced by elastic forces,
197-8; produced by electricity, 214-
17; produced by heat, 198-202,
204-5; produced by velocity of
moving masses, 194-7; thermal
equivalent of, 207-9

Works, Luther on justification by,
xxxvi, 363-4, 365-6, 367, 368-9,
372, 375, 377, 378-97; Jesus on,
xliv, 375 (47-9); tested by time,
xxxix, 219

World, the, Arnold on, xlii, 1184;
beauty of, i, 379 (485); Browne
on, iii, 341; Buddha on eternity
of, xlv, 662-7; changes in, xxxix,
112; Drummond on, xl, 336 (196,
197); end of, Browne on, iii, 310-
12, 316; end of, Buddhistic, xlv,
617; end of, Hayes on, xxxiii,
274-5; end of, Raleigh on, xxxix,
111-13; end of, Stoic belief of,
ix, 304 note; idea of eternity of,
xxxix, 106, 107-13; in a grain of
sand, xli, 601; Hume on origin of,
xxxvii, 418-19; indestructibility of,
xix, 54; Socrates's conception of,
ii, 105-10; Tennyson on mystery
of, xlii, 1059; undivine conceptions of, xlv, 871; visible, a picture of the invisible, iii, 275 (12)
(see also Earth, Universe)

WORLD, THE, IS TOO MUCH WITH
Us, xli, 693-4

WORLD WELL LOST, Dryden's, xviii,
11-101

World-citizenship, Epictetus on, ii,
122 (15, 16); Marcus Aurelius on,
211 (11), 214 (4)

Worldliness, aspirations and, xix,
30; Bacon on, lll, 111; Bunyan
on, xv, 312-13; Jesus on, xliv, 394
(22-34); Raleigh on, xxxix, 94,
98-100

Worldling, in FAUST, xix, 181

Worldly Goods, Kempis on, vii, 237
(2), 288 (1, 2); Marcus Aurelius
on, 227 (10), 228 (12), 229 (15)

WORLDLY PLACE, by Arnold, xlii,
1185

Worldly Things, transitoriness of,
xvi, 315-18, 326-7, 334-5, 331-2,
334-6

Worldly Wisdom, Penn on, i, 392-5

Worldly Wiseman, Mr., in PIL-
GRIM'S PROGRESS, xv, 21-4, 26-7

WORLD'S WANDERERS, THE, xli, 879
WORM, THE CONQUEROR, xlii, 1291-2
Worm, Shakespeare on the, xlvi, 162
Worry, Epictetus on, ii, 123 (19) (see also Anxiety)
Worship, better than knowing, xlv, 858; Calvin on splendor in, xxxix, 38-9; Confucius on, xliv, 10 (12); Emerson on loss of, v, 38; natural forms of, xxxiv, 393-4; Penn on, i, 380-1; Rousseau on, xxxiv, 263-4, 291-2; in Utopia, xxxvi, 247-50
WORSHIP, ESSAY ON, v, 283-305
Worth, Confucius on, xliv, 13 (14), 14 (17), 51 (39), 52 (3); Emerson on, v, 196; Jonson on, xl, 298 (152); Hobbes on, xxxiv, 375, 378, 383-4; moral, tests of, xxxii, 327-34, 370-1; Pope on, xl, 446; is worth wherever found, xxvi, 404
Worthilake, Capt., ballad on, i, 15
Worthington, Dr., xxxvii, 143
Wortley, Mr., quoted, v, 408-9
Wotton, Edward, xxvii, 7
Wotton, Sir Henry, George Herbert and, xv, 388; poems by, xl, 294-6; Walton on, xv, 358; Walton's Life of, 326
WOUND-DRESSER, THE, xlii, 1491-4
WOUNDED HARE, THE, vi, 359
Wounds, antiseptic care of, xxxviii, 271-7, 280-1; gunshot, Lister on, 280; gunshot, Paré on, 11-12, 40, 55; cause of suppuration in, 271
Wrath, Dante on, xx, 51; the sin of, in FAUSTUS, xix, 221; punishment of, in Hell, xx, 32-3, 48 (see also Anger)
Wratislaus, Duke of Bohemia, xxxv, 278
WRECK OF THE HESPERUS, xlii, 1321
WREN'S NEST, THE, vi, 580
Wrens, nests of, xi, 296
Wrestler, life of a, Epictetus on, ii, 155 (104)
Wrestling, Milton advises, iii, 257
Wright, Dr., Franklin on, i, 155
Wrightington, Tom, xxiii, 410
Writers, pecuniary rewards of, x, 141
Writing, among the Egyptians, xxxiii, 22; extempore, Carlyle on, xxv, 460-4; extempore, Shelley on, xxvii, 372; invention of, x, 465; Locke on instruction in, xxxvii, 143-4; maketh an exact man, iii, 128; natural, Pascal on, xlviii, 12 (14); for the press, Mill on, xxv, 57-8; the primary art, xxvii, 269; for subsistence, Mill on, xxv, 57-8; Stevenson on difficulty of, xxviii, 288
Writings, Arabian verses on, xvi, 88; Franklin on, i, 108; virtue of, tested by time, xxxix, 218-19

Wrong, right and, Emerson on, v, 66; right and, Pope on, xl, 419-25; Rousseau on, xxxiv, 276; Socrates on, ii, 38
Wrong-doing, Manzoni on, xxi, 34-5; Marcus Aurelius on, ii, 202 (10); Marcus Aurelius on patience under, 248 (22), 249 (26), 293 (18), 271 (11), 272 (20), 275 (38), 276 (42), 282 (13), 301 (16); Mohammed on punishment of, xlv, 905 note 8; punishment of, Emerson on, v, 104-5; punishment of, Epictetus on, ii, 120 (12); reason of, iii, 15
Wrongs, "in se," and "prohibita," xxv, 122
Wu King, xliv, 27 (20), 69 note
Wulf, Eofor and, xlix, 75 note 1, 88-9
Wulfgar, in BEOWULF, xlix, 15-16
Wu-ma Chí, xliv, 24 (30)
Wyatt, Sir Thomas, Jonson on, xxvii, 60; LOVER'S APPEAL, xl, 195; A SUPPLICATION, 194
Wycherley, Taine on, xxxix, 452; Voltaire on, xxxiv, 139-41, 142
Wyclif, Milton on, iii, 234; rise of, 206
Wye, lines composed on banks of the, xli, 500-4
Wygate, Franklin and, i, 49
Wyndham, Sir William, i, 50-1
Wyrd, xlix, 18 note 6; references to, 19, 21, 26, 40, 73, 76, 78, 84
Xanthias, in THE FROGS, viii, 419-25, 427-38, 441-3
Xanthippe, in prison with Socrates, ii, 47; Socrates and, 297 (28)
Xanthippus, father of Pericles, xii, 38; dog of, 15
Xanthippus, son of Pericles, xii, 62; reviles Pericles, 75-6
Xenien, satirized, xix, 180
Xenocles, of Cholargus, xii, 51
Xenophilus, the Musitian, xxxii, 11
Xenophon, on agriculture, ix, 67; Memorabilia, Franklin on, i, 18; Sainte-Beuve on, xxxii, 137; Sidney on, xxvii, 15; Spenser on, xxxix, 65; the Ten Thousand and, xii, 371; v, 198
Xerxes, bridge of, iv, 302; Burns on, vi, 433; Dante on, xx, 262 and note 3; defeat of, xii, 8-9; invasion of, 13-20; memory of, xxxvii, 162; prophecy of, xlviii, 252; regrets death of soldiers, ix, 248; Themistocles and, xii, 29-31; iii, 149
Ximines, Gonzalez, xxxiii, 335-6
Xiphias, reference to, xli, 508
Yak Cow, Buddha on the, xlv, 608
Yakshas, xlv, 873 note
Yama, ruler of the dead, xlv, 701, 704
Yang Fu, xliv, 67 (19)

Yang Huo, xliv, 59 (1)

Yao, Emperor, xliv, 21 note 18, 27 (19), 52 (45), 68 (1) note

Yarrow, The Braes of, by Hamilton, xli, 586

Yarrow, The Braes of, by Logan, xli, 512

Yarrow, The Dowy Houms O, xl, 116-18

Yarrow Revisited, xli, 647-50

Yarrow Unvisited, xli, 642-4

Yarrow Visited, xli, 644-7

Ye Shall Walk in Silk Attire, xli, 593-4

Year 1788, Elegy on the, vi, 341-2

Year That's Awa', xli, 595

Years, cheap and dear, effect on labor, x, 87-91

Yeast, action of, xxxviii, 364-7, 371; Liebig on, 369; relations of, to oxygen, 289-317, 329-32; pencillium and, 378-9

Yen P'ing, xliv, 16 (16)

Yen Yüan, disciple of Confucius, xliv, 7, note 4, 15 note 7, 18 (25), 18 note 2, 19 (5, 9), 22 (10), 26 note 4, 29 (10), 30 (19, 20), 34 (2, 3, 6, 7, 8, 9), 35 (10), 36 (18, 22), 38 (1), 53 (10)

Yeoman, Chaucer's, xl, 14

Yeomen, Harrison on, of England, xxxv, 238-9, 241

Yggdrasil, the tree, xlix, 291 note

Yi, death of, xliv, 47 note

Yi-yi, xliv, 64 (8)

Yi-yin, xliv, 42 note 9

Yngve, Alf and, v, 357

Yôg, xlv, 809, 810, 813, 823, 829

Yon Wild Mossy Mountains, vi, 263-4

Yorick, the skull of, xlvi, 184

York, and Lancaster, xxxix, 78

York, the See of, xxxv, 264; archbishop of, 268-9

York, Minster, the Fuugian, xxix, 222-4, 230, 237, 238, 242, 244-5

Yorktown, Articles of Capitulation, xliii, 180-4

You Ask Me Why, xlii, 1032

Youatt, on selection, iii, 46, 50

You'll Love Me Yet, xlii, 1115

Young, Edward, Night Thoughts of, xxxix, 314

Young, James, Burns on, vi, 373

Young, Stephen, Burns on, vi, 373

Young Bicham: a ballad, xl, 85-8

Young Friend, Epistle to a, vi, 212-14

Young Highland Rover, vi, 305

Young Jamie, Pride of a' the Plain, vi, 515

Young Jockie was the Blyhest Lad, vi, 362

Young Lady, To a, xli, 547

Young May Moon, xli, 842

Young and Old, xlii, 1103

Young Peggy Blooms, vi, 114-15

Yount, John, xxiii, 416

You're Welcome, Willie Stewart, vi, 438

Youth, age and, Shakespeare on, xl, 273; aspirations of, xix, 31; beauty of, iii, 112; Byron on glories of, xli, 809; Carlyle on, xxv, 334; confidence of, v, 65; Confucius on, xliv, 30 (22); determines course of life, i, 73; Ecclesiastes on, xliv, 353 (9-10); education best begun in, iii, 104; faith of, xix, 34-5; Goethe on, 13-14; Kingsley on, xlii, 1103; nature's recipe of, xix, 95; needs guidance, 379; plasticity of, xxv, 377-8; Pliny on leniency with, ix, 354; reason of pleasantness of, xxiv, 67-8; poetry and, xxxix, 327-8; Shakespeare on, xl, 268; Shakespeare on lightness of, xlvi, 176; son of Cupid and Psyche, iv, 73; Stevenson on, xxviii, 314; virtue and, i, 219; Wordsworth on, xli, 611

Youth and Age, Essay on, Bacon's, iii, 110-11

Youth and Age, by Byron, xli, 803-4

Youth and Age, by Coleridge, xli, 719-20

Youth, My Lost, xlii, 1343-5

Yspaddaden, Penkawr, xxxii, 156

Yu, Emperor, xliv, 68 (1) note

Yu, the historian, xliv, 53 (6)

Yu Jo, disciple of Confucius, xliv, 40 (9)

Yuan Jang, xliv, 52 (46)

Yuan Ssu, disciple of Confucius, xliv, 19 (3), 46 (1) note

Yu-chung, xliv, 64 (8), 65

Yu-tzu, disciple of Confucius, xliv, 5 (2), 6 (12, 13)

Yukta, xlv, 825, 826, 827

Yunan, King, story of, xvi, 33-43

Yunani Sage, story of the, v, 202

Zacchæus, the publican, xliv, 409 (1-10)

Zachariah, the prophet, xliv, 392 (51)

Zacharias, the priest, xliv, 357-8, 360-1; Mohammed on, xlv, 919-20, 965

Zâid, freedman of Mohammed, xlv, 1003 note

Zainab, wife of Mohammed, xlv, 999 note 2, 1003 note

Zaleucus, Cicero on, ix, 155

Zalih, xlv, 916-17

Zalmunna, reference to, xliv, 253 (11)

Zanche, Michel, in Hell, xx, 93 and note 5; murder of, 142 note 6

Zanoguera, John, xiv, 407

Zapoletes, More on the, xxxvi, 232-3

Zarate, Francisco de, xxxiii, 220 note

Zarephath, the widow of, xliv, 369 (26)

Zeal, "excessive, but little wisdom shows," viii, 245; excessive, Browne on, iii, 269; excessive, Penn on, i, 398 (76-8), 353 (142-3); knowledge and, Pascal on, xlviii, 308 (868); More on, xxxvi, 165; on occasion waits, iv, 392; Raleigh on, xl, 208; without charity, i, 383 (541)

Zebah, reference to, xliv, 253 (11)

Zebra, descent of the, xi, 173-4

Zedechias, physician, xxxix, 86

Zedekiah, King, xxxvi, 333

Zeeb, reference to, xliv, 253 (11)

Zeno, the Eleatic, xii, 40; in Athens, xxviii, 59; in Limbo, xx, 20; mission of, ii, 157 (108); native of Cyprus, xxviii, 60; Newman on, 53; on Pericles, xii, 41; on two kinds of pupils, xxxii, 67

Zephon, in PARADISE LOST, iv, 177-178

Zephyr, and Aurora, iv, 31

Zertusht, and the Yunani sage, v, 202

Zeruiah, sons of, xliii, 100

Zethus, founder of Thebes, xxii, 158

Zeus, Æschylus on, viii, 62; throne of, on Athos, 16; Cronos and, 157 note 2; has power over everything but death, 140; subject to the Fates, 174; guardian of the hearth and board, 7, 30; Io and, 178-9, 185 and note 59; guardian of marriage-bed, 123; Odysseus and, xxii, 10-11, 72, 179-80, 344; overthrow prophesied, viii, 182, 187-8; orders Phæacians punished, xxii, 184-5; Prometheus and, viii, 164; why represented with ram's face, xxxiii, 26; Semele and, viii, 307; god of strangers and beggars, xxii, 127; Thetis and, viii, 182 note 49; thunderbolts of, controlled by

Athena, 147 (see also Jove, Jupiter)

Zeuxidamus, on the Spartans, xxxii, 61

Zeuxis, Agatharchus and, xii, 51; Cervantes on, xiv, 9

Ziba, and David, xli, 498

Zikrs, xvi, 85 note 7

Zinc, action of, on water, xxx, 127-8

"Zingara," statue called, xxxi, 332 note 1

Zion, beauty and glory of, xliv, 205; Bernard of Morlaix on, xlv, 561; Bunyan on, xv, 159; chosen of God, xliv, 318 (13-18); description of a citizen of, 160; privileges of citizenship in, 257; Milton on, iv, 139

Zion, Mount, xliv, 247 (68)

Ziphites, David on the, xliv, 212

Zipporah, reference to, vi, 172

Zisca, John, skin of, xxiv, 402

Zoilus, Apollo and, xxviii, 395; Cervantes on, xiv, 9

Zoology, Locke on study of, xxxvii, 157

Zoophytes, in Falkland Islands, xxix, 216-18; Harvey on, xxxviii, 137

Zoospores, Pasteur on, xxxviii, 359

Zophar the Naamathite, xliv, 75, 89, 103, 143

Zophiel, the cherub, iv, 220

Zopyrus, teacher of Alcibiades, xii, 110

Zopyrus, servant of Darius, xxvii, 23

Zoraida, Lela, xiv, 392; story of, 417-44

Zorillo, Darwin on the, xxix, 92

Zoroaster, on God, xxxix, 106; on perseverance, v, 82

Zosimus, freedman of Pliny, ix, 289-90

Zounds, meaning of, xix, 210 note 1

Zubeydeh, wife of Harun Er-Rashid, xvi, 145

Zwinglius, Voltaire on, xxxiv, 85

CHRONOLOGICAL INDEX

(Names printed in SMALL CAPITALS refer to entries in the *General Index*)

447

400 A. D.—GLORIA IN EXCELSIS, great Latin hymn, written (supposed date)

430 A. D.—Death of Saint AUGUSTINE

450-500 A. D.—Birth of BEOWULF, hero of the Saxon epic (supposed date)

571 A. D.—Birth of MOHAMMED, the prophet of Arabia, founder of Mohammedanism

622-624 A. D.—Beginning of the MOHAMMEDAN Era and Holy War

632 A. D.—Death of MOHAMMED

673 A. D.—Birth of the venerable BEDE, Saxon writer in England, most distinguished scholar of his age

676 A. D.—Birth of St. JOHN OF DAMASCUS, great theologian of the Greek Church

725 A. D.—Birth of St. STEPHEN the Sabaite, hymnist.

735 A. D.—Death of the Venerable BEDE

742 A. D.—Birth of CHARLEMAGNE (Charles the Great), king of the Franks and Roman Emperor

778 A. D.—CHARLEMAGNE returns from Spain. The rear-guard of his army is annihilated at Roncesvalles by the Basques. Subject of "The SONG OF ROLAND"

814 A. D.—Death of CHARLEMAGNE

935 A. D.—Birth of FIRDOUSI (Abul Kasim Mausur), Persian epic poet

1000 A. D.—Discovery of North America by LEIF (Ericsson) THE LUCKY (supposed date)

1012 A. D.—Death of FIRDOUSI

1050 A. D.—Birth of OMAR KHAYYAM, Persian astronomer and poet. Author of the "RUBAIYAT"

1091 A. D.—Birth of St. BERNARD OF CLAIRVAUX, mystical theologian and hymnist

1100 A. D.—Period assigned to Irish epic the DESTRUCTION OF DA DERGAS HOSTEL (supposed date)

1112 A. D.—Birth of WACE, Anglo-Norman poet

1125 A. D.—Birth of BERNARD OF MORLAIX (or of Cluny), Benedictine monk; author of Latin poem, basis of JERUSALEM THE GOLDEN (supposed date)

1180 A. D.—Death of WACE, Anglo-Norman poet

1200 A. D.—Period assigned to the composition of the VOLSUNGA SAGA

1200 A. D.—History of the Danes by SAXE GRAMMATICUS written

1200-1275 A. D.—Period of Thomas à CELANO, author of DIES IRÆ

1200-1300 A. D.—Period of JACOBUS DE BENEDICTIS, author of "STABAT MATER"

1265 A. D.—Birth of DANTE Alighieri, Italian poet, author of "THE DIVINE COMEDY"

1300-1350 A. D.—Period of Sir John MANDEVILLE, hero and reputed author of the famous work "Travels of Sir John Mandeville"

CHRONOLOGICAL INDEX

(Names printed in SMALL CAPITALS refer to entries in the *General Index*)

1316-1307 B. C.—Siege of TROY by the Greeks under AGAMEMNON, King of Argos

900-800 B. C.—Birth of HOMER, Greek epic poet. There is great uncertainty regarding both the date and place of his birth

557 B. C.—Birth of Siddhartha GAUTAMA, known as BUDDHA, founder of Buddhism, the "Light of Asia"

551 B. C.—Birth of CONFUCIUS, Chinese philosopher and moralist

550 B. C.—Birth of ÆSOP, Greek fabulist (supposed date)

525 B. C.—Birth of ÆSCHYLUS, father of classic Greek tragedy

500-300 B. C.—The MAHA BHARATA, Hindu epic, probable date of writing, according to the claims of most scholars

495 B.C.—Birth of SOPHOCLES, the "most perfectly balanced among the three great masters of Greek tragedy"

492 B. C.—CORIOLANUS (Gnæus Marcius), defeats the Volsci, an Italic tribe, capturing their town Corioli, whence his surname

491 B. C.—CORIOLANUS banished from Rome for demanding the deposition of the plebeian tribunes

490 D. C. Battle of MARATHON between the Athenians and Platæans under Miltiades and the Persian army of Darius

490 B. C.—Birth of HERODOTUS, the "father of history" (supposed date)

480 B. C.—Birth of EURIPIDES, Greek tragedian, the youngest of the great trio

479 B. C.—The battle of MYCALE, between the Greeks under Leotychides, King of Sparta, and the army of Xerxes

478 B. C.—Death of CONFUCIUS

477 B. C.—Death of BUDDHA

466 B. C.—PERICLES, General of Athenian forces, subdues revolts in Eubœa and Megara

470-460 B. C.—Birth of HIPPOCRATES, Greek physician, the "father of medicine"

469 B. C.—Birth of SOCRATES, Athenian philosopher, the central figure in the history of Greek thought

468 B. C.—Death of ARISTIDES, called "The Just," Athenian statesman and general (supposed date)

456 B. C.—Death of ÆSCHYLUS (supposed date)

455 B. C.—PERICLES overruns the Peloponnesus

447

450 B. C.—Birth of ALCIBIADES, Athenian statesman and general

450 B. C.—Birth of ARISTOPHANES, "the greatest of the comic writers in Greek" (supposed date)

444-429 B. C.—PERICLES serves as ruler of the Athenian Commonwealth

428 B. C.—Birth of PLATO, Athenian philosopher, disciple of Socrates

426 B. C.—Death of HERODOTUS (supposed date)

407 B. C.—ALCIBIADES, Athenian statesman, deposed

406 B. C.—Death of EURIPIDES

405 B. C.—Death of SOPHOCLES

404 B. C.—Death of ALCIBIADES

400 B. C.—BOOK OF JOB written, according to many scholars

399 B. C.—Death of SOCRATES

388 B. C.—Death of ARISTOPHANES

384 B. C.—Birth of DEMOSTHENES, Athenian orator

384 B. C.—Birth of ARISTOTLE of Stagira, the famous Greek philosopher, whose theories long dominated the learned world

380-360 B. C.—Death of HIPPOCRATES, Greek physician

356 B. C.—Birth of ALEXANDER THE GREAT, King of Macedon, conqueror of most of the then known world

337 B. C.—DEMOSTHENES chosen as foremost statesman at Athens

323 B. C.—Death of ALEXANDER THE GREAT

322 B. C.—Death of DEMOSTHENES

322 B. C.—Death of ARISTOTLE

106 B. C.—Birth of Marcus Tullius CICECO, the great Roman orator

100 B. C.—Birth of Julius CÆSAR, Roman general and statesman (supposed date)

83 B. C.—Birth of Marcus Antonius (Mark ANTONY), Roman triumvir and general

76 B. C.—CICERO elected quæstor to the province of Lilybæum, Sicily

70 B. C.—Birth of Publius Vergilius Maro (VIRGIL), Roman epic poet; author of the ÆNEID

69 B. C.—Birth of CLEOPATRA, Queen of Egypt, famous for her intrigues and extravagance

64 B. C.—CICERO elected Consul. Crushes the conspiracy of CATILINE

58-50 B. C.—CÆSAR conquers Gaul

58 B. C.—CICERO banished from Rome by the Triumvirate

51 B. C.—CICERO proconsul of Cilicia

49 B. C.—War for supremacy between CÆSAR and POMPEY. Cæsar crosses the Rubicon

48 B. C.—OCTAVIUS defeats Mark ANTONY in naval battle at Actium

48-44 B. C.—Julius CÆSAR made dictator

48 B. C.—POMPEY defeated by CÆSAR in the battle of Pharsalia. Later murdered in Egypt

45 B. C.—CLEOPATRA marries Mark ANTONY

44 B. C.—Julius CÆSAR assassinated in Rome

43 B. C.—CICERO killed by agents of ANTONY

43 B. C.—The second Triumvirate formed by Mark ANTONY, OCTAVIUS and Marcus Æmilius LEPIDUS

42 B. C.—Battle of PHILIPPI; Brutus and Cassius defeated by Antony and Octavius

42 B. C.—CLEOPATRA meets Mark ANTONY by his order at Tarsus

37 B. C.—VIRGIL'S "Eclogues" completed

31 B. C.—Battle of ACTIUM between OCTAVIUS and Mark ANTONY

30 B. C.—Death of CLEOPATRA, Queen of Egypt, by suicide at Alexandria. ANTONY commits suicide

30 B. C.—VIRGIL'S "Georgics" first issued

19 B. C.—Death of VIRGIL, Roman poet

7-2 B. C.—Birth of CHRIST

46-51 A. D.—Birth of PLUTARCH, Greek biographer—the "great biographer of Antiquity"

50 A. D.—Birth of EPICTETUS, Græco-Roman Stoic philosopher (supposed date)

54-58 A. D.—PAUL'S First and Second Epistles to the CORINTHIANS written (supposed date)

62 A. D.—Gaius Plinius Cæcilius Secundus, known as PLINY THE YOUNGER, born

69-70 A. D.—Period covered by the fragments of the "ANNALS" and "Histories" of TACITUS

70 A. D.—The Gospel according to St. LUKE written (supposed date)

80-90 A. D.—ACTS OF THE APOSTLES written, according to accepted chronologies

90 A. D.—EPICTETUS banished from Rome by the Emperor DOMITIAN, who abhorred his Stoic sentiments

100 A. D.—PLINY THE YOUNGER made consul by TRAJAN and governor of Bithynia

113 A. D.—Death of PLINY THE YOUNGER

120-130 A. D.—Death of PLUTARCH, the biographer

121 A. D.—Birth of MARCUS AURELIUS Antoninus, Roman emperor and moralist. Adopted son of the Emperor Aurelius Antoninus

161 A. D.—MARCUS AURELIUS Antoninus succeeds to Imperial throne

170-220 A. D.—Birth of St. CLEMENT of Alexandria, one of the "Fathers" of the Christian Church (supposed date)

180 A. D.—Death of MARCUS AURELIUS Antoninus

354 A. D.—Birth of Aurelius Augustinus, known as Saint AUGUSTINE, Bishop of Hippo, the greatest theologian of the ancient Church

387 A. D.—Saint AUGUSTINE converted to Catholic Christianity from the errors of the Manichæan sect

1302 A. D.—DANTE Alighieri, condemned to death by his political enemies, saves himself by exile

1313 A. D.—Birth of Giovanni BOCCACCIO, Italian poet and novelist; author of the "Decameron"

1321 A. D.—Death of DANTE Alighieri

1326 A. D.—Birth of John GOWER, English poet (supposed date)

1337 A. D.—Birth of Sir John FROISSART, French poet and historian

1340 A. D.—Birth of Geoffrey CHAUCER, English poet

1346 A. D.—The battle of CRECY in which King EDWARD III of England defeated the French Army under PHILIP VI

1356 A. D.—Battle of POITIERS in which Edward the BLACK PRINCE gained a great victory over the French and captured the French king, JOHN II

1356 A. D.—"Voyage and Travaile of Sir John MANDEVILLE" written

1364 A. D.—CHAUCER's "Canterbury Tales" written

1372 A. D.—Date assigned to death of Sir John MANDEVILLE, hero of book of travels

1375 A. D.—Death of Giovanni BOCCACCIO, "creator of the classic Italian prose and father of the modern novel"

1379-1380 A. D.—Birth of Thomas HAEMMERLEIN, known as Thomas à KEMPIS

1381 A. D.—Wat TYLER's Rebellion. The name usually applied to the English social revolt of 1381, from Wat Tyler its chief leader

1388 A. D.—Battle of OTTERBURN, between the forces of PERCY, surnamed Hotspur, and DOUGLAS, in which both leaders fell. The battle is commemorated by the ballad "CHEVY CHASE"

1400 A. D.—Death of Geoffrey CHAUCER

1408 A. D.—Death of John GOWER

1410 A. D.—Death of Sir John FROISSART

1422 A. D.—Birth of William CAXTON, the first English printer (supposed date)

1469 A. D.—Birth of Niccolo di Bernardo MACHIAVELLI

1471 A. D.—Death of Thomas à KEMPIS

1471 A. D.—Birth of Albrecht DURER, German painter, engraver and designer, the "greatest master of the German Renaissance"

1472 A. D.—DANTE's "DIVINE COMEDY" first printed

1474 A. D.—CAXTON's translation of "The RECUYELL OF THE HISTORIES OF TROY" published, the first book printed in the English language

1475 A. D.—Birth of Thomas WOLSEY, English Cardinal and statesman (supposed date)

1478 A. D.—Birth of Sir Thomas MORE, English author and statesman

1480-1537 A. D.—Birth of Alessandro de MEDICI, Duke of Florence (supposed date)

1483 A. D.—Birth of Martin LUTHER, the "Founder of Protestant Civilization"

1485 A. D.—Sir Thomas MALORY's "Morte D'Arthur" published

1491 A. D.—Death of William CAXTON

1492 A. D.—The discovery of the West Indies by Christopher COLUMBUS

1495 A. D.—Birth of François RABELAIS, French humorist

1497 A. D.—John CABOT discovers the mainland of North America, probably Labrador

1500 A. D.—Birth of Raphael HOLINSHED, English chronicler

1500 A. D.—Birth of Benvenuto CELLINI, Italian sculptor and goldsmith

1503 A. D.—Birth of Sir Thomas WYATT, English diplomatist and poet (supposed date)

1505 A. D.—Birth of John KNOX, Scottish reformer, statesman and writer

1506 A. D.—Birth of St. FRANCIS XAVIER, Spanish Jesuit missionary

1509 A. D.—Birth of John CALVIN, French reformer and theologian

1513 A. D.—Niccolo MACHIAVELLI imprisoned and tortured

1516 A. D.—Birth of Roger ASCHAM, English classical scholar and author

1516 A. D.—"UTOPIA" by Thomas MORE written

1516 A. D.—"Orlando Furioso" published

1517 A. D.—Birth of Ambroise PARE, French surgeon

1517 A. D.—Birth of Henry HOWARD, Earl of Surrey, English poet (supposed date)

1517 A. D.—Martin LUTHER posts "THE NINETY-FIVE THESES" on the church door at Wittenberg

1519 A. D.—Birth of Cosimo de MEDICI, Grand Duke of Tuscany

1520 A. D.—Martin LUTHER publishes the fundamental principles of the Reformation and is expelled from the Church

1523 A. D.—Pope CLEMENT VII elected

1523 A. D.—Birth of Richard EDWARDS, English dramatist

1526 A. D.—Sack of Rome by the Ghibelline house of Colonna

1527 A. D.—Death of Niccolo MACHIAVELLI

1528 A. D.—Death of Albrecht DURER

1529 A. D.—Sir Thomas MORE made Lord Chancellor of England

1530 A. D.—Death of Cardinal WOLSEY

1533 A. D.—Birth of Michel Eyquem de MONTAIGNE, French philosopher and essayist

1533 A. D.—Death of Ludovico ARIOSTO

1533 A. D.—John CALVIN banished from Paris

1534 A. D.—Martin LUTHER's translation of the BIBLE published

1535 A. D.—Birth of George GASCOIGNE, English poet (supposed date)

1535 A. D.—Sir Thomas MORE executed on Tower Hill

1536 A. D.—CALVIN's "INSTITUTES OF THE CHRISTIAN RELIGION" published

1536 A. D.—Birth of Thomas SACKVILLE, Earl of Dorset, English poet

1537 A. D.—Death of Alessandro, Duke de MEDICI

1537 A. D.—Triumphal entry of the Emperor CHARLES V into Rome

1539 A. D.—Birth of Sir Humphrey GILBERT, founder of the first English colony in North America

1540 A. D.—Birth of Sir Francis DRAKE, English navigator (supposed date)

1542 A. D.—John KNOX becomes a convert to Protestant doctrines

1542 A. D.—Death of Sir Thomas WYATT

1544 A. D.—Birth of Torquato TASSO, Italian epic poet

1545 A. D.—Birth of Nicholas BRETON, English poet (supposed date)

1547 A. D.—John KNOX a prisoner in France

1547 A. D.—Birth of Miguel CERVANTES Saavedra, Spanish novelist and poet, author of "DON QUIXOTE"

1547 A. D.—Henry HOWARD, Earl of Surrey, English poet and courtier, beheaded

1549 A. D.—First English prayer-book composed

1550 A. D.—Birth of Edward DE VERE, Earl of Oxford, English poet and courtier

1552 A. D.—Birth of Sir Walter RALEIGH, English navigator, author, courtier and soldier

1552 A. D.—Death of St. FRANCIS XAVIER

1552-1555 A. D.—Period of the War of SIENA, when Piero Strozzi acted as general for Henry II of France against the Spaniards

1553 A. D.—Birth of Anthony MUNDAY, English dramatist, poet and compiler

1553 A. D.—Birth of John FLORIO, English lexicographer, author and translator

1553 A. D.—Birth of Edmund SPENSER, English poet

1553 A. D.—Birth of John LYLY, English dramatist

1553 A. D.—Death of François RABELAIS

1554 A. D.—Birth of Sir Philip SIDNEY, English soldier and author

1556 A. D.—Birth of Thomas LODGE, English novelist, dramatist and poet (supposed date)

1558 A. D.—John KNOX's "First Blast of the Trumpet against the Monstrous Regiment of Women" published

1558 A. D.—Birth of George PEELE, English dramatist and poet

1558-1566 A. D.—Period covered by the "Autobiography of Benvenuto CELLINI"

1558-1603 A. D.—Reign of ELIZABETH, Queen of England

1560 A. D.—Birth of Robert GREENE, English dramatist, novelist and poet (supposed date)

1561 A. D.—Birth of Francis BACON, English philosopher, jurist and statesman

1561 A. D.—Birth of Robert SOUTHWELL, English poet and Jesuit martyr (supposed date)

1562 A. D.—Lope de VEGA, the "Spanish Shakespeare," born

1562 A. D.—Birth of Henry CONSTABLE, English poet

1562 A. D.—Birth of Samuel DANIEL, English poet and historian

1563 A. D.—Birth of Joshua SYLVESTER, English poet

1563 A. D.—Birth of Michael DRAYTON, English poet

1564 A. D.—Death of John CALVIN

1564 A. D.—Birth of William SHAKESPEARE, English poet and dramatist

1564 A. D.—Birth of Christopher MARLOWE, English poet and dramatist

1565 A. D.—Birth of Richard ROWLANDS, English poet

1566 A. D.—Death of Richard EDWARDS

1567 A. D.—Birth of William ALEXANDER, Earl of Stirling, Scottish poet and statesman (supposed date)

1567 A. D.—Sir Francis DRAKE commanding a ship under Sir John Hawkins is defeated by the Spaniards

1567 A. D.—Birth of Robert DEVEREUX, Earl of Essex, English courtier and soldier

1567 A. D.—Birth of Thomas CAMPION, English poet (supposed date)

1568 A. D.—Birth of Sir Henry WOTTON, English diplomatist and author

1568 A. D.—Death of Roger ASCHAM

1569-1574 A. D.—Sir Walter RALEIGH serves in the Huguenot Army in France

1569 A. D.—Death of Bernardo Tasso, Italian poet

1570 A. D.—Birth of Thomas DEKKER, English dramatist (supposed date)

1571 A. D.—Death of Benvenuto CELLINI

1572 A. D.—Death of John KNOX

1573 A. D.—Birth of John DONNE, English poet and divine

1574 A. D.—Birth of Ben JONSON, English dramatist (supposed date)

1574 A. D.—Death of Cosimo de' MEDICI

1574 A. D.—Birth of Richard BARNFIELD, English poet

1575 A. D.—Miguel CERVANTES Saavedra, maimed for life in the battle of Lepanto, is captured by the Moors. He was a slave for five years among them

1575 A. D.—Birth of Thomas HEYWOOD, English dramatist and miscellaneous writer (supposed date)

1577 A. D.—Birth of Robert BURTON, English writer

1577 A. D.—Death of George GASCOIGNE

1577 A. D.—Sir Francis DRAKE's voyage in "The Golden Hind"

1578 A. D.—"Chronicles of England," by Raphael HOLINSHED, published

1578 A. D.—Sir Humphrey GILBERT receives from Queen Elizabeth a charter to plant a colony in North America

1578 A. D.—Birth of William HARVEY, English physiologist and anatomist

1578 A. D.—Sir Walter RALEIGH engages with his half-brother Sir Humphrey GILBERT in his first expedition against the Spaniards

1579 A. D.—Birth of John FLETCHER, English dramatist and poet

1579 A. D.—Birth of Captain John SMITH, English adventurer

1579 A. D.—"The Shepherds Calendar," by Edmund SPENSER, published

1580 A. D.—Birth of John WEBSTER, English dramatist (supposed date)

1580 A. D.—Death of Raphael HOLINSHED

1582 A. D.—Birth of Richard CORBET, English prelate and poet

1583 A. D.—Birth of Philip MASSINGER, English dramatist

1584 A. D.—Birth of Francis BEAUMONT, English dramatist and poet

1585 A. D.—Birth of Cornelius JANSEN, who gave his name to the Jansenist school

1585 A. D.—Birth of William DRUMMOND, Scottish poet

1586 A. D.—Birth of Martin RINKART, German hymn writer

1586 A. D.—DRAKE brings home the despairing Virginian colony

1586 A. D.—Death of Sir Philip SIDNEY

1587 A. D.—Christopher MARLOWE's first tragedy "Tamburlaine" produced

1588 A. D.—Birth of George WITHER, English poet

1588 A. D.—Birth of Thomas HOBBES, English philosopher

1588 A. D.—Christopher MARLOWE's "Doctor FAUSTUS" first produced

1590 A. D.—"The FAERIE QUEENE," by Edmund SPENSER, published

1590 A. D.—Death of Ambroise PARE

1591 A. D.—Christopher MARLOWE's tragedy of "EDWARD II" is produced

1591 A. D.—Birth of William BROWNE

1591 A. D.—Birth of Robert HERRICK, English lyric poet

1592 A. D.—Death of Michel de MONTAIGNE

1592 A. D.—Birth of Francis QUARLES, English poet

1592 A. D.—Sir Walter RALEIGH a prisoner in the Tower

1592 A. D.—Death of Robert GREENE

1593 A. D.—Death of Christopher MARLOWE

1593 A. D.—Birth of Izaak WALTON, English author; noted for his "Compleat Angler"

1593 A. D.—Birth of George HERBERT, English poet

1594 A. D.—Birth of GUSTAVUS ADOLPHUS, King of Sweden

1595 A. D.—Death of Torquato TASSO at Rome

1595 A. D.—Sir Walter RALEIGH discovers Guiana

1595 A. D.—Death of Robert SOUTHWELL

1596 A. D.—Birth of James SHIRLEY, English dramatist

1596 A. D.—Death of Sir Francis DRAKE

1596 A. D.—Birth of René DESCARTES, French philosopher

1597 A. D.—Death of George PEELE (supposed date)

1597 A. D.—Francis BACON's Essays first published

1598 A. D.—Birth of Thomas CAREW, English poet

1599 A. D.—Thomas DEKKER's play, "The SHOEMAKER'S HOLIDAY," first acted

1599 A. D.—Death of Edmund SPENSER

1600 A. D.—Birth of Don Pedro CALDERON, Spanish dramatist and poet

1601 A. D.—Death of Robert DEVEREUX, second Earl of Essex, chief favorite of Queen Elizabeth

1603 A. D.—First edition of SHAKESPEARE's "HAMLET" published

1604 A. D.—Death of Edward DE VERE, Earl of Oxford

1604 A. D.—Beginning of Sir Walter RALEIGH's imprisonment of twelve years for treason against James I. During this period he wrote his "History of the World"

1605 A. D.—"KING LEAR" first acted

1605 A. D.—The first part of "DON QUIXOTE" published in Madrid

1605 A. D.—Birth of Sir Thomas BROWNE, scholar and antiquary; author of "RELIGIO MEDICI"

1605 A. D.—Birth of William HABINGTON, English poet

1606 A. D.—Birth of Edmund WALLER, English poet

1606 A. D.—Birth of Sir William D'AVENANT, English poet and play-writer

1606 A. D.—Death of John LYLY, English romancer and dramatist

1606 A. D.—Birth of Pierre CORNEILLE, French dramatist. The works of Corneille represent most fully the ideal of French classical tragedy

1608 A. D.—Birth of Thomas FULLER, English author and divine, famous for his work, the "Worthies of England"

1608 A. D.—Birth of John MILTON, English poet and statesman

1608 A. D.—Death of Thomas SACKVILLE, Earl of Dorset, English poet and statesman

1609 A. D.—Birth of Sir John SUCKLING, English poet

1610 A. D.—Ben JONSON's play, "The ALCHEMIST," first acted

1610 A. D.—SHAKESPEARE's tragedy, "MACBETH," first produced

1611 A. D.—Birth of William CARTWRIGHT, English poet and divine

1611 A. D.—SHAKESPEARE's play, "The TEMPEST," first produced

1611 A. D.—First English translation of "DON QUIXOTE" (first part) by Thomas Shelton is published

1612 A. D.—Birth of Thomas JORDAN, English poet

1612 A. D.—Birth of James GRAHAM, first Marquis of Montrose

1612 A. D.—Birth of Samuel BUTLER, English satirist

1613 A. D.—Birth of Duke de LA ROCHEFOUCAULD, French epigrammatic moralist

1613 A. D.—Birth of Richard CRASHAW, English poet (supposed date)

1615 A. D.—CERVANTES's "DON QUIXOTE" (second part) published

1616 A. D.—Death of Francis BEAUMONT, English poet and dramatist. In collaboration with FLETCHER wrote fifty-four plays

1616 A. D.—Death of Miguel CERVANTES Saavedra

1616 A. D.—Death of William SHAKESPEARE

1618 A. D.—Birth of Abraham COWLEY, English poet and essayist

1618 A. D.—Birth of Richard LOVELACE, English poet

1618 A. D.—Execution of Sir Walter RALEIGH

1618 A. D.—Francis BACON, philosopher and statesman, made Lord Chancellor and Baron Verulam

1619 A. D.—Death of Thomas CAMPION

1620 A. D.—Lord BACON's "NOVUM ORGANUM" published

1620 A. D.—The MAYFLOWER COMPACT signed

1620 A. D.—Birth of Alexander BROME, English poet and dramatist

1620 A. D.—Birth of John EVELYN, English author

1621 A. D.—Francis BACON, statesman and philosopher, made Viscount St. Albans; convicted of bribery. Sentenced by House of Lords to loss of offices, imprisonment, and fine

1621 A. D.—Birth of Andrew MARVELL, English poet and politician

1621 A. D.—Birth of Jean de LA FONTAINE, French poet and fable writer

1622 A. D.—Birth of Henry VAUGHAN, English poet

1622 A. D.—Birth of Jean Baptiste MOLIERE, the "greatest of French dramatists"

1623 A. D.—Birth of Blaise PASCAL, French philosopher and author

1623 A. D.—John WEBSTER's play, "The DUCHESS OF MALFI," published

1623 A. D.—First folio edition of Shakespeare's plays published by HEMINGE and CONDELL

1624 A. D.—John SMITH's "General Historie of Virginia and New England" published

1625 A. D.—MASSINGER's play, "A NEW WAY TO PAY OLD DEBTS," first acted

1625 A. D.—Death of John WEBSTER (supposed date)

1625 A. D.—Death of John FLETCHER

1625 A. D.—Death of Thomas LODGE

1626 A. D.—Death of Nicholas BRETON (supposed date)

1626 A. D.—Death of Francis BACON

1627 A. D.—Birth of Jacques Benigne BOSSUET, French pulpit orator

1627 A. D.—BACON's "NEW ATLANTIS" published

1628 A. D.—William HARVEY's work on "The Circulation of the Blood" published in Latin at Frankfort

1628 A. D.—Birth of Sir William TEMPLE, English statesman and essayist

1631 A. D.—Death of Michael DRAYTON

1631 A. D.—Death of Captain John SMITH

1631 A. D.—Birth of John DRYDEN, English dramatist, poet, and critic

1632 A. D.—Death of GUSTAVUS ADOLPHUS

1632 A. D.—Birth of John LOCKE, English philosopher

1633 A. D.—Birth of Samuel PEPYS, English diarist

1633 A. D.—Death of George HERBERT

1633 A. D.—Death of Anthony MUNDAY

1633 A. D.—Abraham COWLEY's "Poetical Blossoms" published

1635 A. D.—Death of LOPE DE VEGA

1636 A. D.—Birth of Nicolas BOILEAU-Despreaux, greatest French critic of the 17th century

1637 A. D.—Death of Ben JONSON

1637 A. D.—René DESCARTES's "DISCOURSE ON METHOD" published

1639 A. D.—The first American constitution of government, adopted by a popular convention of the towns, Windsor, Wethersfield, and Hartford

1639 A. D.—Birth of Sir Charles SEDLEY, English poet and dramatist

1639 A. D.—Birth of Jean Baptiste RACINE, greatest of French classical dramatists

1640 A. D.—Death of Philip MASSINGER

1640 A. D.—Death of Robert BURTON

1641 A. D.—Death of Thomas DEKKER (supposed date)

1641 A. D.—MILTON's "Prelatical Episcopacy" published

1641 A. D.—MILTON's "Reformation of England" published

1641 A. D.—The first code of laws established in New England; known as "THE BODY OF LIBERTIES"

1642 A. D.—Death of Sir John SUCKLING (supposed date)

1642 A. D.—Sir Thomas BROWNE's "RELIGIO MEDICI" published

1642 A. D.—The Long Parliament closes the theaters

1642 A. D.—Birth of Sir Isaac NEWTON, "The greatest English mathematician and physicist"

1644 A. D.—John WINTHROP, Deputy Governor of Massachusetts, publishes a document on "ARBITRARY GOVERNMENT"

1644 A. D.—Birth of William PENN, the founder of Pennsylvania

1644 A. D.—MILTON's "AREOPAGITICA" and "TRACTATE ON EDUCATION" published

1647 A. D.—Abraham COWLEY's "The Wish" published

1649 A. D.—King CHARLES I of England executed

1650 A. D.—Death of René DESCARTES

1651 A. D.—Thomas HOBBES's "LEVIATHAN" published

1653 A. D.—CROMWELL and his council of Officers adopt "The INSTRUMENT OF GOVERNMENT"

1653 A. D.—Oliver CROMWELL becomes Lord Protector of England

1653 A. D.—Izaak WALTON's "The Compleat Angler" published

1656 A. D.—Sir Henry VANE published "A HEALING QUESTION" on the subject of civil and religious liberty

1656-1657 A. D.—PASCAL's "LETTERS" published

1657 A. D.—Death of William HARVEY

1657 A. D.—Birth of John DENNIS, English critic and dramatist

1660-1672 A. D.—John BUNYAN in prison

1661 A. D.—Birth of Charles Montague, Earl of HALIFAX, English statesman and financier

1661 A. D.—Birth of Daniel DEFOE, English novelist, author of "Robinson Crusoe"

1662 A. D.—Death of Blaise PASCAL

1664 A. D.—Birth of Matthew PRIOR, English poet and diplomatist

1665 A. D.—Birth of Lady Grisel BAILLIE, Scottish poet

1666 A. D.—John DRYDEN'S "Annus Mirabilis" published. It procured for him in 1670 the Poet Laureateship

1667 A. D.—Birth of Jonathan SWIFT, "Greatest of English satirists"

1667 A. D.—MILTON'S "PARADISE LOST" published

1667 A. D.—Death of Jeremy TAYLOR

1667 A. D.—Death of George WITHER

1668 A. D.—William PENN a prisoner in the Tower

1670 A. D.—John DRYDEN appointed Poet Laureate

1670 A. D.—John ELIOT'S "BRIEF NARRATIVE" on the Indians published

1670 A. D.—Izaak WALTON'S "LIFE OF GEORGE HERBERT" published

1671 A. D.—Birth of Anthony Ashley Cooper, third Earl of SHAFTESBURY, moralist

1671 A. D.—Birth of Colley CIBBER, English actor and dramatist

1672 A. D.—Birth of Richard STEELE, English essayist and dramatist

1672 A. D.—Birth of Joseph ADDISON, English poet and essayist

1673 A. D.—Death of Jean Baptiste Poquelin MOLIERE

1674 A. D.—Birth of Isaac WATTS, English nonconformist theologian, hymn writer and author

1674 A. D.—Death of Robert HERRICK

1674 A. D.—Death of John MILTON

1675 A. D.—Birth of Ambrose PHILIPS, English poet and dramatist (supposed date)

1678 A. D.—Birth of Henry St. John, first Viscount BOLINGBROKE, English statesman, author and orator

1678 A. D.—First edition of John BUNYAN'S "PILGRIM'S PROGRESS" appears

1679 A. D.—Death of Thomas HOBBES

1680 A. D.—Death of Samuel BUTLER

1681 A. D.—Birth of Esther JOHNSON, Swift's "Stella"

1681 A. D.—Death of Pedro CALDERON de la Barca

1681 A. D.—William PENN obtains a charter creating him proprietor and governor of East New Jersey and Pennsylvania

1682 A. D.—Death of Sir Thomas BROWNE

1683 A. D.—Death of Izaak WALTON

1684 A. D.—Death of Pierre CORNEILLE

1685 A. D.—Birth of George BERKELEY, Bishop of Cloyne, English metaphysical philosopher

1685 A. D.—Birth of John GAY, English poet
1686 A. D.—Birth of Allan RAMSAY, Scottish pastoral poet
1687 A. D.—Sir Isaac NEWTON's "PRINCIPIA" published
1687 A. D.—Death of Edmund WALLER
1688 A. D.—Birth of Alexander POPE, English poet and critic
1688 A. D.—Death of John BUNYAN
1689 A. D.—Birth of Lady Mary Wortley MONTAGU, English poet and letter writer
1689 A. D.—Birth of Samuel RICHARDSON, "the founder of the English domestic novel"
1690 A. D.—John LOCKE's "Essay Concerning Human Understanding" published
1694 A. D.—Birth of Lord CHESTERFIELD (Philip Dormer Stanhope), English courtier, wit and orator
1694 A. D.—Birth of VOLTAIRE (François Marie Arouet), French philosopher
1695 A. D.—Death of Jean de LA FONTAINE
1699 A. D.—Birth of Alexander ROSS, Scottish poet
1699 A. D.—Death of Jean Baptiste RACINE
1700 A. D.—Death of John DRYDEN
1700 A. D.—Birth of James THOMSON, Scottish poet
1703 A. D.—Death of Samuel PEPYS
1704 A. D.—Death of Jacques Benigne BOSSUET
1704 A. D.—Birth of William HAMILTON of Bangour, Scottish poet
1704 A. D.—Death of John LOCKE
1706 A. D.—Birth of Benjamin FRANKLIN, American statesman, scientist and author
1707 A. D.—Birth of Henry FIELDING, English novelist
1707 A. D.—Birth of Charles WESLEY, English hymn writer
1709 A. D.—Birth of Samuel JOHNSON, English lexicographer, essayist and poet
1711 A. D.—Alexander POPE's "Essay on Criticism" written
1711 A. D.—Birth of David HUME, English philosopher and historian
1711 A. D.—"The Spectator" commenced publication
1711 A. D.—Death of Nicolas BOILEAU-Despreaux
1712 A. D.—Birth of Alison Rutherford COCKBURN, Scottish ballad writer
1712 A. D.—Birth of Jean Jacques ROUSSEAU, French author
1713 A. D.—Bishop George BERKELEY's "DIALOGUES BETWEEN HYLAS AND PHILONOUS" published
1713 A. D.—Joseph ADDISON's drama "Cato" appeared
1713 A. D.—Death of Lord SHAFTESBURY (Anthony Ashley Cooper)
1713 A. D.—Birth of Laurence STERNE, English author
1713 A. D.—Jonathan SWIFT appointed Dean of St. Patrick's, Dublin, Ireland
1715 A. D.—Alexander POPE's translations from Homer published
1715 A. D.—Death of Charles Montague, Earl of HALIFAX

1716 A. D.—Birth of Thomas GRAY, English poet
1718 A. D.—Death of William PENN
1719 A. D.—Death of Joseph ADDISON
1721 A. D.—Birth of William COLLINS, English poet
1720 A. D.—Birth of John WOOLMAN, English Quaker preacher and social reformer
1721 A. D.—Birth of John SKINNER, Scottish poet
1721 A. D.—Death of Matthew PRIOR
1722 A. D.—Birth of Christopher SMART, English poet
1723 A. D.—Birth of Adam SMITH, political economist and moral philosopher
1723 A. D.—Death of Esther VANHOMRIGH, Swift's "Vanessa"
1724 A. D.—Birth of Immanuel KANT, German metaphysician
1726 A. D.—Birth of Adam AUSTIN, English poet (supposed date)
1727 A. D.—Birth of Jane ELLIOT, English poet
1727 A. D.—Death of Sir Isaac NEWTON
1728 A. D.—Death of Esther JOHNSON ("Stella")
1728 A. D.—Birth of Oliver GOLDSMITH, English author and poet
1729 A. D.—Birth of Edmund BURKE, English statesman and orator
1729 A. D.—Death of Sir Richard STEELE
1729 A. D.—Birth of Gotthold Ephraim LESSING, German critic and dramatist
1731 A. D.—Death of Daniel DEFOE
1731 A. D.—Birth of William COWPER, English poet
1732 A. D.—"Poor Richard's Almanac" by FRANKLIN is commenced
1732 A. D.—Death of John GAY
1733 A. D.—Alexander POPE's "ESSAY ON MAN" published
1734 A. D.—Death of John DENNIS
1735 A. D.—Birth of Robert GRAHAM of Gartmore
1739-40 A. D.—David HUME's "Treatise of Human Nature" published
1740 A. D.—Birth of James BOSWELL, "the greatest of English biographers"
1741 A. D.—Birth of Isobel PAGAN, Scottish poet
1742 A. D.—Henry FIELDING's "Joseph Andrews" published
1742 A. D.—Birth of Anne HUNTER, English poet
1742 A. D.—David HUME's Essays (first part) published
1743 A. D.—Birth of Anna Letitia BARBAULD, English poet
1744 A. D.—Death of Alexander POPE
1745 A. D.—Birth of Charles DIBDIN, English song writer and dramatist
1745 A. D.—Death of Jonathan SWIFT
1745 A. D.—Birth of Hannah MORE, English religious writer
1746 A. D.—Birth of Sir William JONES, English Orientalist and linguist
1746 A. D.—Birth of Hector MACNEIL, Scottish poet
1747 A. D.—Birth of Susanna BLAMIRE
1748 A. D.—Death of Isaac WATTS

1748 A. D.—Death of James THOMSON

1748 A. D.—Birth of John LOGAN, Scottish poet

1749 A. D.—Birth of Edward JENNER, English physician and discoverer of vaccination

1749 A. D.—Birth of Johann Wolfgang von GOETHE, German poet and critic

1750 A. D.—Birth of Lady Anne LINDSAY

1750 A. D.—Samuel JOHNSON's "Rambler" started

1751 A. D.—Thomas GRAY's "ELEGY WRITTEN IN A COUNTRY CHURCHYARD" published

1751 A. D.—Birth of Richard Brinsley SHERIDAN, English dramatist, orator, and statesman

1751 A. D.—Death of Henry St. John, Viscount BOLINGBROKE

1752 A. D.—Birth of Thomas CHATTERTON, English poet

1753 A. D.—Death of Bishop George BERKELEY

1754 A. D.—Death of Henry FIELDING

1754-1762 A. D.—David HUME's "History of England" published

1755 A. D.—Birth of John DUNLOP, English poet

1755 A. D.—Dr. Samuel JOHNSON's Dictionary published

1756 A. D.—Edmund BURKE's Essay on the "SUBLIME AND BEAUTIFUL" published

1757 A. D.—Thomas GRAY's "Pindaric Odes" published

1757 A. D.—Birth of William BLAKE, English poet and painter

1757 A. D.—Benjamin FRANKLIN is sent to England to protest against the proprietary government of the colony of Pennsylvania

1758 A. D.—Samuel JOHNSON's "Idler" started

1759 A. D.—Birth of Robert BURNS, the greatest of Scottish poets

1759 A. D.—Birth of Johann Christoph Friedrich von SCHILLER, German poet, dramatist, and historian

1761 A. D.—Birth of August Friedrich Ferdinand von KOTZEBUE, German dramatist

1761 A. D.—Death of Samuel RICHARDSON

1762 A. D.—Birth of William COBBETT, English political writer

1762 A. D.—Birth of William Lisle BOWLES, English poet and antiquary

1762 A. D.—J. J. ROUSSEAU's "Contrat Social" published

1762 A. D.—Death of Lady Mary Wortley MONTAGU

1763 A. D.—Birth of Samuel ROGERS, English poet

1764 A. D.—FRANKLIN petitions George III to resume the government of the colony from the hands of the proprietors

1765 A. D.—Samuel JOHNSON's edition of Shakespeare's works published

1766 A. D.—Birth of Caroline Oliphant, Lady NAIRNE, a Scottish poet known as "The Flower of Strathearn"

1766 A. D.—Oliver GOLDSMITH's "Vicar of Wakefield" published

1767 A. D.—Birth of August Wilhelm von SCHLEGEL, German poet and critic; translator of Shakespeare

1768 A. D.—Oliver GOLDSMITH's first dramatic attempt, "The Good-Natured Man," produced

1768 A. D.—Death of Laurence STERNE
1770 A. D.—Oliver Goldsmith's "DESERTED VILLAGE" published
1770 A. D.—Death of Thomas CHATTERTON
1770 A. D.—Birth of James HOGG, Scottish poet
1770 A. D.—Birth of William WORDSWORTH, English poet
1771 A. D.—Birth of Sir Walter SCOTT, Scottish novelist and poet
1771 A. D.—Death of Thomas GRAY
1771 A. D.—Birth of Sydney SMITH, English wit and essayist
1772 A. D.—Death of John WOOLMAN
1772 A. D.—Birth of Samuel Taylor COLERIDGE, English poet, philosopher and critic
1773 A. D.—Johann Wolfgang von GOETHE's first important work, "Goetz von Berlichingen," produced
1773 A. D.—Death of Lord CHESTERFIELD (Philip Dormer Stanhope)
1773 A. D.—Oliver GOLDSMITH's comedy, "SHE STOOPS TO CONQUER," first produced
1774 A. D.—Birth of Robert TANNAHILL, Scottish poet
1774 A. D.—Birth of Robert SOUTHEY, English poet and prose writer
1774 A. D.—Death of Oliver GOLDSMITH
1775 A. D.—Birth of Charles LAMB, English essayist and critic
1775 A. D.—Birth of Joseph Blanco WHITE, English clergyman and author
1775 A. D.—Birth of Walter Savage LANDOR, English poet and prose writer
1775 A. D.—Richard Brinsley SHERIDAN's "The Rivals" first produced
1775 A. D.—Benjamin FRANKLIN chosen a member of the Continental Congress
1776 A. D.—The DECLARATION OF INDEPENDENCE adopted by the second Continental Congress
1776 A. D.—Death of David HUME
1776 A. D.—FRANKLIN sent to France as commissioner for the United States
1776 A. D.—Adam SMITH's "WEALTH OF NATIONS" published
1777 A. D.—Richard Brinsley SHERIDAN's "SCHOOL FOR SCANDAL" produced
1777 A. D.—Birth of Thomas CAMPBELL, English poet
1778 A. D.—Birth of William HAZLITT, English critic and essayist
1778 A. D.—Death of J. J. ROUSSEAU
1778 A. D.—Death of Jean François Marie Arouet, called VOLTAIRE
1779 A. D.—Birth of Robert SURTEES, English author
1779 A. D.—Birth of Thomas MOORE, Irish poet
1780 A. D.—Richard Brinsley SHERIDAN enters Parliament
1780 A. D.—Birth of William Ellery CHANNING, American clergyman, essayist and philanthropist
1781 A. D.—The surrender of Lord CORNWALLIS at Yorktown

1781 A. D.—Immanuel KANT's "Critique of Pure Reason" published

1781 A. D.—Death of Gotthold Ephraim LESSING

1783 A. D.—TREATY OF PEACE BETWEEN THE UNITED STATES AND GREAT BRITAIN, by which the War of the Revolution was ended and the United States recognized by Great Britain as a free and independent nation

1783 A. D.—Birth of Reginald HEBER, English prelate and hymn writer

1783 A. D.—Birth of Washington IRVING, American historian, essayist and novelist

1784 A. D.—Death of Samuel JOHNSON

1784 A. D.—Birth of Allan CUNNINGHAM, Scottish poet and general writer

1784 A. D.—Birth of Leigh HUNT, English essayist and poet

1785 A. D.—Birth of Count Alessandro MANZONI, Italian novelist and poet

1785 A. D.—William COWPER's "Task" published

1785 A. D.—"FUNDAMENTAL PRINCIPLES OF THE METAPHYSICS OF MORALS," by Immanuel KANT, published

1785 A. D.—Birth of Jakob GRIMM, German philologist and writer

1785 A. D.—Birth of Thomas DE QUINCEY, English essayist and miscellaneous writer

1786 A. D.—Birth of Wilhelm GRIMM, German philologist and writer

1787 A. D.—Birth of François Pierre Guillaume GUIZOT, French historian and statesman

1787 A. D.—Johann Wolfgang von GOETHE's play of "EGMONT" begun, published twelve years later

1787 A. D.—"The FEDERALIST," articles by Alexander HAMILTON, James MADISON and John JAY, begun in "The Independent Journal," New York

1787 A. D.—The CONSTITUTION OF THE UNITED STATES is drawn up at Philadelphia

1788 A. D.—Death of Charles WESLEY

1788 A. D.—Birth of Lord BYRON (George Gordon), English poet

1788 A. D.—Birth of Sir Aubrey DE VERE, Irish poet

1788 A. D.—Richard Brinsley SHERIDAN delivers his great speech at the trial of Warren Hastings

1789 A. D.—WASHINGTON delivers his first inaugural address

1789 A. D.—Nine of the thirteen United States ratify the CONSTITUTION

1790 A. D.—Edmund BURKE's "REFLECTIONS ON THE REVOLUTION IN FRANCE" published

1790 A. D.—Death of Benjamin FRANKLIN

1791 A. D.—Birth of Charles WOLFE, British clergyman and poet

1791 A. D.—Birth of Michael FARADAY, English physicist and chemist

1792 A. D.—Birth of John KEBLE, English clergyman and religious poet

1792-1793 A. D.—Johann Wolfgang von GOETHE takes part in the wars against France

1792 A. D.—Birth of Percy Bysshe SHELLEY, English poet

1793 A. D.—Birth of Henry Francis LYTE, British hymn writer

1793 A. D.—Queen MARIE ANTOINETTE of France guillotined

1794 A. D.—Birth of John Gibson LOCKHART, Scottish author

1794 A. D.—The United States TREATY WITH THE SIX NATIONS OF INDIANS concluded

1794 A. D.—Edmund BURKE delivers a nine days' speech in the Warren Hastings trial

1794 A. D.—Birth of William Cullen BRYANT, American poet and journalist

1795 A. D.—Birth of George DARLEY, English poet

1795 A. D.—Birth of Thomas CARLYLE, Scottish essayist and historian

1795 A. D.—Birth of John KEATS, English poet

1795 A. D.—Death of James BOSWELL

1796 A. D.—WASHINGTON'S FAREWELL ADDRESS read in the House of Representatives

1796 A. D.—"A LETTER FROM THE RIGHT HON. EDMUND BURKE TO A NOBLE LORD" appears

1796 A. D.—Edward JENNER makes his first experiment in vaccination

1796 A. D.—Death of Robert BURNS

1796 A. D.—Birth of Hartley COLERIDGE, English poet

1797 A. D.—Birth of Sir Charles LYELL, English geologist

1797 A. D.—Death of Edmund BURKE

1798 A. D.—JENNER'S FIRST TREATISE ON THE SMALL-POX published

1798 A. D.—Birth of Thomas HOOD, English poet and humorist

1798 A. D.—COLERIDGE'S "ANCIENT MARINER" published

1799 A. D.—Birth of Heinrich HEINE, German poet and critic

1800 A. D.—Death of William COWPER

1800 A. D.—Birth of Thomas Babington MACAULAY, English historian, essayist, poet and statesman

1801 A. D.—Birth of Sir Henry LYTTON, Earl Bulwer

1802 A. D.—Birth of Hugh MILLER, Scottish geologist and writer

1802 A. D.—Birth of Victor Marie HUGO, French lyric poet and novelist

1803 A. D.—TREATY WITH FRANCE, FOR THE CESSION OF LOUISIANA, concluded

1803 A. D.—Birth of Ralph Waldo EMERSON, American essayist, lecturer and poet

1804 A. D.—Death of Immanuel KANT

1804 A. D.—Birth of Robert Stephen HAWKER, English poet and divine

1804 A. D.—Birth of Charles Augustin SAINTE-BEUVE, French critic

1805 A. D.—Death of Johann Christoph Friedrich SCHILLER

1805 A. D.—Birth of Sarah Flower ADAMS, English poet, author of "Nearer, my God, to Thee"

1805 A. D.—Birth of Hans Christian ANDERSEN, Danish novelist, poet and writer of fairy tales

1806 A. D.—Birth of Elizabeth Barrett BROWNING, English poet

1806 A. D.—Birth of John Stuart MILL, English philosopher and economist

1807 A. D.—Birth of Lady DUFFERIN, Irish poet

1807 A. D.—Birth of Henry Wadsworth LONGFELLOW, American poet

1807 A. D.—Birth of John Greenleaf WHITTIER, American poet

1808 A. D.—Birth of Ray PALMER, American hymn writer

1808 A. D.—Birth of Giuseppe MAZZINI, Italian patriot and writer

1808 A. D.—Birth of Charles Tennyson TURNER, English poet

1809 A. D.—Birth of Edgar Allan POE, American poet and story writer

1809 A. D.—Birth of Oliver Wendell HOLMES, American poet, essayist and novelist

1809 A. D.—Birth of Richard Monckton MILNES, Lord Houghton, English statesman, poet and miscellaneous writer

1809 A. D.—Birth of Alfred TENNYSON, English poet

1809 A. D.—Birth of Charles Robert DARWIN, English naturalist, founder of the "Darwinian" theory of evolution

1809 A. D.—Birth of Edward FITZGERALD, English poet, translator of the "RUBAIYAT" of Omar Khayyam

1810 A. D.—Birth of Sir Samuel FERGUSON, Irish poet

1811 A. D.—Birth of William Makepeace THACKERAY, English novelist, satirist and critic

1812-1815 A. D.—"Kinder- und Hausmärchen," fairy stories by the Brothers GRIMM, published

1812 A. D.—Birth of Robert BROWNING, English poet and dramatist

1812 A. D.—Birth of Charles DICKENS, English novelist

1813 A. D.—Birth of William Edmondstoune AYTOUN, Scottish lawyer, poet and editor

1814 A. D.—Birth of Frederick William FABER, English hymn writer

1816 A. D.—Death of Richard Brinsley SHERIDAN, English orator, wit and dramatist

1817 A. D.—Lord BYRON's first poetic drama "MANFRED" appears

1817 A. D.—AGREEMENT BETWEEN GREAT BRITAIN AND THE UNITED STATES REGARDING THE NAVAL FORCE TO BE MAINTAINED ON THE GREAT LAKES

1817 A. D.—Birth of Henry David THOREAU, American author

1818 A. D.—Birth of Emily BRONTE, English poet and novelist

1819 A. D.—SPAIN cedes Florida to the United States

1819 A. D.—Birth of Arthur Hugh CLOUGH, English poet

1819 A. D.—Chief Justice John MARSHALL delivers his opinion in the case of McCULLOCH VS. MARYLAND

1819 A. D.—Birth of Walt WHITMAN, American poet

1819 A. D.—Birth of James Russell LOWELL, American poet, critic and scholar

1819 A. D.—Birth of John RUSKIN, English art critic

1821 A. D.—Death of John KEATS

1822 A. D.—Death of Percy Bysshe SHELLEY

1822 A. D.—Birth of Louis PASTEUR, French chemist and bacteriologist, founder of modern stereo-chemistry and discoverer of cure for hydrophobia

1822 A. D.—Birth of Matthew ARNOLD, English poet and critic

1823 A. D.—President James MONROE promulgates his doctrine, the so-called MONROE DOCTRINE, against foreign encroachment and interference in the Americas

1823 A. D.—Birth of William Johnson CORY, English poet

1823 A. D.—Birth of Coventry PATMORE, English poet and writer

1823 A. D.—Thomas CARLYLE's first long work, "Life of Schiller" published

1823 A. D.—Death of Edward JENNER

1823 A. D.—Birth of Professor Max MULLER, German-English philologist

1823 A. D.—Birth of Ernest RENAN, French philologist and religious historian

1823 A. D.—Birth of Edward Augustus FREEMAN, English historian

1824 A. D.—Birth of Sydney DOBELL, English poet

1824 A. D.—Death of Lord BYRON

1824 A. D.—Birth of George MACDONALD, Scottish novelist and poet

1824 A. D.—Birth of William ALLINGHAM, Irish poet

1823 A. D.—Charles LAMB's "Essays of Elia" published

1825-1826 A. D.—Alessandro MANZONI's masterpiece, the novel, "I PROMESSI SPOSI" ("The Betrothed"), published

1825 A. D.—Birth of Thomas Henry HUXLEY, English biologist

1825 A. D.—Lord MACAULAY's Essays published

1826 A. D.—Death of Reginald HEBER

1826 A. D.—Birth of Walter BAGEHOT, English economist, publicist and journalist

1827 A. D.—Birth of Joseph LISTER, founder of antiseptic surgery

1828 A. D.—Birth of Dante Gabriel ROSSETTI, English poet and painter

1828 A. D.—Birth of George MEREDITH, English novelist and poet

1828 A. D.—Birth of Hippolyte Adolphe TAINE, French historian

1829 A. D.—Birth of Alexander SMITH, Scottish poet

1830 A. D.—Birth of Thomas Edward BROWN, English poet

1830 A. D.—Birth of Christina ROSSETTI, English poet

1830 A. D.—LYELL's "Principles of Geology" published

1830 A. D.—Death of William HAZLITT

1831 A. D.—Birth of Edward, Earl of LYTTON, English poet

1831 A. D.—On the 27th of December Charles DARWIN started on his famous voyage around the world in Her Majesty's ship "Beagle"

1832 A. D.—Death of Sir Walter SCOTT

1832 A. D.—Death of Wolfgang von GOETHE

1832 A. D.—MAZZINI exiled from France

1833 A. D.—BROWNING's first published poem, "Pauline," appears

1833 A. D.—John Henry NEWMAN cooperates with Froude and others in founding the "Oxford Movement"

1834 A. D.—Death of Samuel Taylor COLERIDGE

1834 A. D.—Birth of William MORRIS, English poet

1834 A. D.—Birth of James THOMSON (B. V.), Scottish poet

1834 A. D.—Death of Charles LAMB

1835 A. D.—Birth of Sir Archibald GEIKIE, Scottish geologist

1835 A. D.—First volume of fairy tales by Hans Christian ANDERSEN is published

1837 A. D.—Birth of Algernon Charles SWINBURNE, English poet

1839 A. D.—Birth of Francis Bret HARTE, American author and poet

1841 A. D.—Birth of Robert BUCHANAN, English poet and novelist

1841 A. D.—EMERSON's Essays published

1842 A. D.—Birth of Sidney LANIER, American poet and author

1842 A. D.—TREATY BETWEEN THE UNITED STATES AND GREAT BRITAIN ON THE BOUNDARIES QUESTION, ratified

1842 A. D.—Death of William Ellery CHANNING

1843 A. D.—John RUSKIN's "Modern Painters" (First volume) appears

1843 A. D.—BROWNING's tragedy, "A BLOT IN THE 'SCUTCHEON, is published and acted

1843 A. D.—Death of Robert SOUTHEY

1844 A. D.—Birth of Arthur O'SHAUGHNESSY, English poet

1844 A. D.—Birth of John Boyle O'REILLY, Irish-American poet and journalist

1845 A. D.—J. H. NEWMAN leaves the Anglican Church for the Catholic

1845 A. D.—POE's "RAVEN" published

1845 A. D.—Death of Sydney SMITH

1846 A. D.—THACKERAY's "Vanity Fair" published

1848-1849 A. D.—MAZZINI returns from banishment to join the Italian revolution when the French besieged Rome and ended the Roman Republic

1848 A. D.—TREATY OF PEACE BETWEEN THE UNITED STATES AND MEXICO, ratified

1848 A. D.—MACAULAY's "History of England" published

1849 A. D.—Birth of William Ernest HENLEY, English author

1849 A. D.—Death of Edgar Allan POE

1850 A. D.—The FUGITIVE SLAVE ACT passed in the United States

1850 A. D.—THACKERAY's "Pendennis" published

1850 A. D.—Death of William Lisle BOWLES

1850 A. D.—Birth of Robert Louis STEVENSON, Scottish author

1850 A. D.—Death of William WORDSWORTH

1852 A. D.—Death of Thomas MOORE

1853 A. D.—Irish text and English translation of "The Battle of Gabra" by Nicholas O'KEARNEY first published

1854 A. D.—THOREAU's "Walden" published

1855 A. D.—Walt WHITMAN's "Leaves of Grass" published

1855 A. D.—THACKERAY's "The Newcomes" published

1856 A. D.—Death of Heinrich HEINE

1857 A. D.—MAZZINI joins the insurrection in Italy fighting under Garibaldi

1857-1859 A. D.—THACKERAY's "The Virginians" published

1859 A. D.—DARWIN's "ORIGIN OF SPECIES" published

1859 A. D.—John Stuart MILL's "ESSAY ON LIBERTY" published

1859 A. D.—Death of Leigh HUNT

1859 A. D.—Death of Lord MACAULAY

1859 A. D.—Death of Thomas DE QUINCEY

1861 A. D.—President LINCOLN delivers his first inaugural address

1861 A. D.—Death of Elizabeth Barrett BROWNING

1862 A. D.—Death of H. D. THOREAU

1863 A. D.—President LINCOLN's GETTYSBURG ADDRESS

1863 A. D.—President LINCOLN's PROCLAMATION OF AMNESTY

1863 A. D.—The EMANCIPATION PROCLAMATION issued by President Abraham Lincoln

1863 A. D.—TAINE's "History of English Literature" published

1863 A. D.—Death of William M. THACKERAY

1864 A. D.—Death of Walter Savage LANDOR

1865 A. D.—General Robert E. LEE surrenders at Appomattox

1865 A. D.—General Lee's FAREWELL TO HIS ARMY

1865 A. D.—President LINCOLN's SECOND INAUGURAL ADDRESS

1865 A. D.—J. R. LOWELL's "Commemoration Ode" published

1866 A. D.—President Johnson's PROCLAMATION DECLARING THE INSURRECTION AT AN END

1866 A. D.—Death of John KEBLE

1867 A. D.—The United States concludes a TREATY WITH RUSSIA, ANNEXING ALASKA by purchase

1867 A. D.—Death of Michael FARADAY

1867 A. D.—John Stuart MILL begins his "AUTOBIOGRAPHY"

1867-1879 A. D.—E. A. FREEMAN's "History of the Norman Conquest" published

1869 A. D.—Death of Charles Augustin SAINTE-BEUVE

1869 A. D.—John Stuart MILL issues his "Subjection of Women," a standard plea for the rights of women

1870 A. D.—Death of Charles DICKENS

1872 A. D.—Death of Giuseppe MAZZINI

1873 A. D.—Death of John Stuart MILL

1874 A. D.—Death of François Pierre GUIZOT

1875 A. D.—Death of Sir Charles LYELL

1875 A. D.—Death of Hans Christian ANDERSEN

1878 A. D.—Death of William Cullen BRYANT

1879 A. D.—John Henry NEWMAN made a Cardinal

1881 A. D.—Death of Thomas CARLYLE

1882 A. D.—Death of Charles DARWIN

1882 A. D.—Death of Henry W. LONGFELLOW

1882 A. D.—Death of Ralph Waldo EMERSON

1882 A. D.—Sir Archibald GEIKIE'S "GEOGRAPHICAL EVOLUTION" published

1885 A. D.—Death of Victor HUGO

1888-1894 A. D.—Ernest RENAN'S "History of Israel" published

1888 A. D.—Death of Matthew ARNOLD

1891 A. D.—Death of James Russell LOWELL

1892 A. D.—Death of Walt WHITMAN

1892 A. D.—Death of John G. WHITTIER

1892 A. D.—Death of Alfred, Lord TENNYSON

1892 A. D.—Death of Ernest RENAN

1892 A. D.—Death of Edward Bulwer, Earl of LYTTON

1893 A. D.—Death of Hippolyte Adolphe TAINE

1894 A. D.—Death of Oliver Wendell HOLMES

1895 A. D.—Death of Louis PASTEUR

1895 A. D.—Death of Thomas Henry HUXLEY

1896 A. D.—Death of William MORRIS

1898 A. D.—ANNEXATION OF THE HAWAIIAN ISLANDS by the United States

1898 A. D.—TREATY OF PEACE signed BETWEEN THE UNITED STATES AND SPAIN

1898 A. D.—RECOGNITION OF THE INDEPENDENCE OF CUBA BY THE UNITED STATES

1904 A. D.—CONVENTION BETWEEN THE UNITED STATES AND THE REPUBLIC OF PANAMA

" ENCLOSED please find a list of selections from The Harvard Classics which I have prepared in consultation with Dr. Neilson for the use of boys and girls of from twelve to eighteen years of age, in answer to your suggestion of October fourth."

Charles W. Eliot

SELECTIONS FROM THE FIVE-FOOT SHELF OF BOOKS

For Boys and Girls from Twelve to Eighteen Years of Age

	VOL.	PAGE
AESOP'S FABLES	XVII	9-46
GRIMM'S TALES	XVII	47-232
ANDERSEN'S TALES	XVII	237-383
HOMER—*The Odyssey*	XXII	
VIRGIL—*The Æneid*	XIII	
THE ARABIAN NIGHTS	XVI	
THE SONG OF ROLAND	XLIX	97-208
ROBIN HOOD	XL	130-189
TRADITIONAL BALLADS — *Selections at pleasure*	XL	
MALORY, SIR THOMAS—*The Holy Grail*	XXXV	109-226
VOYAGES AND TRAVELS	XXXIII	
BENJAMIN FRANKLIN — *Autobiography*	I	5-170
JOHN BUNYAN — *The Pilgrim's Progress*	XV	5-324
SHAKESPEARE — *Macbeth* and *The Tempest*	XLVI	303-442
THOMAS DEKKER — *The Shoemaker's Holiday*	XLVII	447-515
PLUTARCH'S LIVES	XII	
FROISSART	XXXV	3-105
AMBROISE PARE—*Journeys*	XXXVIII	9-61
MANZONI—*The Betrothed*	XXI	
R. H. DANA — *Two Years before the Mast*	XXIII	
DARWIN — *The Voyage of the Beagle*	XXIX	
JOSEPH ADDISON — *The Vision of Mirza*	XXVII	77-81

	VOL.	PAGE
GOLDSMITH—*She Stoops to Conquer*	XVIII	197-260
The Deserted Village.	XLI	521-532
SCHILLER—*William Tell*..........	XXVI	369-474
GOETHE—*Hermann and Dorothea*..	XIX	335-431
MICHAEL DRAYTON—*Agincourt* and		
The Virginian Voyage.........	XL	226-232
COWPER—*John Gilpin*............	XLI	559-567
WORDSWORTH—*Michael*..........	XLI	630-642
SIR WALTER SCOTT—*Poems*.......	XLI	755-774
MACAULAY—*Poems*..............	XLI	940-943
COLERIDGE—*The Ancient Mariner*..	XLI	698-718
JAMES HOGG—*Kilmeny*...........	XLI	774-783
THOMAS CAMPBELL—*Poems*......	XLI	789-801
LORD BYRON — *The Prisoner of*		
Chillon.......................	XLI	821-831
LORD BYRON — *The Destruction of*		
Sennacherib...................	XLI	804-805
LORD BYRON—*The Isles of Greece*.	XLI	833-835
THOMAS MOORE—*Poems*..........	XLI	837-843
LEIGH HUNT—*Abou Ben Adhem*.	XLI	893-894
KEATS—*The Eve of St. Agnes*....	XLI	907-917
TENNYSON—*Morte d'Arthur*......	XLII	1019-1026
Sir Galahad.........	XLII	1036-1038
Charge of the Light		
Brigade..........	XLII	1039
The Revenge........	XLII	1041-1046
RUSKIN—*Sesame and Lilies*.......	XXVIII	95-168
THACKERAY — *The End of the*		
Play.........................	XLII	1099
ROBERT BROWNING — *How They*		
Brought the Good News........	XLII	1107
SYDNEY DOBELL — *Ballad of Keith*		
of Ravelston..................	XLII	1160
DANTE GABRIEL ROSSETTI — *The*		
King's Tragedy................	XLII	1200-1225
WILLIAM E. HENLEY — *England,*		
My England..................	XLII	1259-1260
BRYANT—*Robert of Lincoln*......	XLII	1264-1266
To a Waterfowl........	XLII	1271-1272

	VOL.	PAGE
HENRY WADSWORTH LONGFELLOW— *Poems*	XLII	1316-1414
JOHN G. WHITTIER—*Randolph of Roanoke*	XLII	1416-1419
JOHN G. WHITTIER — *Barclay of Ury*	XLII	1424-1427
JOHN G. WHITTIER—*The Barefoot Boy*	XLII	1431-1434
JOHN G. WHITTIER—*The Pipes at Lucknow*	XLII	1437
JOHN G. WHITTIER — *B a r b a r a Frietchie*	XLII	1439-1441
OLIVER WENDELL HOLMES — *The Chambered Nautilus*	XLII	1442
OLIVER WENDELL HOLMES — *Old Ironsides*	XLII	1443
SIDNEY LANIER — *The Revenge of Hamish*	XLII	1474-1479
FRANK A. HASKELL—*The Battle of Gettysburg*	XLIII	347
ABRAHAM LINCOLN—*Speech at Gettysburg*	XLIII	441
SELECTIONS—*From Sacred Writings*	XLIV	
Some representation of each of the six religions	XLV	